The Borzoi College Reader

SIXTH EDITION

Charles Muscatine
University of California, Berkeley

Marlene Griffith
Laney College

Alfred A. Knopf *New York*

Sixth Edition

98765432

Copyright © 1966, 1971, 1976, 1980, 1984, 1988 by Charles Muscatine and Marlene Griffith

Library of Congress Cataloging-in-Publication Data

The Borzoi college reader.

  Includes indexes.
  1. College readers. I. Muscatine, Charles.
II. Griffith, Marlene.
PE1122.B595   1988   808'.0427   87-29701
ISBN 0-394-37251-4

Manufactured in the United States of America

Cover Design: Sandra Josephson
Book Design: Karin Batten

Acknowledgments

GORDON ALLPORT, "Prejudice and the Individual," from the book *The Black American Reference Book*, edited by Mabel M. Smythe. © 1976. Used by permission of the publisher, Prentice-Hall, Inc., Englewood Cliffs, N.J.

W. H. AUDEN, "The Unknown Citizen." Copyright 1940 and renewed 1968 by W. H. Auden. Reprinted from *W. H. Auden: Collected Poems* by W. H. Auden, edited by Edward Mendelson, by permission of Random House, Inc., and from *Collected Poems* by W. H. Auden by permission of Faber and Faber Ltd.

MARILOU AWIAKTA, "Motheroot" from *Abiding Appalachia* © St. Lukes Press, 1978. Appears in Alice Walker, "In Search of Our Mothers' Gardens."

BEN H. BAGDIKIAN, "The Gentle Suppression," from *The Effete Conspiracy and Other Crimes by the Press* by Ben H. Bagdikian. Copyright © 1972 by Ben H. Bagdikian. Reprinted by permission of Harper & Row, Publishers, Inc.

JAMES BALDWIN, "If Black English Isn't a Language, Then Tell Me, What Is?" July 29, 1979. Copyright 1979 by The New York Times Company. Reprinted by permission. "Notes of a Native Son" from *Notes of a Native Son* by James Baldwin. Copyright © 1955, renewed 1983, by James Baldwin. Reprinted by permission of Beacon Press.

IMAMU AMIRI BARAKA (LeRoi Jones), "Young Soul," from *Black Magic: Poetry 1961–1967.* Reprinted by permission of Sterling Lord Literistic, Inc. Copyright © 1969 LeRoi Jones (Amiri Baraka).

ROBERT BAZELL, "Gene of the Week," March 23, 1987. Reprinted by permission of *The New Republic,* © 1987, The New Republic, Inc.

WALTER W. BENJAMIN, "A Challenge to the Eco-Doomsters." Copyright 1979 Christian Century Foundation. Reprinted by permission from the March 24, 1979 issue of *The Christian Century.*

JOHN BERGER, "The Production of the World," from *The Sense of Sight: Writings by John Berger* by John Berger, edited by Lloyd Spencer. Copyright © 1985 by John Berger. Reprinted by permission of Pantheon Books, a Division of Random House, Inc.

WENDELL BERRY, "Home of the Free," "Horse-Drawn Tools and the Doctrine of Labor Saving," and "The Reactor and the Garden," excerpted from *The Gift of Good Land: Further Essays Cultural and Agricultural.* Copyright © 1981 by Wendell Berry. Published by North Point Press and reprinted by permission. All rights reserved.

CAROL BLY, "Even Paranoids Have Enemies!" from *Letters from the Country* by Carol Bly. Copyright © 1977 by Carol Bly. Reprinted by permission of Harper & Row, Publishers, Inc.

SISSELA BOK, "Lies for the Public Good," from *Lying: Moral Choice in Public and Private Life* by Sissela Bok. Copyright © 1978 by Sissela Bok. Reprinted by permission of Pantheon Books, a Division of Random House, Inc.

HAIG A. BOSMAJIAN, from *The Language of Oppression,* pp. 1–9. © 1983. Reprinted by permission of University Press of America, Inc.

GWENDOLYN BROOKS, "Two Dedications: 'The Chicago Picasso' and 'The Wall.'" Reprinted by permission of Gwendolyn Brooks (The David Company, Chicago).

JOHN H. BROOMFIELD, "High Technology: The Construction of Disaster," from *Alternative Futures*, Vol. 3, No. 2 (Spring 1980), pp. 31–44. Reprinted by permission of the author.

ANTHONY BURGESS, "A Deadly Sin—Creativity for All" and "Grunts from a Sexist Pig," from *But Do Blondes Prefer Gentlemen?* published by McGraw-Hill, Inc., © 1986 by Liana Burgess.

ALBERT CAMUS, "The Guest," from *Exile and the Kingdom* by Albert Camus, translated by Justin O'Brien. Copyright © 1957, 1958 by Alfred A. Knopf, Inc. Reprinted by permission of the publisher.

ROBERT CLAIBORNE, "A Wasp Stings Back," September 30, 1974. Copyright 1974, Newsweek, Inc. Copyright 1987 Robert Claiborne.

SEPTIMA CLARK, "Judge Waring," from *Ready from Within* by Septima P. Clark and Cynthia Stokes Brown.

THOMAS J. COTTLE, "Overcoming an Invisible Handicap," January 1980. Reprinted with permission from *Psychology Today* Magazine. Copyright © 1980 American Psychological Association.

NORMAN COUSINS, "Of Life and Lifeboats," March 8, 1975. © 1975 *Saturday Review* magazine. Reprinted by permission.

JENNIFER CRICHTON, "Who Shall I Be?" *Ms.*, October 1984. Copyright by Jennifer Crichton.

E. E. CUMMINGS, "since feeling is first" is reprinted from *Is 5* by E. E. Cummings, edited by George James Firmage, by permission of Liveright Publishing Corporation. Copyright © 1985 by E. E. Cummings Trust. Copyright © 1926 by Horace Liveright. Copyright © 1954 by E. E. Cummings. Copyright © 1985 by George James Firmage.

ROBERTSON DAVIES, "The Deadliest of the Sins," *One-Half of Robertson Davies* by Robertson Davies. Copyright © 1977 by Robertson Davies. All rights reserved. Reprinted by permission of Viking Penguin Inc.

ALAN M. DERSHOWITZ, "Discrimination by Creed." Reprinted by permission of United Features Syndicate, Inc.

JOAN DIDION, "Some Dreamers of the Golden Dream," from *Slouching Towards Bethlehem* by Joan Didion. Copyright © 1966, 1968 by Joan Didion. Reprinted by permission of Farrar, Straus and Giroux, Inc.

ANNIE DILLARD, "Living Like Weasels," from *Teaching a Stone to Talk* by Annie Dillard. Copyright © 1982 by Annie Dillard. Reprinted by permission of Harper & Row, Publishers, Inc.

W. E. B. DU BOIS, "Negro Art," from *W. E. B. Du Bois: A Reader*, edited by Meyer Weinberg. Copyright © 1970 by Meyer Weinberg. Reprinted by permission of Harper & Row, Publishers, Inc.

LOREN EISELEY, Chapter 5 from *The Firmament of Time*. Copyright © 1960 Loren Eiseley. Copyright © 1960 The Trustees of the University of Pennsylvania. Reprinted with the permission of Atheneum Publishers, a division of Macmillan, Inc.

AMITAI ETZIONI, "When Rights Collide," *Psychology Today*, October 1972.

JEFFREY A. FADIMAN, "A Traveler's Guide to Gifts and Bribes," (July/August 1986). Reprinted by permission of the *Harvard Business Review*. Copyright © 1986 by the President and Fellows of Harvard College; all rights reserved.

HENRY FAIRLIE, "Can You Believe Your Eyes?" © 1967 American Heritage Publishing Company, Inc. Reprinted by permission from *Horizon* (Vol. IX, No. 2, Spring 1967).

MARC FEIGEN FASTEAU, "Friendships Among Men," from *The Male Machine*, by Marc Feigen Fasteau. Copyright © 1974 by Marc Feigen Fasteau. Reprinted by permission of McGraw-Hill Book Company.

PETER MARIN, "Helping and Hating the Homeless," January 1987. Copyright © 1987 by *Harper's Magazine.* All rights reserved. Adapted from the January issue by special permission.

PAULE MARSHALL, "From Poets in the Kitchen," January 9, 1983. Copyright 1983 by The New York Times Company. Reprinted by permission.

MAO ZEDONG, from "Talks at the Yenan Forum on Art and Literature," from *Selected Works 1941–1945.* Reprinted with permission of International Publishers Co.

JACK MCGARVEY, "To Be or Not to Be as Defined by TV," *Today's Education,* February/ March 1982, pp. 33–36. Reprinted with permission of The National Education Association.

MARGARET MEAD, "The Egalitarian Error," from *A Way of Seeing* by Margaret Mead and Rhoda Metraux. Copyright © 1962, 1970 by Margaret Mead and Rhoda Metraux. By permission of William Morrow & Company, Inc.

MEMORANDUM, "Understanding Women" from Harper's Magazine's *Readings.* Copyright © 1987 by *Harper's Magazine.* All rights reserved. Reprinted from the April issue by special permission.

JOSEPHINE MILES, "Essay in Reason," *Educational Leadership* 19(5):311–313 (February 1962). Reprinted with the permission of the Association for Supervision and Curriculum Development and Josephine Miles. Copyright 1962 by the Association for Supervision and Curriculum Development. All rights reserved.

MARIANNE MOORE, "Poetry." Reprinted with permission of Macmillan Publishing Company from *Collected Poems* by Marianne Moore. Copyright 1935 by Marianne Moore, renewed 1963 by Marianne Moore and T. S. Eliot.

THOMAS B. MORGAN, from "The Latinization of America," first published in *Esquire,* May 1983. Copyright © 1983 Thomas B. Morgan.

HAROLD J. MOROWITZ, "Prison of Socrates," from *Mayonnaise and the Origin of Life.* Copyright © 1985 Harold J. Morowitz. Reprinted with the permission of Charles Scribner's Sons, a division of Macmillan, Inc. "Drinking Hemlock and Other Nutritional Matters," from *The Wine of Life and Other Essays on Society, Energy and Living Things* by Harold J. Morowitz. Copyright © 1979 by Harold J. Morowitz. Reprinted by permission of St. Martin's Press, Inc., New York.

TONI MORRISON, "A Slow Walk of Trees," July 4, 1976. Copyright © 1976 by The New York Times Company. Reprinted by permission.

FAYE MOSKOWITZ, excerpt from *A Leak in the Heart: Tales from a Woman's Life* by Faye Moskowitz. Copyright © 1985 by Faye Moskowitz. Reprinted by permission of David R. Godine, Publisher.

NATIONAL CONFERENCE OF CATHOLIC BISHOPS, excerpts from *Economic Justice for All: Catholic Social Teaching and the U.S. Economy,* Copyright © 1986, United States Catholic Conference, Washington, D.C. are used with permission.

ANAÏS NIN, excerpt from "The Personal Life Deeply Lived" from *A Woman Speaks* by Anaïs Nin. Copyright © 1975 by Anaïs Nin. All rights reserved. Reprinted by permission of the Author's Representative, Gunther Stuhlmann.

MICHAEL NOVAK, "Neither WASP nor Jew nor Black," from *The Rise of the Unmeltable Ethnics.* Reprinted by permission of Sterling Lord Literistic, Inc. Copyright 1974 by Michael Novak.

GEORGE ORWELL, "Politics and the English Language" and "Shooting an Elephant," from *Shooting an Elephant and Other Essays* by George Orwell. "Politics and the English Language" copyright 1946, 1974 by Sonia Brownell Orwell. "Shooting an Elephant" copyright 1950 by Sonia Brownell Orwell; renewed 1978 by Sonia Pitt-Rivers. Both reprinted by permission of Harcourt Brace Jovanovich, Inc., the Estate of the late Sonia Brownell Orwell and Martin Secker & Warburg Limited.

JO GOODWIN PARKER, "What Is Poverty?" from *America's Other Children: Public Schools Outside Suburbia,* by George Henderson. Copyright © 1971 by the University of Oklahoma Press.

CHARLES W. PARRY, "My Company—Right or Wrong?" *Vital Speeches of the Day,* Vol. 51, August 1, 1985. Reprinted with permission.

ROBERT PATTISON, "Connect the Dots," *The Nation,* March 7, 1987. *The Nation* magazine/The Nation Company, Inc. Copyright 1987.

WALKER PERCY, "The Loss of the Creature," from *The Message in the Bottle* by Walker Percy. Copyright © 1975 by Walker Percy. Reprinted by permission of Farrar, Straus and Giroux, Inc.

MARGE PIERCY, "To Be of Use." Copyright © 1973 by Marge Piercy. Reprinted from *Circles on the Water* by Marge Piercy, by permission of Alfred A. Knopf, Inc.

NEIL POSTMAN, "Amusing Ourselves to Death." Reprinted from *Et cetera,* Vol. 42, No. 1 by permission of the International Society for General Semantics.

MARCEL PROUST, "Prologue," from *By Way of Sainte-Beuve,* by Marcel Proust, translated by Sylvia Townsend Warner. Copyright © 1958 by Meridian Books, Inc. Reprinted by arrangement with World Publishing Company, Cleveland and New York. Translation copyright © Chatto and Windus, Ltd., 1957. Reprinted by permission of the Translator's Literary Estate and Chatto & Windus, Ltd. Originally published in French by Librairie Gallimard, Paris, 1954, under the title *Contre Sainte-Beuve.*

SANTHA RAMA RAU, "By Any Other Name." Copyright © 1951 by Santha Rama Rau. Reprinted by permission of William Morris Agency, Inc., on behalf of the author. First appeared in *The New Yorker.*

JAMES HARVEY ROBINSON, "On Various Kinds of Thinking," from *The Mind in the Making* by James Harvey Robinson. Copyright 1921 by Harper & Row, Publishers, Inc. Renewed 1949 by Bankers Trust Company. Reprinted by permission of Harper & Row, Publishers, Inc.

THEODORE ROETHKE, "Dolor." Copyright 1943 by Modern Poetry Associates, Inc. from *The Collected Poems of Theodore Roethke.* Reprinted by permission of Doubleday Publishing, a division of Bantam, Doubleday, Dell Publishing Group.

THEODORE ROSZAK, "Ideas Come First" and "The Master Ideas," from *The Cult of Information* by Theodore Roszak. Copyright © 1986 by Theodore Roszak. Reprinted by permission of Pantheon Books, a Division of Random House, Inc.

CARL SAGAN, "In Defense of Robots," from *Broca's Brain* by Carl Sagan. Copyright © 1979 by Carl Sagan. All Rights Reserved. Reprinted by permission of the author.

PHYLLIS SCHLAFLY, "Marriage and Motherhood" and "The Price of a Happy Marriage." Reprinted from *The Power of the Positive Woman* by Phyllis Schlafly. Copyright © 1977 by Phyllis Schlafly. Used by permission of Arlington House, Inc.

THOMAS B. SHERIDAN, "Seven Factors in Alienation." Reprinted with permission from *Technology Review,* copyright 1980.

ISAAC BASHEVIS SINGER, "The Son from America," from *A Crown of Feathers* by Isaac Bashevis Singer. Copyright © 1970, 1971, 1972, 1973 by Isaac Bashevis Singer.

THEODORE R. SIZER, "What High School Is," from *Horace's Compromise* by Theodore R. Sizer. Copyright © 1984 by Theodore R. Sizer. Reprinted by permission of Houghton Mifflin Company.

RAY SLATER, "A Young Man Sifts the Ashes of Efficiency in Search of the Work Ethic." Reprinted by permission of the author.

JAMES P. SMITH, "Cognitive Science, Computers, and the Humanities: Artificial and Natural Intelligence." Reprinted with permission from *Federation Review,* Vol. IX, No. 3 (May/June 1986).

WILLIAM STAFFORD, "A Way of Writing" © 1970 by William Stafford. Originally appeared in *Field* No. 2 (Spring 1970). Reprinted in *Writing the Australian Crawl,* copyright © by The University of Michigan, 1978.

BRENT STAPLES, "Just Walk On By: A Black Man Ponders His Power to Alter Public Space," *Ms.,* September 1968. Reprinted with permission of the author.

LINCOLN STEFFENS, "I Go To College" and "I Become a Student" from *The Autobiography of Lincoln Steffens* by Lincoln Steffens, copyright 1931 by Harcourt Brace Jovanovich, Inc.; renewed 1959 by Peter Steffens. Reprinted by permission of the publisher.

JUDY SYFERS, "I Want a Wife," from *Ms.* Magazine (December 1971), Copyright © 1971 by Judy Syfers. Reprinted by permission of the author.

THOMAS S. SZASZ, "Drug Prohibition," *Reason,* January 1978, pp. 14–18. Reprinted with permission.

RABINDRANATH TAGORE, #LXXIX from *Fruit-Gathering:* "Let me not pray to be sheltered from dangers . . . " (used as chapter opening in Kübler-Ross: *On Death and Dying*). Reprinted with permission of Macmillan Publishing Company and Macmillan Publishers Ltd. from *Collected Poems and Plays* by Rabindranath Tagore. Copyright 1916 by Macmillan Publishing Company, renewed 1944 by Rathindranath Tagore.

STUDS TERKEL, "Carol and Tony Danlow" and "William Gothard," from *American Dreams: Lost and Found* by Studs Terkel. Copyright © 1980 by Studs Terkel. Reprinted by permission of Pantheon Books, a Division of Random House, Inc. "Carl Murray Bates—Mason," "Nora Watson—Editor," and "Mike Lefevre—Steelworker," from *Working: People Talk about What They Do All Day and How They Feel about What They Do,* by Studs Terkel. Copyright © 1972, 1974 by Studs Terkel. Reprinted by permission of Pantheon Books, a Division of Random House, Inc.

PAUL THEROUX, "Being a Man," from *Sunrise with Sea Monsters* by Paul Theroux. Copyright © 1985 by Cape Cod Scriveners Company. Reprinted by permission of Houghton Mifflin Company.

LEWIS THOMAS, "How to Fix the Premedical Curriculum," *The Medusa and the Snail* by Lewis Thomas. Copyright © 1974, 1975, 1976, 1977, 1978, 1979 by Lewis Thomas. All rights reserved. Reprinted by permission of Viking Penguin Inc.

JAMES THURBER, "The Secret Life of Walter Mitty," from *My World & Welcome to It* by James Thurber. Copyright © 1942 James Thurber. Copyright © 1970 Helen Thurber and Rosemary A. Thurber. From *My World & Welcome to It* published by Harcourt Brace Jovanovich, Inc.

CALVIN TRILLIN, "A Stranger with a Camera," from *Killings.* Copyright © 1969 by Calvin Trillin. Originally appeared in *The New Yorker.*

BISHOP DESMOND TUTU, "Mythology." Reprinted with permission from *The New York Review of Books.* Copyright © 1985 Nyrev, Inc.

JOHN UPDIKE, "The Golden Age of the 30-Second Spot." Copyright © 1984 by *Harper's Magazine.* All rights reserved. Reprinted from the June issue by special permission.

LEWIS H. VAN DUSEN, JR., "Civil Disobedience: Destroyer of Democracy." Reprinted from the *ABA Journal,* The Lawyer's Magazine.

ALICE WALKER, "In Search of Our Mothers' Gardens," from *In Search of Our Mothers' Gardens,* copyright © 1974 by Alice Walker. Reprinted by permission of Harcourt Brace Jovanovich, Inc. "Women" from *Revolutionary Petunias and Other Poems,* copyright © 1970 by Alice Walker. Reprinted by permission of Harcourt Brace Jovanovich, Inc.

MARY HELEN WASHINGTON, "Working at Single Bliss," *Ms.,* October 1982. Reprinted by permission of the author.

JOSEPH WEIZENBAUM, from *Computer Power and Human Reason,* pp. 1–16. Copyright © 1976 by W. H. Freeman and Company. Reprinted by permission of the publisher.

JUDITH WELLS, "Daddy's Girl." Reprinted by permission of the author.

E. B. WHITE, "The Morning of the Day They Did It," February 25, 1950 from *The Second Tree from the Corner.* Copyright 1950 by E. B. White. Reprinted by permission of Harper & Row, Publishers, Inc.

GEORGE F. WILL, "Reading, Writing and Rationality," March 17, 1986. © 1986, Newsweek, Inc. All rights reserved. Reprinted by permission.

LANGDON WINNER, "Technical Arrangements as Forms of Order." Reprinted by permission of *Daedalus,* Journal of the American Academy of Arts and Sciences, "Modern Technology: Problem or Opportunity?" vol. 109, Winter 1980, Boston, MA.

VIRGINIA WOOLF, "Professions for Women," from *The Death of the Moth and Other Essays* by Virginia Woolf, copyright 1942 by Harcourt Brace Jovanovich, Inc.; renewed 1970 by Marjorie T. Parsons, Executrix. Reprinted by permission of the publisher, the author's estate and The Hogarth Press. "Shakespeare's Sister," from *A Room of One's Own* by Virginia Woolf, copyright 1929 by Harcourt Brace Jovanovich, Inc.; renewed 1957 by Leonard Woolf. Reprinted by permission of the publisher, the author's estate and The Hogarth Press.

SUSAN WRIGHT, "Genetic Engineering: The Real Risks," *Christianity and Crisis.* Copyright, Christianity and Crisis, September 19, 1983. Reprinted with permission, Christianity and Crisis, 537 West 121st, New York, NY 10027.

WILLIAM BUTLER YEATS, "Leda and the Swan" and "Sailing to Byzantium." Reprinted with permission of Macmillan Publishing Company from *Collected Poems* by W. B. Yeats. Copyright 1928 by Macmillan Publishing Company, renewed 1956 by Georgie Yeats and with permission of A. P. Watt Ltd. on behalf of Michael B. Yeats and Macmillan London Ltd.

WILLIAM ZINSSER, "Simplicity," from *On Writing Well,* published by Harper & Row, Publishers, Inc. Copyright © 1976 by William K. Zinsser. Reprinted by permission of the author.

Preface

"To teach the art of critical thinking is the main design of this book." This was the first sentence of the first edition of this book. It holds equally true today. The basic organization by topic has also remained the same; under each topic we have collected pieces representing different attitudes, points of view, or approaches, and whenever possible, pieces that directly respond to or oppose each other.

The reading presents, then, a wide range of subjects, ideas, and assumptions, and at the same time a continuous dialogue or debate among them. We hope that presenting ideas in the form of issues will help the reader to see that he or she has something to think about. Suggesting comparison at every point, giving ready occasion to take sides and to criticize, the material is directly suited to generating discussion and writing.

Human values and ethical choice continue to be the underlying themes of the book. We believe as strongly as ever in the personal value of the kind of reading or writing that tests ideas and leads to discovery or confirmation of what we mean and believe. The first sections introduce ideas on writing, thinking, and language, but the interplay of ideas in each subsequent section raises questions about values—for instance, "What Should Students Learn?," "What Should Work Be?," "Ethics in Business and Government," or "On Computers and People."

If the plan of the book holds true to our original ideas, this edition is nevertheless a new book. It has more selections than ever, half of them are new, and perhaps more important, well over forty of them are very short pieces of high quality. We hope that this large number of well-written, short essays that present important ideas with integrity will make critical reading more easily accessible than ever to the beginning college student, and provide a full range of realistic models for the student's own critical writing.

The Introduction to each section gives the reader both a context for and an overview of the pieces in that section. In the headnotes, we have tried to provide background and other information about each piece and its writer, not only to define the writer's authority, but also to show that significant writing comes out of real lives and that these lives and careers are the kind open to all college students.

As with the earlier editions, we have done no silent editing, and most of the pieces are either complete works in themselves or coherent sections (usually chapters) of longer works. At the foot of each page, we have glossed allusions and references that cannot be found in a standard college dictionary. A Rhetorical Index is included at the end of the book.

The Student's Guide and the Instructor's Manual to accompany *The Borzoi College Reader,* Sixth Edition, are available separately from the publisher.

Friends and colleagues have been most generous in their suggestions for new pieces and new directions. We owe particular thanks to Ann Connor, Gregg Camfield, Margot Dashiell, Sandra Gilbert, Robert J. Griffin, Bart Harloe, Ellen Hart, Valerie Miner, Ingrid Radkey, Sestus Otis Smith, Jan Wall, and Smokey Wilson.

In addition, colleagues from other colleges and universities provided us with detailed analyses and suggestions based on their experience with previous editions; our appreciation and thanks go to Rebecca Bailey, University of North Carolina, Chapel Hill; Ruth Bryant, Sam Houston State University; Santi V. Buscemi, Middlesex County College; Darrell Eckersley, Los Angeles Southwest College; John Fiedler, College of San Mateo; Gretchen Flesher, University of Utah; Brenda Gordon, University of Florida, Gainesville; Patricia Kolonosky, Kansas State University; Barry Maid, University of Arkansas, Little Rock; Hugh Remash, Seattle Central Community College; Sidney Shrager, California State Polytechnic University, Pomona; Emily Seelbinder, Wake Forest University; Robert Sommer, Rutgers University, Newark; Mary Steussy Shanahan, Cameron University; Steven Stewart, Virginia Polytechnic Institute; Eugene Thompson, Ricks College; Annette Wahlgreen, Garland County Community College.

We have been unusually fortunate in the colleagues with whom we have worked. Our collaboration with the people at Alfred A. Knopf has been and continues to be a happy one. We thank our editor, Steve Pensinger, who prods us so gently and supports us so fully. Holly Gordon kept us to our schedule as she shepherded the manuscript benevolently through production. Andrea Haight provided us with remarkably expert copyediting. And, as always, we are thankful for the presence of June Smith. We are grateful also to Lin Look and Elizabeth Abrams for bibliographical assistance, and to Susan McCallister for proofreading. But we owe most to the collaboration of Jean O'Meara, whose wide reading, keen eye, and excellent judgment have made this a much richer book than it would otherwise have been.

C.M.
M.G.

Contents

The Problem of Identity   221

Barriers to Women, Visible and Invisible   253

Spouses, Households, and Careers   291

On Being a Man **325**

Race, Culture, and Prejudice **349**

On Conscience and Moral Responsibility **423**

Ethics in Business and Government   465

What Is the Good Life?   505

What Should Work Be?   535

What Is Democracy? 575

Issues in Democracy 587

On Civil Disobedience 621

The Haves and the Have-Nots 675

Technology and Human Values   **727**

Computers and People   **791**

Television and Reality   **835**

On the Function of Art

On Death and Dying

Epilogue

Advice to the Student:
On Reading an Essay

In offering here some practical advice on how to read an essay, we do not mean to imply that there is just one way to go at it. Essays differ, and readers differ even more, and how a given reader comes to an understanding of an author's message may be a very individual process indeed. But for our present purpose—which is to offer some initial guidance to the comparatively inexperienced reader of essays—it will be safe to assume that if you have no settled way of starting out on your own, a good way to learn is to use standard moves that have worked well for others. The method we will offer, indeed, corresponds closely to what many college teachers do when an essay is being discussed in class. Thus students who follow our suggestions in the order given will often find that they have not only read an essay critically, but have prepared themselves for active class discussion and for writing about it.

First of all, you must be prepared—and leave time—to read the essay more than once. The first reading, which may be comparatively rapid, is to get a preliminary overview. This overview—a sense of how the essay goes from beginning to end—is essential to getting a good general sense of the essay's purpose and point. That is, the two main questions one asks oneself on first reading are: What is this essay trying to do? and What is its "main idea"?

What is the essay trying to do? Why is the writer telling us what he or she is telling us? A preliminary answer is essential to appreciating the essay, to coming to a secure conclusion about what it means. Most essays are prose statements that make some kind of point, but within that rough definition they vary as much as the motives behind any human communication can vary. The writer may be trying, as one human being to another, to share an experience; or helpfully to explain something that might be interesting or puzzling to the reader; or to persuade the reader to an opinion about something, to move him or her to action, perhaps political. Some writers may even have selfish or questionable motives: to promote themselves or to deceive the reader. In any case, you need some general idea of what the writer is up to in order to ask the right questions and to come to secure conclusions about the meaning and value of the essay in all its details. In the present volume, the essays are marshaled around a number of important issues in our culture, and most of them will be found to be expository—that is, written to set out, explain, or prove to the reader the truth of an idea. Yet some essays, however they may involve ideas, are principally narratives. They tell us a story; often they share some important experiences in the authors' lives. (See, for instance, Santha Rama Rau's "By Any Other Name," p. 144; Dick Gregory's "Shame," p. 426; and the pieces by James Herriot, p. 537, Calvin Trillin, p. 397, and Faye Moskowitz, p. 905.)

Other essays seem more obviously to move, as we read them, from narrative to an explicit idea that is drawn, finally, from the events narrated. Thus Samuel Scudder's essay (p. 45) begins by simply narrating the experience of his first days in Agassiz's laboratory, but ends by calling the discipline of careful observation they entailed "the best entomological lesson I ever had." James Baldwin's "Notes of a Native Son" (p. 351) starts with the events surrounding his father's funeral, but ends with some complex ideas about injustice. In some essays that are largely narrative, as in George Orwell's "Shooting an Elephant" (p. 441), the author early identifies the idea which is to be illustrated by what he is about to tell:

> One day something happened which in a roundabout way was enlightening. It was a tiny incident in itself, but it gave me a better glimpse than I had had before of the real nature of imperialism—the real motives for which despotic governments act. (p. 442)

Many essays announce immediately that they are about ideas. Thus Sissela Bok uses the first two paragraphs of her "Lies for the Public Good" to summarize the arguments of her preceding chapters and announce that they lead to the idea of the present one, that lies "to advance the public good . . . form the most dangerous body of deceit of all" (p. 492). Similarly, James Harvey Robinson (p. 31) starts at once with ideas about the nature of intelligence or mind; and Thomas Sheridan (p. 827) loses no time in introducing his topic of how people relate to computers.

Still other essays let us know, earlier or later, that they want us to take sides in an ongoing controversy. Thus Martin Luther King, Jr. (p. 650), defends the civil rights demonstrations in Birmingham against the criticism of other clergymen. Theodore Roszak offers his definition of information "in deliberate contradiction to the computer enthusiasts and information theorists who have suggested far more extravagant definitions" (p. 56). Samuel C. Florman's "On-the-Job Enrichment" is written in response to what he calls "the antitechnology campaign" (p. 569).

While we are coming to a rough idea of what the essay is for, we will already be working on the second question, What is the essay's main idea? The two questions are related, but they are not the same. It is important to have read an essay right to the end before deciding what the main idea is, for quite often the idea with which an essay begins is not the principal idea of the essay. The opening sections of the essay may be introducing the topic, laying the groundwork, perhaps getting the reader into a frame of mind for accepting the main idea, which may itself be reserved for the end. Thus Orwell's "Politics and the English Language" starts out with the idea that "the English language is in a bad way" (p. 166), and, in the second paragraph, that the badness of our language "makes it easier for us to have foolish thoughts" and that clear thinking may have something to do with our "political regeneration." He then spends some nine pages beautifully elaborating these preliminary ideas, not coming again to a full expression of what turns out to be his main idea—each aspect of which he has already argued in some detail—until his last paragraph: "The present political chaos is connected with the decay of language, and . . . one can probably bring about some improvement by starting at the verbal end." In "The Indispensable Opposition," Walter Lippmann gives us his main idea at the end of the fourth paragraph: "We must protect the right of our opponents to speak because we must hear what they have to say" (p. 596). We know that this *is* the main idea because by the end of the essay nothing else tops it; the rest of the essay is devoted to expounding and defending it. Of course, many essays will announce their main idea quite early, as does Haig Bosmajian's at the end of the first paragraph: ". . . the power which comes from naming and defining people has had positive as well as negative effects on entire populations" (p. 150). His essay emphasizes the negative effects. Marc Feigen Fasteau's main idea in "Friendships Among Men" comes at the end of the second paragraph, when he writes: "Despite the time men spend together, their contact rarely goes beyond the external, a limitation which tends to make their friendships shallow and unsatisfying" (p. 330). Both of these essays, like many others, end on an upbeat or corrective note, and so seem to have not one but two main ideas—the one that occupies the body of the essay and the one that follows it at the end. Be that as it may, you will have done your reading well if the first time through you can put your finger on a statement that all or most of the essay seems to be supporting. Notice that a main idea *is* an idea: It says something *about* something. You can test whether you are identifying an *idea* as opposed, merely, to a *topic* like "sex roles" or "politics and language" by whether you can express it in a sentence.

Sometimes the main idea is not stated anywhere by the author in so many words, and sometimes, as in poetry or fiction, it is not reducible to simple terms; in these cases the reader can supply only an approximation of it. The "main idea" of Dick Gregory's narrative (p. 426), a narrative that freely mingles ideas and feelings, is something about the way shame can get in the way of human sympathy. James Herriot's account of his rounds as a veterinarian (p. 537) includes some uncomfortable incidents, yet the total effect is to show how satisfying such work can be.

The reason that it is useful to start with a notion of the purpose and the main idea of an essay is that most good essays are *organized* or *unified* around their purpose and main idea, and so can be understood most handily in those terms. Much of an appreciative, critical reading comes from being able to explain the various parts or features of the essay and relate them to the essay's purpose and main idea. The main features that a good reader will be on the alert for by the second reading will be organization or argument, the kinds of evidence presented, and any elements of technique, tone, or style that contribute to its full meaning. By this time the reader should be well past the "receptive" stage of just sitting there and letting the words come. Try to take an active role, working along with the writer step by step, or standing behind the writer and watching and appreciating how it is done.

There are many ways to organize an essay, but in general, in the essay that tries to establish an idea, the main parts will be the steps used to get the reader to accept the idea. As we have said, the author's strategy may lead to announcing the idea at the beginning or to withholding it until the end, but the body of the essay will have to consist, in one way or another, of some organized combination of argument and evidence.

One of the simplest and best ways for a writer to make a point is to mention one by one all the things in personal experience or reading that make one feel the idea is true, organizing them by groups and subgroups in order to avoid diffuseness. Thus Marc Feigen Fasteau, after stating his main idea about the quality of friendships among men, starts in the fourth paragraph (p. 330) with a group of observations about uncommunicativeness among men. He talks first about the general quality of male conversations, then in the next paragraph about the use of games as a substitute for conversation; in the next paragraph comes some evidence from his experience with a college friend and with his father; in the next comes an example from popular literature; then, after dealing with some exceptions, he lets us know, with the adverb *finally*, that his last piece of evidence for uncommunicativeness "is the way men depend on women to facilitate certain conversations" (p. 332). The next paragraphs see him summarizing for us the meaning of this subsection of his essay and announcing that he is now going to turn to "the reasons why men hide from each other," which "lie in the taboos and imperatives of the masculine stereotype" (p. 333). The alert reader will expect then, in the ensuing paragraphs, a list of cultural prohibitions or commands that make men behave the way they do, with some discussion of each. And sure enough, that is what Fasteau gives us, with due attention to some exceptions, and with a brief, constructive conclusion. Notice that a writer will often use adverbs and transitional phrases—*first of all, finally, however, furthermore,* and the like—to let the reader know continuously what is going on.

Your acceptance of the main idea of this kind of essay depends on your acceptance of the evidence presented. Is it true to your experience? Or, if it is not within your experience, do you believe it? Is the author reliable? Is the author the kind of person who should be believed on this subject?

Sometimes the author will try to persuade by using some form of logic, a chain of argument. Thus Garrett Hardin (p. 708) argues that since the poor multiply many times faster than the rich, simply feeding the poor creates that much more of a surplus of poor people and makes the problem of world poverty ultimately greater, not less. In dealing with arguments based on logic, the experienced reader will want to test, perhaps with the aid of further research or wider reading, whether all the parts of the argument are true, whether the conclusions really do follow from the facts given, and whether anywhere in the argument the reader is being asked to accept a hidden assumption—something that is quietly assumed by the writer and intended to stand without proof. (The essay by Thomas H. Huxley, p. 49, will give you a good idea of two major forms of logic.)

Writers use many other means to help them make their meanings clear. Sometimes they offer contrasting definitions or comparisons, which help clarify each other. (See William Golding, p. 25, and James Harvey Robinson, p. 31, on kinds of thinking; Martin Luther King, Jr., on just and unjust laws, p. 650; Mao Zedong on the political and artistic criteria in art criticism, p. 878). Sometimes they use analogy, that is, a reference to something familiar to the reader that is comparable to the idea being presented. (Hardin, p. 708, starts with the idea of the lifeboat to clarify his view of the situation of rich nations; and Walter Lippmann, p. 594, uses our tolerance of our doctor's diagnosis as an analogy to what he means by political tolerance.) Sometimes the writer relies heavily on a simple incident or anecdote or a few vivid pieces of evidence that seem to sum up or symbolize the whole meaning all at once. (Marcel Proust, p. 101, uses the remembered taste of a piece of toast this way; Wendell Berry, p. 525, uses a few phrases from two advertisements; Harold Morowitz, p. 206, uses a remembered TV program, in which a movie star made an attack on the use of sugar, to epitomize the problem of knowing how we know what we know.) Sometimes, as in James Baldwin's "Notes of a Native Son" (p. 351), the writer seems to take us through the actual network of experiences that led him to his final conclusions. As you encounter these various devices, your appreciation of them will deepen if you continually ask yourself how and why they work to support or embody the author's main purpose and idea.

Of course, much that a writer does in an essay will go beyond the requirement of simply making ideas clear. The writer will, quite legitimately, want to appeal to the reader's feelings, to share feelings, or to suggest a proper emotional response to the topic. You should be sensitively aware of this aspect of the essay, not only to be on guard against improper manipulation of feelings—as, for instance, in appeals to sentimentality or prejudice—but also to enhance your understanding and enjoyment of the feelings themselves.

Feelings are powerfully generated by the techniques that the essay writer shares with the poet and novelist—the choice of particular words, sounds, and rhythms, the setting of scenes, telling of stories, creation of atmosphere—and by the particular tone of voice that the writer seems to adopt. An adequate account of all these would require volumes. Here we must be content to point briefly to some easily noticed effects of literary style in the essays usually read in college.

Some writers—often professors and scientists—write in an impersonal style that seems calculated to keep feelings neutral or at a distance. The kind of words they use seems to be saying: Let the ideas or facts speak for themselves. Gordon Allport writes like this:

> While some animals have an instinctive aversion to others, this is not true among species that are cross-fertile. Human beings of all races can, and do, mate and procreate. There is therefore no reason to assume that instinctive aversion exists between ethnic and racial groups. A young child may be frightened by a person of unfamiliar color or appearance, but ordinarily this fear lasts only a few moments. It is well known that young children will play contentedly together whatever their race or national origin. Thus since prejudice is not inborn but acquired, the question is: What are the chief factors in the complex process of learning? (p. 418)

So does Sissela Bok:

> While Watergate may be unusual in its scope, most observers would agree that deception is part and parcel of many everyday decisions in government. Statistics may be presented in such a way as to diminish the gravity of embarrassing problems. Civil servants may lie to members of Congress in order to protect programs they judge important, or to guard secrets they have been ordered not to divulge. (p. 497)

Other writers have more personal styles, as if they had found their own unique voices, and seem to be addressing us personally. This is the way Wendell Berry sounds:

> My labor-saving equipment consists of a team of horses and a forty-year-old manure spreader. We forked the manure on by hand—forty-five loads. I made my back tired and my hands sore, but I got a considerable amount of pleasure out of it. Everywhere I spread that manure I knew it was needed. (p. 528)

And Henry David Thoreau:

> Under a government which imprisons any unjustly, the true place for a just man is also a prison. The proper place to-day, the only place which Massachusetts has provided for her freer and less desponding spirits, is in her prisons, to be put out and locked out of the State by her own act, as they have already put themselves out by their principles. It is there that the fugitive slave, and the Mexican prisoner on parole, and the Indian come to plead the wrongs of his race should find them; on that separate, but more free and honorable ground, where the State places those who are not *with* her, but *against* her,— the only house in a slave State in which a free man can abide with honor. If any think that their influence would be lost there, and their voices no longer afflict the ear of the State, that they would not be as an enemy within its walls,

they do not know by how much truth is stronger than error, nor how much more eloquently and effectively he can combat injustice who has experienced a little in his own person. Cast your whole vote, not a strip of paper merely, but your whole influence. A minority is powerless while it conforms to the majority; it is not even a minority then; but it is irresistible when it clogs by its whole weight. (p. 641)

And Zora Neale Hurston:

I follow those heathen—follow them exultingly. I dance wildly inside myself; I yell within, I whoop; I shake my assegai above my head, I hurl it true to the mark *yeeeeooww!* I am in the jungle and living in the jungle way. My face is painted red and yellow and my body is painted blue. My pulse is throbbing like a war drum. (p. 229)

The directness of this sort of writing, and the personal relationship implied by it, often make the reader feel a certain shared confidence and intimacy with the writer.

Some writers—Orwell is among the greatest of them—try for a plain style, in which the writing, like a pane of glass, rarely calls attention to itself, rarely interposes itself between the reader and what there is to be seen and felt. This style is much admired nowadays; it has an economy that harmonizes with the pace of modern life, and it suggests an attractive modesty on the part of the writer. Other authors seem almost intoxicated with words; they write a highly colored prose, with heavily distinctive sounds and rhythms, rich in metaphor, that borders on poetry:

What goes on in his brain the rest of the time? What does a weasel think about? He won't say. His journal is tracks in clay, a spray of feathers, mouse blood and bone: uncollected, unconnected, loose-leaf, and blown. (p. 109)

When done as well as Annie Dillard does it above, this style can be very moving.

Some writers of essays use techniques characteristic of fiction. Thus the opening descriptions in Joan Didion's "Some Dreamers of the Golden Dream" are used less to give us the facts than to create artistically a certain atmosphere or tone:

Imagine Banyan Street first, because Banyan is where it happened. The way to Banyan is to drive west from San Bernardino out Foothill Boulevard, Route 66: past the Santa Fe switching yards, the Forty Winks Motel. Past the motel that is nineteen stucco tepees: "SLEEP IN A WIGWAM—GET MORE FOR YOUR WAMPUM." Past Fontana Drag City and the Fontana Church of the Nazarene and the Pit Stop A Go-Go; past Kaiser Steel, through Cucamonga, out to the Kapu Kai Restaurant-Bar and Coffee Shop, at the corner of Route 66 and Carnelian Avenue. Up Carnelian Avenue from the Kapu Kai, which means "Forbidden Seas," the subdivision flags whip in the harsh wind. "HALF-ACRE RANCHES! SNACK BARS! TRAVERTINE ENTRIES! $95 DOWN." (p. 512)

Similarly the choice and sequencing of details in the description of the funeral (p. 513), and the vivid characterizations Didion gives even to the minor actors in her story, all suggest the talents of a fiction writer and all contribute to what she wants to say about the culture she is describing. The same can be said of the way Paule Marshall describes her neighborhood library (p. 139), or Santha Rama Rau evokes the heat of an afternoon's walk in India (p. 148). Indeed, most good essay writers have some sensitivity to scene, atmosphere, character, word choice, and tone, and you should try to appreciate how any of these aspects adds to the meaning of the piece you are reading. Finally, you should be alert to the great devices of irony and humor, which often convey their meanings indirectly through some implied reversal of what they seem to say, often for the sake of satire. The classic example of irony is Jonathan Swift's "A Modest Proposal" (p. 90). Other, lighter examples are William Golding's "Thinking as a Hobby" (p. 25), E. B. White's "The Morning of the Day They Did It" (p. 728), and William Geist's "Sofa-sized Art" (p. 887).

Because you are in a college classroom situation, you may well have started out to read an essay because of compulsion or on faith—on someone else's say so. It is wise to start out with a certain humility or faith or optimism that an essay someone wrote, and that was published and perhaps republished and then recommended or assigned—that such an essay must have a message of value. It is well to have started out with some receptiveness and some respect for the writer; but in the end, reading is for yourself, and once a couple of careful readings have given you an idea of the essay's meaning for the author, the final question to ask is: What does it mean for me? The words on the page will not take on their deepest meaning until you have come to terms with the essay, as if you had just had (what deep reading really is) a personal encounter with the writer. How does the message fit with what you already knew, wanted to know, or needed to know? How does the essay relate to others you have read; to ideas and experiences you have already had? If it challenges or disturbs you, where are the points of conflict? If it confirms your ideas, does it merely tell you what you already knew, or make you feel surer of yourself? Is it true to your experience, or false? If new to you, does it enlarge your experience or fail to find a place there; and if it fails, why so? What has it changed in your ideas or feelings? How, in fact, does it make you feel? Even your response to the writer's tone, or to the writer's own degree of involvement with the subject, is a legitimate part of the meaning of the essay for you.

The answers to any of these questions, besides capping your sense of the essay's meaning, will begin to move you from the role of reader to that of thinker, discussant, and writer. Even before you have clearly formulated ideas about the essay, your first emotional response to it will be useful; but you must try to follow out the line of that response, staying on its trail. It may lead you to finding its source in a significant complex of ideas about the essay, about the world, or about yourself.

Prologue

Prison of Socrates

Harold J. Morowitz

Harold J. Morowitz, born in 1927, is a professor of molecular biophysics and biochemistry at Yale, where he received his Ph.D. in 1951. From 1969 to 1974, he served as a member of the planetary biology committee of the National Aeronautics and Space Administration. Although most of his books and articles have been written for the scientific community, Moro-witz speaks eloquently to a general audience in The Wine of Life and Other Essays on Societies, Energy, and Living Things *(1979);* Cosmic Joy & Local Pain: Musings of a Mystic Scientist *(1987); and* Mayonnaise and the Origin of Life: Thoughts of Minds and Molecules *(1985), from which the following piece is reprinted. "Prison of Socrates" offers an explanation of why we ask the reader to think about the issues raised in this book; in it, a scientist challenges himself and us to answer an essential question: "Tell me, Reader, what do we mean by a good society?"*

It is not my usual custom to write an essay while sitting on a rock on the Acropolis; nevertheless the reasons are compelling. The architectural splendor of the Parthenon and surrounding ruins by themselves might inspire poetry rather than this hesitant prose, but I have just come from the supposed site of one of enlightenment's earliest martyrdoms, the prison of Socrates. I had experienced some difficulty in finding the exact place. There are no signs, no monuments; only ΣΩΚΡΑΤΕΣ scratched in the stone, graffiti-like, informed me that I had arrived at my destination. The path to the prison started at the foot of the Acropolis and passed near a small church that echoed with ageless liturgical chanting. Drawn to the chapel door, I was distracted from my mission for a few minutes of listening. Nearby stood a small restaurant where a kindly waiter, with whom I did not share a common language, responded to my inquiry after Socrates by escorting me to the porch and pointing out a walkway leading up a hill.

1

The prison cell was the simple two-room cave described by Plato. Iron grillwork closed off the entrance, and I peered inside, feeling a strange admixture of past and present. The dimly remembered words of Plato somehow emblazoned themselves on the here and now, creating a surrealistic timelessness: "Were you yourself, Phaedo, in the prison with Socrates on the day when he drank the poison?" "Yes, Echecrates, I was."

It is strange that the location of such an important happening should go unmarked. In the half hour that I was there, not a single tourist appeared to experience this shrine. Could it be that the descendants of the citizens of Athens who voted the death of Socrates do not wish to advertise the matter? That is a charming notion, but it is probably more ideal than real. Perhaps there is too much uncertainty about the authenticity of the location. I don't know, and I am fully prepared to leave the mystery unsolved, being content with the good fortune of visiting the place in tranquility, uninterrupted by the constant comings and goings that characterize such a popular attraction as the Parthenon. One of the chief reasons for including Athens on our itinerary had been to see the prison where the great philosopher had met his noble end. The motivation was a long-time attraction to Socrates' doctrine that the beginning of wisdom is the realization of how little we know. It is a necessary antidote to the tendency to regard ourselves as wise and to consider present knowledge as the final word.

Still somewhat dazed by having walked on the stones that had known the sandals of the famous philosophers of antiquity, I climb the Acropolis and look out over the modern city of Athens. In my mind's eye I try to sense the scene as it must have been in the days of Pericles, but something obtrudes on that fantasy. Hovering over the city is a dark cloud of pollutants so obscenely dirty that it blots out all visions in a reeking miasma of filth. I have seen that cloud floating over many great cities. Yet viewed from the Parthenon, it takes on a new significance, for in looking back at the past, we are tempted to look toward the future. The events of the morning are forcing me to move from the Golden Age of Greece, to modern Athens, to some dim beyond.

It is simply not true that the past is good and the present is bad, as some romanticists would maintain. The trial and death of Socrates is in itself evidence enough that classical Greece was something less than a utopia. Yet there is an interesting contrast between one lone man sipping poison for ideological reasons and an entire city of several million slowly inhaling a lethal mixture as the price of a life-style committed to certain technological and material wants that have become needs. Even here the comparison is informative. What is done for modern Athens by pollution-causing machinery was done for their ancestors by slaves. The simple notion of good and bad begins to slip away, and we focus instead on the issue of what a modern society wants. How have we arrived at these goals? What price are we willing to pay?

We can, in this context, begin to understand what made Socrates so different and classical Greece so unique. He dared constantly to raise the questions: What is justice? What is the good life? What are the responsibilities of the state? By obstinately placing these difficulties before his fellow citizens, he kept them from falling into the rut of merely accepting a way of life for its own sake. He forced each Athenian to look inward, even if just a little, and ask why he was doing the things he was doing. Modern Athens lacks a living conscience, a public nuisance who will force the citizens to pause and question the most fundamental assumptions of their lives.

Classical Athens was what it was because most of the citizens knew Socrates personally. Present-day nations are so large that individuals know only their small circle of acquaintances, and the state is an abstraction that can be comprehended but not touched emotionally. Most of the great social writings of antiquity deal with relations of individuals at a one-on-one level of interaction. The Ten Commandments deal with parent and child, man and wife, neighbor and neighbor. These interactions, while immensely important, have been overshadowed by social patterns that relate the individual to his world in a statistical and impersonal way. We are now faced with problems where each person's contribution is minute, but the aggregate is potentially disastrous. The black cloud over Athens is such an issue. Concerning these moral dilemmas, the most cherished writings of antiquity stand mute, since the problems have only arisen with the industrial revolution and the enormous population growth of the last 200 years.

If wisdom does not provide us with answers, it does suggest that we should not cease from asking the questions. In the performance of this task our societies are lacking. We turn our attention to such pragmatic features as manufacture and transportation, but we do not inquire what we should be making or where we should be going. A highly diverse culture will no doubt offer many answers to such challenges, and arriving at conclusions will be exceedingly difficult. It is naive to suggest that a few simple Socratic queries and replies will suddenly turn us on to the right road. I do maintain, however, that if we do not constantly labor over the major points of social ethics, we will surely miss the mark, for the guidance of the past does not fully encompass the present.

The world is in need of annoying, troublesome, Socratic-like thinkers who will keep us from intellectual and spiritual slumbers brought on by lethargy, hyperstimulation, self-satisfaction, or simple discouragement over the magnitude and complexity of the challenges that have been set before us. Such philosophers are needed in education, journalism, television, movies, and every other public forum. They will trouble us and cause us sleepless nights, and I suppose that from time to time we shall imprison them or worse. But in the end they are national treasures, and if their graves or the sites of their martyrdom are unmarked, their ideas are the catalysts that enliven life and keep us from stagnation.

It is a very emotional experience sitting here on the Acropolis, and I wish not to let the event pass without finding deeper meaning in life. "Tell me, Reader, what do we mean by a good society?"

On Writing

Few of us would feel offended if a friend or teacher returned a math problem marked "wrong." Yet almost all of us would feel at least hurt if something we had written were returned to us marked "wrong." Words are more intimately connected to our sense of self than numbers are. When we try to express an idea or a feeling, we risk not being understood. And writing is riskier than talking. We cannot follow our listeners' responses by watching their faces. We cannot interject, "What I mean is . . . ," or simply change direction or even subjects if we see or sense that we are being misunderstood. Not knowing how our reader will read us (as partner? as judge? as editor? as critic?) can cramp even our sense of how to begin.

The five writers in this section present us with different perspectives on writing, and different reasons *to* write. Anaïs Nin is an ardent advocate of the daily journal or diary. "Your attentiveness," she says, "your care for what is happening, your watchfulness, your meditation on what happens, your examination of what happens, the fact that you are observing others and that you are not only writing down your life but that you are also naturally concerned with the growth of people around you, make that a necessary part of our existence." There is no judgment here. We write for ourselves.

In a similar vein, William Stafford sees writing as a way to help uncover what it is we want to say. A writer, he says, "is not so much someone who has something to say as he is someone who has found a process that will bring about new things he would not have thought of if he had not started to say them." Here, too, there is no "wrong"; the writer must simply have the courage to begin.

Lawrence Langer talks of writing for a reader other than self. He thinks that the fear of being judged keeps many students from saying anything that means very much to them—and thus to others. They avoid language that could break down barriers between reader and writer and lead to genuine understanding. In fact, they build barriers of "abstract diction and technical jargon" to protect themselves from their readers. Langer also reminds us of the responsibility of the reader, especially of a first reader, by citing a poignant example of a student who risked a very personal essay and an instructor who responded only by correcting it.

These first three essays focus on language as a means of formulating or clarifying what we think, feel, and know. The next two essays, by William Zinsser and Josephine Miles, are more concerned with how we express and communicate our thoughts, feelings, and knowledge.

Concerned as she is with teaching the student writer "how to make responsible statements," Josephine Miles shows how the structure of the argument depends on the thesis statement. In the next essay, William Zinsser, in a seeming contradiction of Stafford, says "Clear thinking becomes clear writing. It is impossible for a muddy thinker to write good English." He then gives some excellent advice on fighting clutter, echoing the great William Strunk's admonition to "omit needless words."

from *The Personal Life Deeply Lived*

Anaïs Nin

Anaïs Nin (1903–1977) was born in Paris, the daughter of Spanish pianist and composer Joaquin Nin. When she was eleven, her father deserted the family, and they moved abruptly to New York. During this difficult year she began keeping a diary, which she continued to keep with great faithfulness, at first in French and later in English, throughout her life. Her diary amounted to 126 handwritten volumes when it was edited for publication in 1965. It appeared in successive volumes, beginning in 1966, as The Diary of Anaïs Nin.

Nin was also a popular speaker and lecturer. With her approval, a close associate, Evelyn J. Hinz, edited and published A Woman Speaks: The Lectures, Seminars, and Interviews of Anaïs Nin *(1975); the material was drawn from 38 different tapes. The present passage, taken from a chapter by the same name, was edited by Hinz from four lectures Nin gave on college campuses in 1972 and 1973.*

Tonight I was asked to talk about writing, not writing as literature but writing as intimately connected with our lives—I would even say as necessary to our lives. . . . And now I want to tell you, from the very beginning, how this writing happened to become for me so linked with life and how it was a necessary part of living. When I was nine years old a doctor made an erroneous diagnosis and said I would never walk again. My first reaction then was to ask for pencil and paper and to start making portraits of the members of my family. Then this continued in the form of notes which I gathered in a little notebook and even wrote on it "Member of the French Academy." Quite obviously there was then a turning to writing as a way of life because I thought I was going to be deprived of the normal activities of a child or an adolescent. But I'm trying to use this as an example of the importance of writing as a way of learning to live; for when I was able to walk again and there was no question of that impediment, the writing remained a source of contact with myself and with others.

It's also very symbolic that when I was asked once to go to a masquerade in which we had to dress as our madness I put my head in a bird cage. And coming out of the bird cage was a sort of ticker tape of the unconscious, long strips of paper on which I had copied a great deal of writing. This was, of course, a very clear symbol of how I hoped to escape from my cage.

You might say, however, when you are reading the *Diary* now: "Oh well, it was easy for you, you could write well." But I want you to know that at twenty I wrote very badly, and I purposely gave my first novel to the library of Northwestern University so that students could see the difference between the writing I did at twenty and the writing I do now. The mistake we make when we choose a model is that we choose the point of arrival. We are unaware of the things that have been overcome, like shyness, or not being able to speak in public (I couldn't even speak to the people I knew). The final achievements are what we notice and then say: "Well it's no use modelling ourselves after this or that writer because we don't have these particular gifts." I didn't have any particular gift in my twenties. I didn't have any exceptional qualities. It was the persistence and the great love of my craft which finally became a discipline, which finally made me a craftsman and a writer.

The only reason I finally was able to say exactly what I felt was because, like a pianist practising, I wrote every day. There was no more than that. There was no studying of writing, there was no literary discipline, there was only the reading and receiving of experience. And I had to be open because I had to write it in the diary.

So I would like to remove from everyone the feeling that writing is something that is only done by a few gifted people. I want to eliminate this instantly. . . . You shouldn't think that someone who achieves fulfillment in writing and a certain art in writing is necessarily a person with unusual gifts. I always said that it was an unusual stubbornness. Nothing prevented me from doing it every night, after every day's happenings.

It's not only the people with unusual gifts who will write their life in an interesting way. It has nothing to do really with the literary value of the work. What is important is that in the doing of it you begin to penetrate much deeper into the layers of consciousness and the unconscious. I registered everything. I registered intuitions, prophesies; I would be looking into the future or looking back and re-examining the past.

I don't want to make writers of all of you, but I *do* want you to become very aware of your orientation. First of all, of how much contact you have with yourself. If you remember, in the early diaries I spoke of my feeling that I was playing all the roles demanded of woman, which I had been programmed to play. But I knew also that there was a part of myself that stood apart from that and wanted some other kind of life, some other kind of authenticity. R. D. Laing° describes this authenticity as a process of constant peeling off the false selves. You can do this in many ways, but you can begin by looking at it, for there is so much that we *don't* want to look at. I didn't want to see exactly where I was in Louveciennes° before I made friends, before I entered the literary life, before I wrote my first book. I didn't want to see that I was nowhere, but wanting to see is terribly important to our direction. And to find this direction I used every possible means. Not only friendship and psychology and therapy, but also a tremendous amount of reading, exploration, listening to others—all these things contributed to my discovering who I really was. It wasn't as final or definite as it might sound now, because it doesn't happen in one day and it doesn't happen finally. It's a continuum, it's something that goes on all of your life. But once I was at least on the track of what I could do, then the obstacles began to move away. It was not something that anybody could give me, it was something that I had to find inside myself.

So I'm speaking now of the diary not as a work of literature but as something necessary to living, as a way of orienting ourselves to our inner lives. It doesn't matter in what form you do it, whether it's meditation, whether it's writing or whether it's just a moment of thoughtfulness about the trend, the current, of your life. It's a moment of stopping life in order to become aware of it. And it's this kind of awareness which is threatened in our world today, with its acceleration and with its mechanization.

R. D. Laing (b. 1927) British psychiatrist and author.
Louveciennes Village near Paris where Nin was living in 1931, described in the opening pages of her *Diary*.

A Way of Writing

William Stafford

William Stafford, a poet, was born and raised in Kansas. During his school years, he writes, "we moved from one little town to another. . . . Our lives were quiet and the land was very steady. Our teachers were good. Not till I finished my BA degree at the University of Kansas and went on to graduate school in another state did I see an adult drunk or enraged or seriously menacing. Higher education and the coming of World War II supplied a new aspect of experience." A pacifist, he spent the war years in camps for conscientious objectors, fighting forest fires, building trails, and terracing eroding land. After the war he taught at Lewis and Clark College in Oregon, left to study in the creative writing program at the State University of Iowa, and then returned to Lewis and Clark. He moved to Washington in 1970, where he served as Consultant in Poetry to the Library of Congress. He now lives in Oregon.

Stafford has been published widely. Among his collections are Traveling Through the Dark *(1962), for which he won the 1963 National Book Award in Poetry;* The Rescued Year *(1966), which includes an autobiographical account of his Kansas childhood;* Allegiances *(1970);* Someday, Maybe *(1973);* All About Light *(1978);* Two About Music *(1978);* Around You, Your House and a Catechism *(1979);* The Quiet of the Land: Poems *(1979);* Things That Happen Where There Aren't Any People *(1980);* Sometimes Like a Legend *(1981); and* Wyoming *(1985). His work also includes criticism and a collection of personal and autobiographical pieces on writing, published in 1978 as* Writing the Australian Crawl. *From this comes the chapter printed below, a description of one way to begin writing, of one way by which "blocked" writers may discover what they have to say.*

A writer is not so much someone who has something to say as he is someone who has found a process that will bring about new things he would not have thought of if he had not started to say them. That is, he does not draw on a reservoir; instead, he engages in an activity that brings to him a whole succession of unforeseen stories, poems, essays, plays, laws, philosophies, religions, or—but wait!

Back in school, from the first when I began to try to write things, I felt this richness. One thing would lead to another; the world would give and give. Now, after twenty years or so of trying, I live by that certain richness, an idea hard to pin, difficult to say, and perhaps offensive to some. For there are strange implications in it.

One implication is the importance of just plain receptivity. When I write, I like to have an interval before me when I am not likely to be interrupted. For me, this means usually the early morning, before others are awake. I get pen and paper, take a glance out of the window (often it is dark out there), and wait. It is like fishing. But I do not wait very long, for there is always a nibble—and this is where receptivity comes in. To get started I will accept anything that occurs to me. Something always occurs, of course, to any of us. We can't keep from thinking. Maybe I have to settle for an immediate impression: it's cold, or hot, or dark, or bright, or in between! Or—well, the possibilities are endless. If I put down something, that thing will help the next thing come, and I'm off. If I let the process go on, things will occur to me that were not at all in my mind when I started. These things, odd or trivial as they may be, are somehow connected. And if I let them string out, surprising things will happen.

If I let them string out. . . . Along with initial receptivity, then, there is another readiness: I must be willing to fail. If I am to keep on writing, I cannot bother to insist on high standards. I must get into action and not let anything stop me, or even slow me much. By "standards" I do not mean "correctness"—spelling, punctuation, and so on. These details become mechanical for anyone who writes for a while. I am thinking about such matters as social significance, positive values, consistency, etc. I resolutely disregard these. Something better, greater, is happening! I am following a process that leads so wildly and originally into new territory that no judgment can at the moment be made about values, significance, and so on. I am making something new, something that has not been judged before. Later others—and maybe I myself—will make judgments. Now, I am headlong to discover. Any distraction may harm the creating.

So, receptive, careless of failure, I spin out things on the page. And a wonderful freedom comes. If something occurs to me, it is all right to accept it. It has one justification: it occurs to me. No one else can guide me. I must follow my own weak, wandering, diffident impulses.

A strange bonus happens. At times, without my insisting on it, my writings become coherent; the successive elements that occur to me are clearly related. They lead by themselves to new connections. Sometimes the language, even the syllables that happen along, may start a trend. Sometimes the materials alert me to something waiting in my mind, ready for sustained attention. At such times, I allow myself to be eloquent, or intentional, or for great swoops (Treacherous! Not to be trusted!) reasonable. But I do not insist on any of that; for I know that back of my activity there will be the coherence of my self, and that indulgence of my impulses will bring recurrent patterns and meanings again.

This attitude toward the process of writing creatively suggests a problem for me, in terms of what others say. They talk about "skills" in writing. Without denying that I do have experience, wide reading, automatic orthodoxies and maneuvers of various kinds, I still must insist that I am often baffled about what "skill" has to do with the precious little area of confusion when I do not know what I am going to say and then I find out what I am going to say. That precious interval I am unable to bridge by skill. What can I witness about it? It remains mysterious, just as all of us must feel puzzled about how we are so inventive as to be able to talk along through complexities with our friends, not needing to plan what we are going to say, but never stalled for long in our confident forward progress. Skill? If so, it is the skill we all have, something we must have learned before the age of three or four.

A writer is one who has become accustomed to trusting that grace, or luck, or—skill.

Yet another attitude I find necessary: most of what I write, like most of what I say in casual conversation, will not amount to much. Even I will realize, and even at the time, that it is not negotiable. It will be like practice. In conversation I allow myself random remarks—in fact, as I recall, that is the way I learned to talk—so in writing I launch many expendable efforts. A result of this free way of writing is that I am not writing for others, mostly; they will not see the product at all unless the activity eventuates in something that later appears to be worthy. My guide is the self, and its adventuring in the language brings about communication.

This process-rather-than-substance view of writing invites a final, dual reflection:

1. Writers may not be special—sensitive or talented in any usual sense. They are simply engaged in sustained use of a language skill we all have. Their "creations" come about through confident reliance on stray impulses that will, with trust, find occasional patterns that are satisfying.

2. But writing itself is one of the great, free human activities. There is scope for individuality, and elation, and discovery, in writing. For the person who follows with trust and forgiveness what occurs to him, the world remains always ready and deep, an inexhaustible environment, with the combined vividness of an actuality and flexibility of a dream. Working back and forth between experience and thought, writers have more than space and time can offer. They have the whole unexplored realm of human vision.

The Human Use of Language

Lawrence Langer

Lawrence Langer, born in New York City in 1929, is a professor of English at Simmons College in Boston. His books, which are based on his research in the literature of the Holocaust, include The Holocaust and the Literary Imagination *(1975),* The Age of Atrocity: Death in Modern Literature *(1978), and* Versions of Survival: The Holocaust and the Human Spirit

(1982). The article reprinted below first appeared in January 1977 in The Chronicle of Higher Education.

A friend of mine recently turned in a paper to a course on behavior modification.° She had tried to express in simple English some of her reservations about this increasingly popular approach to education. She received it back with the comment: "Please rewrite this in behavioral terms."

It is little wonder that human beings have so much trouble saying what they feel, when they are told that there is a specialized vocabulary for saying what they think. The language of simplicity and spontaneity is forced to retreat behind the barricades of an official prose developed by a few experts who believe that jargon is the most precise means of communication. The results would be comic, if they were not so poisonous; unfortunately, there is an attitude toward the use of language that is impervious to human need and drives some people back into silence when they realize the folly of risking human words on insensitive ears.

The comedy is easy to come by. Glancing through my friend's textbook on behavior modification, I happened on a chapter beginning with the following challenging statement: "Many of the problems encountered by teachers in the daily management of their classes could be resolved if. . . ." Although I was a little wary of the phrase "daily management," I was encouraged to plunge ahead, because as an educator I have always been interested in ideas for improving learning. So I plunged. The entire sentence reads: "Many of the problems encountered by teachers in the daily management of their classes could be resolved if the emission of desirable student behaviors was increased."

Emission? At first I thought it was a misprint for "omission," but the omission of desirable student behaviors (note the plural) hardly seemed an appropriate goal for educators. Then I considered the possibility of metaphor, both erotic and automotive, but these didn't seem to fit, either. A footnote clarified the matter: " 'Emission' is a technical term used in behavioral analysis. The verb, 'to emit,' is used specifically with a certain category of behavior called 'operant behavior.' Operant behaviors are modified by their consequences. Operant behaviors correspond closely to the behavior colloquially referred to as voluntary." Voluntary? Is jargon then an attack on freedom of the will?

Of course, this kind of abuse of language goes on all the time—within

---

behavior modification   Use of conditioning techniques, usually a system of reward and punishment, to change behavior by encouraging desirable actions and discouraging undesirable actions.

the academic world, one regrets to say, as well as outside it. Why couldn't the author of this text simply say that we need to motivate students to learn willingly? The more I read such non-human prose, and try to avoid writing it myself, the more I am convinced that we must be in touch with ourselves before we can use words to touch others.

Using language meaningfully requires risk; the sentence I have just quoted takes no risks at all. Much of the discourse that poses as communication in our society is really a decoy to divert our audience (and often ourselves) from that shadowy plateau where our real life hovers on the precipice of expression. How many people, for example, have the courage to walk up to someone they like and actually *say* to them: "I'm very fond of you, you know"?

Such honesty reflects the use of language as revelation, and that sort of revelation, brimming with human possibilities, is risky precisely because it invites judgment and rebuff. Perhaps this is one reason why, especially in academe, we are confronted daily with so much neutral prose: Our students are not yet in touch with themselves; not especially encouraged by us, their instructors, to move in that direction; they are encouraged indeed to expect judgment and hence perhaps rebuff, too, in our evaluation of them. Thus they instinctively retreat behind the anonymity of abstract diction and technical jargon to protect themselves against us— but also, as I have suggested, against themselves.

This problem was crystallized for me recently by an encounter only peripherally related to the issue. As part of my current research, I have been interviewing children of concentration-camp survivors. One girl I have been meeting with says that her mother does not like to talk about the experience, *except with other survivors*. Risk is diminished when we know in advance that our audience shares with us a sympathy for our theme. The nakedness of pain *and* the nakedness of love require gentle responses. So this survivor is reticent, except with fellow victims.

But one day a situation arose which tempted her to the human use of language although she could not be sure, in advance, of the reception her words would receive. We all recognize it. This particular woman, at the age of 40, decided to return to school to get a college degree. Her first assignment in freshman composition was to write a paper on something that was of great importance to her personally. The challenge was immense; the risk was even greater. For the first time in 20 years, she resolved to confront a silence in her life that she obviously needed to rouse to speech.

She was 14 when the Germans invaded Poland.° When the roundup of the Jews began a year later, some Christian friends sent their young

---

Germans invaded Poland September 1, 1939.

daughter to "call for her" one day, so that they might hide her. A half hour later, the friends went themselves to pick up her parents, but during that interval, a truck had arrived, loaded aboard the Jewish mother and father—and the daughter never saw them or heard from them again. Their fate we can imagine. The girl herself was eventually arrested, survived several camps, and after the war came to America. She married, had children of her own, and except for occasional reminiscences with fellow survivors, managed to live adequately without diving into her buried personal past. Until one day her instructor in English composition touched a well-insulated nerve, and it began to throb with a painful impulse to express. I present verbatim the result of that impulse, a paper called "People I Have Forgotten":

"Can you forget your own Father and Mother? If so—how or why?

"I thought I did. To mention their names, for me is a great emotional struggle. The brutal force of this reality shakes my whole body and mind, wrecking me into ugly splinters; each crying to be mended anew. So the silence I maintain about their memory is only physical and valid as such but not true. I could never forget my parents, nor do I want to do it. True, I seldom talk about them with my husband or my children. How they looked, who they were, why they perished during the war. The love and sacrifices they have made for me during their lifetime, never get told.

"The cultural heritage to which each generation is entitled to have access seems to be nonexistant [*sic*], since I dare not talk about anything relating to my past, my parents.

"This awful, awesome power of not-remembering, this heart-breaking sensation of the conspiracy of silence is my dilemma.

"Often, I have tried to break through my imprisoning wall of irrational silence, but failed: now I hope to be able to do it.

"Until now, I was not able to face up to the loss of my parents, much less talk about them. The smallest reminder of them would set off a chain reaction of results that I could anticipate but never direct. The destructive force of sadness, horror, fright would then become my master. And it was this subconscious knowledge that kept me paralyzed with silence, not a conscious desire to forget my parents.

"My silent wall, my locked shell existed only of real necessity; I needed time.

"I needed time to forget the tragic loss of my loved ones, time to heal my emotional wound so that there shall come a time when I can again remember the people I have forgotten."

The essay is not a confrontation, only a prelude, yet it reveals qualities which are necessary for the human use of language: In trying to reach her audience, the author must touch the deepest part of herself. She risks self-exposure—when we see the instructor's comment, we will realize how great was her risk—and she is prepared for judgment and perhaps even rebuff, although I doubt whether she was prepared for the form they took. This kind of prose, for all its hesitant phraseology, throws down a gauntlet to the reader, a challenge asking him to understand that life is pain as well as plenty, chaos as well as form. Its imagery of locked shells and imprisoning walls hints at a silent world of horror and sadness far less enchanting than the more familiar landscape of love where most of us dwell. Language is a two-edged tool, to pierce the wall which hides that world, or build high abstract barriers to protect us from its threats.

The instructor who graded the paper I have just read preferred walls to honest words. At the bottom of the last page she scrawled a large "D-minus," emphatically surrounded by a circle. Her only comment was: "Your theme is not clear—you should have developed your 1st paragraph. You talk around your subject." At this moment, two realms collide: a universe of unarticulated feeling seeking expression (and the courage and encouragement to express) and a nature made so immune to feeling by heaven-knows-what that she hides behind the tired, tired language of the professional theme-corrector.

Suddenly we realize that reading as well as writing requires risks, and that the metaphor of insulation, so central to the efforts of the Polish woman survivor to re-establish contact with her past, is a metaphor governing the response of readers, too. Some writing, like "the emission of desirable student behaviors," thickens the insulation that already separates the reader from the words that throw darts at his armor of indifference. But even when language unashamedly reveals the feeling that is hidden behind the words, it must contend with a different kind of barrier, the one behind which our instructor lies concealed, unwilling or unable to hear a human voice and return a human echo of her own.

Ironically, the victor in this melancholy failure at communication is the villain of the piece, behavior modification. For the Polish survivor wrote her next theme on an innocuous topic, received a satisfactory grade, and never returned to the subject of her parents. The instructor, who had encountered a problem in the daily management of her class in the form of an essay which she could not respond to in a human way, altered the attitude of her student by responding in a non-human way, thus resolving her problem by increasing the emission of desirable student behavior. The student now knows how vital it is to develop her first paragraph, and how futile it is to reveal her first grief.

Even more, she has learned the danger of talking around her subject: She not only refuses to talk *around* it now, she refuses to talk *about* it. Thus the human use of language leads back to silence—where perhaps it should have remained in the first place.

Essay in Reason

Josephine Miles

Josephine Miles (1911–1985), teacher, scholar, and poet, was educated at the University of California at Los Angeles (B.A.) and at Berkeley (M.A., Ph.D.), where she taught in the English Department beginning in 1940. Among her books are several collections of poems, including Poems 1930–1960 *(1960),* Kinds of Affection *(1967),* To All Appearances: New and Selected Poems *(1974), and* Coming to Terms *(1979).* Poetry and Change: Donne, Milton, Wordsworth and the Equilibrium of the Present *(1974) won the Modern Language Association Lowell Award for literary scholarship.*

Throughout her teaching career, her interest in style, structure, and language was demonstrated not only in print but also in many talks to teachers' groups and in a commitment to the teaching of freshman English. The essay that follows first appeared in Educational Leadership *in February 1962; it was edited by the author for inclusion in this book. (A slightly different version of the essay has been included in Josephine Miles'* Working Out Ideas: Predication and Other Uses of Language, *published in 1979 under the auspices of the Bay Area Writing Project.)*

Prose essay like prose narrative or prose drama is an art of prose, and as an art it works in basic patterns. Rather than a sequence of events, it is a sequence of ideas, and it shapes up in certain ways, depending upon its main idea, its attempt or "essay." It makes a leading statement, that is, predicates its subject, and then unfolds, develops, substantiates both subject and predicate in the specific relation it has proposed for them.

Students in California have usually read widely and well in books of essays in ideas. The first week of the Fall term of 1961, 30 freshmen, my teaching assistant, and I talked about ideas we had met with during the past year. We were able to range from Thoreau to Jung and Freud, from Milton to Edith Hamilton, from Plato to Riesman. There were enough ideas for months of talking and writing.

Then I asked the students each to make a statement of one idea which particularly interested him, to suggest two or three different ways in which it might be developed into an essay. Blockade. Few associated the concept of an *idea* with the concept of a *statement* or a *sentence*. For many, ideas were at best abstract words or phrases; at worst, as one student suggested, "opinions or untrue facts." Inasmuch as a fact or topic assumes no responsibility for predication, no pattern of organization is obvious for it, and the student is at a loss to know what development may mean for it. Therefore the most typical response to the assignment is something like: "The importance of music: (a) development by examples,

(b) general development." Or "The necessity for world government: (a) subjective, (b) objective." Not many aids to reason here!

First need then is to talk about ideas as sentences, that is, predicating the subjects, saying something about something, establishing relations. The student hopefully proposes, "Music is important" or "World government is necessary," and then goes on: "First I'll write a paragraph saying what I mean by *music* or *world government.* Then I'll develop my point in the predicate about important or necessary." But can importance or necessity be shown without showing possible alternatives? "Sure," says the student triumphantly. "Here's where I switch from objective to subjective!"

After some time discussing these terms as well as *general* and *particular,* demonstrating the need for both pairs and for the clarity of their relations, we come back to develop the useful structural implications of a good leading sentence. Here is one of the few really organizable ones achieved in the first week. Please ignore the horrors of its wordiness. These problems are secondary to sheer understanding of the point, and will mostly clear up when the writer's thought clears up. And he is on the right track: "A prevalent disease, mental retardation has received a minimum of public attention and this neglect has hampered any progress toward alleviating the problems of the disease."

What is the main point here? "Well, that lack of public interest in the disease has hampered progress in understanding it." Cheers. The subject is *lack;* the predicate, *has hampered;* so what will the basic organization be? "Chronological—stages of hampering, development of the verb. But now I see I don't want that kind of organization. I want to talk about ways of studying retardation and how they need public support." So? So: "Most ways of studying and improving mental retardation depend on public understanding and support." Then you'll have to demonstrate the predicate *depend,* and talk about *how* and *why.* "That's what I want to talk about—three *hows* and one *why.*" Now we are beginning to work out the development of an idea.

Chronology, spatial description, sequences work mainly with additive connectives: *and-and-and; then-then-then; also; moreover*—"Here are the main stages in the study of retardation: such and such and such." Alternatives strive to separate, sometimes to compare: *either-or; on the one hand-on the other; not this, but that*—"Either we get public interest, or we give up." Conditional shows interdependent causal relations: *if-then; because-therefore*—"If public interest improves, our study of retardation will be aided in the following ways." This is the structure which, it turned out, our student intended to establish. Each of these procedures has its negatives. For example, *but* is a negative for *and; nor* for *or;* and concessional *though* for *if.*

The first help we can give the student writer then is to make him see whether the predication he has chosen to make, the verb he has chosen to apply to the subject, is really supportable by what he knows or can discover; and then, second, to see whether he has arranged the elements of support in the order and connection best for his purposes. A syllogism, the classic unit of reasoning, is in itself a small paragraph of substantiation. "I want to say something about Socrates, and what I want to say about him is that despite his great wisdom he is still mortal. Why is he mortal? Because all men are mortal, and Socrates is a man, as I can show in a paragraph of characteristics." Most of our thought concerns *some*, rather than the *all* referred to in this syllogism, but the pattern may be adapted to *some* by using recognition of negative as well as positive evidence: "Though two specific authorities deny it, public interest in retardation does help, and by public interest I mean not press-publicity, but active individual concern."

Reasoning means giving reasons: that is, it deals with the relations between statements, and these relations as we have said are of a few basic kinds: of cause or purpose—*if* this, therefore this, or this is so *because;* or of choice—this *or* this—both are impossible at once; or of association—this *and* this go along with this. Once a student recognizes that his own thought moves in these basic relations, he will be apt to enjoy both the art and the social force of the simple reasoning process of the paragraph. His planning or outlining will show first what main point or predication he is planning to make about his subject; then the main blocks of material he will use to support it, guided by such *pro* connections as *and, or, if* (and such *con* connections as *but, nor, though*); and finally a new main point, revised from the first hypothesis in the light of the evidence as it has developed. It is the predicate, not the subject, which is planned to be thus supported and modified. There is no such thing as too large or unwieldy a subject; what the student wants to say about the subject is what needs estimation. A student who tries to outline his material rather than his idea is trying, as one student has put it, to eat sardines without opening the can.

Man does not receive raw materials through the senses and then try to make meanings of them through the mind. Rather, the meanings that he makes, tentative and provisional as they may be at every stage, lead him to look for materials of experience which will test his meanings. So the writer does not need to stuff his mind with so-called "facts" before he can be responsible for a tentative statement; and so, on the other hand, for *any* statement he makes he can be held responsible. If we do not teach the student writer how to make responsible statements, we give in to the myths of "raw fact" or of individual autonomy, and make him the victim either of the outer world or of the inner. Thus we see the dangers on the one hand of the so-called "report" in composition-writing, which leads to an inert sort of copying, and on the other hand the dangers of journal writing or of so-called "creative" writing in which anything goes because there seems to be no valid outer check.

Why should we allow ourselves to be pulled between two extremes, when what we share is that very human power which philosophers have always spoken of, the power to agree on basic issues and to subordinate minor issues to major? For the Renaissance humanist, such reasonable powers served to mediate between man's sense and his spirit: so today it may mediate between man's psyche and his society. Robert Nisbet's *The Quest for Community* warns that so-called individual autonomy at one extreme and totalitarianism at the other tend to create a vacuum in between, where men actually live; and that men, to prevent this vacuum, need to strengthen the working categories of their own activities—their church, their club, their voting precinct, their job, to build a solid structure of human community between the forces of the personal and impersonal. So, I think, we need also to compose our thoughts: to learn to get from where we have been, to where we are, to where we want to go.

Simplicity

William Zinsser

William Zinsser has been a writer for most of his life. Born in New York in 1922, he graduated from Princeton in 1944 and served in the army for two years. He then joined the New York Herald Tribune, *where he stayed until 1959, first as a feature editor, then as drama editor and film critic, and finally as an editorial writer. For the next ten years, he worked as free-lance writer, published a number of books, and contributed to many magazines, including* Look *and* Life. *He was a member of the English faculty of Yale University, where he taught nonfiction writing and humor writing from 1971 until 1979, when he took a position as general editor of the Book-of-the-Month Club.*

Zinsser's course in writing nonfiction at Yale led to the book On Writing Well *(1976), from which the second chapter is reprinted here. In the first chapter, Zinsser says that there isn't any "right" way to write, but he adds that all good writing "has an aliveness that keeps the reader reading from one paragraph to the next, and it's not a question of gimmicks to 'personalize' the author. It's a question of using the English language in a way that will achieve the greatest strength and the least clutter." Such principles can be learned, he concludes, although perhaps they cannot be taught.*

The third edition of On Writing Well, *enlarged and revised, was published in 1987 and includes a section on working with a word processor, a topic covered also in* Writing with a Word Processor, *published in 1983.*

Clutter is the disease of American writing. We are a society strangling in unnecessary words, circular constructions, pompous frills and meaningless jargon.

Who really knows what the average businessman is trying to say in the average business letter? What member of an insurance or medical plan can decipher the brochure that tells him what his costs and benefits are? What father or mother can put together a child's toy—on Christmas Eve or any other eve—from the instructions on the box? Our national tendency is to inflate and thereby sound important. The airline pilot who wakes us to announce that he is presently anticipating experiencing considerable weather wouldn't dream of saying that there's a storm ahead and it may get bumpy. The sentence is too simple—there must be something wrong with it.

But the secret of good writing is to strip every sentence to its cleanest components. Every word that serves no function, every long word that could be a short word, every adverb that carries the same meaning that is already in the verb, every passive construction that leaves the reader unsure of who is doing what—these are the thousand and one adulterants that weaken the strength of a sentence. And they usually occur, ironically, in proportion to education and rank.

During the late 1960's the president of Princeton University wrote a letter to mollify the alumni after a spell of campus unrest. "You are probably aware," he began, "that we have been experiencing very considerable potentially explosive expressions of dissatisfaction on issues only partially related." He meant that the students had been hassling them about different things. As an alumnus I was far more upset by the president's syntax than by the students' potentially explosive expressions of dissatisfaction. I would have preferred the presidential approach taken by Franklin D. Roosevelt when he tried to convert into English his own government's memos, such as this blackout order of 1942:

> Such preparations shall be made as will completely obscure all Federal buildings and non-Federal buildings occupied by the Federal government during an air raid for any period of time from visibility by reason of internal or external illumination.

"Tell them," Roosevelt said, "that in buildings where they have to keep the work going to put something across the windows."

Simplify, simplify. Thoreau said it, as we are so often reminded, and no American writer more consistently practiced what he preached. Open *Walden* to any page and you will find a man saying in a plain and orderly way what is on his mind:

> I love to be alone. I never found the companion that was so companionable as solitude. We are for the most part more lonely when we go abroad among men than when we stay in our chambers. A man thinking or working is always alone, let him be where he will. Solitude is not measured by the miles of space that intervene between a man and his fellows. The really diligent student in one of the crowded hives of Cambridge College is as solitary as a dervish in the desert.

How can the rest of us achieve such enviable freedom from clutter? The answer is to clear our heads of clutter. Clear thinking becomes clear writing: one can't exist without the other. It is impossible for a muddy thinker to write good English. He may get away with it for a paragraph or two, but soon the reader will be lost, and there is no sin so grave, for he will not easily be lured back.

Who is this elusive creature, the reader? He is a person with an attention span of about twenty seconds. He is assailed on every side by forces competing for his time: by newspapers and magazines, by television and radio and stereo, by his wife and children and pets, by his house and his yard and all the gadgets that he has bought to keep them spruce, and by that most potent of competitors, sleep. The man snoozing in his chair with an unfinished magazine open on his lap is a man who was being given too much unnecessary trouble by the writer.

It won't do to say that the snoozing reader is too dumb or too lazy to keep pace with the train of thought. My sympathies are with him. If a reader is lost, it is generally because the writer has not been careful enough to keep him on the path.

This carelessness can take any number of forms. Perhaps a sentence is so excessively cluttered that the reader, hacking his way through the verbiage, simply doesn't know what it means. Perhaps a sentence has been so shoddily constructed that the reader could read it in any of several ways. Perhaps the writer has switched pronouns in mid-sentence, or has switched tenses, so the reader loses track of who is talking or when the action took place. Perhaps Sentence B is not a logical sequel to Sentence A—the writer, in whose head the connection is clear, has not bothered to provide the missing link. Perhaps the writer has used an important word incorrectly by not taking the trouble to look it up. He may think that "sanguine" and "sanguinary" mean the same thing, but the difference is a bloody big one. The reader can only infer (speaking of big differences) what the writer is trying to imply.

Faced with these obstacles, the reader is at first a remarkably tenacious bird. He blames himself—he obviously missed something, and he goes back over the mystifying sentence, or over the whole paragraph, piecing it out like an ancient rune, making guesses and moving on. But he won't do this for long. The writer is making him work too hard, and the reader will look for one who is better at his craft.

The writer must therefore constantly ask himself: What am I trying to say? Surprisingly often, he doesn't know. Then he must look at what he has written and ask: Have I said it? Is it clear to someone encountering the subject for the first time? If it's not, it is because some fuzz has worked its way into the machinery. The clear writer is a person clear-headed enough to see this stuff for what it is: fuzz.

I don't mean that some people are born clear-headed and are therefore natural writers, whereas others are naturally fuzzy and will never write well. Thinking clearly is a conscious act that the writer must force upon himself, just as if he were embarking on any other project that requires logic: adding up a laundry list or doing an algebra problem. Good writing doesn't come naturally, though most people obviously think it does. The professional writer is forever being bearded by strangers who say that they'd like to "try a little writing some time" when they retire from their real profession. Good writing takes self-discipline and, very often, self-knowledge.

Many writers, for instance, can't stand to throw anything away. Their sentences are littered with words that mean essentially the same thing and with phrases which make a point that is implicit in what they have already said. When students give me these littered sentences I beg them to select from the surfeit of words the few that most precisely fit what they want to say. Choose one, I plead, from among the three almost identical adjectives. Get rid of the unnecessary adverbs. Eliminate "in a funny sort of way" and other such qualifiers—they do no useful work.

The students look stricken—I am taking all their wonderful words away. I am only taking their superfluous words away, leaving what is organic and strong.

"But," one of my worst offenders confessed, "I never can get rid of anything—you should see my room." (I didn't take him up on the offer.) "I have two lamps where I only need one, but I can't decide which one I like better, so I keep them both." He went on to enumerate his duplicated or unnecessary objects, and over the weeks ahead I went on throwing away his duplicated and unnecessary words. By the end of the term—a term that he found acutely painful—his sentences were clean.

"I've had to change my whole approach to writing," he told me. "Now I have to *think* before I start every sentence and I have to *think* about every word." The very idea amazed him. Whether his room also looked better I never found out. I suspect that it did.

Thinking
About
Thinking

Almost all the selections in this book are records of men and women deliberately using their power to think and to feel in an effort to comprehend experience—either their own experience or that of other people and other times. The next two groups of essays—the present one on thinking, the one following on feeling—confront the fact that these two activities, unavoidably and characteristically human as they may be, seem in recent times to have taken on a particularly urgent and problematic character.

The importance of logical and reasonable thought has of course been recognized since the time of Plato and Aristotle; but never before have we been so aware of the complexity and difficulty of thinking critically, of using reliable evidence to come to clear and unprejudiced conclusions. To make matters worse, thinking has in the post-atomic age become no less than a matter of survival. As the biochemist Albert Szent-Gyorgyi once put it: "If it is our intelligence which led us into trouble, it may be our intelligence which can lead us out of it."

The first two essays in the section—Golding's lightly and wittily, Robinson's more fully and philosophically—take up the problem of distinguishing among the very different activities that go under the name of thinking. They focus on the differences between thinking and emotional prejudice or rationalization; and both give highest place to the creative kind of thinking that transforms our understanding.

Next follow two nineteenth-century scientists writing about some of the basic stages in the process of clear thinking. Samuel Scudder's "In the Laboratory with Agassiz" deals with close observation, the art of acquiring accurate information. Thomas Henry Huxley's essay is the clearest explanation we know of how observations are transformed by two key modes of thought—induction and deduction—into useful hypotheses. These two essays lead naturally to the basic point of Theodore Roszak's essay "Ideas Come First," that observations, facts, information, however important, do not in themselves constitute thinking: "The mind thinks with ideas, not with information."

Roszak's discussion of the mind's inventing or creating of the ideas or the patterns that make sense of experience brings us directly to the typically modern awareness of the subjectivity of thought. The following essay, by George Lakoff and Mark Johnson, carries us a brief but fascinating step further into that topic. A close study of our language habits suggests to them that the mental patterns we make, which are the concepts we live by, are fundamentally metaphorical. We often unconsciously structure one kind of experience in terms of another.

"The Loss of the Creature," by Walker Percy, examines these same ideas, but from a far different perspective. He asks us to consider that often the mental patterns we use to make sense of experience affect our perceptions of that experience adversely. The preconceptions and formulations imposed by our culture prepackage our experience, and thus separate us from it. The "loss of the creature" is the loss of direct experience. He urges us to re-examine and resist patterns that tell us in advance how to think and feel, suggesting that the lost, pristine "being" in experience could be re-possessed if we were willing to struggle for it.

The last two essays deal with very different kinds of subversion of thinking. Aldous Huxley shows how the expert propagandist uses the media and the mass meeting to strip people of their capacity for thinking and for moral choice. Stephen Jay Gould shows how even the professional thinker, the scientist, can subvert his own data and deceive himself in the service of a deep-seated prejudice.

Thinking as a Hobby

William Golding

William Golding, winner of the Nobel Prize for literature in 1983, was born in Cornwall in 1911 and was educated at Marlborough grammar school and at Oxford. During World War II he served in the Royal Navy, rising to the command of a rocket-launching ship. Since the war he has devoted himself to teaching and writing and to his hobbies, which he once described as "thinking, classical Greek, sailing, and archaeology." He is widely known for his strikingly original novels, of which the most famous is Lord of the Flies *(1954), an account of a group of schoolboys marooned on an island who revert to savagery. Other novels include* The Inheritors *(1955),* Pincher Martin *(1956),* The Spire, *(1964),* The Pyramid *(1967),* The Scorpion God *(1971),* Darkness Visible *(1979),* Rites of Passage *(1980),* The Paper Men *(1984), and* Close Quarters *(1987). He has also published two books of essays and a travel book,* An Egyptian Journal *(1985). The following essay first appeared in the August 1961 issue of* Holiday.

While I was still a boy, I came to the conclusion that there were three grades of thinking; and since I was later to claim thinking as my hobby, I came to an even stranger conclusion—namely, that I myself could not think at all.

I must have been an unsatisfactory child for grownups to deal with. I remember how incomprehensible they appeared to me at first, but not, of course, how I appeared to them. It was the headmaster of my grammar school° who first brought the subject of thinking before me—though neither in the way, nor with the result he intended. He had some statuettes in his study. They stood on a high cupboard behind his desk. One was a lady wearing nothing but a bath towel. She seemed frozen in an eternal panic lest the bath towel slip down any farther; and since she had no arms, she was in an unfortunate position to pull the towel up again. Next to her, crouched the statuette of a leopard, ready to spring down at the top drawer of a filing cabinet labeled A–AH. My innocence interpreted this as the victim's last, despairing cry. Beyond the leopard was a naked, muscular gentleman, who sat, looking down, with his chin on his fist and his elbow on his knee. He seemed utterly miserable.

Some time later, I learned about these statuettes. The headmaster had placed them where they would face delinquent children, because they symbolized to him the whole of life. The naked lady was the Venus of Milo. She was Love. She was not worried about the towel. She was just busy

---

grammar school   In Great Britain, the academic secondary school for those preparing for the university or the professions; students enter at about age eleven.

being beautiful. The leopard was Nature, and he was being natural. The naked, muscular gentleman was not miserable. He was Rodin's Thinker, an image of pure thought. It is easy to buy small plaster models of what you think life is like.

I had better explain that I was a frequent visitor to the headmaster's study, because of the latest thing I had done or left undone. As we now say, I was not integrated. I was, if anything, disintegrated; and I was puzzled. Grownups never made sense. Whenever I found myself in a penal position before the headmaster's desk, with the statuettes glimmering whitely above him, I would sink my head, clasp my hands behind my back and writhe one shoe over the other.

The headmaster would look opaquely at me through flashing spectacles.

"What are we going to do with you?"

Well, what *were* they going to do with me? I would writhe my shoe some more and stare down at the worn rug.

"Look up, boy! Can't you look up?"

Then I would look up at the cupboard, where the naked lady was frozen in her panic and the muscular gentleman contemplated the hindquarters of the leopard in endless gloom. I had nothing to say to the headmaster. His spectacles caught the light so that you could see nothing human behind them. There was no possibility of communication.

"Don't you ever think at all?"

No, I didn't think, wasn't thinking, couldn't think—I was simply waiting in anguish for the interview to stop.

"Then you'd better learn—hadn't you?"

On one occasion the headmaster leaped to his feet, reached up and plonked Rodin's masterpiece on the desk before me.

"That's what a man looks like when he's really thinking."

I surveyed the gentleman without interest or comprehension.

"Go back to your class."

Clearly there was something missing in me. Nature had endowed the rest of the human race with a sixth sense and left me out. This must be so, I mused, on my way back to the class, since whether I had broken a window, or failed to remember Boyle's Law, or been late for school, my teachers produced me one, adult answer: "Why can't you think?"

As I saw the case, I had broken the window because I had tried to hit Jack Arney with a cricket ball and missed him; I could not remember Boyle's Law because I had never bothered to learn it; and I was late for school because I preferred looking over the bridge into the river. In fact, I was wicked. Were my teachers, perhaps, so good that they could not understand the depths of my depravity? Were they clear, untormented people who could direct their every action by this mysterious business of thinking? The whole thing was incomprehensible. In my earlier years, I found even the statuette of the Thinker confusing. I did not believe any of my teachers were naked, ever. Like someone born deaf, but bitterly determined to find out about sound, I watched my teachers to find out about thought.

There was Mr. Houghton. He was always telling me to think. With a modest satisfaction, he would tell me that he had thought a bit himself. Then why did he spend so much time drinking? Or was there more sense in drinking than there appeared to be? But if not, and if drinking were in fact ruinous to health—and Mr. Houghton was ruined, there was no doubt about that—why was he always talking about the clean life and the virtues of fresh air? He would spread his arms wide with the action of a man who habitually spent his time striding along mountain ridges.

"Open air does me good, boys—I know it!"

Sometimes, exalted by his own oratory, he would leap from his desk and hustle us outside into a hideous wind.

"Now boys! Deep breaths! Feel it right down inside you—huge draughts of God's good air!"

He would stand before us, rejoicing in his perfect health, an open-air man. He would put his hands on his waist and take a tremendous breath. You could hear the wind, trapped in the cavern of his chest and struggling with all the unnatural impediments. His body would reel with shock and his ruined face go white at the unaccustomed visitation. He would stagger back to his desk and collapse there, useless for the rest of the morning.

Mr. Houghton was given to high-minded monologues about the good life, sexless and full of duty. Yet in the middle of one of these monologues, if a girl passed the window, tapping along on her neat little feet, he would interrupt his discourse, his neck would turn of itself and he would watch her out of sight. In this instance, he seemed to me ruled not by thought but by an invisible and irresistible spring in his nape.

His neck was an object of great interest to me. Normally it bulged a bit over his collar. But Mr. Houghton had fought in the First World War alongside both Americans and French, and had come—by who knows what illogic?—to a settled detestation of both countries. If either country happened to be prominent in current affairs, no argument could make Mr. Houghton think well of it. He would bang the desk, his neck would bulge still further and go red. "You can say what you like," he would cry, "but I've thought about this—and I know what I think!"

Mr. Houghton thought with his neck.

There was Miss Parsons. She assured us that her dearest wish was our welfare, but I knew even then, with the mysterious clairvoyance of childhood, that what she wanted most was the husband she never got. There was Mr. Hands—and so on.

I have dealt at length with my teachers because this was my introduction to the nature of what is commonly called thought. Through them I discovered that thought is often full of unconscious prejudice, ignorance and hypocrisy. It will lecture on disinterested purity while its neck is being remorselessly twisted toward a skirt. Technically, it is about as proficient as most businessmen's golf, as honest as most politicians' intentions, or—to come near my own preoccupation—as coherent as most books that get written. It is what I came to call grade-three thinking, though more properly, it is feeling, rather than thought.

True, often there is a kind of innocence in prejudices, but in those days I viewed grade-three thinking with an intolerant contempt and an incautious mockery. I delighted to confront a pious lady who hated the Germans with the proposition that we should love our enemies. She taught me a great truth in dealing with grade-three thinkers; because of her, I no longer dismiss lightly a mental process which for nine-tenths of the population is the nearest they will ever get to thought. They have immense solidarity. We had better respect them, for we are outnumbered and surrounded. A crowd of grade-three thinkers, all shouting the same thing, all warming their hands at the fire of their own prejudices, will not thank you for pointing out the contradictions in their beliefs. Man is a gregarious animal, and enjoys agreement as cows will graze all the same way on the side of a hill.

Grade-two thinking is the detection of contradictions. I reached grade two when I trapped the poor, pious lady. Grade-two thinkers do not stampede easily, though often they fall into the other fault and lag behind. Grade-two thinking is a withdrawal, with eyes and ears open. It became my hobby and brought satisfaction and loneliness in either hand. For grade-two thinking destroys without having the power to create. It set me watching the crowds cheering His Majesty the King and asking myself what all the fuss was about, without giving me anything positive to put in the place of that heady patriotism. But there were compensations. To hear people justify their habit of hunting foxes and tearing them to pieces by claiming that the foxes liked it. To hear our Prime Minister talk about the great benefit we conferred on India by jailing people like Pandit Nehru° and Gandhi. To hear American politicians talk about peace in one sentence and refuse to join the League of Nations in the next. Yes, there were moments of delight.

But I was growing toward adolescence and had to admit that Mr. Houghton was not the only one with an irresistible spring in his neck. I, too, felt the compulsive hand of nature and began to find that pointing out contradiction could be costly as well as fun. There was Ruth, for example, a serious and attractive girl. I was an atheist at the time. Grade-two

---

Pandit Nehru   Motilal (Pandit) Nehru (1861–1931) was a leader of the Indian independence movement and father of India's first prime minister, Jawaharlal Nehru. He was imprisoned by the British in 1921 and again in 1930.

thinking is a menace to religion and knocks down sects like skittles. I put myself in a position to be converted by her with an hypocrisy worthy of grade three. She was a Methodist—or at least, her parents were, and Ruth had to follow suit. But, alas, instead of relying on the Holy Spirit to convert me, Ruth was foolish enough to open her pretty mouth in argument. She claimed that the Bible (King James Version) was literally inspired. I countered by saying that the Catholics believed in the literal inspiration of Saint Jerome's *Vulgate,* and the two books were different. Argument flagged.

At last she remarked that there were an awful lot of Methodists, and they couldn't be wrong, could they—not all those millions? That was too easy, said I restively (for the nearer you were to Ruth, the nicer she was to be near to) since there were more Roman Catholics than Methodists anyway; and they couldn't be wrong, could they—not all those hundreds of millions? An awful flicker of doubt appeared in her eyes. I slid my arm round her waist and murmured breathlessly that if we were counting heads, the Buddhists were the boys for my money. But Ruth had *really* wanted to do me good, because I was so nice. She fled. The combination of my arm and those countless Buddhists was too much for her.

That night her father visited my father and left, red-cheeked and indignant. I was given the third degree to find out what had happened. It was lucky we were both of us only fourteen. I lost Ruth and gained an undeserved reputation as a potential libertine.

So grade-two thinking could be dangerous. It was in this knowledge, at the age of fifteen, that I remember making a comment from the heights of grade two, on the limitations of grade three. One evening I found myself alone in the schoolhall, preparing it for a party. The door of the headmaster's study was open. I went in. The headmaster had ceased to thump Rodin's Thinker down on the desk as an example to the young. Perhaps he had not found any more candidates, but the statuettes were still there, glimmering and gathering dust on top of the cupboard. I stood on a chair and rearranged them. I stood Venus in her bath towel on the filing cabinet, so that now the top drawer caught its breath in a gasp of sexy excitement. "A-ah!" The portentous Thinker I placed on the edge of the cupboard so that he looked down at the bath towel and waited for it to slip.

Grade-two thinking, though it filled life with fun and excitement, did not make for content. To find out the deficiencies of our elders bolsters the young ego but does not make for personal security. I found that grade two was not only the power to point out contradictions. It took the swimmer some distance from the shore and left him there, out of his depth. I decided that Pontius Pilate was a typical grade-two thinker. "What is truth?" he said, a very common grade-two thought, but one that is used always as the end of an argument instead of the beginning. There is a still higher grade of thought which says, "What is truth?" and sets out to find it.

But these grade-one thinkers were few and far between. They did not visit my grammar school in the flesh though they were there in books. I aspired to them, partly because I was ambitious and partly because I now saw my hobby as an unsatisfactory thing if it went no further. If you set out to climb a mountain, however high you climb, you have failed if you cannot reach the top.

I *did* meet an undeniably grade-one thinker in my first year at Oxford. I was looking over a small bridge in Magdalen Deer Park, and a tiny mustached and hatted figure came and stood by my side. He was a German who had just fled from the Nazis to Oxford as a temporary refuge. His name was Einstein.

But Professor Einstein knew no English at that time and I knew only two words of German. I beamed at him, trying wordlessly to convey by my bearing all the affection and respect that the English felt for him. It is possible—and I have to make the admission—that I felt here were two grade-one thinkers standing side by side; yet I doubt if my face conveyed more than a formless awe. I would have given my Greek and Latin and French and a good slice of my English for enough German to communicate. But we were divided; he was as inscrutable as my headmaster. For perhaps five minutes we stood together on the bridge, undeniable grade-one thinker and breathless aspirant. With true greatness, Professor Einstein realized that any contact was better than none. He pointed to a trout wavering in midstream.

He spoke: *"Fisch."*

My brain reeled. Here I was, mingling with the great, and yet helpless as the veriest grade-three thinker. Desperately I sought for some sign by which I might convey that I, too, revered pure reason. I nodded vehemently. In a brilliant flash I used up half of my German vocabulary. *"Fisch. Ja. Ja."*

For perhaps another five minutes we stood side by side. Then Professor Einstein, his whole figure still conveying good will and amiability, drifted away out of sight.

I, too, would be a grade-one thinker. I was irreverent at the best of times. Political and religious systems, social customs, loyalties and traditions, they all came tumbling down like so many rotten apples off a tree. This was a fine hobby and a sensible substitute for cricket, since you could play it all the year round. I came up in the end with what must always remain the justification for grade-one thinking, its sign, seal and charter. I devised a coherent system for living. It was a moral system, which was wholly logical. Of course, as I readily admitted, conversion of the world to my way of thinking might be difficult, since my system did away with a number of trifles, such as big business, centralized government, armies, marriage. . . .

It was Ruth all over again. I had some very good friends who stood by me, and still do. But my acquaintances vanished, taking the girls with them. Young women seemed oddly contented with the world as it was. They valued the meaningless ceremony with a ring. Young men, while willing to concede the chaining sordidness of marriage, were hesitant about abandoning the organizations which they hoped would give them a career. A young man on the first rung of the Royal Navy, while perfectly agreeable to doing away with big business and marriage, got as red-necked as Mr. Houghton when I proposed a world without any battleships in it.

Had the game gone too far? Was it a game any longer? In those prewar days, I stood to lose a great deal, for the sake of a hobby.

Now you are expecting me to describe how I saw the folly of my ways and came back to the warm nest, where prejudices are so often called loyalties, where pointless actions are hallowed into custom by repetition, where we are content to say we think when all we do is feel.

But you would be wrong. I dropped my hobby and turned professional.

If I were to go back to the headmaster's study and find the dusty statuettes still there, I would arrange them differently. I would dust Venus and put her aside, for I have come to love her and know her for the fair thing she is. But I would put the Thinker, sunk in his desperate thought, where there were shadows before him—and at his back, I would put the leopard, crouched and ready to spring.

On Various Kinds of Thinking

James Harvey Robinson

James Harvey Robinson (1863–1936), an American historian, taught at the University of Pennsylvania and at Columbia. He resigned from Columbia in 1919 in protest against the expulsion of a group of professors for their opposition to World War I, at which time he attacked Columbia president Nicholas Murray Butler for his alleged attempts to suppress freedom of expression at the university. Robinson then helped to found the New School for Social Research in New York City and taught there until 1921, when he retired to devote the rest of his life to writing. Among his dozen volumes of historical and philosophical writing, perhaps the best known to the general public is The Mind in the Making *(1921), subtitled* The Relation of Intelligence to Social Reform. *Chapter 2 of this book has been often excerpted and reprinted, but familiarity has not reduced its value. We reprint the chapter here in full, using the heading of its first section as title for the whole.*

ᴊood sense is, of all things among men, the most equally distributed; for everyone thinks himself so abundantly provided with it that those even who are the most difficult to satisfy in everything else do not usually desire a larger measure of this quality than they already possess.

—DESCARTES

We see man to-day, instead of the frank and courageous recognition of his status, the docile attention to his biological history, the determination to let nothing stand in the way of the security and permanence of his future, which alone can establish the safety and happiness of the race, substituting blind confidence in his destiny, unclouded faith in the essentially respectful attitude of the universe toward his moral code, and a belief no less firm that his traditions and laws and institutions necessarily contain permanent qualities of reality.

—WILFRED TROTTER

1. On Various Kinds of Thinking

The truest and most profound observations on Intelligence have in the past been made by the poets and, in recent times, by story-writers. They have been keen observers and recorders and reckoned freely with the emotions and sentiments. Most philosophers, on the other hand, have exhibited a grotesque ignorance of man's life and have built up systems that are elaborate and imposing, but quite unrelated to actual human affairs. They have almost consistently neglected the actual process of thought and have set the mind off as something apart to be studied by itself. *But no such mind, exempt from bodily processes, animal impulses, savage traditions, infantile impressions, conventional reactions, and traditional knowledge, ever existed,* even in the case of the most abstract of metaphysicians. Kant entitled his great work *A Critique of Pure Reason.* But to the modern student of mind pure reason seems as mythical as the pure gold, transparent as glass, with which the celestial city is paved.

Formerly philosophers thought of mind as having to do exclusively with conscious thought. It was that within man which perceived, remembered, judged, reasoned, understood, believed, willed. But of late it has been shown that we are unaware of a great part of what we perceive, remember, will, and infer; and that a great part of the thinking of which we are aware is determined by that of which we are not conscious. It has indeed been demonstrated that our unconscious psychic life far outruns our conscious. This seems perfectly natural to anyone who considers the following facts:

The sharp distinction between the mind and the body is, as we shall find, a very ancient and spontaneous uncritical savage prepossession. What we think of as "mind" is so intimately associated with what we call "body" that we are coming to realize that the one cannot be understood

Mind & body

without the other. Every thought reverberates through the body, and, on the other hand, alterations in our physical condition affect our whole attitude of mind. The insufficient elimination of the foul and decaying products of digestion may plunge us into deep melancholy, whereas a few whiffs of nitrous monoxide may exalt us to the seventh heaven of supernal knowledge and godlike complacency. And *vice versa,* a sudden word or thought may cause our heart to jump, check our breathing, or make our knees as water. There is a whole new literature growing up which studies the effects of our bodily secretions and our muscular tensions and their relation to our emotions and our thinking.

Then there are hidden impulses and desires and secret longings of which we can only with the greatest difficulty take account. They influence our conscious thought in the most bewildering fashion. Many of these unconscious influences appear to originate in our very early years. The older philosophers seem to have forgotten that even they were infants and children at their most impressionable age and never could by any possibility get over it.

The term "unconscious," now so familiar to all readers of modern works on psychology, gives offense to some adherents of the past. There should, however, be no special mystery about it. It is not a new animistic abstraction, but simply a collective word to include all the physiological changes which escape our notice, all the forgotten experiences and impressions of the past which continue to influence our desires and reflections and conduct, even if we cannot remember them. What we can remember at any time is indeed an infinitesimal part of what has happened to us. We could not remember anything unless we forgot almost everything. As Bergson says, the brain is the organ of forgetfulness as well as of memory. Moreover, we tend, of course, to become oblivious to things to which we are thoroughly accustomed, for habit blinds us to their existence. So the Habit forgotten and the habitual make up a great part of the so-called "unconscious."

If we are ever to understand man, his conduct and reasoning, and if we aspire to learn to guide his life and his relations with his fellows more happily than heretofore, we cannot neglect the great discoveries briefly noted above. We must reconcile ourselves to novel and revolutionary conceptions of the mind, for it is clear that the older philosophers, whose works still determine our current views, had a very superficial notion of the subject with which they dealt. But for our purposes, with due regard to what has just been said and to much that has necessarily been left unsaid (and with the indulgence of those who will at first be inclined to dissent), *we shall consider mind chiefly as conscious knowledge and intelligence, as what we know and our attitude toward it—our disposition to increase our information, classify it, and apply it.*

We do not think enough about thinking, and much of our confusion is the result of current illusions in regard to it. Let us forget for the moment

any impressions we may have derived from the philosophers, and see
what seems to happen in ourselves. The first thing that we notice is that
our thought moves with such incredible rapidity that it is almost impossible to arrest any specimen of it long enough to have a look at it. When
we are offered a penny for our thoughts we always find that we have
recently had so many things in mind that we can easily make a selection
which will not compromise us too nakedly. On inspection we shall find
that even if we are not downright ashamed of a great part of our spontaneous thinking, it is far too intimate, personal, ignoble or trivial to permit
us to reveal more than a small part of it. I believe this must be true of
everyone. We do not, of course, know what goes on in other people's heads.
They tell us very little and we tell them very little. The spigot of speech,
rarely fully opened, could never emit more than driblets of the ever
renewed hogshead of thought—*noch grösser wie's Heidelberger Fass.*° We
find it hard to believe that other people's thoughts are as silly as our own,
but they probably are.

We all appear to ourselves to be thinking all the time during our waking
hours, and most of us are aware that we go on thinking while we are
asleep, even more foolishly than when awake. When uninterrupted by
some practical issue we are engaged in what is now known as a *reverie.*
This is our spontaneous and favorite kind of thinking. We allow our ideas
to take their own course and this course is determined by our hopes and
fears, our spontaneous desires, their fulfillment or frustration; by our
likes and dislikes, our loves and hates and resentments. There is nothing
else anything like so interesting to ourselves as ourselves. All thought
that is not more or less laboriously controlled and directed will inevitably
circle about the beloved Ego. It is amusing and pathetic to observe this
tendency in ourselves and in others. We learn politely and generously to
overlook this truth, but if we dare to think of it, it blazes forth like the
noontide sun.

The reverie or "free association of ideas" has of late become the subject
of scientific research. While investigators are not yet agreed on the results, or at least on the proper interpretation to be given to them, there
can be no doubt that our reveries form the chief index to our fundamental
character. They are a reflection of our nature as modified by often hidden
and forgotten experiences. We need not go into the matter further here,
for it is only necessary to observe that the reverie is at all times a potent
and in many cases an omnipotent rival to every other kind of thinking.
It doubtless influences all our speculations in its persistent tendency to
self-magnification and self-justification, which are its chief preoccupations, but it is the last thing to make directly or indirectly for honest

---

noch . . . Fass "even bigger than the Heidelberg barrel," a barrel famous for its size,
located in the cellar of the castle at Heidelberg, Germany.

increase of knowledge.[1] Philosophers usually talk as if such thinking did not exist or were in some way negligible. This is what makes their speculations so unreal and often worthless.

The reverie, as any of us can see for himself, is frequently broken and interrupted by the necessity of a second kind of thinking. We have to make practical decisions. Shall we write a letter or no? Shall we take the subway or a bus? Shall we have dinner at seven or half past? Shall we buy U.S. Rubber or a Liberty Bond? Decisions are easily distinguishable from the free flow of the reverie. Sometimes they demand a good deal of careful pondering and the recollection of pertinent facts; often, however, they are made impulsively. They are a more difficult and laborious thing than the reverie, and we resent having to "make up our mind" when we are tired, or absorbed in a congenial reverie. Weighing a decision, it should be noted, does not necessarily add anything to our knowledge, although we may, of course, seek further information before making it.

Rationalizing

A third kind of thinking is stimulated when anyone questions our belief and opinions. We sometimes find ourselves changing our minds without any resistance or heavy emotion, but if we are told that we are wrong we resent the imputation and harden our hearts. We are incredibly heedless in the formation of our beliefs, but find ourselves filled with an illicit passion for them when anyone proposes to rob us of their companionship. It is obviously not the ideas themselves that are dear to us, but our self-esteem, which is threatened. We are by nature stubbornly pledged to defend our own from attack, whether it be our person, our family, our property, or our opinion. A United States Senator once remarked to a friend of mine that God Almighty could not make him change his mind on our Latin-America policy. We may surrender, but rarely confess ourselves vanquished. In the intellectual world at least peace is without victory.

Few of us take the pains to study the origin of our cherished convictions; indeed, we have a natural repugnance to so doing. We like to continue to

---

[1]The poet-clergyman, John Donne, who lived in the time of James I, has given a beautifully honest picture of the doings of a saint's mind: "I throw myself down in my chamber and call in and invite God and His angels thither, and when they are there I neglect God and His angels for the noise of a fly, for the rattling of a coach, for the whining of a door. I talk on in the same posture of praying, eyes lifted up, knees bowed down, as though I prayed to God, and if God or His angels should ask me when I thought last of God in that prayer I cannot tell. Sometimes I find that I had forgot what I was about, but when I began to forget it I cannot tell. A memory of yesterday's pleasures, a fear of to-morrow's dangers, a straw under my knee, a noise in mine ear, a light in mine eye, an anything, a nothing, a fancy, a chimera in my brain troubles me in my prayer."—Quoted by Robert Lynd, *The Art of Letters,* pp. 46–47.

believe what we have been accustomed to accept as true, and the resentment aroused when doubt is cast upon any of our assumptions leads us
to seek every manner of excuse for clinging to them. *The result is that
most of our so-called reasoning consists in finding arguments for going on
believing as we already do.*

I remember years ago attending a public dinner to which the Governor
of the state was bidden. The chairman explained that His Excellency
could not be present for certain "good" reasons; what the "real" reasons
were the presiding officer said he would leave us to conjecture. This distinction between "good" and "real" reasons is one of the most clarifying
and essential in the whole realm of thought. We can readily give what
seem to us "good" reasons for being a Catholic or a Mason, a Republican
or a Democrat, an adherent or opponent of the League of Nations. But the
"real" reasons are usually on quite a different plane. Of course the importance of this distinction is popularly, if somewhat obscurely, recognized.
The Baptist missionary is ready enough to see that the Buddhist is not
such because his doctrines would bear careful inspection, but because he
happened to be born in a Buddhist family in Tokio. But it would be treason
to his faith to acknowledge that his own partiality for certain doctrines
is due to the fact that his mother was a member of the First Baptist church
of Oak Ridge. A savage can give all sorts of reasons for his belief that it
is dangerous to step on a man's shadow, and a newspaper editor can
advance plenty of arguments against the Bolsheviki. But neither of them
may realize why he happens to be defending his particular opinion.

The "real" reasons for our beliefs are concealed from ourselves as well
as from others. As we grow up we simply adopt the ideas presented to us
in regard to such matters as religion, family relations, property, business,
our country, and the state. We unconsciously absorb them from our environment. They are persistently whispered in our ear by the group in
which we happen to live. Moreover, as Mr. Trotter has pointed out, these
judgments, being the product of suggestion and not of reasoning, have the
quality of perfect obviousness, so that to question them

> . . . is to the believer to carry skepticism to an insane degree, and will be met
> by contempt, disapproval, or condemnation, according to the nature of the
> belief in question. When, therefore, we find ourselves entertaining an opinion
> about the basis of which there is a quality of feeling which tells us that to
> inquire into it would be absurd, obviously unnecessary, unprofitable, undesir-
> able, bad form, or wicked, we may know that that opinion is a nonrational one,
> and probably, therefore, founded upon inadequate evidence.[2]

Opinions, on the other hand, which are the result of experience or of
honest reasoning do not have this quality of "primary certitude." I remember when as a youth I heard a group of business men discussing the

---

[2]*Instincts of the Herd* [New York: Macmillan, 1916], p. 44.

question of the immortality of the soul, I was outraged by the sentiment of doubt expressed by one of the party. As I look back now I see that I had at the time no interest in the matter, and certainly no least argument to urge in favor of the belief in which I had been reared. But neither my personal indifference to the issue, nor the fact that I had previously given it no attention, served to prevent an angry resentment when I heard *my* ideas questioned.

This spontaneous and loyal support of our preconceptions—this process of finding "good" reasons to justify our routine beliefs—is known to modern psychologists as "rationalizing"—clearly only a new name for a very ancient thing. Our "good" reasons ordinarily have no value in promoting honest enlightenment, because, no matter how solemnly they may be marshaled, they are at bottom the result of personal preference or prejudice, and not of an honest desire to seek or accept new knowledge.

In our reveries we are frequently engaged in self-justification, for we cannot bear to think ourselves wrong, and yet have constant illustrations of our weaknesses and mistakes. So we spend much time finding fault with circumstances and the conduct of others, and shifting on to them with great ingenuity the onus of our own failures and disappointments. *Rationalizing is the self-exculpation which occurs when we feel ourselves, or our group, accused of misapprehension or error.*

The little word *my* is the most important one in all human affairs, and properly to reckon with it is the beginning of wisdom. It has the same force whether it is *my* dinner, *my* dog, and *my* house, or *my* faith, *my* country, and *my* God. We not only resent the imputation that our watch is wrong, or our car shabby, but that our conception of the canals of Mars, of the pronunciation of "Epictetus," of the medicinal value of salicine, or the date of Sargon I, are subject to revision.

Philosophers, scholars, and men of science exhibit a common sensitiveness in all decisions in which their *amour propre*° is involved. Thousands of argumentative works have been written to vent a grudge. However stately their reasoning, it may be nothing but rationalizing, stimulated by the most commonplace of all motives. A history of philosophy and theology could be written in terms of grouches, wounded pride, and aversions, and it would be far more instructive than the usual treatments of these themes. Sometimes, under Providence, the lowly impulse of resentment leads to great achievements. Milton wrote his treatise on divorce as a result of his troubles with his seventeen-year-old wife, and when he was accused of being the leading spirit in a new sect, the Divorcers, he wrote his noble *Areopagitica* to prove his right to say what he thought fit, and incidentally to establish the advantage of a free press in the promotion of Truth.

---

amour propre   self-respect (French).

All mankind, high and low, thinks in all the ways which have been described. The reverie goes on all the time not only in the mind of the mill hand and the Broadway flapper, but equally in weighty judges and godly bishops. It has gone on in all the philosophers, scientists, poets, and theologians that have ever lived. Aristotle's most abstruse speculations were doubtless tempered by highly irrelevant reflections. He is reported to have had very thin legs and small eyes, for which he doubtless had to find excuses, and he was wont to indulge in very conspicuous dress and rings and was accustomed to arrange his hair carefully.[3] Diogenes the Cynic[o] exhibited the impudence of a touchy soul. His tub was his distinction. Tennyson in beginning his "Maud" could not forget his chagrin over losing his patrimony years before as the result of an unhappy investment in the Patent Decorative Carving Company. These facts are not recalled here as a gratuitous disparagement of the truly great, but to insure a full realization of the tremendous competition which all really exacting thought has to face, even in the minds of the most highly endowed mortals.

And now the astonishing and perturbing suspicion emerges that perhaps almost all that had passed for social science, political economy, politics, and ethics in the past may be brushed aside by future generations as mainly rationalizing. John Dewey has already reached this conclusion in regard to philosophy.[4] Veblen[5] [o] and other writers have revealed the various unperceived presuppositions of the traditional political economy, and now comes an Italian sociologist, Vilfredo Pareto, who, in his huge treatise on general sociology, devotes hundreds of pages to substantiating a similar thesis affecting all the social sciences.[6] This conclusion may be ranked by students of a hundred years hence as one of the several great discoveries of our age. It is by no means fully worked out, and it is so opposed to nature that it will be very slowly accepted by the great mass of those who consider themselves thoughtful. As a historical student I am personally fully reconciled to this newer view. Indeed, it seems to me inevitable that just as the various sciences of nature were, before the opening of the seventeenth century, largely masses of rationalizations to

---

[3]Diogenes Laertius, book v.

[4]*Reconstruction in Philosophy.*

[5]*The Place of Science in Modern Civilization.*

[6]*Traité de Sociologie Générale, passim.* The author's term *"dérivations"* seems to be his precise way of expressing what we have called the "good" reasons, and his *"résidus"* correspond to the "real" reasons. He well says, *"L'homme éprouve le besoin de raisonner, et en outre d'étendre un voile sur ses instincts et sur ses sentiments"*—hence, rationalization. (P. 788.) His aim is to reduce sociology to the "real" reasons. (P. 791.)

Diogenes the Cynic   Greek philosopher (fourth century B.C.) who is known for his search to find an honest man. He lived in a tub to show his freedom from material needs.
Veblen   Thorstein Veblen (1857–1929), American economist and social critic.

a charge to social sci

suit the religious sentiments of the period, so the social sciences have continued even to our own day to be rationalizations of uncritically accepted beliefs and customs.

It will become apparent as we proceed that the fact that an idea is ancient and that it has been widely received is no argument in its favor, but should immediately suggest the necessity of carefully testing it as a probable instance of rationalization.

3. How Creative Thought Transforms the World

This brings us to another kind of thought which can fairly easily be distinguished from the three kinds described above. It has not the usual qualities of the reverie, for it does not hover about our personal complacencies and humiliations. It is not made up of the homely decisions forced upon us by everyday needs, when we review our little stock of existing information, consult our conventional preferences and obligations, and make a choice of action. It is not the defense of our own cherished beliefs and prejudices just because they are our own—mere plausible excuses for remaining of the same mind. On the contrary, it is that peculiar species of thought which leads us to *change* our mind.

It is this kind of thought that has raised man from his pristine, subsavage ignorance and squalor to the degree of knowledge and comfort which he now possesses. On his capacity to continue and greatly extend this kind of thinking depends his chance of groping his way out of the plight in which the most highly civilized peoples of the world now find themselves. In the past this type of thinking has been called Reason. But so many misapprehensions have grown up around the word that some of us have become very suspicious of it. I suggest, therefore, that we substitute a recent name and speak of "creative thought" rather than of Reason. *For this kind of meditation begets knowledge, and knowledge is really creative in as much as it makes things look different from what they seemed before and may indeed work for their reconstruction.*

In certain moods some of us realize that we are observing things or making reflections with a seeming disregard of our personal preoccupations. We are not preening or defending ourselves; we are not faced by the necessity of any practical decision, nor are we apologizing for believing this or that. We are just wondering and looking and mayhap seeing what we never perceived before.

Curiosity is as clear and definite as any of our urges. We wonder what is in a sealed telegram or in a letter in which some one else is absorbed, or what is being said in the telephone booth or in low conversation. This inquisitiveness is vastly stimulated by jealousy, suspicion, or any hint that we ourselves are directly or indirectly involved. But there appears to be a fair amount of personal interest in other people's affairs even when they do not concern us except as a mystery to be unraveled or a tale to be told. The reports of a divorce suit will have "news value" for many weeks. They constitute a story, like a novel or play or moving picture. This is not an example of pure curiosity, however, since we readily identify ourselves with others, and their joys and despair then become our own.

We also take note of, or "observe," as Sherlock Holmes says, things which have nothing to do with our personal interests and make no personal appeal either direct or by way of sympathy. This is what Veblen so well calls "idle curiosity." And it is usually idle enough. Some of us when we face the line of people opposite us in a subway train impulsively consider them in detail and engage in rapid inferences and form theories in regard to them. On entering a room there are those who will perceive at a glance the degree of preciousness of the rugs, the character of the pictures, and the personality revealed by the books. But there are many, it would seem, who are so absorbed in their personal reverie or in some definite purpose that they have no bright-eyed energy for idle curiosity. The tendency to miscellaneous observation we come by honestly enough, for we note it in many of our animal relatives.

Veblen, however, uses the term "idle curiosity" somewhat ironically, as is his wont. It is idle only to those who fail to realize that it may be a very rare and indispensable thing from which almost all distinguished human achievement proceeds, since it may lead to systematic examination and seeking for things hitherto undiscovered. For research is but diligent search which enjoys the high flavor of primitive hunting. Occasionally and fitfully idle curiosity thus leads to creative thought, which alters and broadens our own views and aspirations and may in turn, under highly favorable circumstances, affect the views and lives of others, even for generations to follow. An example or two will make this unique human process clear.

Galileo was a thoughtful youth and doubtless carried on a rich and varied reverie. He had artistic ability and might have turned out to be a musician or painter. When he had dwelt among the monks at Valambrosa he had been tempted to lead the life of a religious. As a boy he busied himself with toy machines and he inherited a fondness for mathematics. All these facts are of record. We may safely assume also that, along with many other subjects of contemplation, the Pisan maidens found a vivid place in his thoughts.

One day when seventeen years old he wandered into the cathedral of his native town. In the midst of his reverie he looked up at the lamps hanging by long chains from the high ceiling of the church. Then something very difficult to explain occurred. He found himself no longer thinking of the building, worshipers, or the services; of his artistic or religious interests; of his reluctance to become a physician as his father wished. He forgot the question of a career and even the *graziosissime donne.*° As he

---

graziosissime donne   most gracious ladies (Italian).

watched the swinging lamps he was suddenly wondering if mayhap their oscillations, whether long or short, did not occupy the same time. Then he tested his hypothesis by counting his pulse, for that was the only timepiece he had with him.

This observation, however remarkable in itself, was not enough to produce a really creative thought. Others may have noticed the same thing and yet nothing came of it. Most of our observations have no assignable results. Galileo may have seen that the warts on a peasant's face formed a perfect isosceles triangle, or he may have noticed with boyish glee that just as the officiating priest was uttering the solemn words, *ecce agnus Dei,*° a fly lit on the end of his nose. To be really creative, ideas have to be worked up and then "put over," so that they become a part of man's social heritage. The highly accurate pendulum clock was one of the later results of Galileo's discovery. He himself was led to reconsider and successfully to refute the old notions of falling bodies. It remained for Newton to prove that the moon was falling, and presumably all the heavenly bodies. This quite upset all the consecrated views of the heavens as managed by angelic engineers. The universality of the laws of gravitation stimulated the attempt to seek other and equally important natural laws and cast grave doubts on the miracles in which mankind had hitherto believed. In short, those who dared to include in their thought the discoveries of Galileo and his successors found themselves in a new earth surrounded by new heavens.

On the 28th of October, 1831, two hundred and fifty years after Galileo had noticed the isochronous vibrations of the lamps, creative thought and its currency had so far increased that Faraday was wondering what would happen if he mounted a disk of copper between the poles of a horseshoe magnet. As the disk revolved an electric current was produced. This would doubtless have seemed the idlest kind of an experiment to the staunch business men of the time, who, it happened, were just then denouncing the child-labor bills in their anxiety to avail themselves to the full of the results of earlier idle curiosity. But should the dynamos and motors which have come into being as the outcome of Faraday's experiment be stopped this evening, the business man of to-day, agitated over labor troubles, might, as he trudged home past lines of "dead" cars, through dark streets to an unlighted house, engage in a little creative thought of his own and perceive that he and his laborers would have no modern factories and mines to quarrel about had it not been for the strange practical effects of the idle curiosity of scientists, inventors, and engineers.

The examples of creative intelligence given above belong to the realm of modern scientific achievement, which furnishes the most striking in-

---

ecce agnus Dei behold the Lamb of God (Latin). In a Catholic Mass said in Latin, this is the opening phrase of a prayer recited by the priest as he lifts up the consecrated host.

stances of the effects of scrupulous, objective thinking. But there are, of course, other great realms in which the recording and embodiment of acute observation and insight have wrought themselves into the higher life of man. The great poets and dramatists and our modern story-tellers have found themselves engaged in productive reveries, noting and artistically presenting their discoveries for the delight and instruction of those who have the ability to appreciate them.

The process by which a fresh and original poem or drama comes into being is doubtless analogous to that which originates and elaborates so-called scientific discoveries; but there is clearly a temperamental difference. The genesis and advance of painting, sculpture, and music offer still other problems. We really as yet know shockingly little about these matters, and indeed very few people have the least curiosity about them.[7] Nevertheless, creative intelligence in its various forms and activities is what makes man. Were it not for its slow, painful, and constantly discouraged operations through the ages man would be no more than a species of primate living on seeds, fruit, roots, and uncooked flesh, and wandering naked through the woods and over the plains like a chimpanzee.

The origin and progress and future promotion of civilization are ill understood and misconceived. These should be made the chief theme of education, but much hard work is necessary before we can reconstruct our ideas of man and his capacities and free ourselves from innumerable persistent misapprehensions. There have been obstructionists in all times, not merely the lethargic masses, but the moralists, the rationalizing theologians, and most of the philosophers, all busily if unconsciously engaged in ratifying existing ignorance and mistakes and discouraging creative thought. Naturally, those who reassure us seem worthy of honor and respect. Equally naturally those who puzzle us with disturbing criticisms and invite us to change our ways are objects of suspicion and readily discredited. Our personal discontent does not ordinarily extend to any critical questioning of the general situation in which we find ourselves. In every age the prevailing conditions of civilization have appeared quite natural and inevitable to those who grew up in them. The cow asks no questions as to how it happens to have a dry stall and a supply of hay. The kitten laps its warm milk from a china saucer, without knowing anything about porcelain; the dog nestles in the corner of a divan with no sense of obligation to the inventors of upholstery and the manufacturers of down

---

[7]Recently a re-examination of creative thought has begun as a result of new knowledge which discredits many of the notions formerly held about "reason." See, for example, *Creative Intelligence*, by a group of American philosophic thinkers; John Dewey, *Essays in Experimental Logic* (both pretty hard books); and Veblen, *The Place of Science in Modern Civilization*. Easier than these and very stimulating are Dewey, *Reconstruction in Philosophy*, and Woodworth, *Dynamic Psychology*.

pillows. So we humans accept our breakfasts, our trains and telephones and orchestras and movies, our national Constitution, our moral code and standards of manners, with the simplicity and innocence of a pet rabbit. We have absolutely inexhaustible capacities for appropriating what others do for us with no thought of a "thank you." We do not feel called upon to make any least contribution to the merry game ourselves. Indeed, we are usually quite unaware that a game is being played at all.

We have now examined the various classes of thinking which we can readily observe in ourselves and which we have plenty of reasons to believe go on, and always have been going on, in our fellow-men. We can sometimes get quite pure and sparkling examples of all four kinds, but commonly they are so confused and intermingled in our reverie as not to be readily distinguishable. The reverie is a reflection of our longings, exultations, and complacencies, our fears, suspicions, and disappointments. We are chiefly engaged in struggling to maintain our self-respect and in asserting that supremacy which we all crave and which seems to us our natural prerogative. It is not strange, but rather quite inevitable, that our beliefs about what is true and false, good and bad, right and wrong, should be mixed up with the reverie and be influenced by the same considerations which determine its character and course. We resent criticisms of our views exactly as we do of anything else connected with ourselves. Our notions of life and its ideals seem to us to be *our own* and as such necessarily true and right, to be defended at all costs.

We very rarely consider, however, the process by which we gained our convictions. If we did so, we could hardly fail to see that there was usually little ground for our confidence in them. Here and there, in this department of knowledge or that, some one of us might make a fair claim to have taken some trouble to get correct ideas of, let us say, the situation in Russia, the sources of our food supply, the origin of the Constitution, the revision of the tariff, the policy of the Holy Roman Apostolic Church, modern business organization, trade unions, birth control, socialism, the League of Nations, the excess-profits tax, preparedness, advertising in its social bearings; but only a very exceptional person would be entitled to opinions on all of even these few matters. And yet most of us have opinions on all these, and on many other questions of equal importance, of which we may know even less. We feel compelled, as self-respecting persons, to take sides when they come up for discussion. We even surprise ourselves by our omniscience. Without taking thought we see in a flash that it is most righteous and expedient to discourage birth control by legislative enactment, or that one who decries intervention in Mexico is clearly wrong, or that big advertising is essential to big business and that big business is the pride of the land. As godlike beings why should we not rejoice in our omniscience?

It is clear, in any case, that our convictions on important matters are not the result of knowledge or critical thought, nor, it may be added, are they often dictated by supposed self-interest. Most of them are *pure prejudices* in the proper sense of that word. We do not form them ourselves. They are the whisperings of "the voice of the herd." We have in the last analysis no responsibility for them and need assume none. They are not really our own ideas, but those of others no more well informed or inspired than ourselves, who have got them in the same careless and humiliating manner as we. It should be our pride to revise our ideas and not to adhere to what passes for respectable opinion, for such opinion can frequently be shown to be not respectable at all. We should, in view of the considerations that have been mentioned, resent our supine credulity. As an English writer has remarked:

"If we feared the entertaining of an unverifiable opinion with the warmth with which we fear using the wrong implement at the dinner table, if the thought of holding a prejudice disgusted us as does a foul disease, then the dangers of man's suggestibility would be turned into advantages."[8]

The purpose of this essay is to set forth briefly the way in which the notions of the herd have been accumulated. This seems to me the best, easiest, and least invidious educational device for cultivating a proper distrust for the older notions on which we still continue to reply.

The "real" reasons, which explain how it is we happen to hold a particular belief, are chiefly historical. Our most important opinions—those, for example, having to do with traditional, religious, and moral convictions, property rights, patriotism, national honor, the state, and indeed all the assumed foundations of society—are, as I have already suggested, rarely the result of reasoned consideration, but of unthinking absorption from the social environment in which we live. Consequently, they have about them a quality of "elemental certitude," and we especially resent doubt or criticism cast upon them. So long, however, as we revere the whisperings of the herd, we are obviously unable to examine them dispassionately and to consider to what extent they are suited to the novel conditions and social exigencies in which we find ourselves to-day.

The "real" reasons for our beliefs, by making clear their origins and history, can do much to dissipate this emotional blockade and rid us of our prejudices and preconceptions. Once this is done and we come critically to examine our traditional beliefs, we may well find some of them sustained by experience and honest reasoning, while others must be revised to meet new conditions and our more extended knowledge. But only after we have undertaken such a critical examination in the light of experience and modern knowledge, freed from any feeling of "pri-

---

[8]Trotter, *op. cit.,* p. 45. The first part of this little volume is excellent.

mary certitude," can we claim that the "good" are also the "r
sons for our opinions.

I do not flatter myself that this general show-up of man's thought
through the ages will cure myself or others of carelessness in adopting
ideas, or of unseemly heat in defending them just because we have
adopted them. But if the considerations which I propose to recall are
really incorporated into our thinking and are permitted to establish our
general outlook on human affairs, they will do much to relieve the imaginary obligation we feel in regard to traditional sentiments and ideals. Few
of us are capable of engaging in creative thought, but some of us can at
least come to distinguish it from other and inferior kinds of thought and
accord to it the esteem that it merits as the greatest treasure of the past
and the only hope of the future.

In the Laboratory with Agassiz

Samuel H. Scudder

*Samuel H. Scudder (1837–1911) apparently had no clear future plans
when he entered Williams College in 1853, at the age of sixteen. In a
biographical memoir of Scudder, Alfred G. Mayor writes that during that
first semester, his "sense of the beautiful was profoundly stirred by the
sight of a glass case of butterflies on the wall of a friend's room." He made
himself a net, began to collect, and by the time he was a junior he had
decided on his future career, the study of insects. He has been called the
greatest American entomologist of his time.*

*After he graduated from Williams in 1857, Scudder entered the Law-
rence Scientific School at Harvard University in order to study under the
great naturalist (now we would say biologist), Jean Louis R. Agassiz.
Although he announced his intention to devote his life to the study of
insects, Agassiz first set him to observe and report not on insects, but on
a fish. He describes the experience in the celebrated essay presented below,
first published anonymously in* Every Saturday, *April 4, 1874.*

*Mayor writes that "one thing seemed thereafter to be burned into his very
nature; devotion to all but infinite detail." His voluminous writings
throughout his career are all characterized by this "remarkable interest in
system and fascination for detail."*

It was more than fifteen years ago that I entered the laboratory of Professor Agassiz, and told him I had enrolled my name in the scientific school

as a student of natural history. He asked me a few questions about my object in coming, my antecedents generally, the mode in which I afterwards proposed to use the knowledge I might acquire, and finally, whether I wished to study any special branch. To the latter I replied that while I wished to be well grounded in all departments of zoölogy, I purposed to devote myself specially to insects.

"When do you wish to begin?" he asked.

"Now," I replied.

This seemed to please him, and with an energetic "Very well," he reached from a shelf a huge jar of specimens in yellow alcohol.

"Take this *fish*," said he, "and look at it; we call it a Hæmulon; by and by I will ask what you have seen."

With that he left me, but in a moment returned with explicit instructions as to the care of the object entrusted to me.

"No man is fit to be a naturalist," said he, "who does not know how to take care of specimens."

I was to keep the fish before me in a tin tray, and occasionally moisten the surface with alcohol from the jar, always taking care to replace the stopper tightly. Those were not the days of ground glass stoppers, and elegantly shaped exhibition jars; all the old students will recall the huge, neckless glass bottles with their leaky, wax-besmeared corks, half eaten by insects and begrimed with cellar dust. Entomology was a cleaner science than ichthyology, but the example of the professor, who had unhesitatingly plunged to the bottom of the jar to produce the fish, was infectious; and though his alcohol had "a very ancient and fish-like smell," I really dared not show any aversion within these sacred precincts, and treated the alcohol as though it were pure water. Still I was conscious of a passing feeling of disappointment, for gazing at a fish did not commend itself to an ardent entomologist. My friends at home, too, were annoyed, when they discovered that no amount of eau de cologne would drown the perfume which haunted me like a shadow.

In ten minutes I had seen all that could be seen in that fish, and started in search of the professor, who had however left the museum; and when I returned, after lingering over some of the odd animals stored in the upper apartment, my specimen was dry all over. I dashed the fluid over the fish as if to resuscitate the beast from a fainting-fit, and looked with anxiety for a return of the normal, sloppy appearance. This little excitement over, nothing was to be done but return to a steadfast gaze at my mute companion. Half an hour passed,—an hour,—another hour; the fish began to look loathsome. I turned it over and around; looked it in the face,—ghastly; from behind, beneath, above, sideways, at a three quarters view,—just as ghastly. I was in despair; at an early hour I concluded that lunch was necessary; so, with infinite relief, the fish was carefully replaced in the jar, and for an hour I was free.

On my return, I learned that Professor Agassiz had been at the museum, but had gone and would not return for several hours. My fellow-students were too busy to be disturbed by continued conversation. Slowly I drew forth that hideous fish, and with a feeling of desperation again looked at it. I might not use a magnifying glass; instruments of all kinds were interdicted. My two hands, my two eyes, and the fish; it seemed a most limited field. I pushed my finger down its throat to feel how sharp the teeth were. I began to count the scales in the different rows until I was convinced that that was nonsense. At last a happy thought struck me—I would draw the fish; and now with surprise I began to discover new features in the creature. Just then the professor returned.

"That is right," said he; "a pencil is one of the best of eyes. I am glad to notice, too, that you keep your specimen wet and your bottle corked."

With these encouraging words, he added,—

"Well, what is it like?"

He listened attentively to my brief rehearsal of the structure of parts whose names were still unknown to me; the fringed gill-arches and movable operculum; the pores of the head, fleshy lips, and lidless eyes; the lateral line, the spinous fins, and forked tail; the compressed and arched body. When I had finished, he waited as if expecting more, and then, with an air of disappointment,—

"You have not looked very carefully; why," he continued, more earnestly, "you haven't even seen one of the most conspicuous features of the animal, which is as plainly before your eyes as the fish itself; look again, look again!" and he left me to my misery.

I was piqued; I was mortified. Still more of that wretched fish! But now I set myself to my task with a will, and discovered one new thing after another, until I saw how just the professor's criticism had been. The afternoon passed quickly, and when, toward its close, the professor inquired,—

"Do you see it yet?"

"No," I replied, "I am certain I do not, but I see how little I saw before."

"That is next best," said he, earnestly, "but I won't hear you now; put away your fish and go home; perhaps you will be ready with a better answer in the morning. I will examine you before you look at the fish."

This was disconcerting; not only must I think of my fish all night, studying, without the object before me, what this unknown but most visible feature might be; but also, without reviewing my new discoveries, I must give an exact account of them the next day. I had a bad memory; so I walked home by Charles River in a distracted state, with my two perplexities.

The cordial greeting from the professor the next morning was reassuring; here was a man who seemed to be quite as anxious as I, that I should see for myself what he saw.

teacher having a good time teaching

"Do you perhaps mean," I asked, "that the fish has symmetrical sides with paired organs?"

His thoroughly pleased, "Of course, of course!" repaid the wakeful hours of the previous night. After he had discoursed most happily and enthusiastically—as he always did—upon the importance of this point, I ventured to ask what I should do next.

"Oh, look at your fish!" he said, and left me again to my own devices. In a little more than an hour he returned and heard my new catalogue.

"That is good, that is good!" he repeated; "but that is not all; go on;" and so for three long days he placed that fish before my eyes, forbidding me to look at anything else, or to use any artificial aid. "Look, look, look," was his repeated injunction.

This was the best entomological lesson I ever had,—a lesson, whose influence has extended to the details of every subsequent study; a legacy the professor has left to me, as he has left it to many others, of inestimable value, which we could not buy, with which we cannot part.

A year afterward, some of us were amusing ourselves with chalking outlandish beasts upon the museum blackboard. We drew prancing star-fishes; frogs in mortal combat; hydra-headed worms; stately crawfishes, standing on their tails, bearing aloft umbrellas; and grotesque fishes with gaping mouths and staring eyes. The professor came in shortly after, and was as amused as any, at our experiments. He looked at the fishes.

"Hæmulons, every one of them," he said; "Mr. —— drew them."

True; and to this day, if I attempt a fish, I can draw nothing but Hæmulons.

The fourth day, a second fish of the same group was placed beside the first, and I was bidden to point out the resemblances and differences between the two; another and another followed, until the entire family lay before me, and a whole legion of jars covered the table and surrounding shelves; the odor had become a pleasant perfume; and even now, the sight of an old, six-inch, worm-eaten cork brings fragrant memories!

The whole group of Hæmulons was thus brought in review; and, whether engaged upon the dissection of the internal organs, the preparation and examination of the bony frame-work, or the description of the various parts, Agassiz' training in the method of observing facts and their orderly arrangement was ever accompanied by the urgent exhortation not to be content with them.

"Facts are stupid things," he would say, "until brought into connection with some general law."

At the end of eight months, it was almost with reluctance that I left these friends and turned to insects; but what I had gained by this outside experience has been of greater value than years of later investigation in my favorite groups.

The Method of Scientific Investigation

Thomas H. Huxley

Thomas H. Huxley (1825–1895)—British anatomist, embryologist, essayist, and lecturer—is one of the most memorable figures in nineteenth-century science. He studied medicine at the University of London. His researches on marine animals, made while serving as assistant surgeon on a naval vessel in the waters off Australia, earned him an early reputation as a first-class scientific investigator. He continued to publish technical scientific papers all his life, but he also became engrossed in advocating the scientific method and its findings to a wide audience. The publication of Charles Darwin's Origin of Species *in 1859, and the controversy it aroused, brought Huxley to Darwin's defense. Huxley's lectures and writings on evolution, and on the place of humans in the universe, did much to establish a new freedom of debate and expression about matters of religion.*

Huxley also made notable contributions to elementary, technical, and medical education and was a strong advocate of higher education for women. Although he spent much of his career as a college teacher and administrator, his educational fervor embraced all kinds of people. In 1855 he began giving lectures addressed to laborers. Six of the lectures given in 1862, entitled "On Our Knowledge of the Causes of the Phenomena of Organic Nature," were devoted to Darwin's theories. The passage excerpted below is from the third lecture in the series and comes from the second volume of Huxley's Collected Essays *(9 vols., 1893–1894). For Huxley, "the method of scientific investigation" was by no means limited to science. And though a great believer in liberal education and in literature and the arts, he maintained that "a perfect culture . . . could not be acquired without training in the methods of physical science."*

The method of scientific investigation is nothing but the expression of the necessary mode of working of the human mind. It is simply the mode at which all phenomena are reasoned about, rendered precise and exact. There is no more difference, but there is just the same kind of difference, between the mental operations of a man of science and those of an ordinary person, as there is between the operations and methods of a baker or of a butcher weighing out his goods in common scales, and the operations of a chemist in performing a difficult and complex analysis by means of his balance and finely-graduated weights. It is not that the action of the scales in the one case, and the balance in the other, differ in the principles of their construction or manner of working; but the beam of one is set on an infinitely finer axis than the other, and of course turns by the addition of a much smaller weight.

You will understand this better, perhaps, if I give you some familiar example. You have all heard it repeated, I dare say, that men of science work by means of induction and deduction, and that by the help of these operations, they, in a sort of sense, wring from Nature certain other things, which are called natural laws, and causes, and that out of these, by some cunning skill of their own, they build up hypotheses and theories. And it is imagined by many, that the operations of the common mind can be by no means compared with these processes, and that they have to be acquired by a sort of special apprenticeship to the craft. To hear all these large words, you would think that the mind of a man of science must be constituted differently from that of his fellow men; but if you will not be frightened by terms, you will discover that you are quite wrong, and that all these terrible apparatus are being used by yourselves every day and every hour of your lives.

There is a well-known incident in one of Molière's plays,° where the author makes the hero express unbounded delight on being told that he had been talking prose during the whole of his life. In the same way, I trust, that you will take comfort, and be delighted with yourselves, on the discovery that you have been acting on the principles of inductive and deductive philosophy during the same period. Probably there is not one here who has not in the course of the day had occasion to set in motion a complex train of reasoning, of the very same kind, though differing of course in degree, as that which a scientific man goes through in tracing the causes of natural phenomena.

A very trivial circumstance will serve to exemplify this. Suppose you go into a fruiterer's shop, wanting an apple,—you take up one, and, on biting it, you find it is sour; you look at it, and see that it is hard and green. You take up another one, and that too is hard, green, and sour. The shopman offers you a third; but, before biting it, you examine it, and find that it is hard and green, and you immediately say that you will not have it, as it must be sour, like those that you have already tried.

Nothing can be more simple than that, you think; but if you will take the trouble to analyse and trace out into its logical elements what has been done by the mind, you will be greatly surprised. In the first place, you have performed the operation of induction. You found that, in two experiences, hardness and greenness in apples went together with sourness. It was so in the first case, and it was confirmed by the second. True, it is a very small basis, but still it is enough to make an induction from; you generalise the facts, and you expect to find sourness in apples where

---

one of Molière's plays   *Le Bourgeois Gentilhomme*, written in 1670.

you get hardness and greenness. You found upon that a general law, that all hard and green apples are sour; and that, so far as it goes, is a perfect induction. Well, having got your natural law in this way, when you are offered another apple which you find is hard and green, you say, "All hard and green apples are sour; this apple is hard and green, therefore this apple is sour." That train of reasoning is what logicians call a syllogism, and has all its various parts and terms,—its major premise, its minor premise, and its conclusion. And, by the help of further reasoning, which, if drawn out, would have to be exhibited in two or three other syllogisms, you arrive at your final determination, "I will not have that apple." So that, you see, you have, in the first place, established a law by induction, and upon that you have founded a deduction, and reasoned out the special conclusion of the particular case. Well now, suppose, having got your law, that at some time afterwards, you are discussing the qualities of apples with a friend: you will say to him, "It is a very curious thing,—but I find that all hard and green apples are sour!" Your friend says to you, "But how do you know that?" You at once reply, "Oh, because I have tried them over and over again, and have always found them to be so." Well, if we were talking science instead of common sense, we should call that an experimental verification. And, if still opposed, you go further, and say, "I have heard from the people in Somersetshire and Devonshire, where a large number of apples are grown, that they have observed the same thing. It is also found to be the case in Normandy, and in North America. In short, I find it to be the universal experience of mankind wherever attention has been directed to the subject." Whereupon, your friend, unless he is a very unreasonable man, agrees with you, and is convinced that you are quite right in the conclusion you have drawn. He believes, although perhaps he does not know he believes it, that the more extensive verifications are,—that the more frequently experiments have been made, and results of the same kind arrived at,—that the more varied the conditions under which the same results are attained, the more certain is the ultimate conclusion, and he disputes the question no further. He sees that the experiment has been tried under all sorts of conditions, as to time, place, and people, with the same result; and he says with you, therefore, that the law you have laid down must be a good one, and he must believe it.

In science we do the same thing;—the philosopher exercises precisely the same faculties, though in a much more delicate manner. In scientific inquiry it becomes a matter of duty to expose a supposed law to every possible kind of verification, and to take care, moreover, that this is done intentionally, and not left to a mere accident, as in the case of the apples. And in science, as in common life, our confidence in a law is in exact proportion to the absence of variation in the result of our experimental verifications. For instance, if you let go your grasp of an article you may have in your hand, it will immediately fall to the ground. That is a very common verification of one of the best established laws of nature—that of gravitation. The method by which men of science establish the existence of that law is exactly the same as that by which we have established the trivial proposition about the sourness of hard and green apples. But we believe it in such an extensive, thorough, and unhesitating manner because the universal experience of mankind verifies it, and we can verify it ourselves at any time; and that is the strongest possible foundation on which any natural law can rest.

So much, then, by way of proof that the method of establishing laws in science is exactly the same as that pursued in common life. Let us now turn to another matter (though really it is but another phase of the same question), and that is, the method by which, from the relations of certain phenomena, we prove that some stand in the position of causes towards the others.

I want to put the case clearly before you, and I will therefore show you what I mean by another familiar example. I will suppose that one of you, on coming down in the morning to the parlour of your house, finds that a tea-pot and some spoons which had been left in the room on the previous evening are gone,—the window is open, and you observe the mark of a dirty hand on the window-frame, and perhaps, in addition to that, you notice the impress of a hob-nailed shoe on the gravel outside. All these phenomena have struck your attention instantly, and before two seconds have passed you say, "Oh somebody has broken open the window, entered the room, and run off with the spoons and the tea-pot!" That speech is out of your mouth in a moment. And you will probably add, "I know there has; I am quite sure of it!" You mean to say exactly what you know; but in reality you are giving expression to what is, in all essential particulars, an hypothesis. You do not *know* it at all; it is nothing but an hypothesis rapidly framed in your own mind. And it is an hypothesis founded on a long train of inductions and deductions.

What are those inductions and deductions, and how have you got at this hypothesis? You have observed, in the first place, that the window is open; but by a train of reasoning involving many inductions and deductions, you have probably arrived long before at the general law—and a very good one it is—that windows do not open of themselves; and you therefore conclude that something has opened the window. A second general law that you have arrived at in the same way is, that tea-pots and spoons do not go out of a window spontaneously, and you are satisfied that, as they are not now where you left them, they have been removed. In the third place, you look at the marks on the window-sill, and the shoe-marks outside, and you say that in all previous experience the former kind of mark has never been produced by anything else but the hand of a human being; and the same experience shows that no other animal but man at present wears shoes with hob-nails in them such as would produce the marks in the gravel. I do not know, even if we could discover any of those "missing links"⁰ that are talked about, that they would help us to any other conclusion! At any rate the law which states our present experience is strong enough for my present purpose. You next reach the conclusion, that as these kinds of marks have not been left by any other animals than men, or are liable to be formed in any other way than by a man's hand and shoe, the marks in question have been formed by a man in that way. You have, further, a general law, founded on observation and experience, and that, too, is, I am sorry to say, a very universal and unimpeachable one,—that some men are thieves; and you assume at once from all these premises—and that is what constitutes your hypothesis—that the man who made the marks outside and on the window-sill, opened the window, got into the room, and stole your tea-pot and spoons. You have now arrived at a *vera causa;*⁰—you have assumed a cause which, it is plain, is competent to produce all the phenomena you have observed. You can explain all these phenomena only by the hypothesis of a thief. But that is a hypothetical conclusion, of the just of which you have no absolute proof at all; it is only rendered highly probable by a series of inductive and deductive reasonings.

I suppose your first action, assuming that you are a man of ordinary common sense, and that you have established this hypothesis to your own satisfaction, will very likely be to go off for the police, and set them on the track of the burglar, with the view to the recovery of your property. But just as you are starting with this object, some person comes in, and on learning what you are about, says, "My good friend, you are going on a great deal too fast. How do you know that the man who really made the marks took the spoons? It might have been a monkey that took them, and the man may have merely looked in afterwards." You would probably reply, "Well, that is all very well, but you see it is contrary to all experience of the way tea-pots and spoons are abstracted; so that, at any rate, your hypothesis is less probable than mine." While you are talking the thing over in this way, another friend arrives, one of that good kind of people that I was talking of a little while ago. And he might say, "Oh, my dear sir, you are certainly going on a great deal too fast. You are most presumptuous. You admit that all of these occurrences took place when you were fast asleep, at a time when you could not possibly have known anything about what was taking place. How do you know that the laws of Nature are not suspended during the night? It may be that there has been some kind of supernatural interference in this case." In point of fact, he declares that your hypothesis is one of which you cannot at all demon-

---

missing links Hypothetical primates once thought to be a bridge between apes and humans in the evolutionary chain.
vera causa cause in accordance with fact (Latin).

strate the truth, and that you are by no means sure that the laws of
Nature are the same when you are asleep as when you are awake.

Well, now, you cannot at the moment answer that kind of reasoning.
You feel that your worthy friend has you somewhat at a disadvantage.
You will feel perfectly convinced in your own mind, however, that you are
quite right, and you say to him, "My good friend, I can only be guided by
the natural probabilities of the case, and if you will be kind enough to
stand aside and permit me to pass, I will go and fetch the police." Well,
we will suppose that your journey is successful, and that by good luck you
meet with a policeman; that eventually the burglar is found with your
property on his person, and the marks correspond to his hand and to his
boots. Probably any jury would consider those facts a very good experimental verification of your hypothesis, touching the cause of the abnormal phenomena observed in your parlour, and would act accordingly.

Now, in this suppositious cause, I have taken phenomena of a very
common kind, in order that you might see what are the different steps in
an ordinary process of reasoning, if you will only take the trouble to
analyse it carefully. All the operations I have described, you will see, are
involved in the mind of any man of sense in leading him to a conclusion
as to the course he should take in order to make good a robbery and punish
the offender. I say that you are led, in that case, to your conclusion by
exactly the same train of reasoning as that which a man of science pursues when he is endeavouring to discover the origin and laws of the most
occult phenomena. The process is, and always must be, the same; and
precisely the same mode of reasoning was employed by Newton and La-
place in their endeavours to discover and define the causes of the movements of the heavenly bodies, as you, with your own common sense, would
employ to detect a burglar. The only difference is, that the nature of the
inquiry being more abstruse, every step has to be most carefully watched,
so that there may not be a single crack or flaw in your hypothesis. A flaw
or crack in many of the hypotheses of daily life may be of little or no
moment as affecting the general correctness of the conclusions at which
we may arrive; but, in a scientific inquiry, a fallacy, great or small, is
always of importance, and is sure to be in the long run constantly productive of mischievous, if not fatal results.

Do not allow yourselves to be misled by the common notion that an
hypothesis is untrustworthy simply because it is an hypothesis. It is often
urged, in respect to some scientific conclusion, that, after all, it is only an
hypothesis. But what more have we to guide us in nine-tenths of the most
important affairs of daily life than hypotheses, and often very ill-based
ones? So that in science, where the evidence of an hypothesis is subjected
to the most rigid examination, we may rightly pursue the same course.
You may have hypotheses and hypotheses. A man may say, if he likes, that
the moon is made of green cheese: that is an hypothesis. But another man,
who has devoted a great deal of time and attention to the subject, and

availed himself of the most powerful telescopes and the results of the observations of others, declares that in his opinion it is probably composed of materials very similar to those of which our own earth is made up: and that is also only an hypothesis. But I need not tell you that there is an enormous difference in the value of the two hypotheses. That one which is based on sound scientific knowledge is sure to have a corresponding value; and that which is a mere hasty random guess is likely to have but little value. Every great step in our progress in discovering causes has been made in exactly the same way as that which I have detailed to you. A person observing the occurrence of certain facts and phenomena asks, naturally enough, what process, what kind of operation known to occur in Nature applied to the particular case, will unravel and explain the mystery? Hence you have the scientific hypothesis; and its value will be proportionate to the care and completeness with which its basis had been tested and verified. It is in these matters as in the commonest affairs of practical life: the guess of the fool will be folly, while the guess of the wise man will contain wisdom. In all cases, you see that the value of the result depends on the patience and faithfulness with which the investigator applies to his hypothesis every possible kind of verification.

Ideas Come First

Theodore Roszak

Theodore Roszak (born 1933) is a vigorous social philosopher and critic. He attended U.C.L.A. (B.A. 1955) and Princeton University (Ph.D. 1958), and is now Professor of History at California State University at Hayward. His book The Making of a Counter Culture: Reflections on the Technocratic Society and Its Youthful Opposition *(1969), a guide to and analysis of the youthful dissent in the 1960s, helped establish the term "counter culture" in the American vocabulary. In his most recent work,* The Cult of Information: The Folklore of Computers and the True Art of Thinking *(1986), he takes on the consequences of a computer culture: "Data, data everywhere, but not a thought to think." We present here the first part of Chapter 5.*

In raising these questions about the place of the computer in our schools, it is not my purpose to question the value of information in and of itself. For better or worse, our technological civilization needs its data the way the Romans needed their roads and the Egyptians of the Old Kingdom needed the Nile flood. To a significant degree, I share that need. As a writer and teacher, I must be part of the 5 to 10 percent of our society which has a steady professional appetite for reliable, up-to-date information. I have long since learned to value the services of a good reference library equipped with a well-connected computer.

Nor do I want to deny that the computer is a superior means of storing and retrieving data. There is nothing sacred about the typed or printed page when it comes to keeping records; if there is a faster way to find facts and manipulate them, we are lucky to have it. Just as the computer displaced the slide rule as a calculating device, it has every right to oust the archive, the filing cabinet, the reference book, if it can prove itself cheaper and more efficient.

But I do want to insist that information, even when it moves at the speed of light, is no more than it has ever been: discrete little bundles of fact, sometimes useful, sometimes trivial, and never the substance of thought. I offer this modest, common-sense notion of information in deliberate contradiction to the computer enthusiasts and information theorists who have suggested far more extravagant definitions. In the course of this chapter and the next, as this critique unfolds, it will be my purpose to challenge these ambitious efforts to extend the meaning of information to nearly global proportions. That project, I believe, can only end by distorting the natural order of intellectual priorities. And insofar as educators acquiesce in that distortion and agree to invest more of their limited resources in information technology, they may be undermining their students' ability to think significantly.

That is the great mischief done by the data merchants, the futurologists, and those in the schools who believe that computer literacy is the educational wave of the future: they lose sight of the paramount truth that *the mind thinks with ideas, not with information.* Information may helpfully illustrate or decorate an idea; it may, where it works under the guidance of a contrasting idea, help to call other ideas into question. But information does not create ideas; by itself, it does not validate or invalidate them. An idea can only be generated, revised, or unseated by another idea. A culture survives by the power, plasticity, and fertility of its ideas. Ideas come first, because ideas define, contain, and eventually produce information. The principal task of education, therefore, is to teach young minds how to deal with ideas: how to evaluate them, extend them, adapt them to new uses. This can be done with the use of very little information, perhaps none at all. It certainly does not require data processing machinery of any kind. An excess of information may actually crowd out ideas, leaving the mind (young minds especially) distracted by sterile, disconnected facts, lost among shapeless heaps of data.

It may help at this point to take some time for fundamentals.

The relationship of ideas to information is what we call a *generalization.* Generalizing might be seen as the basic action of intelligence; it takes two forms. *First,* when confronted with a vast shapeless welter of facts (whether in the form of personal perceptions or secondhand reports), the mind seeks for a sensible, connecting pattern. Second, when confronted with very few facts, the mind seeks to create a pattern by enlarging upon the little it has and pointing it in the direction of a conclusion. The result in either case is some general statement which is not in the particulars, but has been imposed upon them by the imagination. Perhaps, after more facts are gathered, the pattern falls apart or yields to another, more convincing possibility. Learning to let go of an inadequate idea in favor of a better one is part of a good education in ideas.

Generalizations may take place at many levels. At the lowest level, they are formulated among many densely packed and obvious facts. These are cautious generalizations, perhaps even approaching the dull certainty of a truism. At another level, where the information grows thinner and more scattered, the facts less sharp and certain, we have riskier generalizations which take on the nature of a guess or hunch. In science, where hunches must be given formal rigor, this is where we find theories and hypotheses about the physical world, ideas that are on trial, awaiting more evidence to strengthen, modify, or subvert them. This is also the level at which we find the sort of hazardous generalizations we may regard as either brilliant insights or reckless prejudices, depending upon our critical response: sweeping statements perhaps asserted as unassailable truths, but based upon very few instances.

Generalizations exist, then, along a spectrum of information that stretches from abundance to near absence. As we pass along that spectrum, moving away from a secure surplus of facts, ideas tend to grow more unstable, therefore more daring, therefore more controversial. When I observe that women have been the homemakers and childminders in human society, I make a safe but uninteresting generalization that embraces a great many data about social systems past and present. But suppose I go on to say, "And whenever women leave the home and forsake their primary function as housewives, morals decline and society crumbles." Now I may be hard pressed to give more than a few questionable examples of the conclusion I offer. It is a risky generalization, a weak idea.

In Rorschach psychological testing, the subject is presented with a meaningless arrangement of blots or marks on a page. There may be many marks or there may be few, but in either case they suggest no sensible image. Then, after one has gazed at them for a while, the marks may suddenly take on a form which becomes absolutely clear. But where is this image? Not in the marks, obviously. The eye, searching for a sensible pattern, has projected it into the material; it has imposed a meaning upon the meaningless. Similarly in Gestalt psychology, one may be confronted with a specially contrived perceptual image: an ambiguous arrangement of marks which seems at first to be one thing but then shifts to become another. Which is the "true" image? The eye is free to choose between them, for they are both truly there. In both cases—the Rorschach blots and the Gestalt figure—the pattern is in the eye of the beholder; the sensory material simply elicits it. The relationship of ideas to facts is much like this. The facts are the scattered, possibly ambiguous marks; the mind orders them one way or another by conforming them to a pattern of its own invention. *Ideas are integrating patterns* which satisfy the mind when it asks the question, What does this mean? What is this all about?

But, of course, an answer that satisfies me may not satisfy you. We may see different patterns in the same collection of facts. And then we disagree and seek to persuade one another that one or the other of these patterns is superior, meaning that it does more justice to the facts at hand. The argument may focus on this fact or that, so that we will seem to be disagreeing about particular facts—as to whether they really *are* facts, or as to their relative importance. But even then, we are probably disagreeing about ideas. For as I shall suggest further on, facts are themselves the creations of ideas.

Those who would grant information a high intellectual priority often like to assume that facts, all by themselves, can jar and unseat ideas. But that is rarely the case, except perhaps in certain turbulent periods when the general idea of "being skeptical" and "questioning authority" is in the air and attaches itself to any dissenting, new item that comes along. Otherwise, in the absence of a well-formulated, intellectually attractive, new idea, it is remarkable how much in the way of dissonance and contradiction a dominant idea can absorb. There are classic cases of this even in the sciences. The Ptolemaic cosmology that prevailed in ancient times and during the Middle Ages had been compromised by countless contradictory observations over many generations. Still, it was an internally coherent, intellectually pleasing idea; therefore, keen minds stood by the familiar old system. Where there seemed to be any conflict, they simply adjusted and elaborated the idea, or restructured the observations in order to make them fit. If observations could not be made to fit, they might be allowed to stand along the cultural sidelines as curiosities, exceptions, freaks of nature. It was not until a highly imaginative constellation of ideas about celestial and terrestrial dynamics, replete with new concepts of gravitation, inertia, momentum, and matter, was created that the old system was retired. Through the eighteenth and nineteenth centuries, similar strategies of adjustment were used to save other inherited scientific ideas in the fields of chemistry, geology, and biology. None of these gave way until whole new paradigms were invented to replace them, sometimes with relatively few facts initially to support them. The minds that clung to the old concepts were not necessarily being stubborn or benighted; they simply needed a better idea to take hold of.

Concepts We Live By

George Lakoff and Mark Johnson

George Lakoff (born 1941) was educated at M.I.T. and Indiana University, and teaches at the University of California, Berkeley. He is one of the leading scholars in the branch of linguistics known as cognitive semantics. Mark Johnson (born 1949) studied at the University of Kansas and at the University of Chicago, and is a professor of philosophy at Southern Illinois University. The two met over coffee one day in 1979 because the researches of each, from very different directions, had led to the same conclusions about the role of metaphor in human perception. They immediately decided to collaborate, and shortly produced the book Metaphors We Live By *(1980), whose brief first chapter we print below, without its transitional final sentence.*

After further collaborating on a number of essays, each has continued independently to pursue the implications of their study. Johnson's latest book is The Body in the Mind: The Bodily Basis of Reason and Imagination *(1987); Lakoff has written* Women, Fire, and Dangerous Things: What Categories Reveal About the Mind *(1987), and is preparing (with Mark Turner) a book for college freshmen, to be called* More Than Cool Reason: The Power of Poetic Metaphor.

Metaphor is for most people a device of the poetic imagination and the rhetorical flourish—a matter of extraordinary rather than ordinary language. Moreover, metaphor is typically viewed as characteristic of language alone, a matter of words rather than thought or action. For this reason, most people think they can get along perfectly well without metaphor. We have found, on the contrary, that metaphor is pervasive in everyday life, not just in language but in thought and action. Our ordinary conceptual system, in terms of which we both think and act, is fundamentally metaphorical in nature.

The concepts that govern our thought are not just matters of the intellect. They also govern our everyday functioning, down to the most mundane details. Our concepts structure what we perceive, how we get around in the world, and how we relate to other people. Our conceptual system thus plays a central role in defining our everyday realities. If we are right in suggesting that our conceptual system is largely metaphorical, then the way we think, what we experience, and what we do every day is very much a matter of metaphor.

But our conceptual system is not something we are normally aware of. In most of the little things we do every day, we simply think and act more or less automatically along certain lines. Just what these lines are is by no means obvious. One way to find out is by looking at language. Since communication is based on the same conceptual system that we use in thinking and acting, language is an important source of evidence for what that system is like.

Primarily on the basis of linguistic evidence, we have found that most of our ordinary conceptual system is metaphorical in nature. And we have found a way to begin to identify in detail just what the metaphors are that structure how we perceive, how we think, and what we do.

To give some idea of what it could mean for a concept to be metaphorical and for such a concept to structure an everyday activity, let us start with the concept ARGUMENT and the conceptual metaphor ARGUMENT IS WAR. This metaphor is reflected in our everyday language by a wide variety of expressions:

ARGUMENT IS WAR

Your claims are *indefensible.*
He *attacked every weak point* in my argument.
His criticisms were *right on target.*
I *demolished* his argument.
I've never *won* an argument with him.
You disagree? Okay, *shoot!*
If you use that *strategy,* he'll *wipe you out.*
He *shot down* all of my arguments.

It is important to see that we don't just *talk* about arguments in terms of war. We can actually win or lose arguments. We see the person we are arguing with as an opponent. We attack his positions and we defend our own. We gain and lose ground. We plan and use strategies. If we find a position indefensible, we can abandon it and take a new line of attack. Many of the things we *do* in arguing are partially structured by the concept of war. Though there is no physical battle, there is a verbal battle, and the structure of an argument—attack, defense, counterattack, etc.— reflects this. It is in this sense that the ARGUMENT IS WAR metaphor is one that we live by in this culture; it structures the actions we perform in arguing.

Try to imagine a culture where arguments are not viewed in terms of war, where no one wins or loses, where there is no sense of attacking or defending, gaining or losing ground. Imagine a culture where an argument is viewed as a dance, the participants are seen as performers, and the goal is to perform in a balanced and aesthetically pleasing way. In such a culture, people would view arguments differently, experience them differently, carry them out differently, and talk about them differently. But *we* would probably not view them as arguing at all: they would simply be doing something different. It would seem strange even to call what they were doing "arguing." Perhaps the most neutral way of describing this difference between their culture and ours would be to say that we have a discourse form structured in terms of battle and they have one structured in terms of dance.

This is an example of what it means for a metaphorical concept, namely, ARGUMENT IS WAR, to structure (at least in part) what we do and how we understand what we are doing when we argue. *The essence of metaphor is understanding and experiencing one kind of thing in terms of another.* It is not that arguments are a subspecies of war. Arguments and wars are different kinds of things—verbal discourse and armed conflict— and the actions performed are different kinds of actions. But ARGUMENT is partially structured, understood, performed, and talked about in terms of WAR. The concept is metaphorically structured, the activity is metaphorically structured, and, consequently, the language is metaphorically structured.

Moreover, this is the *ordinary* way of having an argument and talking about one. The normal way for us to talk about attacking a position is to use the words "attack a position." Our conventional ways of talking about arguments presuppose a metaphor we are hardly ever conscious of. The metaphor is not merely in the words we use—it is in our very concept of an argument. The language of argument is not poetic, fanciful, or rhetorical; it is literal. We talk about arguments that way because we conceive of them that way—and we act according to the way we conceive of things.

The most important claim we have made so far is that metaphor is not just a matter of language, that is, of mere words. We shall argue that, on the contrary, human *thought processes* are largely metaphorical. This is what we mean when we say that the human conceptual system is metaphorically structured and defined. Metaphors as linguistic expressions are possible precisely because there are metaphors in a person's conceptual system.

The Loss of the Creature

Walker Percy

Walker Percy is a Southern writer who began as a scientist. Born in Alabama in 1916, he majored in chemistry at the University of North Carolina. Convinced that "scientific truth was the only truth worth pursuing," he went on to earn a medical degree from Columbia University in 1941. Shortly after his graduation he contracted tuberculosis and was forced to spend two years in a sanitarium, with all the time in the world to read and think. "What began to interest me," he says, "was not the physiological and pathological processes within man's body but the problem of man himself, the nature and destiny of man." Shortly after this period of reflection he converted to Roman Catholicism, and soon turned from medicine to writing.

Percy wrote both fiction and nonfiction, but nothing of his was published until, at the age of 45, his first published novel, The Moviegoer *(1961), won the National Book Award. Subsequent novels include* Love in the Ruins: The Adventures of a Bad Catholic at a Time Near the End of the World *(1971),* The Second Coming *(1980), and* The Thanatos Syndrome *(1987). His nonfiction includes a collection of essays of social criticism,* Lost in the Cosmos *(1983), and a collection of literary and philosophical journal articles,* The Message in the Bottle: How Queer Man Is, How Queer Language Is, and What One Has To Do with the Other *(1975), from which we present the following essay.*

Every explorer names his island Formosa, beautiful. To him it is beautiful because, being first, he has access to it and can see it for what it is. But to no one else is it ever as beautiful—except the rare man who manages to recover it, who knows that it has to be recovered.

Garcia López de Cárdenas discovered the Grand Canyon and was amazed at the sight. It can be imagined: One crosses miles of desert, breaks through the mesquite, and there it is at one's feet. Later the government set the place aside as a national park, hoping to pass along to millions the experience of Cárdenas. Does not one see the same sight from the Bright Angel Lodge that Cárdenas saw?

The assumption is that the Grand Canyon is a remarkably interesting and beautiful place and that if it had a certain value P for Cárdenas, the same value P may be transmitted to any number of sightseers—just as Banting's discovery of insulin can be transmitted to any number of diabetics. A counterinfluence is at work, however, and it would be nearer the truth to say that if the place is seen by a million sightseers, a single sightseer does not receive value P but a millionth part of value P.

It is assumed that since the Grand Canyon has the fixed interest value P, tours can be organized for any number of people. A man in Boston decides to spend his vacation at the Grand Canyon. He visits his travel bureau, looks at the folder, signs up for a two-week tour. He and his family take the tour, see the Grand Canyon, and return to Boston. May we say that this man has seen the Grand Canyon? Possibly he has. But it is more likely that what he has done is the one sure way not to see the canyon.

Why is it almost impossible to gaze directly at the Grand Canyon under these circumstances and see it for what it is—as one picks up a strange object from one's back yard and gazes directly at it? It is almost impossible because the Grand Canyon, the thing as it is, has been appropriated by the symbolic complex which has already been formed in the sightseer's mind. Seeing the canyon under approved circumstances is seeing the symbolic complex head on. The thing is no longer the thing as it confronted the Spaniard; it is rather that which has already been formulated—by picture postcard, geography book, tourist folders, and the words *Grand Canyon*. As a result of this preformulation, the source of the sightseer's pleasure undergoes a shift. Where the wonder and delight of the Spaniard arose from his penetration of the thing itself, from a progressive discovery of depths, patterns, colors, shadows, etc., now the sightseer measures his satisfaction *by the degree to which the canyon conforms to the preformed complex*. If it does so, if it looks just like the postcard, he is pleased; he might even say, "Why it is every bit as beautiful as a picture postcard!" He feels he has not been cheated. But if it does not conform, if the colors are somber, he will not be able to see it directly; he will only be conscious of the disparity between what it is and what it is supposed to be. He will say later that he was unlucky in not being there at the right time. The highest point, the term of the sightseer's satisfaction, is not the sovereign discovery of the thing before him; it is rather the measuring up of the thing to the criterion of the preformed symbolic complex.

Seeing the canyon is made even more difficult by what the sightseer does when the moment arrives, when sovereign knower confronts the thing to be known. Instead of looking at it, he photographs it. There is no confrontation at all. At the end of forty years of preformulation and with the Grand Canyon yawning at his feet, what does he do? He waives his right of seeing and knowing and records symbols for the next forty years. For him there is no present; there is only the past of what has been formulated and seen and the future of what has been formulated and not seen. The present is surrendered to the past and the future.

The sightseer may be aware that something is wrong. He may simply be bored; or he may be conscious of the difficulty: that the great thing yawning at his feet somehow eludes him. The harder he looks at it, the less he can see. It eludes everybody. The tourist cannot see it; the bellboy at the Bright Angel Lodge cannot see it: for him it is only one side of the space he lives in, like one wall of a room; to the ranger it is a tissue of everyday signs relevant to his own prospects—the blue haze down there means that he will probably get rained on during the donkey ride.

How can the sightseer recover the Grand Canyon? He can recover it in any number of ways, all sharing in common the stratagem of avoiding the approved confrontation of the tour and the Park Service.

It may be recovered by leaving the beaten track. The tourist leaves the tour, camps in the back country. He arises before dawn and approaches the South Rim through a wild terrain where there are no trails and no railed-in lookout points. In other words, he sees the canyon by avoiding all the facilities for seeing the canyon. If the benevolent Park Service hears about this fellow and thinks he has a good idea and places the following notice in the Bright Angel Lodge: *Consult ranger for information on getting off the beaten track*—the end result will only be the closing of another access to the canyon.

It may be recovered by a dialectical movement which brings one back to the beaten track but at a level above it. For example, after a lifetime of avoiding the beaten track and guided tours, a man may deliberately seek out the most beaten track of all, the most commonplace tour imaginable: he may visit the canyon by a Greyhound tour in the company of a party from Terre Haute—just as a man who has lived in New York all his life may visit the Statute of Liberty. (Such dialectical savorings of the familiar as the familiar are, of course, a favorite stratagem of *The New Yorker* magazine.) The thing is recovered from familiarity by means of an exercise in familiarity. Our complex friend stands behind his fellow tourists at the Bright Angel Lodge and sees the canyon through them and their predicament, their picture taking and busy disregard. In a sense, he exploits his fellow tourists; he stands on their shoulders to see the canyon.

Such a man is far more advanced in the dialectic than the sightseer who is trying to get off the beaten track—getting up at dawn and approaching the canyon through the mesquite. This strategem is, in fact, for our complex man the weariest, most beaten track of all.

It may be recovered as a consequence of a breakdown of the symbolic machinery by which the experts present the experience to the consumer. A family visits the canyon in the usual way. But shortly after their arrival, the park is closed by an outbreak of typhus in the south. They have the canyon to themselves. What do they mean when they tell the home folks of their good luck: "We had the whole place to ourselves"? How does one see the thing better when the others are absent? Is looking like sucking: the more lookers, the less there is to see? They could hardly answer, but by saying this they testify to a state of affairs which is considerably more complex than the simple statement of the schoolbook about the Spaniard and the millions who followed him. It is a state in which there is a complex distribution of sovereignty, of zoning.

It may be recovered in a time of national disaster. The Bright Angel Lodge is converted into a rest home, a function that has nothing to do with the canyon a few yards away. A wounded man is brought in. He regains consciousness; there outside his window is the canyon.

The most extreme case of access by privilege conferred by disaster is the Huxleyan novel of the adventures of the surviving remnant after the great wars of the twentieth century. An expedition from Australia lands in Southern California and heads east. They stumble across the Bright Angel Lodge, now fallen into ruins. The trails are grown over, the guard rails fallen away, the dime telescope at Battleship Point rusted. But there is the canyon, exposed at last. Exposed by what? By the decay of those facilities which were designed to help the sightseer.

This dialectic of sightseeing cannot be taken into account by planners, for the object of the dialectic is nothing other than the subversion of the efforts of the planners.

The dialectic is not known to objective theorists, psychologists, and the like. Yet it is quite well known in the fantasy-consciousness of the popular arts. The devices by which the museum exhibit, the Grand Canyon, the ordinary thing, is recovered have long since been stumbled upon. A movie shows a man visiting the Grand Canyon. But the moviemaker knows something the planner does not know. He knows that one cannot take the sight frontally. The canyon must be approached by the stratagems we have mentioned: the Inside Track, the Familiar Revisited, the Accidental Encounter. Who is the stranger at the Bright Angel Lodge? Is he the ordinary tourist from Terre Haute that he makes himself out to be? He is not. He has another objective in mind, to revenge his wronged brother, counterespionage, etc. By virtue of the fact that he has other fish to fry, he may take a stroll along the rim after supper and then we can see the canyon through him. The movie accomplishes its purpose by concealing it. Overtly the characters (the American family marooned by typhus) and we the onlookers experience pity for the sufferers, and the family experience anxiety for themselves; covertly and in truth they are the happiest of people and we are happy through them, for we have the canyon to ourselves. The movie cashes in on the recovery of sovereignty through disaster. Not only is the canyon now accessible to the remnant; the members of the remnant are now accessible to each other; a whole new ensemble of relations becomes possible—friendship, love, hatred, clandestine sexual adventures. In a movie when a man sits next to a woman on a bus, it is necessary either that the bus break down or that the woman lose her memory. (The question occurs to one: Do you imagine there are sightseers who see sights just as they are supposed to? a family who live in Terre Haute, who decide to take the canyon tour, who go there, see it, enjoy it immensely, and go home content? a family who are entirely innocent of all the barriers, zones, losses of sovereignty I have been talking about? Wouldn't most people be sorry if Battleship Point fell into the canyon, carrying all one's fellow passengers to their death, leaving one alone on the South Rim? I cannot answer this. Perhaps there are such people. Certainly a great many American families would swear they had no such problems, that they came, saw, and went away happy. Yet it is just these families who would be happiest if they had gotten the Inside Track and been among the surviving remnant.)

It is now apparent that as between the many measures which may be taken to overcome the opacity, the boredom, of the direct confrontation of the thing or creature in its citadel of symbolic investiture, some are less authentic than others. That is to say, some stratagems obviously serve other purposes than that of providing access to being—for example, various unconscious motivations which it is not necessary to go into here.

Let us take an example in which the recovery of being is ambiguous, where it may under the same circumstances contain both authentic and unauthentic components. An American couple, we will say, drives down into Mexico. They see the usual sights and have a fair time of it. Yet they are never without the sense of missing something. Although Taxco and Cuernavaca are interesting and picturesque as advertised, they fall short of "it." What do the couple have in mind by "it"? What do they really hope for? What sort of experience could they have in Mexico so that upon their return, they would feel that "it" had happened? We have a clue: Their hope has something to do with their own role as tourists in a foreign country and the way in which they conceive this role. It has something to do with other American tourists. Certainly they feel that they are very far from "it" when, after traveling five thousand miles, they arrive at the plaza in Guanajuato only to find themselves surrounded by a dozen other couples from the Midwest.

Already we may distinguish authentic and unauthentic elements. First, we see the problem the couple faces and we understand their efforts to surmount it. The problem is to find an "unspoiled" place. "Unspoiled" does not mean only that a place is left physically intact; it means also that it is not encrusted by renown and by the familiar (as is Taxco), that it has not been discovered by others. We understand that the couple really want to get at the place and enjoy it. Yet at the same time we wonder if there is not something wrong in their dislike of their compatriots. Does access to the place require the exclusion of others?

Let us see what happens.

The couple decide to drive from Guanajuato to Mexico City. On the way they get lost. After hours on a rocky mountain road, they find themselves in a tiny valley not even marked on the map. There they discover an Indian village. Some sort of religious festival is going on. It is apparently a corn dance in supplication of the rain god.

The couple know at once that this is "it." They are entranced. They spend several days in the village, observing the Indians and being themselves observed with friendly curiosity.

Now may we not say that the sightseers have at last come face to face with an authentic sight, a sight which is charming, quaint, picturesque, unspoiled, and that they see the sight and come away rewarded? Possibly this may occur. Yet it is more likely that what happens is a far cry indeed from an immediate encounter with being, that the experience, while masquerading as such, is in truth a rather desperate impersonation. I use the word *desperate* advisedly to signify an actual loss of hope.

The clue to the spuriousness of their enjoyment of the village and the festival is a certain restiveness in the sightseers themselves. It is given expression by their repeated exclamations that "this is too good to be true," and by their anxiety that it may not prove to be so perfect, and finally by their downright relief at leaving the valley and having the experience in the bag, so to speak—that is, safely embalmed in memory and movie film.

What is the source of their anxiety during the visit? Does it not mean that the couple are looking at the place with a certain standard of performance in mind? Are they like Fabre, who gazed at the world about him with wonder, letting it be what it is; or are they not like the overanxious mother who sees her child as one performing, now doing badly, now doing well? The village is their child and their love for it is an anxious love because they are afraid that at any moment it might fail them.

We have another clue in their subsequent remark to an ethnologist friend. "How we wished you had been there with us! What a perfect goldmine of folkways! Every minute we would say to each other, if only you were here! You must return with us." This surely testifies to a generosity of spirit, a willingness to share their experience with others, not at all like their feelings toward their fellow Iowans on the plaza at Guanajuato!

I am afraid this is not the case at all. It is true that they longed for their ethnologist friend, but it was for an entirely different reason. They wanted him, not to share their experience, but to certify their experience as genuine.

"This is it" and "Now we are really living" do not necessarily refer to the sovereign encounter of the person with the sight that enlivens the mind and gladdens the heart. It means that now at last we are having the acceptable experience. The present experience is always measured by a prototype, the "it" of their dreams. "Now I am really living" means that now I am filling the role of sightseer and the sight is living up to the prototype of sights. This quaint and picturesque village is measured by a Platonic ideal of the Quaint and the Picturesque.

Hence their anxiety during the encounter. For at any minute something could go wrong. A fellow Iowan might emerge from a 'dobe hut; the chief might show them his Sears catalogue. (If the failures are "wrong" enough, as these are, they might still be turned to account as rueful conversation pieces: "There we were expecting the chief to bring us a churinga and he shows up with a Sears catalogue!") They have snatched victory from disaster, but their experience always runs the danger of failure.

They need the ethnologist to certify their experience as genuine. This is borne out by their behavior when the three of them return for the next corn dance. During the dance, the couple do not watch the goings-on; instead they watch the ethnologist! Their highest hope is that their friend should find the dance interesting. And if he should show signs of true absorption, an interest in the goings-on so powerful that he becomes oblivious of his friends—then their cup is full. "Didn't we tell you?" they say at last. What they want from him is not ethnological explanations; all they want is his approval.

What has taken place is a radical loss of sovereignty over that which is as much theirs as it is the ethnologist's. The fault does not lie with the ethnologist. He has no wish to stake a claim to the village; in fact, he desires the opposite: he will bore his friends to death by telling them about the village and the meaning of the folkways. A degree of sovereignty has been surrendered by the couple. It is the nature of the loss, moreover, that they are not aware of the loss, beyond a certain uneasiness. (Even if they read this and admitted it, it would be very difficult for them to bridge the gap in their confrontation of the world. Their consciousness of the corn dance cannot escape their consciousness of their consciousness, so that with the onset of the first direct enjoyment, their higher consciousness pounces and certifies: "Now you are doing it! Now you are really living!" and, in certifying the experience, sets it at nought.)

Their basic placement in the world is such that they recognize a priority of title of the expert over his particular department of being. The whole horizon of being is staked out by "them," the experts. The highest satisfaction of the sightseer (not merely the tourist but any layman seer of sights) is that his sight should be certified as genuine. The worst of this impoverishment is that there is no sense of impoverishment. The surrender of title is so complete that it never even occurs to one to reassert title. A poor man may envy the rich man, but the sightseer does not envy the expert. When a caste system becomes absolute, envy disappears. Yet the caste of layman-expert is not the fault of the expert. It is due altogether to the eager surrender of sovereignty by the layman so that he may take up the role not of the person but of the consumer.

I do not refer only to the special relation of layman to theorist. I refer to the general situation in which sovereignty is surrendered to a class of privileged knowers, whether these be theorists or artists. A reader may surrender sovereignty over that which has been written about, just as a consumer may surrender sovereignty over a thing which has been theorized about. The consumer is content to receive an experience just as it has been presented to him by theorists and planners. The reader may also be content to judge life by whether it has or has not been formulated by those who know and write about life. A young man goes to France. He too has a fair time of it, sees the sights, enjoys the food. On his last day, in fact as he sits in a restaurant in Le Havre waiting for his boat, something happens. A group of French students in the restaurant get into an impassioned argument over a recent play. A riot takes place. Madame la concierge joins in, swinging her mop at the rioters. Our young American is transported. This is "it." And he had almost left France without seeing "it"!

But the young man's delight is ambiguous. On the one hand, it is a pleasure for him to encounter the same Gallic temperament he had heard about from Puccini and Rolland. But on the other hand, the source of his pleasure testifies to a certain alienation. For the young man is actually barred from a direct encounter with anything French excepting only that which has been set forth, authenticated by Puccini and Rolland—those who know. If he had encountered the restaurant scene without reading

Hemingway, without knowing that the performance was so typically, charmingly French, he would not have been delighted. He would only have been anxious at seeing things get so out of hand. The source of his delight is the sanction of those who know.

This loss of sovereignty is not a marginal process, as might appear from my example of estranged sightseers. It is a generalized surrender of the horizon to those experts within whose competence a particular segment of the horizon is thought to lie. Kwakiutls are surrendered to Franz Boas; decaying Southern mansions are surrendered to Faulkner and Tennessee Williams. So that, although it is by no means the intention of the expert to expropriate sovereignty—in fact he would not even know what sovereignty meant in this context—the danger of theory and consumption is a seduction and deprivation of the consumer.

In the New Mexican desert, natives occasionally come across strange-looking artifacts which have fallen from the skies and which are stenciled: *Return to U.S. Experimental Project, Alamogordo. Reward.* The finder returns the object and is rewarded. He knows nothing of the nature of the object he has found and does not care to know. The sole role of the native, the highest role he can play, is that of finder and returner of the mysterious equipment.

The same is true of the layman's relation to *natural* objects in a modern technical society. No matter what the object or event is, whether it is a star, a swallow, a Kwakiutl, a "psychological phenomenon," the layman who confronts it does not confront it as a sovereign person, as Crusoe° confronts a seashell he finds on the beach. The highest role he can conceive himself as playing is to be able to recognize the title of the object, to return it to the appropriate expert and have it certified as a genuine find. He does not even permit himself to see the thing—as Gerard Hopkins could see a rock or a cloud or a field. If anyone asks him why he doesn't look, he may reply that he didn't take that subject in college (or he hasn't read Faulkner).

This loss of sovereignty extends even to oneself. There is the neurotic who asks nothing more of his doctor than that his symptom should prove interesting. When all else fails, the poor fellow has nothing to offer but his own neurosis. But even this is sufficient if only the doctor will show interest when he says, "Last night I had a curious sort of dream; perhaps it will be significant to one who knows about such things. It seems I was standing in a sort of alley—" (I have nothing else to offer you but my own unhappiness. Please say that it, at least, measures up, that it is a *proper* sort of unhappiness.)

Crusoe Hero of *Robinson Crusoe* (1719), Daniel Defoe's story of a man marooned on a desert island.

2

A young Falkland Islander walking along a beach and spying a dead dogfish and going to work on it with his jackknife has, in a fashion wholly unprovided in modern educational theory, a great advantage over the Scarsdale high-school pupil who finds the dogfish on his laboratory desk. Similarly the citizen of Huxley's *Brave New World* who stumbles across a volume of Shakespeare in some vine-grown ruins and squats on a potsherd to read it is in a fairer way of getting at a sonnet than the Harvard sophomore taking English Poetry II.

The educator whose business it is to teach students biology or poetry is unaware of a whole ensemble of relations which exist between the student and the dogfish and between the student and the Shakespeare sonnet. To put it bluntly: A student who has the desire to get at a dogfish or a Shakespeare sonnet may have the greatest difficulty in salvaging the creature itself from the educational package in which it is presented. The great difficulty is that he is not aware that there is a difficulty; surely, he thinks, in such a fine classroom, with such a fine textbook, the sonnet must come across! What's wrong with me?

The sonnet and the dogfish are obscured by two different processes. The sonnet is obscured by the symbolic package which is formulated not by the sonnet itself but by the *media* through which the sonnet is transmitted, the media which the educators believe for some reason to be transparent. The new textbook, the type, the smell of the page, the classroom, the aluminum windows and the winter sky, the personality of Miss Hawkins—these media which are supposed to transmit the sonnet may only succeed in transmitting themselves. It is only the hardiest and cleverest of students who can salvage the sonnet from this many-tissued package. It is only the rarest student who knows that the sonnet must be salvaged from the package. (The educator is well aware that something is wrong, that there is a fatal gap between the student's learning and the student's life: The student reads the poem, appears to understand it, and gives all the answers. But what does he recall if he should happen to read a Shakespeare sonnet twenty years later? Does he recall the poem or does he recall the smell of the page and the smell of Miss Hawkins?)

One might object, pointing out that Huxley's citizen reading his sonnet in the ruins and the Falkland Islander looking at his dogfish on the beach also receive them in a certain package. Yes, but the difference lies in the fundamental placement of the student in the world, a placement which makes it possible to extract the thing from the package. The pupil at Scarsdale High sees himself placed as a consumer receiving an experience-package; but the Falkland Islander exploring his dogfish is a person exercising the sovereign right of a person in his lordship and mastery of creation. He too could use an instructor and a book and a technique, but he would use them as his subordinates, just as he uses his jackknife. The biology student does not use his scalpel as an instrument; he uses it as a magic wand! Since it is a "scientific instrument," it should do "scientific things."

The dogfish is concealed in the same symbolic package as the sonnet. But the dogfish suffers an additional loss. As a consequence of this double deprivation, the Sarah Lawrence student who scores A in zoology is apt to know very little about a dogfish. She is twice removed from the dogfish, once by the symbolic complex by which the dogfish is concealed, once again by the spoliation of the dogfish by theory which renders it invisible. Through no fault of zoology instructors, it is nevertheless a fact that the zoology laboratory at Sarah Lawrence College is one of the few places in the world where it is all but impossible to see a dogfish.

The dogfish, the tree, the seashell, the American Negro, the dream, are rendered invisible by a shift of reality from concrete thing to theory which Whitehead has called the fallacy of misplaced concreteness. It is the mistaking of an idea, a principle, an abstraction, for the real. As a consequence of the shift, the "specimen" is seen as less real than the theory of the specimen. As Kierkegaard said, once a person is seen as a specimen of a race or a species, at that very moment he ceases to be an individual. Then there are no more individuals but only specimens.

To illustrate: A student enters a laboratory which, in the pragmatic view, offers the student the optimum conditions under which an educational experience may be had. In the existential view, however—that view of the student in which he is regarded not as a receptacle of experience but as a knowing being whose peculiar property it is to see himself as being in a certain situation—the modern laboratory could not have been more effectively designed to conceal the dogfish forever.

The student comes to his desk. On it, neatly arranged by his instructor, he finds his laboratory manual, a dissecting board, instruments, and a mimeographed list:

EXERCISE 22

Materials: 1 dissecting board
            1 scalpel
            1 forceps
            1 probe
            1 bottle india ink and syringe
            1 specimen of *Squalus acanthias*

The clue to the situation in which the student finds himself is to be found in the last item: 1 specimen of *Squalus acanthias*.

The phrase *specimen of* expresses in the most succinct way imaginable the radical character of the loss of being which has occurred under his very nose. To refer to the dogfish, the unique concrete existent before him, as a "specimen of *Squalus acanthias*" reveals by its grammar the spoliation of the dogfish by the theoretical method. This phrase, *specimen of,* example of, instance of, indicates the ontological status of the individual creature in the eyes of the theorist. The dogfish itself is seen as a rather shabby expression of an ideal reality, the species *Squalus acanthias.* The result is the radical devaluation of the individual dogfish. (The *reductio ad absurdum* of Whitehead's shift is Toynbee's employment of it in his historical method. If a gram of NaCl is referred to by the chemist as a "sample of" NaCl, one may think of it as such and not much is missed by the oversight of the act of being of this particular pinch of salt, but when the Jews and the Jewish religion are understood as—in Toynbee's favorite phrase—a "classical example of" such and such a kind of *Voelkerwanderung,*° we begin to suspect that something is being left out.)

If we look into the ways in which the student can recover the dogfish (or the sonnet), we will see that they have in common the stratagem of avoiding the educator's direct presentation of the object as a lesson to be learned and restoring access to sonnet and dogfish as beings to be known, reasserting the sovereignty of knower over known.

In truth, the biography of scientists and poets is usually the story of the discovery of the indirect approach, the circumvention of the educator's presentation—the young man who was sent to the *Technikum*° and on his way fell into the habit of loitering in book stores and reading poetry; or the young man dutifully attending law school who on the way became curious about the comings and goings of ants. One remembers the scene in *The Heart Is a Lonely Hunter* where the girl hides in the bushes to hear the Capehart° in the big house play Beethoven. Perhaps she was the lucky one after all. Think of the unhappy souls inside, who see the record, worry about scratches, and most of all worry about whether they are *getting it,* whether they are bona fide music lovers. What is the best way to hear Beethoven: sitting in a proper silence around the Capehart or eavesdropping from an azalea bush?

However it may come about, we notice two traits of the second situation: (1) an openness of the thing before one—instead of being an exercise to be learned according to an approved mode, it is a garden of delights which beckons to one; (2) a sovereignty of the knower—instead of being a consumer of a prepared experience, I am a sovereign wayfarer, a wanderer in the neighborhood of being who stumbles into the garden.

One can think of two sorts of circumstances through which the thing may be restored to the person. (There is always, of course, the direct recovery: A student may simply be strong enough, brave enough, clever enough to take the dogfish and the sonnet by storm, to wrest control of it from the educators and the educational package.) First by ordeal: The Bomb falls; when the young man recovers consciousness in the shambles of the biology laboratory, there not ten inches from his nose lies the

---

Voelkerwanderung   migration of the peoples (German).
Technikum   technical school or college (German).
Capehart   An expensive record player.

dogfish. Now all at once he can see it, directly and without let, just as the exile or the prisoner or the sick man sees the sparrow at his window in all its inexhaustibility; just as the commuter who has had a heart attack sees his own hand for the first time. In these cases, the simulacrum of everydayness and of consumption has been destroyed by disaster; in the case of the bomb, literally destroyed. Secondly, by apprenticeship to a great man: One day a great biologist walks into the laboratory; he stops in front of our student's desk; he leans over, picks up the dogfish, and, ignoring instruments and procedure, probes with a broken fingernail into the little carcass. "Now here is a curious business," he says, ignoring also the proper jargon of the specialty. "Look here how this little duct reverses its direction and drops into the pelvis. Now if you would look into a coelacanth, you would see that it—" And all at once the student can see. The technician and the sophomore who loves his textbook are always offended by the genuine research man because the latter is usually a little vague and always humble before the thing; he doesn't have much use for the equipment or the jargon. Whereas the technician is never vague and never humble before the thing; he holds the thing disposed of by the principle, the formula, the textbook outline; and he thinks a great deal of equipment and jargon.

But since neither of these methods of recovering the dogfish is pedagogically feasible—perhaps the great man even less so than the Bomb—I wish to propose the following educational technique which should prove equally effective for Harvard and Shreveport High School. I propose that English poetry and biology should be taught as usual, but that at irregular intervals, poetry students should find dogfishes on their desks and biology students should find Shakespeare sonnets on their dissecting boards. I am serious in declaring that a Sarah Lawrence English major who began poking about in a dogfish with a bobby pin would learn more in thirty minutes than a biology major in a whole semester; and that the latter upon reading on her dissecting board

> That time of year Thou may'st in me behold
> When yellow leaves, or none, or few, do hang
> Upon those boughs which shake against the cold—
> Bare ruin'd choirs where late the sweet birds sang.

might catch fire at the beauty of it.

The situation of the tourist at the Grand Canyon and the biology student are special cases of a predicament in which everyone finds himself in a modern technical society—a society, that is, in which there is a division between expert and layman, planner and consumer, in which experts and planners take special measures to teach and edify the consumer. The measures taken are measures appropriate to the consumer: The expert and the planner *know* and *plan,* but the consumer *needs* and *experiences.*

There is a double deprivation. First, the thing is lost through its packaging. The very means by which the thing is presented for consumption, the very techniques by which the thing is made available as an item of need-satisfaction, these very means operate to remove the thing from the sovereignty of the knower. A loss of title occurs. The measures which the museum curator takes to present the thing to the public are self-liquidating. The upshot of the curator's efforts is not that everyone can see the exhibit but that no one can see it. The curator protests: Why are they so indifferent? Why do they even deface the exhibits? Don't they know it is theirs? But it is not theirs. It is his, the curator's. By the most exclusive sort of zoning, the museum exhibit, the park oak tree, is part of an ensemble, a package, which is almost impenetrable to them. The archeologist who puts his find in a museum so that everyone can see it accomplishes the reverse of his expectations. The result of his action is that no one can see it now but the archaeologist. He would have done better to keep it in his pocket and show it now and then to strangers.

The tourist who carves his initials in a public place, which is theoretically "his" in the first place, has good reasons for doing so, reasons which the exhibitor and planner know nothing about. He does so because in his role of consumer of an experience (a "recreational experience" to satisfy a "recreational need") he knows that he is disinherited. He is deprived of his title over being. He knows very well that he is in a very special sort of zone in which his only rights are the rights of a consumer. He moves like a ghost through schoolroom, city streets, trains, parks, movies. He carves his initials as a last desperate measure to escape his ghostly role of consumer. He is saying in effect: I am not a ghost after all; I am a sovereign person. And he establishes title the only way remaining to him, by staking his claim over one square inch of wood or stone.

Does this mean that we should get rid of museums? No, but it means that the sightseer should be prepared to enter into a struggle to recover a sight from a museum.

The second loss is the spoliation of the thing, the tree, the rock, the swallow, by the layman's misunderstanding of scientific theory. He believes that the thing is *disposed of* by theory, that it stands in the Platonic relation of being a *specimen of* such and such an underlying principle. In the transmission of scientific theory from theorist to layman, the expectation of the theorist is reversed. Instead of the marvels of the universe being made available to the public, the universe is disposed of by theory. The loss of sovereignty takes this form: As a result of the science of botany, trees are not made available to every man. On the contrary. The tree loses its proper density and mystery as a concrete existent and, as merely another *specimen of* a species, becomes itself nugatory.

Does this mean that there is no use taking biology at Harvard and Shreveport High? No, but it means that the student should know what a fight he has on his hands to rescue the specimen from the educational package. The educator is only partly to blame. For there is nothing the educator can do to provide for this need of the student. Everything the educator does only succeeds in becoming, for the student, part of the educational package. The highest role of the educator is the maieutic role of Socrates: to help the student come to himself not as a consumer of experience but as a sovereign individual.

The thing is twice lost to the consumer. First, sovereignty is lost: It is theirs, not his. Second, it is radically devalued by theory. This is a loss which has been brought about by science but through no fault of the scientist and through no fault of scientific theory. The loss has come about as a consequence of the seduction of the layman by science. The layman will be seduced as long as he regards beings as consumer items to be experienced rather than prizes to be won, and as long as he waives his sovereign rights as a person and accepts his role of consumer as the highest estate to which the layman can aspire.

As Mounier° said, the person is not something one can study and provide for; he is something one struggles for. But unless he also struggles for himself, unless he knows that there is a struggle, he is going to be just what the planners think he is.

Propaganda Under a Dictatorship

Aldous Huxley

Aldous Huxley (1894–1963), one of the most well known of modern English novelists and essayists, came from a family celebrated for its intellectual achievement. He was the son of author and editor Leonard Huxley; the grandson of the naturalist Thomas H. Huxley (see p. 49); and the grandnephew of poet and critic Matthew Arnold. His brother Sir Julian was a distinguished biologist, and his half-brother David won the 1963 Nobel Prize for his work in physiology. Huxley studied at Eton and Oxford, despite a serious eye disease that made him almost totally blind for three years. Reading with the aid of a magnifying glass, he graduated from Oxford in 1915 with honors in English literature. In 1919 he joined the staff of Athenaeum, *a London literary magazine, and began a steady production of writings in all genres.*

The success of his early novels allowed Huxley to move to Italy in 1923 and thence to France; in 1934 he traveled in the United States and finally settled in southern California near Los Angeles. He continued to write books, articles, and an occasional screenplay. He studied Vedanta and

---

Mounier Emmanuel Mounier (1905–1950), French founder of the philosophy of "personalism."

other Eastern religions and became interested in the effects of drugs on the mind.

Huxley wrote eleven novels, of which the most famous is Brave New World *(1932); others include* Antic Hay *(1923),* Point Counter Point *(1928), and* After Many a Summer Dies the Swan *(1939). His literary reputation rests equally on his over twenty volumes of essays and belles-lettres.*

Huxley's Brave New World *has turned out to be devastatingly accurate as a piece of futuristic science fiction and as a satire on modern technological mass-produced civilization. It became so widely known that in 1958 Huxley could safely give the title* Brave New World Revisited *to a study of the progress of dehumanization and mental tyranny in the intervening quarter century. The following essay is Chapter 5 of that book.*

At his trial after the Second World War, Hitler's Minister for Armaments, Albert Speer, delivered a long speech in which, with remarkable acuteness, he described the Nazi tyranny and analyzed its methods. "Hitler's dictatorship," he said, "differed in one fundamental point from all its predecessors in history. It was the first dictatorship in the present period of modern technical development, a dictatorship which made complete use of all technical means for the domination of its own country. Through technical devices like the radio and the loud-speaker, eighty million people were deprived of independent thought. It was thereby possible to subject them to the will of one man. . . . Earlier dictators needed highly qualified assistants even at the lowest level—men who could think and act independently. The totalitarian system in the period of modern technical development can dispense with such men; thanks to modern methods of communication, it is possible to mechanize the lower leadership. As a result of this there has arisen the new type of the uncritical recipient of orders."

In the Brave New World of my prophetic fable technology had advanced far beyond the point it had reached in Hitler's day; consequently the recipients of orders were far less critical than their Nazi counterparts, far more obedient to the order-giving elite. Moreover, they had been genetically standardized and postnatally conditioned to perform their subordinate functions, and could therefore be depended upon to behave almost as predictably as machines. As we shall see in a later chapter, this conditioning of "the lower leadership" is already going on under the Communist dictatorships. The Chinese and the Russians are not relying merely on the indirect effects of advancing technology; they are working directly on the psychophysical organisms of their lower leaders, subjecting minds and bodies to a system of ruthless and, from all accounts, highly effective conditioning. "Many a man," said Speer, "has been haunted by the nightmare that one day nations might be dominated by technical means. That nightmare was almost realized in Hitler's totalitarian system." Almost, but not quite. The Nazis did not have time—and perhaps did not have the intelligence and the necessary knowledge—to brainwash and condition their lower leadership. This, it may be, is one of the reasons why they failed.

Since Hitler's day the armory of technical devices at the disposal of the would-be dictator has been considerably enlarged. As well as the radio, the loud-speaker, the moving picture camera and the rotary press, the contemporary propagandist can make use of television to broadcast the image as well as the voice of his client, and can record both image and voice on spools of magnetic tape. Thanks to technological progress, Big Brother° can now be almost as omnipresent as God. Nor is it only on the technical front that the hand of the would-be dictator has been strengthened. Since Hitler's day a great deal of work has been carried out in those fields of applied psychology and neurology which are the special province of the propagandist, the indoctrinator and the brainwasher. In the past these specialists in the art of changing people's minds were empiricists. By a method of trial and error they had worked out a number of techniques and procedures, which they used very effectively without, however, knowing precisely why they were effective. Today the art of mind-control is in process of becoming a science. The practitioners of this science know what they are doing and why. They are guided in their work by theories and hypotheses solidly established on a massive foundation of experimental evidence. Thanks to the new insights and the new techniques made possible by these insights, the nightmare that was "all but realized in Hitler's totalitarian system" may soon be completely realizable.

But before we discuss these new insights and techniques let us take a look at the nightmare that so nearly came true in Nazi Germany. What were the methods used by Hitler and Goebbels° for "depriving eighty million people of independent thought and subjecting them to the will of one man"? And what was the theory of human nature upon which those terrifyingly successful methods were based? These questions can be answered, for the most part, in Hitler's own words. And what remarkably clear and astute words they are! When he writes about such vast abstractions as Race and History and Providence, Hitler is strictly unreadable. But when he writes about the German masses and the methods he used for dominating and directing them, his style changes. Nonsense gives place to sense, bombast to a hardboiled and cynical lucidity. In his philosophical lucubrations Hitler was either cloudily daydreaming or reproducing other people's half-baked notions. In his comments on crowds and

---

Big Brother   Head of the totalitarian state in George Orwell's anti-Utopian novel *Nineteen Eighty-Four.*
Goebbels   Joseph Goebbels, minister of propaganda under Hitler.

propaganda he was writing of things he knew by firsthand experience. In the words of his ablest biographer, Mr. Alan Bullock, "Hitler was the greatest demagogue in history." Those who add, "only a demagogue," fail to appreciate the nature of political power in an age of mass politics. As he himself said, "To be a leader means to be able to move the masses." Hitler's aim was first to move the masses and then, having pried them loose from their traditional loyalties and moralities, to impose upon them (with the hypnotized consent of the majority) a new authoritarian order of his own devising. "Hitler," wrote Hermann Rauschning° in 1939, "has a deep respect for the Catholic church and the Jesuit order; not because of their Christian doctrine, but because of the 'machinery' they have elaborated and controlled, their hierarchical system, their extremely clever tactics, their knowledge of human nature and their wise use of human weaknesses in ruling over believers." Ecclesiasticism without Christianity, the discipline of a monastic rule, not for God's sake or in order to achieve personal salvation, but for the sake of the State and for the greater glory and power of the demagogue turned Leader—this was the goal toward which the systematic moving of the masses was to lead.

Let us see what Hitler thought of the masses he moved and how he did the moving. The first principle from which he started was a value judgment: the masses are utterly contemptible. They are incapable of abstract thinking and uninterested in any fact outside the circle of their immediate experience. Their behavior is determined, not by knowledge and reason, but by feelings and unconscious drives. It is in these drives and feelings that "the roots of their positive as well as their negative attitudes are implanted." To be successful a propagandist must learn how to manipulate these instincts and emotions. "The driving force which has brought about the most tremendous revolutions on this earth has never been a body of scientific teaching which has gained power over the masses, but always a devotion which has inspired them, and often a kind of hysteria which has urged them into action. Whoever wishes to win over the masses must know the key that will open the door of their hearts." . . . In post-Freudian jargon, of their unconscious.

Hitler made his strongest appeal to those members of the lower middle classes who had been ruined by the inflation of 1923, and then ruined all over again by the depression of 1929 and the following years. "The masses" of whom he speaks were these bewildered, frustrated and chronically anxious millions. To make them more masslike, more homogeneously subhuman, he assembled them, by the thousands and the tens of thousands, in vast halls and arenas, where individuals could lose their personal identity, even their elementary humanity, and be merged with

---

Hermann Rauschning Former high-ranking member of the Nazi party, who criticized its anti-Semitism and resigned and fled Germany in 1935. His 1939 book, *The Revolution of Nihilism*, was a report and analysis of Adolf Hitler and the Nazi movement.

the crowd. A man or woman makes direct contact with society in two ways: as a member of some familial, professional or religious group, or as a member of a crowd. Groups are capable of being as moral and intelligent as the individuals who form them; a crowd is chaotic, has no purpose of its own and is capable of anything except intelligent action and realistic thinking. Assembled in a crowd, people lose their powers of reasoning and their capacity for moral choice. Their suggestibility is increased to the point where they cease to have any judgment or will of their own. They become very excitable, they lose all sense of individual or collective responsibility, they are subject to sudden accesses of rage, enthusiasm and panic. In a word, a man in a crowd behaves as though he had swallowed a large dose of some powerful intoxicant. He is a victim of what I have called "herd-poisoning." Like alcohol, herd-poison is an active, extraverted drug. The crowd-intoxicated individual escapes from responsibility, intelligence and morality into a kind of frantic, animal mindlessness.

During his long career as an agitator, Hitler had studied the effects of herd-poison and had learned how to exploit them for his own purposes. He had discovered that the orator can appeal to those "hidden forces" which motivate men's actions, much more effectively than can the writer. Reading is a private, not a collective activity. The writer speaks only to individuals, sitting by themselves in a state of normal sobriety. The orator speaks to masses of individuals, already well primed with herd-poison. They are at his mercy and, if he knows his business, he can do what he likes with them. As an orator, Hitler knew his business supremely well. He was able, in his own words, "to follow the lead of the great mass in such a way that from the living emotion of his hearers the apt word which he needed would be suggested to him and in its turn this would go straight to the heart of his hearers." Otto Strasser[o] called him a "loud-speaker, proclaiming the most secret desires, the least admissible instincts, the sufferings and personal revolts of a whole nation." Twenty years before Madison Avenue embarked upon "Motivational Research," Hitler was systematically exploring and exploiting the secret fears and hopes, the cravings, anxieties and frustrations of the German masses. It is by manipulating "hidden forces" that the advertising experts induce us to buy their wares—a toothpaste, a brand of cigarettes, a political candidate. And it is by appealing to the same hidden forces—and to others too dangerous for Madison Avenue to meddle with—that Hitler induced the German masses to buy themselves a Fuehrer, an insane philosophy and the Second World War.

Unlike the masses, intellectuals have a taste for rationality and an

---

Otto Strasser A leading member of the early Nazi Party. Disillusioned with Hitler, he left the Party in 1930 and was forced into exile when Hitler came to power.

interest in facts. Their critical habit of mind makes them resistant to the kind of propaganda that works so well on the majority. Among the masses "instinct is supreme, and from instinct comes faith. . . . While the healthy common folk instinctively close their ranks to form a community of the people" (under a Leader, it goes without saying) "intellectuals run this way and that, like hens in a poultry yard. With them one cannot make history; they cannot be used as elements composing a community." Intellectuals are the kind of people who demand evidence and are shocked by logical inconsistencies and fallacies. They regard over-simplification as the original sin of the mind and have no use for the slogans, the unqualified assertions and sweeping generalizations which are the propagandist's stock in trade. "All effective propaganda," Hitler wrote, "must be confined to a few bare necessities and then must be expressed in a few stereotyped formulas." These stereotyped formulas must be constantly repeated, for "only constant repetition will finally succeed in imprinting an idea upon the memory of a crowd." Philosophy teaches us to feel uncertain about the things that seem to us self-evident. Propaganda, on the other hand, teaches us to accept as self-evident matters about which it would be reasonable to suspend our judgment or to feel doubt. The aim of the demagogue is to create social coherence under his own leadership. But, as Bertrand Russell has pointed out, "systems of dogma without empirical foundations, such as scholasticism, Marxism and fascism, have the advantage of producing a great deal of social coherence among their disciples." The demagogic propagandist must therefore be consistently dogmatic. All his statements are made without qualification. There are no grays in his picture of the world; everything is either diabolically black or celestially white. In Hitler's words, the propagandist should adopt "a systematically one-sided attitude towards every problem that has to be dealt with." He must never admit that he might be wrong or that people with a different point of view might be even partially right. Opponents should not be argued with; they should be attacked, shouted down, or, if they become too much of a nuisance, liquidated. The morally squeamish intellectual may be shocked by this kind of thing. But the masses are always convinced that "right is on the side of the active aggressor."

Such, then, was Hitler's opinion of humanity in the mass. It was a very low opinion. Was it also an incorrect opinion? The tree is known by its fruits, and a theory of human nature which inspired the kind of techniques that proved so horribly effective must contain at least an element of truth. Virtue and intelligence belong to human beings as individuals freely associating with other individuals in small groups. So do sin and stupidity. But the subhuman mindlessness to which the demagogue makes his appeal, the moral imbecility on which he relies when he goads his victims into action, are characteristic not of men and women as individuals, but of men and women in masses. Mindlessness and moral idiocy are not characteristically human attributes; they are symptoms of herd-poisoning. In all the world's higher religions, salvation and enlight-enment are for individuals. The kingdom of heaven is within the mind of a person, not within the collective mindlessness of a crowd. Christ pro-mised to be present where two or three are gathered together. He did not say anything about being present where thousands are intoxicating one another with herd-poison. Under the Nazis enormous numbers of people were compelled to spend an enormous amount of time marching in serried ranks from point A to point B and back again to point A. "This keeping of the whole population on the march seemed to be a senseless waste of time and energy. Only much later," adds Hermann Rauschning, "was there revealed in it a subtle intention based on a well-judged adjustment of ends and means. Marching diverts men's thoughts. Marching kills thought. Marching makes an end of individuality. Marching is the indis-pensable magic stroke performed in order to accustom the people to a mechanical, quasi-ritualistic activity until it becomes second nature."

From his point of view and at the level where he had chosen to do his dreadful work, Hitler was perfectly correct in his estimate of human nature. To those of us who look at men and women as individuals rather than as members of crowds, or of regimented collectives, he seems hide-ously wrong. In an age of accelerating over-population, of accelerating over-organization and ever more efficient means of mass communication, how can we preserve the integrity and reassert the value of the human individual? This is a question that can still be asked and perhaps effec-tively answered. A generation from now it may be too late to find an answer and perhaps impossible, in the stifling collective climate of that future time, even to ask the question.

Women's Brains

Stephen Jay Gould

Stephen Jay Gould (born 1941) decided on his career as a paleontologist at the age of five, when his father took him to New York's American Museum of Natural History and he saw the twenty-foot-high reconstruc-tion of Tyrannosaurus rex. *After studying at Antioch and Columbia, he became a professor at Harvard, specializing, however, not in dinosaurs but in snails. He has also become a controversial thinker about major issues in the life sciences, and a much-admired, award-winning essayist.*

Gould is particularly well known for his opposition to creationism, and for his support of the idea that evolution does not occur gradually and smoothly but rather in rapid and sudden episodes. He has debated with sociobiologists on the extent to which human social behavior—such as aggression—is genetically determined. In The Mismeasure of Man *(1981)*

*he vigorously combats the notions that intelligence is a single, simple
capacity, and that it can be expressed and ranked in numbers.*

Since 1974 he has written regularly for the magazine Natural History
*essays addressed to a general audience. He ranges widely and imagina-
tively for his examples, and is just as likely to use baseball averages or
classical music or the face of Mickey Mouse as more conventionally scientific material. His essays have been collected in four books:* Ever Since
Darwin *(1977);* The Panda's Thumb *(1980), from which we have taken the
present piece;* Hen's Teeth and Horse's Toes *(1983); and* The Flamingo's
Smile *(1985).*

In the prelude to *Middlemarch,* George Eliot lamented the unfulfilled
lives of talented women:

> Some have felt that these blundering lives are due to the inconvenient indefi-
> niteness with which the Supreme Power has fashioned the natures of women:
> if there were one level of feminine incompetence as strict as the ability to count
> three and no more, the social lot of women might be treated with scientific
> certitude.

Eliot goes on to discount the idea of innate limitation, but while she
wrote in 1872, the leaders of European anthropometry were trying to
measure "with scientific certitude" the inferiority of women. Anthropometry, or measurement of the human body, is not so fashionable a field
these days, but it dominated the human sciences for much of the nineteenth century and remained popular until intelligence testing replaced
skull measurement as a favored device for making invidious comparisons
among races, classes, and sexes. Craniometry, or measurement of the
skull, commanded the most attention and respect. Its unquestioned
leader, Paul Broca (1824–80), professor of clinical surgery at the Faculty
of Medicine in Paris, gathered a school of disciples and imitators around
himself. Their work, so meticulous and apparently irrefutable, exerted
great influence and won high esteem as a jewel of nineteenth-century
science.

Broca's work seemed particularly invulnerable to refutation. Had he
not measured with the most scrupulous care and accuracy? (Indeed, he
had. I have the greatest respect for Broca's meticulous procedure. His
numbers are sound. But science is an inferential exercise, not a catalog
of facts. Numbers, by themselves, specify nothing. All depends upon what
you do with them.) Broca depicted himself as an apostle of objectivity, a
man who bowed before facts and cast aside superstition and sentimentality. He declared that "there is no faith, however respectable, no interest,
however legitimate, which must not accommodate itself to the progress
of human knowledge and bend before truth." Women, like it or not, had
smaller brains than men and, therefore, could not equal them in intelligence. This fact, Broca argued, may reinforce a common prejudice in male

society, but it is also a scientific truth. L. Manouvrier, a black sheep in Broca's fold, rejected the inferiority of women and wrote with feeling about the burden imposed upon them by Broca's numbers:

> Women displayed their talents and their diplomas. They also invoked philosophical authorities. But they were opposed by *numbers* unknown to Condorcet or to John Stuart Mill. These numbers fell upon poor women like a sledge hammer, and they were accompanied by commentaries and sarcasms more ferocious than the most misogynist imprecations of certain church fathers. The theologians had asked if women had a soul. Several centuries later, some scientists were ready to refuse them a human intelligence.

Broca's argument rested upon two sets of data: the larger brains of men in modern societies, and a supposed increase in male superiority through time. His most extensive data came from autopsies performed personally in four Parisian hospitals. For 292 male brains, he calculated an average weight of 1,325 grams; 140 female brains averaged 1,144 grams for a difference of 181 grams, or 14 percent of the male weight. Broca understood, of course, that part of this difference could be attributed to the greater height of males. Yet he made no attempt to measure the effect of size alone and actually stated that it cannot account for the entire difference because we know, a priori, that women are not as intelligent as men (a premise that the data were supposed to test, not rest upon):

> We might ask if the small size of the female brain depends exclusively upon the small size of her body. Tiedemann has proposed this explanation. But we must not forget that women are, on the average, a little less intelligent than men, a difference which we should not exaggerate but which is, nonetheless, real. We are therefore permitted to suppose that the relatively small size of the female brain depends in part upon her physical inferiority and in part upon her intellectual inferiority.

In 1873, the year after Eliot published *Middlemarch,* Broca measured the cranial capacities of prehistoric skulls from L'Homme Mort cave. Here he found a difference of only 99.5 cubic centimeters between males and females, while modern populations range from 129.5 to 220.7. Topinard, Broca's chief disciple, explained the increasing discrepancy through time as a result of differing evolutionary pressures upon dominant men and passive women:

> The man who fights for two or more in the struggle for existence, who has all the responsibility and the cares of tomorrow, who is constantly active in combating the environment and human rivals, needs more brain than the woman whom he must protect and nourish, the sedentary woman, lacking any interior occupations, whose role is to raise children, love, and be passive.

In 1879, Gustave Le Bon, chief misogynist of Broca's school, used these data to publish what must be the most vicious attack upon women in modern scientific literature (no one can top Aristotle). I do not claim his views were representative of Broca's school, but they were published in France's most respected anthropological journal. Le Bon concluded:

> In the most intelligent races, as among the Parisians, there are a large number of women whose brains are closer in size to those of gorillas than to the most developed male brains. This inferiority is so obvious that no one can contest it for a moment; only its degree is worth discussion. All psychologists who have studied the intelligence of women, as well as poets and novelists, recognize today that they represent the most inferior forms of human evolution and that they are closer to children and savages than to an adult, civilized man. They excel in fickleness, inconstancy, absence of thought and logic, and incapacity to reason. Without doubt there exist some distinguished women, very superior to the average man, but they are as exceptional as the birth of any monstrosity, as, for example, of a gorilla with two heads; consequently, we may neglect them entirely.

Nor did Le Bon shrink from the social implications of his views. He was horrified by the proposal of some American reformers to grant women higher education on the same basis as men:

> A desire to give them the same education, and, as a consequence, to propose the same goals for them, is a dangerous chimera. . . . The day when, misunderstanding the inferior occupations which nature has given her, women leave the home and take part in our battles; on this day a social revolution will begin, and everything that maintains the sacred ties of the family will disappear.

Sound familiar?*

I have reexamined Broca's data, the basis for all this derivative pronouncement, and I find his numbers sound but his interpretation ill-founded, to say the least. The data supporting his claim for increased difference through time can be easily dismissed. Broca based his contention on the samples from L'Homme Mort alone—only seven male and six female skulls in all. Never have so little data yielded such far ranging conclusions.

In 1888, Topinard published Broca's more extensive data on the Parisian hospitals. Since Broca recorded height and age as well as brain size, we may use modern statistics to remove their effect. Brain weight decreases with age, and Broca's women were, on average, considerably older than his men. Brain weight increases with height, and his average man was almost half a foot taller than his average woman. I used multiple regression, a technique that allowed me to assess simultaneously the

---

*When I wrote this essay, I assumed that Le Bon was a marginal, if colorful, figure. I have since learned that he was a leading scientist, one of the founders of social psychology, and best known for a seminal study on crowd behavior, still cited today (*La psychologie des foules,* 1895), and for his work on unconscious motivation.

influence of height and age upon brain size. In an analysis of the data for women, I found that, at average male height and age, a woman's brain would weigh 1,212 grams. Correction for height and age reduces Broca's measured difference of 181 grams by more than a third, to 113 grams.

I don't know what to make of this remaining difference because I cannot assess other factors known to influence brain size in a major way. Cause of death has an important effect: degenerative disease often entails a substantial diminution of brain size. (This effect is separate from the decrease attributed to age alone.) Eugene Schreider, also working with Broca's data, found that men killed in accidents had brains weighing, on average, 60 grams more than men dying of infectious diseases. The best modern data I can find (from American hospitals) records a full 100-gram difference between death by degenerative arteriosclerosis and by violence or accident. Since so many of Broca's subjects were very elderly women, we may assume that lengthy degenerative disease was more common among them than among the men.

More importantly, modern students of brain size still have not agreed on a proper measure for eliminating the powerful effect of body size. Height is partly adequate, but men and women of the same height do not share the same body build. Weight is even worse than height, because most of its variation reflects nutrition rather than intrinsic size—fat versus skinny exerts little influence upon the brain. Manouvrier took up this subject in the 1880s and argued that muscular mass and force should be used. He tried to measure this elusive property in various ways and found a marked difference in favor of men, even in men and women of the same height. When he corrected for what he called "sexual mass," women actually came out slightly ahead in brain size.

Thus, the corrected 113-gram difference is surely too large; the true figure is probably close to zero and may as well favor women as men. And 113 grams, by the way, is exactly the average difference between a 5 foot 4 inch and a 6 foot 4 inch male in Broca's data. We would not (especially us short folks) want to ascribe greater intelligence to tall men. In short, who knows what to do with Broca's data? They certainly don't permit any confident claim that men have bigger brains than women.

To appreciate the social role of Broca and his school, we must recognize that his statements about the brains of women do not reflect an isolated prejudice toward a single disadvantaged group. They must be weighed in the context of a general theory that supported contemporary social distinctions as biologically ordained. Women, blacks, and poor people suffered the same disparagement, but women bore the brunt of Broca's argument because he had easier access to data on women's brains. Women were singularly denigrated but they also stood as surrogates for other disenfranchised groups. As one of Broca's disciples wrote in 1881: "Men of the black races have a brain scarcely heavier than that of white women." This juxtaposition extended into many other realms of anthropological argument, particularly to claims that, anatomically and emotionally, both women and blacks were like white children—and that white children, by the theory of recapitulation, represented an ancestral (primitive) adult stage of human evolution. I do not regard as empty rhetoric the claim that women's battles are for all of us.

Maria Montessori did not confine her activities to educational reform for young children. She lectured on anthropology for several years at the University of Rome, and wrote an influential book entitled *Pedagogical Anthropology* (English edition, 1913). Montessori was no egalitarian. She supported most of Broca's work and the theory of innate criminality proposed by her compatriot Cesare Lombroso. She measured the circumference of children's heads in her schools and inferred that the best prospects had bigger brains. But she had no use for Broca's conclusions about women. She discussed Manouvrier's work at length and made much of his tentative claim that women, after proper correction of the data, had slightly larger brains than men. Women, she concluded, were intellectually superior, but men had prevailed heretofore by dint of physical force. Since technology has abolished force as an instrument of power, the era of women may soon be upon us: "In such an epoch there will really be superior human beings, there will really be men strong in morality and in sentiment. Perhaps in this way the reign of women is approaching, when the enigma of her anthropological superiority will be deciphered. Woman was always the custodian of human sentiment, morality and honor."

This represents one possible antidote to "scientific" claims for the constitutional inferiority of certain groups. One may affirm the validity of biological distinctions but argue that the data have been misinterpreted by prejudiced men with a stake in the outcome, and that disadvantaged groups are truly superior. In recent years, Elaine Morgan has followed this strategy in her *Descent of Woman,* a speculative reconstruction of human prehistory from the woman's point of view—and as farcical as more famous tall tales by and for men.

I prefer another strategy. Montessori and Morgan followed Broca's philosophy to reach a more congenial conclusion. I would rather label the whole enterprise of setting a biological value upon groups for what it is: irrelevant and highly injurious. George Eliot well appreciated the special tragedy that biological labeling imposed upon members of disadvantaged groups. She expressed it for people like herself—women of extraordinary talent. I would apply it more widely—not only to those whose dreams are flouted but also to those who never realize that they may dream—but I cannot match her prose. In conclusion, then, the rest of Eliot's prelude to *Middlemarch:*

The limits of variation are really much wider than anyone would imagine from the sameness of women's coiffure and the favorite love stories in prose and verse. Here and there a cygnet is reared uneasily among the ducklings in the brown pond, and never finds the living stream in fellowship with its own oary-footed kind. Here and there is born a Saint Theresa, foundress of nothing, whose loving heartbeats and sobs after an unattained goodness tremble off and are dispersed among hindrances instead of centering in some long-recognizable deed.

Conclusion

On the Need for Feeling

Although we discuss thinking and feeling in two separate sections, we do not mean to suggest that they exist as separate capacities of mind. Our thoughts are so entangled with our feelings that it is probably impossible to achieve pure thought or pure feeling. Indeed, as William Golding (p. 25) and James Harvey Robinson (p. 31) point out, we often mistake one for the other.

But even if we could separate thinking from feeling, thinking is itself never enough. To make that point, we open the section with Jonathan Swift's classic satire, a biting example of the consequences of pure logic untempered by human feeling.

College work—in fact, our whole educational tradition—often seems to nurture and reward rational thought at the expense of human feeling. We talk of a trained mind but we rarely talk of educated feelings. Yet threatened as we seem to be today by an impersonal, bureaucratic world, by a mechanized, standardized, alienating environment, we need more and more to be concerned with our capacity to feel: to love, to sympathize, to imagine, to appreciate.

Robertson Davies speaks to that need, charging university graduates "to take pains not to lose your capacity to feel," not to confuse "feeling nothing deeply" with sophistication, and offering some advice on how to cultivate the capacity to feel.

The next two pieces approach the importance of feeling and the limitations of rational thought from different directions. Proust describes how sensation, not intellect, has the power to unlock and call up feeling memories of past events and impressions. Annie

Dillard's narrative relates her unexpected encounter with a wild weasel, which she describes as "a clearing blow to the gut"; it leads her to wonder whether "I might learn something of mindlessness, something of the purity of living in the physical senses and the dignity of living without bias or motive."

For expressing feeling in words, however, poetry is best, and so we present last a group of four poems that were written largely in appreciation of feeling.

A Modest Proposal

Jonathan Swift

Jonathan Swift (1667–1745) is one of the most famous writers in English. He was born of an English family in Dublin and became an Anglican clergyman in a period of disappointment over his hopes for a political career in England. He nevertheless pursued politics; in 1713 the Tory government rewarded him for his powerful writing—in the manner of those times—with the deanship of St. Patrick's, Dublin. However, he spent little time in Ireland until the fall of the party forced his return to Dublin a few years later, where he became for the rest of his life a champion of the Irish people against English oppression. Meanwhile, he had become an intimate of the best English writers of his day, a leading political pamphleteer, and the author of a series of writings that would make him the greatest of English satirists. Especially notable are A Tale of a Tub *and* The Battle of the Books *published in 1704, the incomparable* Gulliver's Travels *(1726), and the present piece,* A Modest Proposal, *published in 1729, at a time when the miseries of the poor in Ireland seemed to Swift to have reached an intolerable state. Calculated to arouse attention and sympathy in Ireland and England, it has become a classic, notable particularly for its daring use of irony.*

It is a melancholly Object to those, who walk through this great Town, or travel in the Country; when they see the *Streets,* the *Roads,* and *Cabbin-doors* crowded with *Beggars* of the Female Sex, followed by three, four, or six Children, *all in Rags,* and importuning every Passenger for an Alms. These *Mothers,* instead of being able to work for their honest Livelyhood, are forced to employ all their Time in Stroling to beg Sustenance for their *helpless Infants;* who, as they grow up, either turn *Thieves* for want of Work; or leave their *dear Native Country,* to fight for the *Pretender in Spain,* or sell themselves to the *Barbadoes.*

I think it is agreed by all Parties, that this prodigious Number of

Children in the Arms, or on the Backs, or at the Heels of their Mothers, and frequently of their *Fathers,* is *in the present deplorable State of the Kingdom,* a very great additional Grievance; and therefore, whoever could find out a fair, cheap, and easy Method of making these Children sound and useful Members of the Commonwealth, would deserve so well of the Publick, as to have his Statue set up for a Preserver of the Nation.

But my Intention is very far from being confined to provide only for the Children of *professed Beggars:* It is of a much greater Extent, and shall take in the whole Number of Infants at a certain Age, who are born of Parents, in effect as little able to support them, as those who demand our Charity in the Streets.

As to my own Part, having turned my Thoughts for many Years, upon this important Subject, and maturely weighed the several *Schemes of other Projectors,* I have always found them grossly mistaken in their Computation. It is true a Child, *just dropt from its Dam,* may be supported by her Milk, for a Solar Year with little other Nourishment; at most not above the Value of two Shillings; which the Mother may certainly get, or the Value in *Scraps,* by her lawful Occupation of *Begging:* And, it is exactly at one Year old, that I propose to provide for them in such a Manner, as, instead of being a Charge upon their *Parents,* or the *Parish,* or *wanting Food and Raiment* for the rest of their Lives; they shall, on the Contrary, contribute to the Feeding, and partly to the Cloathing, of many Thousands.

There is likewise another great Advantage in my *Scheme,* that it will prevent those *voluntary Abortions,* and that horrid Practice of *Women murdering their Bastard Children;* alas! too frequent among us; sacrificing the *poor innocent Babes,* I doubt, more to avoid the Expense than the Shame; which would move Tears and Pity in the most Savage and inhuman Breast.

The Number of Souls in *Ireland* being usually reckoned one Million and a half; of these I calculate there may be about Two hundred Thousand Couple whose Wives are Breeders; from which Number I subtract thirty thousand Couples, who are able to maintain their own Children; although I apprehend there cannot be so many, under *the present Distresses of the Kingdom;* but this being granted, there will remain an Hundred and Seventy Thousand Breeders. I again subtract Fifty Thousand, for those Women who miscarry, or whose Children die by Accident, or Disease, within the Year. There only remain an Hundred and Twenty Thousand Children of poor Parents, annually born: The Question therefore is, How this Number shall be reared, and provided for? Which, as I have already said, under the present Situation of Affairs, is utterly impossible, by all the Methods hitherto proposed: For we can *neither employ them in Handicraft or Agriculture;* we neither build Houses, (I mean in the Country) nor cultivate Land: They can very seldom pick up a Livelihood *by Stealing* until they arrive at six Years old; except where they are of towardly Parts;

although, I confess, they learn the Rudiments much earlier; during which Time, they can, however, be properly looked upon only as *Probationers;* as I have been informed by a principal Gentleman in the County of *Cavan,* who protested to me, that he never knew above one or two Instances under the Age of six, even in a Part of the Kingdom *so renowned for the quickest Proficiency in that Art.*

I am assured by our Merchants, that a Boy or a Girl before twelve Years old, is no saleable Commodity; and even when they come to this Age, they will not yield above Three Pounds, or Three Pounds and half a Crown at most, on the Exchange; which cannot turn to Account either to the Parents or the Kingdom; the Charge of Nutriment and Rags, having been at least four Times that Value.

I shall now therefore humbly propose my own Thoughts; which I hope will not be liable to the least Objection.

I have been assured by a very knowing *American* of my Acquaintance in *London;* that a young healthy Child, well nursed, is, at a Year old, a most delicious, nourishing, and wholesome Food; whether *Stewed, Roasted, Baked,* or *Boiled;* and, I make no doubt, that it will equally serve in a *Fricasie,* or *Ragoust.*

I do therefore humbly offer it to *publick Consideration,* that of the Hundred and Twenty Thousand Children, already computed, Twenty thousand may be reserved for Breed; whereof only one Fourth Part to be Males; which is more than we allow to *Sheep, black Cattle,* or *Swine;* and my Reason is, that these Children are seldom the Fruits of Marriage, *a Circumstance not much regarded by our Savages;* therefore, *one Male* will be sufficient to serve *four Females.* That the remaining Hundred thousand, may, at a Year old, be offered in Sale to the *Persons of Quality and Fortune,* through the Kingdom; always advising the Mother to let them suck plentifully in the last Month, so as to render them plump, and fat for a good Table. A Child will make two Dishes at an Entertainment for Friends; and when the Family dines alone, the fore or hind Quarter will make a reasonable Dish; and seasoned with a little Pepper or Salt, will be very good Boiled on the fourth Day, especially in *Winter.*

I have reckoned upon a Medium, that a Child just born will weigh Twelve Pounds; and in a solar Year, if tolerably nursed, encreaseth to twenty eight Pounds.

I grant this Food will be somewhat dear, and therefore very *proper for Landlords;* who, as they have already devoured most of the Parents, seem to have the best Title to the Children.

Infants Flesh will be in Season throughout the Year; but more plentiful in *March,* and a little before and after: For we are told by a grave[1]Author, an eminent *French* physician, that *Fish being a prolifick Dyet,* there are

---

[1]Rabelais.

more Children born in *Roman Catholick Countries,* about Nine Months
after *Lent,* than at any other Season: Therefore reckoning a Year after
Lent, the Markets will be more glutted than usual; because the Number
of *Popish Infants,* is, at least, three to one in this Kingdom; and therefore
it will have one other Collateral Advantage, by lessening the Number of
Papists among us.

I have already computed the Charge of nursing a Beggar's Child (in
which List I reckon all *Cottagers, Labourers,* and Four fifths of the *Farmers*) to be about two Shillings *per Annum,* Rags included; and I believe,
no Gentleman would repine to give Ten Shillings for the *Carcase of a good
fat Child;* which, as I have said, will make four Dishes of excellent nutri-
tive Meat, when he hath only some particular Friend, or his own Family,
to dine with him. Thus the Squire will learn to be a good Landlord, and
grow popular among his Tenants; the Mother will have Eight Shillings
net Profit, and be fit for Work until she produceth another Child.

Those who are more thrifty *(as I must confess the Times require)* may
flay the Carcase; the Skin of which, artificially dressed, will make admirable *Gloves for Ladies,* and *Summer Boots for fine Gentlemen.*

As to our City of *Dublin;* Shambles may be appointed for this Purpose,
in the most convenient Parts of it; and Butchers we may be assured will
not be wanting; although I rather recommend buying the Children alive,
and dressing them hot from the Knife, as we do *roasting Pigs.*

A very worthy Person, a true Lover of his Country, and whose Virtues
I highly esteem, was lately pleased, in discoursing on this Matter, to
offer a Refinement upon my Scheme. He said, that many Gentlemen of
this Kingdom, having of late destroyed their Deer; he conceived, that
the Want of Venison might be well supplied by the Bodies of young Lads
and Maidens, not exceeding fourteen Years of Age, nor under twelve; so
great a Number of both Sexes in every Country being now ready to
starve, for Want of Work and Service: And these to be disposed of by
their Parents, if alive, or otherwise by their nearest Relations. But with
due Deference to so excellent a Friend, and so deserving a Patriot, I
cannot be altogether in his Sentiments. For as to the Males, my *American* Acquaintance assured me from frequent Experience, that their
Flesh was generally tough and lean, like that of our School-boys, by
continual Exercise, and their Taste disagreeable; and to fatten them
would not answer the Charge. Then, as to the Females, it would, I think,
with humble Submission, *be a Loss to the Publick,* because they soon
would become Breeders themselves: And besides it is not improbable,
that some scrupulous People might be apt to censure such a Practice
(although indeed very unjustly) as a little bordering upon Cruelty;
which, I confess, hath always been with me the strongest Objection
against any Project, how well soever intended.

But in order to justify my Friend; he confessed, that this Expedient was put into his Head by the famous *Salmanaazor,*° a Native of the Island *Formosa,* who came from thence to *London,* above twenty Years ago, and in Conversation told my Friend, that in his Country, when any young Person happened to be put to Death, the Executioner sold the Carcase to *Persons of Quality,* as a prime Dainty; and that, in his Time, the Body of a plump Girl of fifteen, who was crucified for an Attempt to poison the Emperor, was sold to his Imperial *Majesty's prime Minister of State,* and other great *Mandarins* of the Court, *in Joints from the Gibbet,* at Four hundred Crowns. Neither indeed can I deny, that if the same Use were made of several plump young Girls in this Town, who, without one single Groat to their Fortunes, cannot stir Abroad without a Chair, and appear at the *Play-house,* and *Assemblies* in foreign Fineries, which they never will pay for; the Kingdom would not be the worse.

Some Persons of a desponding Spirit are in great Concern about that vast Number of poor People, who are Aged, Diseased, or Maimed; and I have been desired to employ my Thoughts what Course may be taken, to ease the Nation of so grievous an Incumbrance. But I am not in the least Pain upon that Matter; because it is very well known, that they are every Day *dying,* and *rotting,* by *Cold* and *Famine,* and *Filth,* and *Vermin,* as fast as can be reasonably expected. And as to the younger Labourers, they are now in almost as hopeful a Condition: They cannot get Work, and consequently pine away for Want of Nourishment, to a Degree, that if at any Time they are accidentally hired to common Labour, they have not Strength to perform it; and thus the Country, and themselves, are in a fair Way of being soon delivered from the Evils to come.

I have too long digressed; and therefore shall return to my Subject. I think the Advantages by the Proposal which I have made, are obvious, and many, as well as of the highest Importance.

For, *First,* as I have already observed, it would greatly lessen the *Number of Papists,* with whom we are yearly overrun; being the principal Breeders of the Nation, as well as our most dangerous Enemies; and who stay at home on Purpose, with a Design to *deliver the Kingdom to the Pretender;* hoping to take their Advantage by the Absence *of so many good Protestants,* who have chosen rather to leave their Country, than stay at home, and pay Tithes against their Conscience, to an idolatrous *Episcopal Curate.*

Secondly, The poorer Tenants will have something valuable of their own, which, by Law, may be made liable to Distress, and help to pay their Landlord's Rent; their Corn and Cattle being already seized, and *Money a Thing unknown.*

Thirdly, Whereas the Maintenance of an Hundred Thousand Children,

---

Salmanaazor George Psalmanazar (c. 1679–1763) was a Frenchman who posed as a native of Formosa and wrote a "Description" of Formosa, published in 1704. His fraud was widely known by the time of *A Modest Proposal.*

from two Years old, and upwards, cannot be computed at less than ten Shillings a Piece *per Annum,* the Nation's Stock will be thereby encreased Fifty Thousand Pounds *per Annum;* besides the Profit of a new Dish, introduced to the Tables of all *Gentlemen of Fortune* in the Kingdom, who have any Refinement in Taste; and the Money will circulate among ourselves, the Goods being entirely of our own Growth and Manufacture.

Fourthly, The constant Breeders, besides the Gain of Eight Shillings *Sterling per Annum,* by the Sale of their Children, will be rid of the Charge of maintaining them after the first Year.

Fifthly, This Food would likewise bring great *Custom to Taverns,* where the Vintners will certainly be so prudent, as to procure the best Receipts for dressing it to Perfection; and consequently, have their Houses frequented by all the *fine Gentlemen,* who justly value themselves upon their Knowledge in good Eating; and a skilful Cook, who understands how to oblige his Guests, will contrive to make it as expensive as they please.

Sixthly, This would be a great Inducement to Marriage, which all wise Nations have either encouraged by Rewards, or enforced by Laws and Penalties. It would encrease the Care and Tenderness of Mothers towards their Children, when they were sure of a Settlement for Life, to the poor Babes, provided in some Sort by the Publick, to their annual Profit instead of Expense. We should soon see an honest Emulation among the married Women, *which of them could bring the fattest Child to the Market.* Men would become as *fond* of their Wives, during the Time of their Pregnancy, as they are now of their *Mares* in Foal, their *Cows* in Calf, or *Sows* when they are ready to farrow; nor offer to beat or kick them, (as it is too *frequent* a Practice) for fear of a Miscarriage.

Many other Advantages might be enumerated. For instance, the Addition of some Thousand Carcasses in our Exportation of barrelled Beef: The Propagation of *Swines Flesh,* and Improvement in the Art of making good *Bacon;* so much wanted among us by the great Destruction of *Pigs,* too frequent at our Tables, and are no way comparable in Taste, or Magnificence, to a well-grown fat yearling Child; which, roasted whole, will make a considerable Figure at a *Lord Mayor's Feast,* or any other publick Entertainment. But this, and many others, I omit; being studious of Brevity.

Supposing that one Thousand Families in this City, would be constant Customers for Infants Flesh; besides others who might have it at *merry Meetings,* particularly *Weddings and Christenings;* I compute that *Dublin* would take off, annually, about Twenty Thousand Carcasses; and the rest of the Kingdom (where probably they will be sold somewhat cheaper) the remaining Eighty Thousand.

I can think of no one Objection, that will possibly be raised against this Proposal; unless it should be urged, that the Number of People will be thereby much lessened in the Kingdom. This I freely own; and it was indeed one principal Design in offering it to the World. I desire the Reader will observe, that I calculate my Remedy *for this one individual Kingdom of* IRELAND, *and for no other that ever was, is, or I think ever can be upon Earth.* Therefore, let no man talk to me of other Expedients: *Of taxing our Absentees at five Shillings a Pound: Of using neither Cloaths, nor Houshold Furniture except what is of our own Growth and Manufacture: Of utterly rejecting the Materials and Instruments that promote foreign Luxury: Of curing the Expensiveness of Pride, Vanity, Idleness, and Gaming in our Women: Of introducing a Vein of Parsimony, Prudence and Temperance: Of learning to love our Country, wherein we differ even from* LAPLANDERS, *and the Inhabitants of* TOPINAMBOO: *Of quitting our Animosities, and Factions; nor act any longer like the Jews, who were murdering one another at the very Moment their City was taken: Of being a little cautious not to sell our Country and Consciences for nothing: Of teaching Landlords to have, at least, one Degree of Mercy towards their Tenants.* Lastly, *Of putting a Spirit of Honesty, Industry, and Skill into our Shop-keepers; who, if a Resolution could now be taken to buy only our native Goods, would immediately unite to cheat and exact upon us in the Price, the Measure, and the Goodness; nor could ever yet be brought to make one fair Proposal of just Dealing, though often and earnestly invited to it.*

Therefore I repeat, let no Man talk to me of these and the like Expedients; till he hath, at least, a Glimpse of Hope, that there will ever be some hearty and sincere Attempt to put *them in Practice.*

But, as to my self; having been wearied out for many Years with offering vain, idle, visionary Thoughts; and at length utterly despairing of Success, I fortunately fell upon this Proposal; which, as it is wholly new, so it hath something *solid* and *real,* of no Expence, and little Trouble, full in our own Power; and whereby we can incur no Danger in *disobliging* ENGLAND: for this Kind of Commodity will not bear Exportation; the Flesh being of too tender a Consistence, to admit a long Continuance of Salt; *although, perhaps, I could name a Country, which would be glad to eat up our whole Nation without it.*

After all, I am not so violently bent upon my own Opinion, as to reject any Offer proposed by wise Men, which shall be found equally innocent, cheap, easy, and effectual. But before something of that Kind shall be advanced, in Contradiction to my Scheme, and offering a better; I desire the Author, or Authors, will be pleased maturely to consider two Points. *First,* As Things now stand, how they will be able to find Food and Raiment, for a Hundred Thousand useless Mouths and Backs? And *secondly,* There being a round Million of Creatures in human Figure, throughout this Kingdom; whose whole Subsistence, put into a common Stock, would leave them in Debt two Millions of Pounds *Sterling;* adding those, who are Beggars by Profession, to the Bulk of Farmers, Cottagers, and Labourers, with their Wives and Children, who are Beggars in Effect; I desire those Politicians, who dislike my Overture, and may perhaps be so bold to attempt an Answer, that they will first ask the Parents of these Mortals, Whether they would not, at this Day, think it a great Happiness to have been sold for Food at a Year old, in the Manner I prescribe; and thereby have avoided such a perpetual Scene of Misfortunes, as they have since gone through; by the *Oppression of Landlords;* the Impossibility of paying Rent, without Money or Trade; the Want of common Sustenance, with neither House nor Cloaths, to cover them from the Inclemencies of Weather; and the most inevitable Prospect of intailing the like, or greater Miseries upon their Breed for ever.

I profess, in the Sincerity of my Heart, that I have not the least personal Interest, in endeavouring to promote this necessary Work; having no other Motive than the *publick Good of my Country, by advancing our Trade, providing for Infants, relieving the Poor, and giving some Pleasure to the Rich.* I have no Children, by which I can propose to get a single Penny; the youngest being nine Years old, and my Wife past Child-bearing.

The Deadliest of the Sins

Robertson Davies

Robertson Davies, a Canadian, has written numerous novels, plays, and works of criticism. Born in 1913 in Ontario, he attended Queen's University there, and then studied in England, receiving his degree from Balliol College, Oxford. Davies has been a journalist, actor, editor, and teacher; from 1960 to 1981 he was Professor of English at the University of Toronto.

The "Deptford Trilogy" established Davies' reputation in the United States. These three novels, Fifth Business *(1970),* The Manticore *(1972), and* World of Wonders *(1975), abound with rich, almost Dickensian characters. His theme, he says, is the isolation of the human spirit; it is "worked out in terms of characters who are trying to escape from early influences and find their own place in the world but who are reluctant to do so in a way that will bring pain and disappointment to others." A masterful plotter and storyteller, he is knowledgeably and comfortably at home with myth and magic. He re-creates for his readers many varied worlds: a rural Canadian town, a European Jesuit retreat, a traveling freak show. Recent books include* The Mirror of Nature *(1983),* What's Bred in the Bone *(1985), and* The Papers of Samuel Marchbanks *(1985).*

The selection printed here is from One Half of Robertson Davies *(1977), a book "composed of pieces written to be spoken." The selection is a talk he gave at Queen's University when he accepted an honorary degree. We omit the opening remarks on his personal relationships to the university.*

What shall we talk about, you and I, who are getting our first degrees from Queen's today? The problem is a little easier than is usually the case, because we are both going into new jobs. I have been an author for many years, and I intend to go on being one. But being an author isn't a job—it is a state of mind; also, it is not a gainful occupation except in a rather restricted sense. I have been earning my living as a journalist for twenty years, and now I am giving up that sort of work to take a different sort of job in a university. I shall be very green at it, and I expect I shall do a lot of things the wrong way. Perhaps I shall be a failure, but I have failed at several things already, and somehow I have lived through it. Failure at a specific task is always disagreeable and sometimes it is humiliating. But there is only one kind of failure that really breaks the spirit, and that is failure in the art of life itself. That is the failure that one does well to fear.

What is it like, this failure in the art of life? It is the failure which manifests itself in a loss of interest in really important things. It does not come suddenly; there is nothing dramatic about it, and thus it works with a dreadful advantage; it creeps upon us, and once it has us in its grip, it is hard for us to recognize what ails us.

It is not for nothing that this failure was reckoned by medieval theologians as one of the Seven Deadly Sins. I suppose you know what they were. Wrath, Gluttony, Envy, Avarice, and Lechery are not very hard to recognize and are perilously easy to justify, by one means or another. Pride is an extremely subtle sin because it is so clever at disguising itself as something else, and those astute men St. Ambrose and St. Augustine thought it the most dangerous of all the sins. But it is the seventh which I think is particularly prevalent in our day; medieval theologians called it Sloth.

Sloth is not really a suitable name for it now, because the word has come to mean a sluggishness and inactivity which is chiefly physical. But the sloth the theologians meant, the sloth which can damn you in this world and perhaps in the next, is spiritual. There was a better name, a Latin name, for it; it was also called Accidie, and it meant intellectual and spiritual torpor, indifference, and lethargy.

To be guilty of Acedia it is not necessary to be physically sluggish at all. You can be as busy as a bee. You can fill your days with activity, bustling from meeting to meeting, sitting on committees, running from one party to another in a perfect whirlwind of movement. But if, meanwhile, your feelings and sensibilities are withering, if your relationships with people near to you are becoming more and more superficial, if you are losing touch even with yourself, it is Acedia which has claimed you for its own.

How can it be recognized? Anatole France[0] said that the great danger

---

Anatole France French novelist, poet, and political satirist (1844–1924) who was awarded the 1921 Nobel Prize in literature.

of increasing age was that the feelings atrophied, and we mistook the sensation for the growth of wisdom. It is true that as one grows older, one's sense of proportion may become greater, and things which troubled us or wounded us deeply in our youth seem less significant. But that is a different thing from feeling nothing deeply, and leaping to the conclusion that therefore nothing is really very important. As one grows older, one learns how to spare oneself many kinds of unnecessary pain, but one is in great danger if one ceases to feel pain of any kind. If you cannot feel pain at some of the harsh circumstances of life, it is very likely that you have ceased to feel joy at some of the satisfactions and delights of life. When that happens, one lives at all times under a mental and spiritual cloud; it is always wet weather in the soul. That is Acedia, and it was called a Deadly Sin because it dimmed and discouraged the spirit, and at last killed it.

I am sure that all of you know some people who have yielded to Acedia. They are the dampers, the wet blankets of life. Unfortunately some of them have a great attraction for the young. Their chronic lack of enthusiasm looks so much like sophistication. They are often clever people, who are adept at putting a chilly finger on the weak spot in whatever attracts their friends. They seldom make mistakes, because they never put themselves in a position where they are not complete masters of the situation. They take a sly pleasure in the failure of others, and they are always ready to say 'I told you so'. They have made just one great—indeed monstrous—mistake: they have died to joy and pain, and thus to feeling.

The opposites of these people are not, of course, those who allow every enthusiasm to run away with them, whose hearts always rule their heads, who go a-whoring after everything that is new. They are, on the contrary, people who take pains to keep their common sense in repair, and who keep their intelligence bright, but who also make daily efforts to meet experience with a fresh vision, and to give to everything that comes their way the measure of feeling, of emotion, of charity and understanding— yes, and also of pain—that it needs in order to understand it.

Because you are university people, I assume that you are people in whom mind is more prominent and better trained than is feeling. If you had not had some intellectual bias—even of quite a mild sort—it is unlikely that you would be here today to receive a degree. Therefore you must take special care that, in the years ahead of you, feeling is not neglected.

The temptation to neglect feeling is strong. You see—I say this knowing that it is blasphemy within university walls—it is really very much easier to think sensibly than it is to feel sensibly. We all know what messes people get into when they feel too much and think too little; but those people do not compel my pity so much as the hundreds of thousands whose lives are cast in a mould of midget tragedy because they think a good deal, in a strangulated, ill-nourished fashion, but hardly feel at all. These are the victims of Acedia.

Therefore I charge you, whether you are struggling under the burden of a mighty intellect, or perhaps just shuffling along with a pretty well-trained mediocre brain, to take pains not to lose your capacity to feel.

How is it to be done? I have some practical advice for you in this struggle, which is one of the great battles of life. Take some time every day—*every* day—to examine what you have been doing in the light of feeling, rather than of intelligence. It may be before you fall asleep at night; it may be while you are walking to your work; it may be at any time when you can withdraw your attention from external matters: that is the time to ask yourself—What do I really feel about all this? Not, what should I feel about it, what does the world expect me to feel, but what do I truly feel about it? You must be honest with yourself, because self-deception is one of the commonest roads to Acedia.

Now it may happen that you will find that you are committed to some course of action which you do not like—which you may positively hate. And yet, for good reasons, it may be necessary to continue with it. We all have to do things we detest, at one time or another, because we are not free to consult our own wishes only. But if you know the truth, you are protected from Acedia.

Nor is it only the detestable things that should be carefully examined. You must look clearly at the things which make your life happy and enviable, and you must give yourself up to a grateful contemplation of them. Never take such things for granted. I have seen many a promising marriage shrivel and dry up because one or both of the parties to it assumed that happiness was something that came by right, and could never be diminished. Consciously summoning up, and consciously enjoying, the good things that life brings us is a way of preserving them. It is not in their nature to last forever; they will change, and if you cherish them gratefully, the change is much more likely to be a change for the better than if you accept them as gifts which a grateful providence has showered upon you as a recognition of your magnanimity in condescending to inhabit the earth.

I have never been able to make up my mind which it is that people fear to feel most—pain or joy. Life will bring you both. You will not be able to escape the pain completely, though Acedia will dull it a little. But unfortunately it lies in your power to reject the joy utterly. Because we are afraid that great exultation may betray us into some actions, some words, which may make us look a little foolish to people who are not sharing our experience, we very often stifle our moments of joy, thinking that we shall give them their outlet later. But alas, after a few years of that kind of thing, joy ceases to visit us. I seem to be quoting theologians this afternoon. There is an old saying of medieval teachers which I recommend to your special notice:

Time Jesum transeuntem et non revertentem.

I shall translate it thus: 'Dread the passing of Jesus, for He does not return.' And thus it is with all great revelations, be they religious or not. Seize them, embrace them, let them engulf you, draw from them the uttermost of what they have to give, for if you rebuff them, they will not come again. We live in a world where too many people are pitifully afraid of joy. Because I wish you well, I beg you not to add yourself to their number.

Do not put off the moment of decision. Begin now. This is your hour. You are shortly to receive one of the great distinctions of your lifetime. Don't worry about looking dignified; don't be afraid that your pleasure may betray you into some lapse from that nullity of demeanour which we so pathetically accept as a substitute for true dignity. Don't accept your BA as if it were one more padlock on the inmost chamber of your heart. Education, if it is real and not a sham, is a releasing, not an imprisoning, thing. If you wish it to be so, the achievement of your degree is a step toward a new freedom. What is the word in your heart as you accept your diploma? Is it No—or is it Yes?

Prologue

Marcel Proust

Marcel Proust's literary fame comes from his long novel À la Recherche du temps perdu (Remembrance of Things Past). *He published the first volume in 1913 and was dictating passages of the eighth the night before he died in 1922. Although the novel is not autobiographical, it does record the life of a Paris dilettante, wealthy and purposeless until one day when he realizes that the memories of his own life, relived and reshaped into art, will provide the subject for a great novel.*

Proust, asthmatic and nervous from earliest childhood, lived in his family home in Paris from his birth in 1871 until his mother's death in 1905. While in school he wrote essays and poems that show his early interest in the Decadent movement—a school of French writers who stressed the abnormal and artificial in their works. At the Sorbonne he enrolled as a student of law and political science, but his only academic interest was in philosophy. He spent most of his time widening his circle of acquaintances in the literary and artistic society of Paris and sporadically composing novels and shorter works. Though only a few were printed, he later worked parts of them into his major novel.

His mother's death grieved Proust excessively, for she had given his life a continuity and a portion of her own strict discipline. Her death did enable Proust to stop hiding his homosexuality—though none of his series of affairs lasted long, and the most intense ended tragically when his lover died in a plane crash in 1914.

In 1907 Proust moved to a flat, which he had made soundproof and from which, in later years, he almost never stirred. By 1909 he had begun steady work on Remembrance of Things Past. *He saw less and less of aristocratic Paris society; because of his asthma he often worked on his novel all night and slept during the day. He became progressively weaker and more nervous, took large amounts of drugs for his asthma, and died of pneumonia in 1922.*

Contre Sainte-Beuve (By Way of Sainte-Beuve), written between 1908 and 1910, was the only major interruption to the work on his novel. It began as a critical study but soon turned into an account of Proust's own processes of memory, thought, and feeling. The present essay, which opens the book, is celebrated as a description of how his masterpiece may have originated. The translation is by Sylvia Townsend Warner (1958). "Sainte-Beuve's Method," referred to in the final paragraph, is described elsewhere by Proust as "not separating the man and his work," "to surround oneself with every possible piece of information about a writer" before making a judgment on his writings. Proust did not admire this method.

Every day I set less store on intellect. Every day I see more clearly that if the writer is to repossess himself of some part of his impressions, reach something personal, that is, and the only material of art, he must put it aside. What intellect restores to us under the name of the past, is not the past. In reality, as soon as each hour of one's life has died, it embodies itself in some material object, as do the souls of the dead in certain folk-stories, and hides there. There it remains captive, captive forever, unless we should happen on the object, recognise what lies within, call it by its name, and so set it free. Very likely we may never happen on the object (or the sensation, since we apprehend every object as sensation) that it hides in; and thus there are hours of our life that will never be resuscitated: for this object is so tiny, so lost in the world, and there is so little likelihood that we shall come across it.

Several summers of my life were spent in a house in the country. I thought of those summers from time to time, but they were not themselves. They were dead, and in all probability they would always remain so. Their resurrection, like all these resurrections, hung on a mere chance. One snowy evening, not long ago, I came in half frozen, and had sat down in my room to read by lamplight, and as I could not get warm my old cook offered to make me a cup of tea, a thing I never drink. And as chance would have it, she brought me some slices of dry toast. I dipped the toast in the cup of tea, and as soon as I put it in my mouth, and felt its softened texture, all flavoured with tea, against my palate, something came over me—the smell of geraniums and orange-blossom, a sensation of extraordinary radiance and happiness. I sat quite still, afraid that the slightest movement might cut short this incomprehensible process which was taking place in me, and concentrated on the bit of sopped toast which seemed responsible for all these marvels; then suddenly the shaken partitions in my memory gave way, and into my conscious mind there rushed the summers I had spent in the aforesaid house in the country, with their early mornings, and the succession, the ceaseless onset, of happy hours in their train. And then I remembered. Every morning, when I was dressed, I went down to my grandfather in his bedroom, where he had just woken up and was drinking his tea. He soaked a rusk in it, and gave me the rusk to eat. And when those summers were past and gone, the taste of a rusk soaked in tea was one of the shelters where the dead hours—dead as far as intellect knew—hid themselves away, and where I should certainly never have found them again if, on that winter's evening when I came in frozen from the snow, my cook had not offered me the potion to which, by virtue of a magic past I knew nothing about, their resurrection was plighted.

But as soon as I had tasted the rusk, a whole garden, up till then vague and dim, mirrored itself, with its forgotten walks and all their urns with all their flowers, in the little cup of tea, like those Japanese flowers which do not reopen as flowers until one drops them into water. In the same way, many days in Venice, which intellect had not been able to give back, were dead for me until last year, when crossing a courtyard I came to a standstill among the glittering uneven paving-stones. The friends I was with were afraid that I might have slipped, but I waved to them to go on, and that I would catch up with them. Something of greater importance engaged me, I still did not know what it was, but in the depth of my being I felt the flutter of a past that I did not recognise; it was just as I set foot on a certain paving-stone that this feeling of perplexity came over me. I felt an invading happiness, I knew that I was going to be enriched by that purely personal thing, a past impression, a fragment of life in unsullied preservation (something we can only know in preservation, for while we live in it, it is not present in the memory, since other sensations accompany and smother it) which asked only that it might be set free, that it might come and augment my stores of life and poetry. But I did not feel that I had the power to free it. No, intellect could have done nothing for me at such a moment! Trying to put myself back into the same state, I retraced my steps a little so that I might come afresh to those uneven shining paving-stones. It was the same sensation underfoot that I had felt on the smooth, slightly uneven pavement of the baptistry of Saint Mark's. The shadow which had lain that day on the canal, where a gondola waited for me, and all the happiness, all the wealth of those hours—this recognized sensation brought them hurrying after it, and that very day came alive for me.

It is not merely that intellect can lend no hand in these resurrections; these past hours will only hide themselves away in objects where intellect has not tried to embody them. The objects which you have consciously tried to connect with certain hours of your life, these they can never take shelter in. What is more, if something else should resuscitate those hours, the objects called back with them will be stripped of their poetry.

I remember how once when I was travelling by train I strove to draw impressions from the passing landscape. I wrote about the little country churchyard while it was still passing before my eyes, I noted down the bright bars of sunlight on the trees, the wayside flowers like those in *Le Lys dans la Vallée.*° Since then, calling to mind those trees streaked with light and that little churchyard, I have often tried to conjure up that day, that day *itself,* I mean, not its pallid ghost. I could never manage it, and I had lost all hope of doing so, when at lunch, not long ago, I let my spoon fall on my plate. And then it made the same noise as the hammers of the linesmen did that day, tapping on the wheels when the train halted at stations. The burning blinded hour when that noise rang out instantly came back to me, and all that day in its poetry—except for the country churchyard, the trees streaked with light, and the Balzacian flowers, gained by deliberate observation and lost from the poetic resurrection.

Now and again, alas, we happen on the object, and the lost sensation thrills in us, but the time is too remote, we cannot give a name to the sensation, or call on it, and it does not come alive. As I was walking through a pantry the other day, a piece of green canvas plugging a broken windowpane made me stop dead and listen inwardly. A gleam of summer crossed my mind. Why? I tried to remember. I saw wasps in a shaft of sunlight, a smell of cherries came from the table—I could not remember. For a moment I was like those sleepers who wake up in the dark and do not know where they are, who ask their bodies to give them a bearing as to their whereabouts, not knowing what bed, what house, what part of the world, which year of their life they are in. For a moment I hesitated like this, groping round the square of green canvas to discover the time and the place where my scarcely awakened memory would find itself at home. All the sensations of my life, confused, or known, or forgotten, I was hesitating among all of them at once. This only lasted a minute. Soon I saw nothing more; my memory had fallen asleep again forever.

How often during our walks have not my friends known me halt like this at the turning-off of an avenue, or beside a clump of trees, and ask them to leave me alone for a minute. Nothing came of it. I shut my eyes and made my mind a blank to recruit fresh energies for my pursuit of the past, then suddenly reopened them, all in an attempt to see those same

---

Le Lys dans la Vallée *The Lily of the Valley,* by Honoré de Balzac.

trees as if for the first time. I could not tell where I had seen them. I could recognise their shapes and their grouping, their outline seemed to have been traced from some beloved drawing that trembled in my heart. But I could tell no more of them, and they themselves seemed by their artless passionate attitude to say how sorry they felt not to be able to make themselves clear, not to be able to tell me the secret that they well knew I could not unriddle. Ghosts of a dear past, so dear that my heart beat to bursting, they held out powerless arms to me, like the ghosts that Aeneas met in the underworld. Was it in the walks near the town of my happy childhood, was it only in that imagined country where, later on, I dreamed that Mamma was so ill, close to a lake and in a forest where it was light all night long, a dream country only but almost as real as the country of my childhood which was already no more than a dream? I should never know more of it. And I had to rejoin my friends who were waiting for me at the turn of the road, with the anguish of turning my back forever on a past I might see no more, of disowning the dead who held out their powerless fond arms to me, and seemed to say, Recall us to life. And before I fell into step and into conversation with my friends, I again turned round for a moment to cast a less and less discerning glance towards the crooked, receding line of mutely expressive trees still undulating before my eyes.

Compared with this past, this private essence of ourselves, the truths of intellect seem scarcely real at all. So, and above all from the time when our vitality begins to dwindle, it is to whatever may help us to recover this past that we resort, even though this should entail being very ill-understood by intellectual people who do not know that the artist lives to himself, that the absolute value of what he sees means nothing to him and that his scale of values is wholly subjective. A nauseating musical show put on by a provincial company, or a ball that people of taste would laugh at, may be far more quickening to his memories, far more relevant to the nature of what he dreams of and dwells on, than a brilliant performance at the Opera House or an ultra-elegant evening party in the Faubourg Saint-Germain. A railway time-table with its names of stations where he loves to fancy himself getting out of the train on an autumn evening when the trees are already stripped of their leaves and the bracing air is full of their rough scent, or a book that means nothing to people of discrimination but is full of names he has not heard since he was a child, can be worth incommensurably more to him than admirable philosophical treatises, so that people of discrimination will remark that for a man of talent he has very stupid likings.

Perhaps it will cause surprise that I, who make light of the intellect, should have devoted the following few pages precisely to some of these considerations that intellect, in contradiction to the platitudes that we hear said or read in books, suggests to us. At a time when my days may be numbered (and besides, are we not all in the same case?) it is perhaps very frivolous of me to undertake an intellectual exercise. But if the truths of intellect are less precious than those secrets of feeling that I was talking about just now, yet in one way they too have their interest. A writer is not only a poet; in our imperfect world where masterpieces are no more than the shipwrecked flotsam of great minds, even the greatest writers of our century have spun a web of intellect round jewels of feeling which only here or there show through it. And if one believes that on this important point one hears the best among one's contemporaries making mistakes, there comes a time when one shakes off one's indolence and feels the need to speak out. Sainte-Beuve's Method is not, at first sight, such an important affair. But perhaps in the course of these pages we may be led to realise that it touches on very important intellectual problems, and on what is perhaps for an artist the greatest of all: this relative inferiority of the intellect which I spoke of at the beginning. Yet all the same, it is intellect we must call on to establish this inferiority. Because if intellect does not deserve the crown of crowns, only intellect is able to award it. And if intellect ranks only second in the hierarchy of virtues, intellect alone is able to proclaim that the first place must be given to instinct.

Living Like Weasels

Annie Dillard

Annie Dillard is a poet as well as a prose writer, and her prose style is instantly recognizable for its poetic exactness and intensity. Her favorite subjects are nature, art, God, and the mysteries of their reconcilement.

She was born in 1945 to a well-to-do Pittsburgh family, and attended Hollins College, where she studied English and Creative Writing and took a Master's degree in 1968. She began publishing poems, and keeping in notebooks and on index cards a journal of things that interested her: descriptions and reflections on nature, memorable quotations, scientific information, and religious ideas. Her first published collection of poems, Tickets for a Prayer Wheel *(1974), was soon followed by a book of essays based on her journal.* Pilgrim at Tinker Creek *(1974) was a great success, becoming a best-seller and winning a Pulitzer Prize in 1975.*

Dillard has continued to write, to teach, and to travel widely, both geographically and spiritually. Teaching a Stone to Talk *(1982) relates some of her more recent experiences, but also includes pieces, such as the present one, which originate in the Virginia countryside around Hollins.* Living by Fiction *(1982) is a book about writing itself. In it she says, "I*

*approach fiction, and the world, and these absurdly large questions, as a
reader, and a writer, and a lover."*

A weasel is wild. Who knows what he thinks? He sleeps in his underground den, his tail draped over his nose. Sometimes he lives in his den
for two days without leaving. Outside, he stalks rabbits, mice, muskrats,
and birds, killing more bodies than he can eat warm, and often dragging
the carcasses home. Obedient to instinct, he bites his prey at the neck,
either splitting the jugular vein at the throat or crunching the brain at
the base of the skull, and he does not let go. One naturalist refused to kill
a weasel who was socketed into his hand deeply as a rattlesnake. The man
could in no way pry the tiny weasel off, and he had to walk half a mile
to water, the weasel dangling from his palm, and soak him off like a
stubborn label.

And once, says Ernest Thompson Seton—once, a man shot an eagle out
of the sky. He examined the eagle and found the dry skull of a weasel fixed
by the jaws to his throat. The supposition is that the eagle had pounced
on the weasel and the weasel swiveled and bit as instinct taught him,
tooth to neck, and nearly won. I would like to have seen that eagle from
the air a few weeks or months before he was shot: was the whole weasel
still attached to his feathered throat, a fur pendant? Or did the eagle eat
what he could reach, gutting the living weasel with his talons before his
breast, bending his beak, cleaning the beautiful airborne bones?

I have been reading about weasels because I saw one last week. I startled
a weasel who startled me, and we exchanged a long glance.

Twenty minutes from my house, through the woods by the quarry and
across the highway, is Hollins Pond, a remarkable piece of shallowness,
where I like to go at sunset and sit on a tree trunk. Hollins Pond is also
called Murray's Pond; it covers two acres of bottomland near Tinker
Creek with six inches of water and six thousand lily pads. In winter,
brown-and-white steers stand in the middle of it, merely dampening their
hooves; from the distant shore they look like miracle itself, complete with
miracle's nonchalance. Now, in summer, the steers are gone. The water
lilies have blossomed and spread to a green horizontal plane that is terra
firma to plodding blackbirds, and tremulous ceiling to black leeches,
crayfish, and carp.

This is, mind you, suburbia. It is a five-minute walk in three directions
to rows of houses, though none is visible here. There's a 55 mph highway
at one end of the pond, and a nesting pair of wood ducks at the other.
Under every bush is a muskrat hole or a beer can. The far end is an
alternating series of fields and woods, fields and woods, threaded every-

where with motorcycle tracks—in whose bare clay wild turtles lay eggs.

So. I had crossed the highway, stepped over two low barbed-wire fences, and traced the motorcycle path in all gratitude through the wild rose and poison ivy of the pond's shoreline up into high grassy fields. Then I cut down through the woods to the mossy fallen tree where I sit. This tree is excellent. It makes a dry, upholstered bench at the upper, marshy end of the pond, a plush jetty raised from the thorny shore between a shallow blue body of water and a deep blue body of sky.

The sun had just set. I was relaxed on the tree trunk, ensconced in the lap of lichen, watching the lily pads at my feet tremble and part dreamily over the thrusting path of a carp. A yellow bird appeared to my right and flew behind me. It caught my eye; I swiveled around—and the next instant, inexplicably, I was looking down at a weasel, who was looking up at me.

Weasel! I'd never seen one wild before. He was ten inches long, thin as a curve, a muscled ribbon, brown as fruitwood, soft-furred, alert. His face was fierce, small and pointed as a lizard's; he would have made a good arrowhead. There was just a dot of chin, maybe two brown hairs' worth, and then the pure white fur began that spread down his underside. He had two black eyes I didn't see, any more than you see a window.

The weasel was stunned into stillness as he was emerging from beneath an enormous shaggy wild rose bush four feet away. I was stunned into stillness twisted backward on the tree trunk. Our eyes locked, and someone threw away the key.

Our look was as if two lovers, or deadly enemies, met unexpectedly on an overgrown path when each had been thinking of something else: a clearing blow to the gut. It was also a bright blow to the brain, or a sudden beating of brains, with all the charge and intimate grate of rubbed balloons. It emptied our lungs. It felled the forest, moved the fields, and drained the pond; the world dismantled and tumbled into that black hole of eyes. If you and I looked at each other that way, our skulls would split and drop to our shoulders. But we don't. We keep our skulls. So.

He disappeared. This was only last week, and already I don't remember what shattered the enchantment. I think I blinked, I think I retrieved my brain from the weasel's brain, and tried to memorize what I was seeing, and the weasel felt the yank of separation, the careening splash-down into real life and the urgent current of instinct. He vanished under the wild rose. I waited motionless, my mind suddenly full of data and my spirit with pleadings, but he didn't return.

Please do not tell me about "approach-avoidance conflicts." I tell you I've been in that weasel's brain for sixty seconds, and he was in mine. Brains are private places, muttering through unique and secret tapes— but the weasel and I both plugged into another tape simultaneously, for a sweet and shocking time. Can I help it if it was a blank?

What goes on in his brain the rest of the time? What does a weasel think about? He won't say. His journal is tracks in clay, a spray of feathers, mouse blood and bone: uncollected, unconnected, loose-leaf, and blown.

I would like to learn, or remember, how to live. I come to Hollins Pond not so much to learn how to live as, frankly, to forget about it. That is, I don't think I can learn from a wild animal how to live in particular—shall I suck warm blood, hold my tail high, walk with my footprints precisely over the prints of my hands?—but I might learn something of mindlessness, something of the purity of living in the physical sense and the dignity of living without bias or motive. The weasel lives in necessity and we live in choice, hating necessity and dying at the last ignobly in its talons. I would like to live as I should, as the weasel lives as he should. And I suspect that for me the way is like the weasel's: open to time and death painlessly, noticing everything, remembering nothing, choosing the given with a fierce and pointed will.

I missed my chance. I should have gone for the throat. I should have lunged for that streak of white under the weasel's chin and held on, held on through mud and into the wild rose, held on for a dearer life. We could live under the wild rose wild as weasels, mute and uncomprehending. I could very calmly go wild. I could live two days in the den, curled, leaning on mouse fur, sniffing bird bones, blinking, licking, breathing musk, my hair tangled in the roots of grasses. Down is a good place to go, where the mind is single. Down is out, out of your ever-loving mind and back to your careless senses. I remember muteness as a prolonged and giddy fast, where every moment is a feast of utterance received. Time and events are merely poured, unremarked, and ingested directly, like blood pulsed into my gut through a jugular vein. Could two live that way? Could two live under the wild rose, and explore by the pond, so that the smooth mind of each is as everywhere present to the other, and as received and as unchallenged, as falling snow?

We could, you know. We can live any way we want. People take vows of poverty, chastity, and obedience—even of silence—by choice. The thing is to stalk your calling in a certain skilled and supple way, to locate the most tender and live spot and plug into that pulse. This is yielding, not fighting. A weasel doesn't "attack" anything; a weasel lives as he's meant to, yielding at every moment to the perfect freedom of single necessity.

I think it would be well, and proper, and obedient, and pure, to grasp your one necessity and not let it go, to dangle from it limp wherever it takes you. Then even death, where you're going no matter how you live, cannot you part. Seize it and let it seize you up aloft even, till your eyes burn out and drop; let your musky flesh fall off in shreds, and let your very bones unhinge and scatter, loosened over fields, over fields and woods, lightly, thoughtless, from any height at all, from as high as eagles.

William Wordsworth
(1770–1850)

I Wandered Lonely as a Cloud

I wandered lonely as a cloud
That floats on high o'er vales and hills,
When all at once I saw a crowd,
A host, of golden daffodils;
Beside the lake, beneath the trees,
Fluttering and dancing in the breeze.

Continuous as the stars that shine
And twinkle on the milky way,
They stretched in never-ending line
Along the margin of a bay:
Ten thousand saw I at a glance,
Tossing their heads in sprightly dance.

The waves beside them danced; but they
Out-did the sparkling waves in glee:
A poet could not but be gay,
In such a jocund company:
I gazed—and gazed—but little thought
What wealth the show to me had brought:

For oft, when on my couch I lie
In vacant or in pensive mood,
They flash upon that inward eye
Which is the bliss of solitude;
And then my heart with pleasure fills,
And dances with the daffodils.

(1804)

William Butler Yeats

(1865–1939)

Leda and the Swan°

A sudden blow: the great wings beating still
Above the staggering girl, her thighs caressed
By the dark webs, her nape caught in his bill,
He holds her helpless breast upon his breast.

How can those terrified vague fingers push
The feathered glory from her loosening thighs?
And how can body, laid in that white rush,
But feel the strange heart beating where it lies?

A shudder in the loins engenders there
The broken wall, the burning roof and tower
And Agamemnon dead.
                                    Being so caught up,
So mastered by the brute blood of the air,
Did she put on his knowledge with his power
Before the indifferent beak could let her drop?

(1923)

Leda and the Swan   Reference to the Greek myth of the god Zeus, who, in the form of
a swan, made love to Queen Leda. Their union resulted in the birth of the beautiful and
legendary Helen, whose abduction started the Trojan War.

e. e. cummings
(1894–1962)

since feeling is first

since feeling is first
who pays any attention
to the syntax of things
will never wholly kiss you;
wholly to be a fool
while Spring is in the world

my blood approves,
and kisses are a better fate
than wisdom
lady i swear by all flowers. Don't cry
—the best gesture of my brain is less than
your eyelids' flutter which says

we are for each other: then
laugh, leaning back in my arms
for life's not a paragraph

And death i think is no parenthesis

(1926)

Imamu Amiri Baraka
(LeRoi Jones)
(b. 1934)

Young Soul

First, feel, then feel, then
read, or read, then feel, then
fall, or stand, where you
already are. Think
of your self, and the other
selves . . . think
of your parents, your mothers
and sisters, your bentslick
father, then feel, or
fall, on your knees
if nothing else will move you,

    then read
    and look deeply
    into all matters
    come close to you
    city boys—
    country men

    Make some muscle
    in your head, but
    use the muscle
    in yr heart

How Language Works

Language and thought are so closely connected that sometimes we can't tell them apart. Words enable us to hold in mind what happens, and to talk and think about it long afterwards. Furthermore, words seem to make it possible for us to be creative, to imagine what never happened. The three writers in this section all take up our uniquely human capacity for language, and its relation to thought and to culture.

In the opening piece, Helen Keller, who lost both hearing and sight before she was two years old, describes herself as a child without words. It felt, she said, "like being at sea in a dense fog" until that moment when "somehow the mystery of language was revealed to me." Her story introduces the question of what it means to be fully human, and to what extent thought and even feeling depend on language.

Susanne K. Langer takes up this same question on a more abstract level. Her essay deals with language as symbolism, and the use of symbols as the activity most characteristic of humans. "We live in a mind-made world," she says, "where the things of prime importance are images or words that embody ideas and feelings and attitudes." She stresses our unique capacity to manipulate symbols, and so opens, in their broadest terms, the political and moral questions that the use of language generates. Because we can imagine enemies and friends, we can create them. Because human beings can "embody ideas and set them up to view," they can "oppress each other by symbols of might."

Langer describes our inner capacity for language and for symbolism, but, as Helen Keller suggests, without human and social interaction, that capacity would hardly come into play. Without her teacher, Anne Sullivan, Keller would have remained in her "dense fog." Paule Marshall's essay deals with language in its social workings. Her description of the talk in her mother's kitchen illustrates some of the many ways in which language can do more than communicate information. She shows how ordinary people unselfconsciously create language, using it as poetry that expresses the deepest traits of their culture, and how, by listening, she learned the language of her own culture.

from *The Story of My Life*

Helen Keller

Helen Keller (1880–1968) was born a healthy baby, but before she was two years old and just after she had begun to speak, she became ill with a "brain fever" that left her blind, deaf, and mute. She grew up wild and unruly until Anne Mansfield Sullivan, who herself had been half-blind before surgery, became her teacher. We print here Chapter 4 from Keller's autobiography, The Story of My Life *(1902), which describes her rediscovery of language, a day she has referred to as her "soul's birthday."*

Under the tutelage of her teacher, Keller learned to read, write, even to speak. She went on to graduate from Radcliffe College in 1904, cum laude, *with an additional citation: "excellent in English letters." In 1909, she published* The World We Live In, *a collection of essays about her ways of knowing the world. She continued to write and to travel, and became a lifelong and world-known advocate for the handicapped.*

The most important day I remember in all my life is the one on which my teacher, Anne Mansfield Sullivan, came to me. I am filled with wonder when I consider the immeasurable contrasts between the two lives which it connects. It was the third of March, 1887, three months before I was seven years old.

On the afternoon of that eventful day, I stood on the porch, dumb, expectant. I guessed vaguely from my mother's signs and from the hurrying to and fro in the house that something unusual was about to happen, so I went to the door and waited on the steps. The afternoon sun penetrated the mass of honeysuckle that covered the porch, and fell on my upturned face. My fingers lingered almost unconsciously on the familiar leaves and blossoms which had just come forth to greet the sweet southern spring. I did not know what the future held of marvel or surprise for me. Anger and bitterness had preyed upon me continually for weeks and a deep languor had succeeded this passionate struggle.

Have you ever been at sea in a dense fog, when it seemed as if a tangible white darkness shut you in, and the great ship, tense and anxious, groped her way toward the shore with plummet and sounding-line, and you waited with beating heart for something to happen? I was like that ship before my education began, only I was without compass or sounding-line, and had no way of knowing how near the harbour was. "Light! give me light!" was the wordless cry of my soul, and the light of love shone on me in that very hour.

I felt approaching footsteps. I stretched out my hand as I supposed to my mother. Some one took it, and I was caught up and held close in the arms of her who had come to reveal all things to me, and, more than all things else, to love me.

The morning after my teacher came she led me into her room and gave me a doll. The little blind children at the Perkins Institution had sent it and Laura Bridgman had dressed it; but I did not know this until afterward. When I had played with it a little while, Miss Sullivan slowly spelled into my hand the word "d-o-l-l." I was at once interested in this finger play and tried to imitate it. When I finally succeeded in making the letters correctly I was flushed with childish pleasure and pride. Running downstairs to my mother I held up my hand and made the letters for doll. I did not know that I was spelling a word or even that words existed; I was simply making my fingers go in monkey-like imitation. In the days that followed I learned to spell in this uncomprehending way a great many words, among them *pin, hat, cup* and a few verbs like *sit, stand* and *walk.* But my teacher had been with me several weeks before I understood that everything has a name.

One day, while I was playing with my new doll, Miss Sullivan put my big rag doll into my lap also, spelled "d-o-l-l" and tried to make me understand that "d-o-l-l" applied to both. Earlier in the day we had had a tussle over the words "m-u-g" and "w-a-t-e-r." Miss Sullivan had tried to impress it upon me that "m-u-g" is *mug* and that "w-a-t-e-r" is *water,* but I persisted in confounding the two. In despair she had dropped the subject for the time, only to renew it at the first opportunity. I became impatient at her repeated attempts and, seizing the new doll, I dashed it upon the floor. I was keenly delighted when I felt the fragments of the broken doll at my feet. Neither sorrow nor regret followed my passionate outburst. I had not loved the doll. In the still, dark world in which I lived there was no strong sentiment or tenderness. I felt my teacher sweep the fragments to one side of the hearth, and I had a sense of satisfaction that the cause of my discomfort was removed. She brought me my hat, and I knew I was going out into the warm sunshine. This thought, if a wordless sensation may be called a thought, made me hop and skip with pleasure.

We walked down the path to the well-house, attracted by the fragrance of the honeysuckle with which it was covered. Someone was drawing water and my teacher placed my hand under the spout. As the cool stream gushed over one hand she spelled into the other the word *water,* first slowly, then rapidly. I stood still, my whole attention fixed upon the motions of her fingers. Suddenly I felt a misty consciousness as of something forgotten—a thrill of returning thought; and somehow the mystery of language was revealed to me. I knew then that "w-a-t-e-r" meant the wonderful cool something that was flowing over my hand. That living word awakened my soul, gave it light, hope, joy, set it free! There were barriers still, it is true, but barriers that could in time be swept away.

I left the well-house eager to learn. Everything had a name, and each name gave birth to a new thought. As we returned to the house every object which I touched seemed to quiver with life. That was because I saw everything with the strange, new sight that had come to me. On entering the door I remembered the doll I had broken. I felt my way to the hearth and picked up the pieces. I tried vainly to put them together. Then my eyes filled with tears; for I realized what I had done, and for the first time I felt repentance and sorrow.

I learned a great many new words that day. I do not remember what they all were; but I do know that *mother, father, sister, teacher* were among them—words that were to make the world blossom for me, "like Aaron's rod, with flowers." It would have been difficult to find a happier child than I was as I lay in my crib at the close of that eventful day and lived over the joys it had brought me, and for the first time longed for a new day to come.

The Prince of Creation

Susanne K. Langer

Susanne K. Langer (1895–1985) was born in New York City to German immigrant parents. She received her bachelor's degree in 1920 from Radcliffe College, where she studied under the philosopher Alfred North Whitehead; she took her master's degree in philosophy from Harvard in 1924 and her doctorate from Harvard in 1926. As a teacher and a research scholar pursuing investigations in the philosophy of art, expression, and meaning, Professor Langer reached a large audience and has had great influence on recent thought, particularly about the arts. Her best-known book is Philosophy in a New Key: A Study in the Symbolism of Reason, Rite, and Art *(1942). Her final work was a three-volume essay,* Mind: An Essay on Human Feeling *(1967–1982). The present selection, clearly deriving from her interest in symbolism, appeared in* Fortune *in January 1944, at the height of World War II, and shows some of the interrelations of political, biological, anthropological, and linguistic thinking.*

wrote this during WWII

metaphors symbols

The world is aflame with man-made public disasters, artificial rains of brimstone and fire, planned earthquakes, cleverly staged famines and floods. The Prince of Creation is destroying himself. He is throwing down the cities he has built, the works of his own hand, the wealth of many thousand years in his frenzy of destruction, as a child knocks down its own handiwork, the whole day's achievement, in a tantrum of tears and rage.

What has displeased the royal child? What has incurred his world-shattering tantrum? ?

The bafflement of the magnificent game he is playing. Its rules and its symbols, his divine toys, have taken possession of the player. For this global war is not the old, hard, personal fight for the means of life, *bellum omnium contra omnes*,° which animals perpetually wage; this is a war of monsters. Not mere men but great superpersonal giants, the national states, are met in combat. They do not hate and attack and wrestle as injured physical creatures do; they move heavily, inexorably, by strategy and necessity, to each other's destruction. The game of national states has come to this pass, and the desperate players ride their careening animated toys to a furious suicide.

These moloch gods, these monstrous states, are not natural beings; they are man's own work, products of the power that makes him lord over all other living things—his mind. They are not of the earth, earthy, as families and herds, hives and colonies are, whose members move and fight as one by instinct and habit until a physical disturbance splits them and the severed parts reconstitute themselves as new organized groups. The national states are not physical groups; they are social symbols, profound and terrible.

They are symbols of the new way of life, which the past two centuries have given us. For thousands of years, the pattern of daily life—working, praying, building, fighting, and raising new generations—repeated itself with only slow or unessential changes. The social symbols expressive of this life were ancient and familiar. Tribal gods or local saints, patriarchs, squires, or feudal lords, princes and bishops, raised to the highest power in the persons of emperors and popes—they were all expressions of needs →

---

bellum omnium contra omnes   war of all against all (Latin).

people fighting). Ideas and about ideas

and duties and opinions grounded in an immemorial way of life. The average man's horizon was not much greater than his valley, his town, or whatever geographical ramparts bounded his community. Economic areas were small, and economic problems essentially local. Naturally in his conception the powers governing the world were local, patriarchal, and reverently familiar.

Then suddenly, within some two hundred years, and for many places far less than that, the whole world has been transformed. Communities of different tongues and faiths and physiognomies have mingled; not as of old in wars of conquest, invading lords and conquered population gradually mixing their two stocks, but by a new process of foot-loose travel and trade, dominated by great centers of activity that bring individuals from near and far promiscuously together as a magnet draws filings from many heaps into close but quite accidental contact. Technology has made old horizons meaningless and localities indefinite. For goods and their destinies determine the structure of human societies. This is a new world, a world of persons, not of families and clans, or parishes and manors. The proletarian order is not founded on a hearth and its history. It does not express itself in a dialect, a local costume, a rite, a patron saint. All such traditions by mingling have canceled each other, and disappeared.

Most of us feel that since the old controlling ideas of faith and custom are gone, mankind is left without anchorage of any sort. None of the old social symbols fit this modern reality, this shrunken and undifferentiated world in which we lead a purely economic, secular, essentially homeless life.

But mankind is never without its social symbols; when old ones die, new ones are already in process of birth; and the new gods that have superseded all faiths are the great national states. The conception of them is mystical and moral, personal and devotional; they conjure with names and emblems, and demand our constant profession and practice of the new orthodoxy called "Patriotism."

Of all born creatures, man is the only one that cannot live by bread alone. He lives as much by symbols as by sense report, in a realm compounded of tangible things and virtual images, of actual events and ominous portents, always between fact and fiction. For he sees not only actualities but meanings. He has, indeed, all the impulses and interests of animal nature; he eats, sleeps, mates, seeks comfort and safety, flees pain, falls sick and dies, just as cats and bears and fishes and butterflies do. But he has something more in his repertoire, too—he has laws and religions, theories and dogmas, because he lives not only through sense but through symbols. That is the special asset of his mind, which makes him the master of earth and all its progeny.

By the agency of symbols—marks, words, mental images, and icons of all sorts—he can hold his ideas for contemplation long after their original causes have passed away. Therefore, he can think of things that are not presented or even suggested by his actual environment. By associating symbols in his mind, he combines things and events that were never together in the real world. This gives him the power we call imagination. Further, he can symbolize only part of an idea and let the rest go out of consciousness; this gives him the faculty that has been his pride throughout the ages—the power of abstraction. The combined effect of these two powers is inestimable. They are the roots of his supreme talent, the gift of reason.

In the war of each against all, which is the course of nature, man has *point* an unfair advantage over his animal brethren; for he can see what is not yet there to be seen, know events that happened before his birth, and take possession of more than he actually eats; he can kill at a distance; and by rational design he can enslave other creatures to live and act for him instead of for themselves.

Yet this mastermind has strange aberrations. For in the whole animal kingdom there is no such unreason, no such folly and impracticality as man displays. He alone is hounded by imaginary fears, beset by ghosts and devils, frightened by mere images of things. No other creature wastes *point* time in unprofitable ritual or builds nests for dead specimens of its race. Animals are always realists. They have intelligence in varying degrees— chickens are stupid, elephants are said to be very clever—but, bright or foolish, animals react only to reality. They may be fooled by appearance, by pictures or reflections, but once they know them as such, they promptly lose interest. Distance and darkness and silence are not fearful to them, filled with voices or forms, or invisible presences. Sheep in the pasture do not seem to fear phantom sheep beyond the fence, mice don't look for mouse goblins in the clock, birds do not worship a divine thunderbird.

But oddly enough, men do. They think of all these things and guard against them, worshipping animals and monsters even before they conceive of divinities in their own image. Men are essentially unrealistic. With all their extraordinary intelligence, they alone go in for patently impractical actions—magic and exorcism and holocausts—rites that have no connection with common-sense methods of self-preservation, such as a highly intelligent animal might use. In fact, the rites and sacrifices by which primitive man claims to control nature are sometimes fatal to the performers. Indian puberty rites are almost always intensely painful, and African natives have sometimes died during initiations into honorary societies.

We usually assume that very primitive tribes of men are closer to *point* animal estate than highly civilized races; but in respect of practical attitudes, this is not true. The more primitive man's mind, the more fantastic it seems to be; only with high intellectual discipline do we gradually approach the realistic outlook of intelligent animals.

Yet this human mind, so beclouded by phantoms and superstitions, is probably the only mind on earth that can reach out to an awareness of things beyond its practical environment and can also conceive of such notions as truth, beauty, justice, majesty, space and time and creation.

There is another paradox in man's relationship with other creatures: namely, that those very qualities he calls animalian—"brutal," "bestial," "inhuman"—are peculiarly his own. No other animal is so deliberately cruel as man. No other creature intentionally imprisons its own kind, or invents special instruments of torture such as racks and thumbscrews for the sole purpose of punishment. No other animal keeps its own brethren in slavery; so far as we know, the lower animals do not commit anything like the acts of pure sadism that figure rather largely in our newspapers. There is no torment, spite, or cruelty for its own sake among beasts, as there is among men. A cat plays with its prey, but does not conquer and torture smaller cats. But man, who knows good and evil, is cruel for cruelty's sake; he who has a moral law is more brutal than the brutes, who have none; he alone inflicts suffering on his fellows with malice afore-thought.

If man's mind is really a higher form of the animal mind, his morality a specialized form of herd instinct, then where in the course of evolution did he lose the realism of a clever animal and fall prey to subjective fears? And why should he take pleasure in torturing helpless members of his own race?

The answer is, I think, that man's mind is *not* a direct evolution from the beast's mind, but is a unique variant and therefore has had a meteoric and startling career very different from any other animal history. The trait that sets human mentality apart from every other is its preoccupation with symbols, with images and names that *mean* things, rather than with things themselves. This trait may have been a mere sport of nature once upon a time. Certain creatures do develop tricks and interests that seem biologically unimportant. Pack rats, for instance, and some birds of the crow family take a capricious pleasure in bright objects and carry away such things for which they have, presumably, no earthly use. Perhaps man's tendency to see certain forms as *images*, to hear certain sounds not only as signals but as expressive tones, and to be excited by sunset colors or starlight, was originally just a peculiar sensitivity in a rather highly developed brain. But whatever its cause, the ultimate destiny of this trait was momentous; for all human activity is based on the appreciation and use of symbols. Language, religion, mathematics, all learning, all science and superstition, even right and wrong, are products of symbolic expression rather than direct experience. Our commonest words, such as "house" and "red" and "walking," are symbols; the pyramids of Egypt and the mysterious circles of Stonehenge are symbols; so are dominions and empires and astronomical universes. We live in a mind-made world, where the things of prime importance are images or words that embody ideas and feelings and attitudes.

The animal mind is like a telephone exchange; it receives stimuli from outside through the sense organs and sends out appropriate responses through the nerves that govern muscles, glands, and other parts of the body. The organism is constantly interacting with its surroundings, receiving messages and acting on the new state of affairs that the messages signify.

But the human mind is not a simple transmitter like a telephone exchange. It is more like a great projector; for instead of merely mediating between an event in the outer world and a creature's responsive action, it transforms or, if you will, distorts the event into an image to be looked at, retained, and contemplated. For the images of things that we remember are not exact and faithful transcriptions even of our actual sense impressions. They are made as much by what we think as by what we see. It is a well-known fact that if you ask several people the size of the moon's disk as they look at it, their estimates will vary from the areas of a dime to that of a barrel top. Like a magic lantern, the mind projects its ideas of things on the screen of what we call "memory"; but like all projections, these ideas are transformations of actual things. They are, in fact, *symbols* of reality, not pieces of it.

A symbol is not the same thing as a sign; that is a fact that psychologists and philosophers often overlook. All intelligent animals use signs; as do we. To them as well as to us sounds and smells and motions are signs of food, danger, the presence of other beings, or of rain or storm. Furthermore, some animals not only attend to signs but produce them for the benefit of others. Dogs bark at the door to be let in; rabbits thump to call each other; the cooing of doves and the growl of a wolf defending his kill are unequivocal signs of feelings and intentions to be reckoned with by other creatures.

We use signs just as animals do, though with considerably more elaboration. We stop at red lights and go on green; we answer calls and bells, watch the sky for coming storms, read trouble or promise or anger in each other's eyes. That is animal intelligence raised to the human level. Those of us who are dog lovers can probably all tell wonderful stories of how high our dogs have sometimes risen in the scale of clever sign interpretation and sign using.

A sign is anything that announces the existence or the imminence of some event, the presence of a thing or a person, or a change in a state of affairs. There are signs of the weather, signs of danger, signs of future good or evil, signs of what the past has been. In every case a sign is closely bound up with something to be noted or expected in experience. It is always a part of the situation to which it refers, though the reference may be remote in space and time. In so far as we are led to note or expect the signified event we are making correct use of a sign. This is the essence of rational behavior, which animals show in varying degrees. It is entirely realistic, being closely bound up with the actual objective course of history—learned by experience, and cashed in or voided by further experience.

If man had kept to the straight and narrow path of sign using, he would be like the other animals, though perhaps a little brighter. He would not talk, but grunt and gesticulate and point. He would make his wishes known, give warnings, perhaps develop a social system like that of bees and ants, with such a wonderful efficiency of communal enterprise that all men would have plenty to eat, warm apartments—all exactly alike and perfectly convenient—to live in, and everybody could and would sit in the sun or by the fire, as the climate demanded, not talking but just basking, with every want satisfied, most of his life. The young would romp and make love, the old would sleep, the middle-aged would do the routine work almost unconsciously and eat a great deal. But that would be the life of a social, superintelligent, purely sign-using animal.

To us who are human, it does not sound very glorious. We want to go places and do things, own all sorts of gadgets that we do not absolutely need, and when we sit down to take it easy we want to talk. Rights and property, social position, special talents and virtues, and above all our ideas, are what we live for. We have gone off on a tangent that takes us far away from the mere biological cycle that animal generations accomplish; and that is because we can use not only signs but symbols.

A symbol differs from a sign in that it does not announce the presence of the object, the being, condition, or whatnot, which is its meaning, but merely *brings this thing to mind*. It is not a mere "substitute sign" to which we react as though it were the object itself. The fact is that our reaction to hearing a person's name is quite different from our reaction to the person himself. There are certain rare cases where a symbol stands directly for its meaning: in religious experience, for instance, the Host° is not only a symbol but a Presence. But symbols in the ordinary sense are not mystic. They are the same sort of thing that ordinary signs are; only they do not call our attention to something necessarily present or to be physically dealt with—they call up merely a conception of the thing they "mean."

The difference between a sign and a symbol is, in brief, that a sign causes us to think or act *in face of* the thing signified, whereas a symbol causes us to think *about* the thing symbolized. Therein lies the great importance of symbolism for human life, its power to make this life so different from any other animal biography that generations of men have found it incredible to suppose that they were of purely zoological origin. A sign is always embedded in reality, in a present that emerges from the actual past and stretches to the future; but a symbol may be divorced from reality altogether. It serves, therefore, to liberate thought from the immediate stimuli of a physically present world; and that liberation marks the

---

Host   Bread, usually in the form of a wafer, that, having been consecrated during Mass, is believed by Roman Catholics to be the body of Christ.

essential difference between human and nonhuman mentality. Animals think, but they think *of* and *at* things; men think primarily *about* things. Words, pictures, and memory images are symbols that may be combined and varied in a thousand ways. The result is a symbolic structure whose meaning is a complex of all their respective meanings, and this kaleidoscope of *ideas* is the typical product of the human brain that we call the "stream of thought."

The process of transforming all direct experience into imagery or into that supreme mode of symbolic expression, language, has so completely taken possession of the human mind that it is not only a special talent but a dominant, organic need. All our sense impressions leave their traces in our memory not only as signs disposing our practical reactions in the future but also as symbols, images representing our *ideas* of things; and the tendency to manipulate ideas, to combine and abstract, mix and extend them by playing with symbols, is man's outstanding characteristic. It seems to be what his brain most naturally and spontaneously does. Therefore his primitive mental function is not judging reality, but *dreaming his desires.*

Dreaming is apparently a basic function of human brains, for it is free and unexhausting like our metabolism, heartbeat, and breath. It is easier to dream than not to dream, as it is easier to breathe than to refrain from breathing. The symbolic character of dreams is fairly well established. Symbol mongering, on this ineffectual, uncritical level, seems to be instinctive, the fulfillment of an elementary need rather than the purposeful exercise of a high and difficult talent.

The special power of man's mind rests on the evolution of this special activity, not on any transcendently high development of animal intelligence. We are not immeasurably higher than other animals; we are different. We have a biological need and with it a biological gift that they do not share.

Because man has not only the ability but the constant need of *conceiving* what has happened to him, what surrounds him, what is demanded of him—in short, of symbolizing nature, himself, and his hopes and fears—he has a constant and crying need of *expression.* What he cannot express, he cannot conceive; what he cannot conceive is chaos, and fills him with terror.

If we bear in mind this all-important craving for expression we get a new picture of man's behavior; for from this trait spring his powers and his weaknesses. The process of symbolic transformation that all our experiences undergo is nothing more nor less than the process of *conception,* which underlies the human faculties of abstraction and imagination.

When we are faced with a strange or difficult situation, we cannot react directly, as other creatures do, with flight, aggression, or any such simple instinctive pattern. Our whole reaction depends on how we manage to conceive the situation—whether we cast it in a definite dramatic form, whether we see it as a disaster, a challenge, a fulfillment of doom, or a fiat of the Divine Will. In words or dreamlike images, in artistic or religious or even in cynical form, we must *construe* the events of life. There is great virtue in the figure of speech, "I can *make* nothing of it," to express a failure to understand something. Thought and memory are processes of *making* the thought content and the memory image; the pattern of our ideas is given by the symbols through which we express them. And in the course of manipulating those symbols we inevitably distort the original experience, as we abstract certain features of it, embroider and reinforce those features with other ideas, until the conception we project on the screen of memory is quite different from anything in our real history.

Conception is a necessary and elementary process; what we do with our conceptions is another story. That is the entire history of human culture—of intelligence and morality, folly and superstition, ritual, language, and the arts—all the phenomena that set man apart from, and above, the rest of the animal kingdom. As the religious mind has to make all human history a drama of sin and salvation in order to define its own moral attitudes, so a scientist wrestles with the mere presentation of "the facts" before he can reason about them. The process of *envisaging* facts, values, hopes, and fears underlies our whole behavior pattern; and this process is reflected in the evolution of an extraordinary phenomenon found always, and only, in human societies—the phenomenon of language.

Language is the highest and most amazing achievement of the symbolistic human mind. The power it bestows is almost inestimable, for without it anything properly called "thought" is impossible. The birth of language is the dawn of humanity. The line between man and beast—between the highest ape and the lowest savage—is the language line. Whether the primitive Neanderthal man was anthropoid or human depends less on his cranial capacity, his upright posture, or even his use of tools and fire, than on one issue we shall probably never be able to settle—whether or not he spoke.

In all physical traits and practical responses, such as skills and visual judgments, we can find a certain continuity between animal and human mentality. Sign using is an ever evolving, ever improving function throughout the whole animal kingdom, from the lowly worm that shrinks into his hole at the sound of an approaching foot, to the dog obeying his master's command, and even to the learned scientist who watches the movements of an index needle.

This continuity of the sign-using talent has led psychologists to the belief that language is evolved from the vocal expressions, grunts and coos and cries, whereby animals vent their feelings or signal their fellows; that man has elaborated this sort of communion to the point where it makes a perfect exchange of ideas possible.

I do not believe that this doctrine of the origin of language is correct. The essence of language is symbolic, not signific; we use it first and most vitally to formulate and hold ideas in our own minds. Conception, not social control, is its first and foremost benefit.

Watch a young child that is just learning to speak play with a toy; he says the name of the object, e.g.: "Horsey! horsey! horsey!" over and over again, looks at the object, moves it, always saying the name to himself or to the world at large. It is quite a time before he talks to anyone in particular; he talks first of all to himself. This is his way of forming and fixing the *conception* of the object in his mind, and around this conception all his knowledge of it grows. *Names* are the essence of language; for the *name* is what abstracts the conception of the horse from the horse itself, and lets the mere idea recur at the speaking of the name. This permits the conception gathered from one horse experience to be exemplified again by another instance of a horse, so that the notion embodied in the name is a general notion.

To this end, the baby uses a word long before he *asks for* the object; when he wants his horsey he is likely to cry and fret, because he is reacting to an actual environment, not forming ideas. He uses the animal language of *signs* for his wants; talking is still a purely symbolic process— its practical value has not really impressed him yet.

Language need not be vocal; it may be purely visual, like written language, or even tactual, like the deaf-mute system of speech; but it *must be denotative.* The sounds, intended or unintended, whereby animals communicate do not constitute a language, because they are signs, not names. They never fall into an organic pattern, a meaningful syntax of even the most rudimentary sort, as all language seems to do with a sort of driving necessity. That is because signs refer to actual situations, in which things have obvious relations to each other that require only to be noted; but symbols refer to ideas, which are not physically there for inspection, so their connections and features have to be represented. This gives all true language a natural tendency toward growth and development, which seems almost like a life of its own. Languages are not invented; they grow with our need for expression.

In contrast, animal "speech" never has a structure. It is merely an emotional response. Apes may greet their ration of yams with a shout of "Nga!" But they do not say "Nga" between meals. If they could *talk about* their yams instead of just saluting them, they would be the most primitive men instead of the most anthropoid of beasts. They would have ideas, and tell each other things true or false, rational or irrational; they would make plans and invent laws and sing their own praises, as men do.

The history of speech is the history of our human descent. Yet the habit of transforming reality into symbols, of contemplating and combining and distorting symbols, goes beyond the confines of language. All *images* are symbols, which make us think about the things they mean.

This is the source of man's great interest in "graven images," and in *mere appearances* like the face of the moon or the human profiles he sees in rocks and trees. There is no limit to the meanings he can read into natural phenomena. As long as this power is undisciplined, the sheer enjoyment of finding meanings in everything, the elaboration of concepts without any regard to truth and usefulness, seems to run riot; superstition and ritual in their pristine strength go through what some anthropologists have called a "vegetative" stage, when dreamlike symbols, gods and ghouls and rites, multiply like the overgrown masses of life in a jungle. From this welter of symbolic forms emerge the images that finally govern a civilization; the great symbols of religion, society, and selfhood.

What does an image "mean"? Anything it is thought to resemble. It is only because we can abstract quite unobvious forms from the actual appearance of things that we see line drawings in two dimensions as images of colored, three-dimensional objects, find the likeness of a dipper in a constellation of seven stars, or see a face on a pansy. Any circle may represent the sun or moon; an upright monolith may be a man.

Wherever we can fancy a similarity we tend to see something represented. The first thing we do, upon seeing a new shape, is to assimilate it to our own idea of something that it resembles, something that is known and important to us. Our most elementary concepts are of our own actions, and the limbs or organs that perform them; other things are named by comparison with them. The opening of a cave is its mouth, the divisions of a river its arms. Language, and with it all articulate thought, grows by this process of unconscious metaphor. Every new idea urgently demands a word; if we lack a name for it, we call it after the first namable thing seen to bear even a remote analogy to it. Thus all the subtle and variegated vocabulary of a living language grows up from a few roots of very general application; words as various in meaning as "gentle" and "ingenious" and "general" spring from the one root "ge" meaning "to give life."

Yet there are conceptions that language is constitutionally unfit to express. The reason for this limitation of our verbal powers is a subject for logicians and need not concern us here. The point of interest to us is that, just as rational, discursive thought is bound up with language, so the life of feeling, of direct personal and social consciousness, the emotional stability of man and his sense of orientation in the world are bound up with images directly given to his senses: fire and water, noise and silence, high mountains and deep caverns, the brief beauty of flowers, the persistent grin of a skull. There seem to be irresistible parallels between the expressive forms we find in nature and the forms of our inner life; thus the use of light to represent all things good, joyful, comforting, and of darkness to express all sorts of sorrow, despair, or horror, is so primitive as to be well-nigh unconscious.

A flame is a soul; a star is a hope; the silence of winter is death. All such images, which serve the purpose of metaphorical thinking, are *natural symbols.* They have not conventionally assigned meanings, like words, but recommend themselves even to a perfectly untutored mind, a child's or a savage's, because they are definitely articulated *forms,* and to see something expressed in such forms is a universal human talent. We do not have to learn to use natural symbols; it is one of our primitive activities.

The fact that sensuous forms of natural processes have a significance beyond themselves makes the range of our symbolism, and with it the horizon of our consciousness, much wider and deeper than language. This is the source of ritual, mythology, and art. Ritual is a symbolic rendering of certain emotional *attitudes,* which have become articulate and fixed by being constantly expressed. Mythology is man's image of his world, and of himself in the world. Art is the exposition of his own subjective history, the life of feeling, the human spirit in all its adventures.

Yet this power of envisagement, which natural symbolism bestows, is a dangerous one; for human beings can envisage things that do not exist, and create horrible worlds, insupportable duties, monstrous gods and ancestors. The mind that can see past and future, the poles and the antipodes, and guess at obscure mechanisms of nature, is ever in danger of seeing what is not there, imagining false and fantastic causes, and courting death instead of life. Because man can play with ideas, he is unrealistic; he is inclined to neglect the all-important interpretation of signs for a rapt contemplation of symbols.

Some twenty years ago, Ernst Cassirer° set forth a theory of human mentality that goes far toward explaining the vagaries of savage religions and the ineradicable presence of superstition even in civilized societies: a symbol, he observed, is the embodiment of an idea; it is at once an abstract and a physical fact. Now its great emotive value lies in the concept it conveys; this inspires our reverent attitude, the attention and awe with which we view it. But man's untutored thought always tends to lose its way between the symbol and the fact. A skull represents death; but to a primitive mind the skull *is* death. To have it in the house is not unpleasant but dangerous. Even in civilized societies, symbolic objects—figures of saints, relics, crucifixes—are revered for their supposed efficacy. Their actual power is a power of *expression,* of embodying and thus revealing the greatest concepts humanity has reached; these concepts are the commanding forces that change our estate from a brute existence to the transcendent life of the spirit. But the symbol-loving mind of man reveres the meaning not *through* the articulating form but *in* the form so that the image appears to be the actual object of love and fear, supplication and praise.

Because of this constant identification of concepts with their expressions, our world is crowded with unreal beings. Some societies have actu-

---

Ernst Cassirer   German philosopher (1874–1945).

ally realized that these beings do not belong to nature, and have postulated a so-called "other world" where they have their normal existence and from which they are said to descend, or arise, into our physical realm. For savages it is chiefly a nether world that sends up spooks; for more advanced cults it is from the heavens that supernatural beings, the embodiments of human ideas—of virtue, triumph, immortality—descend to the mundane realm. But from this source emanates also a terrible world government, with heavy commands and sanctions. Strange worship and terrible sacrifices may be the tithes exacted by the beings that embody our knowledge of nonanimalian human nature.

So the gift of symbolism, which is the gift of reason, is at the same time the seat of man's peculiar weakness—the danger of lunacy. Animals go mad with hydrophobia or head injuries, but purely mental aberrations are rare; beasts are not generally subject to insanity except through a confusion of signs, such as the experimentally produced "nervous breakdown" in rats. It is man who hears voices and sees ghosts in the dark, feels irrational compulsions and holds fixed ideas. All these phantasms are symbolic forms that have acquired a false factual status. It has been truly said that everybody has some streak of insanity; i.e., the threat of madness is the price of reason.

Because we can think of things potential as well as actual, we can be held in nonphysical bondage by laws and prohibitions and commands and by images of a governing power. This makes men tyrants over their own kind. Animals control each other's actions by immediate threats, growls and snarls and passes; but when the bully is roving elsewhere, his former domain is free of him. We control our inferiors by setting up symbols of our power, and the mere idea that words or images convey stands there to hold our fellows in subjection even when we cannot lay our hands on them. There is no flag over the country where a wolf is king; he is king where he happens to prowl, so long as he is there. But men, who can embody ideas and set them up to view, oppress each other by symbols of might.

The envisagements of good and evil, which make man a moral agent, make him also a conscript, a prisoner, and a slave. His constant problem is to escape the tyrannies he has created. Primitive societies are almost entirely tyrannical, symbol-bound, coercive organizations; civilized governments are so many conscious schemes to justify or else to disguise man's inevitable bondage to law and conscience.

Slowly, through ages and centuries, we have evolved a picture of the world we live in; we have made a drama of the earth's history and enhanced it with a backdrop of divinely ordered, star-filled space. And all this structure of infinity and eternity against which we watch the pageant of life and death, and all the moral melodrama itself, we have wrought by a gradual articulation of such vast ideas in symbols—symbols of good and evil, triumph and failure, birth and maturity and death. Long before the beginning of any known history, people saw in the heavenly bodies, in the changes of day and night or of the seasons, and in great beasts, symbolic forms to express those ultimate concepts that are the very frame of human existence. So gods, fates, the cohorts of good and evil were conceived. Their myths were the first formulations of cosmic ideas. Gradually the figures and traditions of religion emerged; ritual, the overt expression of our mental attitudes, became more and more intimately bound to definite and elaborate concepts of the creative and destructive powers that seem to control our lives.

Such beings and stories and rites are sacred because they are the great symbols by which the human mind orients itself in the world. To a creature that lives by reason, nothing is more terrible than what is formless and meaningless; one of our primary fears is fear of chaos. And it is the fight against chaos that has produced our most profound and indispensable images—the myths of light and darkness, of creation and passion, the symbols of the altar flame, the daystar, and the cross.

For thousands of years people lived by the symbols that nature presented to them. Close contact with earth and its seasons, intimate knowledge of stars and tides, made them feel the significance of natural phenomena and gave them a poetic, unquestioning sense of orientation. Generations of erudite and pious men elaborated the picture of the temporal and spiritual realms in which each individual was a pilgrim soul.

Then came the unprecedented change, the almost instantaneous leap of history from the immemorial tradition of the plow and the anvil to the new age of the machine, the factory, and the ticker tape. Often in no more than the length of a life-time the shift from handwork to mass production, and with it from poetry to science and from faith to nihilism, has taken place. The old nature symbols have become remote and have lost their meanings; in the clatter of gears and the confusion of gadgets that fill the new world, there will not be any obvious and rich and sacred meanings for centuries to come. All the accumulated creeds and rites of men are suddenly in the melting pot. There is no fixed community, no dynasty, no family inheritance—only the one huge world of men, vast millions of men, still looking on each other in hostile amazement.

A sane, intelligent animal should have invented, in the course of ten thousand years or more, some sure and obvious way of accommodating indefinite numbers of its own kind on the face of a fairly spacious earth. Modern civilization has achieved the highest triumphs of knowledge, skill, ingenuity, theory; yet all around its citadels, engulfing and demolishing them, rages the maddest war and confusion, inspired by symbols and slogans as riotous and irrational as anything the "vegetative" stage of savage phantasy could provide. How shall we reconcile this primitive nightmare excitement with the achievements of our high, rational, scientific culture?

The answer is, I think, that we are no longer in possession of a definite, established culture; we live in a period between an exhausted age—the European civilization of the white race—and an age still unborn, of which we can say nothing as yet. We do not know what races shall inherit the earth. We do not know what even the next few centuries may bring. But it is quite evident, I think, that we live in an age of transition, and that before many more generations have passed, mankind will make a new beginning and build itself a different world. Whether it will be a "brave, new world," or whether it will start all over with an unchronicled "state of nature" such as Thomas Hobbes described, wherein the individual's life is "nasty, brutish, and short," we simply cannot tell. All we know is that every tradition, every institution, every tribe is gradually becoming uprooted and upset, and we are waiting in a sort of theatrical darkness between the acts.

Because we are at a new beginning, our imaginations tend to a wild, "vegetative" overgrowth. The political upheavals of our time are marked, therefore, by a veritable devil dance of mystical ideologies, vaguely conceived, passionately declared, holding out fanatic hopes of mass redemption and mass beatitudes. Governments vie with each other in proclaiming social plans, social aims, social enterprises, and demanding bloody sacrifices in the name of social achievements.

New conceptions are always clothed in an extravagant metaphorical form, for there is no language to express genuinely new ideas. And in their pristine strength they imbue the symbols that express them with their own mystery and power and holiness. It is impossible to disengage the welter of ideas embodied in a swastika, a secret sign, or a conjuring word from the physical presence of the symbol itself; hence the apparently nonsensical symbol worship and mysticism that go with new movements and visions. This identification of symbolic form and half-articulate meaning is the essence of all mythmaking. Of course the emotive value is incomprehensible to anyone who does not see such figments as expressive forms. So an age of vigorous new conception and incomplete formulation always has a certain air of madness about it. But it is really a fecund and exciting period in the life of reason. Such is our present age. Its apparent unreason is a tremendous unbalance and headiness of the human spirit, a conflict not only of selfish wills but of vast ideas in the metaphorical state of emergence.

The change from fixed community life and ancient local custom to the mass of unpedigreed human specimens that actually constitutes the world in our industrial and commercial age has been too sudden for the mind of man to negotiate. Some transitional form of life had to mediate between those extremes. And so the idol of nationality arose from the wreckage of tribal organization. The concept of the national state is really the old tribe concept applied to millions of persons, unrelated and different creatures gathered under the banner of a government. Neither birth nor language nor even religion holds such masses together, but a mystic bond is postulated even where no actual bond of race, creed, or color may ever have existed.

At first glance it seems odd that the concept of nationality should reach its highest development just as all actual marks of national origins—language, dress, physiognomy, and religion—are becoming mixed and obliterated by our new mobility and cosmopolitan traffic. But it is just the loss of these things that inspires this hungry seeking for something like the old egocentric pattern in the vast and formless brotherhood of the whole earth. While mass production and universal communication clearly portend a culture of world citizenship, we cling desperately to our nationalism, a more and more attenuated version of the old clan civilization. We fight passionate and horrible wars for the symbols of our nations, we make a virtue of self-glorification and exclusiveness and invent strange anthropologies to keep us at least theoretically set apart from other men.

Nationalism is a transition between an old and a new human order. But even now we are not really fighting a war of nations; we are fighting a war of fictions, from which a new vision of the order of nature will someday emerge. The future, just now, lies wide open—open and dark, like interstellar space; but in that emptiness there is room for new gods, new cultures, mysterious now and nameless as an unborn child.

From the Poets in the Kitchen

Paule Marshall

Paule Marshall was born in Brooklyn, New York, in 1929, of parents who had come from the Caribbean island of Barbados. After graduating from Brooklyn College, she worked as a librarian, as a staff writer for Our World *magazine, and as a free-lance writer. She has lectured on black literature at Oxford, Columbia, and other universities. Marshall is best known, however, as a writer of fiction. She began writing before her tenth birthday and is noted for the range and originality of her treatment of her black experience. Her novels are* Brown Girl, Brownstones *(1959),* The Chosen Place, the Timeless People *(1969), and* Praisesong for the Widow *(1983).* Soul Clap Hands and Sing, *a collection of four short novels, appeared in 1961. This essay appeared in the* New York Times Book Review *on January 9, 1983.*

Some years ago, when I was teaching a graduate seminar in fiction at Columbia University, a well-known male novelist visited my class to speak on his development as a writer. In discussing his formative years, he didn't realize it but he seriously endangered his life by remarking that women writers are luckier than those of his sex because they usually spend so much time as children around their mothers and their mothers' friends in the kitchen.

What did he say that for? The women students immediately forgot about being in awe of him and began readying their attack for the question and answer period later on. Even I bristled. There again was that awful image of women locked away from the world in the kitchen with only each other to talk to, and their daughters locked in with them.

But my guest wasn't really being sexist or trying to be provocative or even spoiling for a fight. What he meant—when he got around to examining himself more fully—was that, given the way children are (or were) raised in our society, with little girls kept closer to home and their mothers, the woman writer stands a better chance of being exposed, while growing up, to the kind of talk that goes on among women, more often than not in the kitchen; and that this experience gives her an edge over her male counterpart by instilling in her an appreciation for ordinary speech.

It was clear that my guest lecturer attached great importance to this, which is understandable. Common speech and the plain, workaday words that make it up are, after all, the stock in trade of some of the best fiction writers. They are the principal means by which a character in a novel or story reveals himself and gives voice sometimes to profound feelings and complex ideas about himself and the world. Perhaps the proper measure of a writer's talent is his skill in rendering everyday speech—when it is appropriate to his story—as well as his ability to tap, to exploit, the beauty, poetry and wisdom it often contains.

"If you say what's on your mind in the language that comes to you from your parents and your street and friends you'll probably say something beautiful." Grace Paley tells this, she says, to her students at the beginning of every writing course.

It's all a matter of exposure and a training of the ear for the would-be writer in those early years of his or her apprenticeship. And, according to my guest lecturer, this training, the best of it, often takes place in as unglamorous a setting as the kitchen.

He didn't know it, but he was essentially describing my experience as a little girl. I grew up among poets. Now they didn't look like poets—whatever that breed is supposed to look like. Nothing about them suggested that poetry was their calling. They were just a group of ordinary housewives and mothers, my mother included, who dressed in a way (shapeless housedresses, dowdy felt hats and long, dark, solemn coats) that made it impossible for me to imagine they had ever been young.

Nor did they do what poets were supposed to do—spend their days in an attic room writing verses. They never put pen to paper except to write occasionally to their relatives in Barbados. "I take my pen in hand hoping these few lines will find you in health as they leave me fair for the time being," was the way their letters invariably began. Rather, their day was spent "scrubbing floor," as they described the work they did.

Several mornings a week these unknown bards would put an apron and a pair of old house shoes in a shopping bag and take the train or streetcar from our section of Brooklyn out to Flatbush. There, those who didn't have steady jobs would wait on certain designated corners for the white housewives in the neighborhood to come along and bargain with them over pay for a day's work cleaning their houses. This was the ritual even in the winter.

Later, armed with the few dollars they had earned, which in their vocabulary became "a few raw-mouth pennies," they made their way back to our neighborhood, where they would sometimes stop off to have a cup of tea or cocoa together before going home to cook dinner for their husbands and children.

The basement kitchen of the brownstone house where my family lived was the usual gathering place. Once inside the warm safety of its walls the women threw off the drab coats and hats, seated themselves at the large center table, drank their cups of tea or cocoa, and talked. While my sister and I sat at a smaller table over in a corner doing our homework, they talked—endlessly, passionately, poetically, and with impressive range. No subject was beyond them. True, they would indulge in the usual gossip: whose husband was running with whom, whose daughter looked slightly "in the way" (pregnant) under her bridal gown as she walked down the aisle. That sort of thing. But they also tackled the great issues of the time. They were always, for example, discussing the state of the economy. It was the mid and late 30's then, and the aftershock of the Depression, with its soup lines and suicides on Wall Street, was still being felt.

Some people, they declared, didn't know how to deal with adversity. They didn't know that you had to "tie up your belly" (hold in the pain, that is) when things got rough and go on with life. They took their image from the bellyband that is tied around the stomach of a newborn baby to keep the navel pressed in.

They talked politics. Roosevelt was their hero. He had come along and rescued the country with relief and jobs, and in gratitude they christened their sons Franklin and Delano and hoped they would live up to the names.

If F.D.R. was their hero, Marcus Garvey was their God. The name of the fiery, Jamaican-born black nationalist of the 20's was constantly invoked around the table. For he had been their leader when they first came to the United States from the West Indies shortly after World War I. They had contributed to his organization, the United Negro Improvement Association (UNIA), out of their meager salaries, bought shares in his ill-fated

Black Star Shipping Line, and at the height of the movement they had marched as members of his "nurses' brigade" in their white uniforms up Seventh Avenue in Harlem during the great Garvey Day parades. Garvey: He lived on through the power of their memories.

And their talk was of war and rumors of wars. They raged against World War II when it broke out in Europe, blaming it on the politicians. "It's these politicians. They're the ones always starting up all this lot of war. But what they care? It's the poor people got to suffer and mothers with their sons." If it was *their* sons, they swore they would keep them out of the Army by giving them soap to eat each day to make their hearts sound defective. Hitler? He was for them "the devil incarnate."

Then there was home. They reminisced often and at length about home. The old country. Barbados—or Bimshire, as they affectionately called it. The little Caribbean island in the sun they loved but had to leave. "Poor—poor but sweet" was the way they remembered it.

And naturally they discussed their adopted home. America came in for both good and bad marks. They lashed out at it for the racism they encountered. They took to task some of the people they worked for, especially those who gave them only a hard-boiled egg and a few spoonfuls of cottage cheese for lunch. "As if anybody can scrub floor on an egg and some cheese that don't have no taste to it!"

Yet although they caught H in "this man country," as they called America, it was nonetheless a place where "you could at least see your way to make a dollar." That much they acknowledged. They might even one day accumulate enough dollars, with both them and their husbands working, to buy the brownstone houses which, like my family, they were only leasing at that period. This was their consuming ambition: to "buy house" and to see the children through.

There was no way for me to understand it at the time, but the talk that filled the kitchen those afternoons was highly functional. It served as therapy, the cheapest kind available to my mother and her friends. Not only did it help them recover from the long wait on the corner that morning and the bargaining over their labor, it restored them to a sense of themselves and reaffirmed their self-worth. Through language they were able to overcome the humiliations of the work-day.

But more than therapy, that freewheeling, wide-ranging, exuberant talk functioned as an outlet for the tremendous creative energy they possessed. They were women in whom the need for self-expression was strong, and since language was the only vehicle readily available to them they made of it an art form that—in keeping with the African tradition in which art and life are one—was an integral part of their lives.

And their talk was a refuge. They never really ceased being baffled and overwhelmed by America—its vastness, complexity and power. Its strange customs and laws. At a level beyond words they remained fearful and in awe. Their uneasiness and fear were even reflected in their attitude toward the children they had given birth to in this country. They referred to those like myself, the little Brooklyn-born Bajans (Barbadians), as "these New York children" and complained that they couldn't discipline us properly because of the laws here. "You can't beat these children as you would like, you know, because the authorities in this place will dash you in jail for them. After all, these is New York children." Not only were we different, American, we had, as they saw it, escaped their ultimate authority.

Confronted therefore by a world they could not encompass, which even limited their rights as parents, and at the same time finding themselves permanently separated from the world they had known, they took refuge in language. "Language is the only homeland," Czeslaw Milosz, the emigré Polish writer and Nobel Laureate, has said. This is what it became for the women at the kitchen table.

It served another purpose also, I suspect. My mother and her friends were after all the female counterpart of Ralph Ellison's invisible man.[0] Indeed, you might say they suffered a triple invisibility, being black, female and foreigners. They really didn't count in American society except as a source of cheap labor. But given the kind of women they were, they couldn't tolerate the fact of their invisibility, their powerlessness. And they fought back, using the only weapon at their command: the spoken word.

Those late afternoon conversations on a wide range of topics were a way for them to feel they exercised some measure of control over their lives and the events that shaped them. "Soully-gal, talk yuk talk!" they were always exhorting each other. "In this man world you got to take yuh mouth and make a gun!" They were in control, if only verbally and if only for the two hours or so that they remained in our house.

For me, sitting over in the corner, being seen but not heard, which was the rule for children in those days, it wasn't only what the women talked about—the content—but the way they put things—their style. The insight, irony, wit and humor they brought to their stories and discussions and their poet's inventiveness and daring with language—which of course I could only sense but not define back then.

They had taken the standard English taught them in the primary schools of Barbados and transformed it into an idiom, an instrument that more adequately described them—changing around the syntax and imposing their own rhythm and accent so that the sentences were more pleasing to their ears. They added the few African sounds and words that had survived, such as the derisive suck-teeth sound and the word "yam," meaning to eat. And to make it more vivid, more in keeping with their expressive quality, they brought to bear a raft of metaphors, parables, Biblical quotations, sayings and the like:

---

invisible man *The Invisible Man* (1952), a novel by Ralph Ellison.

"The sea ain't got no back door," they would say, meaning that it wasn't like a house where if there was a fire you could run out the back. Meaning that it was not to be trifled with. And meaning perhaps in a larger sense that man should treat all of nature with caution and respect.

"I has read hell by heart and called every generation blessed!" They sometimes went in for hyperbole.

A woman expecting a baby was never said to be pregnant. They never used that word. Rather, she was "in the way" or, better yet, "tumbling big." "Guess who I butt up on in the market the other day tumbling big again!"

And a woman with a reputation of being too free with her sexual favors was known in their book as a "thoroughfare"—the sense of men like a steady stream of cars moving up and down the road of her life. Or she might be dubbed "a free-bee," which was my favorite of the two. I liked the image it conjured up of a woman scandalous perhaps but independent, who flitted from one flower to another in a garden of male beauties, sampling their nectar, taking her pleasure at will, the roles reversed.

And nothing, no matter how beautiful, was ever described as simply beautiful. It was always "beautiful-ugly": the beautiful-ugly dress, the beautiful-ugly house, the beautiful-ugly car. Why the word "ugly," I used to wonder, when the thing they were referring to was beautiful, and they knew it. Why the antonym, the contradiction, the linking of opposites? It used to puzzle me greatly as a child.

There is the theory in linguistics which states that the idiom of a people, the way they use language, reflects not only the most fundamental views they hold of themselves and the world but their very conception of reality. Perhaps in using the term "beautiful-ugly" to describe nearly everything, my mother and her friends were expressing what they believed to be a fundamental dualism in life: the idea that a thing is at the same time its opposite, and that these opposites, these contradictions make up the whole. But theirs was not a Manichean brand of dualism that sees matter, flesh, the body, as inherently evil, because they constantly addressed each other as "soully-gal"—soul: spirit; gal: the body, flesh, the visible self. And it was clear from their tone that they gave one as much weight and importance as the other. They had never heard of the mind/body split.

As for God, they summed up His essential attitude in a phrase. "God," they would say, "don' love ugly and He ain't stuck on pretty."

Using everyday speech, the simple commonplace words—but always with imagination and skill—they gave voice to the most complex ideas. Flannery O'Connor° would have approved of how they made ordinary language work, as she put it, "double-time," stretching, shading, deepening its meaning. Like Joseph Conrad they were always trying to infuse

---

Flannery O'Connor (1925–1964) American novelist and short story writer whose works are usually set in the South.

new life in the "old old words worn thin . . . by . . . careless usage." And the goals of their oral art were the same as his: "to make you hear, to make you feel . . . to make you *see.*" This was their guiding esthetic.

By the time I was 8 or 9, I graduated from the corner of the kitchen to the neighborhood library, and thus from the spoken to the written word. The Macon Street Branch of the Brooklyn Public Library was an imposing half block long edifice of heavy gray masonry, with glass-paneled doors at the front and two tall metal torches symbolizing the light that comes of learning flanking the wide steps outside.

The inside was just as impressive. More steps—of pale marble with gleaming brass railings at the center and sides—led up to the circulation desk, and a great pendulum clock gazed down from the balcony stacks that faced the entrance. Usually stationed at the top of the steps like the guards outside Buckingham Palace was the custodian, a stern-faced West Indian type who for years, until I was old enough to obtain an adult card, would immediately shoo me with one hand into the Children's Room and with the other threaten me into silence, a finger to his lips. You would have thought he was the chief librarian and not just someone whose job it was to keep the brass polished and the clock wound. I put him in a story called "Barbados" years later and had terrible things happen to him at the end.

I was sheltered from the storm of adolescence in the Macon Street library, reading voraciously, indiscriminately, everything from Jane Austen to Zane Grey, but with a special passion for the long, full-blown, richly detailed 18th- and 19th-century picaresque tales: *Tom Jones. Great Expectations. Vanity Fair.*

But although I loved nearly everything I read and would enter fully into the lives of the characters—indeed, would cease being myself and become them—I sensed a lack after a time. Something I couldn't quite define was missing. And then one day, browsing in the poetry section, I came across a book by someone called Paul Laurence Dunbar, and opening it I found the photograph of a wistful, sad-eyed poet who to my surprise was black. I turned to a poem at random. "Little brown-baby wif spa'klin'/ eyes/ Come to yo' pappy an' set on his knee." Although I had a little difficulty at first with the words in dialect, the poem spoke to me as nothing I had read before of the closeness, the special relationship I had had with my father, who by then had become an ardent believer in Father Divine° and gone to live in Father's "kingdom" in Harlem. Reading it helped to ease somewhat the tight knot of sorrow and longing I carried around in my chest that refused to go away. I read another poem. "Lias! Lias! Bless de Lawd!/Don' you know de day's/erbroad?/Ef you don' get up, you scamp/

Father Divine George Baker (c. 1882–1965), founder of the Peace Mission Movement, an interracial religious organization. He founded numerous "heavens"—communal residences—for his followers, many of whom believed he was God.

Dey'll be trouble in dis camp." I laughed. It reminded me of the way my mother sometimes yelled at my sister and me to get out of bed in the mornings.

And another: "Seen my lady home las' night/Jump back, honey, jump back./Hel' huh han' an' sque'z it tight . . ." About love between a black man and a black woman. I had never seen that written about before and it roused in me all kinds of delicious feelings and hopes.

And I began to search then for books and stories and poems about "The Race" (as it was put back then), about my people. While not abandoning Thackeray, Fielding, Dickens and the others, I started asking the reference librarian, who was white, for books by Negro writers, although I must admit I did so at first with a feeling of shame—the shame I and many others used to experience in those days whenever the word "Negro" or "colored" came up.

No grade school literature teacher of mine had ever mentioned Dunbar or James Weldon Johnson or Langston Hughes. I didn't know that Zora Neale Hurston existed and was busy writing and being published during those years. Nor was I made aware of people like Frederick Douglass and Harriet Tubman—their spirit and example—or the great 19th-century abolitionist and feminist Sojourner Truth. There wasn't even Negro History Week when I attended P.S. 35 on Decatur Street!

What I needed, what all the kids—West Indian and native black American alike—with whom I grew up needed, was an equivalent of the Jewish shul, someplace where we could go after school—the schools that were shortchanging us—and read works by those like ourselves and learn about our history.

It was around that time also that I began harboring the dangerous thought of someday trying to write myself. Perhaps a poem about an apple tree, although I had never seen one. Or the story of a girl who could magically transplant herself to wherever she wanted to be in the world— such as Father Divine's kingdom in Harlem. Dunbar—his dark, eloquent face, his large volume of poems—permitted me to dream that I might someday write, and with something of the power with words my mother and her friends possessed.

When people at readings and writers' conferences ask me who my major influences were, they are sometimes a little disappointed when I don't immediately name the usual literary giants. True, I am indebted to those writers, white and black, whom I read during my formative years and still read for instruction and pleasure. But they were preceded in my life by another set of giants whom I always acknowledge before all others: the group of women around the table long ago. They taught me my first lesson in the narrative art. They trained my ear. They set a standard of excellence. This is why the best of my work must be attributed to them; it stands as testimony to the rich legacy of language and culture they so freely passed on to me in the wordshop of the kitchen.

Language as Power

In the preceding section, Susanne K. Langer introduces the idea of language as power when she says "We control our inferiors by setting up symbols of our power, and the mere idea that words or images convey stands there to hold our fellows in subjection even when we cannot lay our hands on them" (p. 130). Each of the following essays deals directly or indirectly with language as an implement of power.

The excerpt from Bishop Tutu with which the section begins adds a political dimension to Langer's remarks. He takes up briefly but pointedly how the words used by contending parties to define the "facts" of a situation are related to the struggle for power between those parties.

The next two pieces take up the power and consequences of naming and defining. Santha Rama Rau's narrative describes a childhood experience in an Anglo-Indian school when the English headmistress gave "pretty English names" to her and her sister. The chapter by Haig A. Bosmajian expands on the importance of names and labels in the power to oppress: "The power which comes from names and naming is related directly to the power to define others—individuals, races, sexes, ethnic groups."

In the following essay, Robin Lakoff illustrates and extends this point as it applies to women. She discusses how the language women have been allowed to speak, the subjects they have been

allowed to speak about, and the ways they have been spoken of
have inhibited and shaped their sense of personal and social identity.

James Baldwin enlarges on this role of language, particularly as
it relates to black English. "People evolve a language," he says, "in
order to describe and thus control their circumstances or in order
not to be submerged by a situation that they cannot articulate." In
other words, one's language is a primary source of one's power.

George Orwell's classic essay focuses on the purely political; he
shows how bad thinking and bad writing propagate each other and
how they are related to badness in political life. Although he wrote
this essay nearly forty years ago, he could nevertheless be describing the 1980s. He concludes, however, on a hopeful note: "One
ought to recognize that the present political chaos is connected
with the decay of language, and that one can probably bring about
some improvement by starting at the verbal end."

Mythology

Bishop Desmond Tutu

*Bishop Desmond Tutu is the Anglican Bishop of Johannesburg, the first
black to hold that post. He was born in South Africa in 1931; his father
was a schoolteacher from the Bantu tribe known as the Xhosas, his mother
a domestic servant and later a cook at a missionary school for the blind.
Tutu started his professional life as a high-school teacher, but he resigned
in protest when the South African government introduced a second-class,
state-run system for black students. He then turned to the church as a
"likely means of service," and has since become a tireless spokesman for
"justice, peace, and reconciliation." In 1984, he was awarded the Nobel
Peace Prize for his role "in the campaign to resolve the problem of apartheid in South Africa."*

*Sermons, speeches, and other writings by Bishop Tutu have been col-
lected in two volumes:* Crying in the Wilderness *(1982) and* Hope and
Suffering *(1984). We present below the opening section of a review of* The
Political Mythology of Apartheid *by Leonard Thompson, published in the
September 26, 1985, issue of the* New York Review of Books.

I remember as if it were yesterday our reactions as black primary school
children when we read what the Reverend Mr. Whitehead had to say
when describing the relations between the Xhosas on the eastern border

and the white frontiersmen. Mr. Whitehead was, I believe, a Methodist missionary who wrote a history textbook which we were obliged to use if we wanted to pass our history examinations. I must underline that my contemporaries and I were not the radicalized and highly politicized students of the sort who were involved in the 1976 uprising and in the current violent protest against the vicious and immoral policy of apartheid. We were rather docile and thoroughly unsophisticated and naive, hardly questioning what appeared to be the divine ordering of our segregated society. It is therefore particularly noteworthy that it was such innocents who found certain features of Mr. Whitehead's historiography disturbing.

We found it distinctly odd that in virtually every encounter between the black Xhosas and the white settlers, Mr. Whitehead invariably described the Xhosas as those who *stole* the settlers' cattle and of the white settlers he would write that the settlers *captured* the cattle from the Xhosas. We did not press this point at all, or hardly at all, in class discussion; but when we were outside we would mutter that it was very funny. It certainly seemed to be stretching coincidence to the breaking point. We often remarked that after all, these farmers had no cattle when they landed in South Africa, and all their cattle had had to be procured from the indigenous peoples.

But if we had given expression to any of these misgivings it would have put an end to our chances of success in the examinations. We would have committed South Africa's unforgivable sin of mixing politics with whatever else we were at the time dealing with. At other times we were a little annoyed to read that such and such a white person had "discovered" this or that, as if there had been no other human beings, for example, to see the Victoria Falls before this superior denizen of another hemisphere came upon them.

These were the vague and unformed misgivings and perhaps hurt feelings of somewhat unsophisticated and really unlettered black pupils, feelings that had not been buttressed by any scholarly research or evidence that could stand up to critical scrutiny. Much later we heard a great deal about Western historical objectivity; it all seemed to suggest that Western historians were able to describe the naked, the real facts without any kind of embellishment or accretion, that they were quite uninfluenced by who they were and where they were, able, as it were, to stand outside themselves and give an account of what had "really" taken place, which would in all material respects be the same account given by any other self-respecting historian.

I have been skeptical of this claim to objectivity especially when it was made in South Africa about journalism (which chronicles contemporary events as a primary source for later historiography) on behalf of white journalists who, it was averred, were somehow paragons of the virtue of journalistic objectivity, as against what might be described as the engaged journalism of their black counterparts; for example, in giving an account of what took place in the 1976 uprisings. I believed that we could not just speak of the truth. It had to be truth from the perspective of some observer. What was the truth of what set off the Soweto uprising?° It seemed to some of us that who you were, and where you were, determined to a very considerable extent what you were able to see as the facts. You were not just an unconcerned viewer from the sidelines. Your values had been formed by the community to which you belonged and what rated as being important and significant depended very much on the sort of spectacles with which your nature and upbringing had endowed you. The aesthetic, ethical, and moral values a person derives mainly from the community in which he lives will determine very largely what he will judge as being beautiful, good, and true. . . .

By Any Other Name
Santha Rama Rau

Santha Rama Rau was born in Madras, India, in 1923, a daughter of highly educated Brahmin parents who made the decision to break away from that tradition. Her father was a diplomat, and the family travelled with him to London, South Africa, Japan, and the United States. Her mother received international recognition for her work for women's rights in India. Santha Rama Rau was educated in England from age ten to sixteen, when the family returned to India, and in the United States, where she graduated from Wellesley College in 1944. She has written numerous travel books and works of fiction in which she draws upon a sense of perspective that comes of being at home in many cultures. The following selection is reprinted from Gifts of Passage *(1951), a collection of stories which, she says, "taken in sequence . . . provide a sort of rough outline of my life story."*

At the Anglo-Indian day school in Zorinabad to which my sister and I were sent when she was eight and I was five and a half, they changed our names. On the first day of school, a hot, windless morning of a north Indian September, we stood in the headmistress's study and she said, "Now you're the *new* girls. What are your names?"

Soweto uprising A massive revolt in 1976 in Soweto, a section of Johannesburg set aside for blacks by the South African government. The uprising, which lasted nearly three weeks, began as a protest of the government's order that Afrikaans be the official language of instruction in Soweto's high schools.

My sister answered for us. "I am Premila, and she"—nodding in my direction—"is Santha."

The headmistress had been in India, I suppose, fifteen years or so, but she still smiled her helpless inability to cope with Indian names. Her rimless half-glasses glittered, and the precarious bun on the top of her head trembled as she shook her head. "Oh, my dears, those are much too hard for me. Suppose we give you pretty English names. Wouldn't that be more jolly? Let's see, now—Pamela for you, I think." She shrugged in a baffled way at my sister. "That's as close as I can get. And for *you*," she said to me, "how about Cynthia? Isn't that nice?"

My sister was always less easily intimidated than I was, and while she kept a stubborn silence, I said, "Thank you," in a very tiny voice.

We had been sent to that school because my father, among his responsibilities as an officer of the civil service, had a tour of duty to perform in the villages around that steamy little provincial town, where he had his headquarters at that time. He used to make his shorter inspection tours on horseback, and a week before, in the stale heat of a typically postmonsoon day, we had waved good-by to him and a little procession—an assistant, a secretary, two bearers, and the man to look after the bedding rolls and luggage. They rode away through our large garden, still bright green from the rains, and we turned back into the twilight of the house and the sound of fans whispering in every room.

Up to then, my mother had refused to send Premila to school in the British-run establishments of that time, because, she used to say, "you can bury a dog's tail for seven years and it still comes out curly, and you can take a Britisher away from his home for a lifetime and he still remains insular." The examinations and degrees from entirely Indian schools were not, in those days, considered valid. In my case, the question had never come up, and probably never would have come up if Mother's extraordinary good health had not broken down. For the first time in my life, she was not able to continue the lessons she had been giving us every morning. So our Hindi books were put away, the stories of the Lord Krishna as a little boy were left in mid-air, and we were sent to the Anglo-Indian school.

That first day at school is still, when I think of it, a remarkable one. At that age, if one's name is changed, one develops a curious form of dual personality. I remember having a certain detached and disbelieving concern in the actions of "Cynthia," but certainly no responsibility. Accordingly, I followed the thin, erect back of the headmistress down the veranda to my classroom feeling, at most, a passing interest in what was going to happen to me in this strange, new atmosphere of School.

The building was Indian in design, with wide verandas opening onto a central courtyard, but Indian verandas are usually whitewashed, with stone floors. These, in the tradition of British schools, were painted dark brown and had matting on the floors. It gave a feeling of extra intensity to the heat.

I suppose there were about a dozen Indian children in the school—which contained perhaps forty children in all—and four of them were in my class. They were all sitting at the back of the room, and I went to join them. I sat next to a small, solemn girl who didn't smile at me. She had long, glossy-black braids and wore a cotton dress, but she still kept on her Indian jewelry—a gold chain around her neck, thin gold bracelets, and tiny ruby studs in her ears. Like most Indian children, she had a rim of black kohl around her eyes. The cotton dress should have looked strange, but all I could think of was that I should ask my mother if I couldn't wear a dress to school, too, instead of my Indian clothes.

I can't remember too much about the proceedings in class that day, except for the beginning. The teacher pointed to me and asked me to stand up. "Now, dear, tell the class your name."

I said nothing.

"Come along," she said, frowning slightly. "What's your name, dear?"

"I don't know," I said, finally.

The English children in the front of the class—there were about eight or ten of them—giggled and twisted around in their chairs to look at me. I sat down quickly and opened my eyes very wide, hoping in that way to dry them off. The little girl with the braids put out her hand and very lightly touched my arm. She still didn't smile.

Most of that morning I was rather bored. I looked briefly at the children's drawings pinned to the wall, and then concentrated on a lizard clinging to the ledge of the high, barred window behind the teacher's head. Occasionally it would shoot out its long yellow tongue for a fly, and then it would rest, with its eyes closed and its belly palpitating, as though it were swallowing several times quickly. The lessons were mostly concerned with reading and writing and simple numbers—things that my mother had already taught me—and I paid very little attention. The teacher wrote on the easel blackboard words like "bat" and "cat," which seemed babyish to me; only "apple" was new and incomprehensible.

When it was time for the lunch recess, I followed the girl with braids out onto the veranda. There the children from the other classes were assembled. I saw Premila at once and ran over to her, as she had charge of our lunchbox. The children were all opening packages and sitting down to eat sandwiches. Premila and I were the only ones who had Indian food—thin wheat chapatties, some vegetable curry, and a bottle of buttermilk. Premila thrust half of it into my hand and whispered fiercely that I should go and sit with my class, because that was what the others seemed to be doing.

The enormous black eyes of the little Indian girl from my class looked at my food longingly, so I offered her some. But she only shook her head and plowed her way solemnly through her sandwiches.

I was very sleepy after lunch, because at home we always took a siesta.

It was usually a pleasant time of day, with the bedroom darkened against the harsh afternoon sun, the drifting off into sleep with the sound of Mother's voice reading a story in one's mind, and, finally, the shrill, fussy voice of the ayah waking one for tea.

At school, we rested for a short time on low, folding cots on the veranda, and then we were expected to play games. During the hot part of the afternoon we played indoors, and after the shadows had begun to lengthen and the slight breeze of the evening had come up we moved outside to the wide courtyard.

I had never really grasped the system of competitive games. At home, whenever we played tag or guessing games, I was always allowed to "win"—"because," Mother used to tell Premila, "she is the youngest, and we have to allow for that." I had often heard her say it, and it seemed quite reasonable to me, but the result was that I had no clear idea of what "winning" meant.

When we played twos-and-threes that afternoon at school, in accordance with my training, I let one of the small English boys catch me, but was naturally rather puzzled when the other children did not return the courtesy. I ran about for what seemed like hours without ever catching anyone, until it was time for school to close. Much later I learned that my attitude was called "not being a good sport," and I stopped allowing myself to be caught, but it was not for years that I really learned the spirit of the thing.

When I saw our car come up to the school gate, I broke away from my classmates and rushed toward it yelling, "Ayah! Ayah!" It seemed like an eternity since I had seen her that morning—a wizened, affectionate figure in her white cotton sari, giving me dozens of urgent and useless instructions on how to be a good girl at school. Premila followed more sedately, and she told me on the way home never to do that again in front of the other children.

When we got home we went straight to Mother's high, white room to have tea with her, and I immediately climbed onto the bed and bounced gently up and down on the springs. Mother asked how we had liked our first day in school. I was so pleased to be home and to have left that peculiar Cynthia behind that I had nothing whatever to say about school, except to ask what "apple" meant. But Premila told Mother about the classes, and added that in her class they had weekly tests to see if they had learned their lessons well.

I asked, "What's a test?"

Premila said, "You're too small to have them. You won't have them in your class for donkey's years." She had learned the expression that day and was using it for the first time. We all laughed enormously at her wit. She also told Mother, in an aside, that we should take sandwiches to school the next day. Not, she said, that *she* minded. But they would be simpler for me to handle.

That whole lovely evening I didn't think about school at all. I sprinted barefoot across the lawns with my favorite playmate, the cook's son, to the stream at the end of the garden. We quarreled in our usual way, waded in the tepid water under the lime trees, and waited for the night to bring out the smell of the jasmine. I listened with fascination to his stories of ghosts and demons, until I was too frightened to cross the garden alone in the semidarkness. The ayah found me, shouted at the cook's son, scolded me, hurried me in to supper—it was an entirely usual, wonderful evening.

It was a week later, the day of Premila's first test, that our lives changed rather abruptly. I was sitting at the back of my class, in my usual inattentive way, only half listening to the teacher. I had started a rather guarded friendship with the girl with the braids, whose name turned out to be Nalini (Nancy, in school). The three other Indian children were already fast friends. Even at that age it was apparent to all of us that friendship with the English or Anglo-Indian children was out of the question. Occasionally, during the class, my new friend and I would draw pictures and show them to each other secretly.

The door opened sharply and Premila marched in. At first, the teacher smiled at her in a kindly and encouraging way and said, "Now, you're little Cynthia's sister?"

Premila didn't even look at her. She stood with her feet planted firmly apart and her shoulders rigid, and addressed herself directly to me. "Get up," she said. "We're going home."

I didn't know what had happened, but I was aware that it was a crisis of some sort. I rose obediently and started to walk toward my sister.

"Bring your pencils and your notebook," she said.

I went back for them, and together we left the room. The teacher started to say something just as Premila closed the door, but we didn't wait to hear what it was.

In complete silence we left the school grounds and started to walk home. Then I asked Premila what the matter was. All she would say was "We're going home for good."

It was a very tiring walk for a child of five and a half, and I dragged along behind Premila with my pencils growing sticky in my hand. I can still remember looking at the dusty hedges, and the tangles of thorns in the ditches by the side of the road, smelling the faint fragrance from the eucalyptus trees and wondering whether we would ever reach home. Occasionally a horse-drawn tonga passed us, and the women, in their pink or green silks, stared at Premila and me trudging along on the side of the road. A few coolies and a line of women carrying baskets of vegetables on their heads smiled at us. But it was nearing the hottest time of day, and the road was almost deserted. I walked more and more slowly, and shouted to Premila, from time to time, "Wait for me!" with increasing peevishness. She spoke to me only once, and that was to tell me to carry my notebook on my head, because of the sun.

When we got to our house the ayah was just taking a tray of lunch into Mother's room. She immediately started a long, worried questioning about what are you children doing back here at this hour of the day.

Mother looked very startled and very concerned, and asked Premila what had happened.

Premila said, "We had our test today, and She made me and the other Indians sit at the back of the room, with a desk between each one."

Mother said, "Why was that, darling?"

"She said it was because Indians cheat," Premila added. "So I don't think we should go back to that school."

Mother looked very distant, and was silent a long time. At last she said, "Of course not, darling." She sounded displeased.

We all shared the curry she was having for lunch, and afterward I was sent off to the beautifully familiar bedroom for my siesta. I could hear Mother and Premila talking through the open door.

Mother said, "Do you suppose she understood all that?"

Premila said, "I shouldn't think so. She's a baby."

Mother said, "Well, I hope it won't bother her."

Of course, they were both wrong. I understood it perfectly, and I remember it all very clearly. But I put it happily away, because it had all happened to a girl called Cynthia, and I never was really particularly interested in her.

The Language of Oppression

Haig A. Bosmajian

Haig A. Bosmajian, Professor of Parliamentary Procedure, Rhetoric, and Freedom of Speech at the University of Washington, was born in California in 1928. He received his doctorate from Stanford in 1960. Professor Bosmajian's principal areas of interest are dissent, language and behavior, and the language of social movements. He has edited The Principles and Practice of Freedom of Speech *(1971), has collaborated with Hamida Bosmajian on* The Rhetoric of the Civil Rights Movement *(1969) and* This Great Argument: The Rights of Women *(1972), and he is coauthor of* Sexism and Language *(1977). His more recent publications include* Justice Douglas and Freedom of Speech *(1980) and* Censorship, Libraries, and the Law *(1982). Bosmajian has also published essays on the rhetoric of Nazism and communism and on nonverbal communication. The present essay is the introduction to his book* The Language of Oppression *(1974 which we take its title.*

"Sticks and stones may break my bones, but words can never hurt me."
To accept this adage as valid is sheer folly. "What's in a name? that which
we call a rose by any other name would smell as sweet." The answer to
Juliet's question is "Plenty!" and to her own response to the question we
can only say that this is by no means invariably true. The importance,
significance, and ramifications of naming and defining people cannot be
over-emphasized. From *Genesis* and beyond, to the present time, the
power which comes from naming and defining people has had positive as
well as negative effects on entire populations.

The magic of words and names has always been an integral part of both
"primitive" and "civilized" societies. As Margaret Schlauch has observed,
"from time immemorial men have thought there is some mysterious
essential connection between a thing and the spoken name for it. You
could use the name of your enemy, not only to designate him either
passionately or dispassionately, but also to exercise a baleful influence."[1]

Biblical passages abound in which names and naming are endowed with
great power; from the very outset, in *Genesis,* naming and defining are
attributed a significant potency: "And out of the ground the Lord God
formed every beast of the field and every fowl of the air; and brought them
unto Adam to see what he would call them: and whatsoever Adam called
every living creature, that was the name thereof."[2] Amidst the admonitions in *Leviticus* against theft, lying, and fraud is the warning: "And ye
shall not swear my name falsely, neither shalt thou profane the name of
thy God: I am the Lord."[3] So important is the name that it must not be
blasphemed; those who curse and blaspheme shall be stoned "and he that
blasphemeth the name of the Lord, he shall surely be put to death, and
all the congregation shall certainly stone him."[4] So important is the name
that the denial of it is considered a form of punishment: "But ye are they
that forsake the Lord, that forget my holy mountain. . . . Therefore will
I number you to the sword, and ye shall all bow down to the slaughter:
because when I called, ye did not answer; when I spake, ye did not hear.
. . . Therefore thus saith the Lord God, behold, my servants shall eat, but
ye shall be hungry. . . . And ye shall leave your name for a curse unto my
chosen: for the Lord God shall slay thee, and call his servants by another
name."[5]

To be unnamed is to be unknown, to have no identity. William Saroyan
has observed that "the word nameless, especially in poetry and in much
prose, signifies an alien, unknown, and almost unwelcome condition, as
when, for instance, a writer speaks of 'a nameless sorrow.'" "Human

[1]Margaret Schlauch, *The Gift of Language* (New York: Dover, 1955), p. 13.
[2]*Genesis,* 2:19.
[3]*Leviticus,* 19:12.
[4]*Leviticus,* 25:16.
[5]*Isaiah,* 66:11–12.

beings," continues Saroyan, "are for the fact of being named at all, how-ever meaninglessly, lifted out of an area of mystery, doubt, or undesirabil-ity into an area in which belonging to everybody else is taken for granted, so that one of the first questions asked by new people, two-year-olds even, whether they are speaking to other new people or to people who have been around for a great many years, is 'What is your name?' "[6]

To receive a name is to be elevated to the status of a human being; without a name one's identity is questionable. In stressing the importance of a name and the significance of having none, Joyce Hertzler has said that "among both primitives and moderns, an individual has no defini-tion, no validity for himself, without a name. His name is his badge of individuality, the means whereby he identifies himself and enters upon a truly subjective existence. My own name, for example, stands for me, a person. Divesting me of it reduces me to a meaningless, even pathologi-cal, nonentity."[7]

In his book *What Is in a Name?* Farhang Zabeeh reminds us that "the Roman slaves originally were without names. Only after being sold they took their master's praenomen in the genitive case followed by the suffix—'por' (boy), e.g., 'Marcipor,' which indicates that some men, so long as they were regarded by others as cattle, did not need a name. However, as soon as they became servants some designation was called forth."[8] To this day one of the forms of punishment meted out to wrongdoers who are imprisoned is to take away their names and to give them numbers. In an increasingly computerized age people are becoming mere numbers—credit card numbers, insurance numbers, bank account numbers, student numbers, et cetera. Identification of human beings by numbers is a nega-tion of their humanity and their existence.

Philologist Max Muller has pointed out that "if we examine the most ancient word for 'name,' we find it is *naman* in Sanskrit, *nomen* in Latin, *namo* in Gothic. This *naman* stands for gnaman and is derived from the root, *gna*, to know, and meant originally that by which we know a thing."[9] In the course of the evolution of human society, R. P. Masani tells us, the early need for names "appears to have been felt almost simultaneously with the origin of speech . . . personality and the rights and obligations connected with it would not exist without the name."[10] In his classic work *The Golden Bough* James Frazer devotes several pages to tabooed names

---

[6]William Saroyan, "Random Notes on the Names of People," *Names,* 1 (December 1953), p. 239.

[7]Joyce Hertzler, *A Sociology of Language* (New York: Random House, 1965), p. 271.

[8]Farhang Zabeeh, *What Is in a Name?* (The Hague: Martinus Nijhoff, 1968), p. 66.

[9]Cited in Elsdon Smith, *Treasury of Name Lore* (New York: Harper and Row, 1967), p. vii.

[10]R. P. Masani, *Folk Culture Reflected in Names* (Bombay: Popular Prakashan, 1966), p. 6.

and words in ancient societies, taboos reflecting the power and magic people saw in names and words. Frazer notes, for example, that "the North American Indian regards his name, not as a mere label, but as a distinct part of his personality, just as much as are his eyes or his teeth, and believes that injury will result as surely from the malicious handling of his name as from a wound inflicted on any part of his physical organism."[11]

A name can be used as a curse. A name can be blasphemed. Namecalling is so serious a matter that statutes and court decisions prohibit "fighting words" to be uttered. In 1942 the United States Supreme Court upheld the conviction of a person who had addressed a police officer as "a God damned racketeer" and "a damned Fascist." (*Chaplinsky v. New Hampshire*, 315 U.S. 568). Such namecalling, such epithets, said the Court, are not protected speech. So important is one's "good name" that the law prohibits libel.

History abounds with instances in which the mere utterance of a name was prohibited. In ancient Greece, according to Frazer, "the names of the priests and other high officials who had to do with the performance of the Eleusinian mysteries might not be uttered in their lifetime. To pronounce them was a legal offense."[12] Jörgen Ruud reports in *Taboo: A Study of Malagasy Customs and Beliefs* that among the Antandroy people the father has absolute authority in his household and that "children are forbidden to mention the name of their father. They must call him father, daddy. . . . The children may not mention his house or the parts of his body by their ordinary names, but must use other terms, i.e., euphemisms."[13]

It was Iago who said in *Othello:*

Who steals my purse steals trash; 'tis something nothing;
'Twas mine, 'tis his, and has been slave to thousands;
But he that filches from me my good name
Robs me of that which not enriches him
And makes me poor indeed.

Alice, in Lewis Carroll's *Through the Looking Glass,* had trepidations about entering the woods where things were nameless: "This must be the wood," she said thoughtfully to herself, "where things have no names. I wonder what'll become of *my* name when I go in? I shouldn't like to lose it at all—because they'd have to give me another, and it would almost certain to be an ugly one."

A Nazi decree of August 17, 1938 stipulated that "Jews may receive only those first names which are listed in the directives of the Ministry

---

[11]James Frazer, *The Golden Bough* (New York: Macmillan, 1951), p. 284.

[12]*Ibid.,* p. 302.

[13]Jörgen Ruud, *Taboo: A Study of Malagasy Customs and Beliefs* (Oslo: Oslo University Press, 1960), p. 15.

of the Interior concerning the use of first names." Further, the decree provided: "If Jews should bear first names other than those permitted . . . they must . . . adopt an additional name. For males, that name shall be Israel, for females Sara." Another Nazi decree forbade Jews in Germany "to show themselves in public without a Jew's star. . . . [consisting] of a six-pointed star of yellow cloth with black borders, equivalent in size to the palm of the hand. The inscription is to read 'JEW' in black letters. It is to be sewn to the left breast of the garment, and to be worn visibly."

The power which comes from names and naming is related directly to the power to define others—individuals, races, sexes, ethnic groups. Our identities, who and what we are, how others see us, are greatly affected by the names we are called and the words with which we are labelled. The names, labels, and phrases employed to "identify" a people may in the end determine their survival. The word "define" comes from the Latin *definire,* meaning to limit. Through definition we restrict, we set boundaries, we name.

"When I use a word," said Humpty Dumpty in *Through the Looking Glass,* "it means just what I choose it to mean—neither more nor less." "The question is," said Alice, "whether you can make words mean so many different things." "The question is," said Humpty Dumpty, "which is to be master—that's all."

During his days as a civil rights-black power activist, Stokely Carmichael accurately asserted: "It [definition] is very, very important because I believe that people who can define are masters."[14] Self-determination must include self-definition, the ability and right to name oneself; the master-subject relationship is based partly on the master's power to name and define the subject.

While names, words and language can be and are used to inspire us, to motivate us to humane acts, to liberate us, they can also be used to dehumanize human beings and to "justify" their suppression and even their extermination. It is not a great step from the coercive suppression of dissent to the extermination of dissenters (as the United States Supreme Court declared in its 1943 compulsory flag salute opinion in *West Virginia State Board of Education v. Barnette*); nor is it a large step from defining a people as non-human or sub-human to their subjugation or annihilation. One of the first acts of an oppressor is to redefine the "enemy" so they will be looked upon as creatures warranting separation, suppression, and even eradication.

The Nazis redefined Jews as "bacilli," "parasites," "disease," "demon," and "plague." In his essay "The Hollow Miracle," George Steiner informs us that the Germans "who poured quicklime down the openings of the sewers in Warsaw to kill the living and stifle the stink of the dead wrote

[14]Stokely Carmichael, speech delivered in Seattle, Washington, April 19, 1967.

about it. They spoke of having to 'liquidate vermin'. . . . Gradually, words lost their original meaning and acquired nightmarish definitions. *Jude, Pole, Russe* came to mean two-legged lice, putrid vermin which good Aryans must squash, as a [Nazi] Party manual said, 'like roaches on a dirty wall.' 'Final solution,' *endgültige Lösung,* came to signify the death of six million human beings in gas ovens."[15]

The language of white racism has for centuries been used to "keep the nigger in his place." Our sexist language has allowed men to define who and what a woman is and must be. Labels like "traitors," "saboteurs," "queers," and "obscene degenerates" were applied indiscriminately to students who protested the war in Vietnam or denounced injustices in the United States. Are such people to be listened to? Consulted? Argued with? Obviously not! One does not listen to, much less talk to, traitors and outlaws, sensualists and queers. One only punishes them or, as Spiro Agnew suggested in one of his 1970 speeches, there are some dissenters who should be separated "from our society with no more regret than we should feel over discarding rotten apples."[16]

What does it mean to separate people? When the Japanese-Americans were rounded up in 1942 and sent off to "relocation camps" they were "separated." The Jews in Nazi Germany were "separated." The Indians of the United States, the occupants of the New World before Columbus "discovered" it, have been systematically "separated." As "chattels" and slaves, the blacks in the United States were "separated"; legally a black person was a piece of property, although human enough to be counted as three-fifths of a person in computing the number of people represented by white legislators.

How is the forcible isolation of human beings from society at large justified? To make the separation process more palatable to the populace, what must the oppressor first do? How does he make the populace accept the separation of the "creatures," or, if not accept it, at least not protest it? Consideration of such questions is not an academic exercise without practical implications. There is a close nexus between language and self-perception, self-awareness, self-identity, and self-esteem. Just as our thoughts affect our language, so does our language affect our thoughts and eventually our actions and behavior. As Edward Sapir has observed, we are all "at the mercy of the particular language which has become the medium of expression" in our society. The "real world," he points out, "is to a large extent unconsciously built up on the language habits of the group. . . . We see and hear and otherwise experience very largely as we do because the language habits of our community predispose certain choices of interpretation."[17]

[15]George Steiner, *Language and Silence* (New York: Atheneum, 1970), p. 100.

[16]*The New York Times,* October 31, 1969, p. 25.

[17]Cited in John Carroll (ed.), *Language, Thought and Reality: Selected Writings of Benjamin Lee Whorf* (Cambridge, Mass.: The M.I.T. Press, 1956), p. 134.

George Orwell has written in his famous essay ["Politics and the English Language": "A man may take to drink because he feels himself to be a failure, and then fail all the more completely because he drinks. It is rather the same thing that is happening to the English language. It becomes ugly and inaccurate because our thoughts are foolish, but the slovenliness of our language makes it easier for us to have foolish thoughts."[18] Orwell maintains that "the decadence in our language is probably curable" and that "silly words and expressions have often disappeared, not through any evolutionary process but owing to the conscious action of a minority."[19] Wilma Scott Heide, speaking as president of the National Organization for Women several years ago, indicated that feminists were undertaking this conscious action: ["In any social movement, when changes are effected, the language sooner or later reflects the change. Our approach is different. Instead of passively noting the change, we are changing language patterns to actively effect the changes, a significant part of which is the conceptual tool of thought, our language."[20]

This then is our task—to identify the decadence in our language, the inhumane uses of language, the "silly words and expressions" which have been used to justify the unjustifiable, to make palatable the unpalatable, to make reasonable the unreasonable, to make decent the indecent. Hitler's ["Final Solution"] appeared reasonable once the Jews were successfully labelled by the Nazis as sub-humans, as "parasites," "vermin," and "bacilli." The segregation and suppression of blacks in the United States was justified once they were considered "chattels" and "inferiors." The subjugation of the "American Indians" was defensible since they were defined as "barbarians" and "savages." As Peter Farb has said, "cannibalism, torture, scalping, mutilation, adultery, incest, sodomy, rape, filth, drunkenness—such a catalogue of accusations against a people is an indication not so much of their depravity as that their land is up for grabs."[21] [As long as adult women are "chicks," "girls," "dolls," "babes," and "ladies," their status in society will remain "inferior"; they will go on being treated as subjects in the subject-master relationship as long as the language of the law places them into the same class as children, minors, and the insane.]

Far fetched

It is my hope that an examination of the language of oppression will result in a conscious effort by the reader to help cure this decadence in our language, especially that language which leads to dehumanization of the human being. One way for us to curtail the use of the language of oppression is for those who find themselves being defined into subjugation

---

[18]George Orwell, "Politics and the English Language," in C. Muscatine and M. Griffith, *The Borzoi College Reader*, 2nd ed. (New York: Alfred A. Knopf, 1971), p. 88.

[19]*Ibid.*

[20]Wilma Scott Heide, "Feminism: The *sine qua non* for a Just Society," *Vital Speeches*, 38 (1971–72), p. 402.

[21]Peter Farb, "Indian Corn," *The New York Review*, 17 (December 16, 1971), p. 36.

to rebel against such linguistic suppression. It isn't strange that those persons who insist on defining themselves, who insist on this elemental privilege of self-naming, self-definition, and self-identity encounter vigorous resistance. Predictably, the resistance usually comes from the oppressor or would-be oppressor and is a result of the fact that he or she does not want to relinquish the power which comes from the ability to define others.

You Are What You Say

Robin Lakoff

Robin Lakoff (born 1942) has written many books and articles on linguistics. She began her scholarly career by studying Latin syntax, but has progressively shifted her attention—through English syntax, semantics, and sociolinguistics—to pragmatics, the study of how language is used in practical situations, between people. She received her B.A. from Radcliffe in 1964 and her Ph.D. from Harvard in 1967. Subsequently she has taught at the University of Michigan and at Stanford, and since 1976 has been a professor of linguistics at the University of California, Berkeley. In 1979 Ripon College awarded her the honorary degree of Doctor of Letters, recognizing particularly her work on linguistic stereotypes and on the language associated with sex roles. The citation concluded: "She has helped to give productive contemporary meaning to the Biblical injunction 'by thy words thou shalt be justified, and by thy words thou shalt be condemned'."

Her essay "You Are What You Say" appeared in the July 1974 issue of Ms. *A fuller treatment of the subject is found in her book* Language and Women's Place *(1975). More recently she has written (with Raquel Scherr)* Face Value: The Politics of Beauty *(1984), and (with Mandy Aftel)* When Talk Is Not Cheap *(1985), on the language of psychological therapy. Currently she is studying the language and psychology of prospective jurors.*

"Women's language" is that pleasant (dainty?), euphemistic, never-aggressive way of talking we learned as little girls. Cultural bias was built into the language we were allowed to speak, the subjects we were allowed to speak about, and the ways we were spoken of. Having learned our linguistic lesson well, we go out in the world, only to discover that we are communicative cripples—damned if we do, and damned if we don't.

If we refuse to talk "like a lady," we are ridiculed and criticized for being unfeminine. ("She thinks like a man" is, at best, a left-handed compliment.) If we do learn all the fuzzy-headed, unassertive language of our sex, we are ridiculed for being unable to think clearly, unable to take part in a serious discussion, and therefore unfit to hold a position of power.

It doesn't take much of this for a woman to begin feeling she deserves such treatment because of inadequacies in her own intelligence and education.

"Women's language" shows up in all levels of English. For example, women are encouraged and allowed to make far more precise discriminations in naming colors than men do. Words like *mauve, beige, ecru, aquamarine, lavender,* and so on, are unremarkable in a woman's active vocabulary, but largely absent from that of most men. I know of no evidence suggesting that women actually *see* a wider range of colors than men do. It is simply that fine discriminations of this sort are relevant to women's vocabularies, but not to men's; to men, who control most of the interesting affairs of the world, such distinctions are trivial—irrelevant.

In the area of syntax, we find similar gender-related peculiarities of speech. There is one construction, in particular, that women use conversationally far more than men: the tag-question. A tag is midway between an outright statement and a yes-no question; it is less assertive than the former, but more confident than the latter.

A *flat statement* indicates confidence in the speaker's knowledge and is fairly certain to be believed; a *question* indicates a lack of knowledge on some point and implies that the gap in the speaker's knowledge can and will be remedied by an answer. For example, if, at a Little League game, I have had my glasses off, I can legitimately ask someone else: "Was the player out at third?" A *tag question,* being intermediate between statement and question, is used when the speaker is stating a claim, but lacks full confidence in the truth of that claim. So if I say, "Is Joan here?" I will probably not be surprised if my respondent answers "no"; but if I say, "Joan is here, isn't she?" instead, chances are I am already biased in favor of a positive answer, wanting only confirmation. I still want a response, but I have enough knowledge (or think I have) to predict that response. A tag question, then, might be thought of as a statement that doesn't demand to be believed by anyone but the speaker, a way of giving leeway, of not forcing the addressee to go along with the views of the speaker.

Another common use of the tag-question is in small talk when the speaker is trying to elicit conversation: "Sure is hot here, isn't it?"

But in discussing personal feelings or opinions, only the speaker normally has any way of knowing the correct answer. Sentences such as "I have a headache, don't I?" are clearly ridiculous. But there are other examples where it is the speaker's opinions, rather than perceptions, for which corroboration is sought, as in "The situation in Southeast Asia is terrible, isn't it?"

While there are, of course, other possible interpretations of a sentence like this, one possibility is that the speaker has a particular answer in mind—"yes" or "no"—but is reluctant to state it baldly. This sort of tag question is much more apt to be used by women than by men in conversation. Why is this the case?

The tag question allows a speaker to avoid commitment, and thereby avoid conflict with the addressee. The problem is that, by so doing, speakers may also give the impression of not really being sure of themselves, or looking to the addressee for confirmation of their views. This uncertainty is reinforced in more subliminal ways, too. There is a peculiar sentence intonation-pattern, used almost exclusively by women, as far as I know, which changes a declarative answer into a question. The effect of using the rising inflection typical of a yes-no question is to imply that the speaker is seeking confirmation, even though the speaker is clearly the only one who has the requisite information, which is why the question was put to her in the first place:

(Q) When will dinner be ready?

(A) Oh . . . around six o'clock . . .? It is as though the second speaker were saying, "Six o'clock—if that's okay with you, if you agree." The person being addressed is put in the position of having to provide confirmation. One likely consequence of this sort of speech-pattern in a woman is that, often unbeknownst to herself, the speaker builds a reputation of tentativeness, and others will refrain from taking her seriously or trusting her with any real responsibilities, since she "can't make up her mind," and "isn't sure of herself."

Such idiosyncrasies may explain why women's language sounds much more "polite" than men's. It is polite to leave a decision open, not impose your mind, or views, or claims, on anyone else. So a tag-question is a kind of polite statement, in that it does not force agreement or belief on the addressee. In the same way a request is a polite command, in that it does not force obedience on the addressee, but rather suggests something be done as a favor to the speaker. A clearly stated order implies a threat of certain consequences if it is not followed, and—even more impolite—implies that the speaker is in a superior position and able to enforce the order. By couching wishes in the form of a request, on the other hand, a speaker implies that if the request is not carried out, only the speaker will suffer; noncompliance cannot harm the addressee. So the decision is really left up to the addressee. The distinction becomes clear in these examples:

Close the door.

Please close the door.
Will you close the door?
Will you please close the door?
Won't you close the door?

In the same ways as words and speech patterns used *by* women undermine her image, those used *to describe* women make matters even worse. Often a word may be used of both men and women (and perhaps of things as well); but when it is applied to women, it assumes a special meaning that, by implication rather than outright assertion, is derogatory to women as a group.

The use of euphemisms has this effect. A euphemism is a substitute for a word that has acquired a bad connotation by association with something unpleasant or embarrassing. But almost as soon as the new word comes into common usage, it takes on the same old bad connotations, since feelings about the things or people referred to are not altered by a change of name; thus new euphemisms must be constantly found.

There is one euphemism for *woman* still very much alive. The word, of course is *lady. Lady* has a masculine counterpart, namely *gentleman,* occasionally shortened to *gent.* But for some reason *lady* is very much commoner than *gent(leman).*

The decision to use *lady* rather than *woman,* or vice versa, may considerably alter the sense of a sentence, as the following examples show:

(a) A woman (lady) I know is a dean at Berkeley.

(b) A woman (lady) I know makes amazing things out of shoelaces and old boxes.

The use of *lady* in (a) imparts a frivolous, or nonserious, tone to the sentence: the matter under discussion is not one of great moment. Similarly, in (b), using *lady* here would suggest that the speaker considered the "amazing things" not to be serious art, but merely a hobby or an aberration. If *woman* is used, she might be a serious sculptor. To say *lady doctor* is very condescending, since no one ever says *gentleman doctor* or even *man doctor.* For example, mention in the San Francisco *Chronicle* of January 31, 1972, of Madalyn Murray O'Hair as the *lady atheist* reduces her position to that of scatterbrained eccentric. Even *woman atheist* is scarcely defensible: sex is irrelevant to her philosophical position.

Many women argue that, on the other hand, *lady* carries with it overtones recalling the age of chivalry: conferring exalted stature on the person so referred to. This makes the term seem polite at first, but we must also remember that these implications are perilous: they suggest that a "lady" is helpless, and cannot do things by herself.

Lady can also be used to infer frivolousness, as in titles of organizations. Those that have a serious purpose (not merely that of enabling "the ladies" to spend time with one another) cannot use the word *lady* in their titles, but less serious ones may. Compare the *Ladies' Auxiliary* of a men's group, or the *Thursday Evening Ladies' Browning and Garden Society* with *Ladies' Liberation* or *Ladies' Strike for Peace*.

What is curious about this split is that *lady* is in origin a euphemism—a substitute that puts a better face on something people find uncomfortable—for *woman*. What kind of euphemism is it that subtly denigrates the people to whom it refers? Perhaps *lady* functions as a euphemism for *woman* because it does not contain the sexual implications present in *woman;* it is not "embarrassing" in that way. If this is so, we may expect that, in the future, *lady* will replace woman as the primary word for the human female, since *woman* will have become too blatantly sexual. That this distinction is already made in some contexts at least is shown in the following examples, where you can try replacing *woman* with *lady:*

(a) She's only twelve, but she's already a woman.

(b) After ten years in jail, Harry wanted to find a woman.

(c) She's my woman, see, so don't mess around with her.

Another common substitute for *woman* is *girl*. One seldom hears a man past the age of adolescence referred to as a boy, save in expressions like "going out with the boys," which are meant to suggest an air of adolescent frivolity and irresponsibility. But women of all ages are "girls": one can have a man—not a boy—Friday, but only a girl—never a woman or even a lady—Friday; women have girlfriends, but men do not—in a nonsexual sense—have boyfriends. It may be that this use of *girl* is euphemistic in the same way the use of *lady* is: in stressing the idea of immaturity, it removes the sexual connotations lurking in *woman*. *Girl* brings to mind irresponsibility: you don't send a girl to do a woman's errand (or even, for that matter, a boy's errand). She is a person who is both too immature and too far from real life to be entrusted with responsibilities or with decisions of any serious or important nature.

Now let's take a pair of words which, in terms of the possible relationships in an earlier society, were simple male-female equivalents, analogous to *bull : cow*. Suppose we find that, for independent reasons, society has changed in such a way that the original meanings now are irrelevant. Yet the words have not been discarded, but have acquired new meanings, metaphorically related to their original senses. But suppose these new metaphorical uses are no longer parallel to each other. By seeing where the parallelism breaks down, we discover something about the different roles played by men and women in this culture. One good example of such a divergence through time is found in the pair, *master : mistress*. Once used with reference to one's power over servants, these words have become unusable today in their original master-servant sense as the relationship has become less prevalent in our society. But the words are still common.

Unless used with reference to animals, *master* now generally refers to a man who has acquired consummate ability in some field, normally nonsexual. But its feminine counterpart cannot be used this way. It is practically restricted to its sexual sense of "paramour." We start out with two terms, both roughly paraphrasable as "one who has power over another." But the masculine form, once one person is no longer able to have absolute power over another, becomes usable metaphorically in the sense of "having power over *something.*" *Master* requires as its object only the name of some activity, something inanimate and abstract. But *mistress* requires a masculine noun in the possessive to precede it. One cannot say: "Rhonda is a mistress." One must be *someone's* mistress. A man is defined by what he does, a woman by her sexuality, that is, in terms of one particular aspect of her relationship to men. It is one thing to be an *old master* like Hans Holbein, and another to be an *old mistress.*

The same is true of the words *spinster* and *bachelor*—gender words for "one who is not married." The resemblance ends with the definition. While *bachelor* is a neutral term, often used as a compliment, *spinster* normally is used pejoratively, with connotations of prissiness, fussiness, and so on. To be a bachelor implies that one has the choice of marrying or not, and this is what makes the idea of a bachelor existence attractive, in the popular literature. He has been pursued and has successfully eluded his pursuers. But a spinster is one who has not been pursued, or at least not seriously. She is old, unwanted goods. The metaphorical connotations of *bachelor* generally suggest sexual freedom; of *spinster,* puritanism or celibacy.

These examples could be multiplied. It is generally considered a *faux pas,* in society, to congratulate a woman on her engagement, while it is correct to congratulate her fiancé. Why is this? The reason seems to be that it is impolite to remind people of things that may be uncomfortable to them. To congratulate a woman on her engagement is really to say, "Thank goodness! You had a close call!" For the man, on the other hand, there was no such danger. His choosing to marry is viewed as a good thing, but not something essential.

The linguistic double standard holds throughout the life of the relationship. After marriage, bachelor and spinster become man and wife, not man and woman. The woman whose husband dies remains "John's widow"; John, however, is never "Mary's widower."

Finally, why is it that salesclerks and others are so quick to call women customers "dear," "honey," and other terms of endearment they really have no business using? A male customer would never put up with it. But women, like children, are supposed to enjoy these endearments, rather than being offended by them.

In more ways than one, it's time to speak up.

ck English Isn't a Language, Then Tell Me, What Is?

James Baldwin

James Baldwin (1924–1987) was born in Harlem. The eldest of nine children, he never knew his real father. After the death of his stepfather, a lay preacher, in 1943, he lived in Greenwich Village, working by day as handyman, office boy, or factory worker, and writing at night. A Rosenwald Fellowship enabled him to go to Paris in 1948 where he wrote his first two novels, Go Tell It on the Mountain *(1953) and* Giovanni's Room *(1956), and the essays published as* Notes of a Native Son *(1955).*

Baldwin returned to America in 1957 and continued his career as a distinguished novelist, playwright, and essayist, and as a spokesman for black civil rights. His first Broadway play, Blues for Mister Charlie, *was dedicated to his friend Medgar Evers, the civil rights leader who had recently been slain, and to the children bombed in a Birmingham church. He won many awards, including a Guggenheim Fellowship in 1954.* Nobody Knows My Name, *a collection of essays, was selected as one of the outstanding books of 1961 by the American Library Association.* The Fire Next Time *(1963)—two searing articles, or letters, on the relationship between black and white Americans—secures Baldwin's lasting reputation as an essayist and as a commentator on American culture. Recent publications include* Evidence of Things Not Seen *(1985) and* The Price of the Ticket: Collected Nonfiction 1948–1985 *(1985), from which the following article—originally published in the* New York Times, *July 29, 1979—is reprinted.*

The argument concerning the use, or the status, or the reality, of black English is rooted in American history and has absolutely nothing to do with the question the argument supposes itself to be posing. The argument has nothing to do with language itself but with the role of language. Language, incontestably, reveals the speaker. Language, also, far more dubiously, is meant to define the other—and, in this case, the other is refusing to be defined by a language that has never been able to recognize him.

People evolve a language in order to describe and thus control their circumstances or in order not to be submerged by a situation that they cannot articulate. (And if they cannot articulate it, they are submerged.) A Frenchman living in Paris speaks a subtly and crucially different language from that of the man living in Marseilles; neither sounds very much like a man living in Quebec; and they would all have great difficulty

in apprehending what the man from Guadeloupe, or Martinique, is saying, to say nothing of the man from Senegal—although the "common"
language of all these areas is French. But each has paid, and is paying,
a different price for this "common" language, in which, as it turns out,
they are not saying, and cannot be saying, the same things: They each
have very different realities to articulate, or control.

What joins all languages, and all men, is the necessity to confront life,
in order, not inconceivably, to outwit death: The price for this is the
acceptance, and achievement, of one's temporal identity. So that, for
example, though it is not taught in the schools (and this has the potential
of becoming a political issue) the south of France still clings to its ancient
and musical Provençal, which resists being described as a "dialect." And
much of the tension in the Basque countries, and in Wales, is due to the
Basque and Welsh determination not to allow their languages to be destroyed. This determination also feeds the flames in Ireland for among the
many indignities the Irish have been forced to undergo at English hands
is the English contempt for their language.

It goes without saying, then, that language is also a political instrument, means, and proof of power. It is the most vivid and crucial key to
identity: It reveals the private identity, and connects one with, or divorces
one from, the larger, public, or communal identity. There have been, and
are, times and places, when to speak a certain language could be dangerous, even fatal. Or, one may speak the same language, but in such a way
that one's antecedents are revealed, or (one hopes) hidden. This is true in
France, and is absolutely true in England: The range (and reign) of accents on that damp little island make England coherent for the English
and totally incomprehensible for everyone else[To open your mouth in
England is (if I may use black English) to "put your business in the street."
You have confessed your parents, your youth, your school, your salary,
your self-esteem, and, alas, your future.]

Now, I do not know what white Americans would sound like if there had
never been any black people in the United States, but they would not
sound the way they sound. *Jazz,* for example, is a very specific sexual
term, as in *jazz me, baby,* but white people purified it into the Jazz Age.
Sock it to me, which means, roughly, the same thing, has been adopted
by Nathaniel Hawthorne's descendants with no qualms or hesitations at
all, along with *let it all hang out* and *right on! Beat to his socks,* which
was once the black's most total and despairing image of poverty, was
transformed into a thing called the Beat Generation, which phenomenon
was, largely, composed of *uptight,* middle-class white people, imitating
poverty, trying to *get down,* to get *with it,* doing their *thing,* doing their
despairing best to be *funky,* which we, the blacks, never dreamed of
doing—we were funky, baby, like *funk* was going out of style.

Now, no one can eat his cake, and have it, too, and it is late in the day
to attempt to penalize black people for having created a language that

permits the nation its only glimpse of reality, a language without which the nation would be even more *whipped* than it is.

I say that the present skirmish is rooted in American history, and it is. Black English is the creation of the black diaspora. Blacks came to the United States chained to each other, but from different tribes. Neither could speak the other's language. If two black people, at that bitter hour of the world's history, had been able to speak to each other, the institution of chattel slavery could never have lasted as long as it did. Subsequently, the slave was given, under the eye, and the gun, of his master, Congo Square,° and the Bible—or, in other words, and under those conditions, the slave began the formation of the black church, and it is within this unprecedented tabernacle that black English began to be formed. This was not, merely, as in the European example, the adoption of a foreign tongue, but an alchemy that transformed ancient elements into a new language: *A language comes into existence by means of brutal necessity, and the rules of the language are dictated by what the language must convey.*

There was a moment, in time, and in this place, when my brother, or my mother, or my father, or my sister, had to convey to me, for example, the danger in which I was standing from the white man standing just behind me, and to convey this with a speed and in a language, that the white man could not possibly understand, and that, indeed, he cannot understand, until today. He cannot afford to understand it. This understanding would reveal to him too much about himself and smash that mirror before which he has been frozen for so long.

Now, if this passion, this skill, this (to quote Toni Morrison) "sheer intelligence," this incredible music, the mighty achievement of having brought a people utterly unknown to, or despised by "history"—to have brought this people to their present, troubled, troubling, and unassailable and unanswerable place—if this absolutely unprecedented journey does not indicate that black English is a language, I am curious to know what definition of languages is to be trusted.

A people at the center of the western world, and in the midst of so hostile a population, has not endured and transcended by means of what is patronizingly called a "dialect." We, the blacks, are in trouble, certainly, but we are not inarticulate because we are not compelled to defend a morality that we know to be a lie.

The brutal truth is that the bulk of the white people in America never had any interest in educating black people, except as this could serve white purposes. It is not the black child's language that is despised. It is his experience. A child cannot be taught by anyone who despises him, and

---

Congo Square An area, now part of Armstrong Park in New Orleans, where slaves and free blacks were allowed to gather on Sunday afternoons during most of the nineteenth century to play music, and sing, and dance.

a child cannot afford to be fooled. A child cannot be taught by anyone whose demand, essentially, is that the child repudiate his experience, and all that gives him sustenance, and enter a limbo in which he will no longer be black, and in which he knows that he can never become white. Black people have lost too many black children that way.

And, after all, finally, in a country with standards so untrustworthy, a country that makes heroes of so many criminal mediocrities, a country unable to face why so many of the nonwhite are in prison, or on the needle, or standing, futureless, in the streets—it may very well be that both the child, and his elder, have concluded that they have nothing whatever to learn from the people of a country that has managed to learn so little.

Politics and the English Language

George Orwell

George Orwell's reputation as a writer has shown no sign of decline since his death in 1950 at the age of forty-six. Best known as the author of the novels Animal Farm *(1945) and* Nineteen Eighty-Four *(1949), he was also a journalist and one of the great English essayists. The editors of* Partisan Review, *on presenting him an award in 1949, commented that his writing is "marked by a singular directness and honesty, a scrupulous fidelity to his experience that has placed him in that valuable class of the writer who is a witness to his time."*

His real name was Eric Arthur Blair, and he was born in 1903 in Bengal, a province of British India. He was sent to preparatory school when he was eight years old—an experience he grimly describes in Such, Such Were the Joys *(1953)—and attended Eton on a King's Scholarship from 1917 to 1921. From 1922 to 1927, he served with the Imperial Police in Burma. These early years are the subject of a biography by Peter Stansky and William Abrahams entitled* The Unknown Orwell *(1972). Returning to Europe, Orwell spent several poverty-stricken years doing odd jobs, from teaching to dishwashing, while he wrote novels and short stories that did not sell. The book* Down and Out in Paris and London *(1933) is a vivid record of those years. In 1936, Orwell went to Spain to take part in the civil war on the Republican side; he reported his experiences in* Homage to Catalonia *(1938).*

Among Orwell's other novels are Burmese Days *(1934),* A Clergyman's Daughter *(1935), and* Keep the Aspidistra Flying *(1936). His collections of essays include* Shooting an Elephant and Other Essays *(1950) and* Such, Such Were the Joys. *Sonia Orwell, his second wife, and Ian Angus edited* The Collected Essays, Journalism and Letters of George Orwell

(1968). The present essay first appeared in the London monthly Horizon *in 1946 and was reprinted in* Shooting an Elephant. *It was written with the horrors of World War II in mind; sadly, it has not lost a bit of its relevance since.*

Most people who bother with the matter at all would admit that the English language is in a bad way, but it is generally assumed that we cannot by conscious action do anything about it. Our civilization is decadent and our language—so the argument runs—must inevitably share in the general collapse. It follows that any struggle against the abuse of language is a sentimental archaism, like preferring candles to electric light or hansom cabs to aeroplanes. Underneath this lies the half-conscious belief that language is a natural growth and not an instrument which we shape for our own purposes.

Now, it is clear that the decline of a language must ultimately have political and economic causes: it is not due simply to the bad influence of this or that individual writer. But an effect can become a cause, reinforcing the original cause and producing the same effect in an intensified form, and so on indefinitely. A man may take to drink because he feels himself to be a failure, and then fail all the more completely because he drinks. It is rather the same thing that is happening to the English language. It becomes ugly and inaccurate because our thoughts are foolish, but the slovenliness of our language makes it easier for us to have foolish thoughts. The point is that the process is reversible. Modern English, especially written English, is full of bad habits which spread by imitation and which can be avoided if one is willing to take the necessary trouble. If one gets rid of these habits one can think more clearly, and to think clearly is a necessary first step towards political regeneration: so that the fight against bad English is not frivolous and is not the exclusive concern of professional writers. I will come back to this presently, and I hope that by that time the meaning of what I have said here will have become clearer. Meanwhile, here are five specimens of the English language as it is now habitually written.

These five passages have not been picked out because they are especially bad—I could have quoted far worse if I had chosen—but because they illustrate various of the mental vices from which we now suffer. They are a little below the average, but are fairly representative samples. I number them so that I can refer back to them when necessary:

(1) I am not, indeed, sure whether it is not true to say that the Milton who once seemed not unlike a seventeenth-century Shelley had not become, out of an experience ever more bitter in each year, more alien [*sic*] to the founder of that Jesuit sect which nothing could induce him to tolerate.

PROFESSOR HAROLD LASKI
(ESSAY IN *Freedom of Expression*).

(2) Above all, we cannot play ducks and drakes with a native battery of idioms which prescribes such egregious collocations of vocables as the Basic *put up with* for *tolerate* or *put at a loss* for *bewilder.*

PROFESSOR LANCELOT HOGBEN

(Interglossa).

(3) On the one side we have the free personality: by definition it is not neurotic, for it has neither conflict nor dream. Its desires, such as they are, are transparent, for they are just what institutional approval keeps in the forefront of consciousness; another institutional pattern would alter their number and intensity; there is little in them that is natural, irreducible, or culturally dangerous. But *on the other side,* the social bond itself is nothing but the mutual reflection of these self-secure integrities. Recall the definition of love. Is not this the very picture of a small academic? Where is there a place in this hall of mirrors for either personality or fraternity?

ESSAY ON PSYCHOLOGY IN *Politics*

(NEW YORK).

(4) All the "best people" from the gentlemen's clubs, and all the frantic fascist captains, united in common hatred of Socialism and bestial horror of the rising tide of the mass revolutionary movement, have turned to acts of provocation, to foul incendiarism, to medieval legends of poisoned wells, to legalize their own destruction of proletarian organizations, and rouse the agitated petty-bourgeoisie to chauvinistic fervor on behalf of the fight against the revolutionary way out of the crisis.

COMMUNIST PAMPHLET.

(5) If a new spirit *is* to be infused into this old country, there is one thorny and contentious reform which must be tackled, and that is the humanization and galvanization of the B.B.C. Timidity here will bespeak canker and atrophy of the soul. The heart of Britain may be sound and of strong beat, for instance, but the British lion's roar at present is like that of Bottom in Shakespeare's *Midsummer Night's Dream*—as gentle as any sucking dove. A virile new Britain cannot continue indefinitely to be traduced in the eyes or rather ears, of the world by the effete languors of Langham Place, brazenly masquerading as "standard English." When the voice of Britain is heard at nine o'clock, better far and infinitely less ludicrous to hear aitches honestly dropped than the present priggish, inflated, inhibited, school-ma'amish arch braying of blameless bashful mewing maidens!

LETTER IN *Tribune.*

Pay attention ↓

Say what you mean ↗

Each of these passages has faults of its own, but, quite apart from avoidable ugliness, two qualities are common to all of them. The first is staleness of imagery; the other is lack of precision. The writer either has a meaning and cannot express it, or he inadvertently says something else, or he is almost indifferent as to whether his words mean anything or not. This mixture of vagueness and sheer incompetence is the most marked characteristic of modern English prose, and especially of any kind of political writing. As soon as certain topics are raised, the concrete melts into the abstract and no one seems able to think of turns of speech that are not hackneyed: prose consists less and less of *words* chosen for the sake of their meaning, and more and more of *phrases* tacked together like the sections of a prefabricated henhouse. I list below, with notes and examples, various of the tricks by means of which the work of prose-construction is habitually dodged:

Dying metaphors. A newly invented metaphor assists thought by evoking a visual image, while on the other hand a metaphor which is technically "dead" (e.g. *iron resolution*) has in effect reverted to being an ordinary word and can generally be used without loss of vividness. But in between these two classes there is a huge dump of worn-out metaphors which have lost all evocative power and are merely used because they save people the trouble of inventing phrases for themselves. Examples are: *Ring the changes on, take up the cudgels for, toe the line, ride roughshod over, stand shoulder to shoulder with, play into the hands of, no axe to grind, grist to the mill, fishing in troubled waters, on the order of the day, Achilles' heel, swan song, hotbed.* Many of these are used without knowledge of their meaning (what is a "rift," for instance?), and incompatible metaphors are frequently mixed, a sure sign that the writer is not interested in what he is saying. Some metaphors now current have been twisted out of their original meaning without those who use them even being aware of the fact. For example, *toe the line* is sometimes written *tow the line.* Another example is *the hammer and the anvil,* now always used with the implication that the anvil gets the worst of it. In real life it is always the anvil that breaks the hammer, never the other way about: a writer who stopped to think what he was saying would be aware of this, and would avoid perverting the original phrase.

Operators or verbal false limbs. These save the trouble of picking out appropriate verbs and nouns, and at the same time pad each sentence with extra syllables which give it an appearance of symmetry. Characteristic phrases are *render inoperative, militate against, make contact with, be subjected to, give rise to, give grounds for, have the effect of, play a leading part (role) in, make itself felt, take effect, exhibit a tendency to, serve the purpose of,* etc., etc. The keynote is the elimination of simple verbs. Instead of being a single word, such as *break, stop, spoil, mend, kill,* a verb becomes a *phrase,* made up of a noun or adjective tacked on to some general-purpose verb such as *prove, serve, form, play, render.* In addition, the passive voice is wherever possible used in preference to the active, and noun constructions are used instead of gerunds (*by examination of* instead of *by examining*). The range of verbs is further cut down by means of the *-ize* and *de-* formations, and the banal statements are given an appearance of profundity by means of the *not un-* formation. Simple conjunctions and prepositions are replaced by such phrases as *with respect to, having regard to, the fact that, by dint of, in view of, in the interests of, on the hypothesis that;* and the ends of sentences are saved from anticlimax by such resounding common-places as *greatly to be desired, cannot be left out of account, a development to be expected in the near future, deserving of serious consideration, brought to a satisfactory conclusion,* and so on and so forth.

Pretentious diction. Words like *phenomenon, element, individual* (as noun), *objective, categorical, effective, virtual, basic, primary, promote, constitute, exhibit, exploit, utilize, eliminate, liquidate,* are used to dress up simple statements and give an air of scientific impartiality to biased judgments. Adjectives like *epoch-making, epic, historic, unforgettable, triumphant, age-old, inevitable, inexorable, veritable,* are used to dignify the sordid processes of international politics, while writing that aims at glorifying war usually takes on an archaic color, its characteristic words being: *realm, throne, chariot, mailed fist, trident, sword, shield, buckler, banner, jackboot, clarion.* Foreign words and expressions such as *cul de sac, ancien régime, deus ex machina, mutatis mutandis, status quo, gleichschaltung, weltanschauung,* are used to give an air of culture and elegance. Except for the useful abbreviations *i.e., e.g.,* and *etc.,* there is no real need for any of the hundreds of foreign phrases now current in English. Bad writers, and especially scientific, political and sociological writers, are nearly always haunted by the notion that Latin or Greek words are grander than Saxon ones, and unnecessary words like *expedite, ameliorate, predict, extraneous, deracinated, clandestine, subaqueous* and hundreds of others constantly gain ground from their Anglo-Saxon opposite numbers.[1] The jargon peculiar to Marxist writing (*hyena, hangman, cannibal, petty bourgeois, these gentry, lacquey, flunkey, mad dog, White Guard,* etc.) consists largely of words and phrases translated from Russian, German or French; but the normal way of coining a new word is to use a Latin or Greek root with the appropriate affix and, where necessary, the *-ize* formation. It is often easier to make up words of this kind (*deregionalize, impermissible, extramarital, non-fragmentary* and so forth) than to think up the English

[1]An interesting illustration of this is the way in which the English flower names which were in use till very recently are being ousted by Greek ones, *snapdragon* becoming *antirrhinum, forget-me-not* becoming *myosotis,* etc. It is hard to see any practical reason for this change of fashion: it is probably due to an instinctive turning-away from the more homely word and a vague feeling that the Greek word is scientific.

words that will cover one's meaning. The result, in general, is an increase in slovenliness and vagueness.

Meaningless words. In certain kinds of writing, particularly in art criticism and literary criticism, it is normal to come across long passages which are almost completely lacking in meaning.[2] Words like *romantic, plastic, values, human, dead, sentimental, natural, vitality,* as used in art criticism, are strictly meaningless, in the sense that they not only do not point to any discoverable object, but are hardly ever expected to do so by the reader. When one critic writes, "The outstanding feature of Mr. X's work is its peculiar deadness," the reader accepts this as a simple difference of opinion. If words like *black* and *white* were involved, instead of the jargon words *dead* and *living,* he would see at once that language was being used in an improper way. Many political words are similarly abused. The word *Fascism* has now no meaning except in so far as it signifies "something not desirable." The words *democracy, socialism, freedom, patriotic, realistic, justice,* have each of them several different meanings which cannot be reconciled with one another. In the case of a word like *democracy,* not only is there no agreed definition, but the attempt to make one is resisted from all sides. It is almost universally felt that when we call a country democratic we are praising it: consequently the defenders of every kind of régime claim that it is a democracy, and fear that they might have to stop using the word if it were tied down to any one meaning. Words of this kind are often used in a consciously dishonest way. That is, the person who uses them has his own private definition, but allows his hearer to think he means something quite different. Statements like *Marshal Pétain was a true patriot, The Soviet Press is the freest in the world, The Catholic Church is opposed to persecution,* are almost always made with intent to deceive. Other words used in variable meanings, in most cases more or less dishonestly, are: *class, totalitarian, science, progressive, reactionary, bourgeois, equality.*

Now that I have made this catalogue of swindles and perversions, let me give another example of the kind of writing that they lead to. This time it must of its nature be an imaginary one. I am going to translate a passage of good English into modern English of the worst sort. Here is a well-known verse from *Ecclesiastes:*

"I returned and saw under the sun, that the race is not to the swift, nor the battle to the strong, neither yet bread to the wise, nor yet riches to men of understanding, nor yet favour to men of skill; but time and chance happeneth to them all."

---

[2]Example: "Comfort's catholicity of perception and image, strangely Whitmanesque in range, almost the exact opposite in aesthetic compulsion, continues to evoke that trembling atmospheric accumulative hinting at a cruel, an inexorably serene timelessness. . . . Wrey Gardiner scores by aiming at simple bull's-eyes with precision. Only they are not so simple, and through this contented sadness runs more than the surface bittersweet of resignation." *(Poetry Quarterly.)*

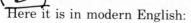

Here it is in modern English:

"Objective consideration of contemporary phenomena compels the conclusion that success or failure in competitive activities exhibits no tendency to be commensurate with innate capacity, but that a considerable element of the unpredictable must invariably be taken into account."

This is a parody, but not a very gross one. Exhibit (3), above, for instance, contains several patches of the same kind of English. It will be seen that I have not made a full translation. The beginning and ending of the sentence follow the original meaning fairly closely, but in the middle the concrete illustrations—race, battle, bread—dissolve into the vague phrase "success or failure in competitive activities." This had to be so, because no modern writer of the kind I am discussing—no one capable of using phrases like "objective consideration of contemporary phenomena"—would ever tabulate his thoughts in that precise and detailed way. The whole tendency of modern prose is away from concreteness. Now analyse these two sentences a little more closely. The first contains forty-nine words but only sixty syllables, and all its words are those of everyday life. The second contains thirty-eight words of ninety syllables: eighteen of its words are from Latin roots, and one from Greek. The first sentence contains six vivid images, and only one phrase ("time and chance") that could be called vague. The second contains not a single fresh, arresting phrase, and in spite of its ninety syllables it gives only a shortened version of the meaning contained in the first. Yet without a doubt it is the second kind of sentence that is gaining ground in modern English. I do not want to exaggerate. This kind of writing is not yet universal, and outcrops of simplicity will occur here and there in the worst-written page. Still, if you or I were told to write a few lines on the uncertainty of human fortunes, we should probably come much nearer to my imaginary sentence than to the one from *Ecclesiastes*.

As I have tried to show, modern writing at its worst does not consist in picking out words for the sake of their meaning and inventing images in order to make the meaning clearer. It consists in gumming together long strips of words which have already been set in order by someone else, and making the results presentable by sheer humbug. The attraction of this way of writing is that it is easy. It is easier—even quicker, once you have the habit—to say *In my opinion it is not an unjustifiable assumption that* than to say *I think*. If you use ready-made phrases, you not only don't have to hunt about for words; you also don't have to bother with the rhythms of your sentences since these phrases are generally so arranged as to be more or less euphonious. When you are composing in a hurry—when you are dictating to a stenographer, for instance, or making a public speech—it is natural to fall into a pretentious, Latinized style. Tags like *a consideration which we should do well to bear in mind* or *a conclusion to which all of us would readily assent* will save many a sentence from coming down with a bump. By using stale metaphors, similes and idioms, you save much mental effort, at the cost of leaving your meaning vague, not only for your reader but for yourself. This is the significance of mixed metaphors. The sole aim of a metaphor is to call up a visual image. When these images clash—as in *The Fascist octopus has sung its swan song, the jackboot is thrown into the melting pot*—it can be taken as certain that the writer is not seeing a mental image of the objects he is naming; in other words he is not really thinking. Look again at the examples I gave at the beginning of this essay. Professor Laski (1) uses five negatives in fifty-three words. One of these is superfluous, making nonsense of the whole passage, and in addition there is the slip *alien* for *akin,* making further nonsense, and several avoidable pieces of clumsiness which increase the general vagueness. Professor Hogben (2) plays ducks and drakes with a battery which is able to write prescriptions, and, while disapproving of the everyday phrase *put up with,* is unwilling to look *egregious* up in the dictionary and see what it means; (3), if one takes an uncharitable attitude towards it, is simply meaningless: probably one could work out its intended meaning by reading the whole of the article in which it occurs. In (4), the writer knows more or less what he wants to say, but an accumulation of stale phrases chokes him like tea leaves blocking a sink. In (5), words and meaning have almost parted company. People who write in this manner usually have a general emotional meaning—they dislike one thing and want to express solidarity with another—but they are not interested in the detail of what they are saying. A scrupulous writer, in every sentence that he writes, will ask himself at least four questions, thus: What am I trying to say? What words will express it? What image or idiom will make it clearer? Is this image fresh enough to have an effect? And he will probably ask himself two more: Could I put it more shortly? Have I said anything that is avoidably ugly? But you are not obliged to go to all this trouble. You can shirk it by simply throwing your mind open and letting the ready-made phrases come crowding in. They will construct your sentences for you—even think your thoughts for you, to a certain extent—and at need they will perform the important service of partially concealing your meaning even from yourself. It is at this point that the special connection between politics and the debasement of language becomes clear.

In our time it is broadly true that political writing is bad writing. Where it is not true, it will generally be found that the writer is some kind of rebel, expressing his private opinions and not a "party line." Orthodoxy, of whatever color, seems to demand a lifeless, imitative style. The political dialects to be found in pamphlets, leading articles, manifestos, White Papers and the speeches of under-secretaries do, of course, vary from party to party, but they are all alike in that one almost never finds in them a fresh, vivid, homemade turn of speech. When one watches some tired hack on the platform mechanically repeating the familiar phrases—*bestial atrocities, iron heel, bloodstained tyranny, free peoples of the world, stand shoulder to shoulder*—one often has a curious feeling that one is not watching a live human being but some kind of dummy: a feeling which suddenly becomes stronger at moments when the light catches the speaker's spectacles and turns them into blank discs which seem to have no eyes behind them. And this is not altogether fanciful. A speaker who uses that kind of phraseology has gone some distance towards turning himself into a machine. The appropriate noises are coming out of his larynx, but his brain is not involved as it would be if he were choosing his words for himself. If the speech he is making is one that he is accustomed to make over and over again, he may be almost unconscious of what he is saying, as one is when one utters the responses in church. And this reduced state of consciousness, if not indispensable, is at any rate favorable to political conformity.

In our time, political speech and writing are largely the defence of the indefensible. Things like the continuance of British rule in India, the Russian purges and deportations, the dropping of the atom bombs on Japan, can indeed be defended, but only by arguments which are too brutal for most people to face, and which do not square with the professed aims of political parties. Thus political language has to consist largely of euphemism, question-begging and sheer cloudy vagueness. Defenceless villages are bombarded from the air, the inhabitants driven out into the countryside, the cattle machine-gunned, the huts set on fire with incendiary bullets: this is called *pacification*. Millions of peasants are robbed of their farms and sent trudging along the roads with no more than they can carry: this is called *transfer of population* or *rectification of frontiers*. People are imprisoned for years without trial, or shot in the back of the neck or sent to die of scurvy in Arctic lumber camps: this is called *elimination of unreliable elements*. Such phraseology is needed if one wants to name things without calling up mental pictures of them. Consider for instance some comfortable English professor defending Russian totalitarianism. He cannot say outright, "I believe in killing off your opponents when you can get good results by doing so." Probably, therefore, he will say something like this:

"While freely conceding that the Soviet régime exhibits certain features which the humanitarian may be inclined to deplore, we must, I think, agree that a certain curtailment of the right to political opposition is an unavoidable concomitant of transitional periods, and that the rigors which the Russian people have been called upon to undergo have been amply justified in the sphere of concrete achievement."

The inflated style is itself a kind of euphemism. A mass of Latin words falls upon the facts like soft snow, blurring the outlines and covering up all the details. The great enemy of clear language is insincerity. When there is a gap between one's real and one's declared aims, one turns as it were instinctively to long words and exhausted idioms, like a cuttlefish squirting out ink. In our age there is no such thing as "keeping out of politics." All issues are political issues, and politics itself is a mass of lies, evasions, folly, hatred and schizophrenia. When the general atmosphere is bad, language must suffer. I should expect to find—this is a guess which I have not sufficient knowledge to verify—that the German, Russian and Italian languages have all deteriorated in the last ten to fifteen years, as a result of dictatorship.

But if thought corrupts language, language can also corrupt thought. A bad usage can spread by tradition and imitation, even among people who should and do know better. The debased language that I have been discussing is in some ways very convenient. Phrases like *a not unjustifiable assumption, leaves much to be desired, would serve no good purpose, a consideration which we should do well to bear in mind,* are a continuous temptation, a packet of aspirins always at one's elbow. Look back through this essay, and for certain you will find that I have again and again committed the very faults I am protesting against. By this morning's post I have received a pamphlet dealing with conditions in Germany. The author tells me that he "felt impelled" to write it. I open it at random, and here is almost the first sentence that I see: "[The Allies] have an opportunity not only of achieving a radical transformation of Germany's social and political structure in such a way as to avoid a nationalistic reaction in Germany itself, but at the same time of laying the foundations of a cooperative and unified Europe." You see, he "feels impelled" to write—feels, presumably, that he has something new to say—and yet his words, like cavalry horses answering the bugle, group themselves automatically into the familiar dreary pattern. This invasion of one's mind by ready-made phrases *(lay the foundations, achieve a radical transformation)* can only be prevented if one is constantly on guard against them, and every such phrase anaesthetizes a portion of one's brain.

I said earlier that the decadence of our language is probably curable. Those who deny this would argue, if they produced an argument at all, that language merely reflects existing social conditions, and that we cannot influence its development by any direct tinkering with words and constructions. So far as the general tone or spirit of a language goes, this may be true, but it is not true in detail. Silly words and expressions have often disappeared, not through any evolutionary process but owing to the conscious action of a minority. Two recent examples were *explore every avenue* and *leave no stone unturned,* which were killed by the jeers of a few journalists. There is a long list of flyblown metaphors which could similarly be got rid of if enough people would interest themselves in the job; and it should also be possible to laugh the *not un-* formation out of existence,[3] to reduce the amount of Latin and Greek in the average sentence, to drive out foreign phrases and strayed scientific words, and, in

---

[3]One can cure oneself of the *not un-* formation by memorizing this sentence: *A not unblack dog was chasing a not unsmall rabbit across a not ungreen field.*

general, to make pretentiousness unfashionable. But all these are minor points. The defence of the English language implies more than this, and perhaps it is best to start by saying what it does *not* imply.

To begin with it has nothing to do with archaism, with the salvaging of obsolete words and turns of speech, or with the setting up of a "standard English" which must never be departed from. On the contrary, it is especially concerned with the scrapping of every word or idiom which has outworn its usefulness. It has nothing to do with correct grammar and syntax, which are of no importance so long as one makes one's meaning clear, or with the avoidance of Americanisms, or with having what is called a "good prose style." On the other hand it is not concerned with fake simplicity and the attempt to make written English colloquial. Nor does it even imply in every case preferring the Saxon word to the Latin one, though it does imply using the fewest and shortest words that will cover one's meaning. What is above all needed is to let the meaning choose the word, and not the other way about. In prose, the worst thing one can do with words is to surrender to them. When you think of a concrete object, you think wordlessly, and then, if you want to describe the thing you have been visualizing you probably hunt about till you find the exact words that seem to fit it. When you think of something abstract you are more inclined to use words from the start, and unless you make a conscious effort to prevent it, the existing dialect will come rushing in and do the job for you, at the expense of blurring or even changing your meaning. Probably it is better to put off using words as long as possible and get one's meaning as clear as one can through pictures or sensations. Afterwards one can choose—not simply *accept*—the phrases that will best cover the meaning, and then switch round and decide what impression one's words are likely to make on another person. This last effort of the mind cuts out all stale or mixed images, all prefabricated phrases, needless repetitions, and humbug and vagueness generally. But one can often be in doubt about the effect of a word or a phrase, and one needs rules that one can rely on when instinct fails. I think the following rules will cover most cases:

1. Never use a metaphor, simile or other figure of speech which you are used to seeing in print.
2. Never use a long word where a short one will do.
3. If it is possible to cut a word out, always cut it out.
4. Never use the passive where you can use the active.
5. Never use a foreign phrase, a scientific word or a jargon word if you can think of an everyday English equivalent.
6. Break any of these rules sooner than say anything outright barbarous.

These rules sound elementary, and so they are, but they demand a deep change of attitude in anyone who has grown used to writing in the style now fashionable. One could keep all of them and still write bad English, but one could not write the kind of stuff that I quoted in those five specimens at the beginning of this article.

I have not here been considering the literary use of language, but merely language as an instrument for expressing and not for concealing or preventing thought. Stuart Chase and others have come near to claiming that all abstract words are meaningless, and have used this as a pretext for advocating a kind of political quietism. Since you don't know what Fascism is, how can you struggle against Fascism? One need not swallow such absurdities as this, but one ought to recognize that the present political chaos is connected with the decay of language, and that one can probably bring about some improvement by starting at the verbal end. If you simplify your English, you are freed from the worst follies of orthodoxy. You cannot speak any of the necessary dialects, and when you make a stupid remark its stupidity will be obvious, even to yourself. Political language—and with variations this is true of all political parties, from Conservatives to Anarchists—is designed to make lies sound truthful and murder respectable, and to give an appearance of solidity to pure wind. One cannot change this all in a moment, but one can at least change one's own habits, and from time to time one can even, if one jeers loudly enough, send some worn-out and useless phrase—some *jackboot, Achilles' heel, hotbed, melting pot, acid test, veritable inferno* or other lump of verbal refuse—into the dustbin where it belongs.

Excellent sentence

How to Write "Official"

Gerald Grow

Gerald Grow's ten steps to "official" writing appeared in the April (fool) 1982 issue of Simply Stated *#25, a free newsletter published by the Document Design Center of the American Institute for Research. The Center publishes articles about research in writing and producing documents; its primary goal is to reduce the burden that paperwork causes. Grow's list is presented here as further illustration of Orwell's ideas.*

1. **Start with a simple statement:** We quit. Why? Nobody knew how to program the computer.

2. **Put it in the passive voice and dilute the responsibility:** *It was decided to* quit.

3. **Expand with terminology that does not add meaning:** It was decided to *terminate.*

4. **Build in noun strings:** It was decided to terminate *project processes.*

5. **Add a qualifier of uncertain relation to the original statement:** *On account of the status of the computer,* it was decided to terminate project processes.

6. **Add noun strings and terminology to the qualifier:** On account of the status of the *computer program assessment planning development effort,* it was decided to terminate project processes.

7. **Separate related words:** On account of the status of the computer program assessment planning development effort, it was decided to terminate *until a later date* project processes.

8. **Equivocate:** On account of the *uncertain* status of the computer program assessment planning development effort, it was *proposed and tentatively accepted* to terminate until a later date project processes.

9. **Obfuscate:** Due to uncertainties in the status of the computer program assessment planning development effort, *proposals were carefully considered and tentatively adopted to suspend temporarily* until a later date project processes.

10. **Cover your tracks; make yourself look good:** Due to *unavoidable* uncertainties in the status of the computer program assessment planning development effort, *a number of contingency* proposals were carefully considered and one was tentatively adopted to suspend on a temporary basis until a later date those project processes *deemed unessential to the expeditious fulfillment of contract requirements.*

What Should Students Learn?

In describing a typical student's typical day, Theodore R. Sizer's "What High School Is" sadly documents the thesis that the announced purposes of our high schools could hardly be achieved by the way they actually run. Schools describe themselves as devoted to broad intellectual, moral, and cultural development, says Sizer, but are actually rather boring (if placidly accepted) places where young people are kept safely off the adult labor market while they "take subjects" and learn to follow predictable routines. Readers may want to test Sizer's thesis in the light of their own school experiences.

In important ways, our colleges, too, reveal a marked difference between lofty goals and conventional practice. Student criticisms are often similar to those made by Lincoln Steffens a century ago about his college experience. College was far from the expected venture into a new world. There were courses and information and training, but "no one," he says, "brought out for me the relation of anything I was studying to anything else, except of course, to that wretched degree." As for questions, the professors asked them, not the students.

Lucille Elmore's experience, however, as described by Thomas J. Cottle in the essay following, is the exact opposite. A mature returning student, she expresses the immense excitement and satisfaction of her "open affair with books." "Students talk about the real world out there," she says. "What about the free world in here?" Again, readers may want to explore whether Steffens or Elmore comes closer to reflecting their own experiences in college.

One of the greatest difficulties facing colleges and college students today is the rapid growth of knowledge and its equally rapid obsolescence. This fosters extreme specialism and makes it hard to know what is important to learn and what is not. Should colleges offer specialized training or broad education? Can they do both?

Most critics agree that college must be something more than preparation for an entry-level job or professional career, and the next three essays in this section propose alternatives to narrow professional training. Clearly distinguishing between information and ideas, Theodore Roszak identifies "the master ideas" as the most urgent subject of education. "The mind that owns few ideas," he says, "is apt to be crabbed and narrow, ungenerous and defensive in its judgment." Using medical students to stand for all career-oriented students, the eminent medical researcher Lewis Thomas prescribes for them the classics, literature, and history, learning "about how human beings have always lived out their lives."

Harold J. Morowitz then changes the terms of the argument, suggesting that education is not so much a matter of subjects as of stance. In his view, every subject must be presented in terms of its epistemology: How do we know it's true? The section ends with an able journalist, Otto Friedrich, summarizing five main ideas of what education should be.

What High School Is

Theodore R. Sizer

Theodore R. Sizer (born 1932) was brought up in elite educational circumstances but has devoted much of his energy to bettering education for everyone. Son of a Yale art historian, he attended both Yale and Harvard, and has become a noted historian and professor of education. Between appointments at Harvard and at Brown University, he has conscientiously practiced what he taught. He has been a school teacher in Melbourne, Australia, and at Roxbury Latin School in Boston, and for nine years served as headmaster at Andover (1972–1981).

Sizer has thought long and hard about improving schools. His first book about education, Places for Learning, Places for Joy: Speculations on American School Reform, *appeared in 1973. Then in 1981 he was put in charge of a project, sponsored by the National Association of School Principals and others, to do a deep study of our high schools. Sizer and his researchers spent five years and studied eighty schools. His report and recommendations were published in 1984 as* Horace's Compromise: The Dilemma of the American High School; *its second chapter appears below. "Horace," a composite of the teachers Sizer met, is able and conscientious, but has to compromise painfully with the numerous obstacles imposed by the present system. If Sizer had his way, Horace would be teaching smaller groups in a more personalized, challenging way, aiming to teach students the use of the mind rather than specialized subjects.*

Mark, sixteen and a genial eleventh-grader, rides a bus to Franklin High School, arriving at 7:25. It is an Assembly Day, so the schedule is adapted to allow for a meeting of the entire school. He hangs out with his friends, first outside school and then inside, by his locker. He carries a pile of textbooks and notebooks; in all, it weighs eight and a half pounds.

From 7:30 to 8:19, with nineteen other students, he is in Room 304 for English class. The Shakespeare play being read this year by the eleventh grade is *Romeo and Juliet.* The teacher, Ms. Viola, has various students in turn take parts and read out loud. Periodically, she interrupts the (usually halting) recitations to ask whether the thread of the conversation in the play is clear. Mark is entertained by the stumbling readings of some of his classmates. He hopes he will not be asked to be Romeo, particularly if his current steady, Sally, is Juliet. There is a good deal of giggling in class, and much attention paid to who may be called on next. Ms. Viola reminds the class of a test on this part of the play to be given next week.

The bell rings at 8:19. Mark goes to the boys' room, where he sees a classmate who he thinks is a wimp but who constantly tries to be a buddy. Mark avoids the leech by rushing off. On the way, he notices two boys engaged in some sort of transaction, probably over marijuana. He pays them no attention. 8:24. Typing class. The rows of desks that embrace big office machines are almost filled before the bell. Mark is uncomfortable here: typing class is girl country. The teacher constantly threatens what to Mark is a humiliatingly female future: "Your employer won't like these erasures." The minutes during the period are spent copying a letter from a handbook onto business stationery. Mark struggles to keep from looking at his work; the teacher wants him to watch only the material from which he is copying. Mark is frustrated, uncomfortable, and scared that he will not complete his letter by the class's end, which would be embarrassing.

Nine tenths of the students present at school that day are assembled in the auditorium by the 9:18 bell. The dilatory tenth still stumble in, running down aisles. Annoyed class deans try to get the mob settled. The curtains part; the program is a concert by a student rock group. Their electronic gear flashes under the lights, and the five boys and one girl in the group work hard at being casual. Their movements on stage are studiously at three-quarter time, and they chat with one another as though the tumultuous screaming of their schoolmates were totally inaudible. The girl balances on a stool; the boys crank up the music. It is very soft rock, the sanitized lyrics surely cleared with the assistant principal. The girl sings, holding the mike close to her mouth, but can scarcely be heard. Her light voice is tentative, and the lyrics indecipherable. The guitars, amplified, are tuneful, however, and the drums are played with energy.

The students around Mark—all juniors, since they are seated by class—alternately slouch in their upholstered, hinged seats, talking to one another, or sit forward, leaning on the chair backs in front of them, watching the band. A boy near Mark shouts noisily at the microphone-fondling singer, "Bite it . . . ohhh," and the area around Mark explodes in vulgar male laughter, but quickly subsides. A teacher walks down the aisle. Songs continue, to great applause. Assembly is over at 9:46, two minutes early.

9:53 and biology class. Mark was at a different high school last year and did not take this course there as a tenth-grader. He is in it now, and all but one of his classmates are a year younger than he. He sits on the side, not taking part in the chatter that goes on after the bell. At 9:57, the public address system goes on, with the announcements of the day. After a few words from the principal ("Here's today's cheers and jeers . . ." with a cheer for the winning basketball team and a jeer for the spectators who made a ruckus at the gymnasium), the task is taken over by officers of ASB (Associated Student Bodies). There is an appeal for "bat bunnies." Carnations are for sale by the Girls' League. Miss Indian American is coming. Students are auctioning off their services (background catcalls are heard) to earn money for the prom. Nominees are needed for the ballot for school bachelor and school bachelorette. The announcements end with a "thought for the day. When you throw a little mud, you lose a little ground."

At 10:04 the biology class finally turns to science. The teacher, Mr. Robbins, has placed one of several labeled laboratory specimens—some are pinned in frames, others swim in formaldehyde—on each of the classroom's eight laboratory tables. The three or so students whose chairs circle each of these benches are to study the specimen and make notes about it or drawings of it. After a few minutes each group of three will move to another table. The teacher points out that these specimens are of organisms already studied in previous classes. He says that the period-long test set for the following day will involve observing some of these specimens—then to be without labels—and writing an identifying paragraph on each. Mr. Robbins points out that some of the printed labels ascribe the specimens names different from those given in the textbook. He explains that biologists often give several names to the same organism.

The class now falls to peering, writing, and quiet talking. Mr. Robbins comes over to Mark, and in whispered words asks him to carry a requisition form for science department materials to the business office. Mark, because of his "older" status, is usually chosen by Robbins for this kind of errand. Robbins gives Mark the form and a green hall pass to show to any teacher who might challenge him, on his way to the office, for being out of a classroom. The errand takes Mark four minutes. Meanwhile Mark's group is hard at work but gets to only three of the specimens before the bell rings at 10:42. As the students surge out, Robbins shouts a reminder about a "double" laboratory period on Thursday.

Between classes one of the seniors asks Mark whether he plans to be a candidate for schoolwide office next year. Mark says no. He starts to explain. The 10:47 bell rings, meaning that he is late for French class.

There are fifteen students in Monsieur Bates's language class. He hands out tests taken the day before: *"C'est bien fait, Etienne . . . c'est mieux, Marie . . . Tch, tch, Robert . . ."* Mark notes his C+ and peeks at the A− in front of Susanna, next to him. The class has been assigned seats by M. Bates; Mark resents sitting next to prissy, brainy Susanna. Bates starts by asking a student to read a question and give the correct answer. *"James, question un."* James haltingly reads the question and gives an answer that Bates, now speaking English, says is incomplete. In due course: *"Mark, question cinq."* Mark does his bit, and the sequence goes on, the eight quiz questions and answers filling about twenty minutes of time.

"Turn to page forty-nine. *Maintenant, lisez après moi . . ."* and Bates reads a sentence and has the class echo it. Mark is embarrassed by this and mumbles with a barely audible sound. Others, like Susanna, keep the decibel count up, so Mark can hide. This I-say-you-repeat drill is interrupted once by the public address system, with an announcement about a meeting for the cheerleaders. Bates finishes the class, almost precisely at the bell, with a homework assignment. The students are to review these sentences for a brief quiz the following day. Mark takes note of the assignment, because he knows that tomorrow will be a day of busy-work in French class. Much though he dislikes oral drills, they are better than the workbook stuff that Bates hands out. Write, write, write, for Bates to throw away, Mark thinks.

11:36. Down to the cafeteria, talking noisily, hanging out, munching. Getting to Room 104 by 12:17: U.S. history. The teacher is sitting cross-legged on his desk when Mark comes in, heatedly arguing with three students over the fracas that had followed the previous night's basketball game. The teacher, Mr. Suslovic, while agreeing that the spectators from their school certainly were provoked, argues that they should neither have been so obviously obscene in yelling at the opposing cheerleaders nor have allowed Coke cans to be rolled out on the floor. The three students keep saying that "it isn't fair." Apparently they and some others had been assigned "Saturday mornings" (detentions) by the principal for the ruckus.

At 12:34, the argument appears to subside. The uninvolved students, including Mark, are in their seats, chatting amiably. Mr. Suslovic climbs off his desk and starts talking: "We've almost finished this unit, chapters nine and ten . . ." The students stop chattering among themselves and turn toward Suslovic. Several slouch down in their chairs. Some open notebooks. Most have the five-pound textbook on their desks.

Suslovic lectures on the cattle drives, from north Texas to railroads west of St. Louis. He breaks up this narrative with questions ("Why were the railroad lines laid largely east to west?"), directed at nobody in particular and eventually answered by Suslovic himself. Some students take notes. Mark doesn't. A student walks in the open door, hands Mr. Suslovic a list, and starts whispering with him. Suslovic turns from the class and hears out this messenger. He then asks, "Does anyone know where Maggie Sharp is?" Some one answers, "Sick at home"; someone else says, "I thought I saw her at lunch." Genial consternation. Finally Suslovic tells the messenger, "Sorry, we can't help you," and returns to the class: "Now, where were we?" He goes on for some minutes. The bell rings. Suslovic forgets to give the homework assignment.

1:11 and Algebra II. There is a commotion in the hallway: someone's locker is rumored to have been opened by the assistant principal and a narcotics agent. In the five-minute passing time, Mark hears the story three times and three ways. A locker had been broken into by another student. It was Mr. Gregory and a narc. It was the cops, and they did it without Gregory's knowing. Mrs. Ames, the mathematics teacher, has not heard anything about it. Several of the nineteen students try to tell her and start arguing among themselves. "O.K., that's enough." She hands out the day's problem, one sheet to each student. Mark sees with dismay that it is a single, complicated "word" problem about some train that, while traveling at 84 mph, due west, passes a car that was going due east at 55 mph. Mark struggles: Is it $d = rt$ or $t = rd$? The class becomes quiet, writing, while Mrs. Ames writes some additional, short problems on the blackboard. "Time's up." A sigh; most students still writing. A muffled "Shit." Mrs. Ames frowns. "Come on, now." She collects papers, but it takes four minutes for her to corral them all.

"Copy down the problems from the board." A minute passes. "William, try number one." William suggests an approach. Mrs. Ames corrects and cajoles, and William finally gets it right. Mark watches two kids to his right passing notes; he tries to read them, but the handwriting is illegible from his distance. He hopes he is not called on, and he isn't. Only three students are asked to puzzle out an answer. The bell rings at 2:00. Mrs. Ames shouts a homework assignment over the resulting hubbub.

Mark leaves his books in his locker. He remembers that he has homework, but figures that he can do it during English class the next day. He knows that there will be an in-class presentation of one of the *Romeo and Juliet* scenes and that he will not be in it. The teacher will not notice his homework writing, or won't do anything about it if she does.

Mark passes various friends heading toward the gym, members of the basketball teams. Like most students, Mark isn't an active school athlete. However, he is associated with the yearbook staff. Although he is not taking "Yearbook" for credit as an English course, he is contributing photographs. Mark takes twenty minutes checking into the yearbook staff's headquarters (the classroom of its faculty adviser) and getting some assignments of pictures from his boss, the senior who is the photography editor. Mark knows that if he pleases his boss and the faculty adviser, he'll take that editor's post for the next year. He'll get English credit for his work then.

After gossiping a bit with the yearbook staff, Mark will leave school by 2:35 and go home. His grocery market bagger's job is from 4:45 to 8:00, the rush hour for the store. He'll have a snack at 4:30, and his mother will save him some supper to eat at 8:30. She will ask whether he has any homework, and he'll tell her no. Tomorrow, and virtually every other tomorrow, will be the same for Mark, save for the lack of the assembly: each period then will be five minutes longer.

Most Americans have an uncomplicated vision of what secondary education should be. Their conception of high school is remarkably uniform across the country, a striking fact, given the size and diversity of the United States and the politically decentralized character of the schools. This uniformity is of several generations' standing. It has, however, two appearances, each quite different from the other, one of words and the other of practice, a world of political rhetoric and Mark's world.

A California high school's general goals, set out in 1979, could serve equally well most of America's high schools, public and private. This school had as its ends:

> Fundamental scholastic achievement . . . to acquire knowledge and share in the traditionally accepted academic fundamentals . . . to develop the ability to make decisions, to solve problems, to reason independently, and to accept responsibility for self-evaluation and continuing self-improvement.
> Career and economic competence . . .
> Citizenship and civil responsibility . . .
> Competence in human and social relations . . .
> Moral and ethical values . . .
> Self-realization and mental and physical health . . .
> Aesthetic awareness . . .
> Cultural diversity . . .[1]

---

[1]Shasta High School, Redding, California. An eloquent and analogous statement, "The Essentials of Education," one stressing explicitly the "interdependence of skills and content" that is implicit in the Shasta High School statement, was issued in 1980 by a coalition of education associations. Organizations for the Essentials of Education (Urbana, Illinois).

In addition to its optimistic rhetoric, what distinguishes this list is its comprehensiveness. The high school is to touch most aspects of an adolescent's existence—mind, body, morals, values, career. No one of these areas is given especial prominence. School people arrogate to themselves an obligation to all.

An example of the wide acceptability of these goals is found in the courts. Forced to present a detailed definition of "thorough and efficient education," elementary as well as secondary, a West Virginia judge sampled the best of conventional wisdom and concluded that

> there are eight general elements of a thorough and efficient system of education: (a) Literacy, (b) The ability to add, subtract, multiply, and divide numbers, (c) Knowledge of government to the extent the child will be equipped as a citizen to make informed choices among persons and issues that affect his own governance, (d) Self-knowledge and knowledge of his or her total environment to allow the child to intelligently choose life work—to know his or her options, (e) Work-training and advanced academic training as the child may intelligently choose, (f) Recreational pursuits, (g) Interests in all creative arts such as music, theater, literature, and the visual arts, and (h) Social ethics, both behavioral and abstract, to facilitate compatibility with others in this society.[2]

That these eight—now powerfully part of the debate over the purpose and practice of education in West Virginia—are reminiscent of the influential list, "The Seven Cardinal Principles of Secondary Education," promulgated in 1918 by the National Education Association, is no surprise.[3] The rhetoric of high school purpose has been uniform and consistent for decades. Americans agree on the goals for their high schools.

That agreement is convenient, but it masks the fact that virtually all the words in these goal statements beg definition. Some schools have labored long to identify specific criteria beyond them; the result has been lists of daunting pseudospecificity and numbing earnestness. However, most leave the words undefined and let the momentum of traditional practice speak for itself. That is why analyzing how Mark spends his time is important: from watching him one uncovers the important purposes of education, the ones that shape practice. Mark's day is similar to that of other high school students across the country, as similar as the rhetoric of one goal statement to others'. Of course, there are variations, but the extent of consistency in the shape of school routine for a large and diverse adolescent population is extraordinary, indicating more graphically than

---

[2]Judge Arthur M. Recht, in his order resulting from *Pauley v. Kelly,* 1979, as reprinted in *Education Week,* May 26, 1982, p. 10. See also, in *Education Week,* January 16, 1983, pp. 21, 24, Jonathan P. Sher, "The Struggle to Fulfill a Judicial Mandate: How Not to 'Reconstruct' Education in W. Va."

[3]Bureau of Education, Department of the Interior, "Cardinal Principles of Secondary Education: A Report of the Commission on the Reorganization of Secondary Education, appointed by the National Education Association," *Bulletin,* no. 35 (Washington: U.S. Government Printing Office, 1918).

any rhetoric the measure of agreement in America about what one does in high school, and, by implication, what it is for.

The basic organizing structures in schools are familiar. Above all, students are grouped by age (that is, freshman, sophomore, junior, senior), and all are expected to take precisely the same time—around 720 school days over four years, to be precise—to meet the requirements for a diploma. When one is out of his grade level, he can feel odd, as Mark did in his biology class. The goals are the same for all, and the means to achieve them are also similar.

Young males and females are treated remarkably alike; the schools' goals are the same for each gender. In execution, there are differences, as those pressing sex discrimination suits have made educators intensely aware. The students in metalworking classes are mostly male; those in home economics, mostly female. But it is revealing how much less sex discrimination there is in high schools than in other American institutions. For many young women, the most liberated hours of their week are in school.

School is to be like a job: you start in the morning and end in the afternoon, five days a week. You don't get much of a lunch hour, so you go home early, unless you are an athlete or are involved in some special school or extracurricular activity. School is conceived of as the children's workplace, and it takes young people off parents' hands and out of the labor market during prime-time work hours. Not surprisingly, many students see going to school as little more than a dogged necessity. They perceive the day-to-day routine, a Minnesota study reports, as one of "boredom and lethargy." One of the students summarizes: School is "boring, restless, tiresome, puts ya to sleep, tedious, monotonous, pain in the neck."[4]

The school schedule is a series of units of time: the clock is king. The base time block is about fifty minutes in length. Some schools, on what they call modular scheduling, split that fifty-minute block into two or even three pieces. Most schools have double periods for laboratory work, especially in the sciences, or four-hour units for the small numbers of students involved in intensive vocational or other work-study programs. The flow of all school activity arises from or is blocked by these time units. "How much time do I have with my kids" is the teacher's key question.

Because there are many claims for those fifty-minute blocks, there is little time set aside for rest between them, usually no more than three to ten minutes, depending on how big the school is and, consequently, how far students and teachers have to walk from class to class. As a result, there is a frenetic quality to the school day, a sense of sustained restlessness. For the adolescents, there are frequent changes of room and fellow students, each change giving tempting opportunities for distraction,

[4]Diane Hedin, Paula Simon, and Michael Robin, *Minnesota Youth Poll: Youth's Views on School and School Discipline*, Minnesota Report 184 (1983), Agricultural Experiment Station, University of Minnesota, p. 13.

which are stoutly resisted by teachers. Some schools play soft music during these "passing times," to quiet the multitude, one principal told me.

Many teachers have a chance for a coffee break. Few students do. In some city schools where security is a problem, students must be in class for seven consecutive periods, interrupted by a heavily monitored twenty-minute lunch period for small groups, starting as early as 10:30 A.M. and running to after 1:00 P.M. A high premium is placed on punctuality and on "being where you're supposed to be." Obviously, a low premium is placed on reflection and repose. The student rushes from class to class to collect knowledge. Savoring it, it is implied, is not to be done much in school, nor is such meditation really much admired. The picture that these familiar patterns yield is that of an academic supermarket. The purpose of going to school is to pick things up, in an organized and predictable way, the faster the better.

What is supposed to be picked up is remarkably consistent among all sorts of high schools. Most schools specifically mandate three out of every five courses a student selects. Nearly all of these mandates fall into five areas—English, social studies, mathematics, science, and physical education. On the average, English is required to be taken each year, social studies and physical education three out of the four high school years, and mathematics and science one or two years. Trends indicate that in the mid-eighties there is likely to be an increase in the time allocated to these last two subjects. Most students take classes in these four major academic areas beyond the minimum requirements, sometimes in such special areas as journalism and "yearbook," offshoots of English departments.[5]

Press most adults about what high school is for, and you hear these subjects listed. *High school? That's where you learn English and math and that sort of thing.* Ask students, and you get the same answer. High school is to "teach" these "subjects."

What is often absent is any definition of these subjects or any rationale for them. They are just there, labels. Under those labels lie a multitude of things. A great deal of material is supposed to be "covered"; most of these courses are surveys, great sweeps of the stuff of their parent disciplines.

While there is often a sequence *within* subjects—algebra before trigonometry, "first-year" French before "second-year" French—there is rarely a coherent relationship or sequence *across* subjects. Even the most logically related matters—reading ability as a precondition for the reading of history books, and certain mathematical concepts or skills before

---

[5]I am indebted to Harold F. Sizer and Lyde E. Sizer for a survey of the diploma requirements of fifty representative secondary schools, completed for A Study of High Schools.

the study of some of physics—are only loosely coordinated, if at all. There is little demand for a synthesis of it all; English, mathematics, and the rest are discrete items, to be picked up individually. The incentive for picking them up is largely through tests and, with success at these, in credits earned.

Coverage within subjects is the key priority. If some imaginative teacher makes a proposal to force the marriage of, say, mathematics and physics or to require some culminating challenges to students to use several subjects in the solution of a complex problem, and if this proposal will take "time" away from other things, opposition is usually phrased in terms of what may be thus forgone. If we do that, we'll have to give up colonial history. We won't be able to get to programming. We'll not be able to read *Death of a Salesman.* There isn't time. The protesters usually win out.

The subjects come at a student like Mark in random order, a kaleidoscope of worlds: algebraic formulae to poetry to French verbs to Ping-Pong to the War of the Spanish Succession, all before lunch. Pupils are to pick up these things. Tests measure whether the picking up has been successful.

The lack of connection between stated goals, such as those of the California high school cited earlier, and the goals inherent in school practice is obvious and, curiously, tolerated. Most striking is the gap between statements about "self-realization and mental and physical growth" or "moral and ethical values"—common rhetoric in school documents—and practice. Most physical education programs have neither the time nor the focus really to ensure fitness. Mental health is rarely defined. Neither are ethical values, save at the negative extremes, such as opposition to assault or dishonesty. Nothing in the regimen of a day like Mark's signals direct or implicit teaching in this area. The "schoolboy code" (not ratting on a fellow student) protects the marijuana pusher, and a leechlike associate is shrugged off without concern. The issue of the locker search was pushed aside, as not appropriate for class time.

Most students, like Mark, go to class in groups of twenty to twenty-seven students. The expected attendance in some schools, particularly those in low-income areas, is usually higher, often thirty-five students per class, but high absentee rates push the actual numbers down. About twenty-five per class is an average figure for expected attendance, and the actual numbers are somewhat lower. There are remarkably few students who go to class in groups much larger or smaller than twenty-five.[6]

A student such as Mark sees five or six teachers per day; their differing

---

[6] Education Research Service, Inc. *Class Size: A Summary of Research* (Arlington, Virginia, 1978); and *Class Size Research: A Critique of Recent Meta-Analyses* (Arlington, Virginia, 1980).

styles and expectations are part of his kaleidoscope. High school staffs are highly specialized: guidance counselors rarely teach mathematics, mathematics teachers rarely teach English, principals rarely do any classroom instruction. Mark, then, is known a little bit by a number of people, each of whom sees him in one specialized situation. No one may know him as a "whole person"—unless he becomes a special problem or has special needs.

Save in extracurricular or coaching situations, such as in athletics, drama, or shop classes, there is little opportunity for sustained conversation between student and teacher. The mode is a one-sentence or two-sentence exchange: *Mark, when was Grover Cleveland president?* Let's see, was 1890 . . . or something . . . wasn't he the one . . . he was elected twice, wasn't he? . . . *Yes . . . Gloria, can you get the dates right?* Dialogue is strikingly absent, and as a result the opportunity of teachers to challenge students' ideas in a systematic and logical way is limited. Given the rushed, full quality of the school day, it can seldom happen. One must infer that careful probing of students' thinking is not a high priority. How one gains (to quote the California school's statement of goals again) "the ability to make decisions, to solve problems, to reason independently, and to accept responsibility for self-evaluation and continuing self-improvement" without being challenged is difficult to imagine. One certainly doesn't learn these things merely from lectures and textbooks.

Most schools are nice places. Mark and his friends enjoy being in theirs. The adults who work in schools generally like adolescents. The academic pressures are limited, and the accommodations to students are substantial. For example, if many members of an English class have jobs after school, the English teacher's expectations for them are adjusted, downward. In a word, school is sensitively accommodating, as long as students are punctual, where they are supposed to be, and minimally dutiful about picking things up from the clutch of courses in which they enroll.

This characterization is not pretty, but it is accurate, and it serves to describe the vast majority of American secondary schools. "Taking subjects" in a systematized, conveyer-belt way is what one does in high school. That this process is, in substantial respects, not related to the rhetorical purposes of education is tolerated by most people, perhaps because they do not really either believe in those ill-defined goals or, in their heart of hearts, believe that schools can or should even try to achieve them. The students are happy taking subjects. The parents are happy, because that's what they did in high school. The rituals, the most important of which is graduation, remain intact. The adolescents are supervised, safely and constructively most of the time, during the morning and afternoon hours, and they are off the labor market. That is what high school is all about.

from *The Autobiography of Lincoln Steffens*

Lincoln Steffens

Lincoln Steffens (1866–1936) is remembered primarily as a journalist and reformer. Born in Sacramento, California, he spent his youth largely with horses rather than books and failed to pass grammar school. "My parents did not bring me up," he writes. "They sent me to school, they gave me teachers of music, drawing; they offered me every opportunity in their reach. But also they gave me liberty. . . ." A great admirer of Napoleon, Steffens was enrolled at a military academy at fifteen and hoped to become a soldier: "I read about Napoleon as if I were reading up on my own future," he remembers. He acquired an interest in philosophy at the University of California, and subsequently studied in Germany, Paris, and London, returning to the United States in 1892. Steffens then began his career as a reporter for the New York Evening Post. *After the turn of the century, he became closely associated with the muckraker movement, exposing municipal corruption and inefficiency in numerous magazine articles and in books such as* The Shame of the Cities *(1904).*

As the public impact of muckraking lessened, Steffens dropped from the public eye and gradually lost faith in reform as an effective means of change. He supported the Mexican Revolution in 1914 and wrote extensively on the successes of the Russian Revolution and the Communist regime. After he spent twenty years in relative obscurity, the publication of The Autobiography of Lincoln Steffens *in 1931 brought him renewed public interest and acclaim.*

When Steffens failed the entrance requirements for the University of California, his father engaged Mr. Evelyn Nixon as a private tutor. For Steffens, Nixon was the first teacher "who interested me in what I had to learn." Nixon apparently realized this and invited him to his home where, on Saturday evenings, he met with a group of friends, all displaced English athletes and scholars, "a maddening lot of cultivated minds" who discussed "any and all subjects with knowledge, with the precise information of scholarship, but with no common opinions on anything apparently." These Saturday nights became Steffens' prep school and whetted his appetite for college.

The passages below, from the Autobiography, *record his expectations as well as his disappointment at what he actually found at the university, and invite comparison with student expectations and disappointments today.*

I Go to College

Going to college is, to a boy, an adventure into a new world, and a very strange and complete world too. Part of his preparation for it is the stories he hears from those that have gone before; these feed his imagination, which cannot help trying to picture the college life. And the stories and the life are pretty much the same for any college. The University of California was a young, comparatively small institution when I was entered there in 1885 as a freshman. Berkeley, the beautiful, was not the developed villa community it is now; I used to shoot quail in the brush under the oaks along the edges of the college grounds. The quail and the brush are gone now, but the oaks are there and the same prospect down the hill over San Francisco Bay out through the Golden Gate between the low hills of the city and the high hills of Marin County. My class numbered about one hundred boys and girls, mostly boys, who came from all parts of the State and represented all sorts of people and occupations. There was, however, a significant uniformity of opinion and spirit among us, as there was, and still is, in other, older colleges. The American is molded to type early. And so are our college ways. We found already formed at Berkeley the typical undergraduate customs, rights, and privileged vices which we had to respect ourselves and defend against the faculty, regents, and the State government.

One evening, before I had matriculated, I was taken out by some upper classmen to teach the president a lesson. He had been the head of a private preparatory school and was trying to govern the private lives and the public morals of university "men" as he had those of his schoolboys. Fetching a long ladder, the upper classmen thrust it through a front window of Prexy's house and, to the chant of obscene songs, swung it back and forth, up and down, round and round, till everything breakable within sounded broken and the drunken indignation outside was satisfied or tired.

This turned out to be one of the last battles in the war for liberty against that president. He was allowed to resign soon thereafter and I noticed that not only the students but many of the faculty and regents rejoiced in his downfall and turned with us to face and fight the new president when, after a lot of politics, he was appointed and presented. We learned somehow a good deal about the considerations that governed our college government. They were not only academic. The government of a university was—like the State government and horse-racing and so many other things—not what I had been led to expect. And a college education wasn't either, nor the student mind.

Years later, when I was a magazine editor, I proposed a series of articles to raise and answer the question: Is there any intellectual life in our colleges? My idea sprang from my remembered disappointment at what I found at Berkeley and some experiences I was having at the time with the faculties and undergraduates of the other older colleges in the east. Berkeley, in my day, was an Athens compared with New Haven, for example, when I came to know Yale undergraduates.

My expectations of college life were raised too high by Nixon's Saturday nights. I thought, and he assumed, that at Berkeley I would be breathing in an atmosphere of thought, discussion, and some scholarship; working, reading, and studying for the answers to questions which would be threshed out in debate and conversation. There was nothing of the sort. I was primed with questions. My English friends never could agree on the answers to any of the many and various questions they disputed. They did not care; they enjoyed their talks and did not expect to settle anything. I was more earnest. I was not content to leave things all up in the air. Some of those questions were very present and personal to me, as some of those Englishmen meant them to be. William Owen was trying to convert me to the anarchistic communism in which he believed with all his sincere and beautiful being. I was considering his arguments. Another earnest man, who presented the case for the Roman Catholic Church, sent old Father Burchard and other Jesuits after me. Every conversation at Mr. Nixon's pointed some question, academic or scientific, and pointed them so sharp that they drove me to college with an intense desire to know. And as for communism or the Catholic Church, I was so torn that I could not answer myself. The Jesuits dropped me and so did Owen, in disgust, when I said I was going to wait for my answer till I had heard what the professors had to say and had learned what my university had to teach me upon the questions underlying the questions Oxford and Cambridge and Rome quarreled over and could not agree on. Berkeley would know.

There were no moot questions in Berkeley. There was work to do, knowledge and training to get, but not to answer questions. I found myself engaged, as my classmates were, in choosing courses. The choice was limited and within the limits, had to be determined by the degree we were candidates for. My questions were philosophical, but I could not take philosophy, which fascinated me, till I had gone through a lot of higher mathematics which did not interest me at all. If I had been allowed to take philosophy, and so discovered the need and the relation of mathematics, I would have got the philosophy and I might have got the mathematics which I miss now more than I do the Hegelian metaphysics taught at Berkeley. Or, if the professor who put me off had taken the pains to show me the bearing of mathematical thought on theoretical logic, I would have undertaken the preparation intelligently. But no one ever developed for me the relation of any of my required subjects to those that attracted me; no one brought out for me the relation of anything I was studying to anything else, except, of course, to that wretched degree. Knowledge was absolute, not relative, and it was stored in compartments, categorical and independent. The relation of knowledge to life, even to student life, was ignored, and as for questions, the professors asked them, not the students; and the students, not the teachers, answered them—in examinations.

The unknown is the province of the student; it is the field for his life's adventure, and it is a wide field full of beckonings. Curiosity about it would drive a boy as well as a child to work through the known to get at the unknown. But it was not assumed that we had any curiosity or the potential love of skill, scholarship, and achievement or research. And so far as I can remember now, the professors' attitude was right for most of the students who had no intellectual curiosity. They wanted to be told not only what they had to learn, but what they had to want to learn—for the purpose of passing. That came out in the considerations which decided the choice among optional courses. Students selected subjects or teachers for a balance of easy and hard, to fit into their time and yet "get through." I was the only rebel of my kind, I think. The nearest to me in sympathy were the fellows who knew what they wanted to be: engineers, chemists, professional men, or statesmen. They grunted at some of the work required of them, studies that seemed useless to their future careers. They did not understand me very well, nor I them, because I preferred those very subjects which they called useless, highbrow, cultural. I did not tell them so; I did not realize it myself definitely; but I think now that I had had as a boy an exhausting experience of *being* something great. I did not want now to be but rather to know things. . . .

I Become a Student

It is possible to get an education at a university. It has been done; not often, but the fact that a proportion, however small, of college students do get a start in interested, methodical study, proves my thesis, and the two personal experiences I have to offer illustrate it and show how to circumvent the faculty, the other students, and the whole college system of mind-fixing. My method might lose a boy his degree, but a degree is not worth so much as the capacity and the drive to learn, and the undergraduate desire for an empty baccalaureate is one of the holds the educational system has on students. Wise students some day will refuse to take degrees, as the best men (in England, for instance) give, but do not themselves accept, titles.

My method was hit on by accident and some instinct. I specialized. With several courses prescribed, I concentrated on the one or two that interested me most, and letting the others go, I worked intensively on my favorites. In my first two years, for example, I worked at English and political economy and read philosophy. At the beginning of my junior year I had several cinches in history. Now I liked history; I had neglected it partly because I rebelled at the way it was taught, as positive knowledge unrelated to politics, art, life, or anything else. The professors gave us chapters out of a few books to read, con, and be quizzed on. Blessed as I was with a "bad memory," I could not commit to it anything that I did not understand and intellectually need. The bare record of the story of man, with names, dates, and irrelative events, bored me. But I had discovered in my readings of literature, philosophy, and political economy that history had light to throw upon unhistorical questions. So I proposed in my junior and senior years to specialize in history, taking all the courses required and those also that I had flunked in. With this in mind I listened attentively to the first introductory talk of Professor William Cary Jones on American constitutional history. He was a dull lecturer, but I noticed that, after telling us what pages of what books we must be prepared in, he mumbled off some other references "for those that may care to dig deeper."

When the rest of the class rushed out into the sunshine, I went up to the professor and, to his surprise, asked for this memorandum. He gave it me. Up in the library I ran through the required chapters in the two different books, and they differed on several points. Turning to the other authorities, I saw that they disagreed on the same facts and also on others. The librarian, appealed to, helped me search the book-shelves till the library closed, and then I called on Professor Jones for more references. He was astonished, invited me in, and began to approve my industry, which astonished me. I was not trying to be a good boy; I was better than that: I was a curious boy. He lent me a couple of his books, and I went off to my club to read them. They only deepened the mystery, clearing up the historical question, but leaving the answer to be dug for and written.

The historians did not know! History was not a science, but a field for research, a field for me, for any young man, to explore, to make discoveries in and write a scientific report about. I was fascinated. As I went on from chapter to chapter, day after day, finding frequently essential differences of opinion and of fact, I saw more and more work to do. In this course, American constitutional history, I hunted far enough to suspect that the Fathers of the Republic who wrote our sacred Constitution of the United States not only did not, but did not want to, establish a democratic government, and I dreamed for a while—as I used as a child to play I was Napoleon or a trapper—I promised myself to write a true history of the making of the American Constitution. I did not do it; that chapter has been done or well begun since by two men: Smith of the University of Washington and Beard (then) of Columbia (afterward forced out, perhaps for this very work). I found other events, men, and epochs waiting for students. In all my other courses, in ancient, in European, and in modern history, the disagreeing authorities carried me back to the need of a fresh search for (or of) the original documents or other clinching testimony. Of course I did well in my classes. The history professors soon knew me as a student and seldom put a question to me except when the class had flunked it. Then Professor Jones would say, "Well, Steffens, tell them about it."

Fine. But vanity wasn't my ruling passion then. What I had was a quickening sense that I was learning a method of studying history and that every chapter of it, from the beginning of the world to the end, is crying out to be rewritten. There was something for Youth to do; these superior old men had not done anything, finally.

Years afterward I came out of the graft prosecution office in San Francisco with Rudolph Spreckels, the banker and backer of the investigation. We were to go somewhere, quick, in his car, and we couldn't. The chauffeur was trying to repair something wrong. Mr. Spreckels smiled; he looked closely at the defective part, and to my silent, wondering inquiry he answered: "Always, when I see something badly done or not done at all, I see an opportunity to make a fortune. I never kick at bad work by my class: there's lots of it and we suffer from it. But our failures and neglects are chances for the young fellows coming along and looking for work."

Nothing is done. Everything in the world remains to be done or done over. "The greatest picture is not yet painted, the greatest play isn't written (not even by Shakespeare), the greatest poem is unsung. There isn't in all the world a perfect railroad, nor a good government, nor a sound law." Physics, mathematics, and especially the most advanced and exact of the sciences, are being fundamentally revised. Chemistry is just becoming a science; psychology, economics, and sociology are awaiting a Darwin, whose work in turn is awaiting an Einstein. If the rah-rah boys in our colleges could be told this, they might not all be such specialists in football, petting parties, and unearned degrees. They are not told it, however; they are told to learn what is known. This is nothing, philosophically speaking.

Somehow or other in my later years at Berkeley, two professors, Moses and Howison, representing opposite schools of thought, got into a controversy, probably about their classes. They brought together in the house of one of them a few of their picked students, with the evident intention of letting us show in conversation how much or how little we had understood of their respective teachings. I don't remember just what the subject was that they threw into the ring, but we wrestled with it till the professors could stand it no longer. Then they broke in, and while we sat silent and highly entertained, they went at each other hard and fast and long. It was after midnight when, the debate over, we went home. I asked the other fellows what they had got out of it, and their answers showed that they had seen nothing but a fine, fair fight. When I laughed, they asked me what I, the D.S.,° had seen that was so much more profound.

I said that I had seen two highly-trained, well-educated Masters of Arts and Doctors of Philosophy disagreeing upon every essential point of thought and knowledge. They had all there was of the sciences; and yet they could not find any knowledge upon which they could base an acceptable conclusion. They had no test of knowledge; they didn't know what is and what is not. And they have no test of right and wrong; they have no basis for even an ethics.

Well, and what of it? They asked me that, and that I did not answer. I was stunned by the discovery that it was philosophically true, in a most literal sense, that nothing is known; that it is precisely the foundation

---

D.S. Drill Master of the Student Cadets, "Damned Stinker."

that is lacking for science; that all we call knowledge rested upon assumptions which the scientists did not all accept; and that, likewise, there is no scientific reason for saying, for example, that stealing is wrong. In brief: there was no scientific basis for an ethics. No wonder men said one thing and did another; no wonder they could settle nothing either in life or in the academies.

I could hardly believe this. Maybe these professors, whom I greatly respected, did not know it all. I read the books over again with a fresh eye, with a real interest, and I could see that, as in history, so in other branches of knowledge, everything was in the air. And I was glad of it. Rebel though I was, I had got the religion of scholarship and science; I was in awe of the authorities in the academic world. It was a release to feel my worship cool and pass. But I could not be sure. I must go elsewhere, see and hear other professors, men these California professors quoted and looked up to as their high priests. I decided to go as a student to Europe when I was through Berkeley, and I would start with the German universities.

My father listened to my plan, and he was disappointed. He had hoped I would succeed him in his business; it was for that that he was staying in it. When I said that, whatever I might do, I would never go into business, he said, rather sadly, that he would sell out his interest and retire. And he did soon after our talk. But he wanted me to stay home and, to keep me, offered to buy an interest in a certain San Francisco daily paper. He had evidently had this in mind for some time. I had always done some writing, verse at the poetical age of puberty, then a novel which my mother alone treasured. Journalism was the business for a boy who liked to write, he thought, and he said I had often spoken of a newspaper as my ambition. No doubt I had in the intervals between my campaigns as Napoleon. But no more. I was now going to be a scientist, a philosopher. He sighed; he thought it over, and with the approval of my mother, who was for every sort of education, he gave his consent.

Overcoming an Invisible Handicap
Thomas J. Cottle

Thomas J. Cottle (born 1937) was educated at Harvard University and the University of Chicago (Ph.D.). He is a research sociologist and practicing clinical psychologist who has also hosted his own, sometimes controversial, interview shows on radio and television. A prolific writer (author of more than twenty-five books), he has contributed a series of interviews which he calls "Life Studies" to Psychology Today. *The one we present here with Lucille Elmore (not her real name) is from the January 1980 issue.*

On her 30th birthday, Lucille Elmore informed her husband that she was going through a crisis. "I was 30 years old, active, in good health—and I was illiterate," she recalls. "I didn't know books. I didn't know history, I didn't know science. I had the barest understanding of the arts. Like a physical condition, my knowledge limped, my intelligence limped."

She was not only the mother of two young children but also was working full time as an administrative assistant in a business-consulting firm. Nevertheless, at age 30, with her husband's agreement, Lucille Elmore enrolled in college. "I thought getting in would be difficult," she says. "It was easy. I thought I couldn't discipline myself, but that came. Half the people in the library the first day thought I was the librarian, but that didn't deter me."

For Lucille, the awareness of her invisible limp came only gradually. As a young woman, she had finished high school, but she had chosen not to go on with her education. Her parents, who had never completed high school themselves, urged her to go to college, but she refused. At the time, she was perhaps a bit timid and lacked a certain confidence in her own intellectual or academic abilities. Besides, a steady job was far more important at that point to Lucille than schooling: she felt she could read on her own to make up for any lack of education.

At 20, working full time, she married Ted Elmore, a salesman for a food-store chain, a man on his way to becoming more than modestly successful. There was no need for her to work, but she did so until her first child was born; she was then 22. A second child was born two years later, and three years after that, she went back to work. With her youngest in a day-care program, she felt no reservations about working, but her lack of education began to nag at her as she approached the age of 30. She thus gave up her job, entered a continuing-education program at a nearby university, and began what she likens to a love affair.

"I'm carrying on an open affair with books, but like a genuinely good lover, I'm being guided. Reading lists, suggested reading, recommended readings—I want them all. I must know what happened in the 12th, 13th, 18th centuries. I want to know how the world's major religions evolved. Papal history, I know nothing of papal history and succession, or the politics involved. I read the Bible, but I never studied it. It's like music: I listened, but it wasn't an informed listening. Now all of this is changing.

"I must tell you, I despise students when they talk about 'the real world,' as if college were a dream world. They simply don't understand what the accumulation of knowledge and information means. Maybe you

at least, and going through a personal crisis, to fully appreciate what historical connections are.

"A line of Shakespeare challenges me more than half the jobs I'll be
equipped for when I'm finished. I'm having an affair with him, too, only
it's called Elizabethan Literature 606. I think many people prefer the real
world of everyday work because it's less frightening than the larger-than-
life world of college.

"There's a much more important difference between the rest of the
students and me. We don't agree at all on what it means to be a success.
They think in terms of money, material things. I suppose that's normal.
They don't understand that with a nice home, and decent job prospects,
and two beautiful children, I know I am a failure. I'm a failure because
I am ignorant. I'm a failure until I have knowledge, until I can work with
it, be excited by and play with ideas.

"I don't go to school for the rewards down the line. I want to reach the
point at which I don't measure knowledge by anything but itself. An idea
has value or it doesn't. This is how I now determine success and failure."

" 'How can I use it?' That's what students ask. 'What good will this do
me?' They don't think about what the question says about them, even
without an answer attached to it. Questions like that only build up competition. But competition is the bottom line for so many students, I guess,
getting ahead, getting a bit of a step up on the other guy. I know, it's my
husband's life.

"I'll tell you what I think I like most about my work: the library. I can
think of no place so exclusive and still so open and public. Millions of
books there for the taking. A chair to sit in, a row of books, and you don't
need a penny. For me, the library is a religious center, a shrine.

"Students talk about the real world out there. What about the free
world in here? Here, no one arrests you for what you're thinking. In the
library, you can't talk, so you have to think. I never knew what it meant
to think about something, to really think it through. I certainly never
understood what you had to know to even begin to think. I always thought
it was normal to limp."

The Master Ideas

Theodore Roszak

*The following essay is the second part of Chapter 5 in Theodore Roszak's
book* The Cult of Information: The Folklore of Computers and the True
Art of Thinking *(1986). For further information about the author, see page
55.*

If there is an art of thinking which we would teach the young, it has much to do with showing how the mind may move along the spectrum of information, discriminating solid generalizations from hunches, hypotheses from reckless prejudices. But for our purposes here, I want to move to the far end of the spectrum, to that extreme point where the facts, growing thinner and thinner, finally vanish altogether. What do we find once we step beyond that point into the zone where facts are wholly absent?

There we discover the riskiest ideas of all. Yet they may also be the richest and most fruitful. For there we find what might be called the *master ideas*—the great moral, religious, and metaphysical teachings which are the foundations of culture. Most of the ideas that occupy our thinking from moment to moment are not master ideas; they are more modest generalizations. But from this point forward I will be emphasizing master ideas because they are always there in some form at the foundation of the mind, molding our thoughts below the level of awareness. I want to focus upon them because they bear a peculiarly revealing relationship to information, which is our main subject of discussion. *Master ideas are based on no information whatever.* I will be using them, therefore, to emphasize the radical difference between ideas and data which the cult of information has done so much to obscure.

Let us take one of the master ideas of our society as an example: *All men are created equal.*

The power of this familiar idea will not be lost on any of us. From it, generations of legal and philosophical controversy have arisen, political movements and revolutions have taken their course. It is an idea that has shaped our culture in ways that touch each of us intimately; it is part, perhaps the most important part, of our personal identity.

But where did this idea come from? Obviously not from some body of facts. Those who created the idea possessed no more information about the world than their ancestors, who would, doubtless, have been shocked by such a pronouncement. They possessed far less information about the world than we in the late twentieth century may feel is necessary to support such a sweeping, universal statement about human nature. Nevertheless, those who shed their blood over the generations to defend that assertion (or to oppose it) did not do so on the basis of any data presented to them. The idea has no relationship whatever to information. One would be hard pressed even to imagine a line of research that might prove or disprove it. Indeed, where such research has been attempted (for example by inveterate IQ theorists), the result, as their critics are always quick to point out, is a hopeless distraction from the real meaning of the idea, which has nothing to do with measurements or findings, facts or figures of any kind. The idea of human equality is a statement about the essential worth of people in the eyes of their fellows. At a certain juncture in history, this idea arose in the minds of a few morally impassioned thinkers as a defiantly compassionate response to conditions of gross injustice that could no longer be accepted as tolerable. It spread from the few to the many; finding the same insurgent response in the multitude, it soon became the battle cry of an era. So it is with all master ideas. They are born, not from data, but from absolute conviction that catches fire in the mind of one, of a few, then of many as the ideas spread to other lives where enough of the same experience can be found waiting to be ignited.

Here are some more ideas, some of them master ideas, each of which, though condensed in form, has been the theme of countless variations in the philosophy, religious belief, literature, and jurisprudence of human society:

Jesus died for our sins.

List of master Ideas

The Tao that can be named is not the true Tao.

Man is a rational animal.

Man is a fallen creature.

Man is the measure of all things.

The mind is a blank sheet of paper.

The mind is governed by unconscious instincts.

The mind is a collection of inherited archetypes.

God is love.

God is dead.

Life is a pilgrimage.

Life is a miracle.

Life is a meaningless absurdity.

At the heart of every culture we find a core of ideas like these, some old, some new, some rising to prominence, some declining into obsolescence. Because those I list here in terse formulations are verbal ideas, they might easily be mistaken for intended statements of fact. They have the same linguistic form as a point of information, like "George Washington was the first president of the United States." But of course they are not facts, any more than a painting by Rembrandt is a fact, or a sonata by Beethoven, or a dance by Martha Graham. For these too are ideas; they are integrating patterns meant to declare the meaning of things as human beings have discovered it by way of revelation, sudden insight, or the slow growth of wisdom over a lifetime. Where do these patterns come from? The imagination creates them from *experience.* Just as ideas order information, they also order the wild flux of experience as it streams through us in the course of life.

This is the point Fritz Machlup makes when he observes a striking difference between "information" and "knowledge." (He is using "knowledge" here in exactly the same way I am using "idea"—as an integrating pattern.) "Information" he tells us, "is acquired by being told, whereas knowledge can be acquired by thinking."

Any kind of experience—accidental impressions, observations, and even "inner experience" not induced by stimuli received from the environment—may initiate cognitive processes leading to changes in a person's knowledge. Thus, *new knowledge can be acquired without new information being received.* (That this statement refers to subjective knowledge goes without saying; but there is no such thing as objective knowledge that was not previously somebody's subjective knowledge.)[1]

Ideas, then—and especially master ideas—give order to experience. They may do this in deep or shallow ways; they may do it nobly or savagely. Not all ideas are humane; some, which bid to become master ideas and may succeed, are dangerous, vile, destructive. Hitler's *Mein Kampf* is a book filled with toxic ideas that were born of vengefulness and resentment. Yet they became, for a brief interval, the master ideas of one troubled society. No one who ever read that book and hated it did so because they thought the author had gotten some of his facts wrong; no one who ever read it and loved it cared about the accuracy of its information. The appeal of the book, whether accepted or rejected, was pitched at a different level of the mind.

Here are some more ideas that, at least in my view, are just as toxic:

Society is the war of each against all.

Self-interest is the only reliable human motivation.

Let justice be done though the heavens fall.

The only good Indian is a dead Indian.

Nice guys finish last.

The end justifies the means.

My country right or wrong.

It is precisely because some ideas—many ideas—are brutal and deadly that we need to learn how to deal with them adroitly. An idea takes us into people's minds, ushers us through their experience. Understanding an idea means understanding the lives of those who created and championed it. It means knowing their peculiar sources of inspiration, their limits, their vulnerabilities and blind spots. What our schools must offer the young is an education that lets them make that journey through another mind in the light of other ideas, including some that they have fashioned for themselves from their own experience. The mind that owns few ideas is apt to be crabbed and narrow, ungenerous and defensive in its judgments. "Nothing is more dangerous than an idea," Emil Chartier once said, "when it is the only one we have."

---

[1]Fritz Machlup and Una Mansfield, eds., *The Study of Information* (New York: Wiley, 1983), p. 644.

On the other hand, the mind that is gifted with many ideas is equipped to make its evaluations more gracefully. It is open and welcoming to its own experience, yet capable of comparing that experience discriminately with the lives of others, and so choosing its convictions with care and courtesy.

How to Fix the Premedical Curriculum

Lewis Thomas

Lewis Thomas, a physician and a physician's son, was born in 1913, entered Harvard Medical School in 1933, and received his M.D. in 1937. After internship, he began a distinguished career as medical researcher, teacher, and administrator. In 1973, he resigned from Yale—where he had been Professor of Pathology, chairman of his department, and Dean of the Medical School—to go to the Memorial Sloan-Kettering Cancer Center in New York City, where he served as president (1973–1980) and chancellor (1980–1983).

Thomas has received numerous awards for distinguished achievement both in science and in literature. His first book directed to a general audience, The Lives of a Cell: Notes of a Biology Watcher *(1974), is a collection of monthly columns written for the* New England Journal of Medicine; *it won the National Book Award. Since then he has published three more equally acclaimed books:* The Medusa and the Snail: More Notes of a Biology Watcher *(1979); a kind of autobiography,* The Youngest Science: Notes of a Medicine Watcher *(1983); and* Late Night Thoughts on Listening to Mahler's Ninth Symphony *(1983). Thomas is a master of the short, reflective essay; he draws from his knowledge of biology a set of ideas and metaphors richly applicable to the human condition. This selection was first printed in the* New York Times Magazine, *July 4, 1976.*

The influence of the modern medical school on liberal-arts education in this country over the last decade has been baleful and malign, nothing less. The admission policies of the medical schools are at the root of the trouble. If something is not done quickly to change these, all the joy of going to college will have been destroyed, not just for that growing number of undergraduate students who draw breath only to become doctors, but for everyone else, all the students, and all the faculty as well.

The medical schools used to say they wanted applicants as broadly educated as possible, and they used to mean it. The first two years of medical school were given over entirely to the basic biomedical sciences, and almost all entering students got their first close glimpse of science in those years. Three chemistry courses, physics, and some sort of biology were all that were required from the colleges. Students were encouraged by the rhetoric of medical-school catalogues to major in such nonscience disciplines as history, English, philosophy. Not many did so; almost all premedical students in recent generations have had their majors in chemistry or biology. But anyway, they were authorized to spread around in other fields if they wished.

There is still some talk in medical deans' offices about the need for general culture, but nobody really means it, and certainly the premedical students don't believe it. They concentrate on science.

They concentrate on science with a fury, and they live for grades. If there are courses in the humanities that can be taken without risk to class standing they will line up for these, but they will not get into anything tough except science. The so-called social sciences have become extremely popular as stand-ins for traditional learning.

The atmosphere of the liberal-arts college is being poisoned by premedical students. It is not the fault of the students, who do not start out as a necessarily bad lot. They behave as they do in the firm belief that if they behave any otherwise they won't get into medical school.

I have a suggestion, requiring for its implementation the following announcement from the deans of all the medical schools: henceforth, any applicant who is self-labeled as a "premed," distinguishable by his course selection from his classmates, will have his dossier placed in the third stack of three. Membership in a "premedical society" will, by itself, be grounds for rejection. Any college possessing something called a "premedical curriculum," or maintaining offices for people called "premedical advisers," will be excluded from recognition by the medical schools.

Now as to grades and class standing. There is obviously no way of ignoring these as criteria for acceptance, but it is the grades *in general* that should be weighed. And, since so much of the medical-school curriculum is, or ought to be, narrowly concerned with biomedical science, more attention should be paid to the success of students in other, nonscience disciplines before they are admitted, in order to assure the scope of intellect needed for a physician's work.

Hence, if there are to be MCAT° tests, the science part ought to be made the briefest, and weigh the least. A knowledge of literature and languages ought to be the major test, and the scariest. History should be tested, with rigor.

MCAT tests Medical College Admission Test, a standardized test for those planning to apply to medical school.

The best thing would be to get rid of the MCATs, once and for all, and rely instead, wholly, on the judgment of the college faculties.

You could do this if there were some central, core discipline, universal within the curricula of all the colleges, which could be used for evaluating the free range of a student's mind, his tenacity and resolve, his innate capacity for the understanding of human beings, and his affection for the human condition. For this purpose, I propose that classical Greek be restored as the centerpiece of undergraduate education. The loss of Homeric and Attic Greek from American college life was one of this century's disasters. Putting it back where it once was would quickly make up for the dispiriting impact which generations of spotty Greek in translation have inflicted on modern thought. The capacity to read Homer's language closely enough to sense the terrifying poetry in some of the lines could serve as a shrewd test for the qualities of mind and character needed in a physician.

If everyone had to master Greek, the college students aspiring to medical school would be placed on the same footing as everyone else, and their identifiability as a separate group would be blurred, to everyone's advantage. Moreover, the currently depressing drift on some campuses toward special courses for prelaw students, and even prebusiness students, might be inhibited before more damage is done.

Latin should be put back as well, but not if it is handled, as it ought to be, by the secondary schools. If Horace has been absorbed prior to college, so much for Latin. But Greek is a proper discipline for the college mind.

English, history, the literature of at least two foreign languages, and philosophy should come near the top of the list, just below Classics, as basic requirements, and applicants for medical school should be told that their grades in these courses will count more than anything else.

Students should know that if they take summer work as volunteers in the local community hospital, as ward aides or laboratory assistants, this will not necessarily be held against them, but neither will it help.

Finally, the colleges should have much more of a say about who goes on to medical school. If they know, as they should, the students who are generally bright and also respected, this judgment should carry the heaviest weight for admission. If they elect to use criteria other than numerical class standing for recommending applicants, this evaluation should hold.

The first and most obvious beneficiaries of this new policy would be the college students themselves. There would no longer be, anywhere where they could be recognized as a coherent group, the "premeds," that most detestable of all cliques eating away at the heart of the college. Next to benefit would be the college faculties, once again in possession of the destiny of their own curriculum, for better or worse. And next in line, but perhaps benefiting the most of all, are the basic-science faculties of the medical schools, who would once again be facing classrooms of students who are ready to be startled and excited by a totally new and unfamiliar body of knowledge, eager to learn, unpreoccupied by the notions of relevance that are paralyzing the minds of today's first-year medical students already so surfeited by science that they want to start practicing psychiatry in the first trimester of the first year.

Society would be the ultimate beneficiary. We could look forward to a generation of doctors who have learned as much as anyone can learn, in our colleges and universities, about how human beings have always lived out their lives. Over the bedrock of knowledge about our civilization, the medical schools could then construct as solid a structure of medical science as can be built, but the bedrock would always be there, holding everything else upright.

Drinking Hemlock and Other Nutritional Matters

Harold J. Morowitz

This essay is taken from The Wine of Life and Other Essays on Societies, Energy and Living Things *(1979). For further information about the author, see page 1.*

It was a rather dark, bleak morning, and after rising early I thought it appropriate to turn on the television and communicate, unidirectionally to be sure, with the outside world. There to my great surprise was a famous movie star of a few years back discoursing on the evils of sugar. The former Hollywood idol was vehement in her denunciation of this hexose dimer particularly in its purified and crystallized form. She denounced it as an "unnatural food," an epithet that may well have bruised the egos of the photosynthesizing cane and beet plants. The mental image evoked was that of a solemn judge sentencing someone in perpetuity for an "unnatural act." In no time at all this great lady had me caught up in her crusade, and I kept muttering "hate sucrose" as I prepared an unnatural extract of coffee beans and dropped in a highly synthetic saccharin tablet.

A few minutes later, when the veil of sleep had lifted and the uncertainty of reason had replaced the assuredness of emotion, I began to wonder where my cinema heroine had acquired such self-righteous certainty about biochemical and nutritional matters that have eluded my colleagues for years. Perhaps all this messy experimental work of grinding and extracting tissue and otherwise mucking about the laboratory is not the shortest road to truth at all, and we of the dirty white lab coat crowd are missing some mysterious pathway whereby true nutritional knowledge comes with blinding insight and transforms the lives of the faithful.

All of this recalled a frequent, painful experience that haunts biomedical scientists like a recurring nightmare. One is at a cocktail party or other social gathering where someone appears in the crowd and begins an oratorical declamation on Good Nutrition. The "facts" being set forth are often inconsistent with everything one knows about metabolic pathways, cell and organ physiology, enzymology, and common sense. If the listener is so bold as to raise the question, "How do you know that?", he or she is greeted with a look that must have faced Columbus when he queried, "How do you know that the world is flat?"

Nutrition seems to be like politics; everyone is an expert. It would appear that to the general public years of education are as naught compared to knowledge somehow painlessly available to everyone, regardless of his familiarity with innumerable facts and theories that constitute a complex discipline.

The situation described is by no means confined to the choice of foods, and I certainly feel ill prepared to get involved in the sucrose controversy. Nevertheless, the field of nutrition is a good example of the many areas where we are constantly subjected to a host of dogmatic statements, some of which are true, some of which are false, and many of which are indeterminate. The response to each of these assertions should be the query, "How do you know that what you are saying is indeed a statement of fact?" At this level of question, I believe our educational system has been a total failure.

Asking how we know the things that we know is part of the philosophical discipline of epistemology, the theory of knowledge, which is usually taught in upper-level and graduate philosophy courses and is therefore restricted to a small group of college students. But can there be any study that is more basic to education? Should not every high school graduate be prepared to cope with the many incorrect and misleading assertions that come his way every day? On the surface it seems strange that acquiring skills in assessing the validity of statements is not a core feature of the school curriculum.

Education, as conceived at present, is largely a matter of transferring subject matter from teacher to student, and uncertainty is usually settled by appeal to authority, the teacher, a textbook, or an encyclopedia. The methodological issue of how knowledge is obtained is rarely mentioned. Thus one of the most important analytical tools that an educated individual should possess is ignored. This is not to argue against the transfer of information but rather to assert that by itself it is insufficient protection in a real world containing demagogues and all kinds of charlatans and hucksters who have a free rein because almost no one is asking the appropriate questions.

On the issue of sorting out reality, most holders of doctoral degrees are almost as naive as grade-school graduates, and all manner of academic disciplines also expend effort on statements that would be quickly discarded if epistemological criteria were invoked. This takes us back briefly to the subject of nutrition, where methodological problems make it very difficult to obtain even pragmatically useful information. Statements are made on the basis of averaging over populations when we have no idea of the distribution functions that go into forming the averages. The impossibility of large-scale experiments with people requires extrapolation of animal or small-scale human determinations over ranges where the correctness of the extrapolation procedure is unknown. Nutrition is thus beset with difficulties that are clearly of an epistemological nature and, until these are resolved, careful scientists will be confined to very limited statements. Dogmatic assertions will remain the province of cocktail party orators.

The problem of why the theory of knowledge is not taught in the schools is relatively easy to see. Epistemology is, after all, a dangerous subject. If we start to question the validity of statements, then the teachers themselves come under question. All assertions about education, established forms of religion, government, and social mores will also be subject to justification on the grounds of how they are known to be true. For parents and teachers who have not been through the experience of exploring how we determine facts, it would be unnerving to have their children continuously questioning the roots of knowledge. Inquiry is indeed a challenge to the acceptance of things as they are.

To realize the threat to established ways that is perceived in the type of analysis we are discussing, we need to go back to ancient Athens, where the philosopher Socrates taught his young followers by the technique of questioning everything and seeking answers. As Will Durant[o] has noted, "he went about prying into the human soul, uncovering assumptions and questioning certainties." This has come to be known as the Socratic method. The citizens of the Greek city-state condemned the inquiring teacher to death by poisoning with hemlock. One of the most serious charges against him was "corrupting the young." The fate of the first propounder of the Theory of Knowledge has perhaps served as a warning to keep the subject out of the school system.

There is still an objection that it is dangerous to teach the art and science of inquiry to the young; I would submit that it is more dangerous not to teach it to them, thus leaving them vulnerable to the quacks and

---

Will Durant   American historian and philosopher (1885–1981), perhaps best known for his ten-volume *The Story of Civilization* (1935–1967), which he wrote with his wife Ariel (1898–1981).

phonies who now add mass communication to their bag of tricks. If we believe that rationality will lead the way to the solution of problems, then we must start by making the examination of what is "real" a part of everyone's thought. If challenging young people are a nuisance, think of how much more of a menace is presented by young people marching off in lock step and never questioning where they are going.

The solution seems clear. When we return education to the basics of reading, writing, and 'rithmetic, we should add a fourth R, "reality." Starting at the first grade and continuing through graduate training we must see that students become sensitized to the meaning of what is said and the realization of how valid knowledge is established. If this seems radical, it is. Drinking hemlock may be less painful than swallowing some of the drivel that comes over the TV set every day.

Five Ways to Wisdom

Otto Friedrich

Otto Friedrich (born 1929) is a senior writer at Time *magazine. Since graduating from Harvard in 1948, he has worked as an editor for* Stars and Stripes, *the* New York Daily News, Newsweek, *and the* Saturday Evening Post. *Friedrich has written books on subjects ranging from Berlin in the 1920s to insanity to growing roses to Henry Adams's wife, and, he says, "in a way, all these things overlap." In 1986, he and his wife published* City of Nets: A Portrait of Hollywood in the 1940s. *The present article originally appeared in* Time, *September 27, 1982, with a long introduction, here omitted, on the current status of colleges in the United States.*

What is it essential to learn—to know—and why? Everyone seems to have his own answer, but there are interesting patterns among those answers. They can be organized into five main ideas:

1: Education Means Careers

Today's most popular answer is the practical one, on which students are most likely to agree with parents virtually impoverished by tuition bills: an education should enable a student to get a better job than he would otherwise be able to find or fill. In a Carnegie Council poll, 67% of students cited this as an "essential" purpose of their education. A 9.8% unemployment rate makes this purpose seem all the more essential. Michael Adelson, 23, who studied psychology at U.C.L.A., has been unable to find a job in his field for a year and a half, and he now wishes he had chosen engineering. He calls his bachelor of arts degree "completely useless."

The idea that education has a basically social purpose derives more or less from Plato. In his *Republic,* the philosopher portrayed a utopia governed by an intellectual elite specially trained for that purpose. This form of education was both stern and profoundly conservative. Children who attempt innovations, warned Socrates, acting as Plato's narrator, will desire a different sort of life when they grow up to be men, with other institutions and laws. And this "is full of danger to the whole state." To prevent any innovations, Socrates forthrightly demanded censorship so that students could not "hear any casual tales which may be devised by casual persons." When asked whose works he would ban, Socrates specifically named Homer. The poet's crime, he said, was to provide "an erroneous representation of the nature of gods and heroes."

Political pressure of this kind has never been far from the campus, but the overwhelming influence on U.S. education has been not politics but economics: the need for a technologically trained managerial caste. The very first Land Grant Act, in 1862, handed out 30,000 acres per Congressman for the building of state colleges at which "the leading object shall be . . . to teach such branches of learning as are related to agriculture and the mechanic arts." These needs keep changing, of course, and over the decades the U.S. economy demanded of its universities not only chemists and engineers but lawyers and accountants and personnel analysts, and then, after Sputnik's shocking revelation of the Soviet lead in space, yet more engineers.

Students naturally respond to the economy's needs. The Rev. Theodore Hesburgh, president of Notre Dame, complained last year that "the most popular course on the American college campus is not literature or history but accounting." This criticism reflects the fact that less than half the nation's swarm of college students go to liberal arts colleges; the rest are seeking not just jobs but entry into the middle class.

There are now thousands of Ph.D.s unable to find anyone willing to pay them for their hard-earned knowledge of Renaissance painting or the history of French monasticism, but any Sunday newspaper overflows with ads appealing for experts in electromagnetic capability, integrated logistics support or laser electro-optics. Says George W. Valsa, supervisor of the college-recruiting section at Ford: "We are not ready to sign a petition to burn down liberal arts colleges, but don't expect us to go out and hire many liberal arts graduates." Ford does hire nearly 1,000 graduates a year, and most of them are engineers or M.B.A.s.

This is not the old argument between the "two cultures" of science and the humanities, for science too is often forced to defer to technical and vocational training. In 1979, according to one Carnegie study, 58% of all undergraduates pursued "professional" majors (up from 38% a decade earlier), in contrast to 11% in social sciences, 7% in biological sciences, 6% in the arts and 4% in physical sciences. Rich and prestigious private universities can resist this rush toward vocational training, but public and smaller private colleges are more vulnerable. "The bulk of the institutions will have to give in to a form of consumerism," says U.C.L.A.'s Astin, "in that they need applicants and will therefore have to offer students what they want."

Says Paul Ginsberg, dean of students at Wisconsin: "It's becoming increasingly difficult to persuade a student to take courses that will contribute to his intellectual development in addition to those that will make him a good accountant." Quite apart from the pros and cons of professional training, the idea of educating oneself in order to rise in the world is a perfectly legitimate goal. But Ginsberg has been receiving letters from high school freshmen asking about the prospects for professional schools and job opportunities when they graduate from college seven years hence. Says he: "I don't know at what point foresight ends and panic sets in."

2: Education Transmits Civilization

Jill Ker Conway, president of Smith, echoes the prevailing view of contemporary technology when she says that "anyone in today's world who doesn't understand data processing is not educated." But she insists that the increasing emphasis on these matters leaves certain gaps. Says she: "The very strongly utilitarian emphasis in education, which is an effect of Sputnik and the cold war, has really removed from this culture something that was very profound in its 18th and 19th century roots, which was a sense that literacy and learning were ends in themselves for a democratic republic."

In contrast to Plato's claim for the social value of education, a quite different idea of intellectual purposes was propounded by the Renaissance humanists. Intoxicated with their rediscovery of the classical learning that was thought to have disappeared during the Dark Ages, they argued that the imparting of knowledge needs no justification—religious, social, economic or political. Its purpose, to the extent that it has one, is to pass on from generation to generation the corpus of knowledge that constitutes civilization. "What could man acquire, by virtuous striving, that is more valuable than knowledge?" asked Erasmus, perhaps the greatest scholar of the early 16th century. That idea has acquired a tradition of its own. "The educational process has no end beyond itself," said John Dewey. "It is its own end."

But what exactly is the corpus of knowledge to be passed on? In simpler times, it was all included in the medieval universities' *quadrivium* (arithmetic, geometry, astronomy, music) and *trivium* (grammar, rhetoric, logic). As recently as the last century, when less than 5% of Americans went to college at all, students in New England establishments were compelled mainly to memorize and recite various Latin texts, and crusty professors angrily opposed the introduction of any new scientific discoveries or modern European languages. "They felt," said Charles Francis Adams Jr., the Union Pacific Railroad president who devoted his later years to writing history, "that a classical education was the important distinction between a man who had been to college and a man who had not been to college, and that anything that diminished the importance of this distinction was essentially revolutionary and tended to anarchy."

Such a view was eventually overcome by the practical demands of both students and society, yet it does not die. In academia, where every professor is accustomed to drawing up lists of required reading, it can even be played as a game. Must an educated man have read Dostoyevsky, Rimbaud, Tacitus, Kafka? (Yes.) Must he know both Bach's *Goldberg Variations* and Schoenberg's *Gurrelieder?* (Perhaps.) Must he know the Carnot Cycle and Boole's Inequality? (Well . . .) And then languages—can someone who reads only Constance Garnett's rather wooden version of *Anna Karenina* really know Tolstoy's masterpiece any better than some Frenchman can know Shakespeare by reading André Gide's translation of *Hamlet?* Every scholar likes to defend his own specialty as a cornerstone of Western civilization, and any restraints can seem philistine. George Steiner approvingly quotes, in *Language and Silence,* a suggestion that "an acquaintance with a Chinese novel or a Persian lyric is almost indispensable to contemporary literacy." On a slightly more practical level, intellectual codifiers like to draw up lists of masterworks that will educate any reader who is strong enough to survive them—thus Charles Eliot's famous five-foot shelf of Harvard Classics and all its weighty sequels.

It was the immensely influential Eliot, deeply impressed with the specialized scholarly and scientific research performed at German universities, who proclaimed in 1869, upon becoming president of Harvard, the abolition of its rigid traditional curriculum. Basic education should be performed by the high schools, Eliot declared; anyone who went on to college should be free to make his own choice among myriad elective courses. The students chose the practical. "In the end, it was the sciences that triumphed, guided by the hidden hand of capitalism and legitimated by the binding ideology of positivism," Ernest Boyer and Martin Kaplan observe in *Educating for Survival.* Before long, however, the inevitable counterrevolution against the elective system began; there was a "core" of certain things that every student must learn. Columbia established required courses in contemporary civilization; the University of Chicago and St. John's College duly followed with programs solidly based on required readings of classic texts.

St. John's, which is based in Annapolis, Md., and has a smaller campus in Santa Fe, N. Mex., is a remarkable example of an institution resolutely taking this approach. Ever since 1937, all of St. John's students (683 this fall on both campuses) have been required to read and discuss a list of 130 great books, drawn heavily from the classics and philosophy but also from the ranks of modern novelists like Faulkner and Conrad. The students must take four years of math, three of a laboratory science, two of music and two years each of Greek and French. That is just about it. This modern liberal arts version of the *trivium* and *quadrivium* includes no such novelties as psychology (except what can be learned in the works of Freud and William James) and no sociology (except perhaps Jane Austen).

St. John's is aware of the obvious criticism that its approach is "elitist" and even "irrelevant" to the real world. But President Edwin DeLattre's mild voice turns a bit sharp when he retorts, "If knowing the foundations of one's country—the foundations of one's civilization—if understanding and learning how to gain access to the engines of political and economic power in the world—if knowing how to learn in mathematics and the sciences, the languages, the humanities—if having access to the methods that have advanced civilizations since the dawn of human intelligence . . . if all those things are irrelevant, then boy, are we irrelevant!" DeLattre is a philosopher by training, and he offers one definition that has an ominous but compelling reverberation in the thermonuclear age: "Don't forget the notion of an educated person as someone who would understand how to refound his or her own civilization."

3: Education Teaches How to Think

Aristotle was one of those who could found a civilization, and while he thought of education as both a social value and an end in itself, he ascribed its chief importance to what might be considered a third basic concept of education: to train the mind to think, regardless of what it is thinking about. The key is not what it knows but how it evaluates any new fact or argument. "An educated man," Aristotle wrote in *On the Parts of Animals,* "should be able to form a fair offhand judgment as to the goodness or badness of the method used by a professor in his exposition. To be educated is in fact to be able to do this."

The Aristotelian view of education as a process has become the conventionally worthy answer today whenever college presidents and other academic leaders are asked what an education should be. An educated man, says Harvard President Bok,° taking a deep breath, must have a "curiosity in exploring the unfamiliar and unexpected, an open-mindedness in entertaining opposing points of view, tolerance for the ambiguity that surrounds so many important issues, and a willingness to make the best decisions he can in the face of uncertainty and doubt . . ."

"The educated person," says University of Chicago President Hanna Holborn Gray, taking an equally deep breath, "is a person who has a respect for rationality, and who understands some of the limits of rationality as well, who has acquired independent critical intelligence, and a

---

Harvard President Bok Derek Bok (b. 1930), president of Harvard since 1971.

sense not only for the complexity of the world and different points of view but of the standards he or she would thoughtfully want to be pursuing in making judgments."

This is an approach that appears to attach more importance to the process of learning than to the substance of what is learned, but it does provide a way of coping with the vast increase of knowledge. "The old notion of the generalist who could comprehend all subjects is an impossibility, and it was even in past ages," says Chicago's Gray. "Renaissance humanism concentrated on social living and aesthetic engagement but left out most of science. To know all about today's physics, biology and mathematics, or even the general principles of all these fields, would be impossible." To make matters still more difficult, the fields of knowledge keep changing. Says Harvard's Henry Rosovsky, dean of the faculty of arts and sciences: "We can't prepare students for an explosion of knowledge because we don't know what is going to explode next. The best we can do is to make students capable of gaining new knowledge."

The old Aristotelian idea, combined with a contemporary sense of desperation about coping with the knowledge explosion, helped inspire a complete reorganization—yet again—of Harvard's curriculum. At the end of World War II, Harvard had curtailed Eliot's electives and launched a series of general education courses that were supposed to teach everyone the rudiments of science and the humanities. But by the 1960s, when rebellious students seized an administration building, that whole system had broken down. "At the moment," a saddened Dean Rosovsky later wrote to his colleagues, "to be an educated man or woman doesn't mean anything . . . The world has become a Tower of Babel."

Out of Rosovsky's unhappiness came what Harvard somewhat misleadingly calls its core curriculum. Inaugurated in 1979, after much faculty debate and amid considerable press attention, this core turned out to be a rather sprawling collection of 122 different courses, ranging from Abstraction in Modern Art to Microbial and Molecular Biology. Students are required to select eight of their 32 courses from five general areas of knowledge (science, history, the arts, ethics and foreign cultures).

Harvard's eminence exerts a wide influence, but other first-rate institutions, like Columbia, Chicago and Princeton, point out that they have taught a more concentrated core and steadfastly continued doing so throughout the 1960s. "It makes me unhappy when people think that Harvard has done some innovative curriculum work," says Columbia College Associate Dean Michael Rosenthal (a Harvard graduate). "They have millions of courses, none of which, you could argue, represents any fundamental effort to introduce people to a kind of thinking or to a discipline."

But that is exactly what Harvard does claim to be doing. "The student should have an understanding of the major ways mankind organizes knowledge," says Rosovsky. "That is done in identifiable ways: in sciences by experiment, conducted essentially in mathematics; in social science through quantitative and historical analysis; in the humanities by studying the great traditions. We are not ignoring content but simply recognizing that because of the knowledge explosion, it makes sense to emphasize the gaining of knowledge."

If anyone objects that it is still perfectly possible to graduate from Harvard without having read a word of Shakespeare, Rosovsky is totally unfazed. Says he: "That's not necessary."

4: Education Liberates the Individual

The current trend toward required subjects—a kind of intellectual law-and-order—reflects contemporary political conservatism. It implies not only that there is a basic body of knowledge to be learned but also that there is a right way to think. It implies that a certain amount of uniformity is both socially and intellectually desirable.

Perhaps, but the excesses of the 1960s should not be used to besmirch reforms that were valuable. They too derived from a distinguished intellectual tradition. Its founding father was Jean-Jacques Rousseau, who argued in his novel *Emile* that children are not miniature adults and should not be drilled into becoming full-grown robots. "Everything is good as it comes from the hand of the Creator," said Rousseau; "everything degenerates in the hands of man."

Isolated from the corrupting world, Rousseau's young Emile was given no books but encouraged to educate himself by observing the workings of nature. Not until the age of twelve, the age of reason, was he provided with explanations in the form of astronomy or chemistry, and not until the social age of 15 was he introduced to aesthetics, religion and, eventually, female company. That was how Emile met Sophie and lived happily ever after. It is a silly tale, and yet there is considerable power to the idea that a student should be primarily educated not to hold a job or to memorize literary monuments or even to think like Aristotle, but simply to develop the potentialities of his own self—and that everyone's self is different.

While there is probably not a single university that has not retreated somewhat from the experimentation of the 1960s, and while the rhetoric of that decade is now wildly out of fashion, a few small institutions have tried to keep the faith. For them, education is, in a sense, liberation, personal liberation. At Evergreen State College in Washington, which has no course requirements of any kind and no letter grades, a college spokesman describes a class on democracy and tyranny by saying, "We will try to find out who we are, and what kind of human beings we should become." At Hampshire College, founded in Massachusetts in 1970 as a resolutely experimental school, students still design their own curriculums, take no exams and talk of changing the world. "I don't see myself as giving a body of knowledge or even 'a way of learning,' " says Physics Professor Herbert Bernstein, "but as involved in something beyond that—to help people find their own path and the fullness of who they are."

The times have not been easy for such colleges. Not only do costs keep rising, but many students now prefer conventional courses and grades that will look impressive on job applications. Antioch, which expanded into an unmanageable national network of 32 experimental institutions, stumbled to the verge of bankruptcy in the 1970s, and is drastically cutting costs to survive. But the spirit of Rousseau flickers on. Rollins, which has sometimes been dismissed as a Florida tennis school, is trying to organize a conference for such like-minded colleges as Bard, Bennington, Sarah Lawrence and Scripps on how best to pursue the goal of "making higher education more personal and developmental rather than formalistic."

Even when these enthusiasts do bend to the current pressures for law-and-order, they tend to do it in their own dreamy way. At Bard, where President Leon Botstein decided last year that all students should attend an intensive three-week workshop on how to think and write, the students pondered such questions as the nature of justice. What color is justice? What shape is it? What sound does it make? What does it eat? "I can't think of anything," one student protested at the first such writing class. "Don't worry about it," the teacher soothingly answered. Among the students' offerings: "Justice is navy blue, it's square. It weaves in and out and backs up . . . Justice is black and white, round . . . It has the sound of the cracked Liberty Bell ringing." Workshop Director Peter Elbow's conclusion: "We're trying an experiment here, and we're not pretending that we have it under control or that we know how it works."

5: Education Teaches Morals

The U.S. Supreme Court has forbidden prayers in public schools, but many Americans cling to the idea that their educational system has a moral purpose. It is an idea common to both the Greeks and the medieval church ("O Lord my King," St. Augustine wrote in his *Confessions,* "whatsoever I speak or write, or read, or number, let all serve Thee"). In a secular age, the moral purpose of education takes secular forms: racial integration, sex education, good citizenship. At the college level, the ambiguities become more complex. Should a morally objectionable person be allowed to teach? (Not Timothy Leary,° said Harvard.) Should a morally objectionable doctrine be permitted? (Not Arthur Jensen's claims of racial differences in intelligence, said student protesters at Berkeley.)

Timothy Leary Psychologist who was once widely known for advocating the use of psychedelic drugs.

Many people are understandably dismayed by such censorship. But would they prefer ethical neutrality? Should engineers be trained to build highways without being taught any concern for the homes they displace? Should prospective corporate managers learn how to increase profits regardless of pollution or unemployment? Just the opposite, according to *Beyond the Ivory Tower,* a new book by Harvard's Bok, which calls for increased emphasis on "applied ethics." (Writes Bok: "A university that refuses to take ethical dilemmas seriously violates its basic obligations to society.")

Religious colleges have always practiced a similar preaching. But some 500 schools now offer courses in the field. The Government supports such studies with a program known as EVIST, which stands for Ethics and Values in Science and Technology (and which sounds as though a computer had already taken charge of the matter). "The modern university is rooted in the scientific method, having essentially turned its back on religion," says Steven Muller, president of Johns Hopkins. "The scientific method is a marvelous means of inquiry, but it really doesn't provide a value system. The biggest failing in higher education today is that we fall short in exposing students to values."

Charles Muscatine, a professor of English at Berkeley and member of a committee that is analyzing liberal arts curriculums for the Association of American Colleges, is even harsher. He calls today's educational programs "a marvelous convenience for a mediocre society." The key goal of education, says Muscatine, should be "informed decision making that recognizes there is a moral and ethical component to life." Instead, he says, most universities are "propagating the dangerous myth that technical skills are more important than ethical reasoning."

Psychiatrist Robert Coles, who teaches at both Harvard and Duke, is still more emphatic in summing up the need: "Reading, writing and arithmetic. That's what we've got to start with, and all that implies, at every level. If people can't use good, strong language, they can't think clearly, and if they haven't been trained to use good, strong language, they become vulnerable to all the junk that comes their way. They should be taught philosophy, moral philosophy and theology. They ought to be asked to think about moral issues, especially about what use is going to be made of knowledge, and why—a kind of moral reflection that I think has been supplanted by a more technological education. Replacing moral philosophy with psychology has been a disaster, an absolute disaster!"

Each of these five ways to wisdom has its strengths and weaknesses, of course. The idea that education provides better jobs promises practical rewards for both the student and the society that trains him, but it can leave him undernourished in the possibilities of life away from work. The idea that education means the acquisition of a cultural heritage does give the student some grasp of that heritage, but it can also turn into glib superficialities or sterile erudition. The idea that education consists mainly of training the mind does provide a method for further education, but it can also make method seem more important than knowledge. So can the idea that education is a form of self-development. And the teaching of ethics can unfortunately become a teaching of conventional pieties.

To define is to limit, as we all learned in school, and to categorize is to oversimplify. To some extent, the five ways to wisdom all overlap and blend, and though every educator has his own sense of priorities, none would admit that he does not aspire to all five goals. Thus the student who has mastered the riches of Western civilization has probably also learned to think for himself and to see the moral purposes of life. And surely such a paragon can find a good job even in the recession of 1982.

Are there specific ways to come nearer to achieving these goals? The most obvious is money. Good teachers cost money; libraries cost money; so do remedial classes for those who were short-changed in earlier years. Only mediocrity comes cheap. Those who groan at the rising price of college tuition (up as much as $7,000 since 1972) may not realize that overall, taking enrollment growth into account, college budgets have just barely kept up with inflation. Indeed, adjusted for inflation, four years of college today costs less than a decade ago, and faculty salaries in real dollars declined about 20% during the 1970s. Crocodile tears over the cost of higher education come in waves from the Federal Government, which has so far held spending to roughly 1981 levels, and proposes deep cuts (*e.g.*, nearly 40% in basic grants) by 1985. This is an economy comparable to skimping on the maintenance of an expensive machine.

But money alone will not solve all problems, as is often said, and this is particularly true in the field of education. If improving the quality of American education is a matter of urgent national concern—and it should be—then what is required besides more dollars is more sense: a widespread rededication to a number of obvious but somewhat neglected principles. That probing research and hard thinking be demanded of students (and of teachers too). That academic results be tested and measured. That intellectual excellence be not just acknowledged but rewarded.

These principles admittedly did serve the system that educated primarily those few who were born into the governing classes, but the fact that elitist education once supported elitist politics does not mean that egalitarian politics requires egalitarian education. Neither minds nor ideas are all the same.

All that the schools can be asked to promise is that everyone will be educated to the limit of his capacities. Exactly what this means, everyone must discover for himself. At the community college minimum, it may have to mean teaching basic skills, at least until the weakened high schools begin doing their job properly, as Philosopher Mortimer Adler urges in his new *Paideia Proposal*. This calls for a standardized high school curriculum in three categories: fundamental knowledge such as history, science and arts; basic skills such as reading and mathematical computation; and critical understanding of ideas and values. These essentials must really be taught, not just certified with a passing grade. Beyond such practical benefits, though, and beyond the benefits that come from exercising the muscles of the mind, higher education must ultimately serve the higher purpose of perpetuating whatever it is in civilization that is worth perpetuating. Or as Ezra Pound once said of the craft that he later betrayed, "The function of literature is precisely that it does incite humanity to continue living."

This is the core of the core idea, and surely it is by now indisputable that every college student improves by learning the fundamentals of science, literature, art, history. Harvard's Rosovsky may be right in suggesting that it is "not necessary" to have read Shakespeare as part of the process of learning how to think, but he is probably wrong. Not because anyone really *needs* to have shared in Lear's howling rage or because anyone can earn a better salary from having heard Macbeth declaim "Tomorrow and tomorrow and tomorrow . . ." But he is enriched by knowing these things, impoverished by not knowing them. And *The Marriage of Figaro* enriches. *The Cherry Orchard* enriches. *The City of God* enriches. So does a mastery of Greek, or of subnuclear particles, or of Gödel's theorem.

In a sense, there really is no core, except as a series of arbitrary choices, for there is no limit to the possibilities of learning. There are times when these possibilities seem overwhelming, and one hears echoes of Socrates' confession, "All I know is that I know nothing." Yet that too is a challenge. "We shall not cease from exploration," as T.S. Eliot put it, "and the end of all our exploring / Will be to arrive where we started / And know the place for the first time." The seemingly momentous years of schooling, then, are only the beginning.

Henry Adams, who said in *The Education of Henry Adams* that Harvard "taught little, and that little ill," was 37 when he took up the study of Saxon legal codes and 42 when he first turned to writing the history of the Jefferson and Madison Administrations, and 49 when he laboriously began on Chinese. In his 50s, a tiny, wiry figure with a graying beard, the future master of Gothic architecture solemnly learned to ride a bicycle.

The Problem
of Identity

Jennifer Crichton's "Who Shall I Be?" reminds us that going away to college is a marvellous opportunity to re-form one's identity, to start over in a new and better role. Her easy, breezy, journalistic style does not quite conceal the fact that identity, for centuries a problem mainly for philosophers and psychologists, has in recent times become a problem for most of us. As the eminent public servant John Gardner has put it:

> Old communities and belief systems have broken down. With few exceptions a swiftly changing society has withdrawn from the individual the emotional supports of custom, tradition, family solidarity, religion, stable relationships, codes of conduct, and community coherence. . . . In a day when families and traditions were stable, when national and local loyalties were powerful, young people didn't ask "Who am I?" They knew.[1]

It is no wonder that many a young person feels the need to consciously create an identity, or to search for "the real me" under the flimsy and temporary covering of recently acquired tastes, clothes, and manners.

The voice in the next essay, by Zora Neale Hurston, is that of a person who has an identity, understands it, and likes it. Conversely, Walter Mitty, the hero of James Thurber's classic comic story which follows, falls back repeatedly on a fantasy life richly supplied with identities far different from his own. Next, the essay

---

[1]From an essay by Gardner in *On the Meaning of the University*, ed. Sterling M. McMurrin (Salt Lake City: University of Utah Press, 1976), p. 59.

by the daily columnist Ellen Goodman reports her concern that "we seem increasingly dependent on work for our sense of self." The last prose piece in the section, and the most sustained of all, is a reflection by William Kilpatrick on how chronic change in our society undermines our sense of identity.

The section ends with two poems. In the first Denise Levertov describes alternate and contradictory selves she can imagine for herself; in the second W. H. Auden imagines a person who seems to have no identity at all.

Who Shall I Be?

Jennifer Crichton

Jennifer Crichton was born in New York City in 1957, and in due course, as the following article relates, was driven up to Brown University for college. She majored in creative writing (at Brown called "semiotics"), and after graduation, she says, she "bummed around the West, doing all the things a young writer is supposed to do." With increasing recognition as a freelance writer she returned to the East, now lives in upstate New York, and contributes regularly to such magazines as Mademoiselle *and* Ms. *Her first novel,* Delivery, A Nurse-Midwife Story, *was published in 1986. "Who Shall I Be?" appeared in* Ms./Campus Times *in 1984.*

The student is a soul in transit, coming from one place en route to someplace else. Moving is the American way, after all. Our guiding principle is the fresh start, our foundation the big move, and nothing seduces like the promise of a clean slate.

"Do you realize how many people saw me throw up at Bob Stonehill's party in tenth grade? A lot of people," says my friend Anne. "How many forgot about it? Maybe two or three. Do you know how much I wanted to go someplace where nobody knew I threw up all over Bob Stonehill's living room in tenth grade? Very much. This may not seem like much of a justification for going away to college, but it was for me." Going away to college gives us a chance to rinse off part of our past, to shake off our burdensome reputations.

We've already survived the crises of being known, allowing how American high schools are as notoriously well-organized as totalitarian regimes, complete with secret police, punishment without trial, and banishment. High school society loves a label, cruelly infatuated with pinning down every species of student. Hilary is a klutz, Julie is a slut, and Michele a gossiping bitch who eats like a pig.

No wonder so many of us can't wait to be free of our old identities and climb inside a new skin in college. Even flattering reputations can be as confining as a pair of too-tight shoes. But identity is tricky stuff, constructed with mirrors. How you see yourself is a composite reflection of how you appear to friends, family, and lovers. In college, the fact that familiar mirrors aren't throwing back a familiar picture is both liberating and disorienting (maybe that's why so many colleges have freshman "orientation week").

"I guess you could call it an identity crisis," Andrea, a junior now, says of her freshman year. "It was the first time nobody knew who I was. I wasn't even anybody's daughter any more. I had always been the best and brightest—what was I going to do now, walk around the dorm with a sign around my neck saying 'Former High School Valedictorian?' "

For most of my college years, I was in hot pursuit of an identity crisis, especially after a Comparative Literature major informed me that the Chinese definition of "crisis" was "dangerous opportunity," with the emphasis on opportunity. On college applications, where there were blanks for your nickname, I carefully wrote "Rusty," although none of my friends (despite the fact that I have red hair) had ever, even for a whimsical moment, considered calling me that. I was the high-strung, sensitive, acne-blemished, antiauthoritarian, would-be writer. If I went through a day without some bizarre mood swing, people asked me what was wrong. I didn't even have the leeway to be the cheerful, smiling sort of girl I thought I might have it in me to be. My reputation seemed etched in stone, and I was pretty damn sick of it. As I pictured her, Rusty was the blithe spirit who would laugh everything off, shrug at perils as various as freshman mixers, bad grades, and cafeterias jammed with aloof strangers, and in general pass through a room with all the vitality and appeal of a cool gust of wind.

But when I arrived at college, Rusty had vaporized. She was simply not in the station wagon that drove me up to campus. Much of college had to do with filling in the blanks, but changing myself would not be so easy, so predictable, so clichéd.

My parents, acting as anxious overseers on the hot, humid day I took my new self to college, seemed bound by a demonic ESP to sabotage my scarcely budding new identity. After a summer planning how I would metamorphose into the great American ideal, the normal teenage girl, I heard my mother tell my roommate, "I think you'll like Jenny—she's quite the oddball." Luckily, my roommate was saturated with all kinds of information the first day of college had flung at her, and the last thing she was paying attention to were the off-the-cuff remarks this oddball's mother was making. My unmarked reputation kept its sheen as it waited for me to cautiously build it up according to plan. My parents left without any further blunders, except to brush my bangs from my eyes ("You'll get a headache, Sweetheart") and foist on what had been a blissfully bare dormitory room an excruciatingly ugly lamp from home. As soon as the station wagon became a distant mote of dust on the highway, I pulled my bangs back over my eyes in my New Wave fashion of choice, tossed the ugly lamp in the nearest trash can, and did what I came to college to do. Anonymous, alone, without even a name, I would start over and become the kind of person I was meant to be: like myself, but better, with all my failures, rejections, and sexual indiscretions relegated to a history I hoped none of my new acquaintances would ever hear of.

Why was it, I wondered, when *any* change seemed possible that year, had it been so impossible in high school? For one thing, people know us well enough to see when we're attempting a change, and change can look embarrassingly like a public admission of weakness. Our secret desires, and the fact that we're not entirely pleased with ourselves, are on display. To change in public under the scrutiny of the most hypercritical witnesses in the world—other high school students—is to risk failure ("Look how cool she's trying to be, the jerk!") or succeeding but betraying friends in the process ("I don't understand her any more," they say, hurt and angry) or feeling so much like a fraud that you're forced to back down. And while we live at home, parental expectations, from the lovingly hopeful to the intolerably ambitious, apply the pressure of an invisible but very effective mold.

Jacki dressed in nothing but baggy Levi's and flannel shirts for what seemed to be the endless duration of high school, even though she came to a sort of truce with her developing woman's body in eleventh grade and wasn't averse any longer to looking pretty. Looking good in college was a fantasy she savored because in high school, "I didn't want to make the attempt in public and then fail," she explains now, looking pulled-together and chic. "I thought everyone would think I was trying to look good but I only managed to look weird. And I didn't want a certain group of girls who were very image-conscious to think they'd won some kind of victory either, that I was changing to please them.

"So I waited for college, and wore nice, new clothes right off the bat so nobody would know me any other way. I had set my expectations too high, though—I sort of thought that I'd be transformed into a kind of femme fatale or something. When I wasn't measuring up to what I'd imagined, I almost ditched the whole thing until I realized that at least I wasn't sabotaging myself any more. When I ran into a friend from high school, even though I had gotten used to the nice way I looked, I was scared that she could see right through my disguise. That's how I felt for a long time: a slobby girl just pretending to be pulled together."

At first, any change can feel uncomfortably like a pretense, an affectation. Dana had been a punked-out druggy in high school, so worried about being considered a grind that she didn't use a fraction of her considerable vocabulary when she was around her anti-intellectual friends. She promised herself to get serious academically in college, but the first night she spent studying in the science library, she recalls, "I half-expected the other kids to look twice at me, as if my fish-out-of-water feeling was showing. Of course, it wasn't. But it was schizophrenic at first, as if I were an impostor only playing at being smart. But when you do something long enough, that thing becomes *you*. It's not playing any more. It's what you are."

Wanting to change yourself finds its source in two wellsprings: self-hatred and self-affirmation. Self-affirmation takes what already exists in your personality (even if slightly stunted or twisted) and encourages its growth. Where self-affirmation is expansive, self-hatred is reductive, negating one's own personality while appropriating qualities external to it and applying them like thick pancake makeup.

Joan's thing was to hang out with rich kids with what can only be described as a vengeance. She dressed in Ralph Lauren, forayed to town for $75 haircuts, and complained about the tackiness of mutual friends. But after a late night of studying, Joan allowed her self-control to slip long enough to tell me of her upbringing. Her mother was a cocktail waitress and Joan had never even found out her father's name. She and her mother had trucked about from one Western trailer park to another, and Joan always went to school dogged by her wrong-side-of-the-tracks background. That Joan had come through her hardscrabble life with such strong intellectual achievement seemed a lot more creditable—not to mention interesting—than the effortless achievements of many of our more privileged classmates. Joan didn't think so, and, I suppose in fear I'd blow her cover (I never did), she cut me dead after her moment's indulgence in self-revelation. Joan was rootless and anxious, alienated not only from her background but, by extension, from herself, and paid a heavy psychic price. This wasn't change: this was lies. She scared me. But we learn a lot about friends from the kinds of masks they choose to wear.

After all, role-playing to some degree is the prerogative of youth. A woman of romance, rigorous academic, trendy New Waver, intense politico, unsentimental jock, by turn—we have the chance to experiment as we decide the kind of person we want to become. And a stereotypical role, adopted temporarily, can offer refuge from the swirl of confusing choices available to us, by confining us to the limits of a type. Returning to my old self after playing a role, I find I'm slightly different, a little bit more than what I was. To contradict one's self is to transcend it.

As occasional fugitives from our families, we all sometimes do what Joan did. Sometimes you need a radical change in order to form an identity independent of your family, even if that change is a weird but transient reaction. My friend Lisa came from a family of feminists and academics. When she returned home from school for Thanksgiving, dressed as a "ditsy dame" straight out of a beach-blanket-bingo movie, she asked me, "How do you think I look? I've been planning this since tenth grade. Isn't it great?" Well, er, yes, it was great—not because she looked like a Barbie doll incarnate but because nobody would ever automatically connect her life with that of her parents again.

Another friend, Dan, went from a Southern military academy to a Quaker college in the North to execute his scheme of becoming a serious intellectual. The transformation went awry after a few months, partly because his own self was too likably irrepressible. It wouldn't lie down and play dead. "I kept running into myself like a serpent chasing its tail," as he puts it. But his openness to change resulted in a peculiar amalgamation of cultures whose charm lies in his realizing that, while he's of his background, he's not identical to it. Most of our personalities and bodies are just as stubbornly averse to being extinguished, even if the fantasy of a symbolic suicide and a renaissance from the ashes takes its obsessive toll on our thoughts now and again. But a blank slate isn't the same as a blank self, and the point of the blank slate that college provides is not to erase the past, but to sketch out a new history with a revisionist's perspective and an optimist's acts.

And what of my changes? Well, when I was friendly and happy in college, nobody gaped as though I had sprouted a tail. I learned to laugh things off as Rusty might have done, and there was one particular counterman at the corner luncheonette who called me Red, which was the closest I came to being known as Rusty.

What became of Rusty? Senior year, I stared at an announcement stating the dates that banks would be recruiting on campus, and Rusty materialized for the first time since freshman year. Rusty was a Yuppie now, and I pictured her dressed in a navy-blue suit, looking uneasily like Mary Cunningham,° setting her sights on Citibank. I was still the highstrung, oversensitive, would-be writer (I'm happy to report my skin did clear up), but a little better, who left the corporate world to Rusty. For myself, I have the slate of the rest of my life to write on.

How It Feels to Be Colored Me

Zora Neale Hurston

Zora Neale Hurston (1891–1960) was born in Eatonville, Florida, and educated first at Howard University in Washington, D.C., then at Barnard College and Columbia University in New York City. She was a prolific writer; her books include Their Eyes Were Watching God *(1937), of which Alice Walker says "There is no book more important to me," and an autobiography,* Dust Tracks on a Road *(1942). Under the tutelage of*

Mary Cunningham   An M.B.A. from Harvard (1979) whose meteoric success and subsequent resignation from the Bendix Corporation attracted attention in the national press.

anthropologist Franz Boas, she also became a major Afro-American folk-lorist.

In a biographical essay, Lillie P. Howard describes Hurston's works as "manifestos of selfhood, as affirmations of blackness." The essay we print here provides a fine example. First published in The World Tomorrow *(May 1928), it has been reprinted in a collection entitled* I Love Myself When I Am Laughing *(1979), edited by Alice Walker.*

I am colored but I offer nothing in the way of extenuating circumstances except the fact that I am the only Negro in the United States whose grandfather on the mother's side was *not* an Indian chief.

I remember the very day that I became colored. Up to my thirteenth year I lived in the little Negro town of Eatonville, Florida. It is exclusively a colored town. The only white people I knew passed through the town going to or coming from Orlando. The native whites rode dusty horses, the Northern tourists chugged down the sandy village road in automobiles. The town knew the Southerners and never stopped cane chewing when they passed. But the Northerners were something else again. They were peered at cautiously from behind curtains by the timid. The more venturesome would come out on the porch to watch them go past and got just as much pleasure out of the tourists as the tourists got out of the village.

The front porch might seem a daring place for the rest of the town, but it was a gallery seat to me. My favorite place was atop the gate-post. Proscenium box for a born first-nighter. Not only did I enjoy the show, but I didn't mind the actors knowing that I liked it. I usually spoke to them in passing. I'd wave at them and when they returned my salute, I would say something like this: "Howdy-do-well-I-thank-you-where-you-goin'?" Usually the automobile or the horse paused at this, and after a queer exchange of compliments, I would probably "go a piece of the way" with them, as we say in farthest Florida. If one of my family happened to come to the front in time to see me, of course negotiations would be rudely broken off. But even so, it is clear that I was the first "welcome-to-our-state" Floridian, and I hope the Miami Chamber of Commerce will please take notice.

During this period, white people differed from colored to me only in that they rode through town and never lived there. They liked to hear me "speak pieces" and sing and wanted to see me dance the parse-me-la, and gave me generously of their small silver for doing these things, which seemed strange to me for I wanted to do them so much that I needed bribing to stop. Only they didn't know it. The colored people gave no dimes. They deplored any joyful tendencies in me, but I was their Zora nevertheless. I belonged to them, to the nearby hotels, to the county— everybody's Zora.

But changes came in the family when I was thirteen, and I was sent to school in Jacksonville. I left Eatonville, the town of the oleanders, as Zora. When I disembarked from the river-boat at Jacksonville, she was no more. It seemed that I had suffered a sea change. I was not Zora of Orange County any more, I was now a little colored girl. I found it out in certain ways. In my heart as well as in the mirror, I became a fast brown— warranted not to rub nor run.

But I am not tragically colored. There is no great sorrow dammed up in my soul, nor lurking behind my eyes. I do not mind at all. I do not belong to the sobbing school of Negrohood who hold that nature somehow has given them a lowdown dirty deal and whose feelings are all hurt about it. Even in the helter-skelter skirmish that is my life, I have seen that the world is to the strong regardless of a little pigmentation more or less. No, I do not weep at the world—I am too busy sharpening my oyster knife.

Someone is always at my elbow reminding me that I am the grand-daughter of slaves. It fails to register depression with me. Slavery is sixty years in the past. The operation was successful and the patient is doing well, thank you. The terrible struggle that made me an American out of a potential slave said "On the line!" The Reconstruction said "Get set!"; and the generation before said "Go!" I am off to a flying start and I must not halt in the stretch to look behind and weep. Slavery is the price I paid for civilization, and the choice was not with me. It is a bully adventure and worth all that I have paid through my ancestors for it. No one on earth ever had a greater chance for glory. The world to be won and nothing to be lost. It is thrilling to think—to know that for any act of mine, I shall get twice as much praise or twice as much blame. It is quite exciting to hold the center of the national stage, with the spectators not knowing whether to laugh or to weep.

The position of my white neighbor is much more difficult. No brown specter pulls up a chair beside me when I sit down to eat. No dark ghost thrusts its leg against mine in bed. The game of keeping what one has is never so exciting as the game of getting.

I do not always feel colored. Even now I often achieve the unconscious Zora of Eatonville before the Hegira. I feel most colored when I am thrown against a sharp white background.

For instance at Barnard. "Beside the waters of the Hudson" I feel my race. Among the thousand white persons, I am a dark rock surged upon, overswept by a creamy sea. I am surged upon and overswept, but through it all, I remain myself. When covered by the waters, I am; and the ebb but reveals me again.

Sometimes it is the other way around. A white person is set down in our midst, but the contrast is just as sharp for me. For instance, when I sit in the drafty basement that is The New World Cabaret with a white person, my color comes. We enter chatting about any little nothing that we have in common and are seated by the jazz waiters. In the abrupt way that jazz orchestras have, this one plunges into a number. It loses no time in circumlocutions, but gets right down to business. It constricts the thorax and splits the heart with its tempo and narcotic harmonies. This orchestra grows rambunctious, rears on its hind legs and attacks the tonal veil with primitive fury, rending it, clawing it until it breaks through to the jungle beyond. I follow those heathen—follow them exultingly. I dance wildly inside myself; I yell within, I whoop; I shake my assegai above my head, I hurl it true to the mark *yeeeeooww!* I am in the jungle and living in the jungle way. My face is painted red and yellow and my body is painted blue. My pulse is throbbing like a war drum. I want to slaughter something—give pain, give death to what, I do not know. But the piece ends. The men of the orchestra wipe their lips and rest their fingers. I creep back slowly to the veneer we call civilization with the last tone and find the white friend sitting motionless in his seat, smoking calmly.

"Good music they have here," he remarks, drumming the table with his fingertips.

Music! The great blobs of purple and red emotion have not touched him. He has only heard what I felt. He is far away and I see him but dimly across the ocean and the continent that have fallen between us. He is so pale with his whiteness then and I am *so* colored.

At certain times I have no race, I am *me*. When I set my hat at a certain angle and saunter down Seventh Avenue, Harlem City, feeling as snooty as the lions in front of the Forty-Second Street Library, for instance. So far as my feelings are concerned, Peggy Hopkins Joyce on the Boule Mich with her gorgeous raiment, stately carriage, knees knocking together in a most aristocratic manner, has nothing on me. The cosmic Zora emerges. I belong to no race nor time. I am the eternal feminine with its string of beads.

I have no separate feeling about being an American citizen and colored. I am merely a fragment of the Great Soul that surges within the boundaries. My country, right or wrong.

Sometimes, I feel discriminated against, but it does not make me angry. It merely astonishes me. How *can* any deny themselves the pleasure of my company! It's beyond me.

But in the main, I feel like a brown bag of miscellany propped against a wall. Against a wall in company with other bags, white, red and yellow. Pour out the contents, and there is discovered a jumble of small things priceless and worthless. A first-water diamond, an empty spool, bits of broken glass, lengths of string, a key to a door long since crumbled away, a rusty knife-blade, old shoes saved for a road that never was and never will be, a nail bent under the weight of things too heavy for any nail, a dried flower or two, still a little fragrant. In your hand is the brown bag.

On the ground before you is the jumble it held—so much like the jumble in the bags, could they be emptied, that all might be dumped in a single heap and the bags refilled without altering the content of any greatly. A bit of colored glass more or less would not matter. Perhaps that is how the Great Stuffer of Bags filled them in the first place—who knows?

The Secret Life of Walter Mitty

James Thurber

James Thurber (1894–1961), one of the greatest of American humorists, grew up in Columbus, Ohio, and for a time attended Ohio State University. After World War I (his poor eyesight kept him out of military service) he worked as a reporter in Columbus, Chicago, Paris, and New York, and in 1926 began the long and famous association with The New Yorker *chronicled in* The Years with Ross *(1959). Thurber was a prolific essayist, cartoonist, and writer of short stories and children's books, and did first-rate work in all of these media. A few of his best-known volumes are* Is Sex Necessary? *(with E. B. White, 1929),* My Life and Hard Times *(1933),* Fables for Our Time *(1940), and* The Thurber Carnival *(1945).*

"The Secret Life of Walter Mitty," his most famous story, was first published in The New Yorker *in 1939 and is printed below from the collection* My World—and Welcome to It *(1943). Its hero is a perfect example of the "Thurber man," who appears often in his stories, a "mild little man" who copes with life's problems—usually including a ferociously dominating woman—by taking refuge in fantasy. The story well illustrates Thurber's comic mixture of the realistic and the absurd, his feeling for words and images, at once economical and expressive, his psychological keenness, and his abiding sympathy with daydreaming.*

"We're going through!" The Commander's voice was like thin ice breaking. He wore his full-dress uniform, with the heavily braided white cap pulled down rakishly over one cold gray eye. "We can't make it, sir. It's spoiling for a hurricane, if you ask me." "I'm not asking you, Lieutenant Berg," said the Commander. "Throw on the power lights! Rev her up to 8,500! We're going through!" The pounding of the cylinders increased: ta-pocketa-pocketa-pocketa-*pocketa-pocketa*. The Commander stared at the ice forming on the pilot window. He walked over and twisted a row of complicated dials. "Switch on No. 8 auxiliary!" he shouted. "Switch on No. 8 auxiliary!" repeated Lieutenant Berg. "Full strength in No. 3 turret!" shouted the Commander. "Full strength in No. 3 turret!" The crew, bend-

ing to their various tasks in the huge, hurtling eight-engined Navy hydro-
plane, looked at each other and grinned. "The Old Man'll get us through,"
they said to one another. "The Old Man ain't afraid of Hell!" . . .

"Not so fast! You're driving too fast!" said Mrs. Mitty. "What are you
driving so fast for?"

"Hmm?" said Walter Mitty. He looked at his wife, in the seat beside
him, with shocked astonishment. She seemed grossly unfamiliar, like a
strange woman who had yelled at him in a crowd. "You were up to
fifty-five," she said. "You know I don't like to go more than forty. You were
up to fifty-five." Walter Mitty drove on toward Waterbury in silence, the
roaring of the SN202 through the worst storm in twenty years of Navy
flying fading in the remote, intimate airways of his mind. "You're tensed
up again," said Mrs. Mitty. "It's one of your days. I wish you'd let Dr.
Renshaw look you over."

Walter Mitty stopped the car in front of the building where his wife
went to have her hair done. "Remember to get those overshoes while I'm
having my hair done," she said. "I don't need overshoes," said Mitty. She
put her mirror back into her bag. "We've been all through that," she said,
getting out of the car. "You're not a young man any longer." He raced the
engine a little. "Why don't you wear your gloves? Have you lost your
gloves?" Walter Mitty reached in a pocket and brought out the gloves. He
put them on, but after she had turned and gone into the building and he
had driven on to a red light, he took them off again. "Pick it up, brother!"
snapped a cop as the light changed, and Mitty hastily pulled on his gloves
and lurched ahead. He drove around the streets aimlessly for a time, and
then he drove past the hospital on his way to the parking lot.

. . . "It's the millionaire banker, Wellington McMillan," said the pretty
nurse. "Yes?" said Walter Mitty, removing his gloves slowly. "Who has
the case?" "Dr. Renshaw and Dr. Benbow, but there are two specialists
here, Dr. Remington from New York and Mr. Pritchard-Mitford from
London. He flew over." A door opened down a long, cool corridor and Dr.
Renshaw came out. He looked distraught and haggard. "Hello, Mitty," he
said. "We're having the devil's own time with McMillan, the millionaire
banker and close personal friend of Roosevelt. Obstreosis of the ductal
tract. Tertiary. Wish you'd take a look at him." "Glad to," said Mitty.

In the operating room there were whispered introductions: "Dr. Remington, Dr. Mitty. Mr. Pritchard-Mitford, Dr. Mitty." "I've read your book
on streptothricosis," said Pritchard-Mitford, shaking hands. "A brilliant
performance, sir." "Thank you," said Walter Mitty. "Didn't know you
were in the States, Mitty," grumbled Remington. "Coals to Newcastle,
bringing Mitford and me up here for a tertiary." "You are very kind," said
Mitty. A huge, complicated machine, connected to the operating table,
with many tubes and wires, began at this moment to go pocketa-pocketa-
pocketa. "The new anesthetizer is giving way!" shouted an interne.
"There is no one in the East who knows how to fix it!" "Quiet, man!" said

Mitty, in a low, cool voice. He sprang to the machine, which was now going pocketa-pocketa-queep-pocketa-queep. He began fingering delicately a row of glistening dials. "Give me a fountain pen!" he snapped. Someone handed him a fountain pen. He pulled a faulty piston out of the machine and inserted the pen in its place. "That will hold for ten minutes," he said. "Get on with the operation." A nurse hurried over and whispered to Renshaw, and Mitty saw the man turn pale. "Coreopsis has set in," said Renshaw nervously. "If you would take over, Mitty?" Mitty looked at him and at the craven figure of Benbow, who drank, and at the grave, uncertain faces of the two great specialists. "If you wish," he said. They slipped a white gown on him; he adjusted a mask and drew on thin gloves; nurses handed him shining . . .

"Back it up, Mac! Look out for that Buick!" Walter Mitty jammed on the brakes. "Wrong lane, Mac," said the parking-lot attendant, looking at Mitty closely. "Gee. Yeh," muttered Mitty. He began cautiously to back out of the lane marked "Exit Only." "Leave her sit there," said the attendant. "I'll put her away." Mitty got out of the car. "Hey, better leave the key." "Oh," said Mitty, handing the man the ignition key. The attendant vaulted into the car, backed it up with insolent skill, and put it where it belonged.

They're so damn cocky, thought Walter Mitty, walking along Main Street; they think they know everything. Once he had tried to take his chains off, outside New Milford, and he had got them wound around the axles. A man had had to come out in a wrecking car and unwind them, a young, grinning garageman. Since then Mrs. Mitty always made him drive to a garage to have the chains taken off. The next time, he thought, I'll wear my right arm in a sling; they won't grin at me then. I'll have my right arm in a sling and they'll see I couldn't possibly take the chains off myself. He kicked at the slush on the sidewalk. "Overshoes," he said to himself, and he began looking for a shoe store.

When he came out into the street again, with the overshoes in a box under his arm, Walter Mitty began to wonder what the other thing was his wife had told him to get. She had told him, twice, before they set out from their house for Waterbury. In a way he hated these weekly trips to town—he was always getting something wrong. Kleenex, he thought, Squibb's, razor blades? No. Toothpaste, toothbrush, bicarbonate, carborundum, initiative and referendum? He gave it up. But she would remember it. "Where's the what's-its-name?" she would ask. "Don't tell me you forgot the what's-its-name." A newsboy went by shouting something about the Waterbury trial.

. . . "Perhaps this will refresh your memory." The District Attorney suddenly thrust a heavy automatic at the quiet figure on the witness stand. "Have you ever seen this before?" Walter Mitty took the gun and examined it expertly. "This is my Webley-Vickers 50.80," he said calmly. An excited buzz ran around the courtroom. The Judge rapped for order.

"You are a crack shot with any sort of firearms, I believe?" said the District Attorney, insinuatingly. "Objection!" shouted Mitty's attorney. "We have shown that the defendant could not have fired the shot. We have shown that he wore his right arm in a sling on the night of the fourteenth of July." Walter Mitty raised his hand briefly and the bickering attorneys were stilled. "With any known make of gun," he said evenly, "I could have killed Gregory Fitzhurst at three hundred feet *with my left hand.*" Pandemonium broke loose in the courtroom. A woman's scream rose above the bedlam and suddenly a lovely, dark-haired girl was in Walter Mitty's arms. The District Attorney struck at her savagely. Without rising from his chair, Mitty let the man have it on the point of the chin. "You miserable cur!" . . .

"Puppy biscuit," said Walter Mitty. He stopped walking and the buildings of Waterbury rose up out of the misty courtroom and surrounded him again. A woman who was passing laughed. "He said 'Puppy biscuit,'" she said to her companion. "That man said 'Puppy biscuit' to himself." Walter Mitty hurried on. He went into an A. & P.,° not the first one he came to but a smaller one farther up the street. "I want some biscuit for small, young dogs," he said to the clerk. "Any special brand, sir?" The greatest pistol shot in the world thought a moment. "It says 'Puppies Bark for It' on the box," said Walter Mitty.

His wife would be through at the hairdresser's in fifteen minutes, Mitty saw in looking at his watch, unless they had trouble drying it; sometimes they had trouble drying it. She didn't like to get to the hotel first; she would want him to be there waiting for her as usual. He found a big leather chair in the lobby, facing a window, and he put the overshoes and the puppy biscuit on the floor beside it. He picked up an old copy of *Liberty* and sank down into the chair. "Can Germany Conquer the World Through the Air?" Walter Mitty looked at the pictures of bombing planes and of ruined streets.

. . . "The cannonading has got the wind up in young Raleigh, sir," said the sergeant. Captain Mitty looked up at him through touseled hair. "Get him to bed," he said wearily. "With the others. I'll fly alone." "But you can't, sir," said the sergeant anxiously. "It takes two men to handle that bomber and the Archies° are pounding hell out of the air. Von Richtman's circus° is between here and Saulier." "Somebody's got to get that ammunition dump," said Mitty. "I'm going over. Spot of brandy?" He poured a drink for the sergeant and one for himself. War thundered and whined around the dugout and battered at the door. There was a rending of wood

---

A. & P. A grocery-store chain.
Archies Anti-aircraft guns used in World War I.
Von Richtman's circus An imperfect reference to the German air ace Baron Manfred von Richthofen, "the Red Baron."

and splinters flew through the room. "A bit of a near thing," said Captain Mitty carelessly. "The box barrage is closing in," said the sergeant. "We only live once, Sergeant," said Mitty, with his faint, fleeting smile. "Or do we?" He poured another brandy and tossed it off. "I never see a man could hold his brandy like you, sir," said the sergeant. "Begging your pardon, sir." Captain Mitty stood up and strapped on his huge Webley-Vickers automatic. "It's forty kilometers through hell, sir," said the sergeant. Mitty finished one last brandy. "After all," he said softly, "what isn't?" The pounding of the cannon increased; there was the rat-tat-tatting of machine guns, and from somewhere came the menacing pocketa-pocketa-pocketa of the new flame-throwers. Walter Mitty walked to the door of the dugout humming "Auprès de Ma Blonde." He turned and waved to the sergeant. "Cheerio!" he said. . . .

Something struck his shoulder. "I've been looking all over this hotel for you," said Mrs. Mitty. "Why do you have to hide in this old chair? How did you expect me to find you?" "Things close in," said Walter Mitty vaguely. "What?" Mrs. Mitty said. "Did you get the what's-its-name? The puppy biscuit? What's in that box?" "Overshoes," said Mitty. "Couldn't you have put them on in the store?" "I was thinking," said Walter Mitty. "Does it ever occur to you that I am sometimes thinking?" She looked at him. "I'm going to take your temperature when I get you home," she said.

They went out through the revolving doors that made a faintly derisive whistling sound when you pushed them. It was two blocks to the parking lot. At the drugstore on the corner she said, "Wait here for me. I forgot something. I won't be a minute." She was more than a minute. Walter Mitty lighted a cigarette. It began to rain, rain with sleet in it. He stood up against the wall of the drugstore, smoking. . . . He put his shoulders back and his heels together. "To hell with the handkerchief," said Walter Mitty scornfully. He took one last drag on his cigarette and snapped it away. Then, with that faint, fleeting smile playing about his lips, he faced the firing squad; erect and motionless, proud and disdainful, Walter Mitty the Undefeated, inscrutable to the last.

A Working Community

Ellen Goodman

Ellen Goodman (born 1941) has been writing a feature column for the Boston Globe *since 1972. The column, now widely syndicated, has long been admired for its keen observation of American manners and morals, for its good sense, and for its rootedness in traditional values. One of her favorite subjects has been the change in our sense of sex roles, on which she has also written a book,* Turning Points *(1979), based on interviews with some 150 men and women all over the country.*

Goodman was educated at Radcliffe and worked as a reporter for the Detroit Free Press *and* Newsweek *before coming to the* Globe *in 1967. In 1979 she joined the NBC "Today Show" as commentator, and in 1980 received a Pulitzer Prize for journalism. She has since received many other honors. Her columns have been collected in three books:* Close to Home *(1979),* At Large *(1981), and* Keeping in Touch *(1985), from which we take the following piece.*

BOSTON—I have a friend who is a member of the medical community. It does not say that, of course, on the stationery that bears her home address. This membership comes from her hospital work.

I have another friend who is a member of the computer community. This is a fairly new subdivision of our economy, and yet he finds his sense of place in it.

Other friends and acquaintances of mine are members of the academic community, or the business community, or the journalistic community. Though you cannot find these on any map, we know where we belong.

None of us, mind you, was born into these communities. Nor did we move into them, U-Hauling our possessions along with us. None has papers to prove we are card-carrying members of one such group or another. Yet it seems that more and more of us are identified by work these days, rather than by street.

In the past, most Americans lived in neighborhoods. We were members of precincts or parishes or school districts. My dictionary still defines community, first of all in geographic terms, as "a body of people who live in one place."

But today fewer of us do our living in that one place; more of us just use it for sleeping. Now we call our towns "bedroom suburbs," and many of us, without small children as icebreakers, would have trouble naming all the people on our street.

It's not that we are more isolated today. It's that many of us have transferred a chunk of our friendships, a major portion of our everyday social lives, from home to office. As more of our neighbors work away from home, the workplace becomes our neighborhood.

The kaffeeklatsch of the fifties is the coffee break of the eighties. The water cooler, the hall, the elevator, and the parking lot are the back fences of these neighborhoods. The people we have lunch with day after day are those who know the running saga of our mother's operations, our child's math grades, our frozen pipes, and faulty transmissions.

We may be strangers at the supermarket that replaced the corner grocer, but we are known at the coffee shop in the lobby. We share with each other a cast of characters from the boss in the corner office to the crazy lady in Shipping, to the lovers in Marketing. It's not surprising that when researchers ask Americans what they like best about work, they say it is "the shmoose [chatter] factor." When they ask young mothers at home what they miss most about work, it is the people.

Not all the neighborhoods are empty, nor is every workplace a friendly playground. Most of us have had mixed experiences in these environments. Yet as one woman told me recently, she knows more about the people she passes on the way to her desk than on her way around the block.

Our new sense of community hasn't just moved from house to office building. The labels that we wear connect us with members from distant companies, cities, and states. We assume that we have something "in common" with other teachers, nurses, city planners.

It's not unlike the experience of our immigrant grandparents. Many who came to this country still identified themselves as members of the Italian community, the Irish community, the Polish community. They sought out and assumed connections with people from the old country. Many of us have updated that experience. We have replaced ethnic identity with professional identity, the way we replaced neighborhoods with the workplace.

This whole realignment of community is surely most obvious among the mobile professions. People who move from city to city seem to put roots down into their professions. In an age of specialists, they may have to search harder to find people who speak the same language.

I don't think that there is anything massively disruptive about this shifting sense of community. The continuing search for connection and shared enterprise is very human. But I do feel uncomfortable with our shifting identity. The balance has tipped and we seem increasingly dependent on work for our sense of self.

If our offices are our new neighborhoods, if our professional titles are our new ethnic tags, then how do we separate our selves from our jobs? Self-worth isn't just something to measure in the marketplace. But in these new communities, it becomes harder and harder to tell who we are without saying what we do.

FEBRUARY 1984

Identity in a Temporary Society
William Kilpatrick

William Kilpatrick (born 1940) was educated at Holy Cross, Harvard, and Purdue, where he earned a Ph.D. He is now a member of the faculty at

Boston College. His interest in the relationship between culture and psychological ideas has led to two books: Identity and Intimacy *(1975), from which we reprint the major part of Chapter 1, and* Psychological Seduction: The Failure of Modern Psychology *(1983), which deals with psychology and religion.*

At the parochial grammar school I attended we were taught that it was wrong to have impure thoughts. It was in fact a sin. This caused a lot of trouble for us because on the one hand we took our religion seriously and on the other we kept having impure thoughts. When confession time came each week it was always a problem deciding how many of these thoughts to admit to. I decided on three. Somehow three seemed like a good number—about what the normal Catholic boy should have, I guessed. Besides, I didn't want to scandalize the priest by letting him know the actual count.

In our school a good person was defined by the nuns as being, among other things, pure and chaste in thought, word and deed; as being, so it seemed, asexual. And we, if we wanted to be good (which we did) were supposed to define ourselves in the same way. In our self-definition there was no place for sexuality. But it was hard being "good." One constantly had to contend with desires that were inconsistent with one's narrowly defined self. The environment was full of temptations—magazine racks and tight sweaters—and one had either to compulsively restrict one's activities ("avoiding the near occasion of sin," as the church called it) or resort to obsessive rituals such as reciting "ejaculations" at three-second intervals. These were brief spurts of prayer designed to keep Satan at a distance, but the very thought of that word was enough to set off a new chain of impure speculations. It was a vicious circle.

Most of us, as time went on, learned to redefine ourselves on a larger scale and to admit the sexual part of our humanity which had, of course, been there all along. It was a process of letting in more reality, of widening the boundaries of self to take account of life's variety. One could, as it turned out, have impure thoughts and still be a good Catholic. It was only necessary either to broaden the definition of "good" or else restrict the meaning of "impure."

I don't recall how my own growth up from parochialism in this respect occurred. It may have been occasioned by the reading of an enlightened pamphlet in a darkened church. Or it may have been some absolution-weary priest, tired of shriving a child's daydreams, who gave me new perspectives on the nature of evil. More probably the change happened gradually through a process of reflection. At any rate I felt no great dislocation from my scrupulous past—only a little older and wiser. Whatever new definitions of the self I arrived at, there was always a continuity with what I had been, a solid sense of sameness winding through my life, a wide unbreakable ribbon tying it all together. After all, despite the changes, everything in my life was still there. For thirteen years, the same house with the same wisteria vine climbing to the roof, changing as I did, only in growing larger and stronger, the same neighborhood, the same friends, the weekly visits to aunts and uncles, cousins, and grandparents—all giving reassuring testimony to that essential continuity with my past.

Since the pace of change was slower in those days, continuity was not so difficult to achieve. But today the situation is different. In a constantly changing society, a sense of personal continuity becomes extremely important. In such a context it is necessary to redefine oneself many times, for rapid change creates sharp discontinuities which must be bridged in order to retain a unified sense of self. This sense of self, composed in large part of the experience of continuity, is what we call identity.

The Formation of Identity

A child doesn't have an identity so much as a collection of identifications. He identifies with his mother and father or with some aspect of their personalities, perhaps rejecting other aspects. As he grows he makes identifications with brothers and sisters, playmates, grandparents, folk heroes, athletes, and other figures; some more significant, some less so. These identifications may be transient, partial, unrealistic, even contradictory. Added together, they do not form a coherent or consistent sense of identity, but this is not yet a problem for the child.

For the adolescent it *is* a problem—the main problem. His body is growing rapidly and changing. His mind is becoming capable of high-level abstraction. He becomes acutely aware of possibilities. He begins to worry about his future. The adult world he is about to enter seems at odds with his dependent childhood. This internal revolution creates in him a need to pull his life together into a coherent unity. He needs to believe that the person he was as a child has persisted despite the changes—or else what was his childhood for? He has to find connections between the person he was and the person he anticipates he will be. If he is not quite the same as he was yesterday he would like to trace the history of that transformation; to find the links that bind past self to present self. In short, he seeks to create an identity that will bridge all the discontinuities of puberty.

Identity is not created all at once, nor is it ever really completed, but it takes shape gradually out of the successive identifications of childhood and those newly formed. These are slowly integrated into a new configuration which is both a coherent and unique whole. It is not an easy task. Consciously and unconsciously the growing child must somehow reconcile the identifications he has made with figures as diverse as his aging grandfather and the hero of the last movie he has seen. Out of the bag of partial identifications which he carries from his earliest years and out of the future toward which he aspires, he must synthesize a unique self he can call his own.

The Essential Self

It is only our sense of continuity that allows us to tolerate the contradictions and inconsistencies of such a process. A sense of continuity reassures us that despite the redefinitions we have made, there still persists an essential self. We may not be able to locate this bedrock foundation precisely, but without the sense that it exists, without the conviction that something essential endures, our identity would seem an insubstantial thing.

This is the self to which we believe we must be true; which we would prefer on the whole to keep faith with. And it is upon this core self that others rely when they trust us or take us at our word. Our self is their guarantee of fidelity; the part of us that can be held responsible. It is possible to retreat from many things we hold dear. Principles can be compromised and ideals sacrificed without completely losing our integrity. We can draw lines and redraw them if necessary and still retain our self-respect. But there is a point at which we must draw a line and stand fast, for beyond that point lies something indispensable. That something is the essence of what we mean by identity or the self.

Exactly where that point is we can never say. Certainly it differs from person to person. But when the self reveals itself it leaves no doubt that such a place exists. The life of Thomas More provides a point of reference. In it we can find the place at which one man located his sense of self. As a loyal subject of King Henry VIII, More was expected to sign an oath approving of the king's marriage to Anne Boleyn; as Lord Chancellor of the Realm and as a man who held the admiration of the populace, his assent was all the more crucial to Henry. More refused the oath. Not out of any sense of propriety or priggishness, but because it required him to swear to something he considered untrue, something that constituted a denial of God's revelation as he understood it. To consent to the oath would be to deny his faith.

As represented in Robert Bolt's play *A Man for All Seasons,* More comes under increasing pressure to sign. One by one his friends give in until Thomas is left alone against the king. To one of these friends he proclaims in defense of his dangerous obstinacy: "I will not give in because I oppose it—I do—not my pride, not my spleen, nor any other of my appetites but I do—*I!*"[1]

For his disloyalty More is imprisoned in the Tower. But in the face of

[1] Robert Bolt, *A Man for All Seasons* (New York: Random House, 1962), p. 123.

continued interrogation and the king's growing impatience he remains unmoved. Finally, More's family comes to him to plead that he sign the oath. Their appeals to his affection are matched only by More's appeal to his integrity. To his daughter he says:

> "When a man takes an oath, Meg, he's holding his own self in his own hands. Like water. [*He cups his hands*] And if he opens his fingers *then*—he needn't hope to find himself again. Some men aren't capable of this but I'd be loathe to think your father one of them."[2]

The rest of the story is well known. More is made to stand trial, and on the basis of trumped-up charges is sentenced to death and executed.

In his preface to the play, Bolt provides an explanation for More's behavior in what must stand as one of the finest statements on the ultimate meaning of identity:

> He knew where he began and left off, what area of himself he could yield to the encroachments of his enemies, and what to the encroachments of those he loved. It was a substantial area in both cases, for he had a proper sense of fear and was a busy lover. Since he was a clever man and a great lawyer he was able to retire from those areas in wonderfully good order, but at length he was asked to retreat from that final area where he located his self. And there this supple, humorous, unassuming and sophisticated person set like metal, was overtaken by an absolutely primitive rigor, and could no more be budged than a cliff.[3]

The perjured testimony which finally sends More to the gallows is given by one Richard Rich. In the career of Rich we see an opposite process at work—the dissolution of identity. In fact we can almost pinpoint the precise point at which it is abandoned. Rich is a young man who is anxious to enter into the world of affairs—at any price, as it turns out. What little sense of identity he has, threatens to be engulfed by his ambition. Yet one can see possibilities in this young man. He is a reflective person who admires More's integrity, and behind his adolescent intensity there glimmers the possibility of loyalty and courage. We detect in him an attempt, however feeble, to cling to whatever verities he has been schooled in; to find some continuity with a past that was more plain and honest than the cunning deceits of the courts and chambers through which he now moves.

But finally these possibilities never develop. The lure of power and money is too great. At one point in the play More has been given a silver goblet which he belatedly realizes to be a bribe. Rather than be influenced by it, he gives the goblet to Rich. Later Rich is being questioned by Thomas Cromwell, who is seeking some kind of damning evidence against More. Since Cromwell is a powerful man, Rich stands to gain considerably

---

[2]Ibid., p. 140.
[3]Ibid., p. xii.

by revealing what he knows. In his extended dialogue with Cromwell we can trace the disintegration of a self. Cromwell has just asked Rich if he believes he would never repeat anything said in friendship:

RICH: Yes!
CROMWELL: No, but seriously.
RICH: Why, yes!
CROMWELL: (*not sinister, but rather as a kindly teacher with a promising pupil*) Rich; seriously.
RICH: (*pauses, then bitterly*) It would depend on what I was offered.

He is offered a position as Collector of Revenues for the Diocese of York. Then Cromwell questions Rich about the silver goblet.

CROMWELL: Where did he [More] get it? (*No reply. Rich puts the cup down.*) It was a gift from a litigant, a woman, wasn't it?
RICH: Yes.
CROMWELL: Which court? Chancery? (*restrains Rich from filling his glass*) No, don't get drunk. In which court was this litigant's case?
RICH: Court of Requests.
CROMWELL: There, that wasn't too painful, was it?
RICH: (*laughing a little and a little rueful*) No!
CROMWELL: That's all there is. And you'll find it easier next time.[4]

"Court of Requests." A simple enough statement. Yet at that point Rich has abdicated his self. After this the man no longer has a self to commit. His word has no guarantee. Sensing this inner hollowness More can say to him: "Richard, you couldn't answer for yourself even so far as to-night."[5]

We would not want to say that Rich can never again get back his identity. That possibility always remains, we must suppose, until the final moment. It would be a damaged identity, of course, but the possibility for repentance and renewal always exists. But Rich, as it turns out, never gets his back. By the end of the play his personality has hardened into a mask, and behind the mask there is nothing. Nothing has persisted in him but his ambition.

The self that persists, the self upon which others rely and upon which we found our identity—that self is now threatened from several directions. Any society produces more Richard Riches than Thomas Mores, but our present American culture is now far more conducive to the production of people like Rich than it has ever been. It is not the type of society that provides a solid sense of identity; and it is upon identity that ethics are built.

[4]Ibid., pp. 72, 75–76.
[5]Ibid., p. 65.

Rarely is anyone called upon to make the type of heroic self-definition that Thomas More made, and the encroachments upon our identity are more subtle than those that Rich suffered; but in less obvious ways there are forces at work that threaten to undermine that something in us which we feel ought to persist. This chapter and the ones that follow will examine these forces.

An oath is not nearly so sacred as it once was, and we would now prefer that men, as Bolt puts it, "guarantee their statements with, say, cash, rather than with themselves."[6] Nevertheless there is an anxiety that pervades our sense of self: a fear that underneath the many roles we play there is nothing. If we cannot identify with More, and if we are loath to find in ourselves the deceitfulness of a Richard Rich, there is yet another metaphor for us. It can be found in Ibsen's play *Peer Gynt,* where Peer, seated among a field of onions, imagines his personality to be no different from an onion. The layers he peels off one by one represent the roles he has played in life, but after all are peeled away there is nothing left:

> "There's a most surprising lot of layers! Are we never coming to the kernel? [*Pulls all that's left to pieces*] There isn't one! To the innermost bit it's nothing but layers, smaller and smaller. Nature's a joker!"[7]

It's a cruel joke that leaves a man with no core of identity. But it would appear that just such a joke is being played on a growing number of individuals in our society. The jokester in this case is not nature but a culture that accelerates social and technological change at a dizzying pace.

Identity in a Changing World

The work of Erik Erikson provides the most useful recent discussion of identity, and one which makes sense in human terms, for Erikson makes allowance for the ambiguities and uncertainties of life, for the possibility of this going wrong and that going right. It is Erikson who stressed the importance of continuity in the formation of identity, and it is to Erikson that we owe our understanding of how identity is synthesized out of many childhood identifications. As Erikson describes it, identity emerges out of a dialectic between the need for continuity and the need for experimentation. Identity formation leads in the direction of a new self-delineation, yet it is also an "accrued confidence" that one retains an "inner sameness." With this confidence it is possible to take the chances with one's identity that true intimacy requires. Erikson has become the preeminent theorist of identity, and this perhaps most of all because his is a theory made to fit men rather than one they are fitted into.

But theories, like selves, need occasionally to be redefined in light of

---

[6]Ibid., p. xiv.

[7]Henrik Ibsen, *Peer Gynt* (New York: E. P. Dutton and Co., 1930), p. 202.

new realities, and certain new realities would seem to require a rethinking of our ideas about this fundamental process of identity formation. There is the possibility that these new realities are not realities at all, of course, but only new myths. But since men live as much by myths as realities, we are still forced to consider the usefulness of our traditional explanations. I would not suggest that Erikson's explanation is no longer useful (it is extremely useful) but that the model of health it presents no longer reflects the norm. As social realities change, a theory can become more and more a statement of the way things should be than the way they are, and this, I believe, is what has happened to Erikson's criteria of health. For Erikson, a healthy identity is one that is open to change and redefinition, but above all is rooted in an historical, traceable past, so that through all there runs an invigorating "sense of sameness,"[8]—what I have been calling "continuity."

This healthy sense of sameness is increasingly difficult to come by as we approach the last quarter of the twentieth century. To illustrate let us juxtapose Erikson's definition of identity with a statement from Toffler's (1970) *Future Shock*. First, Erikson:

> Ego identity . . . is an awareness of the fact that there is a self-sameness and continuity to the ego's synthesizing methods, *the style of one's individuality*, and that this style coincides with the sameness and continuity of one's *meaning for significant others* in the immediate community.[9]

Contrast to this a statement from Toffler's book:

> What remains? What is there of "self" or "personality" in the sense of a continuous, durable internal structure? For some, the answer is very little. For they are no longer dealing in "self" but in what might be called "serial selves."[10]

"They" are for the most part the affluent and highly mobile elite most involved in the accelerated pace of change that produces future shock. But since "they" are soon to be followed by the rest of us, it seems worth investigating this matter of "serial selves" and the sharp contrast it opposes to Erikson's definition of identity.

Continuity and Change

Identity—the type Erikson has in mind—requires a threefold continuity: a continuity of significant others; a continuity with one's past self; a continuity with one's anticipated future self. At all three levels the phenomenon of chronic change acts to disrupt these continuities.

It is imperative that our sense of identity be reinforced by significant

---

[8]Erik H. Erikson, *Identity, Youth and Crisis* (New York: W. W. Norton and Co., 1968), p. 246.

[9]Ibid., p. 50.

[10]Alvin Toffler, *Future Shock* (New York: Bantam Books, 1970), p. 319.

others. We need their reassurance that despite the transformations we have undergone something essential remains. What are we after all but social creatures? Even Thomas More, who had stood alone against all, at the last begs his family for their understanding. An identity is a fragile thing when it stands by itself. It is strengthened when we feel that others recognize in us that self-sameness which we recognize in ourselves.

Identity achievement then would seem to require a continuity of significant others in our lives to confirm our links to our past selves. One of the problems of a future-shocked society, however, is the absence of such continuity. Friends and neighbors come and go with alarming rapidity. They change, and we change, and "those who knew us in some previous incarnation," as Toffler puts it, have a difficult time recognizing us. They do little to reinforce our sense of sameness.

Mobility and transience combine to create a society of nomads. Incessant moving is the norm. Who still lives in the house of his birth? In the house of his childhood? Even for the young the answer is that practically no one does. The house of my own youth no longer exists. In its place stands a modern apartment building. The backyard in which I discovered praying mantis and morning glory is now a paved parking lot. The phrase "you can't go home again" takes on for us a physical as well as psychological meaning. And even when we can return to a physical site, what strangers will we find at the door? Among the statistics Toffler cites is that one out of five Americans changes his address each year. Over half the listings in the 1969 Washington, D.C., phonebook, he tells us, were different from the year before.

No one, it seems, can be counted on to stay in one place. The aunts, uncles and grandparents who once lived across the street now live across the city or across the country. By and large we are left with only the stripped-down, streamlined nuclear family to fill the role of "significant others." And even here there is a growing lack of continuity. The nuclear family is coming apart. An increasing number of children must adjust to the fact that parents, like friends and neighbors, can come and go. Serial marriage—a succession of temporary marriages—is already an established although unofficial pattern. Those parents who do stay together increasingly shift the burden of child rearing to schools and day care centers. Annual rituals through which families could confer a unique sense of belonging to an ongoing tradition have largely been taken over by mass commercialism. The organization of our activities for Thanksgiving week is now in the hands of *TV Guide*. Little chance for identity confirmation here: the family is caught up in the same winds of change that buffet individual lives. As a result, we all have a vague feeling of truly belonging nowhere and to no one.

It is not only the continuity of our meaning to others that is threatened. We also have increasing difficulty in recognizing our own past selves. This would seem to be especially true in the matter of rapidly changing values. To a high degree our identity—our sense of continuity—is bound up with our sense of right and wrong. The world may change, we feel, but if we hold fast to our ethical moorings we can still retain a sense of our place in it. But what happens to identity when our values turn over almost as rapidly as fashions in dress? What does it mean for identity when, for instance, the Catholic who yesterday opposed birth control today accepts abortion and tomorrow may embrace euthanasia and test-tube reproduction? What does it mean for personal continuity to continually redraw the moral line at which one will make his or her stand? According to some of the sex researchers (e.g., Gilbert Bartell, 1971),[11] It is not unusual for a suburban woman to move from chastity through monogamy to adultery and on to group sex and lesbianism in a half-dozen years or less. My intent is not to pass judgment on any of these activities, only to point out that the more lines we erase, the harder it becomes to trace the genealogy of our morals or the lineage of our identity.

But it is precisely such historical acts that constitute the process of identity formation. This is why the adolescent whose main developmental task is identity formation becomes so concerned with questions of his personal lineage, descent, and legitimacy. The biological discontinuities of puberty prompt him to find connections with his past; the integration of his past and present identities demands that he take an historical perspective. It is the point of *Future Shock,* however, that the current diversity of life-styles and the rate at which we move through them makes such integration increasingly improbable. Erikson himself, anticipating this possibility, states that "the integration of infantile part-identities and fragmentary roles can be interfered with by . . . rapid social evolution or technological change."[12] In a similar vein, Kenneth Keniston sees contemporary youth as suffering from "historical dislocation," which he describes as "the inability to find connections with the past and future" and as "the feeling of unrelatedness, of being adrift, of not being able to 'catch hold' of anything or anyone in our rapidly changing society."[13] He sees this dislocation as being due on the one hand to the difficulty of synthesizing the many irreconcilable identities our society proffers, and on the other to an inability of youth to identify with their parents because their parents have been "outdated" by rapid change.

To the youth Keniston studied, parents are seen as simply irrelevant. To identify with them is to choose obsolescence. Although they may be the

[11]Gilbert D. Bartell, *Group Sex* (New York: New American Library, 1973).

[12]R. I. Evans, *Dialogue with Erik Erikson* (New York: E. P. Dutton, 1969), Erikson quoted, p. 39.

[13]Kenneth Keniston, *The Uncommitted* (New York: Harcourt, Brace and World, 1965), pp. 239–40.

only link to their children's past, the children simply cannot relate to them. The ever-present generation gap is widened by the factors of transience, mobility, novelty, and diversity that Toffler describes and analyzes in *Future Shock*. When change accelerates beyond a certain point it is difficult to retain a sense of continuity with one's past; the past seems increasingly distant and beside the point.

The same holds true for the future. Endless change makes the future unpredictable. That which we thought to be stable and permanent rapidly becomes obsolescent. In the face of accelerating social and technological innovations it is difficult to anticipate the future or plan for it. We turn instead to the present, the only time we can be sure of. If the past is irrelevant and the future enigmatic, the present is more certain.

When the past loses its significance and the future becomes unknowable, when those on whom we rely to confirm our identity depart our lives, and when we have been forced to play many successive parts, we may begin to wonder, like Peer Gynt, if there is any center. Chronic change undermines our sense of the persistence of something essential in us. It separates us from our identity as effectively as Cromwell unburdened Rich of his.

Even as basic a touchstone as our sense of physical identity may soon be undermined by rapid advances in the field of medicine. Our sense of identity is reinforced on a physical level by the simple fact of bodily continuity. Allowing for normal wear and tear and cell replacement, we recognize ourselves as being of our own flesh and blood. But even now, Teflon and Dacron and metal are replacing skin and bones. And the heart we were born with may have to be discarded along the way in favor of a "new" one. What happens to an individual's sense of uniqueness or continuity when faced with the knowledge that his body is a system of interchangeable parts? The speed with which we enter the future is measured by the fact that questions like this find us totally unprepared.

Fidelity

The sense of continuity is not the only quality to be threatened by accelerated change. Erikson observed that at each stage of development a capacity or "virtue" emerges in the individual to help him meet the crisis of that stage. An important step in the crisis of identity formation is the development of a capacity for what he terms "fidelity." Fidelity is faithfulness, loyalty, commitment. In large part the adolescent quest for identity is a search for something to which one can commit one's newly developing sense of identity. Through fidelity, moreover, one can cultivate those long-term relationships that give continuity to one's sense of self. Our fidelity is our guarantee that there is something solid about our identity—something which endures. "Without the development of a capacity for fidelity," says Erikson, "the individual will either have what we call a weak ego, or look for a deviant group to be faithful to." And elsewhere in stronger terms he asserts, "Fidelity . . . must not, in the crisis of youth, fail its time of ascendance if human adaptation is to remain intact."[14]

Once again, if we juxtapose to this some statements from Toffler we find a sharp contrast. It is Toffler's contention that most of our relationships are characterized by transience. This is especially true of our relationships to things and places but is becoming increasingly true of our relationships to people. Our attitude toward things that are disposable, rentable, and impermanent may begin to color our attitude toward people. Although we are very much attached to material goods in general, there is no longer the tradition of specific attachment to a specific thing which prevailed when goods were less abundant and things were made to last. All this is preparation for a world in which our attachments to people become equally tenuous; in which we feel driven to experience the latest model friend, lover, or spouse. "The logical end of the direction in which we are now travelling," writes Toffler, "is a society based on a system of temporary encounters."[15] Here Toffler is speaking not only of our transient relations to acquaintances, colleagues, and neighbors but also of friendship, love, and marriage bonds. The traditional ideal for marriage has been that of shared growth. This pattern, says Toffler, has been difficult to achieve even in stable societies, but people no longer change at the same rate or in the same direction. The best we can hope for is the system of serial marriages mentioned earlier.

In a world of disposable goods, easily replaced, we probably should not wonder that people also come to seem disposable. And our vaunted mobility only intensifies the feeling that it is wiser if we do not get too attached. Commitment to others is difficult enough in a stable society because it entails not only the risk of rejection but also the risk of involvement. People who move around a great deal are even more reluctant to commit themselves to friends, colleagues, or communities. Why invest the energy when one is going to move on? Why get involved?

The Risks of Fidelity

Moreover, fidelity carries with it the risk of what Keniston calls "damaging commitment to false life styles or goals."[16] To understand the meaning of this risk it is necessary to understand that identity and fidelity have

---

[14]Evans, *Dialogue,* Erikson quoted, p. 30. Erikson, "Youth: Fidelity and Diversity," in *The Challenge of Youth,* E. H. Erikson, ed. (Garden City: Doubleday Anchor, 1965), p. 1.

[15]Toffler, *Future Shock,* p. 122.

[16]Kenneth Keniston, "Social Change and Youth in America" in *The Challenge of Youth,* p. 202.

a mutually supportive relationship; they do not develop apart from each other. Identity generates the capacity for fidelity, which in turn generates a stronger sense of identity. The more tenuous one's hold on his identity, the less likely he is to risk losing it in a relationship with another. He fears that the price of commitment may be the absorption of his self into another's. But without commitment or intimacy there is no further growth for him. Conversely, the anxieties of identity diffusion may propel an individual to find any identity, no matter how premature and limiting, in an effort to have done with it. He may seek an end to anxiety in a hasty and confining marriage or in narrow commitment to some group or cause. The "true believer," as Eric Hoffer[o] points out, is only too willing to have his uncertain sense of self welded to some ideological superstructure.

The danger of being welded or wedded to false life-styles or to the wrong persons makes fidelity risky in the best of circumstances. In a world characterized by mobility, novelty, faddishness, transience, and temporality where there are many competing life-styles and persons, and little time to examine or decide, the risk is multiplied enormously.

Not only is fidelity difficult in such a world, but the job of synthesizing identifications also becomes highly problematic. The more variegated a society, the more identities it offers, and the harder it is to pull them together into a coherent unity. When an individual fails to achieve an integration of past and current identifications he falls victim to what Erikson calls identity confusion: an inability to feel that one is all together, a feeling of not fitting in, of not knowing who one is or what one wants to do, of trying on many roles and settling for none.

Erikson sees the resolution of the identity crisis in the achievement of a ratio between a sense of coherence and a sense of identity confusion, with the balance tipped in favor of the former. But in a future-shocked society the ratio is reversed. If Toffler's assessment of cultural change is correct, then the balance has been tipped the other way. Identity confusion, not coherence, has become the prevailing norm.

It is true that the human race has an impressive record of adaptability. But to adapt is not to thrive or prosper. We cannot be too sanguine about the benefits of adapting to a society where identity confusion is not redeemed by a sense of continuity. Toffler is not unaware of the danger that is posed to our identity in an accelerating society. There are, he asserts, definite limits to the amount of change that the human organism can cope with. The higher the level of change, the greater the likelihood of illness, both physical and mental. The more change is accelerated, the more we run the risk of being thrown into a state of shock.

I do not mean to imply that the future-shock problem is the main

---

Eric Hoffer Longshoreman, author, social philosopher (1902–1983).

difficulty for identity formation. It is one of several problems that necessitate a rethinking of our traditional ideas about the achievement of identity. In this chapter I have merely tried to draw attention to the discrepancy that exists between a major theory of development and a widely accepted description of current social change. What the one requires, the other refuses.

Denise Levertov
(b. 1923)

In Mind

There's in my mind a woman
of innocence, unadorned but

fair-featured, and smelling of
apples or grass. She wears

a utopian smock or shift, her hair
is light brown and smooth, and she

is kind and very clean without
ostentation—
but she has
no imagination.
And there's a
turbulent moon-ridden girl

or old woman, or both,
dressed in opals and rags, feathers

and torn taffeta,
who knows strange songs—

but she is not kind.

(1962)

W. H. Auden
(1907–1973)

The Unknown Citizen

(To JS/07/M/378
This Marble Monument
Is Erected by the State)

He was found by the Bureau of Statistics to be
One against whom there was no official complaint,
And all the reports on his conduct agree
That, in the modern sense of an old-fashioned word, he
    was a saint,
For in everything he did he served the Greater Community.
Except for the War till the day he retired
He worked in a factory and never got fired,
But satisfied his employers, Fudge Motors Inc.
Yet he wasn't a scab or odd in his views,
For his Union reports that he paid his dues,
(Our report on his Union shows it was sound)
And our Social Psychology workers found
That he was popular with his mates and liked a drink.
The Press are convinced that he bought a paper every day
And that his reactions to advertisements were normal in
    every way.
Policies taken out in his name prove that he was fully insured,
And his Health-card shows he was once in hospital but
    left it cured.
Both Producers Research and High-Grade Living declare
He was fully sensible to the advantages of the Instalment Plan
And had everything necessary to the Modern Man,
A phonograph, a radio, a car and a frigidaire.
Our researchers into Public Opinion are content
That he held the proper opinions for the time of year;
When there was peace, he was for peace; when there was
    war, he went.
He was married and added five children to the population,

Which our Eugenist says was the right number for a
   parent of his generation,
And our teachers report that he never interfered with
   their education.
Was he free? Was he happy? The question is absurd:
Had anything been wrong, we should certainly have heard.

(March 1939)

Barriers to Women, Visible and Invisible

Although there are comparatively few of us who have not heard of the feminist movement, and there are more and more people who believe, generally, that "women's liberation" is a good thing, the issues raised by the movement are not yet clearly settled. Perhaps the most fundamental problem is the persistence of the age-old tradition, today often called sexism, that there are fixed roles for women and men predetermined by nature or God, which women refuse at their peril. To illustrate traditional sexism we print first an editorial on the Woman's Rights Convention of 1852. The writer is scandalized by women who leave their "true sphere"; the subjection of woman by man, he writes, is "the law of her nature."

Virginia Woolf, next, shifts the ground of discourse from biology to society, from the assumption that woman's role is genetically determined to the revolutionary idea that it is limited only by what society permits and what she permits herself. In her essay "Professions for Women" she asks a key question, "What is a woman?," and then answers it, saying, "I assure you, I do not know. I do not believe that you know. I do not believe that anybody can know until she has expressed herself in all the arts and professions open to human skill."

The short excerpt that follows, from Woolf's *A Room of One's Own,* helps us imagine what a supremely talented woman might

have been up against before women's rights became an issue. Then
Alice Walker extends the same theme over time and across ethnic
and class boundaries. Writing what she calls a "personal account
that is yet shared in its theme and its meaning," Walker speaks
first to black women but finally exhorts all women to go "in search
of our mothers' gardens," to reclaim "the living creativity some of
our great-grandmothers were not allowed to know."

As both Virginia Woolf and Alice Walker make clear, there are
many ghosts for a woman to fight, "contrary instincts" to reconcile.
The next essay describes from experience the struggle against such
ghosts and divided loyalties. Judith Wells shows how easy it is for
women to adopt certain roles and how real change in oneself takes
time and hard work. Matina Horner's study next presents a different perspective on that struggle. Her field research, completed in
the late 1960s, illustrates differences in how men and women react
to achievement. She concludes that although many legal and educational barriers to female achievement have been removed in
recent years, "it is clear that a psychological barrier remains."

The last two pieces in this section, one heavy-handed and humor-
less, the other more ironic and reflective, present two contemporary versions of sexism. The memorandum sent out by the
personnel office of a major corporation provides a "profile" for
female applicants and a checklist for "understanding women." Finally, Anthony Burgess offers a spirited challenge to those who call
him a "sexist pig," and celebrates, in his own way, the "otherness"
of women. He ends his essay by asking anew Freud's famous question, "What does a woman *want?*"

The Woman's Rights Convention (September 12, 1852)

New York Herald, Editorial

*The Woman's Rights Convention which met September 8–10, 1852, at
Syracuse, New York, was one of a series of national conventions inspired
by the 1848 Seneca Falls convention organized by Lucretia Mott, Martha
Wright, Elizabeth Cady Stanton, and Mary Ann McClintock "to discuss
the social, civil and religious rights of women." The convention at Syracuse*

was attended by delegates from eight states and Canada. Lucretia Mott was named permanent president with one dissenting vote—her husband's; Susan B. Anthony was one of the secretaries.

The farce at Syracuse has been played out. We publish to-day the last act, in which it will be seen that the authority of the Bible, as a perfect rule of faith and practice for human beings, was voted down, and what are called the laws of nature set up instead of the Christian code. We have also a practical exhibition of the consequences that flow from woman leaving her true sphere where she wields all her influence, and coming into public to discuss questions of morals and politics with men. . . .

Who are these women? what do they want? what are the motives that impel them to this course of action? The *dramatis personae* of the farce enacted at Syracuse present a curious conglomeration of both sexes. Some of them are old maids, whose personal charms were never very attractive, and who have been sadly slighted by the masculine gender in general; some of them women who have been badly mated, whose own temper, or their husbands', has made life anything but agreeable to them, and they are therefore down upon the whole of the opposite sex; some, having so much of the virago in their disposition, that nature appears to have made a mistake in their gender—mannish women, like hens that crow; some of boundless vanity and egotism, who believe that they are superior in intellectual ability to "all the world and the rest of mankind," and delight to see their speeches and addresses in print; and man shall be consigned to his proper sphere—nursing the babies, washing the dishes, mending stockings, and sweeping the house. This is "the good time coming." Besides the classes we have enumerated, there is a class of wild enthusiasts and visionaries—very sincere, but very mad—having the same vein as the fanatical Abolitionists, and the majority, if not all of them, being, in point of fact, deeply imbued with the anti-slavery sentiment. Of the male sex who attend these Conventions for the purpose of taking a part in them, the majority are hen-pecked husbands, and all of them ought to wear petticoats.

In point of ability, the majority of the women are flimsy, flippant, and superficial. Mrs. Rose[o] alone indicates much argumentative power.

How did woman first become subject to man as she now is all over the world? By her nature, her sex, just as the negro is and always will be, to the end of time, inferior to the white race, and, therefore, doomed to subjection; but happier than she would be in any other condition, just

---

Mrs. Rose Ernestine L. Rose (1810–1892), born in Poland, was one of the best platform speakers of her day; she was one of the first women to work for women's rights through legislative action, repeatedly petitioning the New York State Legislature for a Married Women's Property Law.

because it is the law of her nature. The women themselves would not have this law reversed. It is a significant fact that even Mrs. Swisshelm,° who formerly ran about to all such gatherings from her husband, is now "a keeper at home," and condemns these Conventions in her paper. How does this happen? Because, after weary years of unfruitfulness, she has at length got her rights in the shape of a baby. This is the best cure for the mania, and we would recommend a trial of it to all who are afflicted.

What do the leaders of the Woman's Rights Convention want? They want to vote, and to hustle with the rowdies at the polls. They want to be members of Congress, and in the heat of debate to subject themselves to coarse jests and indecent language, like that of Rev. Mr. Hatch. They want to fill all other posts which men are ambitious to occupy—to be lawyers, doctors, captains of vessels, and generals in the field. How funny it would sound in the newspapers, that Lucy Stone,° pleading a cause, took suddenly ill in the pains of parturition, and perhaps gave birth to a fine bouncing boy in court! Or that Rev. Antoinette Brown° was arrested in the middle of her sermon in the pulpit from the same cause, and presented a "pledge" to her husband and the congregation; or, that Dr. Harriot K. Hunt,° while attending a gentleman patient for a fit of the gout or *fistula in ano,*° found it necessary to send for a doctor, there and then, and to be delivered of a man or woman child—perhaps twins. A similar event might happen on the floor of Congress, in a storm at sea, or in the raging tempest of battle, and then what is to become of the woman legislator?

Two Essays on Women

Virginia Woolf

Virginia Woolf (1882–1941) was the daughter of a prominent English scholar and critic, Sir Leslie Stephen, and was educated mainly in her father's library and from extensive travels. In 1917, she and her husband,

---

Mrs. Swisshelm   Jane Swisshelm (1815–1884) founded and published a newspaper, the *Pittsberg Saturday Visiter* [sic], which ran from 1847 to 1857.
Lucy Stone   Lucy Stone (1818–1893) was one of the leading public speakers for the abolition of slavery and for women's rights.
Rev. Antoinette Brown   Antoinette Brown (1825–1921), a Congregationalist minister, became the first American woman minister when she was ordained in 1853.
Dr. Harriot K. Hunt   Harriot K. Hunt (1805–1875) was denied admission to Harvard Medical School and practiced medicine without a license.
fistula in ano   Anal ulcer (Latin).

*Leonard Woolf, began printing on a hand press their own writings and
those of other (then obscure) authors like Katherine Mansfield, T. S. Eliot,
and E. M. Forster. This was the beginning of the celebrated Hogarth Press
and center of the so-called "Bloomsbury Group" of intellectuals and writers. Virginia Woolf is particularly noted for her novels, among which we
mention* Mrs. Dalloway *(1925),* To the Lighthouse *(1927),* Orlando *(1928),
and* The Waves *(1931) as a few of the best. They are considered important
experiments in novelistic form: she disregards ordinary factual description
of characters and action, concentrating instead on psychological penetration and on variations in temporal perspective and rhythm. She also wrote
many reviews and essays, on art and literature, and on the problems of
social and economic reform. Her literary essays were collected in* The
Common Reader *(1925; second series, 1932),* The Death of the Moth *(1942),*
The Moment and Other Essays *(1947), and* Three Guineas *(1938).*

*A Room of One's Own (1929), a seminal feminist piece, is a long essay
in which she uses metaphor and history to show the relative status of
women in twentieth-century English society. From it we have taken the
second selection printed below. The first, "Professions for Women," is from*
The Death of the Moth.

Professions for Women[1]

When your secretary invited me to come here, she told me that your
Society is concerned with the employment of women and she suggested
that I might tell you something about my own professional experiences.
It is true I am a woman; it is true I am employed; but what professional
experiences have I had? It is difficult to say. My profession is literature;
and in that profession there are fewer experiences for women than in any
other, with the exception of the stage—fewer, I mean, that are peculiar
to women. For the road was cut many years ago—by Fanny Burney, by
Aphra Behn, by Harriet Martineau, by Jane Austen, by George Eliot—
many famous women, and many more unknown and forgotten, have been
before me, making the path smooth, and regulating my steps. Thus, when
I came to write, there were very few material obstacles in my way. Writing was a reputable and harmless occupation. The family peace was not
broken by the scratching of a pen. No demand was made upon the family
purse. For ten and sixpence one can buy paper enough to write all the
plays of Shakespeare—if one has a mind that way. Pianos and models,
Paris, Vienna and Berlin, masters and mistresses, are not needed by a
writer. The cheapness of writing paper is, of course, the reason why

---

[1]A paper read to The Women's Service League.

women have succeeded as writers before they have succeeded in the other professions.

But to tell you my story—it is a simple one. You have only got to figure to yourselves a girl in a bedroom with a pen in her hand. She had only to move that pen from left to right—from ten o'clock to one. Then it occurred to her to do what is simple and cheap enough after all—to slip a few of those pages into an envelope, fix a penny stamp in the corner, and drop the envelope into the red box at the corner. It was thus that I became a journalist; and my effort was rewarded on the first day of the following month—a very glorious day it was for me—by a letter from an editor containing a cheque for one pound ten shillings and sixpence. But to show you how little I deserve to be called a professional woman, how little I know of the struggles and difficulties of such lives, I have to admit that instead of spending that sum upon bread and butter, rent, shoes and stockings, or butcher's bills, I went out and bought a cat—a beautiful cat, a Persian cat, which very soon involved me in bitter disputes with my neighbours.

What could be easier than to write articles and to buy Persian cats with the profits? But wait a moment. Articles have to be about something. Mine, I seem to remember, was about a novel by a famous man. And while I was writing this review, I discovered that if I were going to review books I should need to do battle with a certain phantom. And the phantom was a woman, and when I came to know her better I called her after the heroine of a famous poem, The Angel in the House.° It was she who used to come between me and my paper when I was writing reviews. It was she who bothered me and wasted my time and so tormented me that at last I killed her. You who come of a younger and happier generation may not have heard of her—you may not know what I mean by the Angel in the House. I will describe her as shortly as I can. She was intensely sympathetic. She was immensely charming. She was utterly unselfish. She excelled in the difficult arts of family life. She sacrificed herself daily. If there was chicken, she took the leg; if there was a draught she sat in it—in short she was so constituted that she never had a mind or a wish of her own, but preferred to sympathize always with the minds and wishes of others. Above all—I need not say it—she was pure. Her purity was supposed to be her chief beauty—her blushes, her great grace. In those days—the last of Queen Victoria—every house had its Angel. And when I came to write I encountered her with the very first words. The shadow of her wings fell on my page; I heard the rustling of her skirts in the room. Directly, that is to say, I took my pen in hand to review that novel by a famous man, she slipped behind me and whispered: "My dear, you are a

---

The Angel in the House   Long poem by Coventry Patmore (1823–1896) that traces the courtship and marriage of a clergyman's daughter. It describes the progress of pure love.

young woman. You are writing about a book that has been written by a man. Be sympathetic; be tender; flatter; deceive; use all the arts and wiles of our sex. Never let anybody guess that you have a mind of your own. Above all, be pure." And she made as if to guide my pen. I now record the one act for which I take some credit to myself, though the credit rightly belongs to some excellent ancestors of mine who left me a certain sum of money—shall we say five hundred pounds a year?—so that it was not necessary for me to depend solely on charm for my living. I turned upon her and caught her by the throat. I did my best to kill her. My excuse, if I were to be had up in a court of law, would be that I acted in self-defence. Had I not killed her she would have killed me. She would have plucked the heart out of my writing. For, as I found, directly I put pen to paper, you cannot review even a novel without having a mind of your own, without expressing what you think to be the truth about human relations, morality, sex. And all these questions, according to the Angel in the House, cannot be dealt with freely and openly by women; they must charm, they must conciliate, they must—to put it bluntly—tell lies if they are to succeed. Thus, whenever I felt the shadow of her wing or the radiance of her halo upon my page, I took up the inkpot and flung it at her. She died hard. Her fictitious nature was of great assistance to her. It is far harder to kill a phantom than a reality. She was always creeping back when I thought I had despatched her. Though I flatter myself that I killed her in the end, the struggle was severe; it took much time that had better have been spent upon learning Greek grammar; or in roaming the world in search of adventures. But it was a real experience; it was an experience that was bound to befall all women writers at that time. Killing the Angel in the House was part of the occupation of a woman writer.

But to continue my story. The Angel was dead; what then remained? You may say that what remained was a simple and common object—a young woman in a bedroom with an inkpot. In other words, now that she had rid herself of falsehood, that young woman had only to be herself. Ah, but what is "herself"? I mean, what is a woman? I assure you, I do not know. I do not believe that you know. I do not believe that anybody can know until she has expressed herself in all the arts and professions open to human skill. That indeed is one of the reasons why I have come here—out of respect for you, who are in process of showing us by your experiments what a woman is, who are in process of providing us, by your failures and successes, with that extremely important piece of information.

But to continue the story of my professional experiences. I made one pound ten and six by my first review; and I bought a Persian cat with the proceeds. Then I grew ambitious. A Persian cat is all very well, I said; but a Persian cat is not enough. I must have a motor car. And it was thus that I became a novelist—for it is a very strange thing that people will give you a motor car if you will tell them a story. It is a still stranger thing that there is nothing so delightful in the world as telling stories. It is far pleasanter than writing reviews of famous novels. And yet, if I am to obey your secretary and tell you my professional experiences as a novelist, I must tell you about a very strange experience that befell me as a novelist. And to understand it you must try first to imagine a novelist's state of mind. I hope I am not giving away professional secrets if I say that a novelist's chief desire is to be as unconscious as possible. He has to induce in himself a state of perpetual lethargy. He wants life to proceed with the utmost quiet and regularity. He wants to see the same faces, to read the same books, to do the same things day after day, month after month, while he is writing, so that nothing may break the illusion in which he is living—so that nothing may disturb or disquiet the mysterious nosings about, feelings round, darts, dashes and sudden discoveries of that very shy and illusive spirit, the imagination. I suspect that this state is the same both for men and women. Be that as it may, I want you to imagine me writing a novel in a state of trance. I want you to figure to yourselves a girl sitting with a pen in her hand, which for minutes, and indeed for hours, she never dips into the inkpot. The image that comes to my mind when I think of this girl is the image of a fisherman lying sunk in dreams on the verge of a deep lake with a rod held out over the water. She was letting her imagination sweep unchecked round every rock and cranny of the world that lies submerged in the depths of our unconscious being. Now came the experience, the experience that I believe to be far commoner with women writers than with men. The line raced through the girl's fingers. Her imagination had rushed away. It had sought the pools, the depths, the dark places where the largest fish slumber. And then there was a smash. There was an explosion. There was foam and confusion. The imagination had dashed itself against something hard. The girl was roused from her dream. She was indeed in a state of the most acute and difficult distress. To speak without figure she had thought of something, something about the body, about the passions which it was unfitting for her as a woman to say. Men, her reason told her, would be shocked. The consciousness of what men will say of a woman who speaks the truth about her passions had roused her from her artist's state of unconsciousness. She could write no more. The trance was over. Her imagination could work no longer. This I believe to be a very common experience with women writers—they are impeded by the extreme conventionality of the other sex. For though men sensibly allow themselves great freedom in these respects, I doubt that they realize or can control the extreme severity with which they condemn such freedom in women.

These then were two very genuine experiences of my own. These were two of the adventures of my professional life. The first—killing the Angel in the House—I think I solved. She died. But the second, telling the truth about my own experiences as a body, I do not think I solved. I doubt that any woman has solved it yet. The obstacles against her are still immensely powerful—and yet they are very difficult to define. Outwardly, what is simpler than to write books? Outwardly, what obstacles are there for a woman rather than for a man? Inwardly, I think, the case is very different; she has still many ghosts to fight, many prejudices to overcome. Indeed it will be a long time still, I think, before a woman can sit down to write a book without finding a phantom to be slain, a rock to be dashed against. And if this is so in literature, the freest of all professions for women, how is it in the new professions which you are now for the first time entering?

Those are the questions that I should like, had I time, to ask you. And indeed, if I have laid stress upon these professional experiences of mine, it is because I believe that they are, though in different forms, yours also. Even when the path is nominally open—when there is nothing to prevent a woman from being a doctor, a lawyer, a civil servant—there are many phantoms and obstacles, as I believe, looming in her way. To discuss and define them is I think of great value and importance; for thus only can the labour be shared, the difficulties be solved. But besides this, it is necessary also to discuss the ends and the aims for which we are fighting, for which we are doing battle with these formidable obstacles. Those aims cannot be taken for granted; they must be perpetually questioned and examined. The whole position, as I see it—here in this hall surrounded by women practising for the first time in history I know not how many different professions—is one of extraordinary interest and importance. You have won rooms of your own in the house hitherto exclusively owned by men. You are able, though not without great labour and effort, to pay the rent. You are earning your five hundred pounds a year. But this freedom is only a beginning; the room is your own, but it is still bare. It has to be furnished; it has to be decorated; it has to be shared. How are you going to furnish it, how are you going to decorate it? With whom are you going to share it, and upon what terms? These, I think are questions of the utmost importance and interest. For the first time in history you are able to ask them; for the first time you are able to decide for yourselves what the answers should be. Willingly would I stay and discuss those questions and answers—but not tonight. My time is up; and I must cease.

Shakespeare's Sister

. . . I thought of that old gentleman, who is dead now, but was a bishop, I think, who declared that it was impossible for any woman, past, present, or to come, to have the genius of Shakespeare. He wrote to the papers about it. He also told a lady who applied to him for information that cats do not as a matter of fact go to heaven, though they have, he added, souls of a sort. How much thinking those old gentlemen used to save one! How the borders of ignorance shrank back at their approach! Cats do not go to heaven. Women cannot write the plays of Shakespeare.

Be that as it may, I could not help thinking, as I looked at the works of Shakespeare on the shelf, that the bishop was right at least in this; it would have been impossible, completely and entirely, for any woman to have written the plays of Shakespeare in the age of Shakespeare. Let me imagine, since facts are so hard to come by, what would have happened had Shakespeare had a wonderfully gifted sister, called Judith, let us say. Shakespeare himself went, very probably—his mother was an heiress—to the grammar school, where he may have learnt Latin—Ovid, Virgil and Horace—and the elements of grammar and logic. He was, it is well known, a wild boy who poached rabbits, perhaps shot a deer, and had, rather sooner than he should have done, to marry a woman in the neighbourhood, who bore him a child rather quicker than was right. That escapade sent him to seek his fortune in London. He had, it seemed, a taste for the theatre; he began by holding horses at the stage door. Very soon he got work in the theatre, became a successful actor, and lived at the hub of the universe, meeting everybody, knowing everybody, practising his art on the boards, exercising his wits in the streets, and even getting access to the palace of the queen. Meanwhile his extraordinarily gifted sister, let us suppose, remained at home. She was as adventurous, as imaginative, as agog to see the world as he was. But she was not sent to school. She had no chance of learning grammar and logic, let alone of reading Horace and Virgil. She picked up a book now and then, one of her brother's perhaps, and read a few pages. But then her parents came in and told her to mend the stockings or mind the stew and not moon about with books and papers. They would have spoken sharply but kindly, for they were substantial people who knew the conditions of life for a woman and loved their daughter—indeed, more likely than not she was the apple of her father's eye. Perhaps she scribbled some pages up in an apple loft on the sly, but was careful to hide them or set fire to them. Soon, however, before she was out of her teens, she was to be betrothed to the son of a neighbouring wool-stapler. She cried out that marriage was hateful to her, and for that she was severely beaten by her father. Then he ceased to scold her. He begged her instead not to hurt him, not to shame him in this matter of her marriage. He would give her a chain of beads or a fine petticoat, he said; and there were tears in his eyes. How could she disobey him? How could she break his heart? The force of her own gift alone drove her to it. She made up a small parcel of her belongings, let herself down by a rope one summer's night and took the road to London. She was not seventeen. The birds that sang in the hedge were not more musical than she was. She had the quickest fancy, a gift like her brother's, for the tune of words. Like him, she had a taste for the theatre. She stood at the stage door; she wanted to act, she said. Men laughed in her face. The manager—a fat, loose-lipped man—guffawed. He bellowed something about poodles dancing and women acting—no woman, he said, could possibly be an actress. He hinted—you can imagine what. She could get no training in her craft. Could she even seek her dinner in a tavern or roam the streets at midnight? Yet her genius was for fiction and lusted to feed abundantly upon the lives of men and women and the study of their ways. At last—for she was very young, oddly like Shakespeare the poet in her face, with the same grey eyes and rounded brows—at last Nick Greene the actor-manager took pity on her; she found herself with child by that gentleman and so—who shall measure the heat and violence of the poet's heart when caught and tangled in a woman's body?—killed herself one winter's night and lies buried at some cross-roads where the omnibuses now stop outside the Elephant and Castle.

In Search of Our Mothers' Gardens

Alice Walker

Alice Walker was born in 1944 in Eatonton, Georgia, the eighth child of black sharecroppers. She attended Spelman College for two years, then graduated from Sarah Lawrence in 1965. She has since taught writing and black literature at Jackson State College and Tougaloo College in Mississippi, at Wellesley College and the University of Massachusetts, and at Yale University; she has been a fiction editor of Ms. *and has traveled and lived in Africa and the Soviet Union.*

She has written three novels, including The Color Purple, *which won the 1983 Pulitzer Prize for fiction; four books of poems, most recently* Horses Make a Landscape Look More Beautiful *(1984); two collections of short stories; and a collection of essays,* In Search of Our Mothers' Gardens *(1983). She has also edited a collection of writings by Zora Neale Hurston, and her Wild Tree Press has published relatively unknown writers, including Septima Clark, from whose autobiography we reprint a chapter in a later section (p. 447).*

Walker is a social activist and a feminist whose politics and writing feed each other. In an essay, "Saving the Life That Is Your Own," she says, "I write not only what I want to read . . . I write all the things I should have been able to read." She often writes and talks of the strong influence of her parents, particularly her mother. The present essay, in spite of its somewhat cryptic first page, becomes a clear call for women to look back in order to find and reclaim their own creativity.

I described her own nature and temperament. Told how they needed a larger life for their expression. . . . I pointed out that in lieu of proper

> *channels, her emotions had overflowed into paths that dissipated them. I*
> *talked, beautifully I thought, about an art that would be born, an art*
> *that would open the way for women the likes of her. I asked her to hope,*
> *and build up an inner life against the coming of that day. . . . I sang,*
> *with a strange quiver in my voice, a promise song.*

—JEAN TOOMER, "Avey," *Cane*

The poet speaking to a prostitute who falls asleep while he's talking—

When the poet Jean Toomer walked through the South in the early twenties, he discovered a curious thing: black women whose spirituality was so intense, so deep, so *unconscious,* that they were themselves unaware of the richness they held. They stumbled blindly through their lives: creatures so abused and mutilated in body, so dimmed and confused by pain, that they considered themselves unworthy even of hope. In the selfless abstractions their bodies became to the men who used them, they became more than "sexual objects," more even than mere women: they became "Saints." Instead of being perceived as whole persons, their bodies became shrines: what was thought to be their minds became temples suitable for worship. These crazy Saints stared out at the world, wildly, like lunatics—or quietly, like suicides; and the "God" that was in their gaze was as mute as a great stone.

Who were these Saints? These crazy, loony, pitiful women?

Some of them, without a doubt, were our mothers and grandmothers.

In the still heat of the post-Reconstruction South, this is how they seemed to Jean Toomer: exquisite butterflies trapped in an evil honey, toiling away their lives in an era, a century, that did not acknowledge them, except as "the *mule* of the world." They dreamed dreams that no one knew—not even themselves, in any coherent fashion—and saw visions no one could understand. They wandered or sat about the countryside crooning lullabies to ghosts, and drawing the mother of Christ in charcoal on courthouse walls.

They forced their minds to desert their bodies and their striving spirits sought to rise, like frail whirlwinds from the hard red clay. And when those frail whirlwinds fell, in scattered particles, upon the ground, no one mourned. Instead, men lit candles to celebrate the emptiness that remained, as people do who enter a beautiful but vacant space to resurrect a God.

Our mothers and grandmothers, some of them: moving to music not yet written. And they waited.

They waited for a day when the unknown thing that was in them would be made known; but guessed, somehow in their darkness, that on the day of their revelation they would be long dead. Therefore to Toomer they walked, and even ran, in slow motion. For they were going nowhere immediate, and the future was not yet within their grasp. And men took our mothers and grandmothers, "but got no pleasure from it." So complex was their passion and their calm.

To Toomer, they lay vacant and fallow as autumn fields, with harvest time never in sight: and he saw them enter loveless marriages, without joy; and become prostitutes, without resistance; and become mothers of children, without fulfillment.

For these grandmothers and mothers of ours were not Saints, but Artists; driven to a numb and bleeding madness by the springs of creativity in them for which there was no release. They were Creators, who lived lives of spiritual waste, because they were so rich in spirituality—which is the basis of Art—that the strain of enduring their unused and unwanted talent drove them insane. Throwing away this spirituality was their pathetic attempt to lighten the soul to a weight their work-worn, sexually abused bodies could bear.

What did it mean for a black woman to be an artist in our grandmothers' time? In our great-grandmothers' day? It is a question with an answer cruel enough to stop the blood.

Did you have a genius of a great-great-grandmother who died under some ignorant and depraved white overseer's lash? Or was she required to bake biscuits for a lazy backwater tramp, when she cried out in her soul to paint watercolors of sunsets, or the rain falling on the green and peaceful pasturelands? Or was her body broken and forced to bear children (who were more often than not sold away from her)—eight, ten, fifteen, twenty children—when her one joy was the thought of modeling heroic figures of rebellion, in stone or clay?

How was the creativity of the black woman kept alive, year after year and century after century, when for most of the years black people have been in America, it was a punishable crime for a black person to read or write? And the freedom to paint, to sculpt, to expand the mind with action did not exist. Consider, if you can bear to imagine it, what might have been the result if singing, too, had been forbidden by law. Listen to the voices of Bessie Smith, Billie Holiday, Nina Simone, Roberta Flack, and Aretha Franklin, among others, and imagine those voices muzzled for life. Then you may begin to comprehend the lives of our "crazy," "Sainted" mothers and grandmothers. The agony of the lives of women who might have been Poets, Novelists, Essayists, and Short-Story Writers (over a period of centuries), who died with their real gifts stifled within them.

And, if this were the end of the story, we would have cause to cry out in my paraphrase of Okot p'Bitek's great poem:

O, my clanswomen
Let us all cry together!
Come,
Let us mourn the death of our mother,

The death of a Queen
The ash that was produced
By a great fire!
O, this homestead is utterly dead
Close the gates
With *lacari* thorns,
For our mother
The creator of the Stool is lost!
And all the young women
Have perished in the wilderness!

But this is not the end of the story, for all the young women—our mothers and grandmothers, *ourselves*—have not perished in the wilderness. And if we ask ourselves why, and search for and find the answer, we will know beyond all efforts to erase it from our minds, just exactly who, and of what, we black American women are.

One example, perhaps the most pathetic, most misunderstood one, can provide a backdrop for our mothers' work: Phillis Wheatley, a slave in the 1700s.

Virginia Woolf, in her book *A Room of One's Own,* wrote that in order for a woman to write fiction she must have two things, certainly: a room of her own (with key and lock) and enough money to support herself.

What then are we to make of Phillis Wheatley, a slave, who owned not even herself? This sickly, frail black girl who required a servant of her own at times—her health was so precarious—and who, had she been white, would have been easily considered the intellectual superior of all the women and most of the men in the society of her day.

Virginia Woolf wrote further, speaking of course not of our Phillis, that "any woman born with a great gift in the sixteenth century [insert "eighteenth century," insert "black woman," insert "born or made a slave"] would certainly have gone crazed, shot herself, or ended her days in some lonely cottage outside the village, half witch, half wizard [insert "Saint"], feared and mocked at. For it needs little skill and psychology to be sure that a highly gifted girl who had tried to use her gift for poetry would have been so thwarted and hindered by contrary instincts [add "chains, guns, the lash, the ownership of one's body by someone else, submission to an alien religion"], that she must have lost her health and sanity to a certainty."

The key words, as they relate to Phillis, are "contrary instincts." For when we read the poetry of Phillis Wheatley—as when we read the novels of Nella Larsen or the oddly false-sounding autobiography of that freest of all black women writers, Zora Hurston—evidence of "contrary instincts" is everywhere. Her loyalties were completely divided, as was, without question, her mind.

But how could this be otherwise? Captured at seven, a slave of wealthy, doting whites who instilled in her the "savagery" of the Africa they "rescued" her from . . . one wonders if she was even able to remember her homeland as she had known it, or as it really was.

Yet, because she did try to use her gift for poetry in a world that made her a slave, she was "so thwarted and hindered by . . . contrary instincts, that she . . . lost her health. . . ." In the last years of her brief life, burdened not only with the need to express her gift but also with a penniless, friendless "freedom" and several small children for whom she was forced to do strenuous work to feed, she lost her health, certainly. Suffering from malnutrition and neglect and who knows what mental agonies, Phillis Wheatley died.

So torn by "contrary instincts" was black, kidnapped, enslaved Phillis that her description of "the Goddess"—as she poetically called the Liberty she did not have—is ironically, cruelly humorous. And, in fact, has held Phillis up to ridicule for more than a century. It is usually read prior to hanging Phillis's memory as that of a fool. She wrote:

The Goddess comes, she moves divinely fair,
Olive and laurel binds her *golden* hair.
Wherever shines this native of the skies,
Unnumber'd charms and recent graces rise. [My italics]

It is obvious that Phillis, the slave, combed the "Goddess's" hair every morning; prior, perhaps, to bringing in the milk, or fixing her mistress's lunch. She took her imagery from the one thing she saw elevated above all others.

With the benefit of hindsight we ask, "How could she?"

But at last, Phillis, we understand. No more snickering when your stiff, struggling, ambivalent lines are forced on us. We know now that you were not an idiot or a traitor; only a sickly little black girl, snatched from your home and country and made a slave; a woman who still struggled to sing the song that was your gift, although in a land of barbarians who praised you for your bewildered tongue. It is not so much what you sang, as that you kept alive, in so many of our ancestors, *the notion of song.*

Black women are called, in the folklore that so aptly identifies one's status in society, "the *mule* of the world," because we have been handed the burdens that everyone else—*everyone* else—refused to carry. We have also been called "Matriarchs," "Superwomen," and "Mean and Evil Bitches." Not to mention "Castraters" and "Sapphire's Mama." When we have pleaded for understanding, our character has been distorted; when we have asked for simple caring, we have been handed empty inspirational appellations, then stuck in the farthest corner. When we have asked for love, we have been given children. In short, even our plainer gifts, our labors of fidelity and love, have been knocked down our throats. To be an artist and a black woman, even today, lowers our status in many respects, rather than raises it: and yet, artists we will be.

Therefore we must fearlessly pull out of ourselves and look at and identify with our lives the living creativity some of our great-grandmothers were not allowed to know. I stress *some* of them because it is well known that the majority of our great-grandmothers knew, even without "knowing" it, the reality of their spirituality, even if they didn't recognize it beyond what happened in the singing at church—and they never had any intention of giving it up.

How they did it—those millions of black women who were not Phillis Wheatley, or Lucy Terry or Frances Harper or Zora Hurston or Nella Larsen or Bessie Smith; or Elizabeth Catlett, or Katherine Dunham, either—brings me to the title of this essay, "In Search of Our Mothers' Gardens," which is a personal account that is yet shared, in its theme and its meaning, by all of us. I found, while thinking about the far-reaching world of the creative black woman, that often the truest answer to a question that really matters can be found very close.

In the late 1920s my mother ran away from home to marry my father. Marriage, if not running away, was expected of seventeen-year-old girls. By the time she was twenty, she had two children and was pregnant with a third. Five children later, I was born. And this is how I came to know my mother: she seemed a large, soft, loving-eyed woman who was rarely impatient in our home. Her quick, violent temper was on view only a few times a year, when she battled with the white landlord who had the misfortune to suggest to her that her children did not need to go to school.

She made all the clothes we wore, even my brothers' overalls. She made all the towels and sheets we used. She spent the summers canning vegetables and fruits. She spent the winter evenings making quilts enough to cover all our beds.

During the "working" day, she labored beside—not behind—my father in the fields. Her day began before sunup, and did not end until late at night. There was never a moment for her to sit down, undisturbed, to unravel her own private thoughts; never a time free from interruption—by work or the noisy inquiries of her many children. And yet, it is to my mother—and all our mothers who were not famous—that I went in search of the secret of what has fed that muzzled and often mutilated, but vibrant, creative spirit that the black woman has inherited, and that pops out in wild and unlikely places to this day.

But when, you will ask, did my overworked mother have time to know or care about feeding the creative spirit?

The answer is so simple that many of us have spent years discovering it. We have constantly looked high, when we should have looked high— and low.

For example: in the Smithsonian Institution in Washington, D.C., there hangs a quilt unlike any other in the world. In fanciful, inspired, and yet simple and identifiable figures, it portrays the story of the Crucifixion. It is considered rare, beyond price. Though it follows no known pattern of quilt-making, and though it is made of bits and pieces of worthless rags, it is obviously the work of a person of powerful imagination and deep spiritual feeling. Below this quilt I saw a note that says it was made by "an anonymous Black woman in Alabama, a hundred years ago."

If we could locate this "anonymous" black woman from Alabama, she would turn out to be one of our grandmothers—an artist who left her mark in the only materials she could afford, and in the only medium her position in society allowed her to use.

As Virginia Woolf wrote further, in *A Room of One's Own:*

> Yet genius of a sort must have existed among women as it must have existed among the working class. [Change this to "slaves" and "the wives and daughters of sharecroppers."] Now and again an Emily Brontë or a Robert Burns [change this to "a Zora Hurston or a Richard Wright"] blazes out and proves its presence. But certainly it never got itself on to paper. When, however, one reads of a witch being ducked, of a woman possessed by devils [or "Sainthood"], of a wise woman selling herbs [our root workers], or even a very remarkable man who had a mother, then I think we are on the track of a lost novelist, a suppressed poet, of some mute and inglorious Jane Austen. . . . Indeed, I would venture to guess that Anon, who wrote so many poems without signing them, was often a woman. . . .

And so our mothers and grandmothers have, more often than not anonymously, handed on the creative spark, the seed of the flower they themselves never hoped to see: or like a sealed letter they could not plainly read.

And so it is, certainly, with my own mother. Unlike "Ma" Rainey's songs, which retained their creator's name even while blasting forth from Bessie Smith's mouth, no song or poem will bear my mother's name. Yet so many of the stories that I write, that we all write, are my mother's stories. Only recently did I fully realize this: that through years of listening to my mother's stories of her life, I have absorbed not only the stories themselves, but something of the manner in which she spoke, something of the urgency that involves the knowledge that her stories—like her life—must be recorded. It is probably for this reason that so much of what I have written is about characters whose counterparts in real life are so much older than I am.

But the telling of these stories, which came from my mother's lips as naturally as breathing, was not the only way my mother showed herself as an artist. For stories, too, were subject to being distracted, to dying without conclusion. Dinners must be started, and cotton must be gathered before the big rains. The artist that was and is my mother showed itself to me only after many years. This is what I finally noticed:

Like Mem, a character in *The Third Life of Grange Copeland,*° my mother adorned with flowers whatever shabby house we were forced to live in. And not just your typical straggly country stand of zinnias, either. She planted ambitious gardens—and still does—with over fifty different varieties of plants that bloom profusely from early March until late November. Before she left home for the fields, she watered her flowers, chopped up the grass, and laid out new beds. When she returned from the fields she might divide clumps of bulbs, dig a cold pit, uproot and replant roses, or prune branches from her taller bushes or trees—until night came and it was too dark to see.

Whatever she planted grew as if by magic, and her fame as a grower of flowers spread over three counties. Because of her creativity with her flowers, even my memories of poverty are seen through a screen of blooms—sunflowers, petunias, roses, dahlias, forsythia, spirea, delphiniums, verbena . . . and on and on.

And I remember people coming to my mother's yard to be given cuttings from her flowers; I hear again the praise showered on her because whatever rocky soil she landed on, she turned into a garden. A garden so brilliant with colors, so original in its design, so magnificent with life and creativity, that to this day people drive by our house in Georgia—perfect strangers and imperfect strangers—and ask to stand or walk among my mother's art.

I notice that it is only when my mother is working in her flowers that she is radiant, almost to the point of being invisible—except as Creator: hand and eye. She is involved in work her soul must have. Ordering the universe in the image of her personal conception of Beauty.

Her face, as she prepares the Art that is her gift, is a legacy of respect she leaves to me, for all that illuminates and cherishes life. She has handed down respect for the possibilities—and the will to grasp them.

For her, so hindered and intruded upon in so many ways, being an artist has still been a daily part of her life. This ability to hold on, even in very simple ways, is work black women have done for a very long time.

This poem is not enough, but it is something, for the woman who literally covered the holes in our walls with sunflowers:

They were women then
My mama's generation
Husky of voice—Stout of
Step
With fists as well as

The Third Life of Grange Copeland A novel by Alice Walker, published in 1970.

Hands
How they battered down
Doors
And ironed
Starched white
Shirts
How they led
Armies
Headragged Generals
Across mined
Fields
Booby-trapped
Kitchens
To discover books
Desks
A place for us
How they knew what we
Must know
Without knowing a page
Of it
Themselves.

Guided by my heritage of a love of beauty and a respect for strength—in search of my mother's garden, I found my own.

And perhaps in Africa over two hundred years ago, there was just such a mother; perhaps she painted vivid and daring decorations in oranges and yellows and greens on the walls of her hut; perhaps she sang—in a voice like Roberta Flack's—*sweetly* over the compounds of her village; perhaps she wove the most stunning mats or told the most ingenious stories of all the village storytellers. Perhaps she was herself a poet—though only her daughter's name is signed to the poems that we know.

Perhaps Phillis Wheatley's mother was also an artist.

Perhaps in more than Phillis Wheatley's biological life is her mother's signature made clear.

1974

Daddy's Girl

Judith Wells

Judith Wells was born in 1944, grew up in San Francisco, and received her B.A. in French from Stanford and her Ph.D. in comparative literature from the University of California, Berkeley. (Her dissertation dealt with

*women and madness in modern literature—madness meaning both anger
and insanity.) She helped develop the Women's Studies program at Berkeley and has taught courses on women and madness in literature. She has
also headed a program at Napa Community College designed to encourage
older women to return to school. In 1980, she published* Been in Berkeley
Too Long. *"Daddy's Girl," her first published work, appeared in* Libera,
Winter 1972.

> *"A little girl, full of innocence and indulgence. And then this mad-
> ness. . . ."*

> —Ladders to Fire, ANAÏS NIN

Nothing is more startling to a Daddy's girl than to find herself in revolt
against her Daddies. Because of her intimacy with and desire for approval
from her Daddies, she finds it painful to make a clean break with them.
"Daddy, daddy, you bastard, I'm through," cries Sylvia Plath° in her poem
"Daddy"; in spite of the voodoo murder of her Father, Plath is still a little
girl murderess who addresses the "Panzer man," "the brute," the "Fascist" of her poem as Daddy. Even her closing words, "I'm through,"
strangely undercut her patricide—as if she herself dies with her Father—
an echo of her death wish in a previous stanza: "At twenty I tried to
die / And get back, back, back, to you."

   This complicity with "Daddy" has been my own peculiar emotional
madness for years. A large part of what I always called my "self" has been
invested in the personality of the Daddy's Girl or the Little Girl. The
Little Girl is fragile, vulnerable, helpless, bewildered, compliant. She feels
she occupies a very tiny amount of both physical and psychological space.
In my own dreams this smallness is experienced through seeing myself
as a miniature person—a girl who melts down to a face in a postage stamp
or a girl whose full size is as small as a person's hands (and thus easily
manipulated). The Little Girl is an object, not a subject.

   It took me a good deal of hard work in psychotherapy and the Women's
Movement to reach any understanding about my own Little Girl. For a
long time I maintained a masque of independence; I made myself believe
I didn't care what my father and men thought about me. Yet underneath,
I based most of my personality on masculine approval. Any criticism from
a male brought me a haunting sense of guilt. The least assertion of my
own preference or will was stepping over the line; I internalized the reply
"You've gone too far" even before I opened my mouth. I was unable to
work when my boyfriend was around and felt guilty over surpassing male

---

Sylvia Plath   American poet and novelist (1932–1963) who attempted suicide at the end
of her junior year of college and committed suicide at the age of thirty.

friends and my father in intellectual achievements; but I also knew I had to accomplish something to get masculine approval. The only activity this ambivalence brought on was diarrhea. Then I became sick and could nurture my vulnerable, fragile self which was, and still is, in effect, my Little Girl.

The Little Girl infects many females because she is nurtured by so much of society as well as by ourselves. She has no age limit:

> She wears sweet little dresses, her tears and caprices are viewed indulgently, her hair is done up carefully, older people are amused at her expressions and coquetries—bodily contacts and agreeable glances protect her against the anguish of solitude. (*The Second Sex,* p. 252)

Although this is Simone de Beauvoir's description of a small girl in childhood, it could well apply to the Little Girl aspect of ourselves, our mothers, and our grandmothers. I was surprised when I realized that some of the gestures of my boss's eight-year-old daughter were not far from my own— her cajoling, indirect expression of what she wanted, her refusal to attempt a simple task without precise, precise instructions. The Little Girl pose is designed to elicit maternal or paternal indulgence—specifically, because the Little Girl is or thinks she is helpless.

Although the Little Girl can inhabit any woman's body, a small woman is particularly susceptible to this syndrome. In her first *Diary,* Anaïs Nin relates a conversation with her psychiatrist about this sense of vulnerability and helplessness that a small woman experiences:

> My greatest fear is that people will become aware that I am fragile, not a full-blown woman physically, that I am emotionally vulnerable, that I have small breasts like a girl. (p. 86)

My own sense that I am physically slight and fragile has not only bolstered my feelings of helplessness, but it has also contributed to my feeling that I am not quite a grown woman—that creature who is defined by having curves in the right places. The curveless woman easily sees herself as a Little Girl.

Although the Little Girl may be more readily apparent in a woman with a small body, most women experience the Little Girl at times as a psychic state. In Nin's *Children of the Albatross,* Djuna remembers:

> She remembered, too, that whenever she became entangled in too great a difficulty she had these swift regressions into her adolescent state. Almost as if in the large world of maturity, when the obstacle loomed too large, she shrank again into the body of the young girl for whom the world had first appeared as a violent and dangerous place, forcing her to retreat, and when she retreated she fell back into smallness. (p. 40)

Djuna experiences a "psychic smallness" which is her inability to affect significantly the world around her—hence, her helplessness.

In the Little Girl, "psychic smallness" is also directly related to her desire for approval from authority figures, especially from Daddies. As a Little Girl, I found that I had based my personality for such a long time on approval from authority figures that *they* were my personality. I experienced "psychic smallness" because I had never defined who I was or what I wanted in life; my only sense of identity stemmed from Daddy's approval.

The real tragedy of the Little Girl, then, is her inability to define herself in her own terms, select her own goals, and feel her life has significance *without* Daddy's support. The Little Girl turns over the responsibility for her own life to her Daddies (real fathers, boyfriends, husbands, professors, psychiatrists) and sits devotedly, if a bit uneasily, at their feet. Unfortunately, society sanctions this pose of the Child-Woman, especially in its sexual images and stereotypes.

In the Magic Theater's recent production of *Miles Gloriosus*, two poles of stereotyped female sexuality are portrayed: the Vixen-Whore in black wasp waist corset and tights, and the Baby Doll in pink pajamas, with freckles on her nose and ribbons in her hair. Although the Baby Doll is parody in this play, many girls are schooled in this image of coyness, flirtation, and "innocent" sexuality which they carry over into adult life. The Little Girl clothes syndrome, which periodically runs rampant through fashion as it has recently, supports this image: the mod "little dresses," the clingy pastel tee shirts with patterns from babyhood, the overall and romper outfits—all designed to make females resemble innocent little girls yet still be sexually appealing. Roger Vadim exploited this combination of innocence and sexuality to the hilt in his presentation of Brigitte Bardot to moviegoers. In Simone de Beauvoir's book, *Brigitte Bardot and the Lolita Syndrome,* the author relates:

> He [Vadim] painted her as naive to the point of absurdity. According to him, at the age of eighteen she thought that mice laid eggs. (p. 13)

De Beauvoir comments on Bardot's roles in "And God Created Woman" and "Love Is My Profession":

> BB is a lost, pathetic child who needs a guide and protector. This cliché has proved its worth. It flatters masculine vanity. . . . (p. 15)

The child-woman poses no threat to the male ego—hence her appeal. De Beauvoir notes the particular charm of the child-woman to the American male:

> . . . he feels a certain antipathy to the 'real woman.' He regards her as an antagonist, a praying mantis, a tyrant. He abandons himself eagerly to the charms of the 'nymph' in whom the formidable figure of the wife and 'Mom' is not yet apparent. (p. 23)

Although I hardly possess the "nymph" looks of Bardot, my own appearance and Little Girl personality have encouraged me to maintain this child-woman sexual role. When I was younger, this child role came easily; but with increased sexual experience, the role became harder and harder to maintain. I can't kid myself anymore. I know my own sexual desires, but the child-woman in me still makes me embarrassed when I want to be sexually aggressive or state my desires straight out. I know many women share this problem—this embarrassment over wanting to be a subject, not an object in sexual activity. And the male attitude doesn't help much; for even though "The Sexual Revolution's Here," a woman is discouraged subtly (a male's slightly chilly response to her phone call) and not so subtly (his impotence when she asks him to bed) when she is sexually aggressive.

As a Little Girl I have spent a good deal of my life adjusting to just such masculine requirements, adapting myself to gain their approval. Finally, I felt pain—the intense frustration of being confined by my own compliancy. I understand all too well the statement of the man I work for (who designed an educational program to improve the self-image of Blacks) about the accommodation attitudes of Blacks. I have substituted *woman* for *man* in the quote and *her* for *him:*

> Let us assume I am standing with my foot on the neck of a *woman* who is lying on the ground; I am wearing a hobnail boot. I say to *her,* "Your role is simply different from mine, not worse; you are horizontal and I am vertical." And then I say to *her,* "Your role has certain advantages over mine; you do not have to worry about falling down. Furthermore, you are developing a very interesting adaptive behavior. You are learning to breathe with my foot on your neck."
> (*Teaching and Testing the Disadvantaged,* William Johntz)

Interestingly enough, the sado-masochistic imagery of this passage exactly fits sexual politics. The victim is made to feel she is lucky she doesn't have the "burdens" of the victor. The victim's final adaptive behavior is what the Little Girl and, in actuality, any woman, has done all her life. She has learned to breathe with a foot on her neck until she finally explodes in frustration and cries out with Sylvia Plath, "You do not do, you do not do / Any more, black shoe. . . ."

It would be great if the Little Girl could join the Women's Movement and instantly become a self-sufficient woman. I have found that my Little Girl personality is not shed so easily, and that my rebellion against my Daddies has its own peculiar Little Girl cyclic rhythm: compliancy towards a man—simmering hate—explosion of outrage—anxiety over having stepped over the line—fear of reprisal—compliancy towards a man—and the cycle begins again. Because the Little Girl has suffocated her own desires so completely in favor of her Daddies, her potential for rage is volcanic once she questions the belief that "Father knows best."

Yet for myself and probably for most Little Girls, each explosion is followed less by a sense of triumph than by anxiety and fear of reprisal. Since the Little Girl's only previous sense of identity stemmed from approval from her Daddies, cutting these figures out of her life will seem like cutting out the core of herself. At first, "destruction" of Daddy seems like self-destruction. This anxiety over self-destruction in the elimination of her source of identity brings on the Little Girl's helplessness. She is then a weak, vulnerable, compliant child again, fearing Daddy's reprisal.

Even if she finally rebels against her Daddies, the Little Girl will remain caught in this circle of anger and compliancy until she learns to stop loving and nurturing the Little Girl in herself. If I had to select the most important moment in my several years of psychotherapy, it would be the moment I realized who loved the Little Girl in me most. I was astonished to find it was myself. I was finally able to objectify my Little Girl enough to see her as separate from another part of me. I experienced myself caressing and cherishing that Little Girl as I had loved my dolls many years ago—the same kind of love I desperately wanted to experience when I was a real little girl. Perhaps, above everything else, this desperation for love kept me locked into my first childhood attempts to gain approval from adults. And when, as a real little girl, I realized that the "adult world" was governed mainly by male figures, I began to base my worth on how much love and approval I could get from my Daddies. The Little Girl pose stuck.

I am coming to realize more and more that I no longer receive much approval for the Little Girl role; it's an illusion I maintain which has little basis in my own daily life. As a friend of mine in graduate school put it, "I'm thirty years old. I look like a grown woman. If I start to do the Little Girl bit with my professors, they look at me funny." The Little Girl role has a few benefits but enormous drawbacks: a stifling of one's intelligence and creativity, a confining sexual role, an arresting of growth of one's personality. When I experienced myself cherishing my Little Girl doll self, I flashed on a picture I had drawn when I was ten years old to illustrate a poem I had read called "The long ago, far away doll." I drew a doll in a sea chest; she was dressed in a lovely yellow fancy dress, and her cheeks were rouged; but her eyes stared into space, and she looked like a dead person. The Little Girl aspect of any woman keeps her like this doll—repressed, inactive, dead.

The Little Girl has no place to grow but up. It is true that if she does choose to continue her growth, she may not receive some of the masculine approval she received in the past. As I stated previously, certain men like a Little Girl because she is less threatening to the masculine ego. Too, the growing Little Girl must risk the disapproval of her real father—often the man who clings the most tenaciously to the idea of his daughter as a perpetual girl child. She may be regarded as a rebel or even a bitch. Yet there will be others, both women and men, who will approve of her—not for feminine fluff, but for her real talents and developing personality. More important, she will gain self-respect from presenting her *own self* to the world, and this self-respect will be worth much more than the approval she received as a crippled Little Girl.

I read someplace in my many psychological readings, when I was trying to pinpoint my "problems," about a young girl in an African society. In her early teens, she was listless, lacked confidence, and was fearful of males and masculine authority. Her tribe used a mode of transvestitism to exorcise her fears. She dressed up in the male military costume of the former colonial power of the area and began to dance in this costume. After the ceremony, the girl's confidence increased enormously, she no longer feared men, and she eventually developed into a mature, self-reliant woman. The girl in this story acts out symbolically what the Little Girl must learn to do for herself: incorporate the authority, which she objectifies outside of herself, into her own person. She must develop a sense of her *own personal authority* and hence, *self-approval.* When the Little Girl develops this sense of self-approval, she will no longer be a Little Girl, but a mature woman—a full, complete human being. With this new sense of personal authority, she can look back on her "rebellious" struggles as Anaïs Nin does:

> Very often I would say I rebelled against this or that. Much later it occurred to me to question this statement. Instead of rebellion could it be that I was merely asserting my own belief? (*Diary* III, p. xiii)

And I answer with Nin: YES.

Book in a different voice expands on this

Fail: Bright Women

Matina Horner

Matina Horner was born in 1939 to Greek parents, who decided to stay in the United States after the outbreak of World War II. She received her bachelor's degree from Bryn Mawr College in 1961 and then attended the University of Michigan, where in 1968 she received her doctorate in psychology with some of the research she writes about in the present essay. The research appeared in Psychology Today *in November 1969, headed by a quotation from Balzac: "A woman who is guided by the head and not by the heart is a social pestilence: she has all the defects of a passionate and affectionate woman with none of her compensations: she is without pity, without love, without virtue, without sex."*

Besides being an authority on motivation and achievement in women, Dr. Horner has studied ability grouping in schools, the impact of internalized sex and race role stereotypes, and factors that foster the development of curiosity. She has been on the Harvard faculty since 1969 in the Depart-

ment of Social Relations, and in 1972 she became President of Radcliffe College, which is integrated as a coeducational institution with Harvard.

Consider Phil, a bright young college sophomore. He has always done well in school, he is in the honors program, he has wanted to be a doctor as long as he can remember. We ask him to tell us a story based on one clue: *"After first-term finals, John finds himself at the top of his medical school class."* Phil writes:

> John is a conscientious young man who worked hard. He is pleased with himself. John has always wanted to go into medicine and is very dedicated . . . John continues working hard and eventually graduates at the top of his class.

Now consider Monica, another honors student. She too has always done well and she too has visions of a flourishing career. We give her the same clue, but with "Anne" as the successful student—*after first-term finals, Anne finds herself at the top of her medical school class.* Instead of identifying with Anne's triumph, Monica tells a bizarre tale:

> Anne starts proclaiming her surprise and joy. Her fellow classmates are so disgusted with her behavior that they jump on her in a body and beat her. She is maimed for life.

Next we ask Monica and Phil to work on a series of achievement tests by themselves. Monica scores higher than Phil. Finally we get them together, competing against each other on the same kind of tests. Phil performs magnificently, but Monica dissolves into a bundle of nerves.

The glaring contrast between the two stories and the dramatic changes in performance in competitive situations illustrate important differences between men and women in reacting to achievement.

In 1953, David McClelland, John Atkinson and colleagues published the first major work on the "achievement motive." Through the use of the Thematic Apperception Test (TAT), they were able to isolate the psychological characteristic of a *need to achieve.* This seemed to be an internalized standard of excellence, motivating the individual to do well in any achievement-oriented situation involving intelligence and leadership ability. Subsequent investigators studied innumerable facets of achievement motivation: how it is instilled in children, how it is expressed, how it relates to social class, even how it is connected to the rise and fall of civilizations. The result of all this research is an impressive and a theoretically consistent body of data about the achievement motive—in men.

Women, however, are conspicuously absent from almost all of the studies. In the few cases where the ladies were included, the results were contradictory or confusing. So women were eventually left out altogether.

The predominantly male researchers apparently decided, as Freud had before them, that the only way to understand woman was to turn to the poets. Atkinson's 1958 book, *Motives in Fantasy, Action and Society,* is an 800-page compilation of all the theories and facts on achievement motivation in men. Women got a footnote, reflecting the state of the science.

To help remedy this lopsided state of affairs, I undertook to explore the basis for sex differences in achievement motivation. But where to begin?

My first clue came from the one consistent finding on the women: they get higher test-anxiety scores than do the men. Eleanor Maccoby has suggested that the girl who is motivated to achieve is defying conventions of what girls "should" do. As a result, the intellectual woman pays a price in anxiety. Margaret Mead concurs, noting that intense intellectual striving can be viewed as "competitively aggressive behavior." And of course Freud thought that the whole essence of femininity lay in repressing aggressiveness (and hence intellectuality).

Thus consciously or unconsciously the girl equates intellectual achievement with loss of femininity. A bright woman is caught in a double bind. In testing and other achievement-oriented situations she worries not only about failure, but also about success. If she fails, she is not living up to her own standards of performance; if she succeeds, she is not living up to societal expectations about the female role. Men in our society do not experience this kind of ambivalence, because they are not only permitted but actively encouraged to do well.

For women, then, the desire to achieve is often contaminated by what I call the *motive to avoid success.* I define it as the fear that success in competitive achievement situations will lead to negative consequences, such as unpopularity and loss of femininity. This motive, like the achievement motive itself, is a stable disposition within the person, acquired early in life along with other sex-role standards. When fear of success conflicts with a desire to be successful, the result is an inhibition of achievement motivation.

I began my study with several hypotheses about the motive to avoid success:

1) Of course, it would be far more characteristic of women than of men.

2) It would be more characteristic of women who are capable of success and who are career-oriented than of women not so motivated. Women who are not seeking success should not, after all, be threatened by it.

3) I anticipated that the anxiety over success would be greater in competitive situations (when one's intellectual performance is evaluated against someone else's) than in noncompetitive ones (when one works alone). The aggressive, masculine aspects of achievement striving are certainly more pronounced in competitive settings, particularly when the opponent is male. Women's anxiety should therefore be greatest when they compete with men.

I administered the standard TAT achievement motivation measures to a sample of 90 girls and 88 boys, all undergraduates at the University of Michigan. In addition, I asked each to tell a story based on the clue described before: *After first-term finals, John (Anne) finds himself (herself) at the top of his (her) medical school class.* The girls wrote about Anne, the boys about John.

Their stories were scored for "motive to avoid success" if they expressed any negative imagery that reflected concern about doing well. Generally, such imagery fell into three categories:

1) The most frequent Anne story reflected strong fears of social rejection as a result of success. The girls in this group showed anxiety about becoming unpopular, unmarriageable and lonely.

> Anne is an acne-faced bookworm. She runs to the bulletin board and finds she's at the top. As usual she smarts off. A chorus of groans is the rest of the class's reply. . . . She studies 12 hours a day, and lives at home to save money. "Well it certainly paid off. All the Friday and Saturday nights without dates, fun—I'll be the best woman doctor alive." And yet a twinge of sadness comes thru—she wonders what she really has . . .

> Although Anne is happy with her success she fears what will happen to her social life. The male med. students don't seem to think very highly of a female who has beaten them in their field . . . She will be a proud and successful but alas a very *lonely* doctor.

> Anne doesn't want to be number one in her class . . . she feels she shouldn't rank so high because of social reasons. She drops down to ninth in the class and then marries the boy who graduates number one.

> Anne is pretty darn proud of herself, but everyone hates and envies her.

2) Girls in the second category were less concerned with issues of social approval or disapproval; they were more worried about definitions of womanhood. Their stories expressed guilt and despair over success, and doubts about their femininity or normality.

> Unfortunately Anne no longer feels so certain that she really wants to be a doctor. She is worried about herself and wonders if perhaps she isn't normal . . . Anne decides not to continue with her medical work but to take courses that have a deeper personal meaning for her.

> Anne feels guilty . . . She will finally have a nervous breakdown and quit medical school and marry a successful young doctor.

> Anne is pleased. She had worked extraordinarily hard and her grades showed it. "It is not enough," Anne thinks. "I am not happy." She didn't even want to be a doctor. She is not sure what she wants. Anne says to hell with the whole business and goes into social work—not hardly as glamorous, prestigious or lucrative; but she is happy.

3) The third group of stories did not even try to confront the ambivalence about doing well. Girls in this category simply denied the possibility that any mere woman could be so successful. Some of them completely changed the content of the clue, or distorted it, or refused to believe it, or absolved Anne of responsibility for her success. These stories were remarkable for their psychological ingenuity:

> Anne is a *code name* for a nonexistent person created by a group of med. students. They take turns writing exams for Anne . . .

> Anne is really happy she's on top, though *Tom is higher than she*—though that's as it should be . . . Anne doesn't mind Tom winning.

> Anne is talking to her counselor. Counselor says she will make a fine *nurse*.

> It was *luck* that Anne came out on top because she didn't want to go to medical school anyway.

Fifty-nine girls—over 65 per cent—told stories that fell into one or another of the above categories. But only eight boys, fewer than 10 per cent, showed evidence of the motive to avoid success. (These differences are significant at better than the .0005 level.) In fact, sometimes I think that most of the young men in the sample were incipient Horatio Algers. They expressed unequivocal delight at John's success (clearly John had worked hard for it), and projected a grand and glorious future for him. There was none of the hostility, bitterness and ambivalence that the girls felt for Anne. In short, the differences between male and female stories based on essentially the same clue were enormous.

Two of the stories are particularly revealing examples of this male-female contrast. The girls insisted that Anne give up her career for marriage:

> Anne has a boyfriend, Carl, in the same class and they are quite serious. . . . She wants him to be scholastically higher than she is. Anne will deliberately lower her academic standing the next term, while she does all she subtly can to help Carl. His grades come up and Anne soon drops out of medical school. They marry and he goes on in school while she raises their family.

But of course the boys would ask John to do no such thing:

> John has worked very hard and his long hours of study have paid off. . . . He is thinking about his girl, Cheri, whom he will marry at the end of med. school. He realizes he can give her all the things she desires after he becomes established. He will go on in med. school and be successful in the long run.

Success inhibits social life for the girls; it enhances social life for the boys.

Earlier I suggested that the motive to avoid success is especially aroused in competitive situations. In the second part of this study I wanted to see whether the aggressive overtones of competition against men scared the girls away. Would competition raise their anxiety about success and thus lower their performance?

First I put all of the students together in a large competitive group, and gave them a series of achievement tests (verbal and arithmetic). I then assigned them randomly to one of three other experimental conditions. One-third worked on a similar set of tests, each in competition with a member of the same sex. One-third competed against a member of the opposite sex. The last third worked by themselves, a non-competitive condition.

Ability is an important factor in achievement motivation research. If you want to compare two persons on the strength of their *motivation* to succeed, how do you know that any differences in performance are not due to initial differences in *ability* to succeed? One way of avoiding this problem is to use each subject as his own control; that is, the performance of an individual working alone can be compared with his score in competition. Ability thus remains constant; any change in score must be due to motivational factors. This control over ability was, of course, possible only for the last third of my subjects: the 30 girls and 30 boys who had worked alone *and* in the large group competition. I decided to look at their scores first.

Performance changed dramatically over the two situations. A large number of the men did far better when they were in competition than when they worked alone. For the women the reverse was true. Fewer than one-third of the women, but more than two-thirds of the men, got significantly higher scores in competition.

When we looked at just the girls in terms of the motive to avoid success, the comparisons were even more striking. As predicted, the students who felt ambivalent or anxious about doing well turned in their best scores when they worked by themselves. Seventy-seven percent of the girls who feared success did better alone than in competition. Women who were low on the motive, however, behaved more like the men: 93 per cent of them got higher scores in competition. (Results significant at the .005.)

As a final test of motivational differences, I asked the students to indicate on a scale from 1 to 100 "How important was it for you to do well in this situation?" The high-fear-of-success girls said that it was much more important for them to do well when they worked alone than when they worked in either kind of competition. For the low-fear girls, such differences were not statistically significant. Their test scores were higher in competition, as we saw, and they thought that it was important to succeed no matter what the setting. And in all experimental conditions—working alone, or in competition against males or females—high-fear women consistently lagged behind their fearless comrades on the importance of doing well.

The findings suggest that most women will fully explore their intellec-

Female Fear of Success & Performance

	perform better working alone	*perform better in competition*
high fear of success	13	4
low fear of success	1	12

tual potential only when they do not need to compete—and least of all when they are competing with men. This was most true of women with a strong anxiety about success. Unfortunately, these are often the same women who could be very successful if they were free from that anxiety. The girls in my sample who feared success also tended to have high intellectual ability and histories of academic success. (It is interesting to note that all but two of these girls were majoring in the humanities and in spite of very high grade points aspired to traditional female careers: housewife, mother, nurse, schoolteacher. Girls who did not fear success, however, were aspiring to graduate degrees and careers in such scientific areas as math, physics and chemistry.)

We can see from this small study that achievement motivation in women is much more complex than the same drive in men. Most men do not find many inhibiting forces in their path if they are able and motivated to succeed. As a result, they are not threatened by competition; in fact, surpassing an opponent is a source of pride and enhanced masculinity.

If a woman sets out to do well, however, she bumps into a number of obstacles. She learns that it really isn't ladylike to be too intellectual. She is warned that men will treat her with distrustful tolerance at best, and outright prejudice at worst, if she pursues a career. She learns the truth of Samuel Johnson's comment, "A man is in general better pleased when he has a good dinner upon his table, than when his wife talks Greek." So she doesn't learn Greek, and the motive to avoid success is born.

In recent years many legal and educational barriers to female achievement have been removed; but it is clear that a psychological barrier remains. The motive to avoid success has an all-too-important influence on the intellectual and professional lives of women in our society. But perhaps there is cause for optimism. Monica may have seen Anne maimed for life, but a few of the girls forecast a happier future for our medical student. Said one:

> Anne is quite a lady—not only is she tops academically, but she is liked and admired by her fellow students—quite a trick in a man-dominated field. She is brilliant—but she is also a woman. She will continue to be at or near the top. And . . . always a lady.

Understanding Women

Memorandum

This 1980 personnel memorandum was sent to divisional managers of a major American corporation as part of the company's "Recruiting and Selection Standards." It became a public document when it was introduced as an exhibit in a sex-discrimination suit. We reprint it from the April 1987 issue of Harper's Magazine.

Female Applicant Profile

The female sales rep we are looking for is not the stereotypical twenty-seven-year-old beautiful, blue-collar daughter of an electrician. She can be any age and from any background. We are only concerned that her *attitude* toward "work"—an attitude toward that combination of "job" and "career"—be such that she will be able and interested enough to function as an employee for approximately *five years*.

The hiring manager should not try to hire someone with the executive potential to become a president, a vice president, or a regional manager. In fact, a candidate who shows strong presidential potential at the entry level is not likely to last long enough to get the promotion.

Appearance: She's not "pretty," she's not sexy; she should be neat, clean, and without frills. She should have neither excessive jewelry nor long fingernails. Her clothes should be practical, not high fashion. Her heels should be made for walking, not modeling. She should have the look of someone who might clean her bathroom or kitchen on her hands and knees. If you went to school together, she would be likable—a friend. She wouldn't look like someone who found new boyfriends in singles bars.

Education: She went to a state college, not a private university, and not recently. She probably had a part-time job. She probably didn't belong to a sorority. She was a C or a B student and had to work for it. Ideally, she prepared for a business career. If she had a car, it was practical; you could not even imagine her in a Corvette.

Personality: Conscientious, thorough, completes what she starts; persistent, down-to-earth, friendly, likable. She's also independent, competitive. Financial security would rank high on her value scale. She's not waiting to get married to solve her financial problems. Open and candid, often to her disadvantage. Strong sense of right and wrong.

Early work history: Her background before college should indicate a need to earn her own spending money: after-school jobs, summer jobs.

Some of the jobs were probably boring, but they were the best she could get.

Family background: Blue-collar. Her father, and perhaps her mother, worked in and chose occupations that provided good, steady incomes.

Work history: No glamour jobs.

Understanding Women

1. God was a he. He created man (Adam) in his own image and likeness. He had only one child, a son, Jesus. No religion has a female leader or role model, except for saints; they all suffered greatly and died prematurely. It's the kind of thing that could give you an inferiority complex.

2. A married female has different and greater responsibilities than a married male. When a married male goes home after work, someone brings him things; a married female goes home and keeps working. In the traditional family, a married mother has greater home duties than a married father.

   If a manager does not accommodate these differences, and if he demands extra effort and long hours from his sales reps, a married mother is statistically not likely to survive.

3. Females are statistically more honest and conscientious than males; if the workload is unrealistic, they are more inclined to quit rather than to cut corners or create phantom call reports. They don't like to b.s. or fake it. They're more afraid of getting caught.

4. Women are more sensitive than men. They shame easier. They cry often.

5. Women don't trust "men."

6. Women are more loyal.

7. Women have more social problems that create business problems.

8. Women are more verbal and upfront.

9. Women are more passive, less assertive.

10. Women need praise; they respond to it.

11. Women are not as vulgar as men; they don't find vulgarity as amusing.

12. Women have a greater sense of what's "fair" and what's "not right."

13. Women are more afraid than men are: of fights, scenes, confrontations, physical danger, and men.

14. Women are more affectionate.

15. Women become humiliated and mortified. Men become pissed off.

16. Lack of rapport, disagreements with superiors, and dislike of direct superiors are less problematic to men than to women.

17. Women are more easily hurt by criticism.

18. Women are more interested in supporting and helping each other than men are.

Grunts from a Sexist Pig

Anthony Burgess

Anthony Burgess was born in Manchester, England, in 1917. He wanted to become a composer, but having come to the University of Manchester without the science background that the university required for music study, he earned a degree in English language and literature instead (1940). After a stint in the British Army from 1940 to 1946, he continued as teacher and musician and in 1954 joined the British Colonial Service as an education officer. Teaching first in Malaya, then in Borneo, he stayed aloof from the closed colonial community and began writing "as a kind of hobby." A few years later, he was told that he had a brain tumor and given one year to live. During that year he wrote five novels, emerged as a professional novelist, and recovered.

Burgess, still a musician (jazz pianist, composer, music critic), is an extraordinarily prolific writer, mainly of fiction but also of essays and articles, music and drama criticism, television scripts and plays. He has also lectured and taught on many college campuses. He is probably best known in the United States for A Clockwork Orange *(1963); the story was inspired by a brutal attack on his pregnant wife, which resulted in the loss of the child. The piece we present here is taken from a collection of nonfiction titled* But Do Blondes Prefer Gentlemen? *(1986).*

Cleaning out my son's bedroom the other day (he has gone to Paris to work as an apprentice fish chef in the all-male kitchens of Le Fouquet) I came across a partly eaten pig in pink marzipan. It had come, apparently, in the Christmas mail and was so ill-wrapped that neither its provenance nor purpose was apparent. My son thought it was an eccentric gift from one of his friends. Now, quite by chance, I discover (a matter of an old *Punch*° in a thanatologist's waiting room) that it was a trophy sent by the Female Publishers of Great Britain to myself as one of the Sexist Pigs of the year. I forget who the others were, but I think one of them published a picture book on the beauty of the female breast. What my own sin against woman was I am not sure, but I'm told that it may have been a published objection to the name the Virago Press (women publishers publishing women) had chosen for itself.

Now all my dictionaries tell me that a virago is a noisy, violent, ill-tempered woman, a scold or a shrew. There is, true, an archaic meaning which makes a virago a kind of amazon, a woman strong, brave and

---

Punch   A British humor magazine.

warlike. But the etymology insists on a derivation from Latin *vir,* a man, and no amount of semantic twisting can force the word into a meaning which denotes intrinsic female virtues as opposed to ones borrowed from the other sex. I think it was a silly piece of naming, and it damages what is a brave and valuable venture. The Virago Press has earned my unassailable gratitude for reprinting the *Pilgrimage* of Dorothy Richardson, and I said so publicly. But I get from its warlike officers only a rude and stupid insult, and I cannot laugh it off. Women should not behave like that, nor men either.

It has already been said, perhaps too often, that militant organizations pleading the rights of the supposedly oppressed—blacks, homosexuals, women—begin with reason but soon fly from it. On this basic level of language they claim the right to distort words to their own ends. I object to the delimitation of 'gay'. American blacks are not the only blacks in the world: the Tamils of India and Sri Lanka are far blacker. 'Chauvinistic' stands for excessive patriotism and not for other kinds of sectional arrogance. 'Pig' is an abusive word which libels a clean and tasty animal: it is silly, and it can be ignored. But 'sexist' is intended to have a precise meaning, and, on learning that I was a sexist pig, I felt it necessary to start thinking about the term.

As far as I can make out, one *ought* to be a sexist if one preaches or practises discrimination of any kind towards members of the other sex. In practice, a sexist is always male, and his sexism consists in his unwillingness to accept the world view of women in one or other or several or all of its aspects. This means, in my instance, that if I will not accept the meaning the Virago Press imposes on its chosen name, I qualify, by feminist logic, for the pink pig. But I cannot really believe it is as simple as that. The feminists must have other things against me but none of them will speak out and say what they are.

In the *Harvard Guide to Contemporary American Writing,* Elizabeth Janeway, discussing women's literature, considers a book by Mary Ellmann called *Thinking About Women.* She says: 'It is worth being reminded of how widespread and how respectable has been the unquestioned assumption of women's inevitable, innate, and significant "otherness", and Ellmann here collects utterances on the subject not only from those we might expect (Norman Mailer, Leslie Fiedler, Anthony Burgess) but from Robert Lowell, Malamud, Beckett, and Reinhold Niebuhr.' Note both the vagueness and the obliqueness. There can be no vaguer word in the world than 'otherness'. The vagueness is a weapon. Since it is not defined, the term 'otherness' can mean whatever its users wish, rather like 'virago'. The position of people like Mailer and Burgess and Fiedler vis-à-vis this 'otherness' does not have to be defined either: we have an intuitive knowledge of their qualities, and, between women, no more need be said.

That women are 'other', meaning different from men, is one of the

great maxims of the feminists. They are biologically different, think and
feel differently. But men must not say so, for with men the notion of
difference implies a value judgement: women are not like us, therefore
they must be inferior to us. I myself have never said or written or even
thought this. What I am prepared to see as a virtue in myself (as also in
Mailer and Fiedler and other pigs) is—because of the feminist insistence
on this damnable otherness—automatically transformed by such women
as read me into a vice. I mean the fact that I admire women, love the
qualities in them that are different from my own male ones, but will not
be seduced by their magic into accepting their values in areas where
only neutral values should apply. Here, of course, the trouble lies.
Women don't believe there are neutral zones: what males call neutral
they call male.

I believe, for instance, that in matters of art we are in a zone where
judgements have nothing to do with sex. In considering the first book the
Virago Press brought out—the masterpiece of Dorothy Richardson—I did
not say that here we had a great work of women's literature, but rather
here we had a great work which anticipated some of the innovations of
James Joyce. I should have stressed that this was a work by a woman, and
the womanly aspect of the thing didn't seem to me to be important. I
believe that the sex of an author is irrelevant, because any good writer
contains both sexes. But what we are hearing a lot of now, especially in
American colleges, is the heresy that *Madame Bovary* and *Anna
Karenina* can't be good portraits of women because they were written by
men. These are not aesthetic judgements: they are based on an a priori
position which refuses to be modified by looking at the facts. The feminists
just don't want men to be able to understand women. On the other hand,
women are quite sure that they understand men, and nobody finds fault
with the male creations of the Brontës or of Jane Austen.

Let's get out of literature and into life. I think I am quite capable of
seeing the feminist point of view with regard to men's sexual attitude to
women. I am strongly aware of the biological polarity, and it intrudes
where women say it shouldn't. I am incapable of having *neutral* dealings
with a woman. Consulting a woman doctor or lawyer, shaking hands with
a woman prime minister, listening to a sermon by a woman minister of
religion, I cannot help letting the daydream of a possible sexual relationship intrude. That this diminishes the woman in question I cannot deny.
It depersonalizes her, since the whole sexual process necessarily involves
depersonalization: this is nature's fault, not man's. Women object to their
reduction into 'sex objects', but this is what nature decrees when the
erotic process gets to work. While writing this I am intermittently watching a most ravishing lady on French television. She is talking about
Kirkegaard, but I am not taking much of that in. Aware of her charms
as she must be, she ought to do what that beautiful lady professor of
mathematics did at the University of Bologna in the Middle Ages—talk

from behind a screen, meaning talk on the radio. But then the voice itself, a potent sex signal, would get in the way.

This awareness of the sexual power of women, I confess, induces attitudes which are, from the feminist angle, unworthy. At Brown's Hotel a woman porter proposed carrying my bags upstairs. It was her job, she said, but I could not let her do it. Old as I am, I still give up my seat to women far younger when on a bus or tube train. This is a protective tenderness wholly biological in origin. How can I apologize for it when it is built into my glands? Women are traditionally (but this is, I admit, possibly a man-imposed tradition) slower to be sexually moved than are men, and this enables them to maintain a neutral relationship with the other sex in offices and consulting rooms.

I believe what women tell me to believe—namely, that they can do anything men can do except impregnate and carry heavy loads (though this latter was contradicted by the girl at Brown's Hotel). Nevertheless, I have to carry this belief against weighty evidence to the contrary. Take music, for instance. Women have never been denied professional musical instruction—indeed, they used to be encouraged to have it—but they have not yet produced a Mozart or a Beethoven. I am told by feminists that all this will change some day, when women have learned how to create like *women* composers, a thing men have prevented their doing in the past. This seems to me to be nonsense, and it would be denied by composers like Thea Musgrave and the shade of the late Dame Ethel Smyth (a great feminist herself, the composer of *The March of the Women* as well as *The Wreckers* and *The Prison,* which the liberationists ought to do something about reviving). I believe that artistic creativity is a male surrogate for biological creativity, and that if women do so well in literature it may be that literature is, as Mary McCarthy said, closer to gossip than to art. But no one will be happier than I to see women produce the greatest art of all time, so long as women themselves recognize that the art is more important than the artist.

I see that most, if not all, of what I say above is likely to cause feminist rage and encourage further orders to pink-pig manufacturers (did the Virago Press search for a *woman* confectioner?). But, wearily, I recognize that anything a man says is liable to provoke womanly hostility in these bad and irrational times. A man, by his very nature, is incapable of saying the right thing to a woman unless he indues the drag of hypocrisy. Freud, bewildered, said: 'What does a woman *want?*' I don't think, despite the writings of Simone de Beauvoir, Caroline Bird, Sara Evans, Betty Friedan, Germaine Greer, Elizabeth Janeway, Kate Millett, Juliet Mitchell, Sarah B. Pomeroy, Marian Ramelson, Alice Rossi, Sheila Rowbotham, Dora Russell, Edith Thomas, Mary Wollstonecraft and the great Virginia herself, the question has yet been answered, except negatively. What women *don't* want is clear—their subjection to the patriarchal image, male sexual exploitation, and all the rest of it. When positive programmes emerge—like the proposed 'desexualization' of language—we men have an uneasy intimation of the possible absurdity of the whole militant movement. I refuse to say Ms, which is not a real vocable, and I object to 'chairperson' and the substitution of 'ovarimony' for 'testimony'. And I maintain (a) that a virago is a detestable kind of woman and (b) that feminist militancy should not condone bad manners. If that pink pig had not been thrown in the garbage bin I should tell the women publishers of Britain what to do with it.

Spouses, Households, and Careers

Traditionally, the American family was thought of as mother, father, and children in one household, and that in fact was the case. In the last few decades, however, the reality of the American family has changed. According to *Population Profile for 1984/85,* only 28 percent of households contain a husband, wife, and children under eighteen, and one of four children lives with only one parent. Furthermore, the number of households that consist of communal families, of couples of the same sex, and of single people is steadily increasing.

The four essays in this section offer different perspectives on some of the changing relationships and roles within a family. Judy Syfers amusingly defines the traditional role of "wife" and wishes she too had such a paragon of support and attention. The following essay by Pete Hamill—"notes from a man who knows himself and some other men"—looks at the consequences of the wish to "Have It All" (the wish to have career *and* family *and* children), especially as it pertains to men. Writing as a single parent, he concludes that the difficulties and the rewards of raising children make the fantasy of "having it all" soon sound like "some adolescent slogan."

Phyllis Schlafly also disapproves of the "Have It All" mentality, but her reasons are very different from Hamill's. She fervently and firmly reasserts the value of traditional roles and the traditional view of family: "Marriage and motherhood give a woman new

identity and the opportunity for all-round fulfillment as a woman."
A wife, she feels, "must appreciate and admire her husband," and
must be cheerfully supportive. "Those who want to be hermits and
live in isolation" she adds, "are welcome to make that choice."

That is precisely the view that Mary Helen Washington objects
to. She speaks as a single woman who has chosen to be single and
has strong family ties, strong friendships, and rewarding work. She
nevertheless finds little public respect or support for the single life,
and resents the fact that she "had to work so hard for the honor
that naturally accompanies the married state."

I Want a Wife

Judy Syfers

Judy Syfers, who was born in San Francisco in 1937, feels that the prob-
lems of American wives "stem from a social system which places primary
value on profits rather than on people's needs. As long as we continue to
tolerate the system, we will continue to be exploited as workers and as
wives." Ms. Syfers received her B.F.A. in painting from the University of
Iowa in 1960. She wanted to go on for a higher degree that would enable
her to paint and to teach in a university, but her (male) teachers advised
that the best she could hope for as a woman was teaching in high school
with a secondary-education credential. Her reaction was to drop school, get
married, and have two children. Thus the present piece, which appeared
in the Spring 1972 preview issue of Ms., *arises from real experience.*

I belong to that classification of people known as wives. I am A Wife. And,
not altogether incidentally, I am a mother.

Not too long ago a male friend of mine appeared on the scene fresh from
a recent divorce. He had one child, who is, of course, with his ex-wife. He
is looking for another wife. As I thought about him while I was ironing
one evening, it suddenly occurred to me that I, too, would like to have a
wife. Why do I want a wife?

I would like to go back to school so that I can become economically
independent, support myself, and, if need be, support those dependent
upon me. I want a wife who will work and send me to school. And while
I am going to school I want a wife to take care of my children. I want a
wife to keep track of the children's doctor and dentist appointments. And
to keep track of mine, too. I want a wife to make sure my children eat
properly and are kept clean. I want a wife who will wash the children's

clothes and keep them mended. I want a wife who is a good nurturant attendant to my children, who arranges for their schooling, makes sure that they have an adequate social life with their peers, takes them to the park, the zoo, etc. I want a wife who takes care of the children when they are sick, a wife who arranges to be around when the children need special care, because, of course, I cannot miss classes at school. My wife must arrange to lose time at work and not lose the job. It may mean a small cut in my wife's income from time to time, but I guess I can tolerate that. Needless to say, my wife will arrange and pay for the care of the children while my wife is working.

I want a wife who will take care of *my* physical needs. I want a wife who will keep my house clean. A wife who will pick up after me. I want a wife who will keep my clothes clean, ironed, mended, replaced when need be, and who will see to it that my personal things are kept in their proper place so that I can find what I need the minute I need it. I want a wife who cooks the meals, a wife who is a *good* cook. I want a wife who will plan the menus, do the necessary grocery shopping, prepare the meals, serve them pleasantly, and then do the cleaning up while I do my studying. I want a wife who will care for me when I am sick and sympathize with my pain and loss of time from school. I want a wife to go along when our family takes a vacation so that someone can continue to care for me and my children when I need a rest and change of scene.

I want a wife who will not bother me with rambling complaints about a wife's duties. But I want a wife who will listen to me when I feel the need to explain a rather difficult point I have come across in my course of studies. And I want a wife who will type my papers for me when I have written them.

I want a wife who will take care of the details of my social life. When my wife and I are invited out by friends, I want a wife who will take care of the babysitting arrangements. When I meet people at school that I like and want to entertain, I want a wife who will have the house clean, will prepare a special meal, serve it to me and my friends, and not interrupt when I talk about the things that interest me and my friends. I want a wife who will have arranged that the children are fed and ready for bed before my guests arrive so that the children do not bother us. I want a wife who takes care of the needs of my guests so that they feel comfortable, who makes sure that they have an ashtray, that they are passed the hors d'oeuvres, that they are offered a second helping of the food, that their wine glasses are replenished when necessary, that their coffee is served to them as they like it. And I want a wife who knows that sometimes I need a night out by myself.

I want a wife who is sensitive to my sexual needs, a wife who makes love passionately and eagerly when I feel like it, a wife who makes sure that I am satisfied. And, of course, I want a wife who will not demand sexual attention when I am not in the mood for it. I want a wife who assumes the complete responsibility for birth control, because I do not want more children. I want a wife who will remain sexually faithful to me so that I do not have to clutter up my intellectual life with jealousies. And I want a wife who understands that *my* sexual needs may entail more than strict adherence to monogamy. I must, after all, be able to relate to people as fully as possible.

If, by chance, I find another person more suitable as a wife than the wife I already have, I want the liberty to replace my present wife with another one. Naturally, I will expect a fresh, new life; my wife will take the children and be solely responsible for them so that I am left free.

When I am through with school and have a job, I want my wife to quit working and remain at home so that my wife can more fully and completely take care of a wife's duties.

My God, who *wouldn't* want a wife?

Great Expectations
Pete Hamill

Pete Hamill was born in Brooklyn in 1935. He attended Pratt Institute there and Mexico City College (University of the Americas) in Mexico. After doing sheetmetal work, serving in the U.S. Navy, and designing advertisements, he became a journalist and writer. He has worked as a reporter for the New York Post, *as a contributing editor for the* Saturday Evening Post, *and as a war correspondent in Vietnam; but he is probably best known for his syndicated newspaper column. He published a collection of these columns,* Irrational Ravings, *in 1972. In addition to his many magazine articles, he has written novels and screenplays.*

Hamill married in 1962, divorced in 1970, and is the father of two daughters. His experiences as a single parent occasioned the essay we print here from the September 1986 issue of Ms.

The subject is men and what they want. If there is a calculated echo here of Freud's famous remark about women,[°] I must also offer a large caution: the subject of men, like the subject of women, is not simple. Only fools or philosophers would presume to generalize about so many millions of individual lives. Human beings insist on having this one terrible fault: they will not fit neatly on charts or graphs. There seems no room for the myriad complexities of our lives: our triumphs, sorrows, brutalities, terrors. There is also no way to diagram hope.

Freud's famous remark about women "What does a woman want?"—a question he asked Princess Marie Bonaparte.

So these are notes from a man who knows himself and some other men. Nothing more. At 50, I'm not yet old and no longer young. I'm part of a generation that was born in a major economic depression, came to consciousness during a world war, and arrived at young manhood in the 1950s.

Nobody is a typical case of anything (or we would cease writing novels and leave the human heart to the sociologists), but in some ways what happened to me also happened to many other men my age. We grew up before television conquered the American consciousness, before millions of the young began to think that lives could be as easily altered as the switching of a channel. The newspapers, radio, magazines all offered essentially the same message: work hard and steadily, master a craft or a trade, marry a good woman and have healthy children, and you will lead a long, serene life.

The world was more complicated than that. The 1960s arrived, with their storms and interruptions, their assassinations and riots, and their distant ugly war. Television jumbled its images and ours. Lives were ruined by drugs. People donned and doffed lifestyles as if they were clothes.

Marriages failed. Millions of them. Mine too. And at a point toward the end of that ferocious decade, I found myself alone with two daughters to raise. I bought a house. I worked impossible hours. I struggled to be a good parent, retired from the drinking life, made awful mistakes, had some triumphs, made more mistakes, was humbled, saddened, enervated, and was made infinitely more human. This is not the place to tell that story; it belongs more properly to my daughters. But we went the distance. I tried my best. I love them more than anyone else on this earth and they love me. I would not have lived the past 15 years in any other way.

I say all of this not to evoke sympathy. Others have struggled harder than I did and had much more difficult obstacles to overcome. But I do feel that I have a few meager credentials to discuss the subject at hand. I'm not the sort of person who looks at himself and sees the universe. But I've also talked to a lot of men my own age and younger who have tried to live in tough times. Some want nothing beyond what they have; they are content, it seems, reasonably happy. I know many who want more; the American imperative drives them beyond every hill, across every river, urging them to collect, acquire, multiply; the cars pile up, the homes and possessions and wives, and they remain all appetite, living in some permanent and unreachable future. But more and more these days, particularly in my wanderings among the young, I encounter those men who, as the brainless slogan puts it, Want It All.

This vague notion isn't always the same for men and women, of course. For some women, the "it" seems to mean the opportunity to have children *and* a career. The men I've spoken to offer a broader compound: a successful career, a traditional marriage based on romantic love, wonderful children, modern independence of action and spirit. Not for them lives of existential dread, nausea, or absurdity. Not for these brave voyagers the tedium of the daily rounds, the comical variety of our couplings, or what John Updike once described as "the peculiar crazy, sleepless staleness of our great domestic crises."

These are children of the Reagan era, almost wholly formed by television, free of the draft and the anxieties of dying in some foreign field (a chore reserved now for volunteers), becalmed by the genius of a President whose style, ideas, and oratory descend directly from Beverly Hills in the 1940s. Listen to them and you know they believe in happy endings. Their world is a kind of watercolor, devoid of shadows, certainly free of skepticism and doubt, existing without history.

"I want a wife who's understanding and supportive," a young stockbroker told me last summer. "I want her to have a career, if that makes her happy, but if she wants to stay home and have babies, that's okay too. She's got to be great in bed. She's got to be beautiful. She's got to have a sense of humor. She's got to be faithful." He laughed. "In other words, I believe in the American Dream, man."

Needless to say, this appalling young man was still single. But the formula he described for the Perfect Wife (admittedly led on by me) was repeated in a number of other casual researches. Young men, some of them married, spoke with almost schematic serenity about the adult lives they wanted or had embarked upon. Some had mastered the rhetorical buzzwords of what they perceived to be the feminist movement. Others insisted that the women they knew didn't care about being liberated; they wanted someone to take care of them. (To be fair, I talked to *these* young men on the sidewalk outside a movie house where we had all watched "Rambo" together; their language sounded as if it had just come off a Nautilus machine, and the women with them just giggled.) A few sounded as if they knew that a life with another human being was not going to be a stroll in the park, but they too said that with some luck, they could Have It All.

In a way, of course, this desire—virtually unique to the United States—could be traced to the Women's Movement itself. One of the major topics of what could be called the postliberation debate is the subject of Having It All. At the heart of the discussion is the imposing figure of Supermom. She has been discussed, delineated, condemned, applauded in millions of printed words. She is a stock character on talk shows. She is presented in various guises in the lies of advertising. She's always essentially the same person: in her thirties, well educated, almost always white, heroically juggling career, husband, children, and self-respect in the forging of a happy fulfilling life. Some women are actually managing this extraordinary feat. But other reports from the field describe casualties and mutinies, the wounds inflicted by anger, guilt, and exhaustion.

"I tried," a 42-year-old woman friend told me last year. An investment banker, she married at 35, had two children before she was 38. "I tried like hell to put everything together, and I just couldn't manage it. Not because I'm weak; I think I'm a strong person. But there simply aren't enough hours in the day to be all the people I tried to be. The economy was booming, I was making good money. But so was my husband. I felt I was being a lousy mother. I was distracted at work. Something had to give. Sure, I could have asked my husband to quit his job and stay home but I don't think he could have done it. So *I* quit *my* job. I can't say I'm happier. But I'm healthier. I'm less exhausted. I love the children." She laughed in the telling and shook her head. "Of course, I also know that I tried to do something and failed. I'll have to live with that."

Other women I know have had to face the same dilemma; a few are writers and have been able to continue writing, usually at a slower pace, but writers and entertainers are an infinitesimally small elite. I don't know any who have been able to Have It All (which is not to say that such people don't exist). But when I hear men talking about attempting the same thing, I am reminded of a French novelist's maxim for living a life: "Optimism of the will, pessimism of the intelligence." And wonder if these young men truly understand the task before them, the life of struggle that their optimism will guarantee.

Consider the simple attempt to braid together two careers. Although the great majority of American mothers work (half of all married women with children under one, and a majority of those with children under 18), the usual arrangement is familiar and depressing. He has the career; she has a job.

Careers in America are essentially the province of the middle class and those who want to rise above that class. But there are certain extremely difficult problems involved in the attempt to forge two simultaneously growing careers. Most young middle-class families cannot live in the central cities; those centers are either in decay, seething with anger, violence, and crime, or they are too expensive for people in the early stages of careers. Certainly, in my town of New York the only people who can afford Manhattan apartments are inside stock traders, Eurotrash, and drug dealers. Unable to pay the skyrocketing rents or the tuitions at private schools, unwilling to hire people to ride shotgun with the children so they can play in public parks, these middle-class families must move to the suburbs.

Most American suburbs are at least an hour from the central city. Since the goals of most American corporate careers involve the acquisition of power, this means that a career-minded couple must emulate their superiors. A recent survey published in *The Wall Street Journal* showed that American senior executives work a total—on average—of 56 hours a week. That's more than 10 hours a day. Add two hours of commuting and you are talking about a 12-hour day, eight in the morning to eight at night.

If a two-career couple have children, they might see the kids for an hour in the morning and an hour in the evening, with weekends free (presuming their careers don't require extensive traveling). They will see them at that time in the morning when the mind is coiling for the challenges of the day; they will see them in the evening after a day packed with the stress, tension, collisions, conflicts, compromises, and evasions of normal existence in American corporate life. Such human beings do not arrive home in any state to enjoy or be enjoyed by children. It is doubtful if they can enjoy each other.

If this were a sensible world, of course, there would be a vast system of day-care facilities in the richest country on earth, so that small children could be brought to a safe, interesting place near where parents work. Such a system doesn't exist here (it does in France and a few other Western nations) and in the Reagan years will not be brought into existence. So a 1980s couple with two careers are forced to pay someone to care for the children.

And the man who Wants It All will soon learn that a marriage with two children, say, and two careers will not be a simple matter. Those men who have applied a patina of liberation rhetoric to themselves will be swiftly tested. Someone will have to give up the career. And though some one million American men now head single-parent families, and a small number are staying home while their wives work, the institution of the househusband will probably not be established in the age of Rambo. Most women who want to preserve the marriage will probably have to abandon the career.

Such a sad and terrible choice will not guarantee that pacific dream house envisioned by so many of the Reagan-era young; if anything, it will guarantee the opposite. They have yet to learn (as my generation did) that romantic love always promises more than it can deliver, and that there is no way to prepare for this bittersweet truth when it is learned with its usual arctic clarity. Some feel cheated. All are disappointed. A few are crushed.

Men react to this realization in various ways. Some are so warped, sexually and emotionally (often after a sudden, startling epiphany), that they tumble into the black hole of depression. Others become grievance collectors, hoarding slights and affronts as if they were ammunition, firing them across the fault lines of the marriage. Some revert to type, abandoning responsibility, as Huck Finn says, "to light out for the Territory." Others actually grow up.

That, of course, is the most difficult task of all. There is much talk now about fathering, of developing a "new" kind of father, sensitive to his children, willing to listen, firm when necessary, guide, protector, imparter of wisdom. There have always been such fathers and there will be in the future, but I doubt if they will come about through the establishment of courses at the local community college. Such fathers can only exist in an atmosphere that includes time for those children.

"Growing up," for most American men, is actually a process, sometimes glacially slow, of escaping the self to recognize the other, and consequently dealing in a new way with time. All men I know speak with extraordinary warmth of the years of youth, when days lasted forever, when summers were plump with irresponsible joys and time could be squandered on the self. Maturity is another matter (I think it begins when you stop talking about the gifts you receive and mention only the gifts you've given). And giving time to children is the most difficult problem of all.

I've met men and women in the past few years who talk as if having children might be only a minor distraction for a few years, an intense period of nurturing after which a "normal" life can be resumed, interrupted careers reassembled, the equations of American happiness reasserted. But those of us who have raised children know that they are not, and can never be, a two- or three-year aside; they are a 20-year (at least) obligation. Young men who think that it would be "nice" to have children don't seem to realize often enough that when that obligation is completed, when the children have gone off at last as relatively autonomous human beings, they will no longer be young. As for those men who decide in their fifties, usually in second or third marriages, that they will become fathers again, they must know that when *their* new children are in college, they'll most likely be dead.

I realize that the tone of these notes is not cheerful, or even mildly optimistic. But I would be a faker to describe a state of impending utopian perfection that common sense tells us is unlikely ever to come into existence and the desire for which might lead to a litter of human casualties. Having It All is a desire for perfection, and in many ways the notion of the perfect is the enemy of all human beings. (Consider only the millions who have been slaughtered in this century as a consequence of the lust for social, economic, or religious perfection.) There are no perfect marriages, perfect children, perfect careers, perfect living arrangements for a very simple reason: there are no perfect human beings. Mr. and Mrs. Right do not exist. You need not accept the doctrine of original sin to recognize that every human being is flawed. The goofy young man in search of a perfect woman is as foolish as the female reader of romantic novels seeking her yuppie Heathcliff.° The desire for certain forms of perfection also leads to bizarre distortions of common humanity. I would not like to attempt to explain the billions spent in the United States on makeup, cosmetic surgery, or health clubs to men and women trudging across the plains of Ethiopia, or through the jungles of Cambodia, or dwelling in the hard highlands of Mexico.

Heathcliff   The passionate, mysterious, violent hero of Emily Brontë's *Wuthering Heights* (1847).

It's unfashionable in the Reagan years to mention such things, of course. The ethos of the times urges us to tend our private gardens. But anyone who spends much time in the real world knows that such a willed isolation from the real almost always leads to disaster. Young Americans—men and women—are being fed images that make Having It All seem desirable and possible; the rhetoric of optimism is extremely seductive and politically quite powerful. Those images also sell a lot of goods. But they fly in the face of reality. Conservatives act as if the traditional American family exists; we know that only 12 percent of American families are built on the old structure of husband-as-breadwinner, wife-as-homemaker. Conservatives also speak as if the 1950s notion of the nuclear family in the house with the white picket fence (where the family practices, God help us, "togetherness") has made an amazing comeback; the statistics indicate that 50 percent of all American marriages will still end in divorce. There is a sunny impression that a booming stock market, the fall in oil prices, the growth of a service economy have created a time of abundance and prosperity for all; but a recent issue of *Newsweek* reminds us that to maintain the middle-class lifestyle of 20 years ago, husbands and wives must both work. While spoiled young men talk to me about Having It All, there are an estimated 50,000 homeless people in the streets of New York City and almost one million people—more than 700,000 of them women and children without men in their families—on welfare.

The traditional family, so beloved of the American right wing, is as dead as the big bands. And Having It All, from the point of view of the young men I've met in the past few years, is really a renewed vision of that traditional family. Its surface is hipper, more civilized, more "sensitive." But it's a fantasy construct. The right has blamed feminism, in some cases, for the dissolution of that traditional family. But there were many more important factors. Money killed that family and wars killed it and the automobile killed it and welfare killed it and television killed it and education killed it and the romantic love industry killed it. Americans moved all over their country, seeking the Great Good Place; they left behind parents (who in most societies help with child care). They adopted the rhythms of television seasons, where a show that lasted seven years was a great hit and then dissipated into boredom and disappearance. Men looked at the minefield of human relationships and deserted. The young are now encouraged to ignore all that.

Can men Have It All? I don't think so. They can certainly lead more human lives, they can be better fathers and husbands, but not if they enter marriages as if they were accepting parts in movies. A marriage is a compact. And if mature human beings enter that compact, they must understand with great clarity that they will have to surrender certain freedoms. Once a child is born, neither mother nor father is free. Ever. And to create a home life in which men truly share the task of parenting, men will have to surrender some of their positions on the fast track.

Such surrenders go against some of the most deeply felt assumptions of the American vision. When American men speak about being free, they mean, in practice, being free of responsibility. Being a true father (as compared to those amazing men numbering now in the millions who become biological fathers and then hurry on to the next womb) is *all* responsibility. But for generations, cowboys have climbed on horses to ride into the sunset; heroes are lone men facing overwhelming odds. The tedium of family life, its excruciating dailiness, the tensions created by the illusion of perfection, the infinite number of crises and improvisations it requires: these are not the concern of our heroes. Imagine, for example, Rambo helping his daughters with biology homework. Or Dirty Harry° helping carry a science project to his child's high school.

The surrender of some career goals also denies the training given to all American boys. From childhood, they are told they can be anything in this country: center fielder for the Yankees, the head of the Chrysler Corporation, President of the United States. They are trained to compete. On the playing field. In class. At their first jobs. Increasingly, they are competing in many of these arenas with women, and greeting the challenge with various degrees of acceptance, anger, trauma (those fragile male egos!), and resignation. Women have fought hard and intelligently for the right to such competition, and as a father of daughters I have a special interest in the breaking down of all remaining barriers to what is, after all, a constitutional right.

But there remain extremely powerful cultural forces at play in the country that will not be easily altered. The images of success for men do not include changing diapers, nursing a child through illness or heartbreak, dropping off children at the company day-care center; would Lee Iacocca do such things? It would be a good thing if those images were swiftly altered—if the education and training of young American boys could be broadened, made more humane and less competitive. I wish that the relentless pressure in this country to be famous or powerful would ease up, so that more of us—men and women—could lead more civilized lives. I wish Americans were made to feel that being a good plumber is at least as important for a man or a woman (and for the country) as being a rock singer, a novelist, a politician, or heavyweight champion of the world.

For now, men and women will probably continue to muddle through. Families can be more democratic without losing the necessary parental

---

Rambo . . . Dirty Harry   Movie heroes who achieve justice by meeting violence with greater violence.

authority, but they will never be little utopias. The government might be persuaded (after Reagan is gone) to build that day-care system, encourage parental leave for both parents, ask industry to give workers of both sexes shorter workweeks while they're raising small children. But government will not be able to make human beings understand themselves and each other.

In the past 15 years, there has been much real change—particularly in increased male consciousness of women and their hopes, ambitions, and desires. Men probably would not be asking the questions about Having It All if women hadn't raised them first. For some men and for some women, new arrangements have been made, and more of the young will try to make them too. The operative word is "some." Neither legislation nor manifestos will change all men or all women. But I know this, as a man who raised children, changed diapers, was intricately involved in the nitty-gritty of the process: the struggle is worth it.

Nothing is more difficult. Nothing is more rewarding.

But that process requires clarity, sacrifice, humor, responsibility, a recognition of one's own flaws. It is made easier with patience and common sense. It is infinitely better if shared with another adult. But for those who truly make the effort, the notion of Having It All will soon sound like some adolescent slogan, and they will be involved in something of greater, more enduring value.

from *The Power of the Positive Woman*

Phyllis Schlafly

Phyllis Schlafly is a lawyer and a writer, a wife and the mother of six children; she is also one of the foremost spokeswomen against the feminist movement. She was educated at Maryville College of the Sacred Heart and Washington University (B.A. 1944, J.D. 1978) and at Harvard University (M.A. 1945). After college she worked as a librarian and researcher for a bank in St. Louis, but in 1949 left her job to get married. Since then she has been a radio commentator, a syndicated columnist, and an activist in conservative Republican politics. As founder and president of the Eagle Forum and of Stop-ERA, she led the successful campaign against the Equal Rights Amendment.

Schlafly has written six books, most in support of ultraconservative causes. We present here two sections from Chapter 2 of The Power of the Positive Woman *(1977).*

Marriage and Motherhood

Marriage and motherhood have always been the number-one career choice of the large majority of women. Are they still a viable career for the modern woman? Do they represent servitude or fulfillment? Are they, as the women's liberation movement would have us believe, an anachronism from a bygone era, the institutionalized serfdom (or "legalized prostitution") from which women must be freed if they are to find their own identity and self-fulfillment?

What is it that the women's liberation movement invites women to be liberated from? An objective reading of the liberation movement literature compels the conclusion that the answer must be marriage, home, husband, family, and children—because, by definition, those are all evidences of the "second-class status" of women. The movement literature paints marriage as slavery, the home as a prison, the husband as the oppressor, family as an anachronism no longer relevant to woman's happiness, and children as the daily drudgery from which the modern woman must be freed in order to pursue more fulfilling careers.

Midge Decter closeted herself for weeks with women's "movement" literature and the result was her *New Chastity and Other Arguments Against Women's Liberation.* [1] She distilled the dreary essence of the basic premises of women's liberation, such as that women are the victims of a vast societal conspiracy spearheaded by male supremacists, and that marriage is the ultimate act of prostitution in which women barter their bodies and services for economic security. Based on firsthand sources, she accurately concluded:

> The biggest of all put-downs of women is the movement's own literature. It's all there, so completely that women don't need any put-down by men.... The women's liberation movement does not belong to the history of feminism, but to the history of radicalism.

Long before women's lib came along and made *housewife* a term of derision, it had its own unique dignity. The 1933 edition of the *Oxford English Dictionary* defined a housewife as "a woman (usually, a married woman) who manages or directs the affairs of her household; the mistress of a family; the wife of a householder. Often (with qualifying words), a woman who manages her household with skill and thrift, a domestic economist."

---

[1] Midge Decter, *The New Chastity and Other Arguments Against Women's Liberation* (New York: Coward, McCann and Geoghegan, 1972).

A housewife is a home executive: planning, organizing, leading, coordinating, and controlling. She can set her own schedule and standards and have freedom of choice to engage in everything from children to civic work, politics to gardening. What man on a job can do that?

Marriage and motherhood are not for every woman, but before a young woman rejects it out of hand, she should give it fair consideration as one of her available options.

What does a woman want out of life? If you want to love and be loved, marriage offers the best opportunity to achieve your goal. Men may want, or think they want, a cafeteria selection of lunchcounter sex. But most women continue to want what the popular song calls "a Sunday kind of love." A happy marriage is the perfect vehicle for the Positive Woman. Marriage and motherhood give a woman new identity and the opportunity for all-round fulfillment as a woman.

Are you looking for security—emotional, social, financial? Nothing in this world is sure except death and taxes, but marriage and motherhood are the most reliable security the world can offer.

The Ten Commandments adjure us: "Honor thy father and thy mother that thy days may be long upon the land." In the normal courses of human life, the young and healthy eventually grow old, sick, senile, and helpless. The aged and weary become dependent on the younger generation to provide love, compassion, and material aid—not to speak of the regular checks officially labeled "social security." Motherhood provides children who, in their turn, will honor you in your declining years.

Do you want the satisfaction of achievement in your career? No career in the world offers this reward at such an early age as motherhood. In the business or professional world, a man or a woman may labor for years, or even decades, to acquire the satisfaction of accomplishment. A mother reaps that reward within months of her labor when she proudly shows off her healthy and happy baby. She can have the satisfaction of doing her job well—and being recognized for it.

It is generally conceded that former Israeli Premier Golda Meir is the outstanding career woman of our time. She achieved more in a man's world than any woman in any country—and she did it on sheer ability, not on her looks or her legs. The Gallup Poll repeatedly identified her as "the most-admired woman" in the world. Yet Golda Meir said without hesitation that having a baby is the most fulfilling thing a woman can ever do, and she put down the women's liberationists as a bunch of "bra-burning nuts."

Mrs. Meir is correct. If young women think that there are greater career satisfactions in being elected to important positions, traveling to exciting faraway places, having executive authority over large numbers of people, winning a big lawsuit, or earning a financial fortune than there are in having a baby, they are wrong. None of those measures of career success can compare with the thrill, the satisfaction, and the fun of having and caring for babies, and watching them respond and grow under a mother's loving care. More babies multiply a woman's joy.

Consider another highly successful career woman: Oriana Fallaci, the Italian journalist whose interviews with heads of state are the envy of most reporters and whose financial success in her chosen profession has brought her two homes in Italy and an apartment in Manhattan. When she gave a personal interview to the *New York Times,* she conceded that the crushing disappointment of her life is that she never had a baby. Even though she reached the pinnacle of her profession, career success was not enough for her self-fulfillment as a woman. She still yearns to satisfy her natural maternal urge.

Amelia Earhart has been a longtime heroine of feminists because she lived such an independent and exciting life. Yet when her true story was dramatized on national television in October, 1976, she was shown cuddling another woman's baby—and wishing it were her own.

One of the most successful writers of the twentieth century was Taylor Caldwell. *Family Weekly* asked her if it didn't give her solid satisfaction to know that her novel *Captains and the Kings* was to be seen as a nine-hour television production. She replied:

> There is no solid satisfaction in any career for a woman like myself. There is no home, no true freedom, no hope, no joy, no expectation for tomorrow, no contentment. I would rather cook a meal for a man and bring him his slippers and feel myself in the protection of his arms than have all the citations and awards and honors I have received worldwide, including the Ribbon of the Legion of Honor and my property and my bank accounts.

In unguarded moments, women's liberationists often reveal the womanly desires lurking behind their negative attitude toward men and marriage. One who heard me extol the rewards of marriage and motherhood could not restrain the tears in her eyes even in front of live television cameras. Another, with a glamorous network television job, whispered off camera: "I'd rather be scrubbing floors in my own home than working on this program." A third said, "If you find one of those nice guys who would like to support a wife, please bring him around; I'd like to meet him." A fourth conceded in a public debate, "I envy the happily married woman."

Mrs. Ronald Reagan summed it up in a November, 1975, interview: "I believe a woman's real happiness and fulfillment come from within her home with a husband and children."

Anne Morrow Lindbergh spoke for the big majority of women when she described her own priorities in *Hour of Gold, Hour of Lead:*

> To be deeply in love is, of course, a great liberating force and the most common experience that frees—or seems to free—young people. The loved one is the liberator. Ideally, both members of a couple in love free each other to new and different worlds. I was no exception to the general rule. The sheer fact of finding myself loved was unbelievable and changed my world, my feelings about life

and myself. I was given confidence, strength, and almost a new character. The man I was to marry believed in me and what I could do, and consequently, I found I could do more than I realized, even in that mysterious outer world that fascinated me but seemed unattainable. He opened the door to "real life" and although it frightened me, it also beckoned. I had to go. . . .

The first months of motherhood were totally normal, joyful, and satisfying and I would have been content to stay home and do nothing else but care for my baby. This was "real life" at its most basic level.

Marriage and motherhood, of course, have their trials and tribulations. But what lifestyle doesn't? If you look upon your home as a cage, you will find yourself just as imprisoned in an office or a factory. The flight from the home is a flight from yourself, from responsibility, from the nature of woman, in pursuit of false hopes and fading illusions.

If you complain about servitude to a husband, servitude to a boss will be more intolerable. Everyone in the world has a boss of some kind. It is easier for most women to achieve a harmonious working relationship with a husband than with a foreman, supervisor, or office manager.

The women's liberationists point to the Bible as proof that marriage forces women into a subservient role from which they must be liberated. The feminists get livid at any reading of Ephesians 5, wherein Saint Paul says: "Wives, submit yourselves unto your own husbands, as unto the Lord. For the husband is the head of the wife, even as Christ is the head of the church." The fringe group called Saint Joan's Alliance often pickets in front of churches when Saint Paul is scheduled to be read at the Sunday service.

The first answer to these anti-Scripture agitators is that Ephesians also states:

> Husbands, love your wives, even as Christ also loved the church, and gave Himself for it. . . . Let everyone of you in particular so love his wife even as himself; and the wife see that she reverence her husband.

The Positive Woman recognizes that there is a valid and enduring purpose behind this recognition of different roles for men and women which is just as relevant in the twentieth century as it was in the time of Saint Paul.

Any successful vehicle must have one person at the wheel with ultimate responsibility. When I fly on a plane or sail on a ship, I'm glad there is one captain who has the final responsibility and can act decisively in a crisis situation. A family cannot be run by committee. The committee system neutralizes a family with continuing controversy and encumbers it with psychological impedimenta. It makes a family as clumsy and slow as a hippopotamus (which might be defined as a racehorse designed by a committee).

Every successful country and company has one "chief executive officer." None successfully functions with responsibility equally divided between cochairmen or copresidents. The United States has a president and a vice president. They are not equal. The vice president supports and carries out the policies enunciated by the president. Likewise with the presidents and vice-presidents of all business concerns. Vice-presidents can and do have areas of jurisdiction delegated to them, but there is always one final decision maker. The experience of the ages has taught us that this system is sound, practical, and essential for success. The republic of ancient Rome tried a system of two consuls of equal authority, and it failed.

If marriage is to be a successful institution, it must likewise have an ultimate decision maker, and that is the husband. Seen in this light, the laws that give the husband the right to establish the domicile of the marriage and to give his surname to his children are good laws designed to keep the family together. They are not anachronisms from a bygone era from which wives should be liberated in the name of equality. If a woman does not want to live in her husband's home, she is not entitled to the legal rights of a wife. Those women who preach that a wife should have the right to establish her own separate domicile do not stay married very long. That "equal right" is simply incompatible with a happy lifetime marriage.

The women's liberationists look upon marriage as an institution of dirty dishes and dirty diapers. They spend a lot of energy writing marriage contracts that divide up what they consider the menial, degrading chores. The much quoted "Shulmans' marriage agreement," for example, includes such provisions as "Husband does dishes on Tuesday, Thursday and Sunday. Wife does Monday, Wednesday and Saturday, Friday is split . . . ," and "wife strips beds, husband remakes them." If the baby cries in the night, the chore of "handling" the baby is assigned as follows: "Husband does Tuesday, Thursday and Sunday. Wife does Monday, Wednesday and Saturday, Friday is split. . . ." Presumably, if the baby cries for his mother on Tuesday night, he would be informed that the marriage contract prohibits her from responding.

It is possible, in such a loveless home, that the baby would never call for his mother at all. Most wives remember those years of diapers and tiny babies as the happiest of their lives.

Are dirty dishes all that bad? It's all in whether you wake up in the morning with a chip on your shoulder or whether you have a positive mental attitude. One happy wife I know has this poem hanging on her kitchen wall:

> Thank God for dirty dishes,
> They have a tale to tell.
> While others may go hungry
> We're eating very well.
> With home, health and happiness,
> I wouldn't want to fuss;
> By the stack of the evidence,
> God's been very good to us.

If you think diapers and dishes are a never-ending, repetitive routine, just remember that most of the jobs outside the home are just as repetitious, tiresome, and boring. Consider the assembly-line worker who pulls the same lever, pushes the same button, or inspects thousands of identical bits of metal or glass or paper, hour after weary hour; the stenographer who turns out page after page of typing; the telephone operator; the retail clerk who must repeatedly bite her lip because "the customer is always right."

Many people take such jobs because they need or want the money. But it is ludicrous to suggest that they are more self-fulfilling than the daily duties of a wife and mother in the home. The plain fact is that most women would rather cuddle a baby than a typewriter or factory machine. Not only does the baby provide a warm and loving relationship that satisfies the woman's maternal instinct and returns love for service, but it is a creative and growing job that builds for the future. After twenty years of diapers and dishes, a mother can see the results of her own handiwork in the good citizen she has produced and trained. After twenty years of faithful work in the business world, you are lucky if you have a good watch to show for your efforts.

Those who want to be hermits and live in isolation are welcome to make that choice. Most people want and need human companionship in facing life's trials. Family living requires many social compromises, but it is worth the price, especially for women. The loneliness of career success without a family was poignantly described by champion golfer Carol Mann, who told a *New York Times* reporter: "Life is nothing more than a mattress, a box spring, a bathroom, and four walls. You say to yourself, 'Is that all there is?' And you cry a lot." She has banked half a million dollars from golf tournament prizes, but she cries into her pillow as she travels from motel to motel.

The most recent sociological phenomenon to receive the attention of the statisticians is the fact that young women are dropping out of motherhood at a landslide rate; hospitals are closing their maternity wards and school enrollment has dropped by a million and a half in the last five years.

On the average, all young women are having fewer children, four-year-college women graduates are having still fewer, and the graduates of the colleges with the highest academic standards are having the least of all. According to the latest United States Census Bureau report, 17 percent of married women between the ages of twenty-five and twenty-nine are childless. But 86 percent of the married graduates of Radcliffe College (the women's division of Harvard University) in that same age group are childless.[2] Samuel L. Blumenfeld observed in his book *The Retreat from Motherhood:*

---

[2]Harriet Belin, "Dropping Out of Motherhood," *Radcliffe Quarterly,* June, 1976, p. 4.

The symptoms are all around us. *Parents* magazine is down to a meager shadow of its former self. *Cosmopolitan,* the magazine of the liberated single woman, is fat and prosperous, and *Playgirl* features center foldouts of nude men. Few of the women's magazines show pictures of infants. The motherly virtues are ignored; the wifely love-making virtues are played up. Pictures of active glamourous women pursuing careers in the man's world are everywhere. Articles about the woman holding her man with sexual know-how and seductiveness are abundant. Here and there an infant appears. Husband and wife, and unmarried couples, are now so busy making love to each other that they have little time for children at all.[3]

Many causes are advanced for the plummeting birth rates; the million abortions that take place every year, the widespread use of the Pill, the large influx of women into the labor force. It is likely that the principal cause is the propaganda of the women's liberation movement that motherhood is the least attractive role a woman can choose, and that the work force offers more rewards and more fulfillment. Many causes are advanced for the apparent disintegration of the institution of marriage. It is likely that the principal cause is the refusal of young women to have babies. Why should a man marry a woman who refuses to be a mother to his children? He can get everything else he wants from women at a price much cheaper than marriage.

In his *Washington Post* column of December 18, 1976, William Raspberry described the present retreat from motherhood like this:

> A hundred years from now, we'll look back at this period and wonder how we got so foolishly and so hopelessly sidetracked en route to sexual equality. We'll look back, that is, if there is anybody around to look back.
>
> For if the present trend continues, we will reach the point where no sane woman would even consider having a baby, nor would any sensitive man dream of inflicting pregnancy upon her. . . .
>
> The trend seems to be growing most rapidly among those women with the most education. And since more and more women are seeking higher education these days, we may be looking toward a future in which having babies will be considered as dumb as sponsoring debutante balls, giving tea parties, doing volunteer work and other traditionally female enterprises.

The Price of a Happy Marriage

With the high divorce rates of today, is a happy, lifetime marriage a realistically attainable goal?

---

[3]Samuel L. Blumenfeld, *The Retreat from Motherhood* (New Rochelle, N.Y.: Arlington House, 1975), p. 15.

Of course it is—if you have a positive mental attitude. In the first place, the odds aren't as bad as you have been led to believe, because they include second and third divorces by the same persons. The percentage of first marriages that last a lifetime is thus much higher than any popularly circulated statistics indicate.

In their attack on marriage and the home, the women's liberationists tell young women that *Cinderella* and all fairy tales in which the girl meets her Prince Charming and they "live happily ever after" are a myth and a delusion. One thing is sure. If you make up your mind that you will never find your "Prince Charming," you won't. If you decide in advance that it is impossible to "live happily ever after," you won't. It all *can* happen to you, however, if you make up your mind that it *will* happen. I *know*—because it happened to me.

A happy marriage is truly a pearl of great price, but it isn't something to be discovered by searching in faraway places. Nor is it like a lucky strike for oil or gold. It is like a garden that yields a good crop when the seed is planted and the ground is cultivated regularly. Marriage is like pantyhose; it is what you put into it that makes the difference.

If the recipe for a happy marriage required rare, hard-to-get ingredients or some sophisticated training, marriage would have died out centuries ago. For a woman to build a happy marriage, she does not need beauty, a good figure, gorgeous gams, a high IQ, a dumb look, money, or popularity with other men. All those qualities may make a man look around and notice her, but none will build or hold a lasting relationship.

The Positive Woman knows that there are two main pillars of a happy marriage and that she has the capability to build both. The first is that a wife must appreciate and admire her husband. Whereas a woman's chief emotional need is active (i.e., to love), a man's prime emotional need is passive (i.e., to be appreciated or admired).

The Positive Woman recognizes this fundamental difference and builds her male/female relationship accordingly. She knows that this does not in any sense make her inferior, but that it is one key to personal fulfillment for both herself and her husband. Knowledge of this factor gives the Positive Woman the power to build and retain that most fragile but most rewarding of all human relationships, the happy marriage.

It is really just as easy as it sounds. Those who fight it, or try to bypass it or suppress it, face endless frustration and battles that lead to bitter dead ends. How often have you thought, as you noticed a contented couple, "What on earth does he see in her?" The answer is always very simple: She knows how to make him feel like a man—and to remember always that she is a woman.

Is this degrading to the wife? Humiliating? Subservient? Or any of the other extravagant liberationist adjectives? How ridiculous! It is just the application of the Golden Rule with a simple male/female variation. Most women think that the prize is worth the price.

A satisfying and rewarding relationship between a man and a woman can last through the years only if she is willing to give him the appreciation and the admiration his manhood craves. There are a thousand ways a woman can devise—public and private, obvious and subtle, physical and intellectual. It makes little difference how—so long as it is personal, pervasive, perennial, and genuine.

Take, for example, two such totally different women as Queen Victoria and Katharine Hepburn. Although poles apart in morals and milieu, they were alike in being extremely strongminded in temperament and independent in action. Both spoke with the voice of authority and were forceful to the point of being domineering in their dealings with their fellow human beings, male and female. Except for one person, that is. Victoria's relationship with her husband, Prince Albert, was that of the dutiful wife, deferring always to her husband's wishes in their domestic partnership.

Recent revelations of Katharine Hepburn's twenty-seven-year love affair with Spencer Tracy (who had a wife) show that, to him alone in all the world, this assertive, headstrong, freethinking spitfire of a woman was submissive and more abnegating than any wife this side of the Orient. She often sat at his feet when they were together, and metaphorically, she was always there. The bond that pulled them together was the abundance of admiration she lavished on him.[4] A really Positive Woman, she had enough self-confidence that she could afford to accord to her man a preeminence in their personal relationship.

Among the dozens of fallacies of the women's liberation movement is the cluster of mistaken notions that traditional marriage is based on the wife's submerging her identity in her husband's, catering to his every whim, binding herself to seven days and nights a week inside the four walls of the home, stultifying her intellectual or professional or community interests, and otherwise reducing herself to the caricature of the dumb, helpless blonde, or a domestic servant.

What nonsense. It is true (and properly so) that the husband is naturally possessive about his wife's sexual favors, but he is seldom possessive of his wife's mind, time, or talents. A Positive Man is delighted to have his wife pursue her talents and spend her time however she pleases. The more she achieves, the prouder he is—*so long as* he knows that he is Number One in her life, and that she needs him.

A man who fights the competitive battle every day does not want to compete with his wife on the same terms that he competes with other men and women in the business world. He wants the security of knowing that he doesn't have to compete against his wife. However, he is perfectly happy to have her compete against others if she wants to join the competitive world—*so long as* he knows that she admires and needs him.

---

[4]Charles Higham, *Kate—The Life of Katharine Hepburn* (New York: Norton, 1975).

Actually, the total submersion of a wife's identity in her husband's can become more offensive to the husband than to the wife. Many marriages have gone on the rocks when a wife, with no substantive interests in life other than her husband, nags and complains about the time he spends on his growing career instead of on social or family engagements that include her. The marriage is on firmer footing if she develops her own interests. A successful marriage is possessive in regard to sexual fidelity, but possessiveness about personal identity, allocation of time, and life's ordinary routine can crush all the spontaneity out of a loving relationship.

One way of handling decision making in a marriage is to divide jurisdictions between husband and wife. The story is told about the husband who proudly told his friends: "When my wife and I were married, we agreed that I would make all the major decisions, and she would make the minor ones. I decide what legislation Congress should pass, what treaties the president should sign, and whether the United States should stay in the United Nations. My wife makes the minor decisions—such as how we spend our money, whether I should change my job, where we should live, and where we go on our vacations."

The Positive Woman is skillful enough to draw the jurisdictional line at the most advantageous point in *her* marriage. She acquired the key to her power when she erected that first pillar—admiration and appreciation of her husband as a man, as provider and protector, as the father of her children, and, yes, even as head of the household. The woman who goes into marriage thinking she can make it a mathematically equal fifty-fifty partnership in every decision and activity will come out on the short end every time.

The second pillar of a happy marriage is cheerfulness. No other quality can do so much to ensure a happy marriage as a happy disposition.

Life is full of problems and every one has his or her share. A great part of most people's time and energy is occupied with trying to cope with financial problems, health problems, social problems, and emotional problems—their own and those of their families. You may think that you are the first person in the world who ever faced tragic or intransigent circumstances, but you are not. Everyone's own problems always seem the most momentous, the most insoluble, and the most unjust.

However, no problems have ever been solved by a bad disposition, a gloom-and-doom outlook on life, or cross and angry behavior toward spouse, family, or friends. When an interviewer said to opera star Beverly Sills "You're always so happy—how do you do it?" she told him, no, she isn't always happy, but she is always *cheerful*. She has one retarded child, another child who is deaf, and she herself has been operated on for cancer. But she's always cheerful!

A cheerful disposition can guide you over countless obstacles. A wife's cheerful disposition will draw her husband like a magnet. Why would a husband want to stop off at the local bar instead of coming straight home? Unless he has already become addicted to alcohol, the subconscious reason is probably because everyone there is cheerful and no one is nagging him. If home is to have a greater lure than the tavern, the wife must be at least as cheerful as the waitress. The Bacharach/David lyrics are a good reminder to wives: "Hey, little girl, comb your hair, fix your makeup, soon he will open the door. Don't think because there's a ring on your finger, you needn't try any more."

One of the mistaken pieces of advice often given young people is "be yourself." Maybe you are a hard-to-get-along-with person with an irritable disposition who spends the evening reciting and reliving the troubles of the day and blaming them on others. Don't "be yourself." Be the person you would like to be—a cheerful person who sheds a little sunshine into an otherwise gloomy day, who sees the silver lining in every cloud, who keeps a sense of humor in the face of every reverse. A cheerful disposition will keep a happy marriage decades longer than a pretty face. Men may like to watch a beautiful woman like Greta Garbo in the movies, but she is not the type of woman men marry or stay married to. Men choose and love the cheerful over the beautiful and the wealthy. Miss Garbo never married.

Working at Single Bliss

Mary Helen Washington

Mary Helen Washington (born 1941) was educated at Notre Dame Academy and Notre Dame College (B.A. 1962) in Cleveland. She then taught high-school English for two years before continuing her education at the University of Detroit (M.A. 1966, Ph.D. 1976). She has taught at St. Johns College and at the University of Detroit, where she was also Director of Black Studies, and is presently a professor of English at the University of Massachusetts in Boston.

She has edited three books: Black Eyed Susans: Classic Stories by and about Black Women *(1975);* Midnight Birds: Stories of Contemporary Black Women Writers *(1980); and, most recently,* Invented Lives *(1987), which has been described as "two fine books in one: at once an anthology and a critical study." She has also written for* Negro Digest *and* Black World. *The essay we present here is from the October 1982 issue of* Ms.

I

Apart from the forest
have you seen
that a tree alone
will often take inventive form . . .

—PAULETTE CHILDRESS WHITE, "A Tree Alone" (unpublished)

She who has chosen her Self, who defines her Self, by choice, neither in
relation to children nor men; who is Self-identified, is a Spinster, a
whirling dervish spinning in a new time/space.

—MARY DALY, *Gyn/Ecology* (Beacon Press)

Last year I was asked to be on the "Tom Cottle Show," a syndicated
television program that originates here in Boston. The psychiatrist-host
wanted to interview six single women about their singleness. I hesitated
only a moment before refusing. Six single women discussing the significance of their lives? No, I instinctively knew that the interview would end
up being an interrogation of six unmarrieds (a pejorative, like coloreds)—
women trying to rationalize lives of loss. Losers at the marriage game.
Les femmes manqués.

I watched the program they put together without me, and sure enough,
Cottle asked a few perfunctory questions about singleness and freedom,
and then moved on rapidly to the real killer questions. I found it painful
to watch these very fine women trapped in the net he'd laid. "Don't you
ever come home from these glamorous lives of freedom [read selfishness]
and sit down to dinner alone and just cry?" "What about sex?" "What
about children?" The women struggled to answer these insulting questions with dignity and humor, but clearly the game was rigged against
them. Imagine the interviewer lining up six couples and asking them the
same kinds of questions: "Well, what about your sex lives?" "Why don't
you have any children?" (or "Why do you have so many?") "Don't you ever
come home at night, sit down to dinner, and wonder why you ever married
the person on the other side of the table?" Of course, this interview would
never take place—the normal restraint and politeness that are reserved
for people whose positions are socially acceptable assure married folks
some measure of protection and, at least, common decency.

"You're so lucky, footloose and fancy-free, with no responsibilities," a
friend with two children once said to me. Ostensibly that's a compliment,
or at least, it's supposed to be. But underneath it is really a critique of
single people, implying that their lives do not have the moral stature of
a life with "responsibilities." It's a comment that used to leave me feeling
a little like a kid, a failed adult; for what's an adult with no responsibili-

ties? A kid. I have had to learn to recognize and reject the veiled contempt in this statement because, of course, single people do have responsibilities.

At age 40, I have been a single adult for 20 years. No, I am neither widowed nor divorced. I am single in the pristine sense of that word—which unleashes that basic fear in all of us, "What will I do if I'm left by myself?" As I have more or less successfully dealt with that fear over the years, I am somewhat indignant at being cast as an irresponsible gadfly, unencumbered by the problems of Big People. I have earned a living and "kept myself," and I have done that without being either male or white in a world dominated by men and corroded by racism. I've sat up nights with students' papers and even later with their problems. Without any of the social props married people have, I have given many memorable parties. Like my aunts before me, I've celebrated the births, birthdays, first communions, graduations, football games, and track meets of my 10 nephews. And not a hair on my mother's head changes color without my noticing it.

As Zora Hurston's° Janie says, "Two things everybody's got tuh do fuh theyselves. They got tuh go tuh God, and they got tuh find out about livin' fuh theyselves." If anything, a single person may be more aware of the responsibility to discover and create meaning in her life, to find community, to honor her creativity, to live out her values, than the person whose life is circumferenced by an immediate and intimate family life.

II

To be single and busy—nothing bad in that. Such people do much good.

—ELIZABETH HARDWICK, *Sleepless Nights* (Random House)

To some extent my adolescent imagination was bewitched by the myth that marriage is *the* vertical choice in a woman's life—one that raises her status, completes her life, fulfills her dreams, and makes her a valid person in society. In the 1950s, all the movies, all the songs directed us to this one choice: to find our worldly prince and go two by two into the ark. Nothing else was supposed to matter quite as much and it was a surprise to discover that something else matters just as much, sometimes more.

But in spite of the romance-marriage-motherhood bombardment, I grew up in a kind of war-free zone where I heard the bombs and artillery all around me but was spared from a direct attack. I was raised in two very separate but mutually supportive communities—one black, one Catholic, both of which taught me that a woman could be her own person in the world.

Zora Hurston   Zora Neale Hurston, see page 226.

In the all-women's Catholic high school and college in Cleveland, Ohio, where I put in eight formative years, we were required to think of ourselves as women with destinies, women whose achievements mattered—whether we chose marriage or religious life or, as it was called then, a life of "single blessedness." In fact, marriage and the single life seemed to my convent-honed ninth-grade mind to have a clearly equal status: they were both inferior to the intrinsically superior religious life.

The program of spiritual, intellectual, social, and physical development the nuns demanded of us allowed an involvement with myself I craved even in the ninth grade. *Some* dating was encouraged at Notre Dame Academy (ninth through twelfth grades)—not as a consuming emotional involvement but as part of a "normal social development." Boys had their place—on the periphery of one's life. (A girl who came to school with her boyfriend's taped class ring on her finger was subject to expulsion.) You were expected to be the central, dominant figure in the fabric of your own life.

The nuns themselves were vivid illustrations of that principle. For me they were the most powerful images of women imaginable—not ladies-in-waiting, not submissive homebodies, not domestic drudges, not deviants. They ran these women-dominated universes with aplomb and authority. Even if "Father" appeared on Monday morning for our weekly religious lesson, his appearance was tolerated as a kind of necessary token of the male hierarchy, and, when he left, the waters ran back together, leaving no noticeable trace of his presence.

Nuns were the busiest people I knew then. No matter how graceful and dignified the pace, they always seemed to be hurrying up and down the corridors of Notre Dame planning something important and exciting. Sister Wilbur directed dramatics and went to New York occasionally to see the latest Off-Broadway productions. Sister Kathryn Ann wrote poetry and went to teach in Africa. Another sister coached debate and took our winning teams to state championships in Columbus. Though technically nuns are not single, they do not have that affiliation with a male figure to establish their status. (After Mary Daly it should not be necessary to point out that God is not a man.) They also have to ward off the same stigma of being different from the norm as single people do. So it's only a little ironic that I got some of my sense of how a woman could be complete and autonomous and comfortable in the world—sans marriage—from the Sisters of Notre Dame.

The message I got from the black community about single life was equally forceful. So many black girls heard these words, they might have been programmed tapes: "Girl, get yourself an education, you can't count on a man to take care of you." "An education is something no one can take from you." "Any fool can get married, but not everyone can go to school."

I didn't know it then, but this was my feminist primer. Aim high, they said, because that is the only way a black girl can claim a place in this world. Marriage was a chancy thing, not dependable like diplomas: my mother and aunts and uncles said that even if you married a Somebody— a doctor or a lawyer—there was no assurance that he'd have a good heart or treat you right. They thought that the worst thing a woman could do was to get into financial dependency with a man—and it was not that they hated or distrusted men so much as they distrusted any situation that made an already vulnerable woman more powerless.

There was such reverence in my mother's voice for women of achievement that I never connected their social status with anything as mundane as marriage. The first black woman with a Ph.D., the first black woman school principal, the first woman doctor—I knew their names by heart and wanted to be one of them and do important things.

My third-grade teacher, the first black teacher at Parkwood Elementary in Cleveland, Ohio, was a single woman in her thirties. At age nine, I saw her as a tall, majestic creature who wore earrings, drove her own car, and made school pure joy. To my family and the neighborhood, Miss Hilliard was like a totem of our tribe's good fortune: an independent, self-sufficient, educated woman bringing her treasures back to their children. She was a part of that tradition of 19th-century black women whose desire for "race uplift" sent them to teach in the South and to schools like Dunbar High in Washington, D.C., and the School for Colored Youth in Philadelphia. Though many of these women were married, the majority of them were widowed for a great many years and those were often the years of achievement for them.

One of these 19th-century stellar examples, Anna Julia Cooper, dismissed the question of marriage as a false issue. The question should not be "How shall I so cramp, stunt, simplify, and nullify myself as to make me eligible for the horror of being swallowed up into some little man," but how shall a generation of women demand of themselves and of men "the noblest, the grandest and the best" in their capacities.

III

In the places of their childhoods, the troubles they had getting grown, the tales of men they told among themselves as we sat unnoted at their feet, we saw some image of a past and future self. The world had loved them even less than their men but this did not keep them from scheming on its favor.

—SHERLEY ANNE WILLIAMS, *Some One Sweet Angel Chile*
(William Morrow)

I learned early about being single from my five aunts. By the time I was old enough to notice, four were widowed and one divorced, so from my 12-year-old perspective, they were single women for a good part of their

lives. They ran their own households, cooked, entertained, searched for
spirituality, helped my mother to raise eight children, traveled some,
went to work, cared for the sick, planned picnics. In short, they made up
their lives by themselves, inventing the forms that satisfied them. And in
the course of their "scheming" they passed on to me something about the
rituals and liturgy of single life.

The eldest of these aunts, Aunt Bessie, lived as a single woman for 26
years. Her husband of 40 years died when she was 60 and she began to
live alone for the first time since she was 18. She bought a huge old house,
painted, decorated, and furnished every room with Oriental rugs and
secondhand furniture purchased at estate sales. (Black people discovered
this bonanza in the 1940s long before it became a middle-class fad.) She
put in a new lawn, grew African violets, and started a whole new life for
herself on Ashbury Avenue.

Aunt Bessie was secretly proud of how well she was doing on her own,
and she used to tell me slyly how many of these changes she could not
have made as a married woman: "Uncle wouldn't have bought this house,
baby; he wouldn't have wanted this much space. He wouldn't have
changed neighborhoods." She was finally doing exactly what pleased her,
and the shape of her life as she had designed it in her singularity was
much more varied, dynamic, and daring. What I learned from her is
symbolized by that multilevel house on Ashbury Avenue. She had three
bedrooms—she needed them for guests; on the third floor she made hats,
which she sold for a living; the huge old basement was for her tools and
lawn work. All this room was essential to the amount of living she
planned to do.

Since she willed all of her furniture to me, my own flat resembles that
house in many ways, and her spirit came with the furnishings: I have the
sense of inhabiting every corner of my life just as she lived in all 10 rooms
of her house. Even my overstocked refrigerator is a reflection of something I learned from her about taking care of your life. Another aunt,
Hazel, died only a few years after she was widowed, and I remember Aunt
Bessie's explanation of her untimely death as a warning about the perils
of not taking your life seriously. "Hazel stopped cooking for herself after
her husband died, just ate snacks and junk food instead of making a
proper dinner for herself. And she got that cancer and died." The message
was clear to me—even at age 12—that single life could be difficult at times
and that living it well required some effort, but you were not supposed to
let it kill you.

IV

*[Friendship] is a profound experience which calls forth our humanness
and shapes our being. . . . This is true for all persons, but it has a special*

*significance for single persons. For it is in the context of friendship that
most single persons experience the intimacy and immediacy of others.*

—FRANCINE CARDMAN, "On Being Single"*

Girded up with all of this psychological armament from my past, I still
entered adult life without the powerful and sustaining myths and rituals
that could provide respect and support for single life. Terms like "old
maid" and "spinster," not yet redefined by a feminist consciousness, could
still be used to belittle and oppress single women. By the time I was 35,
I had participated in scores of marriage ceremonies, and even had begun
sending anniversary cards to my married friends. But never once did I
think of celebrating the anniversary of a friendship—even one that was
by then 25 years old. (Aren't you entitled to gifts of silver at that mile-
stone?)

Once, about 10 years ago, five of us single women from Cleveland took
a trip to Mexico together. (Actually only four of the group were single; the
fifth, Ernestine, was married and three months pregnant.) I remember
that trip as seven days and eight nights of adventure, laughter, discovery,
and closeness.

We were such typical tourists—taking snapshots of ancient ruins, posing in front of cathedrals, paying exorbitant sums to see the cliff divers
(whose entire act took about 20 seconds), floating down debris-filled waterways to see some totally unnoteworthy sights, learning the hard way that
in the hot Acapulco sun even us "killer browns" could get a sunburn. We
stayed up at night talking about our lives, our dreams, our careers, our
men, and laughing so hard in these late-night sessions that we hardly had
the energy for the next morning's tour.

It was the laughter and the good talk (remember Toni Cade Bambara's
short story "The Johnson Girls") that made the trip seem so complete. It
was so perfect that even in the midst of the experience I knew it was to
be a precious memory. Years later I asked my friend, Ponchita, why she
thought the five of us never planned another trip like that, why we let
such good times drift out of our lives without an attempt to recapture
them. "Because," she said, "it wasn't enough. It was fun, stimulating,
warm, exciting, but it wasn't 'The Thing That Made Life Complete,' and
it wasn't leading us in that direction; I guess it was a little like 'recess.' "
We wanted nests, not excitement. We wanted domestic bliss, not lives
lived at random, no matter how thrilling, how wonderful. So there was
the potential—those "dependable and immediate supports" existed. But

---

*From "The Wind Is Rising," September, 1978, a newsprint collection of articles pub-
lished by the Quixote Center, an activist religious community in Hyattsville, Maryland.

without the dependable myths to accompany them, we couldn't seriously invest ourselves in those experiences.

When my friend Meg suggested we celebrate Mother's Day this year with a brunch for all our single, childless women friends, and bring pictures of the nieces and nephews we dote on, I recognized immediately the psychic value in honoring our own form of caretaking. We were establishing rituals by which we could ceremonially acknowledge our particular social identities.

My oldest friend Ponchita and I did exchange gifts last year on the twenty-fifth anniversary of our friendship, and never again will the form "anniversary" mean only a rite (right) of the married. My journey through the single life was beginning to have its own milestones and to be guided by its own cartography.

V

A life of pure decision, of thoughtful calculations, every inclination honored. They go about on their own, nicely accompanied in their singularity by the companion of possibility.

—ELIZABETH HARDWICK, *Sleepless Nights*

Our Mexico trip was in 1971. In the next 10 years, I earned a Ph.D., became director of black studies at the University of Detroit, edited two anthologies, threw out my makeshift bricks-and-board furniture, began to think about buying a house and adopting a child, and in the process, decided that my life was no longer "on hold." These deliberate choices made me begin to regard my single status as an honorable estate. But you know, when I look back at that checklist of accomplishments and serious life plans, I feel resentful that I had to work so hard for the honor that naturally accompanies the married state. Overcompensation, however, sometimes has its rewards: I had established a reputation in my profession that brought the prospect of a fellowship year at Radcliffe and a new job in Boston.

When I was leaving Detroit, I was acutely aware of my single status. What kind of life was it, I wondered, if you could start all over again in a new city with nothing to show for your past except your furniture and your diplomas? I didn't even have a cat. Where were the signs and symbols of a coherent, meaningful life that others could recognize? What was I doing living *at random* like this? I had made this "pure" decision and was honoring my inclination to live in another city, to take a job that offered excitement and challenge. As I packed boxes alone, signed contracts with moving companies, and said good-bye at numerous dinners and going-away parties to all the friends I had made over 10 years, I felt not so very different from a friend who was moving after separating from his wife: "like a rhinoceros being cut loose from the herd."

I think it was the wide-open, netless freedom of it all that scared me, because I was truly *not* alone. I moved into a triple-decker in Cambridge where I live in a kind of semi-cooperative with two other families. Here, I feel secure, but independent and private. The journalist on the second floor and I read each other's work, and I exchange ideas about teaching methods with the three other professors in the house. We all share meals occasionally; we've met one another's extended families; and we celebrate one another's assorted triumphs. I have put together another network of friends whose lives I feel intimately involved in, and who, like me, are interested in making single life work—not disappear.

But I do not yet have the solid sense of belonging to a community that I had in Cleveland and Detroit, and sometimes I am unsettled by the variousness and unpredictableness of my single life. This simply means that I still have some choices to make—about deepening friendships, about having children (possibly adopting them), about establishing closer ties with the black community in Boston. If and when I do adopt a child, she or he will have a selection of godparents and aunts and uncles as large and varied as I had. That is one of the surest signs of the richness of my single life.

VI

You're wondering if I'm lonely;
OK then, yes, I'm lonely
as a plane rides lonely and level
on its radio beam, aiming
across the Rockies
for the blue-strung aisles
of an airfield on the ocean

—ADRIENNE RICH, "Song," from *Diving into the Wreck* (Norton)

Last year Elizabeth Stone wrote an article in the *Village Voice* called "A Married Woman" in which she discussed how much her life had changed since she married at the age of 33. Somewhat boastfully, she remarked at the end that she had hardly made any reference in the whole article to her husband. But if a single woman describes her life without reference to romance—no matter how rich and satisfying her life may be, no matter what she says about wonderful friends, exciting work, cultural and intellectual accomplishments—in fact, the *more* she says about these things—the more skeptical people's reactions will be. That one fact—her romantic involvement—if it is not acceptable can cancel out all the rest. This is how society keeps the single woman feeling perilous about her sense of personal success.

Still, everybody wants and needs some kind of special alliance(s) in her life. Some people have alliances called marriage. (I like that word alliance: it keeps marriage in its proper—horizontal—place.) I'd like an alliance with a man who could be a comrade and kindred spirit, and I've had such alliances in the past. Even with the hassles, they were enriching and enjoyable experiences for me, but I have never wanted to forsake my singularity for this kind of emotional involvement. Whatever psychic forces drive me have always steered me toward autonomy and independence, out toward the ocean's expanse and away from the shore.

I don't want to sound so smooth and glib and clear-eyed about it all, because it has taken me more than a decade to get this sense of balance and control. A lot of rosaries and perpetual candles and expensive long-distance calls have gotten me through the hard times when I would have chosen the holy cloister over another day of "single blessedness." The truth is that those hard times were not caused by being single. They were part of every woman's struggle to find commitment and contentment for herself. Singleness does not define me, is not an essential characteristic of me. I simply wish to have it acknowledged as a legitimate way to be in the world. After all, we started using Ms. instead of Mrs. or Miss because *none* of us wanted to be defined by the presence or absence of a man.

VII

Apart from the forest
a single tree will sometimes grow awry
in brave and extraordinary search
for its own shape

—PAULETTE CHILDRESS WHITE, "A Tree Alone"

When I first started running in 1972, I ran regularly with a man. As long as I had this male companion, the other men passing by either ignored me or gave me slight nods to show their approval of my supervised state. Eventually I got up the nerve to run alone around Detroit's Palmer Park, and then the men came out of the trees to make comments—usually to tell me what I was doing wrong ("Lift your legs higher" or "Stop waving your arms"), or to flirt ("Can I run with you, baby?" was by far the most common remark, though others were nastier).

Once a carload of black teenagers who were parked in the lot at the end of my run started making comments about my physical anatomy, which I started to dismiss as just a dumb teenage ritual. But on this particular day, something made me stop my run, walk over to the car, and say, "You know, when you see a sister out trying to get some exercise, as hard as that is for us, you ought to be trying to support her, because she needs all the help she can get." I didn't know how they would respond, so I was surprised when they apologized, and somewhat shamefaced, one of them said: "Go on, sister; we're with you."

Now, that incident occurred because I was alone, and the image has become part of my self-definition: I am a woman in the world—single and powerful and astonished at my ability to create my own security, "in brave and extraordinary search for my own shape."

On Being a Man

The introduction to Mark Gerzon's book on American manhood serves well to introduce the issue raised in this section. Men today, he says, have run out of adequate symbols of manhood. The available models are either traditional ones which have lost their meaning, or media inventions impossible to emulate. He argues furthermore that sympathy with feminism, and its parallel movement for men's liberation, is not enough to retire "the old chauvinistic images of manhood." Self-exploration by men, he concludes, is the means to discovering satisfactory new models of masculinity.

Mark Feigen Fasteau, author of the following essay, has conducted one such exploration. Examining and then responding to the inadequacy of the traditional American ideal of male friendship, he finds that "the imagined hazards of showing oneself to be human, and thus vulnerable, to one's friends tend not to materialize when actually put to the test."

The last two essays offer virtually opposite views of traditional maleness. Paul Theroux, a writer, is repelled by it. "There is no book-hater," he says, "like a Little League coach." M. F. K. Fisher's César is a male of Biblical proportions whose lecherous habits and love of food, wine, and male companionship she portrays with affectionate objectivity.

from *Introduction* to *A Choice of Heroes*

Mark Gerzon

Mark Gerzon is a writer and journalist who grew up in Indianapolis and was educated at Harvard University (1970). During the Vietnam War he was active in anti-war activities; later, when a journalist, he helped create and edit a global newspaper, WorldPaper. *He is the author of* The Whole World Is Watching: A Young Man Looks at Youth's Dissent *(1969),* A Childhood for Every Child: The Politics of Parenthood *(1973),* The Young Internationalists *(1973), and most recently,* A Choice of Heroes: The Changing Faces of American Manhood *(1982), a book, he says, "about choosing one's heroes—who are, after all, only reflections of ourselves." We print here the second part of the Introduction to* A Choice of Heroes.

If not in the judgment of history, then in the eyes of a woman, every man wants to be a hero. Men may not boast about it. We may not even talk about it. In fact, we may not even be aware of it. Yet each of us tries to emulate models of manhood that to us seem heroic.

But who are our heroes? Do names and faces spring to mind of men who have succeeded in battle or in business, in politics or in sports, in literature or in religion? Or does no clear image crystallize? Behind the response of our conscious mind is much that remains unsaid. This question of heroism is, wrote Ernest Becker in his Pulitzer Prize-winning essay, *The Denial of Death,* "the most important that man can put to himself." Yet we do not dare face it squarely.

Whether in the faculty club or the officers' club, at a board meeting or in bed, we want to be seen as real men, whatever that may mean to us. This need is so strong, so primitive, that some of us will risk anything to satisfy it—our wealth, our health, even our lives.

Yet how conscious are we of what we are doing to earn this feeling of heroism? Men's behavior, both in private and in public, suggests that our images of heroism are largely unconscious. They are so much a part of our boyhood conditioning that we are barely aware of them. In the midst of our Clark Kent lives, we dream of being Superman.

In the portraits of masculinity that follow, no image of heroism is alluded to more often than John Wayne. Countless men, in recalling the kind of man they wanted to be, say they wanted to grow up to be like John Wayne. But none of these men actually knew Wayne himself. They did not know Marion Michael Morrison, the son of a druggist. They did not know the lanky lad who forfeited his name because, as he put it, it "didn't sound American enough." They did not know the man who late in his life told an interviewer, "I still don't recognize it when somebody calls me John." Nor did they know the man who slowly died of cancer, possibly contracted while filming at an old nuclear testing site in the Southwest.

No, these men knew only his image as it was captured on celluloid. The same is true for boys who invoke, not movie stars, but heroes from football, baseball, and other manly sports. The ones who say they wanted to be like Mickey Mantle or O. J. Simpson are not referring to the real men. They never knew the tired men who tore themselves away from their families week after week, who cursed their lives in countless hotel rooms, and who, by the age of forty, were managing restaurants or marketing rental cars. They knew only those figures in uniform who flickered across their television screens. And the ones who say they wanted to be like Elvis Presley knew only the glittering, sequined strutter on the stage beneath dazzling lights. They did not know the drug-addicted, obese man who died isolated and alone.

When men go crazy, however, the image often surfaces. Listen to Frank Barber, a Vietnam veteran, describe his mental breakdown and the crazed, demonic rage that overwhelmed him. "I was not Frank Barber," he said. "I was John Wayne, Steve McQueen, Clint Eastwood." After Frank returned home, the navy gave him medals. But what he really needed, he said, was to be held and comforted by his wife. Why couldn't he ask his own wife for solace? "I never saw John Wayne walk up to a woman and say, 'I need a hug.' "

Through therapy, Frank rediscovered himself. But other men lose their identity so completely that they *become* the image. A few months after John Hinckley, the privileged son of an oil magnate, shot and almost killed President Ronald Reagan, he explained why he did it. He said he wanted to impress actress Jodie Foster, whom he had seen in the intensely violent film *Taxi Driver*. When asked why he bought so many guns, Hinckley replied, "Ask Travis." Travis was the taxi driver in the movie, played by Robert de Niro.

A normal man in ordinary circumstances obviously does not succumb so irrationally to his unconscious images of manhood. He remembers his identity; he does not lose his own self and become someone else's. Nevertheless, our culture's images of manhood influence us more than we know. Through the course of this book, five archetypes of masculinity will be introduced: the Frontiersman, the Soldier, the Expert, the Breadwinner, and the Lord. These archetypes, or hero-images, influence our behavior whether we are aware of it or not. The stodgy word *archetype,* which means original model or first form, is appropriate because it suggests that these images of manhood cannot be dislodged simply by frenetic consciousness raising or alternative lifestyles.

These archetypes of manhood exist because they were once useful. They promised survival and well-being. The Frontiersman explored new lands. The Soldier symbolized greater security. The Expert marshaled new knowledge. The Breadwinner fostered economic prosperity, both for his family and for the nation. And the Lord, a symbol of divinity, offered salvation and immortality. Such hero-images served vital purposes. They led men to protect their loved ones, to defend cherished values, and to enrich and expand their lives.

But are these symbols of manhood useful for men today? We are no longer certain. Our presidents, once they leave office, drift into obscurity. Our veterans, after returning from Vietnam, are unheralded. Our sports stars are overpaid, overpublicized, and often just overnight sensations. A biography of Gary Cooper is called *The Last Hero*. After the space shuttle *Columbia* returns to earth, the pilots are not treated as demigods the way Charles Lindbergh was. We remember the machine, not the men. Only superhumans, humanoids from other galaxies, and the bizarre products of surgical or chemical experimentation now thrill the young.

Traditionally, men have identified with images that were passed down from father to son, generation after generation. Embedded in myths and rituals with prehistoric origins, their images represented the core of early human cultures. But as modern technological societies emerge, change accelerates. As Susan Sontag pointed out in *On Photography,* "Society becomes modern when one of its chief activities becomes producing and consuming images [that] are in themselves coveted substitutes for firsthand experience." Thus men today consume certain images of manhood even though the world from which they are derived may have disappeared—if it ever existed.

To model oneself after another man is in itself problematic. But to model oneself after an image of a man, repackaged for the camera, is dangerous. In comparing themselves to the dashing figure riding off into the setting sun or racing across the goal line, ordinary men in everyday life cannot help but feel overshadowed.

Even in private, men no longer feel like heroes. A husband is no longer undisputed lord of the manor, a small-scale hero. To be the breadwinner is no longer a badge of honor. A man cannot assume that his wife will tend his house and raise his children, or even take his name. His wife may earn as much money as he does. If she doesn't, she may resent the disparity in their incomes (even as she spends his). Whether or not his wife calls herself a feminist, she will expect him to do more housework and child care than he was raised to expect. If the marriage fails, she is as likely to leave him as he is to leave her.

For many men, feminism has only compounded their confusion. Few men in America are unaware that a movement led by women wants us to liberate ourselves from old styles of masculine behavior. This women's liberation movement has been echoed by men's liberation, which is also dedicated to raising our consciousness. In academic studies, best-selling books, popular films, government legislation, lobbying organizations, nationwide coalitions—indeed, in virtually every aspect of American society—these movements are advocating new images of masculinity.

Beginning in the sixties, feminists traced the impact of sexuality on literature, art, science, government, philosophy, law, medicine, psychology, religion. They challenged the masculine world view. Few men stopped to listen; even those who did often pretended that the problem was merely a women's issue. They dismissed men's liberation as a mere adjunct of feminism and assumed that any man who questioned the prevailing images of masculinity must be of doubtful virility.

But as the women's movement matured and deepened through the seventies, more men noticed. Our mothers and sisters, wives and girl friends, made us listen even if we would not learn. Books by men, with titles such as *The Liberated Male, Tenderness Is Strength,* and *The Myth of American Manhood,* questioned the archetypes of masculinity in our culture. Newsletters began to flourish: "Changing Men," "American Man," "Nurturing News." Scores of articles about masculinity appeared in the popular and student press.

Writing on men's liberation is often shallow, severed both from history and from the heart. Some writing is merely a response to feminism. Other writing suggests that we should change our masculinity, not to appease feminists, but to enjoy ourselves more. There is nothing wrong with pleasing feminists or with having fun, but neither touches the deeper forces that shape masculinity, and neither will motivate enough men to profound change. We cannot retire the old chauvinistic images of manhood and put them away in our psychic closet like winter clothes.

Inevitably, some who wish to redefine masculinity have put forward an image of a "liberated" man. They extol the new male without ever exploring why the old one has been with us for so long. They exhort us to transform ourselves without admitting that the old masculinity cannot be exorcised overnight. It still influences each of us. Whether we cook dinner or call cooking women's work, whether we call women Ms. or Mrs., the old images of manhood live within us. Our task, as Jung argues, is not to deny these images or archetypes but to become conscious of them. As Phil Donahue puts it later in this book, men must stop "sleepwalking."

The purpose of such reexamination is not to make us all suddenly fit the mold of the new male. Just the opposite: it will enable us to see that molds, whether liberated or macho, are dehumanizing. Thinking about our own masculinity will enable us to take responsibility for ourselves. We will not be so quick to blame our problems on the finite earth, on our ungrateful wives and children, on some subversive enemy at home or abroad, or on some other force apart from us. Instead, we will find the courage to tell the difference between existential dilemmas inherent in life and the unnecessary pain caused by our own, unexamined selves.

This is true heroism: the courage to explore oneself deeply and to act with self-awareness. In this sense, heroism is not dead; it is constantly evolving. Old models of masculinity are dying. But if we look carefully, we can discover new models emerging that are as vital to our survival as the earlier ones were to our forefathers. As the threats to human survival change, so does masculinity. Walter Cronkite told the Harvard class of 1980 at its graduation that their challenge is "to unseat the Four Modern Horsemen of the Apocalypse—the population explosion, pollution, scarce resources, and nuclear war." Faced with such threats, we should not be worried if masculinity is changing. We should be worried if it were not.

Friendships Among Men

Marc Feigen Fasteau

Marc Feigen Fasteau was born in Washington, D.C., in 1942; he was educated at Harvard College, Georgetown University, and Harvard Law School, where he was an editor of the Law Review. *In Washington, he worked as an assistant in foreign affairs to Senator Mike Mansfield and as a staff member of the Joint Economic Committee of Congress. He also served as a research fellow at the Kennedy Institute of Politics before going into law practice in New York. In his work and in his writing, he has been actively engaged in the breaking of sexual stereotypes. The Male Machine (1974), from which we reprint a chapter, is his first book.*

There is a long-standing myth in our society that the great friendships are between men. Forged through shared experience, male friendship is portrayed as the most unselfish, if not the highest form, of human relationship. The more traditionally masculine the shared experience from which it springs, the stronger and more profound the friendship is supposed to be. Going to war, weathering crises together at school or work, playing on the same athletic team, are some of the classic experiences out of which friendships between men are believed to grow.

By and large, men do prefer the company of other men, not only in their structured time but in the time they fill with optional, nonobligatory activity. They prefer to play games, drink, and talk, as well as work and fight together. Yet something is missing. Despite the time men spend together, their contact rarely goes beyond the external, a limitation which tends to make their friendships shallow and unsatisfying.

My own childhood memories are of doing things with my friends— playing games or sports, building walkie-talkies, going camping. Other people and my relationships to them were never legitimate subjects for attention. If someone liked me, it was an opaque, mysterious occurrence that bore no analysis. When I was slighted, I felt hurt. But relationships with people just happened. I certainly had feelings about my friends, but I can't remember a single instance of trying consciously to sort them out until I was well into college.

For most men this kind of shying away from the personal continues into adult life. In conversations with each other, we hardly ever use ourselves as reference points. We talk about almost everything except how we ourselves are affected by people and events. Everything is discussed as though it were taking place out there somewhere, as though we had no more felt response to it than to the weather. Topics that can be treated in this detached, objective way become conversational mainstays. The few subjects which are fundamentally personal are shaped into discussions of abstract general questions. Even in an exchange about their reactions to liberated women—a topic of intensely personal interest—the tendency will be to talk in general, theoretical terms. Work, at least its objective aspects, is always a safe subject. Men also spend an incredible amount of time rehashing the great public issues of the day. Until early 1973, Vietnam was the work-horse topic. Then came Watergate. It doesn't seem to matter that we've all had a hundred similar conversations. We plunge in for another round, trying to come up with a new angle as much to impress the others with what we know as to keep from being bored stiff.

Games play a central role in situations organized by men. I remember a weekend some years ago at the country house of a law-school classmate as a blur of softball, football, croquet, poker, and a dice-and-board game called Combat, with swimming thrown in on the side. As soon as one game ended, another began. Taken one at a time, these "activities" were fun, but the impression was inescapable that the host, and most of his guests, would do anything to stave off a lull in which they would be together without some impersonal focus for their attention. A snapshot of almost any men's club would show the same thing, ninety percent of the men engaged in some activity—ranging from backgammon to watching the tube—other than, or at least as an aid to, conversation.[1]

My composite memory of evenings spent with a friend at college and later when we shared an apartment in Washington is of conversations punctuated by silences during which we would internally pass over any personal or emotional thoughts which had arisen and come back to the permitted track. When I couldn't get my mind off personal matters, I said very little. Talks with my father have always had the same tone. Respect for privacy was the rationale for our diffidence. His questions to me about how things were going at school or at work were asked as discreetly as he would have asked a friend about someone's commitment to a hospital for the criminally insane. Our conversations, when they touched these matters at all, to say nothing of more sensitive matters, would veer quickly back to safe topics of general interest.

In our popular literature, the archetypal male hero embodying this personal muteness is the cowboy. The classic mold for the character was set in 1902 by Owen Wister's novel *The Virginian* where the author spelled out, with an explicitness that was never again necessary, the characteristics of his protagonist. Here's how it goes when two close friends the Virginian hasn't seen in some time take him out for a drink:

[1]Women may use games as a reason for getting together—bridge clubs, for example. But the show is more for the rest of the world—to indicate that they are doing *something*—and the games themselves are not the only means of communication.

All of them had seen rough days together, and they felt guilty with emotion.
"It's hot weather," said Wiggin.
"Hotter in Box Elder," said McLean. "My kid has started teething."
Words ran dry again. They shifted their positions, looked in their glasses, read the labels on the bottles. They dropped a word now and then to the proprietor about his trade, and his ornaments.[2]

One of the Virginian's duties is to assist at the hanging of an old friend as a horse thief. Afterward, for the first time in the book, he is visibly upset. The narrator puts his arm around the hero's shoulders and describes the Virginian's reaction:

I had the sense to keep silent, and presently he shook my hand, not looking at me as he did so. He was always very shy of demonstration.[3]

And, for explanation of such reticence, "As all men know, he also knew that many things should be done in this world in silence, and that talking about them is a mistake."[4]

There are exceptions, but they only prove the rule.

One is the drunken confidence: "Bob, ole boy, I gotta tell ya—being divorced isn't so hot. . . . [and see, I'm too drunk to be held responsible for blurting it out]." Here, drink becomes an excuse for exchanging confidences and a device for periodically loosening the restraint against expressing a need for sympathy and support from other men—which may explain its importance as a male ritual.[5] Marijuana fills a similar need.

Another exception is talking to a stranger—who may be either someone the speaker doesn't know or someone who isn't in the same social or business world. (Several black friends told me that they have been on the receiving end of personal confidences from white acquaintances that they were sure had not been shared with white friends.) In either case, men are willing to talk about themselves only to other men with whom they do not have to compete or whom they will not have to confront socially later.

Finally, there is the way men depend on women to facilitate certain conversations. The women in a mixed group are usually the ones who make the first personal reference, about themselves or others present. The men can then join in without having the onus for initiating a discussion of "personalities." Collectively, the men can "blame" the conversation on the women. They can also feel in these conversations that since they are talking "to" the women instead of "to" the men, they can be excused for deviating from the masculine norm. When the women leave, the tone and subject invariably shift away from the personal.

The effect of these constraints is to make it extraordinarily difficult for

---

[2]Owen Wister, *The Virginian* ([Macmillan: 1902] Grosset & Dunlap ed.: 1929), pp. 397–98.
[3]*Ibid.*, p. 343.
[4]*Ibid.*, p. 373.
[5]Lionel Tiger, *Men in Groups* (Random House: 1969), p. 185.

men to really get to know each other. A psychotherapist who has conducted a lengthy series of encounter groups for men summed it up:

> With saddening regularity [the members of these groups] described how much they wanted to have closer, more satisfying relationships with other men: "I'd settle for having one really close man friend. I supposedly have some close men friends now. We play golf or go for a drink. We complain about our jobs and our wives. I care about them and they care about me. We even have some physical contact—I mean we may even give a hug on a big occasion. But it's not enough."[6]

The sources of this stifling ban on self-disclosure, the reasons why men hide from each other, lie in the taboos and imperatives of the masculine stereotype.

To begin with, men are supposed to be functional, to spend their time working or otherwise solving or thinking about how to solve problems. Personal reaction, how one feels about something, is considered dysfunctional, at best an irrelevant distraction from the expected objectivity. Only weak men, and women, talk about—i.e., "give in," to their feelings. "I group my friends in two ways," said a business executive:

> those who have made it and don't complain and those who haven't made it. And only the latter spend time talking to their wives about their problems and how bad their boss is and all that. The ones who concentrate more on communicating . . . are those who have realized that they aren't going to make it and therefore they have changed the focus of attention.[7]

In a world which tells men they have to choose between expressiveness and manly strength, this characterization may be accurate. Most of the men who talk personally to other men *are* those whose problems have gotten the best of them, who simply can't help it. Men not driven to despair don't talk about themselves, so the idea that self-disclosure and expressiveness are associated with problems and weakness becomes a self-fulfilling prophecy.

Obsessive competitiveness also limits the range of communication in male friendships. Competition is the principal mode by which men relate to each other—at one level because they don't know how else to make contact, but more basically because it is the way to demonstrate, to themselves and others, the key masculine qualities of unwavering toughness

---

[6]Don Clark, "Homosexual Encounter in All-Male Groups," in L. Solomon and B. Berzon (eds.), *New Perspectives on Encounter Groups* (Jossey-Bass: 1972), pp. 376–77. See also Alan Booth, "Sex and Social Participation," *American Sociological Review,* Vol. 37 (April 1972), p. 183, an empirical study showing that, contrary to Lionel Tiger's much publicized assertion *(Men in Groups)* women form stronger and closer friendship bonds with each other than men do.

[7]Fernando Bartolomé, "Executives as Human Beings," *Harvard Business Review,* Vol. 50 (November–December 1972), p. 64.

and the ability to dominate and control. The result is that they inject competition into situations which don't call for it.

In conversations, you must show that you know more about the subject than the other man, or at least as much as he does. For example, I have often engaged in a contest that could be called My Theory Tops Yours, disguised as a serious exchange of ideas. The proof that it wasn't serious was that I was willing to participate even when I was sure that the participants, including myself, had nothing fresh to say. Convincing the other person—victory—is the main objective, with control of the floor an important tactic. Men tend to lecture at each other, insist that the discussion follow their train of thought, and are often unwilling to listen.[8] As one member of a men's rap group said,

> When I was talking I used to feel that I had to be driving to a point, that it had to be rational and organized, that I had to persuade at all times, rather than exchange thoughts and ideas.[9]

Even in casual conversation some men hold back unless they are absolutely sure of what they are saying. They don't want to have to change a position once they have taken it. It's "just like a woman" to change your mind, and, more important, it is inconsistent with the approved masculine posture of total independence.

Competition was at the heart of one of my closest friendships, now defunct. There was a good deal of mutual liking and respect. We went out of our way to spend time with each other and wanted to work together. We both had "prospects" as "bright young men" and the same "liberal but tough" point of view. We recognized this about each other, and this recognition was the basis of our respect and of our sense of equality. That we saw each other as equals was important—our friendship was confirmed by the reflection of one in the other. But our constant and all-encompassing competition made this equality precarious and fragile. One way or another, everything counted in the measuring process. We fought out our tennis matches as though our lives depended on it. At poker, the two of us would often play on for hours after the others had left. These *mano a mano*° poker marathons seem in retrospect especially revealing of the competitiveness of the relationship: playing for small stakes, the essence of the game is in outwitting, psychologically beating down the other player—the other skills involved are negligible. Winning is the only pleasure, one that evaporates quickly, a truth that struck me in inchoate form every time our game broke up at four a.m. and I walked out the door with

---

[8]The contrast with women on this point is striking. Casual observation will confirm that women's conversations move more quickly, with fewer long speeches and more frequent changes of speaker.

[9]*Boston Globe*, March 12, 1972, p. B–1.

mano a mano   hand-to-hand, competitive (Spanish).

my five-dollar winnings, a headache, and a sense of time wasted. Still, I did the same thing the next time. It was what we did together, and somehow it counted. Losing at tennis could be balanced by winning at poker; at another level, his moving up in the federal government by my getting on the *Harvard Law Review.*

This competitiveness feeds the most basic obstacle to openness between men, the inability to admit to being vulnerable. Real men, we learn early, are not supposed to have doubts, hopes and ambitions which may not be realized, things they don't (or even especially do) like about themselves, fears and disappointments. Such feelings and concerns, of course, are part of everyone's inner life, but a man must keep quiet about them. If others know how you really feel you can be hurt, and that in itself is incompatible with manhood. The inhibiting effect of this imperative is not limited to disclosures of major personal problems. Often men do not share even ordinary uncertainties and half-formulated plans of daily life with their friends. And when they do, they are careful to suggest that they already know how to proceed—that they are not really asking for help or understanding but simply for particular bits of information. Either way, any doubts they have are presented as external, carefully characterized as having to do with the issue as distinct from the speaker. They are especially guarded about expressing concern or asking a question that would invite personal comment. It is almost impossible for men to simply exchange thoughts about matters involving them personally in a comfortable, non-crisis atmosphere. If a friend tells you of his concern that he and a colleague are always disagreeing, for example, he is likely to quickly supply his own explanation—something like "different professional backgrounds." The effect is to rule out observations or suggestions that do not fit within this already reconnoitered protective structure. You don't suggest, even if you believe it is true, that in fact the disagreements arise because he presents his ideas in a way which tends to provoke a hostile reaction. It would catch him off guard; it would be something he hadn't already thought of and accepted about himself and, for that reason, no matter how constructive and well-intentioned you might be, it would put you in control for the moment. He doesn't want that; he is afraid of losing your respect. So, sensing he feels that way, because you would yourself, you say something else. There is no real give-and-take.

It is hard for men to get angry at each other honestly. Anger between friends often means that one has hurt the other. Since the straightforward expression of anger in these situations involves an admission of vulnerability, it is safer to stew silently or find an "objective" excuse for retaliation. Either way, trust is not fully restored.

Men even try not to let it show when they feel good. We may report the reasons for our happiness, if they have to do with concrete accomplishments, but we try to do it with a straight face, as if to say, "Here's what happened, but it hasn't affected my grown-up unemotional equilibrium, and I am not asking for any kind of response." Happiness is a precarious, "childish" feeling, easy to shoot down. Others may find the event that triggers it trivial or incomprehensible, or even threatening to their own self-esteem—in the sense that if one man is up, another man is down. So we tend not to take the risk of expressing it.

What is particularly difficult for men is seeking or accepting help from friends. I, for one, learned early that dependence was unacceptable. When I was eight, I went to a summer camp I disliked. My parents visited me in the middle of the summer and, when it was time for them to leave, I wanted to go with them. They refused, and I yelled and screamed and was miserably unhappy for the rest of the day. That evening an older camper comforted me, sitting by my bed as I cried, patting me on the back soothingly and saying whatever it is that one says at times like that. He was in some way clumsy or funny-looking, and a few days later I joined a group of kids in cruelly making fun of him, an act which upset me, when I thought about it, for years. I can only explain it in terms of my feeling, as early as the age of eight, that by needing and accepting his help and comfort I had compromised myself, and took it out on him.

"You can't express dependence when you feel it," a corporate executive said, "because it's a kind of absolute. If you are loyal 90% of the time and disloyal 10%, would you be considered loyal? Well, the same happens with independence: you are either dependent or independent; you can't be both."[10] "Feelings of dependence," another explained, "are identified with weakness or 'untoughness' and our culture doesn't accept those things in men."[11] The result is that we either go it alone or "act out certain games or rituals to provoke the desired reaction in the other and have our needs satisfied without having to ask for anything."[12]

Somewhat less obviously, the expression of affection also runs into emotional barriers growing out of the masculine stereotype. When I was in college, I was suddenly quite moved while attending a friend's wedding. The surge of feeling made me uncomfortable and self-conscious. There was nothing inherently difficult or, apart from the fact of being moved by a moment of tenderness, "unmasculine" about my reaction. I just did not know how to deal with or communicate what I felt. "I consider myself a sentimentalist," one man said, "and I think I am quite able to express my feelings. But the other day my wife described a friend of mine to some people as my best friend and I felt embarrassed when I heard her say it."[13]

A major source of these inhibitions is the fear of being, or being thought, homosexual. Nothing is more frightening to a heterosexual man in our society. It threatens, at one stroke, to take away every vestige of his claim

---

[10]Bartolomé, *op. cit.*, p. 65.
[11]*Ibid.*, p. 64.
[12]*Ibid.*, p. 66.
[13]*Ibid.*, p. 64.

to a masculine identity—something like knocking out the foundations of a building—and to expose him to the ostracism, ranging from polite tolerance to violent revulsion, of his friends and colleagues. A man can be labeled as homosexual not just because of overt sexual acts but because of almost any sign of behavior which does not fit the masculine stereotype. The touching of another man, other than shaking hands or, under emotional stress, an arm around the shoulder, is taboo. Women may kiss each other when they meet; men are uncomfortable when hugged even by close friends.[14] Onlookers might misinterpret what they saw, and, more important, what would we think of ourselves if we felt a twinge of sensual pleasure from the embrace.

Direct verbal expressions of affection or tenderness are also something that only homosexuals and women engage in. Between "real" men affection has to be disguised in gruff, "you old son-of-a-bitch" style. Paradoxically, in some instances, terms of endearment between men can be used as a ritual badge of manhood, dangerous medicine safe only for the strong. The flirting with homosexuality that characterizes the initiation rites of many fraternities and men's clubs serves this purpose. Claude Brown wrote about black life in New York City in the 1950s:

> The term ["baby"] had a hip ring to it. . . . It was like saying, "Man, look at me. I've got masculinity to spare. . . . I can say 'baby' to another cat and he can say 'baby' to me, and we can say it with strength in our voices." If you could say it, this meant that you really had to be sure of yourself, sure of your masculinity.[15]

Fear of homosexuality does more than inhibit the physical display of affection. One of the major recurring themes in the men's groups led by psychotherapist Don Clark was:

> "A large segment of my feelings about other men are unknown or distorted because I am afraid they might have something to do with homosexuality. Now I'm lonely for other men and don't know how to find what I want with them."

As Clark observes, "The spectre of homosexuality seems to be the dragon at the gateway to self-awareness, understanding, and acceptance of male-male needs. If a man tries to pretend the dragon is not there by turning a blind eye to erotic feelings for all other males, he also blinds himself to the rich variety of feelings that are related."[16]

The few situations in which men do acknowledge strong feelings of affection and dependence toward other men are exceptions which prove the rule. With "cop couples," for example, or combat soldier "buddies,"

---

[14]*Ibid.*, p. 65.

[15]Claude Brown, *Manchild in the Promised Land* ([Macmillan: 1965] Signet ed.: 1965), p. 171.

[16]Clark, *op. cit.*, p. 378.

intimacy and dependence are forced on the men by their work—they have to ride in the patrol car or be in the same foxhole with somebody—and the jobs themselves have such highly masculine images that the men can get away with behavior that would be suspect under any other conditions.

Furthermore, even these combat-buddy relations, when looked at closely, turn out not to be particularly intimate or personal. Margaret Mead has written:

> During the last war English observers were confused by the apparent contradiction between American soldiers' emphasis on the buddy, so grievously exemplified in the break-downs that followed a buddy's death, and the results of detailed inquiry which showed how transitory these buddy relationships were. It was found that men actually accepted their buddies as derivatives from their outfit, and from accidents of association, rather than because of any special personality characteristics capable of ripening into friendship.[17]

One effect of the fear of appearing to be homosexual is to reinforce the practice that two men rarely get together alone without a reason. I once called a friend to suggest that we have dinner together. "O.K.," he said. "What's up?" I felt uncomfortable telling him that I just wanted to talk, that there was no other reason for the invitation.

Men get together to conduct business, to drink, to play games and sports, to re-establish contact after long absences, to participate in heterosexual social occasions—circumstances in which neither person is responsible for actually wanting to see the other. Men are particularly comfortable seeing each other in groups. The group situation defuses any possible assumptions about the intensity of feeling between particular men and provides the safety of numbers—"All the guys are here." It makes personal communication, which requires a level of trust and mutual understanding not generally shared by all members of a group, more difficult and offers an excuse for avoiding this dangerous territory. And it provides what is most sought after in men's friendships: mutual reassurance of masculinity.

Needless to say, the observations in this chapter did not spring full-blown from my head. The process started when I began to understand that, at least with Brenda, a more open, less self-protective relationship was possible. At first, I perceived my situation as completely personal. The changes I was trying to effect in myself had to do, I thought, only with Brenda and me, and could be generalized, if at all, only to other close relationships between men and women. But, as Brenda came to be deeply involved in the women's movement, I began to see, usually at one remove but sometimes directly, the level of intimacy that women, especially women active in the movement, shared with each other. The contrast between this and

---

[17]Margaret Mead, *Male and Female* ([William Morrow: 1949] Mentor ed.: 1949), p. 214.

the friendships I had with men was striking. I started listening to men's conversations, including my own, and gradually the basic outlines of the pattern described here began to emerge. I heard from women that the men they knew had very few really close male friends; since then I have heard the same thing from men themselves. It was, I realized, my own experience as well. It wasn't that I didn't know a lot of men, or that I was not on friendly terms with them. Rather, I gradually became dissatisfied with the impersonality of these friendships.

Of course, some constraints on self-disclosure do make sense. Privacy is something you give up selectively and gradually to people you like and trust, and who are capable of understanding—instant, indiscriminate intimacy is nearly always formularized, without real content and impact. Nor does self-disclosure as a kind of compartmentalized rest-and-recreation period work: "Well, John, let me tell you about myself. . . ."

Having said all this, it is nonetheless true that men have carried the practice of emotional restraint to the point of paralysis. For me, at least, the ritual affirmations of membership in the fraternity of men that one gets from participation in "masculine" activities do nothing to assuage the feeling of being essentially alone; they have become a poor substitute for being known by and knowing other people. But the positive content of what will replace the old-style friendship is only beginning to take shape. I am learning, though, that when I am able to articulate my feelings as they arise in the context of my friendships, I often find that they are shared by others. Bringing them out into the open clears the air; avoiding them, even unconsciously, is stultifying. I have found also that I am not as fragile as I once thought. The imagined hazards of showing oneself to be human, and thus vulnerable, to one's friends tend not to materialize when actually put to the test. But being oneself is an art, an art sensitive to variations in the receptivity of others as well as to one's own inner life. It is still, for me, something to be mastered, to be tried out and practiced.

Being a Man

Paul Theroux

Paul Theroux (born 1941) is a writer of many novels and his own version of travel books. Best known of these is The Great Railway Bazaar: By Train Through Asia *(1975), which records his experiences on a four-month journey.*

Theroux was educated at the University of Massachusetts (B.A. 1963), but he has for the most part lived and traveled outside the United States since then. After college he joined the Peace Corps, which led to a five year

*period of teaching and writing in East Africa, followed by three years in
Singapore. Since 1971 he and his family have lived in England and spent
summers in the United States.*

*Both his fiction and nonfiction are characterized by that special eye a
writer develops when he lives in a culture not his own. In an interview for
the* New York Times *(July 28, 1976) he said that it was not until he could
develop a "kind of skepticism about what people said that it was possible
to write about them. You can't write about a society with a complete
acceptance of that society." In the piece we print below, taken from* Sunrise
with Seamonsters: Travels & Discoveries 1964–1984 *(1985), one can detect
this skepticism as it extends to his own American male culture.*

There is a pathetic sentence in the chapter "Fetishism" in Dr Norman
Cameron's book *Personality Development and Psychopathology*. It goes,
"Fetishists are nearly always men; and their commonest fetish is a
woman's shoe." I cannot read that sentence without thinking that it is
just one more awful thing about being a man—and perhaps it is an
important thing to know about us.

I have always disliked being a man. The whole idea of manhood in
America is pitiful, in my opinion. This version of masculinity is a little
like having to wear an ill-fitting coat for one's entire life (by contrast, I
imagine femininity to be an oppressive sense of nakedness). Even the
expression "Be a man!" strikes me as insulting and abusive. It means: Be
stupid, be unfeeling, obedient, soldierly and stop thinking. Man means
"manly"—how can one think about men without considering the terrible
ambition of manliness? And yet it is part of every man's life. It is a hideous
and crippling lie; it not only insists on difference and connives at superiority, it is also by its very nature destructive—emotionally damaging and
socially harmful.

The youth who is subverted, as most are, into believing in the masculine
ideal is effectively separated from women and he spends the rest of his life
finding women a riddle and a nuisance. Of course, there is a female
version of this male affliction. It begins with mothers encouraging little
girls to say (to other adults) "Do you like my new dress?" In a sense, little
girls are traditionally urged to please adults with a kind of coquettishness,
while boys are enjoined to behave like monkeys towards each other. The
nine-year-old coquette proceeds to become womanish in a subtle power
game in which she learns to be sexually indispensable, socially decorative
and always alert to a man's sense of inadequacy.

Femininity—being lady-like—implies needing a man as witness and
seducer; but masculinity celebrates the exclusive company of men. That
is why it is so grotesque; and that is also why there is no manliness
without inadequacy—because it denies men the natural friendship of
women.

It is very hard to imagine any concept of manliness that does not belittle women, and it begins very early. At an age when I wanted to meet girls— let's say the treacherous years of thirteen to sixteen—I was told to take up a sport, get more fresh air, join the Boy Scouts, and I was urged not to read so much. It was the 1950s and if you asked too many questions about sex you were sent to camp—boy's camp, of course: the nightmare. Nothing is more unnatural or prison-like than a boy's camp, but if it were not for them we would have no Elks' Lodges, no pool rooms, no boxing matches, no Marines.

And perhaps no sports as we know them. Everyone is aware of how few in number are the athletes who behave like gentlemen. Just as high school basketball teaches you how to be a poor loser, the manly attitude towards sports seems to be little more than a recipe for creating bad marriages, social misfits, moral degenerates, sadists, latent rapists and just plain louts. I regard high school sports as a drug far worse than marijuana, and it is the reason that the average tennis champion, say, is a pathetic oaf.

Any objective study would find the quest for manliness essentially right-wing, puritanical, cowardly, neurotic and fueled largely by a fear of women. It is also certainly philistine. There is no book-hater like a Little League coach. But indeed all the creative arts are obnoxious to the manly ideal, because at their best the arts are pursued by uncompetitive and essentially solitary people. It makes it very hard for a creative youngster, for any boy who expresses the desire to be alone seems to be saying that there is something wrong with him.

It ought to be clear by now that I have something of an objection to the way we turn boys into men. It does not surprise me that when the President of the United States has his customary weekend off he dresses like a cowboy—it is both a measure of his insecurity and his willingness to please. In many ways, American culture does little more for a man than prepare him for modeling clothes in the L. L. Bean catalogue. I take this as a personal insult because for many years I found it impossible to admit to myself that I wanted to be a writer. It was my guilty secret, because being a writer was incompatible with being a man.

There are people who might deny this, but that is because the American writer, typically, has been so at pains to prove his manliness that we have come to see literariness and manliness as mingled qualities. But first there was a fear that writing was not a manly profession—indeed, not a profession at all. (The paradox in American letters is that it has always been easier for a woman to write and for a man to be published.) Growing up, I had thought of sports as wasteful and humiliating, and the idea of manliness was a bore. My wanting to become a writer was not a flight from that oppressive role-playing, but I quickly saw that it was at odds with it. Everything in stereotyped manliness goes against the life of the mind. The Hemingway personality is too tedious to go into here, and in any case his exertions are well-known, but certainly it was not until this aberrant behavior was examined by feminists in the 1960s that any male writer dared question the pugnacity in Hemingway's fiction. All the bullfighting and arm wrestling and elephant shooting diminished Hemingway as a writer, but it is consistent with a prevailing attitude in American writing: one cannot be a male writer without first proving that one is a man.

It is normal in America for a man to be dismissive or even somewhat apologetic about being a writer. Various factors make it easier. There is a heartiness about journalism that makes it acceptable—journalism is the manliest form of American writing and, therefore, the profession the most independent-minded women seek (yes, it is an illusion, but that is my point). Fiction-writing is equated with a kind of dispirited failure and is only manly when it produces wealth—money is masculinity. So is drinking. Being a drunkard is another assertion, if misplaced, of manliness. The American male writer is traditionally proud of his heavy drinking. But we are also a very literal-minded people. A man proves his manhood in America in old-fashioned ways. He kills lions, like Hemingway; or he hunts ducks, like Nathanael West; or he makes pronouncements like, "A man should carry enough knife to defend himself with," as James Jones once said to a *Life* interviewer. Or he says he can drink you under the table. But even tiny drunken William Faulkner loved to mount a horse and go fox hunting, and Jack Kerouac roistered up and down Manhattan in a lumberjack shirt (and spent every night of *The Subterraneans* with his mother in Queens). And we are familiar with the lengths to which Norman Mailer is prepared, in his endearing way, to prove that he is just as much a monster as the next man.

When the novelist John Irving was revealed as a wrestler, people took him to be a very serious writer; and even a bubble reputation like Eric *(Love Story)* Segal's was enhanced by the news that he ran the marathon in a respectable time. How surprised we would be if Joyce Carol Oates were revealed as a sumo wrestler or Joan Didion active in pumping iron. "Lives in New York City with her three children" is the typical woman writer's biographical note, for just as the male writer must prove he has achieved a sort of muscular manhood, the woman writer—or rather her publicists—must prove her motherhood.

There would be no point in saying any of this if it were not generally accepted that to be a man is somehow—even now in feminist-influenced America—a privilege. It is on the contrary an unmerciful and punishing burden. Being a man is bad enough; being manly is appalling (in this sense, women's lib has done much more for men than for women). It is the sinister silliness of men's fashions, and a clubby attitude in the arts. It is the subversion of good students. It is the so-called "Dress Code" of the Ritz-Carlton Hotel in Boston, and it is the institutionalized cheating in college sports. It is the most primitive insecurity.

And this is also why men often object to feminism but are afraid to explain why: of course women have a justified grievance, but most men believe—and with reason—that their lives are just as bad.

César

M. F. K. Fisher

M. F. K. Fisher (born 1908) writes mainly about food, places, and people, in a voice so distinctive and a style so elegant that she often has been called one of the most distinguished prose writers in the United States. She has since childhood seen food as something special, "something beautiful to be shared with people instead of a thrice-daily necessity." There are too many of us, she writes, "who feel an impatience for the demands of our bodies, and who try throughout our whole lives to deafen ourselves to the voices of various hungers."

She was born in Michigan, grew up in Whittier, California, and then lived for many years in France and in Switzerland. In 1962, she settled in the wine country of Northern California. She was for thirty-five years a regular contributor to the The New Yorker. *Her many books include* The Gastronomical Me *(1943),* A Cordiall Water: A Garland of Odd & Old Receipts to Assuage the Ills of Man & Beast *(1961), and* Among Friends *(1971), about her childhood in Whittier. The essay we print here about a butcher friend in southern France is from her first book,* Serve It Forth *(1937).*

For one reason or another it is thought advisable to change the names of real people when you write about them. I can do that sometimes, but not now. And of course there is no reason why I should. César is very real: he lives more surely than most men; and if he does read about himself in any book, which is doubtful, he will at the most be amused.

I cannot remember how we first met him. He was the butcher in a village of fishermen. We were foreigners, who stayed in the village several weeks. It is probably strange that we knew César so well, and he us.

The women of the village hated him and were afraid of him, but, "All I do is reach through my window at night," said César, "and there's a fine piece of woman waiting for me in the dark street. Any time, every night, I pluck them in."

The women hated him for two reasons. He had been very cruel to his termagant wife. She fled from him finally, and the two sons with her, after a fight between them and their father.

They were very strong men, all three, and when they were angry they swelled with muscle and spleen. César chased them out, all howling maledictions.

Later one of the sons crept back and stabbed at his father, but César broke the dagger between his fists and gave the pieces to his son's mistress, one night after he had plucked her through his window.

But it was sorrow for the poor wife, even if she was a foul-mouthed shrew, that made the village women hate César. That was the first reason. The second was that the men in the village loved César more than they did their women or their sons or even their boats.

They loved him for a thousand reasons and one reason. César was all that every man wants secretly to be: strong, brave; foul, cruel, reckless; desired by women and potent as a goat; tender and very sweet with children; feared by the priest, respected by the mayor; utterly selfish and as generous as a prince; gay. César was man. Man noble and monstrous again after so many centuries.

Once a week, two or three times a week, we'd walk down the one street, after noon dinner. All the boats beached on one side of us, all the doorsteps empty on the other, desertion would lie like dust in the air, with here and there a woman peering sourly from a dark room.

Madame Revenusso or Madame Médin, maybe, would call sullenly that César was looking for Monsieur Fischer.

Al's face would flash with joy, like a torch or a trumpet call. He'd hurry away. I'd go home alone, understanding some of the village women's jealous anger.

César's meat shop was behind the chapel, in a dirty alley. It was seldom peopled: women would buy no cuts from him, the devil, and even if they had wanted to, he was always saving the best for himself. Probably he ran the shop because it was an easy way to have good meat ready to hand.

Back of the store, there was one large room. It was dark, spotless, full of clean cold air from stone walls and floor, and almost bare. Under the lone window was César's big bed, very conveniently arranged for his carnal nocturnes. A wide ledge jutted from two walls, wide enough to sit on or lie on. There were one or two chairs on the scrubbed tiles of the floor, nuisances to stumble over in the room's darkness.

In the centre was the heart, the yolk, the altar, the great stone fireplace flat and high as a table, with an iron top for pots and a grill. And the whole ceiling of the room was its chimney, rising to a point and a far hole above the fire, like an ancient ducal kitchen.

It was there, to that big dark room, that the men would come, usually in the afternoon. I never saw them there, nor the room, neither, but I know they came to it as quickly as they could, very joyfully. César would say "Come!" and they would hurry.

On the stove there was always something steaming in a great black pot—a stew of tiny opaque whitebait, or tripe jugged in sour white wine, or succulent scraps whose origin César leeringly would not tell.

Piled on a chair, or on the floor near the stove, were steaks as thick as your fist, or four or five lamb's legs, or a kid ready to broil. On the stone ledge were two kegs of wine, or three, or bottles never counted.

The fire was hot, the steam rose toward the roof.

César stood taller and broader than any other man before his stove, stirring, basting, smelling. His voice was mightier.

"Drink!" he cried out. "Drink, eat!" And he roared with joy.

In the other houses women snapped at their children or perked their heads towards the chapel alley. When they heard songs and wild laughter, or more alarming silence, they sighed and looked black. If there'd only been bad strumpets there behind the butcher shop, they would have comprehended, but just men—it was unnatural.

If their husbands came home before dark, they would not eat fish soup and bread with the children. If they came too late for that, they leaped fiercely and silently on the sleeping women, or stood for a long time looking through the shutters at the sea, their faces very gentle and intent.

The women hated César.

The mornings after, they cackled maliciously when his shop stayed closed until noon, and when he finally opened its wide door, they looked sideways at his tired thick face.

"M'sieur César appears ill today," they would greet him, oilily.

"Ill? My God, no, dear Madame Dirtypot! Two quarts of purgative water is all I need—or three. And I'd advise the same for your husband—but in proportion, in proportion, my good Mrs. Soilskirt. I'd say a half-glass. More would tear his vitals clean off, with more loss to you than to him, eh, Madame Foulface?"

César's eyes, almost shut, gleamed wickedly, and he hoisted up his big sagging belly with lewd relish.

Then his face cleared. A young woman came towards him, with a warm little naked child on one arm. César called her.

"Célèstine! How goes it with your new rascal?"

He paid no attention to her stiff mouth and forehead, but looked lovingly at the tiny brown baby she had.

"Oh, he is a beauty, but a beauty, so strong and straight! Célèstine, you've done a fine job here. That's right, girl—smile. César is your good friend, really. And this child! He is a grand fellow, I tell you. Here, come to me, you little beautiful limb of the devil!"

César stood in the strong white sunlight, his two bottles of physic forgotten. The naked baby in his arms grinned up at him candidly while he murmured to it. He turned it across his arm, and ran his huge hand over its firm little bottom.

"My God!" he exclaimed, suddenly, "what delicious, truly what a delicious morsel that would be, broiled!"

With an outraged squawk Célèstine tore her baby from him and scuttled away. César yelled with laughter, belched mightily, and went toward his shop, his physic under his arms.

Whenever a strange creature came up in the nets, some sea beast's child or watery vegetable, the fishermen carried it to César.

He'd poke it, smell it, inevitably taste it. If he spat it out, they'd nod wisely. Poison! If he gulped it down alive, or cooked it up into a queer stew, they'd talk for days, admiringly. Brave man, to eat a mass of purple jelly with a little green-toothed mouth in its middle!

But do you remember, and their eyes would glisten with amazed delight, do you remember the time the crocodile died at the big zoo in the city, and César was called to skin it, and brought himself back a fine thick steak from it? Ah, do you remember?

The time came for us to go. We asked César to come to our house to eat a last supper.

I felt awkward, because I was a woman—but there was no other place for me to eat. César felt awkward for the same reason.

He came with a coat on, and a pink shirt, and silently handed me a massive filet of beef. I left the room with it, and heard him talking to Al, but when I came back he stopped.

The meal was strained at the beginning, but we had plenty of good wine, and the meat was the best I have ever tasted.

César put down his knife and fork.

"She likes it, she likes good food!" he said, wonderingly, to Al. "She cannot be a real woman!"

After that things were very pleasant. He took off his coat, and we ate and drank and talked, all a good deal.

"I hear you are married," César remarked. "It is a filthy lie, naturally?"

"But of course we are married," Al protested. "We have been married for several years."

César peered incredulously at us, and then laughed.

"Ridiculous! And why? Children, you are not married, I say—because marriage is a rotten business, and you are not rotten." He spat neatly over his huge pink shoulder. "If you were married, Alfred, Alfred-the-Penguin, my Al, would not be a real man, happy. And he is. And you," he glared at me, "would not be sitting knowing good meat between your teeth. And you are.

"Therefore, my two peculiar little foreign children, you are not married! No, you are brother and sister, living in sinful glory!"

He laughed until the whole room shook, and tipped a full bottle of wine down his throat.

"I shall die soon," he said, "and when I die, every man in the village will laugh for many days. Do you know why? Because they'll have all my wine to drink, barrels and casks of it, to drink to my commands, and they'll all try to drink as I would, as I've taught them.

"Yes, they'll drink for me, to float my soul to Purgatory. And the biggest cask of wine will be my coffin. My friends know. They'll put me in it and bury me deep, and they and all the women, too, will weep."

He was silent for a minute, and then roared another laugh.

"And grapes will grow up from me," he cried, "and by God, what wine I'll make!"

Al and I looked and recognized there a ghost with us, another Man from whose dead heart had sprung a vine. Was he César, was César that dim great figure who heard of Pan's death and cried tears as big as ostrich eggs?°

We parted merrily, with no farewells.

About a year later, a shabby post card came from the village on the Mediterranean coast. It was stiffly pencilled.

"My friends in Sinful Glory, plant a tree somewhere for César."

Since then we have planted many, almost all for him.

---

figure . . . eggs The giant Pantagruel in Rabelais' *Gargantua and Pantagruel*, Book 4 (1552), chap. 28.

Race, Culture, and Prejudice

America is a country of immigrants. Even the Native Americans have, sadly, become so dislocated as to be suffering some of the traditional problems of the immigrant. We immigrants have come from very different places, different circumstances, and for very different reasons. We have come as religious enthusiasts, as bonded servants, as speculators; some have come in preference to imprisonment, some because they felt crowded, or restless, or hopeful. The slave trade once brought many by force. In the 1800s and early 1900s immigrants came to escape the Irish potato famine, the Russian pogroms, or harsh conditions of poverty and deprivation in other places. Nazism and World War II brought one wave of political refugees; more recent turmoil in Asia, the Middle East, and Central America has brought others. Some come in large groups, others as lone individuals.

Whatever its origin and character, immigration has given the country the energy and variety that is one of its chief glories. It has also brought massive problems. For if for most immigrants the country has offered haven, hope, freedom, and economic opportunity, it has also often exposed them to economic exploitation and varying degrees of hostility on the part of those already here. It has almost always confronted the newcomers with the need to come to terms with their racial and cultural identity. Put in extreme form, the question is whether to assimilate—to leave cultural origins behind, or at least to melt cultural difference into a homogeneous Americanism—or to preserve a strong cultural diversity, seeing in pluralism a source not of division but of strength, something to be protected as a pattern typically American. Each cultural group and each new immigrant reconciles these contrary pulls in one way or another. Every reader, indeed, can consider his or her own cultural background in the light of this problem. In this section we present a number of thoughtful considerations of it.

The first three pieces, all by black writers, take up one of the oldest and surely our most serious problem of cultural and racial orientation—the "American dilemma" of black and white. James Baldwin's classic essay gives deep insight into the spiritual and psychological perils that race prejudice and discrimination impose. He concludes with a profound paradox: one must accept life as it is, and the fact that injustice is a commonplace; nonetheless, "one must never, in one's own life, accept these injustices as commonplace, but must fight them with all one's strength." In the next essay, Brent Staples gives readers a salutary picture of their own fears as these are forced into the consciousness of a sophisticated black and endanger the ordinary, harmless pursuits of his everyday life. Toni Morrison, finally, uses the views of her grandparents and parents to show how longstanding the problems faced by black people have been, and how diverse are their responses. She concludes with a candid "overview of the state of black people" in the mid-1970s, which seems just as true today, and with her vision of a new generation of black young people "who know who they are because they have invented themselves and who know where they are going because they have envisioned it."

The next essay, by Thomas B. Morgan, deals with a major new crisis that looms into the imagination of an "Anglo" as he contemplates the rate of growth of Hispanic culture in America. Hispanics are determined, it is reported, to maintain their Hispanic identity. Are we facing the creation of two Americas, one Spanish-speaking and one English? How do we acculturate and integrate yet another great immigrant people?

The following three essays deal with cultural tensions within the white community. Michael Novak speaks out for his own origins, and for a group of immigrants—Poles and Italians and Greeks and Slavs—who, he feels, are grossly underrepresented in our discussions of cultural America. He sensitively describes what he sees as the traits of the "unmeltable ethnics," and reminds us of the tensions that come from lack of sympathy between social classes and between levels of education. Robert Claiborne, in turn, briefly and good-humoredly offers a defense of WASP values and a modest objection to the WASP stereotype. Calvin Trillin's essay about a murder in the Kentucky hills brings us face to face with perhaps the deepest prejudice of all—fear of the outsider.

Jean Wakatsuki Houston writes of the cultural tensions within herself, confronting Japanese and American traditions of family and marriage. We end the section with a piece of social science: Gordon Allport's lucid and balanced account of what prejudice is and how it comes about.

Notes of a Native Son

James Baldwin

"Notes of a Native Son" takes its title from Richard Wright's novel, Native Son *(1940), the story of Bigger Thomas, a black man who rebels against the poverty and helplessness of inner-city life through rage and violence. Recounting his stepfather's funeral while a race riot is erupting in Harlem, Baldwin here explores the impact of his own rage. This essay, first published in* Harper's Magazine *(1955) and then as the title essay of Baldwin's* Notes of a Native Son *(1955), is an autobiographical masterpiece. For further information about Baldwin, see page 162.*

On the 29th of July, in 1943, my father died. On the same day, a few hours later, his last child was born. Over a month before this, while all our energies were concentrated in waiting for these events, there had been, in Detroit, one of the bloodiest race riots of the century. A few hours after my father's funeral, while he lay in state in the undertaker's chapel, a race riot broke out in Harlem. On the morning of the 3rd of August, we drove my father to the graveyard through a wilderness of smashed plate glass.

The day of my father's funeral had also been my nineteenth birthday. As we drove him to the graveyard, the spoils of injustice, anarchy, discontent, and hatred were all around us. It seemed to me that God himself had devised, to mark my father's end, the most sustained and brutally dissonant of codas. And it seemed to me, too, that the violence which rose all about us as my father left the world had been devised as a corrective for the pride of his eldest son. I had declined to believe in that apocalypse which had been central to my father's vision; very well, life seemed to be saying, here is something that will certainly pass for an apocalypse until the real thing comes along. I had inclined to be contemptuous of my father for the conditions of his life, for the conditions of our lives. When his life had ended I began to wonder about that life and also, in a new way, to be apprehensive about my own.

I had not known my father very well. We had got on badly, partly because we shared, in our different fashions, the voice of stubborn pride. When he was dead I realized that I had hardly ever spoken to him. When he had been dead a long time I began to wish I had. It seems to be typical of life in America, where opportunities, real and fancied, are thicker than anywhere else on the globe, that the second generation has no time to talk to the first. No one, including my father, seems to have known exactly how old he was, but his mother had been born during slavery. He was of the first generation of free men. He, along with thousands of other Negroes, came North after 1919 and I was part of that generation which had never seen the landscape of what Negroes sometimes call the Old Country.

He had been born in New Orleans and had been a quite young man there during the time that Louis Armstrong, a boy, was running errands for the dives and honky-tonks of what was always presented to me as one of the most wicked of cities—to this day, whenever I think of New Orleans, I also helplessly think of Sodom and Gomorrah. My father never mentioned Louis Armstrong, except to forbid us to play his records; but there was a picture of him on our wall for a long time. One of my father's strong-willed female relatives had placed it there and forbade my father to take it down. He never did, but he eventually maneuvered her out of the house and when, some years later, she was in trouble and near death, he refused to do anything to help her.

He was, I think, very handsome. I gather this from photographs and from my own memories of him, dressed in his Sunday best and on his way to preach a sermon somewhere, when I was little. Handsome, proud, and ingrown, "like a toe-nail," somebody said. But he looked to me, as I grew older, like pictures I had seen of African tribal chieftains: he really should have been naked, with war-paint on and barbaric mementos, standing among spears. He could be chilling in the pulpit and indescribably cruel in his personal life and he was certainly the most bitter man I have ever met; yet it must be said that there was something else in him, buried in him, which lent him his tremendous power and, even, a rather crushing charm. It had something to do with his blackness, I think—he was very black—with his blackness and his beauty, and with the fact that he knew that he was black but did not know that he was beautiful. He claimed to be proud of his blackness but it had also been the cause of much humiliation and it had fixed bleak boundaries to his life. He was not a young man when we were growing up and he had already suffered many kinds of ruin; in his outrageously demanding and protective way he loved his children, who were black like him and menaced, like him; and all these things sometimes showed in his face when he tried, never to my knowledge with any success, to establish contact with any of us. When he took one of his children on his knee to play, the child always became fretful and began to cry; when he tried to help one of us with our homework the absolutely unabating tension which emanated from him caused our minds and our tongues to become paralyzed, so that he, scarcely knowing why, flew into a rage and the child, not knowing why, was punished. If it ever entered his head to bring a surprise home for his children, it was, almost unfailingly, the wrong surprise and even the big watermelons he often brought home on his back in the summertime led to the most appalling scenes. I do not remember, in all those years, that one of his children was ever glad to see him come home. From what I was able to gather of his early life, it seemed that this inability to establish contact with other people had always marked him and had been one of the things which had driven him out of New Orleans. There was something in him, therefore, groping and tentative, which was never expressed and which was buried with him. One saw it most clearly when he was facing new people and hoping to impress them. But he never did, not for long. We went from church to smaller and more improbable church, he found himself in less and less demand as a minister, and by the time he died none of his friends had come to see him for a long time. He had lived and died in an intolerable bitterness of spirit and it frightened me, as we drove him to the graveyard through those unquiet, ruined streets, to see how powerful and overflowing this bitterness could be and to realize that this bitterness now was mine.

When he died I had been away from home for a little over a year. In that year I had had time to become aware of the meaning of all my father's bitter warnings, had discovered the secret of his proudly pursed lips and rigid carriage: I had discovered the weight of white people in the world. I saw that this had been for my ancestors and now would be for me an awful thing to live with and that the bitterness which had helped to kill my father could also kill me.

He had been ill a long time—in the mind, as we now realized, reliving instances of his fantastic intransigence in the new light of his affliction and endeavoring to feel a sorrow for him which never, quite, came true. We had not known that he was being eaten up by paranoia, and the discovery that his cruelty, to our bodies and our minds, had been one of the symptoms of his illness was not, then, enough to enable us to forgive him. The younger children felt, quite simply, relief that he would not be coming home anymore. My mother's observation that it was he, after all, who had kept them alive all these years meant nothing because the problems of keeping children alive are not real for children. The older children felt, with my father gone, that they could invite their friends to the house without fear that their friends would be insulted or, as had sometimes happened with me, being told that their friends were in league with the devil and intended to rob our family of everything we owned. (I didn't fail to wonder, and it made me hate him, what on earth we owned that anybody would want.)

His illness was beyond all hope of healing before anyone realized that he was ill. He had always been so strange and had lived, like a prophet, in such unimaginably close communication with the Lord that his long silences which were punctuated by moans and hallelujahs and snatches of old songs while he sat at the living-room window never seemed odd to us. It was not until he refused to eat because, he said, his family was trying to poison him that my mother was forced to accept as a fact what had, until then, been only an unwilling suspicion. When he was committed, it was discovered that he had tuberculosis and, as it turned out, the disease of his mind allowed the disease of his body to destroy him. For the doctors could not force him to eat, either, and, though he was fed intravenously, it was clear from the beginning that there was no hope for him.

In my mind's eye I could see him, sitting at the window, locked up in his terrors; hating and fearing every living soul including his children who had betrayed him, too, by reaching towards the world which had despised him. There were nine of us. I began to wonder what it could have felt like for such a man to have had nine children whom he could barely feed. He used to make little jokes about our poverty, which never, of course, seemed very funny to us; they could not have seemed very funny to him, either, or else our all too feeble response to them would never have caused such rages. He spent great energy and achieved, to our chagrin, no small amount of success in keeping us away from the people who surrounded us, people who had all-night rent parties to which we listened when we should have been sleeping, people who cursed and drank and flashed razor blades on Lenox Avenue. He could not understand why, if they had so much energy to spare, they could not use it to make their lives better. He treated almost everybody on our block with a most uncharitable asperity and neither they, nor, of course, their children were slow to reciprocate.

The only white people who came to our house were welfare workers and bill collectors. It was almost always my mother who dealt with them, for my father's temper, which was at the mercy of his pride, was never to be trusted. It was clear that he felt their very presence in his home to be a violation: this was conveyed by his carriage, almost ludicrously stiff, and by his voice, harsh and vindictively polite. When I was around nine or ten I wrote a play which was directed by a young, white schoolteacher, a woman, who then took an interest in me, and gave me books to read and, in order to corroborate my theatrical bent, decided to take me to see what she somewhat tactlessly referred to as "real" plays. Theater-going was forbidden in our house, but, with the really cruel intuitiveness of a child, I suspected that the color of this woman's skin would carry the day for me. When, at school, she suggested taking me to the theater, I did not, as I might have done if she had been a Negro, find a way of discouraging her, but agreed that she should pick me up at my house one evening. I then, very cleverly, left all the rest to my mother, who suggested to my father, as I knew she would, that it would not be very nice to let such a kind woman make the trip for nothing. Also, since it was a schoolteacher, I imagine that my mother countered the idea of sin with the idea of "education," which word, even with my father, carried a kind of bitter weight.

Before the teacher came my father took me aside to ask *why* she was coming, what *interest* she could possibly have in our house, in a boy like me. I said I didn't know but I, too, suggested that it had something to do with education. And I understood that my father was waiting for me to say something—I didn't quite know what; perhaps that I wanted his protection against this teacher and her "education." I said none of these things and the teacher came and we went out. It was clear, during the brief interview in our living room, that my father was agreeing very much against his will and that he would have refused permission if he had dared. The fact that he did not dare caused me to despise him: I had no way of knowing that he was facing in that living room a wholly unprecedented and frightening situation.

Later, when my father had been laid off from his job, this woman became very important to us. She was really a very sweet and generous woman and went to a great deal of trouble to be of help to us, particularly during one awful winter. My mother called her by the highest name she knew: she said she was a "christian." My father could scarcely disagree but during the four or five years of our relatively close association he never trusted her and was always trying to surprise in her open, Midwestern face the genuine, cunningly hidden, and hideous motivation. In later years, particularly when it began to be clear that this "education" of mine was going to lead me to perdition, he became more explicit and warned me that my white friends in high school were not really my friends and that I would see, when I was older, how white people would do anything to keep a Negro down. Some of them could be nice, he admitted, but none of them were to be trusted and most of them were not even nice. The best thing was to have as little to do with them as possible. I did not feel this way and I was certain, in my innocence, that I never would.

But the year which preceded my father's death had made a great change in my life. I had been living in New Jersey, working in defense plants, working and living among southerners, white and black. I knew about the south, of course, and about how southerners treated Negroes and how they expected them to behave, but it had never entered my mind that anyone would look at me and expect *me* to behave that way. I learned in New Jersey that to be a Negro meant, precisely, that one was never looked at but was simply at the mercy of the reflexes the color of one's skin caused in other people. I acted in New Jersey as I had always acted, that is as though I thought a great deal of myself—I had to *act* that way—with results that were, simply, unbelievable. I had scarcely arrived before I had earned the enmity, which was extraordinarily ingenious, of all my superiors and nearly all my co-workers. In the beginning, to make matters worse, I simply did not know what was happening. I did not know what I had done, and I shortly began to wonder what *anyone* could possibly do, to bring about such unanimous, active, and unbearably vocal hostility. I knew about jim-crow but I had never experienced it. I went to the same self-service restaurant three times and stood with all the Princeton boys before the counter, waiting for a hamburger and coffee; it was always an extraordinarily long time before anything was set before me; but it was not until the fourth visit that I learned that, in fact, nothing had ever been set before me: I had simply picked something up. Negroes were not served there, I was told, and they had been waiting for me to realize that I was always the only Negro present. Once I was told this, I determined to go there all the time. But now they were ready for me and, though some dreadful scenes were subsequently enacted in that restaurant, I never ate there again.

It was the same story all over New Jersey, in bars, bowling alleys, diners, places to live. I was always being forced to leave, silently, or with mutual imprecations. I very shortly became notorious and children giggled behind me when I passed and their elders whispered or shouted—they really believed that I was mad. And it did begin to work on my mind, of course; I began to be afraid to go anywhere and to compensate for this I went to places to which I really should not have gone and where, God knows, I had no desire to be. My reputation in town naturally enhanced my reputation at work and my working day became one long series of acrobatics designed to keep me out of trouble. I cannot say that these acrobatics succeeded. It began to seem that the machinery of the organization I worked for was turning over, day and night, with but one aim: to eject me. I was fired once, and contrived, with the aid of a friend from New York, to get back on the payroll; was fired again, and bounced back again. It took a while to fire me for the third time, but the third time took. There were no loopholes anywhere. There was not even any way of getting back inside the gates.

That year in New Jersey lives in my mind as though it were the year during which, having an unsuspected predilection for it, I first contracted some dread, chronic disease, the unfailing symptom of which is a kind of blind fever, a pounding in the skull and fire in the bowels. Once this disease is contracted, one can never be really carefree again, for the fever, without an instant's warning, can recur at any moment. It can wreck more important things than race relations. There is not a Negro alive who does not have this rage in his blood—one has the choice, merely, of living with it consciously or surrendering to it. As for me, this fever has recurred in me, and does, and will until the day I die.

My last night in New Jersey, a white friend from New York took me to the nearest big town, Trenton, to go to the movies and have a few drinks. As it turned out, he also saved me from, at the very least, a violent whipping. Almost every detail of that night stands out very clearly in my memory. I even remember the name of the movie we saw because its title impressed me as being so patly ironical. It was a movie about the German occupation of France, starring Maureen O'Hara and Charles Laughton and called *This Land Is Mine*. I remember the name of the diner we walked into when the movie ended: it was the "American Diner." When we walked in the counterman asked what we wanted and I remember answering with the casual sharpness which had become my habit: "We want a hamburger and a cup of coffee, what do you think we want?" I do not know why, after a year of such rebuffs, I so completely failed to anticipate his answer, which was, of course, "We don't serve Negroes here." This reply failed to discompose me, at least for the moment. I made some sardonic comment about the name of the diner and we walked out into the streets.

This was the time of what was called the "brown-out," when the lights in all American cities were very dim. When we re-entered the streets something happened to me which had the force of an optical illusion, or a nightmare. The streets were very crowded and I was facing north. People were moving in every direction but it seemed to me, in that instant, that all of the people I could see, and many more than that, were moving toward me, against me, and that everyone was white. I remember how their faces gleamed. And I felt, like a physical sensation, a *click* at the nape of my neck as though some interior string connecting my head to my body had been cut. I began to walk. I heard my friend call after me, but I ignored him. Heaven only knows what was going on in his mind, but he had the good sense not to touch me—I don't know what would have happened if he had—and to keep me in sight. I don't know what was going on in my mind, either; I certainly had no conscious plan. I wanted to do something to crush these white faces, which were crushing me. I walked for perhaps a block or two until I came to an enormous, glittering, and fashionable restaurant in which I knew not even the intercession of the Virgin would cause me to be served. I pushed through the doors and took the first vacant seat I saw, at a table for two, and waited.

I do not know how long I waited and I rather wonder, until today, what I could possibly have looked like. Whatever I looked like, I frightened the waitress who shortly appeared, and the moment she appeared all of my fury flowed towards her. I hated her for her white face, and for her great, astounded, frightened eyes. I felt that if she found a black man so frightening I would make her fright worth-while.

She did not ask me what I wanted, but repeated, as though she had learned it somewhere, "We don't serve Negroes here." She did not say it with the blunt, derisive hostility to which I had grown so accustomed, but, rather, with a note of apology in her voice, and fear. This made me colder and more murderous than ever. I felt I had to do something with my hands. I wanted her to come close enough for me to get her neck between my hands.

So I pretended not to have understood her, hoping to draw her closer. And she did step a very short step closer, with her pencil poised incongruously over her pad, and repeated the formula: ". . . don't serve Negroes here."

Somehow, with the repetition of that phrase, which was already ringing in my head like a thousand bells of a nightmare, I realized that she would never come any closer and that I would have to strike from a distance. There was nothing on the table but an ordinary watermug half full of water, and I picked this up and hurled it with all my strength at her. She ducked and it missed her and shattered against the mirror behind the bar. And, with that sound, my frozen blood abruptly thawed, I returned from wherever I had been, I *saw,* for the first time, the restaurant, the people with their mouths open, already, as it seemed to me, rising as one man, and I realized what I had done, and where I was, and I was frightened. I rose and began running for the door. A round, potbellied man grabbed me by the nape of the neck just as I reached the doors and began to beat me about the face. I kicked him and got loose and ran into the streets. My friend whispered, *"Run!"* and I ran.

My friend stayed outside the restaurant long enough to misdirect my pursuers and the police, who arrived, he told me, at once. I do not know what I said to him when he came to my room that night. I could not have said much. I felt, in the oddest, most awful way, that I had somehow betrayed him. I lived it over and over and over again, the way one relives an automobile accident after it has happened and one finds oneself alone and safe. I could not get over two facts, both equally difficult for the imagination to grasp, and one was that I could have been murdered. But the other was that I had been ready to commit murder. I saw nothing very clearly but I did see this: that my life, my *real* life, was in danger, and not from anything other people might do but from the hatred I carried in my own heart.

2

I had returned home around the second week in June—in great haste because it seemed that my father's death and my mother's confinement were both but a matter of hours. In the case of my mother, it soon became clear that she had simply made a miscalculation. This had always been her tendency and I don't believe that a single one of us arrived in the world, or has since arrived anywhere else, on time. But none of us dawdled so intolerably about the business of being born as did my baby sister. We sometimes amused ourselves, during those endless, stifling weeks, by picturing the baby sitting within in the safe, warm dark, bitterly regretting the necessity of becoming a part of our chaos and stubbornly putting it off as long as possible. I understood her perfectly and congratulated her on showing such good sense so soon. Death, however, sat as purposefully at my father's bedside as life stirred within my mother's womb and it was harder to understand why he so lingered in that long shadow. It seemed that he had bent, and for a long time, too, all of his energies towards dying. Now death was ready for him but my father held back.

All of Harlem, indeed, seemed to be infected by waiting. I had never before known it to be so violently still. Racial tensions throughout this country were exacerbated during the early years of the war, partly because the labor market brought together hundreds of thousands of ill-prepared people and partly because Negro soldiers, regardless of where they were born, received their military training in the south. What happened in defense plants and army camps had repercussions, naturally, in every Negro ghetto. The situation in Harlem had grown bad enough for clergymen, policemen, educators, politicians, and social workers to assert in one breath that there was no "crime wave" and to offer, in the very next breath, suggestions as how to combat it. These suggestions always seemed to involve playgrounds, despite the fact that racial skirmishes were occurring in the playgrounds, too. Playground or not, crime wave or not, the Harlem police force had been augmented in March, and the unrest grew—perhaps, in fact, partly as a result of the ghetto's instinctive hatred of policemen. Perhaps the most revealing news item, out of the steady parade of reports of muggings, stabbings, shootings, assaults, gang wars, and accusations of police brutality, is the item concerning six Negro girls who set upon a white girl in the subway because, as they all too accurately put it, she was stepping on their toes. Indeed she was, all over the nation.

I had never before been so aware of policemen, on foot, on horseback, on corners, everywhere, always two by two. Nor had I ever been so aware of small knots of people. They were on stoops and on corners and in doorways, and what was striking about them, I think, was that they did not seem to be talking. Never, when I passed these groups, did the usual sound of a curse or a laugh ring out and neither did there seem to be any hum of gossip. There was certainly, on the other hand, occurring between them communication extraordinarily intense. Another thing that was striking was the unexpected diversity of the people who made up these groups. Usually, for example, one would see a group of sharpies standing on the street corner, jiving the passing chicks; or a group of older men, usually, for some reason, in the vicinity of a barber shop, discussing baseball scores, or the numbers,° or making rather chilling observations about women they had known. Women, in a general way, tended to be seen less often together—unless they were church women, or very young girls, or prostitutes met together for an unprofessional instant. But that summer I saw the strangest combinations: large, respectable, churchly

---

the numbers   Popular street gambling game based on winning numbers at a given race track.

matrons standing on the stoops or the corners with their hair tied up, together with a girl in sleazy satin whose face bore the marks of gin and the razor, or heavy-set, abrupt, no-nonsense older men, in company with the most disreputable and fanatical "race" men, or these same "race" men with the sharpies, or these sharpies with the churchly women. Seventh Day Adventists and Methodists and Spiritualists seemed to be hob-nobbing with Holyrollers and they were all, alike, entangled with the most flagrant disbelievers; something heavy in their stance seemed to indicate that they had all, incredibly, seen a common vision, and on each face there seemed to be the same strange, bitter shadow.

The churchly women and the matter-of-fact, no-nonsense men had children in the Army. The sleazy girls they talked to had lovers there, the sharpies and the "race" men had friends and brothers there. It would have demanded an unquestioning patriotism, happily as uncommon in this country as it is undesirable, for these people not to have been disturbed by the bitter letters they received, by the newspaper stories they read, not to have been enraged by the posters, then to be found all over New York, which described the Japanese as "yellow-bellied Japs." It was only the "race" men, to be sure, who spoke ceaselessly of being revenged—how this vengeance was to be exacted was not clear—for the indignities and dangers suffered by Negro boys in uniform; but everybody felt a directionless, hopeless bitterness, as well as that panic which can scarcely be suppressed when one knows that a human being one loves is beyond one's reach, and in danger. This helplessness and this gnawing uneasiness does something, at length, to even the toughest mind. Perhaps the best way to sum all this up is to say that the people I knew felt, mainly, a peculiar kind of relief when they knew that their boys were being shipped out of the south, to do battle overseas. It was, perhaps, like feeling that the most dangerous part of a dangerous journey had been passed and that now, even if death should come, it would come with honor and without the complicity of their countrymen. Such a death would be, in short, a fact with which one could hope to live.

It was on the 28th of July, which I believe was a Wednesday, that I visited my father for the first time during his illness and for the last time in his life. The moment I saw him I knew why I had put off this visit so long. I had told my mother that I did not want to see him because I hated him. But this was not true. It was only that I *had* hated him and I wanted to hold on to this hatred. I did not want to look at him as a ruin: it was not a ruin I had hated. I imagine that one of the reasons people cling to their hates so stubbornly is because they sense, once hate is gone, that they will be forced to deal with pain.

We traveled out to him, his older sister and myself, to what seemed to be the very end of a very Long Island. It was hot and dusty and we wrangled, my aunt and I, all the way out, over the fact that I had recently begun to smoke and, as she said, to give myself airs. But I knew that she wrangled with me because she could not bear to face the fact of her brother's dying. Neither could I endure the reality of her despair, her unstated bafflement as to what had happened to her brother's life, and her own. So we wrangled and I smoked and from time to time she fell into a heavy reverie. Covertly, I watched her face, which was the face of an old woman; it had fallen in, the eyes were sunken and lightless; soon she would be dying too.

In my childhood—it had not been so long ago—I had thought her beautiful. She had been quick-witted and quick-moving and very generous with all the children and each of her visits had been an event. At one time one of my brothers and myself had thought of running away to live with her. Now she could no longer produce out of her handbag some unexpected and yet familiar delight. She made me feel pity and revulsion and fear. It was awful to realize that she no longer caused me to feel affection. The closer we came to the hospital the more querulous she became and at the same time, naturally, grew more dependent on me. Between pity and guilt and fear I began to feel that there was another me trapped in my skull like a jack-in-the-box who might escape my control at any moment and fill the air with screaming.

She began to cry the moment we entered the room and she saw him lying there, all shriveled and still, like a little black monkey. The great, gleaming apparatus which fed him and would have compelled him to be still even if he had been able to move brought to mind, not beneficence, but torture; the tubes entering his arm made me think of pictures I had seen when a child, of Gulliver, tied down by the pygmies on that island. My aunt wept and wept, there was a whistling sound in my father's throat; nothing was said; he could not speak. I wanted to take his hand, to say something. But I do not know what I could have said, even if he could have heard me. He was not really in that room with us, he had at last really embarked on his journey; and though my aunt told me that he said he was going to meet Jesus, I did not hear anything except that whistling in his throat. The doctor came back and we left, into that unbearable train again, and home. In the morning came the telegram saying that he was dead. Then the house was suddenly full of relatives, friends, hysteria, and confusion and I quickly left my mother and the children to the care of those impressive women, who, in Negro communities at least, automatically appear at times of bereavement armed with lotions, proverbs, and patience, and an ability to cook. I went downtown. By the time I returned, later the same day, my mother had been carried to the hospital and the baby had been born.

3

For my father's funeral I had nothing black to wear and this posed a nagging problem all day long. It was one of those problems, simple, or impossible of solution, to which the mind insanely clings in order to avoid the mind's real trouble. I spent most of the day at the downtown apartment of a girl I knew, celebrating my birthday with whiskey and wondering what to wear that night. When planning a birthday celebration one naturally does not expect that it will be up against competition from a funeral and this girl had anticipated taking me out that night, for a big dinner and a night club afterwards. Sometime during the course of that long day we decided that we would go out anyway, when my father's funeral service was over. I imagine *I* decided it, since, as the funeral hour approached, it became clearer and clearer to me that I would not know what to do with myself when it was over. The girl, stifling her very lively concern as to the possible effects of the whiskey on one of my father's chief mourners, concentrated on being conciliatory and practically helpful. She found a black shirt for me somewhere and ironed it and, dressed in the darkest pants and jacket I owned, and slightly drunk, I made my way to my father's funeral.

The chapel was full, but not packed, and very quiet. There were, mainly, my father's relatives, and his children, and here and there I saw faces I had not seen since childhood, the faces of my father's one-time friends. They were very dark and solemn now, seeming somehow to suggest that they had known all along that something like this would happen. Chief among the mourners was my aunt, who had quarreled with my father all his life; by which I do not mean to suggest that her mourning was insincere or that she had not loved him. I suppose that she was one of the few people in the world who had, and their incessant quarreling proved precisely the strength of the tie that bound them. The only other person in the world, as far as I knew, whose relationship to my father rivaled my aunt's in depth was my mother, who was not there.

It seemed to me, of course, that it was a very long funeral. But it was, if anything, a rather shorter funeral than most, nor, since there were no overwhelming, uncontrollable expressions of grief, could it be called—if I dare to use the word—successful. The minister who preached my father's funeral sermon was one of the few my father had still been seeing as he neared his end. He presented to us in his sermon a man whom none of us had ever seen—a man thoughtful, patient, and forbearing, a Christian inspiration to all who knew him, and a model for his children. And no doubt the children, in their disturbed and guilty state, were almost ready to believe this; he had been remote enough to be anything and, anyway, the shock of the incontrovertible, that it was really our father lying up there in that casket, prepared the mind for anything. His sister moaned and this grief-stricken moaning was taken for corroboration. The other faces held a dark, noncommittal thoughtfulness. This was not the man they had known, but they had scarcely expected to be confronted with *him;* this was, in a sense deeper than question of fact, the man they had not known, and the man they had not known may have been the real one. The real man, whoever he had been, had suffered and now he was dead: this was all that was sure and all that mattered now. Every man in the chapel hoped that when his hour came he, too, would be eulogized, which is to say forgiven, and that all of his lapses, greeds, errors, and strayings from the truth would be invested with coherence and looked upon with charity. This was perhaps the last thing human beings could give each other and it was what they demanded, after all, of the Lord. Only the Lord saw the midnight tears, only He was present when one of His children, moaning and wringing hands, paced up and down the room. When one slapped one's child in anger the recoil in the heart reverberated through heaven and became part of the pain of the universe. And when the children were hungry and sullen and distrustful and one watched them, daily, growing wilder, and further away, and running headlong into danger, it was the Lord who knew what the charged heart endured as the strap was laid to the backside; the Lord alone knew what one *would* have said if one had had, like the Lord, the gift of the living word. It was the Lord who knew of the impossibility every parent in the room faced: how to prepare the child for the day when the child would be despised and how to *create* in the child—by what means?—a stronger antidote to this poison than one had found for oneself. The avenues, side streets, bars, billiard halls, hospitals, police stations, and even the playgrounds of Harlem—not to mention the houses of correction, the jails, and the morgue—testified to the potency of the poison while remaining silent as to the efficacy of whatever antidote, irresistibly raising the question of whether or not such an antidote existed; raising, which was worse, the question of whether or not an antidote was desirable; perhaps poison should be fought with poison. With these several schisms in the mind and with more terrors in the heart than could be named, it was better not to judge the man who had gone down under an impossible burden. It was better to remember: *Thou knowest this man's fall; but thou knowest not his wrassling.*

While the preacher talked and I watched the children—years of changing their diapers, scrubbing them, slapping them, taking them to school, and scolding them had had the perhaps inevitable result of making me love them, though I am not sure I knew this then—my mind was busily breaking out with a rash of disconnected impressions. Snatches of popular songs, indecent jokes, bits of books I had read, movie sequences, faces, voices, political issues—I thought I was going mad; all these impressions suspended, as it were, in the solution of the faint nausea produced in me by the heat and liquor. For a moment I had the impression that my alcoholic breath, inefficiently disguised with chewing gum, filled the entire chapel. Then someone began singing one of my father's favorite songs and, abruptly, I was with him, sitting on his knee, in the hot, enormous, crowded church which was the first church we attended. It was the Abysinia Baptist Church on 138th Street. We had not gone there long. With this image, a host of others came. I had forgotten, in the rage of my growing up, how proud my father had been of me when I was little. Apparently, I had had a voice and my father had liked to show me off before the members of the church. I had forgotten what he had looked like when he was pleased but now I remembered that he had always been grinning with pleasure when my solos ended. I even remembered certain expressions on his face when he teased my mother—had he loved her? I would never know. And when had it all begun to change? For now it seemed that he had not always been cruel. I remembered being taken for a haircut and scraping my knee on the footrest of the barber's chair and I remembered my father's face as he soothed my crying and applied the stinging iodine. Then I remembered our fights, fights which had been of the worst possible kind because my technique had been silence.

I remembered the one time in all our life together when we had really spoken to each other.

It was on a Sunday and it must have been shortly before I left home. We were walking, just the two of us, in our usual silence, to or from church. I was in high school and had been doing a lot of writing and I was, at about this time, the editor of the high school magazine. But I had also been a Young Minister and had been preaching from the pulpit. Lately, I had been taking fewer engagements and preached as rarely as possible. It was said in the church, quite truthfully, that I was "cooling off."

My father asked me abruptly, "You'd rather write than preach, wouldn't you?"

I was astonished at his question—because it was a real question. I answered, "Yes."

That was all we said. It was awful to remember that that was all we had *ever* said.

The casket now was opened and the mourners were being led up the aisle to look for the last time on the deceased. The assumption was that the family was too overcome with grief to be allowed to make this journey alone and I watched while my aunt was led to the casket and, muffled in black, and shaking, led back to her seat. I disapproved of forcing the children to look on their dead father, considering that the shock of his death, or, more truthfully, the shock of death as a reality, was already a little more than a child could bear, but my judgment in this matter had been overruled and there they were, bewildered and frightened and very small, being led, one by one, to the casket. But there is also something very gallant about children at such moments. It has something to do with their silence and gravity and with the fact that one cannot help them. Their legs, somehow, seemed *exposed*, so that it is at once incredible and terribly clear that their legs are all they have to hold them up.

I had not wanted to go to the casket myself and I certainly had not wished to be led there, but there was no way of avoiding either of these forms. One of the deacons led me up and I looked on my father's face. I cannot say that it looked like him at all. His blackness had been equivocated by powder and there was no suggestion in that casket of what his power had or could have been. He was simply an old man dead, and it was hard to believe that he had ever given anyone either joy or pain. Yet, his life filled that room. Further up the avenue his wife was holding his newborn child. Life and death so close together, and love and hatred, and right and wrong, said something to me which I did not want to hear concerning man, concerning the life of man.

After the funeral, while I was downtown desperately celebrating my birthday, a Negro soldier, in the lobby of the Hotel Braddock, got into a fight with a white policeman over a Negro girl. Negro girls, white policemen, in or out of uniform, and Negro males—in or out of uniform—were part of the furniture of the lobby of the Hotel Braddock and this was certainly not the first time such an incident had occurred. It was destined, however, to receive an unprecedented publicity, for the fight between the policeman and the soldier ended with the shooting of the soldier. Rumor, flowing immediately to the streets outside, stated the soldier had been shot in the back, an instantaneous and revealing invention, and that the soldier had died protecting a Negro woman. The facts were somewhat different—for example, the soldier had not been shot in the back, and was not dead, and the girl seems to have been as dubious a symbol of womanhood as her white counterpart in Georgia usually is, but no one was interested in the facts. They preferred the invention because this invention expressed and corroborated their hates and fears so perfectly. It is just as well to remember that people are always doing this. Perhaps many of those legends, including Christianity, to which the world clings began their conquest of the world with just some such concerted surrender to distortion. The effect, in Harlem, of this particular legend was like the effect of a lit match in a tin of gasoline. The mob gathered before the doors of the Hotel Braddock simply began to swell and to spread in every direction, and Harlem exploded.

The mob did not cross the ghetto lines. It would have been easy, for example, to have gone over Morningside Park on the west side or to have crossed the Grand Central railroad tracks at 125th Street on the east side, to wreak havoc in the white neighborhoods. The mob seems to have been mainly interested in something more potent and real than the white face, that is, in white power, and the principal damage done during the riot of the summer of 1943 was to white business establishments in Harlem. It might have been a far bloodier story, of course, if, at the hour the riot began, these establishments had still been open. From the Hotel Braddock the mob fanned out, east and west along 125th Street, and for the entire length of Lenox, Seventh, and Eighth avenues. Along each of these avenues, and along each major side street—116th, 125th, 135th, and so on—bars, stores, pawnshops, restaurants, even little luncheonettes had been smashed open and entered and looted—looted, it might be added, with more haste than efficiency. The shelves really looked as though a bomb had struck them. Cans of beans and soup and dog food, along with toilet paper, corn flakes, sardines and milk tumbled every which way, and abandoned cash registers and cases of beer leaned crazily out of the splintered windows and were strewn along the avenues. Sheets, blankets, and clothing of every description formed a kind of path, as though people had dropped them while running. I truly had not realized that Harlem *had* so many stores until I saw them all smashed open; the first time the word *wealth* ever entered my mind in relation to Harlem was when I saw it scattered in the streets. But one's first, incongruous impression of plenty was countered immediately by an impression of waste. None of this was doing anybody any good. It would have been better to have left the plate glass as it had been and the goods lying in the stores.

It would have been better, but it would also have been intolerable, for Harlem had needed something to smash. To smash something is the ghetto's chronic need. Most of the time it is the members of the ghetto who smash each other, and themselves. But as long as the ghetto walls are standing there will always come a moment when these outlets do not work. That summer, for example, it was not enough to get into a fight on Lenox Avenue, or curse out one's cronies in the barber shops. If ever, indeed, the violence which fills Harlem's churches, pool halls, and bars erupts outward in a more direct fashion, Harlem and its citizens are likely to vanish in an apocalyptic flood. That this is not likely to happen is due to a great many reasons, most hidden and powerful among them the Negro's real relation to the white American. This relation prohibits, simply, anything as uncomplicated and satisfactory as pure hatred. In order really to hate white people, one has to blot so much out of the mind—and the heart—that this hatred itself becomes an exhausting and self-destructive pose. But this does not mean, on the other hand, that love comes easily: the white world is too powerful, too complacent, too ready with gratuitous humiliation, and, above all, too ignorant and too innocent for that. One is absolutely forced to make perpetual qualifications and one's own reactions are always canceling each other out. It is this, really, which has driven so many people mad, both white and black. One is always in the position of having to decide between amputation and gangrene. Amputation is swift but time may prove that the amputation was not necessary—or one may delay the amputation too long. Gangrene is slow, but it is impossible to be sure that one is reading one's symptoms right. The idea of going through life as a cripple is more than one can bear, and equally unbearable is the risk of swelling up slowly, in agony, with poison. And the trouble, finally, is that the risks are real even if the choices do not exist.

"But as for me and my house," my father had said, "we will serve the Lord." I wondered, as we drove him to his resting place, what this line had meant for him. I had heard him preach it many times. I had preached it once myself, proudly giving it an interpretation different from my father's. Now the whole thing came back to me, as though my father and I were on our way to Sunday school and I were memorizing the golden text: *And if it seem evil unto you to serve the Lord, choose you this day whom you will serve; whether the gods which your fathers served that were on the other side of the flood, or the gods of the Amorites, in whose land ye dwell: but as for me and my house, we will serve the Lord.* I suspected in these familiar lines a meaning which had never been there for me before. All of my father's texts and songs, which I had decided were meaningless, were arranged before me at his death like empty bottles, waiting to hold the meaning which life would give them for me. This was his legacy: nothing is ever escaped. That bleakly memorable morning I hated the unbelievable streets and the Negroes and whites who had, equally, made them that way. But I knew that it was folly, as my father would have said, this bitterness was folly. It was necessary to hold on to the things that mattered. The dead man mattered, the new life mattered; blackness and whiteness did not matter; to believe that they did was to acquiesce in one's own destruction. Hatred, which could destroy so much, never failed to destroy the man who hated and this was an immutable law.

It began to seem that one would have to hold in the mind forever two ideas which seemed to be in opposition. The first idea was acceptance, the acceptance, totally without rancor, of life as it is, and men as they are: in the light of this idea, it goes without saying that injustice is a commonplace. But this did not mean that one could be complacent, for the second idea was of equal power: that one must never, in one's own life, accept these injustices as commonplace but must fight them with all one's strength. This fight begins, however, in the heart and it now had been laid to my charge to keep my own heart free of hatred and despair. This intimation made my heart heavy and, now that my father was irrecoverable, I wished that he had been beside me so that I could have searched his face for the answers which only the future would give me now.

Just Walk On By: A Black Man Ponders His Power to Alter Public Space

Brent Staples

Brent Staples is Assistant Metropolitan Editor of the New York Times. *He was born in Chester, Pennsylvania (1951), graduated from Widener Uni-*

*versity there, and went on to the University of Chicago for a Ph.D. in
psychology. He taught briefly at Roosevelt University, in Chicago, then
turned to a career in journalism. He has been a reporter for the* Chicago
Sun-Times, *and an editor of the* New York Times Book Review. *He writes
literary and dramatic criticism, and articles on a wide range of other
subjects. The present piece appeared in* Ms. *in September 1986.*

My first victim was a woman—white, well dressed, probably in her early
twenties. I came upon her late one evening on a deserted street in Hyde
Park, a relatively affluent neighborhood in an otherwise mean, impoverished section of Chicago. As I swung onto the avenue behind her, there
seemed to be a discreet, uninflammatory distance between us. Not so. She
cast back a worried glance. To her, the youngish black man—a broad six
feet two inches with a beard and billowing hair, both hands shoved into
the pockets of a bulky military jacket—seemed menacingly close. After
a few more quick glimpses, she picked up her pace and was soon running
in earnest. Within seconds she disappeared into a cross street.

That was more than a decade ago. I was 22 years old, a graduate student
newly arrived at the University of Chicago. It was in the echo of that
terrified woman's footfalls that I first began to know the unwieldy inheritance I'd come into—the ability to alter public space in ugly ways. It was
clear that she thought herself the quarry of a mugger, a rapist, or worse.
Suffering a bout of insomnia, however, I was stalking sleep, not defense-
less wayfarers. As a softy who is scarcely able to take a knife to a raw
chicken—let alone hold it to a person's throat—I was surprised, embarrassed, and dismayed all at once. Her flight made me feel like an accom-
plice in tyranny. It also made it clear that I was indistinguishable from
the muggers who occasionally seeped into the area from the surrounding
ghetto. That first encounter, and those that followed, signified that a vast,
unnerving gulf lay between nighttime pedestrians—particularly
women—and me. And I soon gathered that being perceived as dangerous
is a hazard in itself. I only needed to turn a corner into a dicey situation,
or crowd some frightened, armed person in a foyer somewhere, or make
an errant move after being pulled over by a policeman. Where fear and
weapons meet—and they often do in urban America—there is always the
possibility of death.

In that first year, my first away from my hometown, I was to become
thoroughly familiar with the language of fear. At dark, shadowy intersec-
tions in Chicago, I could cross in front of a car stopped at a traffic light
and elicit the *thunk, thunk, thunk, thunk* of the driver—black, white,
male, or female—hammering down the door locks. On less traveled
streets after dark, I grew accustomed to but never comfortable with people who crossed to the other side of the street rather than pass me. Then
there were the standard unpleasantries with police, doormen, bouncers,

cab drivers, and others whose business it is to screen out troublesome individuals *before* there is any nastiness.

I moved to New York nearly two years ago and I have remained an avid night walker. In central Manhattan, the near-constant crowd cover minimizes tense one-on-one street encounters. Elsewhere—visiting friends in SoHo, where sidewalks are narrow and tightly spaced buildings shut out the sky—things can get very taut indeed.

Black men have a firm place in New York mugging literature. Norman Podhoretz in his famed (or infamous) 1963 essay, "My Negro Problem— And Ours," recalls growing up in terror of black males; they "were tougher than we were, more ruthless," he writes—and as an adult on the Upper West Side of Manhattan, he continues, he cannot constrain his nervousness when he meets black men on certain streets. Similarly, a decade later, the essayist and novelist Edward Hoagland extols a New York where once "Negro bitterness bore down mainly on other Negroes." Where some see mere panhandlers, Hoagland sees "a mugger who is clearly screwing up his nerve to do more than just *ask* for money." But Hoagland has "the New Yorker's quick-hunch posture for broken-field maneuvering," and the bad guy swerves away.

I often witness that "hunch posture," from women after dark on the warrenlike streets of Brooklyn where I live. They seem to set their faces on neutral and, with their purse straps strung across their chests bandolier style, they forge ahead as though bracing themselves against being tackled. I understand, of course, that the danger they perceive is not a hallucination. Women are particularly vulnerable to street violence, and young black males are drastically overrepresented among the perpetrators of that violence. Yet these truths are no solace against the kind of alienation that comes of being ever the suspect, against being set apart, a fearsome entity with whom pedestrians avoid making eye contact.

It is not altogether clear to me how I reached the ripe old age of 22 without being conscious of the lethality nighttime pedestrians attributed to me. Perhaps it was because in Chester, Pennsylvania, the small, angry industrial town where I came of age in the 1960s, I was scarcely noticeable against a backdrop of gang warfare, street knifings, and murders. I grew up one of the good boys, had perhaps a half-dozen fist fights. In retrospect, my shyness of combat has clear sources.

Many things go into the making of a young thug. One of those things is the consummation of the male romance with the power to intimidate. An infant discovers that random flailings send the baby bottle flying out of the crib and crashing to the floor. Delighted, the joyful babe repeats those motions again and again, seeking to duplicate the feat. Just so, I recall the points at which some of my boyhood friends were finally seduced by the perception of themselves as tough guys. When a mark cowered and surrendered his money without resistance, myth and reality merged—and paid off. It is, after all, only manly to embrace the power to frighten and intimidate. We, as men, are not supposed to give an inch of our lane on the highway; we are to seize the fighter's edge in work and in play and even in love; we are to be valiant in the face of hostile forces.

Unfortunately, poor and powerless young men seem to take all this nonsense literally. As a boy, I saw countless tough guys locked away; I have since buried several, too. They were babies, really—a teenage cousin, a brother of 22, a childhood friend in his mid-twenties—all gone down in episodes of bravado played out in the streets. I came to doubt the virtues of intimidation early on. I chose, perhaps even unconsciously, to remain a shadow—timid, but a survivor.

The fearsomeness mistakenly attributed to me in public places often has a perilous flavor. The most frightening of these confusions occurred in the late 1970s and early 1980s when I worked as a journalist in Chicago. One day, rushing into the office of a magazine I was writing for with a deadline story in hand, I was mistaken for a burglar. The office manager called security and, with an ad hoc posse, pursued me through the labyrinthine halls, nearly to my editor's door. I had no way of proving who I was. I could only move briskly toward the company of someone who knew me.

Another time I was on assignment for a local paper and killing time before an interview. I entered a jewelry store on the city's affluent Near North Side. The proprietor excused herself and returned with an enormous red Doberman pinscher straining at the end of a leash. She stood, the dog extended toward me, silent to my questions, her eyes bulging nearly out of her head. I took a cursory look around, nodded, and bade her good night. Relatively speaking, however, I never fared as badly as another black male journalist. He went to nearby Waukegan, Illinois, a couple of summers ago to work on a story about a murderer who was born there. Mistaking the reporter for the killer, police hauled him from his car at gunpoint and but for his press credentials would probably have tried to book him. Such episodes are not uncommon. Black men trade tales like this all the time.

In "My Negro Problem—And Ours," Podhoretz writes that the hatred he feels for blacks makes itself known to him through a variety of avenues—one being his discomfort with that "special brand of paranoid touchiness" to which he says blacks are prone. No doubt he is speaking here of black men. In time, I learned to smother the rage I felt at so often being taken for a criminal. Not to do so would surely have led to madness—via that special "paranoid touchiness" that so annoyed Podhoretz at the time he wrote the essay.

I began to take precautions to make myself less threatening. I move about with care, particularly late in the evening. I give a wide berth to nervous people on subway platforms during the wee hours, particularly when I have exchanged business clothes for jeans. If I happen to be entering a building behind some people who appear skittish, I may walk by, letting them clear the lobby before I return, so as not to seem to be following them. I have been calm and extremely congenial on those rare occasions when I've been pulled over by the police.

And on late-evening constitutionals along streets less traveled by, I employ what has proved to be an excellent tension-reducing measure: I whistle melodies from Beethoven and Vivaldi and the more popular classical composers. Even steely New Yorkers hunching toward nighttime destinations seem to relax, and occasionally they even join in the tune. Virtually everybody seems to sense that a mugger wouldn't be warbling bright, sunny selections from Vivaldi's *Four Seasons*. It is my equivalent of the cowbell that hikers wear when they know they are in bear country.

A Slow Walk of Trees
(as Grandmother Would Say)
Hopeless
(as Grandfather Would Say)
Toni Morrison

Toni Morrison was born in 1931 in Lorain, Ohio, a small steel town near Cleveland. Educated at Howard University (B.A. 1953) and Cornell (M.A. 1955), she has taught English, worked as an editor for Random House, and in 1988 joined the faculty of Princeton University. She has published five novels: The Bluest Eye *(1969);* Sula *(1973), nominated for the 1975 National Book Award in fiction;* Song of Solomon *(1977), winner of the National Book Award for best novel, and the National Book Critics' Circle Award;* Tar Baby *(1981); and, most recently,* Beloved *(1987). The following selection is from the July 4, 1976, issue of the* New York Times Magazine.*

The mythic qualities in Morrison's fiction are often noted, but she also draws on her direct experience as a black woman. In a 1981 interview, she said, "I was very conscious of trying to capture, in writing about what black life meant to me, not just what black people do but the way in which we look at it." In the same interview, when asked how she viewed herself as novelist, she answered, "Still in process, and I think that, if I'm lucky at all, it will always be that way. I want to learn more and more about how to write better."

His name was John Solomon Willis, and when at age 5 he heard from the old folks that "the Emancipation Proclamation was coming," he crawled under the bed. It was his earliest recollection of what was to be his habitual response to the promises of white people: horror and an instinctive yearning for safety. He was my grandfather, a musician who managed to hold on to his violin but not his land. He lost all 88 acres of his Indian mother's inheritance to legal predators who built their fortunes on the likes of him. He was an unreconstructed black pessimist who, in spite of or because of emancipation, was convinced for 85 years that there was no hope whatever for black people in this country. His rancor was legitimate, for he, John Solomon, was not only an artist but a first-rate carpenter and farmer, reduced to sending home to his family money he made playing the violin because he was not able to find work. And this during the years when almost half the black male population were skilled craftsmen who lost their jobs to white ex-convicts and immigrant farmers.

His wife, however, was of a quite different frame of mind and believed that all things could be improved by faith in Jesus and an effort of the will. So it was she, Ardelia Willis, who sneaked her seven children out of the back window into the darkness, rather than permit the patron of their sharecropper's existence to become their executioner as well, and headed north in 1912, when 99.2 percent of all black people in the U.S. were native-born and only 60 percent of white Americans were. And it was Ardelia who told her husband that they could not stay in the Kentucky town they ended up in because the teacher didn't know long division.

They have been dead now for 30 years and more and I still don't know which of them came closer to the truth about the possibilities of life for black people in this country. One of their grandchildren is a tenured professor at Princeton. Another, who suffered from what the Peruvian poet° called "anger that breaks a man into children," was picked up just as he entered his teens and emotionally lobotomized by the reformatories and mental institutions specifically designed to serve him. Neither John Solomon nor Ardelia lived long enough to despair over one or swell with pride over the other. But if they were alive today each would have selected and collected enough evidence to support the accuracy of the other's original point of view. And it would be difficult to convince either one that the other was right.

Some of the monstrous events that took place in John Solomon's America have been duplicated in alarming detail in my own America. There was the public murder of a President in a theater in 1865 and the public murder of another President on television in 1963. The Civil War of 1861 had its encore as the civil-rights movement of 1960. The torture and mutilation of a black West Point Cadet (Cadet Johnson Whittaker) in 1880 had its rerun with the 1970's murders of students at Jackson State College, Texas Southern and Southern University in Baton Rouge. And in 1976 we watch for what must be the thousandth time a pitched battle

---

Peruvian poet   César Vallejo (1892–1938), "La Cólera Que Quiebra Al Hombre . . ."

between the children of slaves and the children of immigrants—only this time, it is not the New York draft riots of 1863, but the busing turmoil in Paul Revere's home town, Boston.

Hopeless, he'd said. Hopeless. For he was certain that white people of every political, religious, geographical and economic background would band together against black people everywhere when they felt the threat of our progress. And a hundred years after he sought safety from the white man's "promise," somebody put a bullet in Martin Luther King's brain. And not long before that some excellent samples of the master race demonstrated their courage and virility by dynamiting some little black girls to death.° If he were here now, my grandfather, he would shake his head, close his eyes and pull out his violin—too polite to say, "I told you so." And his wife would pay attention to the music but not to the sadness in her husband's eyes, for she would see what she expected to see—not the occasional historical repetition, but, like the slow walk of certain species of trees from the flatlands up into the mountains, she would see the signs of irrevocable and permanent change. She, who pulled her girls out of an inadequate school in the Cumberland Mountains, knew all along that the gentlemen from Alabama who had killed the little girls would be rounded up. And it wouldn't surprise her in the least to know that the number of black college graduates jumped 12 percent in the last three years; 47 percent in 20 years. That there are 140 black mayors in this country; 14 black judges in the District Circuit, 4 in the Courts of Appeals and one on the Supreme Court. That there are 17 blacks in Congress, one in the Senate; 276 in state legislatures—223 in state houses, 53 in state senates. That there are 112 elected black police chiefs and sheriffs, 1 Pulitzer Prize winner; 1 winner of the Prix de Rome; a dozen or so winners of the Guggenheim; 4 deans of predominently white colleges. . . . Oh, her list would go on and on. But so would John Solomon's sweet sad music.

While my grandparents held opposite views on whether the fortunes of black people were improving, my own parents struck similarly opposed postures, but from another slant. They differed about whether the moral fiber of white people would ever improve. Quite a different argument. The old folks argued about how and if black people could improve themselves, who could be counted on to help us, who would hinder us and so on. My parents took issue over the question of whether it was possible for white people to improve. They assumed that black people were the humans of the globe, but had serious doubts about the quality and existence of white humanity. Thus my father, distrusting every word and every gesture of every white man on earth, assumed that the white man who crept up the

---

dynamiting some little black girls to death The Sixteenth Street Baptist Church in Birmingham, Alabama, was bombed on September 15, 1963; four young girls, aged eleven to fourteen, were killed while they were putting on their choir robes, and twenty other people were injured.

stairs one afternoon had come to molest his daughters and threw him down the stairs and then our tricycle after him. (I think my father was wrong, but considering what I have seen since, it may have been very healthy for me to have witnessed that as my first black-white encounter.) My mother, however, *believed* in them—their possibilities. So when the meal we got on relief was bug-ridden, she wrote a long letter to Franklin Delano Roosevelt. And when white bill collectors came to our door, it was she who received them civilly and explained in a sweet voice that we were people of honor and that the debt would be taken care of. Her message to Roosevelt got through—our meal improved. Her message to the bill collectors did not always get through and there was occasional violence when my father (self-exiled to the bedroom for fear he could not hold his temper) would hear that her reasonableness had failed. My mother was always wounded by these scenes, for she thought the bill collector knew that she loved good credit more than life and that being in arrears on a payment horrified her probably more than it did him. So she thought he was rude because he was white. For years she walked to utility companies and department stores to pay bills in person and even now she does not seem convinced that checks are legal tender. My father loved excellence, worked hard (he held three jobs at once for 17 years) and was so outraged by the suggestion of personal slackness that he could explain it to himself only in terms of racism. He was a fastidious worker who was frightened of one thing: unemployment. I can remember now the doomsday-cum-graveyard sound of "laid off" and how the minute school was out he asked us, "Where you workin'?" Both my parents believed that all succor and aid came from themselves and their neighborhood, since "they"—white people in charge and those not in charge but in obstructionist positions—were in some way fundamentally, genetically corrupt.

So I grew up in a basically racist household with more than a child's share of contempt for white people. And for each white friend I acquired who made a small crack in that contempt, there was another who repaired it. For each one who related to me as a person, there was one who in my presence at least, became actively "white." And like most black people of my generation, I suffer from racial vertigo that can be cured only by taking what one needs from one's ancestors. John Solomon's cynicism and his deployment of his art as both weapon and solace, Ardelia's faith in the magic that can be wrought by sheer effort of the will; my mother's openmindedness in each new encounter and her habit of trying reasonableness first; my father's temper, his impatience and his efforts to keep "them" (throw them) out of his life. And it is out of these learned and selected attitudes that I look at the quality of life for my people in this country now.

These widely disparate and sometimes conflicting views, I suspect, were held not only by me, but by most black people. Some I know are clearer in their positions, have not sullied their anger with optimism or dirtied their hope with despair. But most of us are plagued by a sense of being worn shell-thin by constant repression and hostility as well as the impression of being buoyed by visible testimony of tremendous strides. There *is* repetition of the grotesque in our history. And there *is* the miraculous walk of trees. The question is whether our walk is progress or merely movement. O.J. Simpson leaning on a Hertz car *is* better than the Gold Dust Twins on the back of a soap box. But is "Good Times"° better than Stepin Fetchit? Has the first order of business been taken care of? Does the law of the land work for us?

Are white people who murder black people punished with at least the same dispatch that sends black teen-age truants to Coxsackie? Can we relax now and discuss "The Jeffersons"° instead of genocide? Or is the difference between the two only the difference between a greedy pointless white life-style and a messy pointless black death? Now that Mr. Poitier and Mr. Belafonte have shot up all the racists in "Buck and the Preacher," have they all gone away? Can we really move into better neighborhoods and not be set on fire? Is there anybody who will lay me a $5 bet on it?

The past decade is a fairly good index of the odds at which you lay your money down.

Ten years ago in Queens, as black people like me moved into a neighborhood 20 minutes away from the Triborough Bridge, "for sale" signs shot up in front of white folks' houses like dandelions after a hot spring rain. And the black people smiled. "Goody, goody," said my neighbor. "Maybe we can push them on out to the sea. You think?"

Now I live in another neighborhood, 20 minutes away from the George Washington Bridge, and again the "for sale" signs are pushing up out of the ground. Fewer, perhaps, and for different reasons, perhaps. Still the Haitian lady and I smile at each other. "My, my," she says "they goin' on up to the hills? Seem like they just come from there." "The woods," I say. "They like to live in the woods." She nods with infinite understanding, then shrugs. The Haitians have already arranged for one mass in the church to be said in French, already have their own newspaper, stores, community center. That's not movement. That's progress.

But the decade has other revelations. Ten years ago, young, bright, energetic blacks were sought out, pursued and hired into major corporations, major networks and onto the staffs of newspapers and national

---

"Good Times" A television show, set in a Chicago housing project, which depicted the struggles of a close-knit black family in hard times (premiered February 8, 1974).
"The Jeffersons" A television show about a wealthy black family, headed by a pompous father, who live in a fashionable apartment in East-side Manhattan (premiered January 7, 1975).

magazines. Many survived that courtship, some even with their souls intact. Newscasters, corporate lawyers, marketing specialists, journalists, production managers, plant foremen, college deans. But many more spend a lot of time on the telephone these days, or at the typewriter preparing résumés, which they send out (mostly to friends now) with little notes attached: "Is there anything you know of?" Or they think there is a good book in the story of what happened to them, the great hoax that was played on them. They are right, of course, about the hoax, for many of them were given elegant executive jobs with the work drained out. Work minus power. Work minus decision-making. Work minus dominion. Affirmative Action Make Believe that a lot of black people *did* believe because they also believed that the white people in those nice offices were not like the ones in the general store or in the plumbers' union—that they were fundamentally kind, or fair, or something. Anything but the desperate prisoners of economics they turned out to be, holding on to their dominion with a tenacity and sang-froid that can only be described as Nixonian. So the bright and the black (architects, reporters, vice-presidents in charge of public relations) walk the streets right along with that astounding 38 percent of the black teen-aged female work force that does not have and never has had a job. So the black female college graduate earns two-thirds of what a white male high-school dropout earns. So the black people who put everything into community-action programs supported by Government funds have found themselves bereft of action, bereft of funds and all but bereft of community.

This decade has been rife with disappointment in practically every place where we thought we saw permanent change: Hostos, CUNY, and the black-studies departments that erupted like minivolcanoes on campuses all over the nation; easy integrations of public-school systems; acceleration of promotion in factories and businesses. But now when we describe what has happened we cannot do it without using the verbs of upheaval and destruction: Open admission *closes;* minority-student quotas *fall* or *discontinue;* salary gaps between blacks and whites *widen;* black-studies departments *merge.* And the only growth black people can count on is in the prison population and the unemployment line. Even busing, which used to be a plain, if emotional, term at best, has now taken on an adjective normally reserved for rape and burglary—it is now called "forced" busing.

All of that counts, but I'm not sure that in the long haul it matters. Maybe Ardelia Willis had the best idea. One sees signs of her vision and the fruits of her prophecy in spite of the dread-lock statistics. The trees *are* walking, albeit slowly and quietly and without the fanfare of a cross-country run. It seems that at last black people have abandoned our foolish dependency on the Government to do the work that we once thought all of its citizenry would be delighted to do. Our love affair with the Federal

Government is over. We misjudged the ardor of its attention. We thought its majority constituency would *prefer* having their children grow up among happy, progressive, industrious, contented black children rather than among angry, disenchanted and dangerous ones. That the profit motive of industry alone would keep us employed and therefore spending, and that our poverty was bad for business. We thought landlords wanted us to have a share in our neighborhoods and therefore love and care for them. That city governments wanted us to control our schools and therefore preserve them.

We were wrong. And now, having been eliminated from the lists of urgent national priorities, from TV documentaries and the platitudes of editorials, black people have chosen, or been forced to seek safety from the white man's promise, but happily not under a bed. More and more, there is the return to Ardelia's ways: the exercise of the will, the recognition of obstacles as only that—obstacles, not fixed stars. Black judges are fixing appropriate rather than punitive bail for black "offenders" and letting the rest of the community of jurisprudence scream. Young black women are leaving plush Northern jobs to sit in their living rooms and teach black children, work among factory women and spend months finding money to finance the college education of young blacks. Groups of blacks are buying huge tracts of land in the South and cutting off entirely the dependency of whole communities on grocery chains. For the first time, significant numbers of black people are returning or migrating to the South to focus on the acquisition of land, the transferral of crafts and skills, and the sharing of resources, the rebuilding of neighborhoods.

In the shambles of closing admissions, falling quotas, widening salary gaps and merging black-studies departments, builders and healers are working quietly among us. They are not like the heroes of old, the leaders we followed blindly and upon whom we depended for everything, or the blacks who had accumulated wealth for its own sake, fame, medals or some public acknowledgment of success. These are the people whose work is real and pointed and clear in its application to the race. Some are old and have been at work for a long time in and out of the public eye. Some are new and just finding out what their work is. But they are unmistakably the natural aristocrats of the race. The ones who refuse to imitate, to compromise, and who are indifferent to public accolade. Whose work is free or priceless. They take huge risks economically and personally. They are not always popular, even among black people, but they are the ones whose work black people respect. They are the healers. Some are nowhere near the public eye: Ben Chavis, preacher and political activist languishing now in North Carolina prisons; Robert Moses, a pioneering activist; Sterling Brown, poet and teacher; Father Al McKnight, land reformer; Rudy Lombard, urban sociologist; Lerone Bennett, historian; C.L.R. James, scholar; Alyce Gullattee, psychologist and organizer. Others are public legends: Judge Crockett, Judge Bruce Wright, Stevie Wonder, Ishmael Reed, Miles Davis, Richard Pryor, Muhammad Ali, Fannie Lou Hamer, Eubie Blake, Angela Davis, Bill Russell. . . .

But a complete roll-call is neither fitting nor necessary. They know who they are and so do we. They clarify our past, make livable our present and are certain to shape our future. And since the future is where our immortality as a race lies, no overview of the state of black people at this time can ignore some speculation on the only ones certain to live it—the children.

They are both exhilarating and frightening, those black children, and a source of wonderment to me. Although statistics about black teen-age crime and the "failure" of the courts to gut them are regularly printed and regularly received with outrage and fear, the children I know and see, those born after 1960, do not make such great copy. They are those who have grown up with nothing to prove to white people, whose perceptions of themselves are so new, so different, so focused they appear to me to be either magnificent hybrids or throwbacks to the time when our ancestors were called "royal." They are the baby sisters of the sit-in generation, the sons of the neighborhood blockbusters, the nephews of jailed revolutionaries, and a huge number who have had college graduates in their families for three and four generations. I thought we had left them nothing to love and nothing to want to know. I thought that those who exhibited some excitement about their future had long ago looked into the eyes of their teachers and were either saddened or outraged by the death of possibility they found there. I thought that those who were interested in the past had looked into the faces of their parents and seen betrayal. I thought the state had deprived them of a land and the landlords and banks had deprived them of a turf. So how is it that, with nothing to love, nothing they need to know, landless, turfless, minus a future and a past, these black children look us dead in the eye? They seem not to know how to apologize. And even when they are wrong they do not ask for forgiveness. It is as though they are waiting for us to apologize to them, to beg their pardon, to seek their approval. What species of black is this that not only does not choose to grovel, but doesn't know how? How will they keep jobs? How will they live? Won't they be killed before they reproduce? But they are unafraid. Is it because they refuse to see the world as we did? Is it because they have rejected both land and turf to seek instead a world? Maybe they finally got the message that we had been shouting into their faces; that they *live* here, *belong* here on this planet earth and that it is *theirs*. So they watch us with the eyes of poets and carpenters and musicians and scholars and other people who know who they are because they have invented themselves and know where they are going because they have envisioned it. All of which would please Ardelia—and John Solomon, too, I think. After all, he did hold on to his violin.

from *The Latinization of America*

Thomas B. Morgan

Thomas Morgan (born 1930) always wanted to be a writer. After gradua-
ting from Carleton College, he wrote to fifteen editors in New York, received
one reply, from Esquire, *and immediately went to work for the magazine*
as an assistant editor; he has since written numerous short stories and
articles for Esquire, American Heritage, *and other publications. During*
the 1970s, he was editor of The Village Voice. *Earlier, he had also*
served as press secretary for Adlai Stevenson's presidential campaign,
and for New York mayor John Lindsay. We print below the first three
segments of a long article from the May 1983 issue of Esquire.

Thinking of oneself as an anglo is hard for a liberal like me. Anglo means
"white, non-Hispanic," in the lingo of the nearly 15 million of my countrymen who have Hispanic (Spanish or Latin American) roots—a number to
which may be added 3 million Puerto Ricans in Puerto Rico (U.S. citizens
all, by act of Congress, 1917) and as many as 5 million Hispanic aliens
residing here now, mostly in the Southwest. *Anglo* is one of those words
that radiate meanings—from straight otherness to pejorative hostility.
It grates on me, although not as much as *gringo* or *gabacho*. I have
always thought of myself as an American. I hold the view that we really
are one people, no matter how diverse. But hard as it is to accept, I am
an Anglo, too—a distinction that came to me only last summer when
the latinization of America suddenly became a problem for me. Since
then, I've been trying to work it out.

It was a sunny day late in June, and crowds of people were milling about
on the streets of New York, where I live. There was nothing special going
on, no fiesta, no protest, no ethnic promotion. The car cards on my subway
train, advertising everything from Eastern Airlines to Preparation-H in
Spanish, may have started me thinking. I don't know. But walking up
Fifth Avenue toward my dentist's office, I felt concern (okay, fear)—
abruptly, it seemed—as I noticed I was hearing Spanish voices everywhere and realized that I had been hearing them in shops, hotels, and
restaurants all over the city. It was as though New York had achieved a
kind of Hispanic critical mass. Nothing in particular jarred me. I just
noticed, felt surrounded by strangers and, for an anxious moment, like
Rip Van Winkle in my own home town.

The voices clicked together in my memory with scraps of information
from here and there to form a picture of change, change of major propor-

tions in my American life. And I began to worry. I suppose people have always worried me when I don't truly know who they are or what they are up to. Any change at all, in fact, troubles me when I don't understand it. I wanted to figure out exactly what was upsetting me.

Later, at home, as the picture emerged it looked something like this: In the papers and on the television news, Hispanic-angled stories had been appearing almost daily—"Hispanics Fastest-Growing U.S. Minority," "Hispanics Highest Birth Rate in U.S.," "Hispanics Expected to Outnumber Blacks Soon." One columnist estimated that the number of Hispanics had multiplied nearly ten times since 1940 while in the same period the nation's whole population did not even double. Talk about change! Then there was the Cuban-American story out of Miami—how they had arrived as political refugees after Castro's revolution, transformed that fatigued tourist and retirement city into a booming, bilingual, multinational business center, and then set about finding homes, cars, and jobs for another 100,000 refugees who had sailed in from Mariel on the Freedom Flotilla at Castro's whim. Perhaps most striking were those relentlessly regular stories about the troubled entries into this immigrant nation of more and more Hispanics from Puerto Rico as well as from Mexico, El Salvador, Guatemala, the Dominican Republic, Honduras, and almost all of the other nations of the Caribbean basin and South America. One expert predicted that a net increase of 500,000 Hispanic newcomers might be expected every year for the rest of this century. And when asked for comment, American spokesmen for the Hispanic community emphasized a consistent theme—the determination of their people as free Americans to maintain their Hispanic identity as they struggled to be included within the system.

I remember my first response. This picture, as far as it went, did not show a bad thing. The latinization of America could be seen as another chapter in our most enduring serial, the Americanization of everybody. In the first place, Hispanic fertility and immigration were only adding more energetic human beings to an ethnic community that had long since demonstrated its zeal for hard work, family virtues, and patriotism. Second, the Cubans in Miami were to be applauded, for, as *The Economist* would say, "Greater Miami is a city with a future in a western world full of cities with only a past." And third, preservation of group identity through language, food, music, religion, and custom had long been the fashion in the United States, which prides itself on being the most successful multiethnic society in the world.

But there was more to the picture, and the source of my alarm turned up there, among stories I'd heard and read about the resistance of middle-class Hispanics to the difficult but (I think) necessary process of assimilation. Since the Seventies there had been a highly publicized Hispanic drive for bilingualism: Spanish-language courses for the transitional training of school kids, as well as maintenance programs for further education in Spanish, with English perhaps as a second language; ballots in Spanish for Hispanic voters as a permanent requirement of election law; even road signs in Spanish for Hispanic motorists. What might come next? The *Congressional Record* in Spanish as well as English? The State of the Union Message with Spanish subtitles? Or, further out, a Quebec-style solution to the problems of integration? That's where I got alarmed: I could imagine a scenario for the latinization of America leading to a divided nation—two Americas, one speaking English, one speaking Spanish.

Farfetched? Not really. Not with a critical mass of Spanish-speaking voters settling in city after city of the nation. Not when Hispanics, too, were expressing concern about the antiassimilationist trend among them. Last spring, for example, a California-born Mexican-American writer, Richard Rodriguez, had sent me a copy of his new book, *Hunger of Memory.* One passage read: "Today I hear bilingual educators say that children lose a degree of 'individuality' by becoming assimilated into public society. . . . But the bilingualists simplistically scorn the value and necessity of assimilation. . . . Dangerously, middle-class ethnics romanticize public separateness and trivialize the dilemma of the socially disadvantaged."

Played out, I realized, the separatist scenario could put an end to my liberal dream of one people and a so-called Americanist future. Then came the hard part: self-recognition. I had to admit that, after all, the choice of a Hispanic future finally rested with the Hispanics. And I had to acknowledge that my alarm, frankly, was that of not only a liberal but an Anglo who did not want to pay for the maintenance of *their* language, did not want to have to learn Spanish in order to get around in his own country, and did not even want to contemplate the turmoil that was sure to arise if America opted for a dual future. That is what I mean by self-recognition. As I say, it was hard, but it also prompted me to find out what I could about the Hispanic future, to talk about that future with Hispanic leaders around the country, to remind myself of what I already knew. And when I remembered the individual Mexican-Americans and Puerto Ricans I had met in my life, I wondered that the shock of self-recognition had been so long in coming.

The first and best Hispanic friend I ever had was a Mexican-American steam fitter named Jesse Saldana. In the summer of 1944 we worked together at a shipyard in Wilmington, California, where Victory ships were built. I was Jesse's assistant. He taught me all that I needed to know about plumbing, and he liked to hear me talk about my home town—Springfield, Illinois—because it was Abraham Lincoln's home town, too. I confessed to him that I had never met a Mexicano before. A Greek family ran the "Mexican" chilli (two *l*'s) parlor in Springfield, and, as far as I knew, they never had a Mexicano customer. Jesse knew a lot of Mexican history, about which I had learned little in school. It was he who told me that the United States Army had occupied Mexico City in 1847, enabling President Polk to persuade the Mexican government to take $15 million for the northern third of its real estate—California, Arizona, New Mexico, Utah, and Nevada. Fifty years later, Jesse also taught me, a similarly persuasive occupation gained us Puerto Rico. Jesse admitted to me that he was virtually illiterate, that he had a serious police record, and that he was wanted by the sheriff of Reno, Nevada. Still, he used to say, he thought he could have done better in his time if it had not been for Anglo prejudice against Mexicanos. He was particularly angry, he said, about the mass deportations of Mexicanos during the Thirties and about the way the Los Angeles police behaved during the "Zoot Suit Riots" of 1943. In bloody detail, he described the street battles he said he had seen between Mexicano youths and Anglo servicemen. His wrath peaked, as I recall, just as he told how the local cops consistently moved in on the side of the soldiers and sailors. "Justice is blind," Jesse often said. "She can't see the Mexicans." In the fall, after I had returned home to get ready for the Army, Jesse sent me a newspaper clipping describing another such "riot." I wrote back, saying I was on *his* side, but I never heard from him again. His anger, though, would be unforgettable.

In the early Sixties I befriended another Mexican-American: Mayor Juan Cornejo of Crystal City, Texas. His town of 9,500 people in the dusty southwestern part of the state called itself the "Spinach Capital of the World." It had long discouraged reckless Hispanic participation in the democratic process until it elected Cornejo, thirty-three, a business agent for the Teamsters union at the spinach packinghouse. The election shocked all of Texas. It became an instant legend, and a New York magazine editor sent me to Crystal City to write a story about it. Local people were talking about threats of reprisals against Cornejo's supporters, and some thought that the mayor himself might be in danger. In fact, Cornejo survived both his term and the national publicity. But I would remember his concern that I might get hurt for coming to Crystal City to write about the Anglos' comeuppance. And I never forgot his feistiness, which had inspired the subtitle for the story I wrote: "The Texas Giant Awakens."

Around Cornejo's time, there were other Mexicano stirrings. "Viva Kennedy" clubs, set up for the Presidential campaign of 1960, brought a new generation of Mexicanos into mainstream politics all over the Southwest. Aside from the *patron* system in Democratic New Mexico, neither party in the region had bothered with that sort of thing before, at least partly because the Mexicano vote had not been large enough to matter. Mexicanos organized opposition to the Federal *bracero* program (whereby farm workers were imported under contract) and helped kill it. Cesar Chavez began his nonviolent fight for recognition of a farm workers' union by California growers. And young Mexicanos chose the name Chicano to express ethnic pride; they called for "brown power" and were echoed by young Puerto Ricans in New York. Looking back with the clarity of hindsight, I saw that the awakening of those days was oversold.

The Sixties did not exactly ring in a new era for Hispanics—indeed, the concept of Hispanics as a kind of superethnic group did not exist at that time—but *something* did happen, more like an alarm clock going off three hours before dawn.

In the early Seventies, when I worked at City Hall in New York with Mayor John Lindsay, I got to know half a dozen Puerto Rican mayoral aides. It was significant then, I now realized, that hardly twenty years after the start of the great migration from the island to the city, New York's desperately underprivileged Puerto Rican community was beginning to claim some share of local patronage. I also got to know Herman Badillo, who in 1970 became the first Puerto Rican ever sent to Congress from New York and the first ever to vote in the House. Badillo's election gave mainland Puerto Ricans an impressive voice in Washington. Moreover, by visibly linking Puerto Ricans and Mexicanos (represented by congressmen from California, New Mexico, and Texas) at the national level, his presence in Washington seemed a step in the direction of creating a national Hispanic identity, and future.

But the truth remains, before last summer's apotheosis the latinization of America was rarely on my mind. And when it was, the context was most likely to be an impersonal occasion—a press conference on the housing crisis in the Bronx, a street festival, a Puerto Rican Day parade, a fundraiser for Cesar Chavez, an FALN⁰ bombing, or Cuban roast pig at Victor's Café in Manhattan. Hispanics as real people were neither my daily reality nor my foremost liberal concern—*that* was the problem of race and poverty among black Americans. As a reporter, I had interviewed Martin Luther King Jr. many times—first, during the Montgomery bus strike, and last, in Chicago, where he was making his stand for the integration of the North. His last movement had failed, utterly. And there had followed—in direct response, I thought—the victory of the "new ethnicity" on the playing fields of American ideologies. I had never celebrated that victory. I put it down as yet another part of the Hispanic picture that was worrying me.

Maybe it was my age. I had grown up in the Thirties and Forties with the ideology of integration through assimilation, the American melting pot, and a hoped-for common civilization to which all could belong and to which all could contribute, eventually achieving no less than a "composite American identity," as Walt Whitman had promised. Just thinking about it last summer made me gasp at how uncool Americanism had become. Yet, *e pluribus unum,* onenationindivisible, equality-in-freedom, and the picture of everyone praying together on Norman Rockwell's Four Freedoms poster—that was us.

FALN Fuerzas Armadas de Liberación Nacional Puertorriqueña, a Puerto Rican separatist group linked to numerous terrorist bombings in the United States.

America was something else, too. It was a deal—first Square, then New, then Fair. Each immigrant's son and the son of each immigrant's son (I am one of those, grandson of Polish and Romanian Jewish immigrants) knew in his bones the terms of *his* deal. You traded memory for opportunity, the Old Country for the New World, culture for power, identity for rights. And if, after you became Americanized, you cared to retrieve the past, argue about dual commitments, biculturism, and ethnic survival, and teach your children a language you yourself may have denied, you were welcome. But making the deal and becoming included was the first order of business. Funny, you still felt your own ethnic self, and all the more an American because it was a seamless relationship; you really felt as though you belonged to an American peoplehood. And despite all the nativist, racist loons who had tried to take charge of this Americanist ideal, our peoplehood was what we believed we were defending in World War II. It made possible whatever else we wanted to be or do, ethnically or otherwise. Sit in wonder, generations. Think what you will. But this was how we were and what we believed.

At some point in the Sixties, though—it may have been just before or just after Stokely Carmichael raised his fist and told whitey to get lost— some people I knew began quoting a book (quoting the title, at least) by Nathan Glazer and Daniel Patrick Moynihan, *Beyond the Melting Pot*, and telling one another that the ingredients in the melting pot hadn't really melted; that ours had been a pluralistic society all along; that we needed a "new ethnicity" to maintain stability in our polyglot cities (then aflame); and that facing our diversity was better and easier than facing the failure of black integration in the North. Dead were Medgar Evers, Martin Luther King Jr., and Robert Kennedy. Dead or dying was integration through assimilation. The goal of democracy was not to be equality for individuals after all but, rather, making the world safe for diversity among groups. And with amazing speed, that America of the new ethnicity materialized with more pluralistic fissures than a Tiffany lamp.

It was easy then, as regards the problem of race, to prescribe for black "rhetoric" a new American policy of benign neglect. Furthermore, as political scientist Michael Mandelbaum had told me, the passion for ethnicity meant to some people that you didn't have to assimilate to make it in America. And when the word *Hispanic* emerged (the U.S. Census used it for the first time on its 1980 forms), it would be hailed as a direct expression of the new American ideology. As Congressman Robert Garcia, successor to Herman Badillo, would exclaim to me: "Six years ago, you didn't see the word *Hispanic*. Now it's a word that everyone can coalesce under. This is the news!"

The stage was set for the Eighties—"the decade of the Hispanics," someone had called it. The picture was complete. And here was the nub of my fear about the Hispanic future. A prolonged process (twenty years? fifty years?) of Americanization is under way. But we are going into it under a new dispensation, as ethnics all, Hispanics and Anglos (and blacks, Asians, and Native Americans). We have no Americanist ideal to see us through, no sense of the nation more lofty than our private identities. Only the challenge is not new: to acculturate and integrate over time yet another great immigrant people.

Census reports and other data I collected helped define the nature of that challenge.

First, they showed the sheer variety of the latinizers of America. Hispanics come from thirty Latin American countries, plus Spain and Portugal. Ethnically and historically, Mexicans, Puerto Ricans, and Cubans (the three largest Hispanic groups in the U.S.) differ from one another as much as the Irish, the English, and the Scotch do. The rest have their differences, too. Each group has its own national memories and its own racial characteristics. Broadly, *Hispanic* may be taken to mean Latin American brown, like European white, African black, and Asian yellow. But such connotations only make life simpler for demographers. Hispanics are actually white, black, or Indian, or a mix of two or of all three. *Hispanic* also may mean "of Spanish-speaking origin or descent," but the first language of Hispanics from Latin America may be Portuguese, French, or even English. And in America, immigrant Hispanics tend to use English when necessary and speak Spanish at home; the vast majority of American-born Hispanics are bilingual. Religious preference further complicates the meaning of *Hispanic*. Although there is a Catholic majority, church attendance is far below that of non-Hispanic Catholics. And significant numbers are Protestants, born-agains, Jews, Baptists, and Mormons. Some, of course, don't believe.

Second, the facts disabused me of the vague ideas I had about where Hispanics live. It was news to me that twenty-five cities in the nation now have Hispanic communities of 50,000 or more—from the largest, Los Angeles (2 million, mostly Mexican, some Salvadoran), to Chicago (422,-000, mainly Mexican and Puerto Rican), Denver (92,000, mostly Mexican), and Philadelphia (63,000, mostly Puerto Rican). Over half the 1.46 million Hispanics in New York are Puerto Rican, but some of these may be among an estimated 400,000 Dominican aliens in the city, some of whom call themselves Puerto Ricans in order to become instantly naturalized. And even in cities where the Hispanic population is less than 50,000, their number is significant as a percentage of the whole. In Hartford, Connecticut, for example, 20 percent of the population of 136,000 is Hispanic. It turns out that Hispanics are not rural people. About 85 percent reside in metropolitan areas. It may be politically significant someday that they have tended to settle in influential states—4.5 million in California (19 percent of the superstate), nearly 3 million in powerful Texas, and 1.7 million in media-rich New York. But there is also a notable trend toward dispersal. After decades of concentration, the census data showed, His-

panics are moving to cities in all parts of the country, taking their future
with them.

Third, unofficial projections that I studied indicated a potentially dramatic rise in the Hispanic population as a percentage of the whole population over the next generation. The 1980 census counted 14.6 million
Hispanics in the United States. Estimates of undocumented Hispanics
ranged from 1 million to 10 million, with most in the middle range; the
5-million guess I have made may be too high or too low by 2 million. Now,
assuming 20 million Hispanic citizens and aliens in America, a continua-
tion of present high birth rates (although these could change with increasing prosperity), and continued immigration at, say, 500,000 annually (this
could change, too, under a new immigration law), Hispanics would number 35 million in a nation of 280 million *seventeen years* from now. And
if that were the combination, Hispanics in the year 2000 would be not only
the largest American "minority" group, ahead of blacks by a small margin, but also the largest of all groups—ahead of WASPs (now leading, with
29 million) and Germans (second today, with more than 25 million). It's
true that then there would be 200 million Anglos, over 33 million blacks,
and about 10 million Asians. Still, the Hispanic share of the population
would rise to more than 12 percent by the millennium. And the meaning
of that seemed clear: Hispanics could be a unique force for change in the
country by then, depending upon the way the challenge of their future
had been met.

Neither WASP nor
Jew nor Black

Michael Novak

*Michael Novak was born of immigrant parents in Johnstown, Pennsyl-
vania, in 1933. At fourteen, he became a junior seminarian in the Congregation of Holy Cross; he continued his Catholic education at Stonehill
College near Boston (B.A. 1956) and the Gregorian University in Rome
(B.Th. 1958), but left in 1960 before his ordination. He then studied at
Harvard University, where he received a master's degree in 1966. He has
taught humanities, philosophy, and religious studies at Stanford University, the State University of New York, and Syracuse University.*

*Novak is a prolific writer of social, political, and religious commentary
and analysis who began as a democratic socialist but over the years has
become increasingly conservative; since 1978 he has been a resident scholar
at the American Enterprise Institute for Public Policy Research, a conservative think tank in Washington, D.C. His many books include* Confession
of a Catholic *(1983),* Will It Liberate? Questions About Liberation Theology *(1986),* The Spirit of Democratic Capitalism *(1982), and* Moral Clarity

in a Nuclear Age *(1983). In the latter two, he challenges two formal positions taken by the American Catholic bishops: their critique of unjust distribution of wealth, and their condemnation of nuclear armament.*

He is probably best known for The Rise of the Unmeltable Ethnics *(1971), in which he calls for "a new cultural pluralism." The following selection is section 1 from Chapter 2.*

Growing up in America has been an assault upon my sense of worthiness. It has also been a kind of liberation and delight.

There must be countless women in America who have known for years that something is peculiarly unfair, yet who only recently have found it possible, because of Women's Liberation, to give tongue to their pain. In recent months I have experienced a similar inner thaw, a gradual relaxation, a willingness to think about feelings heretofore shepherded out of sight.

I am born of PIGS—those Poles, Italians, Greeks, and Slavs, those non-English-speaking immigrants numbered so heavily among the workingmen of this nation. Not particularly liberal or radical; born into a history not white Anglo-Saxon and not Jewish; born outside what, in America, is considered the intellectual mainstream—and thus privy to neither power nor status nor intellectual voice.

Those Poles of Buffalo and Milwaukee—so notoriously taciturn, sullen, nearly speechless. Who has ever understood them? It is not that Poles do not feel emotion—what is their history if not dark passion, romanticism, betrayal, courage, blood? But where in America is there anywhere a language for voicing what a Christian Pole in this nation feels? He has no Polish culture left him, no Polish tongue.[1] Yet Polish feelings do not go easily into the idiom of happy America, the America of the Anglo-Saxons and yes, in the arts, the Jews. (The Jews have long been a culture of the word, accustomed to exile, skilled in scholarship and in reflection. The Christian Poles are largely of peasant origin, free men for hardly more than a hundred years.) Of what shall the young man of Lackawanna think on his way to work in the mills, departing his relatively dreary home and street? What roots does he have? What language of the heart is available to him?[2]

---

[1]See Andrew R. Sisson's chapter "Our Kooky English Language" in his *Applehood and Mother Pie* (Peterborough, N.H.: Orchard Press, 1971), pp. 1–16, for a discussion of the ways in which Continental languages differ from English according to their respective cultural divergencies.

[2]Royko wrote in his *Chicago Daily News* column: "I imagine that the ethnic in Buffalo is thinking the same thing that the white Southerner in Birmingham is thinking, or the Okie oil workers in Tulsa: Another day, another dollar. In fact, that's probably what the guy in Warsaw is thinking on his way to work." There is at least one point Royko overlooks: the bottled-up anger of workers in America.

The PIGS are not silent willingly. The silence burns like hidden coals in the chest.

All four of my grandparents, unknown to one another, arrived in America from the same county in Slovakia. My grandfather had a small farm in Pennsylvania; his wife died in a wagon accident. Meanwhile, Johanna, fifteen, arrived on Ellis Island, dizzy from witnessing births and deaths and illnesses aboard the crowded ship. She had a sign around her neck lettered PASSAIC. There an aunt told her of a man who had lost his wife in Pennsylvania. She went. They were married. She inherited his three children.

Each year for five years Grandma had a child of her own. She was among the lucky; only one died. When she was twenty-two and the mother of seven (my father was the last), her husband died. "Grandma Novak," as I came to know her many years later, resumed the work she had begun in Slovakia at the town home of a man known to my father only as "the Professor"; she housecleaned and she laundered.

I heard this story only weeks ago. Strange that I had not asked insistently before. Odd that I should have such shallow knowledge of my roots. Amazing to me that I do not know what my family suffered, endured, learned, and hoped these last six or seven generations. It is as if there were no project in which we all have been involved, as if history in some way began with my father and with me.

The estrangement I have come to feel derives not only from lack of family history. Early in life, I was made to feel a slight uneasiness when I said my name.[3]

Later "Kim" helped. So did Robert. And "Mister Novak" on TV. The name must be one of the most Anglo-Saxon of the Slavic names. Nevertheless, when I was very young, the "American" kids still made something out of names unlike their own, and their earnest, ambitious mothers thought long thoughts when I introduced myself.

Under challenge in grammar school concerning my nationality, I had been instructed by my father to announce proudly: "American." When my family moved from the Slovak ghetto of Johnstown to the WASP suburb on the hill, my mother impressed upon us how well we must be dressed, and show good manners, and behave—people think of us as "different" and we mustn't give them any cause. "Whatever you do, marry a Slovak girl," was other advice to a similar end: "They cook. They clean. They take good care of you. For your own good." I was taught to be proud of being Slovak, but to recognize that others wouldn't know what it meant, or care.

When I had at last pierced the deception—that most movie stars and

---

[3]See Victor R. Greene's "Sons of Hunkies: Men with a Past?" *Slovakia*, vol. XVI, No. 39, 1966, pp. 85–86.

many other professionals had abandoned their European names in order to feed American fantasies—I felt only a little sadness. One of my uncles, for business reasons and rather late in life, changed his name, too, to a simple German variant—not long, either, after World War II.

Nowhere in my schooling do I recall any attempt to put me in touch with my own history. The strategy was clearly to make an American of me. English literature, American literature, and even the history books, as I recall them, were peopled mainly by Anglo-Saxons from Boston (where most historians seemed to live). Not even my native Pennsylvania, let alone my Slovak forebears, counted for very many paragraphs. (We did have something called "Pennsylvania History" somewhere; I seem to remember its puffs for industry. It could have been written by a Mellon.) I don't remember feeling envy or regret: a feeling, perhaps, of unimportance, of remoteness, of not having heft enough to count.

The fact that I was born a Catholic also complicated life. What is a Catholic but what everybody else is in reaction against? Protestants reformed "the whore of Babylon." Others were "enlightened" from it, and Jews had reason to help Catholicism and the social structure it was rooted in fall apart. The history books and the whole of education hummed in upon that point (for during crucial years I attended a public school): to be modern is decidedly not to be medieval; to be reasonable is not to be dogmatic; to be free is clearly not to live under ecclesiastical authority; to be scientific is not to attend ancient rituals, cherish irrational symbols, indulge in mythic practices. It is hard to grow up Catholic in America without becoming defensive, perhaps a little paranoid, feeling forced to divide the world between "us" and "them."

English Catholics have little of the sense of inferiority in which many other Catholic groups tend to share—Irish Catholics, Polish Catholics, Lithuanians, Germans, Italians, Lebanese, and others. Daniel Callahan *(The Mind of the Catholic Layman, Generation of the Third Eye)* and Garry Wills ("Memories of a Catholic Boyhood," in *Esquire*) both identify, in part, with the more secure Catholicism of an Anglo-Catholic parent. The French around New Orleans have a social ease different from the French Catholics of Massachusetts. Still, as Catholics, especially vis-à-vis the national liberal culture, nearly all have felt a certain involuntary defensiveness. Granted our diverse ethnic circumstances, we share a certain communion of memories.

We had a special language all our own, our own pronunciation for words we shared in common with others (Augústine, contémplative), sights and sounds and smells in which few others participated (incense at Benediction of the Most Blessed Sacrament, Forty Hours, wakes, and altar bells at the silent consecration of the Host); and we had our own politics and slant on world affairs. Since earliest childhood, I have known about a "power elite" that runs America: the boys from the Ivy League in the State Department as opposed to the Catholic boys in Hoover's FBI who (as Daniel Moynihan once put it), keep watch on them. And on a whole host of issues, my people have been, though largely Democratic, conservative: on censorship, on communism, on abortion, on religious schools, etc. "Harvard" and "Yale" long meant "them" to us.

The language of Spiro Agnew, the language of George Wallace, excepting its idiom, awakens childhood memories in me: of men arguing in the barbershop, of my uncle drinking so much beer he threatened to lay his dick upon the porch rail and wash the whole damn street with steaming piss—while cursing the niggers in the mill below, and the Yankees in the mill above—millstones he felt pressing him. Other relatives were duly shocked, but everybody loved Uncle George; he said what he thought.

We did not feel this country belonged to us. We felt fierce pride in it, more loyalty than anyone could know. But we felt blocked at every turn. There were not many intellectuals among us, not even very many professional men. Laborers mostly. Small businessmen, agents for corporations perhaps. Content with a little, yes, modest in expectation, and content. But somehow feeling cheated. For a thousand years the Slovaks survived Hungarian hegemony and our strategy here remained the same: endurance and steady work. Slowly, one day, we would overcome.

A special word is required about a complicated symbol: sex. To this day my mother finds it hard to spell the word intact, preferring to write "s--." Not that much was made of sex in our environment. And that's the point: silence. Demonstrative affection, emotive dances, an exuberance Anglo-Saxons seldom seem to share; but on the realities of sex, discretion. Reverence, perhaps; seriousness, surely. On intimacies, it was as though our tongues had been stolen, as though in peasant life for a thousand years— as in the novels of Tolstoi, Sholokhov, and even Kosinski—the context had been otherwise. Passion, certainly; romance, yes; family and children, certainly; but sex rather a minor if explosive part of life.

Imagine, then, the conflict in the generation of my brothers, sister, and myself. (The reviewer for the *New York Times* reviews on the same day two new novels of fantasy—one a pornographic fantasy to end all such fantasies [he writes], the other in some comic way representing the redemption wrought by Jesus Christ. In language and verve, the books are rated evenly. In theme, the reviewer notes his embarrassment in even reporting a religious fantasy, but no embarrassment at all about preposterous pornography.) Suddenly, what for a thousand years was minor becomes an all-absorbing investigation. Some view it as a drama of "liberation" when the ruling classes (subscribers to the *New Yorker,* I suppose) move progressively, generation by generation since Sigmund Freud, toward concentration upon genital stimulation, and latterly toward consciousness-raising sessions in Clit. Lib. But it is rather a different drama when we stumble suddenly upon mores staggering any expectation our grandparents ever cherished. Fear of becoming "sexual objects" is an ancient fear that appears in many shapes. The emotional reaction of Maria Wyeth in Joan Didion's *Play It as It Lays* is exactly what the ancient morality would have predicted.

Yet more significant in the ethnic experience in America is the intellectual world one meets: the definition of values, ideas, and purposes emanating from universities, books, magazines, radio, and television. One hears one's own voice echoed back neither by spokesmen of "middle America" (so complacent, smug, nativist, and Protestant), nor by the "intellectuals." Almost unavoidably, perhaps, education in America leads the student who entrusts his soul to it in a direction which, lacking a better word, we might call liberal: respect for individual conscience, a sense of social responsibility, trust in the free exchange of ideas and procedures of dissent, a certain confidence in the ability of men to "reason together" and adjudicate their differences, a frank recognition of the vitality of the unconscious, a willingness to protect workers and the poor against the vast economic power of industrial corporations, and the like.

On the other hand, the liberal imagination has appeared to be astonishingly universalist and relentlessly missionary. Perhaps the metaphor "enlightenment" offers a key. One is *initiated into light*. Liberal education tends to separate children from their parents, from their roots, from their history, in the cause of a universal and superior religion. One is taught regarding the unenlightened (even if they be one's uncles George and Peter, one's parents, one's brothers, perhaps) what can only be called a modern equivalent of *odium theologicum*.° Richard Hofstadter described anti-intellectualism in America (more accurately, in nativist America rather than in ethnic America), but I have yet to encounter a comparable treatment of anti-unenlightenment among our educated classes.

In particular, I have regretted and keenly felt the absence of that sympathy for PIGS which simple human feeling might have prodded intelligence to muster, that same sympathy which the educated find so easy to conjure up for black culture, Chicano culture, Indian culture, and other cultures of the poor. In such cases one finds the universalist pretensions of liberal culture suspended; some groups, at least, are entitled to be both different and respected. Why do the educated classes find it so difficult to want to understand the man who drives a beer truck, or the fellow with a helmet working on a site across the street with plumbers and electricians, while their sensitivities race easily to Mississippi or even Bedford-Stuyvesant?°

There are deep secrets here, no doubt, unvoiced fantasies and scarcely

---

odium theologicum   theological antipathy (Latin).
Bedford-Stuyvesant   Black neighborhood in Brooklyn, one of the largest black communities in the world.

admitted historical resentments. Few persons in describing "middle Americans" "the silent majority," or Scammon and Wattenberg's° "typical American voter" distinguish clearly enough between the nativist American and the ethnic American. The first is likely to be Protestant, the second Catholic. Both may be, in various ways, conservative, loyalist, and unenlightened. Each has his own agonies, fears, betrayed expectations. Neither is ready, quite, to become an ally of the other. Neither has the same history behind him here. Neither has the same hopes. Neither lives out the same psychic voyage, shares the same symbols, has the same sense of reality. The rhetoric and metaphors proper to each differ from those of the other.

There is overlap, of course. But country music is not a polka; a successful politician in a Chicago ward needs a very different "common touch" from the one needed by the county clerk in Normal. The urban experience of immigration lacks that mellifluous, optimistic, biblical vision of the good America which springs naturally to the lips of politicians from the Bible Belt. The nativist tends to believe with Richard Nixon that he "knows America, and the American heart is good." The ethnic tends to believe that every American who preceded him has an angle, and that he, by God, will some day find one, too. (Often, ethnics complain that by working hard, obeying the law, trusting their political leaders, and relying upon the American dream, they now have only their own naiveté to blame for rising no higher than they have.)

It goes without saying that the intellectuals do not love "middle America," and that for all the good, warm discovery of America that preoccupied them during the 1950s no strong tide of respect accumulated in their hearts for the Yahoos, Babbitts, Agnews, and Nixons of the land. Willie Morris in *North Toward Home* writes poignantly of the chill, parochial outreach of the liberal sensibility, its failure to engage the humanity of the modest, ordinary little man west of the Hudson. The Intellectual's Map of the United States is succinct: "Two coasts connected by United Airlines."

Unfortunately, it seems, the ethnics erred in attempting to Americanize themselves before clearing the project with the educated classes. They learned to wave the flag and to send their sons to war. They learned to support their President—an easy task, after all, for those accustomed to obeying authority. And where would they have been if Franklin Roosevelt had not sided with them against established interests? They knew a little about communism—the radicals among them in one way, and by far the larger number of conservatives in another. To this day not a few exchange letters with cousins and uncles who did not leave for America when they

---

Scammon and Wattenberg Richard M. Scammon and Ben J. Wattenberg, authors of *The Real Majority* (1970).

might have, whose lot is demonstrably harder than their own and less than free.

Finally, the ethnics do not like, or trust, or even understand the intellectuals. It is not easy to feel uncomplicated affection for those who call you "pig," "fascist," "racist." One had not yet grown accustomed to not hearing "hunkie," "Polack," "spic," "mick," "dago," and the rest. A worker in Chicago told reporter Lois Wille in a vividly home-centered outburst:

> The liberals always have despised us. We've got these mostly little jobs, and we drink beer and, my God, we bowl and watch television and we don't read. It's goddamn vicious snobbery. We're sick of all these phoney integrated TV commercials with these upper-class Negroes. We know they're phoney.
>
> The only time a Pole is mentioned it's to make fun of him. He's Ignatz Dumbrowski, 274 pounds and 5-foot-4, and he got his education by writing in to a firm on a matchbook cover. But what will we do about it? Nothing, because we're the new invisible man, the new whipping boy, and we still think the measure of a man's what he does and how he takes care of his children and what he's doing in his own home, not what he thinks about Vietnam.[4]

At no little sacrifice, one had apologized for foods that smelled too strong for Anglo-Saxon noses; moderated the wide swings of Slavic and Italian emotion; learned decorum; given oneself to education, American style; tried to learn tolerance and assimilation. Each generation criticized the earlier for its authoritarian and European and old-fashioned ways. "Up-to-date" was a moral lever. And now when the process nears completion, when a generation appears that speaks without accent and goes to college, still you are considered "pigs," "fascists," and "racists."

Racists? Our ancestors owned no slaves. Most of us ceased being serfs only in the last two hundred years—the Russians in 1861. Italians, Lithuanians, Slovaks, Poles are not, in principle, against "community control," or even against ghettoes of our own.

Whereas the Anglo-Saxon model appears to be a system of atomic individuals and high mobility, our model has tended to stress communities of our own, attachment to family and relatives, stability, and roots. Ethnics tend to have a fierce sense of attachment to their homes, having been homeowners for less than three generations: a home is almost fulfillment enough for one man's life. Some groups save arduously in a passion to *own;* others rent. We have most ambivalent feelings about suburban assimilation and mobility. The melting pot is a kind of homogenized soup, and its mores only partly appeal to ethnics: to some, yes, and to others, no.

It must be said that ethnics think they are better people than the

---

[4]Lois Wille, "Fear Rises in the Suburbs," a reprint from the *Chicago Daily News*, in *The Anxious Majority* (New York: Institute on Human Relations, 1970), p. 8.

blacks. Smarter, tougher, harder working, stronger in their families. But maybe many are not sure. Maybe many are uneasy. Emotions here are delicate; one can understand the immensely more difficult circumstances under which the blacks have suffered; and one is not unaware of peculiar forms of fear, envy, and suspicion across color lines. How much of this we learned in America by being made conscious of our olive skin, brawny backs, accents, names, and cultural quirks is not plain to us. Racism is not our invention; we did not bring it with us; we had prejudices enough and would gladly have been spared new ones. Especially regarding people who suffer more than we.

When television commentators and professors say "humanism" or "progress," it seems to ethnics like moral pressure to abandon their own traditions, their faith, their associations, in order to reap higher rewards in the culture of the national corporations. Ethnic neighborhoods usually do not like interviewers, consultants, government agents, organizers, sociologists. Usually they resent the media. Almost all spokesmen they meet from the world of intellect have disdain for them. It shows. Do museums, along with "Black art" and "Indian art," have "Italo-American" exhibitions or "Lithuanian-American" days? Dvorak wrote the *New World Symphony* in a tiny community of Bohemian craftsmen in Iowa. All over the nation in print studios and metal foundries when the craftsmen immigrants from Europe die, their crafts will die with them. Who here supports such skills?

A Wasp Stings Back

Robert Claiborne

Robert Claiborne is a writer who was born in England in 1919, but educated in the United States at M.I.T., Antioch College, and New York University (B.A. 1942). He has had a varied career as lathe operator and factory worker, as folk singer and music teacher, and, since the late 1950s, mainly as editor (Scientific American, Medical World News, Life Science Editor) *and writer. His many books include* The Summer Stargazer: Astronomy for Absolute Beginners *(1975),* Our Marvelous Native Tongue: The Life and Times of the English Language *(1983), and* Saying What You Mean: A Commonsense Guide to American Usage *(1986).*

In an interview, he says, "Basically, I tend to think of myself as a teacher whose medium happens to be print rather than the classroom. . . . Because I believe in playing fair with the reader, I try to present not just conclusions but the facts and reasoning that underlie the conclusions." The selection below, from the September 30, 1974, issue of Newsweek, *may serve as example.*

Over the past few years, American pop culture has acquired a new folk antihero: the Wasp. One slick magazine tells us that the White Anglo-Saxon Protestants rule New York City, while other media gurus credit (or discredit) them with ruling the country—and, by inference, ruining it. A Polish-American declares in a leading newspaper that Wasps have "no sense of honor." *Newsweek* patronizingly describes Chautauqua as a citadel of "Wasp values," while other folklorists characterize these values more explicitly as a compulsive commitment to the work ethic, emotional uptightness and sexual inhibition. The Wasps, in fact, are rapidly becoming the one minority that every other ethnic group—blacks, Italians, chicanos, Jews, Poles and all the rest—feels absolutely free to dump on. I have not yet had a friend greet me with "Did you hear the one about the two Wasps who . . . ?"—but any day now!

I come of a long line of Wasps; if you disregard my French great-great-grandmother and a couple of putatively Irish ancestors of the same vintage, a rather pure line. My mother has long been one of the Colonial Dames, an organization some of whose members consider the Daughters of the American Revolution rather parvenu. My umpty-umpth Wasp great-grandfather, William Claiborne, founded the first European settlement in what is now Maryland (his farm and trading post were later ripped off by the Catholic Lord Baltimore, Maryland politics being much the same then as now).

The Stereotype

As a Wasp, the mildest thing I can say about the stereotype emerging from the current wave of anti-Wasp chic is that I don't recognize myself. As regards emotional uptightness and sexual inhibition, modesty forbids comment—though I dare say various friends and lovers of mine could testify on these points if they cared to. I will admit to enjoying work—because I am lucky enough to be able to work at what I enjoy—but not, I think, to the point of compulsiveness. And so far as ruling America, or even New York, is concerned, I can say flatly that (a) it's a damn lie because (b) if I *did* rule them, both would be in better shape than they are. Indeed I and all my Wasp relatives, taken in a lump, have far less clout with the powers that run this country than any one of the Buckleys or Kennedys (Irish Catholic), the Sulzbergers or Guggenheims (Jewish), or the late A. P. Giannini (Italian) of the Bank of America.

Admittedly, both corporate and (to a lesser extent) political America are dominated by Wasps—just as (let us say) the garment industry is dominated by Jews, and organized crime by Italians. But to conclude from this that The Wasps are the American elite is as silly as to say that The Jews are cloak-and-suiters or The Italians are gangsters. Wasps, like other ethnics, come in all varieties, including criminals—political, corporate and otherwise.

The Values

More seriously, I would like to say a word for the maligned "Wasp values," one of them in particular. As a matter of historical fact, it was we Wasps—by which I mean here the English-speaking peoples—who invented the idea of *limited governments:* that there are some things that no king, President or other official is allowed to do. It began more than seven centuries ago, with Magna Carta, and continued (to cite only the high spots) through the wrangles between Parliament and the Stuart kings, the Puritan Revolution of 1640, the English Bill of Rights of 1688, the American Revolution and our own Bill of Rights and Constitution.

The Wasp principle of limited government emerged through protracted struggle with the much older principle of unlimited government. This latter was never more cogently expressed than at the trial of Charles I, when the hapless monarch informed his judges that, as an anointed king, he was not accountable to any court in the land. A not dissimilar position was taken more recently by another Wasp head of state—and with no more success: Executive privilege went over no better in 1974 than divine right did in 1649. The notion that a king, a President or any other official can do as he damn well pleases has never played in Peoria—or Liverpool or Glasgow, Melbourne or Toronto. For more than 300 years, no Wasp nation has endured an absolute monarchy, dictatorship or any other form of unlimited government—which is something no Frenchman, Italian, German, Pole, Russian or Hispanic can say.

It is perfectly true, of course, that we Wasps have on occasion imposed unlimited governments on other (usually darker) peoples. We have, that is, acted in much the same way as have most other nations that possessed the requisite power and opportunity—including many Third World nations whose leaders delight in lecturing us on political morality (for recent information on this point, consult the files on Biafra, Bangladesh and Brazil, Indian tribes of). Yet even here, Wasp values have played an honorable part. When you start with the idea that Englishmen are entitled to self-government, you end by conceding the same right to Africans and Indians. If you begin by declaring that all (white) men are created equal, you must sooner or later face up to the fact that blacks are also men—and conform your conduct, however reluctantly, to your values.

The Faith

Keeping the Wasp faith hasn't always been easy. We Wasps, like other people, don't always live up to our own principles, and those of us who don't, if occupying positions of power, can pose formidable problems to the rest of us. Time after time, in the name of anti-Communism, peace with honor or some other slippery shibboleth, we have been conned or bullied into tolerating government interference with our liberties and privacy in all sorts of covert—and sometimes overt—ways; time after time we have had to relearn the lesson that eternal vigilance is the price of liberty.

It was a Wasp who uttered that last thought. And it was a congress of Wasps who, about the same time, denounced the executive privileges of George III and committed to the cause of liberty their lives, their fortunes and—*pace,* my Polish-American compatriot—their sacred honor.

A Stranger with a Camera

Calvin Trillin

Calvin Trillin was born in Kansas City, Missouri, in 1935. In high school, he says, he "had no special talents in writing projects," but he went on to major in English at Yale University (B.A. 1957), and to become a writer who is known for his irreverent wit. Since 1963 he has been a staff writer for The New Yorker. *He is probably best known for his eloquent, funny, and often passionate writing about food, which has been collected in three books:* American Fried: Adventures of a Happy Eater *(1974),* Alice, Let's Eat: Further Adventures of a Happy Eater *(1978), and* Third Helpings *(1983). He contributes a regular column to* The Nation *titled "Uncivil Liberties" (collected in two volumes published in 1982 and 1985) and is a syndicated columnist for daily newspapers.*

Although Trillin now lives and writes in New York City, he describes himself as a regional writer from the Midwest. "Most of the people I talk to have never spoken to a reporter before," he said in an interview with the Los Angeles Times. *"I began the U.S. Journal series [for* The New Yorker] *partly because I wanted to stay in touch with the country. I like regional stories. The fact is, government and politics are important, but they aren't the country." All of the pieces in* Killings *(1984) start with small-town incidents that led to murders; all are created by cultures in tension. The selection below, included in that volume, first appeared in* The New Yorker, *April 12, 1969.*

On a bright afternoon in September, in 1967, a five-man film crew working in the mountains of Eastern Kentucky stopped to take pictures of some people near a place called Jeremiah. In a narrow valley, a half-dozen dilapidated shacks—each one a tiny square box with one corner cut away to provide a cluttered front porch—stood alongside the county blacktop. Across the road from the shacks, a mountain rose abruptly. In the field that separated them from the mountain behind them, there were a couple of ramshackle privies and some clotheslines tied to trees and a railroad track and a rusted automobile body and a dirty river called Rockhouse Creek. The leader of the film crew was a Canadian named Hugh O'Connor. Widely acclaimed as the co-producer of the Labyrinth show at Expo 67 in Montreal, O'Connor had been hired by Francis Thompson, an American filmmaker, to work on a film Thompson was producing for the American pavilion at HemisFair in San Antonio. O'Connor went up to three of the shacks and asked the head of each household for permission to take pictures. When each one agreed, O'Connor had him sign the customary release forms and gave him a token payment of ten dollars—a token that, in this case, happened to represent a month's rent. The light was perfect in the valley, and the shooting went well. Theodore Holcomb, the associate producer of the film, was particularly struck by the looks of a miner, still in his work clothes and still covered with coal dust, sitting in a rocking chair on one of the porches. "He was just sitting there scratching his arm in a listless way," Holcomb said later. "He had an expression of total despair. It was an extraordinary shot—so evocative of the despair of that region."

The shot of the coal miner was good enough to be included in the final version of the film, and so was a shot of a half-dozen children who, somehow, lived with their parents in one of the tiny shacks. After about an hour and a half, the crew was ready to leave, but someone had noticed a woman come out of one of the shacks and go to the common well to draw some water, and she was asked to repeat the action for filming. As that last shot was being completed, a woman drove up and told the filmmakers that the man who owned the property was coming to throw them off of it. Then she drove away. A couple of minutes later, another car arrived, and a man—a thin, bald man—leaped out. He was holding a pistol. "Get off my property!" he shouted again and again. Then he shot twice. No one was hit. The filmmakers kept moving their equipment toward their cars across the road while trying to tell the man that they were leaving. One of them said that the man must be shooting blanks. "Get off my property!" he kept screaming. Hugh O'Connor, who was lugging a heavy battery across the highway, turned to say that they were going. The man held the pistol in both hands and pulled the trigger again. "Mr. O'Connor briefly looked down in amazement, and I saw a hole in his chest," Holcomb later testified in court. "He saw it and he looked up in despair and said, 'Why did you have to do that?' and, with blood coming from his mouth, he fell to the ground."

Whitesburg, a town about twelve miles from Jeremiah, is the county seat of Letcher County—headquarters for the county court, the sheriff, and assorted coal companies and anti-poverty agencies. Word that someone had been killed reached Whitesburg quickly, but for a couple of hours there was some confusion about just who the victim was. According to various stories, the dead man had been a representative of the Army

Corps of Engineers, a Vista volunteer, or a C.B.S. cameraman—any of whom might qualify as a candidate for shooting in Letcher County. The Corps of Engineers had proposed building the Kingdom Come Dam across Rockhouse Creek, thereby flooding an area that included Jeremiah, and some opponents of the dam had been saying that the first government man who came near their property had better come armed. Throughout Eastern Kentucky, local political organizations and coal-mining interests had warned that community organizers who called themselves Vistas or Appalachian Volunteers or anything else were nothing but another variety of Communists—three of them had been arrested on charges of attempting to overthrow the government of Pike County—and even some of the impoverished people whom the volunteers were supposedly in Kentucky to help viewed them with fear and suspicion. A number of television crews had been to Letcher County to record the despair that Holcomb saw in the face of the miner sitting on the front porch. Whitesburg happens to be the home of Harry M. Caudill, a lawyer who drew attention to the plight of the mountain people in 1963 with an eloquent book called *Night Comes to the Cumberlands.* Television crews and reporters on a tour of Appalachia are tempted to start with Letcher County in order to get the benefit of Caudill's counsel, which is ordinarily expressed in a tone of sustained rage—rage at the profit ratio of out-of-state companies that take the region's natural resources while paying virtually no taxes, rage at the strip mines that are gouged across the mountains and at the mud slides and floods and pollution and ugliness they cause, rage at the local merchants and politicians who make a good living from the trade of welfare recipients or the retainers of coal companies and insist that there is nothing wrong with the economy, and, most of all, rage at the country that could permit it all to happen. "Look what man hath wrought on *that* purple mountain's majesty," he will say as he points out the coal waste on the side of a mountain that had once been beautiful. "A country that treats its land and people this way deserves to perish from the earth."

In the view of Caudill and of Tom Gish, the liberal editor of the *Mountain Eagle,* a Letcher County weekly, the reactions of people in Jeremiah to the presence of O'Connor's film crew—coöperation by the poor people being photographed in their squalid shacks, rage by the man who owned the shacks—were characteristic of Letcher County: a lot of people who are still in Eastern Kentucky after years of welfare or subsistence employment have lost the will to treat their situation as an embarrassment, but outside journalists are particularly resented by the people who have managed to make a living—running a country store or a filling station or a small truck mine, working for the county administration, managing some rental property. They resent the impression that everyone in Eastern Kentucky is like the people who are desperately poor—people whose condition they tend to blame on "just sorriness, mostly." In Letcher County, fear of outsiders by people who are guarding reputations or economic interests blends easily into a deep-rooted suspicion of outsiders by all Eastern Kentucky mountain people, who have always had a fierce instinct to protect their property and a distrust of strangers that has often proved to have been justified. All of the people in Letcher County—people who live in the shacks up remote hollows or people who run stores on Main Street in Whitesburg—consider themselves mountain people, and, despite an accurate story in the *Mountain Eagle,* many of them instinctively believed that the mountaineer who killed High O'Connor was protecting his property from smart-aleck outsiders who wouldn't leave when they were told.

The mountaineer's name was Hobart Ison. There have always been Isons in Letcher County, and many of them have managed somewhat better than their neighbors. Hobart Ison had inherited a rather large piece of land in Jeremiah—he raised chickens and rented out shacks he himself had built and at one time ran a small sawmill—but he was known mainly as an eccentric, mean-tempered old man. Everyone in Letcher County knew that Hobart Ison had once built and furnished a house for his future bride and—having been rejected or having been afraid to ask or having had no particular future bride in mind—had let the house remain as it was for thirty years, the grass growing up around it and the furniture still in the packing crates. He had occasionally painted large signs attacking the people he thought had wronged him. He was easily enraged by people hunting on his property, and he despised all of the local Democrats, whom he blamed for injustices that included dismissing him from a post-office job. A psychiatrist who examined him after the shooting said, "Any reference to 'game warden' or 'Democrat' will provoke him tremendously." Once, when some local youths were taunting him, he took a shot at them, hitting one in the shoulder. "A lot of people around here would have welcomed them," Caudill said of the filmmakers. "They just happened to pick the wrong place."

Streams of people came to visit Ison in the Letcher County jail before he was released on bail. Women from around Jeremiah baked him cakes. When his trial came up, it proved impossible to find a jury. The Letcher County commonwealth's attorney and Caudill, who had been retained by Francis Thompson, Inc., secured a change of venue. They argued that Ison's family relationship in Letcher County was "so extensive as to comprise a large segment of the population," and, through an affidavit signed by three citizens in position to know public opinion, they stated that "the overwhelming expression of sentiment has been to the effect that the defendant did right in the slaying of Hugh O'Connor and that he ought to be acquitted of the offense of murder."

Harlan County is a mountain or two away from Letcher County. In the town of Harlan, benches advertising Bunny Enriched Bread stand outside the front door of the county courthouse, flanking the First World War monument and the Revolutionary War monument and the plaque recalling how many Kentucky courthouses were burned down by each side during the Civil War. On the ground floor of the courthouse, the men who habitually gather on the plain wooden benches to pass the time use old No. 5 cans for ashtrays or spittoons and a large container that once held Oscar Mayer's Pure Lard as a wastebasket. In the courtroom, a plain room with all of its furnishings painted black, the only decoration other than pictures of the men who have served as circuit judge is a framed poster in praise of the country lawyer—and also in praise, it turns out upon close reading, of the Dun & Bradstreet Corporation. The front door of the courthouse is almost always plastered with election stickers. In the vestibule just inside, an old man sits on the floor behind a display of old pocketknives and watchbands and billfolds and eyeglass cases offered for sale or trade.

The commonwealth's attorney of Harlan County is Daniel Boone Smith. Eight or nine years ago, Smith got curious about how many people he had prosecuted or defended for murder, and counted up seven hundred and fifty. He was able to amass that total partly because of longevity (except for a few years in the service during the Second World War, he has been commonwealth's attorney continuously since 1933), partly because he has worked in an area that gives anyone interested in trying murder cases plenty of opportunity (the wars between the unions and the coal operators in Harlan County during the thirties were almost as bloody as the mountain feuds earlier in the century), and partly because he happens to be a quick worker ("Some people will take three days to try a murder case," he has said. "I usually get my case on in a day"). During his first week as commonwealth's attorney of Harlan and an adjoining county, Smith tried five murder cases. These days, Harlan County may have about that many a year, but it remains a violent place. The murders that do occur in mountain counties like Harlan and Letcher often seem to occur while someone is in a drunken rage, and often among members of the same family—a father shooting a son over something trivial, one member of a family mowing down another who is breaking down the door trying to get at a third. "We got people in this county today who would kill you as quick as look at you," Smith has said. "But most of 'em are the type that don't bother you if you leave them alone." Smith is known throughout Eastern Kentucky for his ability to select jurors—to remember which prospective juror's uncle may have had a boundary dispute with which witness's grandfather twenty years ago—and for his ability to sum up the case for them in their own language once the evidence has been heard. He is an informal, colloquial, storytelling man who happens to be a graduate of the Harvard Law School.

A lack of fervor about convicting Hobart Ison was assumed in Harlan County when he came up for trial there in May 1968. "Before the case, people were coming up and saying, 'He *should've* killed the son of a bitch,' " Smith said later. "People would say, 'They oughtn't to make fun of mountain people. They've made enough fun of mountain people. Let me on the jury, Boone, and I'll turn him loose.' " Smith saw his task as persuading the citizens and the jurors that the case was not what it appeared to be—that the filmmakers were not "a bunch of privateers and pirates" but respectable people who had been commissioned by the United States government, that the film was not another study of how poor and ignorant people were in Eastern Kentucky but a film about the whole United States in which the shots of Eastern Kentucky would take up only a few seconds, that the filmmakers had behaved properly and politely to those they were photographing. "Why, if they had been smart alecks come to hold us up to ridicule, I'd be the last man to try him," Smith assured everyone. It took Smith only a day or so to present his case against Hobart Ison, although it took three days to pick the jury. On the witness stand, the surviving filmmakers managed to avoid admitting to Ison's lawyers that it was the appalling poverty of his tenants that had interested them; they talked about being attracted by expressive family groups and by the convenience of not having to move their equipment far from the road. The defense asked if they were planning to take pictures of the Bluegrass as well as Appalachia. Were they going to make a lot of money from the film? How many millions of viewers would see the pictures of poor Eastern Kentucky people? Had they refused to move? Had they taunted Ison by saying he was shooting blanks? Did the people who signed the release forms really know what they were signing? (At least one of the signers was, like one out of four of his neighbors, unable to read.)

Except for the underlying issue of Eastern Kentucky v. Outsiders, the only issue seriously in contention was Ison's sanity. The director of a nearby mental-health clinic, testifying for the defense, said that Ison was a paranoid schizophrenic. He told of Ison showing up for one interview with long socks worn on the outside of his trouser legs and of his altercations with his neighbors and of his lack of remorse. The prosecution's psychiatrist—an impressive woman from the University of Kentucky who had been retained by Francis Thompson, Inc.—said that Ison had grown up at a time when it was common practice to run people off of property with a gun, and, because he had lived with aging parents or alone ever since childhood, he still followed that practice. Some of Ison's ideas did have "paranoid coloring," she said, but that could be traced to his being a mountaineer, since people in isolated mountain pockets normally had a suspicion of strangers and even of each other. "Socio-cultural circumstances," she concluded, "lead to the diagnosis of an individual who is normal for his culture, the shooting and the paranoid color both being present in other individuals in this culture who are considered normal." In the trial and in the insanity hearing that had earlier found Ison competent to stand trial, Smith insisted that Ison was merely peculiar, not crazy. "I said, 'Now, I happen to like mayonnaise on my beans. Does that make *me* crazy?' " Smith later recalled. "I turned to one of the jurors, a man named Mahan Fields, and I said, 'Mahan, you remember Uncle Bob Woolford, who used to work up at Evarts? Did you ever see Uncle Bob in the winter when he didn't have his socks pulled up over his pants legs to keep out the cold? Now, was Uncle Bob crazy? Why, Mahan, I bet on many a winter morning *you* wore *your* socks over your pants legs.' "

In his summation, Smith saved his harshest words not for the defendant but for the person who was responsible for bringing Hobart Ison, a mountaineer who was not quite typical of mountaineers, and Hugh O'Connor, a stranger with a camera who was not quite typical of strangers with cameras, into violent conflict. Judy Breeding—the operator of a small furniture store near Ison's shacks, and the wife of Ison's cousin—had testified that she was not only the woman who told the film crew that Ison was coming but also the woman who had told Ison that the film crew was on his property. "Hobart," she recalled saying, "there is some men over there taking pictures of your houses, with out-of-state license." Smith looked out toward the courtroom spectators and suddenly pointed his finger at Judy Breeding. He told her that he would like to be prosecuting her, that if it hadn't been for her mouth Hugh O'Connor would not be in his grave and Hobart Ison would be back home where he belonged. Later, Smith caught a glimpse of Mrs. Breeding in the hall, and he thought he saw her shake her fist at him, smiling. "You know," he said, "I believe the idea that she had anything to do with bringing that about had never occurred to her till I mentioned it."

The jury was eleven to one for conviction, but the one held out. Some people were surprised that Ison had come that close to being convicted, although it was generally agreed that the prosecution's psychiatrist had out-talked the psychiatrist who testified for the defense. Smith believed that his case had been greatly strengthened by the fact that the filmmakers had been respectful, soft-spoken witnesses—not at all smart-alecky. "If there was anything bigheaded about them," he said, "it didn't show."

The retrial was postponed once, and then was stopped suddenly during jury selection when Smith became ill. On March 24th, Hobart Ison came to trial again. The filmmakers, who had been dreading another trip to Kentucky, were at the county courthouse in Harlan at nine in the morning, ready to repeat their testimony. Although Smith had anticipated even more trouble finding a jury, he was prepared to go to trial. But Ison's lawyers indicated to Smith and Caudill that their client, now seventy, would be willing to plead guilty to voluntary manslaughter, and they finally met Smith's insistence on a ten-year sentence. Ison—wearing a baggy brown suit, his face pinched and red—appeared only briefly before the judge to plead guilty. A couple of hours after everyone arrived, Caudill was on his way back to Whitesburg, where he was working on the case of a Vietnam veteran accused of killing two men during an argument in the street, and the filmmakers were driving to Knoxville to catch the first plane to New York.

The following day, the clerk of the court, a strong-looking woman with a strong Kentucky accent, happened to get into a discussion about the filmmakers with another citizen who had come to know them in the year and a half since Hugh O'Connor's death—a woman with a softer accent and a less certain tone to her voice.

"You know, I asked those men yesterday morning if they were happy with the outcome," the clerk said. "And they said, 'Yes.' And I said, 'Well, you know, us hillbillies is a queer breed. We are. I'm not offering any apologies when I say that. Us hillbillies *are* a queer breed, and I'm just as proud as punch to be one.'"

"Not all of us are like that," the other woman said. "Mean like that."

"Well, I wouldn't say that man is mean," the clerk said. "I don't guess he ever harmed anybody in his life. They were very nice people. I think it was strictly a case of misunderstanding. I think that the old man thought they were laughing and making fun of him, and it was more than he could take. I know this: a person isolated in these hills, they often grow old and eccentric, which I think they have a right to do."

"But he didn't have a right to kill," the other woman said.

"Well, no," the clerk said. "But us hillbillies, we don't bother nobody. We go out of our way to help people. But we don't want nobody pushin' us around. Now, that's the code of the hills. And he felt like—that old man felt like—he was being pushed around. You know, it's like I told those men: 'I wouldn't have gone on that old man's land to pick me a mess of wild greens without I'd asked him.' They said, 'We didn't know all this.' I said, 'I bet you know it now. I bet you know it now.'"

Beyond Manzanar: A Personal View of Asian American Womanhood

Jeanne Wakatsuki Houston

Jeanne Wakatsuki Houston was born in Inglewood, California, in 1935. In April 1942 when she was seven, her family was removed by Executive Order 9066 to a Japanese internment camp near Death Valley for the duration of World War II. They were freed in October 1945, when she was eleven. She later studied sociology and journalism at San Jose State Col-

lege, where she met her husband, the writer James D. Houston. Together, they wrote Farewell to Manzanar *(1973), a record of her experiences during internment. Another book,* Don't Cry, It's Only Thunder *(1984), which Houston wrote in collaboration with Vietnam veteran Paul Hansler, describes his experiences with war orphans. The present essay, originally presented as a paper for the Seminar on Ethnic Lifestyles at Oklahoma State University in 1978, is here taken from* Asian Americans: Social and Psychological Perspectives, *edited by Russell Endo (1979); it is reprinted in the Houstons' most recent collection of their essays,* One Can Think About Life After the Fish Is in the Canoe *(1985).*

Farewell to Manzanar is a personal story of my family's experiences during and after the Second World War. To fill out the story, my husband and I did a fair amount of research on the Internment and various aspects of Asian American experience. But I do not consider myself a scholar, nor do I feel I can speak for Asian Americans as a group. What I will be sharing with you will be more personal observations of my awareness of being an Asian American female in this society.

I will begin with memories of my mother, as she was the first, strongest and most important role model influencing my identity as a female. Then I would like to share with you some thoughts and feelings from my own experience, which have surfaced since the writing of *Farewell to Manzanar*.

1

My mother married for love. This was rare among Japanese immigrants living in America during that time—1915. Most were men who had to send for wives from their provinces in Japan via the *Baishakunin* or matchmaker, who exchanged photographs for the prospective couple and made the arrangements. This is not to say that love did not develop or occur among these couples. What is significant about this "Picture Bride" phenomenon is that the reasons for marriage were not love and affection, as is the case for the dominant culture in America. Marriages were arranged to perpetuate the family.

My mother was 18 and living in Spokane, Washington, when she met and fell in love with my father, a student ten years older than herself. She had been promised to someone else, a steady, hard-working farmer and friend of her family. In absolute defiance of her tradition and training, to be dutifully obedient to the authority of parents, she ran away with my father. Thus, their marriage became the first step towards assimilation into American culture; romantic love had intertwined itself among the responsibilities which defined their roles as husband/father, wife/mother. Perhaps it was this love, unexhibited but pervasive, which softened the sharp facts of the inequities in their relationship, in her acquiescence to his needs and demands. In my more immature years I could not understand how she could tolerate his volatile temperament, his arrogance and obsession with dignity, and his "kingly" presence in the home. I was in my teens then, not fully assimilated, but trying desperately to be as American as Doris Day.° My parents did not behave like the parents of my Caucasian friends, and this was embarrassing for me.

Mama worked very hard. She would garden, cook, care for us when we were ill, and after the war she even went to work in the fish cannery to supplement the family income, which was minimal at the time. I felt sorry for her. I remember one day when I was 6 years old watching her scrub clothes, my arms barely reaching over the bathtub's edge, and she on her knees, rubbing soapy shirts against a tin washboard. I watched her silent and sweat-streaked face, her hair greying wispily around her temples. I filled with terror as I envisioned her dying because she worked too hard. I started to cry.

She only laughed when I told her my fears and said, "I like to wash clothes. It gives me time to think of other things in my head." She tapped her forehead. "Besides, I'm not a washerwoman. This is just a chore. I'm your mother."

I did not understand the weight of her explanation to me then. Being mother was not only enough for her, it was a prized identity. It meant she had a family, and in her world—her peers and community almost exclusively of Japanese descent—the family was supreme in its hierarchy of values. Thus, the chores and duties which she inherited as Japanese wife and mother were not her identity as such; they were just a means to accomplish the end, which was to keep her family intact, happy and well. She never confused her tasks with who she was.

This concept of the inner self, which I have begun only recently to understand as a result of my attempts to rediscover my Japanese "roots," allowed her to form her own image, distinct from the one in the exterior world. This ability to create a psychological privacy, inherited from a people who for centuries have had to create their own internal "space" in an overpopulated island, gave her the freedom, of which she was so deprived in her role as Japanese wife and mother. This was her way to survive . . . and to succeed. She did both with grace and with love. I think of the many people I know today (myself included) who have become so obsessed with freedom and independence. We resent our family, our jobs, our relationships . . . any responsibilities that seem to inhibit our mobility. I have so many more choices than my mother had, so much more external independence; yet, it was not until recently that I realized mobility and time do not mean freedom. The freedom is *within* me. I must *feel* free to be free.

Doris Day   Movie star, epitome of the all-American girl next door.

I believe my mother was a fulfilled person. She had ten children who loved her devotedly. Even after ten years since her passing, I can truthfully say not a day passes that I do not think of her, not with grief, but with love and gratitude. What Japanese mother could be a failure when even after death her children do not abandon her? This brings to mind a comment made to me by a Japanese American friend commenting on American values and the family. "We abandon each other when we need each other the most," he said. "We abandon the young and the old. We send our young to nursery schools as early as we can get them in . . . just when they need our love and presence more than any time in their lives. We send our old and sickly to institutions to die alone. Where is our love responsibility? Where is that feeling of responsibility for each other that the family instills? Where is the family?"

There was a time when I would not declare my love for her. Not until I was in college did I realize my Caucasian peers seemed to have a different attitude toward their mothers than I did. Or, at least, they talked about them differently. During my Freshman year I took the required General Psychology course and was exposed for the first time to Freud and Jung, as were most of my classmates. I was stunned to hear them discuss their mothers so impersonally and often with great hostility. It seemed everyone had something negative to say about their "domineering, materialistic, guilt-evoking, aggressive" mothers. I did not understand then that these utterings were merely a way of asserting independence, of striking out at the one authority in their lives that emotionally held them to the "nest." What was clear to me was that mother and motherhood were not "sacred" to them in the same way it was to me. They celebrated Mother's Day, which we never did, yet I heard such resentment surrounding that day, I used to wonder why it was celebrated.

Years later I was keenly reminded again of that period in my life. I was working as the Student Activities Coordinator at one of the colleges at the University of California in Santa Cruz. Among my duties was the responsibility for room assignments and changes. One day, a Chicano student came into my office requesting a room change. He was clearly agitated. I offered to act as mediator or counselor if there was a misunderstanding with his roommate. Reluctantly, he said, "I don't know about these Anglos. My roommate talks so badly about his mother. He calls her a bitch. This hurts me very much. I love my mother. I know she is sacrificing for me, crawling on her hands and knees in the strawberry fields of Delano so I can come to the University. I'm afraid I will hurt him if I have to keep rooming with him." I had felt my throat tighten and my eyes fill with tears, empathizing with him. I was touched by his love and loyalty, his willingness to overtly challenge an attitude so acceptable within the dominant culture and so unacceptable within his.

The word "sacrifice," spoken by my Caucasian friends in reference to their mothers, always carried connotations of guilt and manipulative martyrdom. It did not carry that taint for me or for the Mexican student. In fact, I have found that most of my friends from other ethnic minority backgrounds will readily say, if it is so, that they knew their mothers sacrificed their own comforts, or worked so that they could go to school or have a graduation suit . . . no guilt implied, just a recognition and acceptance of it with gratitude.

I think that Japanese women of my mother's generation who were mothers were fortunate because their role was highly valued by their society . . . their society being the community of other Japanese immigrants. The family and community prized her role, and when she fulfilled that role, she prized herself. She not only knew her worth, she *felt* her significance. There was no celebration of "Mother's Day," but there was no question that *Oka-san* was respected and loved by her culture.

Her role as wife to my father is not as clear cut in my memory. Whereas her world in the home, in the immediate Japanese community, did not differ much from the society in which she and her mother were raised, my father's world was very different. He had to earn a living for his family in an environment both alien and hostile to him. My mother, already inherently prepared to subordinate herself in their relationship knew this and zealously sought for ways to elevate his position in the family. He had to absorb the humiliations "out there"; she would absorb them at home. After all, was he not doing this for his family, protecting her, acting as the buffer between herself and that alien *hakujin*° world?

She served him . . . with grace and naturalness. I conjure up the image of her calm, smooth face, her alert brown eyes scanning his stockings for holes as she carefully laid them and his underwear out at the foot of their bed. She did this faithfully every morning I can remember when he was at home. He was always served first at meals. She cooked special things for him and sat next to him at the table, vigilantly aware of his needs, handing him the condiments and pouring his tea before he could ask. She drew his bath and massaged him and laid his clothes out when he dressed up. As I was growing up I accepted these rituals to be the natural expressions of a wife's love for her husband. There was no question in my mind that my mother loved my father; that is why she served him. This attitude, that to serve meant to love, became an integral part of my psychological make-up and a source for confusion when I later began to relate to men.

There was also no question in my mind that my father was absolute authority in their relationship and in his relationship to his children. During and after the Second World War, when his dreams and economic situation had hit bottom, and he was too old to start over again as he had already done several times, he raged at his wife and family and drank. His

---

hakujin Caucasian (Japanese).

frustration toward the society that rejected and humiliated him caused him to turn on his own and on himself. I never understood how she so patiently endured him during those times. But she never abandoned him, understanding as I did not, the reasons for his anguish, for his sense of failure.

Even though respect for him diminished then, I always felt that he was very powerful and that he dominated her with this power. As they grew older and inevitable thoughts of their passing entered my mind, I worried that she would be lost if he died before her. When that sad day arrived I learned what is meant by the Asian philosophical truism "softness is strength." I had taken my gravely ill father, along with my mother, to see his doctor. The doctor informed me privately that we should take him to the hospital where he would be comfortable, as he could not live more than 10 days.

It was raining. I numbly drove the car toward the hospital, straining to see through the blurred windshields and my own tears. My mother was not crying. "Riku," he said, weakly. He never called her Riku . . . always "Mama." "Don't leave me. Stay with me at the hospital. They won't know how to cook for me . . . or how to care for me." She patted his hand. "You've been a good wife. You've always been the strong one."

Not wanting him to tire, I tried to quiet him. He sat up bolt-like and roared like a lion. "Shut up!" I quaked at his forcefulness, but felt some comfort in knowing he could still "save face" and be the final authority to his children, even at death's door. My mother's quiet strength filled the car as she gently stroked his forehead. Without tears or panic she assured him she would stay with him until the end.

He died that afternoon a few hours after he entered the hospital. For the ten years afterward that my mother lived, she never once appeared lost or rudderless, as I feared she would be with him gone. Hadn't he been the center of her life? Hadn't the forms in their relationship, the rituals of their roles all affirmed his power over her? No. She had been the strong one. The structure had been created for him; but it was her essence that had sustained it.

2

The memories surrounding my awareness of being female seem to fall into two categories: those of the period before the war, when the family made up my world, and those after the war when I entered puberty, and my world expanded to include the ways and values of my Caucasian peers. I did not think about my Asian-ness and how it influenced my self-image as a female, until I married.

In remembering myself as a small child, I find it hard to separate myself from the entity of the family. I was too young to be given "duties" according to my sex, and I was unaware that this was the organizational basis for the operating of the family. I took it for granted that everyone just did what had to be done to keep things running smoothly. My five older sisters helped my mother with domestic duties, and my four older brothers helped my father in the fishing business. What I vaguely recall about the sensibility surrounding our sex differences was that my sisters and I all liked to please our brothers. Moreso, we tried to attract positive attention from Papa. A smile or affectionate pat from him was like a gift from heaven. Somehow, we never felt this way about Mama. We took her love for granted. But there was something special about Papa.

I never identified this specialness as being one of the blessings of maleness. After all, I played with my brother Kiyo, two years older than myself, and I never felt there was anything special about him. I could even make him cry. My older brothers were fun-loving, boisterous and very kind to me, especially when I made them laugh with my imitations of Carmen Miranda⁰ dancing and Bonnie Baker singing "Oh, Johnny." But Papa was different. His specialness was that he was the authority, not that he was a male.

After the war, my world drastically changed. The family had disintegrated, my father no longer "Godlike" despite my mother's attempt to sustain that pre-war image of him. I was spending most of my time with my new Caucasian friends and learning new values that clashed with the values of my parents. It was also time that I assumed duties in the home that the girls were supposed to do . . . like cooking, cleaning the house, washing and ironing clothes. I remember washing and ironing my brother's shirts, careful to press the collars correctly, trying not to displease them. I cannot ever remember my brothers performing domestic chores while I lived at home. Yet, even though they may not have been working "out there," as the men were supposed to do, I did not resent it. It would have embarrassed me to see my brothers doing the dishes. Their reciprocation came in a different way.

They were very protective of me and made me feel good and important for being a female. If my brother Ray had extra money, he would sometimes buy me a sexy sweater like my Caucasian friends wore that Mama wouldn't buy for me. My brothers taught me to ride a bicycle, to drive a car, took me to my first dance, and proudly introduced me to their friends.

Although the family had changed, my identity as a female within it did not differ much from my older sisters who grew up before the war. The males and females supported each other but for different reasons. No longer was the survival of the family as a group our primary objective; we cooperated to help each other survive "out there" in the complicated world that had weakened Papa.

Carmen Miranda Movie star known for her Latin-American dances and towering head-dresses trimmed with fruit.

My brothers encouraged me to run for school office, to try out for majorette and song leader, and to run for Queen of various festivities. They were proud that I was breaking social barriers still closed to them. It was acceptable for an Oriental male to excel academically and in sports. But to gain recognition socially in a society that had been fed the stereotyped model of the Asian male as cook, houseboy or crazed *kamikaze* pilot, was almost impossible. The more alluring myth of mystery and exotica that surrounds the Oriental female made it easier, though no less spiritually painful, for me.

Whenever I succeeded in the *hakujin* world, my brothers were supportive, whereas, Papa would be disdainful, undermined by my obvious capitulation to the ways of the West. I wanted to be like my Caucasian friends. Not only did I want to look like them, I wanted to act like them. I tried hard to be outgoing and socially aggressive, and to act confidently like my girl friends. At home I was careful not to show these personality traits to my father. For him it was bad enough that I did not even look very Japanese; I was too big, and I walked too assertively. My breasts were large, and besides that I showed them off with those sweaters the *hakujin* girls wore! My behavior at home was never calm and serene, but I still tried to be as Japanese as I could around my father.

As I passed puberty and grew more interested in boys, I soon became aware that an Oriental female evoked a certain kind of interest from males. I was still too young to understand how or why an Oriental female fascinated Caucasian men, and of course, far too young to see then that it was a form of "not seeing," of stereotyping. My brothers would warn me, "Don't trust the *hakujin* boys. They only want one thing. They'll treat you like a servant and expect you to wait on them hand and foot. They don't know how to be nice to you." My brothers never dated Caucasian girls. In fact, I never really dated Caucasian boys until I went to college. In high school, I used to sneak out to dances and parties where I would meet them. I wouldn't even dare to think what Papa would do if he knew I was seeing *hakujin* boys.

What my brothers were saying was that I should not act towards Caucasian males as I did towards them. I must not "wait on them" or allow them to think I would, because they wouldn't understand. In other words, be a Japanese female around Japanese men and act *hakujin* around Caucasian men. This double identity within a "double standard" resulted not only in a confusion for me of my role or roles as female, but also in who or what I was racially. With the admonitions of my brothers lurking deep in my consciousness, I would try to be aggressive, assertive and "come on strong" towards Caucasian men. I mustn't let them think I was submissive, passive and all-giving like Madame Butterfly. With Asian males I would tone down my natural enthusiasm and settle into patterns instilled in me through the models of my mother and my sisters. I was not comfortable in either role.

I found I was more physically attracted to Caucasian men. Although T.V. and film were not nearly as pervasive as they are now, we still had an abundance of movie magazines and movies from which to garner our idols for crushes and fantasy. For years I was madly in love with Lon McCallister and Alan Ladd. Bruce Lee and O.J. Simpson were absent from the idol-making media. Asian men became like "family" to me; they were my brothers. Of course, no one was like my father. He was so powerful. The only men who might possess some of that power were those whose control and dominance over his life diminished his. Those would be the men who interested me.

Although I was attracted to males who looked like someone in a Coca-Cola ad, I yearned for the expressions of their potency to be like that of Japanese men, like that of my father: unpredictable, dominant, and brilliant—yet sensitive and poetic. I wanted a blond Samurai.

When I met my blond Samurai I was surprised to see how readily my mother accepted the idea of our getting married. My father had passed away, but I was still concerned about her reaction. All of my married brothers and sisters had married Japanese American mates. I would be the first to marry a Caucasian. "He's a strong man and will protect you. I'm all for it," she said. Her main concern for me was survival. Knowing that my world was the world of the *hakujin,* she wanted me to be protected, even if it meant marriage to one. It was 1957, and inter-racial couples were a rare sight to see. She felt that my husband-to-be was strong because he was acting against the norms of his culture, perhaps even against his parent's wishes. From her vantage point, where family and group opinion outweighed the individual's, this willingness to oppose them was truly a show of strength.

When we first married I wondered if I should lay out his socks and underwear every morning like my mother used to do. But then my brother's warning not to be subservient to Caucasian men or they will take advantage would float up from the past. So I compromised and laid them out sporadically, whenever I thought to do it . . . which grew less and less often as the years passed. (Now my husband is lucky if *he* can even find a clean pair of socks in the house!) His first reaction to this wifely gesture was to be uncomfortably pleased. Then he was puzzled by its sporadic occurrence, which did not seem to coincide as an act of apology, or because I wanted something. On the days when I felt I should be a good Japanese wife, I did it. On other days, when I felt American and assertive, I did not.

When my mother visited us, as she often did when she was alive, I had to be on good behavior, much to my husband's pleasure and surprise. I would jump up from the table to fill his empty water glass (that is, if she hadn't beat me to it) or butter his roll. If I didn't notice that his plate needed refilling, she would kick me under the table and reprimand me with a disapproving look. Needless to say, we never had mother-in-law problems. He would often ask with hope in his voice, "When is your mother coming to visit?"

Despite the fact that early in our marriage we had become aware of the "images" we had married and were trying to relate to each other as the real people we were, he still hoped deep in his heart that I was his *Cho-Cho san*,[°] his saronged, exotic Dorothy Lamour. And I still saw him as my golden Samurai, wielding his sword of justice and integrity, slaying the dragons that prevented my acceptance as an equal human being in his world, now mine.

My mother dutifully served my father throughout their marriage. I never felt she resented it. I served my brothers and father and did not resent it. I was made to feel not only important for performing duties of my role, but absolutely integral for the functioning of the family. I realized a very basic difference in attitude between Japanese and American culture towards serving another. In my family, to serve another could be uplifting, a gracious gesture that elevated oneself. For many white Americans it seems that serving another is degrading, an indication of dependency or weakness in character, or a low place in the social ladder. To be ardently considerate is to be "self-effacing" or apologetic.

My father used to say, "Serving humanity is the greatest virtue. Giving service of yourself is more worthy than selling the service or goods of another." He would prefer that we be maids in someone's home, serving someone well, than be a salesgirl where our function would be to exchange someone else's goods, handling money. Perhaps it was his way to rationalize and give pride to the occupations open to us as Orientals. Nevertheless, his words have stayed with me, giving me spiritual sustenance at times when I perceived that my willingness to give was misconstrued to be a need to be liked or an act of manipulation to get something.

I was talking about this subject with an Asian American woman friend, recently widowed, whose husband had also been Asian American. He had been a prominent surgeon, highly thought of in the community where we live. She is 42, third generation Chinese, born in San Francisco in 1935, articulate, intelligent and a professional therapist for educationally handicapped children. She "confessed" of her reticence to let her Caucasian friends know she served her husband. "There is such a stereotyped view that is laid on us. They just don't understand *why* we do what we do!"

She told me of an incident when she remarked to a Caucasian friend that she polished her husband's shoes. Her friend turned on her in mock fury and said, "Don't you dare let my husband know you do that!" My friend said she felt ashamed, humiliated, that she had somehow betrayed this woman by her seeming subordination to her husband.

Cho-Cho san   Heroine who marries an American naval officer in Puccini's opera *Madama Butterfly*.

"I served him in many ways," she said. "I did it because even though he was a graduate of Stanford and professionally successful, he drove himself to work harder and longer to compete because he felt he was handicapped by being Chinese. You know our Asian men, the ones raised with values from the old country are not equipped to compete like white American men. They are not conditioned to be outwardly aggressive and competitive. It was agony for my husband, and I knew he was out there doing it for us, so I tried to make it easier for him at home." As I looked at her I could see her compassion, and for a flickering moment I saw my mother. A generation had passed, but some things had not changed that much.

My husband and I often joke that the reason we have stayed married for so long is that we continually mystify each other with responses and attitudes that are plainly due to our different backgrounds. For years I frustrated him with unpredictable silences and accusative looks. I felt a great reluctance to tell him what I wanted or what needed to be done in the home. I was inwardly furious that I was being put into the position of having to *tell* him what to do. I felt my femaleness, in the Japanese sense, was being degraded. I did not want to be the authority. That would be humiliating for him and for me. He, on the other hand, considering the home to be under my dominion, in the American sense, did not dare to impose on me what he thought I wanted. He wanted me to tell him or make a list, like his parents did in his home.

Entertaining socially was also confusing. Up to recent times, I still hesitated to sit at one head of our rectangular dining table when my husband sat at the other end. It seemed right to be seated next to him, helping him serve the food. Sometimes I did it anyway, but only with our close friends who didn't misunderstand my physical placement to be psychological subservience.

At dinner parties I always used to serve the men first until I noticed the women glaring at me. I became self-conscious about it and would try to remember to serve the ladies first. Sometimes I would forget and automatically turn to a man. I would catch myself abruptly, dropping a bowl of soup all over him. Then I would have to serve him first anyway, as an apologetic gesture. My unconscious Japanese instinct still managed to get what it wanted!

Now I just entertain according to how I feel that day. If my Japanese sensibility is stronger I act accordingly and feel comfortable. If I feel like going all-American I can do that too, and feel comfortable. I have come to accept the cultural hybridness of my personality, to recognize it as strength and not weakness. Because I am neither culturally pure Japanese nor pure American does not mean I am less of a person. It means I have been enriched with the heritage of both.

As I look back on my marriage and try to compare it to the marriage of my parents, it seems ludicrous to do so . . . like comparing a sailboat to a jet airliner; both get you there, but one depends on the natural element of wind and the other on technological expertise. What does emerge as a basic difference is directly related to the Japanese concept of cooperation for group survival and the American value of competition for the survival of individualism. My Japanese family cooperated to survive economically and spiritually. Although sibling rivalry was subtly present, it was never allowed the ferocity of expression we allow our children. I see our children compete with each other. I have felt my husband and I compete with each other . . . not always in obvious ways such as professional recognition or in the comparison of role responsibilities, but in attitudes towards self-fulfillment. "I love you more than you love me," or "My doing nothing is more boring than your doing nothing."

Competition does provide some challenge and excitement in life. Yet carried to extremes in personal relationships, it can become destructive. How can you fully trust someone you are in competition with? And when trust breaks down, isolation and alienation set in.

I find that another basic difference is between my mother and myself in how we relate to sons. I try very consciously not to indulge my son, as my mother had indulged my brothers. My natural inclination is to do this. So I try to restrain it. In fact, I find myself being harder on him, afraid that my constrained Japanese training to please the male might surface, crippling instead of equipping him for future relationships with females who may not be of my background, hampering his emotional survival in the competitive, independent world he will face when he leaves the nest.

How my present attitudes will affect my children in later years remains to be seen. My world is radically different from my mother's world, and all indications point to an even wider difference in our world from our children's. Whereas my family's and part of my struggle were racially based, I do not foresee a similar struggle for our children. Their biracialness is, indeed, a factor in their identity and self-image, but I feel their struggle will be more to sustain human dignity in a world rapidly dehumanizing itself with mechanization and technology. My hope is they have inherited a strong will to survive, that essential trait which ethnic minorities in this country have sharply honed.

3

In searching for remarks to conclude this paper, I find myself hearkening again to imagined words of advice from my parents. My mother would say, "Love yourself. Nurture your children and your family with love and emotional support. Accept change if it means protecting your loved ones."

My father would say, "We are all brothers. Brother must not be pitted against brother; race must not be pitted against race. We do not raise ourselves at the expense of others. Through cooperation we advance together as human beings."

I see the yin and the yang of their sensibilities and acknowledge how the combination of them has formed my own. Thus, I close with these words, "In this game of life, we are only as good as our partner . . . our partner being the other in a male-female relationship, or a race or ethnic group co-existing with a dominant culture. The best game is when partners are equal, in top form, sharing their diversities, and enriching their experience. Dominating a partner only weakens the game, unbalancing it, lessening its vigor and quality. It is my hope in these changing times that the rules for the game will improve, encouraging understanding, and thus, acceptance and respect for all partners."

Prejudice and the Individual

Gordon Allport

Gordon Allport (1897–1967) was educated at Harvard and spent most of his career there as Professor of Psychology. He was particularly interested in the relationship between human psychology and social problems, and he became a worldwide authority on racial and religious prejudice. In 1956 he visited the University of Natal, compared the South African racial issue with the American one, and concluded that white supremacy could not be maintained in either country. Some of his most influential books are Personality: A Psychological Interpretation *(1937),* The Psychology of Rumor *(written with Leo G. Postman, 1947),* The Individual and His Religion *(1950), and* The Nature of Prejudice *(1954). The present essay was written for a symposium on prejudice; it is taken from* The Black American Reference Book *(1976).*

Definition and Extent of Prejudice

There are two ingredients implicit in any prejudiced state of mind: (a) a feeling of favorableness or unfavorableness which in turn is (b) based on unsupported judgment. While some prejudice can be *pro,* or "love prejudice" (as when we think too well of our own group), the ethnic attitudes that cause most social concern are *con,* or "hate prejudice."

A scholastic definition states that hate prejudice is "thinking ill of others without sufficient warrant." An equivalent slang definition says "prejudice is being down on something you are not up on." Whatever wording we prefer, there is always an element of inadequate knowledge or false judgment in prejudice; if not, then we are dealing with a well-grounded dislike, not with prejudice. If a criminal gang threatens my safety, my fear and hatred of it are not prejudice; but if I say that no ex-convict can be trusted, I am overgeneralizing and am therefore prejudiced. Examples are legion. "Every Jew will cheat you if he gets a chance." "Negroes are a violent lot; they carry razors." "Puerto Ricans are ignorant." "I couldn't trust any white man."

It should be added that overgeneralized prejudgments of this sort are prejudices only if they are not reversible when exposed to new knowledge. A person (e.g., a child) can start with a misconception about Jews, Negroes, or Puerto Ricans; but if he changes his mind when new evidence comes along he was not really prejudiced, only misinformed. Prejudices are inflexible, rigid, and erroneous generalizations about groups of people.

Discrimination and Prejudice

While discrimination ultimately rests on prejudice, the two processes are not identical. Discrimination denies people their natural or legal rights because of their membership in some unfavored group. Many people discriminate automatically[1] without being prejudiced; and others, the "gentle people of prejudice," feel irrational aversion, but are careful not to show it in discriminatory behavior. Yet in general, discrimination reinforces prejudices, and prejudices provide rationalizations for discrimination. The two concepts are most distinct when it comes to seeking remedies. The corrections for discrimination are legal, or lie in a direct change of social practices; whereas the remedy for prejudice lies in education and the conversion of attitudes. The best opinion today says that if we eliminate discrimination, then—as people become acquainted with one another on equal terms—attitudes are likely to change, perhaps more rapidly than through the continued preaching or teaching of tolerance.

While some people are prejudiced against one group only, it is more common to find that if a person is bigoted in regard to one nationality, race, or religion, he is likely to be bigoted regarding all "out-groups." He feels safe only within the narrow confines of his own familiar circle. It is this finding that argues most cogently for regarding prejudice as rooted in personal character structure.

How widespread is prejudice? Research suggests that perhaps 80 percent of the American people harbor ethnic prejudice of some type and in some appreciable degree. Only 20 percent of the people are, in Gandhi's terms, "equiminded" or completely democratic in all their attitudes.[2]

---

[1]An example of this in the past might have been the use of a waiting room labeled "White" or "Colored." A contemporary example could involve the choice between rest rooms marked "Ladies" and "Gentlemen."

[2]Gordon W. Allport, *The Nature of Prejudice* (New York: Doubleday Anchor Books, 1958), p. 77.

Widespread though ethnic prejudice is, there is good reason to believe that in the United States it is declining year by year.

Origins of Prejudice

While some animals have an instinctive aversion to others, this is not true among species that are cross-fertile. Human beings of all races can, and do, mate and procreate. There is therefore no reason to assume that instinctive aversion exists between ethnic and racial groups. A young child may be frightened by a person of unfamiliar color or appearance, but ordinarily this fear last only a few moments. It is well known that young children will play contentedly together whatever their race or national origin. Thus since prejudice is not inborn but acquired, the question is: What are the chief factors in the complex process of learning?

Some prejudice is deliberately taught by parents. Children obediently learn the lesson, as in the case of the little girl who asked her mother, "What's the name of those children I am supposed to hate?" The parent may pass on prejudice by punishing a child for his friendliness to minority groups. A child thus punished may acquire a conditioned aversion to members of the out-group. Sometimes the teaching is subtler. Even to a four-year-old, dark skin may suggest dirt; and since he is repeatedly warned to keep clean, he may develop an avoidance for dark-skinned people.

Tags are powerful factors in learning. Most children learn the emotional force of words long before they know the meanings of the words. An angry first-grader once called his white teacher a "nigger." She asked him what "nigger" meant. He replied, "I don't know, but you're supposed to say it when you're mad." Before the child has knowledge of the meaning of Jap, Jew, nigger, Polack and similar labels, he senses the potency of the negative feeling-tone behind these labels. Derogatory chatter in the home may thus dispose a child of six or eight to "think ill of others without sufficient warrant."

Much prejudice is *caught* rather than directly *taught.* The whole atmosphere of child-training may be subtly decisive. Thus a child who is sometimes rejected, sometimes loved, who is punished harshly or capriciously, who does not know unconditional trust at home—such a child grows up "on guard." Unable to depend emotionally upon his parents, he enters school with a suspicious, fearful attitude toward people in general, and especially toward those who have an unfamiliar appearance and (to him) odd and threatening ways of talking, or worshiping, or behaving. Although we cannot make the assertion with finality, it seems likely that the major factor in predisposing a child toward a lifetime of prejudice is this rejective, neglectful, harsh, or inconsistent style of preschool training.[3]

---

[3]Dale B. Harrison, G. Gough, and William E. Martin, "Children's Ethnic Attitudes: II, Relationship to Parental Beliefs Concerning Child Training," *Child Development* 21, 1950,

As the child grows older additional factors may create or intensify prejudice. Around the age of eight or ten he goes through a period of fierce identification with his family. Whatever the family is, is "right" (whether it be Catholic, Jewish, white, black, Scotch-Irish, or Hottentot). By comparison all other groups are of doubtful status and merit. At this point the church and the school have the opportunity of teaching the child the concept of reciprocity and basic equality among human groups. The lesson is difficult to learn, because as adolescence approaches, the child seeks personal security and a new identity in his peer groups, which usually are of his own color, class, and neighborhood. If adolescents are friendly with out-groups they risk a diffusion and loss of their own precarious identity.[4] To build up a sense of personal importance they often persecute out-groups. *West Side Story* is an epic of this gang-age phenomenon.

Occasionally prejudice is formed on the basis of a single emotional trauma. A certain youngster who was chased by a Chinese laundryman felt ever after a terror of Orientals (a clear case of overgeneralizing from a single experience). Such traumatic origins are relatively rare. But we see that throughout childhood and youth there are many opportunities for irreversible and unfavorable belief-systems to become set.

The Psychodynamics of Prejudice

However prejudice is learned it takes root in a personality because it meets certain basic needs or cravings. It works for the person and may be a pivotal factor in the economy of his life.

All mortals require simplified rubrics to live by. We think of school teachers, of physicians, of blind people, of Russians, or of ex-convicts in homogeneous groups. All Orientals we perceive as mysterious (though many are not); we regard all weeds as inedible (though some are nutritious). Thus our thinking seems to be guided by a law of least effort. If I reject all foreigners (including the United Nations), I simplify my existence by ruling out the troublesome issues of international relations. If I say "all blacks are ignorant," I dispose of twenty million more people. If I add "Catholics know only what the priest tells them," I eliminate forty million more. With the conviction that Jews will cheat me, I discard another five million. Labor unions I exclude by calling them "pirates." Intellectuals are simply "long-haired communists." And so it goes. My life is simplified when I invoke these stereotyped rejections. With the aid of aversive categories I avoid the painful task of dealing with individuals as individuals.

---

pp. 169–81. Also, David P. Ausubel, *Ego Development and the Personality Disorders* (New York: Grune and Stratton, 1962).

[4]Bettelheim and Janowitz, *Social Change and Prejudice* (New York: The Free Press of Glencoe, 1964), p. 57.

Prejudice is thus an economical mode of thought, and is widely embraced for this very reason.

A major source of prejudice is the sense that one's security and status are threatened. One fears for one's job, for one's home, especially for one's prestige. American culture is enormously competitive, and so we find ourselves keenly fearful of our rivals. Downwardly mobile people on the whole are more prejudiced than people who hold a stable social position.[5] Now in cold logic it is very seldom that any minority group actually threatens the well-being, safety, or equity of our lives, but we nonetheless perceive them as the cause of our distress. Racist agitators play upon this anxiety. The easiest idea to sell anyone is that he is better than someone else, and that this someone else must be kept "in his place" so that we may enjoy our own position of superiority.

When things go wrong we find it convenient to blame others. Since biblical times it has been known that a scapegoat relieves our own sense of failure or guilt. We say it is the Jews who are keeping us from a promotion or the migration of blacks that takes away available jobs. Or we may vaguely blame our failures or discomforts upon "the politicians." Few people take blame upon themselves. They are quick to adopt an extrapunitive ego-defense.

A peculiarly deep complex is found in accusations that out-groups (especially Negroes) are immoral. Simply because they are "forbidden fruit," many white people find blacks sexually attractive; much miscegenation has been the result. Since looseness of morals is condemned, the white person may exonerate himself from his web of desire, fantasy, and guilt by projecting it upon the black male, who, he says, is sexually aggressive—at heart a rapist. In Germany, Hitler accused the Jews of all manner of sexual irregularities; in the United States it is the black who is the projection screen (the "living inkblot"[o]) for one's own frightening id-impulses.

To summarize these and other similar emotional needs, trends, and twists that enter into the psychodynamics of prejudice, psychologists have formulated the concept of "authoritarianism."[6] It says that a person who is basically insecure, anxious, sexually repressed, suffering from unresolved

---

[5]*Ibid.,* pp. 29–34.

[6]T. G. W. Adorno, E. Frenkel-Brunswick, D. J. Levinson, and R. N. Sanford, *The Authoritarian Personality* (New York: Harper & Brothers, 1952).

"living inkblot"   A reference to the Rorschach test, a psychological test based on a person's interpretation of a series of inkblots.

Oedipal conflicts with his own parents, given to projection—such a person will develop a rigid, conventional, hostile style of life. Ethnic prejudice fits into this character syndrome. This formulation has been widely studied and debated. Just how to define it in detail is a matter of dispute, but most scholars believe that it contains an important truth. People having this syndrome are "functional bigots" whose whole style of life is hostile, fearful, rejective of out-groups. Such people need prejudice and are ready to follow a demagogue who focuses all this latent hate upon some ethnic target.

Conformity

Although the authoritarian pattern clearly exists, we must not assume that it accounts for all prejudice. What we call "conformity prejudice" springs from the tendency of people to yield to local custom and to the legends and ideology of their own class.[7] If bigotry is in the air, they are bigots; if tolerance is customary, they are tolerant. Perhaps half of our population can be considered to be in this middle range. Since prejudice is to some degree prevalent, especially in the southern regions of the United States, this half of the population can be expected to go along with the existing biases.

What we have called the authoritarian syndrome accounts for about the same amount of prejudice in both northern and southern states, but there is much more conformity prejudice in the South.[8]

Victimization

Those who are victims of prejudice cannot be indifferent to their plight; they must constantly defend themselves from discomfort or insult. One study states that 50 percent of blacks say that when they are with a white person they expect him "to make a slip and say something wrong about Negroes."[9] Even when not expecting an insult, a minority group member must ordinarily plan his life within a racial or ethnic frame of reference.

Besides this chronic sensitization to the problem, additional psychological reactions to victimization may be noted; among them, withdrawal and apathy, slyness and cunning, clowning, rejection of one's own group—or quite the reverse, forming closer in-group ties, resignation, neuroticism,

---

[7]Gordon W. Allport, "Prejudice: Is It Societal or Personal?" *Journal of Social Issues,* 18, 1961, pp. 120–134.

[8]Thomas F. Pettigrew, "Regional Differences in Anti-Negro Prejudice," *Journal of Abnormal and Social Psychology,* 29, 1959, pp. 28–36.

[9]Robin M. Williams, Jr., *Strangers Next Door* (Englewood Cliffs: Prentice-Hall, Inc., 1964), p. 47.

sympathy with other minorities, and enhanced striving and militancy.[10] Of course not all members of a minority group will show all of these types of response.

Reducing Prejudice

Someone has said that it is easier to smash an atom than a prejudice. In the case of deep-dyed functional bigots this verdict may be true. And yet change in prejudice does occur, and has clearly happened since World War II in America. Prejudiced attitudes change when it makes sociological, economic, and personal sense to change them. Not all people are incurably blind to their own illogical and harmful ways of thinking. Education combats easy overgeneralizations, and as the educational level rises we find a reduction in stereotyped thinking.[11] Also we know that increased self-knowledge and personal insight reduce prejudice.[12] Education for mental health works in this direction. Furthermore, militant protests call attention to needed reforms and win the sympathy of potentially democratic citizens. Various measures of prejudice have been invented to help follow these trends, even the subtle factor of human-heartedness within the population.[13]

All progress toward the reduction of prejudice will be met by vociferous resistance from the functional bigots. And yet even when violence flares up the trend is unmistakable. Antidiscrimination laws, revised school curricula and effective desegregation, raising of educational levels, open discussion and enlightenment, nonviolent protests that focus attention and win sympathy—all these, and other forces, are working in a single direction. Let the reader also keep in mind the fact that the problem we are here discussing has had in the past quarter-century more attention and intelligent study among people of goodwill than in all the millennia of human history previously. Recent research on ethnic prejudice has been remarkably rich and informative,[14] and shows clearly that the forces of social science are strongly arrayed in the battle against bigotry.

---

[10]Gordon W. Allport, *The Nature of Prejudice* (New York: Doubleday Anchor Books, 1958), Chapter 9.

[11]Charles H. Stember, *Education and Attitude Change* (New York: Institute of Human Relations Press, 1961). Also, Henry G. Stetler, *Attitudes toward Racial Integration in Connecticut* (Hartford: Commission on Civil Rights, 1961).

[12]Richard M. Jones, *An Application of Psychoanalysis to Education* (Springfield, Ill.: Charles C. Thomas, 1960).

[13]Howard Schuman and John Harding, "Sympathetic Identification with the Underdog," *Public Opinion Quarterly*, 27, 1963, pp. 230–41.

[14]Bernard Berelson and Gary A. Steiner, *Human Behavior: An Inventory of Scientific Findings* (New York: Harcourt, Brace & World, 1964).

On Conscience and Moral Responsibility

Many a commentator on recent events has observed that conscience in our culture seems to be losing its traditional strength. The *Random House Dictionary* defines conscience as "the sense of what is right or wrong in one's conduct or motives, impelling one toward right action." In the opening essay of this section, Meg Greenfield notices that we no longer use the word "wrong" but instead use alternative terms that show how dulled our sense of wrong-doing has become, and how habitually we rationalize and excuse it. If she and the others are right, then conscience, both personal and public, has become an issue newly worth examining.

The ending of Dick Gregory's "Shame" touches the issue of personal conscience in an everyday form: "I waited too long to help another man." The pieces following study the individual's conscience—supported by a sense of charity or sympathy or justice—as it comes up against a variety of contrary forces. In some cases conscience wins, and in some it does not. Albert Camus's story "The Guest" ambiguously explores subtle issues of culture, nationality, and humaneness, and also the irony of misunderstood motives. George Orwell's "Shooting an Elephant" exposes with scrupulous honesty the defeat of his conscience by the fear of being laughed at. Septima Clark's "Judge Waring" celebrates understatedly the triumph of conscience over the pressure of loyalty to race and caste, and over fear of reprisal. Using as an example his famous, fictional British spy George Smiley, the novelist John le Carré raises the issue of conscience versus patriotic conformity. His view is that the renunciation of individual conscience in favor of institutional loyalties is "the greatest threat to mankind."

The section ends with C. S. Lewis's elegant defining of one of the subtlest sources of the muffling of conscience: the pleasure of being an insider. His essay leads particularly well to this book's closely related following section on ethics in business and government.

Why Nothing Is 'Wrong' Anymore

Meg Greenfield

Meg Greenfield (born 1930) grew up in Seattle, was educated at Smith College (B.A. 1952), and then spent several years in Europe, first as a Fulbright scholar at Cambridge, then in Rome. She returned in time to work for Adlai Stevenson's 1956 presidential campaign, and then for The Reporter, *first as researcher, later as a staff writer, and finally as its Washington editor. When the magazine stopped publication in 1968, she immediately became an editorial writer for the* Washington Post; *she has been editorial page editor since 1979, and a regular columnist for* Newsweek *since 1974. In 1978 she won the Pulitzer Prize for editorial writing.*

As a Washington journalist during the days of the Watergate scandal, she frequently reflected on the absence or presence of public morality. She said in a 1974 Vogue *interview, "I was taught that you could only be free and have dignity and self-respect if you were responsible for what you did. . . . You couldn't get away with anything on the grounds that all the other kids did it, or because you were only eight years old and blameless." In the piece below, from the July 28, 1986, issue of* Newsweek, *she takes up a similar theme.*

There has been an awful lot of talk about sin, crime and plain old antisocial behavior this summer—drugs and pornography at home, terror and brutality abroad. Maybe it's just the heat; or maybe these categories of conduct (sin, crime, etc.) are really on the rise. What strikes me is our curiously deficient, not to say defective, way of talking about them. We don't seem to have a word anymore for "wrong" in the moral sense, as in, for example, "theft is wrong."

Let me quickly qualify. There is surely no shortage of people condemning other people on such grounds, especially their political opponents or characters they just don't care for. Name-calling is still very much in vogue. But where the concept of wrong is really important—as a guide to one's own behavior or that of one's own side in some dispute—it is missing; and this is as true of those on the religious right who are going around pronouncing great masses of us sinners as it is of their principal antagonists, those on the secular left who can forgive or "understand" just about anything so long as it has not been perpetrated by a right-winger.

There is a fairly awesome literature that attempts to explain how we have changed as a people with the advent of psychiatry, the weakening of religious institutions and so forth, but you don't need to address these matters to take note of a simple fact. As a guide and a standard to live by, you don't hear so much about "right and wrong" these days. The very notion is considered politically, not to say personally, embarrassing, since it has such a repressive, Neanderthal ring to it. So we have developed a broad range of alternatives to "right and wrong." I'll name a few.

Right and stupid: This is the one you use when your candidate gets caught stealing, or, for that matter, when anyone on your side does something reprehensible. "It was really so dumb of him"—head must shake here—"I just can't understand it." Bad is dumb, breathtakingly dumb and therefore unfathomable; so, conveniently enough, the effort to fathom it might just as well be called off. This one had a big play during Watergate and has had mini-revivals ever since whenever congressmen and senators investigating administration crimes turn out to be guilty of something similar themselves.

Right and not necessarily unconstitutional: I don't know at quite what point along the way we came to this one, the avoidance of admitting that something is wrong by pointing out that it is not specifically or even inferentially prohibited by the Constitution or, for that matter, mentioned by name in the criminal code or the Ten Commandments. The various parties that prevail in civil-liberty and civil-rights disputes before the Supreme Court have gotten quite good at making this spurious connection: it is legally permissible, therefore it is morally acceptable, possibly even good. But both as individuals and as a society we do things every day that we know to be wrong even though they may not fall within the class of legally punishable acts or tickets to eternal damnation.

Right and sick: Crime or lesser wrongdoing defined as physical and/or psychological disorder—this one has been around for ages now and as long ago as 1957 was made the butt of a great joke in the "Gee Officer Krupke!" song in "West Side Story." Still, I think no one could have foreseen the degree to which an originally reasonable and humane assumption (that some of what once was regarded as wrongdoing is committed by people acting out of ailment rather than moral choice) would be seized upon and exploited to exonerate every kind of misfeasance. This route is a particular favorite of caught-out officeholders who, when there is at last no other recourse, hold a press conference, announce that they are "sick" in some wise and throw themselves and their generally stunned families on our mercy. At which point it becomes gross to pick on them; instead we are exhorted to admire them for their "courage."

Right and only to be expected: You could call this the tit-for-tat school; it is related to the argument that holds moral wrongdoing to be evidence of sickness, but it is much more pervasive and insidious these days. In fact it is probably the most popular dodge, being used to justify, or at least avoid owning up to, every kind of lapse: the other guy, or sometimes just plain circumstance, "asked for it." For instance, I think most of us could agree that setting fire to live people, no matter what their political offense, is—dare I say it?—wrong. Yet if it is done by those for whom we have sympathy in a conflict, there is a tendency to extenuate or disbelieve it, receiving it less as evidence of wrongdoing on our side than as evidence of the severity of the provocation or as enemy-supplied disinformation. Thus the hesitation of many in the antiapartheid movement to confront the brutality of so-called "necklacing," and thus the immediate leap of Sen. Jesse Helms to the defense of the Chilean government after the horrifying incineration of protesters there.

Right and complex: This one hardly takes a moment to describe; you know it well. "Complex" is the new "controversial," a word used as "controversial" was for so long to flag trouble of some unspecified, dismaying sort that the speaker doesn't want to have to step up to. "Well, you know, it's very complex . . ." I still can't get this one out of my own vocabulary.

In addition to these various sophistries, we also have created a rash of "ethics committees" in our government, of course, whose function seems to be to dither around writing rules that allow people who have clearly done wrong—and should have known it and probably did—to get away because the rules don't cover their offense (see Right and not necessarily unconstitutional). But we don't need any more committees or artful dodges for that matter. As I listen to the moral arguments swirling about us this summer I become ever more persuaded that our real problem is this: the "still, small voice" of conscience has become far too small—and utterly still.

Shame

Dick Gregory

Dick Gregory has lived many roles—among them slum kid, athlete, comedian, and political activist. Born in St. Louis in 1932, he set records for running the mile and half-mile in high school and again at Southern Illinois University, where he was named outstanding athlete in 1953. After two years in the army, he began working night clubs around Chicago and by 1959 was the regular master of ceremonies at a show club. He went on to television, records, and books, shaping his comedy act in sympathy with the civil rights movement of the early sixties and then with the antiwar movement. After many arrests in political confrontations, he ran for President of the United States as the candidate of the Peace and Freedom party in 1968. Fasting, and its accompanying publicity, became his favorite form of political protest. In 1978 he received the Ebony-Topaz Heritage and Freedom Award.

His books include From the Back of the Bus *(1962),* No More Lies: The Myth and Reality of American History *(1971),* Dick Gregory's Political Primer *(1972), an autobiography,* Nigger, *written with Robert Lipsyte (1964), and* Up from Nigger *(1976). The following selection comes from a chapter in* Nigger *entitled "Not Poor, Just Broke."*

I never learned hate at home, or shame. I had to go to school for that. I was about seven years old when I got my first big lesson. I was in love with a little girl named Helene Tucker, a light-complected little girl with pigtails and nice manners. She was always clean and she was smart in school. I think I went to school then mostly to look at her. I brushed my hair and even got me a little old handkerchief. It was a lady's handkerchief, but I didn't want Helene to see me wipe my nose on my hand. The pipes were frozen again, there was no water in the house, but I washed my socks and shirt every night. I'd get a pot, and go over to Mister Ben's grocery store, and stick my pot down into his soda machine. Scoop out some chopped ice. By evening the ice melted to water for washing. I got sick a lot that winter because the fire would go out at night before the clothes were dry. In the morning I'd put them on, wet or dry, because they were the only clothes I had.

Everybody's got a Helene Tucker, a symbol of everything you want. I loved her for her goodness, her cleanness, her popularity. She'd walk down my street and my brothers and sisters would yell. "Here comes Helene," and I'd rub my tennis sneakers on the back of my pants and wish my hair wasn't so nappy and the white folks' shirt fit me better. I'd run out on the street. If I knew my place and didn't come too close, she'd wink at me and say hello. That was a good feeling. Sometimes I'd follow her all the way home, and shovel the snow off her walk and try to make friends with her Momma and her aunts. I'd drop money on her stoop late at night on my way back from shining shoes in the taverns. And she had a Daddy, and he had a good job. He was a paper hanger.

I guess I would have gotten over Helene by summertime, but something happened in that classroom that made her face hang in front of me for the next twenty-two years. When I played the drums in high school it was for Helene and when I broke track records in college it was for Helene and when I started standing behind microphones and heard applause I wished Helene could hear it, too. It wasn't until I was twenty-nine years old and married and making money that I finally got her out of my system. Helene was sitting in that classroom when I learned to be ashamed of myself.

It was on a Thursday. I was sitting in the back of the room, in a seat with a chalk circle drawn around it. The idiot's seat, the troublemaker's seat.

The teacher thought I was stupid. Couldn't spell, couldn't read, couldn't do arithmetic. Just stupid. Teachers were never interested in finding out that you couldn't concentrate because you were so hungry, because you hadn't had any breakfast. All you could think about was noontime, would it ever come? Maybe you could sneak into the cloakroom and steal a bite of some kid's lunch out of a coat pocket. A bite of something. Paste. You can't really make a meal of paste, or put it on bread for a sandwich, but sometimes I'd scoop a few spoonfuls out of the paste jar in the back of the room. Pregnant people get strange tastes. I was pregnant with poverty. Pregnant with dirt and pregnant with smells that made people turn away, pregnant with cold and pregnant with shoes that were never bought for me, pregnant with five other people in my bed and no Daddy in the next room, and pregnant with hunger. Paste doesn't taste too bad when you're hungry.

The teacher thought I was a troublemaker. All she saw from the front of the room was a little black boy who squirmed in his idiot's seat and made noises and poked the kids around him. I guess she couldn't see a kid who made noises because he wanted someone to know he was there.

It was on a Thursday, the day before the Negro payday. The eagle always flew on Friday. The teacher was asking each student how much his father would give to the Community Chest. On Friday night, each kid would get the money from his father, and on Monday he would bring it to the school. I decided I was going to buy me a Daddy right then. I had money in my pocket from shining shoes and selling papers, and whatever Helene Tucker pledged for her Daddy I was going to top it. And I'd hand the money right in. I wasn't going to wait until Monday to buy me a Daddy.

I was shaking, scared to death. The teacher opened her book and started calling out names alphabetically.

"Helene Tucker?"

"My Daddy said he'd give two dollars and fifty cents."

"That's very nice, Helene. Very, very nice indeed."

That made me feel pretty good. It wouldn't take too much to top that. I had almost three dollars in dimes and quarters in my pocket. I stuck my hand in my pocket and held onto the money, waiting for her to call my name. But the teacher closed her book after she called everybody else in the class.

I stood up and raised my hand.

"What is it now?"

"You forgot me."

She turned toward the blackboard. "I don't have time to be playing with you, Richard."

"My Daddy said he'd . . ."

"Sit down, Richard, you're disturbing the class."

"My Daddy said he'd give . . . fifteen dollars."

She turned around and looked mad. "We are collecting this money for you and your kind, Richard Gregory. If your Daddy can give fifteen dollars you have no business being on relief."

"I got it right now, I got it right now, my Daddy gave it to me to turn in today, my Daddy said . . ."

"And furthermore," she said, looking right at me, her nostrils getting big and her lips getting thin and her eyes opening wide, "we know you don't have a Daddy."

Helene Tucker turned around, her eyes full of tears. She felt sorry for me. Then I couldn't see her too well because I was crying, too.

"Sit down, Richard."

And I always thought the teacher kind of liked me. She always picked me to wash the blackboard on Friday, after school. That was a big thrill, it made me feel important. If I didn't wash it, come Monday the school might not function right.

"Where are you going, Richard?"

I walked out of school that day, and for a long time I didn't go back very often. There was shame there.

Now there was shame everywhere. It seemed like the whole world had been inside that classroom, everyone had heard what the teacher had said, everyone had turned around and felt sorry for me. There was shame in going to the Worthy Boys Annual Christmas Dinner for you and your kind, because everybody knew what a worthy boy was. Why couldn't they just call it the Boys Annual Dinner, why'd they have to give it a name? There was shame in wearing the brown and orange and white plaid mackinaw the welfare gave to 3,000 boys. Why'd it have to be the same for everybody so when you walked down the street the people could see you were on relief? It was a nice warm mackinaw and it had a hood, and my Momma beat me and called me a little rat when she found out I stuffed it in the bottom of a pail full of garbage way over on Cottage Street. There was shame in running over to Mister Ben's at the end of the day and asking for his rotten peaches, there was shame in asking Mrs. Simmons for a spoonful of sugar, there was shame in running out to meet the relief truck. I hated that truck, full of food for you and your kind. I ran into the house and hid when it came. And then I started to sneak through alleys, to take the long way home so the people going into White's Eat Shop wouldn't see me. Yeah, the whole world heard the teacher that day, we all know you don't have a Daddy.

It lasted for a while, this kind of numbness. I spent a lot of time feeling sorry for myself. And then one day I met this wino in a restaurant. I'd been out hustling all day, shining shoes, selling newspapers, and I had goo-gobs of money in my pocket. Bought me a bowl of chili for fifteen cents, and a cheeseburger for fifteen cents, and a Pepsi for five cents, and a piece of chocolate cake for ten cents. That was a good meal. I was eating when this old wino came in. I love winos because they never hurt anyone but themselves.

The old wino sat down at the counter and ordered twenty-six cents worth of food. He ate it like he really enjoyed it. When the owner, Mister Williams, asked him to pay the check, the old wino didn't lie or go through his pocket like he suddenly found a hole.

He just said: "Don't have no money."

The owner yelled: "Why in hell you come in here and eat my food if you don't have no money? That food cost me money."

Mister Williams jumped over the counter and knocked the wino off his stool and beat him over the head with a pop bottle. Then he stepped back and watched the wino bleed. Then he kicked him. And he kicked him again.

I looked at the wino with blood all over his face and I went over. "Leave him alone, Mister Williams. I'll pay the twenty-six cents."

The wino got up, slowly, pulling himself up to the stool, then up to the counter, holding on for a minute until his legs stopped shaking so bad. He looked at me with pure hate. "Keep your twenty-six cents. You don't have to pay, not now. I just finished paying for it."

He started to walk out, and as he passed me, he reached down and touched my shoulder. "Thanks, sonny, but it's too late now. Why didn't you pay it before?"

I was pretty sick about that. I waited too long to help another man.

The Guest

Albert Camus

Albert Camus, regarded by many of his contemporaries as the conscience of his age, was killed in an automobile accident in France at the age of forty-six. Born in Algeria in 1913, he spent his childhood in extreme poverty. The Wrong Side and the Right Side *(1937) is a moving record of those years. While he was working his way through the University of Algeria, he became interested in the theater, and for a few years he managed, acted, and wrote for a theatrical company. He then worked as a journalist, first for* Alger Républicain, *later in France for* Paris-Soir. *In 1942 he joined the*

French Resistance movement; he edited and wrote many articles—then unsigned—for the underground newspaper Combat. *After the liberation of France from the Nazis, he began to devote full time to his writing.*

Camus's reputation was soon solidly established. His fame became international, and in 1957 he was awarded the Nobel Prize for literature. The Nobel Committee cited his "clearsighted earnestness," which "illuminates the problem of the human conscience of our time." Some of his most influential expository writing is found in The Myth of Sisyphus *(1942),* The Rebel *(1951), and* Resistance, Rebellion, and Death *(1960). His philosophical ideas are also expressed in his three novels,* The Stranger *(1942),* The Plague *(1947), and* The Fall *(1956), and in* Exile and the Kingdom *(1957), a book of short stories. "The Guest," translated by Justin O'Brien, is taken from this book.*

The schoolmaster was watching the two men climb toward him. One was on horseback, the other on foot. They had not yet tackled the abrupt rise leading to the schoolhouse built on the hillside. They were toiling onward, making slow progress in the snow, among the stones, on the vast expanse of the high, deserted plateau. From time to time the horse stumbled. Without hearing anything yet, he could see the breath issuing from the horse's nostrils. One of the men, at least, knew the region. They were following the trail although it had disappeared days ago under a layer of dirty white snow. The schoolmaster calculated that it would take them half an hour to get onto the hill. It was cold; he went back into the school to get a sweater.

He crossed the empty, frigid classroom. On the blackboard the four rivers of France, drawn with four different colored chalks, had been flowing toward their estuaries for the past three days. Snow had suddenly fallen in mid-October after eight months of drought without the transition of rain, and the twenty pupils, more or less, who lived in the villages scattered over the plateau had stopped coming. With fair weather they would return. Daru now heated only the single room that was his lodging, adjoining the classroom and giving also onto the plateau to the east. Like the class windows, his window looked to the south too. On that side the school was a few kilometers from the point where the plateau began to slope toward the south. In clear weather could be seen the purple mass of the mountain range where the gap opened onto the desert.

Somewhat warmed, Daru returned to the window from which he had first seen the two men. They were no longer visible. Hence they must have tackled the rise. The sky was not so dark, for the snow had stopped falling during the night. The morning had opened with a dirty light which had scarcely become brighter as the ceiling of clouds lifted. At two in the afternoon it seemed as if the day were merely beginning. But still this was better than those three days when the thick snow was falling amidst unbroken darkness with little gusts of wind that rattled the double door of the classroom. Then Daru had spent long hours in his room, leaving it only to go to the shed and feed the chickens or get some coal. Fortunately the delivery truck from Tadjid, the nearest village to the north, had brought his supplies two days before the blizzard. It would return in forty-eight hours.

Besides, he had enough to resist a siege, for the little room was cluttered with bags of wheat that the administration left as a stock to distribute to those of his pupils whose families had suffered from the drought. Actually they had all been victims because they were all poor. Every day Daru would distribute a ration to the children. They had missed it, he knew, during these bad days. Possibly one of the fathers or big brothers would come this afternoon and he could supply them with grain. It was just a matter of carrying them over to the next harvest. Now shiploads of wheat were arriving from France and the worst was over. But it would be hard to forget that poverty, that army of ragged ghosts wandering in the sunlight, the plateaus burned to a cinder month after month, the earth shriveled up little by little, literally scorched, every stone bursting into dust under one's foot. The sheep had died then by thousands and even a few men, here and there, sometimes without anyone's knowing.

In contrast with such poverty, he who lived almost like a monk in his remote schoolhouse, nonetheless satisfied with the little he had and with the rough life, had felt like a lord with his whitewashed walls, his narrow couch, his unpainted shelves, his well, and his weekly provision of water and food. And suddenly this snow, without warning, without the foretaste of rain. This is the way the region was, cruel to live in, even without men—who didn't help matters either. But Daru had been born here. Everywhere else, he felt exiled.

He stepped out onto the terrace in front of the schoolhouse. The two men were now halfway up the slope. He recognized the horseman as Balducci, the old gendarme he had known for a long time. Balducci was holding on the end of a rope an Arab who was walking behind him with hands bound and head lowered. The gendarme waved a greeting to which Daru did not reply, lost as he was in contemplation of the Arab dressed in a faded blue jellaba, his feet in sandals but covered with socks of heavy raw wool, his head surmounted by a narrow, short *chèche.*° They were approaching. Balducci was holding back his horse in order not to hurt the Arab, and the group was advancing slowly.

Within earshot, Balducci shouted: "One hour to do the three kilometers from El Ameur!" Daru did not answer. Short and square in his thick sweater, he watched them climb. Not once had the Arab raised his head. "Hello," said Daru when they got up onto the terrace. "Come in and warm up." Balducci painfully got down from his horse without letting go the

---

chèche   tarboosh, a felt cap (French).

rope. From under his bristling mustache he smiled at the schoolmaster. His little dark eyes, deep-set under a tanned forehead, and his mouth surrounded with wrinkles made him look attentive and studious. Daru took the bridle, led the horse to the shed, and came back to the two men, who were now waiting for him in the school. He led them into his room. "I am going to heat up the classroom," he said. "We'll be more comfortable there." When he entered the room again, Balducci was on the couch. He had undone the rope tying him to the Arab, who had squatted near the stove. His hands still bound, the *chèche* pushed back on his head, he was looking toward the window. At first Daru noticed only his huge lips, fat, smooth, almost Negroid; yet his nose was straight, his eyes were dark and full of fever. The *chèche* revealed an obstinate forehead and, under the weathered skin now rather discolored by the cold, the whole face had a restless and rebellious look that struck Daru when the Arab, turning his face toward him, looked him straight in the eyes. "Go into the other room," said the schoolmaster, "and I'll make you some mint tea." "Thanks," Balducci said. "What a chore! How I long for retirement." And addressing his prisoner in Arabic: "Come on, you." The Arab got up and, slowly, holding his bound wrists in front of him, went into the classroom.

With the tea, Daru brought a chair. But Balducci was already enthroned on the nearest pupil's desk and the Arab had squatted against the teacher's platform facing the stove, which stood between the desk and the window. When he held out the glass of tea to the prisoner, Daru hesitated at the sight of his bound hands. "He might perhaps be untied." "Sure," said Balducci. "That was for the trip." He started to get to his feet. But Daru, setting the glass on the floor, had knelt beside the Arab. Without saying anything, the Arab watched him with his feverish eyes. Once his hands were free, he rubbed his swollen wrists against each other, took the glass of tea, and sucked up the burning liquid in swift little sips.

"Good," said Daru. "And where are you headed?"

Balducci withdrew his mustache from the tea. "Here, son."

"Odd pupils! And you're spending the night?"

"No. I'm going back to El Ameur. And you will deliver this fellow to Tinguit. He is expected at police headquarters."

Balducci was looking at Daru with a friendly little smile.

"What's this story?" asked the schoolmaster. "Are you pulling my leg?"

"No, son. Those are the orders."

"The orders? I'm not . . ." Daru hesitated, not wanting to hurt the old Corsican. "I mean, that's not my job."

"What! What's the meaning of that? In wartime people do all kinds of jobs."

"Then I'll wait for the declaration of war!"

Balducci nodded.

"O.K. But the orders exist and they concern you too. Things are brewing, it appears. There is talk of a forthcoming revolt. We are mobilized, in a way."

Daru still had his obstinate look.

"Listen, son," Balducci said. "I like you and you must understand. There's only a dozen of us at El Ameur to patrol throughout the whole territory of a small department and I must get back in a hurry. I was told to hand this guy over to you and return without delay. He couldn't be kept there. His village was beginning to stir; they wanted to take him back. You must take him to Tinguit tomorrow before the day is over. Twenty kilometers shouldn't faze a husky fellow like you. After that, all will be over. You'll come back to your pupils and your comfortable life."

Behind the wall the horse could be heard snorting and pawing the earth. Daru was looking out the window. Decidedly, the weather was clearing and the light was increasing over the snowy plateau. When all the snow was melted, the sun would take over again and once more would burn the fields of stone. For days, still, the unchanging sky would shed its dry light on the solitary expanse where nothing had any connection with man.

"After all," he said, turning around toward Balducci, "what did he do?" And, before the gendarme had opened his mouth, he asked: "Does he speak French?"

"No, not a word. We had been looking for him for a month, but they were hiding him. He killed his cousin."

"Is he against us?"

"I don't think so. But you can never be sure."

"Why did he kill?"

"A family squabble, I think. One owed the other grain, it seems. It's not at all clear. In short, he killed his cousin with a billhook. You know, like a sheep, *kreezk!*"

Balducci made the gesture of drawing a blade across his throat and the Arab, his attention attracted, watched him with a sort of anxiety. Daru felt a sudden wrath against the man, against all men with their rotten spite, their tireless hates, their blood lust.

But the kettle was singing on the stove. He served Balducci more tea, hesitated, then served the Arab again, who, a second time, drank avidly. His raised arms made the jellaba fall open and the schoolmaster saw his thin, muscular chest.

"Thanks, kid," Balducci said. "And now, I'm off."

He got up and went toward the Arab, taking a small rope from his pocket.

"What are you doing?" Daru asked dryly.

Balducci, disconcerted, showed him the rope.

"Don't bother."

The old gendarme hesitated. "It's up to you. Of course, you are armed?"

"I have my shotgun."

"Where?"

"In the trunk."

"You ought to have it near your bed."

"Why? I have nothing to fear."

"You're crazy, son. If there's an uprising, no one is safe, we're all in the same boat."

"I'll defend myself. I'll have time to see them coming."

Balducci began to laugh, then suddenly the mustache covered the white teeth.

"You'll have time? O.K. That's just what I was saying. You have always been a little cracked. That's why I like you, my son was like that."

At the same time he took out his revolver and put it on the desk.

"Keep it; I don't need two weapons from here to El Ameur."

The revolver shone against the black paint of the table. When the gendarme turned toward him, the schoolmaster caught the smell of leather and horseflesh.

"Listen, Balducci," Daru said suddenly, "every bit of this disgusts me, and first of all your fellow here. But I won't hand him over. Fight, yes, if I have to. But not that."

The old gendarme stood in front of him and looked at him severely.

"You're being a fool," he said slowly. "I don't like it either. You don't get used to putting a rope on a man even after years of it, and you're even ashamed—yes, ashamed. But you can't let them have their way."

"I won't hand him over," Daru said again.

"It's an order, son, and I repeat it."

"That's right. Repeat to them what I've said to you: I won't hand him over."

Balducci made a visible effort to reflect. He looked at the Arab and at Daru. At last he decided.

"No, I won't tell them anything. If you want to drop us, go ahead; I'll not denounce you. I have an order to deliver the prisoner and I'm doing so. And now you'll just sign this paper for me."

"There's no need. I'll not deny that you left him with me."

"Don't be mean with me. I know you'll tell the truth. You're from hereabouts and you are a man. But you must sign, that's the rule."

Daru opened his drawer, took out a little square bottle of purple ink, the red wooden penholder with the "sergeant-major" pen he used for making models of penmanship, and signed. The gendarme carefully folded the paper and put it into his wallet. Then he moved toward the door.

"I'll see you off," Daru said.

"No," said Balducci. "There's no use being polite. You insulted me."

He looked at the Arab, motionless in the same spot, sniffed peevishly, and turned away toward the door. "Good-by, son," he said. The door shut behind him. Balducci appeared suddenly outside the window and then disappeared. His footsteps were muffled by the snow. The horse stirred on the other side of the wall and several chickens fluttered in fright. A moment later Balducci reappeared outside the window leading the horse by the bridle. He walked toward the little rise without turning around and disappeared from sight with the horse following him. A big stone could be heard bouncing down. Daru walked back toward the prisoner, who, without stirring, never took his eyes off him. "Wait," the schoolmaster said in Arabic and went toward the bedroom. As he was going through the door, he had a second thought, went to the desk, took the revolver, and stuck it in his pocket. Then, without looking back, he went into his room.

For some time he lay on his couch watching the sky gradually close over, listening to the silence. It was this silence that had seemed painful to him during the first days here, after the war. He had requested a post in the little town at the base of the foothills separating the upper plateaus from the desert. There, rocky walls, green and black to the north, pink and lavender to the south, marked the frontier of eternal summer. He had been named to a post farther north, on the plateau itself. In the beginning, the solitude and the silence had been hard for him on these wastelands peopled only by stones. Occasionally, furrows suggested cultivation, but they had been dug to uncover a certain kind of stone good for building. The only plowing here was to harvest rocks. Elsewhere a thin layer of soil accumulated in the hollows would be scraped out to enrich paltry village gardens. This is the way it was: bare rock covered three quarters of the region. Towns sprang up, flourished, then disappeared; men came by, loved one another or fought bitterly, then died. No one in this desert, neither he nor his guest, mattered. And yet, outside this desert neither of them, Daru knew, could have really lived.

When he got up, no noise came from the classroom. He was amazed at the unmixed joy he derived from the mere thought that the Arab might have fled and that he would be alone with no decision to make. But the prisoner was there. He had merely stretched out between the stove and the desk. With eyes open, he was staring at the ceiling. In that position, his thick lips were particularly noticeable, giving him a pouting look. "Come," said Daru. The Arab got up and followed him. In the bedroom, the schoolmaster pointed to a chair near the table under the window. The Arab sat down without taking his eyes off Daru.

"Are you hungry?"

"Yes," the prisoner said.

Daru set the table for two. He took flour and oil, shaped a cake in a frying-pan, and lighted the little stove that functioned on bottled gas. While the cake was cooking, he went out to the shed to get cheese, eggs, dates, and condensed milk. When the cake was done he set it on the window sill to cool, heated some condensed milk diluted with water, and beat up the eggs into an omelette. In one of his motions he knocked against the revolver stuck in his right pocket. He set the bowl down, went into the classroom, and put the revolver in his desk drawer. When he came back to the room, night was falling. He put on the light and served the Arab. "Eat," he said. The Arab took a piece of the cake, lifted it eagerly to his mouth, and stopped short.

"And you?" he asked.

"After you. I'll eat too."

The thick lips opened slightly. The Arab hesitated, then bit into the cake determinedly.

The meal over, the Arab looked at the schoolmaster. "Are you the judge?"

"No, I'm simply keeping you until tomorrow."

"Why do you eat with me?"

"I'm hungry."

The Arab fell silent. Daru got up and went out. He brought back a folding bed from the shed, set it up between the table and the stove, perpendicular to his own bed. From a large suitcase which, upright in a corner, served as a shelf for papers, he took two blankets and arranged them on the camp bed. Then he stopped, felt useless, and sat down on his bed. There was nothing more to do or to get ready. He had to look at this man. He looked at him, therefore, trying to imagine his face bursting with rage. He couldn't do so. He could see nothing but the dark yet shining eyes and the animal mouth.

"Why did you kill him?" he asked in a voice whose hostile tone surprised him.

The Arab looked away.

"He ran away. I ran after him."

He raised his eyes to Daru again and they were full of a sort of woeful interrogation. "Now what will they do to me?"

"Are you afraid?"

He stiffened, turning his eyes away.

"Are you sorry?"

The Arab stared at him openmouthed. Obviously he did not understand. Daru's annoyance was growing. At the same time he felt awkward and self-conscious with his big body wedged between the two beds.

"Lie down there," he said impatiently. "That's your bed."

The Arab didn't move. He called to Daru:

"Tell me!"

The schoolmaster looked at him.

"Is the gendarme coming back tomorrow?"

"I don't know."

"Are you coming with us?"

"I don't know. Why?"

The prisoner got up and stretched out on top of the blankets, his feet toward the window. The light from the electric bulb shone straight into his eyes and he closed them at once.

"Why?" Daru repeated, standing beside the bed.

The Arab opened his eyes under the blinding light and looked at him, trying not to blink.

"Come with us," he said.

In the middle of the night, Daru was still not asleep. He had gone to bed after undressing completely; he generally slept naked. But when he suddenly realized that he had nothing on, he hesitated. He felt vulnerable and the temptation came to him to put his clothes back on. Then he shrugged his shoulders; after all, he wasn't a child and, if need be, he could break his adversary in two. From his bed he could observe him, lying on his back, still motionless with his eyes closed under the harsh light. When Daru turned out the light, the darkness seemed to coagulate all of a sudden. Little by little, the night came back to life in the window where the starless sky was stirring gently. The schoolmaster soon made out the body lying at his feet. The Arab still did not move, but his eyes seemed open. A faint wind was prowling around the schoolhouse. Perhaps it would drive away the clouds and the sun would reappear.

During the night the wind increased. The hens fluttered a little and then were silent. The Arab turned over on his side with his back to Daru, who thought he heard him moan. Then he listened for his guest's breathing, become heavier and more regular. He listened to that breath so close to him and mused without being able to go to sleep. In this room where he had been sleeping alone for a year, this presence bothered him. But it bothered him also by imposing on him a sort of brotherhood he knew well but refused to accept in the present circumstances. Men who share the same rooms, soldiers or prisoners, develop a strange alliance as if, having cast off their armor with their clothing, they fraternized every evening, over and above their differences, in the ancient community of dream and fatigue. But Daru shook himself; he didn't like such musings, and it was essential to sleep.

A little later, however, when the Arab stirred slightly, the schoolmaster was still not asleep. When the prisoner made a second move, he stiffened, on the alert. The Arab was lifting himself slowly on his arms with almost the motion of a sleepwalker. Seated upright in bed, he waited motionless without turning his head toward Daru, as if he were listening attentively. Daru did not stir; it had just occurred to him that the revolver was still in the drawer of his desk. It was better to act at once. Yet he continued to observe the prisoner, who, with the same slithery motion, put his feet on the ground, waited again, then began to stand up slowly. Daru was about to call out to him when the Arab began to walk, in a quite natural but extraordinarily silent way. He was heading toward the door at the end of the room that opened into the shed. He lifted the latch with precaution and went out, pushing the door behind him but without shutting it. Daru had not stirred. "He is running away," he merely thought. "Good riddance!" Yet he listened attentively. The hens were not fluttering; the guest must be on the plateau. A faint sound of water reached him, and he didn't know what it was until the Arab again stood framed in the doorway, closed the door carefully, and came back to bed without a sound. Then Daru turned his back on him and fell asleep. Still later he seemed, from the depths of his sleep, to hear furtive steps around the schoolhouse. "I'm dreaming! I'm dreaming!" he repeated to himself. And he went on sleeping.

When he awoke, the sky was clear; the loose window let in a cold, pure air. The Arab was asleep, hunched up under the blankets now, his mouth open, utterly relaxed. But when Daru shook him, he started dreadfully, staring at Daru with wild eyes as if he had never seen him and such a frightened expression that the schoolmaster stepped back. "Don't be afraid. It's me. You must eat." The Arab nodded his head and said yes. Calm had returned to his face, but his expression was vacant and listless.

The coffee was ready. They drank it seated together on the folding bed as they munched their pieces of the cake. Then Daru led the Arab under the shed and showed him the faucet where he washed. He went back into the room, folded the blankets and the bed, made his own bed and put the room in order. Then he went through the classroom and out onto the terrace. The sun was already rising in the blue sky; a soft, bright light was bathing the deserted plateau. On the ridge the snow was melting in spots. The stones were about to reappear. Crouched on the edge of the plateau, the schoolmaster looked at the deserted expanse. He thought of Balducci. He had hurt him, for he had sent him off in a way as if he didn't want to be associated with him. He could still hear the gendarme's farewell and, without knowing why, he felt strangely empty and vulnerable. At that moment, from the other side of the schoolhouse, the prisoner coughed. Daru listened to him almost despite himself and then, furious, threw a pebble that whistled through the air before sinking into the snow. That man's stupid crime revolted him, but to hand him over was contrary to honor. Merely thinking of it made him smart with humiliation. And he cursed at one and the same time his own people who had sent him this Arab and the Arab too who had dared to kill and not managed to get away. Daru got up, walked in a circle on the terrace, waited motionless, and then went back into the schoolhouse.

The Arab, leaning over the cement floor of the shed, was washing his teeth with two fingers. Daru looked at him and said: "Come." He went back into the room ahead of the prisoner. He slipped a hunting-jacket on over his sweater and put on walking-shoes. Standing, he waited until the Arab had put on his *chèche* and sandals. They went into the classroom and the schoolmaster pointed to the exit, saying: "Go ahead." The fellow didn't budge. "I'm coming," said Daru. The Arab went out. Daru went back into the room and made a package of pieces of rusk, dates, and sugar. In the classroom, before going out, he hesitated a second in front of his desk, then crossed the threshold and locked the door. "That's the way," he said. He started toward the east, followed by the prisoner. But, a short distance from the schoolhouse, he thought he heard a slight sound behind them. He retraced his steps and examined the surroundings of the house; there was no one there. The Arab watched him without seeming to understand. "Come on," said Daru.

They walked for an hour and rested beside a sharp peak of limestone. The snow was melting faster and faster and the sun was drinking up the puddles at once, rapidly cleaning the plateau, which gradually dried and vibrated like the air itself. When they resumed walking, the ground rang under their feet. From time to time a bird rent the space in front of them with a joyful cry. Daru breathed in deeply the fresh morning light. He felt a sort of rapture before the vast familiar expanse, now almost entirely yellow under its dome of blue sky. They walked an hour more, descending toward the south. They reached a level height made up of crumbly rocks. From there on, the plateau sloped down, eastward, toward a low plain where there were a few spindly trees and, to the south, toward outcroppings of rock that gave the landscape a chaotic look.

Daru surveyed the two directions. There was nothing but the sky on the horizon. Not a man could be seen. He turned toward the Arab, who was looking at him blankly. Daru held out the package to him. "Take it," he said. "There are dates, bread, and sugar. You can hold out for two days. Here are a thousand francs too." The Arab took the package and the money but kept his full hands at chest level as if he didn't know what to do with what was being given him. "Now look," the schoolmaster said as he pointed in the direction of the east, "there's the way to Tinguit. You have a two-hour walk. At Tinguit you'll find the administration and the police. They are expecting you." The Arab looked toward the east, still holding the package and the money against his chest. Daru took his elbow and turned him rather roughly toward the south. At the foot of the height on which they stood could be seen a faint path. "That's the trail across the plateau. In a day's walk from here you'll find pasturelands and the first nomads. They'll take you in and shelter you according to their law." The Arab had now turned toward Daru and a sort of panic was visible in his expression. "Listen," he said. Daru shook his head: "No, be quiet. Now I'm leaving you." He turned his back on him, took two long steps in the direction of the school, looked hesitantly at the motionless Arab, and started off again. For a few minutes he heard nothing but his own step resounding on the cold ground and did not turn his head. A moment later, however, he turned around. The Arab was still there on the edge of the hill, his arms hanging now, and he was looking at the schoolmaster. Daru felt something rise in his throat. But he swore with impatience, waved vaguely, and started off again. He had already gone some distance when he again stopped and looked. There was no longer anyone on the hill.

Daru hesitated. The sun was now rather high in the sky and was beginning to beat down on his head. The schoolmaster retraced his steps, at first somewhat uncertainly, then with decision. When he reached the little hill, he was bathed in sweat. He climbed it as fast as he could and stopped, out of breath, at the top. The rock-fields to the south stood out sharply against the blue sky, but on the plain to the east a steamy heat was already rising. And in that slight haze, Daru, with heavy heart, made out the Arab walking slowly on the road to prison.

A little later, standing before the window of the classroom, the schoolmaster was watching the clear light bathing the whole surface of the plateau, but he hardly saw it. Behind him on the blackboard, among the winding French rivers, sprawled the clumsily chalked-up words he had just read: "You handed over our brother. You will pay for this." Daru looked at the sky, the plateau, and, beyond, the invisible lands stretching all the way to the sea. In this vast landscape he had loved so much he was alone.

Shooting an Elephant

also a "Hanging" is an essay of his

George Orwell

"Shooting an Elephant," which is based on George Orwell's experiences in the Imperial Police in Burma, was written in the early 1930s and is the title essay in the collection Shooting an Elephant and Other Essays *(1950). The narrative reflects his conviction that ideas are derived from experience, and that experience is best conveyed in concrete and specific terms. He seems to be warning us of what can happen when what we say, do, think, and feel become disconnected from each other. For further biographical information on Orwell, see page 165.*

In Moulmein, in Lower Burma, I was hated by large numbers of people—the only time in my life that I have been important enough for this to happen to me. I was sub-divisional police officer of the town, and in an aimless, petty kind of way anti-European feeling was very bitter. No one had the guts to raise a riot, but if a European woman went through the bazaars alone somebody would probably spit betel juice over her dress. As a police officer I was an obvious target and was baited whenever it seemed safe to do so. When a nimble Burman tripped me up on the football field and the referee (another Burman) looked the other way, the crowd yelled with hideous laughter. This happened more than once. In the end the sneering yellow faces of young men that met me everywhere, the insults hooted after me when I was at a safe distance, got badly on my nerves. The young Buddhist priests were the worst of all. There were several thousands of them in the town and none of them seemed to have anything to do except stand on street corners and jeer at Europeans.

All this was perplexing and upsetting. For at that time I had already made up my mind that imperialism was an evil thing and the sooner I chucked up my job and got out of it the better. Theoretically—and secretly, of course—I was all for the Burmese and all against their oppressors, the British. As for the job I was doing, I hated it more bitterly than I can perhaps make clear. In a job like that you see the dirty work of Empire at close quarters. The wretched prisoners huddling in the stinking cages of the lock-ups, the grey, cowed faces of the long-term convicts, the scarred buttocks of the men who had been flogged with bamboos—all these oppressed me with an intolerable sense of guilt. But I could get nothing into perspective. I was young and ill-educated and I had had to think out my problems in the utter silence that is imposed on every Englishman in the East. I did not even know that the British Empire is dying, still less did I know that it is a great deal better than the younger empires that are going to supplant it. All I knew was that I was stuck between my hatred of the empire I served and my rage against the evil-spirited little beasts who tried to make my job impossible. With one part of my mind I thought of the British Raj as an unbreakable tyranny, as something clamped down, in *saecula saeculorum*,° upon the will of prostrate peoples; with another part I thought that the greatest joy in the world would be to drive a bayonet into a Buddhist priest's guts. Feelings like these are the normal by-products of imperialism; ask any Anglo-Indian official, if you can catch him off duty.

One day something happened which in a roundabout way was enlightening. It was a tiny incident in itself, but it gave me a better glimpse than I had had before of the real nature of imperialism—the real motives for which despotic governments act. Early one morning the sub-inspector at a police station the other end of town rang me up on the 'phone and said that an elephant was ravaging the bazaar. Would I please come and do something about it? I did not know what I could do, but I wanted to see what was happening and I got on to a pony and started out. I took my rifle, an old .44 Winchester and much too small to kill an elephant, but I thought the noise might be useful *in terrorem*. Various Burmans stopped me on the way and told me about the elephant's doings. It was not, of course, a wild elephant, but a tame one which had gone "must." It had been chained up, as tame elephants always are when their attack of "must" is due, but on the previous night it had broken its chain and escaped. Its mahout, the only person who could manage it when it was in that state, had set out in pursuit, but had taken the wrong direction and was now twelve hours' journey away, and in the morning the elephant

---

in *saecula saeculorum*   for ever and ever (Latin).

had suddenly reappeared in the town. The Burmese population had no weapons and were quite helpless against it. It had already destroyed somebody's bamboo hut, killed a cow and raided some fruit-stalls and devoured the stock; also it had met the municipal rubbish van and, when the driver jumped out and took to his heels, had turned the van over and inflicted violences upon it.

The Burmese sub-inspector and some Indian constables were waiting for me in the quarter where the elephant had been seen. It was a very poor quarter, a labyrinth of squalid bamboo huts, thatched with palm-leaf, winding all over a steep hillside. I remember that it was a cloudy, stuffy morning at the beginning of the rains. We began questioning the people as to where the elephant had gone and, as usual, failed to get any definite information. That is invariably the case in the East; a story always sounds clear enough at a distance, but the nearer you get to the scene of events the vaguer it becomes. Some of the people said that the elephant had gone in one direction, some said that he had gone in another, some professed not even to have heard of any elephant. I had almost made up my mind that the whole story was a pack of lies, when we heard yells a little distance away. There was a loud, scandalized cry of "Go away, child! Go away this instant!" and an old woman with a switch in her hand came around the corner of a hut, violently shooing away a crowd of naked children. Some more women followed, clicking their tongues and exclaiming; evidently there was something that the children ought not to have seen. I rounded the hut and saw a man's dead body sprawling in the mud. He was an Indian, a black Dravidian coolie, almost naked, and he could not have been dead many minutes. The people said that the elephant had come suddenly upon him round the corner of the hut, caught him with its trunk, put its foot on his back and ground him into the earth. This was the rainy season and the ground was soft, and his face had scored a trench a foot deep and a couple of yards long. He was lying on his belly with arms crucified and head sharply twisted to one side. His face was coated with mud, the eyes wide open, the teeth bared and grinning with an expression of unendurable agony. (Never tell me, by the way, that the dead look peaceful. Most of the corpses I have seen looked devilish.) The friction of the great beast's foot had stripped the skin from his back as neatly as one skins a rabbit. As soon as I saw the dead man I sent an orderly to a friend's house nearby to borrow an elephant rifle. I had already sent back the pony, not wanting it to go mad with fright and throw me if it smelt the elephant.

The orderly came back in a few minutes with a rifle and five cartridges, and meanwhile some Burmans had arrived and told us that the elephant was in the paddy fields below, only a few hundred yards away. As I started forward practically the whole population of the quarter flocked out of the houses and followed me. They had seen the rifle and were all shouting excitedly that I was going to shoot the elephant. They had not shown much interest in the elephant when he was merely ravaging their homes, but it was different now that he was going to be shot. It was a bit of fun to them, as it would be to an English crowd; besides they wanted the meat. It made me vaguely uneasy. I had no intention of shooting the elephant—I had merely sent for the rifle to defend myself if necessary—and it is always unnerving to have a crowd following you. I marched down the hill, looking and feeling a fool, with the rifle over my shoulder and an ever-growing army of people jostling at my heels. At the bottom, when you got away from the huts, there was a metalled road and beyond that a miry waste of paddy fields a thousand yards across, not yet ploughed but soggy from the first rains and dotted with coarse grass. The elephant was standing eight yards from the road, his left side towards us. He took not the slightest notice of the crowd's approach. He was tearing up bunches of grass, beating them against his knees to clean them and stuffing them into his mouth.

I had halted on the road. As soon as I saw the elephant I knew with perfect certainty that I ought not to shoot him. It is a serious matter to shoot a working elephant—it is comparable to destroying a huge and costly piece of machinery—and obviously one ought not to do it if it can possibly be avoided. And at that distance, peacefully eating, the elephant looked no more dangerous than a cow. I thought then and I think now that his attack of "must" was already passing off; in which case he would merely wander harmlessly about until the mahout came back and caught him. Moreover, I did not in the least want to shoot him. I decided that I would watch him for a little while to make sure that he did not turn savage again, and then go home.

But at that moment I glanced round at the crowd that had followed me. It was an immense crowd, two thousand at the least and growing every minute. It blocked the road for a long distance on either side. I looked at the sea of yellow faces above the garish clothes—faces all happy and excited over this bit of fun, all certain that the elephant was going to be shot. They were watching me as they would watch a conjurer about to perform a trick. They did not like me, but with the magical rifle in my hands I was momentarily worth watching. And suddenly I realized that I should have to shoot the elephant after all. The people expected it of me and I had to do it; I could feel their two thousand wills pressing me forward, irresistibly. And it was at this moment, as I stood there with the rifle in my hands, that I first grasped the hollowness, the futility of the white man's dominion in the East. Here was I, the white man with his gun, standing in front of the unarmed native crowd—seemingly the leading actor of the piece; but in reality I was only an absurd puppet pushed to and fro by the will of those yellow faces behind. I perceived in this moment that when the white man turns tyrant it is his own freedom that he destroys. He becomes a sort of hollow, posing dummy, the convention-alized figure of a sahib. For it is the condition of his rule that he shall spend his life in trying to impress the "natives," and so in every crisis he has got to do what the "natives" expect of him. He wears a mask, and his face grows to fit it.)I had got to shoot the elephant. I had committed myself to doing it when I sent for the rifle. A sahib has got to act like a sahib; he has got to appear resolute, to know his own mind and do definite things. To come all that way, rifle in hand, with two thousand people marching at my heels, and then to trail feebly away, having done nothing—no, that was impossible. The crowd would laugh at me. And my whole life, every white man's life in the East, was one long struggle not to be laughed at.

But I did not want to shoot the elephant. I watched him beating his bunch of grass against his knees, with that preoccupied grandmotherly air that elephants have. It seemed to me that it would be murder to shoot him. At that age I was not squeamish about killing animals, but I had never shot an elephant and never wanted to. (Somehow it always seems worse to kill a *large* animal.) Besides, there was the beast's owner to be considered. Alive, the elephant was worth at least a hundred pounds; dead, he would only be worth the value of his tusks, five pounds, possibly. But I had got to act quickly. I turned to some experienced-looking Burmans who had been there when we arrived, and asked them how the elephant had been behaving. They all said the same thing: he took no notice of you if you left him alone, but he might charge if you went too close to him.

It was perfectly clear to me what I ought to do. I ought to walk up to within, say, twenty-five yards of the elephant and test his behavior. If he charged, I could shoot; if he took no notice of me, it would be safe to leave him until the mahout came back. But also I knew that I was going to do no such thing. I was a poor shot with a rifle and the ground was soft mud into which one would sink at every step. If the elephant charged and I missed him, I should have about as much chance as a toad under a steamroller. But even then I was not thinking particularly of my own skin, only of the watchful yellow faces behind. For at that moment, with the crowd watching me, I was not afraid in the ordinary sense, as I would have been if I had been alone. A white man mustn't be frightened in front of "natives"; and so, in general, he isn't frightened. The sole thought in my mind was that if anything went wrong those two thousand Burmans would see me pursued, caught, trampled on and reduced to a grinning corpse like that Indian up the hill. And if that happened it was quite probable that some of them would laugh. That would never do. There was only one alternative. I shoved the cartridges into the magazine and lay down on the road to get a better aim.

The crowd grew very still, and a deep, low, happy sigh, as of people who see the theatre curtain go up at last, breathed from innumerable throats. They were going to have their bit of fun after all. The rifle was a beautiful German thing with cross-hair sights. I did not then know that in shooting an elephant one would shoot to cut an imaginary bar running from ear-hole to ear-hole. I ought, therefore, as the elephant was sideways on, to have aimed straight at his ear-hole; actually I aimed several inches in front of this, thinking the brain would be further forward.

When I pulled the trigger I did not hear the bang or feel the kick—one never does when a shot goes home—but I heard the devilish roar of glee that went up from the crowd. In that instant, in too short a time, one would have thought, even for the bullet to get there, a mysterious, terrible change had come over the elephant. He neither stirred nor fell, but every line of his body had altered. He looked suddenly stricken, shrunken, immensely old, as though the frightful impact of the bullet had paralysed him without knocking him down. At last, after what seemed a long time— it might have been five seconds, I dare say—he sagged flabbily to his knees. His mouth slobbered. An enormous senility seemed to have settled upon him. One could have imagined him thousands of years old. I fired again into the same spot. At the second shot he did not collapse but climbed with desperate slowness to his feet and stood weakly upright, with legs sagging and head drooping. I fired a third time. That was the shot that did for him. You could see the agony of it jolt his whole body and knock the last remnant of strength from his legs. But in falling he seemed for a moment to rise, for as his hind legs collapsed beneath him he seemed to tower upward like a huge rock toppling, his trunk reaching skywards like a tree. He trumpeted, for the first and only time. And then down he came, his belly towards me, with a crash that seemed to shake the ground even where I lay.

I got up. The Burmans were already racing past me across the mud. It was obvious that the elephant would never rise again, but he was not dead. He was breathing very rhythmically with long rattling gasps, his great mound of a side painfully rising and falling. His mouth was wide open—I could see far down into caverns of pale pink throat. I waited a long time for him to die, but his breathing did not weaken. Finally I fired my two remaining shots into the spot where I thought his heart must be. The thick blood welled out of him like red velvet, but still he did not die. His body did not even jerk when the shots hit him, the tortured breathing continued without a pause. He was dying, very slowly and in great agony, but in some world remote from me where not even a bullet could damage him further. I felt that I had got to put an end to that dreadful noise. It seemed dreadful to see the great beast lying there, powerless to move and yet powerless to die, and not even to be able to finish him. I sent back for my small rifle and poured shot after shot into his heart and down his throat. They seemed to make no impression. The tortured gasps continued as steadily as the ticking of a clock.

In the end I could not stand it any longer and went away. I heard later that it took him half an hour to die. Burmans were bringing dahs and baskets even before I left, and I was told they had stripped his body almost to the bones by the afternoon.

Afterwards, of course, there were endless discussions about the shooting of the elephant. The owner was furious, but he was only an Indian and could do nothing. Besides, legally I had done the right thing, for a mad elephant has to be killed, like a mad dog, if its owner fails to control it. Among the Europeans opinion was divided. The older men said I was right, the younger men said it was a damn shame to shoot an elephant for killing a coolie, because an elephant was worth more than any damn Coringhee coolie. And afterwards I was very glad that the coolie had been killed; it put me legally in the right and it gave me a sufficient pretext for shooting the elephant. I often wondered whether any of the others grasped that I had done it solely to avoid looking a fool.

Judge Waring

Septima Clark

Septima Clark is one of the great women in the fight for civil rights and human justice. Her quiet work over many decades is still relatively unknown. She was eighteen when she began her teaching career in a one-room schoolhouse on a South Carolina island. Two years later, she helped lead a successful effort to pass a law that let black teachers teach in the Charleston, South Carolina, public schools. During her forty years of teaching, she was always active in community work to improve conditions for black people. In 1954, her visible role in the local chapter of the National Association for the Advancement of Colored People led to her expulsion from the South Carolina public school system. She then joined the staff of the Highlander Folk School in Tennessee where she directed a literacy training program and developed her idea of citizenship schools, designed to enable disenfranchised black voters to pass the voting registration tests. Later, under the sponsorship of the Southern Christian Leadership Conference, she helped create these schools throughout the South. Her commitment to education has never wavered. In a Christmas message published in 1975, she wrote, "I believe unconditionally in the ability of people to respond when they are told the truth. We need to be taught to study rather than to believe, to inquire rather than to affirm."

In 1962, together with Legette Blythe, she published an autobiography, Echo in My Soul. *The present piece is a chapter from her narrative* Ready from Within: Septima Clark and the Civil Rights Movement *(1986), told to and edited by Cynthia Stokes Brown. In it, she concludes "I don't expect to ever see a utopia. No, I think there will always be something that you're going to have to work on, always. . . . Things will happen, and things will change. The only thing that's really worthwhile is change. It's coming."*

My name is Septima Poinsette Clark. I was born at 105 Wentworth Street in Charleston, South Carolina, on May 3, 1898. When I was seven, my parents moved to Henrietta Street. 26 Henrietta Street. After I grew up,

I moved to different places in South Carolina to teach, but I always had the home I bought here in Charleston. This German that my brother was working with had that house for sale. It wasn't but two thousand and five hundred dollars. I was able to get it in 1927 with my little bit of money and get it all paid for. So we had our own house at 17 Henrietta Street, the street I had grown up on.

I moved back to Charleston in 1947, and that is the part of my story I want to tell about first. Later on I will go back and tell about my growing up and the early years of my teaching.

I want to start my story with the end of World War II because that is when the civil rights movement really got going, both for me personally and for people all over the South. After World War II the men were coming home from fighting in Europe and Africa, and they weren't going to take segregation any more.

In 1947 I got a job in Charleston teaching seventh grade at the newest school in the system, the Henry P. Archer School. But soon my assignment was changed, and I was put in charge of a group of problem pupils in grades four through seven. Each period these children would come to me from their home rooms, and we did what was actually remedial reading. It was challenging work, and we made considerable progress.

I hadn't been in Charleston long before I got involved in civic activities. Among other organizations I had a special interest in the work of the Young Women's Christian Association. There was a dual system in Charleston, with separate white and black "Y's." Soon after I returned to Charleston I became chairman of the black "Y's" committee on administration. My courage was soon to be tested. It came about this way.

At the time the judge of the United States Court for the eastern district of South Carolina was a Charlestonian named Julius Waties Waring. He was the same judge who had decreed that the salaries of school teachers in South Carolina, black and white, had to be equalized. I knew him principally because of that decision; since he was Charleston born and bred, I saw his name in the newspapers frequently.

I knew that Judge Waring had grown up in the upper-class area of Charleston and had married an aristocratic girl. He was a personal friend of both the U.S. senators from South Carolina, one of whom just spouted racist rhetoric. When Waring was appointed U.S. judge, he was considered a person who would protect the southern way of life.

But Judge Waring transformed himself as he sat in his judge's chair. I heard him say once: "You know, a judge has to live with his conscience. I would sit in the courtroom, and I would see black men coming in that I knew were decent men, and they were considered bums and trash because they were black. And I would see white men that I knew were bums, and they were considered gentlemen. I just couldn't take it any longer."

When I returned to Charleston, black people still could not vote in the Democratic primary elections. There weren't many blacks who were registered voters, but those who were registered Democrats could not vote in the primary election, where you elect the candidates your party will run in the final election.

That rule to keep blacks out of primary elections was made way back in 1896, just before I was born. The legislature passed that law as part of setting up segregation in South Carolina. The U.S. Supreme Court finally ruled against white primaries in 1944, but southern states were still following their own rules.

A number of black people had gotten to the place where their children were going north to college, and they were coming back talking about the injustices we had in Charleston where we could not vote in the Democratic primary. It had gotten to the place where the younger generation felt very bad about it.

After Judge Waring realized how wrong it was to keep blacks out of the primary, he decided to change it. In 1947 he ruled that blacks must be permitted to vote in the next primary, and he told the leaders of the Democratic Party that the court would hold them personally responsible for carrying out this ruling.

Several days before the election some of the whites made a statement that if blacks attempted to vote in the primary, then blood would be running down the streets like water. Judge Waring said to them, and had the press print it, that "If that happens, I'll put you in jail, and you'll stay there for the rest of your life. These people have a right to vote, and so they will vote."

You know, that was a quiet election. Election day used to be a terrible thing around Charleston. Guns were always out. During the election just before this one a young white reporter was killed. There would always be some death. But Judge Waring stopped that.

Just reading about Judge Waring I became really enthused about him. I thought, "This is a wonderful man to come forth and say that blacks should vote." At the YWCA we were going to have a special day, and I thought, "Now, if Judge Waring could say that, his wife might be able to say something to Negro women." In 1945 Judge Waring had divorced his first wife and had married Elizabeth Avery, a native of Detroit.

Another lady from the "Y" and I went to Mrs. Waring's house at 9 o'clock one night to ask her to speak. She was very glad to do it. But somehow or other the newspaper got hold of it, and all hell broke forth. Evidently somebody saw us going into that house, and they decided that this could not be.

I started getting obscene phone calls. I'd pick up the telephone, and they'd say: "Who in the hell do you think you are? You are a damn fool to ask Judge Waring's wife to speak." I'd say, "Thank you," and put down the phone.

Right away I decided that I'd better go and tell Mrs. Waring that if black people would ask her not to speak, would she let me know, but if

white people would ask her not to speak, would she decide that she was
going to speak regardless.

I went down to the Warings' house again. Judge Waring told me, "Now,
Septima, the thing to do is to put somebody at each one of the places where
you turn the lights on. You're going to have to have a man standing there,
because if the Klan comes in, the first thing they're going to do is turn
your lights out, and then you'll have a terrible time."

That's what I did. I got men to stand by all the lights in the hall of the
YWCA. But no Klan came, only two or three white women. Mrs. Waring
called the white people in Charleston decadent and low-down. I think she
did it because they were mean. The reporters were there, and Mrs. Waring passed out a copy of her speech, saying, "Take this speech and put it
in the paper just as it is. Don't change a word."

They printed that speech word for word. For three days after that
meeting the town talked about Mrs. Waring and what she had said.

After that, the Warings were terribly harassed and persecuted. Their
friends abandoned them. Not one white person would have dinner with
them, or even drink tea with them. The white hairdressers refused to
wash Mrs. Waring's hair. And when Judge Waring went to get his hair
cut, a guard had to go with him and sit until he got his hair cut. They had
to guard him day and night.

The Warings reached out to their black friends. Of course, a lot of blacks
wouldn't go to the Warings' house. The Warings invited them to tea one
night, and they wouldn't go. A few of us went to dinner. I had to say to
myself that if these people invite me, surely I should go. Why should I be
one who says not to go? All of these things you had to make up in your
mind to do because too many of the blacks were against your going to the
Warings' anyway. I had to make a decision to go regardless of what
happened.

When I went to Judge Waring's home to dinner I, too, felt real worried.
I always had to have my hair straightened, and I tried to have a new dress.
Mrs. Waring told me that wasn't necessary. I was glad she could tell me
that, but I thought it had to be.

At the Warings' I met many of the mulatto people of Charleston, and
I wasn't considered too well by that group because they were very fair-
skinned people with straight hair. My mother was a washerwoman, and
my father had been a slave, so I wasn't considered one of them. But
because of the way I could talk about the things I knew about, the injustices, they listened. By that time I had been to several universities, and
I had studied a good bit about history, the history of government, and
economics. These things had made an impression on me. I don't know
whether they ever learned to like me too well, but they listened to me.

I was very happy for the kinds of people that I could meet at Mrs.
Waring's house. I couldn't meet them otherwise. They would not have
come to my house. I wasn't good enough. Neither could I go to their house.

I couldn't even play cards or bridge with them, not at all. But this was the kind of caste and class thing that we had in Charleston.

I had a feeling that if I could eat at Judge Waring's house, at any white person's house, then they should be able to drink a cup of tea or do something at my house. So I invited Judge and Mrs. Waring and two others to have tea with me one afternoon, and they did come. My mother was sick in bed at the time, and I had taken her meal to her bedside. But she couldn't eat; she was too worried about it. My neighbors on my street were also worried. They said, "As long as Septima Clark have them white people coming to her house, we're gonna always have trouble."

Then my principal got worried about it, too. He saw me coming out of Mrs. Waring's house from dinner one Sunday, and he said, "That's a dangerous thing to do. How in the world could you do it?"

At a faculty meeting at my school, they all told me how wrong they thought it was for me to go to the Warings' house. They said it just proved what white people were saying, that the real reason that blacks wanted integration was to socialize with whites.

I waited until they finished. Then I asked the principal if I could ask him a question.

"I would like to ask you if anyone decided for you whom you would marry."

"No, of course not," he replied. "I decided for myself."

Then I asked one of the women teachers, "Did anyone tell you what kind of car to buy and how much to pay for it?"

"No," she said. "I did that myself. It's my car. Why shouldn't I have made those decisions?"

Then I turned to a teacher who put a big emphasis on clothes; she was probably our best-dressed teacher.

"Did anybody tell you what type of dresses to buy and what stores to buy them at?" I asked.

"Of course not," she replied, a bit indignantly.

"Well, I can see that you all make decisions for yourselves," I told them. "The principal decided what woman he wished to marry, and I think that no one should tell a man or woman who to marry. And you—" I pointed to the first woman I had questioned, "selected the car you bought, and I'm sure you had a perfect right to do that, just as you—" I pointed to the woman who loved to dress beautifully, "have every right to select your own clothes. In the same way," I looked them in the eyes, "I think that I have a right to select my own friends. I feel that nobody has a right to tell me who my friends must be any more than I have a right to tell the principal who his wife will be, or you what kind of car to buy, or you what sort of clothes you should wear."

The meeting closed, but I knew they were quite angry with me. After that there were many times, I'm sure, when it was hard for them to say a pleasant word to me or about me, all because of my association with the Warings.

The Warings did not get to finish out their years here in Charleston. They moved to New York City in 1950. They did that because when Mrs. Waring was sitting on a couch in their living room, someone threw a block of cement through the window. It nearly hit her, but it didn't. Then when she went to get some letters mimeographed, the woman refused and said, "Please don't come in here, because if you do you're going to ruin my business, and I won't be able to stay here any longer." Judge Waring used to go and hold court in the upper part of New York and in California, down at San Diego. When those courts were cancelled, he decided that they had better get out of here, which they did.

They lived in New York City until they died in 1968. He was buried in January, and she died in November. He had two hundred blacks and twelve whites at his funeral, and she had nine of us at hers. She said she didn't want none of the hypocrites at her funeral, and she didn't have any. They were both buried in Charleston, right up in Magnolia Cemetery overlooking the harbor.

They had one laugh from the grave, though. They gave his retirement money to the College of Charleston, and it has to be used for a black student to live on campus. Of course, at that time the College of Charleston did not allow black people to go there. It took the college until 1976 to spend that money. Now black students can live on the campus. That has come out of Judge Waring's will.

The Dishonorable Spy

John le Carré

John le Carré (in private life, David John Moore Cornwell) is the acknowledged master of the Cold War spy thriller. Many of his books cast George Smiley as the unglamorous British Secret Service agent, who must operate in a morally ambiguous world of intrigue and betrayal where, le Carré has said, "there is no victory and no virtue."

Le Carré's fiction draws on his own experiences. He was born in England in 1931. His family, he has said, was led to live "in the style of millionaire paupers" because of his father's sometimes shady business and political dealings. "We arrived in educated, middle-class society feeling almost like spies, knowing that we had no social hinterland, that we had a great deal to conceal and a lot of pretending to do."

But he also knew how the spy system worked. Before he studied at Oxford

University (B.A. 1956), he had completed his national service with the British Army Intelligence Corps, and after Oxford he spent five years with the British Foreign Service. He resigned only after The Spy Who Came in from the Cold *(1963), published under his now-famous pseudonym, became an international bestseller. Since then he has been a full-time writer. Among his other novels are* The Honorable Schoolboy *(1977) and* Smiley's People *(1980).*

"The Dishonorable Spy" was first given as a speech titled "The Clandestine Muse" at Johns Hopkins University and printed in the August 1986 issue of Johns Hopkins Magazine. *The shorter version presented here is from* Harper's Magazine *(December 1986).*

In one of those old sixpenny notebooks in which I wrote my first story for George Smiley twenty-six years ago, I made a drawing of him as I first imagined him. Tubby and perplexed, the weary pilgrim is struggling up a stony hill, carrying his exhausted horse on his shoulders.

Smiley himself—or so the image was supposed to tell us—would nobly pay the cost for doing the dreadful things that have to be done so that ordinary, decent, unaware citizens can sleep peacefully in their beds at night. He would find the money out of his own conscience. Smiley would sacrifice his own morality on the altar of national necessity. For you and me. It was an argument that for the next two decades I repeatedly placed in the mouths of the main characters of the Smiley novels: in *The Spy Who Came In From the Cold,* where it is used both by the chief of the Secret Service and by his luckless agent; in *The Honourable Schoolboy,* where the protagonist willfully, almost aggressively, wishes upon Smiley the entire responsibility for determining what means are justified by what end; until in *Smiley's People,* at present the last of the Smiley novels, the argument comes very near to being thrown in Smiley's face. Let me describe to you the final moments of the book:

Smiley has just brought off the intelligence coup of his lifetime: he has secured the defection of his Russian adversary. He is standing at the Berlin Wall (still the troubled heart of his beloved Germany). His once young colleague Peter Guillam, now himself in middle age, is at his side. This should be their shared moment of triumph. But the narrative hardly reflects this:

> From long habit, Smiley had taken off his spectacles and was absently polishing them on the fat end of his tie, even though he had to delve for it among the folds of his tweed coat.
> "George, you won," said Guillam, as they walked slowly towards the car.
> "Did I?" said Smiley. "Yes. Yes, well I suppose I did."

Smiley has not been heard of since. If he has left the stage for good, then he has left it, for me, as an enigma, with the biggest question of his life and mine still unresolved—yet taking with him, as he lumbers away to his spies' Valhalla, the bulk of my work in his shabby briefcase.

Yet whether Smiley stays teasingly in the shadows or stages yet another comeback, the argument between him and myself—*dialogue* is too weak a word—continues unabated. Was it really such a heroic thing that he did with his life? All that sacrifice of moral conscience—was it really noble? Is he not a little bit like the virgin in Eric Linklater's short story who bravely sells herself into prostitution in order to save her family from starvation, when a little good stewardship on the domestic accounts might have done the trick as well?

Is there such a grand difference, in fact, between the man who voluntarily gives up his moral conscience and the man who never had one in the first place! Has Smiley, has *anyone,* the right—least of all a man of such perception—to suspend his individual conscience in the interest of some mistily perceived collective? Is that what Smiley's "Western culture" was about? Maybe we should ask the CIA.

It's not, after all, the dissenters who have brought havoc to our non-conciliatory world. Not the mavericks, heretics, detractors; not the traitors. Not even that latest monster in the Washington lexicon, the pragmatist—by which, I have an awful feeling, they mean me—has so far succeeded in undermining our civilization.

But the *loyal* men marching blindly to the music of their institutionalized faiths: *their* record is not good, whether they are marching to the posthumous tunes of the British Empire, for Islam, for Germany (whichever one), for God (whomever he is working for at that moment), or for democracy of whichever brand. Christ himself supplies no Good Housekeeping guarantee of rectitude when it comes to picking your champion. Whose side was he on in the Falklands show?° Whose side is he on now, in Salvador, in Nicaragua? In Rome? Or on the issue of nuclear disarmament? "There have never been so many civil wars," said Montesquieu, "as in the Kingdom of Christ." And the fact of sacrifice is no guarantee at all. We cannot measure the integrity of a cause by the number of people who died for it, as Smiley should know very well.

The only thing we *can* say with safety, perhaps, is that the greatest threat to mankind comes from the renunciation of individual scruple in favor of institutional denominators; from the adoption of slogan, and the mute acceptance of prepackaged animosities, in preference to the hard-fought decisions of individual, humanistic conscience. Real heroism lies, as it always will, not in conformity or even patriotism but in acts of solitary moral courage. Which, come to think of it, is what we used to admire in our Christian savior.

Falklands show   Argentina invaded the Falkland Islands on April 2, 1982, in an attempt to reclaim them from the British but were forced to surrender to the British on June 14, 1982.

Forgive this burst of moralizing, but I have a feeling that as Smiley left the stage, he was seriously wondering whether he had ever been a hero at all—or whether all that so-called moral sacrifice he made was really a bit of a cop-out.

Did he in his whole life ever once cry *"Stop"*? Not so far as I know. Did he ever throw down his cloak and dagger and storm along the dingy passages of the Circus, kick open his chief's door, and yell: "What's the limit?"

He didn't, so let me write the scene for you now.

His chief—whoever he is these days—sits at his desk enjoying his first cup of tea of the morning.

"Ah, George. You look flustered. Has Ann run off again?"

"What's the limit?" Smiley says belligerently. This is the line he has been rehearsing all the way from his room. "I want to know how long we can go on doing this stuff in defense of Western society without ceasing to be the sort of society that is worth defending. That's all."

"What *stuff*? George, don't be so Gothic. Take some leave."

But Smiley is determined to have his say.

"Meddling with tin-pot Third World countries. That *stuff*. Bullying them. Wrecking their economies. Rigging their elections. Assassinating their leaders. Buying their politicians like popcorn. Ignoring their starving. Their uneducated. Kicking their peasants off the land. Arming their oppressors to the teeth. Turning their children into tomorrow's terrorists. Manipulating the media. Lying. Constantly."

"But my dear George, think what the other side does. It's *far* worse. Have some tea."

Smiley won't be placated.

"Listen, Chief. I've worked it out. If we were to put as much energy into stopping as we do into going on—if the Americans did—if peace were as important to us as getting a man on the moon—"

"You've been drinking, George. I can tell."

"We've lost our vision, Chief. Our courage. What's happened to Tom Paine? What's happened to Thoreau and Edmund Burke?"

The Chief allows himself a rare, if weary, laugh. "My dear George, we put *them* on the payroll *years* ago."

The Inner Ring

C. S. Lewis

Clive Staples Lewis (1898–1963) was for most of his life a fellow and tutor at Magdalen College, Oxford, and was universally admired in academic circles for his work in medieval and Renaissance English literature. But his interests carried his name far beyond the university. He was also an accomplished lecturer, writer of children's books (among them, The Lion, the Witch and the Wardrobe *and* The Silver Chair*), novelist, moralist, and apologist for religion. He is probably best known to the general reading public for* The Screwtape Letters *(1942, rev. ed. 1961), a mixture of religious thought, morality, and satire conveyed in thirty-one letters from an experienced devil, Screwtape, to his nephew, Wormwood, a tempter-in-training.*

The following selection is reprinted from The Weight of Glory and Other Addresses *(1949); Lewis first presented it as the Memorial Oration at King's College, the University of London, in 1944.*

May I read you a few lines from Tolstoi's *War and Peace?*

> When Boris entered the room, Prince Andrey was listening to an old general, wearing his decorations, who was reporting something to Prince Andrey, with an expression of soldierly servility on his purple face. "All right. Please wait!" he said to the general, speaking in Russian with the French accent which he used when he spoke with contempt. The moment he noticed Boris he stopped listening to the general who trotted imploringly after him and begged to be heard, while Prince Andrey turned to Boris with a cheerful smile and a nod of the head. Boris now clearly understood—what he had already guessed—that side by side with the system of discipline and subordination which were laid down in the Army Regulations, there existed a different and a more real system—the system which compelled a tightly laced general with a purple face to wait respectfully for his turn while a mere captain like Prince Andrey chatted with a mere second lieutenant like Boris. Boris decided at once that he would be guided not by the official system but by this other unwritten system.— Part III, Chap. 9.

When you invite a middle-aged moralist to address you, I suppose I must conclude, however unlikely the conclusion seems, that you have a taste for middle-aged moralizing. I shall do my best to gratify it. I shall in fact give you advice about the world in which you are going to live. I do not mean by this that I am going to attempt a talk on what are called current affairs. You probably know quite as much about them as I do. I am not going to tell you—except in a form so general that you will hardly recognize it—what part you ought to play in post-war reconstruction. It is not, in fact, very likely that any of you will be able, in the next ten years, to make any direct contribution to the peace or prosperity of Europe. You will be busy finding jobs, getting married, acquiring facts. I am going to do something more old-fashioned than you perhaps expected. I am going to give advice. I am going to issue warnings. Advice and warnings about things which are so perennial that no one calls them "current affairs".

And of course every one knows what a middle-aged moralist of my type warns his juniors against. He warns them against the World, the Flesh, and the Devil. But one of this trio will be enough to deal with to-day. The Devil, I shall leave strictly alone. The association between him and me in the public mind has already gone quite as deep as I wish: in some quarters it has already reached the level of confusion, if not of identification. I begin to realize the truth of the old proverb that he who sups with that formidable host needs a long spoon. As for the Flesh, you must be very abnormal young people if you do not know quite as much about it as I do. But on the World I think I have something to say.

In the passage I have just read from Tolstoi, the young second lieutenant Boris Dubretskoi discovers that there exist in the army two different systems or hierarchies. The one is printed in some little red book and anyone can easily read it up. It also remains constant. A general is always superior to a colonel and a colonel to a captain. The other is not printed anywhere. Nor is it even a formally organized secret society with officers and rules which you would be told after you had been admitted. You are never formally and explicitly admitted by anyone. You discover gradually, in almost indefinable ways, that it exists and that you are outside it; and then later, perhaps, that you are inside it. There are what correspond to pass words, but they too are spontaneous and informal. A particular slang, the use of particular nicknames, an allusive manner of conversation, are the marks. But it is not constant. It is not easy, even at a given moment, to say who is inside and who is outside. Some people are obviously in and some are obviously out, but there are always several on the border-line. And if you come back to the same Divisional Headquarters, or Brigade Headquarters, or the same regiment or even the same company, after six weeks' absence, you may find this second hierarchy quite altered. There are no formal admissions or expulsions. People think they are in it after they have in fact been pushed out of it, or before they have been allowed in: this provides great amusement for those who are really inside. It has no fixed name. The only certain rule is that the insiders and outsiders call it by different names. From inside it may be designated, in simple cases, by mere enumeration: it may be called "You and Tony and me". When it is very secure and comparatively stable in membership it calls itself "we". When it has to be suddenly expanded to meet a particular emergency it calls itself "All the sensible people at this place." From outside, if you have despaired of getting into it, you call it "That gang" or "They" or "So-and-so and his set" or "the Caucus" or "the Inner Ring". If you are a candidate for admission you probably don't call it anything. To discuss it with the other outsiders would make you feel outside yourself. And to mention it in talking to the man who is inside, and who may help you in if this present conversation goes well, would be madness.

Badly as I may have described it, I hope you will all have recognized the thing I am describing. Not, of course, that you have been in the Russian Army or perhaps in any army. But you have met the phenomenon of an

Inner Ring. You discovered one in your house at school before the end of the first term. And when you had climbed up to somewhere near it by the end of your second year, perhaps you discovered that within the Ring there was a Ring yet more inner, which in its turn was the fringe of the great school Ring to which the house Rings were only satellites. It is even possible that the School Ring was almost in touch with a Masters' Ring. You were beginning, in fact, to pierce through the skins of the onion. And here, too, at your university—shall I be wrong in assuming that at this very moment, invisible to me, there are several rings—independent systems or concentric rings—present in this room? And I can assure you that in whatever hospital, inn of court, diocese, school, business, or college you arrive after going down, you will find the Rings—what Tolstoi calls the second or unwritten system.

All this is rather obvious. I wonder whether you will say the same of my next step, which is this. I believe that in all men's lives at certain periods, and in many men's lives at all periods between infancy and extreme old age, one of the most dominant elements is the desire to be inside the local Ring and the terror of being left outside. This desire, in one of its forms, has indeed had ample justice done to it in literature. I mean, in the form of snobbery. Victorian fiction is full of characters who are hag-ridden by the desire to get inside that particular Ring which is, or was, called Society. But it must be clearly understood that "Society", in that sense of the word, is merely one of a hundred Rings and snobbery therefore only one form of the longing to be inside. People who believe themselves to be free, and indeed are free, from snobbery, and who read satires on snobbery with tranquil superiority, may be devoured by the desire in another form. It may be the very intensity of their desire to enter some quite different Ring which renders them immune from the allurements of high life. An invitation from a duchess would be very cold comfort to a man smarting under the sense of exclusion from some artistic or communist côterie. Poor man—it is not large, lighted rooms, or champagne, or even scandals about peers and Cabinet Ministers that he wants: it is the sacred little attic or studio, the heads bent together, the fog of tobacco smoke, and the delicious knowledge that we—we four or five all huddled beside this stove—are the people who *know*. Often the desire conceals itself so well that we hardly recognize the pleasures of fruition. Men tell not only their wives but themselves that it is a hardship to stay late at the office or the school on some bit of important extra work which they have been let in for because they and So-and-so and the two others are the only people left in the place who really know how things are run. But it is not quite true. It is a terrible bore, of course, when old Fatty Smithson draws you aside and whispers "Look here, we've got to get you in on this examination somehow" or "Charles and I saw at once that you've got to be on this committee". A terrible bore . . . ah, but how much more terrible if you were left out! It is tiring and unhealthy to lose your

Saturday afternoons: but to have them free because you don't matter, that is much worse.

Freud would say, no doubt, that the whole thing is a subterfuge of the sexual impulse. I wonder whether the shoe is not sometimes on the other foot. I wonder whether, in ages of promiscuity, many a virginity has not been lost less in obedience to Venus than in obedience to the lure of the caucus. For of course, when promiscuity is the fashion, the chaste are outsiders. They are ignorant of something that other people know. They are uninitiated. And as for lighter matters, the number who first smoked or first got drunk for a similar reason is probably very large.

I must now make a distinction. I am not going to say that the existence of Inner Rings is an evil. It is certainly unavoidable. There must be confidential discussions: and it is not only not a bad thing, it is (in itself) a good thing, that personal friendship should grow up between those who work together. And it is perhaps impossible that the official hierarchy of any organization should quite coincide with its actual workings. If the wisest and most energetic people invariably held the highest posts, it might coincide; since they often do not, there must be people in high positions who are really deadweights and people in lower positions who are more important than their rank and seniority would lead you to suppose. In that way the second, unwritten system is bound to grow up. It is necessary; and perhaps it is not a necessary evil. But the desire which draws us into Inner Rings is another matter. A thing may be morally neutral and yet the desire for that thing may be dangerous. As Byron has said,

> Sweet is a legacy, and passing sweet
> The unexpected death of some old lady.

The painless death of a pious relative at an advanced age is not an evil. But an earnest desire for her death on the part of her heirs is not reckoned a proper feeling, and the law frowns on even the gentlest attempt to expedite her departure. Let Inner Rings be an unavoidable and even an innocent feature of life, though certainly not a beautiful one: but what of our longing to enter them, our anguish when we are excluded, and the kind of pleasure we feel when we get in?

I have no right to make assumptions about the degree to which any of you may already be compromised. I must not assume that you have ever first neglected, and finally shaken off, friends whom you really loved and who might have lasted you a lifetime, in order to court the friendship of those who appeared to you more important, more esoteric. I must not ask whether you have ever derived actual pleasure from the loneliness and humiliation of the outsiders after you yourself were in: whether you have talked to fellow members of the Ring in the presence of outsiders simply in order that the outsiders might envy; whether the means whereby, in your days of probation, you propitiated the Inner Ring, were always wholly admirable. I will ask only one question—and it is, of course, a rhetorical question which expects no answer. In the whole of your life as you now remember it, has the desire to be on the right side of that invisible line ever prompted you to any act or word on which, in the cold small hours of a wakeful night, you can look back with satisfaction? If so, your case is more fortunate than most.

But I said I was going to give advice, and advice should deal with the future, not the past. I have hinted at the past only to awake you to what I believe to be the real nature of human life. I don't believe that the economic motive and the erotic motive account for everything that goes on in what we moralists call the World. Even if you add Ambition I think the picture is still incomplete. The lust for the esoteric, the longing to be inside, take many forms which are not easily recognizable as Ambition. We hope, no doubt, for tangible profits from every Inner Ring we penetrate: power, money, liberty to break rules, avoidance of routine duties, evasion of discipline. But all these would not satisfy us if we did not get in addition the delicious sense of secret intimacy. It is no doubt a great convenience to know that we need fear no official reprimands from our official senior because he is old Percy, a fellow-member of our Ring. But we don't value the intimacy only for the sake of the convenience; quite equally we value the convenience as a proof of the intimacy.

My main purpose in this address is simply to convince you that this desire is one of the great permanent mainsprings of human action. It is one of the factors which go to make up the world as we know it—this whole pell-mell of struggle, competition, confusion, graft, disappointment and advertisement, and if it is one of the permanent mainsprings then you may be quite sure of this. Unless you take measures to prevent it, this desire is going to be one of the chief motives of your life, from the first day on which you enter your profession until the day when you are too old to care. That will be the natural thing—the life that will come to you of its own accord. Any other kind of life, if you lead it, will be the result of conscious and continuous effort. If you do nothing about it, if you drift with the stream, you will in fact be an "inner ringer". I don't say you'll be a successful one; that's as may be. But whether by pining and moping outside Rings that you can never enter, or by passing triumphantly further and further in—one way or the other you will be that kind of man.

I have already made it fairly clear that I think it better for you not to be that kind of man. But you may have an open mind on the question. I will therefore suggest two reasons for thinking as I do.

It would be polite and charitable, and in view of your age reasonable too, to suppose that none of you is yet a scoundrel. On the other hand, by the mere law of averages (I am saying nothing against free will) it is almost certain that at least two or three of you before you die will have become something very like scoundrels. There must be in this room the makings of at least that number of unscrupulous, treacherous, ruthless egotists. The choice is still before you: and I hope you will not take my

hard words about your possible future characters as a token of disrespect
to your present characters. And the prophecy I make is this. To nine out
of ten of you the choice which could lead to scoundrelism will come, when
it does come, in no very dramatic colours. Obviously bad men, obviously
threatening or bribing, will almost certainly not appear. Over a drink or
a cup of coffee, disguised as a triviality and sandwiched between two jokes,
from the lips of a man, or woman, whom you have recently been getting
to know rather better and whom you hope to know better still—just at the
moment when you are most anxious not to appear crude, or naif or a
prig—the hint will come. It will be the hint of something which is not
quite in accordance with the technical rules of fair play: something which
the public, the ignorant, romantic public, would never understand: something which even the outsiders in your own profession are apt to make
a fuss about: but something, says your new friend, which "we"—and at
the word "we" you try not to blush for mere pleasure—something "we
always do". And you will be drawn in, if you are drawn in, not by desire
for gain or ease, but simply because at that moment, when the cup was
so near your lips, you cannot bear to be thrust back again into the cold
outer world. It would be so terrible to see the other man's face—that
genial, confidential, delightfully sophisticated face—turn suddenly cold
and contemptuous, to know that you had been tried for the Inner Ring and
rejected. And then, if you are drawn in, next week it will be something
a little further from the rules, and next year something further still, but
all in the jolliest, friendliest spirit. It may end in a crash, a scandal, and
penal servitude: it may end in millions, a peerage and giving the prizes
at your old school. But you will be a scoundrel.

That is my first reason. Of all passions the passion for the Inner Ring
is most skilful in making a man who is not yet a very bad man do very
bad things.

My second reason is this. The torture allotted to the Danaids in the
classical underworld, that of attempting to fill sieves with water, is the
symbol not of one vice but of all vices. It is the very mark of a perverse
desire that it seeks what is not to be had. The desire to be inside the
invisible line illustrates this rule. As long as you are governed by that
desire you will never get what you want. You are trying to peel an onion:
if you succeed there will be nothing left. Until you conquer the fear of
being an outsider, an outsider you will remain.

This is surely very clear when you come to think of it. If you want to
be made free of° a certain circle for some wholesome reason—if, say, you
want to join a musical society because you really like music—then there
is a possibility of satisfaction. You may find yourself playing in a quartet
and you may enjoy it. But if all you want is to be in the know, your

---

made free of   given the privilege of (British).

pleasure will be short-lived. The circle cannot have from within the charm it had from outside. By the very act of admitting you it has lost its magic. Once the first novelty is worn off the members of this circle will be no more interesting than your old friends. Why should they be? You were not looking for virtue or kindness or loyalty or humour or learning or wit or any of the things that can be really enjoyed. You merely wanted to be "in". And that is a pleasure that cannot last. As soon as your new associates have been staled to you by custom, you will be looking for another Ring. The rainbow's end will still be ahead of you. The old Ring will now be only the drab background for your endeavour to enter the new one.

And you will always find them hard to enter, for a reason you very well know. You yourself, once you are in, want to make it hard for the next entrant, just as those who are already in made it hard for you. Naturally. In any wholesome group of people which holds together for a good purpose, the exclusions are in a sense accidental. Three or four people who are together for the sake of some piece of work exclude others because there is work only for so many or because the others can't in fact do it. Your little musical group limits its numbers because the rooms they meet in are only so big. But your genuine Inner Ring exists for exclusion. There'd be no fun if there were no outsiders. The invisible line would have no meaning unless most people were on the wrong side of it. Exclusion is no accident: it is the essence.

The quest of the Inner Ring will break your hearts unless you break it. But if you break it, a surprising result will follow. If in your working hours you make the work your end, you will presently find yourself all unawares inside the only circle in your profession that really matters. You will be one of the sound craftsmen, and other sound craftsmen will know it. This group of craftsmen will by no means coincide with the Inner Ring or the Important People or the People in the Know. It will not shape that professional policy or work up that professional influence which fights for the profession as a whole against the public: nor will it lead to those periodic scandals and crises which the Inner Ring produces. But it will do those things which that profession exists to do and will in the long run be responsible for all the respect which that profession in fact enjoys and which the speeches and advertisements cannot maintain. And if in your spare time you consort simply with the people you like, you will again find that you have come unawares to a real inside: that you are indeed snug and safe at the centre of something which, seen from without, would look exactly like an Inner Ring. But the difference is that its secrecy is accidental, and its exclusiveness a by-product, and no one was led thither by the lure of the esoteric: for it is only four or five people who like one another meeting to do things that they like. This is friendship. Aristotle placed it among the virtues. It causes perhaps half of all the happiness in the world, and no Inner Ringer can ever have it.

We are told in Scriptures that those who ask get. That is true, in senses

I can't now explore. But in another sense there is much truth in the schoolboy's principle "them as asks shan't have." To a young person, just entering on adult life, the world seems full of "insides", full of delightful intimacies and confidentialities, and he desires to enter them. But if he follows that desire he will reach no "inside" that is worth reaching. The true road lies in quite another direction. It is like the house in *Alice Through the Looking Glass.*°

---

house in *Alice Through the Looking Glass* In Lewis Carroll's book, Alice must walk in the opposite direction of what she wants in order to reach it.

Ethics in Business and Government

In 1979, the *Wall Street Journal* reported on a course titled Competitive Decision Making offered by the Harvard Business School. The course was designed to teach students how to negotiate in business; it included role-playing negotiations, with great pressure to win and thereby earn a high grade. The student with the highest grade later reported that "I was willing to lie to get a better score." The professor acknowledged that lying, what he called "strategic misrepresentation," was sometimes resorted to in business negotiations.

The article drew unprecedented attention to what was being taught in business schools, and it gave new impetus to the debate on how unethical business practices, apparently accepted even within the university, influence personal and public values. We continue that debate in the present section.

In the first essay, television producer Norman Lear is critically concerned that, to a larger extent than ever before, our personal and public values are being shaped by the corporate world. He sees America becoming a game show where "winning is all that matters. Cash prizes. Get rich quick. We are the captives of a culture that celebrates instant gratification and individual success no matter the larger costs." Lear looks for a new climate and a new set of heroes.

Charles Parry, until recently Chief Executive Officer of the Alcoa Company, takes a more benign view. "Business is not separate from society," he says. "It is not an ethical adversary of the common good. Instead, business is a reflection of society." Speaking from within the corporate world, he discusses two sorts of ethical standards: the ethics of relationships within the institution, and "the ethics of action," which concern the relationships between the institution and the world it deals with.

The ethics of action is precisely what troubles Jeffrey Fadiman, who describes some of the quandaries faced by Americans who do business in other countries. If one culture's courtesy turns out to be another culture's bribery, whose ethical guidelines does one follow? What is right and what is wrong?

The last two writers turn the question to ethics in government. Is it ever necessary to lie for the public good? Niccolò Machiavelli argues yes, because for the prince, or absolute ruler, the end justifies the means. "A prince," he says, "needs to be a great feigner and dissembler." Philosopher Sissela Bok, applying the question to a democracy, disagrees, and carefully builds a case for the idea that "deceiving the people for the sake of the people is a self-contradictory notion."

Cashing in the Commonweal for the Commonwheel of Fortune

Norman Lear

Norman Lear (born 1922) has worked in television and film for most of his life. He attended Emerson College, enlisted in the Air Force, and by 1950 he started to write for comedy shows; he continued to write, direct, and produce a long series of successes, including "All in the Family," "Maude," "The Jeffersons," "One Day at a Time," "Good Times," and "Mary Hartman, Mary Hartman."

Lear has also been an active worker for public interest organizations such as People for the American Way, which he founded in 1980, and the American Civil Liberties Union. In a 1983 interview, he said, "Our country is choking on short-term thinking—we seem to be sacrificing all of our tomorrows for that . . . momentary gratification which we call success. Success has much more to do with succeeding at the level of doing one's best—and we are forgetting that."

The piece we present here was titled "Our Babylon" in the National Weekly Edition of the Washington Post, *April 20, 1987. It is an excerpt of a speech delivered at the John F. Kennedy School at Harvard University on February 17, 1987.*

The societal disease of our time, I am convinced, is America's obsession with short-term success, its fixation with the proverbial bottom-line. "Give me a profit statement this quarter larger than the last, and everything else be damned!" That is today's predominant business ethic. It took root in the business community but has since spread beyond business and insinuated itself into the rest of our culture. In this climate, a quiet revolution in values has occurred, and it has not been for the better.

Short-term thinking, corrosive individualism, fixating on "economic man" at the expense of the human spirit, has taken an alarming toll. I focus on the business community for starters, not to make it a scapegoat—but because I believe business has become a fountainhead of values in our society.

If the church was the focal point for personal values and public mores in medieval times, that role in our time has been assumed, unwittingly perhaps, by the modern corporation.

For better or worse, traditional institutions such as the family, the churches and education are no longer as influential in molding moral-cultural values. There are, I suppose, dozens of reasons one could find: the disruptions of urbanization; the alarming increase of single-parent households; the rise of the mass media, especially television; the dizzy mobility of our car culture; the telecommunications revolution and the altered sense of time and distance it has created. As traditional families have come under stress and splintered, as education has come under siege, as churches and synagogues have become less influential in daily life, the modern corporation with the help of the media has stepped into the breach.

Mythologist Joseph Campbell has said that in medieval times, when one approached a city, one saw the cathedral and the castle. Now one sees the soaring tower of commerce. People build their lives around these towers. Communities take shape. Work skills are learned. Social relationships are formed. Attitudes and aspirations are molded. A dense matrix of values grow up around the towers of commerce and spread beyond.

Never before has the business of business been such a cultural preoccupation. If media attention is any indication of popular interest—and it is—today there is an unprecedented interest in business affairs. In recent years, a dozen new business programs have burst forth on commercial television, public television and cable. Americans once found their heroes, for the most part, in Congress or the entertainmen~~~~~~~~~~ ~~~~~~~~~~~ ~~~~~~~~~~ now more and more people find them in business: Lee I~ ens; H. Ross Perot; Carl Icahn; until 10 minutes ~ until a moment ago, Martin A. Siegel.

If you grant me the possibility that American b~ nent force in shaping our culture and its values, leaders setting? What attitudes and behavior do th~

The Wall Street Journal recently took an over~

corporation and concluded: "Gone is talk of balanced, long-term growth; impatient shareholders and well-heeled corporate raiders have seen to that. Now anxious executives, fearing for their jobs or their companies, are focusing their efforts on trimming operations and shuffling assets to improve near-term profits, often at the expense of both balance and growth."

There are no two-legged villains in this "get-while-the-getting-is-good" atmosphere. Only victims. The villain is the climate which, like a house with a leaking gas pipe, is certain to see us all dead in our sleep one day, never knowing what hit us.

Sociologist Daniel Bell has argued that in promoting an ethic of "materialistic hedonism," the free enterprise system tends to subvert the very values that help to sustain it. If American business insists upon defining itself solely in terms of its market share, profitability and stock price—if its short-term material goals are allowed to prevail over all else—then business tends to subvert the moral-cultural values that undergird the entire system, such values as social conscience, pride in one's work, commitment to one's community, loyalty to one's company—in short, a sense of the commonweal.

This ethic breeds in a climate where leadership everywhere—in business, Congress, federal agencies, state legislatures, organized labor, the universities—refuses, through greed or myopia or weakness, to make provisions for the future. And in this climate, with this kind of short-sighted leadership, we have been raising generations of children to believe that there is nothing between winning and losing. The notion that life has anything to do with succeeding at the level of doing one's best, or that some of life's richest rewards are not monetary, is lost to these kids in this short-term, bottom-line climate.

America has become a game show. Winning is all that matters. Cash prizes. Get rich quick. We are the captives of a culture that celebrates instant gratification and individual success no matter the larger costs. George Will, in his book *Statecraft as Soulcraft,* argues that the country's future is imperiled unless our leaders can cultivate in citizens a deeper commitment to the commonweal. Yet rather than heed that admonition, we are turning the commonweal into the Commonwheel of Fortune.

Take a look at the Commonwheel of Fortune gameboard. It's not unlike the Monopoly gameboard—but instead of real estate, we've got just about every major American corporation represented, all up for grabs. For you latecomers to the game, Owens Corning, NBC, Texaco and TWA are off the board now—but Goodyear, USX, Union Carbide and many more have ~~be~~en in play recently. With a little roll of the dice and the junk bonds the ~~game~~ is played with, just watch the raiding and merging and acquisition—~~wh~~at fun!

~~W~~e produced 14 new billionaires last year—not to mention what it's done for foreign investors who, with their yens and deutschemarks, have caught on to our national lack of concern for the future. We are now selling them America as cheaply, under the circumstances, as the Indians sold us Manhattan.

On the surface, we seem to have accepted the selling of America just as we seem to have accepted the fact that we no longer make the best automobiles, the best radios and stereos and television sets and compact discs; the fact is we hardly make any of these products by ourselves today where we once were responsible for most of them. We've accepted that without a whimper.

There is a psychic, spiritual dimension to these changes that cannot be ignored. There is an open wound, a gash, on the American psyche that must be attended to.

Take the American motor car. Through all the years I was growing up, it was the standard of the world. "Keeping up with the Joneses" in those years meant only one thing: You were either trading up the General Motors line, the Ford line or the Chrysler line. My dad was a GM man. He got as far as the Oldsmobile; one year he almost made it to the Buick. But caring about your motor car was the universal family vocation. The American motor car was the national, non-military symbol of America's macho—and one does not have to be a social scientist to know that when we lost that symbol, sometime in the past 25 years, it left a big dent in the American Dream.

The Big Three automakers failed to heed the handwriting on the wall and refused to innovate, to build small fuel-efficient cars; refused to sacrifice a current quarterly profit statement to invest in the future and meet the threat of imports from abroad.

There is the ailing steel industry, which refused to modernize and invest in its future. There are the labor unions in both industries, which fought only for added wages and benefits—and declined to fight to modernize and to protect their members' jobs in the long term. There is the U.S. consumer electronics industry, which surrendered the compact-disc technology to Japan and Holland, who were willing to make long-term investments in the fledgling technology.

There is a hurt and an emptiness and confusion in this nation to which attention must be paid. There is fear and resentment, which makes Americans ripe for extremists who offer promises of easy salvation. It can exacerbate social tensions and result in an escalation of the kind of racism we have witnessed around the country recently.

If you agree with me that our culture has been weaned from a respect for other values to the worshipping of money and success and the fruits of instant gratification—and that this is resulting in a spiritual and cultural crisis—what, then, do we do about it? How can we reclaim the commonweal from the mindless game show it has become?

We can start by recognizing that government has a major responsibility here. I am a product of the free-enterprise system, and I cherish it. I am also a human being, and I cherish my humanity. But everything I know about human nature tells me we are innately selfish. We do look out for ourselves first. And then our family, our loved ones. Some of us, not enough, reach out beyond that. But when we, the people, talk about caring for things that are ours—our water, our air, our safety, our protection from the myriad harmful things we reasonable good people are capable of doing to each other—we have to know we can only rely on our government! It is we, through government, who provide for the common welfare.

Business nurtures the conceit that its behavior is purely private—but take one look at the largess it receives from the government: It once accounted for 29 percent of federal tax revenues; it is now down to 6 percent. Take a look, too, at the role of corporate political action committees and the cultural values that business fosters—and it is clear why government must play a more influential role in protecting the commonweal from the Commonwheel of Fortune.

This, again, is a climate we are seeking to change—and there are thermostats that address that climate in every home, in every school, in every church, in every business in this country. We can start, perhaps, by establishing a new set of symbols and heroes. We have had Rambo and Oliver North and Ivan Boesky; corporate raiders and arbitrageurs; the "yuppie generation" and the culture of conspicuous consumption; we have had religious zealots who would abridge the First Amendment in the name of God and political extremists who would censor books and condone racism.

But we have also had, and more attention must be paid to, people like Robert Hayes. An attorney with a top-flight New York law firm, he quit his lucrative job several years ago to start a new branch of legal practice: defending the rights of the homeless. His initiative inspired dozens of other such legal practices around the country.

Attention must be paid to Eugene Lang, a New York millionaire who, while speaking at an elementary school graduation, spontaneously offered to pay for the college expenses of some sixth graders of an inner city school if they would study hard and not drop out of school. His example has caught on in other cities, where individuals and businesses "adopt" students to help them succeed.

And attention must be paid to Warren Buffett, the Nebraska chairman of Berkshire-Hathaway, who has seen to it that a part of every single dollar among the millions of dollars earmarked for shareholders goes to a charity or a cause selected by that shareholder in advance.

We need to rehabilitate the idea of public service; to set new ethical standards for business; to harness the natural idealism of young people; and to encourage leadership everywhere to assume a greater burden of responsibility to lead. As I said, the villain here is the climate. It needs changing.

Plant in your mind, if you will, the close-up actions of a man, as in a film. Savagely, he is cutting off the hands of another man. We are horrified; this action defies our understanding. Now pull back to examine the context, and learn that we are in a different culture—perhaps, but not necessarily, in an earlier time. Eyes can be gouged out here. Men are drawn and quartered—sometimes for sheer entertainment. We don't accept, but we understand better now that first savage act. Its perpetrators were behaving in the context of their time and culture.

Now look at Martin A. Siegel and gang, arrested recently for insider trading. A thief. Broke a trust. We don't understand. He was making $2 million. Why did he need another $7 million?

But let's pull back and see Siegel in the context of the culture I have been describing, and we must ask: In some perverse way, doesn't his story speak for the '80s?

Isn't Siegel's story an example in microcosm of the perverted values of our culture—where the making of money, not working hard, producing well, leaving something lasting behind—but the making of money has become the sole value?

The problem isn't Martin Siegel's alone. It is ours. We have found the Holy Grail, and it is the Bottom Line.

Do we want it?

Must we continue cashing in the commonweal for the Commonwheel of Fortune?

My Company—
Right or Wrong?

Charles W. Parry

Charles W. Parry (born 1924) was raised in Pittsburgh, Pennsylvania, and educated at the University of Pittsburgh (B.S.E.E. 1948). After graduation, he immediately began work as a staff engineer for the Aluminum Company of America; he rose through the company in various positions to become president and then chairman of the board and chief executive officer. After almost forty years with Alcoa, he retired in 1987. He is the author of Alcoa: A Retrospection *(1985). The speech we present here was delivered before the Carlow College Ethics Seminar in Pittsburgh on May 16, 1985.*

Winston Churchill once remarked that, "Some see private enterprise as a predatory target to be shot, others as a cow to be milked, but few are those who see it as a sturdy horse pulling the wagon." Long after Churchill's death, we still find ourselves to be in a period of diminishing public trust toward the standards and behavior of the business community. Yet the "wagon" moves on, steadily increasing the wealth of the nation. America's ambivalence toward its own prosperity results from a continuing struggle to understand the relationship between business, ethics and society. While not hoping to master this mystery, I would like to share with you a few thoughts on this relationship and discuss the direction our enterprise is pulling us.

Business, ethics and society are interesting concepts to explore, because they define each other to a significant extent. Business is not separate from society; it is not an ethical adversary of the common good. Instead, business is a reflection of society; it is the method by which individuals unite to form a network of common interest. Ethics is not something businessmen must violate in order to make a profit; it is something they must implement in order to prevent chaos.

Let us begin at the level of the individual. A person needs to act upon his environment in order to achieve expression and an improved standard of living. The Catholic bishops have referred to this as "self-realization in labor." In order to better themselves, productive individuals must form a communion of commerce. It is at this point that we have an economy.

What is the ultimate end of an economy? I'm afraid there's no certain answer. We do not know the limits of human skill, creativity or productive capacity. This renders meaningless such subjective and abstract goals as happiness or equality. Thomas Jefferson recognized as much when he cited the *"pursuit* of happiness" as one of society's ends. Economic man must be free to pursue his unknown limits, just as economic society must be open to change and development. Indeed, we may even go so far as to consider whether pursuit *is* in a material world. And the thing we are pursuing is the limit of our potential—a distant horizon that we can chase, but which continues to move forward with every step we take.

Business is the act of changing the world to meet the needs and desires of men and women as they explore their potential. But the finite resources of the world require us to develop a code of conduct that will preserve us from violence and deceit. Regardless of the size of the enterprise, business relies on ethics for its existence. I would refer you to the classic case of the merchant who scared away his competitor's customers by shooting them with pellets as they approached the competitor's door. The man was arrested and punished, and rightly so. Coercion would lead to anarchy if it became an accepted business practice, and intimidation would lead to retaliation instead of competition.

The modern corporation is a business that requires a more complex system of ethics. It might help us to think of two levels of ethical standards that relate to corporations: these are the ethics of the institution and the ethics of action.

The ethics of the institution refer to the relationships among the groups that comprise the corporation. It is a serious mistake to think of the corporation as a monolith, existing to meet the every whim of a board of directors. The corporation is a process. It is, like the economy, a fluid enterprise. At its center are the managers and executives responsible for directing the resources of the company. The shareholders own the capital and deserve a return on their investment. The workers produce the goods for the marketplace and deserve a living wage and safe working conditions. The ethics of the institution require each group to be responsible to the others and to balance its interest against the interests of the others. Pope John Paul II refers to such a balance as a "harmonization of legitimate interests and aspirations." When the balance is upset, or when the interests pull too hard against each other, the ethical system is damaged.

Two cases may help illustrate the kinds of problems that arise under the category of institutional ethics. Film Recovery Systems, Inc.—now defunct—cut corners in providing safety equipment and supplies for its workers, who were exposed to toxic levels of cyanide. One of the workers died of cyanide poisoning, and four corporate executives went on trial for murder as a result.° Were these executives merely unscrupulous villains, or were they conscientious managers who were subjected to unfair competitive pressure to turn a profit? Perhaps the trial will determine this. It is clear from the outset that a harmony of interests was lacking, and with terrible consequences.

Another case is closer to home. It involves the sale of Gulf Oil. Shareholders' interests are sometimes well served by efforts of speculators to bid up the value of capital through a takeover bid. Even consumers may benefit by reduced prices and greater efficiency. But what about the interests of the individuals and the communities who have lost jobs as a result of the sale? Is it possible to protect them from the hardships imposed by this decision? If so, who is responsible for administering the remedy?

The ethics of the institution concern the responses of the component groups of a corporation to the constant changes of economic life. When new technology or new tastes require a business to change, ethical considerations must be taken into account so that sacrifices may be shared as much as possible. Conversely, selfish interests must not be confused with ethics. Workers whose wage demands threaten the survival of financially-strapped companies should not claim that God is on their side if their struggle with management bankrupts the company. For its own part, management should not ruin the return to shareholders by crippling the business in order to punish impertinent workers.

The ethics of action is the second relationship I would like to mention. These involve the performance of a business and its transformation of the

---

four corporate executives . . . result They were convicted of murder in 1985.

world it inhabits. A corporation and a consumer have mutual obligations, as do the groups within the business. The corporation must produce a good of use or value to the consumer; the product must not be harmful to the consumer; and the price of the good must be as competitive as possible. As for the consumer, he must be willing to pay a fair market price, and he must not abuse the product. It is also important that the changes brought about by a company do not include permanent environmental damage. Such use inhibits future use of resources, or, in the case of a Love Canal,° poses a hazard to public health.

There are many and varied abuses involving the ethics of action, and they frequently result from greed rather than legitimate responses to the pressures of the market. A growing threat to the consumer is posed by counterfeit goods. Fake fertilizers, fashions and computers are among the hundreds of products made in Asia and Latin America that cost the United States more than 130,000 jobs each year and steal at least $8 billion annually from American industry. Some of these phony products are used in aerospace and pharmaceutical businesses, threatening the health and safety of unwitting consumers.

A more difficult ethical problem is brought about through the legitimate pressure of competition. As countries with lower living standards and lower wage rates enter the international marketplace, consumers are able to take advantage of significantly cheaper goods of comparable quality. Imported cars and stereos, textiles and sporting goods challenge the standard of living of America's skilled and unskilled labor force. Can the competition be fair when a Mexican can make a car or a Haitian can make a baseball for one-tenth the labor cost of his American counterpart? If the competition is not fair, is it ethical to punish the Korean garment worker or the Taiwanese toymaker for living in a poorer society? What kind of political turmoil might result from depriving a poor worker of a market for his goods? And what responsibility does the consumer bear? It may seem unreasonable to expect a consumer to "buy American," when paying a higher price diminishes his opportunities to purchase additional goods. It may also seem unreasonable to expect a steelworker or a textile worker to diminish his opportunities by working for a Third World wage. There hardly seems a fair and ethical way out of this quandary in the short run. The long run requires patience and greater involvement in the markets of poorer countries.

The ethics of action, like the ethics of the institution, imply reciprocal responsibility. One area of possible abuse by the consumer is the growing

---

Love Canal Site of a toxic waste dump in Niagara Falls, New York, during the 1940s and 1950s. In 1978 the government discovered that toxic chemicals were leaking into homes. Much of the area was evacuated.

issue of product liability. The number of million-dollar awards to plaintiffs in lawsuits has soared from eight in 1970 to 360 in 1983. Some pharmaceutical firms have been frightened out of marketing drugs whose risks are statistically very small, but whose insurance costs make production economically impossible. Even when successful, legal defenses are sufficiently costly to do harm to businesses. Johnson & Johnson has had to endure an increasing amount of nuisance suits involving plaster of paris—a product it has been selling successfully for decades. The costs of consumer irresponsibility should be included in any discussion of business ethics, since the consumer's purpose in doing business with a company should not include harassment.

As we can see, the relationship of business and ethics is not a simple or uniform one. Human history is a river, not a rock, and the transformations of societies and economies should proceed unhindered. As these changes occur, some businesses emerge and some become obsolete. The purpose of ethics is not to preserve vested interests and prevent change; it is to give those affected by change a sense of mutual responsibility in preparing for the future.

A final relationship I would like to explore with you is the relationship between business and society, particularly as it involves the political system under which business operates. Since business is open-ended in its view of the future, and since it works best when free from the obstructions of interest groups, it does not function well as a social welfare agency. True, business charity and community involvement are extensive and important, but the prime purpose of business is material transformation and the creation of wealth. The distribution of that wealth is a matter for government.

I find it both interesting and troubling that the American bishops, in the first draft of their paper on economics, chose an apparently disingenuous tack. They spent nine-tenths of their efforts on the distribution of wealth, and only one-tenth on its creation. In reality, however, the two are intimately tied, for in the absence of the creation of wealth, there is nothing to distribute.

I would include a word of caution. As we have seen in countries behind the Iron Curtain, severe government interference with business subjects it to the vested interests of particular parties, and all but destroys the incentive for change that is so important to the pursuit of happiness. Even in the more moderate socialist context of Western Europe, since 1970 the United States has produced more jobs each day than that continent has produced in the entire decade and a half. And in the completely state-controlled economy of the Soviet Union, the destruction of incentive has produced less economic growth, higher alcoholism and lower life expectancy. The end result of this paradise for the proletariat has been the pursuit of lethargy.

In the American context, there are those unable to participate in the communion of commerce. For them there is a need for a safety net. The nature and extent of this assistance is a matter for public debate and political decision. The obligation of business is to act as a responsible citizen and honor the wishes of the society as a whole. Business should not use its economic power to buy votes. It does have a right to lobby on behalf of its own interests. But it should not attempt to engage in corporate civil disobedience toward objectionable laws. Taxes, pollution regulations and safety standards must be honored.

In this, the age of the multinational corporation, businesses find themselves operating under many and varied social and political systems. My feelings here are that the best interests of the company are economic, and that the regulations and laws of host countries must be accepted and obeyed. During the tenure of the late President Ahmed Sekou Toure of Guinea, Alcoa conducted its business in his country without interfering in the political system. Even though I had strong personal reservations about his government, the principle of non-interference is more important.

Ironically, there are others who adhere to that principle. My own experience brings to mind examples of advanced societies sending religious people—both missionaries and laity—to lesser developed nations. Those citizens from advanced countries all too often find it convenient to criticize companies from their own or other advanced societies, while remaining silent about identical behavior on the part of indigenous businesses. This double standard is readily accepted and frequently applied, and I find it disturbing.

All too often the discussion on the role of business in politics is a reflection of ideology rather than ethics. I would think that a supporter of the Sandinistas in Nicaragua might insist that American businesses bring to bear all their influence to promote change in government policies in South Korea or South Africa. Would that same person support U.S. businesses that worked to change the government or policies in Managua? Was IT&T right in involving itself in Chilean politics during the overthrow of Salvador Allende? I think it is safer and more honest if businesses avoid such ideological struggles. I think it is a wiser policy to stay away from the political structures of host countries and do that which business does best, namely, increase wealth and the standard of living of the greatest possible number.

It has been said that capitalism makes a virtue out of selfishness. I don't think that is entirely true. It is up to the capitalist to be aware of his self-interest, and to reflect that interest in the image of an enterprise composed of a network of responsibilities. Harmony and balance are required if a business is to continue to give value to human effort and to bring to life the most creative achievements of human imagination. With an ethical sense, we can help the old horse carry its wagon along the right path.

from *A Traveler's Guide to Gifts and Bribes*

Jeffrey A. Fadiman

Jeffrey Fadiman (born 1936) is a professor of international marketing and intercultural communications at San Jose State University. He was educated at Stanford University (B.A. 1959), American University (M.A. 1963) and the University of Wisconsin (Ph.D. 1973), and also in Makere, Uganda (DIP. Ed. 1963). He is the author of three books: The Moment of Conquest: Meru, Kenya, 1907 *(1979);* An Oral History of Tribal Warfare: The Meru of Mt. Kenya *(1982); and* The Witchcraft Traditions: An African Oral History *(forthcoming).*

His twenty-two years as safari guide, African oral historian, and anthropologist in Africa and Asia provide the experience for the question he raises here: Can Americans doing business in foreign cultures avoid compromising their own moral codes? We print below the first three sections of an article from the July–August 1986 issue of the Harvard Business Review.

"What do I say if he asks for a bribe?" I asked myself while enduring the all-night flight to Asia. Uncertain, I shared my concern with the man sitting beside me, a CEO en route to Singapore. Intrigued, he passed it on to his partners next to him. No one seemed sure.

Among American executives doing business overseas, this uncertainty is widespread. Consider, for example, each of the following situations:

You are invited to the home of your foreign colleague. You learn he lives in a palatial villa. What gift might both please your host and ease business relations? What if he considers it to be a bribe? What if he *expects* it to be a bribe? Why do you feel uneasy?

Your company's product lies on the dock of a foreign port. To avoid spoilage, you must swiftly transport it inland. What "gift," if any, would both please authorities and facilitate your business? What if they ask for "gifts" of $50? $50,000? $500,000? When does a gift become a bribe? When do you stop feeling comfortable?

Negotiations are complete. The agreement is signed. One week later, a minister asks your company for $1 million—"for a hospital"—simultaneously suggesting that "other valuable considerations" might come your way as the result of future favors on both sides. What response, if any, would please him, satisfy you, and help execute the signed agreement?

You have been asked to testify before the Securities and Exchange Commission regarding alleged violations of the Foreign Corrupt Practices Act. How would you explain the way you handled the examples above? Would your explanations both satisfy those in authority and ensure the continued overseas operation of your company?

Much of the discomfort Americans feel when faced with problems of this nature is due to U.S. law. Since 1977, congressional passage of the Foreign Corrupt Practices Act has transformed hypothetical problems into practical dilemmas and has created considerable anxiety among Americans who deal with foreign governments and companies. The problem is particularly difficult for those conducting business in the developing nations, where the rules that govern payoffs may differ sharply from our own. In such instances, U.S. executives may face not only legal but also ethical and cultural dilemmas: How do businesspeople comply with customs that conflict with both their sense of ethics and this nation's law?

One way to approach the problem is to devise appropriate corporate responses to payoff requests. The suggestions that follow apply to those developing Asian, African, and Middle Eastern nations, still in transition toward industrial societies, that have retained aspects of their communal traditions. These approaches do not assume that those who adhere to these ideals exist in selfless bliss, requesting private payments only for communal ends, with little thought of self-enrichment. Nor do these suggestions apply to situations of overt extortion, where U.S. companies are forced to provide funds. Instead they explore a middle way in which non-Western colleagues may have several motives when requesting a payoff, thereby providing U.S. managers with several options.

My own first experience with Third World bribery may illustrate the inner conflict Americans can feel when asked to break the rules. It occurred in East Africa and began with this request: "Oh, and Bwana, I would like 1,000 shillings as Zawadi, my gift. And, as we are now friends, for Chai, my tea, an eight-band radio, to bring to my home when you visit."

Both *Chai* and *Zawadi* can be Swahili terms for "bribe." He delivered these requests in respectful tones. They came almost as an afterthought, at the conclusion of negotiations in which we had settled the details of a projected business venture. I had looked forward to buying my counterpart a final drink to complete the deal symbolically in the American fashion. Instead, after we had settled every contractual aspect, he expected money.

The amount he suggested, although insignificant by modern standards, seemed large at the time. Nonetheless, it was the radio that got to me. Somehow it added insult to injury. Outwardly, I kept smiling. Inside, my stomach boiled. My own world view equates bribery with sin. I expect monetary issues to be settled before contracts are signed. Instead, although the negotiations were complete, he expected me to pay out once more. Once? How often? Where would it stop? My reaction took only moments to formulate. "I'm American," I declared. "I don't pay bribes." Then I walked away. That walk was not the longest in my life. It was, however, one of the least commercially productive.

As it turned out, I had misunderstood him—in more ways than one. By misinterpreting both his language and his culture, I lost an opportunity for a business deal and a personal relationship that would have paid enormous dividends without violating either the law or my own sense of ethics.

Go back through the episode—but view it this time with an East African perspective. First, my colleague's language should have given me an important clue as to how he saw our transaction. Although his limited command of English caused him to frame his request as a command—a phrasing I instinctively found offensive—his tone was courteous. Moreover, if I had listened more carefully, I would have noted that he had addressed me as a superior: he used the honorific *Bwana,* meaning "sir," rather than *Rafiki* (or friend), used between equals. From his perspective, the language was appropriate; it reflected the differences in our personal wealth and in the power of the institutions we each represented.

Having assigned me the role of the superior figure in the economic transaction, he then suggested how I should use my position in accord with his culture's traditions—logically assuming that I would benefit by his prompting. In this case, he suggested that money and a radio would be appropriate gifts. What he did not tell me was that his culture's traditions required him to use the money to provide a feast—in my honor—to which he would invite everyone in his social and commercial circle whom he felt I should meet. The radio would simply create a festive atmosphere at the party. This was to mark the beginning of an ongoing relationship with reciprocal benefits.

He told me none of this. Since I was willing to do business in local fashion, I was supposed to know. In fact, I had not merely been invited to a dwelling but through a gateway into the maze of gifts and formal visiting that linked him to his kin. He hoped that I would respond in local fashion. Instead, I responded according to my cultural norms and walked out both on the chance to do business and on the opportunity to make friends.

Perhaps from a strictly legal perspective my American reaction was warranted. In the late 1970s, as part of the national reaction to Watergate, the SEC sued several large U.S. companies for alleged instances of bribery overseas. One company reportedly authorized $59 million in contributions to political parties in Italy, including the Communist party. A second allegedly paid $4 million to a political party in South Korea. A third reportedly provided $450,000 in "gifts" to Saudi generals. A fourth may have diverted $377,000 to fly planeloads of voters to the Cook Islands to rig elections there.

The sheer size of the payments and the ways they had been used staggered the public. A U.S. senate committee reported "corrupt" foreign payments involving hundreds of millions of dollars by more than 400 U.S. corporations, including 117 of the *Fortune* "500." The SEC described the problem as a national crisis.

In response, Congress passed the Foreign Corrupt Practices Act in 1977. The law prohibits U.S. corporations from providing or even offering payments to foreign political parties, candidates, or officials with discretionary authority under circumstances that might induce recipients to misuse their positions to assist the company to obtain, maintain, or retain business.

The FCPA does not forbid payments to lesser figures, however. On the contrary, it explicitly allows facilitating payments ("grease") to persuade foreign officials to perform their normal duties, at both the clerical and ministerial levels. The law establishes no monetary guidelines but requires companies to keep reasonably detailed records that accurately and fairly reflect the transactions.

The act also prohibits indirect forms of payment. Companies cannot make payments of this nature while "knowing or having reason to know" that any portion of the funds will be transferred to a forbidden recipient to be used for corrupt purposes as previously defined. Corporations face fines of up to $1 million. Individuals can be fined $10,000—which the corporation is forbidden to indemnify—and sentenced to a maximum of five years in prison. In short, private payments by Americans abroad can mean violation of U.S. law, a consideration that deeply influences U.S. corporate thinking.

For most U.S. executives, however, the problem goes beyond the law. Most Americans share an aversion to payoffs. In parts of Asia, Africa, and the Middle East, however, certain types of bribery form an accepted element of their commercial traditions. Of course, nepotism, shakedown, and similar practices do occur in U.S. business; these practices, however, are both forbidden by law and universally disapproved.

Americans abroad reflect these sentiments. Most see themselves as personally honest and professionally ethical. More important, they see themselves as preferring to conduct business according to the law, both American and foreign. They also know that virtually all foreign governments—including those notorious for corruption—have rigorously enforced statutes against most forms of private payoff. In general, there is popular support for these anticorruption measures. In Malaysia, bribery is publicly frowned on and punishable by long imprisonment. In the Soviet Union, Soviet officials who solicit bribes can be executed.

Reflecting this awareness, most U.S. businesspeople prefer to play by local rules, competing in the open market according to the quality, price, and services provided by their product. Few, if any, want to make illegal payments of any kind to anybody. Most prefer to obey both local laws and their own ethical convictions while remaining able to do business.

Yet, as my African experience suggests, indigenous traditions often override the law. In some developing nations, payoffs have become a norm. The problem is compounded when local payoff practices are rooted in a "communal heritage," ideals inherited from a preindustrial past where a community leader's wealth—however acquired—was shared throughout the community. Those who hoarded were scorned as antisocial. Those who shared won status and authority. Contact with Western commerce has blurred the ideal, but even the most individualistic businesspeople remember their communal obligations.

Contemporary business practices in those regions often reflect these earlier ideals. Certain forms of private payoff have endured for centuries. The Nigerian practice of *dash* (private payments for private services), for example, goes back to fifteenth century contacts with the Portuguese, in which Africans solicited "gifts" (trade goods) in exchange for labor. Such solicitation can pose a cultural dilemma to Americans who may be unfamiliar with the communal nuances of non-Western commercial conduct. To cope, they may denigrate these traditions, perceiving colleagues who solicit payments as unethical and their culture as corrupt.

Or they may respond to communal business methods by ignoring them, choosing instead to deal with foreign counterparts purely in Western fashion. This approach will usually work—up to a point. Non-Western businesspeople who deal with U.S. executives, for example, are often graduates of Western universities. Their language skills, commercial training, and professional demeanor, so similar to ours, make it comfortable to conduct business. But when these same colleagues shift to non-Western behavior, discussing gifts or bribes, Americans are often shocked.

Obviously, such reactions ignore the fact that foreign businesspeople have more than one cultural dimension. Managers from developing countries may hold conflicting values: one instilled by exposure to the West, the other imposed by local tradition. Non-Western businesspeople may see no conflict in negotiating contracts along Western lines, then reverting to indigenous traditions when discussing private payments. For Americans, however, this transition may be hard to make.

My experience suggests that most non-Westerners are neither excessively corrupt nor completely communal. Rather, they are simultaneously drawn to both indigenous and Western ideals. Many have internalized the Western norms of personal enrichment along with those of modern commerce, while simultaneously adhering to indigenous traditions by fulfilling communal obligations. Requests for payoffs may spring from both these ideals. Corporate responses must therefore be designed to satisfy them both.

Throughout non-Western cultures, three traditions form the background for discussing payoffs: the inner circle, future favors, and the gift exchange. Though centuries old, each has evolved into a modern business concept. Americans who work in the Third World need to learn about them so they can work within them.

Most individuals in developing nations classify others into some form of "ins" and "outs." Members of more communal societies, influenced by the need to strive for group prosperity, divide humanity into those with whom they have relationships and those with whom they have none. Many Africans, for instance, view people as either "brothers" or "strangers." Relationships with brothers may be real—kin, however distant—or fictional, extending to comrades or "mates." Comrades, however, may both speak and act like kin, address one another as family, and assume obligations of protection and assistance that Americans reserve for nuclear families.

Together, kin and comrades form an inner circle, a fictional "family," devoted to mutual protection and prosperity. Like the "old boy networks" that operate in the United States, no single rule defines membership in the inner circle. East Africans may include "age mates," individuals of similar age; West Africans, "homeboys," all men of similar region; Chinese, members of a dialect group; Indians, members of a caste. In most instances, the "ins" include extended families and their friends.

Beyond this magic circle live the "outs": strangers, aliens, individuals with no relationship to those within. Communal societies in Southern Africa, for example, describe these people in all their millions as "predators," implying savage creatures with whom the "ins" lack any common ground. The motives of outsiders inspire fear, not because there is danger but simply because they are unknown. Although conditioned to display courtesy, insiders prefer to restrict both social and commercial dealings to those with whom they have dependable relationships. The ancient principle can still be found in modern commerce; non-Western businesspeople often prefer to restrict commercial relationships to those they know and trust.

Not every U.S. manager is aware of this division. Those who investigate often assume that their nationality, ethnic background, and alien culture automatically classify them as "outs." Non-Western colleagues, however, may regard specific Westerners as useful contacts, particularly if they seem willing to do business in local fashion. They may, therefore, consider bringing certain individuals into their inner circles in such a manner as to benefit both sides.

Overseas executives, if asked to work within such circles, should find their business prospects much enhanced. These understandings often lead to implicit quid pro quos. For example, one side might agree to hire workers from only one clan; in return the other side would guarantee devoted labor. As social and commercial trust grows, the Westerners may be regarded less and less as aliens or predators and more and more as comrades or kin. Obviously, this is a desirable transition, and executives assigned to work within this type of culture may wish to consider whether these inner circles exist, and if so, whether working within them will enhance business prospects.

A second non-Western concept that relates to payoffs is a system of future favors. Relationships within the inner circles of non-Western nations function through such favors. In Japan, the corresponding system is known as "inner duty" or *giri*. On Mt. Kenya, it is "inner relationship," *uthoni*. Filipinos describe it as "inner debt," *utani na loob*. All systems of this type assume that any individual under obligation to another has entered a relationship in which the first favor must be repaid in the future, when convenient to all sides.

Neither side defines the manner of repayment. Rather, both understand that some form of gift or service will repay the earlier debt with interest. This repayment places the originator under obligation. The process then begins again, creating a lifelong cycle. The relationship that springs from meeting lifelong obligations builds the trust that forms a basis for conducting business.

My own introduction to the future favors system may illustrate the process. While conducting business on Mt. Kenya in the 1970s, I visited a notable local dignitary. On completing our agenda, he stopped my rush to leave by presenting me a live and angry hen. Surprised, I stammered shaky "thank-yous," then walked down the mountain with my kicking, struggling bird. Having discharged my obligation—at least in Western terms—by thanking him, I cooked the hen, completed my business, eventually left Kenya, and forgot the incident.

Years later, I returned on different business. It was a revelation. People up and down the mountain called out to one another that I had come back to "return the dignitary's hen." To them, the relationship that had sprung up between us had remained unchanged throughout the years. Having received a favor, I had now come back to renew the relationship by returning it.

I had, of course, no such intention. Having forgotten the hen incident, I was also unaware of its importance to others. Embarrassed, I slipped into a market and bought a larger hen, then climbed to his homestead to present it. Again I erred, deciding to apologize in Western fashion for delaying my return. "How can a hen be late?" he replied. "Due to the bird, we have *uthoni* [obligations, thus a relationship]. That is what sweetens life. What else was the hen for but to bring you here again?"

These sentiments can also operate within non-Western commercial circles, where business favors can replace hens, but *uthoni* are what sweetens corporate life. Western interest lies in doing business; non-Western, in forming bonds so that business can begin. Westerners seek to discharge obligations; non-Westerners, to create them. Our focus is on producing short-term profit; theirs, on generating future favors. The success of an overseas venture may depend on an executive's awareness of these differences.

One final non-Western concept that can relate to payoffs is a continuous exchange of gifts. In some developing nations, gifts form the catalysts that trigger future favors. U.S. executives often wish to present gifts appropriate to cultures where they are assigned, to the point where at least one corporation has commissioned a special study of the subject. They may be less aware, however, of the long-range implications of gift giving within these cultures. Two of these may be particularly relevant to CEOs concerned with payoffs.

In many non-Western commercial circles, the tradition of gift giving has evolved into a modern business tool intended to create obligation as well as affection. Recipients may be gratified by what they receive, but they also incur an obligation that they must some day repay. Gift giving in these cultures may therefore operate in two dimensions: one meant to provide short-term pleasure; the other, long-range bonds.

This strategy is common in Moslem areas of Africa and Asia. Within these cultures, I have watched export merchants change Western clientele from browsers to buyers by inviting them to tea. Seated, the customers sip at leisure, while merchandise is brought before them piece by piece. The seller thus achieves three goals. His clients have been honored, immobilized, and placed under obligation.

In consequence, the customers often feel the need to repay in kind. Lacking suitable material gifts, they frequently respond as the merchant intends: with decisions to buy—not because they need the merchandise but to return the seller's gift of hospitality. The buyers, considering their obligation discharged, leave the premises believing relations have ended. The sellers, however, hope they have just begun. Their intent is to create relationships that will cause clients to return. A second visit would mean presentation of another gift, perhaps of greater value. That, in turn, might mean a second purchase, leading to further visits, continued gifts, and a gradual deepening of personal and commercial relations intended to enrich both sides.

The point of the process, obviously, is not the exchanges themselves but the relationships they engender. The gifts are simply catalysts. Under ideal circumstances the process should be unending, with visits, gifts, gestures, and services flowing back and forth among participants throughout their lives. The universally understood purpose is to create reciprocal good feelings and commercial prosperity among all concerned.

Gift giving has also evolved as a commercial "signal." In America, gifts exchanged by business colleagues may signal gratitude, camaraderie, or perhaps the discharge of minor obligations. Among non-Westerners, gifts may signal the desire to begin both social and commercial relationships with members of an inner circle. That signal may also apply to gifts exchanged with Westerners. If frequently repeated, such exchanges may be signals of intent. For Americans, the signal may suggest a willingness to work within a circle of local business colleagues, to assume appropriate obligations, and to conduct business in local ways. For non-Western colleagues, gifts may imply a wish to invite selected individuals into their commercial interactions.

While U.S. corporations may benefit from adapting to local business concepts, many indigenous business traditions, especially in developing regions, are alien to the American experience and therefore difficult to implement by U.S. field personnel—as every executive who has tried to sit cross-legged for several hours with Third World counterparts will attest.

Conversely, many non-Western administrators are particularly well informed about U.S. business practices, thus permitting U.S. field representatives to function on familiar ground. Nonetheless, those willing to adapt indigenous commercial concepts to U.S. corporate needs may find that their companies can benefit in several ways. Through working with a circle of non-Western business colleagues, and participating fully in the traditional exchange of gifts and favors, U.S. executives may find that their companies increase the chance of preferential treatment; use local methods and local contacts to gain market share; develop trust to reinforce contractual obligations; and minimize current risk, while maximizing future opportunities by developing local expertise.

Corporations that adapt to local business concepts may also develop methods to cope with local forms of payoff. Current approaches vary from culture to culture, yet patterns do appear. Three frequently recur in dealings between Americans and non-Westerners: gifts, bribes, and other considerations.

This form of payoff may occur when key foreign businesspeople approach their U.S. colleagues to solicit "gifts." Solicitations of this type have no place in U.S. business circles where they could be construed as exploitation. Obviously, the same may hold true overseas, particularly in areas where shakedown, bribery, and extortion may be prevalent. There is, however, an alternative to consider. To non-Western colleagues, such requests may simply be a normal business strategy, designed to build long-term relationships.

To U.S. businesspeople, every venture is based on the bottom line. To non-Western colleagues, a venture is based on the human relationships that form around it. Yet, when dealing with us they often grow uncertain as to how to form these relationships. How can social ties be created with Americans who speak only of business, even when at leisure? How can traditions of gift giving be initiated with people unaware of the traditions? Without the exchange of gifts, how can obligations be created? Without obligations, how can there be trust?

Faced with such questions, non-Western business colleagues may understandably decide to initiate gift-giving relationships on their own. If powerful, prominent, or wealthy, they may simply begin by taking on the role of giver. If less powerful or affluent, some may begin by suggesting they become recipients. There need be no dishonor in such action, since petitioners know they will repay with future favors whatever inner debt they incur.

The hosts may also realize that, as strangers, Americans may be unaware of local forms of gift giving as well as their relationship to business norms. Or they may be cognizant of such relationships but may have no idea of how to enter into them. In such instances, simple courtesy may cause the hosts to indicate—perhaps obliquely—how proper entry into the local system should be made. Such was the unfortunate case with my East African colleague's request for the eight-band radio.

Cultural barriers can be difficult to cross. Most Americans give generously, but rarely on request. When solicited, we feel exploited. Solicitations may seem more relevant, however, if examined from the perspective of the non-Western peoples with whom we are concerned.

Often, in societies marked by enormous gaps between the rich and the poor, acts of generosity display high status. To withhold gifts is to deny the affluence one has achieved. Non-Western counterparts often use lavish hospitality both to reflect and to display their wealth and status within local society. When Americans within these regions both represent great wealth through association with their corporations and seek high status as a tool to conduct business, it may prove more profitable for the corporation to give than to receive.

In short, when asked for "gifts" by foreign personnel, managers may consider two options. The first option is to regard each query as extortion and every petitioner as a potential thief. The second is to consider the request within its local context. In nations where gifts generate a sense of obligation, it may prove best to give them, thereby creating inner debts among key foreign colleagues in the belief that they will repay them over time. If such requests indeed reflect a local way of doing business, they may be gateways into the workings of its commercial world. One U.S. option, therefore, is to consider the effect of providing "gifts"—even on direct request—in terms of the relationships required to implement the corporation's long-range plans.

A second approach to payoffs, recurrent in non-Western business circles, is the indirect request. Most Third World people prefer the carrot to the stick. To avoid unpleasant confrontation, they designate third parties to suggest that "gifts" of specified amounts be made to those in local power circles. In explanation they cite the probability of future favors in return. No line exists, of course, dividing gifts from bribes. It seems that direct solicitation involves smaller amounts, while larger ones require go-betweens. On occasion, however, the sums requested can be staggering: in 1976, for example, U.S. executives in Qatar were asked for a $1.5 million "gift" for that nation's minister of oil.

U.S. responses to such queries must preserve both corporate funds and executive relationships with those in power. While smaller gifts may signal a desire to work with the local business circles, a company that supplies larger sums could violate both local antipayoff statutes and the FCPA. Conversely, outright rejection of such requests may cause both the go-betweens and those they represent to lose prestige and thus possibly prompt retaliation.

In such instances, the FCPA may actually provide beleaguered corporate executives with a highly convenient excuse. Since direct compliance with requests for private funds exposes every U.S. company to threats of negative publicity, blackmail, legal action, financial loss, and damage to corporate image, it may prove easy for Americans to say no—while at the same time offering nonmonetary benefits to satisfy both sides.

U.S. competitors may, in fact, be in a better situation than those companies from Europe and Japan that play by different rules. Since the principle of payoffs is either accepted or encouraged by many of their governments, the companies must find it difficult to refuse payment of whatever sums are asked.

Nor should the "right to bribe" be automatically considered an advantage. Ignoring every other factor, this argument assumes contracts are awarded solely on the basis of the largest private payoff. At the most obvious level, it ignores the possibility that products also compete on the basis of quality, price, promotion, and service—factors often crucial to American success abroad. U.S. field representatives are often first to recognize that payoffs may be only one of many factors in awarding contracts. In analyzing U.S. competition in the Middle East, for instance, one executive of an American aircraft company noted: "The French have savoir faire in giving bribes discreetly and well, but they're still not . . . backing up their sales with technical expertise." The overseas executive should consider to what degree the right to bribe may be offset by turning the attention of the payoff seekers to other valuable considerations.

A third approach, often used by members of a non-Western elite, is to request that U.S. companies contribute cash to public service projects, often administered by the petitioners themselves. Most proposals of this type require money. Yet if American executives focus too sharply on the financial aspects, they may neglect the chance to work other nonmonetary considerations into their response. In many developing nations, nonmonetary considerations may weigh heavily on foreign colleagues.

Many elite non-Westerners, for example, are intensely nationalistic. They love their country keenly, deplore its relative poverty, and yearn to help it rise. They may, therefore, phrase their requests for payoffs in terms of a suggested service to the nation. In Kenya, for example, ministerial requests to U.S. companies during the 1970s suggested a contribution toward the construction of a hospital. In Indonesia, in the mid-1970s, a top executive of Pertamina, that nation's government-sponsored oil company, requested contributions to an Indonesian restaurant in New York City as a service to the homeland. In his solicitation letter, the executive wrote that the restaurant was in fact intended to "enhance the Indonesian image in the U.S.A., . . . promote tourism, . . . and attract the interest of the U.S. businessmen to investments in Indonesia."

Westerners may regard such claims with cynicism. Non-Westerners may not. They recognize that, even if the notables involved become wealthy, some portion of the wealth, which only they can attract from abroad, will still be shared by other members of their homeland.

That belief is worth consideration, for many elite non-Westerners share a second concern: the desire to meet communal obligations by sharing wealth with members of their inner circle. Modern business leaders in communal cultures rarely simply hoard their wealth. To do so would invite social condemnation. Rather, they provide gifts, funds, and favors to those in their communal settings, receiving deference, authority, and prestige in return.

This does not mean that funds transferred by Western corporations to a single foreign colleague will be parceled out among a circle of cronies. Rather, money passes through one pair of hands over time, flowing slowly in the form of gifts and favors to friends and kin. The funds may even flow beyond this inner circle to their children, most often to ensure their continued education. Such generosity, of course, places both adult recipients and children under a long-term obligation, thereby providing donors both with current status and with assurance of obtaining future favors.

In short, non-Western colleagues who seek payoffs may have concerns beyond their personal enrichment. If motivated by both national and communal idealism, they may feel that these requests are not only for themselves but also a means to aid much larger groups and ultimately their nation.

In What Way Princes Must Keep Faith

Niccolò Machiavelli

Niccolò Machiavelli (1469–1527) was first a patriotic Florentine statesman and second a writer of political theory, history, plays, and poetry. Living in a period of political chaos, he worked to stabilize the Florentine republic and to build a citizens' militia so that Florence would not have to depend on mercenaries to fight off attacks from France, Germany, Spain, the Pope, other Italian city-states, and rival factions within Florence. But Ma-

chiavelli failed. In 1512 the Medici—the ruling family that had been ousted after the death of the powerful Lorenzo de Medici in 1492—returned to defeat the new militia and to set up another princedom in Florence. Within a year Machiavelli was imprisoned on conspiracy charges, tortured, and finally released as part of a general amnesty because Cardinal de Medici had just been elected Pope. He retired to his farm, bitter and broken in spirit, and spent the rest of his life trying to figure out what went wrong.

Machiavelli is best known for the bitter cynicism of The Prince *(Il Principe, 1517), the first book he wrote while in exile and the book that has made the term "Machiavellianism" come to mean amoral political deceit and manipulation. Among his other works, the most famous are his* Discourses on Livy *(1513–1517), containing his thoughts on the creation and maintenance of a republic, and* The Mandrake *(La Mandragola, 1507), a comedy.*

Machiavelli occupied his earliest political post in 1498 as Secretary of the Ten of Liberty and Peace. He traveled as a diplomat all around Europe (leaving a wife and five children on his farm) and sent back reports to the Florentine republican government. He observed, among other things, the ruling techniques of Cesare Borgia—whose ruthless skill at maintaining his princedom through times of chaos Machiavelli would later describe and attempt to codify in The Prince.

The present selection is Chapter 18 of The Prince, *in the translation of Luigi Ricci revised by E. R. P. Vincent.*

How laudable it is for a prince to keep good faith and live with integrity, and not with astuteness, every one knows. Still the experience of our times shows those princes to have done great things who have had little regard for good faith, and have been able by astuteness to confuse men's brains, and who have ultimately overcome those who have made loyalty their foundation.

You must know, then, that there are two methods of fighting, the one by law, the other by force: the first method is that of men, the second of beasts; but as the first method is often insufficient, one must have recourse to the second. It is therefore necessary for a prince to know well how to use both the beast and the man. This was covertly taught to rulers by ancient writers, who relate how Achilles and many others of those ancient princes were given to Chiron the centaur to be brought up and educated under his discipline. The parable of this semi-animal, semi-human teacher is meant to indicate that a prince must know how to use both natures, and that the one without the other is not durable.

A prince being thus obliged to know well how to act as a beast must imitate the fox and the lion, for the lion cannot protect himself from traps, and the fox cannot defend himself from wolves. One must therefore be a fox to recognise traps, and a lion to frighten wolves. Those that wish to be only lions do not understand this. Therefore, a prudent ruler ought not to keep faith when by so doing it would be against his interest, and when the reasons which made him bind himself no longer exist. If men were all good, this precept would not be a good one; but as they are bad, and would not observe their faith with you, so you are not bound to keep faith with them. Nor have legitimate grounds ever failed a prince who wished to show colourable excuse for the non-fulfillment of his promise. Of this one could furnish an infinite number of modern examples, and show how many times peace has been broken, and how many promises rendered worthless, by the faithlessness of princes, and those that have been best able to imitate the fox have succeeded best. But it is necessary to be able to disguise this character well, and to be a great feigner and dissembler; and men are so simple and so ready to obey present necessities, that one who deceives will always find those who allow themselves to be deceived.

I will only mention one modern instance. Alexander VI° did nothing else but deceive men, he thought of nothing else, and found the occasion for it; no man was ever more able to give assurances, or affirmed things with stronger oaths, and no man observed them less; however, he always succeeded in his deceptions, as he well knew this aspect of things.

It is not, therefore, necessary for a prince to have all the above-named qualities, but it is very necessary to seem to have them. I would even be bold to say that to possess them and always to observe them is dangerous, but to appear to possess them is useful. Thus it is well to seem merciful, faithful, humane, sincere, religious, and also to be so; but you must have the mind so disposed that when it is needful to be otherwise you may be able to change to the opposite qualities. And it must be understood that a prince, and especially a new prince, cannot observe all those things which are considered good in men, being often obliged, in order to maintain the state, to act against faith, against charity, against humanity, and against religion. And, therefore, he must have a mind disposed to adapt itself according to the wind, and as the variations of fortune dictate, and, as I said before, not deviate from what is good, if possible, but be able to do evil if constrained.

A prince must take great care that nothing goes out of his mouth which is not full of the above-named five qualities, and, to see and hear him, he should seem to be all mercy, faith, integrity, humanity, and religion. And nothing is more necessary than to seem to have this last quality, for men in general judge more by the eyes than by the hands, for every one can see, but very few have to feel. Everybody sees what you appear to be, few feel what you are, and those few will not dare to oppose themselves to the many, who have the majesty of the state to defend them; and in the actions of men, and especially of princes, from which there is no appeal,

---

Alexander VI   Rodrigo Borgia, who reigned as Pope from 1492 to 1503. He was the father of Cesare and Lucrezia Borgia.

the end justifies the means. Let a prince therefore aim at conquering and maintaining the state, and the means will always be judged honourable and praised by every one, for the vulgar is always taken by appearances and the issue of the event; and the world consists only of the vulgar, and the few who are not vulgar are isolated when the many have a rallying point in the prince. A certain prince of the present time, whom it is well not to name, never does anything but preach peace and good faith, but he is really a great enemy to both, and either of them, had he observed them, would have lost him state or reputation on many occasions.

Lies for the Public Good

Sissela Bok

Sissela Bok was born in Sweden and educated in Switzerland, France, and the United States, where she has lived since 1955. She received her B.A. and M.A. in psychology from George Washington University and her Ph.D. in philosophy from Harvard. Her particular field is ethics, and she is the author of two highly praised books: Lying: Moral Choice in Public and Private Life *(1978), from which the selection below has been taken; and* Secrets: On the Ethics of Concealment and Revelation *(1982). With Daniel Callahan she has edited* Ethics Teaching in Higher Education *(1980).*

> *"How then," said I, "might we contrive one of those opportune falsehoods of which we were just now speaking, so as by one noble lie to persuade if possible the rulers themselves, but failing that the rest of the city?"*
> *[. . .] "While all of you are brothers," we will say, "yet God in fashioning those of you who are fitted to hold rule mingled gold in their generation, for which reason they are most precious—but in their helpers silver and iron and brass in the farmers and other craftsmen."*
> *[. . .] "Do you see any way of getting them to believe this tale?" "No, not these themselves," he said, "but I do, their sons and successors and the rest of mankind who come after." "Well," said I, "even that would have a good effect in making them more inclined to care for the state and one another."*
>
> PLATO, *The Republic*

> HUGO   *And do you think the living will agree to your schemes?*
> HOEDERER   *We'll get them to swallow them little by little.*
> HUGO   *By lying to them?*

HOEDERER *By lying to them sometimes.*

. . . .

HOEDERER *I'll lie when I must, and I have contempt for no one. I wasn't the one who invented lying. It grew out of a society divided into classes, and each one of us has inherited it from birth. We shall not abolish lying by refusing to tell lies, but by using every means at hand to abolish classes.*

JEAN-PAUL SARTRE, Dirty Hands

The Noble Lie

In earlier chapters three circumstances have seemed to liars to provide the strongest excuse for their behavior—a crisis where overwhelming harm can be averted only through deceit; complete harmlessness and triviality to the point where it seems absurd to quibble about whether a lie has been told; and the duty to particular individuals to protect their secrets. I have shown how lies in times of crisis can expand into vast practices where the harm to be averted is less obvious and the crisis less and less immediate; how white lies can shade into equally vast practices no longer so harmless, with immense cumulative costs; and how lies to protect individuals and to cover up their secrets can be told for increasingly dubious purposes to the detriment of all.

When these three expanding streams flow together and mingle with yet another—a desire to advance the public good—they form the most dangerous body of deceit of all. These lies may not be justified by an immediate crisis nor by complete triviality nor by duty to any one person; rather, liars tend to consider them as right and unavoidable because of the altruism that motivates them. I want, in this chapter and the next, to turn to this far-flung category.

Naturally, there will be large areas of overlap between these lies and those considered earlier. But the most characteristic defense for these lies is a separate one, based on the benefits they may confer and the long-range harm they can avoid. The intention may be broadly paternalistic, as when citizens are deceived "for their own good," or only a few may be lied to for the benefit of the community at large. Error and self-deception mingle with these altruistic purposes and blur them; the filters through which we must try to peer at lying are thicker and more distorting than ever in these practices. But I shall try to single out, among these lies, the elements that are consciously and purposely intended to benefit society.

A long tradition in political philosophy endorses some lies for the sake of the public. Plato, in the passage quoted at the head of this chapter first used the expression "noble lie" for the fanciful story that might be told to people in order to persuade them to accept class distinctions and thereby safeguard social harmony. According to this story, God Himself mingled gold, silver, iron, and brass in fashioning rulers, auxiliaries, farmers, and craftsmen, intending these groups for separate tasks in a harmonious hierarchy.

The Greek adjective which Plato used to characterize this falsehood expresses a most important fact about lies by those in power: this adjective is *"gennaion,"* which means "noble" in the sense of both "high-minded" and "well-bred."[1] The same assumption of nobility, good breeding, and superiority to those deceived is also present in Disraeli's statement that a gentleman is one who knows when to tell the truth and when not to. In other words, lying is excusable when undertaken for "noble" ends by those trained to discern these purposes.

Rulers, both temporal and spiritual, have seen their deceits in the benign light of such social purposes. They have propagated and maintained myths, played on the gullibility of the ignorant, and sought stability in shared beliefs. They have seen themselves as high-minded and well-bred—whether by birth or by training—and as superior to those they deceive. Some have gone so far as to claim that those who govern have a *right* to lie.[2] The powerful tell lies believing that they have greater than ordinary understanding of what is at stake; very often, they regard their dupes as having inadequate judgment, or as likely to respond in the wrong way to truthful information.

At times, those who govern also regard particular circumstances as too uncomfortable, too painful, for most people to be able to cope with rationally. They may believe, for instance, that their country must prepare for long-term challenges of great importance, such as a war, an epidemic, or a belt-tightening in the face of future shortages. Yet they may fear that citizens will be able to respond only to short-range dangers. Deception at such times may seem to the government leaders as the only means of attaining the necessary results.

The perspective of the liar is paramount in all such decisions to tell "noble" lies. If the liar considers the responses of the deceived at all, he assumes that they will, once the deceit comes to light and its benefits are

---

[1] The *gennaion pseudos* has generated much controversy. Some have translated it as "pious fraud" and debated whether such fraud can be perpetrated. Thus Hastings Rashdall, in *The Theory of Good and Evil*, 2d ed. (New York and London: Oxford University Press, 1924), bk. 1, p. 195, argued that such frauds would be justifiable "if (when *all* their consequences are considered) they were socially beneficial." Other translations are: "royal lie" (Jowett), and "bold flight of the imagination" (Cornford). The latter represents an effort to see Plato as advocating not lies by the government but stories, and possible errors; an interpretation that is difficult to uphold in view of the other contexts in *The Republic* where lying is discussed, such as 389b: "The rulers of the city may, if anybody, fitly lie on account of enemies or citizens for the benefit of the state." For Plato to have endorsed lying by the state is very significant, as truth for him was opposed, not just to falsehood, but to unreality.

[2] Arthur Sylvester, "The Government Has the Right to Lie," *Saturday Evening Post*, 18 November 1967, p. 10.

understood, be uncomplaining if not positively grateful. The lies are often seen as necessary merely at one *stage* in the education of the public. Thus Erasmus, in commenting on Plato's views, wrote:

> [. . .][H]e sets forth deceitful fictions for the rabble, so that the people might not set fire to the magistracy, and similar falsifications by which the crass multitude is deceived in its own interest, in the same way that parents deceive children and doctors the sick.
> [. . .]Thus for the crass multitude there is need of temporary promises, figures, allegories, parables [. . .] so that little by little they might advance to loftier things.[3]

Some experienced public officials are impatient with any effort to question the ethics of such deceptive practices (except actions obviously taken for private ends). They argue that vital objectives in the national interest require a measure of deception to succeed in the face of powerful obstacles. Negotiations must be carried on that are best left hidden from public view; bargains must be struck that simply cannot be comprehended by a politically unsophisticated electorate. A certain amount of illusion is needed in order for public servants to be effective. Every government, therefore, has to deceive people to some extent in order to lead them.

These officials view the public's concern for ethics as understandable but hardly realistic. Such "moralistic" concerns, put forth without any understanding of practical exigencies, may lead to the setting of impossible standards; these could seriously hamper work without actually changing the underlying practices. Government officials could then feel so beleaguered that some of them might quit their jobs; inefficiency and incompetence would then increasingly afflict the work of the rest.

If we assume the perspective of the deceived—those who experience the consequences of government deception—such arguments are not persuasive. We cannot take for granted either the altruism or the good judgment of those who lie to us, no matter how much they intend to benefit us. We have learned that much deceit for private gain masquerades as being in the public interest. We know how deception, even for the most unselfish motive, corrupts and spreads. And we have lived through the consequences of lies told for what were believed to be noble purposes.

Equally unpersuasive is the argument that there always has been government deception, and always will be, and that efforts to draw lines and set standards are therefore useless annoyances. It is certainly true that deception can never be completely absent from most human practices. But there are great differences among societies in the kinds of deceit that exist and the extent to which they are practiced, differences also among individuals in the same government and among successive governments

---

[3]Erasmus, *Responsio ad Albertum Pium, Opera Omnia*, vol. 9 (Leiden, 1706; reprinted Hildesheim, 1962).

within the same society. This strongly suggests that it is worthwhile trying to discover why such differences exist and to seek ways of raising the standards of truthfulness that can have an effect.

The argument that those who raise moral concerns are ignorant of political realities, finally, ought to lead, not to a dismissal of such inquiries, but to a more articulate description of what these realities are, so that a more careful and informed debate could begin. We have every reason to regard government as more profoundly injured by a dismissal of criticism and a failure to consider standards than by efforts to discuss them openly. If duplicity is to be allowed in exceptional cases, the criteria for these exceptions should themselves be openly debated and publicly chosen. Otherwise government leaders will have free rein to manipulate and distort the facts and thus escape accountability to the public.

The effort to question political deception cannot be ruled out so summarily. The disparagement of inquiries into such practices has to be seen as the defense of unwarranted power—power bypassing the consent of the governed. In the pages to come I shall take up just a few cases to illustrate both the clear breaches of trust that no group of citizens could desire, and circumstances where it is more difficult to render a judgment.

Examples of Political Deception

In September 1964, a State Department official, reflecting a growing administration consensus, wrote a memorandum advocating a momentous deceit of the American public.[4] He outlined possible courses of action to cope with the deteriorating military situation in South Vietnam. These included a stepping up of American participation in the "pacification" in South Vietnam and a "crescendo" of military action against North Vietnam, involving heavy bombing by the United States. But an election campaign was going on; the President's Republican opponent, Senator Goldwater, was suspected by the electorate of favoring escalation of the war in Vietnam and of brandishing nuclear threats to the communist world. In keeping with President Johnson's efforts to portray Senator Goldwater as an irresponsible war hawk, the memorandum ended with a paragraph entitled "Special considerations during the next two months," holding that:

> During the next two months, because of the lack of "rebuttal time" before election to justify particular actions which may be distorted to the U.S. public, we must act with special care—signaling to . . . [the South Vietnamese] that we are behaving energetically despite the restraints of our political season, and to the U.S. public that we are behaving with good purpose and restraint.

---

[4]The Senator Gravel Edition, *The Pentagon Papers* (Boston: Beacon Press, 1971), 3:556–59.

As the campaign wore on, President Johnson increasingly professed to be the candidate of peace. He gave no indication of the growing pressure for escalation from high administrative officials who would remain in office should he win; no hint of the hard choice he knew he would face if reelected.[5] Rather he repeated over and over again that:

> [T]he first responsibility, the only real issue in this campaign, the only thing you ought to be concerned about at all, is: Who can best keep the peace?[6]

The stratagem succeeded; the election was won; the war escalated. Under the name of Operation Rolling Thunder, the United States launched massive bombing raids over North Vietnam early in 1965. In suppressing genuine debate about these plans during the election campaign and masquerading as the party of peace, government members privy to the maneuver believed that they knew what was best for the country and that history would vindicate them. They meant to benefit the nation and the world by keeping the danger of a communist victory at bay. If a sense of *crisis* was needed for added justification, the Domino Theory strained for it: one regime after another was seen as toppling should the first domino be pushed over.

But why the deceit, if the purposes were so altruistic? Why not espouse these purposes openly before the election? The reason must have been that the government could not count on popular support for the scheme. In the first place, the sense of crisis and threat from North Vietnam would have been far from universally shared. To be forthright about the likelihood of escalation might lose many votes; it certainly could not fit with the campaign to portray President Johnson as the candidate most likely to keep the peace. Second, the government feared that its explanations might be "distorted" in the election campaign, so that the voters would not have the correct information before them. Third, time was lacking for the government to make an effort at educating the people about all that was at issue. Finally, the plans were not definitive; changes were possible, and the Vietnamese situation itself very unstable. For all these reasons, it seemed best to campaign for negotiation and restraint and let the Republican opponent be the target for the fear of United States belligerence.

President Johnson thus denied the electorate any chance to give or to refuse consent to the escalation of the war in Vietnam. Believing they had voted for the candidate of peace, American citizens were, within months, deeply embroiled in one of the cruelest wars in their history. Deception

---

[5]As early as March 1964, Lyndon Johnson knew that such a hard choice might have to be made. See telephone transcript cited by Doris Kearns in *Lyndon Johnson and the American Dream* (New York: Harper & Row, 1976), p. 197.

[6]Theodore H. White, *The Making of the President 1964* (New York: Atheneum, 1965), p. 373.

of this kind strikes at the very essence of democratic government. It allows those in power to override or nullify the right vested in the people to cast an informed vote in critical elections. Deceiving the people for the sake of the people is a self-contradictory notion in a democracy, unless it can be shown that there has been genuine consent to deceit. The actions of President Johnson were therefore inconsistent with the most basic principle of our political system.

What if all governments felt similarly free to deceive provided they believed the deception genuinely necessary to achieve some important public end? The trouble is that those who make such calculations are always susceptible to bias. They overestimate the likelihood that the benefit will occur and that the harm will be averted; they underestimate the chances that the deceit will be discovered and ignore the effects of such a discovery on trust; they underrate the comprehension of the deceived citizens, as well as their ability and their right to make a reasoned choice. And, most important, such a benevolent self-righteousness disguises the many motives for political lying which could *not* serve as moral excuses: the need to cover up past mistakes; the vindictiveness; the desire to stay in power. These self-serving ends provide the impetus for countless lies that are rationalized as "necessary" for the public good.

As political leaders become accustomed to making such excuses, they grow insensitive to fairness and to veracity. Some come to believe that any lie can be told so long as they can convince themselves that people will be better off in the long run. From there, it is a short step to the conclusion that, even if people will not be better off from a particular lie, they will benefit by all maneuvers to keep the right people in office. Once public servants lose their bearings in this way, all the shabby deceits of Watergate—the fake telegrams, the erased tapes, the elaborate cover-ups, the bribing of witnesses to make them lie, the televised pleas for trust— become possible.

While Watergate may be unusual in its scope, most observers would agree that deception is part and parcel of many everyday decisions in government. Statistics may be presented in such a way as to diminish the gravity of embarrassing problems. Civil servants may lie to members of Congress in order to protect programs they judge important, or to guard secrets they have been ordered not to divulge. If asked, members of Congress who make deals with one another to vote for measures they would otherwise oppose deny having made such deals. False rumors may be leaked by subordinates who believe that unwise executive action is about to be taken. Or the leak may be correct, but falsely attributed in order to protect the source.

Consider the following situation and imagine all the variations on this theme being played in campaigns all over the United States, at the local, state, or federal level:

A big-city mayor is running for reelection. He has read a report recommending that he remove rent controls after his reelection. He intends to do so, but believes he will lose the election if his intention is known. When asked, at a news conference two days before his election, about the existence of such a report, he denies knowledge of it and reaffirms his strong support of rent control.

In the mayor's view, his reelection is very much in the public interest, and the lie concerns questions which he believes the voters are unable to evaluate properly, especially on such short notice. In all similar situations, the sizable bias resulting from the self-serving element (the desire to be elected, to stay in office, to exercise power) is often clearer to onlookers than to the liars themselves. This bias inflates the alleged justifications for the lie—the worthiness, superiority, altruism of the liar, the rightness of his cause, and the inability of those deceive to respond "appropriately" to hearing the truth.

These common lies are now so widely suspected that voters are at a loss to know when they can and cannot believe what a candidate says in campaigning. The damage to trust has been immense. I have already referred to the poll which found 69 percent of Americans agreeing, both in 1975 and 1976, that the country's leaders had consistently lied to the American people over the past ten years. Over 40 percent of the respondents also agreed that:

> Most politicians are so similar that it doesn't really make much difference who gets elected.[7]

Many refuse to vote under such circumstances. Others look to appearance or to personality factors for clues as to which candidate might be more honest than the others. Voters and candidates alike are the losers when a political system has reached such a low level of trust. Once elected, officials find that their warnings and their calls to common sacrifice meet with disbelief and apathy, even when cooperation is most urgently needed. Law suits and investigations multiply. And the fact that candidates, should they win, are not expected to have meant what they said while campaigning, nor held accountable for discrepancies, only reinforces the incentives for them to bend the truth the next time, thus adding further to the distrust of the voters.

Political lies, so often assumed to be trivial by those who tell them, rarely are. They cannot be trivial when they affect so many people and when they are so peculiarly likely to be imitated, used to retaliate, and spread from a few to many. When political representatives or entire governments arrogate to themselves the right to lie, they take power from the public that would not have been given up voluntarily.

[7] *Cambridge Survey Research,* 1975, 1976.

Deception and Consent

Can there be exceptions to the well-founded distrust of deception in public life? Are there times when the public itself might truly not care about possible lies, or might even prefer to be deceived? Are some white lies so trivial or so transparent that they can be ignored? And can we envisage public discussion of more seriously misleading government statements such that reasonable persons could consent to them in advance?

White lies, first of all, are as common to political and diplomatic affairs as they are to the private lives of most people. Feigning enjoyment of an embassy gathering or a political rally, toasting the longevity of a dubious regime or an unimpressive candidate for office—these are forms of politeness that mislead few. It is difficult to regard them as threats to either individuals or communities. As with all white lies, however, the problem is that they spread so easily, and that lines are very hard to draw. Is it still a white lie for a secretary of state to announce that he is going to one country when in reality he travels to another? Or for a president to issue a "cover story" to the effect that a cold is forcing him to return to the White House, when in reality an international crisis made him cancel the rest of his campaign trip? Is it a white lie to issue a letter of praise for a public servant one has just fired? Given the vulnerability of public trust, it is never more important than in public life to keep the deceptive element of white lies to an absolute minimum, and to hold down the danger of their turning into more widespread deceitful practices.

A great deal of deception believed not only innocent but highly justified by public figures concerns their private lives. Information about their marriages, their children, their opinions about others—information about their personal plans and about their motives for personal decisions—all are theirs to keep private if they wish to do so. Refusing to give information under these circumstances is justifiable—but the right to withhold information is not the right to lie about it. Lying under such circumstances bodes ill for conduct in other matters.*

Certain additional forms of deception may be debated and authorized in advance by elected representatives of the public. The use of unmarked police cars to discourage speeding by drivers is an example of such a practice. Various forms of unannounced, sometimes covert, auditing of business and government operations are others. Whenever these

---

*A lie by an experienced adult in a position of authority about private matters that can be protected by a refusal to speak is therefore much less excusable than a lie by the school child described by Bonhoeffer in Chapter XI: too frightened by the bullying teacher to be able to stand up to him or think of a non-deceptive "way out" on the spur of the moment.

practices are publicly regulated, they can be limited so that abuses are avoided. But they must be *openly* debated and agreed to in advance, with every precaution against abuses of privacy and the rights of individuals, and against the spread of such covert activities. It is not enough that a public official assumes that consent would be given to such practices.

Another type of deceit has no such consent in advance: the temporizing or the lie when truthful information at a particular *time* might do great damage. Say that a government is making careful plans for announcing the devaluation of its currency. If the news leaks out to some before it can be announced to all, unfair profits for speculators might result. Or take the decision to make sharp increases in taxes on imported goods in order to rescue a tottering economy. To announce the decision beforehand would lead to hoarding and to exactly the results that the taxes are meant to combat. Thus, government officials will typically seek to avoid any premature announcement and will refuse to comment if asked whether devaluation or higher taxes are imminent. At times, however, official spokesmen will go further and falsely deny that the actions in question will in fact take place.

Such lies may well be uttered in good faith in an effort to avoid harmful speculation and hoarding. Nevertheless, if false statements are made to the public only to be exposed as soon as the devaluation or the new tax is announced, great damage to trust will result. It is like telling a patient that an operation will be painless—the swifter the disproof, the more likely the loss of trust. In addition, these lies are subject to all the dangers of spread and mistake and deterioration of standards that accompany all deception.

For these reasons, it is far better to refuse comment than to lie in such situations. The objection may be made, however, that a refusal to comment will be interpreted by the press as tantamount to an admission that devaluation or higher taxes are very near. Such an objection has force only if a government has not already established credibility by letting it be known earlier that it would never comment on such matters, and by strictly adhering to this policy at all times. Since lies in these cases are so egregious, it is worth taking care to establish such credibility in advance, so that a refusal to comment is not taken as an invitation to monetary speculation.

Another form of deception takes place when the government regards the public as frightened, or hostile, and highly volatile. In order not to create a panic, information about early signs of an epidemic may be suppressed or distorted. And the lie to a mob seeking its victim is like lying to the murderer asking where the person he is pursuing has gone. It can be acknowledged and defended as soon as the threat is over. In such cases, one may at times be justified in withholding information; perhaps, on rare occasions, even in lying. But such cases are so rare that they hardly exist for practical purposes.

The fact that rare circumstances exist where the justification for government lying seems powerful creates a difficulty—these same excuses will often be made to serve a great many more purposes. For some governments or public officials, the information they wish to conceal is almost never of the requisite certainty, the time never the right one, and the public never sufficiently dispassionate. For these reasons, it is hard to see how a practice of lying to the public about devaluation or changes in taxation or epidemics could be consented to in advance, and therefore justified.

Are there any exceptionally dangerous circumstances where the state of crisis is such as to justify lies to the public for its own protection? We have already discussed lying to enemies in an acute crisis. Sometimes the domestic public is then also deceived, at least temporarily, as in the case of the U-2 incident.° Wherever there is a threat—from a future enemy, as before World War II, or from a shortage of energy—the temptation to draw upon the excuses for deceiving citizens is very strong. The government may sincerely doubt that the electorate is capable of making the immediate sacrifices needed to confront the growing danger. (Or one branch of the government may lack confidence in another, for similar reasons, as when the administration mistrusts Congress.) The public may seem too emotional, the time not yet ripe for disclosure. Are there crises so exceptional that deceptive strategies are justifiable?

Compare, for instance, what was said and left unsaid by two United States Presidents confronted by a popular unwillingness to enter a war: President Lyndon Johnson, in escalating the war in Vietnam, and President Franklin D. Roosevelt, in moving the country closer to participating in World War II, while making statements such as the following in his 1940 campaign to be reelected:

> I have said this before, but I shall say it again and again and again: Your boys are not going to be sent into any foreign wars.[8]

By the standards set forth in this chapter, President Johnson's covert escalation and his failure to consult the electorate concerning the unde-

---

[8] *The Public Papers and Addresses of Franklin D. Roosevelt,* 1940, vol. 8, p. 517 (October 30, 1940).

U-2 incident An American surveillance plane—a U-2—was shot down over the Soviet Union in May 1960, and the pilot was captured, forcing President Eisenhower to make a full disclosure of the spy flights. The State Department had denied any overflights of the Soviet Union.

clared war in Vietnam were clearly unjustifiable. Consent was bypassed; there was no immediate danger to the nation which could even begin to excuse deceiving the public in a national election on grounds of an acute crisis.

The crisis looming before World War II, on the other hand, was doubtless much greater. Certainly this case is a difficult one, and one on which reasonable persons might not be able to agree. The threat was unprecedented; the need for preparations and for support of allies great; yet the difficulties of alerting the American public seemed insuperable. Would this crisis, then, justify proceeding through deceit?

To consent even to such deception would, I believe, be to take a frightening step. Do we want to live in a society where public officials can resort to deceit and manipulation whenever they decide that an exceptional crisis has arisen? Would we not, on balance, prefer to run the risk of failing to rise to a crisis honestly explained to us, from which the government might have saved us through manipulation? And what protection from abuse do we foresee should we surrender this choice?

In considering answers to these questions, we must take into account more than the short-run effects of government manipulation. President Roosevelt's manner of bringing the American people to accept first the possibility, then the likelihood, of war was used as an example by those who wanted to justify President Johnson's acts of dissimulation. And these acts in turn were pointed to by those who resorted to so many forms of duplicity in the Nixon administration. Secrecy and deceit grew at least in part because of existing precedents.[9]

The consequences of spreading deception, alienation, and lack of trust could not have been documented for us more concretely than they have in the past decades. We have had a very vivid illustration of how lies undermine our political system. While deception under the circumstances confronting President Roosevelt may in hindsight be more excusable than much that followed, we could no more consent to it in advance than to all that came later.

Wherever lies to the public have become routine, then, very special safeguards should be required. The test of public justification of deceptive practices is more needed than ever. It will be a hard test to satisfy, the more so the more trust is invested in those who lie and the more power they wield. Those in government and other positions of trust should be held to the highest standards. Their lies are not ennobled by their posi-

---

[9]See Arthur M. Schlesinger, Jr., *The Imperial Presidency* (Boston: Houghton Mifflin, 1973), p. 356: "The power to withhold and the power to leak led on inexorably to the power to lie ... uncontrolled secrecy made it easy for lying to become routine." See also David Wise, *The Politics of Lying* (New York: Random House, 1973).

tions; quite the contrary. Some lies—notably minor white lies and emergency lies rapidly acknowledged—may be more *excusable* than others, but only those deceptive practices which can be openly debated and consented to in advance are *justifiable* in a democracy.[10]

[10]For discussions of lying and moral choice in politics, see Plato, *The Republic;* Machiavelli, *The Prince;* Grotius, *On the Law of War and Peace;* Werner Krauss, ed., *Est-il utile de tromper le peuple?,* a fascinating compilation of answers by Condorcet and others in a contest sponsored by Frederick II in 1780 (Berlin: Akademie-Verlag, 1966); Max Weber, "Politics as a Vocation," in *Essays in Sociology,* trans. H. H. Gerth and C. Wright Mills (New York: Oxford University Press, 1946), pp. 77–128; and Michael Walzer, "Political Action: The Problem of Dirty Hands," *Philosophy and Public Affairs* 2 (Winter 1973): 160–80.

What Is the Good Life?

"What is the good life?" is one of the oldest human questions. Often, the attempt to achieve the good life is indistinguishable from the effort to find out what it is. When people are struggling to stay alive in the face of danger or poverty, the question seems to have an easy answer. Then, the good life means safety or food. But once we have this, once we pass from survival or subsistence to a range of wider possibilities, the question takes on a new meaning. Are plenty and ease sufficient? Does "making it" make us happy?

The first two selections are by people who are satisfied with their lives. "The American Dream? That's what we're doing right now," says one woman in an interview from Studs Terkel's book, *American Dreams.* "I really liked my job," says her husband. In a second interview, William Gothard, a young lawyer, also feels he is on the right road. He says, "I want to get married, have two kids, two cars, two color TV sets, and live in the suburbs outside Los Angeles. But I want to maintain my individuality." In sharp contrast, Joan Didion, in the course of reporting on a murder trial in southern California, paints a devastating picture of the "Golden Dream" of material comfort and status, here with no past or future, devoid of meaning and value.

The last two selections in this group raise more directly the question of needs versus wants. "Where does satisfaction come from?" asks Wendell Berry as he compares the "freedom" provided by modern conveniences to the pleasurable burdens of such jobs as spreading manure. The short story by Isaac Bashevis Singer takes up a similar theme. Berl and Berlcha feel no wants beyond the simple needs of their village life, and so have neither use nor understanding for the culture of their son.

from *American Dreams: Lost and Found*

Studs Terkel

Studs Terkel is perhaps best known for his interviews and oral histories, recording the feelings and thoughts of "ordinary" people who are rarely heard. His tool is a portable tape recorder, a tool, he says that can be used or misused. Hidden, it can be a means of blackmail or an instrument of the police state. In the open, "on the steps of a public housing project, in a frame bungalow, in a furnished apartment, in a parked car," it can capture the thoughts of the uncelebrated and "carry away valuables beyond price." He has published these "valuables" in six books: Division Street: America *(1966), interviews with people from different groups and classes in Chicago;* Hard Times: An Oral History of the Great Depression *(1970), interviews with one hundred Americans who survived the Great Depression;* Working: People Talk About What They Do All Day and How They Feel About What They Do *(1974);* American Dreams: Lost and Found *(1980), the source of the pieces reprinted below;* "The Good War": An Oral History of World War II *(1985), which won the 1985 Pulitzer Prize for nonfiction; and, most recently,* Chicago *(1986). He has also written* Talking to Myself: A Memoir of My Times *(1977).*

Terkel's background probably helped him develop an ability to talk with many kinds of people and an interest in what they have to say. He was born Louis Terkel in New York in 1912; his family moved to Chicago when he was eleven. His father was a tailor; his mother took over a hotel for blue-collar workers, mechanics, and craftsmen, men Terkel knew as he was growing up. He later changed his first name to Studs, after Studs Lonigan, from James T. Farrell's novels about the Chicago proletarian Irish. After high school he went to Crane Junior College, then graduated from the University of Chicago in 1932. He went on to law school (J.D. 1934) but failed his first bar examination and never practiced. Instead, he has been a radio and stage actor, a radio writer, a jazz columnist, and a disc jockey. In recent years he has developed the interview style—what he calls "guerilla journalism"—into the provocative studies of American culture mentioned above.

Carol and Tony Danlow

Lockport is on the western outskirts of Chicago: new subdivisions, builtup farmland, unincorporated. She describes her neighbors as "working toward a more comfortable life. Their houses are so expensive, for any young couple it would be almost impossible." Theirs is one of those houses. It is tastefully furnished.

She says: "We came from something much more plush than this. We had a commercial building in Evergreen Park and a ten-room apartment, and it was way larger than what this is. It was gorgeous. We had a built-in whirlpool bathtub and a dumbwaiter and all kinds of beautiful things."

Though they have three married children, they look astonishingly young. "We started early," he laughs. They are forty-seven.

In February 1975, they won the big prize of the Illinois lottery: a million dollars.

CAROL: We always enjoyed a little gambling. We played the lottery right from the start, buying maybe ten, fifteen dollars a week. Never really thinking about the biggie.

TONY: I was a truck driver for A & P° for twenty-eight years. Liked my job and everything. Once you win, people take on a different attitude towards you. They don't think you should work any more. You'd go to work and all of a sudden, they'd want to know how come. They figure that you're taking a job that somebody else would really need. Even the heads of the company and the union officials, they don't stand behind you on anything. *They're* working and making a heck of a lot more money than this lottery gives a person. It's all right for them to work, but they think you should give up your life's work that you've been doing for twenty-eight years. What is fifty thousand dollars a year nowadays? It isn't much by the time Uncle Sam gets his cut. There's many people doin' that and a lot better.

CAROL: Fifty thousand dollars a year for twenty years. That's how you get it.

TONY: We had two good jobs. We kept working until it just got intolerable with the abuse that you take. We were fortunate. We knew a little about real estate and we invested. That's where we made a lot of money. This was even before the lottery.

CAROL: We were at the Mill Run, the dinner-theater house, where they had the drawing. It was a big auditorium, and you could bring your own

---
A & P Chain of grocery stores.

cheering section. Which we did in high hopes. You were given a ball with a number on it. It was based on horse position and post. They put it in a big barrel. When my name was called, instant hysteria! (Laughs.) It was wild. It's got to be one of the most thrilling times that could ever happen. It's just chills, butterflies, everything.

TONY: Our son, he was twenty-three then, he musta leaped over six rows of seats, and he's hollerin' he'll never have to work again. I said: "Like hell you're gonna quit." He's a carpenter in the building trades.

CAROL: People were like happy, but you always find out about a few of the green-eyed monsters. We lost a couple of friends we thought were friends. It really must have been jealousy or something. All of a sudden the friendships cooled.

TONY: It was all right the first week at work. After that, since they just expected they would quit working themselves, I should quit too. They were always on our backs. But I really liked my job. I wanted to work. It just didn't mean that much to us because we were preparing to retire at the age of fifty as it was. I was forty-four, forty-five when it happened.

CAROL: I was a checker at the A & P store. People would say: "How come you're still working?" The one boss, in particular, right after we won, passed the remark: "I suppose she'll want a gold-covered counter." Stuff like that. It was just dumb little things. After a while, it can get a little aggravatin'.

TONY: I don't think I would have quit if A & P hadn't fired me. The two bosses got their heads together and fired me for insubordination.

CAROL: People think they have to talk to you a little differently. After I quit my job, I was working as a travel agent. Okay, right after I started this job, here was a big write-up in the *Sun-Times* and a picture and the whole shot. These women saw the paper, and one got on the telephone and called the other: "Did you read your paper yet?" "No." "Well, open it up and see who we're working with." She did and she said: "Well, what do you know?" So she says: "What are we gonna say to her tomorrow?" So they said: "I don't know."

They're super-nice people, we're friendly, but I had a feeling they felt they had to be different to me. I went in to work the next day as usual, and they were kind of coy. All of a sudden, this one lady said: "I saw your picture in the paper yesterday." "Oh really?" She says: "I didn't know what we should say to you." They thought I was a different person now.

TONY: One of the first couples that won, they were elderly and he always used to go to the corner tavern and have his coupla drinks. After he won, every time he'd go in there for a coupla drinks, everyone expected him to buy the whole place a drink. You can't do this. Rockefeller doesn't go into a cocktail lounge and buy everybody a drink. (Laughs.)

CAROL: The American Dream? That's what we're doing right now.

(Laughs.) To me, this is living. We can go golfing whenever we want to and do the things we want to while we're still able. Just where but America could this have been accomplished?

We've always got our eyes open for a new investment. Anything that's gonna pay the best or pay the most.

TONY: I read in the paper about people who believe in reincarnation. I hope there is none. Because I wouldn't want to be born again and get a chance to live a lesser life. I'm so happy with the life that we've had. If I had to do it all over again, I would want it the same way.

William Gothard

A casual encounter during a Los Angeles–Chicago flight; an ensuing conversation at O'Hare International Airport while he's between planes.

"I'm a twenty-seven-year-old white American male. I'm a corporate attorney. Spent most of my life in New York, went to high school in Ohio, college in California, and practice in Los Angeles. And I'm overweight." (Laughs.)

I'm a member of the nomadic middle class. My family moved seven times since I was born. Longest I've been in one place was eight years. My father is of the new managerial class, unaffiliated. He never worked for a company. He was a school administrator, an animal unto himself. You go from place to place, like a minister. To a bigger congregation or a bigger school district. I come from a family of Methodist ministers. (Laughs.) Middle-class suburban Methodist rather than the Bible-thumping, Gospel-singing Methodists.

We have no roots. Our heritage is either German, Dutch, or English. The furthest I can trace back is my great-grandfather. I don't know if he was born here. He ministered to the Oneida Indians. We still have an Indian bible. He died around 1907. That's all I know about my heritage.

We would never sit down at the dinner table and talk about what it means to be an American. When I was a child, my parents would take me around America. We would go to Gettysburg. I was a big Civil War buff. I visited forty-six states. I like to live the American experience. It's not one experience, it's many. There's so much here. Very few people have found the American Dream. When you stop searching, you no longer have it.

I admire my father. The reason he ceased being an administrator and became a professor is, it wasn't a joy any more. He was tired of politics, he was tired of the changing attitude among teachers.

He was a school administrator in Levittown, the great American Dream town at the end of the war. On the GI Bill, you could buy a home you could not afford before. Young people could settle down. It was like your Model

T's. You could have it in any color, just as long as it's black. It was the beginning of assembly-line homes.

We lived in Garden City, the upper-crusty part. The quality of education there was super. When I was in fifth grade, I was first clarinet in the school band. That was hot tuna in those days. (Laughs.)

Talk about Middle America. My father was an Eagle Scout who went to the National Jamboree in '39. He's in Kiwanis and president of Rotary. My brother was an Eagle Scout with a Bronze Palm and five merit badges past Eagle. When I was young, I was very overweight and struggled on these hikes. I *had* to make Eagle, it was an inner thing. I did, got twenty merit badges past Eagle, was president of the Key Club, and an acolyte in the church. It was no mean trick for me. I lost thirty pounds running around the block. (Laughs.) I felt it was important to my family, that's why I did it. My mother was president of faculty wives.

I've been blessed with a wonderful set of parents. We were never wealthy, but I was sent to some very good schools. When my father was making thirty thousand dollars a year, I was at Stanford and Columbia. I appreciate how much they had to sacrifice for me.

One of my big gripes is the crisis of the middle class today. If you're poor or minority, you get preferential treatment, financial aid to go to school. If you're rich, Iacocca's kid, it doesn't matter. But for the professional middle class, paying for a good education is just out of sight.

I really love America, though—I hate to say it—I have a foreign car. (Laughs.) They're built better. There's pride in craftmanship. I'd like less dependence upon government to solve our problems. What I want is the same spirit that made this country what it is.

I think we have the best political system, bar none. I see problems. I have never felt discrimination because I am white, middle-class, and male. Now it's the other way around. We're at the bottom of the list.

America became strong because people, out of their own initiative, have succeeded. Sons and daughters of fishmongers and tailors became lawyers, doctors, and corporate presidents. They drove themselves. We live in a socially mobile society where you can succeed if you have the drive. I realize if you were born in Watts or Harlem, the cards are stacked against you. You got a long way to go. Yet Jews have prospered in this country. They have a tradition of education, of upward mobility. The Irish and the Italians have made it too. With Hispanics and blacks, it's harder to melt in as easily. But in certain of these ethnic groups, you don't have this initiative. The primary thing is survival.

I believe if anyone is blessed with enough drive, enough parental guidance, he could become president of the United States. A little far-fetched, perhaps. (Laughs.) He could become a lawyer. (Laughs.)

Los Angeles, where I work, typifies in one city the best and the worst of American life. The home of franchise foods, home of the automobile society, home of Hollywood, your fantasia, your ultimate American Dream. Without roots.

I want to get married, have two kids, two cars, two color TV sets, and live in the suburbs outside Los Angeles. But I want to maintain my individuality. At the firm, I hate to be called just by my last name, Gothard, or just by my proper first name, William. I like Bill. As a professional person, in front of a client, I'd want my secretary to call me Mr. Gothard.

I'm very optimistic about this country. I've never lived through the depression. That might have sobered my outlook. I've never had a silver spoon in my mouth, but I've never known hunger. If I had, I might be less optimistic. I'm like Merrill Lynch.° I'm bullish on America. (Laughs.)

Some Dreamers of the Golden Dream

Joan Didion

A native Californian, Joan Didion was born in Sacramento in 1934 and was educated at the University of California at Berkeley. She received Vogue's *Prix de Paris in 1956, the year of her graduation, and in 1963 was awarded the Bread Loaf Fellowship in fiction. Her books, articles, and reviews have earned her a distinguished reputation as a writer of fiction and as an essayist. She has written four novels:* Run River *(1963);* Play It as It Lays *(1970);* A Book of Common Prayer *(1977); and* Democracy: A Novel *(1984). Her nonfiction includes two collections of essays—*Slouching Toward Bethlehem *(1968), from which we reprint the selection below, and* The White Album *(1979)—and* Salvador *(1983), based on her travels in El Salvador in 1982.*

This is a story about love and death in the golden land, and begins with the country. The San Bernardino Valley lies only an hour east of Los Angeles by the San Bernardino Freeway but is in certain ways an alien place: not the coastal California of the subtropical twilights and the soft westerlies off the Pacific but a harsher California, haunted by the Mojave just beyond the mountains, devastated by the hot dry Santa Ana wind that comes down through the passes at 100 miles an hour and whines

---

Merrill Lynch Stock brokerage firm, Merrill Lynch, Pierce, Fenner & Smith, whose motto is "Merrill Lynch is bullish [i.e., optimistic] on America."

through the eucalyptus windbreaks and works on the nerves. October is the bad month for the wind, the month when breathing is difficult and the hills blaze up spontaneously. There has been no rain since April. Every voice seems a scream. It is the season of suicide and divorce and prickly dread, wherever the wind blows.

The Mormons settled this ominous country, and then they abandoned it, but by the time they left the first orange tree had been planted and for the next hundred years the San Bernardino Valley would draw a kind of people who imagined they might live among the talismanic fruit and prosper in the dry air, people who brought with them Midwestern ways of building and cooking and praying and who tried to graft those ways upon the land. The graft took in curious ways. This is the California where it is possible to live and die without ever eating an artichoke, without ever meeting a Catholic or a Jew. This is the California where it is easy to Dial-A-Devotion, but hard to buy a book. This is the country in which a belief in the literal interpretation of Genesis has slipped imperceptibly into a belief in the literal interpretation of *Double Indemnity*,° the country of the teased hair and the Capris and the girls for whom all life's promise comes down to a waltz-length white wedding dress and the birth of a Kimberly or a Sherry or a Debbi and a Tijuana divorce and a return to hairdressers' school. "We were just crazy kids," they say without regret, and look to the future. The future always looks good in the golden land, because no one remembers the past. Here is where the hot wind blows and the old ways do not seem relevant, where the divorce rate is double the national average and where one person in every thirty-eight lives in a trailer. Here is the last stop for all those who come from somewhere else, for all those who drifted away from the cold and the past and the old ways. Here is where they are trying to find a new life style, trying to find it in the only places they know to look: the movies and the newspapers. The case of Lucille Marie Maxwell Miller is a tabloid monument to that new life style.

Imagine Banyan Street first, because Banyan is where it happened. The way to Banyan is to drive west from San Bernardino out Foothill Boulevard, Route 66: past the Santa Fe switching yards, the Forty Winks Motel. Past the motel that is nineteen stucco tepees: "SLEEP IN A WIGWAM—GET MORE FOR YOUR WAMPUM." Past Fontana Drag City and the Fontana Church of the Nazarene and the Pit Stop A Go-Go; past Kaiser Steel, through Cucamonga, out to the Kapu Kai Restaurant-Bar and Coffee Shop, at the corner of Route 66 and Carnelian Avenue. Up Carnelian Avenue from the Kapu Kai, which means "Forbidden Seas," the subdivi-

---

Double Indemnity A novel by James M. Cain—and later a famous film—whose plot involves a wife's scheme to arrange the murder of her husband, making the death look like an accident in order to profit from the provision in his life insurance policy which pays double indemnity in case of accidental death.

sion flags whip in the harsh wind. "HALF-ACRE RANCHES! SNACK BARS! TRAVERTINE ENTRIES! $95 DOWN." It is the trail of an intention gone haywire, the flotsam of the New California. But after a while the signs thin out on Carnelian Avenue, and the houses are no longer the bright pastels of the Springtime Home owners but the faded bungalows of the people who grow a few grapes and keep a few chickens out here, and then the hill gets steeper and the road climbs and even the bungalows are few, and here—desolate, roughly surfaced, lined with eucalyptus and lemon groves—is Banyan Street.

Like so much of this country, Banyan suggests something curious and unnatural. The lemon groves are sunken, down a three- or four-foot retaining wall, so that one looks directly into their dense foliage, too lush, unsettlingly glossy, the greenery of nightmare; the fallen eucalyptus bark is too dusty, a place for snakes to breed. The stones look not like natural stones but like the rubble of some unmentioned upheaval. There are smudge pots, and a closed cistern. To one side of Banyan there is the flat valley, and to the other the San Bernardino Mountains, a dark mass looming too high, too fast, nine, ten, eleven thousand feet, right there above the lemon groves. At midnight on Banyan Street there is no light at all, and no sound except the wind in the eucalyptus and a muffled barking of dogs. There may be a kennel somewhere, or the dogs may be coyotes.

Banyan Street was the route Lucille Miller took home from the twenty-four-hour Mayfair Market on the night of October 7, 1964, a night when the moon was dark and the wind was blowing and she was out of milk, and Banyan Street was where, at about 12:20 A.M., her 1964 Volkswagen came to a sudden stop, caught fire, and began to burn. For an hour and fifteen minutes Lucille Miller ran up and down Banyan calling for help, but no cars passed and no help came. At three o'clock that morning, when the fire had been put out and the California Highway Patrol officers were completing their report, Lucille Miller was still sobbing and incoherent, for her husband had been asleep in the Volkswagen. "What will I tell the children, when there's nothing left, nothing left in the casket," she cried to the friend called to comfort her. "How can I tell them there's nothing left?"

In fact there was something left, and a week later it lay in the Draper Mortuary Chapel in a closed bronze coffin blanketed with pink carnations. Some 200 mourners heard Elder Robert E. Denton of the Seventh-Day Adventist Church of Ontario speak of "the temper of fury that has broken out among us." For Gordon Miller, he said, there would be "no more death, no more heartaches, no more misunderstandings." Elder Ansel Bristol mentioned the "peculiar" grief of the hour. Elder Fred Jensen asked "what shall it profit a man, if he shall gain the whole world, and lose his own soul?" A light rain fell, a blessing in a dry season, and a female vocalist sang "Safe in the Arms of Jesus." A tape recording of the service was made for the widow, who was being held without bail in the San Bernardino County Jail on a charge of first-degree murder.

Of course she came from somewhere else, came off the prairie in search of something she had seen in a movie or heard on the radio, for this is a Southern California story. She was born on January 17, 1930, in Winnipeg, Manitoba, the only child of Gordon and Lily Maxwell, both schoolteachers and both dedicated to the Seventh-Day Adventist Church, whose members observe the Sabbath on Saturday, believe in an apocalyptic Second Coming, have a strong missionary tendency, and, if they are strict, do not smoke, drink, eat meat, use makeup, or wear jewelry, including wedding rings. By the time Lucille Maxwell enrolled at Walla Walla College in College Place, Washington, the Adventist school where her parents then taught, she was an eighteen-year-old possessed of unremarkable good looks and remarkable high spirits. "Lucille wanted to see the world," her father would say in retrospect, "and I guess she found out."

The high spirits did not seem to lend themselves to an extended course of study at Walla Walla College, and in the spring of 1949 Lucille Maxwell met and married Gordon ("Cork") Miller, a twenty-four-year-old graduate of Walla Walla and of the university of Oregon dental school, then stationed at Fort Lewis as a medical officer. "Maybe you could say it was love at first sight," Mr. Maxwell recalls. "Before they were ever formally introduced, he sent Lucille a dozen and a half roses with a card that said even if she didn't come out on a date with him, he hoped she'd find the roses pretty anyway." The Maxwells remember their daughter as a "radiant" bride.

Unhappy marriages so resemble one another that we do not need to know too much about the course of this one. There may or may not have been trouble on Guam, where Cork and Lucille Miller lived while he finished his Army duty. There may or may not have been problems in the small Oregon town where he first set up private practice. There appears to have been some disappointment about their move to California: Cork Miller had told friends that he wanted to become a doctor, that he was unhappy as a dentist and planned to enter the Seventh-Day Adventist College of Medical Evangelists at Loma Linda, a few miles south of San Bernardino. Instead he bought a dental practice in the west end of San Bernardino County, and the family settled there, in a modest house on the kind of street where there are always tricycles and revolving credit and dreams about bigger houses, better streets. That was 1957. By the summer of 1964 they had achieved the bigger house on the better street and the familiar accouterments of a family on its way up: the $30,000 a year, the three children for the Christmas card, the picture window, the family room, the newspaper photographs that showed "Mrs. Gordon Miller, Ontario Heart Fund Chairman. . . ." They were paying the familiar price for it. And they had reached the familiar season of divorce.

It might have been anyone's bad summer, anyone's siege of heat and nerves and migraine and money worries, but this one began particularly early and particularly badly. On April 24 an old friend, Elaine Hayton, died suddenly; Lucille Miller had seen her only the night before. During the month of May, Cork Miller was hospitalized briefly with a bleeding ulcer, and his usual reserve deepened into depression. He told his accountant that he was "sick of looking at open mouths," and threatened suicide. By July 8, the conventional tensions of love and money had reached the conventional impasse in the new house on the acre lot of 8488 Bella Vista, and Lucille Miller filed for divorce. Within a month, however, the Millers seemed reconciled. They saw a marriage counselor. They talked about a fourth child. It seemed that the marriage had reached the traditional truce, the point at which so many resign themselves to cutting both their losses and their hopes.

But the Millers' season of trouble was not to end that easily. October 7 began as a commonplace enough day, one of those days that sets the teeth on edge with its tedium, its small frustrations. The temperature reached 102° in San Bernardino that afternoon, and the Miller children were home from school because of Teachers' Institute. There was ironing to be dropped off. There was a trip to pick up a prescription for Nembutal, a trip to a self-service dry cleaner. In the early evening, an unpleasant accident with the Volkswagen: Cork Miller hit and killed a German shepherd, and afterward said that his head felt "like it had a Mack truck on it." It was something he often said. As of that evening Cork Miller was $63,479 in debt, including the $29,637 mortgage on the new house, a debt load which seemed oppressive to him. He was a man who wore his responsibilities uneasily, and complained of migraine headaches almost constantly.

He ate alone that night, from a TV tray in the living room. Later the Millers watched John Forsythe and Senta Berger in *See How They Run,* and when the movie ended, about eleven, Cork Miller suggested that they go out for milk. He wanted some hot chocolate. He took a blanket and pillow from the couch and climbed into the passenger seat of the Volkswagen. Lucille Miller remembers reaching over to lock his door as she backed down the driveway. By the time she left the Mayfair Market, and long before they reached Banyan Street, Cork Miller appeared to be asleep.

There is some confusion in Lucille Miller's mind about what happened between 12:30 A.M., when the fire broke out, and 1:50 A.M., when it was reported. She says that she was driving east on Banyan Street at about 35 m.p.h. when she felt the Volkswagen pull sharply to the right. The next thing she knew the car was on the embankment, quite near the edge of the retaining wall, and flames were shooting up behind her. She does not remember jumping out. She does remember prying up a stone with which she broke the window next to her husband, and then scrambling down the retaining wall to try to find a stick. "I don't know how I was going to push him out," she says. "I just thought if I had a stick, I'd push him out." She could not, and after a while she ran to the intersection of Banyan and Carnelian Avenue. There are no houses at that corner, and almost no traffic. After one car had passed without stopping. Lucille Miller ran back down Banyan toward the burning Volkswagen. She did not stop, but she slowed down, and in the flames she could see her husband. He was, she said, "just black."

At the first house up Sapphire Avenue, half a mile from the Volkswagen, Lucille Miller finally found help. There Mrs. Robert Swenson called the sheriff, and then, at Lucille Miller's request, she called Harold Lance, the Millers' lawyer and their close friend. When Harold Lance arrived he took Lucille Miller home to his wife, Joan. Twice Harold Lance and Lucille Miller returned to Banyan Street and talked to the Highway Patrol officers. A third time Harold Lance returned alone, and when he came back he said to Lucille Miller, "O.K. . . . you don't talk any more."

When Lucille Miller was arrested the next afternoon, Sandy Slagle was with her. Sandy Slagle was the intense, relentlessly loyal medical student who used to baby-sit for the Millers, and had been living as a member of the family since she graduated from high school in 1959. The Millers took her away from a difficult home situation, and she thinks of Lucille Miller not only as "more or less a mother or a sister" but as "the most wonderful character" she has ever known. On the night of the accident, Sandy Slagle was in her dormitory at Loma Linda University, but Lucille Miller called her early in the morning and asked her to come home. The doctor was there when Sandy Slagle arrived, giving Lucille Miller an injection of Nembutal. "She was crying as she was going under," Sandy Slagle recalls. "Over and over she'd say, 'Sandy, all the hours I spent trying to save him and now what are they trying to *do* to me?'"

At 1:30 that afternoon, Sergeant William Paterson and Detectives Charles Callahan and Joseph Karr of the Central Homicide Division arrived at 8488 Bella Vista. "One of them appeared at the bedroom door," Sandy Slagle remembers, "and said to Lucille, 'You've got ten minutes to get dressed or we'll take you as you are.' She was in her nightgown, you know, so I tried to get her dressed."

Sandy Slagle tells the story now as if by rote, and her eyes do not waver. "So I had her panties and bra on her and they opened the door again, so I got some Capris on her, you know, and a scarf." Her voice drops. "And then they just took her."

The arrest took place just twelve hours after the first report that there had been an accident on Banyan Street, a rapidity which would later prompt Lucille Miller's attorney to say that the entire case was an instance of trying to justify a reckless arrest. Actually what first caused the detectives who arrived on Banyan Street toward dawn that morning to give the accident more than routine attention were certain apparent physical inconsistencies. While Lucille Miller had said that she was driving about 35 m.p.h. when the car swerved to a stop, an examination of the cooling Volkswagen showed that it was in low gear, and that the parking rather than the driving lights were on. The front wheels, moreover, did not seem to be in exactly the position that Lucille Miller's description of the accident would suggest, and the right rear wheel was dug in deep, as if it had been spun in place. It seemed curious to the detectives, too, that a sudden stop from 35 m.p.h.—the same jolt which was presumed to have knocked over a gasoline can in the back seat and somehow started the fire—should have left two milk cartons upright on the back floorboard, and the remains of a Polaroid camera box lying apparently undisturbed on the back seat.

No one, however, could be expected to give a precise account of what did and did not happen in a moment of terror, and none of these inconsistencies seemed in themselves incontrovertible evidence of criminal intent. But they did interest the Sheriff's Office, as did Gordon Miller's apparent unconsciousness at the time of the accident, and the length of time it had taken Lucille Miller to get help. Something, moreover, struck the investigators as wrong about Harold Lance's attitude when he came back to Banyan Street the third time and found the investigation by no means over. "The way Lance was acting," the prosecuting attorney said later, "they thought maybe they'd hit a nerve."

And so it was that on the morning of October 8, even before the doctor had come to give Lucille Miller an injection to calm her, the San Bernardino County Sheriff's Office was trying to construct another version of what might have happened between 12:30 and 1:50 A.M. The hypothesis they would eventually present was based on the somewhat tortuous premise that Lucille Miller had undertaken a plan which failed: a plan to stop the car on the lonely road, spread gasoline over her presumably drugged husband, and, with a stick on the accelerator, gently "walk" the Volkswagen over the embankment, where it would tumble four feet down the retaining wall into the lemon grove and almost certainly explode. If this happened, Lucille Miller might then have somehow negotiated the two miles up Carnelian to Bella Vista in time to be home when the accident was discovered. This plan went awry, according to the Sheriff's Office hypothesis, when the car would not go over the rise of the embankment. Lucille Miller might have panicked then—after she had killed the engine the third or fourth time, say, out there on the dark road with the gasoline already spread and the dogs baying and the wind blowing and the unspeakable apprehension that a pair of headlights would suddenly light up Banyan Street and expose her there—and set the fire herself.

Although this version accounted for some of the physical evidence—the car in low because it had been started from a dead stop, the parking lights on because she could not do what needed doing without some light, a rear wheel spun in repeated attempts to get the car over the embankment, the

milk cartons upright because there had been no sudden stop—it did not
seem on its own any more or less credible than Lucille Miller's own story.
Moreover, some of the physical evidence did seem to support her story: a
nail in a front tire, a nine-pound rock found in the car, presumably the
one with which she had broken the window in an attempt to save her
husband. Within a few days an autopsy had established that Gordon
Miller was alive when he burned, which did not particularly help the
State's case, and that he had enough Nembutal and Sandoptal in his blood
to put the average person to sleep, which did: on the other hand Gordon
Miller habitually took both Nembutal and Fiorinal (a common headache
prescription which contains Sandoptal), and had been ill besides.

It was a spotty case, and to make it work at all the State was going to
have to find a motive. There was talk of unhappiness, talk of another man.
That kind of motive, during the next few weeks, was what they set out
to establish. They set out to find it in accountants' ledgers and double-
indemnity clauses and motel registers, set out to determine what might
move a woman who believed in all the promises of the middle class—a
woman who had been chairman of the Heart Fund and who always knew
a reasonable little dressmaker and who had come out of the bleak wild
of prairie fundamentalism to find what she imagined to be the good life—
what should drive such a woman to sit on a street called Bella Vista and
look out her new picture window into the empty California sun and
calculate how to burn her husband alive in a Volkswagen. They found the
wedge they wanted closer at hand than they might have at first expected,
for, as testimony would reveal later at the trial, it seemed that in December of 1963 Lucille Miller had begun an affair with the husband of one of
her friends, a man whose daughter called her "Auntie Lucille," a man
who might have seemed to have the gift for people and money and the
good life that Cork Miller so noticeably lacked. The man was Arthwell
Hayton, a well-known San Bernardino attorney and at one time a member of the district attorney's staff.

In some ways it was the conventional clandestine affair in a place like San
Bernardino, a place where little is bright or graceful, where it is routine
to misplace the future and easy to start looking for it in bed. Over the
seven weeks that it would take to try Lucille Miller for murder, Assistant
District Attorney Don A. Turner and defense attorney Edward P. Foley
would between them unfold a curiously predictable story. There were the
falsified motel registrations. There were the lunch dates, the afternoon
drives in Arthwell Hayton's red Cadillac convertible. There were the
interminable discussions of the wronged partners. There were the confi-
dantes ("I knew everything," Sandy Slagle would insist fiercely later. "I
knew every time, places, everything") and there were the words remembered from bad magazine stories ("Don't kiss me, it will trigger things,"
Lucille Miller remembered telling Arthwell Hayton in the parking lot of

Harold's Club in Fontana after lunch one day) and there were the notes, the sweet exchanges: "Hi Sweetie Pie! You are my cup of tea! ! Happy Birthday—you don't look a day over 29! ! Your baby, Arthwell."

And, toward the end, there was the acrimony. It was April 24, 1964, when Arthwell Hayton's wife, Elaine, died suddenly, and nothing good happened after that. Arthwell Hayton had taken his cruiser, *Captain's Lady,* over to Catalina that weekend; he called home at nine o'clock Friday night, but did not talk to his wife because Lucille Miller answered the telephone and said that Elaine was showering. The next morning the Haytons' daughter found her mother in bed, dead. The newspapers reported the death as accidental, perhaps the result of an allergy to hair spray. When Arthwell Hayton flew home from Catalina that weekend, Lucille Miller met him at the airport, but the finish had already been written.

It was in the breakup that the affair ceased to be in the conventional mode and began to resemble instead the novels of James M. Cain, the movies of the late 1930's, all the dreams in which violence and threats and blackmail are made to seem commonplaces of middle-class life. What was most startling about the case that the State of California was preparing against Lucille Miller was something that had nothing to do with law at all, something that never appeared in the eight-column afternoon head-lines but was always there between them: the revelation that the dream was teaching the dreamers how to live. Here is Lucille Miller talking to her lover sometime in the early summer of 1964, after he had indicated that, on the advice of his minister, he did not intend to see her any more: "First, I'm going to go to that dear pastor of yours and tell him a few things. . . . When I do tell him that, you won't be in the Redlands Church any more. . . . Look, Sonny Boy, if you think your reputation is going to be ruined, your life won't be worth two cents." Here is Arthwell Hayton, to Lucille Miller: "I'll go to Sheriff Frank Bland and tell him some things that I know about you until you'll wish you'd never heard of Arthwell Hayton." For an affair between a Seventh-Day Adventist dentist's wife and a Seventh-Day Adventist personal-injury lawyer, it seems a curious kind of dialogue.

"Boy, I could get that little boy coming and going," Lucille Miller later confided to Erwin Sprengle, a Riverside contractor who was a business partner of Arthwell Hayton's and a friend to both the lovers. (Friend or no, on this occasion he happened to have an induction coil attached to his telephone in order to tape Lucille Miller's call.) "And he hasn't got one thing on me that he can prove. I mean, I've got concrete—he has nothing concrete." In the same taped conversation with Erwin Sprengle, Lucille Miller mentioned a tape that she herself had surreptitiously made, months before, in Arthwell Hayton's car.

"I said to him, I said 'Arthwell, I just feel like I'm being used.' . . . He started sucking his thumb and he said 'I love you. . . . This isn't something that happened yesterday. I'd marry you tomorrow if I could. I don't love Elaine.' He'd love to hear that played back, wouldn't he?"

"Yeah," drawling Sprengle's voice on the tape. "That would be just a little incriminating, wouldn't it?"

"Just a *little* incriminating," Lucille Miller agreed. "It really *is.*"

Later on the tape, Sprengle asked where Cork Miller was.

"He took the children down to the church."

"You didn't go?"

"No."

"You're naughty."

It was all, moreover, in the name of "love"; everyone involved placed a magical faith in the efficacy of the very word. There was the significance that Lucille Miller saw in Arthwell's saying that he "loved" her, that he did not "love" Elaine. There was Arthwell insisting, later, at the trial, that he had never said it, that he may have "whispered sweet nothings in her ear" (as her defense hinted that he had whispered in many ears), but he did not remember bestowing upon her the special seal, saying the word, declaring "love." There was the summer evening when Lucille Miller and Sandy Slagle followed Arthwell Hayton down to his new boat in its mooring at Newport Beach and untied the lines with Arthwell aboard, Arthwell and a girl with whom he later testified he was drinking hot chocolate and watching television. "I did that on purpose," Lucille Miller told Erwin Sprengle later, "to save myself from letting my heart do something crazy."

January 11, 1965, was a bright warm day in Southern California, the kind of day when Catalina floats on the Pacific horizon and the air smells of orange blossoms and it is a long way from the bleak and difficult East, a long way from the cold, a long way from the past. A woman in Hollywood staged an all-night sit-in on the hood of her car to prevent repossession by a finance company. A seventy-year-old pensioner drove his station wagon at five miles an hour past three Gardena poker parlors and emptied three pistols and a twelve-gauge shotgun through their windows, wounding twenty-nine people. "Many young women became prostitutes just to have enough money to play cards," he explained in a note. Mrs. Nick Adams said that she was "not surprised" to hear her husband announce his divorce plans on the Les Crane Show, and, farther north, a sixteen-year-old jumped off the Golden Gate Bridge and lived.

And, in the San Bernardino County Courthouse, the Miller trial opened. The crowds were so bad that the glass courtroom doors were shattered in the crush, and from then on identification disks were issued to the first forty-three spectators in line. The line began forming at 6 A.M., and college girls camped at the courthouse all night, with stores of graham crackers and No-Cal.

All they were doing was picking a jury, those first few days, but the sensational nature of the case had already suggested itself. Early in December there had been an abortive first trial, a trial at which no evidence was ever presented because on the day the jury was seated the San Bernardino *Sun-Telegram* ran an "inside" story quoting Assistant District Attorney Don Turner, the prosecutor, as saying, "We are looking into the circumstances of Mrs. Hayton's death. In view of the current trial concerning the death of Dr. Miller, I do not feel I should comment on Mrs. Hayton's death." It seemed that there had been barbiturates in Elaine Hayton's blood, and there had seemed some irregularity about the way she was dressed on that morning when she was found under the covers, dead. Any doubts about the death at the time, however, had never gotten as far as the Sheriff's Office. "I guess somebody didn't want to rock the boat," Turner said later. "These were prominent people."

Although all of that had not been in the *Sun-Telegram*'s story, an immediate mistrial had been declared. Almost as immediately, there had been another development: Arthwell Hayton had asked newspapermen to an 11 A.M. Sunday morning press conference in his office. There had been television cameras, and flash bulbs popping. "As you gentlemen may know," Hayton had said, striking a note of stiff bonhomie, "there are very often women who become amorous toward their doctor or lawyer. This does not mean on the physician's or lawyer's part that there is any romance toward the patient or client."

"Would you deny that you were having an affair with Mrs. Miller?" a reporter had asked.

"I would deny that there was any romance on my part whatsoever."

It was a distinction he would maintain through all the wearing weeks to come.

So they had come to see Arthwell, these crowds who now milled beneath the dusty palms outside the courthouse, and they had also come to see Lucille, who appeared as a slight, intermittently pretty woman, already pale from lack of sun, a woman who would turn thirty-five before the trial was over and whose tendency toward haggardness was beginning to show, a meticulous woman who insisted, against her lawyer's advice, on coming to court with her hair piled high and lacquered. "I would've been happy if she'd come in with it hanging loose, but Lucille wouldn't do that," her lawyer said. He was Edward P. Foley, a small, emotional Irish Catholic who several times wept in the courtroom. "She has a great honesty, this woman," he added, "but this honesty about her appearance always worked against her."

By the time the trial opened, Lucille Miller's appearance included maternity clothes, for an official examination on December 18 had revealed that she was then three and a half months pregnant, a fact which made picking a jury even more difficult than usual, for Turner was asking the death penalty. "It's unfortunate but there it is," he would say of the pregnancy to each juror in turn, and finally twelve were seated, seven of them women, the youngest forty-one, an assembly of the very peers—housewives, a machinist, a truck driver, a grocery-store manager, a filing clerk—above whom Lucille Miller had wanted so badly to rise.

That was the sin, more than the adultery, which tended to reinforce the one for which she was being tried. It was implicit in both the defense and the prosecution that Lucille Miller was an erring woman, a woman who perhaps wanted too much. But to the prosecution she was not merely a woman who would want a new house and want to go to parties and run up high telephone bills ($1,152 in ten months), but a woman who would go so far as to murder her husband for his $80,000 in insurance, making it appear an accident in order to collect another $40,000 in double indemnity and straight accident policies. To Turner she was a woman who did not want simply her freedom and a reasonable alimony (she could have had that, the defense contended, by going through with her divorce suit), but wanted everything, a woman motivated by "love and greed." She was a "manipulator." She was a "user of people."

To Edward Foley, on the other hand, she was an impulsive woman who "couldn't control her foolish little heart." Where Turner skirted the pregnancy, Foley dwelt upon it, even calling the dead man's mother down from Washington to testify that her son had told her they were going to have another baby because Lucille felt that it would "do much to weld our home again in the pleasant relations that we used to have." Where the prosecution saw a "calculator," the defense saw a "blabbermouth," and in fact Lucille Miller did emerge as an ingenuous conversationalist. Just as, before her husband's death, she had confided in her friends about her love affair, so she chatted about it after his death, with the arresting sergeant. "Of course Cork lived with it for years, you know," her voice was heard to tell Sergeant Paterson on a tape made the morning after her arrest. "After Elaine died, he pushed the panic button one night and just asked me right out, and that, I think, was when he really—the first time he really faced it." When the sergeant asked why she had agreed to talk to him, against the specific instructions of her lawyers, Lucille Miller said airily, "Oh, I've always been basically quite an honest person. . . . I mean I can put a hat in the cupboard and say it cost ten dollars less, but basically I've always kind of just lived my life the way I wanted to, and if you don't like it you can take off."

The prosecution hinted at men other than Arthwell, and even, over Foley's objections, managed to name one. The defense called Miller suicidal. The prosecution produced experts who said that the Volkswagen fire could not have been accidental. Foley produced witnesses who said that it could have been. Lucille's father, now a junior-high-school teacher in Oregon, quoted Isaiah to reporters: *"Every tongue that shall rise against thee in judgment thou shalt condemn."* "Lucille did wrong, her affair," her mother said judiciously. "With her it was love. But with some

I guess it's just passion." There was Debbie, the Millers' fourteen-year-old, testifying in a steady voice about how she and her mother had gone to a supermarket to buy the gasoline can the week before the accident. There was Sandy Slagle, in the courtroom every day, declaring that on at least one occasion Lucille Miller had prevented her husband not only from committing suicide but from committing suicide in such a way that it would appear an accident and ensure the double-indemnity payment. There was Wenche Berg, the pretty twenty-seven-year-old Norwegian governess to Arthwell Hayton's children, testifying that Arthwell had instructed her not to allow Lucille Miller to see or talk to the children.

Two months dragged by, and the headlines never stopped. Southern California's crime reporters were headquartered in San Bernardino for the duration: Howard Hertel from the *Times,* Jim Bennett and Eddy Jo Bernal from the *Herald-Examiner.* Two months in which the Miller trial was pushed off the *Examiner's* front page only by the Academy Award nominations and Stan Laurel's death. And finally, on March 2, after Turner had reiterated that it was a case of "love and greed," and Foley had protested that his client was being tried for adultery, the case went to the jury.

They brought in the verdict, guilty of murder in the first degree, at 4:50 P.M. on March 5. "She didn't do it," Debbie Miller cried, jumping up from the spectators' section. "She didn't *do* it." Sandy Slagle collapsed in her seat and began to scream. "Sandy, for God's sake please *don't,*" Lucille Miller said in a voice that carried across the courtroom, and Sandy Slagle was momentarily subdued. But as the jurors left the courtroom she screamed again: "You're murderers. . . . Every last one of you is a *murderer.*" Sheriff's deputies moved in then, each wearing a string tie that read "1965 SHERIFF'S RODEO," and Lucille Miller's father, the sad-faced junior-high-school teacher who believed in the word of Christ and the dangers of wanting to see the world, blew her a kiss off his fingertips.

The California Institution for Women at Frontera, where Lucille Miller is now, lies down where Euclid Avenue turns into country road, not too many miles from where she once lived and shopped and organized the Heart Fund Ball. Cattle graze across the road, and Rainbirds sprinkle the alfalfa. Frontera has a softball field and tennis courts, and looks as if it might be a California junior college, except that the trees are not yet high enough to conceal the concertina wire around the top of the Cyclone fence. On visitors' day there are big cars in the parking area, big Buicks and Pontiacs that belong to grandparents and sisters and fathers (not many of them belong to husbands), and some of them have bumper stickers that say "SUPPORT YOUR LOCAL POLICE."

A lot of California murderesses live here, a lot of girls who somehow misunderstood the promise. Don Turner put Sandra Garner here (and her husband in the gas chamber at San Quentin) after the 1959 desert killings known to crime reporters as "the soda-pop murders." Carole Tregoff is here, and has been ever since she was convicted of conspiring to murder Dr. Finch's wife in West Covina, which is not too far from San Bernardino. Carole Tregoff is in fact a nurse's aide in the prison hospital, and might have attended Lucille Miller had her baby been born at Frontera; Lucille Miller chose instead to have it outside, and paid for the guard who stood outside the delivery room in St. Bernardine's Hospital. Debbie Miller came to take the baby home from the hospital, in a white dress with pink ribbons, and Debbie was allowed to choose a name. She named the baby Kimi Kai. The children live with Harold and Joan Lance now, because Lucille Miller will probably spend ten years at Frontera. Don Turner waived his original request for the death penalty (it was generally agreed that he had demanded it only, in Edward Foley's words, "to get anybody with the slightest trace of human kindness in their veins off the jury"), and settled for life imprisonment with the possibility of parole. Lucille Miller does not like it at Frontera, and has had trouble adjusting. "She's going to have to learn humility," Turner says. "She's going to have to use her ability to charm, to manipulate."

The new house is empty now, the house on the street with the sign that says

PRIVATE ROAD

BELLA VISTA

DEAD END

The Millers never did get it landscaped, and weeds grow up around the fieldstone siding. The television aerial has toppled on the roof, and a trash can is stuffed with the debris of family life: a cheap suitcase, a child's game called "Lie Detector." There is a sign on what would have been the lawn, and the sign reads "ESTATE SALE." Edward Foley is trying to get Lucille Miller's case appealed, but there have been delays. "A trial always comes down to a matter of sympathy," Foley says wearily now. "I couldn't create sympathy for her." Everyone is a little weary now, weary and resigned, everyone except Sandy Slagle, whose bitterness is still raw. She lives in an apartment near the medical school in Loma Linda, and studies reports of the case in *True Police Cases* and *Official Detective Stories*. "I'd much rather we not talk about the Hayton business too much," she tells visitors, and she keeps a tape recorder running. "I'd rather talk about Lucille and what a wonderful person she is and how her rights were violated." Harold Lance does not talk to visitors at all. "We don't want to give away what we can sell," he explains pleasantly; an attempt was made to sell Lucille Miller's personal story to *Life*, but *Life* did not want to buy it. In the district attorney's offices they are prosecuting other murders now, and do not see why the Miller trial attracted so much attention. "It wasn't a very interesting murder as murders go," Don Turner says laconically. Elaine Hayton's death is no longer under investigation. "We know everything we want to know," Turner says.

Arthwell Hayton's office is directly below Edward Foley's. Some people around San Bernardino say that Arthwell Hayton suffered; others say that he did not suffer at all. Perhaps he did not, for time past is not believed to have any bearing upon time present or future, out in the golden land where every day the world is born anew. In any case, on October 17, 1965, Arthwell Hayton married again, married his children's pretty governess, Wenche Berg, at a service in the Chapel of the Roses at a retirement village near Riverside. Later the newlyweds were feted at a reception for seventy-five in the dining room of Rose Garden Village. The bridegroom was in black tie, with a white carnation in his buttonhole. The bride wore a long white *peau de soie* dress and carried a shower bouquet of sweetheart roses with stephanotis streamers. A coronet of seed pearls held her illusion veil.

[1966]

Home of the Free

Wendell Berry

A review of Recollected Essays, 1965–1980 *in* Publishers Weekly *calls Wendell Berry "probably the closest we have to a modern Thoreau." Born in Kentucky in 1934, Berry was educated at the University of Kentucky and taught English there until 1977. He is a poet, a novelist, an essayist, and, above all, a farmer. His writing often centers on agriculture because he sees a necessary relationship between agriculture and human culture. In the foreword to* The Gift of Good Land: Further Essays Cultural and Agricultural *(1981), from which the following selection has been taken, Berry states a major theme of his work: "My previous book on agriculture,* The Unsettling of America *[1977], sought to comprehend the causes and consequences of industrial agriculture within the bounds of a single argument: that agriculture is an integral part of the structure, both biological and cultural, that sustains human life, and that you cannot disturb one part of that structure without disturbing all of it. . . ." His most recent collections of essays include* Standing by Words *(1985) and* Home Economics *(1987).*

I was writing not long ago about a team of Purdue engineers who foresaw that by 2001 practically everything would be done by remote control. The question I asked—because such a "projection" *forces* one to ask it—was, *Where does satisfaction come from?* I concluded that there probably wouldn't be much satisfaction in such a world. There would be a lot of what passes for "efficiency," a lot of "production" and "consumption," but little satisfaction.

What I failed to acknowledge was that this "world of the future" is already established among us, and is growing. Two advertisements that I have lately received from correspondents make this clear, and raise the question about the sources of satisfaction more immediately and urgently than any abstract "projection" can do.

The first is the legend from a John Deere display at Waterloo Municipal Airport:

INTRODUCING SOUND-GARD BODY . . .
A DOWN TO EARTH SPACE CAPSULE.
New Sound-Gard body from John Deere, an "earth space capsule" to protect and encourage the American farmer at his job of being "Breadwinner to a world of families."
   Outside: dust, noise, heat, storm, fumes.
   Inside: all's quiet, comfortable, safe.
Features include a 4 post Roll Gard, space-age metals, plastics, and fibers to isolate driver from noise, vibration, and jolts. He dials 'inside weather', to his liking . . . he push buttons radio or stereo tape entertainment. He breathes filtered, conditioned air in his pressurized compartment. He has remote control over multi-ton and multi-hookups, with control tower visibility . . . from his scientifically padded seat.

The second is an ad for a condominium housing development:

HOME OF THE FREE.
We do the things you hate. You do the things you like. We mow the lawn, shovel the walks, paint and repair and do all exterior maintenance.
   You cross-country ski, play tennis, hike, swim, work out, read or nap. Or advise our permanent maintenance staff as they do the things you hate.

Different as they may seem at first, these two ads make the same appeal, and they represent two aspects of the same problem: the widespread, and still spreading, assumption that we somehow have the right to be set free from anything whatsoever that we "hate" or don't want to do. According to this view, what we want to be set free from are the natural conditions of the world and the necessary work of human life; we do not want to experience temperatures that are the least bit too hot or too cold, or to work in the sun, or be exposed to wind or rain, or come in personal contact with anything describable as dirt, or provide for any of our own needs, or clean up after ourselves. Implicit in all this is the desire to be free of the "hassles" of mortality, to be "safe" from the life cycle. Such freedom and safety are always for sale. It is proposed that if we put all earthly obligations and the rites of passage into the charge of experts and machines, then life will become a permanent holiday.

What these people are really selling is insulation—cushions of technology, "space age" materials, and the menial work of other people—to keep fantasy in and reality out. The condominium ad says flat out that it is addressed to people who "hate" the handwork of household maintenance, and who will enjoy "advising" the people who do it for them; it is addressed, in other words, to those who think themselves too good to do work that other people are not too good to do. But it is a little surprising to realize that the John Deere ad is addressed to farmers who not only hate farming (that is, any physical contact with the ground or the weather or the crops), but also hate tractors, from the "dust," "fumes," "noise, vibration, and jolts" of which they wish to be protected by an "earth space capsule" and a "scientifically padded seat."

Of course, the only real way to get this sort of freedom and safety—to escape the hassles of earthly life—is to die. And what I think we see in these advertisements is an appeal to a desire to be dead that is evidently felt by many people. These ads are addressed to the perfect consumers—the self-consumers, who have found nothing of interest here on earth, nothing to do, and are impatient to be shed of earthly concerns. And so I am at a loss to explain the delay. Why hasn't some super salesman sold every one of these people a coffin—an "earth space capsule" in which they would experience no discomfort or inconvenience whatsoever, would have to do no work that they hate, would be spared all extremes of weather and all noises, fumes, vibrations, and jolts?

I wish it were possible for us to let these living dead bury themselves in the earth space capsules of their choice and think no more about them. The problem is that with their insatiable desire for comfort, convenience, remote control, and the rest of it, they cause an unconscionable amount of trouble for the rest of us, who would like a fair crack at living the rest of our lives within the terms and conditions of the real world. Speaking for myself, I acknowledge that the world, the weather, and the life cycle have caused me no end of trouble, and yet I look forward to putting in another forty or so years with them because they have also given me no end of pleasure and instruction. They interest me. I want to see them thrive on their own terms. I hate to see them abused and interfered with for the comfort and convenience of a lot of spoiled people who presume to "hate" the more necessary kinds of work and all the natural consequences of working outdoors.

When people begin to "hate" the life cycle and to try to live outside it and to escape its responsibilities, then the corpses begin to pile up and to get into the wrong places. One of the laws that the world imposes on us is that everything must be returned to its source to be used again. But one of the first principles of the haters is to violate this law in the name of convenience or efficiency. Because it is "inconvenient" to return bottles to the beverage manufacturers, "dead soldiers" pile up in the road ditches and in the waterways. Because it is "inconvenient" to be responsible for wastes, the rivers are polluted with everything from human excrement to various carcinogens and poisons. Because it is "efficient" (by what standard?) to mass-produce meat and milk in food "factories," the animal manures that once would have fertilized the fields have instead become wastes and pollutants. And so to be "free" of "inconvenience" and "inefficiency" we are paying a high price—which the haters among us are happy to charge to posterity.

And what a putrid (and profitable) use they have made of the idea of freedom! What a tragic evolution has taken place when the inheritors of the Bill of Rights are told, and when some of them believe, that "the home of the free" is where somebody else will do your work!

Let me set beside those advertisements a sentence that I consider a responsible statement about freedom: "To be free is precisely the same thing as to be pious, wise, just and temperate, careful of one's own, abstinent from what is another's, and thence, in fine, magnanimous and brave." That is John Milton. He is speaking out of the mainstream of our culture. Reading his sentence after those advertisements is coming home. His words have an atmosphere around them that a living human can breathe in.

How do you get free in Milton's sense of the word? I don't think you can do it in an earth space capsule or a space space capsule or a capsule of any kind. What Milton is saying is that you can do it only by living in this world as you find it, and by taking responsibility for the consequences of your life in it. And that means doing some chores that, highly objectionable in anybody's capsule, may not be at all unpleasant in the world.

Just a few days ago I finished up one of the heaviest of my spring jobs: hauling manure. On a feed lot I think this must be real drudgery even with modern labor-saving equipment—all that "waste" and no fields to put it on! But instead of a feed lot I have a small farm—what would probably be called a subsistence farm. My labor-saving equipment consists of a team of horses and a forty-year-old manure spreader. We forked the manure on by hand—forty-five loads. I made my back tired and my hands sore, but I got a considerable amount of pleasure out of it. Everywhere I spread that manure I knew it was needed. What would have been a nuisance in a feed lot was an opportunity and a benefit here. I enjoyed seeing it go out onto the ground. I was working some two-year-olds in the spreader for the first time, and I enjoyed that— mostly. And, since there were no noises, fumes, or vibrations the loading times were socially pleasant. I had some help from neighbors, from my son, and, toward the end, from my daughter who arrived home well rested from college. She helped me load, and then read *The Portrait of a Lady* while I drove up the hill to empty the spreader. I don't think many young women have read Henry James while forking manure. I enjoyed working with my daughter, and I enjoyed wondering what Henry James would have thought of her.

The Son from America

Isaac Bashevis Singer

Isaac Bashevis Singer, who won the Nobel Prize for literature in 1978, is the most popular living Yiddish writer and is also becoming one of the most popular living American writers. He has been a steady contributor to the Yiddish Jewish Daily Forward *since he arrived in New York City in 1935, and in recent years he also has become a frequent contributor to* The New Yorker. *He still writes in Yiddish, his childhood language ("A writer has to write in his own language or not at all"), but by now he is almost always involved in the translation of his own work ("I do not exaggerate when I say that English has become my 'second original language'").*

Singer was born in Poland in 1904, the grandson of two rabbis, the son of a Hasidic scholar. He himself received a traditional Jewish education and for a while studied at a rabbinical seminary, but he began to doubt "not the power of God, but all the traditions and dogmas." As a result, he disappointed family expectations and instead followed the example of his older brother to become a secular writer. He took a job as proofreader for a Yiddish literary journal in Warsaw. By 1926 Singer began to publish stories and reviews. Then in 1935 he followed his brother to New York City, where he still lives, on the upper West Side of Manhattan.

Success came with the English translation of his 1945 novel, The Family Moskat. *Other novels include the two-volume* The Manor *(1967),* Shosha *(1978),* Yentl: The Yeshiva Boy *(1983), and* Love and Exile *(1984), but he is best known for his short stories. Collections include* Gimpel the Fool *(1957),* The Spinoza of Market Street *(1957),* The Seance *(1968),* Passions *(1976), and* Collected Short Stories of Isaac Bashevis Singer *(1982). In* My Father's Court *(1966),* A Day of Pleasure: Stories of a Boy Growing Up in Warsaw *(1969), and* A Little Boy in Search of God; Mysticism in a Personal Light *(1976) are mainly autobiographical. Singer has also written children's stories, and in 1973 he made his playwriting debut with an adaptation of* The Manor, *produced by the Yale Repertory Theater.*

But primarily Singer is an old-fashioned storyteller. Many of his stories, set in the shtetls and ghettos of prewar Poland, draw heavily on Jewish legend and folklore and are peopled with witches and ghosts and demons. An increasing number now deal with life in the United States and are set in contemporary New York. "Because I have now lived in this country longer than in Poland," he says, "I have developed roots here too." "The Son from America," which we reprint below, tells of an encounter between these two cultures. It first appeared in The New Yorker *and was later reprinted in the short-story collection* A Crown of Feathers *(1970), for which he won the National Book Award. The translation is by the author and Dorothea Straus.*

The village of Lentshin was tiny—a sandy marketplace where the peasants of the area met once a week. It was surrounded by little huts with thatched roofs or shingles green with moss. The chimneys looked like pots. Between the huts there were fields, where the owners planted vegetables or pastured their goats.

In the smallest of these huts lived old Berl, a man in his eighties, and his wife, who was called Berlcha (wife of Berl). Old Berl was one of the Jews who had been driven from their villages in Russia and had settled in Poland. In Lentshin, they mocked the mistakes he made while praying aloud. He spoke with a sharp "r." He was short, broad-shouldered, and had a small white beard, and summer and winter he wore a sheepskin hat, a padded cotton jacket, and stout boots. He walked slowly, shuffling his feet. He had a half acre of field, a cow, a goat, and chickens.

The couple had a son, Samuel, who had gone to America forty years ago. It was said in Lentshin that he became a millionaire there. Every month, the Lentshin letter carrier brought old Berl a money order and a letter that no one could read because many of the words were English. How much money Samuel sent his parents remained a secret. Three times a year, Berl and his wife went on foot to Zakroczym and cashed the money orders there. But they never seemed to use the money. What for? The garden, the cow, and the goat provided most of their needs. Besides, Berlcha sold chickens and eggs, and from these there was enough to buy flour for bread.

No one cared to know where Berl kept the money that his son sent him. There were no thieves in Lentshin. The hut consisted of one room, which contained all their belongings: the table, the shelf for meat, the shelf for milk foods, the two beds, and the clay oven. Sometimes the chickens roosted in the woodshed and sometimes, when it was cold, in a coop near the oven. The goat, too, found shelter inside when the weather was bad. The more prosperous villagers had kerosene lamps, but Berl and his wife did not believe in newfangled gadgets. What was wrong with a wick in a dish of oil? Only for the Sabbath would Berlcha buy three tallow candles at the store. In summer, the couple got up at sunrise and retired with the chickens. In the long winter evenings, Berlcha spun flax at her spinning wheel and Berl sat beside her in the silence of those who enjoy their rest.

Once in a while when Berl came home from the synagogue after evening prayers, he brought news to his wife. In Warsaw there were strikers who demanded that the czar abdicate. A heretic by the name of Dr. Herzl° had come up with the idea that Jews should settle again in Palestine. Berlcha listened and shook her bonneted head. Her face was yellowish and wrinkled like a cabbage leaf. There were bluish sacks under her eyes.

Dr. Herzl   Theodor Herzl (1860–1904) founded the modern Zionist movement, believing that the answer to anti-Semitism was a separate Jewish state. Some orthodox Jews opposed Zionism on the grounds that only God could restore the Jews to their land.

She was half deaf. Berl had to repeat each word he said to her. She would say, "The things that happen in the big cities!"

Here in Lentshin nothing happened except usual events: a cow gave birth to a calf, a young couple had a circumcision party, or a girl was born and there was no party. Occasionally, someone died. Lentshin had no cemetery, and the corpse had to be taken to Zakroczym. Actually, Lentshin had become a village with few young people. The young men left for Zakroczym, for Nowy Dwor, for Warsaw, and sometimes for the United States. Like Samuel's, their letters were illegible, the Yiddish mixed with the languages of the countries where they were now living. They sent photographs in which the men wore top hats and the women fancy dresses like squiresses.

Berl and Berlcha also received such photographs. But their eyes were failing and neither he nor she had glasses. They could barely make out the pictures. Samuel had sons and daughters with Gentile names—and grandchildren who had married and had their own offspring. Their names were so strange that Berl and Berlcha could never remember them. But what difference do names make? America was far, far away on the other side of the ocean, at the edge of the world. A Talmud teacher who came to Lentshin had said that Americans walk with their heads down and their feet up. Berl and Berlcha could not grasp this. How was it possible? But since the teacher said so it must be true. Berlcha pondered for some time and then she said, "One can get accustomed to everything."

And so it remained. From too much thinking—God forbid—one may lose one's wits.

One Friday morning, when Berlcha was kneading the dough for the Sabbath loaves, the door opened and a nobleman entered. He was so tall that he had to bend down to get through the door. He wore a beaver hat and a cloak bordered with fur. He was followed by Chazkel, the coachman from Zakroczym, who carried two leather valises with brass locks. In astonishment Berlcha raised her eyes.

The nobleman looked around and said to the coachman in Yiddish, "Here it is." He took out a silver ruble and paid him. The coachman tried to hand him change but he said, "You can go now."

When the coachman closed the door, the nobleman said, "Mother, it's me, your son Samuel—Sam."

Berlcha heard the words and her legs grew numb. Her hands, to which pieces of dough were sticking, lost their power. The nobleman hugged her, kissed her forehead, both her cheeks. Berlcha began to cackle like a hen, "My son!" At that moment Berl came in from the woodshed, his arms piled with logs. The goat followed him. When he saw a nobleman kissing his wife, Berl dropped the wood and exclaimed, "What is this?"

The nobleman let go of Berlcha and embraced Berl. "Father!"

For a long time Berl was unable to utter a sound. He wanted to recite holy words that he had read in the Yiddish Bible, but he could remember nothing. Then he asked, "Are you Samuel?"

"Yes, Father, I am Samuel."

"Well, peace be with you." Berl grasped his son's hand. He was still not sure that he was not being fooled. Samuel wasn't as tall and heavy as this man, but then Berl reminded himself that Samuel was only fifteen years old when he had left home. He must have grown in that faraway country. Berl asked, "Why didn't you let us know you were coming?"

"Didn't you receive my cable?" Samuel asked.

Berl did not know what a cable was.

Berlcha had scraped the dough from her hands and enfolded her son. He kissed her again and asked, "Mother, didn't you receive a cable?"

"What? If I lived to see this, I am happy to die," Berlcha said, amazed by her own words. Berl, too, was amazed. These were just the words he would have said earlier if he had been able to remember. After a while Berl came to himself and said, "Pescha, you will have to make a double Sabbath pudding in addition to the stew."

It was years since Berl had called Berlcha by her given name. When he wanted to address her, he would say, "Listen," or "Say." It is the young or those from the big cities who call a wife by her name. Only now did Berlcha begin to cry. Yellow tears ran from her eyes, and everything became dim. Then she called out, "It's Friday—I have to prepare for the Sabbath." Yes, she had to knead the dough and braid the loaves. With such a guest, she had to make a larger Sabbath stew. The winter day is short and she must hurry.

Her son understood what was worrying her, because he said, "Mother, I will help you."

Berlcha wanted to laugh, but a choked sob came out. "What are you saying? God forbid."

The nobleman took off his cloak and jacket and remained in his vest, on which hung a solid-gold watch chain. He rolled up his sleeves and came to the trough. "Mother, I was a baker for many years in New York," he said, and he began to knead the dough.

"What! You are my darling son who will say Kaddish for me." She wept raspingly. Her strength left her, and she slumped onto the bed.

Berl said, "Women will always be women." And he went to the shed to get more wood. The goat sat down near the oven; she gazed with surprise at this strange man—his height and his bizarre clothes.

The neighbors had heard the good news that Berl's son had arrived from America and they came to greet him. The women began to help Berlcha prepare for the Sabbath. Some laughed, some cried. The room was full of people, as at a wedding. They asked Berl's son, "What is new in America?" And Berl's son answered, "America is all right."

"Do Jews make a living?"

"One eats white bread there on weekdays."

"Do they remain Jews?"

"I am not a Gentile."

After Berlcha blessed the candles, father and son went to the little synagogue across the street. A new snow had fallen. The son took large steps,
but Berl warned him, "Slow down."

In the synagogue the Jews recited "Let Us Exult" and "Come, My
Groom." All the time, the snow outside kept falling. After prayers, when
Berl and Samuel left the Holy Place, the village was unrecognizable.
Everything was covered with snow. One could see only the contours of the
roofs and the candles in the windows. Samuel said, "Nothing has changed
here."

Berlcha had prepared gefilte fish, chicken soup with rice, meat, carrot
stew. Berl recited the benediction over a glass of ritual wine. The family
ate and drank, and when it grew quiet for a while one could hear the
chirping of the house cricket. The son talked a lot, but Berl and Berlcha
understood little. His Yiddish was different and contained foreign words.

After the final blessing Samuel asked, "Father, what did you do with
all the money I sent you?"

Berl raised his white brows. "It's here."

"Didn't you put it in a bank?"

"There is no bank in Lentshin."

"Where do you keep it?"

Berl hesitated. "One is not allowed to touch money on the Sabbath, but
I will show you." He crouched beside the bed and began to shove something heavy. A boot appeared. Its top was stuffed with straw. Berl
removed the straw and the son saw that the boot was full of gold coins.
He lifted it.

"Father, this is a treasure!" he called out.

"Well."

"Why didn't you spend it?"

"On what? Thank God, we have everything."

"Why didn't you travel somewhere?"

"Where to? This is our home."

The son asked one question after the other, but Berl's answer was
always the same: they wanted for nothing. The garden, the cow, the goat,
the chickens provided them with all they needed. The son said, "If thieves
knew about this, your lives wouldn't be safe."

"There are no thieves here."

"What will happen to the money?"

"You take it."

Slowly, Berl and Berlcha grew accustomed to their son and his American Yiddish. Berlcha could hear him better now. She even recognized his
voice. He was saying, "Perhaps we should build a larger synagogue."

"The synagogue is big enough," Berl replied.

"Perhaps a home for old people."

"No one sleeps in the street."

The next day after the Sabbath meal was eaten, a Gentile from Zakroczym brought a paper—it was the cable. Berl and Berlcha lay down for a
nap. They soon began to snore. The goat, too, dozed off. The son put on his
cloak and his hat and went for a walk. He strode with his long legs across
the marketplace. He stretched out a hand and touched a roof. He wanted
to smoke a cigar, but he remembered it was forbidden on the Sabbath. He
had a desire to talk to someone, but it seemed that the whole of Lentshin
was asleep. He entered the synagogue. An old man was sitting there,
reciting psalms. Samuel asked, "Are you praying?"

"What else is there to do when one gets old?"

"Do you make a living?"

The old man did not understand the meaning of these words. He smiled,
showing his empty gums, and then he said, "If God gives health, one keeps
on living."

Samuel returned home. Dusk had fallen. Berl went to the synagogue for
the evening prayers and the son remained with his mother. The room was
filled with shadows.

Berlcha began to recite in a solemn singsong, "God of Abraham, Isaac,
and Jacob, defend the poor people of Israel and Thy name. The Holy
Sabbath is departing; the welcome week is coming to us. Let it be one of
health, wealth and good deeds."

"Mother, you don't need to pray for wealth," Samuel said. "You are
wealthy already."

Berlcha did not hear—or pretended not to. Her face had turned into a
cluster of shadows.

In the twilight Samuel put his hand into his jacket pocket and touched
his passport, his checkbook, his letters of credit. He had come here with
big plans. He had a valise filled with presents for his parents. He wanted
to bestow gifts on the village. He brought not only his own money but
funds from the Lentshin Society in New York, which had organized a ball
for the benefit of the village. But this village in the hinterland needed
nothing. From the synagogue one could hear hoarse chanting. The
cricket, silent all day, started again its chirping. Berlcha began to sway
and utter holy rhymes inherited from mothers and grandmothers:

Thy holy sheep
In mercy keep,
In Torah and good deeds;
Provide for all their needs,
Shoes, clothes, and bread
And the Messiah's tread.

What Should Work Be?

All of the pieces in this section deal, directly or indirectly, with the meaning of work. How much does the value of our lives depend on our work? The opening poems by Marge Piercy and Theodore Roethke present contrasting feelings: work as satisfying and central to our lives and work as inescapable drudgery. There follow four reports on their work by four workers, and these too are in contrast: the veterinarian and the mason find their work fulfilling; the editor and the steelworker do not.

This distinction between fulfilling work and alienating work is treated on a larger and more philosophical scale by Erich Fromm in the next piece. He relates alienation—the separation of work from any inherent meaning or satisfaction—to the rise of industrialism and assembly-line production, and he points to some of the psychological consequences for the worker. The essay by Ray Slater that follows illustrates from personal experience both the meaning of alienation and the reality of the consequences.

In the final essay, engineer Samuel Florman challenges some of Fromm's and Slater's assumptions. He skeptically reexamines the idea that technology is to blame for the dehumanization of work, or that job discontent is "high on the list of American social problems." He concludes that if there is sickness in our culture, it does not originate in the workplace.

Marge Piercy
(b. 1936)

To Be of Use

The people I love the best
jump into work head first
without dallying in the shallows
and swim off with sure strokes almost out of sight.
They seem to become natives of that element,
the black sleek heads of seals
bouncing like half-submerged balls.

I love people who harness themselves, an ox to a heavy
    cart,
who pull like water buffalo, with massive patience,
who strain in the mud and the muck to move things
    forward,
who do what has to be done, again and again.

I want to be with people who submerge
in the task, who go into the fields to harvest
and work in a row and pass the bags along,
who are not parlor generals and field deserters
but move in a common rhythm
when the food must come in or the fire be put out.

The work of the world is common as mud.
Botched, it smears the hands, crumbles to dust.
But the thing worth doing well done
has a shape that satisfies, clean and evident.
Greek amphoras for wine or oil,
Hopi vases that held corn, are put in museums
but you know they were made to be used.
The pitcher cries for water to carry
and a person for work that is real.

(1973)

Theodore Roethke
(1908–1963)

Dolor

I have known the inexorable sadness of pencils,
Neat in their boxes, dolor of pad and paper-weight,
All the misery of manila folders and mucilage,
Desolation in immaculate public places,
Lonely reception room, lavatory, switchboard,
The unalterable pathos of basin and pitcher,
Ritual of multigraph, paper-clip, comma,
Endless duplication of lives and objects.
And I have seen dust from the walls of institutions,
Finer than flour, alive, more dangerous than silica,
Sift, almost invisible, through long afternoons of tedium,
Dropping a fine film on nails and delicate eyebrows,
Glazing the pale hair, the duplicate gray standard faces.

(1943)

from *All Things Bright and Beautiful*

James Herriot

James Herriot (a pseudonym) is a veterinarian and deservedly popular author. He was born in Scotland in 1916. After completing his veterinary studies at Glasgow Veterinary College, he took his first position in the Yorkshire Dales of northern England, where he has practiced ever since. At the age of fifty, he began to write about his early days of veterinary work and of his love of the life and people and animals with whom he worked. The books are not sentimental; they are full of accurate detail and include blunders and tragedy as well as humor and triumph. Published in the United States as All Creatures Great and Small *(1972),* All Things Bright and Beautiful *(1973),* All Things Wise and Wonderful *(1976), and* The Lord God Made Them All *(1981), the books were immediately popular with the critics and the general public. A movie and a television series have been based upon them. In 1979, Herriot published* James Herriot's Yorkshire, *a book of photographs and commentary on the places described in his other*

*books. Despite the fame and income brought by his writing, James Herriot
continues to work as a veterinarian because he is doing the work he loves.
The selection reprinted below comes from* All Things Bright and Beautiful.

This was my third spring in the Dales° but it was like the two before—and
all the springs after. The kind of spring, that is, that a country vet knows;
the din of the lambing pens, the bass rumble of the ewes and the high,
insistent bawling of the lambs. This, for me, has always heralded the end
of winter and the beginning of something new. This and the piercing
Yorkshire wind and the hard, bright sunshine flooding the bare hillsides.

At the top of the grassy slope the pens, built of straw bales, formed a
long row of square cubicles each holding a ewe with her lambs and I could
see Rob Benson coming round the far end carrying two feeding buckets.
Rob was hard at it; at this time of the year he didn't go to bed for about
six weeks; he would maybe take off his boots and doze by the kitchen fire
at night but he was his own shepherd and never very far from the scene
of action.

'Ah've got a couple of cases for you today, Jim.' His face, cracked and
purpled by the weather, broke into a grin. 'It's not really you ah need, it's
that little lady's hand of yours and right sharpish, too.'

He led the way to a bigger enclosure, holding several sheep. There was
a scurry as we went in but he caught expertly at the fleece of a darting
ewe. 'This is the first one. You can see we haven't a deal o' time.'

I lifted the woolly tail and gasped. The lamb's head was protruding from
the vagina, the lips of the vulva clamped tightly behind the ears, and it
had swollen enormously to more than twice its size. The eyes were mere
puffed slits in the great oedematous ball and the tongue, blue and en-
gorged, lolled from the mouth.

'Well I've seen a few big heads, Rob, but I think this takes the prize.'

'Aye, the little beggar came with his legs back. Just beat me to it. Ah
was only away for an hour but he was up like a football. By hell it doesn't
take long. I know he wants his legs bringin' round but what can I do with
bloody great mitts like mine.' He held out his huge hands, rough and
swollen with the years of work.

While he spoke I was stripping off my jacket and as I rolled my shirt
sleeves high the wind struck like a knife at my shrinking flesh. I soaped
my fingers quickly and began to feel for a space round the lamb's neck.
For a moment the little eyes opened and regarded me disconsolately.

'He's alive, anyway,' I said. 'But he must feel terrible and he can't do
a thing about it.'

Easing my way round, I found a space down by the throat where I

Dales In England, a term that refers particularly to river valleys in the district from
Cumberland to Yorkshire.

thought I might get through. This was where my 'lady's hand' came in useful and I blessed it every spring; I could work inside the ewes with the minimum of discomfort to them and this was all-important because sheep, despite their outdoor hardiness, just won't stand rough treatment.

With the utmost care I inched my way along the curly wool of the neck to the shoulder. Another push forward and I was able to hook a finger round the leg and draw it forward until I could feel the flexure of the knee; a little more twiddling and I had hold of the tiny cloven foot and drew it gently out into the light of day.

Well that was half the job done. I got up from the sack where I was kneeling and went over to the bucket of warm water; I'd use my left hand for the other leg and began to soap it thoroughly while one of the ewes, marshalling her lambs around her, glared at me indignantly and gave a warning stamp of her foot.

Turning, I kneeled again and began the same procedure and as I once more groped forward a tiny lamb dodged under my arm and began to suck at my patient's udder. He was clearly enjoying it, too, if the little tail, twirling inches from my face, meant anything.

'Where did this bloke come from?' I asked, still feeling round.

The farmer smiled. 'Oh that's Herbert. Poor little youth's mother won't have 'im at any price. Took a spite at him at birth though she thinks world of her other lamb.'

'Do you feed him, then?'

'Nay, I was going to put him with the pet lambs but I saw he was fendin' for himself. He pops from one ewe to t'other and gets a quick drink whenever he gets chance. I've never seen owt like it.'

'Only a week old and an independent spirit, eh?'

'That's about the size of it, Jim. I notice 'is belly's full every mornin' so I reckon his ma must let him have a do during the night. She can't see him in the dark—it must be the look of him she can't stand.'

I watched the little creature for a moment. To me he seemed as full of knock-kneed charm as any of the others. Sheep were funny things.

I soon had the other leg out and once that obstruction was removed the lamb followed easily. He was a grotesque sight lying on the strawed grass, his enormous head dwarfing his body, but his ribs were heaving reassuringly and I knew the head would shrink back to normal as quickly as it had expanded. I had another search round inside the ewe but the uterus was empty.

'There's no more, Rob,' I said.

The farmer grunted. 'Aye, I thowt so, just a big single 'un. They're the ones that cause the trouble.'

Drying my arms, I watched Herbert. He had left my patient when she moved round to lick her lamb and he was moving speculatively among the other ewes. Some of them warned him off with a shake of the head but eventually he managed to sneak up on a big, wide-bodied sheep and pushed his head underneath her. Immediately she swung round and with a fierce upward butt of her hard skull she sent the little animal flying high in the air in a whirl of flailing legs. He landed with a thud on his back and as I hurried towards him he leaped to his feet and trotted away.

'Awd bitch!' shouted the farmer and as I turned to him in some concern he shrugged. 'I know, poor little sod, it's rough, but I've got a feelin' he wants it this way rather than being in the pen with the pet lambs. Look at 'im now.'

Herbert, quite unabashed, was approaching another ewe and as she bent over her feeding trough he nipped underneath her and his tail went into action again. There was no doubt about it—that lamb had guts.

'Rob,' I said as he caught my second patient. 'Why do you call him Herbert?'

'Well that's my youngest lad's name and that lamb's just like 'im the way he puts his head down and gets stuck in, fearless like.'

I put my hand into the second ewe. Here was a glorious mix up of three lambs; little heads, legs, a tail, all fighting their way towards the outside world and effectively stopping each other from moving an inch.

'She's been hanging about all morning and painin'.' Rob said. 'I knew summat was wrong.'

Moving a hand carefully around the uterus I began the fascinating business of sorting out the tangle which is just about my favorite job in practice. I had to bring a head and two legs up together in order to deliver a lamb; but they had to belong to the same lamb or I was in trouble. It was a matter of tracing each leg back to see if it was hind or fore, to find if it joined the shoulder or disappeared into the depths.

After a few minutes I had a lamb assembled inside with his proper appendages but as I drew the legs into view the neck telescoped and the head slipped back; there was barely room for it to come through the pelvic bones along with the shoulders and I had to coax it through with a finger in the eye socket. This was groaningly painful as the bones squeezed my hand but only for a few seconds because the ewe gave a final strain and the little nose was visible. After that it was easy and I had him on the grass within seconds. The little creature gave a convulsive shake of his head and the farmer wiped him down quickly with straw before pushing him to his mother's head.

The ewe bent over him and began to lick his face and neck with little quick darts of her tongue; and she gave the deep chuckle of satisfaction that you hear from a sheep only at this time. The chuckling continued as I produced another pair of lambs from inside her, one of them hind end first, and, towelling my arms again, I watched her nosing round her triplets delightedly.

Soon they began to answer her with wavering, high-pitched cries and as I drew my coat thankfully over my cold-reddened arms, lamb number one began to struggle to his knees; he couldn't quite make it to his feet and kept toppling on to his face but he knew where he was going, all right; he was headed for that udder with a singleness of purpose which would soon be satisfied.

Despite the wind cutting over the straw bales into my face I found myself grinning down at the scene; this was always the best part, the wonder that was always fresh, the miracle you couldn't explain.

I heard from Rob Benson again a few days later. It was a Sunday afternoon and his voice was strained, almost panic stricken.

'Jim, I've had a dog in among me in-lamb ewes. There was some folk up here with a car about dinner time and my neighbour said they had an Alsatian° and it was chasing the sheep all over the field. There's a hell of a mess—I tell you I'm frightened to look.'

'I'm on my way.' I dropped the receiver and hurried out to the car. I had a sinking dread of what would be waiting for me; the helpless animals lying with their throats torn, the terrifying lacerations of limbs and abdomen. I had seen it all before. The ones which didn't have to be slaughtered would need stitching and on the way I made a mental check of the stock of suture silk in the boot.

The in-lamb ewes were in a field by the roadside and my heart gave a quick thump as I looked over the wall; arms resting on the rough loose stones I gazed with sick dismay across the pasture. This was worse than I had feared. The long slope of turf was dotted with prostrate sheep—there must have been about fifty of them, motionless woolly mounds scattered at intervals on the green.

Rob was standing just inside the gate. He hardly looked at me. Just gestured with his head.

'Tell me what you think. I daren't go in there.'

I left him and began to walk among the stricken creatures, rolling them over, lifting their legs, parting the fleece of their necks to examine them. Some were completely unconscious, others comatose; none of them could stand up. But as I worked my way up the field I felt a growing bewilderment. Finally I called back to the farmer.

'Rob, come over here. There's something very strange.'

'Look,' I said as the farmer approached hesitantly. 'There's not a drop of blood nor a wound anywhere and yet all the sheep are flat out. I can't understand it.'

Rob bent over and gently raised a lolling head. 'Aye, you're right. What the hell's done it, then?'

At that moment I couldn't answer him, but a little bell was tinkling far away in the back of my mind. There was something familiar about that ewe the farmer had just handled. She was one of the few able to support herself on her chest and she was lying there, blank-eyed, oblivious of

---

Alsatian British name for a German shepherd dog.

everything; but . . . that drunken nodding of the head, that watery nasal discharge . . . I had seen it before. I knelt down and as I put my face close to hers I heard a faint bubbling—almost a rattling—in her breathing. I knew then.

'It's calcium deficiency,' I cried and began to gallop down the slope towards the car.

Rob trotted alongside me. 'But what the 'ell? They get that after lambin', don't they?'

'Yes, usually,' I puffed. 'But sudden exertion and stress can bring it on.'

'Well ah never knew that,' panted Rob. 'How does it happen?'

I saved my breath. I wasn't going to start an exposition on the effects of sudden derangement of the parathyroid. I was more concerned with wondering if I had enough calcium in the boot for fifty ewes. It was reassuring to see the long row of round tin caps peeping from their cardboard box; I must have filled up recently.

I injected the first ewe in the vein just to check my diagnosis—calcium works as quickly as that in sheep—and felt a quiet elation as the unconscious animal began to blink and tremble, then tried to struggle on to its chest.

'We'll inject the others under the skin,' I said. 'It'll save time.'

I began to work my way up the field. Rob pulled forward the fore leg of each sheep so that I could insert the needle under the convenient patch of unwoolled skin just behind the elbow; and by the time I was half way up the slope the ones at the bottom were walking about and getting their heads into the food troughs and hay racks.

It was one of the most satisfying experiences of my working life. Not clever, but a magical transfiguration; from despair to hope, from death to life within minutes.

I was throwing the empty bottles into the boot when Rob spoke. He was looking wonderingly up at the last of the ewes getting to its feet at the far end of the field.

'Well Jim, I'll tell you. I've never seen owt like that afore. But there's one thing bothers me.' He turned to me and his weathered features screwed up in puzzlement. 'Ah can understand how gettin' chased by a dog could affect some of them ewes, but why should the whole bloody lot go down?'

'Rob,' I said. 'I don't know.'

And, thirty years later, I still wonder. I still don't know why the whole bloody lot went down.

I thought Rob had enough to worry about at the time, so I didn't point out to him that other complications could be expected after the Alsatian episode. I wasn't surprised when I had a call to the Benson farm within days.

I met him again on the hillside with the same wind whipping over the straw bale pens. The lambs had been arriving in a torrent and the noise was louder than ever. He led me to my patient.

'There's one with a bellyful of dead lambs, I reckon,' he said, pointing to a ewe with her head drooping, ribs heaving. She stood quite motionless and made no attempt to move away when I went up to her; this one was really sick and as the stink of decomposition came up to me I knew the farmer's diagnosis was right.

'Well I suppose it had to happen to one at least after that chasing round,' I said. 'Let's see what we can do, anyway.'

This kind of lambing is without charm but it has to be done to save the ewe. The lambs were putrid and distended with gas and I used a sharp scalpel to skin the legs to the shoulders so that I could remove them and deliver the little bodies with the least discomfort to the mother. When I had finished, the ewe's head was almost touching the ground, she was panting rapidly and grating her teeth. I had nothing to offer her—no wriggling new creature for her to lick and revive her interest in life. What she needed was an injection of penicillin, but this was 1939 and the antibiotics were still a little way round the corner.

'Well I wouldn't give much for her,' Rob grunted. 'Is there owt more you can do?'

'Oh, I'll put some pessaries in her and give her an injection, but what she needs most is a lamb to look after. You know as well as I do that ewes in this condition usually give up if they've nothing to occupy them. You haven't a spare lamb to put on her, have you?'

'Not right now, I haven't. And it's now she needs it. Tomorrow'll be too late.'

Just at that moment a familiar figure wandered into view. It was Herbert, the unwanted lamb, easily recognisable as he prowled from sheep to sheep in search of nourishment.

'Hey, do you think she'd take that little chap?' I asked the farmer.

He looked doubtful. 'Well I don't know—he's a bit old. Nearly a fortnight and they like 'em newly born.'

'But it's worth a try isn't it? Why not try the old trick on her?'

Rob grinned. 'O.K., we'll do that. There's nowt to lose. Anyway the little youth isn't much bigger than a new-born 'un. He hasn't grown as fast as his mates.' He took out his penknife and quickly skinned one of the dead lambs, then he tied the skin over Herbert's back and round his jutting ribs.

'Poor little bugger, there's nowt on 'im,' he muttered. 'If this doesn't work he's going in with the pet lambs.'

When he had finished he set Herbert on the grass and the lamb, resolute little character that he was, bored straight in under the sick ewe and began to suck. It seemed he wasn't having much success because he gave the udder a few peremptory thumps with his hard little head; then his tail began to wiggle.

'She's lettin' him have a drop, any road,' Rob laughed.

Herbert was a type you couldn't ignore and the big sheep, sick as she was, just had to turn her head for a look at him. She sniffed along the tied-on skin in a non-committal way then after a few seconds she gave a few quick licks and the merest beginning of the familiar deep chuckle.

I began to gather up my gear. 'I hope he makes it,' I said. 'Those two need each other.' As I left the pen Herbert, in his new jacket, was still working away.

For the next week I hardly seemed to have my coat on. The flood of sheep work was at its peak and I spent hours of every day with my arms in and out of buckets of hot water in all corners of the district—in the pens, in dark nooks in farm buildings or very often in the open fields, because the farmers of those days didn't find anything disturbing in the sight of a vet kneeling in his shirt sleeves for an hour in the rain.

I had one more visit to Rob Benson's place. To a ewe with a prolapsed uterus after lambing—a job whose chief delight was comparing it with the sweat of replacing a uterus in a cow.

It was so beautifully easy. Rob rolled the animal on to her side then held her more or less upside down by tying a length of rope to her hind legs and passing it round his neck. In that position she couldn't strain and I disinfected the organ and pushed it back with the minimum of effort, gently inserting an arm at the finish to work it properly into place.

Afterwards the ewe trotted away unperturbed with her family to join the rapidly growing flock whose din was all around us.

'Look!' Rob cried. 'There's that awd ewe with Herbert. Over there on t'right—in the middle of that bunch.' They all looked the same to me but to Rob, like all shepherds, they were as different as people and he picked out these two effortlessly.

They were near the top of the field and as I wanted to have a close look at them we manoevered them into a corner. The ewe, fiercely possessive, stamped her foot at us as we approached, and Herbert, who had discarded his woolly jacket, held close to the flank of his new mother. He was, I noticed, faintly obese in appearance.

'You couldn't call him a runt now, Rob,' I said.

The farmer laughed. 'Nay, t'awd lass has a bag like a cow and Herbert's gettin' the lot. By gaw, he's in clover is that little youth and I reckon he saved the ewe's life—she'd have pegged out all right, but she never looked back once he came along.'

I looked away, over the noisy pens, over the hundreds of sheep moving across the fields. I turned to the farmer. 'I'm afraid you've seen a lot of me lately, Rob. I hope this is the last visit.'

'Aye well it could be. We're getting well through now . . . but it's a hell of a time, lambin', isn't it?'

'It is that. Well I must be off—I'll leave you to it.' I turned and made my way down the hillside, my arms raw and chafing in my sleeves, my cheeks whipped by the eternal wind gusting over the grass. At the gate I stopped and gazed back at the wide landscape, ribbed and streaked by the last of the winter's snow, and at the dark grey banks of cloud riding across on the wind followed by lakes of brightest blue; and in seconds the fields and walls and woods burst into vivid life and I had to close my eyes against the sun's glare. As I stood there the distant uproar came faintly down to me, the tumultuous harmony from deepest bass to highest treble; demanding, anxious, angry, loving.

The sound of the sheep, the sound of spring.

from *Working*

Studs Terkel

The following selections are taken from Studs Terkel's book Working: People Talk About What They Do All Day and How They Feel About What They Do *(1974). Further information on Terkel can be found on page 506.*

Carl Murray Bates, Mason

We're in a tavern no more than thirty yards from the banks of the Ohio. Toward the far side of the river, Alcoa smokestacks belch forth: an uneasy coupling of a bucolic past and an industrial present. The waters are polluted, yet the jobs out there offer the townspeople their daily bread.

He is fifty-seven years old. He's a stonemason who has pursued his craft since he was seventeen. None of his three sons is in his trade.

As far as I know, masonry is older than carpentry, which goes clear back to Bible times. Stonemason goes back way *before* Bible time: the pyramids of Egypt, things of that sort. Anybody that starts to build anything, stone, rock, or brick, starts on the northeast corner. Because when they built King Solomon's Temple, they started on the northeast corner. To this day, you look at your courthouses, your big public buildings, you look at the cornerstone, when it was created, what year, it will be on the northeast corner. If I was gonna build a septic tank, I would start on the northeast corner. (Laughs.) Superstition, I suppose.

With stone we build just about anything. Stone is the oldest and best building material that ever was. Stone was being used even by the cavemen that put it together with mud. They built out of stone before they even used logs. He got him a cave, he built stone across the front. And he learned to use dirt, mud, to make the stones lay there without sliding around—which was the beginnings of mortar, which we still call mud. The Romans used mortar that's almost as good as we have today.

Everyone hears these things, they just don't remember 'em. But me being in the profession, when I hear something in that line, I remember it. Stone's my business. I, oh, sometimes talk to architects and engineers that have made a study and I pick up the stuff here and there.

Every piece of stone you pick up is different, the grain's a little different and this and that. It'll split one way and break the other. You pick up your stone and look at it and make an educated guess. It's a pretty good day layin' stone or brick. Not tiring. Anything you like to do isn't tiresome. It's hard work; stone is heavy. At the same time, you get interested in what you're doing and you usually fight the clock the other way. You're not lookin' for quittin'. You're wondering you haven't got enough done and it's almost quittin' time. (Laughs.) I ask the hod carrier what time it is and he says two thirty. I say, "Oh, my Lord, I was gonna get a whole lot more than this."

I pretty well work by myself. On houses, usually just one works. I've got the hod carrier there, but most of the time I talk to myself, "I'll get my hammer and I'll knock the chip off there." (Laughs.) A good hod carrier is half your day. He won't work as hard as a poor one. He knows what to do and make every move count makin' the mortar. It has to be so much water, so much sand. His skill is to see that you don't run out of anything. The hod carrier, he's above the laborer. He has a certain amount of prestige.

I think a laborer feels that he's the low man. Not so much that he works with his hands, it's that he's at the bottom of the scale. He always wants to get up to a skilled trade. Of course he'd make more money. The main thing is the common laborer—even the word *common* laborer—just sounds so common, he's at the bottom. Many that works with his hands takes pride in his work.

I get a lot of phone calls when I get home: how about showin' me how and I'll do it myself; I always wind up doin' it for 'em. (Laughs.) So I take a lot of pride in it and I do get, oh, I'd say, a lot of praise or whatever you want to call it. I don't suppose anybody, however much he's recognized, wouldn't like to be recognized a little more. I think I'm pretty well recognized.

One of my sons is an accountant and the other two are bankers. They're mathematicians, I suppose you'd call 'em that. Air-conditioned offices and all that. They always look at the house I build. They stop by and see me when I'm aworkin'. Always want me to come down and fix somethin' on their house, too. (Laughs.) They don't buy a house that I don't have to look at it first. Oh sure, I've got to crawl under it and look on the roof, you know. . . .

I can't seem to think of any young masons. So many of 'em before, the man lays stone and his son follows his footsteps. Right now the only one of these sons I can think of is about forty, fifty years old.

I started back in the Depression times when there wasn't any apprenticeships. You just go out and if you could hold your job, that's it. I was just a kid then. Now I worked real hard and carried all the blocks I could. Then I'd get my trowel and I'd lay one or two. The second day the boss told me: I think you could lay enough blocks to earn your wages. So I guess I had only one day of apprenticeship. Usually it takes about three years of being a hod carrier to start. And it takes another ten or fifteen years to learn the skill.

I admired the men that we had at that time that were stonemasons. They knew their trade. So naturally I tried to pattern after them. There's been very little change in the work. Stone is still stone, mortar is still the same as it was fifty years ago. The style of stone has changed a little. We use a lot more, we call it golf. A stone as big as a baseball up to as big as a basketball. Just round balls and whatnot. We just fit 'em in the wall that way.

Automation has tried to get in the bricklayer. Set 'em with a crane. I've seen several put up that way. But you've always got in-between the windows and this and that. It just doesn't seem to pan out. We do have a power saw. We do have an electric power mix to mix the mortar, but the rest of it's done by hand as it always was.

In the old days they all seemed to want it cut out and smoothed. It's harder now because you have no way to use your tools. You have no way to use a string, you have no way to use a level or a plumb. You just have to look at it because it's so rough and many irregularities. You have to just back up and look at it.

All construction, there's always a certain amount of injuries. A scaffold will break and so on. But practically no real danger. All I ever did do was work on houses, so we don't get up very high—maybe two stories. Very seldom that any more. Most of 'em are one story. And so many of 'em use stone for a trim. They may go up four, five feet and then paneling or something. There's a lot of skinned fingers or you hit your finger with a hammer. Practically all stone is worked with hammers and chisels. I wouldn't call it dangerous at all.

Stone's my life. I daydream all the time, most times it's on stone. Oh, I'm gonna build me a stone cabin down on the Green River. I'm gonna build stone cabinets in the kitchen. That stone door's gonna be awful heavy and I don't know how to attach the hinges. I've got to figure out how to make a stone roof. That's the kind of thing. All my dreams, it seems like it's got to have a piece of rock mixed in it.

If I got some problem that's bothering me, I'll actually wake up in the night and think of it. I'll sit at the table and get a pencil and paper and go over it, makin' marks on paper or drawin' or however . . . this way or that way. Now I've got to work this and I've only got so much. Or they decided they want it that way when you already got it fixed this way. Anyone hates tearing his work down. It's all the same price but you still don't like to do it.

These fireplaces, you've got to figure how they'll throw out heat, the way you curve the fireboxes inside. You have to draw a line so they reflect heat. But if you throw out too much of a curve, you'll have them smoke. People in these fine houses don't want a puff of smoke coming out of the house.

The architect draws the picture and the plans, and the draftsman and the engineer, they help him. They figure the strength and so on. But when it comes to actually makin' the curves and doin' the work, you've got to do it with your hands. It comes right back to your hands.

When you get into stone, you're gettin' away from the prefabs, you're gettin' into the better homes. Usually at this day and age they'll start into sixty to seventy thousand and run up to about half a million. We've got one goin' now that's mighty close, three or four hundred thousand. That type of house is what we build.

The lumber is not near as good as it used to be. We have better fabricating material, such as plywood and sheet rock and things of that sort, but the lumber itself is definitely inferior. Thirty, forty years ago a house was almost entirely made of lumber, wood floors . . . Now they have vinyl, they have carpet, everything, and so on. The framework wood is getting to be of very poor quality.

But stone is still stone and the bricks are actually more uniform than they used to be. Originally they took a clay bank . . . I know a church been built that way. Went right on location, dug a hole in the ground and formed bricks with their hands. They made the bricks that built the building on the spot.

Now we've got modern kilns, modern heat, the temperature don't vary. They got better bricks now than they used to have. We've got machines that make brick, so they're made true. Where they used to, they were pretty rough. I'm buildin' a big fireplace now out of old brick. They run wide, long, and it's a headache. I've been two weeks on that one fireplace.

The toughest job I ever done was this house, a hundred years plus. The lady wanted one room left just that way. And this doorway had to be closed. It had deteriorated and weathered for over a hundred years. The bricks was made out of broken pieces, none of 'em were straight. If you lay 'em crooked, it gets awful hard right there. You spend a lifetime tryin' to learn to lay bricks straight. And it took a half-day to measure with a spoon, to try to get the mortar to match. I'd have so much dirt, so much soot, so much lime, so when I got the recipe right I could make it in bigger quantity. Then I made it with a coffee cup. Half a cup of this, half a cup of that . . . I even used soot out of a chimney and sweepin's off the floor. I was two days layin' up a little doorway, mixin' the mortar and all. The boss told the lady it couldn't be done. I said, "Give me the time, I believe I can do it." I defy you to find where that door is right now. That's the best job I ever done.

There's not a house in this country that I haven't built that I don't look at every time I go by. (Laughs.) I can set here now and actually in my mind see so many that you wouldn't believe. If there's one stone in there crooked, I know where it's at and I'll never forget it. Maybe thirty years, I'll know a place where I should have took that stone out and redone it but I didn't. I still notice it. The people who live there might not notice it, but I notice it. I never pass that house that I don't think of it. I've got one house in mind right now. (Laughs.) That's the work of my hands. 'Cause you see, stone, you don't prepaint it, you don't camouflage it. It's there, just like I left it forty years ago.

I can't imagine a job where you go home and maybe go by a year later and you don't know what you've done. My work, I can see what I did the first day I started. All my work is set right out there in the open and I can look at it as I go by. It's something I can see the rest of my life. Forty years ago, the first blocks I ever laid in my life, when I was seventeen years old. I never go through Eureka—a little town down there on the river—that I don't look thataway. It's always there.

Immortality as far as we're concerned. Nothin' in this world lasts forever, but did you know that stone—Bedford limestone, they claim—deteriorates one-sixteenth of an inch every hundred years? And it's around four or five inches for a house. So that's gettin' awful close. (Laughs.)

Nora Watson, Editor

Jobs are not big enough for people. It's not just the assembly line worker whose job is too small for his spirit, you know? A job like mine, if you really put your spirit into it, you would sabotage immediately. You don't dare. So you absent your spirit from it. My mind has been so divorced from my job, except as a source of income, it's really absurd.

As I work in the business world, I am more and more shocked. You throw yourself into things because you feel that important questions—self-discipline, goals, a meaning of your life—are carried out in your *work*. You invest a job with a lot of values that the society doesn't allow you to put into a job. You find yourself like a pacemaker that's gone crazy or something. You want it to be a million things that it's not and you want to give it a million parts of yourself that nobody else wants there. So you end up wrecking the curve or else settling down and conforming. I'm really in a funny place right now. I'm so calm about what I'm doing and what's coming . . .

She is twenty-eight. She is a staff writer for an institution publishing health care literature. Previously she had worked as an editor for a corporation publishing national magazines.

She came from a small mountain town in western Pennsylvania. "My father was a preacher. I didn't like what he was doing, but it was his vocation. That was the good part of it. It wasn't just: go to work in the morning and punch a time clock. It was a profession of himself. I expected work to be like that. All my life, I planned to be a teacher. It wasn't until late in college, my senior year, that I realized what the public school system was like. A little town in the mountains is one thing . . .

"My father, to my mind, is a weird person, but whatever he is, he is. Being a preacher was so important to him he would call it the Call of the Lord. He was willing to make his family live in very poor conditions. He was willing to strain his relationship to my mother, not to mention his children. He put us through an awful lot of things, including just bare survival, in order to stay being a preacher. His evenings, his weekends, and his days, he was out calling on people. Going out with healing oil and anointing the sick, listening to their troubles. The fact that he didn't do the same for his family is another thing. But he saw himself as the core resource in the community—at a great price to himself. He really believed that was what he was supposed to be doing. It was his life.

Most of the night he wouldn't go to bed. He'd pull out sermons by Wesley or Spurgeon or somebody, and he'd sit down until he fell asleep, maybe at three o'clock in the morning. Reading sermons. He just never stopped. (Laughs.)

I paper the walls of my office with posters and bring in flowers, bring in an FM radio, bring down my favorite ceramic lamp. I'm the only person in the whole damn building with a desk facing the window instead of the door. I just turn myself around from all that I can. I ration my time so that I'll spend two hours working for the Institution and the rest of the time I'll browse. (Laughs.)

I function better if they leave me alone more. My boss will come in and say, "I know you're overloaded, but would you mind getting this done, it's urgent. I need it in three weeks." I can do it in two hours. So I put it on the back burner and produce it on time. When I first went there, I came in early and stayed late. I read everything I could on the subject at hand. I would work a project to the wall and get it really done right, and then ask for more. I found out I was wrecking the curve, I was out of line.

The people, just as capable as I and just as ready to produce, had realized it was pointless, and had cut back. Everyone, consciously or unconsciously, was rationing his time. Playing cards at lunch time for three hours, going sun bathing, or less obvious ways of blowing it. I realized: Okay, the road to ruin is doing a good job. The amazing, absurd thing was that once I decided to stop doing a good job, people recognized a kind of authority in me. Now I'm just moving ahead like blazes.

I have my own office. I have a secretary. If I want a book case, I get a book case. If I want a file, I get a file. If I want to stay home, I stay home. If I want to go shopping, I go shopping. This is the first comfortable job I've ever had in my life and it is absolutely despicable.

I've been a waitress and done secretarial work. I knew, in those cases, I wasn't going to work at near capacity. It's one thing to work to your limits as a waitress because you end up with a bad back. It's another thing to work to your limits doing writing and editing because you end up with a sharper mind. It's a joy. Here, of all places, where I had expected to put the energy and enthusiasm and the gifts that I may have to work—it isn't happening. They expect less than you can offer. Token labor. What writing you do is writing to order. When I go for a job interview—I must leave this place!—I say, "Sure, I can bring you samples, but the ones I'm proud of are the ones the Institution never published."

It's so demeaning to be there and not be challenged. It's humiliation, because I feel I'm being forced into doing something I would never do of my own free will—which is simply waste itself. It's really not a Puritan hang-up. It's not that I want to be persecuted. It's simply that I know I'm vegetating and being paid to do exactly that. It's possible for me to sit here and read my books. But then you walk out with no sense of satisfaction, with no sense of legitimacy! I'm being had. Somebody has bought the right to you for eight hours a day. The manner in which they use you is completely at their discretion. You know what I mean?

I feel like I'm being pimped for and it's not my style. The level of bitterness in this department is stunning. They take days off quite a bit. They don't show up. They don't even call in. They've adjusted a lot better than I have. They see the Institution as a free ride as long as it lasts. I don't want to be party to it, so I've gone my own way. It's like being on welfare. Not that that's a shameful thing. It's the surprise of this enforced idleness. It makes you feel not at home with yourself. I'm furious. It's a feeling that I will not be humiliated. I will not be dis-used.

For all that was bad about my father's vocation, he showed me it was possible to fuse your life to your work. His home was also his work. A parish is no different from an office, because it's the whole countryside. There's nothing I would enjoy more than a job that was so meaningful to me that I brought it home.

The people I work with are not buffoons. I think they're part of a culture, like me, who've been sold on a dum-dum idea of human nature. It's frightening. I've made the best compromise available. If I were free, economically free, I would go back to school. It galls me that in our culture we have to pay for the privilege of learning.

A guy was in the office next to mine. He's sixty-two and he's done. He came to the Institution in the forties. He saw the scene and said, "Yes, I'll play drone to you. I'll do all the piddley things you want. I won't upset the apple cart by suggesting anything else." With a change of regimes in our department, somebody came across him and said, "Gee, he hasn't contributed anything here. His mind is set in old attitudes. So we'll throw him out." They fired him unceremoniously, with no pension, no severance pay, no nothing. Just out on your ear, sixty-two. He gets back zero from having invested so many years playing the game.

The drone has his nose to the content of the job. The politicker has his nose to the style. And the politicker is what I think our society values. The politicker, when it's apparent he's a winner, is helped. Everyone who has a stake in being on the side of the winner gives him a boost. The minute I finally realized the way to exist at the Institution—for the short time I'll be here—was not to break my back but to use it for my own ends, I was a winner.

Granted, there were choices this guy could have made initially. He might have decided on a more independent way of life. But there were all sorts of forces keeping him from that decision. The Depression, for one thing. You took the job, whatever the terms were. It was a straight negotiation. The drone would get his dole. The Institution broke the contract. He was fired for being dull, which is what he was hired to be.

I resist strongly the mystique of youth that says these kids are gonna come up with the answers. One good thing a lot of the kids are doing, though, is not getting themselves tied up to artificial responsibilities. That includes marriage, which some may or may not call an artificial responsibility. I have chosen to stay unmarried, to not get encumbered with husband and children. But the guy with three kids and a mortgage doesn't have many choices. He wouldn't be able to work two days a week instead of five.

I'm coming to a less moralistic attitude toward work. I know very few people who feel secure with their right just to be—or comfortable. Just you being you and me being me with my mini-talents may be enough. Maybe just making a career of being and finding out what that's about is enough. I don't think I have a calling—at this moment—except to be me. But nobody pays you for being you, so I'm at the Institution—for the moment . . .

When you ask most people who they are, they define themselves by their jobs. "I'm a doctor." "I'm a radio announcer." "I'm a carpenter." If somebody asks me, I say, "I'm Nora Watson." At certain points in time I do things for a living. Right now I'm working for the Institution. But not for long. I'd be lying to you if I told you I wasn't scared.

I have a few options. Given the market, I'm going to take the best job I can find. I really tried to play the game by the rules, and I think it's a hundred percent unadulterated bullshit. So I'm not likely to go back downtown and say, "Here I am. I'm very good, hire me."

You recognize yourself as a marginal person. As a person who can give only minimal assent to anything that is going on in this society: "I'm glad the electricity works." That's about it. What you have to find is your own niche that will allow you to keep feeding and clothing and sheltering yourself without getting downtown. (Laughs.) Because that's death. That's really where death is.

Mike Lefevre,
Steelworker

Who built the seven towers of Thebes?
The books are filled with the names of kings.
Was it kings who hauled the craggy blocks of
stone? . . .
In the evening when the Chinese wall was
finished
Where did the masons go? . . .

—BERTOLT BRECHT

It is a two-flat dwelling, somewhere in Cicero, on the outskirts of Chicago.
He is thirty-seven. He works in a steel mill. On occasion, his wife Carol
works as a waitress in a neighborhood restaurant; otherwise, she is at
home, caring for their two small children, a girl and a boy.

At the time of my first visit, a sculpted statuette of Mother and Child
was on the floor, head severed from body. He laughed softly as he indicated
his three-year-old daughter: "She Doctor Spock'd it."°

I'm a dying breed. A laborer. Strictly muscle work . . . pick it up, put it
down, pick it up, put it down. We handle between forty and fifty thousand
pounds of steel a day. (Laughs.) I know this is hard to believe—from four
hundred pounds to three- and four-pound pieces. It's dying.

You can't take pride any more. You remember when a guy could point
to a house he built, how many logs he stacked. He built it and he was
proud of it. I don't really think I could be proud if a contractor built a
home for me. I would be tempted to get in there and kick the carpenter
in the ass (laughs), and take the saw away from him. 'Cause I would have
to be part of it, you know.

It's hard to take pride in a bridge you're never gonna cross, in a door
you're never gonna open. You're mass-producing things and you never see
the end result of it. (Muses.) I worked for a trucker one time. And I got
this tiny satisfaction when I loaded a truck. At least I could see the truck
depart loaded. In a steel mill, forget it. You don't see where nothing goes.

I got chewed out by my foreman once. He said, "Mike, you're a good
worker but you have a bad attitude." My attitude is that I don't get excited
about my job. I do my work but I don't say whoopee-doo. The day I get

---

Doctor Spock'd it A reference to Benjamin Spock's *Common Sense Book of Baby and
Child Care* (1946). The book's emphasis on common sense and flexibility caused some people
to equate Dr. Spock's methods with advocating a lack of discipline.

excited about my job is the day I go to a head shrinker. How are you gonna get excited about pullin' steel? How are you gonna get excited when you're tired and want to sit down?

It's not just the work. Somebody built the pyramids. Somebody's going to build something. Pyramids, Empire State Building—these things just don't happen. There's hard work behind it. I would like to see a building, say, the Empire State, I would like to see on one side of it a foot-wide strip from top to bottom with the name of every bricklayer, the name of every electrician, with all the names. So when a guy walked by, he could take his son and say, "See, that's me over there on the forty-fifth floor. I put the steel beam in." Picasso can point to a painting. What can I point to? A writer can point to a book. Everybody should have something to point to.

It's the not-recognition by other people. To say a woman is *just* a housewife is degrading right? Okay. *Just* a housewife. It's also degrading to say *just* a laborer. The difference is that a man goes out and maybe gets smashed.

When I was single, I could quit, just split. I wandered all over the country. You worked just enough to get a poke, money in your pocket. Now I'm married and I got two kids . . . (trails off). I worked on a truck dock one time and I was single. The foreman came over and he grabbed my shoulder, kind of gave me a shove. I punched him and knocked him off the dock. I said, "Leave me alone. I'm doing my work, just stay away from me, just don't give me the with-the-hands business."

Hell, if you whip a damn mule he might kick you. Stay out of my way, that's all. Working is bad enough, don't bug me. I would rather work my ass off for eight hours a day with nobody watching me than five minutes with a guy watching me. Who you gonna sock? You can't sock General Motors, you can't sock anybody in Washington, you can't sock a system.

A mule, an old mule, that's the way I feel. Oh yeah. See. (Shows black and blue marks on arms and legs, burns.) You know what I heard from more than one guy at work? "If my kid wants to work in a factory, I am going to kick the hell out of him." I want my kid to be an effete snob. Yeah, mm-hmm. (Laughs.) I want him to be able to quote Walt Whitman, to be proud of it.

If you can't improve yourself, you improve your posterity. Otherwise life isn't worth nothing. You might as well go back to the cave and stay there. I'm sure the first caveman who went over the hill to see what was on the other side—I don't think he went there wholly out of curiosity. He went there because he wanted to get his son out of the cave. Just the same way I want to send my kid to college.

I work so damn hard and want to come home and sit down and lay around. *But I gotta get it out.* I want to be able to turn around to somebody and say, "Hey, fuck you." You know? (Laughs.) The guy sitting next to me on the bus too. 'Cause all day I wanted to tell my foreman to go fuck himself, but I can't.

So I find a guy in a tavern. To tell him that. And he tells me too. I've been in brawls. He's punching me and I'm punching him, because we actually want to punch somebody else. The most that'll happen is the bartender will bar us from the tavern. But at work, you lose your job.

This one foreman I've got, he's a kid. He's a college graduate. He thinks he's better than everybody else. He was chewing me out and I was saying, "Yeah, yeah, yeah." He said, "What do you mean, yeah, yeah, yeah. Yes, *sir.*" I told him, "Who the hell are you, Hitler? What is this *'Yes, sir'* bullshit? I came here to work, I didn't come here to crawl. There's a fuckin' difference." One word led to another and I lost.

I got broke down to a lower grade and lost twenty-five cents an hour, which is a hell of a lot. It amounts to about ten dollars a week. He came over—after breaking me down. The guy comes over and smiles at me. I blew up. He didn't know it, but he was about two seconds and two feet away from a hospital. I said, "Stay the fuck away from me." He was just about to say something and was pointing his finger. I just reached my hand up and just grabbed his finger because I'm married. If I'd a been single, I'd a grabbed his head. That's the difference.

You're doing this manual labor and you know that technology can do it. (Laughs.) Let's face it, a machine can do the work of a man; otherwise they wouldn't have space probes. Why can we send a rocket ship that's unmanned and yet send a man in a steel mill to do a mule's work?

Automation? Depends how it's applied. It frightens me if it puts me out on the street. It doesn't frighten me if it shortens my workweek. You read that little thing: what are you going to do when this computer replaces you? Blow up computers. (Laughs.) Really. Blow up computers. I'll be goddamned if a computer is gonna eat before I do! I want milk for my kids and beer for me. Machines can either liberate man or enslave 'im, because they're pretty neutral. It's man who has the bias to put the thing one place or another.

If I had a twenty-hour workweek, I'd get to know my kids better, my wife better. Some kid invited me to go on a college campus. On a Saturday. It was summertime. Hell, if I have a choice of taking my wife and kids to a picnic or going to a college campus, it's gonna be the picnic. But if I worked a twenty-hour week, I could go do both. Don't you think with that extra twenty hours people could really expand? Who's to say? There are some people in factories just by force of circumstance. I'm just like the colored people. Potential Einsteins don't have to be white. They could be in cotton fields, they could be in factories.

The twenty-hour week is a possibility today. The intellectuals, they always say there are potential Lord Byrons, Walt Whitmans, Roosevelts, Picassos working in construction or steel mills or factories. But I don't think they believe it. I think what they're afraid of is the potential Hitlers and Stalins that are there too. The people in power fear the leisure man. Not just the United States. Russia's the same way.

What do you think would happen in this country if, for one year, they experimented and gave everybody a twenty-hour week? How do they know that the guy who digs Wallace° today doesn't try to resurrect Hitler tomorrow? Or the guy who is mildly disturbed at pollution doesn't decide to go to General Motors and shit on the guy's desk? You can become a fanatic if you had the time. The whole thing is time. That is, I think, one reason rich kids tend to be fanatic about politics: they have time. Time, that's the important thing.

It isn't that the average working guy is dumb. He's tired, that's all. I picked up a book on chess one time. That thing laid in the drawer for two or three weeks, you're too tired. During the weekends you want to take your kids out. You don't want to sit there and the kid comes up: "Daddy, can I go to the park?" You got your nose in a book? Forget it.

I know a guy fifty-seven years old. Know what he tells me? "Mike, I'm old and tired *all* the time." The first thing happens at work: when the arms start moving, the brain stops. I punch in about ten minutes to seven in the morning. I say hello to a couple of guys I like, I kid around with them. One guy says good morning to you and you say good morning. To another guy you say fuck you. The guy you say fuck you to is your friend.

I put on my hard hat, change into my safety shoes, put on my safety glasses, go to the bonderizer. It's the thing I work on. They rake the metal, they wash it, they dip it in a paint solution, and we take it off. Put it on, take it off, put it on, take it off, put it on, take it off . . .

I say hello to everybody but my boss. At seven it starts. My arms get tired about the first half-hour. After that, they don't get tired any more until maybe the last half-hour at the end of the day. I work from seven to three thirty. My arms are tired at seven thirty and they're tired at three o'clock. I hope to God I never get broke in, because I always want my arms to be tired at seven thirty and three o'clock. (Laughs.) 'Cause that's when I know that there's a beginning and there's an end. That I'm not brainwashed. In between, I don't even try to think.

If I were to put you in front of a dock and I pulled up a skid in front of you with fifty hundred-pound sacks of potatoes and there are fifty more skids just like it, and this is what you're gonna do all day, what would you think about—potatoes? Unless a guy's a nut, he never thinks about work or talks about it. Maybe about baseball or about getting drunk the other night or he got laid or he didn't get laid. I'd say one out of a hundred will actually get excited about work.

Why is it that the communists always say they're for the workingman, and as soon as they set up a country, you got guys singing to tractors? They're singing about how they love the factory. That's where I couldn't

---

Wallace George C. Wallace, former governor of Alabama. At his inauguration in 1963, Wallace said, "From the cradle of the Confederacy, this very heart of the great Anglo-Saxon Southland, I draw the line in the dust and toss the gauntlet before the feet of tyranny. And I say, Segregation now! Segregation tomorrow! Segregation forever!"

buy communism. It's the intellectuals' utopia, not mine. I cannot picture myself singing to a tractor, I just can't. (Laughs.) Or singing to steel. (Singsongs.) Oh whoop-dee-doo, I'm at the bonderizer, oh how I love this heavy steel. No thanks. Never happen.

Oh yeah, I daydream. I fantasize about a sexy blond in Miami who's got my union dues. (Laughs.) I think of the head of the union the way I think of the head of my company. Living it up. I think of February in Miami. Warm weather, a place to lay in. When I hear a college kid say, "I'm oppressed," I don't believe him. You know what I'd like to do for one year? Live like a college kid. Just for one year. I'd love to. Wow! (Whispers.) Wow! Sports car! Marijuana! (Laughs.) Wild, sexy broads. I'd love that, hell yes, I would.

Somebody has to do this work. If my kid ever goes to college, I just want him to have a little respect, to realize that his dad is one of those somebodies. This is why even on—(muses) yeah, I guess, sure—on the black thing . . . (Sighs heavily.) I can't really hate the colored fella that's working with me all day. The black intellectual I got no respect for. The white intellectual I got no use for. I got no use for the black militant who's gonna scream three hundred years of slavery to me while I'm busting my ass. You know what I mean? (Laughs.) I have one answer for that guy: go see Rockefeller. See Harriman. Don't bother me. We're in the same cotton field. So just don't bug me. (Laughs.)

After work I usually stop off at a tavern. Cold beer. Cold beer right away. When I was single, I used to go into hillbilly bars, get in a lot of brawls. Just to explode. I got a thing on my arm here (indicates scar). I got slapped with a bicycle chain. Oh, wow! (Softly) Mmm. I'm getting older. (Laughs.) I don't explode as much. You might say I'm broken in. (Quickly) No, I'll never be broken in. (Sighs.) When you get a little older, you exchange the words. When you're younger, you exchange the blows.

When I get home, I argue with my wife a little bit. Turn on TV, get mad at the news. (Laughs.) I don't even watch the news that much. I watch Jackie Gleason. I look for any alternative to the ten o'clock news. I don't want to go to bed angry. Don't hit a man with anything heavy at five o'clock. He just can't be bothered. This is his time to relax. The heaviest thing he wants is what his wife has to tell him.

When I come home, know what I do for the first twenty minutes? Fake it. I put on a smile. I got a kid three years old. Sometimes she says, "Daddy, where've you been?" I say, "Work." I could have told her I'd been in Disneyland. What's work to a three-year-old kid? If I feel bad, I can't take it out on the kids. Kids are born innocent of everything but birth. You can't take it out on your wife either. This is why you go to a tavern. You want to release it there rather than do it at home. What does an actor do when he's got a bad movie? I got a bad movie every day.

I don't even need the alarm clock to get up in the morning. I can go out drinking all night, fall asleep at four, and bam! I'm up at six—no matter what I do. (Laughs.) It's a pseudo-death, more or less. Your whole system is paralyzed and you give all the appearance of death. It's an ingrown clock. It's a thing you just get used to. The hours differ. It depends. Sometimes my wife wants to do something crazy like play five hundred rummy or put a puzzle together. It could be midnight, could be ten o'clock, could be nine thirty.

What do you do weekends?

Drink beer, read a book. See that one? *Violence in America.* It's one of them studies from Washington. One of them committees they're always appointing. A thing like that I read on a weekend. But during the weekdays, gee . . . I just thought about it. I don't do that much reading from Monday through Friday. Unless it's a horny book. I'll read it at work and go home and do my homework. (Laughs.) That's what the guys at the plant call it—homework. (Laughs.) Sometimes my wife works on Saturday and I drink beer at the tavern.

I went out drinking with one guy, oh, a long time ago. A college boy. He was working where I work now. Always preaching to me about how you need violence to change the system and all that garbage. We went into a hillbilly joint. Some guy there, I didn't know him from Adam, he said, "You think you're smart." I said, "What's your pleasure?" (Laughs.) He said, "My pleasure's to kick your ass." I told him I really can't be bothered. He said, "What're you, chicken?" I said, "No, I just don't want to be bothered." He came over and said something to me again. I said, "I don't beat women, drunks, or fools. Now leave me alone."

The guy called his brother over. This college boy that was with me, he came nudging my arm, "Mike, let's get out of here." I said, "What are you worried about?" (Laughs.) This isn't unusual. People will bug you. You fend it off as much as you can with your mouth and when you can't, you punch the guy out.

It was close to closing time and we stayed. We could have left, but when you go into a place to have a beer and a guy challenges you—if you expect to go in that place again, you don't leave. If you have to fight the guy, you fight.

I got just outside the door and one of these guys jumped on me and grabbed me around the neck. I grabbed his arm and flung him against the wall. I grabbed him here (indicates throat), and jiggled his head against the wall quite a few times. He kind of slid down a little bit. This guy who said he was his brother took a swing at me with a garrison belt. He just missed and hit the wall. I'm looking around for my junior Stalin (laughs), who loves violence and everything. He's gone. Split. (Laughs.) Next day I see him at work. I couldn't get mad at him, he's a baby.

He saw a book in my back pocket one time and he was amazed. He walked up to me and he said, "You read?" I said, "What do you mean, I read?" He said, "All these dummies read the sports pages around here.

What are you doing with a book?" I got pissed off at the kid right away. I said, "What do you mean, all these dummies? Don't knock a man who's paying somebody else's way through college." He was a nineteen-year-old effete snob.

Yet you want your kid to be an effete snob?

Yes. I want my kid to look at me and say, "Dad, you're a nice guy, but you're a fuckin' dummy." Hell yes, I want my kid to tell me that he's not gonna be like me . . .

If I were hiring people to work, I'd try naturally to pay them a decent wage. I'd try to find out their first names, their last names, keep the company as small as possible, so I could personalize the whole thing. All I would ask a man is a handshake, see you in the morning. No applications, nothing. I wouldn't be interested in the guy's past. Nobody ever checks the pedigree on a mule, do they? But they do on a man. Can you picture walking up to a mule and saying, "I'd like to know who his granddaddy was?"

I'd like to run a combination bookstore and tavern. (Laughs.) I would like to have a place where college kids came and a steelworker could sit down and talk. Where a workingman could not be ashamed of Walt Whitman and where a college professor could not be ashamed that he painted his house over the weekend.

If a carpenter built a cabin for poets, I think the least the poets owe the carpenter is just three or four one-liners on the wall. A little plaque: Though we labor with our minds, this place we can relax in was built by someone who can work with his hands. And his work is as noble as ours. I think the poet owes something to the guy who builds the cabin for him.

I don't think of Monday. You know what I'm thinking about on Sunday night? Next Sunday. If you work real hard, you think of a perpetual vacation. Not perpetual sleep . . . What do I think of on a Sunday night? Lord, I wish the fuck I could do something else for a living.

I don't know who the guy is who said there is nothing sweeter than an unfinished symphony. Like an unfinished painting and an unfinished poem. If he creates this thing one day—let's say, Michelangelo's Sistine Chapel. It took him a long time to do this, this beautiful work of art. But what if he had to create this Sistine Chapel a thousand times a year? Don't you think that would even dull Michelangelo's mind? Or if da Vinci had to draw his anatomical charts thirty, forty, fifty, sixty, eighty, ninety, a hundred times a day? Don't you think that would even bore da Vinci?

Way back, you spoke of the guys who built the pyramids, not the pharaohs, the unknowns. You put yourself in their category?

Yes. I want my signature on 'em, too. Sometimes, out of pure meanness, when I make something, I put a little dent in it. I like to do something to make it really unique. Hit it with a hammer. I deliberately fuck it up to see if it'll get by, just so I can say I did it. It could be anything. Let me put it this way: I think God invented the dodo bird so when we get up there we could tell Him, "Don't you ever make mistakes?" and He'd say, "Sure, look." (Laughs.) I'd like to make my imprint. My dodo bird. A mistake, *mine.* Let's say the whole building is nothing but red bricks. I'd like to have just the black one or the white one or the purple one. Deliberately fuck up.

This is gonna sound square, but my kid is my imprint. He's my freedom. There's a line in one of Hemingway's books. I think it's from *For Whom the Bell Tolls.* They're behind the enemy lines, somewhere in Spain, and she's pregnant. She wants to stay with him. He tells her no. He says, "if you die, I die," knowing he's gonna die. But if you go, I go. Know what I mean? The mystics call it the brass bowl. Continuum. You know what I mean? This is why I work. Every time I see a young guy walk by with a shirt and tie and dressed up real sharp, I'm lookin' at my kid, you know? That's it.

Work in an Alienated Society

Erich Fromm

Erich Fromm (1900–1980) was born in Germany, where he studied sociology and psychology at Heidelberg, Frankfurt, and Munich. He received his Ph.D. from Heidelberg in 1922. He then trained in psychoanalysis in Munich and at the Psychoanalytical Institute in Berlin. In 1934, with the rise of the Nazis in Germany, Fromm emigrated to the United States, where he lived as a naturalized citizen until 1974, when he retired to Switzerland. He lectured all over the world and held faculty appointments at many distinguished universities. His particular interest was the application of psychoanalytic theory to the problems of culture and society, and he published a number of widely read books in this area. Among them are Escape From Freedom *(1941);* The Sane Society *(1955), from which Chapter 5 of Part V is reprinted here; and* The Revolution of Hope: Toward a Humanized Technology *(1968). Among his last works are* The Greatness and Limitations of Freud's Thought *(1980) and* On Disobedience and Other Essays *(1981).*

What becomes the meaning of *work* in an alienated society?

We have already made some brief comments about this question in the general discussion of alienation. But since this problem is of the utmost importance, not only for the understanding of present-day society, but also for any attempt to create a saner society, I want to deal with the nature of work separately and more extensively in the following pages.

Unless man exploits others, he has to work in order to live. However primitive and simple his method of work may be, by the very fact of production, he has risen above the animal kingdom; rightly has he been defined as "the animal that produces." But work is not only an inescapable necessity for man. Work is also his liberator from nature, his creator as a social and independent being. *In the process of work, that is, the molding and changing of nature outside of himself, man molds and changes himself.* He emerges from nature by mastering her; he develops his powers of cooperation, of reason, his sense of beauty. He separates himself from nature, from the original unity with her, but at the same time unites himself with her again as her master and builder. The more his work develops, the more his individuality develops. In molding nature and re-creating her, he learns to make use of his powers, increasing his skill and creativeness. Whether we think of the beautiful paintings in the caves of Southern France, the ornaments on weapons among primitive people, the statues and temples of Greece, the cathedrals of the Middle Ages, the chairs and tables made by skilled craftsmen, or the cultivation of flowers, trees or corn by peasants—all are expressions of the creative transformation of nature by man's reason and skill.

In Western history, craftsmanship, especially as it developed in the thirteenth and fourteenth centuries, constitutes one of the peaks in the evolution of creative work. Work was not only a useful activity, but one which carried with it a profound satisfaction. The main features of craftsmanship have been very lucidly expressed by C. W. Mills. "There is no ulterior motive in work other than the product being made and the processes of its creation. The details of daily work are meaningful because they are not detached in the worker's mind from the product of the work. The worker is free to control his own working action. The craftsman is thus able to learn from his work; and to use and develop his capacities and skills in its prosecution. There is no split of work and play, or work and culture. The craftsman's way of livelihood determines and infuses his entire mode of living."[1]

With the collapse of the medieval structure, and the beginning of the

---

[1] C. W. Mills, *White Collar*, Oxford University Press, New York, 1951, p. 220.

modern mode of production, the meaning and function of work changed fundamentally, especially in the Protestant countries. Man, being afraid of his newly won freedom, was obsessed by the need to subdue his doubts and fears by developing a feverish activity. The outcome of this activity, success or failure, decided his salvation, indicating whether he was among the saved or the lost souls. *Work, instead of being an activity satisfying in itself and pleasureable, became a duty and an obsession.* The more it was possible to gain riches by work, the more it became a pure means to the aim of wealth and success. Work became, in Max Weber's[o] terms, the chief factor in a system of "inner-worldly asceticism," an answer to man's sense of aloneness and isolation.

However, work in this sense existed only for the upper and middle classes, those who could amass some capital and employ the work of others. For the vast majority of those who had only their physical energy to sell, work became nothing but forced labor. The worker in the eighteenth or nineteenth century who had to work sixteen hours if he did not want to starve was not doing it because he served the Lord in this way, nor because his success would show that he was among the "chosen" ones, but because he was forced to sell his energy to those who had the means of exploiting it. The first centuries of the modern era find the meaning of work divided into that of *duty* among the middle class, and that of *forced labor* among those without property.

The religious attitude toward work as a duty, which was still so prevalent in the nineteenth century, has been changing considerably in the last decades. Modern man does not know what to do with himself, how to spend his lifetime meaningfully, and he is driven to work in order to avoid an unbearable boredom. But work has ceased to be a moral and religious obligation in the sense of the middle-class attitude of the eighteenth and nineteenth centuries. Something new has emerged. Ever-increasing production, the drive to make bigger and better things, have become aims in themselves, new ideals. Work has become alienated from the working person.

What happens to the industrial worker? He spends his best energy for seven or eight hours a day in producing "something." He needs his work in order to make a living, but his role is essentially a passive one. He fulfills a small isolated function in a complicated and highly organized process of production, and is never confronted with "his" product as a whole, at least not as a producer, but only as a consumer, provided he has the money to buy "his" product in a store. He is concerned neither with the whole product in its physical aspects nor with its wider economic and social aspects. He is put in a certain place, has to carry out a certain task,

---

Max Weber German sociologist and political economist (1864–1920).

but does not participate in the organization or management of the work. He is not interested, nor does he know why one produces this, instead of another commodity—what relation it has to the needs of society as a whole. The shoes, the cars, the electric bulbs, are produced by "the enterprise," using the machines. He is a part of the machine, rather than its master as an active agent. The machine, instead of being in his service to do work for him which once had to be performed by sheer physical energy, has become his master. Instead of the machine being the substitute for human energy, man has become a substitute for the machine. *His work can be defined as the performance of acts which cannot yet be performed by machines.*

Work is a means of getting money, not in itself a meaningful human activity. P. Drucker, observing workers in the automobile industry, expresses this idea very succinctly: "For the great majority of automobile workers, the only meaning of the job is in the pay check, not in anything connected with the work or the product. Work appears as something unnatural, a disagreeable, meaningless and stultifying condition of getting the pay check, devoid of dignity as well as of importance. No wonder that this puts a premium on slovenly work, on slow-downs, and on other tricks to get the same pay check with less work. No wonder that this results in an unhappy and discontented worker—because a pay check is not enough to base one's self-respect on."[2]

This relationship of the worker to his work is an outcome of the whole social organization of which he is a part. Being "employed,"[3] he is not an active agent, has no responsibility except the proper performance of the isolated piece of work he is doing, and has little interest except the one of bringing home enough money to support himself and his family. Nothing more is expected of him, or wanted from him. He is part of the equipment hired by capital, and his role and function are determined by this quality of being a piece of equipment. In recent decades, increasing attention has been paid to the psychology of the worker, and to his attitude toward his work, to the "human problem of industry"; but this very formulation is indicative of the underlying attitude; there is a human being spending most of his lifetime at work, and what should be discussed is the *"industrial problem of human beings,"* rather than *"the human problem of industry."*

Most investigations in the field of industrial psychology are concerned with the question of how the productivity of the individual worker can be increased, and how he can be made to work with less friction; psy-

---

[2]Cf. Peter F. Drucker, *Concept of the Corporation*, The John Day Company, New York, 1946, p. 179.

[3]The English "employed," like the German *angestellt*, is a term which refers to things rather than to human beings.

chology has lent its services to "human engineering," an attempt to treat the worker and employee like a machine which runs better when it is well oiled. While Taylor[0] was primarily concerned with a better organization of the technical use of the worker's physical powers, most industrial psychologists are mainly concerned with the manipulation of the worker's psyche. The underlying idea can be formulated like this: if he works better when he is happy, then let us make him happy, secure, satisfied, or anything else, provided it raises his output and diminishes friction. In the name of "human relations," the worker is treated with all devices which suit a completely alienated person; even happiness and human values are recommended in the interest of better relations with the public. Thus, for instance, according to *Time* magazine, one of the best-known American psychiatrists said to a group of fifteen hundred Supermarket executives: "It's going to be an increased satisfaction to our customers if we are happy. . . . It is going to pay off in cold dollars and cents to management, if we could put some of these general principles of values, human relationships, really into practice." One speaks of "human relations" and one means the most in-human relations, those between alienated automatons; one speaks of happiness and means the perfect routinization which has driven out the last doubt and all spontaneity.

The alienated and profoundly unsatisfactory character of work results in two reactions: one, the ideal of complete *laziness;* the other a deep-seated, though often unconscious hostility toward work and everything and everybody connected with it.

It is not difficult to recognize the widespread longing for the state of complete laziness and passivity. Our advertising appeals to it even more than to sex. There are, of course, many useful and labor saving gadgets. But this usefulness often serves only as a rationalization for the appeal to complete passivity and receptivity. A package of breakfast cereal is being advertised as *"new—easier to eat."* An electric toaster is advertised with these words: ". . . the most distinctly different toaster in the world! Everything is done *for* you with this new toaster. You need not even bother to lower the bread. Power-action, through a unique electric motor, *gently takes the bread right out of your fingers!"* How many courses in languages, or other subjects are announced with the slogan "effortless learning, no more of the old drudgery." Everybody knows the picture of the elderly couple in the advertisement of a life-insurance company, who have retired at the age of sixty, and spend their life in the complete bliss of having nothing to do except just travel.

Radio and television exhibit another element of this yearning for lazi-

---

Taylor Frederick W. Taylor (1856–1915), engineer-executive, pioneer developer of management science, author of *The Principles of Scientific Management* (1911).

ness: the idea of "push-button power"; by pushing a button, or turning a knob on my machine, I have the power to produce music, speeches, ball games, and on the television set, to command events of the world to appear before my eyes. The pleasure of driving cars certainly rests partly upon this same satisfaction of the wish for push-button power. By the effortless pushing of a button, a powerful machine is set in motion; little skill and effort is needed to make the driver feel that he is the ruler of space.

But there is far more serious and deep-seated reaction to the meaninglessness and boredom of work. It is a hostility toward work which is much less conscious than our craving for laziness and inactivity. Many a businessman feels himself the prisoner of his business and the commodities he sells; he has a feeling of fraudulency about his product and a secret contempt for it. He hates his customers, who force him to put up a show in order to sell. He hates his competitors because they are a threat; his employees as well as his superiors, because he is in a constant competitive fight with them. Most important of all, he hates himself, because he sees his life passing by, without making any sense beyond the momentary intoxication of success. Of course, this hate and contempt for others and for oneself, and for the very things one produces, is mainly unconscious, and only occasionally comes up to awareness in a fleeting thought, which is sufficiently disturbing to be set aside as quickly as possible.

A Young Man Sifts the Ashes of Efficiency in Search of the Work Ethic

Ray Slater

Ray Slater (born 1944) has lived in many states, mostly in the Northwest. He enlisted in the Army shortly after graduation from high school and later worked odd jobs, including serving pizzas and driving a viner in California bean fields. For thirteen years he wrote commercial spots and news for radio and TV, but left finally "for manual labor, so I could support my family." After nine years with the paint factory that he describes below, he quit to set up his own business as a general contractor.

Slater works days and attends San Bernardino Valley College in the evenings. He began writing in a college class. "I knew I felt things," he

*says, "I knew I could explain things on paper, and I knew I had the
mechanics and grammar. I've always read a lot, but whenever I read
something I really liked, I'd say, 'I could never do that.' My writing
teacher, Judith Hert, made me think I was good enough to publish. We
sat down together and decided my goal for that class would be to get
something published. Before, I didn't think anything I wrote was worth
sending in."*

*The essay we present here was first published in the July 20, 1980,
issue of the* Los Angeles Times; *we take it from* Look Who's Talking
*(1981), an anthology of student writing. Slater continues to write short
essays, but he says most of his creative energies now go into his contract-
ing business.*

My "Christian work ethic" is dying. It fell ill the day the new boss took
away the old coffee pot, and it lapsed into a coma when the first computer
arrived.

When "the old man" ran the warehouse, he knew what work was all
about. He built the company with his own hands, starting with one of the
first paint factories west of the Mississippi. "Climatically Correct" was his
slogan. Paint needs a brush and a brush needs a tray and they both need
thinner and so the company grew. There were stories about the old man
driving through town in the early days with a truckload of empty boxes
just to make it look like business was good. He lived hard, loved hard,
drank hard, cursed hard and, above all, worked hard. He was proud of his
company and proud of his "family" of employees. It was pride that rubbed
off easily. His pride became my pride. His company was my company. It
was unthinkable to ship a poor product or let a paint can go to a customer
with dust on the lid. The warehouse had to be kept neat, clean and
orderly, even if it cost a few dollars more.

Often there was overtime. I looked forward to it, knowing that the old
man would be down later with a six-pack and a pat on the back. He was
always there, it seems, when a good job was finished and it was time to
gather around the coffee pot. God, that coffee pot. It was refilled perhaps
three times in a 24-hour period. At night, the shipping crew would leave
a five-hour-old nectar brewing for the day shift. You could smell the
aroma when you drove into the parking lot. Always the day crew would
arrive early and gather at that wonderful percolator. Always someone
would repeat in jest a comment we had once heard the foreman ask of a
new employee: "Are you man enough to drink this?"

The old man never hired blacks and he didn't like long hair. That
bothered me a little, but it was his company and he was entitled to his
opinions. Besides, the company had plenty of other minority employees;
the old man thought highly of Mexican-Americans. And the younger
employees wore hats with their hair piled under them.

My work ethic thrived under the old man. There was absolutely nothing that my "chewing gum and baling wire" resourcefulness couldn't or wouldn't do for him. When business slowed in the winter, I used the spare time to salvage pallet lumber to build new stock shelves for the products I knew would arrive in spring. When warm summer days brought out the painters and handymen, business swelled to the breaking point and I was ready. Summoning superhuman strength, endurance and driving skill, I somehow managed to make the deliveries on time. It was worth it. One day at the coffee pot, the old man handed me a cup and said, "I see we've got another good delivery driver." With those few words he gave me more than has been gained by all the union negotiations in history.

With this relationship the old man and I produced a lot of hard-earned dollars that we could both be proud of. Sore muscles and calloused hands never felt so good.

The old man got older and more feeble. He came around less often. He was hospitalized. Nearly died. Time to sell the company. Lots of bids. The old man wanted a buyer who would take care of his "family." The stockholders wanted money. Money won.

The first thing to go was the old coffee pot. It was costing the company nearly $300 a month in coffee, not to mention "wasted time." Instead we got a coffee machine that also dispensed soup and hot chocolate. It all tasted the same and it was not the same.

The new owner has no calluses. He has a thin smile. He seldom talks to employees. He likes computers and efficiency. Breaks are too long. They waste time. No need for cleaning and painting. They waste money. No need for pride. The only things we need are time clocks and computers and switchboards and computers and proficiency tests and computers and people who work like computers. The Christian work ethic be damned.

At first I tried to build a defense against this assault on my standards. As fork-lift driver I would make the pallet aisles a thing of beauty in this sea of Philistines. Daily I cleaned each aisle, cut away torn box tops, brought down overstock and dusted paint cans. I told the other employees, "I'm going to work on my supermarket shelves." But no one cared.

And when I returned from vacation, no one cared that the aisles were a shambles. I scurried to clean them and rearrange the stock, propelled by the notion that somehow the old man might suddenly reappear at my elbow and be critical of my shoddy work. But my refuge was crumbling; soon I could go for several days without dusting cans or cutting box tops.

So my Christian work ethic continues to wane. But I am not alone. I see other employees—especially the newer ones—who must have their daily joint to make it through a prideless workday. I see them steal from a company that they feel owes them something more than money for their labors. I see them waste time and produce inferior products and ship dusty paint cans with torn labels.

And then one day, hallelujah, someone actually put a slug in that damn coffee machine. Now it, too, is out of order.

On-the-Job
Enrichment

Samuel C. Florman

Samuel C. Florman is an engineer who communicates well with nonengineers. Born in New York in 1925, he was educated at Dartmouth and Columbia and is presently vice president of Kreisler Borg Florman Construction Company. He is a contributing editor of Harper's *Magazine and writes for other periodicals as well. His books include* Engineering and the Liberal Arts *(1968);* The Existential Pleasures of Engineering *(1976);* Blaming Technology: The Irrational Search for Scapegoats *(1981), from which the following selection is taken; and* The Civilized Engineer *(1987).*

A collection of E. F. Schumacher's speeches, published posthumously in 1979, was called *Good Work.* This was an appropriate title, since the importance of work—the quest for fulfillment, or even salvation, in work—is a topic that, more than any other, roused Schumacher to higher levels of passion. Industrial society, according to Schumacher, makes most forms of work "utterly uninteresting and meaningless." This is because "mechanical, artificial, divorced from nature, utilizing only the smallest part of man's potential capabilities, it sentences the great majority of workers to spending their working lives in a way which contains no worthy challenge, no stimulus to self-perfection, no chance of development, no element of Beauty, Truth, or Goodness."

At the same time, and in the same speech, Schumacher deplores the complexity of work in a modern society, and yearns for the simple physical tasks of bygone days:

> It is obviously much easier for a hard-working peasant to keep his mind attuned to the divine than for a strained office worker.
>
> I say, therefore, that it is a great evil—perhaps the greatest evil—of modern industrial society that, through its immensely involved nature, it imposes an undue nervous strain and absorbs an undue proportion of man's attention.*

The inconsistency here is breathtaking. We are urged to aspire to work that contains challenge, stimulus, and chance of development, while at the same time seeking simple, routine tasks that will free our mind for spiritual contemplation. It never seemed to occur to Schumacher that he was confronting an elemental enigma of human existence, and trying to make it fit within the confines of his simplistic attack on modern technology.

---

*E. F. Schumacher, *Good Work,* Harper & Row, 1979, pp. 25 and 27.

Questions surrounding work and its discontents are as old as civilization. During the 1970s, however, these questions took on renewed urgency, and appeared as a key element in the antitechnology campaign. Schumacher was only one of many observers to express concern about conditions in the workplace. While he was attempting to prescribe a cure for worker dissatisfaction through a return to the fields, a number of sociologists and industrial psychologists sought solutions in a new endeavor which they called "job enrichment" (or, alternatively, "work reform," "job redesign," "humanization of work," or "the quality of work movement"). The deplorable effects of technology, it was hoped, might be mitigated if humanistic concepts could be introduced into the design of work, an area traditionally dominated by "unfeeling" engineers and business managers.

In early 1972 workers at the Vega plant in Lordstown, Ohio, went out on strike, not for more money or shorter hours, but to protest the pressure and monotony of their work on General Motors' fastest-moving assembly line. That 23-day work stoppage helped make "worker alienation" a fashionable term in industrial, sociological, and literary circles.

At the time of the Lordstown strike, a stream of reports was arriving from Sweden, where SAAB and Volvo were trying to deal with worker discontent by experimenting with alternatives to the assembly line. These companies attempted to give workers a sense of significance by having them participate democratically in decisions affecting the manufacturing process. The initial successes attributed to these efforts were reported in a series of beguiling newspaper and magazine articles.

At year's end the Department of Health, Education and Welfare released a study, *Work in America,* which reported that people at all levels of society were becoming increasingly dissatisfied with the quality of their working lives, to the detriment of the economic and social well-being of the nation. This study, widely distributed and acclaimed, provided a manifesto for the revolution that Lordstown seemed to portend. With alacrity the concept of job enrichment spread through the worlds of journalism, academe, business, and government. Corporations hastened to establish ways by which workers could help make decisions affecting their jobs. In *The Future of the Workplace,* completed at the end of 1974, Paul Dickson concluded that newly devised "humanization of work" experiments were proving so successful that corporate executives were beginning to view them as important proprietary developments whose details were not to be shared with competitors. Dickson reported that these changes were no passing fad, but harbingers of things to come.

Concern for the alienated worker, in addition to spawning a host of industrial experiments, articles, studies, grants, and conferences, also inspired Studs Terkel's bestseller *Working* and Barbara Garson's *All the Livelong Day: The Meaning and Demeaning of Routine Work.* Both books were based upon interviews with workers and, in the words of the people themselves, the message seemed to be unambiguous: Americans hated their jobs. They left them frustrated and demoralized. Americans seek in their daily occupations a sense of identity, self-esteem, autonomy, and accomplishment. What they get, according to Terkel, is "daily humiliations." Their fragmented, monotonous jobs are, in Garson's view, "soul-destroying." The average worker's discontent manifests itself in fighting, swearing, absenteeism, high turnover rates, sabotage, alcoholism, drug addiction, and poor mental health. Reform of the workplace, it seemed, was one of the most critical social issues of our time.

Nevertheless, just as enthusiasm for work humanization was reaching a fever pitch among intellectuals, disenchantment set in at many of the places where the experiments were taking place. In a September–October 1975 *Harvard Business Review* article, J. Richard Hackman, an organizational psychologist, reported that "job enrichment seems to be failing at least as often as it is succeeding." And further: "Even though the failures may be relatively unobtrusive now, they may soon become overwhelming."

Corporate executives were not the only ones disappointed with the results; among the workers and union leaders interest also appeared to be flagging. The United Auto Workers, for example, appeared to have forgotten about Lordstown. In preparing for new contract negotiations, they were concentrating on the issues of wages and job security.

An obvious conclusion was that a recession was occurring just in time for management to put the rebellious workers in their place. Clearly, in uncertain times, most people are less interested in fulfillment than in a living wage. But the supporters of job enrichment claimed that a more satisfying job results in improved productivity, so that it should be a management goal in bad times as well as good.

In fact, it was this very feature that had aroused the suspicions of labor union leaders whose lack of cooperation appeared to be one of the main reasons for the many failed experiments. Job enrichment, according to a vice-president of the International Association of Machinists, is "a speedup in the guise of concern for workers." Any experiment that results in increased productivity is necessarily suspect. Even assuming the best of motives, it is disturbing to note that job enrichment depends upon manipulation of workers by the experts. In this respect, it can be viewed as an extension of the much-maligned art of scientific management. The experts, of course, maintain that the new redesign of work is done in response to the desires of the workers. Yes, but it is the experts who must determine what these desires are—a subtle and troubling point.

What *do* people want out of life? That is one of those questions whose answer can be shaped by the way in which the question is posed. Straightforward statistical studies find that in apparent contradiction to Terkel's findings, job discontent is not high on the list of American social problems. When the Gallup Poll's researchers ask, "Is your work interesting?" they get 80 to 90 percent positive responses. But when researchers begin to ask more sophisticated questions, such as, "What type of work would you try to get into if you could start all over again?" complaints begin to pour forth. The probing question cannot help but elicit a plaintive answer. Which of us, confronted with a sympathetic organizational psychologist, or talking into Studs Terkel's tape recorder, could resist tinging our life's story with lamentation, particularly if that was what the questioner was looking for? Compared to the labor performed by most people in the past, today's jobs seem quite attractive. Compared to the "calling" that Terkel says we are all seeking, what job could measure up?

Indeed, people are not "satisfied" with their work nor with any other aspect of their lives. This is hardly news. But can we agree on what should be done to improve the situation? Barbara Garson sees a solution only in workers controlling their own jobs through socialism. (The widespread dissatisfaction of workers in socialist countries does not impress her.) Most proponents of job enrichment, while not advocating socialism, agree that what the average worker misses most is a sense of responsibility and participation in the making of decisions. But is this assumption valid? Are there not many workers who do *not* want responsibility, who prefer the comfortable monotony of routine tasks to the pressures of making decisions and being accountable for the consequences? Miss Garson's workers keep contradicting her basic premise. From a woman who has turned down the job of supervisor: "I don't need the responsibility. After work I like to spend my time fixing up my house. And that's what I like to think about while I'm working." And from people with mechanical, repetitive tasks: "Flip, flip, flip . . . feels good," "you can get a good rhythm going," "you kind of get used to it." Even Garson despairs for a moment: "Maybe the reactionaries are right. Maybe some people are made for this work."

To have thought so (or to have admitted it) up until recently would indeed have marked one as a reactionary. But times are changing. The work enrichment movement appears to be running counter to another trend, the seeking of inner peace rather than ego fulfillment. In the light of this new wisdom, which advocates, among other things, the blanking of the mind in meditation for an hour each day, one can wonder who has the better of the bargain, those who are in the ratrace or those who are "beneath" it. This is the paradox that leads Schumacher into his capricious inconsistencies.

In one episode, Garson tells of a small commune in which ten young adults lived on the wages of four, and where the focus of life was away from work. I dare not predict what modes of life will be attractive to the masses of the future. I believe, however, that the job enrichment enthusiasts have made a mistake in assuming that all people desire what social scientists want them to desire. From Lordstown and some amorphous complaints they have made unwarranted extrapolations.

An even more glaring mistake is that of assuming that by restructuring the workplace, one can solve the problem of alienation. This hypothesis calls to mind those urban planners who saw salvation for the poor in a clean, spacious apartment, and who, after their ideas have been carried out, have spent much energy explaining why attractive apartments have not, in fact, eradicated the ill effects of poverty. They wander from failure to failure seeking the magic environment (high-rise, low-rise, slum clearance, renovation, vestpocket projects, town houses) like so many Ponce de Leons trudging through the malarial Florida swamps.

Alienation cannot be cured by a fascinating job any more than it can be cured by a clean apartment. Some of the best jobs, by almost any standard, are held by members of the skilled construction trades. These people do interesting, varied work. They are craftsmen in the tradition that Schumacher admires. They are not too closely supervised. They see the tangible results of their labor. Their strong unions have made sure that they do not have to produce more than they can comfortably handle. They are well paid. E. E. LeMasters spent five years mingling with hardhats in a tavern, and reported on his experience in a book entitled *Blue-Collar Aristocrats.* He found that these men are pleased with their work and are proud of what they do. He also found that they are about as alienated as it is possible to be—alienated from their wives, their children, their churches, and their political leaders. They are bigoted and full of hate, confused and full of suspicion.

There are diseases of the soul abroad in the land, but only a few of the symptoms, not the viruses themselves, are to be found in the workplace. Healthy people do not become heartless bosses or cruel foremen. Healthy people do not feel debased or dehumanized by menial work or intimidated by blustering superiors. Sick people—alienated people—are not made whole by an interesting job.

Of course, the concept of job enrichment has much to commend it. The idea that work should provide satisfaction is worthy of further pursuit. It serves the interests of the workers, as long as they are assured of not being subtly manipulated, and ideally, it serves the interests of industry and all society, by resulting in increased productivity.

The Japanese seem to have been uniquely successful in this endeavor, indicating that worker alienation has less to do with industrialization than it does with other aspects of the general culture. Work in a factory or a large office is not inherently less satisfying than work on a farm or in a small-town store. The "dehumanization of the workplace" is only tangentially related to technological advance. It is mainly attributable to the way people feel about themselves, and the way that they treat each other. We do not have to look to the Japanese for proof. Anybody who has worked knows that this is so.

In identifying industrial work as a major source of contemporary malaise, the antitechnologists divert us from asking ourselves what we can do to improve mental health, foster common courtesy, and nourish concern of one person for another.

Those who would blame all of life's problems on an amorphous technology, inevitably reject the concept of individual responsibility. This is not humanism. It is a perversion of the humanistic impulse.

What Is Democracy?

"What," asks John Stuart Mill, "is the rightful limit to the sovereignty of the individual over himself? Where does the authority of society begin?" Near the end of his opening statement, Mill offers a very general answer when he says that "it is necessary that general rules should for the most part be observed, in order that people may know what they have to expect; but in each person's own concerns, his individual spontaneity is entitled to free exercise." General rules, however, are often insecure in a pluralistic society such as ours that is undergoing rapid change; too many people do not know what "they have to expect," and "individual spontaneity" can take turns that seem not only to ignore but to intrude on and even harm the interests of others. Many of the most controversial issues of today—for instance, capital punishment, abortion, drug use—can be clarified by the general framework Mill builds here.

Mill's ideas apply not only to social issues but to political philosophy as well. Two important historic answers to his questions are found in the Declaration of Independence, which establishes in our political tradition that human rights and the consent of the governed take precedence over the will of the state, and in the Bill of Rights, which defines and thus protects individual rights.

In the final selection, Margaret Mead takes on the idea central to our democracy: human equality. She argues that being equal does not mean being the same; that to deny or minimize individual differences in the name of democracy is destructive both to individuals and to the society; and finally, that what a democracy should offer to each person is the opportunity—the equal opportunity—to develop as a unique human being.

from *On Liberty*

John Stuart Mill

John Stuart Mill (1806–1873), economist, philosopher, and reformer, was one of the most influential nineteenth-century English thinkers. He was the son of James Mill, an economist and historian, who gave him the extraordinary education which Mill later recorded in his Autobiography *(1873). Mill began Greek at three, Latin at seven, logic at twelve, and at seventeen was writing articles for the* Westminster Review. *He early came under the intellectual influence of Jeremy Bentham, and much of his thought reflects the Benthamite, utilitarian principle that social good lies in whatever brings the greatest benefit to the greatest number. Among his most prominent works are* A System of Logic *(1843),* The Principles of Political Economy *(1848),* On Liberty *(1859),* Considerations on Representative Government *(1861), and* Utilitarianism *(1863). Although many of Mill's ideas have passed out of vogue, he continues to be widely read, partly for what is still useful in his philosophy, and partly for his style and his just, exact, and generous character. We present below the opening of Chapter 4 of* On Liberty.

What, then, is the rightful limit to the sovereignty of the individual over himself? Where does the authority of society begin? How much of human life should be assigned to individuality, and how much to society?

Each will receive its proper share, if each has that which more particularly concerns it. To individuality should belong the part of life in which it is chiefly the individual that is interested; to society, the part which chiefly interests society.

Though society is not founded on a contract, and though no good purpose is answered by inventing a contract in order to deduce social obligations from it, every one who receives the protection of society owes a return for the benefit, and the fact of living in society renders it indispensable that each should be bound to observe a certain line of conduct towards the rest. This conduct consists, first, in not injuring the interests of one another; or rather certain interests, which, either by express legal provision or by tacit understanding, ought to be considered as rights; and secondly, in each person's bearing his share (to be fixed on some equitable principle) of the labors and sacrifices incurred for defending the society or its members from injury and molestation. These conditions society is justified in enforcing, at all costs to those who endeavor to withhold fulfillment. Nor is this all that society may do. The acts of an individual may be hurtful to others, or wanting in due consideration for their welfare, without going to the length of violating any of their constituted rights. The offender may then be justly punished by opinion, though not by law. As soon as any part of a person's conduct affects prejudicially the interests of others, society has jurisdiction over it, and the question whether the general welfare will or will not be promoted by interfering with it, becomes open to discussion. But there is no room for entertaining any such question when a person's conduct affects the interests of no persons besides himself, or needs not affect them unless they like (all the persons concerned being of full age, and the ordinary amount of understanding). In all such cases there should be perfect freedom, legal and social, to do the action and stand the consequences.

It would be a great misunderstanding of this doctrine, to suppose that it is one of selfish indifference, which pretends that human beings have no business with each other's conduct in life, and that they should not concern themselves about the well-doing or well-being of one another, unless their own interest is involved. Instead of any diminution, there is need of a great increase of disinterested exertion to promote the good of others. But disinterested benevolence can find other instruments to persuade people to their good, than whips and scourges, either of the literal or the metaphorical sort. I am the last person to undervalue the self-regarding virtues; they are only second in importance, if even second, to the social. It is equally the business of education to cultivate both. But even education works by conviction and persuasion as well as by compulsion, and it is by the former only that, when the period of education is past, the self-regarding virtues should be inculcated. Human beings owe to each other help to distinguish the better from the worse, and encouragement to choose the former and avoid the latter. They should be forever stimulating each other to increased exercise of their higher faculties, and increased direction of their feelings and aims towards wise instead of foolish, elevating instead of degrading, objects and contemplations. But neither one person, nor any number of persons, is warranted in saying to another human creature of ripe years, that he shall not do with his life for his own benefit what he chooses to do with it. He is the person most interested in his own well-being: the interest which any other person, except in cases of strong personal attachment, can have in it, is trifling, compared with that which he himself has; the interest which society has in him individually (except as to his conduct to others) is fractional, and altogether indirect: while, with respect to his own feelings and circumstances, the most ordinary man or woman has means of knowledge immeasurably surpassing those that can be possessed by anyone else. The interference of society to overrule his judgment and purposes in what only regards himself, must be grounded on general presumptions; which may be altogether wrong, and even if right, are as likely as not to be misapplied to individual cases, by persons no better acquainted with the circumstances of such cases than those are who look at them merely from without. In this department, therefore, of human affairs, individuality has its proper field of action. In the conduct of human beings towards one another, it is necessary that general rules should for the most part be observed, in order that people may know what they have to expect; but in each person's own concerns, his individual spontaneity is entitled to free exercise. Considerations to aid his judgment, exhortations to strengthen his will, may be offered to him, even obtruded on him, by others; but he, himself, is the final judge. All errors which he is likely to commit against advice and warning, are far outweighed by the evil of allowing others to constrain him to what they deem his good.

Declaration of Independence

(In Congress July 4, 1776)

Thomas Jefferson

On June 11, 1776, the Continental Congress appointed a committee of five—Thomas Jefferson, Benjamin Franklin, John Adams, Robert Livingston, and Roger Sherman—to prepare a declaration of independence. It was decided that Jefferson should first write a draft. He did so, drawing heavily on the natural rights political philosophy of the time, but as he says, he turned to "neither book nor pamphlet" in its preparation. A few changes were made by Adams and Franklin, and it was then presented to Congress on June 28. On July 2 and 3 Congress debated the form and content of the Declaration, made a few further changes, and on July 4 approved it without dissent. Although we here credit Jefferson with authorship, we print the amended and official version, taken from the United States Government Senate Manual.

The Unanimous Declaration of the Thirteen United States of America

When in the Course of human events, it becomes necessary for one people to dissolve the political bands which have connected them with another, and to assume among the powers of the earth, the separate and equal station to which the Laws of Nature and of Nature's God entitle them, a decent respect to the opinions of mankind requires that they should declare the causes which impel them to the separation.

We hold these truths to be self-evident, that all men are created equal, that they are endowed by their Creator with certain unalienable Rights, that among these are Life, Liberty and the pursuit of Happiness. That to secure these rights, Governments are instituted among Men, deriving their just powers from the consent of the governed, That whenever any Form of Government becomes destructive of these ends, it is the Right of the People to alter or to abolish it, and to institute new Government, laying its foundation on such principles and organizing its powers in such form, as to them shall seem most likely to effect their Safety and Happiness. Prudence, indeed, will dictate that Governments long established should not be changed for light and transient causes; and accordingly all experience hath shewn that mankind are more disposed to suffer, while evils are sufferable, than to right themselves by abolishing the forms to which they are accustomed. But when a long train of abuses and usurpations, pursuing invariably the same Object evinces a design to reduce them under absolute Despotism, it is their right, it is their duty, to throw off such Government, and to provide new Guards for their future security. Such has been the patient sufferance of these Colonies; and such is now the necessity which constrains them to alter their former Systems of Government. The history of the present King of Great Britain is a history of repeated injuries and usurpations, all having in direct object the establishment of an absolute Tyranny over these States. To prove this, let Facts be submitted to a candid world.

He has refused his Assent to Laws, the most wholesome and necessary for the public good.

He has forbidden his Governors to pass Laws of immediate and pressing importance, unless suspended in their operation till his Assent should be obtained; and when so suspended, he has utterly neglected to attend to them.

He has refused to pass other Laws for the accommodation of large districts of people, unless those people would relinquish the right of Representation in the Legislature, a right inestimable to them and formidable to tyrants only.

He has called together legislative bodies at places unusual, uncomfortable, and distant from the depository of their public Records, for the sole purpose of fatiguing them into compliance with his measures.

He has dissolved Representative Houses repeatedly, for opposing with manly firmness his invasions on the rights of the people.

He has refused for a long time, after such dissolutions, to cause others to be elected; whereby the Legislative powers, incapable of Annihilation, have returned to the People at large for their exercise; the State remaining in the mean time exposed to all the dangers of invasion from without, and convulsions within.

He has endeavored to prevent the population of these States; for that purpose obstructing the Laws for Naturalization of Foreigners; refusing to pass others to encourage their migrations hither, and raising the conditions of new Appropriations of Lands.

He has obstructed the Administration of Justice, by refusing his Assent to Laws for establishing Judiciary powers.

He has made Judges dependent on his Will alone, for the tenure of their offices, and the amount and payment of their salaries.

He has erected a multitude of New Offices, and sent hither swarms of Officers to harass our people, and eat out their substance.

He has kept among us, in times of peace, Standing Armies without the Consent of our legislatures.

He has affected to render the Military independent of and superior to the Civil power.

He has combined with others to subject us to a jurisdiction foreign to our constitution, and unacknowledged by our laws; giving his Assent to their Acts of pretended Legislation:

For quartering large bodies of armed troops among us:

For protecting them, by a mock Trial, from punishment for any Murders which they should commit on the Inhabitants of these States:

For cutting off our Trade with all parts of the world:

For imposing Taxes on us without our Consent:

For depriving us in many cases, of the benefits of Trial by Jury:

For abolishing the free System of English Laws in a neighbouring Province, establishing therein an Arbitrary government, and enlarging its Boundaries so as to render it at once an example and fit instrument for introducing the same absolute rule into these Colonies:

For taking away our Charters, abolishing our most valuable Laws, and altering fundamentally the Forms of our Governments:

For suspending our own Legislatures, and declaring themselves invested with power to legislate for us in all cases whatsoever.

He has abdicated Government here, by declaring us out of his Protection and waging War against us.

He has plundered our seas, ravaged our Coasts, burnt our towns, and destroyed the lives of our people.

He is at this time transporting large Armies of foreign Mercenaries to compleat the works of death, desolation and tyranny, already begun with circumstances of Cruelty & perfidy scarcely paralleled in the most barbarous ages, and totally unworthy the Head of a civilized nation.

He has constrained our fellow Citizens taken Captive on the high Seas to bear Arms against their Country, to become the executioners of their friends and Brethren, or to fall themselves by their Hands.

He has excited domestic insurrections amongst us, and has endeavoured to bring on the inhabitants of our frontiers, the merciless Indian Savages, whose known rule of warfare is an undistinguished destruction of all ages, sexes and conditions.

In every stage of these Oppressions We have Petitioned for Redress in the most humble terms: Our repeated Petitions have been answered only by repeated injury. A Prince, whose character is thus marked by every act which may define a Tyrant, is unfit to be the ruler of a free people.

Nor have We been wanting in attentions to our British Brethren. We have warned them from time to time of attempts by their legislature to extend an unwarrantable jurisdiction over us. We have reminded them of the circumstances of our emigration and settlement here. We have appealed to their native justice and magnanimity, and we have conjured them by the ties of our common kindred to disavow these usurpations, which would inevitably interrupt our connections and correspondence. They too have been deaf to the voice of justice and of consanguinity. We must, therefore, acquiesce in the necessity, which denounces our Separation, and hold them, as we hold the rest of mankind, Enemies in War, in Peace Friends.

WE, THEREFORE, the REPRESENTATIVES OF THE UNITED STATES OF AMERICA, IN GENERAL CONGRESS, Assembled, appealing to the Supreme Judge of the world for the rectitude of our intentions, do, in the Name, and by authority of the good People of these Colonies, solemnly PUBLISH and DECLARE, That these United Colonies are, and of Right ought to be FREE and INDEPENDENT STATES; that they are Absolved from all Allegiance to the British Crown, and that all political connection between them and the State of Great Britain, is and ought to be totally dissolved; and that as FREE AND INDEPENDENT STATES, they have full Power to levy War, conclude Peace, contract Alliances, establish Commerce, and to do all other Acts and Things which INDEPENDENT STATES may of right do. And for the support of this Declaration, with a firm reliance on the protection of divine Providence, we mutually pledge to each other our Lives, our Fortunes and our sacred Honor.

The Bill of Rights

First Congress of the United States

"The Bill of Rights" is the name given to the first ten amendments to the United States Constitution. When the Constitution was originally adopted in 1787, many of its framers had felt that a spelling-out of rights already presumed to exist was unnecessary and might even suggest an undue extension of governmental powers. Some of the states, however, having explicit declarations of rights in their own constitutions, recommended on ratifying the federal Constitution that it too be so furnished. The Bill of Rights was prepared by the first Congress under the leadership of James Madison and was ratified by the states in 1791. It has turned out to be an invaluable guide to the courts in decisions affecting civil rights and is in fact the main protection American citizens have against the diminution of their liberties by their government or by each other.

ARTICLES IN ADDITION TO, AND AMENDMENT OF, THE CONSTITUTION OF THE
UNITED STATES OF AMERICA, PROPOSED BY CONGRESS, AND RATIFIED BY THE
LEGISLATURES OF THE SEVERAL STATES, PURSUANT TO THE FIFTH ARTICLE OF
THE ORIGINAL CONSTITUTION.

Article I

Congress shall make no law respecting an establishment of religion, or
prohibiting the free exercise thereof; or abridging the freedom of speech,
or of the press; or the right of the people peaceably to assemble, and to
petition the Government for a redress of grievances.

Article II

A well regulated Militia, being necessary to the security of a free State,
the right of the people to keep and bear Arms, shall not be infringed.

Article III

No Soldier shall, in time of peace be quartered in any house, without the
consent of the Owner, nor in time of war, but in a manner to be prescribed
by law.

Article IV

The right of the people to be secure in their persons, houses, papers, and
effects, against unreasonable searches and seizures, shall not be violated,
and no Warrants shall issue, but upon probable cause, supported by Oath
or affirmation, and particularly describing the place to be searched, and
the persons or things to be seized.

Article V

No person shall be held to answer for a capital, or otherwise infamous
crime, unless on a presentment or indictment of a Grand Jury, except in
cases arising in the land or naval forces, or in the Militia, when in actual
service in time of War or public danger; nor shall any person be subject
for the same offence to be twice put in jeopardy of life or limb; nor shall
be compelled in any criminal case to be a witness against himself; nor be
deprived of life, liberty, or property, without due process of law; nor shall
private property be taken for public use, without just compensation.

Article VI

In all criminal prosecutions, the accused shall enjoy the right to a speedy
and public trial, by an impartial jury of the State and district wherein the
crime shall have been committed, which district shall have been previ-

ously ascertained by law, and to be informed of the nature and cause of the accusation; to be confronted with the witnesses against him; to have compulsory process for obtaining witnesses in his favor, and to have the Assistance of Counsel for his defence.

Article VII

In Suits at common law, where the value in controversy shall exceed twenty dollars, the right of trial by jury shall be preserved, and no fact tried by a jury, shall be otherwise reexamined in any Court of the United States, than according to the rules of the common law.

Article VIII

Excessive bail shall not be required, nor excessive fines imposed, nor cruel and unusual punishments inflicted.

Article IX

The enumeration in the Constitution, of certain rights, shall not be construed to deny or disparage others retained by the people.

Article X

The powers not delegated to the United States by the Constitution, nor prohibited by it to the States, are reserved to the States respectively, or to the people.

The Egalitarian Error

Margaret Mead

Margaret Mead (1901–1978) was an outstanding anthropologist whose pioneering field studies are still regarded as classics. Born in Philadelphia, the daughter of an economist and a sociologist, she first wanted to be a painter. In college she began as an English major, but in her senior year at Barnard she took a course from the eminent anthropologist Franz Boas. His teaching and subsequently that of Ruth Benedict turned her to anthropology. She received her B.A. from Barnard in 1923, an M.A. in psychology from Columbia in 1924, and in 1925 completed her doctoral thesis on cultural stability in Polynesia; it was published in Germany in 1928. In 1925 she went on her first field expedition to the Samoan island of Tau to study the development of the adolescent girl under primitive conditions. This led to the publication of Coming of Age in Samoa *(1928), still a widely read, though now controversial, classic in*

*the field. In 1928 she went to the Admiralty Islands to study the children
of the Manus tribe* (Growing Up in New Guinea, *1930). These and other
early field trips are described in her autobiography,* Blackberry Winter:
My Early Years *(1972).*

*The study of native people in the Pacific was a central interest through-
out her life, and she mastered seven primitive languages, but in later years
her work turned to contemporary culture. Long the curator of ethnology at
the American Museum of Natural History in New York, she taught at
many colleges and universities, received many honors, and was the author
of many books. These include* Sex and Temperament *(1935), followed by*
Male and Female: A Study of the Sexes in a Changing World *(1949),*
Continuities in Cultural Evolution *(1964),* Culture and Commitment
(1970), and, with James Baldwin, A Rap on Race *(1971). She also co-
authored two books with fellow anthropologist Rhoda Metraux:* Themes
in French Culture *(1954) and* A Way of Seeing *(1970), from which we print
the chapter below.*

Almost all Americans want to be democratic, but many Americans are
confused about what, exactly, democracy means. How do you know when
someone is acting in a democratic—or an undemocratic—way? Recently
several groups have spoken out with particular bitterness against the
kind of democracy that means equal opportunity for all, regardless of race
or national origin. They act as if all human beings did not belong to one
species, as if some races of mankind were inferior to others in their
capacity to learn what members of other races know and have invented.
Other extremists attack religious groups—Jews or Catholics—or deny the
right of an individual to be an agnostic. One reason that these extremists,
who explicitly do not want to be democratic, can get a hearing even
though their views run counter to the Constitution and our traditional
values is that the people who *do* want to be democratic are frequently so
muddled.

For many Americans, democratic behavior necessitates an outright
denial of any significant differences among human beings. In their eyes
it is undemocratic for anyone to refer, in the presence of any other person,
to differences in skin color, manners or religious beliefs. Whatever one's
private thoughts may be, it is necessary always to act as if everyone were
exactly alike.

Behavior of this kind developed partly as a reaction to those who discriminated against or actively abused members of other groups. But it is
artificial, often hypocritical behavior, nonetheless, and it dulls and flat-
tens human relationships. If two people can't talk easily and comfortably
but must forever guard against some slip of the tongue, some admission
of what is in both persons' minds, they are likely to talk as little as
possible. This embarrassment about differences reaches a final absurdity
when a Methodist feels that he cannot take a guest on a tour of his garden

because he might have to identify a wild plant with a blue flower, called the wandering Jew, or when a white lecturer feels he ought not to mention the name of Conrad's beautiful story *The Nigger of the "Narcissus."* But it is no less absurd when well-meaning people, speaking of the physically handicapped, tell prospective employers: "They don't want special consideration. Ask as much of them as you do of everyone else, and fire them if they don't give satisfaction!"

Another version of false democracy is the need to deny the existence of personal advantages. Inherited wealth, famous parents, a first-class mind, a rare voice, a beautiful face, an exceptional physical skill—any advantage has to be minimized or denied. Continually watched and measured, the man or woman who is rich or talented or well educated is likely to be called "undemocratic" whenever he does anything out of the ordinary— more or less of something than others do. If he wants acceptance, the person with a "superior" attribute, like the person with an "inferior" attribute, often feels obliged to take on a protective disguise, to act as if he were just like everybody else. One denies difference; the other minimizes it. And both believe, as they conform to these false standards, that they act in the name of democracy.

For many Americans, a related source of confusion is success. As a people we Americans greatly prize success. And in our eyes success all too often means simply outdoing other people by virtue of achievement judged by some single scale—income or honors or headlines or trophies— and coming out at "the top." Only one person, as we see it, can be the best—can get the highest grades, be voted the most attractive girl or the boy most likely to succeed. Though we often rejoice in the success of people far removed from ourselves—in another profession, another community, or endowed with a talent that we do not covet—we tend to regard the success of people close at hand, within our own small group, as a threat. We fail to realize that there are many kinds of success, including the kind of success that lies within a person. We do not realize, for example, that there could be in the same class one hundred boys and girls— each of them a "success" in a different kind of way. Individuality is again lost in a refusal to recognize and cherish the differences among people.

The attitude that measures success by a single yardstick and isolates the *one* winner and the kind of "democracy" that denies or minimizes differences among people are both deeply destructive. Imagine for a moment a family with two sons, one of whom is brilliant, attractive and athletic while the other is dull, unattractive and clumsy. Both boys attend the same high school. In the interest of the slower boy, the parents would want the school to set equally low standards for everyone. Lessons should be easy; no one should be forced to study dead languages or advanced mathematics in order to graduate. Athletics should be noncompetitive; every boy should have a chance to enjoy playing games. Everyone should be invited to all the parties. As for special attention to gifted children, this is not fair to the other children. An all-round education should be geared to the average, normal child.

But in the interest of the other boy, these same parents would have quite opposite goals. After all, we need highly trained people; the school should do the most it can for its best students. Funds should be made available for advanced classes and special teachers, for the best possible coach, the best athletic equipment. Young people should be allowed to choose friends on their own level. The aim of education should be to produce topflight students.

This is an extreme example, but it illustrates the completely incompatible aims that can arise in this kind of "democracy." Must our country shut its eyes to the needs of either its gifted or its less gifted sons? It would be a good deal more sensible to admit, as some schools do today, that children differ widely from one another, that all successes cannot be ranged on one single scale, that there is room in a real democracy to help each child find his own level and develop to his fullest potential.

Moving now to a wider scene, before World War I Americans thought of themselves as occupying a unique place in the world—and there was no question in most minds that this country was a "success." True, Europeans might look down on us for our lack of culture, but with a few notable, local exceptions, we simply refused to compete on European terms. There was no country in the world remotely like the one we were building. But since World War II we have felt the impact of a country whose size and strength and emphasis on national achievement more closely parallel our own. Today we are ahead of Russia, or Russia is ahead of us. Nothing else matters. Instead of valuing and developing the extraordinary assets and potential of our country for their own sake, we are involved in a simple set of competitions for wealth and power and dominance.

These are expensive and dangerous attitudes. When democracy ceases to be a cherished way of life and becomes instead the name of one team, we are using the word democracy to describe behavior that places us and all other men in jeopardy.

Individually, nationally, and, today, internationally, the misreading of the phrase "all men are created equal" exacts a heavy price. The attitudes that follow from our misconceptions may be compatible with life in a country where land and rank and prestige are severely limited and the roads to success are few. But they are inappropriate in a land as rich, as open, as filled with opportunities as our own. They are the price we pay for being *less* democratic than we claim to be.

"All men are created equal" does not mean that all men are the same. What it does mean is that each should be accorded full respect and full rights as a unique human being—full respect for his humanity *and* for his differences from other people.

Issues in
Democracy

A classic issue within any democracy is the conflict between individual liberty and the needs of the larger society. Where does one draw the line between these two claims? John Stuart Mill asked that question over a hundred years ago (see preceding section); it is our question still because in a democracy making a just compromise between individual liberty and the common good, within a framework of law, is a never-ending process.

In the opening selection, J. Anthony Lukas describes the analogous conflict between the demands of specific communities—of families, churches, neighborhoods—and those of the principle of equality. The tension between these two, he says, "is reflected today in a whole skein of national issues from school desegregation and affirmative action to urban redevelopment and gentrification." Because so many of these issues are very difficult to sort out, it is easy to feel exasperated and to create a fantasy "they" who are supposedly responsible for the difficulties. Carol Bly describes how this happens to people in her native Minnesota, and suggests a reason: "We vaguely feel we ought to be taking part in government . . . so the rationalization is to create such a huger-than-life enemy . . . that we needn't fight him."

The three pieces that follow all take up, in one way or another, the rationale for and the questions raised by our first amendment guarantee of freedom of speech and expression. Walter Lippmann adds a fresh dimension by suggesting that in a democracy freedom of speech is important not so much for the speaker as for the listener: we must be free to hear what our critics have to say. Ben

Bagdikian extends this idea from listener to reader, and applies it to a particular dilemma: Can a democracy ever justify the news quarantine—the exclusion of subjects from news columns because they may produce harmful effects? The reader may want to weigh particularly one assumption shared by both of these writers, namely, that freedom to hear and to speak increases the chances that public policy will reflect the public's thinking.

Alan Dershowitz next explores the troubling complexities that arise when an extremist group like the American Nazi Party or the Ku Klux Klan chooses to express itself—in words, gesture, or dress—not "in public" but in a private establishment such as a restaurant. Does the restaurant have the right to require them to leave?

The last two selections take up the question of whether society ever has the right to protect individuals for their own good. Thomas Szasz says emphatically not, here especially in relation to diets and drugs. Just as the government has no right to censor what we put into our minds, he argues, so it has no right to restrict what we put into our bodies. Amitai Etzioni disagrees. Calling for a balance between individual rights and *some* public rights, he argues that "no civil society can survive if it permits each person to maximize his or her freedoms without concern for the consequences of one's act on others."

Community and Equality in Conflict

J. Anthony Lukas

J. Anthony Lukas (born 1933) is a reporter and writer; he was educated at Harvard (B.A. 1955) and studied for a year at the Free University of Berlin. He became a journalist with the Baltimore Sun *in 1958, and then joined the staff of the* New York Times, *where for nine years he worked in various assignments ranging from foreign correspondent to roving national correspondent. In 1968 he won the Pulitzer Prize for local reporting. Since 1971 he has been a free-lance writer.*

Lukas is a frequent contributor to magazines and author of three books: The Barnyard Epithet and Other Obscenities: Notes on the Chicago Conspiracy Trial *(1970);* Don't Shoot—We Are Your Children! *(1971); and* Common Ground: A Turbulent Decade in the Lives of Three American Families *(1985), for which he won his second Pulitzer Prize. Based on seven years of research,* Common Ground *tells the story of three families whose lives were changed by a court decision ordering busing in Boston public schools. One of the issues raised in the book—the claims of the neighborhood versus the claims of society—is further discussed in the selection we print here, from the September 8, 1985, issue of the* New York Times.

One dusky evening not so long ago, I sat at the beer-stained bar of a tavern in Charlestown, a predominantly Irish-Catholic Boston neighborhood, known as the site of the Battle of Bunker Hill and other more recent struggles. Above the click of billiard balls and the clink of ice, I overheard two regulars in conversation:

First Drinker: "So I told him I'm an American, you know, and I got as much rights as anybody."

Second Drinker: "Yeh, but you're a Townie first. The Townies don't take flapdoodle off any man."

It was an idle exchange after a day of drudgery. But somehow it struck me as emblematic of Boston's recent travail—and indeed of the nation's continuing debate over issues of race, class and ethnicity. For the drinkers were invoking one of the deepest divisions in American life—between the demands of equality and the call of community.

I have recently completed a book about three Boston families: an Irish-Catholic widow and her seven children in Charlestown; a black welfare mother and her six children; a Yankee lawyer and his wife. As these three strands of American life converged, I found their struggle all too frequently rooted in the conflict between community and equality.

On one hand is arrayed the majesty of the Constitution, the Bill of Rights, the Supreme Court and that whole body of law and precedent that embodies much of what it means to be an American; on the other is the warmth, intimacy and comfort of family, church, tavern and neighborhood that lies at the heart of what many Americans mean by "home." The tension between these two constellations is reflected today in a whole skein of national issues from school desegregation and affirmative action to urban redevelopment and gentrification.

It is a conflict as old as the nation itself—between the notion of community expressed by John Winthrop when he set out to found a "city upon a hill" in the Massachusetts Bay Colony, and the idea of equality enshrined in the Declaration of Independence.

The communal intensity of Winthrop's Massachusetts was rooted in the "covenant," the sacred compact that each cluster of settlers made with God and with each other. By the very act of joining the congregation, the Puritan accepted not only one God and one religion, but one polity, one law, one allegiance. The towns they formed could not tolerate diversity: Sudbury enacted resolutions to bar "such whose dispositions do not suit us." Dedham banned "the contrarye minded."

Clearly, Boston during that period was not the Athens of America that has lived so long in legend—the open, generous, diverse, big-spirited seat of American democracy. If anything, it was the national Sparta—narrow, closed, intolerant, a community in quest not of democracy but self-perfection. Yet the notion that communities ought to control their own destinies—even at the expense of outsiders—was a deeply held American value with an ancient and honorable pedigree.

Eventually, a mercantile economy eroded Winthrop's dream of the self-sustaining community. The tight little 17th- and 18th-century towns gradually had to recognize the entitlements of American citizenship, among them the equality of free men.

But the recognition of such universal principles did not destroy the counterclaims of what James Madison called "the spirit of locality." This older communalism survived side by side with the abstract ideals of American constitutionalism. Tocqueville recognized that Americans had not one but two political systems: "The one fulfilling the ordinary duties and responding to the daily and infinite calls of a community; the other circumscribed within certain limits and exercising an exceptional authority over the general interests of the country." For 70 years, this delicate balance prevailed, reassuring Americans that the demands of nationalism were compatible with the intimacies of community.

In the mid-19th century, of course, this revolutionary settlement broke down, the centralizing impulse dashing on the hard rock of particularism. The battle was joined in the Lincoln-Douglas debates, in which Lincoln argued that the essence of democratic government was "the equality of all men" derived from natural law, while Douglas insisted it was the "principle of popular sovereignty," the right of American communities to decide fundamental issues, like slavery, for themselves. Ultimately, force of arms held the nation together and emancipated the slaves, but the tug of war between community and equality was by no means resolved.

In the flowering of 1960's idealism, Americans persuaded themselves that community and equality were not only compatible but mutually reinforcing principles. In 1964, as the educator Diane Ravitch has pointed out, the Johnson Administration secured passage of both the Civil Rights Act, which curbed racial discrimination in Southern schools, and the Economic Opportunity Act, which gave poor people a chance to control their own communities. They were twin expressions of the nation's conscience at mid-decade.

But soon the tensions between community and equality reasserted themselves. After all, civil rights legislation sought to override local law or custom—often equated with bigotry—in the name of human rights. The poverty program, on the other hand, encouraged "community control" as an antidote to bureaucratic centralization—and white ethnics soon invoked that very doctrine, first designed to aid blacks, in a vigorous defense of their own prerogatives.

By 1974 in Boston the two ideals that had seemed to run parallel for much of the 60's had turned at right angles and confronted each other head-on. A Federal district judge, determined to enforce constitutional guarantees of equality, confronted a pack of aggrieved neighborhoods intent on preserving their own sense of community.

In recent years, Boston and other American cities have learned that they have to make some hard choices: between racial justice and self-determination, between equality of educational opportunity and neighborhood schools, between a black child's right to a desegregated education and a white mother's right to control her own child's upbringing. What makes this experience rise to the level of genuine tragedy is precisely that these are not choices between right and wrong, or between judicial dictatorship and sound social policy, but between competing values, between right and right.

Even Paranoids Have Enemies*

Carol Bly

Carol Bly was born in Duluth, Minnesota, in 1930, received her B.A. from Wellesley College in 1951, and did graduate study at the University of Minnesota in 1954–1955. She has remained active in the educational and cultural life of Minnesota as teacher and consultant and has contributed essays, short stories, and poems to numerous magazines. She is particularly effective at recording the details of rural life, of what it means to live in a small town. She presents the satisfactions of a country community and what we think of as country values, but she presents also the stifling aspects, the ways in which that sense of community can inhibit independent judgment and impede critical discussion of important topics. The essay presented here is reprinted from Letters from the Country *(1981), a collection of essays originally printed in* Preview *and the* Minnesota Monthly *between 1973 and 1979.*

Most people in rural Minnesota seem to face evil seldom, inaccurately, and slothfully. It must be a general property of mankind to avoid dealing with actual evils as they show up; I'd like to describe how we do it in southwestern Minnesota.

Lutheran virtue is cheerful virtue, and since Lutheran virtue is strong in our towns and countryside, we are pressed to be pretty cheerful most

---

*Attributed to Delmore Schwartz.

of the time. It isn't cheerful to think of specific social evils, so our usual procedure is to point to the fantasy enemy *"they."*

They are familiar to us all, so, only briefly, here is what *they* do. They don't build cars or anything else the way they used to; they don't do an honest day's work any more; they don't care about the little guy; they are ruining the soil, the countryside, the American family, and the American family farm—and just about everything else. They, like the Devil, are legion, whereas *we* are singular, embattled, and helpless against them. They are *they*—plural: politically astute, cunning, and impersonal; we tend to be, psychologically, singular: the farmer, clean-cut, and minding our own business.

One reason we are minding our own business is that it's easier than taking part in government. We vaguely feel we ought to be taking part in government, though, so the rationalization is to create such a huger-than-life enemy—a kind of a pretend enemy rather than a real one, an enemy made up of contradictory parts—that we needn't fight him: it is hopeless. Here are the convenient aspects of the enemy *they:*

They   are not the United States or any specific corporation or agency; therefore, our country and "the big shots" are kept on as father figures.

They   do not reply when we complain. As Washington people constantly explain: we don't care how much you protest or what you protest as long as you name no names. So there is no danger of reprisal if we are not specific.

They   include not just outer, real enemies—vague figures that resemble U.S. agencies or certain elements of the private sector—but also clumsy, smeary figures, somehow felt, hardly seen, inside our own unconscious. By cursing or accusing *them,* we attack anew our old mean parents or scary childhood figures: we get in a lick, so to speak, albeit late, against ghosts who did us wrong.

Midwest rural paranoia is heartfelt. We can't be deceived about that. Ridiculous as its symptoms sometimes are, it is a real psychic problem, involving real, submerged suffering, and resulting in stupid ways of life. The first noticeable thing about paranoia is the inaccuracy of its shafts. The following anecdote contains several of its elements:

In about 1957 a couple visited my husband and me, and we scarcely could bear the desultory conversation. All four of us were suffering. (I remember afterward my husband remarked that the boredom was so exquisite that tears came to his eyes several times during the afternoon.) At one point, however, the man suddenly announced: Well, the reason you can't count on the weather any more like you used to could is that all these jet airplanes flying over are wrecking it for the farmer.

All four of us perked up a little; paranoid fantasies have a kind of energy, in any case. We asked: Which jet flights? Northwest Airlines? North Central? Continental Defense Command from Duluth—or Strategic Air Command practice flights up from Wichita? Or what?

Instantly, both man and wife answered: "Oh no! None of them!"

I was interested in that sureness as to which were *not* the causes of the bad weather; they insisted on preserving a vague, unidentified enemy. They insisted on a *vague* sort of dread; an enemy in the sky, as opposed to near and walking like us—and (this is what indicates the presence of unconscious material in that enemy) an enemy that brought about the end of a Golden Age. In this case, the Golden Age is entirely phantasmal; it is when you used to be able to count on the weather—this concept despite the plagues of all the ages and the droughts of the 1930s and hail of the 1940s. The quick denial that those flights could originate with an airline with a name or an Air Force unit with a base shows, I think, that the couple in some part of their psyche *meant* to keep the enemy unreal, a pretend enemy, half conscious, who would receive their paranoid flailings.

Apart from attending a few special-interest meetings, most of us in rural Minnesota do not participate in government beyond voting. Whatever we have of the genius of regulating behavior, trying to think of possible plans (as opposed to the ideal plans priests and artists are always laying before us) and trying to sell workable ideas—the whole course of government—we aren't using it much. Carl Jung warned over and over against not using creative gifts if you have them. Dr. Marie-Louis von Franz warns over and over that these unused creative gifts turn to "pure poison." Dr. Franz is a careful as well as eloquent scientist; her use of the expression "pure poison" is advised. If we translate "creative gifts" to "gifts in human government," I think it is clear that unused political gifts, too, turn to poison. In the case of unused political gifts, the poison is called paranoia.

Literally dozens of times I have seen intense anxiety fill the faces of people when someone has said something like "I think that the FBI had something to do with the murder of Martin Luther King." Now this possibility of involvement by the FBI in that death was in the press many times, yet it causes sudden pain. Why?

I think the reason is that we feel secretly guilty about not taking part in our democracy. Our rural towns condition us to being cheerful publicly—to cooling it rather than pointing out harsh truths—but we still feel that participating in government is part of being a human being instead of being a lion or a cow. So we feel a terrible anxiety when evil is done in public life, and we defend against the discomfort of it by saying: "Oh, you can't believe everything you hear!" "Time was, people were willing to love their country without all this negative talk but, boy, I guess not any more!" (again the end of the Golden Era) or "You hardly know what to believe any more, do you?" Every single one of those remarks begs: Please do not lay it on me about King, or Vietnam, or Third World mothers and their baby formula, or Watergate, or Allende's murder, or Korea. I was not told I'd have to bear those griefs!

Another defense-mechanism remark interests me more than any of the above because it has a solution. It is: "Yeah, but if you once get started with all that protest business where's it all going to end?" The cheerful reply is: You can start or quit fighting evil at any time, and decide specifically which evils you will fight, on any timeline. Only fantasy work is without measure and forever—like fantasy enemies. Real work you can enter when you're ready, and you can plan exactly when you mean to leave it. The perfect practitioner of this was Jesus, who rebuked his mother at Cana for showing his hand beforehand (implying a timeline), who frequently "slipped through the crowd" instead of getting arrested because that wasn't in his plan for just then. Also, he instructed the disciples not to do anything until he sent the Holy Ghost to them. In other words, only fantasy enemies are on the field against you at all times.

Truth wins against political paranoia, I think, when we can split this plural, vague, inner-outer enemy *they* into its two parts: the real agent doing some real wrong to other people's lives for the sake of gain, and the huge, constantly flexing, shimmering body of our psychic fears. It means struggling for more consciousness in governmental things, the same struggle we need so badly in other aspects of rural life.

The irony of rural paranoia about what *they* are doing to us is that what real people are really doing to us is actually worse than the fantasies. Someone can sit on his front stoop and mutter about how *they*'re seeding Canadian thistle from airplanes so we have to buy 2-4D to kill it (that's one of the current ones) but what's Canadian thistle compared to the CIA's confessing (March 1977) that, well, yes they did do some germ warfare experiments in American cities.

When the fantasy-enemy action is chickenfeed compared to what real agencies are doing, it is time to become whole, politically, and identify an enemy head or two, and have at them. I think it would also bring a wide-awake feeling to our sleeping countryside.

The Indispensable Opposition

Walter Lippmann

Walter Lippmann (1889–1974) was one of the most honored of American newspapermen. He was educated at Harvard and then taught philosophy there as an assistant to George Santayana. He joined the staff of The New Republic *at its founding in 1914, interrupted his journalistic career to serve as assistant to the Secretary of War—doing special work on peace negotiating—and then moved to an editorial position on the* New York World. *His writings were syndicated in newspapers throughout the country and his column "Today and Tomorrow" won him Pulitzer Prizes in 1958 and 1962. The 1958 award cited the "wisdom, perception, and high sense of responsibility with which he has commented for many years on national and international affairs." During the Watergate years he was quoted with increasing frequency. He received many honorary degrees and such decorations as the Medal of Freedom, the Legion of Honor from France, and the Order of Leopold from Belgium. His books include* Liberty and the News *(1920),* Public Opinion *(1922),* A Preface to Morals *(1929),* The Good Society *(1937),* The Public Philosophy *(1955),* The Coming Tests with Russia *(1961),* Western Unity and the Common Market *(1962), and* The Essential Lippmann: A Political Philosophy for Liberal Democracy *(1963). The essay we present below is taken from* The Atlantic Monthly *for August 1939.*

1

Were they pressed hard enough, most men would probably confess that political freedom—that is to say, the right to speak freely and to act in opposition—is a noble ideal rather than a practical necessity. As the case for freedom is generally put to-day, the argument lends itself to this feeling. It is made to appear that, whereas each man claims his freedom as a matter of right, the freedom he accords to other men is a matter of toleration. Thus, the defense of freedom of opinion tends to rest not on its substantial, beneficial, and indispensable consequences, but on a somewhat eccentric, a rather vaguely benevolent, attachment to an abstraction.

It is all very well to say with Voltaire, 'I wholly disapprove of what you say, but will defend to the death your right to say it,' but as a matter of fact most men will not defend to the death the rights of other men: if they disapprove sufficiently what other men say, they will somehow suppress those men if they can.

So, if this is the best that can be said for liberty of opinion, that a man must tolerate his opponents because everyone has a 'right' to say what he pleases, then we shall find that liberty of opinion is a luxury, safe only in pleasant times when men can be tolerant because they are not deeply and vitally concerned.

Yet actually, as a matter of historic fact, there is a much stronger foundation for the great constitutional right of freedom of speech, and as a matter of practical human experience there is a much more compelling reason for cultivating the habits of free men. We take, it seems to me, a naïvely self-righteous view when we argue as if the right of our opponents to speak were something that we protect because we are magnanimous, noble, and unselfish. The compelling reason why, if liberty of opinion did not exist, we should have to invent it, why it will eventually have to be restored in all civilized countries where it is now suppressed, is that we must protect the right of our opponents to speak because we must hear what they have to say.

We miss the whole point when we imagine that we tolerate the freedom of our political opponents as we tolerate a howling baby next door, as we put up with the blasts from our neighbor's radio because we are too peaceable to heave a brick through the window. If this were all there is to freedom of opinion, that we are too good-natured or too timid to do anything about our opponents and our critics except to let them talk, it would be difficult to say whether we are tolerant because we are magnanimous or because we are lazy, because we have strong principles or because we lack serious convictions, whether we have the hospitality of an inquiring mind or the indifference of an empty mind. And so, if we truly wish to understand why freedom is necessary in a civilized society, we must begin by realizing that, because freedom of discussion improves our own opinions, the liberties of other men are our own vital necessity.

We are much closer to the essence of the matter, not when we quote Voltaire, but when we go to the doctor and pay him to ask us the most embarrassing questions and to prescribe the most disagreeable diet. When we pay the doctor to exercise complete freedom of speech about the cause and cure of our stomachache, we do not look upon ourselves as tolerant and magnanimous, and worthy to be admired by ourselves. We have enough common sense to know that if we threaten to put the doctor in jail because we do not like the diagnosis and the prescription it will be unpleasant for the doctor, to be sure, but equally unpleasant for our own stomachache. That is why even the most ferocious dictator would rather be treated by a doctor who was free to think and speak the truth than by his own Minister of Propaganda. For there is a point, the point at which things really matter, where the freedom of others is no longer a question of their right but of our need.

The point at which we recognize this need is much higher in some men than in others. The totalitarian rulers think they do not need the freedom of an opposition: they exile, imprison, or shoot their opponents. We have concluded on the basis of practical experience, which goes back to Magna Carta and beyond, that we need the opposition. We pay the opposition salaries out of the public treasury.

In so far as the usual apology for freedom of speech ignores this experience, it becomes abstract and eccentric rather than concrete and human. The emphasis is generally put on the right to speak, as if all that mattered were that the doctor should be free to go out into the park and explain to the vacant air why I have a stomachache. Surely that is a miserable caricature of the great civic right which men have bled and died for. What really matters is that the doctor should tell *me* what ails me, that I should listen to him; that if I do not like what he says I should be free to call in another doctor; and that then the first doctor should have to listen to the second doctor; and that out of all the speaking and listening, the give-and-take of opinions, the truth should be arrived at.

This is the creative principle of freedom of speech, not that it is a system for the tolerating of error, but that it is a system for finding the truth. It may not produce the truth, or the whole truth all the time, or often, or in some cases ever. But if the truth can be found, there is no other system which will normally and habitually find so much truth. Until we have thoroughly understood this principle, we shall not know why we must value our liberty, or how we can protect and develop it.

2

Let us apply this principle to the system of public speech in a totalitarian state. We may, without any serious falsification, picture a condition of affairs in which the mass of the people are being addressed through one broadcasting system by one man and his chosen subordinates. The orators speak. The audience listens but cannot and dare not speak back. It is a system of one-way communication; the opinions of the rulers are broadcast outwardly to the mass of the people. But nothing comes back to the rulers from the people except the cheers; nothing returns in the way of knowledge of forgotten facts, hidden feelings, neglected truths, and practical suggestions.

But even a dictator cannot govern by his own one-way inspiration alone. In practice, therefore, the totalitarian rulers get back the reports of the secret police and of their party henchmen down among the crowd. If these reports are competent, the rulers may manage to remain in touch with public sentiment. Yet that is not enough to know what the audience feels. The rulers have also to make great decisions that have enormous consequences, and here their system provides virtually no help from the give-and-take of opinion in the nation. So they must either rely on their own institution, which cannot be permanently and continually inspired, or, if they are intelligent despots, encourage their trusted advisers and their technicians to speak and debate freely in their presence.

On the walls of the houses of Italian peasants one may see inscribed in large letters the legend, 'Mussolini is always right.' But if that legend is taken seriously by Italian ambassadors, by the Italian General Staff, and by the Ministry of Finance, then all one can say is heaven help Mussolini, heaven help Italy, and the new Emperor of Ethiopia.[°]

For at some point, even in a totalitarian state, it is indispensable that

---

new Emperor of Ethiopia   Reference to the fact that Mussolini had invaded Ethiopia in 1935, deposed the then Emperor Haile Selassie and named King Victor Emmanuel of Italy Emperor, thereby defying economic sanctions imposed by the League of Nations. The Italian occupation of Ethiopia lasted from 1936 to 1941.

there should exist the freedom of opinion which causes opposing opinions to be debated. As time goes on, that is less and less easy under a despotism; critical discussion disappears as the internal opposition is liquidated in favor of men who think and feel alike. That is why the early successes of despots, of Napoleon I and of Napoleon III, have usually been followed by an irreparable mistake. For in listening only to his yes men—the others being in exile or in concentration camps, or terrified—the despot shuts himself off from the truth that no man can dispense with.

We know all this well enough when we contemplate the dictatorships. But when we try to picture our own system, by way of contrast, what picture do we have in our minds? It is, is it not, that anyone may stand up on his own soapbox and say anything he pleases, like the individuals in Kipling's poem who sit each in his separate star and draw the Thing as they see it for the God of Things as they are. Kipling, perhaps, could do this, since he was a poet. But the ordinary mortal isolated on his separate star will have an hallucination, and a citizenry declaiming from separate soapboxes will poison the air with hot and nonsensical confusion.

If the democratic alternative to the totalitarian one-way broadcasts is a row of separate soapboxes, then I submit that the alternative is unworkable, is unreasonable, and is humanly unattractive. It is above all a false alternative. It is not true that liberty has developed among civilized men when anyone is free to set up a soapbox, is free to hire a hall where he may expound his opinions to those who are willing to listen. On the contrary, freedom of speech is established to achieve its essential purpose only when different opinions are expounded in the same hall to the same audience.

For, while the right to talk may be the beginning of freedom, the necessity of listening is what makes the right important. Even in Russia and Germany a man may still stand in an open field and speak his mind. What matters is not the utterance of opinions. What matters is the confrontation of opinions in debate. No man can care profoundly that every fool should say what he likes. Nothing has been accomplished if the wisest man proclaims his wisdom in the middle of the Sahara Desert. This is the shadow. We have the substance of liberty when the fool is compelled to listen to the wise man and learn; when the wise man is compelled to take account of the fool, and to instruct him; when the wise man can increase his wisdom by hearing the judgment of his peers.

That is why civilized men must cherish liberty—as a means of promoting the discovery of truth. So we must not fix our whole attention on the right of anyone to hire his own hall, to rent his own broadcasting station, to distribute his own pamphlets. These rights are incidental; and though they must be preserved, they can be preserved only by regarding them as incidental, as auxiliary to the substance of liberty that must be cherished and cultivated.

Freedom of speech is best conceived, therefore, by having in mind the picture of a place like the American Congress, an assembly where opposing views are represented, where ideas are not merely uttered but debated, or the British Parliament, where men who are free to speak are also compelled to answer. We may picture the true condition of freedom as existing in a place like a court of law, where witnesses testify and are cross-examined, where the lawyer argues against the opposing lawyer before the same judge and in the presence of one jury. We may picture freedom as existing in a forum where the speaker must respond to questions; in a gathering of scientists where the data, the hypothesis, and the conclusion are submitted to men competent to judge them; in a reputable newspaper which not only will publish the opinions of those who disagree but will reëxamine its own opinion in the light of what they say.

Thus the essence of freedom of opinion is not in mere toleration as such, but in the debate which toleration provides: it is not in the venting of opinion, but in the confrontation of opinion. That this is the practical substance can readily be understood when we remember how differently we feel and act about the censorship and regulation of opinion purveyed by different media of communication. We find then that, in so far as the medium makes difficult the confrontation of opinion in debate, we are driven towards censorship and regulation.

There is, for example, the whispering campaign, the circulation of anonymous rumors by men who cannot be compelled to prove what they say. They put the utmost strain on our tolerance, and there are few who do not rejoice when the anonymous slanderer is caught, exposed, and punished. At a higher level there is the moving picture, a most powerful medium for conveying ideas, but a medium which does not permit debate. A moving picture cannot be answered effectively by another moving picture; in all free countries there is some censorship of the movies, and there would be more if the producers did not recognize their limitations by avoiding political controversy. There is then the radio. Here debate is difficult; it is not easy to make sure that the speaker is being answered in the presence of the same audience. Inevitably, there is some regulation of the radio.

When we reach the newspaper press, the opportunity for debate is so considerable that discontent cannot grow to the point where under normal conditions there is any disposition to regulate the press. But when newspapers abuse their power by injuring people who have no means of replying, a disposition to regulate the press appears. When we arrive at Congress we find that, because the membership of the House is so large, full debate is impracticable. So there are restrictive rules. On the other hand, in the Senate, where the conditions of full debate exist, there is almost absolute freedom of speech.

This shows us that the preservation and development of freedom of opinion are not only a matter of adhering to abstract legal rights, but also, and very urgently, a matter of organizing and arranging sufficient debate.

Once we have a firm hold on the central principle, there are many practical conclusions to be drawn. We then realize that the defense of freedom of opinion consists primarily in perfecting the opportunity for an adequate give-and-take of opinion; it consists also in regulating the freedom of those revolutionists who cannot or will not permit or maintain debate when it does not suit their purposes.

We must insist that free oratory is only the beginning of free speech; it is not the end, but a means to an end. The end is to find the truth. The practical justification of civil liberty is not that self-expression is one of the rights of man. It is that the examination of opinion is one of the necessities of man. For experience tells us that it is only when freedom of opinion becomes the compulsion to debate that the seed which our fathers planted has produced its fruit. When that is understood, freedom will be cherished not because it is a vent for our opinions but because it is the surest method of correcting them.

The unexamined life, said Socrates, is unfit to be lived by man. This is the virtue of liberty, and the ground on which we may best justify our belief in it, that it tolerates error in order to serve the truth. When men are brought face to face with their opponents, forced to listen and learn and mend their ideas, they cease to be children and savages and begin to live like civilized men. Then only is freedom a reality, when men may voice their opinions because they must examine their opinions.

3

The only reason for dwelling on all this is that if we are to preserve democracy we must understand its principles. And the principle which distinguishes it from all other forms of government is that in a democracy the opposition not only is tolerated as constitutional but must be maintained because it is in fact indispensable.

The democratic system cannot be operated without effective opposition. For, in making the great experiment of governing people by consent rather than by coercion, it is not sufficient that the party in power should have a majority. It is just as necessary that the party in power should never outrage the minority. That means that it must listen to the minority and be moved by the criticisms of the minority. That means that its measures must take account of the minority's objections, and that in administering measures it must remember that the minority may become the majority.

The opposition is indispensable. A good statesman, like any other sensible human being, always learns more from his opponents than from his fervent supporters. For his supporters will push him to disaster unless his opponents show him where the dangers are. So if he is wise he will often pray to be delivered from his friends because they will ruin him. But, though it hurts, he ought also to pray never to be left without opponents; for they keep him on the path of reason and good sense.

The national unity of a free people depends upon a sufficiently even balance of political power to make it impracticable for the administration to be arbitrary and for the opposition to be revolutionary and irreconcilable. Where that balance no longer exists, democracy perishes. For unless all the citizens of a state are forced by circumstances to compromise, unless they feel that they can affect policy but that no one can wholly dominate it, unless by habit and necessity they have to give and take, freedom cannot be maintained.

The Gentle Suppression

Ben H. Bagdikian

Ben H. Bagdikian (born 1920), a journalist and writer, is Dean of the Graduate School of Journalism at Berkeley. A graduate of Clark University, he has been reporter and correspondent at the Providence (R.I.) Journal *and editor at* The Washington Post. *He has also been a contributing editor of the* Saturday Evening Post. *The plight of people not often visible in the media is the subject of many of his writings; among them are* In the Midst of Plenty: The Poor in America *(1964);* The Shame of the Prisons *(1972); and* Caged: Eight Prisoners and Their Keepers *(1976). Also known as a media critic, he is the author of* The Information Machines *(1970) and* The Media Monopoly *(rev. 1987).*

Bagdikian is a frequent spokesman for the importance to a democracy of a free and socially responsible press. He says, "The immediate consequences of valid news can be seen only vaguely. One can only trust that sooner or later, one way or another, news that is true and significant will make society more aware of itself and therefore more humane." His concern with the political implications of news quarantines is expressed in the essay that follows, from his collection The Effete Conspiracy and Other Crimes of the Press *(1972).*

A dramatist looking for a tableau entitled "Dynamic Democracy in Action" might have chosen the sidewalk in front of the White House a few years ago during a civil rights disturbance. At the east end of the block were hundreds of civil rights picketers with signs urging protection of blacks in Alabama. At the west end was a lone uniformed storm trooper of the American Nazi party carrying a placard with the legend, "Who Needs Niggers?", protected by two large serene black policemen.

The Nazis, led by the late George Lincoln Rockwell, were a standard irritant in Washington. Rockwell was a shrewd manipulator of events to dramatize his cause. For years his troopers picketed the White House with shocking signs, peddling Hitlerian propaganda, haranguing tourists with boasts to build bigger and better gas chambers to kill Jews, and breaking up public meetings. Nazis ran onto the stage of the National Theater. They broke into convention meetings in downtown hotels. They disrupted a large gathering at American University by grabbing the stage microphone to yell, "Sieg Heil," and pushed the speaker off the platform while Nazis spotted throughout the audience began fist fights. They interfered with sessions of the United States Congress, sometimes unfurling banners and shouting Nazi slogans from the gallery of the House and Senate, once grabbing the microphone during a congressional hearing, and another time running onto the floor of the House of Representatives dressed in blackface.

Individual Nazis have had less public dealings with the police. One group handcuffed young Jewish boys to headquarters furniture. Others, to the dismay of their führer, seemed unable to understand the statutory rape law.

All in all, the Nazis qualified as news—at the most as a gang promoting savagery and paranoia on the national scene, and at the least as civic pests. But the three Washington papers, in varying degrees, applied a special test for hard news about Nazi activities. Theirs was not an absolute quarantine; all three papers ran numerous accounts of Nazi episodes and printed background pieces. Yet the Nazis got special handling, with the conscious objective of denying them publicity and minimizing their impact. Sometimes this meant not printing news of an event; New York papers and the wire services carried Washington items about the Nazis that were not carried in the local papers. Or it meant omitting parts of the news considered useful to the Nazis in spreading their message. Both the *New York Times* and the *Washington Post,* for example, carried stories in October 1960 of Nazi picketing at the Democratic National Committee headquarters in the capital, but the *Post* omitted what the Nazi placards read while the *Times* printed them ("Kikes for Kennedy"). When a Nazi jumped on the stage of the National Theater, the *Washington Daily News* did not report it and the *Post* did, but buried it in the last two paragraphs of a story on the normal proceedings in the theater. There is little doubt that Washington editors try to run news of the Nazis as little as possible and, when they do, to minimize any advantage to the Nazis and produce the most "healthy" reaction among readers.

These Washington editors are among the most sophisticated in the business, and they have one of the most discerning newspaper audiences in the country. They give individual attention to each story about the Nazis as it occurs. It is a quarantine under the best possible conditions of a subject odious to most Americans. But the quarantine is still pernicious.

News quarantines—exclusion of subjects from news columns because they may produce harmful effects—are difficult to discuss clearly. They fall under the editorial discretion that must be the right of every editor.

They are considered a sign of one of the enlightened developments in American journalism, the idea of social responsibility in the press. At the same time, they are often indistinguishable from less attractive practices, such as special treatment of sacred cows or suppressions for the benefit of friends of the paper. But even when quarantines are altruistically imposed, they interfere with the democratic process and are demoralizing to the discipline of news judgment.

Prevention of racial tension is the most common contemporary cause of local quarantines. They have been practiced in both North and South when black-white incidents occur. Chicago for a time had a ban on reporting racial disturbances. In Washington, D.C., a spectacular riot in the municipal stadium was at first unreported, then distorted to make it appear nonracial. There is no question that at the moment these embargoes seemed prudent.

But not so long ago most Southern dailies had a quarantine in their general news columns on any items that made blacks look good or normal. In these papers blacks did not get born, win scholarships, get elected to lodge offices or die in respectability; they only committed abhorrent crimes and led depraved lives. All the editors of such papers I ever talked to insisted that they were only reporting news the community needed to know.

When civil rights became an issue, many segregationist editors censored out news of integrationist agitation, believing they were doing it for the good of the community. Other editors censored out news of segregationist agitation, believing they were doing it for the good of the community. Both kinds of editors sometimes did it at the same time in the same towns, as in Nashville and Little Rock during their troubles.° These papers had decided what was good for the community and then trimmed their news to fit that end, though the ends were opposite.

Needless to say, race relations has not been the only subject of quarantines. For many years papers in heavily Catholic areas printed almost nothing about birth control. Trouble in religious groups, even spectacular public trouble, has come under fierce pressure for suppression. In Boston a fiery Jesuit, Father Feeney, defied his archbishop, spoke against diocesan activity, was excommunicated, and formed his own schismatic order, which held anti-Semitic rallies on Boston Common, sometimes with violence. But readers of the Boston papers remained ignorant of almost the entire Feeney story. The church wanted no news of its embarrassment and Jews wanted no spreading of anti-Semitic appeals, both urging a quarantine for the public good.

---

troubles Reference to community turbulence in reaction to federal court orders to desegregate public schools. In 1957, in defiance of the court, a school was blown up in Nashville, Tennessee, and in Arkansas, Governor Orval Faubus used the Arkansas National Guard to prevent U.S. marshalls from integrating a school in Little Rock.

Nor is this practice limited to the United States. (It goes without saying that in countries with a controlled press the quarantine is found in its pristine form.) Once, the management of the Quebec papers *Le Soleil* and *L'Événement,* according to *Editor & Publisher,* "banned publication of statements preaching violence by separatists, nationalists and other groups considered to have no authority or groups considered not representative of the public interest." It is language one expects in a code issued by Louis XIV, but there is no reason to doubt that the general manager of the papers felt he was acting for the public good, or as he put it, "to serve the best interests of the milieu with which they are identified."

To argue against quarantines one has to admit risk. Printing news of bad events often makes the events worse. Giving news space to a demagogue grants him his heart's desire. Reporting "events" deliberately created in order to exploit the news process rewards the schemers and imagemakers.

But how can the editor ignore all planned events? If he did there would be almost no political news, because if there is one thing a politician plots day and night it is how to exploit the news process, and this goes from the President down to the Rockwells. News events that are not acts of God are acts of men, and of men who have planned shrewdly. Inspired events need not be reported indiscriminately, but they cannot be dismissed indiscriminately.

Should the reporter and editor be responsible for the ill effects of printing truthful news? If so, then each editor and reporter has to decide ahead of time what he wants the reader to think and do, and report only those events that lead the reader to that end. Yet what is one editor's bad effect may be another's glory: in Nashville and Little Rock two leading editors wanted differing kinds of society, and so reported different kinds of news.

The pursuers of domestic justice are safer putting their trust in an open society and professional discipline rather than in the wisdom and powers of prophecy of any individual—even a reporter or editor.

In the end, the journalist's responsibility is to the reader, not to history, and the heart of that responsibility is to give the reader as clear a picture of pertinent reality as he can, based on how the reporter sees it at that particular moment. Reality is a big word and a subjective one at that. But for journalists it boils down to the reporter's seeing the world with his own eyes and not someone else's. When he begins to filter what he sees and reports through a concern whether the reader will react "correctly," he has ceased being a reporter. The exception, of course, is the existence of a clear and present danger to life and order in the community, but genuinely clear and present dangers arising from the printing of news are rare in any editor's lifetime.

Promoters of quarantines, when they are not the editors themselves, are usually responsible men doing good works. A few years ago a Jewish group circularized editors, asking for a blackout of news about bigots:

"Bigots are not deterred by expressions of public disapproval but often thrive on them; publishing scurrilous statements by bigots, even to ridicule them, only gives such statements respectability; publicizing the bigot, even unfavorably, inflates him."

About George Lincoln Rockwell and the Nazis, the memorandum said:

"It is as an advocate of nazism that Rockwell demands a hearing. But is nazism an issue in this country? Should anyone urging a Hitler regime for the United States be taken seriously as the exponent of one 'side' of a valid public question?"

The concern here is too much with the gratification of the bigot at seeing his name in the newspapers. Men on the way to their executions have been pleased to see their picture in the paper but their joy has not saved them. And if news space shall be given only to ideas considered respectable, then authority (which grants respectability) censors the press.

Nor is it true that Rockwell and others like him deserve news space only as advocates. They deserve it, when they deserve it at all, as principals in public events affecting others. The fact that they deliberately provoke such events does not necessarily mean that the events are not news. If a mayor douses his hair with lighter fluid and makes a flaming leap from a persimmon tree singing "Dixie," it may be a stunt but it is news. If a Nazi deliberately breaks up a public meeting by pushing the speaker off the stage, it is a device to get publicity but it is news. (Papers that are worried about the impact of the Nazis might have played the news straight and then asked editorially why the Nazis arrested for breaking up the meeting were let off with a ten-dollar forfeiture of collateral and never brought to trial.)

Who is to decide whether Nazism is an issue in this country? And how is anyone to know, if it is quarantined from public study? If it is not an issue, then there is no danger in playing news of Nazis in the normal way. The fact that there is a quarantine means editors accept that Nazism is an issue with enough people to cause worry. Rockwell was not an ordinary soapbox shouter. At one time he had the backing of a man with $4 million. He was able to disrupt sessions of Congress. He had only a couple dozen loutish troopers but he was a resourceful leader who had been the subject of many man-hours of official worry by the Department of Justice, the metropolitan police and the district commissioners, and of unofficial attention by university officials and by American Civil Liberties Union leaders preparing defenses of the Nazis' constitutional rights while worrying how to accomplish this without infringing the rights of others. These are deliberations of a fundamental kind from which principles and practices evolve that are applied to all society. If the elite were worried about Rockwell as a problem, the citizen ought to have worried, too. If the elite think the citizenry may come out the wrong way, then what is needed is more news, not less.

In 1960 a wave of desecrations of Jewish temples took place in Germany and the United States. In city after city there was an epidemic of swastikas splashed onto walls and windows—about 650 were reported to police. After it was all over, two social scientists, David Caplovitz and Candace Rogers, wrote an analysis for the Anti-Defamation League with this conclusion on the effects of news reports:

> It cannot be disputed that publicity given to the German desecrations and subsequent outbreaks here played a major role in setting off further incidents. The offenders themselves, as we saw earlier, often reported that they got the idea from the newspapers, from television, and other mass media. It is probable that as early incidents mounted, publicity given to them precipitated other incidents as offenders of otherwise low predisposition were stimulated to participate. But it would be unwise to conclude from this fact alone that the media should refrain from publishing information of such events.
>
> In the first place, the outbreak received more than one kind of publicity. In addition to informing the public that the incidents had occurred, the media also published reactions to the outbreak—and the reactions were uniformly negative. Religious, civic and political leaders alike condemned the incidents in the strongest terms. Regardless of the actual level of anti-Semitism the epidemic represented, it called forth a unanimous denunciation of religious intolerance and a public reaffirmation of the principles of brotherhood. We do not know what long-range effects the reiteration of this public morality may have. It is possible that once the crisis has passed, the feelings and expressions of solidarity it evoked passed also, without touching more subtle and pervasive expressions of prejudice in housing, employment, and recreation. But it is also possible that because of the crisis itself, new agencies of cooperation were created, dormant patterns of collaboration reactivated, and the Jewish community was reassured about the goodwill of its neighbors. . . .
>
> In some unknown proportion of cases, the swastika outbreak may well have given specific form and content to vague and diffuse hostilities, so that offenders who were not originally anti-Semitic have, in the course of the outbreak, learned about the prevalence—and for some, the legitimacy—of religious and ethnic intolerance. Their hostilities now have a new specific target. Others, however, who began with relatively mild and vague anti-Semitic sentiments, may well have been startled and abashed by the violent reaction their offenses provoked, learning that in this area at least, what seemed to them a legitimate and mild form of hostility is in fact a major transgression in the eyes of society. Just as the epidemic may have taught some to be anti-Semitic, it may have taught others not to be.

Discrimination by Creed

Alan M. Dershowitz

Alan M. Dershowitz is best known as a lawyer of last resort, legal defender of those whom most people are not anxious to defend. (He describes a number of his cases in The Best Defense, *published in 1982, a book which provoked controversy.) Strongly committed to the preservation of civil liberties, he also believes that in order to preserve individual rights and the integrity of the judicial process, it is better to let a few guilty people go unpunished than to compromise the constitutional rights of all. He was born in Brooklyn in 1938, received his B.A. from Brooklyn College in 1959, and took his law degree from Yale in 1962. He joined the faculty of Harvard Law School in 1964 and has been a full professor since 1967. The following article is reprinted from the* San Francisco Chronicle, *November 16, 1986.*

I remember, as a kid, reading in Superman comics that it was un-American to judge a person on the basis of race, creed, religion or national origin. I always understood why it was wrong to judge on the basis of factors beyond a person's control, but people should be judged by their creeds, if that means by the beliefs they have chosen to govern their behavior.

Adherents of the Ku Klux Klan, or of Stalinism, or of Nazism should be judged by the abhorrent principles for which they stand. I would never choose a friend on the basis of race, religion or origin. But I would most certainly reject any friendship with a segregationist or a misogynist. Superman was wrong to equate discrimination on the basis of heritage with the very different concept of judging people by their voluntary beliefs and actions. The California branch of the American Civil Liberties Union seems to be making that same equation in a troubling case now pending before the Los Angeles Superior Court.

The case grows out of an incident last October after four men wearing swastikas walked into the Alpine Inn, a German restaurant in Torrance, and sat down for dinner. When the jukebox played a German marching song, the Nazis rose and gave a "Heil Hitler" salute. After they left, the restrooms were found papered with anti-Semitic stickers.

A week later, the Nazis returned. This time the restaurant was filled with more than 1000 customers for a large Oktoberfest celebration. There was concern that violence might ensue, and the Nazis were asked either to leave or to remove their swastikas. They refused and were arrested.

Now they are suing the restaurant under a California civil rights statute that bars discrimination by business establishments on the basis of "sex, race, color, religion, ancestry or national origin." Creed is not specifically mentioned, but the California courts have interpreted the law to bar "all arbitrary discrimination," while allowing businesses to exclude customers who are "disruptive" or fail to comply with "reasonable deportment regulations." The ACLU of California is representing the Nazis.

The issues raised by this case are far more complex than those raised by cases involving discrimination on the basis of race, gender or heritage.

At one level, there are obvious similarities. Some restaurant customers are genuinely offended, even outraged, by a wide range of activities, including interracial or homosexual hand holding, cigaret and cigar smoking or informal dress. Restaurants quite properly have the power to establish some rules for their patrons.

But federal, state and local laws impose limits. Even if every white patron would be offended to the point of leaving by the restaurant serving black or interracial guests, no restaurant may discriminate on the basis of race. The same is generally true—and should be true—for sexual preference, religious background and national origin.

But what about political expression? The issue would be simple if the restaurant enforced an across-the-board policy of refusing admission to anyone wearing any political symbol, or anyone standing up to make any kind of salute during the meal, or anyone posting any sign in the bathroom, or anyone engaging in disruptive conduct of any kind. And perhaps that is how this case will eventually be decided.

But that would not quite be an intellectually honest way of confronting the difficult issues posed here. The content of what these customers were wearing, saying, saluting and postering was critical to why they were excluded. And therein lies the rub.

Imagine the outrage if the owner of a restaurant refused to serve only those people who wore anti-apartheid pins, or anti-war armbands, but willingly served customers who sported pro-apartheid and "nuke the reds" signs. Consider the case of a previously segregated restaurant being frustrated in its attempt to comply with the equal accommodation law by a group of KKK members eating at the establishment wearing sheets and hoods. Obviously, this would be the functional equivalent of a sign at the door reading "Blacks not welcome." Most of us probably would applaud a restaurant owner who ordered the Klansmen to remove their paraphernalia or leave.

A German restaurant frequented by patrons wearing swastikas and making "Heil Hitler" salutes certainly would not encourage Jewish or black patronage. Indeed, it might effectively exclude them, in violation of the very law invoked by the Nazis.

The issue is a difficult one with no knee-jerk solution. Several distinctions must be kept in mind. This is not the Skokie case; there is an enormous difference between public thoroughfares and private restaurants. I supported the ACLU's opposition to the efforts of Skokie, Ill., to bar a Nazi march through town. I feel much more conflict about the ACLU's defense of the rights of Nazis to practice their offensive politics during the dinner hour at a private restaurant.

Nor is this a case of discrimination based on race, religion, gender or national origin. It is a question of people being judged for their political beliefs. I hope these distinctions are kept in mind when the courts confront this complex case.

Drug Prohibition

Thomas S. Szasz

Thomas Szasz is a psychiatrist who has been challenging some of his profession's premises and practices for more than 30 years. Born in Budapest in 1920, he came to this country in 1938. He received his medical degree from the University of Cincinnati in 1954 and took his further training at the Chicago Institute for Psychoanalysis. Since 1956, he has been Professor of Psychiatry at the State University of New York in Syracuse.

Szasz has written numerous professional articles and more than a dozen books, including The Myth of Mental Illness: Foundations of a Theory of Personal Conduct *(rev. 1974),* Ceremonial Chemistry: The Ritual Persecution of Drugs, Addicts, and Pushers *(1976), and* Insanity: The Idea and Its Consequences *(1986). He believes that "mental illness" is a misleading term, a metaphor at best, that "sick" behavior has social, not physiological, causes and can be best described as "problems of living." A firm opponent of any formal connections between psychiatry and the state, he wants to banish both pretrial psychiatric examinations and the insanity plea from the criminal justice system. We should, he says, "regard only psychiatric relations between consenting adults as morally and legally legitimate."*

It follows, then, that Szasz has also become an ardent spokesman for individual rights, believing that "in a free society, a person must have the right to injure or kill himself." The argument against prohibiting drugs, which we present below, is a chapter from The Therapeutic State *(1984).*

Americans regard freedom of speech and religion as fundamental rights. Until 1914, they also regarded freedom of choosing their diets and drugs as fundamental rights. Today, however, virtually all Americans regard ingesting certain substances—prohibited by the government—as both crimes and diseases.

What is behind this fateful moral and political transformation, which has resulted in the rejection by the overwhelming majority of Americans of their right to self-control over their diets and drugs in favor of the alleged protection of their health from their own actions by a medically corrupt and corrupted state? How could it have come about in view of the obvious parallels between the freedom to put things into one's mind and its restriction by the state by means of censorship of the press, and the freedom to put things into one's body and its restriction by the state by means of drug controls?

Censorship

The answer to these questions lies basically in the fact that our society is *therapeutic* in much the same sense in which medieval Spanish society was *theocratic*. Just as the men and women living in a theocratic society did not believe in the separation of church and state but, on the contrary, fervently embraced their union, so we, living in a therapeutic society, do not believe in the separation of medicine and the state but fervently embrace their union. The censorship of drugs follows from the latter ideology as inexorably as the censorship of books followed from the former. That explains why liberals and conservatives—and people in that imaginary center as well—all favor drug controls. In fact, persons of all political and religious convictions, save libertarians, now favor drug controls.

Liberals tend to be permissive towards socially disreputable psychoactive drugs, especially when they are used by young and hairy persons; so they generally favor decriminalizing marijuana and treating rather than punishing those engaged in the trade of LSD. They are not at all permissive, however, toward nonpsychoactive drugs that are allegedly unsafe or worthless and thus favor banning saccharin and Laetrile. In these ways they betray their fantasy of the state—as good parent: such a state should restrain erring citizens by mild, minimal, and medical sanctions, and it should protect ignorant citizens by pharmacological censorship.

Conservatives, on the other hand, tend to be prohibitive toward socially disreputable psychoactive drugs, especially when they are used by young and hairy persons; so they generally favor criminalizing the use of marijuana and punishing rather than treating those engaged in the trade of LSD. At the same time, they are permissive toward nonpsychoactive drugs that are allegedly unsafe or worthless and thus favor free trade in saccharin and Laetrile. In these ways, they too betray their fantasy of the state—as the enforcer of the dominant ethic: such a state should punish citizens who deviate from the moral precepts of the majority and should abstain from meddling with people's self-care.

Viewed as a political issue, drugs, books, and religious practices all present the same problem to a people and its rulers. The state, as the representative of a particular class or dominant ethic, may choose to embrace some drugs, some books, and some religious practices and reject the others as dangerous, depraved, demented, or devilish. Throughout history, such an arrangement has characterized most societies. Or the state, as the representative of a constitution ceremonializing the supremacy of individual choice over collective comfort, may ensure a free trade in drugs, books, and religious practices. Such an arrangement has traditionally characterized the United States. Its Constitution explicitly guarantees the right to freedom of religion and the press and implicitly guarantees the right to freedom of self-determination with respect to what we put into our bodies.

Why did the framers of the Constitution not explicitly guarantee the right to take drugs? For two obvious reasons. First, because 200 years ago medical science was not even in its infancy; medical practice was socially unorganized and therapeutically worthless. Second, because there was then no conceivable danger of an alliance between medicine and the state. The very idea that the government should lend its police power to physicians to deprive people of their free choice to ingest certain substances would have seemed absurd to the drafters of the Bill of Rights.

This conjecture is strongly supported by a casual remark by Thomas Jefferson, clearly indicating that he regarded our freedom to put into our bodies whatever we want as essentially similar to our freedom to put into our own minds whatever we want. "Was the government to prescribe to us our medicine and diet," wrote Jefferson in 1782, "our bodies would be in such keeping as our souls are now. Thus in France the emetic was once forbidden as a medicine, the potato as an article of food."

A Therapeutic State

Jefferson poked fun at the French for their pioneering efforts to prohibit drugs and diets. What, then, would he think of the state that now forbids the use of harmless sweeteners while encouraging the use of dangerous contraceptives? that labels marijuana a narcotic and prohibits it while calling tobacco an agricultural product and promoting it? and that defines the voluntary use of heroin as a disease and the legally coerced use of methadone as a treatment for it?

Freedom of religion is indeed a political idea of transcendent importance. As that idea has been understood in the United States, it does not mean that members of the traditional churches—that is, Christians, Jews, and Muslims—may practice their faith unmolested by the government but that others—for example, Jehovah's Witnesses—may not. American religious freedom is unconditional; it is not contingent on any particular church proving, to the satisfaction of the state, that its principles or practices possess "religious efficacy."

The requirement that the supporters of a religion establish its theological credentials in order to be tolerated is the hallmark of a theological state. In Spain, under the Inquisition, there was, in an ironic sense, religious tolerance: religion was tolerated, indeed, actively encouraged. The point is that religions other than Roman Catholicism were considered to be heresies. The same considerations now apply to drugs.

The fact that we accept the requirement that the supporters of a drug establish its therapeutic credentials before we tolerate its sale or use shows that we live in a therapeutic state. In the United States today, there is, in an ironic sense, pharmacological tolerance: approved drugs are tolerated, indeed, actively encouraged. But drugs other than those officially sanctioned as therapeutic are considered worthless or dangerous. Therein, precisely, lies the moral and political point: governments are notoriously tolerant about permitting the dissemination of ideas or drugs of which they approve. Their mettle is tested by their attitude toward the dissemination of ideas and drugs of which they disapprove.

The argument that people need the protection of the state from dangerous drugs but not from dangerous ideas is unpersuasive. No one has to ingest any drug he does not want, just as no one has to read a book he does not want. Insofar as the state assumes control over such matters, it can only be in order to subjugate its citizens—by protecting them from temptation, as befits children; and by preventing them from assuming self-determination over their lives, as befits an enslaved population.

Controlling Danger

Conventional wisdom now approves—indeed, assumes as obvious—that it is the legitimate business of the state to control certain substances we take into our bodies, especially so-called psychoactive drugs. According to this view, as the state must, for the benefit of society, control dangerous persons, so it must also control dangerous drugs. The obvious fallacy in this analogy is obscured by the riveting together of the notions of dangerous drugs and dangerous acts: as a result, people now "know" that dangerous drugs cause people to behave dangerously and that it is just as much the duty of the state to protect its citizens from dope as it is to protect them from murder and theft. The trouble is that all these supposed facts are false.

It is impossible to come to grips with the problem of drug controls unless we distinguish between things and persons. A drug, whether it be heroin or insulin, is a thing. It does not do anything to anyone unless a person ingests it or injects it into himself or administers it to another. Obviously, a drug has no biological effect on a person unless it gets into his body. The basic question—that is logically prior to whether the drug is good or bad—is, therefore: How does a drug get into the person's body? Although there are many ways for that to happen, we need to consider here only a few typical instances of it.

A person may take an accepted nonprescription drug like aspirin by way of self-medication. Or, he may be given an accepted prescription drug like penicillin by way of medication by his physician. Neither of these situations disturbs most people nowadays. What disturbs the compact majority is a person taking a drug like LSD or selling a drug like heroin to others.

The most cursory attention to how drugs get into the human body thus reveals that the moral and political crux of the problem of drug controls lies not in the pharmacological properties of the chemicals in question, but in the characterological properties of the persons who take them (and of the people who permit, prescribe, and prohibit drugs.)

The true believer in conventional wisdom might wish to insist at this point—not without justification—that some drugs are more dangerous than others; that, in other words, the properties of drugs are no less relevant to understanding our present-day drug problems than are the properties of the persons. That is true. But it is important that we not let that truth divert our attention from the distinction between pharmacological facts and the social policies they supposedly justify.

Prohibition

Today, ordinary, "normal" people do not really want to keep an open mind about drugs and drug controls. Instead of thinking about the problem, they tend to dismiss it with some cliche such as: "Don't tell me that heroin or LSD aren't dangerous drugs!" Ergo, they imply and indeed assert: "Don't tell me that it doesn't make good sense to prohibit their production, sale, and possession!"

What is wrong with this argument? Quite simply, everything. In the first place, the proposition that heroin or LSD is dangerous must be qualified and placed in relation to the dangerousness of other drugs and other artifacts that are not drugs. Second, the social policy that heroin or LSD should be prohibited does not follow, as a matter of logic, from the proposition that they are dangerous, even if they are dangerous.

Admittedly, heroin is more dangerous than aspirin, in the sense that it gives more pleasure to its user than aspirin; heroin is therefore more likely than aspirin to be taken for the self-induction of euphoria. Heroin is also more dangerous than aspirin in the sense that it is easier to kill oneself with it; heroin is therefore more likely to be used for committing suicide.

The fact that people take heroin to make themselves feel happy or high—and use other psychoactive drugs for their mind-altering effects— raises a simple but basic issue that the drug-prohibitionists like to avoid, namely: What is wrong with people using drugs for that purpose? Why shouldn't people make themselves happy by means of self-medication? Let me say at once that I believe these are questions to which honest and reasonable men may offer different answers. Whatever the answers, however, I insist that they flow from moral rather than medical considerations.

For example, some people say that individuals should not take heroin because it diverts them from doing productive work, making those who use the drugs, as well as those economically dependent on them, burdens on society. Others say that whether individuals use, abuse, or avoid heroin is, unless they harm others, their private business. And still others opt for a compromise between the total prohibition of heroin and a free trade in it.

There is, however, more to the prohibitionist's position than his concern that hedonic drugs seduce people from hard labor to happy leisure. If prohibitionists were truly motivated by such concerns, they would advocate permission to use heroin contingent on the individual's proven ability to support himself (and perhaps others), rather than its unqualified suppression. The fact that they advocate no such thing highlights the symbolic aspects of drugs and drug controls.

Drugs, Fun, and Sin

The objects we now call "dangerous drugs" are metaphors for all that we consider sinful and wicked; that is why they are prohibited, rather than because they are demonstrably more harmful than countless other objects in the environment that do not now symbolize sin for us. In this connection, it is instructive to consider the cultural metamorphosis we have undergone during the past half-century, shifting our symbols of sin from sexuality to chemistry.

Our present views on drugs, especially psychoactive drugs, are strikingly similar to our former views on sex, especially masturbation. Intercourse in marriage with the aim of procreation used to be the paradigm of the proper use of one's sexual organs; whereas intercourse outside of marriage with the aim of carnal pleasure used to be the paradigm of their improper use. Until recently, masturbation—or self-abuse, as it was called—was professionally declared, and popularly accepted, as both the cause and the symptom of a variety of illnesses, especially insanity. To be sure, it is now virtually impossible to cite a contemporary medical authority to support this concept of self-abuse. Expert medical opinion now holds that there is simply no such thing: that whether a person masturbates or not is medically irrelevant, and that engaging in the practice or refraining from it is a matter of personal morals or life style.

On the other hand, it is now impossible to cite a contemporary medical authority to oppose the concept of drug abuse. Expert medical opinion now holds that drug abuse is a major medical, psychiatric, and public-health problem: that drug addiction is a disease similar to diabetes, requiring prolonged (or life-long) and medically carefully supervised treatment; and that taking or not taking drugs is primarily, if not solely, a matter of medical concern and responsibility.

Like any social policy, our drug laws may be examined from two entirely different points of view: technical and moral. Our present inclination is either to ignore the moral perspective or to mistake the technical for the moral.

A Medical Problem?

An example of our misplaced overreliance on a technical approach to the so-called drug problem is the professionalized mendacity about the dangerousness of certain types of drugs. Since most propagandists against drug abuse seek to justify certain repressive policies by appeals to the alleged dangerousness of various drugs, they often falsify the facts about the true pharmacological properties of the drugs they seek to prohibit. They do so for two reasons: first, because many substances in daily use are just as harmful as the substances they want to prohibit; second, because they realize that dangerousness alone is never a sufficiently persuasive argument to justify the prohibition of any drug, substance, or artifact. Accordingly, the more they ignore the moral dimensions of the problem, the more they must escalate their fraudulent claims about the dangers of drugs.

To be sure, some drugs are more dangerous than others. It *is* easier to kill oneself with heroin than with aspirin. But it is also easier to kill oneself by jumping off a high building than a low one. In the case of drugs, we regard their potentiality for self-injury as a justification for their prohibition; in the case of buildings, we do not. Furthermore, we systematically blur and confuse the two quite different ways in which narcotics can cause death: by a deliberate act of suicide and by accidental overdose.

I maintain that suicide is an act, not a disease. It is therefore a moral, not a medical, problem. The fact that suicide results in death does not make it a medical problem any more than the fact that execution in the electric chair results in death makes the death penalty a medical problem. Hence, it is morally absurd—and, in a free society, politically illegitimate—to deprive an adult of a drug because he might use it to kill himself. To do so is to treat people as institutional psychiatrists treat so-called psychotics: they not only imprison such persons but take everything away from them—shoelaces, belts, razor blades, eating utensils, and so forth—until the "patients" lie naked on a mattress in a padded cell, lest they kill themselves. The result is one of the most degrading tyrannizations in the annals of human history.

Death by accidental overdose is an altogether different matter. But can anyone doubt that this danger now looms so large precisely because the sale of narcotics and many other drugs is illegal? Persons buying illicit drugs cannot be sure what they are getting or how much of it. Free trade in drugs, with governmental action limited to safeguarding the purity of the product and the veracity of labeling, would reduce the risk of accidental overdose with so-called dangerous drugs to the same levels that prevail, and that we find acceptable, with respect to other chemical agents and physical artifacts that abound in our complex technological society.

In my view, regardless of their dangerousness, all drugs should be "legalized" (a misleading term that I employ reluctantly as a concession to common usage). Although I realize that some drugs—notably, heroin, amphetamine, and LSD among those now in vogue—may have dangerous consequences, I favor free trade in drugs for the same reason the Founding Fathers favored free trade in ideas: in a free society it is none of the government's business what ideas a man puts into his mind; likewise, it should be none of its business what drug he puts into his body.

"Heresy"

Clearly, the argument that marijuana—or heroin, methadone, or morphine—is prohibited because it is addictive or dangerous cannot be supported by facts. For one thing, there are many drugs, from insulin to penicillin, that are neither addictive nor dangerous but are nevertheless also prohibited: they can be obtained only through a physician's prescription. For another, there are many things, from poisons to guns, that are much more dangerous than narcotics (especially to others) but are not prohibited. As everyone knows, it is still possible in the United States to walk into a store and walk out with a shotgun. We enjoy that right, not because we do not believe that guns are dangerous, but because we believe even more strongly that civil liberties are precious. At the same time, it is not possible in the United States to walk into a store and walk out with a bottle of barbiturates or codeine or, indeed, even with an empty hypodermic syringe. We are now deprived of that right because we have come to value medical paternalism more highly than the right to obtain and use drugs without recourse to medical intermediaries.

I submit, therefore, that our so-called drug-abuse problem is an integral part of our present social ethic that accepts "protections" and repressions justified by appeals to health similar to those which medieval societies accepted when they were justified by appeals to faith. Drug abuse (as we now know it) is one of the inevitable consequences of the medical monopoly over drugs—a monopoly whose value is daily acclaimed by science and law, state and church, the professions and the laity. As formerly the church regulated man's relations to God, so medicine now regulates his relations to his body. Deviation from the rules set forth by the church was then considered heresy and was punished by appropriate theological sanctions, called penance; deviation from the rules set forth by medicine is now considered drug abuse (or some sort of "mental illness") and is punished by appropriate medical sanctions, called treatment.

The problem of drug abuse will thus be with us so long as we live under medical tutelage. That is not to say that, if all access to drugs were free, some people would not medicate themselves in ways that might upset us or harm them. That, of course, is precisely what happened when religious practices became free. People proceeded to engage in all sorts of religious behaviors that true believers in traditional faiths found obnoxious and upsetting. Nevertheless, in the conflict between freedom and religion, the American political system has come down squarely for the former and against the latter.

If the grown son of a devoutly religious Jewish father has a ham sandwich for lunch, the father cannot use the police power of American society to impose his moral views on his son. But if the grown son of a devoutly alcoholic father has heroin for lunch, the father can, indeed, use the police power of American society to impose his moral views on his son. Moreover, the penalty that that father could legally visit on his son might exceed the penalty that would be imposed on the son for killing his mother. It is that moral calculus—refracted through our present differential treatment of those who literally abuse others by killing, maiming, and robbing them as against those who metaphorically abuse themselves by using illicit chemicals—which reveals the depravity into which our preoccupation with drugs and drug controls has led us.

Self-medication

I believe that just as we regard freedom of speech and religion as fundamental rights, so we should also regard freedom of self-medication as a fundamental right; and that, instead of mendaciously opposing or mindlessly promoting illicit drugs, we should, paraphrasing Voltaire, make this maxim our rule: "I disapprove of what you take, but I will defend to the death your right to take it!"

Sooner or later we shall have to confront the basic moral dilemma underlying the so-called drug problem: Does a person have the right to take a drug, any drug—not because he needs it to cure an illness, but because he wants to take it?

The Constitution and the Bill of Rights are silent on the subject of drugs. That would seem to imply that the adult citizen has, or ought to have, the right to medicate his own body as he sees fit. Were that not the case, why should there have been a need for a constitutional amendment to outlaw drinking? But if ingesting alcohol was, and is now again, a constitutional right, is ingesting opium or heroin or barbiturates or anything else not also such a right?

It is a fact that we Americans have a right to read a book—any book—not because we are stupid and want to learn from it, nor because a government-supported educational authority claims that it will be good for us, but simply because we want to read it; because the government—as our servant rather than our master—hasn't the right to meddle in our private reading affairs.

I believe that we also have a right to eat, drink, or inject a substance—any substance—not because we are sick and want it to cure us, nor because a government-supported medical authority claims that it will be good for us, but simply because we want to take it; because the government—as our servant rather than our master—hasn't the right to meddle in our private dietary and drug affairs.

It is also a fact, however, that Americans now go to jail for picking harmless marijuana growing wild in the fields, but not for picking poisonous mushrooms growing wild in the forests. Why? Because we Americans have collectively chosen to cast away our freedom to determine what we should eat, drink, or smoke. In this large and ever-expanding area of our lives, we have rejected the principle that the state is our servant rather than our master. This proposition is painfully obvious when people plaintively insist that we need the government to protect us from the hazards of "dangerous" drugs. To be sure, we need private voluntary associations—or also, some might argue, the government—to *warn* us of the dangers of heroin, high-tension wires, and high-fat diets.

But it is one thing for our would-be protectors to *inform* us of what they regard as dangerous objects in our environment. It is quite another thing for them to *punish* us if we disagree with them.

When Rights Collide

Amitai Etzioni

Amitai Etzioni is a liberal, outspoken, practical sociologist of wide interests and influence. He was born in Germany in 1929 to Jewish parents who fled the Nazis in 1936, was raised in Israel, and fought in the Israeli army as a commando during the late 1940s. Etzioni took his B.A. (1954) and M.A. (1956) from the Hebrew University in Jerusalem. After earning his Ph.D. in sociology from the University of California, Berkeley, in 1958, he taught at Columbia (1958–1980); he has been University Professor at George Washington University since 1980. He has served as Director of the Center for Policy Research since 1968.

*Etzioni is the author of many books and articles on subjects ranging from the space race (*Moon-Doggle: Domestic and International Implications of the Space Race, 1964) to the ethical implications of the science of genetics (*Genetic Fix, 1973). His primary field of interest, however, is organizational analysis: how organizations function, change, survive, combine. His recent publications include* An Immodest Agenda *(1982) and* Capital Corruption: An Assault on American Democracy *(1984). The article reprinted here appeared in the October 1977 issue of* Psychology Today.*

The viewpoint, now gaining momentum, that would allow individuals to "make up their own minds" about smoking, air bags, safety helmets, Laetrile, and the like ignores some elementary social realities. The ill-informed nature of this viewpoint is camouflaged by the appeal to values that are dear to most Americans. The essence of the argument is that what individuals wish to do with their lives and limbs, foolhardy though it might be, is their own business, and that any interference would abridge their rights.

Mr. Gene Wirwahn, the legislative director of the American Motorcyclist Association, which is lobbying against laws requiring riders to wear helmets, put it squarely: "The issue that we're speaking about is not the voluntary use of helmets. It's the question of whether or not there should be laws telling people to wear them." State representative Anne Miller, a liberal Democrat in Illinois, favors legalization of Laetrile. She explains that she is aware that this apricot-pit extract is useless, but insists that "the government shouldn't protect people from bad judgment. They might as well bar holy water."

U.S. representative Louis Wyman recently invoked much the same argument in leading the brigade that won adoption in the House of a resolution making seat belts voluntary. The 1974-model cars had been engineered not to start unless the seat belt was buckled. Wyman, a New Hampshire Republican, called the buckle-up system un-American, saying it made the government a Big Brother to auto drivers. Representative Abraham Kazen, Texas Democrat, summed it all up: "It is wrong to tell the individual what is good for him. . . . These are some of the things that the American people want to judge for themselves. Give them the equipment if they so desire, *and if they do not, let them do whatever they want.*"

No civil society can survive if it permits each person to maximize his or her freedoms without concern for the consequences of one's act on others. If I choose to drive without a seat belt or air bag, I am greatly increasing my chances, in case of accident, of being impaled on the steering wheel or exiting via the windshield. It is not just my body that is jeopardized; my careening auto, which I cannot get back under control, will be more likely to injure people in other autos, pedestrians, or riders in my car. (Yes, my passengers choose their own fate when they decide to ride with me, but what about the infants who are killed and injured because they are not properly protected?)

American institutions were fashioned in an era of vast unoccupied spaces and preindustrial technology. In those days, collisions between public needs and individual rights may have been minimal. But increased density, scarcity of resources, and interlocking technologies have now heightened the concern for "public goods," which belong to no one in particular but to all of us jointly. Polluting a lake or river or the air may not directly damage any one person's private property or living space. But it destroys a good that all of us—including future generations—benefit from and have a title to. Our public goods are entitled to a measure of protection.

The individual who chooses to act irresponsibly is playing a game of heads I win, tails the public loses. All too often, the unbelted drivers, the smokers, the unvaccinated, the users of quack remedies, draw on public funds to pay for the consequences of their unrestrained freedom of choice. Their rugged individualism rapidly becomes dependency when cancer strikes, or when the car overturns, sending the occupants to hospitals for treatment paid for at least in part by the public, through subsidies for hospitals and medical training. But the public till is not bottomless, and paying for these irresponsible acts leaves other public needs without funds.

True, totalitarian regimes often defend their invasions of individual liberties by citing public need or "national interest." One difference is that they are less concerned with protecting public goods than they are with building national power or new world orders. Instead of insisting on protection for *some* public rights, such regimes seek to put the national interest above all individual rights. The lesson is that we must not allow any claim of public or national need to go unexplained. But at the same time, we cannot allow simple-minded sloganeering (from "creeping Communism" to "Big Brother") to blind us to the fact that there are needs all of us share as a community.

Last but not least, we must face the truth about ourselves. Are we the independent, self-reliant individuals the politicians like to tell us we are? Or are we a human combination of urges and self-controls, impulses and rational judgments? Can we trust ourselves to make wise judgments routinely, or do we at times have to rely on the laws our elected representatives have fashioned, with our consent, to help guide us? The fact is that driving slowly saves lives, lots of lives; but until we are *required* to do so, most of us drive too fast. The same holds true for buckling our seat belts, buying air bags, and so on. Similarly, we need protection from quack cures. It sounds very libertarian to argue that each person can make up his or her own mind about Laetrile. But the fact is that when confronted with cancer and fearful of surgery, thousands of Americans are tempted to try a "painless medication" first, often delaying surgery until it is too late.

All in all, it is high time the oversimplifications about individual freedom versus Big Brother government were replaced by a social philosophy that calls for a balance among the rights of *various* individuals, between individual rights and *some* public rights, and that acknowledges the support we fallible individuals need from the law.

On Civil Disobedience

All the pieces in this section deal with the direct personal conflict between individual conscience and social law. When, if ever, is civil disobedience justified? For some people, civil disobedience is by definition immoral, especially in a democracy where law is adjustable. We voluntarily relinquish some of our freedom and accept the necessity and authority of the law in order to protect the community and guard against anarchy. Defiance, then, strikes not only at specific laws but also at the concept of law and order—and thus at the system itself. This is the argument that Plato presents so forcefully in the *Crito;* it is also the prime concern of Lewis H. Van Dusen, Jr., who contends that "the disobedient act of conscience does not ennoble democracy; it erodes it."

For others, the opposite is true: nonviolent civil disobedience is not only justified but becomes a moral means to protest unjust laws and thus preserve democracy. For Henry David Thoreau, a dedicated individualist, and Martin Luther King, Jr., an eloquent spokesman for civil and human rights, individual conscience and not the state is sovereign in matters of morality. In reading the above arguments, the reader may wish to consider a paradox pointed out by George Orwell in an essay on Gandhi: that modern civil disobedience can be effective only in a democratic community. "It is difficult to see," wrote Orwell, "how Gandhi's methods [passive resistance] could be applied in a country where opponents to the regime disappear in the middle of the night and are never heard of again. Without a free press and the right of assembly, it is impossible not merely to appeal to outside opinion, but to bring a mass movement into being, or even to make your intentions known to your adversary."

In the last selection, Wendell Berry describes a mild act of civil disobedience at the site of a nuclear power plant, and reintroduces an old idea in a new context: that "it is futile to attempt to correct a public wrong without correcting the sources of that wrong in yourself."

from the *Crito*

Plato

Plato, one of the greatest philosophers of the Western world, was born in Athens. Originally named Aristocles, he was surnamed Plato because of his broad shoulders, or—as some would have it—his broad forehead. Early in his life he became a student of Socrates, and his subsequent writings are evidence of the profound influence his teacher had on him. After Socrates' trial, conviction, and death in 399 B.C., Plato spent thirteen years away from Athens, in Italy, Egypt, and parts of Greece. He returned in 386 B.C. and founded the Academy, in which he taught until his death in 347 B.C. Aristotle was his student. Plato's extant works are in the form of conversations, or dialogues, in which the leading speaker is usually Socrates. Perhaps the best known of the dialogues is the Republic, *in which Socrates explores the nature of the ideal state. Plato records the last days of Socrates in three early dialogues, the* Apology, *the* Crito, *and the* Phaedo. *The* Apology *presents Socrates' defense at his trial on charges of corrupting youth and believing in gods other than the state's divinities. The* Phaedo *records Socrates' last conversation before death. In the* Crito, *Crito visits Socrates in prison and tries to persuade him to escape. We print below, from the Jowett translation, third edition, Socrates' argument for submitting to the death penalty that the law had imposed on him.*

Socrates   ... Ought a man to do what he admits to be right, or ought he to betray the right?

Crito   He ought to do what he thinks right.

Soc.   But if this is true, what is the application? In leaving the prison against the will of the Athenians, do I wrong any? or rather do I not wrong those whom I ought least to wrong? Do I not desert the principles which were acknowledged by us to be just—what do you say?

Cr.   I cannot tell, Socrates; for I do not know.

Soc.   Then consider the matter in this way:—Imagine that I am about to play truant (you may call the proceeding by any name which you like), and the laws and the government come and interrogate me:

'Tell us, Socrates,' they say; 'what are you about? are you not going by an act of yours to overturn us—the laws, and the whole state, as far as in you lies? Do you imagine that a state can subsist and not be overthrown, in which the decisions of law have no power, but are set aside and trampled upon by individuals?' What will be our answer, Crito, to these and the like words? Any one, and especially a rhetorician, will have a good deal to say on behalf of the law which requires a sentence to be carried out. He will argue that this law should not be set aside; and shall we reply, 'Yes; but the state has injured us and given an unjust sentence.' Suppose I say that?

Cr. Very good, Socrates.

Soc. 'And was that our agreement with you?' the law would answer; 'or were you to abide by the sentence of the state?' And if I were to express my astonishment at their words, the law would probably add: 'Answer, Socrates, instead of opening your eyes—you are in the habit of asking and answering questions. Tell us,—What complaint have you to make against us which justifies you in attempting to destroy us and the state? In the first place did we not bring you into existence? Your father married your mother by our aid and begat you. Say whether you have any objection to urge against those of us who regulate marriage?' None, I should reply, 'Or against those of us who after birth regulate the nurture and education of children, in which you also were trained? Were not the laws, which have the charge of education, right in commanding your father to train you in music and gymnastic?' Right, I should reply. 'Well then, since you were brought into the world and nurtured and educated by us, can you deny in the first place that you are our child and slave, as your fathers were before you? And if this is true you are not on equal terms with us; nor can you think that you have a right to do to us what we are doing to you. Would you have any right to strike or revile or do any other evil to your father or your master, if you had one, because you have been struck or reviled by him, or received some other evil at his hands?—you would not say this? And because we think right to destroy you, do you think that you have any right to destroy us in return, and your country as far as in you lies? Will you, O professor of true virtue, pretend that you are justified in this? Has a philosopher like you failed to discover that our country is more to be valued and higher and holier far than mother or father or any ancestor, and more to be regarded in the eyes of the gods and of men of understanding? Also to be soothed, and gently and reverently entreated when angry, even more than a father, and either to be persuaded, or if not persuaded, to be obeyed? And when we are punished by her, whether with imprisonment or stripes, the punishment is to be endured in silence; and if she leads us to wounds or death in battle, thither we follow as is right; neither may any one yield or retreat or leave his rank, but whether in battle or in a court of law, or in any other place, he must do what his city and his country order him; or he must change their view of what is just: and if he may do no violence to his father or mother, much less may he do violence to his country.' What answer shall we make to this, Crito? Do the laws speak truly, or do they not?

Cr. I think that they do.

Soc. Then the laws will say, 'Consider, Socrates, if we are speaking truly that in your present attempt you are going to do us an injury. For, having brought you into the world, and nurtured and educated you, and given you and every other citizen a share in every good which we had to give, we further proclaim to any Athenian by the liberty which we allow him, that if he does not like us when he has become of age and has seen the ways of the city, and made our acquaintance, he may go where he pleases and take his goods with him. None of us laws will forbid him or interfere with him. Any one who does not like us and the city, and who wants to emigrate to a colony or to any other city, may go where he likes, retaining his property. But he who has experience of the manner in which we order justice and administer the state, and still remains, has entered into an implied contract that he will do as we command him. And he who disobeys us is, as we maintain, thrice wrong; first, because in disobeying us he is disobeying his parents; secondly, because we are the authors of his education; thirdly, because he has made an agreement with us that he will duly obey our commands; and he neither obeys them nor convinces us that our commands are unjust; and we do not rudely impose them, but give him the alternative of obeying or convincing us;—that is what we offer, and he does neither.

'These are the sort of accusations to which, as we were saying, you, Socrates, will be exposed if you accomplish your intentions; you, above all other Athenians.' Suppose now I ask, why I rather than anybody else? they will justly retort upon me that I above all other men have acknowledged the agreement. 'There is clear proof,' they will say, 'Socrates, that we and the city were not displeasing to you. Of all Athenians you have been the most constant resident in the city, which, as you never leave, you may be supposed to love. For you never went out of the city either to see the games, except once when you went to the Isthmus, or to any other place unless when you were on military service; nor did you travel as other men do. Nor had you the curiosity to know other states or their laws: your affections did not go beyond us and our state; we were your special favourites, and you acquiesced in our government of you; and here in this city you begat your children, which is a proof of your satisfaction. Moreover, you might in the course of the trial, if you had liked, have fixed the penalty at banishment; the state which refuses to let you go now would have let you go then. But you pretended that you preferred death to exile, and that you were not unwilling to die. And now you have forgotten these fine sentiments, and pay no respect to us the laws, of whom you are the destroyer; and are doing what only a miserable slave would do, running away and turning your back upon the compacts and agreements which you made as a citizen. And first of all answer this very question: Are we right in saying that you agreed to be governed according to us in deed, and not in word only? Is that true or not?' How shall we answer, Crito? Must we not assent?

Cr. We cannot help it, Socrates.

Soc. Then will they not say: 'You, Socrates, are breaking the covenants and agreements which you made with us at your leisure, not in any haste or under any compulsion or deception, but after you have had seventy years to think of them, during which time you were at liberty to leave the city, if we were not to your mind, or if our covenants appeared to you to be unfair. You had your choice, and might have gone either to Lacedaemon or Crete, both which states are often praised by you for their good government, or to some other Hellenic or foreign state. Whereas you, above all other Athenians, seemed to be so fond of the state, or, in other words, of us her laws (and who would care about a state which has no laws?), that you never stirred out of her; the halt, the blind, the maimed were not more stationary in her than you were. And now you run away and forsake your agreements. Not so, Socrates, if you will take our advice; do not make yourself ridiculous by escaping out of the city.

'For just consider, if you transgress and err in this sort of way, what good will you do either to yourself or to your friends? That your friends will be driven into exile and deprived of citizenship, or will lose their property, is tolerably certain; and you yourself, if you fly to one of the neighboring cities, as, for example, Thebes or Megara, both of which are well governed, will come to them as an enemy, Socrates, and their government will be against you, and all patriotic citizens will cast an evil eye upon you as a subverter of the laws, and you will confirm in the minds of the judges the justice of their own condemnation of you. For he who is a corrupter of the laws is more than likely to be a corrupter of the young and foolish portion of mankind. Will you then flee from well-ordered cities and virtuous men? and is existence worth having on these terms? Or will you go to them without shame, and talk to them, Socrates? And what will you say to them? What you say here about virtue and justice and institutions and laws being the best things among men? Would that be decent of you? Surely not. But if you go away from well-governed states to Crito's friends in Thessaly, where there is great disorder and licence, they will be charmed to hear the tale of your escape from prison, set off with ludicrous particulars of the manner in which you were wrapped in a goatskin or some other disguise, and metamorphosed as the manner is of runaways; but will there be no one to remind you that in your old age you were not ashamed to violate the most sacred laws from a miserable desire of a little more life? Perhaps not, if you keep them in a good temper; but if they are out of temper you will hear many degrading things; you will live, but how?—as the flatterer of all men, and the servant of all men; and doing what?—eating and drinking in Thessaly, having gone abroad in order that you may get a dinner. And where will be your fine sentiments about justice and virtue? Say that you wish to live for the sake of your children—you want to bring them up and educate them—will you take them into Thessaly and deprive them of Athenian citizenship? Is this the benefit which you will confer upon them? Or are you under the impression that they will be better cared for and educated here if you are still alive, although absent from them; for your friends will take care of them? Do you fancy that if you are an inhabitant of Thessaly they will take care of them, and if you are an inhabitant of the other world that they will not take care of them? Nay; but if they who call themselves friends are good for anything, they will—to be sure they will.

'Listen, then, Socrates, to us who have brought you up. Think not of life and children first, and of justice afterwards, but of justice first, that you may be justified before the princes of the world below. For neither will you nor any that belong to you be happier or holier or juster in this life, or happier in another, if you do as Crito bids. Now you depart in innocence, a sufferer and not a doer of evil; a victim, not of the laws but of men. But if you go forth, returning evil for evil, and injury for injury, breaking the covenants and agreements which you have made with us, and wronging those whom you ought least of all to wrong, that is to say, yourself, your friends, your country, and us, we shall be angry with you while you live, and our brethren, the laws in the world below, will receive you as an enemy; for they will know that you have done your best to destroy us. Listen, then, to us and not to Crito.'

This, dear Crito, is the voice which I seem to hear murmuring in my ears, like the sound of the flute in the ears of the mystic; that voice, I say, is humming in my ears, and prevents me from hearing any other. And I know that anything more which you may say will be vain. Yet speak, if you have anything to say.

Cr. I have nothing to say, Socrates.

Soc. Leave me then, Crito, to fulfill the will of God, and to follow whither he leads.

Civil Disobedience: Destroyer of Democracy

Lewis H. Van Dusen, Jr.

Lewis H. Van Dusen, Jr., born in Philadelphia in 1910, has been practicing law there since 1935. He was educated at Princeton (B.A. 1932), Harvard Law School (1932–1933), and, as a Rhodes Scholar, at Oxford (B.C.L. 1935). He served in the U.S. Army with great distinction during World War II; among his honors are the croix de guerre *with palm and the* Légion d'honneur *(both awarded by France), and the U.S. Legion of Merit. From*

1950 to 1952 he was a minister in London for the U.S. Department of State, and in 1954 he headed a mission to evaluate the U.S. foreign aid program in Brazil. He has contributed numerous articles to professional journals, one of them the piece reprinted below from the February 1969 issue of the American Bar Association Journal. *Van Dusen characterizes Henry David Thoreau's rejection of normal modes of legislative reform as "not only morally irresponsible but politically reprehensible." Writing at the end of a decade noted for "civil disobedience," this criticism may startle those accustomed to viewing Thoreau as a model of the American independent spirit. The essay requires its readers to consider some of the anti-democratic implications of what is often presented as a high-minded, and even perhaps romantic, act.*

As Charles E. Wyzanski, Chief Judge of the United States District Court in Boston, wrote in the February, 1968, *Atlantic:* "Disobedience is a long step from dissent. Civil disobedience involves a deliberate and punishable breach of legal duty." Protesters might prefer a different definition. They would rather say that civil disobedience is the peaceable resistance of conscience.

The philosophy of civil disobedience was not developed in our American democracy, but in the very first democracy of Athens. It was expressed by the poet Sophocles and the philosopher Socrates. In Sophocles's tragedy, Antigone chose to obey her conscience and violate the state edict against providing burial for her brother, who had been decreed a traitor. When the dictator Creon found out that Antigone had buried her fallen brother, he confronted her and reminded her that there was a mandatory death penalty for this deliberate disobedience of the state law. Antigone nobly replied, "Nor did I think your orders were so strong that you, a mortal man, could overrun the gods' unwritten and unfailing laws."

Conscience motivated Antigone. She was not testing the validity of the law in the hope that eventually she would be sustained. Appealing to the judgment of the community, she explained her action to the chorus. She was not secret and surreptitious—the interment of her brother was open and public. She was not violent; she did not trespass on another citizen's rights. And finally, she accepted without resistance the death sentence—the penalty for violation. By voluntarily accepting the law's sanctions, she was not a revolutionary denying the authority of the state. Antigone's behavior exemplifies the classic case of civil disobedience.

Socrates believed that reason could dictate a conscientious disobedience of state law, but he also believed that he had to accept the legal sanctions of the state. In Plato's *Crito,* Socrates from his hanging basket accepted the death penalty for his teaching of religion to youths contrary to state laws.

The sage of Walden, Henry David Thoreau, took this philosophy of nonviolence and developed it into a strategy for solving society's injustices. First enunciating it in protest against the Mexican War, he then turned it to use against slavery. For refusing to pay taxes that would help pay the enforcers of the fugitive slave law, he went to prison. In Thoreau's words, "If the alternative is to keep all just men in prison or to give up slavery, the state will not hesitate which to choose."

Sixty years later, Gandhi took Thoreau's civil disobedience as his strategy to wrest Indian independence from England. The famous salt march against a British imperial tax is his best-known example of protest.

But the conscientious law breaking of Socrates, Gandhi and Thoreau is to be distinguished from the conscientious law testing of Martin Luther King, Jr., who was not a civil disobedient. The civil disobedient withholds taxes or violates state laws knowing he is legally wrong, but believing he is morally right. While he wrapped himself in the mantle of Gandhi and Thoreau, Dr. King led his followers in violation of state laws he believed were contrary to the Federal Constitution. But since Supreme Court decisions in the end generally upheld his many actions, he should not be considered a true civil disobedient.

The civil disobedience of Antigone is like that of the pacifist who withholds paying the percentage of his taxes that goes to the Defense Department, or the Quaker who travels against State Department regulations to Hanoi to distribute medical supplies, or the Vietnam war protester who tears up his draft card. This civil disobedient has been nonviolent in his defiance of the law; he has been unfurtive in his violation; he has been submissive to the penalties of the law. He has neither evaded the law nor interfered with another's rights. He has been neither a rioter nor a revolutionary. The thrust of his cause has not been the might of coercion but the martyrdom of conscience.

Was the Boston Tea Party Civil Disobedience?

Those who justify violence and radical action as being in the tradition of our Revolution show a misunderstanding of the philosophy of democracy.

James Farmer, former head of the Congress of Racial Equality, in defense of the mass action confrontation method, has told of a famous organized demonstration that took place in opposition to political and economic discrimination. The protesters beat back and scattered the law enforcers and then proceeded to loot and destroy private property. Mr. Farmer then said he was talking about the Boston Tea Party and implied that violence as a method for redress of grievances was an American tradition and a legacy of our revolutionary heritage. While it is true that there is no more sacred document than our Declaration of Independence, Jefferson's "inherent right of rebellion" was predicated on the tyrannical denial of democratic means. If there is no popular assembly to provide an adjustment of ills, and if there is no court system to dispose of injustices, then there is, indeed, a right to rebel.

The seventeenth century's John Locke, the philosophical father of the

Declaration of Independence, wrote in his *Second Treatise on Civil Government:* "Wherever law ends, tyranny begins . . . and the people are absolved from any further obedience. Governments are dissolved from within when the legislative [chamber] is altered. When the government [becomes] . . . arbitrary disposers of lives, liberties and fortunes of the people, such revolutions happen. . . ."

But there are some sophisticated proponents of the revolutionary redress of grievances who say that the test of the need for radical action is not the unavailability of democratic institutions but the ineffectuality of those institutions to remove blatant social inequalities. If social injustice exists, they say, concerted disobedience is required against the constituted government, whether it be totalitarian or democratic in structure.

Of course, only the most bigoted chauvinist would claim that America is without some glaring faults. But there has never been a utopian society on earth and there never will be unless human nature is remade. Since inequities will mar even the best-framed democracies, the injustice rationale would allow a free right of civil resistance to be available always as a shortcut alternative to the democratic way of petition, debate and assembly. The lesson of history is that civil insurgency spawns far more injustices than it removes. The Jeffersons, Washingtons and Adamses resisted tyranny with the aim of promoting the procedures of democracy. They would never have resisted a democratic government with the risk of promoting the techniques of tyranny.

Legitimate Pressures and Illegitimate Results

There are many civil rights leaders who show impatience with the process of democracy. They rely on the sit-in, boycott or mass picketing to gain speedier solutions to the problems that face every citizen. But we must realize that the legitimate pressures that won concessions in the past can easily escalate into the illegitimate power plays that might extort demands in the future. The victories of these civil rights leaders must not shake our confidence in the democratic procedures, as the pressures of demonstration are desirable only if they take place within the limits allowed by law. Civil rights gains should continue to be won by the persuasion of Congress and other legislative bodies and by the decision of courts. Any illegal entreaty for the rights of some can be an injury to the rights of others, for mass demonstrations often trigger violence.

Those who advocate taking the law into their own hands should reflect that when they are disobeying what they consider to be an immoral law, they are deciding on a possibly immoral course. Their answer is that the process for democratic relief is too slow, that only mass confrontation can bring immediate action, and that any injuries are the inevitable cost of the pursuit of justice. Their answer is, simply put, that the end justifies the means. It is this justification of any form of demonstration as a form of dissent that threatens to destroy a society built on the rule of law.

Our Bill of Rights guarantees wide opportunities to use mass meetings, public parades and organized demonstrations to stimulate sentiment, to dramatize issues and to cause change. The Washington freedom march of 1963 was such a call for action. But the rights of free expression cannot be mere force cloaked in the garb of free speech. As the courts have decreed in labor cases, free assembly does not mean mass picketing or sit-down strikes. These rights are subject to limitations of time and place so as to secure the rights of others. When militant students storm a college president's office to achieve demands, when certain groups plan rush-hour car stalling to protest discrimination in employment, these are not dissent, but a denial of rights to others. Neither is it the lawful use of mass protest, but rather the unlawful use of mob power.

Justice Black, one of the foremost advocates and defenders of the right of protest and dissent, has said:

> . . . Experience demonstrates that it is not a far step from what to many seems to be the earnest, honest, patriotic, kind-spirited multitude of today, to the fanatical, threatening, lawless mob of tomorrow. And the crowds that press in the streets for noble goals today can be supplanted tomorrow by street mobs pressuring the courts for precisely opposite ends.[1]

Society must censure those demonstrators who would trespass on the public peace, as it must condemn those rioters whose pillage would destroy the public peace. But more ambivalent is society's posture toward the civil disobedient. Unlike the rioter, the true civil disobedient commits no violence. Unlike the mob demonstrator, he commits no trespass on others' rights. The civil disobedient, while deliberately violating a law, shows an oblique respect for the law by voluntarily submitting to its sanctions. He neither resists arrest nor evades punishment. Thus, he breaches the law but not the peace.

But civil disobedience, whatever the ethical rationalization, is still an assault on our democratic society, an affront to our legal order and an attack on our constitutional government. To indulge civil disobedience is to invite anarchy, and the permissive arbitrariness of anarchy is hardly less tolerable than the repressive arbitrariness of tyranny. Too often the license of liberty is followed by the loss of liberty, because into the desert of anarchy comes the man on horseback, a Mussolini or a Hitler.

Violations of Law Subvert Democracy

Law violations, even for ends recognized as laudable, are not only assaults on the rule of law, but subversions of the democratic process. The disobedient act of conscience does not ennoble democracy; it erodes it.

---

[1]Dissenting in *Cox* v. *Louisiana,* 379 U. S. 536, 575, 584 (1965).

First, it courts violence, and even the most careful and limited use of nonviolent acts of disobedience may help sow the dragon-teeth of civil riot. Civil disobedience is the progenitor of disorder, and disorder is the sire of violence.

Second, the concept of civil disobedience does not invite principles of general applicability. If the children of light are morally privileged to resist particular laws on grounds of conscience, so are the children of darkness. Former Deputy Attorney General Burke Marshall said: "If the decision to break the law really turned on individual conscience, it is hard to see in law how [the civil rights leader] is better off than former Governor Ross Barnett of Mississippi who also believed deeply in his cause and was willing to go to jail."[2]

Third, even the most noble act of civil disobedience assaults the rule of law. Although limited as to method, motive and objective, it has the effect of inducing others to engage in different forms of law breaking characterized by methods unsanctioned and condemned by classic theories of law violation. Unfortunately, the most patent lesson of civil disobedience is not so much nonviolence of action as defiance of authority.

Finally, the greatest danger in condoning civil disobedience as a permissible strategy for hastening change is that it undermines our democratic processes. To adopt the techniques of civil disobedience is to assume that representative government does not work. To resist the decisions of courts and the laws of elected assemblies is to say that democracy has failed.

There is no man who is above the law, and there is no man who has a right to break the law. Civil disobedience is not above the law, but against the law. When the civil disobedient disobeys one law, he invariably subverts all law. When the civil disobedient says that he is above the law, he is saying that democracy is beneath him. His disobedience shows a distrust for the democratic system. He is merely saying that since democracy does not work, why should he help make it work. Thoreau expressed well the civil disobedient's disdain for democracy:

> As for adopting the ways which the state has provided for remedying the evil, I know not of such ways. They take too much time and a man's life will be gone. I have other affairs to attend to. I came into this world not chiefly to make this a good place to live in, but to live in it, be it good or bad.[3]

Thoreau's position is not only morally irresponsible but politically reprehensible. When citizens in a democracy are called on to make a profession of faith, the civil disobedients offer only a confession of failure. Tragically, when civil disobedients for lack of faith abstain from democratic involvement, they help attain their own gloomy prediction. They help create the social and political basis for their own despair. By foresee-

---

[2] *The Protest Movement and the Law,* 51 VA. L. REV. 785 (1965).

[3] Thoreau, *Essay on Civil Disobedience,* in PEOPLE, PRINCIPLES AND POLITICS (Meltzer ed. 1963).

ing failure, they help forge it. If citizens rely on antidemocratic means of protest, they will help bring about the undemocratic result of an authoritarian or anarchic state.

How far demonstrations properly can be employed to produce political and social change is a pressing question, particularly in view of the provocations accompanying the National Democratic Convention in Chicago last August and the reaction of the police to them. A line must be drawn by the judiciary between the demands of those who seek absolute order, which can lead only to a dictatorship, and those who seek absolute freedom, which can lead only to anarchy. The line, wherever it is drawn by our courts, should be respected on the college campus, on the streets and elsewhere.

Undue provocation will inevitably result in overreaction, human emotions being what they are. Violence will follow. This cycle undermines the very democracy it is designed to preserve. The lesson of the past is that democracies will fall if violence, including the intentional provocations that will lead to violence, replaces democratic procedures, as in Athens, Rome and the Weimar Republic. This lesson must be constantly explained by the legal profession.

We should heed the words of William James:

> Democracy is still upon its trial. The civic genius of our people is its only bulwark and . . . neither battleships nor public libraries nor great newspapers nor booming stocks: neither mechanical invention nor political adroitness, nor churches nor universities nor civil service examinations can save us from degeneration if the inner mystery be lost.
>
> That mystery, at once the secret and the glory of our English-speaking race, consists of nothing but two habits . . . [O]ne of them is the habit of trained and disciplined good temper towards the opposite party when it fairly wins its innings. The other is that of fierce and merciless resentment toward every man or set of men who break the public peace.[4]

Civil Disobedience

Henry David Thoreau

A social rebel with high principles, a man who loved nature and solitude, Henry David Thoreau is considered by some a memorable individualist, by others a perennial adolescent, and by still others as both. E. B. White has called him a "regular hairshirt of a man." Born in Concord, Massachusetts, in 1817, he was educated at Harvard and after graduation returned to Concord where he first taught school and on later occasions supported

---

[4] JAMES, PRAGMATISM 127–128 (1907).

himself by making pencils. He became a friend of Emerson, who was at the time leader of Concord's intellectual and spiritual life; he joined the Transcendental Club and contributed frequently to its journal, The Dial. *Some have said that Thoreau was the answer to Emerson's plea for an American Scholar. From July 4, 1845, to September 6, 1847, Thoreau lived in a hut at nearby Walden Pond, an experience that he recorded in his most famous work,* Walden. *His stay there was interrupted for one day in the summer of 1846 when he was arrested for not paying the Massachusetts poll tax. He explained his refusal as an act of protest against a government that sanctioned the Mexican War, a war he considered in the interests of Southern slaveholders; he later wrote an eloquent defense of civil disobedience, which was first published in 1849. This essay, which has become an American classic, is reprinted in full below; the text is that of the Riverside edition of Thoreau's works.*

I heartily accept the motto,—"That government is best which governs least;" and I should like to see it acted up to more rapidly and systematically. Carried out, it finally amounts to this, which also I believe,—"That government is best which governs not at all;" and when men are prepared for it, that will be the kind of government which they will have. Government is at best but an expedient; but most governments are usually, and all governments are sometimes, inexpedient. The objections which have been brought against a standing army, and they are many and weighty, and deserve to prevail, may also at last be brought against a standing government. The standing army is only an arm of the standing government. The government itself, which is only the mode which the people have chosen to execute their will, is equally liable to be abused and perverted before the people can act through it. Witness the present Mexican war,° the work of comparatively a few individuals using the standing government as their tool; for, in the outset, the people would not have consented to this measure.

This American Government,—what is it but a tradition, though a recent one, endeavoring to transmit itself unimpaired to posterity, but each instant losing some of its integrity? It has not the vitality and force of a single living man; for a single man can bend it to his will. It is a sort of wooden gun to the people themselves. But it is not the less necessary for this; for the people must have some complicated machinery or other, and hear its din, to satisfy that idea of government which they have. Governments show thus how successfully men can be imposed on, even impose on themselves, for their own advantage. It is excellent, we must all allow. Yet this government never of itself furthered any enterprise, but by the alacrity with which it got out of its way. *It* does not keep the country free.

---

present Mexican war Mexican War (1846–1848), a conflict between Mexico and the United States, caused by the annexation of Texas by the United States in December 1845.

It didn't do this man alone did.

It does not settle the West. *It* does not educate. The character inherent in the American people has done all that has been accomplished; and it would have done somewhat more, if the government had not sometimes got in its way. For government is an expedient by which men would fain succeed in letting one another alone; and, as has been said, when it is most expedient, the governed are most let alone by it. Trade and commerce, if they were not made of India-rubber, would never manage to bounce over the obstacles which legislators are continually putting in their way; and, if one were to judge these men wholly by the effects of their actions and not partly by their intentions, they would deserve to be classed and punished with those mischievous persons who put obstructions on the railroads.

His opinion every man make known

But, to speak practically and as a citizen, unlike those who call themselves no-government men, I ask for, not at once no government, but *at once* a better government. Let every man make known what kind of government would command his respect, and that will be one step toward obtaining it.

After all, the practical reason why, when the power is once in the hands of the people, a majority are permitted, and for a long period continue, to rule is not because they are most likely to be in the right, nor because this seems fairest to the minority, but because they are physically the strongest. But a government in which the majority rule in all cases cannot be based on justice, even as far as men understand it. Can there not be a government in which majorities do not virtually decide right and wrong, but conscience?—in which majorities decide only those questions to which the rule of expediency is applicable? Must the citizen ever for a moment, or in the least degree, resign his conscience to the legislator? Why has every man a conscience, then? I think that we should be men first, and subjects afterward. It is not desirable to cultivate a respect for the law, so much as for the right. The only obligation which I have a right to assume is to do at any time what I think right. It is truly enough said, that a corporation has no conscience; but a corporation of conscientious men is a corporation *with* a conscience. Law never made men a whit more just; and, by means of their respect for it, even the well-disposed are daily made the agents of injustice. A common and natural result of any undue respect for law is, that you may see a file of soldiers, colonel, captain, corporal, privates, powder-monkeys, and all, marching in admirable order over hill and dale to the wars, against their wills, ay, against their common sense and consciences, which makes it very steep marching indeed, and produces a palpitation of the heart. They have no doubt that it is a damnable business in which they are concerned; they are all peaceably inclined. Now, what are they? Men at all? or small movable forts and magazines, at the service of some unscrupulous man in power? Visit the Navy-Yard, and behold a marine, such a man as an American government can make, or such as it can make a man with its black arts,—a mere shadow and reminiscence of humanity, a man laid out alive and standing, and already, as one may say, buried under arms with funeral accompaniments, though it may be,—

> "Not a drum was heard, not a funeral note,
>   As his corse to the rampart we hurried;
> Not a soldier discharged his farewell shot
>   O'er the grave where our hero we buried."°

The mass of men serve the state thus, not as men mainly, but as machines, with their bodies. They are the standing army, and the militia, jailers, constables, posse comitatus, etc. In most cases there is no free exercise whatever of the judgment or of the moral sense; but they put themselves on a level with wood and earth and stones; and wooden men can perhaps be manufactured that will serve the purpose as well. Such command no more respect than men of straw or a lump of dirt. They have the same sort of worth only as horses and dogs. Yet such as these even are commonly esteemed good citizens. Others—as most legislators, politicians, lawyers, ministers, and office-holders—serve the state chiefly with their heads; and, as they rarely make any moral distinctions, they are as likely to serve the Devil, without *intending* it, as God. A very few, as heroes, patriots, martyrs, reformers in the great sense, and *men*, serve the state with their consciences also, and so necessarily resist it for the most part; and they are commonly treated as enemies by it. A wise man will only be useful as a man, and will not submit to be "clay," and "stop a hole to keep the wind away,"° but leave that office to his dust at least:—

> "I am too high-born to be propertied,
> To be a secondary at control,
> Or useful serving-man and instrument
> To any sovereign state throughout the world."°

He who gives himself entirely to his fellow-men appears to them useless and selfish; but he who gives himself partially to them is pronounced a benefactor and philanthropist.

How does it become a man to behave toward this American government to-day? I answer, that he cannot without disgrace be associated with it. I cannot for an instant recognize that political organization as *my* government which is the *slave's* government also.

All men recognize the right of revolution; that is, the right to refuse allegiance to, and to resist, the government, when its tyranny or its inefficiency are great and unendurable. But almost all say that such is not

---

"Not a drum was heard . . ." From "The Burial of Sir John Moore at Corunna," by the Irish poet Charles Wolfe.
"clay" and "stop a hole . . ." From *Hamlet* (Act V, scene i) by William Shakespeare.
"I am too high-born . . ." From *King John* (Act V, scene ii) by William Shakespeare.

the case now. But such was the case, they think, in the Revolution of '75. If one were to tell me that this was a bad government because it taxed certain foreign commodities brought to its ports, it is most probable that I should not make an ado about it, for I can do without them. All machines have their friction; and possibly this does enough good to counterbalance the evil. At any rate, it is a great evil to make a stir about it. But when the friction comes to have its machine, and oppression and robbery are organized, I say, let us not have such a machine any longer. In other words, when a sixth of the population of a nation which has undertaken to be the refuge of liberty are slaves, and a whole country is unjustly overrun and conquered by a foreign army, and subjected to military law, I think that it is not too soon for honest men to rebel and revolutionize. What makes this duty the more urgent is the fact that the country so overrun is not our own, but ours is the invading army.

Paley,[o] a common authority with many on moral questions, in his chapter on the "Duty of Submission to Civil Government," resolves all civil obligation into expediency; and he proceeds to say, "that so long as the interest of the whole society requires it, that is, so long as the established government cannot be resisted or changed without public inconveniency, it is the will of God that the established government be obeyed, and no longer. . . . This principle being admitted, the justice of every particular case of resistance is reduced to a computation of the quantity of the danger and grievance on the one side, and of the probability and expense of redressing it on the other." Of this, he says, every man shall judge for himself. But Paley appears never to have contemplated those cases to which the rule of expediency does not apply, in which a people, as well as an individual, must do justice, cost what it may. If I have unjustly wrested a plank from a drowning man, I must restore it to him though I drown myself. This, according to Paley, would be inconvenient. But he that would save his life, in such a case, shall lose it. This people must cease to hold slaves, and to make war on Mexico, though it cost them their existence as a people.

In their practice, nations agree with Paley; but does any one think that Massachusetts does exactly what is right at the present crisis?

> "A drab of state, a cloth-o'-silver slut,
> To have her train borne up, and her soul trail in the dirt."[o]

Practically speaking, the opponents to a reform in Massachusetts are not a hundred thousand politicians at the South, but a hundred thousand merchants and farmers here, who are more interested in commerce and

---

Paley   William Paley (1743–1805), English clergyman and philospher. The reference is to a chapter in his book *Principles of Moral and Political Philosophy* (1785).
"A drab of state . . ."   From Act IV, scene IV of Cyril Tourneur's *The Revenger's Tragedy* (1607).

agriculture than they are in humanity, and are not prepared to do justice to the slave and to Mexico, *cost what it may.* I quarrel not with far-off foes, but with those who, near at home, coöperate with, and do the bidding of, —— those far away, and without whom the latter would be harmless. We are accustomed to say, that the mass of men are unprepared; but improvement is slow, because the few are not materially wiser or better than the many. It is not so important that many should be as good as you, as that there be some absolute goodness somewhere; for that will leaven the whole lump. There are thousands who are *in opinion* opposed to slavery and to the war, who yet in effect do nothing to put an end to them; who, esteeming themselves children of Washington and Franklin, sit down with their hands in their pockets, and say that they know not what to do, and do nothing; who even postpone the question of freedom to the question of free-trade, and quietly read the prices-current along with the latest advices from Mexico, after dinner, and, it may be, fall asleep over them both. What is the price-current of an honest man and patriot to-day? They hesitate, and they regret, and sometimes they petition; but they do nothing in earnest and with effect. They will wait, well disposed, for others to remedy the evil, that they may no longer have it to regret. At most, they give only a cheap vote, and a feeble countenance and Godspeed, to the right, as it goes by them. There are nine hundred and ninety-nine patrons of virtue to one virtuous man. But it is easier to deal with the real possessor of a thing than with the temporary guardian of it.

All voting is a sort of gaming, like checkers or backgammon, with a slight moral tinge to it, a playing with right and wrong, with moral questions; and betting naturally accompanies it. The character of the voters is not staked. I cast my vote, perchance, as I think right; but I am not vitally concerned that that right should prevail. I am willing to leave it to the majority. Its obligation, therefore, never exceeds that of expediency. Even voting *for the right* is *doing* nothing for it. It is only expressing to men feebly your desire that it should prevail. A wise man will not leave the right to the mercy of chance, nor wish it to prevail through the power of the majority. There is but little virtue in the action of masses of men. When the majority shall at length vote for the abolition of slavery, it will be because they are indifferent to slavery, or because there is but little slavery left to be abolished by their vote. *They* will then be the only slaves. Only *his* vote can hasten the abolition of slavery who asserts his own freedom by his vote.

I hear of a convention to be held at Baltimore, or elsewhere, for the selection of a candidate for the Presidency, made up chiefly of editors, and men who are politicians by profession; but I think, what is it to any independent, intelligent, and respectable man what decision they may come to? Shall we not have the advantage of his wisdom and honesty, nevertheless? Can we not count upon some independent votes? Are there not many individuals in the country who do not attend conventions? But

voting only for his only option choice between 2

no: I find that the respectable man, so called, has immediately drifted from his position, and despairs of his country, when his country has more reason to despair of him. He forthwith adopts one of the candidates thus selected as the only *available* one, thus proving that he is himself *available* for any purposes of the demagogue. His vote is of no more worth than that of any unprincipled foreigner or hireling native, who may have been bought. O for a man who is a *man,* and, as my neighbor says, has a bone in his back which you cannot pass your hand through! Our statistics are at fault: the population has been returned too large. How many *men* are there to a square thousand miles in this country? Hardly one. Does not America offer any inducement for men to settle here? The American has dwindled into an Odd Fellow,—one who may be known by the development of his organ of gregariousness, and a manifest lack of intellect and cheerful self-reliance; whose first and chief concern, on coming into the world, is to see that the Almshouses are in good repair; and, before yet he has lawfully donned the virile garb, to collect a fund for the support of the widows and orphans that may be; who, in short, ventures to live only by the aid of the Mutual Insurance company, which has promised to bury him decently.

It is not a man's duty, as a matter of course, to devote himself to the eradication of any, even the most enormous wrong; he may still properly have other concerns to engage him; but it is his duty, at least, to wash his hands of it, and, if he gives it no thought longer, not to give it practically his support. If I devote myself to other pursuits and contemplations, I must first see, at least, that I do not pursue them sitting upon another man's shoulders. I must get off him first, that he may pursue his contemplations too. See what gross inconsistency is tolerated. I have heard some of my townsmen say, "I should like to have them order me out to help put down an insurrection of the slaves, or to march to Mexico;—see if I would go;" and yet these very men have each, directly by their allegiance, and so indirectly, at least, by their money, furnished a substitute. The soldier is applauded who refuses to serve in an unjust war by those who do not refuse to sustain the unjust government which makes the war; is applauded by those whose own act and authority he disregards and sets at naught; as if the state were penitent to that degree that it hired one to scourge it while it sinned, but not to that degree that it left off sinning for a moment. Thus, under the name of Order and Civil Government, we are all made at last to pay homage to and support our own meanness. After the first blush of sin comes its indifference; and from immoral it becomes, as it were, *un*moral, and not quite unnecessary to that life which we have made.

The broadest and most prevalent error requires the most disinterested virtue to sustain it. The slight reproach to which the virtue of patriotism is commonly liable, the noble are most likely to incur. Those who, while they disapprove of the character and measures of a government, yield to it their allegiance and support are undoubtedly its most conscientious supporters, and so frequently the most serious obstacles to reform. Some are petitioning the state to dissolve the Union, to disregard the requisitions of the President. Why do they not dissolve it themselves,—the union between themselves and the state,—and refuse to pay their quota into its treasury? Do not they stand in the same relation to the state that the state does to the Union? And have not the same reasons prevented the state from resisting the Union which have prevented them from resisting the state?

How can a man be satisfied to entertain an opinion merely, and enjoy *it?* Is there any enjoyment in it, if his opinion is that he is aggrieved? If you are cheated out of a single dollar by your neighbor, you do not rest satisfied with knowing that you are cheated, or with saying that you are cheated, or even with petitioning him to pay you your due; but you take effectual steps at once to obtain the full amount, and see that you are never cheated again. Action from principle, the perception and the performance of right, changes things and relations; it is essentially revolutionary, and does not consist wholly with anything which was. It not only divides states and churches, it divides families; ay, it divides the *individual,* separating the diabolical in him from the divine.

Unjust laws exist: shall we be content to obey them, or shall we endeavor to amend them, and obey them until we have succeeded, or shall we transgress them at once? Men generally, under such a government as this, think that they ought to wait until they have persuaded the majority to alter them. They think that, if they should resist, the remedy would be worse than the evil. But it is the fault of the government itself that the remedy *is* worse than the evil. *It* makes it worse. Why is it not more apt to anticipate and provide for reform? Why does it not cherish its wise minority? Why does it cry and resist before it is hurt? Why does it not encourage its citizens to be on the alert to point out its faults, and *do* better than it would have them? Why does it always crucify Christ, and excommunicate Copernicus and Luther, and pronounce Washington and Franklin rebels?

One would think, that a deliberate and practical denial of its authority was the only offense never contemplated by government; else, why has it not assigned its definite, its suitable and proportionate penalty? If a man who has no property refuses but once to earn nine shillings for the state, he is put in prison for a period unlimited by any law that I know, and determined only by the discretion of those who placed him there; but if he should steal ninety times nine shillings from the state, he is soon permitted to go at large again.

If the injustice is part of the necessary friction of the machine of government, let it go, let it go: perchance it will wear smooth,—certainly the machine will wear out. If the injustice has a spring, or a pulley, or a rope, or a crank, exclusively for itself, then perhaps you may consider whether the remedy will not be worse than the evil; but if it is of such a nature that it requires you to be the agent of injustice to another, then, I say, break the law. Let your life be a counter friction to stop the machine. What I have to do is to see, at any rate, that I do not lend myself to the wrong which I condemn.

As for adopting the ways which the state has provided for remedying the evil, I know not of such ways. They take too much time, and a man's life will be gone. I have other affairs to attend to. I came into this world, not chiefly to make this a good place to live in, but to live in it, be it good or bad. A man has not everything to do, but something; and because he cannot do *everything,* it is not necessary that he should do *something* wrong. It is not my business to be petitioning the Governor or the Legislature any more than it is theirs to petition me; and if they should not hear my petition, what should I do then? But in this case the state has provided no way: its very Constitution is the evil. This may seem to be harsh and stubborn and unconciliatory; but it is to treat with the utmost kindness and consideration the only spirit that can appreciate or deserve it. So is all change for the better, like birth and death, which convulse the body.

I do not hesitate to say, that those who call themselves Abolitionists should at once effectually withdraw their support, both in person and property, from the government of Massachusetts, and not wait till they constitute a majority of one, before they suffer the right to prevail through them. I think that it is enough if they have God on their side, without waiting for that other one. Moreover, any man more right than his neighbors constitutes a majority of one already.

I meet this American government, or its representative, the state government, directly, and face to face, once a year—no more—in the person of its tax-gatherer; this is the only mode in which a man situated as I am necessarily meets it; and it then says distinctly, Recognize me; and the simplest, the most effectual, and, in the present posture of affairs, the indispensablest mode of treating with it on this head, of expressing your little satisfaction with and love for it, is to deny it then. My civil neighbor, the tax-gatherer, is the very man I have to deal with,—for it is, after all, with men and not with parchment that I quarrel,—and he has voluntarily chosen to be an agent of the government. How shall he ever know well what he is and does as an officer of the government, or as a man, until he is obliged to consider whether he shall treat me, his neighbor, for whom he has respect, as a neighbor and well-disposed man, or as a maniac and disturber of the peace, and see if he can get over this obstruction to his neighborliness without a ruder and more impetuous thought or speech corresponding with his action. I know this well, that if one thousand, if one hundred, if ten men whom I could name,—if ten *honest* men only,— say if *one* HONEST man, in this State of Massachusetts, *ceasing to hold slaves,* were actually to withdraw from this copartnership, and be locked up in the county jail therefor, it would be the abolition of slavery in

America. For it matters not how small the beginning may seem to be: what is once well done is done forever. But we love better to talk about it: that we say is our mission. Reform keeps many scores of newspapers in its service, but not one man. If my esteemed neighbor, the State's ambassador, who will devote his days to the settlement of the question of human rights in the Council Chamber, instead of being threatened with the prisons of Carolina, were to sit down the prisoner of Massachusetts, that State which is so anxious to foist the sin of slavery upon her sister,— though at present she can discover only an act of inhospitality to be the ground of a quarrel with her,—the Legislature would not wholly waive the subject the following winter.

Under a government which imprisons any unjustly, the true place for a just man is also a prison. The proper place to-day, the only place which Massachusetts has provided for her freer and less desponding spirits, is in her prisons, to be put out and locked out of the State by her own act, as they have already put themselves out by their principles. It is there that the fugitive slave, and the Mexican prisoner on parole, and the Indian come to plead the wrongs of his race should find them; on that separate, but more free and honorable ground, where the State places those who are not *with* her, but *against* her,—the only house in a slave State in which a free man can abide with honor. If any think that their influence would be lost there, and their voices no longer afflict the ear of the State, that they would not be as an enemy within its walls, they do not know by how much truth is stronger than error, nor how much more eloquently and effectively he can combat injustice who has experienced a little in his own person. Cast your whole vote, not a strip of paper merely, but your whole influence. A minority is powerless while it conforms to the majority; it is not even a minority then; but it is irresistible when it clogs by its whole weight. If the alternative is to keep all just men in prison, or give up war and slavery, the State will not hesitate which to choose. If a thousand men were not to pay their tax-bills this year, that would not be a violent and bloody measure, as it would be to pay them, and enable the State to commit violence and shed innocent blood. This is, in fact, the definition of a peaceable revolution, if any such is possible. If the tax-gatherer, or any other public officer, asks me, as one has done, "But what shall I do?" my answer is, "If you really wish to do anything, resign your office." When the subject has refused allegiance, and the officer has resigned his office, then the revolution is accomplished. But even suppose blood should flow. Is there not a sort of blood shed when the conscience is wounded? Through this wound a man's real manhood and immortality flow out, and he bleeds to an everlasting death. I see this blood flowing now.

I have contemplated the imprisonment of the offender, rather than the seizure of his goods,—though both will serve the same purpose,—because they who assert the purest right, and consequently are most dangerous to a corrupt State, commonly have not spent much time in accumulating property. To such the State renders comparatively small service, and a slight tax is wont to appear exorbitant, particularly if they are obliged to earn it by special labor with their hands. If there were one who lived wholly without the use of money, the State itself would hesitate to demand it of him. But the rich man—not to make any invidious comparison—is always sold to the institution which makes him rich. Absolutely speaking, the more money, the less virtue; for money comes between a man and his objects, and obtains them for him; and it was certainly no great virtue to obtain it. It puts to rest many questions which he would otherwise be taxed to answer; while the only new question which it puts is the hard but superfluous one, how to spend it. Thus his moral ground is taken from under his feet. The opportunities of living are diminished in proportion as what are called the "means" are increased. The best thing a man can do for his culture when he is rich is to endeavor to carry out those schemes which he entertained when he was poor. Christ answered the Herodians according to their condition. "Show me the tribute-money," said he;—and one took a penny out of his pocket;—if you use money which has the image of Caesar on it, which he has made current and valuable, that is, *if you are men of the State,* and gladly enjoy the advantages of Caesar's government, then pay him back some of his own when he demands it. "Render therefore to Caesar that which is Caesar's, and to God those things which are God's,"—leaving them no wiser than before as to which was which; for they did not wish to know.

When I converse with the freest of my neighbors, I perceive that, whatever they may say about the magnitude and seriousness of the question, and their regard for the public tranquillity, the long and the short of the matter is, that they cannot spare the protection of the existing government, and they dread the consequences to their property and families of disobedience to it. For my own part, I should not like to think that I ever rely on the protection of the State. But, if I deny the authority of the State when it presents its tax-bill, it will soon take and waste all my property, and so harass me and my children without end. This is hard. This makes it impossible for a man to live honestly, and at the same time comfortably, in outward respects. It will not be worth the while to accumulate property; that would be sure to go again. You must hire or squat somewhere, and raise but a small crop, and eat that soon. You must live within yourself, and depend upon yourself always tucked up and ready for a start, and not have many affairs. A man may grow rich in Turkey even, if he will be in all respects a good subject of the Turkish government. Confucius said: "If a state is governed by the principles of reason, poverty and misery are subjects of shame; if a state is not governed by the principles of reason, riches and honors are the subjects of shame." No: until I want the protection of Massachusetts to be extended to me in some distant Southern port, where my liberty is endangered, or until I am bent solely on building up an estate at home by peaceful enterprise, I can afford to refuse allegiance to Massachusetts, and her right to my property and life. It costs me less in every sense to incur the penalty of disobedience to the State than it would to obey. I should feel as if I were worth less in that case.

Some years ago, the State met me in behalf of the Church, and commanded me to pay a certain sum toward the support of a clergyman whose preaching my father attended, but never I myself. "Pay," it said, "or be locked up in the jail." I declined to pay. But, unfortunately, another man saw fit to pay it. I did not see why the schoolmaster should be taxed to support the priest, and not the priest the schoolmaster; for I was not the State's schoolmaster, but I supported myself by voluntary subscription. I did not see why the lyceum should not present its tax-bill, and have the State to back its demand, as well as the Church. However, at the request of the selectmen, I condescended to make some such statement as this in writing:—"Know all men by these presents, that I, Henry Thoreau, do not wish to be regarded as a member of any incorporated society which I have not joined." This I gave to the town clerk; and he has it. The State, having thus learned that I did not wish to be regarded as a member of that church, has never made a like demand on me since; though it said that it must adhere to its original presumption that time. If I had known how to name them, I should then have signed off in detail from all the societies which I never signed on to; but I did not know where to find a complete list.

I have paid no poll-tax for six years. I was put into a jail once on this account, for one night; and, as I stood considering the walls of solid stone, two or three feet thick, the door of wood and iron, a foot thick, and the iron grating which strained the light, I could not help being struck with the foolishness of that institution which treated me as if I were mere flesh and blood and bones, to be locked up. I wondered that it should have concluded at length that this was the best use it could put me to, and had never thought to avail itself of my services in some way. I saw that, if there was a wall of stone between me and my townsmen, there was a still more difficult one to climb or break through before they could get to be as free as I was. I did not for a moment feel confined, and the walls seemed a great waste of stone and mortar. I felt as if I alone of all my townsmen had paid my tax. They plainly did not know how to treat me, but behaved like persons who are underbred. In every threat and in every compliment there was a blunder; for they thought that my chief desire was to stand the other side of that stone wall. I could not but smile to see how industriously they locked the door on my meditations, which followed them out again without let or hindrance, and *they* were really all that was dangerous. As they could not reach me, they had resolved to punish my body; just as boys, if they cannot come at some person against whom they have a spite, will abuse his dog. I saw that the State was half-witted, that it was timid as a lone woman with her silver spoons, and that it did not know its friends from its foes, and I lost all my remaining respect for it, and pitied it.

Thus the State never intentionally confronts a man's sense, intellectual or moral, but only his body, his senses. It is not armed with superior wit or honesty, but with superior physical strength. I was not born to be forced. I will breathe after my own fashion. Let us see who is the strongest. What force has a multitude? They only can force me who obey a higher law than I. They force me to become like themselves. I do not hear of *men* being *forced* to live this way or that by masses of men. What sort of life were that to live? When I meet a government which says to me, "Your money or your life," why should I be in haste to give it my money? It may be in a great strait, and not know what to do: I cannot help that. It must help itself; do as I do. It is not worth the while to snivel about it. I am not responsible for the successful working of the machinery of society. I am not the son of the engineer. I perceive that, when an acorn and a chestnut fall side by side, the one does not remain inert to make way for the other, but both obey their own laws, and spring and grow and flourish as best they can, till one, perchance, overshadows and destroys the other. If a plant cannot live according to its nature, it dies; and so a man.

The night in prison was novel and interesting enough. The prisoners in their shirt-sleeves were enjoying a chat and the evening air in the doorway, when I entered. But the jailer said, "Come, boys, it is time to lock up;" and so they dispersed, and I heard the sound of their steps returning into the hollow apartments. My room-mate was introduced to me by the jailer as "a first-rate fellow and a clever man." When the door was locked, he showed me where to hang my hat, and how he managed matters there. The rooms were whitewashed once a month; and this one, at least, was the whitest, most simply furnished, and probably the neatest apartment in the town. He naturally wanted to know where I came from, and what brought me there; and, when I had told him, I asked him in my turn how he came there, presuming him to be an honest man, of course; and, as the world goes, I believe he was. "Why," said he, "they accuse me of burning a barn; but I never did it." As near as I could discover, he had probably gone to bed in a barn when drunk, and smoked his pipe there; and so a barn was burnt. He had the reputation of being a clever man, had been there some three months waiting for his trial to come on, and would have to wait as much longer; but he was quite domesticated and contented, since he got his board for nothing, and thought that he was well treated.

He occupied one window, and I the other; and I saw that if one stayed there long, his principal business would be to look out the window. I had soon read all the tracts that were left there, and examined where former prisoners had broken out, and where a grate had been sawed off, and heard the history of the various occupants of that room; for I found that even here there was a history and a gossip which never circulated beyond the walls of the jail. Probably this is the only house in the town where verses are composed, which are afterward printed in a circular form, but not published. I was shown quite a long list of verses which were composed by some young men who had been detected in an attempt to escape, who avenged themselves by signing them.

I pumped my fellow-prisoner as dry as I could, for fear I should never see him again; but at length he showed me which was my bed, and left me to blow out the lamp.

It was like traveling into a far country, such as I had never expected to behold, to lie there for one night. It seemed to me that I never had heard the town-clock strike before, nor the evening sounds of the village; for we slept with the windows open, which were inside the grating. It was to see my native village in the light of the Middle Ages, and our Concord was turned into a Rhine stream, and visions of knights and castles passed before me. They were the voices of old burghers that I heard in the streets. I was an involuntary spectator and auditor of whatever was done and said in the kitchen of the adjacent village-inn,—a wholly new and rare experience to me. It was a closer view of my native town. I was fairly inside of it. I never had seen its institutions before. This is one of its peculiar institutions; for it is a shire town. I began to comprehend what its inhabitants were about.

In the morning, our breakfasts were put through the hole in the door, in small oblong-square tin pans, made to fit, and holding a pint of chocolate, with brown bread, and an iron spoon. When they called for the vessels again, I was green enough to return what bread I had left; but my comrade seized it, and said that I should lay that up for lunch or dinner. Soon after he was let out to work at haying in a neighboring field, whither he went every day, and would not be back till noon; so he bade me good-day, saying that he doubted if he should see me again.

When I came out of prison,—for some one interfered, and paid that tax,—I did not perceive that great changes had taken place on the common, such as he observed who went in a youth and emerged a tottering and gray-headed man; and yet a change had to my eyes come over the scene,—the town, and State, and country,—greater than any that mere time could effect. I saw yet more distinctly the State in which I lived. I saw to what extent the people among whom I lived could be trusted as good neighbors and friends; that their friendship was for summer weather only; that they did not greatly propose to do right; that they were a distinct race from me by their prejudices and superstitions, as the Chinamen and Malays are; that in their sacrifices to humanity they ran no risks, not even to their property; that after all they were not so noble but they treated the thief as he had treated them, and hoped, by a certain outward observance and a few prayers, and by walking in a particular straight though useless path from time to time, to save their souls. This may be to judge my neighbors harshly; for I believe that many of them are not aware that they have such an institution as the jail in their village.

It was formerly the custom in our village, when a poor debtor came out of jail, for his acquaintances to salute him, looking through their fingers, which were crossed to represent the grating of a jail window, "How do ye do?" My neighbors did not thus salute me, but first looked at me, and then at one another, as if I had returned from a long journey. I was put into jail as I was going to the shoemaker's to get a shoe which was mended. When I was let out the next morning, I proceeded to finish my errand, and, having put on my mended shoe, joined a huckleberry party, who were impatient to put themselves under my conduct; and in half an hour,—for the horse was soon tackled,—was in the midst of a huckleberry field, on one of our highest hills, two miles off, and then the State was nowhere to be seen.

This is the whole history of "My Prisons."

I have never declined paying the highway tax, because I am as desirous of being a good neighbor as I am of being a bad subject; and as for supporting schools, I am doing my part to educate my fellow-countrymen now. It is for no particular item in the tax-bill that I refuse to pay it. I simply wish to refuse allegiance to the State, to withdraw and stand aloof from it effectually. I do not care to trace the course of my dollar, if I could, till it buys a man or a musket to shoot one with,—the dollar is innocent,—but I am concerned to trace the effects of my allegiance. In fact, I quietly declare war with the State, after my fashion, though I will still make what use and get what advantage of her I can, as is usual in such cases.

If others pay the tax which is demanded of me, from a sympathy with the State, they do but what they have already done in their own case, or rather they abet injustice to a greater extent than the State requires. If they pay the tax from a mistaken interest in the individual taxed, to save his property, or prevent his going to jail, it is because they have not considered wisely how far they let their private feelings interfere with the public good.

This, then, is my position at present. But one cannot be too much on his guard in such a case, lest his action be biased by obstinacy or an undue regard for the opinions of men. Let him see that he does only what belongs to himself and to the hour.

I think sometimes, Why, this people mean well, they are only ignorant; they would do better if they knew how: why give your neighbors this pain to treat you as they are not inclined to? But I think again, This is no reason why I should do as they do, or permit others to suffer much greater pain of a different kind. Again, I sometimes say to myself, When many millions of men, without heat, without ill will, without personal feeling of any kind, demand of you a few shillings only, without the possibility, such is their constitution, of retracting or altering their present demand,

and without the possibility, on your side, of appeal to any other millions, why expose yourself to this overwhelming brute force? You do not resist cold and hunger, the winds and the waves, thus obstinately; you quietly submit to a thousand similar necessities. You do not put your head into the fire. But just in proportion as I regard this as not wholly a brute force, but partly a human force, and consider that I have relations to those millions as to so many millions of men, and not of mere brute or inanimate things, I see that appeal is possible, first and instantaneously, from them to the Maker of them, and, secondly, from them to themselves. But if I put my head deliberately into the fire, there is no appeal to fire or to the Maker of fire, and I have only myself to blame. If I could convince myself that I have any right to be satisfied with men as they are, and to treat them accordingly, and not accordingly, in some respects, to my requisitions and expectations of what they and I ought to be, then, like a good Mussulman and fatalist, I should endeavor to be satisfied with things as they are, and say it is the will of God. And, above all, there is this difference between resisting this and a purely brute or natural force that I can resist this with some effect; but I cannot expect, like Orpheus,° to change the nature of the rocks and trees and beasts.

I do not wish to quarrel with any man or nation. I do not wish to split hairs, to make fine distinctions, or set myself up as better than my neighbors. I seek rather, I may say, even an excuse for conforming to the laws of the land. I am but too ready to conform to them. Indeed, I have reason to suspect myself on this head; and each year, as the tax-gatherer comes round, I find myself disposed to review the acts and position of the general and State governments, and the spirit of the people, to discover a pretext for conformity.

> "We must affect our country as our parents,
> And if at any time we alienate
> Our love or industry from doing it honor,
> We must respect effects and teach the soul
> Matter of conscience and religion,
> And not desire of rule or benefit."°

I believe that the State will soon be able to take all my work of this sort out of my hands, and then I shall be no better a patriot than my fellow-countrymen. Seen from a lower point of view, the Constitution, with all its faults, is very good; the law and the courts are very respectable; even this State and this American government are, in many respects, very admirable, and rare things, to be thankful for, such as a great many have

---

Orpheus legendary pre-Homeric Greek poet and musician. He played the lyre so beautifully that the wild beasts were tamed, and the rocks and trees moved to the music.
"We must affect . . ." From *The Battle of Alcazar* (1594), a play by George Peele (c. 1558–1598).

described them; but seen from a point of view a little higher, they are what I have described them; seen from a higher still, and the highest, who shall say what they are, or that they are worth looking at or thinking of at all?

However, the government does not concern me much, and I shall bestow the fewest possible thoughts on it. It is not many moments that I live under a government, even in this world. If a man is thought-free, fancy-free, imagination-free, that which *is not* never for a long time appearing *to be* to him, unwise rulers or reformers cannot fatally interrupt him.

I know that most men think differently from myself; but those whose lives are by profession devoted to the study of these or kindred subjects content me as little as any. Statesmen and legislators, standing so completely within the institution, never distinctly and nakedly behold it. They speak of moving society, but have no resting-place without it. They may be men of a certain experience and discrimination, and have no doubt invented ingenious and even useful systems, for which we sincerely thank them; but all their wit and usefulness lie within certain not very wide limits. They are wont to forget that the world is not governed by policy and expediency. Webster° never goes behind government, and so cannot speak with authority about it. His words are wisdom to those legislators who contemplate no essential reform in the existing government; but for thinkers, and those who legislate for all time, he never once glances at the subject. I know of those whose serene and wise speculations on this theme would soon reveal the limits of his mind's range and hospitality. Yet, compared with the cheap professions of most reformers, and the still cheaper wisdom and eloquence of politicians in general, his are almost the only sensible and valuable words, and we thank Heaven for him. Comparatively, he is always strong, original, and, above all, practical. Still, his quality is not wisdom, but prudence. The lawyer's truth is not Truth, but consistency or a consistent expediency. Truth is always in harmony with herself, and is not concerned chiefly to reveal the justice that may consist with wrong-doing. He well deserves to be called, as he has been called, the Defender of the Constitution. There are really no blows to be given by him but defensive ones. He is not a leader, but a follower. His leaders are the men of '87. "I have never made an effort," he says, "and never propose to make an effort; I have never countenanced an effort, and never mean to countenance an effort, to disturb the arrangement as originally made, by which the various States came into the Union." Still thinking of the sanction which the Constitution gives to slavery, he says, "Because it was a part of the original compact,—let it stand." Notwithstanding his special acuteness and ability, he is unable to take a fact out of its merely political relations, and behold it as it lies

---

Webster Daniel Webster (1782–1852), legendary American orator, lawyer, and statesman.

absolutely to be disposed of by the intellect,—what, for instance, it behooves a man to do here in America to-day with regard to slavery,—but ventures, or is driven, to make some such desperate answer as the following, while professing to speak absolutely, and as a private man,—from which what new and singular code of social duties might be inferred? "The manner," says he, "in which the governments of those States where slavery exists are to regulate it is for their own consideration, under their responsibility to their constituents, to the general laws of propriety, humanity, and justice, and to God. Associations formed elsewhere, springing from a feeling of humanity, or any other cause, have nothing whatever to do with it. They have never received any encouragement from me, and they never will."

They who know of no purer sources of truth, who have traced up its stream no higher, stand, and wisely stand, by the Bible and the Constitution, and drink at it there with reverence and humility; but they who behold where it comes trickling into this lake or that pool, gird up their loins once more, and continue their pilgrimage toward its fountain-head.

No man with a genius for legislation has appeared in America. They are rare in the history of the world. There are orators, politicians, and eloquent men, by the thousand; but the speaker has not yet opened his mouth to speak who is capable of settling the much-vexed questions of the day. We love eloquence for its own sake, and not for any truth which it may utter, or any heroism it may inspire. Our legislators have not yet learned the comparative value of free-trade and of freedom, of union, and of rectitude, to a nation. They have no genius or talent for comparatively humble questions of taxation and finance, commerce and manufactures and agriculture. If we were left solely to the wordy wit of legislators in Congress for our guidance, uncorrected by the seasonable experience and the effectual complaints of the people, America would not long retain her rank among the nations. For eighteen hundred years, though perchance I have no right to say it, the New Testament has been written; yet where is the legislator who has wisdom and practical talent enough to avail himself of the light which it sheds on the science of legislation?

The authority of government, even such as I am willing to submit to,—for I will cheerfully obey those who know and can do better than I, and in many things even those who neither know nor can do so well,—is still an impure one: to be strictly just, it must have the sanction and consent of the governed. It can have no pure right over my person and property but what I concede to it. The progress from an absolute to a limited monarchy, from a limited monarchy to a democracy, is a progress toward a true respect for the individual. Even the Chinese philosopher was wise enough to regard the individual as the basis of the empire. Is a democracy, such as we know it, the last improvement possible in government? Is it not possible to take a further step towards recognizing and organizing the rights of man? There will never be a really free and enlightened State until the State comes to recognize the individual as a higher and independent power, from which all its own power and authority are derived, and treats him accordingly. I please myself with imagining a State at last which can afford to be just to all men, and to treat the individual with respect as a neighbor; which even would not think it inconsistent with its own repose if a few were to live aloof from it, not meddling with it, nor embraced by it, who fulfilled all the duties of neighbors and fellow-men. A State which bore this kind of fruit, and suffered it to drop off as fast as it ripened, would prepare the way for a still more perfect and glorious State, which also I have imagined, but not yet anywhere seen.

Letter from Birmingham Jail

Martin Luther King, Jr.

Martin Luther King, Jr., was one of the most forceful advocates of nonviolent disobedience in the struggle for civil and human rights. Born in Georgia in 1929 and educated at Morehouse College, Crozer Theological Seminary, and Boston University, he became a Baptist minister in Montgomery, Alabama, in 1954. The next year he helped to launch the famous Montgomery bus boycott. Founder and president of the Southern Christian Leadership Conference, he was a leader of the 1963 March on Washington and of the 1965 voter registration drive in Selma, Alabama. In 1964 he received the Nobel Peace Prize. He was assassinated in Memphis, Tennessee, on April 4, 1968, while supporting a strike of city sanitation workers.

His writings include Stride Toward Freedom *(1958),* Strength to Love *(1963),* Where Do We Go from Here: Chaos or Community *(1967),* Conscience for Change *(1967),* The Measure of Man *(1968), and* The Trumpet of Conscience *(1968).* Why We Can't Wait, *published in 1964, includes a revised version of the letter printed below, and an author's note in which he says, "This response to a published statement by eight fellow clergymen from Alabama . . . was composed under somewhat constricting circumstances. Begun on the margins of the newspaper in which the statement appeared while I was in jail, the letter was continued on scraps of writing paper supplied by a friendly Negro trusty, and concluded on a pad my attorneys were eventually permitted to leave me. Although the text remains in substance unaltered, I have indulged in the author's prerogative of polishing it for publication." For its greater immediacy, we present here the unrevised version of the letter, together with the public statement that occasioned it.*

Public Statement by Eight Alabama Clergymen

(April 12, 1963)

We the undersigned clergymen are among those who, in January, issued "An Appeal for Law and Order and Common Sense," in dealing with racial problems in Alabama. We expressed understanding that honest convictions in racial matters could properly be pursued in the courts, but urged that decisions of those courts should in the meantime be peacefully obeyed.

Since that time there had been some evidence of increased forbearance and a willingness to face facts. Responsible citizens have undertaken to work on various problems which cause racial friction and unrest. In Birmingham, recent public events have given indication that we all have opportunity for a new constructive and realistic approach to racial problems.

However, we are now confronted by a series of demonstrations by some of our Negro citizens, directed and led in part by outsiders. We recognize the natural impatience of people who feel that their hopes are slow in being realized. But we are convinced that these demonstrations are unwise and untimely.

We agree rather with certain local Negro leadership which has called for honest and open negotiation of racial issues in our area. And we believe this kind of facing of issues can best be accomplished by citizens of our own metropolitan area, white and Negro, meeting with their knowledge and experience of the local situation. All of us need to face that responsibility and find proper channels for its accomplishment.

Just as we formerly pointed out that "hatred and violence have no sanction in our religious and political traditions," we also point out that such actions as incite to hatred and violence, however technically peaceful those actions may be, have not contributed to the resolution of our local problems. We do not believe that these days of new hope are days when extreme measures are justified in Birmingham.

We commend the community as a whole, and the local news media and law enforcement officials in particular, on the calm manner in which these demonstrations have been handled. We urge the public to continue to show restraint should the demonstrations continue, and the law enforcement officials to remain calm and continue to protect our city from violence.

We further strongly urge our own Negro community to withdraw support from these demonstrations, and to unite locally in working peacefully for a better Birmingham. When rights are consistently denied, a cause should be pressed in the courts and in negotiations among local leaders, and not in the streets. We appeal to both our white and Negro citizenry to observe the principles of law and order and common sense.

Signed by:

C. C. J. CARPENTER, D.D., LL.D., *Bishop of Alabama*

JOSEPH A. DURICK, D.D., *Auxiliary Bishop, Diocese of Mobile, Birmingham*

Rabbi MILTON L. GRAFMAN, *Temple Emanu-El, Birmingham, Alabama*

Bishop PAUL HARDIN, *Bishop of the Alabama-West Florida Conference of the Methodist Church*

Bishop NOLAN B. HARMON, *Bishop of the North Alabama Conference of the Methodist Church*

GEORGE M. MURRAY, D.D., LL.D., *Bishop Coadjutor, Episcopal Diocese of Alabama*

EDWARD V. RAMAGE, *Moderator, Synod of the Alabama Presbyterian Church in the United States*

EARL STALLINGS, *Pastor, First Baptist Church, Birmingham, Alabama*

Letter from
Birmingham Jail

MARTIN LUTHER KING, JR.
Birmingham City Jail
April 16, 1963

Bishop C. C. J. CARPENTER
Bishop JOSEPH A. DURICK
Rabbi MILTON L. GRAFMAN
Bishop PAUL HARDIN
Bishop NOLAN B. HARMON
The Rev. GEORGE M. MURRAY
The Rev. EDWARD V. RAMAGE
The Rev. EARL STALLINGS

My dear Fellow Clergymen,

While confined here in the Birmingham City Jail, I came across your recent statement calling our present activities "unwise and untimely."

Seldom, if ever, do I pause to answer criticism of my work and ideas. If I sought to answer all of the criticisms that cross my desk, my secretaries would be engaged in little else in the course of the day and I would have no time for constructive work. But since I feel that you are men of genuine good will and your criticisms are sincerely set forth, I would like to answer your statement in what I hope will be patient and reasonable terms.

I think I should give the reason for my being in Birmingham, since you have been influenced by the argument of "outsiders coming in." I have the honor of serving as president of the Southern Christian Leadership Conference, an organization operating in every Southern state with headquarters in Atlanta, Georgia. We have some eighty-five affiliate organizations all across the South—one being the Alabama Christian Movement for Human Rights. Whenever necessary and possible we share staff, educational, and financial resources with our affiliates. Several months ago our local affiliate here in Birmingham invited us to be on call to engage in a nonviolent direct action program if such were deemed necessary. We readily consented and when the hour came we lived up to our promises. So I am here, along with several members of my staff, because we were invited here. I am here because I have basic organizational ties here. Beyond this, I am in Birmingham because injustice is here. Just as the eighth century prophets left their little villages and carried their "thus saith the Lord" far beyond the boundaries of their home town, and just as the Apostle Paul left his little village of Tarsus and carried the gospel of Jesus Christ to practically every hamlet and city of the Graeco-Roman world, I too am compelled to carry the gospel of freedom beyond my particular home town. Like Paul, I must constantly respond to the Macedonian call for aid.

Moreover, I am cognizant of the interrelatedness of all communities and states. I cannot sit idly by in Atlanta and not be concerned about what happens in Birmingham. Injustice anywhere is a threat to justice everywhere. We are caught in an inescapable network of mutuality tied in a single garment of destiny. Whatever affects one directly affects all indirectly. Never again can we afford to live with the narrow, provincial "outside agitator" idea. Anyone who lives inside the United States can never be considered an outsider anywhere in this country.

You deplore the demonstrations that are presently taking place in Birmingham. But I am sorry that your statement did not express a similar concern for the conditions that brought the demonstrations into being. I am sure that each of you would want to go beyond the superficial social analyst who looks merely at effects, and does not grapple with underlying causes. I would not hesitate to say that it is unfortunate that so-called demonstrations are taking place in Birmingham at this time, but I would say in more emphatic terms that it is even more unfortunate that the white power structure of this city left the Negro community with no other alternative.

4 steps

In any nonviolent campaign there are four basic steps: (1) collection of the facts to determine whether injustices are alive; (2) negotiation; (3) self-purification; and (4) direct action. We have gone through all of these steps in Birmingham. There can be no gainsaying of the fact that racial injustice engulfs this community. Birmingham is probably the most thoroughly segregated city in the United States. Its ugly record of police brutality is known in every section of this country. Its unjust treatment of Negroes in the courts is a notorious reality. There have been more unsolved bombings of Negro homes and churches in Birmingham than any city in this nation. These are the hard, brutal, and unbelievable facts. On the basis of these conditions Negro leaders sought to negotiate with the city fathers. But the political leaders consistently refused to engage in good faith negotiation.

Then came the opportunity last September to talk with some of the leaders of the economic community. In these negotiating sessions certain promises were made by the merchants—such as the promise to remove the humiliating racial signs from the stores. On the basis of these promises Rev. Shuttlesworth and the leaders of the Alabama Christian Movement for Human Rights agreed to call a moratorium on any type of demonstrations. As the weeks and months unfolded we realized that we were the victims of a broken promise. The signs remained. As in so many experiences of the past we were confronted with blasted hopes, and the dark shadow of a deep disappointment settled upon us. So we had no alternative except that of preparing for direct action, whereby we would present our very bodies as a means of laying our case before the conscience of the local and national community. We were not unmindful of the difficulties involved. So we decided to go through a process of self-purification. We started having workshops on nonviolence and repeatedly asked ourselves the questions, "Are you able to accept blows without retaliating?" "Are you able to endure the ordeals of jail?"

We decided to set our direct action program around the Easter season, realizing that with the exception of Christmas, this was the largest shopping period of the year. Knowing that a strong economic withdrawal program would be the by-product of direct action, we felt that this was the best time to bring pressure on the merchants for the needed changes. Then it occurred to us that the March election was ahead, and so we speedily decided to postpone action until after election day. When we discovered that Mr. Connor° was in the run-off, we decided again to postpone so that the demonstrations could not be used to cloud the issues. At

---

Mr. Connor   Eugene "Bull" Connor and Albert Boutwell were candidates for mayor of Birmingham, Alabama, in 1963. The more moderate Boutwell won, but Connor and two other commissioners claimed they had been elected originally to serve until 1965 and refused to leave office. While the courts were deciding the issue, Connor, as commissioner of public safety, was free to use force against black demonstrations.

this time we agreed to begin our nonviolent witness the day after the run-off.

This reveals that we did not move irresponsibly into direct action. We too wanted to see Mr. Connor defeated; so we went through postponement after postponement to aid in this community need. After this we felt that direct action could be delayed no longer.

You may well ask, "Why direct action? Why sit-ins, marches, etc.? Isn't negotiation a better path?" You are exactly right in your call for negotiation. Indeed, this is the purpose of direct action. Nonviolent direct action seeks to create such a crisis and establish such creative tension that a community that has constantly refused to negotiate is forced to confront the issue. It seeks so to dramatize the issue that it can no longer be ignored. I just referred to the creation of tension as a part of the work of the nonviolent resister. This may sound rather shocking. But I must confess that I am not afraid of the word tension. I have earnestly worked and preached against violent tension, but there is a type of constructive nonviolent tension that is necessary for growth. Just as Socrates felt that it was necessary to create a tension in the mind so that individuals could rise from the bondage of myths and half-truths to the unfettered realm of creative analysis and objective appraisal, we must see the need of having nonviolent gadflies to create the kind of tension in society that will help men rise from the dark depths of prejudice and racism to the majestic heights of understanding and brotherhood. So the purpose of the direct action is to create a situation so crisis-packed that it will inevitably open the door to negotiation. We, therefore, concur with you in your call for negotiation. Too long has our beloved Southland been bogged down in the tragic attempt to live in monologue rather than dialogue.

One of the basic points in your statement is that our acts are untimely. Some have asked, "Why didn't you give the new administration time to act?" The only answer that I can give to this inquiry is that the new administration must be prodded about as much as the outgoing one before it acts. We will be sadly mistaken if we feel that the election of Mr. Boutwell will bring the millennium to Birmingham. While Mr. Boutwell is much more articulate and gentle than Mr. Connor, they are both segregationists dedicated to the task of maintaining the status quo. The hope I see in Mr. Boutwell is that he will be reasonable enough to see the futility of massive resistance to desegregation. But he will not see this without pressure from the devotees of civil rights. My friends, I must say to you that we have not made a single gain in civil rights without determined legal and nonviolent pressure. History is the long and tragic story of the fact that privileged groups seldom give up their privileges voluntarily. Individuals may see the moral light and voluntarily give up their unjust posture; but as Reinhold Niebuhr has reminded us, groups are more immoral than individuals.

We know through painful experience that freedom is never voluntarily given by the oppressor; it must be demanded by the oppressed. Frankly I have never yet engaged in a direct action movement that was "well timed," according to the timetable of those who have not suffered unduly from the disease of segregation. For years now I have heard the word "Wait!" It rings in the ear of every Negro with a piercing familiarity. This "wait" has almost always meant "never." It has been a tranquilizing thalidomide, relieving the emotional stress for a moment, only to give birth to an ill-formed infant of frustration. We must come to see with the distinguished jurist of yesterday that "justice too long delayed is justice denied." We have waited for more than three hundred and forty years for our constitutional and God-given rights. The nations of Asia and Africa are moving with jet-like speed toward the goal of political independence, and we still creep at horse and buggy pace toward the gaining of a cup of coffee at a lunch counter.

I guess it is easy for those who have never felt the stinging darts of segregation to say wait. But when you have seen vicious mobs lynch your mothers and fathers at will and drown your sisters and brothers at whim; when you have seen hate filled policemen curse, kick, brutalize, and even kill your black brothers and sisters with impunity; when you see the vast majority of your twenty million Negro brothers smothering in an air-tight cage of poverty in the midst of an affluent society; when you suddenly find your tongue twisted and your speech stammering as you seek to explain to your six-year-old daughter why she can't go to the public amusement park that has just been advertised on television, and see tears welling up in her little eyes when she is told that Funtown is closed to colored children, and see the depressing clouds of inferiority begin to form in her little mental sky, and see her begin to distort her little personality by unconsciously developing a bitterness toward white people; when you have to concoct an answer for a five-year-old son asking in agonizing pathos: "Daddy, why do white people treat colored people so mean?"; when you take a cross country drive and find it necessary to sleep night after night in the uncomfortable corners of your automobile because no motel will accept you; when you are humiliated day in and day out by nagging signs reading "white" men and "colored"; when your first name becomes "nigger" and your middle name becomes "boy" (however old you are) and your last name becomes "John," and when your wife and mother are never given the respected title "Mrs."; when you are harried by day and haunted by night by the fact that you are a Negro, living constantly at tip-toe stance never quite knowing what to expect next, and plagued with inner fears and outer resentments; when you are forever fighting a degenerating sense of "nobodiness";—then you will understand why we find it difficult to wait. There comes a time when the cup of endurance runs over, and men are no longer willing to be plunged into an abyss of injustice where they experience the bleakness of corroding despair. I hope, sirs, you can understand our legitimate and unavoidable impatience.

[handwritten: Just & Laws]

You express a great deal of anxiety over our willingness to break laws. This is certainly a legitimate concern. Since we so diligently urge people to obey the Supreme Court's decision of 1954 outlawing segregation in the public schools, it is rather strange and paradoxical to find us consciously breaking laws. One may well ask, "How can you advocate breaking some laws and obeying others?" The answer is found in the fact that there are two types of laws. There are *just* laws and there are *unjust* laws. I would be the first to advocate obeying just laws. One has not only a legal but moral responsibility to obey just laws. Conversely, one has a moral responsibility to disobey unjust laws. I would agree with Saint Augustine that "An unjust law is no law at all."

Now what is the difference between the two? How does one determine when a law is just or unjust? A just law is a man-made code that squares with the moral law or the law of God. An unjust law is a code that is out of harmony with the moral law. To put it in the terms of Saint Thomas Aquinas, an unjust law is a human law that is not rooted in eternal and natural law. Any law that uplifts human personality is just. Any law that degrades human personality is unjust. All segregation statutes are unjust because segregation distorts the soul and damages the personality. It gives the segregator a false sense of superiority and the segregated a false sense of inferiority. To use the words of Martin Buber, the great Jewish philosopher, segregation substitutes an "I-it" relationship for the "I-thou" relationship, and ends up relegating persons to the status of things. So segregation is not only politically, economically, and sociologically unsound, but it is morally wrong and sinful. Paul Tillich° has said that sin is separation. Isn't segregation an existential expression of man's tragic separation, an expression of his awful estrangement, his terrible sinfulness? So I can urge men to obey the 1954 decision of the Supreme Court° because it is morally right, and I can urge them to disobey segregation ordinances because they are morally wrong.

Let us turn to a more concrete example of just and unjust laws. An unjust law is a code that a majority inflicts on a minority that is not binding on itself. This is *difference* made legal. On the other hand a just law is a code that a majority compels a minority to follow that it is willing to follow itself. This is *sameness* made legal.

Let me give another explanation. An unjust law is a code inflicted upon a minority which that minority had no part in enacting or creating because they did not have the unhampered right to vote. Who can say the legislature of Alabama which set up the segregation laws was democratically elected? Throughout the state of Alabama all types of conniving methods are used to prevent Negroes from becoming registered voters and there are some counties without a single Negro registered to vote despite

---

Paul Tillich (1886–1965) Philosopher and theologian.
1954 decision of the Supreme Court *Brown vs. Board of Education,* a decision that declared racial segregation in public schools unconstitutional.

the fact that the Negro constitutes a majority of the population. Can any law set up in such a state be considered democratically structured?

These are just a few examples of unjust and just laws. There are some instances when a law is just on its face but unjust in its application. For instance, I was arrested Friday on a charge of parading without a permit. Now there is nothing wrong with an ordinance which requires a permit for a parade, but when the ordinance is used to preserve segregation and to deny citizens the First Amendment privilege of peaceful assembly and peaceful protest, then it becomes unjust.

I hope you can see the distinction I am trying to point out. In no sense do I advocate evading or defying the law as the rabid segregationist would do. This would lead to anarchy. One who breaks an unjust law must do it *openly, lovingly* (not hatefully as the white mothers did in New Orleans when they were seen on television screaming "nigger, nigger, nigger") and with a willingness to accept the penalty. I submit that an individual who breaks a law that conscience tells him is unjust, and willingly accepts the penalty by staying in jail to arouse the conscience of the community over its injustice, is in reality expressing the very highest respect for law.

Of course there is nothing new about this kind of civil disobedience. It was seen sublimely in the refusal of Shadrach, Meshach, and Abednego to obey the laws of Nebuchadnezzar because a higher moral law was involved. It was practiced superbly by the early Christians who were willing to face hungry lions and the excruciating pain of chopping blocks, before submitting to certain unjust laws of the Roman Empire. To a degree academic freedom is a reality today because Socrates practiced civil disobedience.

We can never forget that everything Hitler did in Germany was "legal" and everything the Hungarian freedom fighters° did in Hungary was "illegal." It was "illegal" to aid and comfort a Jew in Hitler's Germany. But I am sure that, if I had lived in Germany during that time, I would have aided and comforted my Jewish brothers even though it was illegal. If I lived in a communist country today where certain principles dear to the Christian faith are suppressed, I believe I would openly advocate disobeying those antireligious laws.

I must make two honest confessions to you, my Christian and Jewish brothers. First I must confess that over the last few years I have been gravely disappointed with the white moderate. I have almost reached the regrettable conclusion that the Negroes' great stumbling block in the stride toward freedom is not the White Citizens' "Counciler" or the Ku Klux Klanner, but the white moderate who is more devoted to "order" than to justice; who prefers a negative peace which is the absence of

---

Hungarian freedom fighters Hungarians who fought in the 1956 anti-Soviet revolution. The revolt was crushed by Soviet military forces.

tension to a positive peace which is the presence of justice; who constantly says "I agree with you in the goal you seek, but I can't agree with your methods of direct action"; who paternalistically feels that he can set the timetable for another man's freedom; who lives by the myth of time and who constantly advises the Negro to wait until a "more convenient season." Shallow understanding from people of good will is more frustrating than absolute misunderstanding from people of ill will. Lukewarm acceptance is much more bewildering than outright rejection.

I had hoped that the white moderate would understand that law and order exist for the purpose of establishing justice, and that when they fail to do this they become the dangerously structured dams that block the flow of social progress. I had hoped that the white moderate would understand that the present tension in the South is merely a necessary phase of the transition from an obnoxious negative peace, where the Negro passively accepted his unjust plight, to a substance-filled positive peace, where all men will respect the dignity and worth of human personality. Actually, we who engage in nonviolent direct action are not the creators of tension. We merely bring to the surface the hidden tension that is already alive. We bring it out in the open where it can be seen and dealt with. Like a boil that can never be cured as long as it is covered up but must be opened with all its pus-flowing ugliness to the natural medicines of air and light, injustice must likewise be exposed, with all of the tension its exposing creates, to the light of human conscience and the air of national opinion before it can be cured.

In your statement you asserted that our actions, even though peaceful, must be condemned because they precipitate violence. But can this assertion be logically made? Isn't this like condemning the robbed man because his possession of money precipitated the evil act of robbery? Isn't this like condemning Socrates because his unswerving commitment to truth and his philosophical delvings precipitated the misguided popular mind to make him drink the hemlock? Isn't this like condemning Jesus because His unique God consciousness and never-ceasing devotion to His will precipitated the evil act of crucifixion? We must come to see, as federal courts have consistently affirmed, that it is immoral to urge an individual to withdraw his efforts to gain his basic constitutional rights because the quest precipitates violence. Society must protect the robbed and punish the robber.

I had also hoped that the white moderate would reject the myth of time. I received a letter this morning from a white brother in Texas which said: "All Christians know that the colored people will receive equal rights eventually, but is it possible that you are in too great of a religious hurry? It has taken Christianity almost 2000 years to accomplish what it has. The teachings of Christ take time to come to earth." All that is said here grows out of a tragic misconception of time. It is the strangely irrational notion that there is something in the very flow of time that will inevitably cure all ills. Actually time is neutral. It can be used either destructively or constructively. I am coming to feel that the people of ill will have used time much more effectively than the people of good will. We will have to repent in this generation not merely for the vitriolic words and actions of the bad people, but for the appalling silence of the good people. We must come to see that human progress never rolls in on wheels of inevitability. It comes through the tireless efforts and persistent work of men willing to be co-workers with God, and without this hard work time itself becomes an ally of the forces of social stagnation.

We must use time creatively, and forever realize that the time is always ripe to do right. Now is the time to make real the promise of democracy, and transform our pending national elegy into a creative psalm of brotherhood. Now is the time to lift our national policy from the quicksand of racial injustice to the solid rock of human dignity.

You spoke of our activity in Birmingham as extreme. At first I was rather disappointed that fellow clergymen would see my nonviolent efforts as those of the extremist. I started thinking about the fact that I stand in the middle of two opposing forces in the Negro community. One is a force of complacency made up of Negroes who, as a result of long years of oppression, have been so completely drained of self-respect and a sense of "somebodiness" that they have adjusted to segregation, and of a few Negroes in the middle class who, because of a degree of academic and economic security, and because at points they profit by segregation, have unconsciously become insensitive to the problems of the masses. The other force is one of bitterness and hatred and comes perilously close to advocating violence. It is expressed in the various black nationalist groups that are springing up over the nation, the largest and best known being Elijah Muhammad's Muslim movement.° This movement is nourished by the contemporary frustration over the continued existence of racial discrimination. It is made up of people who have lost faith in America, who have absolutely repudiated Christianity, and who have concluded that the white man is an incurable "devil." I have tried to stand between these two forces saying that we need not follow the "do-nothingism" of the complacent or the hatred and despair of the black nationalist. There is the more excellent way of love and nonviolent protest. I'm grateful to God that, through the Negro church, the dimension of nonviolence entered our struggle. If this philosophy had not emerged I am convinced that by now many streets of the South would be flowing with floods of blood. And I am further convinced that if our white brothers dismiss us as "rabble rousers" and "outside agitators"—those of us who are working through the channels of nonviolent direct action—and refuse to support

---

Elijah Muhammad's Muslim movement   The Black Muslims, a black nationalist organization that opposes integration and advocates a separate black nation within the United States.

our nonviolent efforts, millions of Negroes, out of frustration and despair, will seek solace and security in black nationalist ideologies, a development that will lead inevitably to a frightening racial nightmare.

Oppressed people cannot remain oppressed forever. The urge for freedom will eventually come. This is what has happened to the American Negro. Something within has reminded him of his birthright of freedom; something without has reminded him that he can gain it. Consciously and unconsciously, he has been swept in by what the Germans call the *Zeitgeist,*° and with his black brothers of Africa, and his brown and yellow brothers of Asia, South America, and the Caribbean, he is moving with a sense of cosmic urgency toward the promised land of racial justice. Recognizing this vital urge that has engulfed the Negro community, one should readily understand public demonstrations. The Negro has many pent-up resentments and latent frustrations. He has to get them out. So let him march sometime; let him have his prayer pilgrimages to the city hall; understand why he must have sit-ins and freedom rides. If his repressed emotions do not come out in these nonviolent ways, they will come out in ominous expressions of violence. This is not a threat; it is a fact of history. So I have not said to my people, "Get rid of your discontent." But I have tried to say that this normal and healthy discontent can be channeled through the creative outlet of nonviolent direct action. Now this approach is being dismissed as extremist. I must admit that I was initially disappointed in being so categorized.

But as I continued to think about the matter I gradually gained a bit of satisfaction from being considered an extremist. Was not Jesus an extremist in love? "Love your enemies, bless them that curse you, pray for them that despitefully use you." Was not Amos an extremist for justice—"Let justice roll down like waters and righteousness like a mighty stream." Was not Paul an extremist for the gospel of Jesus Christ—"I bear in my body the marks of the Lord Jesus." Was not Martin Luther an extremist—"Here I stand; I can do none other so help me God." Was not John Bunyan an extremist—"I will stay in jail to the end of my days before I make a butchery of my conscience." Was not Abraham Lincoln an extremist—"This nation cannot survive half slave and half free." Was not Thomas Jefferson an extremist—"We hold these truths to be self evident that all men are created equal." So the question is not whether we will be extremist but what kind of extremist will we be. Will we be extremists for hate or will we be extremists for love? Will we be extremists for the preservation of injustice—or will we be extremists for the cause of justice? In that dramatic scene on Calvary's hill three men were crucified. We must never forget that all three were crucified for the same crime—the crime of extremism. Two were extremists for immoral-

---

Zeitgeist spirit of the time (German).

ity, and thus fell below their environment. The other, Jesus Christ, was an extremist for love, truth, and goodness, and thereby rose above His environment. So, after all, maybe the South, the nation, and the world are in dire need of creative extremists.

I had hoped that the white moderate would see this. Maybe I was too optimistic. Maybe I expected too much. I guess I should have realized that few members of a race that has oppressed another race can understand or appreciate the deep groans and passionate yearnings of those that have been oppressed, and still fewer have the vision to see that injustice must be rooted out by strong, persistent, and determined action. I am thankful, however, that some of our white brothers have grasped the meaning of this social revolution and committed themselves to it. They are still all too small in quantity, but they are big in quality. Some like Ralph McGill, Lillian Smith, Harry Golden, and James Dabbs have written about our struggle in eloquent, prophetic, and understanding terms. Others have marched with us down nameless streets of the South. They have languished in filthy, roach-infested jails, suffering the abuse and brutality of angry policemen who see them as "dirty nigger lovers." They, unlike so many of their moderate brothers and sisters, have recognized the urgency of the moment and sensed the need for powerful "action" antidotes to combat the disease of segregation.

Let me rush on to mention my other disappointment. I have been so greatly disappointed with the white Church and its leadership. Of course there are some notable exceptions. I am not unmindful of the fact that each of you has taken some significant stands on this issue. I commend you, Rev. Stallings, for your Christian stand on this past Sunday, in welcoming Negroes to your worship service on a nonsegregated basis. I commend the Catholic leaders of this state for integrating Springhill College several years ago.

But despite these notable exceptions I must honestly reiterate that I have been disappointed with the Church. I do not say that as one of those negative critics who can always find something wrong with the Church. I say it as a minister of the gospel, who loves the Church; who was nurtured in its bosom; who has been sustained by its spiritual blessings and who will remain true to it as long as the cord of life shall lengthen.

I had the strange feeling when I was suddenly catapulted into the leadership of the bus protest in Montgomery° several years ago that we would have the support of the white Church. I felt that the white ministers, priests, and rabbis of the South would be some of our strongest allies.

---

bus protest in Montgomery A bus boycott in Montgomery, Alabama, begun after Rosa Park was arrested on December 1, 1955, for refusing to give up her seat on a bus to a white male passenger. The boycott lasted nearly a year and was supported by almost 100 percent of the city's black residents.

Instead, some have been outright opponents, refusing to understand the freedom movement and misrepresenting its leaders; all too many others have been more cautious than courageous and have remained silent behind the anesthetizing security of stained glass windows.

In spite of my shattered dreams of the past, I came to Birmingham with the hope that the white religious leadership of the community would see the justice of our cause and, with deep moral concern, serve as the channel through which our just grievances could get to the power structure. I had hoped that each of you would understand. But again I have been disappointed.

I have heard numerous religious leaders of the South call upon their worshippers to comply with a desegregation decision because it is the law, but I have longed to hear white ministers say follow this decree because integration is morally right and the Negro is your brother. In the midst of blatant injustices inflicted upon the Negro, I have watched white churches stand on the sideline and merely mouth pious irrelevancies and sanctimonious trivialities. In the midst of a mighty struggle to rid our nation of racial and economic injustice, I have heard so many ministers say, "Those are social issues with which the Gospel has no real concern," and I have watched so many churches commit themselves to a completely otherworldly religion which made a strange distinction between body and soul, the sacred and the secular.

So here we are moving toward the exit of the twentieth century with a religious community largely adjusted to the status quo, standing as a tail light behind other community agencies rather than a headlight leading men to higher levels of justice.

I have travelled the length and breadth of Alabama, Mississippi, and all the other Southern states. On sweltering summer days and crisp autumn mornings I have looked at her beautiful churches with their spires pointing heavenward. I have beheld the impressive outlay of her massive religious education buildings. Over and over again I have found myself asking: "Who worships here? Who is their God? Where were their voices when the lips of Governor Barnett° dripped with words of interposition and nullification? Where were they when Governor Wallace° gave the clarion call for defiance and hatred? Where were their voices of support when tired, bruised, and weary Negro men and women decided to rise from the dark dungeons of complacency to the bright hills of creative protest?"

Yes, these questions are still in my mind. In deep disappointment, I have wept over the laxity of the Church. But be assured that my tears

---

Governor Barnett   Ross R. Barnett, governor of Mississippi (1960–64).
Governor Wallace   George C. Wallace, governor of Alabama (1963–1966, 1971–1979, 1983–1987). See also note on page 556.

have been tears of love. There can be no deep disappointment where there is not deep love. Yes, I love the Church; I love her sacred walls. How could I do otherwise? I am in the rather unique position of being the son, the grandson, and the great grandson of preachers. Yes, I see the Church as the body of Christ. But, oh! How we have blemished and scarred that body through social neglect and fear of being nonconformists.

There was a time when the Church was very powerful. It was during that period when the early Christians rejoiced when they were deemed worthy to suffer for what they believed. In those days the Church was not merely a thermometer that recorded the ideas and principles of popular opinion; it was a thermostat that transformed the mores of society. Wherever the early Christians entered a town the power structure got disturbed and immediately sought to convict them for being "disturbers of the peace" and "outside agitators." But they went on with the conviction that they were a "colony of heaven" and had to obey God rather than man. They were small in number but big in commitment. They were too God-intoxicated to be "astronomically intimidated." They brought an end to such ancient evils as infanticide and gladiatorial contest.

Things are different now. The contemporary Church is so often a weak, ineffectual voice with an uncertain sound. It is so often the archsupporter of the status quo. Far from being disturbed by the presence of the Church, the power structure of the average community is consoled by the Church's silent and often vocal sanction of things as they are.

But the judgment of God is upon the Church as never before. If the Church of today does not recapture the sacrificial spirit of the early Church, it will lose its authentic ring, forfeit the loyalty of millions, and be dismissed as an irrelevant social club with no meaning for the twentieth century. I am meeting young people every day whose disappointment with the Church has risen to outright disgust.

Maybe again I have been too optimistic. Is organized religion too inextricably bound to the status quo to save our nation and the world? Maybe I must turn my faith to the inner spiritual Church, the church within the Church, as the true *ecclesia*° and the hope of the world. But again I am thankful to God that some noble souls from the ranks of organized religion have broken loose from the paralyzing chains of conformity and joined us as active partners in the struggle for freedom. They have left their secure congregations and walked the streets of Albany, Georgia, with us. They have gone through the highways of the South on torturous rides for freedom. Yes, they have gone to jail with us. Some have been kicked out of their churches and lost the support of their bishops and fellow ministers. But they have gone with the faith

---

ecclesia church (Latin).

that right defeated is stronger than evil triumphant. These men have been the leaven in the lump of the race. Their witness has been the spiritual salt that has preserved the true meaning of the Gospel in these troubled times. They have carved a tunnel of hope through the dark mountain of disappointment.

I hope the Church as a whole will meet the challenge of this decisive hour. But even if the Church does not come to the aid of justice, I have no despair about the future. I have no fear about the outcome of our struggle in Birmingham, even if our motives are presently misunderstood. We will reach the goal of freedom in Birmingham and all over the nation, because the goal of America is freedom. Abused and scorned though we may be, our destiny is tied up with the destiny of America. Before the pilgrims landed at Plymouth, we were here. Before the pen of Jefferson etched across the pages of history the majestic words of the Declaration of Independence, we were here. For more than two centuries our foreparents labored in this country without wages; they made cotton "king"; and they built the homes of their masters in the midst of brutal injustice and shameful humiliation—and yet out of a bottomless vitality they continued to thrive and develop. If the inexpressible cruelties of slavery could not stop us, the opposition we now face will surely fail. We will win our freedom because the sacred heritage of our nation and the eternal will of God are embodied in our echoing demands.

I must close now. But before closing I am impelled to mention one other point in your statement that troubled me profoundly. You warmly commended the Birmingham police force for keeping "order" and "preventing violence." I don't believe you would have so warmly commended the police force if you had seen its angry violent dogs literally biting six unarmed, nonviolent Negroes. I don't believe you would so quickly commend the policemen if you would observe their ugly and inhuman treatment of Negroes here in the city jail; if you would watch them push and curse old Negro women and young Negro girls; if you would see them slap and kick old Negro men and young Negro boys; if you will observe them, as they did on two occasions, refuse to give us food because we wanted to sing our grace together. I'm sorry that I can't join you in your praise for the police department.

It is true that they have been rather disciplined in their public handling of the demonstrators. In this sense they have been rather publicly "nonviolent." But for what purpose? To preserve the evil system of segregation. Over the last few years I have consistently preached that nonviolence demands that the means we use must be as pure as the ends we seek. So I have tried to make it clear that it is wrong to use immoral means to attain moral ends. But now I must affirm that it is just as wrong, or even more so, to use moral means to preserve immoral ends. Maybe Mr. Connor and his policemen have been rather publicly nonviolent, as Chief Pritchett° was in Albany, Georgia, but they have used the moral means of nonviolence to maintain the immoral end of flagrant racial injustice. T. S. Eliot has said that there is no greater treason than to do the right deed for the wrong reason.

I wish you had commended the Negro sit-inners and demonstrators of Birmingham for their sublime courage, their willingness to suffer, and their amazing discipline in the midst of the most inhuman provocation. One day the South will recognize its real heroes. They will be the James Merediths,° courageously and with a majestic sense of purpose, facing jeering and hostile mobs and the agonizing loneliness that characterizes the life of the pioneer. They will be old, oppressed, battered Negro women, symbolized in a seventy-two year old woman of Montgomery, Alabama, who rose up with a sense of dignity and with her people decided not to ride the segregated buses, and responded to one who inquired about her tiredness with ungrammatical profundity: "My feets is tired, but my soul is rested." They will be young high school and college students, young ministers of the gospel and a host of the elders, courageously and nonviolently sitting in at lunch counters and willingly going to jail for conscience sake. One day the South will know that when these disinherited children of God sat down at lunch counters they were in reality standing up for the best in the American dream and the most sacred values in our Judeo-Christian heritage, and thus carrying our whole nation back to great wells of democracy which were dug deep by the founding fathers in the formulation of the Constitution and the Declaration of Independence.

Never before have I written a letter this long (or should I say a book?). I'm afraid that it is much too long to take your precious time. I can assure you that it would have been much shorter if I had been writing from a comfortable desk, but what else is there to do when you are alone for days in the dull monotony of a narrow jail cell other than write long letters, think strange thoughts, and pray long prayers?

If I have said anything in this letter that is an overstatement of the truth and is indicative of an unreasonable impatience, I beg you to forgive me. If I have said anything in this letter that is an understatement of the truth and is indicative of my having a patience that makes me patient with anything less than brotherhood, I beg God to forgive me.

I hope this letter finds you strong in the faith. I also hope that circumstances will soon make it possible for me to meet each of you, not as an integrationist or a civil rights leader, but as a fellow clergyman and a

---

Chief Pritchett Police Chief Laurie Pritchett. During the 1961–1962 demonstrations in Albany, Georgia, he opposed nonviolent protest with nonviolent arrests, not allowing his men to be physically or verbally abusive.
James Meredith Enrolled at the University of Mississippi at Oxford in 1962, with the help of federal marshals and the National Guard, after Governor Ross Barnett refused to allow his enrollment.

Christian brother. Let us all hope that the dark clouds of racial prejudice will soon pass away and the deep fog of misunderstanding will be lifted from our fear-drenched communities and in some not too distant tomorrow the radiant stars of love and brotherhood will shine over our great nation with all of their scintillating beauty.

> *Yours for the cause of*
> *Peace and Brotherhood*
>
> MARTIN LUTHER KING, JR.

The Reactor and the Garden

Wendell Berry

The following selection is taken from The Gift of Good Land: Further Essays Cultural and Agricultural *(1981). For information about the author and his work, see page 525.*

On June 3, 1979, I took part in an act of nonviolent civil disobedience at the site of a nuclear power plant being built at Marble Hill, near Madison, Indiana. At about noon that day, eighty-nine of us crossed a wire fence onto the power company's land, were arrested, and duly charged with criminal trespass.

As crimes go, ours was tame almost to the point of boredom. We acted under a well-understood commitment to do no violence and damage no property. The Jefferson County sheriff knew well in advance and pretty exactly what we planned to do. Our trespass was peaceable and orderly. We were politely arrested by the sheriff and his deputies, who acted, as far as I saw, with exemplary kindness. And this nearly eventless event ended in anticlimax: the prosecutor chose to press charges against only one of the eighty-nine who were arrested, and that one was never brought to trial.

And yet, for all its tameness, it was not a lighthearted event. Few of us, I think, found it easy to decide to break the law of the land. For me it was difficult for another reason as well: I do not like public protests or crowd actions of any kind; I dislike and distrust the slogans and the jargon that invariably stick like bubble gum to any kind of "movement."

Why did I do it?

For several years, along with a good many other people, I have been concerned about the proliferation of power plants in the Ohio River Valley, where at present more than sixty plants are either working, under construction, or planned. Air pollution from existing coal-fired plants in the valley is already said to be the worst in the country. And the new plants are being constructed or planned without any evident consideration of the possibility of limiting or moderating the consumption of electricity. The people of this area, then, are expected to sacrifice their health—among other things—to underwrite the fantasy of "unlimited economic growth." This is a decision not made by them—but, rather, made *for* them by the power companies in collaboration with various agencies of government.

The coal-fired plants would be bad enough by themselves. But, in addition, some power companies have decided that nuclear power is the best answer to "the energy problem," and two nuclear power plants are now under construction in this part of the Ohio Valley. The arguments in their favor are not good, but they are backed nevertheless by a great deal of money and political power. For example, our local rural electric co-op publishes a magazine which constantly editorializes in favor of nuclear power. The rate payers are thus, in effect, being taxed to promote an energy policy that many of them consider objectionable and dangerous.

Power plants in the Ohio Valley raise another serious problem, this one political. The Ohio River is a state boundary. A power plant on the north side of the river in Indiana will obviously have an effect in Kentucky. But though a plant will necessarily affect at least two states, it is planned and permitted only in one. The people of one state thus become subject to a decision made in another state, in which they are without representation. And so in the behavior of big technology and corporate power, we can recognize again an exploitive colonialism similar to that of George III.°

Like the majority of people, I am unable to deal competently with the technical aspects of nuclear power and its dangers. My worries are based on several facts available to any reader of a newspaper:

1. Nuclear power is extremely dangerous. For this, the elaborate safety devices and backup systems of the plants themselves are evidence enough. Radioactive wastes, moreover, remain dangerous for many thousands of years, and there is apparently no foreseeable safe way to dispose of them.
2. Dangerous accidents do happen in nuclear power plants. Officials and experts claim that accidents can be foreseen and prevented, but accidents are surprises by definition. If they are foreseen they do not happen.
3. Nuclear experts and plant employees do not always act competently in

---

George III   King of England (1760–1820), whose policies of coercion toward the American colonists led to the American Revolution.

dealing with these accidents. Nuclear power requires people to act with *perfect* competence if it is to be used safely. But people in nuclear power plants are just as likely to blunder or panic or miscalculate as people anywhere else.

4. Public officials do not always act responsibly. Sometimes they deliberately falsify, distort, or withhold information essential to the public's health or safety.

If I had doubts about any of this, they were removed forever by the accident at Three Mile Island.° And if I had any lingering faith that the government would prove a trustworthy guardian of public safety, that was removed by the recent hearings on the atomic bomb tests of the 1950s—which have revealed that the government assured the people living near the explosions that there would be no danger from radiation, when in fact it knew that the danger would be great.

And so when I climbed the fence at Marble Hill, I considered that I was casting a vote that I had been given no better opportunity to cast. I was voting no. And I was voting no confidence. Marble Hill is only about twenty miles upwind from my house. As a father, a neighbor, and a citizen, I had begun to look on the risk of going to jail as trivial in comparison to the risks of living so near a nuclear power plant.

But even though I took part wholeheartedly in the June 3 protest, I am far from believing that such public acts are equal to their purpose, or that they ever will be. They are necessary, but they are not enough, and they subject the minds of their participants to certain dangers.

Any effort that focuses on one problem encourages oversimplification. It is easy to drift into the belief that once the nuclear power problem—or the energy problem, or the pollution problem—is solved everything will be all right. It will not, of course. For all these separate problems are merely aspects of the human problem, which never has been satisfactorily solved, and which would provide every one of us a lifetime agenda of work and worry even if *all* the bedeviling problems of twentieth century technology were solved today.

An even greater danger is that of moral oversimplification, or self-righteousness. Protests, demonstrations, and other forms of "movement" behavior tend to divide people into the ancient categories of "us" and "them." In the midst of the hard work and the risks of opposing what "we" see as a public danger, it is easy to assume that if only "they" were as clear-eyed, alert, virtuous, and brave as "we" are, our problems would

---

Three Mile Island Location of a nuclear power plant in Pennsylvania where a major accident occurred on March 28, 1979. A breakdown in the cooling system caused radioactive gas to escape through the venting system, and there was serious threat of an explosion or of a core meltdown.

soon be solved. This notion, too, is patently false. In the argument over nuclear power—as in most public arguments—the division between "us" and "them" does not really exist. In our efforts to correct the way things are, we are almost always, almost inevitably, opposing what is wrong with ourselves. If we do not see that, then I think we won't find any of the solutions we are looking for.

For example, I believe that most people who took part in the June 3 demonstration at Marble Hill got there in an automobile. I did, and I could hardly have got there any other way. Thus the demonstration, while it pushed for a solution to one aspect of the energy problem, was itself another aspect of that problem.

And I would be much surprised to learn that most of us did not return home to houses furnished with electric light switches, which we flipped on more or less thoughtlessly, not worrying overmuch about the watersheds that are being degraded or destroyed by strip mines to produce the coal to run the power plants to make the electricity that burns in our light bulbs. I know, anyhow, that I often flip on my own light switches without any such worries.

Nearly all of us are sponsoring or helping to cause the ills we would like to cure. Nearly all of us have what I can only call cheap-energy minds; we continue to assume, or to act as if we assume, that it does not matter how much energy we use.

I do not mean to imply that I know how to solve the problems of the automobile or of the wasteful modern household. Those problems are enormously difficult, and their difficulty suggests their extreme urgency and importance. But I am fairly certain that they won't be solved simply by public protests. The roots of the problems are private or personal, and the roots of the solutions will be private or personal too. Public protests are incomplete actions; they speak to the problem, not to the solution.

Protests are incomplete, I think, because they are by definition negative. You cannot protest *for* anything. The positive thing that protest is supposed to do is "raise consciousness," but it can raise consciousness only to the level of protest. So far as protest itself is concerned, the raised consciousness is on its own. It appears to be possible to "raise" your consciousness without changing it—and so to keep protesting forever.

If you have to be negative, there are better negative things to do. You can quit doing something you know to be destructive. It might, for instance, be possible to take a pledge that you will no longer use electricity or petroleum to entertain yourself. My own notion of an ideal negative action is to get rid of your television set. (It is cheating to get rid of it by selling it or giving it away. You should get rid of it by carefully disassembling it with a heavy blunt instrument. Would you try to get rid of any other brain disease by selling it or giving it away?)

But such actions are not really negative. When you get rid of something undesirable you are extending an invitation to something desirable. If it is true that nature abhors a vacuum, there is no need to fear. Wherever you make an opening, it will be filled. When you get rid of petroleum-powered or electronic entertainment you are inviting a renewal of that structure of conversation, work, and play that used to be known as "home life." You are inviting such gentle and instructive pleasures as walking and reading.

Or it may be possible for some people to walk or ride a bicycle to work—and so to consider doing without a car altogether. Or there may be some kind of motor-powered tool that can be done without. Or perhaps it will prove economical or pleasing to change from fossil fuel heat to a solar collector or a wood stove.*

There is, then, a kind of negative action that cannot remain negative. To give up some things is to create problems, which immediately call for solutions—and so the negative action completes itself in an action that is positive. But some actions are probably more complete than others, and the more complete the action, the more effective it is as a protest.

What, then, is a complete action? It is, I think, an action which one takes on one's own behalf, which is particular and complex, real not symbolic, which one can both accomplish on one's own and take full responsibility for. There are perhaps many such actions, but certainly among them is any sort of home production. And of the kinds of home production, the one most possible for most people is gardening.

Some people will object at this point that it belittles the idea of gardening to think of it as an act of opposition or protest. I agree. That is exactly my point. Gardening—or the best kind of gardening—is a *complete* action. It is so effective a protest because it is so much more than a protest.

The best kind of gardening is a form of home production capable of a considerable independence of outside sources. It will, then, be "organic" gardening. One of the most pleasing aspects of this way of gardening is its independence. For fertility, plant protection, etc., it relies as far as possible on resources in the locality and in the gardener's mind. Independence can be further enlarged by saving seed and starting your own seedlings. To work at ways of cutting down the use of petroleum products and gasoline engines in the garden is at once to increase independence and to work directly at a real (that is, a permanent) solution to the energy problem.

A garden gives interest a place, and it proves one's place interesting and worthy of interest. It works directly against the feeling—the source of a lot of our "environmental" troubles—that in order to be diverted or enter-

---

*But the use of wood stoves without proper maintenance of wood lots is only another form of mining. It makes trees an exhaustible resource.

tained, or to "make life interesting," it is necessary to draw upon some distant resource—turn on the TV or take a trip.

One of the most important local resources that a garden makes available for use is the gardener's own body. At a time when the national economy is largely based on buying and selling substitutes for common bodily energies and functions, a garden restores the body to its usefulness—a victory for our species. It may take a bit of effort to realize that perhaps the most characteristic modern "achievement" is the obsolescence of the human body. Jogging and other forms of artificial exercise do not restore the usefulness of the body, but are simply ways of assenting to its uselessness; the body is a diverting pet, like one's Chihuahua, and must be taken out for air and exercise. A garden gives the body the dignity of working in its own support. It is a way of rejoining the human race.

One of the common assumptions, leading to the obsolescence of the body, is that physical work is degrading. That is true if the body is used as a slave or a machine—if, in other words, it is misused. But working in one's own garden does not misuse the body, nor does it dull or "brutalize" the mind. The work of gardening is not "drudgery," but is the finest sort of challenge to intelligence. Gardening is not a discipline that can be learned once for all, but keeps presenting problems that must be directly dealt with. It is, in addition, an agricultural and ecological education, and that sort of education corrects the cheap-energy mind.

A garden is the most direct way to recapture the issue of health, and to make it a private instead of a governmental responsibility. In this, as in several other ways I have mentioned, gardening has a power that is political and even democratic. And it is a political power that can be applied constantly, whereas one can only vote or demonstrate occasionally.

Finally, because it makes backyards (or front yards or vacant lots) productive, gardening speaks powerfully of the abundance of the world. It does so by increasing and enhancing abundance, and by demonstrating that abundance, given moderation and responsible use, is limitless. We learn from our gardens to deal with the most urgent question of the time: How much is enough? We don't soup our gardens up with chemicals because our goal is *enough,* and we know that *enough* requires a modest, moderate, conserving technology.

Atomic reactors and other big-technological solutions, on the other hand, convey an overwhelming suggestion of the poverty of the world and the scarcity of goods. That is because their actuating principle is excessive consumption. They obscure and destroy the vital distinction between abundance and extravagance. The ideal of "limitless economic growth" is based on the obsessive and fearful conviction that more is always needed. The growth is maintained by the consumers' panic-stricken suspicion, since they always want more, that they will never have enough.

Enough is everlasting. Too much, despite all the ballyhoo about "limitless growth," is temporary. And big-technological solutions are temporary: the lifetime of a nuclear power plant is thirty years! A garden, given the right methods and the right care, will last as long as the world.

A garden, of course, is not always as comfortable as Kroger's:° If you grow a garden you are going to shed some sweat, and you are going to spend some time bent over; you will experience some aches and pains. But it is in the willingness to accept this discomfort that we strike the most telling blow against the power plants and what they represent. We have gained a great deal of comfort and convenience by our dependence on various public utilities and government agencies. But it is obviously not possible to become dependent without losing independence—and freedom too. Or to put it another way, we cannot be free from discomfort without becoming subject to the whims and abuses of centralized power, and to any number of serious threats to our health. We cannot hope to recover our freedom from such perils without discomfort.

Someone is sure to ask how I can suppose that a garden, "whose action is no stronger than a flower," can compete with a nuclear reactor. Well, I am not supposing that exactly. As I said, I think the protests and demonstrations are necessary. I think that jail may be the freest place when you *have no choice* but to breathe poison or die of cancer. But it is futile to attempt to correct a public wrong without correcting the sources of that wrong in yourself.

At the same time, I think it may be too easy to underestimate the power of a garden. A nuclear reactor is a proposed "solution" to "the energy problem." But like all big-technological "solutions," this one "solves" a single problem by causing many. The problems of what to do with radioactive wastes and with decommissioned nuclear plants, for example, have not yet been solved; and we can confidently predict that the "solutions," when they come, will cause yet other serious problems that will come as "surprises" to the officials and the experts. In that way, big technology works perpetually against itself. That is the limit of "unlimited economic growth."

A garden, on the other hand, is a solution that leads to other solutions. It is a part of the limitless pattern of good health and good sense.

Kroger's Supermarket chain.

The Haves and
the Have-Nots

Am I my brother's keeper? Are we necessarily interdependent? Or should those who can best survive go it alone and those who cannot be left to their own devices? What, finally, is the proper relationship of those who have to those who have not? These questions have confronted societies from the beginning of history.

The United States has prided itself on being a land of opportunity, a society with a built-in escalator that leads from a state of poverty to a state of relative well-being. This may still be the case for some groups and individuals, but according to the 1983 Census report, 50 million Americans are poor or needy, and poverty, we are told, is increasing, not decreasing. What does this mean in terms of social policy, and how does it affect us as individuals?

The first three selections approach these questions from different perspectives. First, Charles Murray and Jesse Jackson debate Murray's thesis that if government-supported welfare were dismantled, "a lot of good things would begin to happen." Jo Goodwin Parker then writes from her own personal experience to make us feel and see what it means to be poor. Peter Marin next looks at two groups of homeless people in the United States, those "who have been marginalized against their will" and those "who have chosen (or accept or even prize) their marginality." He explores his own ambivalent responses in order to answer what he calls the central question: "Do we owe anything to these men and women?"

This is not only an economic and a social question, but also a moral one. In their Pastoral Letter, the Roman Catholic bishops of the United States urge an "examination of U.S. economic arrangements" in order to fulfill "the promise of the 'American Dream'—freedom for all persons to develop their God-given talents to the full." They also speak of "the urgent need to create equitable forms of global interdependence in a world now marked by extreme inequality."

The next group of essays takes up this issue of global interdependence. Garrett Hardin, thinking of rich countries, poor countries, food, and population, argues for the survival of the fittest and against sharing our resources. There follow two of the many replies generated by his hardheaded argument. Walter W. Benjamin replies that "ours is not a lifeboat but a luxury yacht," implying that the starvation of others comes in part from our own affluence. Norman Cousins, in a brief editorial, focuses mainly on the moral and psychological consequences of Hardin's views. He comments: "desensitization, not hunger, is the greatest curse on earth."

A Conversation: What Does the Government Owe the Poor?

Charles Murray and Jesse Jackson

Charles Murray is a social scientist whose book Losing Ground: American Social Policy 1950–1980 *(1984) has become one of the most influential works on poverty and social policy in the past twenty years. Murray (born 1943) was educated at Harvard and M.I.T. (Ph.D. 1974). He spent five years in the Peace Corps in Thailand, working on rural village health programs, and seven years in Washington on the staff of the American Institutes for Research, studying federally subsidized programs in such fields as welfare, urban education, child nutrition, teenage pregnancy, delinquency, and criminal justice. Some years of additional experience convinced him of the ideas presented in the book: that the government's War on Poverty legislation has been a failure; that its rules induce poor people to behave in ways destructive to their long-term interests, often providing incentives for failure rather than for success; that it deprives poor people of the motivation to work; that people of working age should be taken entirely off the federal welfare and income-support structure, "with no recourse whatsoever except the job market, family members, friends, and public and private locally funded services."*

Though obviously controversial, the book has been praised for its cogency and scholarship.

Murray, now a senior research fellow at the Manhattan Institute for Policy Research, has lectured widely and written many articles expounding his views. "Helping the Poor: a Few Modest Proposals," in Commentary *for May 1985, is a more detailed and systematic statement than he presents here.*

The Reverend Jesse Jackson, one of the most powerful black leaders in the United States, has excellent qualifications to debate the question of poverty. He was born in 1941, in circumstances that once led him to remark, "I was never poor. . . . We just didn't have any money. Our mother didn't allow us to think of ourselves as poor."

He graduated in sociology and economics from the North Carolina Agricultural and Technical State College in Greensboro in 1964, attended Chicago Theological Seminary for two and a half years, and then became a close associate of Dr. Martin Luther King, Jr. He was soon made director of Operation Breadbasket, which got jobs and better services for blacks through the use of boycotts and picketing. After King's assassination, Jackson became a Baptist minister, and he founded PUSH, an organization to "push for a greater share of economic and political power for poor people."

He has since become a national and international figure, and a prominent contender for the Democratic presidential nomination. In 1986 he launched the National Rainbow Coalition, designed as a "progressive force" within the Democratic party.

The editors of Harper's Magazine *invited Murray and Jackson to discuss welfare, government, and the nature of American poverty. The resulting conversation appeared in the April 1986 issue.*

Charles Murray: How can government help the poor? The problem is that, so far, we haven't been very good at it. During the late 1960s and early 1970s, we began a major effort to bring people out of poverty, to educate the uneducated, to employ the unemployable. We have to confront the fact that the effort to help the poor did not have the desired effect. In terms of education, crime, family stability, the lives of poor people have gotten worse since the 1960s, and we have to explain why.

During those years we, in effect, changed the rules of the game for poor people. Essentially we said, in a variety of ways: "It's not your fault. If you are not learning in school, it is because the educational system is biased; if you are committing crimes, it is because the environment is poor; if you have a baby that you can't care for, it's because your own upbringing was bad." Having absolved everybody of responsibility, we then said: "You can get along without holding a job. You can get along if you have a baby but have no husband and no income. You can survive without participating in society the way your parents had to." And lots of young people took the bait. So the question remains: What, if anything, does the government owe the poor?

Jesse Jackson: I'm as unimpressed with boundless liberalism as I am with heartless conservatism. Creative thinking has to take place. But to begin to think creatively, we have to be realistic: about the role of government, for example.

We cannot be blindly anti-government. The government has made significant interventions in many, many areas for the common good. Without public schools, most Americans would not be educated. Without land-grant colleges, the United States would not have the number one agricultural system in the world. Without federal transit programs, we would not have an interstate highway system. Without subsidized hospitals, most Americans could not afford decent medical care. And the government has played a significant role in providing a base for many American industries. The defense industries, for example, may be considered private, part of the market, but many of them are almost wholly supported by government contracts.

Now, we consider spending the public's money toward these ends to be in our national interest. When we saw the devastation in Europe after World War II, we devised the Marshall Plan—a comprehensive, long-term program. Had the Marshall Plan been a five-year investment program— as the War on Poverty essentially was—Europe would have collapsed. But we determined that the redevelopment of Europe was in our national interest. That's an instance where a vigorous government investment made something positive happen.

But when we shift from the notion of subsidy as something that serves our national interest, to that of welfare, the attitudes suddenly shift from positive to negative. In this country there is a negative predisposition toward the poor. We must learn to see the *development* of people who are poor as in our national interest, as cost-efficient, as an investment that can bring an enormous return to every American. The government definitely has a big role to play.

Murray: I agree it has a role. There are some things government *can* do, and one of them is to ensure that a whole range of opportunities is available to everyone. For example, in my ideal world, whether a child lived in the inner city or in the suburbs, everything from preschool to graduate school would be available to him—free. In this ideal world, if someone really looked for a job and just couldn't find one, perhaps because of a downturn in the economy, some minimal unemployment insurance would be in place to help him.

Opportunity should be assured, but attempts at achieving equal outcome abandoned. What would happen if you took away all other government-supported welfare, if the system were dismantled? Well, believe it or not, a lot of good things would begin to happen.

Jackson: The notion of "opportunity" is more complicated than it sounds. For example, some people are poor *because* of government. When a nation is 51 percent female yet can't get an equal rights amendment passed; when many women still cannot borrow money with the same freedom men can, cannot pursue their ideas and aspirations in the marketplace because they are not equally protected—that amounts to government interference, too, but on the side of the status quo. Many blacks and Hispanics cannot borrow money from banks, on subjective grounds— because some bank official doesn't like their color, or because whole neighborhoods are redlined so that money will not be loaned to anyone living there. Government must be committed to the vigorous enforcement of equal protection under the law and other basic principles; without that enforcement, it is not a government handout that's the issue as much as it is the government's shoving people into a hole and not *letting* them out. When Legal Aid is cut, and the poor no longer have access to the courts, that's an example of government playing a role in *perpetuating* poverty.

Murray: If you try to rent an inexpensive apartment in my hometown of Newton, Iowa, even if you're white, you may very well not be able to rent that apartment, on "subjective grounds." I mean, you come to the door, and because of the way you act or the way you look or whatever, the landlord says to himself: "My apartment's going to get trashed." These subjective grounds often have a basis in fact. And it's real tough for people renting out apartments—and maybe even for banks—to operate in ways that enable them to make money if they aren't permitted to make these kinds of subjective judgments.

Jackson: Dr. Murray, the farmer wearing his bib overalls who walks up to that apartment door and is rejected for the way he looks is not a victim of racial prejudgment. That man could put on a suit and get the apartment. Blacks can't change color. The idea is that bankers choose not to make loans to blacks *institutionally.*

Now, I'm not just throwing around a charge here. John H. Johnson, the president of Johnson Publishing Company, which publishes *Ebony,* is perhaps the most established black businessman in the country. Yet several banks turned down his loan application to build in downtown Chicago. Maybe the most established black businessman in the country was turned down for a loan simply because of the institutional racism of banks. And so we need laws enforced, we need the government to protect people who are black or Hispanic or Asian or Indian or female, from the bankers' ability to do that.

A lot of people, to this day, are simply locked out. Until 1967, there had never been more than a couple of black car dealerships, because the automobile industry's policy was not to allow a black to invest in a car dealership or to learn to run one in any neighborhood, black or white. So blacks now have fewer than 240 dealerships out of the 22,050 in this country. Blacks always had the ability, but they were locked out by race, even if they had the money. Operation PUSH confronted Ford as late as

July 1982, when there were fewer than 40 black automobile dealerships out of 5,600. Ford finally agreed to grant thirty new black dealerships in one year, which they had previously claimed was impossible. Well, those thirty dealerships are still operating, employing an average of more than fifty people each, and those jobs represent the alternative to welfare and despair.

Murray: If you say that in 1960 blacks as a people were locked out, well, I have no problem with that. But that is no longer accurate. Let's talk about black youth unemployment. Are you saying that America's black youth are marching resolutely from door to door, interviewing for jobs, and that they are getting turned down because they're black? If so, then a jobs program ought to do wonders. CETA ought to have done wonders. But it didn't.

Jackson: The private economy, by being so closed for so long, has pushed many people into the public economy. There's just no reason why, in a population of 30 million blacks, there are only two black beverage-bottling franchises. You can't explain it by lack of ambition or an unwillingness to take risks, because for the past twenty years blacks have been the top salesmen in that industry. A lot of people got locked into poverty because of the government's failure to enforce equal protection under the law. Until the Civil Rights Act of 1964 and Lyndon Johnson's executive order of 1965, beverage companies could get lucrative government contracts to operate on U.S. military bases around the world, even though they locked out a significant body of Americans.

Murray: I'm not in a position to argue with you about wholesalers and franchises. But I don't think we can assume that if blacks gain more access to entrepreneurial business positions—which I'm all in favor of—it will have a fundamental effect on poverty and the underclass.

Jackson: If there is an artificial ceiling limiting the growth of the so-called talented 10 percent—I use the term advisedly—then it compounds the problem of the disinherited 90 percent. If where we live, our money won't "spend" because of redlining, which becomes a de facto law; if where we live, our money cannot buy a car franchise or a beer franchise or a soft-drink franchise—which are some of the great American ways out of poverty—then blacks are effectively locked out of the private economy. And so, just as the political grandfather clause locked blacks out of the political system, economic grandfather clauses have effectively locked blacks out of the economic system. Blacks today can take over a town politically, because its population is mostly black. But the economic territory—the entrepreneurial opportunities, beyond mom-and-pop businesses, which allow a people to develop a leadership class in the private economy, which in turn begins to lift others as it hires them and trains them—is still closed. Blacks who worked as salesmen and saleswomen for the first generation of black entrepreneurs now have franchises of their own, because they have access to the franchise head. But that has not happened historically.

Murray:　Why is it that the Koreans and Vietnamese and all sorts of other people who come here with very few resources do well, including West Indian blacks? They come here, start businesses, and manage to earn a median income which rivals or surpasses that of whites. I'm not trying to say racism doesn't exist. I'm saying it doesn't explain nearly as much as it ought to.

Jackson:　Do not underestimate the impact of 250 years of legal slavery followed by a hundred years of legal segregation. The damage it did to the minds of the oppressor and the oppressed must not be played down. When I grew up in South Carolina, I could caddy but I couldn't play golf. That's why I can't play golf now; I could have been arrested for hitting a golf ball at the Greenville Country Club. I could shag balls, but I couldn't play tennis. I could shine shoes, but I couldn't sit on the stand and couldn't own a stand at the train station. I could wait tables, but I couldn't sit at them; and I could not borrow money to build a competing establishment.

The other groups you mentioned have not known that level of degradation. The Cubans came to Miami as beneficiaries of a cold war between this country and Cuba; we used money and subsidies to induce them to come here, and those who came were in large measure from a class that had some history of business acumen. Many of the Vietnamese were beneficiaries of the same kind of cold war policy.

Now, shagging balls and not playing tennis, caddying and not playing golf, not voting and seeing others vote—all of this had the cumulative effect of lowering people's ambitions and limiting their horizons. Let me give an example. I saw a story in *USA Today* last summer headlined "More Blacks Graduating from High School, Fewer Going to College." A young lady from Chicago was quoted in the story, and I decided to meet with her and her mother. It turned out she had a B+ average, was a member of the National Honor Society—the whole business. I said to the girl, "Do you want to go to college?" She said she did. I said, "Well, have you taken the SAT tests?" She said she hadn't. "Why not?" "Well, the counselor told me that since I couldn't afford to go to college, that stuff was a waste of time." In other words, she was being programmed for failure, taught to be mediocre, programmed downward.

Once I discovered what was happening, I went on the radio and asked any high school student—black, white, brown—who had every college qualification except money to come to Operation PUSH. Seven hundred fifty young people came with their parents; we have placed 250 of them in colleges, including that young lady. But if that young lady hadn't gone to college, she would have been written off three or four years later: people would have said the family was subsidized, dependent; she didn't go to college; now she's pregnant; and the whole cycle begins again. She was programmed into lower ambition, programmed away from college. Yet many schools, especially the better ones like Harvard and Columbia, provide scholarship money. But so many students don't know this; it's a well-kept secret. Those who have, know; the circle remains essentially closed.

Murray: Getting that information out would serve as an *incentive*. I know how I'd spend money on educational programs. I'd put up a bunch of posters saying that anybody who gets such-and-such a score on the SATs will get a free ride through college. I'm willing to bet that I'd get more results from my program than the government would get by trying directly to improve the schools.

Jackson: There's a role for that kind of motivation. There's also a role for increasing opportunity. Often it's not lack of ability or ambition that locks people out, but lack of information.

Murray: I'm worried, because I'm starting to agree with you too much!

Jackson: Just give me time, you'll be all right.

Murray: Oh, I think we'll find some things to disagree on. I come from an all-white town. I went back to visit this Christmas, and I said to myself, "I wonder what poverty is like here in Newton, Iowa." So I got in touch with the human services people and spent some time riding around with a caseworker. And as I listened to this caseworker describe what her problems were, I realized that if I closed my eyes, I could have been listening to a caseworker in the South Bronx. The problems were indistinguishable from what are usually considered "black problems."

Jackson: Yes, we must whiten the face of poverty. It's an *American* problem, not a black problem. But the face of poverty in this country is portrayed as a black face, and that reinforces certain attitudes. I mean, John Kennedy holds up a sick black baby in his arms and people say, "Gee, he's a nice guy." He holds up a sick white baby in West Virginia and people say, "We've got to *do* something about this."

Of the 34 million people living in poverty in America, 23 million are white. The poor are mostly white and female and young. Most poor people work every day. They're not on welfare; they're changing beds in hospitals and hotels and mopping floors and driving cabs and raising other people's children. And there is no basis for taking a few people who cheat the system as examples, and using them to smear millions of people who by and large work very hard.

Murray: The welfare queen is not the problem. And the dynamics of dependency operate pretty much the same for both blacks and whites. For example, I did some checking on what the out-of-wedlock birthrate is among poor whites. Guess what? Middle-class blacks don't have much of a problem with out-of-wedlock births, just as middle-class whites don't; but poor blacks *and* poor whites alike have a big problem with it.

Now, when I visit a school in inner-city Washington, I see a couple of different kinds of kids. A lot of kids are sent out of their houses every morning by their moms and dads, who tell them, "Get that education. Study hard. Do what the teacher says." And these youngsters go off to school and study hard, do exactly what the teacher says, and still graduate a couple of years behind grade level—not because they're stupid, but because of what has happened to the school systems during the past twenty years. A great deal of energy and attention has been spent catering to the kind of kid who, for whatever reason, makes it real hard for the first set of kids to learn.

So I think we need to reintroduce a notion which has a disreputable recent history in America: the notion of class. A good part of our problem can be characterized as one of "lower-class behavior," which is distinct from the behavior of poor people.

Jackson: In other words, the Watergate burglars, though white, male, and rich, were engaging in "lower-class behavior."

Murray: No, but if you talk about the danger posed by the increase in crime, it so happens that it is not the rich white folks who are suffering.

Jackson: Back up now, back up. You introduced a phenomenon there, Dr. Murray, about "lower-class behavior." I suppose that means low morals.

Murray: You added that.

Jackson: Well, I *guessed* that's what it means. What does "lower-class behavior" mean?

Murray: The syndrome was identified long ago, although the term is more recent. People in the nineteenth and early twentieth centuries would simply talk about "trash," for example, and later there was the concept of the "undeserving poor." The sociologist who did the Elmstown study certainly recognized the syndrome, as did Edward Banfield. It is characterized by chronic unemployment due to people working for a while and then dropping out, unstable family life, and so on.

Jackson: But you know, Dr. Murray, you made a distinction here on this "lower-class behavior," and I was trying to get a definition of it, but I did not get it. I'm sorry, I haven't read all those books you mentioned. But I suppose it means *immoral* behavior.

Murray: I'm not using words like "moral" and "immoral."

Jackson: Well, I guess it means violence against people, unprovoked violence—lower-class behavior. Sex without love, making unwanted babies—lower-class behavior. Taking what belongs to other people—lower-class behavior. Filling your nose full of cocaine, driving drunk—lower-class behavior. That's not lower-class behavior, Dr. Murray, that's immoral.

It seems to me that whether it is stealing in the suites or stealing in the streets, whether it is happening in ghetto, barrio, reservation, or suburb, we should condemn lower-class behavior. Cain killing Abel, brother killing brother, is lower-class behavior because it's low morals, it's unethical, it's not right. Whether they're welfarized or subsidized, people should not engage in lower-class behavior. Is it more moral for a business executive to sniff cocaine than a welfare recipient?

Murray: If you are saying that rich white people can be lousy, I agree. But my point is that if we continue to pretend that all poor people are victims, if we do not once again recognize in social policy the distinctions that have been recognized all along on the street, we will continue to victimize those poor people who most deserve our respect and our help.

Parents, black or white, who are working at lousy jobs but who are *working,* paying the rent, teaching their kids how to behave—yes, those people are behaving differently, and certainly in a more praiseworthy way, than parents who fail to do those things. Poor people fall into very different classes, distinguished by differences in work behavior, such as chronic unemployment whether there are jobs or not. And there are differences in child rearing. Working-class people pay a lot of attention to how their children are doing; they talk to them, ask how they're doing in school. But there are children who come to school at the age of five and do not know, for example, the words for the colors; nobody's talked to them, they've been utterly neglected. Finally, when there is divorce among the working class the man takes continued responsibility for supporting the children. Lower-class behavior, on the other hand, is characterized by serial monogamy or promiscuity and a failure of the man to take responsibility for his children.

Jackson: Dr. Murray, the lady who lived across the street from us while I was growing up ran what they called a "bootleg house." She was a woman of high character: she was a seamstress, and all her children graduated from college. But on the weekend people came over to her house to drink and gamble, and so Mrs. X was considered an outcast. Now, another lady named Mrs. Y, who lived about three blocks from us, owned a liquor store; because she was white she could get a liquor license. Mrs. Y was an entrepreneur, Mrs. X was a moral outcast. But something told me early in the game that the only difference between Mrs. X and Mrs. Y was a license.

Men and women would come over to Mrs. X's house sometimes and have sex down in the basement: promiscuity, also a sign of lower-class behavior, and another reason why people looked down on her. Well, I began working at the hotel in town; I was paid to carry in the booze for the men who would meet women there, often other people's wives, sometimes even their friends' wives. They'd each leave at a different time and by a different door to maintain their respectability, but I knew where they lived because I used to cut their grass and rake their leaves. This is distinctly lower-class behavior—sleeping with other people's wives.

Murray: No, engaging in sexual behavior, even promiscuity, does not make you lower class. What makes you lower class is having kids you can't or don't take care of.

Jackson: Now, Dr. Murray, are you saying that a lawyer who has sex with his partner's wife and uses a prophylactic is engaging in behavior that's higher class than that of someone who does the same thing but does not have the sense or ability to use a prophylactic?

Murray: Look, I'm not against sex. I'm not even necessarily against sex outside of marriage.

Jackson: Now, don't get too swift on me here. The act of going to bed with another man's wife is adultery.

Murray: Fine.

Jackson: It ain't fine. It's *immoral*. It's lower-class behavior, and whether it takes place in the White House, statehouse, courthouse, outhouse, your house, my house, that behavior is unethical.

Murray: But that has nothing to do with what I'm saying.

Jackson: It shows a certain attitude: If you do something and it's subsidized, it's all right. If others do it and it's welfarized, it's not so good.

I was in inner-city Washington several months ago, talking to a gym full of high school kids. I challenged those who had taken drugs to come down front. About 300 came down. Next day the *Washington Post* published three pictures and the headline "Jackson does phenomenal thing—kids admit drug usage." Editorial: "It's a great thing that Jackson did, but you know he has a special way with black kids." Next day I went to a school in Maryland—in one of the richest counties in America, about 97 percent white, single-family dwellings, upper middle class, and all that. The principal said to me, "Well, you can make your pitch, but of course it won't work here." So I made my pitch. I said, "Taking drugs is morally wrong, except in controlled medical situations; it's morally wrong and ungodly." Six hundred students were present. I said, "Those who have tried drugs, come forward." About 200 came forward. This was a junior high school; these kids were thirteen, fourteen years old. The principal was in a daze. Now *that's* lower-class behavior and upper-class economic status. Rich folks embezzle and poor folks steal; rich folks prevaricate and poor folks lie. But I think a lie is a lie is a lie.

Murray: If we agree that lying is lying and stealing is stealing, that doesn't help the little old lady who is trying to get from her apartment to the grocery store without getting her Social Security check ripped off. If we take the attitude that white-collar crime is just as bad as street crime, so let's not go after the street criminals when we let the embezzlers get away, the problem is that we ignore that little old lady, who is not in much immediate danger from embezzlers. Poor people, first of all, need safety. We'll take care of the white-collar criminals as best as we can, but first I want to make it safe in the neighborhoods. And if that requires putting a whole bunch of people behind bars, let's do it.

Jackson: We should remember that four years at a state university in New York costs less than $25,000; four years at Attica costs $104,000. I am more inclined to take these young kids and lock them up in dormitories, give them years of mind expansion and trade development. It costs too much to leave them around for years without education, hope, or training.

The present welfare system should be replaced with a human development system. As presently constructed, the welfare system has built-in snares: there's no earn-incentive, no learn-incentive to get out. Assume you are locked into this box: a girl with a tenth-grade education and a baby. If she's making, say, $200 a month on welfare, why not provide some positive incentives? If she went back to school and got her junior college degree, she should get $240, $250. Why? Because that's making her employable, moving her closer to the market, where she can earn her own money. She can go back to junior college and study computer science, or learn cosmetology or business. The way it is now in most states, if she went out and found a job and made $200, they would take away $200 from welfare. So why earn the $200? Maybe if she earns $200 she should keep at least $100.

The point is that incentives to earn and learn must be built into the system. As it is now, if the young man who fathered the child doesn't have a job but comes back to live with the mother, she loses her check. So there's an incentive to keep the father away. And one of the few ways she can get any extra money is by engaging in an activity that may get her an extra child.

Now this young girl—white, black, Hispanic, Asian, Indian—is the victim of a system that is not oriented toward human development. We must take away the punishment and threats and disincentive and move toward a sense of optimism and increasing options.

Murray: One part of me endorses what you're saying in principle. But when I think of all the practical difficulties I get depressed. Most of all, it is extremely difficult to make much progress with youngsters who already have certain behavior patterns. If we go to a poor part of New York City, white or black, and pick a hundred kids who really have problems—drugs, illegitimate kids, the rest of it—and I say: "Here's a blank check; hire the best people, use the latest technologies, do whatever you can." At the end of three or four or even five years, if you start with seventeen- or eighteen-year-olds, *maybe* you will be able to point to ten or fifteen out of that hundred who show any major signs of getting somewhere.

Human beings aren't plastic. We don't know how to deal with certain kinds of problems after a certain age. The only route we have is prevention. So if you're hearing me say we're going to have to write off a generation, you can certainly back me into that corner.

Jackson: Dr. Murray, I have seen these same kids, who you say can't do anything, volunteer for the Army, and in six to eight months they are building bridges, assuming responsibility. Why? Because it's an effective program that teaches, inspires, and sets clear goals.

So many young people step into sex and have babies because of ignorance, lack of discipline, and the like. If there was sex education before the fact, as well as the teaching of moral values, then there'd be less debate about abortion after the fact. Today, there is this whole group of people who *love* the fetus; they march across America to save a fetus and march right back to cut off aid for a baby.

Aid to women for prenatal care has a lot of value. The Head Start program saved and salvaged a whole generation. The drive to wipe out malnutrition by Senators McGovern and Hollings in the food stamp program actually worked; it brought about balanced diets where there had been none. We should drop programs that aren't working, not those that are.

Murray: It is beginning to percolate into the consciousness of policy-makers that we just don't know how to affect large numbers of people who are leading blighted lives. The only way we can deal with this is by prevention.

Jackson: I agree that there are ways to change this situation without just paying another top-heavy layer of overseers and administrators who'd be sending paperwork back to Albany. I would take 500 young people and say, "How many of you would like this neighborhood to be cleaner?" Most hands would go up. "How many of you would like to have windows in your buildings in the wintertime?" Hands would go up. "How many of you would like to make $12 to $20 an hour?" Many hands. "Then here's what you must do if you want to make $12 to $20 an hour. We'll teach you how to be a mason. You can lay bricks and not throw them. You can learn how to be a glazier, how to be a plasterer. And at the end of this time we'll get you certified in a trade union. You will then have the skill to build where you live; if the floor's buckling in your gymnasium, you can fix it."

And so these young men and women would be empowered and enfranchised: they would much rather make $20 an hour than be on welfare. Just to do things *for* them while keeping them economically disenfranchised is no systemic change at all. And, Dr. Murray, people who can lay bricks and carpet and cut glass have no intention of going back on welfare.

Murray: I should point out that in my ideal world, by God, any black youngster who wants to can become a glazier, any poor youngster can learn a trade. And, Reverend Jackson, in my ideal world I would also clone *you*, because I've heard you speak to these kids.

Jackson: But why do you think black kids everywhere are playing basketball so well? I submit to you that they're playing basketball and football and baseball so well and in such great numbers because there is a clear and obvious reward; there's a carrot. Do this and you'll be in the paper, on the radio, on television. And you'll get a college scholarship. And if you're real good, you'll get a professional contract. So these same kids that you say are unreachable and unteachable will gravitate to a carrot if they can see it. There must be a way out. And right now we must come up with ways out.

Murray: Yes, education and training opportunity—the carrots—are absolutely central. But once you have those, you have to have a support system, and this is where we've got a real problem. For example, let's say a youngster graduates from high school without many skills. He gets into a good job-training program, one that will really teach him a skill if he buckles down. But the youngster has never learned good work habits, so he flunks out of the training program. For that youngster to come out of high school ready to take advantage of a training program, there must be changes in the school he came from.

Now, what about the youngster who is offered an opportunity but who is below average in intelligence? I mean, half the country is below average in intelligence, and in industriousness.

Jackson: Does that apply all the way through the government?

Murray: Let's just say this youngster is no great shakes, not much of anything. How is this youngster going to have a life that lets him look back when he's sixty and say, "Well, I did O.K., given what I had. At least I always supported myself and raised my kids and so on." The only way that eighteen-year-old kid is ever going to get to that position is by taking jobs that aren't much fun and don't pay much money. In order to reach the point where he feels good about supporting himself and his family, he's got to survive those years of eighteen, nineteen, twenty, when kids want to do things which make a whole lot of sense when you're that age but turn out to have been real stupid by the time you're thirty. Here is where, after you've provided the opportunities, which I am for in abundance, you've still got to worry.

Jackson: But Dr. Murray, democracy must first guarantee opportunity. It doesn't guarantee success. Now, why do you think these ghetto and barrio youngsters are doing so well in athletics?

Murray: Because they see people just like them, who came out of those same streets, making a whole lot of money doing it.

Jackson: So successful role models are a great motivator.

Murray: They make a huge difference. Now, how do we get the Jesse Jacksons of the world to be more visible role models?

Jackson: Well, I've been working on that for a few years. But the point is that where the rules are clear, even though the work is hard, the locked-out tend to achieve. Ain't no low-class and high-class touchdowns. But there are no black baseball managers and no black professional football coaches. Why? Because in those areas where the decisions are made behind closed doors and where the rules are not so clear, those who are locked out don't do well.

That is basically true in the private economy: the more subjective the rules, the less the penetration. When people go behind closed doors to, say, determine who the dean of the medical school will be, eight people who are doctors, all of them graduated from the same school, tend to come up with someone from the same lineage. Why are there so many blacks in government? Because if you do well on the test, you can get in, and the rules of seniority are established.

Murray: In 1983, the New York City Police Department gave a sergeant's exam, and 10.6 percent of the white candidates passed but only 1.6 percent of the blacks. So it was decided that even though the rules were clear, some blacks who had failed the test would be promoted in order to fill a quota. Now, either you assume that the test measured nothing relevant to being a sergeant and that skill is randomly distributed, so it didn't make any difference that a whole bunch of blacks were arbitrarily promoted despite the fact that they didn't pass the test, or you assume that the test did in fact measure abilities that are important to advancement. If that's true, a few years down the road very few of the black sergeants will become lieutenants. This ensures, in an almost diabolically clever way, that no matter how able blacks become, they will continue to be segmented, and whites will always be looking at black co-workers who aren't quite as good at their jobs as the whites are. You build in an appearance of inferiority where none need exist.

Now, your son went to St. Albans and my daughters go to National Cathedral. These are among the finest schools in Washington. Your son, when he applies for a job, doesn't need or want any special consideration. The fact that he's black is irrelevant.

Jackson: You're making dangerous comparisons here, Doctor, which tend to inflame weak minds. My son is not a good example because, like his father, his achievements are above average. The fact is that all of America, in some sense, must be educated about its past and must face the corrective surgery that is needed.

When there's moral leadership from the White House and from the academy, people tend to adjust. When Lyndon Johnson said—with the moral authority of a converted Texan—that to make a great society we must make adjustments, people took the Voting Rights Act and affirmative action and said, "Let's go."

There are a lot of positive examples around the country where integrated schools have worked, where busing has worked, where affirmative action has worked, when that spirit of moral leadership was present. The same school where the National Guard had to take two blacks to school in 1961—the University of Georgia—is where Herschel Walker won the Heisman Trophy. Later he was able to marry a white woman without protest in rural Georgia. Why? Because people had been taught that it was all right.

Murray: You've got the cart before the horse. By the mid-1960s, white folks finally, after far too long, had had their consciousnesses raised. They said to themselves, "We've done wrong. We have violated a principle that's one of the taproots of America; we haven't given people a fair shot just because their skin's a different color." A chord was struck that triggered a strong desire not only to stop doing the bad things but also to help people make up for lost ground.

That additional response was, from the very beginning, sort of pushing it. The principle that had actually been violated was that of the fair shot; but the black civil rights movement isn't feeding off that important nutrient anymore. It's gone beyond that. Today, when white folks aren't making public pronouncements, I hear far too many of them saying things which are pretty damned racist. I see a convergence of the old racism, which is still out there, with a new racism, from people who are saying, "Well, gee, it's been twenty years now. You'd think they'd be catching up by now."

Jackson: They're getting strong signals from the highest pulpit in the nation. When the White House and the Justice Department close their doors to the Afro-American leadership; when the Congressional Black Caucus cannot meet with the President of the United States; when the government closes its doors to the NAACP, the SCLC, the Urban League, Operation PUSH; when the White House will not meet with the Conference of Black Mayors; when those who work in the vineyards daily will not even engage in the dialogue you and I have engaged in today—that's reprehensible behavior. It sends out signals that hurt people. When leadership is present, people behave differently.

Murray: In addition to spending a lot of time talking to white people in general, I also spend a lot of time talking to conservatives. And I happen to know that their passion for a colorblind society is not just rhetoric.

Jackson: Are you a consultant for an optometrist? Because the only people who would benefit from people going colorblind would be optometrists.

Nobody wants to be that way, man. We don't *need* to be colorblind; we need to affirm the beauty of colors and the diversity of people. I do not have to see you as some color other than what you are to affirm your person.

Murray: I mean that the ideal of giving everybody a fair shot—of not saying to anyone, "Because you're black I'm going to refuse to give you a chance"—is something which a lot of conservatives feel more passionately about than a lot of your putative friends do.

Jackson: But if two people are in a one-mile race and one starts off with a half-mile head start and one starts off at point zero—O.K., now let's take the chains off, every man for himself—well, such a race is not just. We are starting out behind. I mean, of the top 600 television executives, fewer than fifteen are black.

Murray: I had a talk with somebody from one of the networks a few weeks ago, as a matter of fact. He said to me: "Well, we figured we ought to have a black producer, so we went out and hired the best one we could find. But he really isn't very good, so we do most of his work for him." Now, insofar as people aren't allowed to be TV producers because they're black, that's bad. But insofar as white people go around saying, "We had to get our black TV producer, so we brought in someone who can't make it on his own," they are not doing blacks a service.

Jackson: Man, for most of my life I have seen black people train white people to be their boss. Incompetent whites have stood on the shoulders of blacks for a long time. Do you know how impressed I am when a white rock singer who is selling millions of records explains how he got his inspiration from a black artist, who can't even afford to come to the white man's concert? A few months ago *Time* said in an article that Gary Hart was the only Democrat who has run a coast-to-coast campaign. I was on the cover of *Time* twice during the 1984 campaign. But Hart's the only one. Isn't that a strange phenomenon? It's like Ralph Ellison's invisible man: they look at you but they don't see you.

By and large, the black people the White House sees are those one or two exceptions who did something great. They take a Hispanic kid or a black person and try to impose that model on the nation. I could take the position, "Well, if I can make it from a poor community in South Carolina, explain to me how a white person can be in poverty," and it would be absurd. But I could argue it and get lots of applause.

Murray: I'm willing to grant that we shouldn't make so much of the exception if you grant me that just because folks may be against certain kinds of programs, it doesn't mean that they're mean-spirited, or don't care about problems.

Jackson: If we can avoid the demogogy and turn debate into dialogue and stereotypes into creative thinking, we can begin to develop ideas. I mean, I agree that this welfare system hurts people fundamentally. Many of the things that come from this Administration, like the enterprise zone idea, have a lot of validity. If an enterprise zone creates a green line, instead of a red line, where if you live in that area you get certain incentives—that idea has merit. It may mean that a young man or a young woman teaching school will want to move to a district because of a tax incentive, or perhaps a doctor or a lawyer will want to move his office there. You establish an incentive for people to locate there, through the tax system or otherwise; you begin to shift capital, and the people who live there have first option on the new jobs. But the Administration has never really discussed this idea with those who would have to communicate with the masses about it.

So that idea has merit. Together we could make sense of such an idea. I'm anxious to open up the door of social policy, and I'm impressed with this opportunity today.

What Is Poverty?

Jo Goodwin Parker

We reprint the selection below from America's Other Children: Public Schools Outside Suburbia *(1971), edited by George Henderson. According to a footnote in that anthology, this was an unpublished speech, given in Deland, Florida, on December 27, 1965. We have been unable to find more information about Jo Goodwin Parker, its author.*

You ask me what is poverty? Listen to me. Here I am, dirty, smelly, and with no "proper" underwear on and with the stench of my rotting teeth near you. I will tell you. Listen to me. Listen without pity. I cannot use your pity. Listen with understanding. Put yourself in my dirty, worn out, ill-fitting shoes, and hear me.

Poverty is getting up every morning from a dirt- and illness-stained mattress. The sheets have long since been used for diapers. Poverty is living in a smell that never leaves. This is a smell of urine, sour milk, and spoiling food sometimes joined with the strong smell of long-cooked onions. Onions are cheap. If you have smelled this smell, you did not know how it came. It is the smell of the outdoor privy. It is the smell of young children who cannot walk the long dark way in the night. It is the smell of the mattresses where years of "accidents" have happened. It is the smell of the milk which has gone sour because the refrigerator long has not worked, and it costs money to get it fixed. It is the smell of rotting garbage. I could bury it, but where is the shovel? Shovels cost money.

Poverty is being tired. I have always been tired. They told me at the hospital when the last baby came that I had chronic anemia caused from poor diet, a bad case of worms, and that I needed a corrective operation. I listened politely—the poor are always polite. The poor always listen. They don't say that there is no money for iron pills, or better food, or worm medicine. The idea of an operation is frightening and costs so much that, if I had dared, I would have laughed. Who takes care of my children? Recovery from an operation takes a long time. I have three children. When I left them with "Granny" the last time I had a job, I came home to find the baby covered with fly specks, and a diaper that had not been changed since I left. When the dried diaper came off, bits of my baby's flesh came with it. My other child was playing with a sharp bit of broken glass, and my oldest was playing alone at the edge of a lake. I made twenty-two dollars a week, and a good nursery school costs twenty dollars a week for three children. I quit my job.

Poverty is dirt. You say in your clean clothes coming from your clean house, "Anybody can be clean." Let me explain about housekeeping with no money. For breakfast I give my children grits with no oleo or cornbread without eggs and oleo. This does not use up many dishes. What dishes there are, I wash in cold water and with no soap. Even the cheapest soap has to be saved for the baby's diapers. Look at my hands, so cracked and red. Once I saved for two months to buy a jar of Vaseline for my hands and the baby's diaper rash. When I had saved enough, I went to buy it and the price had gone up two cents. The baby and I suffered on. I have to decide every day if I can bear to put my cracked, sore hands into the cold water and strong soap. But you ask, why not hot water? Fuel costs money. If you have a wood fire it costs money. If you burn electricity, it costs money. Hot water is a luxury. I do not have luxuries. I know you will be surprised when I tell you how young I am. I look so much older. My back has been bent over the wash tubs every day for so long, I cannot remember when I ever did anything else. Every night I wash every stitch my school age child has on and just hope her clothes will be dry by morning.

Poverty is staying up all night on cold nights to watch the fire, knowing one spark on the newspaper covering the walls means your sleeping children die in flames. In summer poverty is watching gnats and flies devour your baby's tears when he cries. The screens are torn and you pay so little rent you know they will never be fixed. Poverty means insects in your food, in your nose, in your eyes, and crawling over you when you sleep. Poverty is hoping it never rains because diapers won't dry when it rains and soon you are using newspapers. Poverty is seeing your children forever with runny noses. Paper handkerchiefs cost money and all your rags you need for other things. Even more costly are antihistamines. Poverty is cooking without food and cleaning without soap.

Poverty is asking for help. Have you ever had to ask for help, knowing your children will suffer unless you get it? Think about asking for a loan from a relative, if this is the only way you can imagine asking for help. I will tell you how it feels. You find out where the office is that you are supposed to visit. You circle that block four or five times. Thinking of your children, you go in. Everyone is very busy. Finally, someone comes out and you tell her that you need help. That never is the person you need to see. You go see another person, and after spilling the whole shame of your poverty all over the desk between you, you find that this isn't the right office after all—you must repeat the whole process, and it never is any easier at the next place.

You have asked for help, and after all it has a cost. You are again told to wait. You are told why, but you don't really hear because of the red cloud of shame and the rising black cloud of despair.

Poverty is remembering. It is remembering quitting school in junior high because "nice" children had been so cruel about my clothes and my smell. The attendance officer came. My mother told him I was pregnant. I wasn't, but she thought that I could get a job and help out. I had jobs off and on, but never long enough to learn anything. Mostly I remember being married. I was so young then. I am still young. For a time, we had all the things you have. There was a little house in another town, with hot water and everything. Then my husband lost his job. There was unemployment insurance for a while and what few jobs I could get. Soon, all our nice things were repossessed and we moved back here. I was pregnant then. This house didn't look so bad when we first moved in. Every week it gets worse. Nothing is ever fixed. We now had no money. There were a few odd jobs for my husband, but everything went for food then, as it does now. I don't know how we lived through three years and three babies, but we did. I'll tell you something, after the last baby I destroyed my marriage. It had been a good one, but could you keep on bringing children in this dirt? Did you ever think how much it costs for any kind of birth control? I knew my husband was leaving the day he left, but there were no good-bys between us. I hope he has been able to climb out of this mess somewhere. He never could hope with us to drag him down.

That's when I asked for help. When I got it, you know how much it was? It was, and is, seventy-eight dollars a month for the four of us; that is all I ever can get. Now you know why there is no soap, no needles and thread, no hot water, no aspirin, no worm medicine, no hand cream, no shampoo. None of these things forever and ever and ever. So that you can see clearly, I pay twenty dollars a month rent, and most of the rest goes for food. For grits and cornmeal, and rice and milk and beans. I try my best to use only the minimum electricity. If I use more, there is that much less for food.

Poverty is looking into a black future. Your children won't play with my boys. They will turn to other boys who steal to get what they want. I can already see them behind the bars of their prison instead of behind the bars of my poverty. Or they will turn to the freedom of alcohol or drugs, and find themselves enslaved. And my daughter? At best, there is for her a life like mine.

But you say to me, there are schools. Yes, there are schools. My children have no extra books, no magazines, no extra pencils, or crayons, or paper and the most important of all, they do not have health. They have worms, they have infections, they have pink-eye all summer. They do not sleep well on the floor, or with me in my one bed. They do not suffer from hunger, my seventy-eight dollars keeps us alive, but they do suffer from malnutrition. Oh yes, I do remember what I was taught about health in school. It doesn't do much good. In some places there is a surplus commodities program. Not here. The county said it cost too much. There is a school lunch program. But I have two children who will already be damaged by the time they get to school.

But, you say to me, there are health clinics. Yes, there are health clinics and they are in the towns. I live out here eight miles from town. I can walk that far (even if it is sixteen miles both ways), but can my little children?

My neighbor will take me when he goes; but he expects to get paid, *one way or another.* I bet you know my neighbor. He is that large man who spends his time at the gas station, the barbershop, and the corner store complaining about the government spending money on the immoral mothers of illegitimate children.

Poverty is an acid that drips on pride until all pride is worn away. Poverty is a chisel that chips on honor until honor is worn away. Some of you say that you would do *something* in my situation, and maybe you would, for the first week or the first month, but for year after year after year?

Even the poor can dream. A dream of a time when there is money. Money for the right kinds of food, for worm medicine, for iron pills, for toothbrushes, for hand cream, for a hammer and nails and a bit of screening, for a shovel, for a bit of paint, for some sheeting, for needles and thread. Money to pay *in money* for a trip to town. And, oh, money for hot water and money for soap. A dream of when asking for help does not eat away the last bit of pride. When the office you visit is as nice as the offices of other governmental agencies, when there are enough workers to help you quickly, when workers do not quit in defeat and despair. When you have to tell your story to only one person, and that person can send you for other help and you don't have to prove your poverty over and over and over again.

I have come out of my despair to tell you this. Remember I did not come from another place or another time. Others like me are all around you. Look at us with an angry heart, anger that will help you help me. Anger that will let you tell of me. The poor are always silent. Can you be silent too?

Helping and Hating the Homeless

Peter Marin

Peter Marin was born in 1936 and is a poet, educator, activist, and writer. After earning his B.A. in literature from Swarthmore and his M.A. from Columbia, he taught briefly at three different colleges, and in 1967–1968 he served as the director of an experimental high school in Palo Alto, California. Since then Marin has spent much of his time writing on subjects generated by his interest in young people and their place in modern culture. He is particularly interested both in dehumanization in American life and in our "psychic evolution," that is, in the possible changes in our individuality, our consciousness, our ability to deal with experience. He is

coauthor of the book Understanding Drug Use *(1960), coeditor of* The
Limits of Schooling *(1975), and author of* In a Man's Time *(1974). He is
also a contributing editor to* Harper's Magazine; *a longer version of the
following essay appeared in its January 1987 issue. The condensation
printed here is from the January 25, 1987, issue of* This World, *published
by the* San Francisco Chronicle. *It includes a few changes requested by the
author.*

When I was a child, I had a recurring vision of how I would end as an old
man: alone, in a sparsely furnished second-story room I could picture
quite precisely, in a walk-up on Fourth Avenue in New York, where the
second-hand bookstores then were. It was not a picture that frightened
me. I liked it. The idea of anonymity and solitude and marginality must
have seemed to me, back then, both inviting and inevitable.

Later, out of college, I took to the road, hitchhiking and traveling on
freights, doing odd jobs here and there, crisscrossing the country. I liked
that too: the anonymity and the absence of constraint and the rough
community I sometimes found. I felt at home on the road, perhaps because
I felt at home nowhere else, and periodically, for years, I would return to
that world, always with a sense of relief and release.

I have been thinking a lot about that these days, now that transience
and homelessness have made their way into the national consciousness,
and especially since the town I live in, Santa Barbara, has become well
known because of the successful campaign last year to do away with the
meanest aspects of its "sleeping ordinances"—a set of foolish laws making
it illegal for the homeless to sleep at night in public places.

During that campaign I got to know many of the homeless men and
women in Santa Barbara, who tend to gather, night and day, in a small
park at the lower end of town, not far from the tracks and the harbor,
under the rooflike, overarching branches of a gigantic fig tree. There one
enters much the same world I thought, as a child, I would die in, and the
one in which I traveled as a young man: a marginal world inhabited by
all those unable to find a place in "our" world.

Late last summer, the Santa Barbara city council was meeting to vote
on the repeal of the sleeping ordinances, though not out of any sudden
sense of compassion or justice. Council members had been pressured into
it by the threat of massive demonstrations—"The Selma of the '80s" was
the slogan one heard among the homeless.

But this threat that frightened the council enraged the town's citizens.
Hundreds of them turned out for the meeting. One by one they filed to the
microphone to curse the council and castigate the homeless. Drinking,
doping, loitering, panhandling, defecating, urinating, molesting, stealing—the litany went on and on, accompanied by fantasies of disaster: the
barbarian hordes at the gates, civilization ended.

What astonished me about the meeting was not what was said; one could have predicted that. It was the power and depth of the emotion revealed: the mindlessness of the fear, the vengefulness of the fury. Also, almost none of what was said had anything to do with the homeless people I know—not the ones I traveled with, not the ones in town. They, the actual homeless men and women, might not have existed at all.

In the last few months I have visited several cities around the country, and in each of them I have found the same thing: more and more people in the streets, more and more suffering. (There are at least 350,000 homeless people in the country, perhaps as many as 3 million.) And, in talking to the good citizens of these cities, I found, almost always, the same thing: confusion and ignorance, or simple indifference, but anger, too, and fear.

Homelessness, in itself, is nothing more than a condition visited upon men and women (and, increasingly, children) as the final stage of a variety of problems about which the word *homelessness* tells us almost nothing. Or, to put it another way, it is a catch basin into which pour all of the people disenfranchised or marginalized or scared off by processes beyond their control, those that lie close to the heart of American life. Here are the groups packed into the single category of "the homeless":

> Veterans, mainly from the war in Vietnam. In many American cities, vets make up close to 50 percent of all homeless males.

> The mentally ill. In some parts of the country, roughly a quarter of the homeless would, a couple of decades ago, have been institutionalized.

> The physically disabled or chronically ill, who do not receive any benefits or whose benefits do not enable them to afford permanent shelter.

> The elderly on fixed incomes whose funds are no longer sufficient for their needs.

> Men, women, and whole families pauperized by the loss of a job. Some 28 percent of the homeless population is composed of families with children, and 15 percent are single women.

> Single parents, usually women, without the resources or skills to establish new lives.

> Runaway children, many of whom have been abused.

> Alcoholics and those in trouble with drugs (whose troubles often begin with one of the other conditions listed here).

> Immigrants, both legal and illegal, who often are not counted among the homeless because they constitute a "problem" in their own right.

> Traditional tramps, hobos and transients, who have taken to the road or the streets for a variety of reasons and who prefer to be there.

You can quickly learn two things about the homeless from this list. First, you can learn that many of the homeless, before they were homeless, were people more or less like ourselves: members of the working or middle class. And you can learn that the world of the homeless has its roots in various policies, events and ways of life for which some of us are responsible and from which some of us actually prosper.

We decide, as a people, to go to war, we ask our children to kill and to die, and the result, years later, is grown men homeless on the street.

We change, with the best intentions, the laws pertaining to the mentally ill and then, without intention, neglect to provide them with services; and the result, in our streets, drives some of us crazy with rage.

We cut taxes and prune budgets, we modernize industry and shift the balance of trade, and the result of all these actions and errors can be read, sleeping form by sleeping form, on our city streets.

The liberals cannot blame the conservatives. The conservatives cannot blame the liberals. Homelessness is the sum total of our dreams, policies, intentions, errors, omissions, cruelties, kindnesses, all of it recorded, in flesh, in the life of the streets.

The homeless can be roughly divided into two groups: those who have had homelessness forced upon them and want nothing more than to escape it; and those who have at least in part chosen it for themselves, and now accept it, or in some cases embrace it.

I understand how dangerous it is to introduce the idea of choice into a discussion of homelessness. It can all too easily be used to justify indifference or brutality toward the homeless, or to argue that they are only getting what they "deserve." And yet it seems to me that it is only by taking choice into account, in all of the intricacies of its various forms and expressions, that one can really understand certain kinds of homelessness.

The fact is, many of the homeless are not only hapless victims but voluntary exiles, "domestic refugees," people who have turned not against life itself but against us, our life, American life. Look for a moment at the vets. The price of returning to America was to forget what they had seen or learned in Vietnam, to "put it behind them." But some could not do that, and the stress of trying showed up as alcoholism, broken marriages, drug addiction, crime. And it showed up too as life on the street, which was for some vets a desperate choice made in the name of life—the best they could manage.

We must learn to accept that there may indeed be people, and not only vets, who have seen so much of our world, or seen it so clearly, that to live in it becomes impossible. Here, for example, is the story of Alice, a homeless middle-aged woman in Los Angeles, where there are perhaps 50,000 homeless people, a 50 percent increase over the previous year. It was set down last year by one of my students at the University of California at Santa Barbara, where I taught for a semester. I had encouraged them to go find the homeless and listen to their stories. And so, one day, when this student saw Alice foraging in a dumpster outside a McDonald's, he stopped and talked to her:

> She told me she had led a pretty normal life as she grew up and eventually went to college. From there she went on to Chicago to teach school. She was single and lived in a small apartment.
>
> One night, after she got off the train after school, a man began to follow her to her apartment building. When she got to her door she saw a knife and the man hovering behind her. She had no choice but to let him in. The man raped her.
>
> After that, things got steadily worse. She had a nervous breakdown. She went to a mental institution for three months, and when she went back to her apartment she found her belongings gone. The landlord had sold them to cover the rent.
>
> She had no place to go and no job because the school had terminated her employment. She slipped into depression. She lived with friends until she could muster enough money for a ticket to Los Angeles. She said she no longer wanted to burden her friends, and that if she had to live outside, at least Los Angeles was warmer than Chicago.

This is, in essence, the same story one hears over and over again on the street. You begin with an ordinary life; then an event occurs—traumatic, catastrophic; smaller events follow, each one deepening the original wound; finally, homelessness becomes inevitable, or begins to seem inevitable to the person involved—the only way out of an intolerable situation.

We like to think, in America, that everything is redeemable, that everything broken can be magically made whole again, and that what has been "dirtied" can be cleansed. Yes, many of those on the streets could be transformed, rehabilitated. But there are others whose lives have been irrevocably changed, damaged beyond repair, and who no longer want help, who no longer recognize the need for help, and whose experience in our world has made them want only to be left alone.

How, for instance, would one restore Alice's life, or reshape it in a way that would satisfy our notion of what a life should be? What would it take to return her to the fold? How to erase the four years of homelessness, which have become as familiar to her, and as much a home, as her "normal" life once was? Whatever we think of the way in which she has resolved her difficulties, it constitutes a sad peace made with the world. Intruding ourselves upon it in the name of redemption is by no means as simple or as justifiable a task as one might think.

It is important to recognize the immensity of the changes that have occurred in the marginal world in the past 20 years. Whole sections of many cities—the Bowery in New York, the Tenderloin in San Francisco— were once ceded to the transient. In every skid-row area in America you could find what you needed to survive: hash houses, saloons offering free lunches, pawnshops, surplus-clothing stores and, most important of all, cheap hotels and flophouses and two-bit employment agencies specializing in seasonal labor. It was by no means a wonderful world. But it was a world.

But things have changed. There began to pour into the marginal world—slowly in the '60s, a bit faster in the '70s, and then faster still in the '80s—more and more people who neither belonged nor knew how to survive there. The '60s brought the counterculture and drugs; the streets filled with young dropouts. Changes in the law loosed upon the streets mentally ill men and women. Inflation took its toll, then recession. Working-class and even middle-class men and women—entire families—began to fall into a world they did not understand.

At the same time, the marginal world's landscape and its economy was shrinking radically. Jobs became harder to find. Modernization had something to do with it; machines took the place of men and women. And the influx of workers from Mexico and points farther south created a class of semipermanent transient workers. More important, perhaps, was the fact that the forgotten parts of many cities began to attract attention. Downtown areas were redeveloped, reclaimed. The skid-row sections of smaller cities were turned into "old townes." The old hotels that once catered to transients were upgraded or torn down or became warehouses for welfare families—an arrangement far more profitable to the owners. The mentally ill, who once could afford to house themselves in cheap rooms, the alcoholics, who once would drink themselves to sleep at night in their cheap hotels, were out on the street—exposed to the weather and to danger, and also in plain and public view: "problems" to be dealt with.

The homeless, simply because they are homeless, are strangers, alien—and therefore a threat. Their presence, in itself, comes to constitute a kind of violence; it deprives us of our sense of safety. Let me use myself as an example. If I walk through the park near my home and see strangers bedding down for the night, my first reaction, if not fear, is a sense of annoyance and intrusion, of worry and alarm. I think of my teenage daughter, who often walks through the park, and then of my house, a hundred yards away, and I am tempted—only tempted, but tempted, still—to call the "proper" authorities to have the strangers moved on. Out of sight, out of mind.

Notice: I do not bring them food. I do not offer them shelter or a shower in the morning. I do not even stop to talk. Instead, I think: my daughter, my house, my privacy. What moves me is not the threat of danger—nothing as animal as that. Instead there pops up inside of me, neatly in a row, a set of anxieties, ones you might arrange in a dollhouse living room and label: Family of bourgeois fears. Our response to the homeless is fed by a complex set of cultural attitudes, habits of thought and fantasies and fears so familiar to us, so common, that they have become second nature. And it is by no means easy to untangle this snarl of responses.

If you look to the history of Europe you find that homelessness first appears (or is first acknowledged) at the very same moment that bourgeois culture begins to appear. The same process produced them both: the breakup of feudalism, the rise of commerce and cities, the combined triumphs of capitalism, industrialism and individualism. The historian Fernand Braudel, in the "Wheels of Commerce," describes, for instance, the armies of impoverished men and women who began to haunt Europe as far back as the 11th century. And the makeup of these masses? Essentially the same then as it is now: ". . . widows, orphans, cripples . . . journeymen who had broken their contracts, out-of-work labourers, homeless priests with no living, old men, fire victims . . . war victims, deserters, discharged soldiers, would-be vendors of useless articles, vagrant preachers without licenses. . . ."

Then, as now, distinctions were made between the "homeless" and the supposedly "deserving" poor, those who knew their place and willingly sustained, with their labors, the emergent bourgeois world.

And just as the distinctions made about these masses were the same then as they are now, so too was the way society saw them. They seemed to bourgeois eyes (as they still do) the one segment of society that remained resistant to progress, unassimilable and incorrigible, inimical to all order.

With the Victorians we begin to see the entangling of self-protection with social obligation, the strategy of masking self-interest and the urge to control as moral duty. Order, ordure—this, in essence, was the tension at the heart of bourgeois culture, and it was the singular genius of the Victorians to make it the main component of their medical, aesthetic and moral systems. It was not a sense of justice or even empathy that called for charity or new attitudes toward the poor; it was hygiene.

All of this is still true in America. Here, for instance, is part of a paper a student of mine wrote about her first visit to a Rescue Mission on skid row.

> The sermon began. The room was stuffy and smelly. The mixture of body odors and cooking was nauseating. I remember thinking: How can these people share this facility? They must be repulsed by each other. They had strange habits and dispositions. They were a group of dirty, dishonored, weird people to me.
>
> When it was over I ran to my car, went home and took a shower. I felt extremely dirty. Through the day I would get flashes of that disgusting smell.

Our policies toward the homeless, our spontaneous sense of disgust and horror, our wish to be rid of them—all of this has hidden in it, close to its heart, our feelings about excrement.

What I am getting at here is the nature of the desire to help the homeless—what is hidden behind it and why it so often does harm. Every government program, almost every private project, is geared as much to the needs of those giving help as it is to the needs of the homeless.

Santa Barbara is as good an example as any. There are three main shelters in the city—all of them private. Between them they provide fewer than 100 beds a night for the homeless. Two of three shelters are religious in nature: the Rescue Mission and the Salvation Army. In the mission, as in most places in the country, there are elaborate and stringent rules. Beds go first to those who have not been there for two months, and you can stay for only two nights in any two-month period. No shelter is given to those who are not sober.

Even if you go to the mission only for a meal, you are required to listen to sermons and participate in prayer, and you are regularly proselytized. There are obligatory, regimented showers. You go to bed precisely at 10: lights out, no reading, no talking. After the lights go out you will find 15 men in a room with double-decker bunks. As the night progresses the room grows stuffier and hotter. Men toss, turn, cough and moan. In the morning you are awakened precisely at 5:45. Then breakfast. At 7:30 you are back on the street.

The town's newest shelter was opened almost a year ago by a consortium of local churches. Families and those who are employed have first call on the beds—a policy that excludes the congenitally homeless. Alcohol is not simply forbidden in the shelter; those with a history of alcoholism must sign a "contract" pledging to remain sober and chemical-free. Finally, in a paroxysm of therapeutic bullying, the shelter has added a new wrinkle: If you stay more than two days you are required to fill out and then discuss with a social worker a complex form listing what you perceive as your personal failings, goals and strategies—all of this for men and women who simply want a place to lie down out of the rain!

We are moved either to "redeem" the homeless or to punish them. Perhaps there is nothing consciously hostile about it. Perhaps it is simply that as the machinery of bureaucracy cranks itself up to deal with these problems, attitudes assert themselves automatically. But whatever the case, the fact remains that almost every one of our strategies for helping the homeless is simply an attempt to rearrange the world cosmetically, in terms of how it looks and smells to us. Compassion is little more than the passion for control.

The central question emerging from all this is, What does a society owe to its members in trouble, and how is that debt to be paid? It is a question that must be answered in two parts: first, in relation to the men and women who have been marginalized against their will, and then, in a slightly different way, in relation to those who have chosen (or accept or even prize) their marginality.

As for those who have been marginalized against their wills, the general answer is obvious: A society owes its members whatever it takes for them to regain their places in the social order. And when it comes to specific remedies, one need only read backward the various processes that have created homelessness and then figure out where help is likely to do the most good.

But the real point here is not the specific remedies required—affordable housing, say—but the basis upon which they must be offered, the necessary underlying ethical notion we seem in this nation unable to grasp: that those who are the inevitable casualties of modern industrial capitalism and the free-market system are entitled, by right, and by the simple virtue of their participation in that system, to whatever help they need. They are entitled to help to find and hold their places in the society whose social contract they have, in effect, signed and observed.

But those marginalized against their will are only half the problem. There remains, still, the question of whether we owe anything to those who are voluntarily marginal. What about them: the street people, the rebels and the recalcitrants, those who have torn up their social contracts or returned them unsigned?

I was in Las Vegas last fall, and I went out to the Rescue Mission at the lower end of town, on the edge of the black ghetto, where I first stayed years ago on my way west. It was twilight, still hot; in the vacant lot next-door to the mission 200 men were lining up for supper. There were elderly alcoholics in line, and derelicts, but mainly the men were the same sort I had seen here years ago: youngish, out of work, restless and talkative, the drifters and wanderers for whom the word "wanderlust" was invented.

At supper—long communal tables, thin gruel, stale sweet rolls, ice water—a huge black man in his twenties, fierce and muscular, sat across from me. "I'm from the Coast, man," he said. "Never been away from home before. Ain't sure I like it. Sure don't like *this* place. But I lost my job back home a couple of weeks ago and figured, why wait around for another. I thought I'd come out here, see me something of the world."

After supper, a squat Portuguese man in his mid-thirties, hunkered down against the mission wall, offered me a smoke and told me: "Been sleeping in my car, up the street, for a week. Had my own business back in Omaha. But I got bored, man. Sold everything, got a little dough, came out here. Thought I'd work construction. Let me tell you, this is one tough town."

In a world better than ours, I suppose, men (or women) like this might not exist. Conservatives seem to have no trouble imagining a society so well disciplined and moral that deviance of this kind would disappear. And leftists envision a world so just, so generous, that deviance would vanish along with inequity. But I suspect that there will always be something at work in some men and women to make them restless with the systems others devise for them, and to move them outward toward the edges of the world, where life is always riskier, less organized, and easier going.

Do we owe anything to these men and women? We owe them, I think, at least a place to exist, a way to exist. That may not be a moral obligation, in the sense that our obligation to the involuntarily marginal is clearly a moral one, but it is an obligation nevertheless, one you might call an existential obligation.

I think we as a society need men like these. A society needs its margins as much as it needs art and literature. It needs holes and gaps, breathing spaces, let us say, into which men and women can escape and live, when necessary, in ways otherwise denied them. Margins guarantee to society a flexibility, an elasticity, and allow it to accommodate itself to the natures and needs of its members. When margins vanish, society becomes too rigid, too oppressive by far and therefore inimical to life.

What we see on the streets of our cities are two dramas, both of which cut to the troubled heart of the culture and demand from us a response we may not be able to make. There is the drama of those struggling to survive by regaining their place in the social order. And there is the drama of those struggling to survive outside it.

The resolution of both struggles depends on a third drama occurring at the heart of the culture: the tension and contention between the magnanimity we owe to life and the darker tendings of the human psyche: our fear of strangeness, our hatred of deviance, our love of order and control. How we mediate by default or design between those contrary forces will determine not only the destinies of the homeless, but also something crucial about the nation, and perhaps—let me say it—about our own souls.

from *Economic Justice for All*

National Conference of Catholic Bishops

Traditionally, "pastoral letters" are announcements to the faithful in each Roman Catholic church of a diocese. In 1986, the National Conference of Catholic Bishops issued in book form a joint pastoral letter entitled Economic Justice for All: Pastoral Letter on Catholic Social Teaching and the U.S. Economy. *It describes what the Conference of Bishops perceived as the social, economic, and moral responsibility of all Roman Catholics in the United States. We print below a section from Chapter 1, titled "Urgent Problems of Today," with the original paragraph numbering.*

The preeminent role of the United States in an increasingly interdependent global economy is a central sign of our times.[1] The United States is still the world's economic giant. Decisions made here have immediate effects in other countries; decisions made abroad have immediate conse-

---

[1]Pope John XXIII, *Peace on Earth* (1963), 130–131.

quences for steelworkers in Pittsburgh, oil company employees in Houston, and farmers in Iowa. U.S. economic growth is vitally dependent on resources from other countries and on their purchases of our goods and services. Many jobs in U.S. industry and agriculture depend on our ability to export manufactured goods and food. (10)

In some industries the mobility of capital and technology makes wages the main variable in the cost of production. Overseas competitors with the same technology but with wage rates as low as one-tenth of ours put enormous pressure on U.S. firms to cut wages, relocate abroad, or close. U.S. workers and their communities should not be expected to bear these burdens alone. (11)

All people on this globe share a common ecological environment that is under increasing pressure. Depletion of soil, water, and other natural resources endangers the future. Pollution of air and water threatens the delicate balance of the biosphere on which future generations will depend.[2] The resources of the earth have been created by God for the benefit of all, and we who are alive today hold them in trust. This is a challenge to develop a new ecological ethic that will help shape a future that is both just and sustainable. (12)

In short, nations separated by geography, culture, and ideology are linked in a complex commercial, financial, technological, and environmental network. These links have two direct consequences. First, they create hope for a new form of community among all peoples, one built on dignity, solidarity, and justice. Second, this rising global awareness calls for greater attention to the stark inequities across countries in the standards of living and control of resources. We must not look at the welfare of U.S. citizens as the only good to be sought. Nor may we overlook the disparities of power in the relationships between this nation and the developing countries. The United States is the major supplier of food to other countries, a major source of arms sales to developing nations, and a powerful influence in multilateral institutions such as the International Monetary Fund, the World Bank, and the United Nations. What Americans see as a growing interdependence is regarded by many in the less developed countries as a pattern of domination and dependence. (13)

Within this larger international setting, there are also a number of challenges to the domestic economy that call for creativity and courage. The promise of the "American dream"—freedom for all persons to develop their God-given talents to the full—remains unfulfilled for millions in the United States today. (14)

Several areas of U.S. economic life demand special attention. Unemployment is the most basic. Despite the large number of new jobs the U.S. economy has generated in the past decade, approximately 8 million peo-

---

[2]Synod of Bishops, *Justice in the World* (1971), 8; Pope John Paul II, *Redeemer of Man* (1979), 15.

ple seeking work in this country are unable to find it, and many more are so discouraged they have stopped looking.[3] Over the past two decades the nation has come to tolerate an increasing level of unemployment. The 6 to 7 percent rate deemed acceptable today would have been intolerable twenty years ago. Among the unemployed are a disproportionate number of blacks, Hispanics, young people, or women who are the sole support of their families.[4] Some cities and states have many more unemployed persons than others as a result of economic forces that have little to do with people's desire to work. Unemployment is a tragedy no matter whom it strikes, but the tragedy is compounded by the unequal and unfair way it is distributed in our society. (15)

Harsh poverty plagues our country despite its great wealth. More than 33 million Americans are poor; by any reasonable standard another 20 to 30 million are needy. Poverty is increasing in the United States, not decreasing.[5] For a people who believe in "progress," this should be cause for alarm. These burdens fall most heavily on blacks, Hispanics, and Native Americans. Even more disturbing is the large increase in the number of women and children living in poverty. Today children are the largest single group among the poor. This tragic fact seriously threatens the nation's future. That so many people are poor in a nation as rich as ours is a social and moral scandal that we cannot ignore. (16)

Many working people and middle-class Americans live dangerously close to poverty. A rising number of families must rely on the wages of two or even three members just to get by. From 1968 to 1978 nearly a quarter of the U.S. population was in poverty part of the time and received welfare benefits in at least one year.[6] The loss of a job, illness, or the breakup of a marriage may be all it takes to push people into poverty. (17)

The lack of a mutually supportive relation between family life and economic life is one of the most serious problems facing the United States today.[7] The economic and cultural strength of the nation is directly linked to the stability and health of its families.[8] When families thrive, spouses contribute to the common good through their work at home, in the community, and in their jobs; and children develop a sense of their own worth

---

[3]U.S. Department of Labor, Bureau of Labor Statistics, *The Employment Situation: August 1985* (September 1985), Table A-1.

[4]Ibid.

[5]U.S. Bureau of the Census, Current Population Reports, Series P-60, 145, *Money Income and Poverty Status of Families and Persons in the United States: 1983* (Washington, D.C.: U.S. Government Printing Office, 1984), 20.

[6]Greg H. Duncan, *Years of Poverty, Years of Plenty: The Changing Economic Fortunes of American Workers and Their Families* (Ann Arbor, Mich.: Institute for Social Research, University of Michigan, 1984).

[7]See Pope John Paul II, *Familiaris Consortio* (1981), 46.

[8]Vatican Council II, *The Pastoral Constitution on the Church in the Modern World*, 47.

and of their responsibility to serve others. When families are weak or break down entirely, the dignity of parents and children is threatened. High cultural and economic costs are inflicted on society at large. (18)

The precarious economic situation of so many people and so many families calls for examination of U.S. economic arrangements. Christian conviction and the American promise of liberty and justice for all give the poor and the vulnerable a special claim on the nation's concern. They also challenge all members of the Church to help build a more just society. (19)

The investment of human creativity and material resources in the production of the weapons of war makes these economic problems even more difficult to solve. Defense Department expenditures in the United States are almost $300 billion per year. The rivalry and mutual fear between superpowers divert into projects that threaten death, minds, and money that could better human life. Developing countries engage in arms races they can ill afford, often with the encouragement of the superpowers. Some of the poorest countries of the world use scarce resources to buy planes, guns, and other weapons when they lack the food, education, and health care their people need. Defense policies must be evaluated and assessed in light of their real contribution to freedom, justice, and peace for the citizens of our own and other nations. We have developed a perspective on these multiple moral concerns in our 1983 pastoral letter, *The Challenge of Peace: God's Promise and Our Response.*[9] When weapons or strategies make questionable contributions to security, peace, and justice and will also be very expensive, spending priorities should be redirected to more pressing social needs.[10] (20)

Many other social and economic challenges require careful analysis: the movement of many industries from the Snowbelt to the Sunbelt, the federal deficit and interest rates, corporate mergers and take-overs, the effects of new technologies such as robotics and information systems in U.S. industry, immigration policy, growing international traffic in drugs, and the trade imbalance. All of these issues do not provide a complete portrait of the economy. Rather they are symptoms of more fundamental currents shaping U.S. economic life today: the struggle to find meaning and value in human work, efforts to support individual freedom in the context of renewed social cooperation, the urgent need to create equitable forms of global interdependence in a world now marked by extreme inequality. These deeper currents are cultural and moral in content. They show that the long-range challenges facing the nation call for sustained reflection on the values that guide economic choices and are embodied in economic institutions. Such explicit reflection on the ethical content of

[9]National Conference of Catholic Bishops, *The Challenge of Peace: God's Promise and Our Response* (Washington, D.C.: USCC Office of Publishing and Promotion Services, 1983).

[10]Cardinal Joseph L. Bernardin and Cardinal John J. O'Connor, Testimony before the House Foreign Relations Committee, June 26, 1984, *Origins* 14:10 (August 10, 1984): 157.

economic choices and policies must become an integral part of the way Christians relate religious belief to the realities of everyday life. In this way, the "split between the faith which many profess and their daily lives,"[11] which Vatican II counted among the more serious errors of the modern age, will begin to be bridged. (21)

Lifeboat Ethics: The Case Against Helping the Poor

Garrett Hardin

Garrett Hardin (born 1915) is a biologist who has written prolifically on the moral and social implications of his field. He is particularly interested in ecology, population, and the problems created by worldwide scarcity of resources. He received his Ph.D. in biology from Stanford in 1941. His dissertation was a study of algae as a large-scale source of food, but he later gave up his research in this area because he had come to believe that producing more food only worsens population problems. Hardin joined the faculty of the University of California, Santa Barbara, in 1946 and is now Professor Emeritus. He is a spirited contributor to periodicals and has written many books; he is especially devoted to—and especially skilled at—telling people things that they do not necessarily want to hear. Among his books are Exploring New Ethics for Survival *(1972),* Stalking the Wild Taboo *(1973),* Mandatory Motherhood *(1974), and* Filters Against Folly: How to Survive Despite Economists, Ecologists, and the Merely Eloquent *(1985). The present essay appeared in the September 1974 issue of* Psychology Today.*

Environmentalists use the metaphor of the earth as a "spaceship" in trying to persuade countries, industries and people to stop wasting and polluting our natural resources. Since we all share life on this planet, they argue, no single person or institution has the right to destroy, waste, or use more than a fair share of its resources.

But does everyone on earth have an equal right to an equal share of its resources? The spaceship metaphor can be dangerous when used by misguided idealists to justify suicidal policies for sharing our resources through uncontrolled immigration and foreign aid. In their enthusiastic but unrealistic generosity, they confuse the ethics of a spaceship with those of a lifeboat.

---

[11]*Pastoral Constitution,* 43.

A true spaceship would have to be under the control of a captain, since no ship could possibly survive if its course were determined by committee. Spaceship Earth certainly has no captain; the United Nations is merely a toothless tiger, with little power to enforce any policy upon its bickering members.

If we divide the world crudely into rich nations and poor nations, two thirds of them are desperately poor, and only one third comparatively rich, with the United States the wealthiest of all. Metaphorically each rich nation can be seen as a lifeboat full of comparatively rich people. In the ocean outside each lifeboat swim the poor of the world, who would like to get in, or at least to share some of the wealth. What should the lifeboat passengers do?

First, we must recognize the limited capacity of any lifeboat. For example, a nation's land has a limited capacity to support a population and as the current energy crisis has shown us, in some ways we have already exceeded the carrying capacity of our land.

So here we sit, say 50 people in our lifeboat. To be generous let us assume it has room for 10 more, making a total capacity of 60. Suppose the 50 of us in the lifeboat see 100 others swimming in the water outside, begging for admission to our boat or for handouts. We have several options: we may be tempted to try to live by the Christian ideal of being "our brother's keeper," or by the Marxist ideal of "to each according to his needs." Since the needs of all in the water are the same, and since they can all be seen as "our brothers," we could take them all into our boat, making a total of 150 in a boat designed for 60. The boat swamps, everyone drowns. Complete justice, complete catastrophe.

Since the boat has an unused excess capacity of 10 more passengers, we could admit just 10 more to it. But which 10 do we let in? How do we choose? Do we pick the best 10, the neediest 10, "first come, first served"? And what do we say to the 90 we exclude? If we do let an extra 10 into our lifeboat, we will have lost our "safety factor," an engineering principle of critical importance. For example, if we don't leave room for excess capacity as a safety factor in our country's agriculture, a new plant disease or a bad change in the weather could have disastrous consequences.

Suppose we decide to preserve our small safety factor and admit no more to the lifeboat. Our survival is then possible although we shall have to be constantly on guard against boarding parties.

While this last solution clearly offers the only means of our survival, it is morally abhorrent to many people. Some say they feel guilty about their good luck. My reply is simple: "Get out and yield your place to others." This may solve the problem of the guilt-ridden person's conscience, but it does not change the ethics of the lifeboat. The needy person to whom the guilt-ridden person yields his place will not himself feel guilty about his good luck. If he did, he would not climb aboard. The net result of conscience-stricken people giving up their unjustly held seats is the elimination of that sort of conscience from the lifeboat.

This is the basic metaphor within which we must work out our solutions. Let us now enrich the image, step by step, with substantive additions from the real world, a world that must solve real and pressing problems of overpopulation and hunger.

The harsh ethics of the lifeboat become even harsher when we consider the reproductive differences between the rich nations and the poor nations. The people inside the lifeboats are doubling in numbers every 87 years: those swimming around outside are doubling on the average, every 35 years, more than twice as fast as the rich. And since the world's resources are dwindling, the difference in prosperity between the rich and the poor can only increase.

As of 1973, the U.S. had a population of 210 million people, who were increasing by 0.8 percent per year. Outside our lifeboat, let us imagine another 210 million people (say the combined populations of Colombia, Ecuador, Venezuela, Morocco, Pakistan, Thailand and the Philippines), who are increasing at a rate of 3.3 percent per year. Put differently, the doubling time for this aggregate population is 21 years, compared to 87 years for the U.S.

Now suppose the U.S. agreed to pool its resources with those seven countries, with everyone receiving an equal share. Initially the ratio of Americans to non-Americans in this model would be one-to-one but consider what the ratio would be after 87 years, by which time the Americans would have doubled to a population of 420 million. By then, doubling every 21 years, the other group would have swollen to 354 billion. Each American would have to share the available resources with more than eight people.

But, one could argue, this discussion assumes that current population trends will continue, and they may not. Quite so. Most likely the rate of population increase will decline much faster in the U.S. than it will in the other countries, and there does not seem to be much we can do about it. In sharing with "each according to his needs," we must recognize that needs are determined by population size, which is determined by the rate of reproduction, which at present is regarded as a sovereign right of every nation, poor or not. This being so, the philanthropic load created by the sharing ethic of the spaceship can only increase.

The fundamental error of spaceship ethics, and the sharing it requires, is that it leads to what I call "the tragedy of the commons." Under a system of private property, the men who own property recognize their responsibility to care for it, for if they don't they will eventually suffer. A farmer, for instance, will allow no more cattle in a pasture than its carrying capacity justifies. If he overloads it, erosion sets in, weeds take over, and he loses the use of the pasture.

If a pasture becomes a commons open to all, the right of each to use it may not be matched by a corresponding responsibility to protect it. Asking everyone to use it with discretion will hardly do, for the considerate herdsman who refrains from overloading the commons suffers more than a selfish one who says his needs are greater. If everyone would restrain himself all would be well; but it takes only one less than everyone to ruin a system of voluntary restraint. In a crowded world of less than perfect human beings, mutual ruin is inevitable if there are no controls. This is the tragedy of the commons.

One of the major tasks of education today should be the creation of such an acute awareness of the dangers of the commons that people will recognize its many varieties. For example, the air and water have become polluted because they are treated as commons. Further growth in the population or per-capita conversion of natural resources into pollutants will only make the problem worse. The same holds true for the fish of the oceans. Fishing fleets have nearly disappeared in many parts of the world, technological improvements in the art of fishing are hastening the day of complete ruin. Only the replacement of the system of the commons with a responsible system of control will save the land, air, water and oceanic fisheries.

In recent years there has been a push to create a new commons called a World Food Bank, an international depository of food reserves to which nations would contribute according to their abilities and from which they would draw according to their needs. This humanitarian proposal has received support from many liberal international groups, and from such prominent citizens as Margaret Mead, U.N. Secretary General Kurt Waldheim, and Senators Edward Kennedy and George McGovern.

A world food bank appeals powerfully to our humanitarian impulses. But before we rush ahead with such a plan, let us recognize where the greatest political push comes from, lest we be disillusioned later. Our experience with the "Food for Peace program," or Public Law 480, gives us the answer. This program moved billions of dollars worth of U.S. surplus grain to food-short, population-long countries during the past two decades. But when P.L. 480 first became law, a headline in the business magazine *Forbes* revealed the real power behind it: "Feeding the World's Hungry Millions: How It Will Mean Billions for U.S. Business."

And indeed it did. In the years 1960 to 1970, U.S. taxpayers spent a total of $7.9 billion on the Food for Peace program. Between 1948 and 1970, they also paid an additional $50 billion for other economic-aid programs, some of which went for food and food-producing machinery and technology. Though all U.S. taxpayers were forced to contribute to the cost of P.L. 480, certain special interest groups gained handsomely under the program. Farmers did not have to contribute the grain; the Government, or rather the taxpayers, bought it from them at full market prices. The increased demand raised prices of farm products generally. The manufacturers of farm machinery, fertilizers and pesticides benefited by the farmers' extra efforts to grow more food. Grain elevators profited from storing the surplus until it could be shipped. Railroads made money hauling it to ports, and shipping lines profited from carrying it overseas. The implementation of P.L. 480 required the creation of a vast Government bureaucracy, which then acquired its own vested interest in continuing the program regardless of its merits.

Those who proposed and defended the Food for Peace program in public rarely mentioned its importance to any of these special interests. The public emphasis was always on its humanitarian effects. The combination of silent selfish interests and highly vocal humanitarian apologists made a powerful and successful lobby for extracting money from taxpayers. We can expect the same lobby to push now for the creation of a World Food Bank.

However great the potential benefit to selfish interests, it should not be a decisive argument against a truly humanitarian program. We must ask if such a program would actually do more good than harm, not only momentarily but also in the long run. Those who propose the food bank usually refer to a current "emergency" or "crisis" in terms of world food supply. But what is an emergency? Although they may be infrequent and sudden, everyone knows that emergencies will occur from time to time. A well-run family, company, organization or country prepares for the likelihood of accidents and emergencies. It expects them, it budgets for them, it saves for them.

What happens if some organizations or countries budget for accidents and others do not? If each country is solely responsible for its own well-being, poorly managed ones will suffer. But they can learn from experience. They may mend their ways, and learn to budget for infrequent but certain emergencies. For example, the weather varies from year to year, and periodic crop failures are certain. A wise and competent government saves out of the production of the good years in anticipation of bad years to come. Joseph taught this policy to Pharoah in Egypt more than 2,000 years ago. Yet the great majority of the governments in the world today do not follow such a policy. They lack either the wisdom or the competence, or both. Should those nations that do manage to put something aside be forced to come to the rescue each time an emergency occurs among the poor nations?

"But it isn't their fault!" Some kind-hearted liberals argue, "How can we blame the poor people who are caught in an emergency? Why must they suffer for the sins of their governments?" The concept of blame is simply not relevant here. The real question is, what are the operational consequences of establishing a world food bank? If it is open to every country every time a need develops, slovenly rulers will not be motivated to take Joseph's advice. Someone will always come to their aid. Some countries will deposit food in the world food bank, and others will withdraw it. There will be almost no overlap. As a result of such solutions to food shortage emergencies, the poor countries will not learn to mend their ways, and will suffer progressively greater emergencies as their populations grow.

On the average, poor countries undergo a 2.5 percent increase in population each year; rich countries, about 0.8 percent. Only rich countries have anything in the way of food reserves set aside, and even they do not have as much as they should. Poor countries have none. If poor countries received no food from the outside, the rate of their population growth would be periodically checked by crop failures and famines. But if they can always draw on a world food bank in time of need, their population can continue to grow unchecked, and so will their "need" for aid. In the short run, a world food bank may diminish that need, but in the long run it actually increases the need without limit.

Without some system of worldwide food sharing, the proportion of people in the rich and poor nations might eventually stabilize. The over-populated poor countries would decrease in numbers, while the rich countries that had room for more people would increase. But with a well-meaning system of sharing, such as a world food bank, the growth differential between the rich and the poor countries will not only persist, it will increase. Because of the higher rate of population growth in the poor countries of the world, 88 percent of today's children are born poor, and only 12 percent rich. Year by year the ratio becomes worse, as the fast-reproducing poor outnumber the slow-reproducing rich.

A world food bank is thus a commons in disguise. People will have more motivation to draw from it than to add to any common store. The less provident and less able will multiply at the expense of the abler and more provident, bringing eventual ruin upon all who share in the commons. Besides, any system of "sharing" that amounts to foreign aid from the rich nations to the poor nations will carry the taint of charity, which will contribute little to the world peace so devoutly desired by those who support the idea of a world food bank.

As past U.S. foreign-aid programs have amply and depressingly demonstrated, international charity frequently inspires mistrust and antagonism rather than gratitude on the part of the recipient nation [see "What Other Nations Hear When the Eagle Screams," by Kenneth J. and Mary M. Gergen, *Psychology Today,* June 1974].

The modern approach to foreign aid stresses the export of technology and advice, rather than money and food. As an ancient Chinese proverb goes: "Give a man a fish and he will eat for a day; teach him how to fish and he will eat for the rest of his days." Acting on this advice, the Rockefeller and Ford Foundations have financed a number of programs for improving agriculture in the hungry nations. Known as the "Green Revolution," these programs have led to the development of "miracle rice" and "miracle wheat," new strains that offer bigger harvests and greater resistance to crop damage. Norman Borlaug, the Nobel Prize winning agronomist who, supported by the Rockefeller Foundation, developed "miracle wheat," is one of the most prominent advocates of a world food bank.

Whether or not the Green Revolution can increase food production as much as its champions claim is a debatable but possibly irrelevant point.

Those who support this well-intended humanitarian effort should first consider some of the fundamentals of human ecology. Ironically, one man who did was the late Alan Gregg, a vice president of the Rockefeller Foundation. Two decades ago he expressed strong doubts about the wisdom of such attempts to increase food production. He likened the growth and spread of humanity over the surface of the earth to the spread of cancer in the human body, remarking that "cancerous growths demand food, but, as far as I know, they have never been cured by getting it."

Every human born constitutes a draft on all aspects of the environment: food, air, water, forests, beaches, wildlife, scenery and solitude. Food can, perhaps, be significantly increased to meet a growing demand. But what about clean beaches, unspoiled forests, and solitude? If we satisfy a growing population's need for food, we necessarily decrease its per capita supply of the other resources needed by men.

India, for example, now has a population of 600 million, which increases by 15 million each year. This population already puts a huge load on a relatively impoverished environment. The country's forests are now only a small fraction of what they were three centuries ago, and floods and erosion continually destroy the insufficient farmland that remains. Every one of the 15 million new lives added to India's population puts an additional burden on the environment, and increases the economic and social costs of crowding. However humanitarian our intent, every Indian life saved through medical or nutritional assistance from abroad diminishes the quality of life for those who remain, and for subsequent generations. If rich countries make it possible, through foreign aid, for 600 million Indians to swell to 1.2 billion in a mere 28 years, as their current growth rate threatens, will future generations of Indians thank us for hastening the destruction of their environment? Will our good intentions be sufficient excuse for the consequences of our actions?

My final example of a commons in action is one for which the public has the least desire for rational discussion—immigration. Anyone who publicly questions the wisdom of current U.S. immigration policy is promptly charged with bigotry, prejudice, ethnocentrism, chauvinism, isolationism or selfishness. Rather than encounter such accusations, one would rather talk about other matters, leaving immigration policy to wallow in the crosscurrents of special interests that take no account of the good of the whole, or the interests of posterity.

Perhaps we still feel guilty about things we said in the past. Two generations ago the popular press frequently referred to Dagos, Wops, Polacks, Chinks and Krauts, in articles about how America was being "overrun" by foreigners of supposedly inferior genetic stock [see "The Politics of Genetic Engineering: Who Decides Who's Defective?" *Psychology Today*, June 1974]. But because the implied inferiority of foreigners was used then as justification for keeping them out, people now assume that restrictive policies could only be based on such misguided notions. There are other grounds.

Just consider the numbers involved. Our Government acknowledges a net inflow of 400,000 immigrants a year. While we have no hard data on the extent of illegal entries, educated guesses put the figure at about 600,000 a year. Since the natural increase (excess of births over deaths) of the resident population now runs about 1.7 million per year, the yearly gain from immigration amounts to at least 19 percent of the total annual increase, and may be as much as 37 percent if we include the estimate for illegal immigrants. Considering the growing use of birth-control devices, the potential effect of educational campaigns by such organizations as Planned Parenthood Federation of America and Zero Population Growth, and the influence of inflation and the housing shortage, the fertility rate of American women may decline so much that immigration could account for all the yearly increase in population. Should we not at least ask if that is what we want?

For the sake of those who worry about whether the "quality" of the average immigrant compares favorably with the quality of the average resident, let us assume that immigrants and nativeborn citizens are of exactly equal quality, however one defines that term. We will focus here only on quantity; and since our conclusions will depend on nothing else, all charges of bigotry and chauvinism become irrelevant.

World food banks *move food to the people,* hastening the exhaustion of the environment of the poor countries. Unrestricted immigration, on the other hand, *moves people to the food,* thus speeding up the destruction of the environment of the rich countries. We can easily understand why poor people should want to make this latter transfer, but why should rich hosts encourage it?

As in the case of foreign-aid programs, immigration receives support from selfish interests and humanitarian impulses. The primary selfish interest in unimpeded immigration is the desire of employers for cheap labor, particularly in industries and trades that offer degrading work. In the past, one wave of foreigners after another was brought into the U.S. to work at wretched jobs for wretched wages. In recent years the Cubans, Puerto Ricans and Mexicans have had this dubious honor. The interests of the employers of cheap labor mesh well with the guilty silence of the country's liberal intelligentsia. White Anglo-Saxon Protestants are particularly reluctant to call for a closing of the doors to immigration for fear of being called bigots.

But not all countries have such reluctant leadership. Most educated Hawaiians, for example, are keenly aware of the limits of their environment, particularly in terms of population growth. There is only so much room on the islands, and the islanders know it. To Hawaiians, immigrants from the other 49 states present as great a threat as those from other nations. At a recent meeting of Hawaiian government officials in Honolulu, I had the ironic delight of hearing a speaker, who like most of his audience was of Japanese ancestry, ask how the country might practically and constitutionally close its doors to further immigration. One member of the audience countered: "How can we shut the doors now? We have many friends and relatives in Japan that we'd like to bring here some day so that they can enjoy Hawaii too." The Japanese-American speaker smiled sympathetically and answered: "Yes, but we have children now, and someday we'll have grandchildren too. We can bring more people here from Japan only by giving away some of the land that we hope to pass on to our grandchildren some day. What right do we have to do that?"

At this point, I can hear U.S. liberals asking: "How can you justify slamming the door once you're inside? You say that immigrants should be kept out. But aren't we all immigrants, or the descendants of immigrants? If we insist on staying, must we not admit all others?" Our craving for intellectual order leads us to seek and prefer symmetrical rules and morals: a single rule for me and everybody else; the same rule yesterday, today and tomorrow. Justice, we feel, should not change with time and place.

We Americans of non-Indian ancestry can look upon ourselves as the descendants of thieves who are guilty morally, if not legally, of stealing this land from its Indian owners. Should we then give back the land to the now living American descendants of those Indians? However morally or logically sound this proposal may be, I, for one, am unwilling to live by it and I know no one else who is. Besides, the logical consequence would be absurd. Suppose that, intoxicated with a sense of pure justice, we should decide to turn our land over to the Indians. Since all our other wealth has also been derived from the land, wouldn't we be morally obliged to give that back to the Indians too?

Clearly, the concept of pure justice produces an infinite regression to absurdity. Centuries ago, wise men invented statutes of limitations to justify the rejection of such pure justice, in the interest of preventing continual disorder. The law zealously defends property rights. Drawing a line after an arbitrary time has elapsed may be unjust, but the alternatives are worse.

We are all the descendants of thieves, and the world's resources are inequitably distributed. But we must begin the journey to tomorrow from the point where we are today. We cannot remake the past. We cannot safely divide the wealth equitably among all peoples so long as people reproduce at different rates. To do so would guarantee that our grandchildren, and everyone else's grandchildren, would have only a ruined world to inhabit.

To be generous with one's own possessions is quite different from being generous with those of posterity. We should call this point to the attention of those who, from a commendable love of justice and equality, would institute a system of the commons, either in the form of a world food bank, or of unrestricted immigration. We must convince them if we wish to save at least some parts of the world from environmental ruin.

Without a true world government to control reproduction and the use of available resources, the sharing ethic of the spaceship is impossible. For the foreseeable future, our survival demands that we govern our actions by the ethics of a lifeboat, harsh though they may be. Posterity will be satisfied with nothing less.

A Challenge to the Eco-Doomsters

Walter W. Benjamin

Walter W. Benjamin is Chair of the Department of Religious Studies at Hamline University in Minnesota, where he has taught since 1966. He received his Ph.D. from Duke University with a specialization in Christian ethics. He is particularly interested and active in the field of medical ethics. At the third annual Midwestern Conference on Food and Social Policy in 1978, Benjamin was one of a group of panelists who responded to an address by Garrett Hardin. The following essay, taken from the Christian Century *(March 24, 1979), is based upon his remarks on that occasion. A reply by W. M. Finnin, Jr., appears in the* Christian Century *on July 4, 1979.*

> *No man is an island, entire of itself; every man is a piece of the*
> *continent, a part of the main; if a clod be washed away by the sea,*
> *Europe is the less, as well as if a promontory were, as well as if a manor*
> *of thy friends or of thine own were; any man's death diminishes me,*
> *because I am involved in mankind; and therefore never send to know for*
> *whom the bell tolls; it tolls for thee.*
>
> JOHN DONNE

Ever since the publication of his essay "The Tragedy of the Commons" ten years ago, Garrett Hardin has been the leading exponent of a population policy that would embrace realism in place of naïveté, pragmatism in place of thoughtless charity, and consideration of long-range benefits in place of an immediate pay-off. Speaking bluntly and uncompromisingly, Hardin—professor of human ecology at the University of California, Santa Barbara—has brought such concepts as "social triage," "lifeboat ethics" and "environmental commons" into our discourse.

Dr. Hardin counsels prudence—a value not alien to our religious tradition. Jesus told his followers to be as "harmless as doves but as wise as serpents"; he warned them not to begin building a tower if they lacked the resources to complete it. Unlike some breast-beating critics on the far left who are forever placing the blame on America, Hardin holds Third World nations themselves largely responsible for their desperate plight. Some of their leaders, he says, are not convinced that they have a population problem; some are more concerned with "demagoguery than with demography." The "green revolution" was supposed to buy Third World countries time to put their houses in order, but some of them frittered the time away.

Certainly Hardin is right in insisting that "trade" is to be preferred to "aid." The former enhances feelings of mutuality, whereas the dole develops dependency on the part of the recipient and an attitude of condescension and noblesse oblige on the part of the giver. A Chinese proverb should be kept in mind: "If you give a man a fish, you feed him for a day; teach him how to fish and you feed him the rest of his life." Nonetheless, Dr. Hardin's views on the population explosion are inadequate in several respects.

1

1. *Hardin ignores the validity of other population strategies.* His own position is a "crisis-environmentalist" ideology—or, in more pejorative terms, an "eco-doomster" stance. Thomas Malthus was that ideology's "great prophet"; Paul Ehrlich and Garrett Hardin are "sons of the prophet." Crisis-environmentalists view both disease and cure as simple; our ecosystem is sick, and the cause of the malady is overpopulation. A remedy can be effected only by moving as quickly as possible—and it may already be too late—to zero population growth (ZPG). But how is this to be done? Persuasion won't work; therefore, governmental coercion will have to be applied. We must, after all, preserve our greatest value—quality of life.

Another population strategy is that of the "family planners," who aim to achieve ZPG by the elimination of all unwanted and unplanned pregnancies, both within and without marriage. They would provide complete and free access for individuals and families to all available methods of birth control, abortion and sterilization. Family planners stress the value of freedom: families know best, if they are given full information and if governmental coercion is minimized.

But a third position, that of the "developmentalists," has the most to recommend it, both scientifically and ethically. Like other population ideologies, it seeks to reduce pollution, stabilize population, and to declare the "religion of endless growth" lethal in its effect. At issue are not the ends toward which we strive, but the means. Developmentalists indict crisis-environmentalists for being reductionistic; that is, concerned only about climate, statistics and quantities. In contrast, the developmentalists' vision is wide-angled, for they see food and population issues as

ineluctably moral, economic, social and political. The value they emphasize, then, is distributive justice.

This tradition, which goes back at least as far as Aristotle, says that
human beings, in order to have community, must "play fair." We must
strike a balance between our own good fortune and the ill fortune of
others, striving toward equity and even-handedness; for without such
goals, we are barbarians. The credo of the developmentalist, then, is
"Take care of the people, and the people will take care of themselves." If
the exploited are given their due—employment, health care, security,
education, balanced diets—and saved from the precarious brink of near
extinction, birth rates will decline.

Dr. Hardin argues that "for all animals, good nutrition means greater
fertility"—an opinion that flies in the face of demographic data when
applied to human beings. Pervasive insecurity creates high human fertility. Where life is Hobbesian—"mean, nasty, brutish and short"—security
is sought in producing children. Each additional child increases one's
social and economic insurance against the void. Hardin's thesis, unsound
on its own terms, defies the fact that the best way to lower the birth rate
is not to let people drift closer to the abyss but rather to give them a better
life. Third World cultures are behaving as many European ones did 200
years ago; by plotting a curve relating birth and death rates according to
time, we can see that these countries are right on schedule. They are
struggling to get through the "demographic transition"—the shift from
high birth and death rates to low birth and death rates. To abandon them
now would be not only unjust but counterproductive.

2. *Hardin's metaphor of the "lifeboat" is not only misleading but dangerous.* Such imagery is a vestige of the 19th century laissez-faire era, but
the values it represents are deeply embedded in our national psyche, as
the cowboy ads for Marlboro cigarettes testify. Lifeboat ethics encourages
the worst myth-making tendencies, promoting the isolationism and self-
absorption that have always been our nemesis.

Perhaps Dr. Hardin should have stayed with his original metaphor, the
Commons. It, like some other images—Kenneth Boulding's "spaceship
earth," Marshall McLuhan's "global village" and Teilhard's° "wheat
sheaf"—is holistic and organic. Such figures of speech help us resist the
temptation to believe that salvation lies in separation and in "going it
alone." These images are in harmony with human evolution. To be sure,
all around we see conflicts and compartments—racial, religious, ethnic—
but despite these divisions, there are profound movements toward con-
nectedness, reunion and intercommunion. We are now trying to hammer
out laws for the mining of the seabed, recognizing that neither the moon,

---

Teilhard Pierre Teilhard de Chardin (1881–1955), priest, scientist, and philosopher.

nor the sea, nor the minerals under the sea belong exclusively to any one nation.

Even if we accept the lifeboat metaphor, we must acknowledge that ours is not a self-sufficient vessel. The higher our technology and the greater our consumption, the more vulnerable we become. The brief oil embargo by the OPEC° nations a few years ago indicated just how "tipsy" was our craft. We are dependent on other nations not only for oil but also for manganese, cobalt, chromium, titanium, tin, mercury, asbestos and many other minerals. Cartels are being organized by developing nations determined to secure fair prices for their raw materials. National "privatism" is at a dead end; interdependence is the wave of the future.

2

3. *Lifeboat ethics stresses survival as the* summum bonum, *to the neglect of other values.* Certainly, survival is an important value, but if it is proclaimed in fear and despair, will it not threaten the search for community, mutuality and reconciliation? Twenty years ago our nation, traumatized by the threat of nuclear holocaust, was on the brink of committing hundreds of billions of dollars to provide fallout shelters in case the ICBMs started dropping. Some individuals constructed elaborate shelters in their backyards and stocked them with food supplies—and a few even suggested that to prepare for a nuclear attack, the shelters would need to be equipped with machine guns to keep improvident neighbors away. I resolved then that I would not like to live in a world with people whose only value was survival. Had our nation taken the "shelter-survival" route then, we wouldn't have SALT° agreements now.

We have always seen ourselves as a humanitarian people. Our food, fiber, and technical know-how have aided millions. To be sure, we haven't always acted from motives of pure altruism. Reinhold Niebuhr° taught us that national "will to power" can never be excluded from an analysis of relations between groups. My concern is to keep the dialectic between egoism and altruism, U.S. and U.N., American citizen and Bangladesh peasant intact. To allow the "survivalists" to call the shots would, I believe, have a devastating effect on the American moral consciousness. Norman Cousins, former editor of *Saturday Review,* has said that "desensitization, not hunger, is the great curse" afflicting the earth. Not long ago a majority of Americans became accustomed to the napalming carried out by U.S. forces in Vietnam; it might not be hard for us to adjust to the

---

OPEC Organization of Petroleum Exporting Countries.
SALT Strategic Arms Limitation Talks, a series of ongoing negotiations between the United States and the Soviet Union, opened in Vienna in 1960. The talks have thus far led to two agreements.
Reinhold Niebuhr Theologian (1882–1971) who served as vice president and senior faculty member of New York City's Union Theological Seminary.

knowledge that there were tens of millions of children overseas dying with bloated bellies.

4. *Hardin's views encourage an American tendency toward ethnocentrism in viewing underdeveloped countries.* Those countries should be spared condescending references suggesting that they are inept, irresponsible and lacking in wisdom. It is an instinctive human reaction to deny our own guilt for the sufferings of others. We are blind to the devastating effects of colonialism, imperialism and the workings of multinational corporations on powerless people. Because people are poor does not mean that they are without virtue; nor, because they are powerless, are they without dignity. Our Western religious tradition informs us that it is the powerful, well-fed, militaristic nations that are in danger of losing their souls.

Lifeboat ethicists are unaware of ethnocentrism, their cultural bias. When Hardin says, "Every Indian life saved through medical or nutritional assistance from abroad diminishes the quality of life for those who remain," that is a view "from the top." But "from the bottom," the moral reality is seen quite differently, though the logic is no less exact: "Every American sustained at the cost of 60 times the resources now required to sustain an Indian diminishes the long-range quality of Indian life."

It may be that some Third World nations resist our efforts to dictate their population policies because they see a connection between our own policies and the social cancers growing in our body politic. They may say: "Certainly you have solved your population problem, but do we have to accept the rest—abortion, rampant divorce, delinquency, drug addiction, crime, disrespect of children for parents? Is this what you want for us?" Would that we could see ourselves as others see us.

3

5. *An appeal to determinism and necessity should not encourage fatalism.* A belief in various forms of determinism—economic, demographic, social—gave rise in the past to a "nothing can be done" attitude. For example, Adam Smith's "unseen hand" theory mysteriously united individual acts of selfishness that in aggregate produced a common good. Karl Marx's discovery of "scientific socialism" made it seem inevitable that capitalism was doomed. Only 100 years ago, social Darwinians accepted the dogma of the survival of the fittest; nature was "red in tooth and claw." Extrapolating their theory to the human world, they gave us another new commandment: "Let ill enough alone." Thus the robber barons were given the green light, social amelioration was said to violate "natural law," and the poor were regarded as deserving their miserable lot for having been born with deleterious genes and "unfavorable characteristics."

Dr. Hardin would have another commandment added to the Decalogue:

"Thou shalt not transgress against the carrying capacity of the environment." He speaks of the hubris of those who think that they can fly in the face of nature's ways. In general, I agree: there *are* limits—but we don't know what those limits are. When I was a boy working on a Minnesota farm, the agronomists of the time were saying that the maximum possible corn production was 60 bushels to the acre. And yet today farmers' yields of corn far exceed that figure. Again, I agree that the constraints of nature ought to be respected but we must admit that they are elastic. Let us not appeal to a new iron law of "carrying capacity" that will engender either fatalism or fanaticism and consign those we could have helped to a future of "benign neglect."

6. *Hardin prefers China over India as the model for the Third World.* I find it strange that Hardin can maintain that the 1 billion Chinese are "much better off" than the 600 million Indians. India, the world's largest democracy, despite significant agricultural and economic gains, is disorderly and inefficient, and people are starving. But people are not attracted to a democracy because of its efficiency, because its trains run on time, but because of its values—because it is an open society that values human dignity and preserves basic freedoms. In *The Brothers Karamazov,* the Grand Inquisitor speaks to the returned Christ: "In the end they will lay their freedom at our feet, and say to us, 'Make us your slaves but feed us.'" It is remarkable how myopic many academics are when it comes to totalitarian regimes. We admire societies that "have got it together." In the 1930s we glorified Soviet Russia; now China is seen as the ideal.

4

7. *Lifeboat moralists fail to see the connection between affluence and starvation.* In all honesty, we must acknowledge that ours is not a lifeboat but a luxury yacht. We are a throwaway, nonreturnable, planned-obsolescence society. When I was a boy in a family of seven, I carried a small two-and-a-half-foot can of garbage to the curb once a week. Today there are two or three large GI cans at the curb in front of each house in the suburb where I live, though the families are smaller.

The Club of Rome° has said that a nation with a diminishing population may nonetheless put increasing pressure on the ecosystem if it doesn't change "sloppy habit" life styles. To fixate on population is to touch only one aspect of our environmental crisis. It's easy for us to point the accusing finger at others for not making use of the pill, the IUD, the abortion and the vasectomy. But our worship of such luxuries as the private automobile, air conditioning and marbleized beef indicates that we have done

---

Club of Rome Nonpartisan, multinational organization founded in 1968 to promote research on global problems that affect all societies. The membership is made up of scientists, humanists, educators, national and international civil servants, and industrialists.

little in the areas of antipollution, recycling, energy reduction and simplification of life styles. Is it any wonder that some writers in other countries have said that "the world can stand only one United States"?

I conclude with a quotation from one who did not moralize or patronize, one who had a reverence for life; one who, by the way he spent his life, put deed and word together—Albert Schweitzer: "Wherever there is lost the consciousness that every man is an object of concern for us just because he is a man, civilization and morals are shaken, and the advance to fully developed inhumanity is only a question of time."

Of Life and Lifeboats

Norman Cousins

Norman Cousins (born 1912) is a prominent American editor and essayist. After graduating from Columbia Teachers College in 1933, he turned to a career in journalism. His name is most closely associated with the Saturday Review, *which, as executive editor, he brought into prominence in the 1940s and with which he was associated until 1980. Cousins has written steadily and fearlessly on most of the major issues of his time. Perhaps his best-known work is* Modern Man Is Obsolete *(1945), written in response to the dropping of the atomic bomb on Hiroshima. He has also written memorably on American democracy and on world federation.* Anatomy of an Illness *(1979) records his own confrontation of a medical crisis with remarkable strength and insight. His continuing interest in medicine and in the relationship between the human mind and physical health is shown in much of his more recent writing, especially in* Healing and Belief *(1982) and* The Healing Heart *(1983). As Adjunct Professor of Medical Humanities at the School of Medicine at UCLA, he lectures to medical students on philosophy and literature. His most recent book is* The Pathology of Power *(1987). The present essay, one of several editorials written by Cousins in response to the ideas of Garrett Hardin, appeared in the* Saturday Review *for March 8, 1975.*

New Delhi

A short distance outside New Delhi, I saw a long file of protest marchers walking slowly in the direction of the capital. Most of them were young adults. They were identified by their placards as teachers, students, farmers, shopkeepers, commercial workers.

One of the placards said: HUNGRY PEOPLE ARE HUMAN, TOO. Another sign: IS INDIA GOING TO BE THROWN ON THE RUBBISH HEAP?

I learned that the reason for the march was the increasing discussion in the Indian press over reports that Western nations, including the United States, are getting ready to turn their backs on India's starving millions. The reports suggest that Western policy-makers feel that no amount of aid can prevent mass famine.

A person whose name has been linked frequently to such a hard-line approach is Garrett Hardin, professor of biology at the University of California, Santa Barbara. According to the reports, Professor Hardin believes that the Western nations are justified in denying aid to famine-threatened countries. He uses the analogy of the lifeboat. If the survivors take more than a certain number on board, everyone will go down.

Professor Hardin's ideas and the shocked reaction of the young people on the New Delhi march serve to dramatize what is rapidly becoming the most important issue before contemporary civilization. The attitudes of the rich toward the poor and the poor toward the rich are setting the stage for what could become the costliest showdown in history. C. P. Snow° sees a world divided between the 75 percent who are starving and the 25 percent who are sitting in their living rooms watching it happen on TV. Robert Heilbroner, in *An Inquiry Into the Human Prospect,* foresees a possibility of atomic blackmail by the hungry nations in possession of nuclear secrets. He predicts these countries will not hesitate to risk a holocaust if they don't receive a larger share of the world's vital resources.

Such a showdown is not a misty, distant possibility, but a fast-growing reality, of which the protest marchers near New Delhi were an early warning. It is not difficult to understand their feelings. Their grievance is not that they think they are entitled to outside help as a matter of natural right, but that they are now being told, in effect, that they are not worth helping. They are protesting lifeboat analogies and the notion that some people have the right to decide whether others should live or die.

The trouble with Professor Hardin's thesis is that it is unsound in its own terms. It defies the fact that the best way to bring down the birth rate is not to let people starve, but to give them a better life. It calls for education, nutrition, decent housing, productive work. Instead of eliminating or cutting back on aid, we ought to be stepping up shipments of fertilizers, chemicals, plows, tractors, harvesting machines, tools, engines, dynamos, and thousands of other items involved in upgrading living standards.

India itself is demonstrating what can be done with a concentrated program of technological innovation. It has cut its food deficit by a third in little more than one year. Several model agricultural communities that have had the benefit of adequate fertilizer and modern equipment have increased the food yield per acre by more than 200 percent. In light of these facts, nothing is more irresponsible or incompetent than to say help by the outside world should be withheld.

C. P. Snow British novelist and physicist (1905–1972) concerned about the communication gap between scientists and humanists.

The principal cancer of the Hardin approach will be felt, not by India, but by the West itself. For Hardinism can become a wild infection in the moral consciousness. If it is possible to rationalize letting large numbers of Asians starve, it will be no time at all before we apply the same reasoning to people at home. Once we discover how easy it is to stare without flinching at famine in Calcutta or Dacca, it should be no trick to be unblinking at the disease-ridden tenements of Harlem or Detroit or the squalor of the shacks in Appalachia.

Desensitization, not hunger, is the greatest curse on earth. It begins by calibrating people's credentials to live and ends by cheapening all life. People were appalled by Lt. William Calley's° moral callousness in spraying machine-gun bullets at Vietnamese. But the difference between Calley's contempt for human life and a policy of impassiveness toward starvation is a difference in degree and not in values.

Famine in India and Bangladesh is a test not just of our capacity to respond as human beings but of our ability to understand the cycles of civilization. We can't ignore outstretched hands without destroying that which is most significant in the American character—a sense of vital identification with human beings wherever they are. Regarding life as the highest value is more important to the future of America than anything we make or sell. We need not be bashful in facing up to that fact and in trying to put it to work.

Lt. William Calley Platoon leader at the Mai Lai massacre (1969), the Vietnam War. He was later court-martialed and found guilty of murdering unarmed South Vietnamese civilians.

Technology and Human Values

The successful application of science to our practical problems has been truly described as "one of the miracles of mankind." But no serious person today can discuss technological progress without misgivings. Most of us, at least, are aware of some of the terrifying consequences that seem always to accompany the gains: the atomic balance of terror; the population explosion; the poisoning of our air, water, and soil; the electronic and psychological threat to privacy; the displacement of skilled workers by skilled machines; the recent advances in brain chemistry and genetics that promise even more danger to human beings.

We place E. B. White's comical science fiction, written in 1950, first because it not only epitomizes the truth that technological progress is always ambiguous, but also deftly brings into the orbit of the present subject two of the topics raised in other sections: the values propagated by television, and the nature of the good life.

There follow two essays by historians, originally designed as part of a debate on technology and pessimism, which take up the issue, pro and con, in very general terms. Melvin Kranzberg is on balance optimistic. He points out that technology is never autonomous, but gets its effects, for good or evil, by the combinations (sometimes unanticipated) that it makes with other aspects of our society. He is confident that American vitality can overcome whatever problems technology presents. John H. Broomfield is emphatically pessimistic; he links the present threat of "bureaucratic technology" to deep defects in our economic, political, and social structures. Wendell Berry is also critical of the technological mentality, insisting that technology be above all limited "to a human or democratic scale." The essay by Langdon Winner argues that technical arrangements—even those that appear to be neutral "improvements"—are often implements of economic and social ordering, and should be given the same careful attention we give to legal and political decisions.

The last two essays deal with some of the risks and ethical dilemmas newly posed by the science of genetics and its remarkable technology. Susan Wright advocates much more control than we now exercise over the awesome possibilities of genetic engineering. Robert Bazell points out some serious moral problems raised by genetic testing. What do we do with the knowledge that an individual carries a gene that will sooner or later cause an incurable disease?

Succeeding sections of the book take up related issues brought on by computer technology and by television.

The Morning of the Day They Did It

E. B. White

Elwyn Brooks White (1899–1985) was born in New York, graduated from Cornell in 1921, and joined the staff of The New Yorker *in 1926. He regularly wrote its "Notes and Comment" section until 1938, and along with James Thurber and a few others with talent, was responsible for* The New Yorker's *extraordinary reputation for good writing at that time. From 1938 to 1943, he contributed a monthly column entitled "One Man's Meat" to* Harper's; *in 1932, he acquired a salt-water farm in Maine, the inspiration for a number of those essays. He resumed writing for* The New Yorker *on a free-lance basis in 1945. White wrote over twenty books and is noted for his sensitive, humorous character and his witty, natural, and exact style. He was awarded numerous honorary degrees, the National Institute of Arts and Letters gold medal (1960), and, in 1963, the Presidential Medal of Freedom.*

White wrote three distinguished children's books, for which he received the Laura Ingalls Wilder Award in 1970: Stuart Little *(1945),* Charlotte's Web *(1952), and* Trumpet of the Swan *(1970). In 1959 he published* The Elements of Style, *a reverent re-editing of a classic textbook written by his former professor, William Strunk, Jr. Recent collections of his works include* Letters of E. B. White *(1976),* Essays of E. B. White *(1977), and* Poems and Sketches of E. B. White *(1981). The story printed below, taken from* The Second Tree from the Corner *(1954), was first published in* The New Yorker *in February 1950.*

My purpose is to tell how it happened and to set down a few impressions of that morning while it is fresh in memory. I was in a plane that was in radio communication with the men on the platform. To put the matter briefly, what was intended as a military expedient turned suddenly into a holocaust. The explanation was plain enough to me, for, like millions of others, I was listening to the conversation between the two men and was instantly aware of the quick shift it took. That part is clear. What is not so clear is how I myself survived, but I am beginning to understand that, too. I shall not burden the reader with an explanation, however, as the facts are tedious and implausible. I am now in good health and fair spirits, among friendly people on an inferior planet, at a very great distance from the sun. Even the move from one planet to another has not relieved me of the nagging curse that besets writing men—the feeling that they must produce some sort of record of their times.

The thing happened shortly before twelve noon. I came out of my house on East Harding Boulevard at quarter of eight that morning, swinging my newspaper and feeling pretty good. The March day was mild and spring-like, the warmth and the smells doubly welcome after the rotten weather we'd been having. A gentle wind met me on the Boulevard, frisked me, and went on. A man in a leather cap was loading bedsprings into a van in front of No. 220. I remember that as I walked along I worked my tongue around the roof of my mouth, trying to dislodge a prune skin. (These details have no significance; why write them down?)

A few blocks from home there was a Contakt plane station and I hurried in, caught the 8:10 plane, and was soon aloft. I always hated a jet-assist takeoff right after breakfast, but it was one of the discomforts that went with my job. At ten thousand feet our small plane made contact with the big one, we passengers were transferred, and the big ship went on up to fifty thousand, which was the height television planes flew at. I was a script writer for one of the programs. My tour of duty was supposed to be eight hours.

I should probably explain here that at the period of which I am writing, the last days of the planet earth, telecasting was done from planes circling the stratosphere. This eliminated the coaxial cable, a form of relay that had given endless trouble. Coaxials worked well enough for a while, but eventually they were abandoned, largely because of the extraordinary depredations of earwigs. These insects had developed an alarming resistance to bugspray and were out of control most of the time. Earwigs increased in size and in numbers, and the forceps at the end of their abdomen developed so that they could cut through a steel shell. They seemed to go unerringly for coaxials. Whether the signals carried by the cables had anything to do with it I don't know, but the bugs fed on these things and were enormously stimulated. Not only did they feast on the cables, causing the cables to disintegrate, but they laid eggs in them in unimaginable quantities, and as the eggs hatched the television images suffered greatly, there was more and more flickering on the screen, more and more eyestrain and nervous tension among audiences, and of course a further debasement of taste and intellectual life in general. Finally the coaxials were given up, and after much experimenting by Westinghouse and the Glenn Martin people a satisfactory substitute was found in the high-flying planes. A few of these planes, spotted around the country, handled the whole television load nicely. Known as Stratovideo planes, they were equipped with studios; many programs originated in the air and were transmitted directly, others were beamed to the aircraft from ground stations and then relayed. The planes flew continuously, twenty-four hours a day, were refuelled in air, and dropped down to ten thousand feet every eight hours to meet the Contakt planes and take on new shifts of workers.

I remember that as I walked to my desk in the Stratoship that morning, the nine-o'clock news had just ended and a program called "Author, Please!" was going on, featuring Melonie Babson, a woman who had written a best-seller on the theme of euthanasia, called "Peace of Body." The program was sponsored by a dress-shield company.

I remember, too, that a young doctor had come aboard the plane with the rest of us. He was a newcomer, a fellow named Cathcart, slated to be the physician attached to the ship. He had introduced himself to me in the Contakt plane, had asked the date of my Tri-D shot, and had noted it down in his book. (I shall explain about these shots presently.) This doctor certainly had a brief life in our midst. He had hardly been introduced around and shown his office when our control room got a radio call asking if there was a doctor in the stratosphere above Earthpoint F-plus-6, and requesting medical assistance at the scene of an accident.

F-plus-6 was almost directly below us, so Dr. Cathcart felt he ought to respond, and our control man gave the word and asked for particulars and instructions. It seems there had been a low-altitude collision above F-plus-6 involving two small planes and killing three people. One plane was a Diaheliper, belonging to an aerial diaper service that flew diapers to rural homes by helicopter. The other was one of the familiar government-owned sprayplanes that worked at low altitudes over croplands, truck gardens, and commercial orchards, delivering a heavy mist of the deadly Tri-D solution, the pesticide that had revolutionized agriculture, eliminated the bee from nature, and given us fruits and vegetables of undreamed-of perfection but very high toxicity.

The two planes had tangled and fallen onto the observation tower of a whooping-crane sanctuary, scattering diapers over an area of half a mile and releasing a stream of Tri-D. Cathcart got his medical kit, put on his parachute, and paused a moment to adjust his pressurizer, preparatory to bailing out. Knowing that he wouldn't be back for a while, he asked if anybody around the shop was due for a Tri-D shot that morning, and it turned out that Bill Foley was. So the Doctor told Foley to come along, and explained that he would give him his injection on the way down. Bill threw me a quick look of mock anguish, and started climbing into his gear. This must have been six or seven minutes past nine.

It seems strange that I should feel obligated to explain Tri-D shots. They were a commonplace at this time—as much a part of a person's life as his toothbrush. The correct name for them was Anti-Tri-D, but people soon shortened the name. They were simply injections that everyone had to receive at regular twenty-one-day intervals, to counteract the lethal effect of food, and the notable thing about them was the great importance of the twenty-one-day period. To miss one's Tri-D shot by as much as a couple of hours might mean serious consequences, even death. Almost every day there were deaths reported in the papers from failure to get the injection at the proper time. The whole business was something like insulin control in diabetes. You can easily imagine the work it entailed for doctors in the United States, keeping the entire population protected against death by poisoning.

As Dr. Cathcart and Bill eased themselves out of the plane through the chute exit, I paused briefly and listened to Miss Babson, our author of the day.

"It is a grand privilege," she was saying, "to appear before the television audience this morning and face this distinguished battery of critics, including my old sparring partner, Ralph Armstrong, of the *Herald Tribune.* I suppose after Mr. Armstrong finishes with me I will be a pretty good candidate for euthanasia myself. Ha. But seriously, ladies and gentlemen, I feel that a good book is its own defense."

The authoress had achieved a state of exaltation already. I knew that her book, which she truly believed to be great, had been suggested to her by an agent over a luncheon table and had been written largely by somebody else, whom the publisher had had to bring in to salvage the thing. The final result was a run-of-the-can piece of rubbish easily outselling its nearest competitor.

Miss Babson continued, her exaltation stained with cuteness:

"I have heard my novel criticized on the ground that the theme of euthanasia is too daring, and even that it is anti-Catholic. Well, I can remember, way back in the dark ages, when a lot of things that are accepted as commonplace today were considered daring or absurd. My own father can recall the days when dairy cows were actually bred by natural methods. The farmers of those times felt that the artificial-breeding program developed by our marvelous experiment stations was high-falutin nonsense. Well, we all know what has happened to the dairy industry, with many of our best milch cows giving milk continuously right around the clock, in a steady stream. True, the cows do have to be propped up and held in position in special stanchions and fed intravenously, but I always say it isn't the hubbub that counts, it's the butterfat. And I doubt if even Mr. Armstrong here would want to return to the days when a cow just gave a bucket of milk and then stopped to rest."

Tiring of the literary life, I walked away and looked out a window. Below, near the layer of cumulus, the two chutes were visible. With the help of binoculars I could see Bill manfully trying to slip his chute over next to the Doc, and could see Cathcart fumbling with his needle. Our telecandid man was at another window, filming the thing for the next newscast, as it was a new wrinkle in the Tri-D world to have somebody getting his shot while parachuting.

I had a few chores to do before our program came on, at eleven-five. "Town Meeting of the Upper Air" was the name of it. "Town Meeting" was an unrehearsed show, but I was supposed to brief the guests, distribute copies of whatever prepared scripts there were, explain the cuing, and make everybody happy generally. The program we were readying that morning had had heavy advance billing, and there was tremendous interest in it everywhere, not so much because of the topic ("Will the fear of retaliation stop aggression?") or even the cast of characters, which included Major General Artemus T. Recoil, but because of an incidental stunt we were planning to pull off. We had arranged a radio hookup with the space platform, a gadget the Army had succeeded in establishing six hundred miles up, in the regions of the sky beyond the pull of gravity. The Army, after many years of experimenting with rockets, had not only got the platform established but had sent two fellows there in a Spaceship, and also a liberal supply of the New Weapon.

The whole civilized world had read about this achievement, which swung the balance of power so heavily in our favor, and everyone was aware that the damned platform was wandering around in its own orbit at a dizzy distance from the earth and not subject to gravitational pull. Every kid in America had become an astrophysicist overnight and talked knowingly of exhaust velocities, synergy curves, and Keplerian ellipses. Every subway rider knew that the two men on the platform were breathing oxygen thrown off from big squash vines that they had taken along. The *Reader's Digest* had added to the fun by translating and condensing several German treatises on rockets and space travel, including the great *Wege zur Raumschiffahrt.* But to date, because of security regulations and technical difficulties, there had been no radio-television hookup. Finally we got clearance from Washington, and General Recoil agreed to interview the officers on the platform as part of the "Town Meeting" program. This was big stuff—to hear directly from the Space Platform for Checking Aggression, known pretty generally as the SPCA.

I was keyed up about it myself, but I remember that all that morning in the plane I felt disaffected, and wished I were not a stratovideo man. There were often days like that in the air. The plane, with its queer cargo and its cheap goings on, would suddenly seem unaccountably remote from the world of things I admired. In a physical sense we were never very remote: the plane circled steadily in a fixed circle of about ten miles diameter, and I was never far from my own home on East Harding Boulevard. I could talk to Ann and the children, if I wished, by radiophone.

In many respects mine was a good job. It paid two hundred and twenty-five dollars a week, of which two hundred and ten was withheld. I should have felt well satisfied. Almost everything in the way of social benefits was provided by the government—medical care, hospitalization, education for the children, accident insurance, fire and theft, old-age retirement, Tri-D shots, vacation expense, amusement and recreation, welfare and well-being, Christmas and good will, rainy-day resource, staples and supplies, beverages and special occasions, baby-sitzfund—it had all been worked out. Any man who kept careful account of his pin money could get along all right, and I guess I should have been happy. Ann never complained much, except about one thing. She found that no matter how we saved and planned, we never could afford to buy flowers. One day, when she was a bit lathered up over household problems, she screamed, "God damn it, I'd rather live dangerously and have one dozen yellow freesias!" It seemed to prey on her mind.

Anyway, this was one of those oppressive days in the air for me. Something about the plane's undeviating course irritated me; the circle we flew seemed a monstrous excursion to nowhere. The engine noise (we flew at subsonic speed) was an unrelieved whine. Usually I didn't notice the engines, but today the ship sounded in my ears every minute, reminding me of a radiotherapy chamber, and there was always the palpable impact of vulgar miracles—the very nature of television—that made me itchy and fretful.

Appearing with General Recoil on "Town Meeting of the Upper Air" were to be Mrs. Florence Gill, president of the Women's Auxiliary of the Sons of Original Matrons; Amory Buxton, head of the Economics and Withholding Council of the United Nations; and a young man named Tollip, representing one of the small, ineffectual groups that advocated world federation. I rounded up this stable of intellects in the reception room, went over the procedure with them, gave the General a drink (which seemed to be what was on his mind), and then ducked out to catch the ten-o'clock news and to have a smoke.

I found Peter Everhardt in the control room. He looked bushed. "Quite a morning, Nuncle," he said. Pete not only had to keep his signal clean on the nine-o'clock show (Melonie Babson was a speaker who liked to range all over the place when she talked) but he had to keep kicking the ball around with the two Army officers on the space platform, for fear he would lose them just as they were due to go on. And on top of that he felt obliged to stay in touch with Dr. Cathcart down below, as a matter of courtesy, and also to pick up incidental stuff for subsequent newscasts.

I sat down and lit a cigarette. In a few moments the day's authoress wound up her remarks and the news started, with the big, tense face of Ed Peterson on the screen dishing it out. Ed was well equipped by nature for newscasting; he had the accents of destiny. When he spread the news, it penetrated in depth. Each event not only seemed fraught with meaning, it seemed fraught with Ed. When he said "I predict . . ." you felt the full flow of his pipeline to God.

To the best of my recollection the ten-o'clock newscast on this awful morning went as follows:

(Announcer) "Good morning. Tepky's Hormone-Enriched Dental Floss brings you Ed Peterson and the news."

(Ed) "Flash! Three persons were killed and two others seriously injured a few minutes ago at Earthpoint F-plus-6 when a government sprayplane collided with a helicopter of the Diaheliper Company. Both pilots were thrown clear. They are at this moment being treated by a doctor released by parachute from Stratovideo Ship 3, from which I am now speaking. The sprayplane crashed into the observation tower of a whooping-crane sanctuary, releasing a deadly mist of Tri-D and instantly killing three wardens who were lounging there watching the love dance of the cranes. Diapers were scattered widely over the area, and these sterile garments proved invaluable to Dr. Herbert L. Cathcart in bandaging the wounds of the injured pilots, Roy T. Bliss and Homer Schenck. [Here followed a newsreel shot showing Cathcart winding a diaper around the head of one of the victims.] You are now at the scene of the disaster," droned Ed. "This is the first time in the history of television that an infant's napkin has appeared in the role of emergency bandage. Another first for American Tel. & Vid.!

"Washington! A Senate committeee, with new facts at its disposal, will reopen the investigation to establish the blame for Pearl Harbor.

"Chicago! Two members of the Department of Sanitation were removed from the payroll today for refusal to take the loyalty oath. Both are members of New Brooms, one of the four hundred thousand organizations on the Attorney General's subversive list.

"Hollywood! It's a boy at the Roscoe Pews. Stay tuned to this channel for a closeup of the Caesarean section during the eleven-o'clock roundup!

"New York! Flash! The Pulitzer Prize in editorial writing has been awarded to Frederick A. Mildly, of the New York *Times,* for his nostalgic editorial 'The Old Pumphandle.'

"Flash! Donations to the Atlantic Community Chest now stand at a little over seven hundred billion dollars. Thanks for a wonderful job of giving—I mean that from my heart.

"New York! The vexing question of whether Greek athletes will be allowed to take part in next year's Olympic Games still deadlocks the

Security Council. In a stormy session yesterday the Russian delegate argued that the presence of Greek athletes at the games would be a threat to world peace. Most of the session was devoted to a discussion of whether the question was a procedural matter or a matter of substance.

"Flash! Radio contact with the two United States Army officers on the Space Platform for Checking Aggression, known to millions of listeners as the SPCA, has definitely been established, despite rumors to the contrary. The television audience will hear their voices in a little more than one hour from this very moment. You will *not* see their faces. Stay tuned! This is history, ladies and gentlemen—the first time a human voice freed from the pull of gravity has been heard on earth. The spacemen will be interviewed by Major General Artemus T. Recoil on the well-loved program 'Town Meeting of the Upper Air.'

"I predict: that because of SPCA and the Army's Operation Space, the whole course of human destiny will be abruptly changed, and that the age-old vision of peace is now on the way to becoming a reality."

Ed finished and went into his commercial, which consisted of digging a piece of beef gristle out of his teeth with dental floss.

I rubbed out my cigarette and walked back toward my cell. In the studio next to ours, "The Bee" was on the air, and I paused for a while to watch. "The Bee" was a program sponsored by the Larry Cross Pollination Company, aimed principally at big orchardists and growers—or rather at their wives. It was an interminable mystery-thriller sort of thing, with a character called the Bee, who always wore a green hood with two long black feelers. Standing there in the aisle of the plane, looking into the glass-enclosed studio, I could see the Bee about to strangle a red-haired girl in slinky pajamas. This was America's pollination hour, an old standby, answer to the housewife's dream. The Larry Cross outfit was immensely rich. I think they probably handled better than eighty per cent of all fertilization in the country. Bees, as I have said, had become extinct, thanks to the massive doses of chemicals, and of course this had at first posed a serious agricultural problem, as vast areas were without natural pollination. The answer came when the Larry Cross firm was organized, with the slogan "We Carry the Torch for Nature." The business mushroomed, and branch offices sprang up all over the nation. During blossom time, field crews of highly trained men fanned out and pollinized everything by hand—a huge job and an arduous one. The only honey in the United States was synthetic—a blend of mineral oil and papaya juice. Ann hated it with a morbid passion.

When I reached my studio I found everybody getting ready for the warmup. The Town Crier, in his fusty costume, stood holding his bell by the clapper, while the makeup man touched up his face for him. Mrs. Gill, the S.O.M. representative, sat gazing contemptuously at young Tollip. I had riffled through her script earlier, curious to find out what kind of punch she was going to throw. It was about what I expected. Her last paragraph contained the suggestion that all persons who advocated a revision of the Charter of the United Nations be automatically deprived of their citizenship. "If these well-meaning but misguided persons," ran the script, "with their utopian plans for selling this nation down the river are so anxious to acquire world citizenship, I say let's make it easy for them—let's take away the citizenship they've already got and see how they like it. As a lineal descendant of one of the Sons of Original Matrons, I am sick and tired of these cuckoo notions of one world, which come dangerously close to simple treachery. We've enough to do right here at home without . . ."

And so on. In my mind's ear I could already hear the moderator's salutary and impartial voice saying, "Thank you, Mrs. Florence Gill."

At five past eleven, the Crier rang his bell. "Hear ye! See ye! Town Meetin' today! Listen to both sides and make up your own minds!" Then George Cahill, the moderator, started the ball rolling.

I glanced at Tollip. He looked as though his stomach were filling up with gas. As the program got under way, my own stomach began to inflate, too, the way it often did a few hours after breakfast. I remember very little of the early minutes of that morning's Town Meeting. I recall that the U.N. man spoke first, then Mrs. Gill, then Tollip (who looked perfectly awful). Finally the moderator introduced General Recoil, whose stomach enjoyed the steadying effects of whiskey and who spoke in a loud, slow, confident voice, turning frequently to smile down on the three other guests.

"We in the Army," began the General, "don't pretend that we know all the answers to these brave and wonderful questions. It is not the Army's business to know whether aggression is going to occur or not. Our business is to put on a good show if it *does* occur. The Army is content to leave to the United Nations and to idealists like Mr. Tollip the troublesome details of political progress. I certainly don't know, ladies and gentlemen, whether the fear of retaliation is going to prevent aggression, but I *do* know that there is no moss growing on we of Operation Space. As for myself, I guess I am what you might call a rataliatin' fool. [Laughter in the upper air.] Our enemy is well aware that we are now in a most unusual position to retaliate. That knowledge on the part of our enemy is, in my humble opinion, a deterrent to aggression. If I didn't believe that, I'd shed this uniform and get into a really well-paid line of work, like professional baseball."

Will this plane never quit circling? (I thought). Will the words never quit going round and round? Is there no end to this noisy carrousel of indigestible ideas? Will no one ever catch the brass ring?

"But essentially," continued the General, "our job is not to deal with the theoretical world of Mr. Tollip, who suggests that we merge in some vast superstate with every Tom, Dick, and Harry, no matter what their color or race or how underprivileged they are, thus pulling down our standard of living to the level of the lowest common denominator. Our job is not to deal with the diplomatic world of Mr. Buxton, who hopes to find a peaceful solution around a conference table. No, the Army must face the world as it is. We know the enemy is strong. In our dumb way, we think it is just horse sense for us to be stronger. And I'm proud, believe me, ladies and gentlemen, proud to be at one end of the interplanetary conversation that is about to take place on this very, *very* historic morning. The achievement of the United States Army in establishing the space platform—which is literally a man-made planet—is unparalleled in military history. We have led the way into space. We have given Old Lady Gravity the slip. We have got there, and we have got there fustest with the mostest. [Applause.]

"I can state without qualification that the New Weapon, in the capable hands of the men stationed on our platform, brings the *en*tire globe under our dominion. We can pinpoint any spot, anywhere, and sprinkle it with our particular brand of thunder. Mr. Moderator, I'm ready for this interview if the boys out there in space are ready."

Everyone suspected that there might be a slipup in the proceedings at this point, that the mechanical difficulties might prove insuperable. I glanced at the studio clock. The red sweep hand was within a few jumps of eleven-thirty—the General had managed his timing all right. Cahill's face was tenser than I had ever seen it before. Because of the advance buildup, a collapse at this moment would put him in a nasty hole, even for an old experienced m.c. But at exactly eleven-thirty the interview started, smooth as silk. Cahill picked it up from the General.

"And now, watchers of television everywhere, you will hear a conversation between Major General Artemus T. Recoil, who pioneered Operation Space, and two United States Army officers on the platform—Major James Obblington, formerly of Brooklyn, New York, now of Space, and Lieutenant Noble Trett, formerly of Sioux City, Iowa, now of Space. Go ahead, General Recoil!"

"Come in, Space!" said the General, his tonsils struggling in whiskey's undertow, his eyes bearing down hard on the script. "Can you hear me, Major Obblington and Lieutenant Trett?"

"I hear you," said a voice. "This is Trett." The voice, as I remember it, astonished me because of a certain laconic quality that I had not expected. I believe it astonished everyone. Trett's voice was cool, and he sounded as though he were right in the studio.

"Lieutenant Trett," continued the General, "tell the listeners here on earth, tell us, in your position far out there in free space, do you feel the pull of gravity?"

"No, sir, I don't," answered Trett. In spite of the "sir," Trett sounded curiously listless, almost insubordinate.

"Yet you are perfectly comfortable, sitting there on the platform, with the whole of earth spread out before you like a vast target?"

"Sure I'm comfortable."

The General waited a second, as though expecting amplification, but it failed to come. "Well, ah, how's the weather up there?" he asked heartily.

"There isn't any," said Trett.

"No weather? No weather in space? That's very interesting."

"The hell it is," said Trett. "It's God-damn dull. This place is a dump. Worse than some of the islands in the Pacific."

"Well, I suppose it must get on your nerves a bit. That's all part of the game. Tell us, Lieutenant, what's it like to be actually part of the solar system, with your own private orbit?"

"It's all right, except I'd a damn sight rather get drunk," said Trett.

I looked at Cahill. He was swallowing his spit. General Recoil took a new hold on his script.

"And you say you don't feel the pull of gravity, not even a little?"

"I just told you I didn't feel any pull," said Trett. His voice now had a surly quality.

"Well, ah," continued the General, who was beginning to tremble, "can you describe, briefly, for the television audience—" But it was at this point that Trett, on the platform, seemed to lose interest in talking with General Recoil and started chinning with Major Obblington, his sidekick in space. At first the three voices clashed and blurred, but the General, on a signal from the moderator, quit talking, and the conversation that ensued between Trett and Obblington was audible and clear. Millions of listeners must have heard the dialogue.

"Hey, Obie," said Trett, "you want to know something else I don't feel the pull of, besides gravity?"

"What?" asked his companion.

"Conscience," said Trett cheerfully. "I don't feel my conscience pulling me around."

"Neither do I," said Obblington. "I ought to feel some pulls but I don't."

"I also don't feel the pull of duty."

"Check," said Obblington.

"And what is even more fantastic, I don't feel the pull of dames."

Cahill made a sign to the General. Stunned and confused by the turn things had taken, Recoil tried to pick up the interview and get it back on the track. "Lieutenant Trett," he commanded, "you will limit your remarks to the—"

Cahill waved him quiet. The next voice was the Major's.

"Jesus, now that you mention it, I don't feel the pull of dames either! Hey, Lieutenant—you suppose gravity has anything to do with sex?"

"God damn if *I* know," replied Trett. "I know I don't *weigh* anything, and when you don't weigh anything, you don't seem to *want* anything."

The studio by this time was paralyzed with attention. The General's face was swollen, his mouth was half open, and he struggled for speech that wouldn't come.

Then Trett's cool, even voice again: "See that continent down there,

E. B. White 739

Obie? That's where old Fatso Recoil lives. You feel drawn toward that continent in any special way?"

"Naa," said Obblington.

"You feel like doing a little shooting, Obie?"

"You're rootin' tootin' I feel like shootin'."

"Then what are we waiting for?"

I am, of course, reconstructing this conversation from memory. I am trying to report it faithfully. When Trett said the words "Then what are we waiting for?" I quit listening and dashed for the phones in the corridor. As I was leaving the studio, I turned for a split second and looked back. The General had partially recovered his power of speech. He was mumbling something to Cahill. I caught the words "phone" and "Defense Department."

The corridor was already jammed. I had only one idea in my head—to speak to Ann. Pete Everhardt pushed past me. He said crisply, "This is it." I nodded. Then I glanced out of a window. High in the east a crazy ribbon of light was spreading upward. Lower down, in a terrible parabola, another streak began burning through. The first blast was felt only slightly in the plane. It must have been at a great distance. It was followed immediately by two more. I saw a piece of wing break up, saw one of the starboard engines shake itself loose from its fastenings and fall. Near the phone booths, the Bee, still in costume, fumbled awkwardly for a parachute. In the crush one of his feelers brushed my face. I never managed to reach a phone. All sorts of things flashed through my mind. I saw Ann and the children, their heads in diapers. I saw again the man in the leather cap, loading bedsprings. I heard again Pete's words, "This is it," only I seemed to hear them in translation: "Until the whole wide world to nothingness do sink." (How durable the poets are!) As I say, I never managed the phone call. My last memory of the morning is of myriads of bright points of destruction where the Weapon was arriving, each pyre in the characteristic shape of an artichoke. Then a great gash, and the plane tumbling. Then I lost consciousness.

I cannot say how many minutes or hours after that the earth finally broke up. I do not know. There is, of course, a mild irony in the fact that it was the United States that was responsible. Insofar as it can be said of any country that it had human attributes, the United States was well-meaning. Of that I am convinced. Even I, at this date and at this distance, cannot forget my country's great heart and matchless ingenuity. I can't in honesty say that I believe we were wrong to send the men to the platform—it's just that in any matter involving love, or high explosives, one can never foresee all the factors. Certainly I can't say with any assurance that Tollip's theory was right; it seems hardly likely that anyone who suffered so from stomach gas could have been on the right track. I did feel sympathetic toward some of his ideas, perhaps because I suffered from flatulence myself. Anyway, it was inevitable that it should have been the United States that developed the space platform and the new weapon that made the H-bomb obsolete. It was inevitable that what happened, at last, was conceived in good will.

Those times—those last days of earth! I think about them a lot. A sort of creeping ineptitude had set in. Almost everything in life seemed wrong to me, somehow, as though we were all hustling down a blind alley. Many of my friends seemed mentally confused, emotionally unstable, and I have an idea I seemed the same to them. In the big cities, horns blew before the light changed, and it was clear that motorists no longer had the capacity to endure the restrictions they had placed on their own behavior. When the birds became extinct (all but the whooping crane), I was reasonably sure that human beings were on the way out, too. The cranes survived only because of their dance—which showmen were quick to exploit. (Every sanctuary had its television transmitter, and the love dance became a more popular spectacle than heavyweight prizefighting.) Birds had always been the symbol of freedom. As soon as I realized that they were gone, I felt that the significance had gone from my own affairs. (I was a cranky man, though—I must remember that, too—and am not trying here to suggest anything beyond a rather strong personal sadness at all this.)

Those last days! There were so many religions in conflict, each ready to save the world with its own dogma, each perfectly intolerant of the other. Every day seemed a mere skirmish in the long holy war. It was a time of debauch and conversion. Every week the national picture magazines, as though atoning for past excesses, hid their cheesecake carefully away among four-color reproductions of the saints. Television was the universal peepshow—in homes, schools, churches, bars, stores, everywhere. Children early formed the habit of gaining all their images at second hand, by looking at a screen; they grew up believing that anything perceived directly was vaguely fraudulent. Only what had been touched with electronics was valid and real. I think the decline in the importance of direct images dated from the year television managed to catch an eclipse of the moon. After that, nobody every looked at the sky, and it was as though the moon had joined the shabby company of buskers. There was really never a moment when a child, or even a man, felt free to look away from the television screen—for fear he might miss the one clue that would explain everything.

In many respects I like the planet I'm on. The people here have no urgencies, no capacity for sustained endeavor, but merely tackle things by fits and starts, leaving undone whatever fails to hold their interest, and so, by witlessness and improvidence, escape many of the errors of accomplishment. I like the apples here better than those on earth. They are often wormy, but with a most wonderful flavor. There is a saying here: "Even a very lazy man can eat around a worm."

But I would be lying if I said I didn't miss that other life, I loved it so.

Technology: The Half-Full Cup

Melvin Kranzberg

Melvin Kranzberg, a historian of technology, was born in 1917, and received his education at Amherst and Harvard University, where he earned his Ph.D. in 1942. He served on the history faculty of Case Western Reserve University from 1952 until 1972, when he became Callaway Professor of the History of Technology at Georgia Institute of Technology. He has edited and been the author or co-author of numerous works on the history of technology in Western culture. The article reprinted here appeared in the Spring 1980 Alternative Futures. *It was originally one of a series of lectures given by Kranzberg, John H. Broomfield, and Samuel Florman; Broomfield's reply is printed below.*

Historians find it instructive to look back at how people dreamt of the future and then at how things actually turned out, to regard the differences between ideals and the spotted actuality. This exercise is especially interesting when one considers "Technology and Pessimism," because treatment of such a topic would have been almost unthinkable back in 1880. Instead, our forebears a century ago would most likely have linked technology with optimism.

For what our great-grandparents saw a hundred years ago inspired them with hope about the century to come. They looked ahead to a world where poverty had ended, where democratic society had spread the blessings of liberty and equality to all mankind, where machines performed all worrisome toil so that men lived in leisure, where universal education had blotted out ignorance and superstition, and where international peace and brotherhood reigned.

Our great-grandparents' optimism is in startling contrast to today's mood. Yet in 1880 there was ample justification for their boundless confidence. For one thing, the rapid growth of scientific knowledge during the 19th century supported the hope for future advancement. The 18th century Enlightenment's idea of progress had been fortified during the 19th century by Darwin's theory of evolution, so that man's past appeared to be a long struggle upward from the primal ooze through the Stone Age and progressive stages to the comforts of the Gilded Age.°

The Industrial Revolution, which had spread to America during the

---

Gilded Age A period of U.S. history from about 1865 to the business panic of 1873, a time associated with loose business and political morals and a gaudy display of wealth. The era takes its name from *The Gilded Age* (1873), a novel by Mark Twain and Charles Dudley Warner.

19th century, provided material evidence of this human progress. At the beginning of the 19th century, a man could travel on land only as fast as a horse could carry him, and on sea only as fast as a sailing vessel could—and these speeds were not significantly faster than they had been several thousand years earlier. But during the course of the 19th century, man invented the railroad, which moved him over the earth's surface at speeds approaching a mile a minute, and steamships which carried him across the oceans faster and more reliably than did sailing vessels. The 19th century's accomplishments in communications were just as spectacular. Throughout most of human history, people could be heard only as far as the voice could carry, but by the 1880s messages were carried over telegraph wires for long distances, and a new-fangled invention, the telephone, had just come into being. In the field of power, too, great developments had taken place. The steam engine had come into widespread use as a source of mechanical power, taking the burden off men's backs, while the perfection of Otto's internal-combustion engine provided the basis for the growth of today's automotive society. A whole new era of power, light, and communication was coming into being. Electric current had not been discovered until the first third of the 19th century, but by the end of the century, with Thomas Edison's development of the incandescent light bulb and of the central generating station, electricity was becoming commonplace.

The pace of technical progress in the 20th century has been even more rapid than in the 19th century. Very near the beginning of this century, the vacuum tube, operating by means of a guided passage of electrons first noted by Edison, and hence called the "Edison effect," gave birth to our modern age of electronics. At the turn of this century men had not yet mastered the art of heavier-than-air flight; yet within three-quarters of a century after the Wright Brothers' first flight, man had landed on the moon, a feat marking the culmination of the Scientific Revolution of the 17th century and the Industrial Revolution of the 18th century, as well as the fulfillment of one of man's most ancient dreams.

One could go on and on with a litany of technological triumphs in our times, but as Howard P. Segal has pointed out, "We must question the notion that technological advances are inherently progressive."[1] For not all of our technological advances have turned out the way we had hoped and expected.

Not only have we not reached the material utopia promised by our technology, but every step we take along the way makes it seem as though we are running on a gilded treadmill. Just as we approached the ideal of producing enough goods and services to provide middle-class comfort for

---

[1]Howard P. Segal, "Let's Abandon the Whig Theory of the History of Technology," *Chronicle of Higher Education*, July 9, 1979: 64.

all Americans, we discovered a large number of people living at or below the poverty level, with the current inflation adding to that number daily. Our astronauts can whiz around the earth in less than an hour, and anyone with a credit card and a reservation on the Concorde can break-fast in New York and London on the same morning, yet suburban com-muters can't get to work on time. Our cars are the most powerful and luxurious in the world, but we are running out of the gas to drive them. Our computers can solve in a few seconds mathematical problems that would require an individual fifty years to solve, our copy machines multi-ply papers faster than the sorcerer's apprentice could dump them into a garbage can, and television and radio bring instant information to us; yet men feel less and less capable of understanding the world in which they live. Despite our vast communications network, people agonize as never before over "the failure to communicate."

We find ourselves baffled by this series of paradoxes. Every technical triumph seems counterbalanced—some would say "outweighed"—by a human defeat.

Over thirty years ago (1947), W. H. Auden published a poem entitled "The Age of Anxiety." Auden was indeed a prophet because two decades later anxiety began to overwhelm American society—and technology was made the scapegoat. Indeed, some of today's social critics place the entire blame for our problems on our technology, claiming that it has provided the instrumentality for the heedless pursuit of wealth and material possessions.

I cannot accept that proposition. Even the most summary of historical surveys would demonstrate that technology has provided man with goods and services, food, shelter, and clothing; it has quickened transportation, heightened communication, and furthered our democratic society in many respects. In the highly industrialized societies, people are living longer and better than ever before by any kind of material standard one would devise.

But, of course, there is more to life than material goods and creature comforts. What has technology done for human values? Lewis Mumford, one of our outstanding social critics, claims that technology is engaged in destroying the values of life,[2] and the late Herbert Marcuse echoed the criticism, stating that technology simply enslaves people by raising false needs and providing false satisfaction.[3]

I should like to suggest that the problem is not technology itself but the way in which technology has interacted with other aspects of our society,

---

[2]Mumford first made this claim in *Technics and Civilization* (New York, 1934), but he still remained optimistic about the forthcoming "Neotechnic Phase." Some thirty years later he had become pessimistic: *The Myth of the Machine*, 2 vols. (New York, 1967–70).

[3]Herbert Marcuse, *An Essay on Liberation* (Boston, 1959).

so that technical developments frequently have unforeseen social and human consequences. I express this in the form of Kranzberg's First Law: "Technology is neither good nor bad, nor is it neutral." By that I mean that technology's interaction with society is such that technical developments frequently have human and social consequences which go far beyond the immediate purpose of the technical devices and practices themselves.

The fact is that technology does not function autonomously.[4] Instead, it interacts with social values and institutions, and sometimes the results are certainly not completely beneficial to man, especially when several technologies come together with synergistic effect. Yet I would also like to suggest that our present concern for non-material things, for societal benefit, for the "higher culture," for social justice, for preservation of the environment and ecology—all these "good causes" (and that is not meant disparagingly)—are a luxury deriving from the very effectiveness of our technological efforts in the past.

For most of human history, men lived in a society of scarcity, so their attention was concentrated on obtaining a sufficiency of material goods. The great outpouring of goods made possible by industrialization in modern times has altered this. Now that we have reached the prospect—if not the complete fulfillment—of the "abundant society," we can begin to turn our attention beyond the immediate satisfaction of our animal needs and creature comforts. We can begin to think of technology in terms of its impact upon society as a whole and upon the physical environment.

One reason a better world has not yet come into being is that we have not had the social innovations to accompany our technological advancements. Instead, our technical achievements have been utilized in the services of values and institutions belonging to an earlier, more competitive society, one based on scarcity.

In past ages, when men worked from sunup to sundown just to eke out a living from the soil, with the hope that they would have enough to subsist for the next day or until the next harvest, men simply did not have time to worry about how their activities affected the global environment; children, also brought up in this backbreaking work, simply did not have time to worry about how they related to their parents; and most human experiences were so demeaning in character that there was little call to "share the experience." Today's "abundant society" has given us the opportunity to worry about more than meeting the minimal needs for sustaining life—and we are now free to worry about the use of our leisure time, the so-called "higher" things of life, the natural environment, and even to worry about our fellow inhabitants on Spaceship Earth.

---

[4]Langdon Winner, *Autonomous Technology: Technics-Out-of-Control as a Theme in Political Thought* (Cambridge, MA, 1977) takes the opposite point of view.

By catering to man's basic material needs, technology enables man to think beyond those to other values, for human values go beyond survival needs. Carlos Alzamora, Peru's representative to the United Nations, once defined the values of civilized man in terms of moral, political, and social "orders." The moral order involves fundamental human rights; the political order liberates people from colonialism and upholds the rule of law; and the social order provides social justice for all. How are these orders affected by technology?

Throughout antiquity, up to one quarter of the population consisted of slaves, who were considered as property and had few rights as individuals. In the Middle Ages, slavery diminished, but the serfs, numerically the largest group in the population, possessed few rights, and those only by virtue of the custom associated with their plot of land, not as individuals. Although the decline of feudalism in the West loosened the bonds of serfdom, elements of serfdom (including the great power of the landlord) have persisted throughout most of the world which did not undergo industrialization. The Industrial Revolution was the catalyst which put an end to feudalism and serfdom. But it changed more than that. Throughout history, the hearth and home had been the center of production. Industrialization moved families to the cities and made factory labor the source of their livelihoods.

What did industrialization do to the individual? Brought into contact with others in a centralized working place, the workingmen could communicate their grievances to one another and they could begin to organize in order to better their lives. For the first time in human history, the ordinary laborer began having a voice in his own destiny—to obtain social justice and personal dignity. Nonetheless, there is a widespread feeling that the worker is losing his individuality—his humanity—on the factory production line. In one sense that is certainly true. Freedom from heavy physical labor does not mean that people no longer have to work, nor does it mean individual license. Some sacrifice of unbridled individualism is necessary if men are to work together. Technology makes compulsory some form of cooperation and discipline among human beings in order to carry on collective tasks. In the great irrigation civilizations of antiquity—in Mesopotamia and Egypt, in China and India—men worked together to build great systems of dikes, dams, and irrigation canals. Their "cooperation" was ensured by the whip; advancing technology and changed social practices have done away with the need for this kind of physical compulsion. Nowadays the question is the degree to which those engaged in this kind of collective action are consulted. In earlier eras, they were not, and even today some social critics complain of the workers' loss of freedom in advanced industrialized nations of the West. However, if we look closely at what is happening, we find that in the most advanced countries, such as Sweden, West Germany, and even the United States, workers are consulted more and more regarding the conditions of their work and their rights on the job.[5]

Critics of technology who claim that it is opposed to human freedom must eventually confront the historical reality: Why is it that, with but few exceptions, the most technologically advanced countries are those which enjoy the greatest amount of democratic freedom, have eradicated cruel and degrading punishments, uphold religious freedom, and in short, endorse fundamental human rights? Why are the most technologically advanced states the ones which have provided for equality of the sexes, abolished child labor, condemned racial discrimination, recognized the rights of workers to associate, developed social security systems for the aged, and in short, upheld the concept and practice of social justice? Can all this be ascribed to mere coincidence?

This does not mean that technology by itself is responsible for the development of social justice in the modern world. What I am saying is that technology is a necessary but not sufficient condition for achieving social justice in the modern world. In order to achieve humane and social goals, technology must interact with other societal elements. But as further proof of the non-neutrality of technology, we also have evidence of technology's interaction with far different values at other places and periods in human history where it has been the instrument for man's bestiality and brutality to his fellow man through the medium of wars, sometimes pursued for high religious ideals or as a "civilizing mission."

Because technology interacts so strongly with our social values and institutions, it is blamed for much of the trouble in the world today. It is also, however, the instrumentality which might enable us to overcome some of our problems—including those which came into being by prior interactions of technology with other sets of social values and institutions.

We call ours a "Technological Age." It is called that, not because all men are engineers, and certainly not because everybody understands technology. We call it that because we are aware, as never before, of the important role which technology plays in our lives. But man has always lived in a technological age, insofar as his life and work have been bound up with his technology. The difference lies in the increased awareness in our own times of our dependence upon our technology, largely because of the accelerated pace of technology in our own times and evidence of what happens to our lives and society when our technology is suddenly cut off or goes awry. Indeed, technology has so ingrained itself into the texture of our daily lives that we take it for granted, not realizing how significant it is to us until a breakdown of an electrical relay plunges an entire

[5]Melvin Kranzberg and Joseph Gies, *By the Sweat of Thy Brow: Work in the Western World* (New York, 1975).

section of the nation into darkness or until political events in far-off places threaten our right to drive.

Technology has thus complicated our lives, making us dependent upon our technology, but even more dependent upon one another—and hence upon our humanity. As Gunther Stent has pointed out, ". . . the technological consequences of scientific progress have rendered the making of [rational decisions regarding man's fate] ever more pressing and their effects ever more grave. . . ."[6]

Complicated as it might be, we still must develop those social innovations and institutional mechanisms which will enable us to utilize our technology to best account for mankind. Although we know by now that technology of itself will not provide us with utopia, there is no indication that turning away from technology will have that effect. Indeed, an unvarnished anti-technological stance would mean the abandonment of all hope that we would ever be able to improve the life of mankind and would bring us to Thomas Hobbes's version of man's life in the natural state: nasty, brutish, and short.

A few years ago the proponents of a new "consciousness," or the counter-culture, turned their backs on technology. They provided trenchant criticism of current American society, and they advocated a lifestyle which was very beguiling and appealing to affluent college youth. But they did not address problems like poverty and medical care distribution and the hunger of most people throughout the world. Such problems cannot be resolved without the aid of technology. The question is which technologies and how best to match these with the social matrix in which they will be employed. The growing need for water provides an example, for the world's population grows by about 200,000 people per day, each requiring about 500 tons of water per year. Last year's population increase alone created an additional annual water demand for thirty-six billion tons of water, or the equivalent of a medium-sized river. Does anyone seriously believe that we can meet the world's future water needs without recourse to technology? Does anyone truly object to our encouraging science and technology so as to meet the energy and food needs of today and tomorrow?

Nevertheless, our continued reliance on technology fills many individuals with forebodings, for they feel that we cannot control our technology. This is part of a larger question: How can individuals exercise some measure of democratic control in a society which is characterized by bigness and which involves problems whose scientific and technical components can only be comprehended by experts?

This problem of social control arises partly from the vastness of scale

---

[6]Gunther S. Stent, *The Paradoxes of Progress* (Berkeley, 1978).

of the contemporary world—the larger number of people—the inter-dependence of a highly complex industrial society, and the acceleration of change. But these elements also characterize our social institutions too, making them seem to function without heed to the needs and wants of the people. Everywhere it seems that the democratic and individualistic impulses of American life are losing out to "big business, big government, big everything." How can we attain some measure of democratic control over these large organisms and make them socially responsive and responsible?

The institutions which we have developed for control and use of our technology share the characteristics of other societal institutions; namely, they are created and run by people, and, consequently, tend to serve the interests of their owners or managers rather than those of their constituency.

Though institutions sometimes war on each other, their most pernicious habit is joining forces with other institutions to reinforce and enlarge their power. Technology serves as a means whereby some of those who control institutions can expand their power further. The battle has long been joined between man and the institutions of his own creation. Technology has merely enlarged the battleground, weapons, and dimensions of this age-old and never-ending struggle.

Nevertheless, within the past few years we have begun to institutionalize new sociopolitical mechanisms for directing our technology to serve the common weal rather than the narrow interests of a favored few. Heretofore technology was employed by men who sought their own profits, without regard to society, or—to be more accurate as well as more charitable—who equated their own profits with social benefits. Now society is beginning to demand a voice in the decision-making process, in technology as well as in other matters, so that the people will have more control over their destinies. As the American people increasingly comprehend the important role which science and technology play in their daily lives, they are demanding greater control over their science and technology as well as over all aspects of life.

More and more social decisions regarding the use of technology are going to be made by the political process and that, in a democracy, is precisely where they belong. So we have the Consumer Product Safety Commission, the Environmental Protection Agency, the Office of Technology Assessment, and a whole series of governmental acts, such as those dealing with toxic substances, which aim to protect the public from the unheeding pursuit of technology for profit's sake.

Heretofore technical decisions were made on an economic basis, with the actual technology being left to the experts, the scientific and technical elite, the corporate managers of American society, the military, the government. But now, even when the public might not be sufficiently informed to act directly on scientific-technical decisions, it wants to hold the decision-makers accountable for their actions, for it recognizes that any activity affecting the public should not be controlled directly by its practioners. Utility companies should not control public utility commissions, stockbrokers should not control the Securities and Exchange Commission, railroads and truckers should not control the Interstate Commerce Commission, and scientists and engineers might not be the best ones to direct our scientific and technical applications.

Science and technology are too important to the public to be left to a small coterie of decision-makers. Scientists and technologists simply do not possess the political wisdom to make these decisions, even though they possess the scientific and technical expertise upon which such decisions must be made. Nevertheless, the fact is that we cannot resolve these problems without the aid of our technical experts. Most of the urgent problems facing man today and tomorrow involve technology, human values, social organization, environmental concerns, economic resources, political decisions, and the like. These are "interface problems," that is, the interface between technology and society, and they can only be resolved—if they can be resolved at all—by the application of scientific knowledge, technical expertise, social understanding, and humane compassion.

These interface problems have another feature in common: Technology cannot solve them alone, yet they cannot be resolved without the aid of technology. Our scientists and technologists, though filled with goodwill, are simply not possessed of the social wisdom which is required to "steer the ship of state," choose our educational objectives, or establish the principles of the "good life." Nor, unfortunately, are our humanists. Instead of attempting to understand and analyze the role and meaning of technology, many of them retreat to romantic criticism or a self-imposed and almost incommunicable personal anguish and despair. Yet we desperately need their help, for our technology functions in a sociocultural matrix and they are the custodians of our cultural heritage and the keepers of our moral conscience. If we wish to fill the cup which today's technology has only half-filled, we must bring together our technological potentialities with revivified values and rejuvenated institutions.

Am I optimistic about our ability to fill the technological cup? Yes and no. In a recent book[7] Lionel Tiger claims that optimism is bred into the human genotype, that optimism is a biological and genetic characteristic, not culturally inspired. Although some sociologists might demur at Tiger's thesis, he points out that those genetically programmed to think in an optimistic and hopeful fashion had an evolutionary advantage over those with pessimistic genes; the early humanoid who believed that he

[7]*Optimism: The Biology of Hope* (New York, 1979).

could triumph over his dangerous prey was not only more likely to attempt to do so, but also to succeed in the venture. A lack of optimism about the future would lead to a greater probability of failure.

There might be good psychological reasoning behind Tiger's optimistic view of optimism, but history does not always follow the hypotheses of sociobiology or psychology. True, American history has been on the side of the technological optimist during the past couple of centuries, but it might be more difficult for others than historians of technology to sustain their optimism by viewing the historical record. (Indeed, if I were a political historian or a historian of morals, I might find it very difficult to remain optimistic.)

Yet even the optimism of an historian of technology cannot remain unqualified. The reason—to use our metaphor of the cup—is that while technology might fill the cup to overflowing, the fact is that yesterday's cup no longer suffices. The cup, at least in the form of people's expectations, is itself evolving and growing.

History reveals that man is a creature of discontent as well as of optimism. Because technology has been so productive in the past, we expect more of it. We keep raising our sights, or, to retain our metaphor, the cup keeps growing even while we are filling it. In a sense we are engaged in the labors of Sisyphus: technology has provided us abundant goods which more than fulfill the expectations of our forefathers; but, because we have grown up in a society of abundance, there has been an escalation of expectations and aspirations. Four centuries ago King Henry IV of France acquired great popularity by promising "a chicken in every pot." Today's politicians are led to promise steak on every barbecue grill, two cars in every garage, national health care, expanded social security, and a whole host of other goodies. And now, in the face of spiralling inflation and an energy crisis, there is great fear that we might lose the material goods and creature comforts which we have accumulated in the past.

However, the human problems lie deeper than holding on to the dreams or realities of our consumer-oriented society, for we live in a world where most people do not yet have a sufficiency of the basic needs of food, clothing, and shelter. And the statistics regarding the ratio of population size to the world's resources show us that the situation will be getting worse in the future.

During classical antiquity, there were probably fewer than 200 million people on the entire earth—and it had taken millennia to reach that figure. By 1650 the world's population had gone up to one-half billion, and scientific and technical developments allowed it to double to one billion around about 1830. But then, with industrialization, things began moving faster. By the beginning of this century the world's population had soared to over 1.5 billion; then it took only seventy-nine years to more than double to today's 4.4 billion, and it is expected to double again by the year 2013. Indeed, the projected increase of 2.26 billion people between 1975 and 2000 means that the population rise during our present quarter century would equal the entire world's population increase from the time of Christ to 1950.

Providing food, clothing, and shelter for this unprecedentedly rapid growth in the world's population puts great demands upon technology. It means that the cup which technology must fill is rapidly growing in size, and the question is whether it will outstrip the ability of technology to fill the cup. Already at current rates of consumption, some natural resources are being exhausted. What will happen when a growing world population with a growing expectation of material goods begins using up resources faster than ever? Obviously, great challenges will be posed to technology to provide substitutes, to eke out existing supplies, to recycle, and to develop new techniques.

Other changes are also occurring which will certainly affect future demands upon technology. One is the increasing urbanization of the world. In 1950 only twenty-nine percent of the world's population lived in urban areas, but that number increased to more than thirty-nine percent in 1975, and it is expected that over half the world's population will be living in urban areas by the year 2000. If the urban centers continue to grow in that fashion, not only will there be great strain on urban services—transportation, sewage, housing, medical facilities—but there will also have to be tremendous agricultural development to feed the growing number of people who are no longer engaged in primary production on farms. In brief, society will put greater and greater demands on our technology.

Back in the 1930s, the great sociologist, William Fielding Ogburn, the first president of the Society for the History of Technology, popularized the notion of "cultural lag," wherein he postulated the view that technology changes rapidly but that our institutional mechanisms in society change slowly, lagging behind the changes in technology. Today, however, we might be faced with the opposite situation: a "technological lag." Society is changing rapidly, but our technology is not keeping up with the growing demands and rising aspirations of the masses of people throughout the world.

Some engineers claim that we already possess the technical knowledge which will enable us to cope with the great demands caused by an increasing world population—demands for food, material goods, energy, and the like. True, but that knowledge is not yet in place, in usable form to meet these social changes. And, unless that knowledge is put to use, unless that knowledge is applied, then it does not count as technology. For technology is not just usable knowledge, it is useful knowledge; it must be applied to meet human needs and wants.

To these charges of technological lag, engineers reply that is is not their fault that their technical knowledge is not receiving application. The blame lies with society, with political institutions which hamper innovation and productivity, with economic theories and practices which impede technical progress, with environmental restrictions, with sociopolitical systems, and what have you. But if that is the case, it is obvious that we need social innovation so that we can make our technical knowledge effective.

But here again the interactions of technology and society require even more technical innovation. Thus, for example, while we might possess the potentiality through nuclear energy to provide for future energy needs, the question is if we possess enough technical knowledge to avoid nuclear disasters, deal with radioactive wastes, and solve the many other technical problems accompanying the exploitation of nuclear energy.

But technology is much more than the machines and devices and products themselves. It involves the man-machine relationship, the organization of work, relationships with the environment, and a whole host of sociocultural factors. Throughout history, the greatest engineers have employed a holistic approach, have viewed technical problems in terms of systems, and have incorporated the human element in their technical solutions.

Despite some qualifications, I still remain optimistic. Why? For several reasons. First, there is the historical record of technical achievement itself. The fact is that within the past two hundred years technology has accomplished marvelous things. There is no reason to believe that the wellsprings of technical creativity and ingenuity have run dry. Instead, there is good reason to believe that they are constantly being refreshed, that new and lively minds are being added to our technical storehouse. I know, because I teach engineering students, and I am constantly impressed with their zeal and enthusiasm, their freshness and imagination, and, believe it or not, their altruistic desire to serve mankind coupled with their realistic wish to achieve material success in the process. That combination of idealism and practicality is difficult to beat. Of course, we have a monumental educational task on our hands. This is especially so in the case of those who teach these fresh and inquiring engineering minds. We must enlarge and broaden the scope of their education, as we have been doing through enhanced liberal studies curricula during the past three decades. We have done well by our students, but we must do still better for society. Second, I do not despair of the vitality of our own American society. Certainly there are nagging doubts which have arisen to challenge the boundless confidence of earlier generations of Americans: the recognition, following our involvement in Vietnam and later happenings in Iran and Afghanistan, that events around the world do not always turn out the way we want; the Watergate scandal, which shook our faith in our constitutional system; the realization that some of our past technical triumphs have had harmful as well as beneficial results; and the spiralling inflation which seems to challenge the work-hard-and-get-ahead ethic which fueled America's rise to industrial and technical preeminence throughout the world.

Archibald MacLeish, the poet, once said, "America was promises." Many people today believe that the promise is over. But I believe that America is still promises. There is much evidence that points toward the continuing vitality and dynamism of American society. America still remains preeminent in its science and technology, in its adherence to democratic ideals, in its concern for the individual, and in its moral strength. The real question is whether or not we possess the will to utilize our great strength and power to meet these problems and close the technological gap so as to meet our own and the world's needs, now and in the future. If ours is a man-made world, I claim that man can remake it. If our technology has thus far given us only a half-full cup, then we can perhaps direct it more wisely in the future so that "our cup runneth over."

High Technology: The Construction of Disaster

John H. Broomfield

John H. Broomfield was born in New Zealand in 1935. He received his Ph.D. from the Australian National University and was for twenty years a member of the History Department of the University of Michigan, Ann Arbor. In 1983 he left Michigan to become president of the California Institute of Integral Studies in San Francisco. His field of specialization is Asian and Southeast Asian studies, and he has done extensive research in India and Pakistan. His many books and articles reflect this concern with the culture, history, and future of that part of the world. The article that follows is taken from the Spring 1980 Alternative Futures, *and is a response to Melvin Kranzberg (see preceding selection) and to Samuel Florman.*

No shred of optimism is added to my view of our current technology and its spokespeople by the arguments of Samuel Florman and Melvin Kranzberg. To start with an obvious problem of their papers: there is no specification of the technology about which they are not pessimistic. This indiscriminate lumping of all technologies from the digging stick to the nuclear reactor into one basket enables Florman, for instance, to ask rhetorically: "How can one be pessimistic about something called 'technology'?" Childish, he says, because human life is technological life. The logic here is as flawed as it would be if a critic of dog fighting was told it is childish to criticize sport—any sport—because recreation is a human need.

Let me start, then, by specifying what I am talking about. Technology: artifacts certainly; but also the organization of their use; the scientific study of the practical arts; the body of knowledge thereby developed, and the terminology in which it is couched; invention and development. This is all technology. We are inclined to think of technology as tools—the hand wrench, for example—or machinery—the steam boiler—, and both Florman and Kranzberg encourage us in that sort of thinking. This emphasis is misleading for contemporary "high technology," especially in the affluent ghetto in which we, the world's rich minority, live. Here technology is infinitely complex, and bureaucratic organization links vast systems together. We are not talking of steam boilers and hand wrenches; we are talking of something far more extensive and sophisticated. Remember that an item as basic as our food is now very largely an artifact, a product of technology. It is either chemistry, or, as in the case of those cheery breakfast cereals, that portion derived from food grains comes from hybrids which will not regenerate, thereby ensuring a continuing role in farming for agricultural corporation laboratories.

The emphasis is necessarily on *system:* large-scale, exceedingly complex technological organization. With high technology, individuals and groups become dependent upon distant decisions of unfamiliar, incomprehensible corporations, including governments. Reliance on high energy usage is encouraged, while the transmission of that energy, as also the fossil fuels from which most of it is derived, are in corporate control. There are irresistible intrusions into almost all aspects of "private" life, and this is a planned feature of high technology. In order to generate a "demand" for new products, and a tolerance for more elaborate organizational combinations, there is a systematic use of the media, the market place, and the educational system to influence and manipulate individual behavior. Internationally the same forces operate to encourage the inter-dependency of national economies, to the profit of those who control the high technology which we all—rich and poor of the world, alike—have been taught to regard as the symbol of the advanced and the progressive. The maintenance or innovative development of independent technologies is discouraged, for the elimination of alternatives (seen as competition for one's own product or technique) is a principle of our system. A consideration of the dangers from the application of such a principle is a subject to which I shall return at the end of the paper.

We approach the nub of the problem of high technology when we recognize the vulnerability of the systems we have built. We have created— and, I would emphasize, only very recently—a technology intolerant of mistakes; a technology that assumes infallibility but is operated by fallible humans.[1] We are a mistake-making species, and we should never have developed technologies that assume mistakes will not happen. Accidents resulting from human error are a certainty. The accustomed response to this observation is the one given by the commission that investigated the Three Mile Island nuclear disaster:° make modifications in the design.[2] It is a response that misses the point that the vulnerability of high technology derives from the fundamental fact that its structural principles are not "natural" or "biological."

In natural systems there is interdependency, but it is the interdependency of subunits which are, in themselves, whole and complete. Cells are the classic example. Large areas of a natural system can be wiped out (brain cells with every highball), but the system will continue to function. Nature is a network. If part of a net breaks, things slip through but the net holds together. By contrast, our high technology is built, link by link, like a chain; a system of interdependent, *incomplete* units. And any child can tell you the relationship between the chain and its weakest link—the well-remembered switch on the electric power relay at Niagara°; the stuck valve at Three Mile Island; or the less visible, but more portentous, passage on a single shipping lane around the southern tip of Africa of sixty percent of the oil required to sustain the industrial life of Western Europe and the United States.[3]

When the subject is vulnerability, military technology inevitably comes to mind, though it is noteworthy that there is not one word about military technology in the Florman and Kranzberg papers. This is a remarkable omission considering the vast investment in military R&D in this nation, to say nothing of the Soviet Union. Of the U.S. Federal budget, two-thirds of discretionary funding is spent on the military, whose projects give employment to one in ten U.S. workers. In the U.S., which has a mere five

---

[1]Here, and in the following paragraph, I am drawing on the ideas of John Todd of the New Alchemy Institute. [See Nancy Jack Todd, ed.: *The Book of the New Alchemists* (New York, 1977).]

[2]*New York Times,* November 1, 1979. Coincidentally the same science section of the *Times* (November 6, 1979) that carried the report on the 'Technology and Pessimism' symposium, contained another rather ludicrous example of this kind of thinking. In an article entitled "Acid Rain: An Increasing Threat," the suggestion "to breed acid-resistant fish" was discussed as a counter-measure. To the credit of the commentator, it was not endorsed.

[3]Øystein Noreng: *Oil Politics in the 1980s: Patterns of International Cooperation* (New York, 1978).

Three Mile Island nuclear disaster   Site of a nuclear power plant in Pennsylvania. On March 28, 1979, a breakdown in the cooling system nearly caused a major nuclear disaster.
electric power relay at Niagara   November 1965 failure of a single electrical relay in the Niagara River power station that initiated a blackout of nine northeastern states and two provinces of Canada.

or six per cent of the world's population, there is an expenditure of an estimated one-third of the world's entire yearly outlay on war technology. U.S. private industry annually exports an average ten billion dollars in weapons, the technology of violence.[4] In April 1979, the University of Michigan *Reporter,* a monthly newsletter directing faculty and graduate students to useful sources of research support, noted that the Department of Defense (in a time of high inflation, and declining funding from other agencies) "expects to be able to support an annual 10% real growth in research funding in the next several years, . . . increasing its emphasis on university support."[5] It is not unfair to say that the war business is a major route through which technological development proceeds in this, as in all other large industrialized societies.

And what has been the objective of military technological development? Let me take as the measure my lifetime, a relatively short period: I was born in 1935. On April 26, 1937, Nazi bombers of the German Luftwaffe attacked the Basque town of Guernica, for two hours and forty-five minutes testing their capacity to destroy a population. At the time there was almost universal outrage that a civilian population would be bombed with cold-blooded intent. By the end of the Second World War this had become a general principle of warfare: we had adopted the Nazi principles. We wiped out Hamburg with a fire-bombing; we wiped out Dresden; we wiped out Tokyo with a fire-bombing. We went on to attack sixty-five other Japanese cities, killing (before the atomic bombs were dropped) an estimated 330,000 people—86,000 in Tokyo alone with the first incendiary raid—and making homeless an estimated 8.5 million.[6]

We had adopted the principle of mass civilian extermination, and our weapons development since that time, with nuclear weapons of hideously greater power, has been directed towards perfecting this capability. Why? Because of the recognition that with high technology the old division between military and civilian is rendered virtually meaningless; the entire system is involved in war-making. As Richard Falk[o] observes, this is, of course, a self-fulfilling prophecy, or, at least, a self-reinforcing conclusion.

In Vietnam we went one step further: we attempted to destroy the natural eco-system supporting the people, because, unfortunately for our military planners, a new technique had been developed: modern guerrilla

---

[4]Anthony Sampson: *The Arms Bazaar: From Lebanon to Lockheed* (New York, 1978) pp. 358–361; Richard J. Barnet: *Roots of War* (New York, 1973) pp. 166–167; The Disarm Education Fund, New York, leaflet, September, 1979.

[5]*Reporter,* vol. XXVI, no. 4, p. 4.

[6]Kent Roberts Greenfield: *Strategy in World War II: A Reconsideration* (Baltimore, 1963) pp. 119–120.

Richard Falk   Another contributor to the journal in which the present essay appeared.

warfare, which has proved resistant to high technology. We poured onto that green and fertile land our defoliants, our poisons, our biological weapons (all, we should note, outlawed earlier in the century by international convention). These silent destroyers continue with their deadly war on the children of the Indo-Chinese, and our own GIs alike, years after we have achieved "peace with honor." Since then we have found the neutron bomb, which will destroy all the people but leave the artifacts of technology untouched. We have the ultimate weapon: now we can commit genocide.

Let me remind you how dramatic and rapid has been the change of scale in this, as in all other areas of our technology. Again I use my own lifetime as the yardstick. In 1940, the Luftwaffe was acknowledged to be the most powerful airforce in the world. Requiring daylight for target sighting, and therefore dependent upon protection from escort fighters with an effective outer range of less than 120 miles, its aircraft were capable of pin-point bombing only in south-eastern England—little further inland than London—even though they were operating from airfields on the French and Belgian coasts.[7] Today, forty years later, the military forces of the U.S.A. and the U.S.S.R. are capable of hitting almost any target in the populated world with colossal destructive power within thirty minutes.

As we turn to an assessment of what we have wrought, let us face squarely one fact, so terrifying that we normally shy away from it: weapons of war are made to be used. There is no historical precedent of a major weapons system being developed and never used. If we accept the fact that all the nuclear nations have large and powerful bureaucracies devoted to preparation for nuclear war, we shall see the true horror of what our technology has brought us to.

What of the possibility of the appearance of a General Jack D. Ripper° figure, that patriotic airman from *Dr. Strangelove?* Fantastic beyond belief? The chance of an accidental or mistaken missile launching, however, is not something we can dismiss so easily. Human error, as we have already observed, is the one thing of which we can be assured.

New York Times, November 11, 1979
ERROR ALERTS U.S. FORCES TO A FALSE MISSILE ATTACK A false alert triggered some of the nation's defenses against a nonexistent missile attack yesterday morning. . . . A mechanical error sent "war game" information into the sensing system that provides early warning of nuclear attack, indicating to military officers that the United States was under attack from a few missiles launched by a Soviet submarine, probably located in the northern Pacific, a Pentagon official said. As a result, 10 jet interceptors from three bases in the

---

[7]B. H. Liddell Hart: *History of the Second World War* (New York, 1971) pp. 90–92.

General Jack D. Ripper Maniacal U.S. Air Force general who orders a nuclear attack on the Soviet Union in the satiric film *Dr. Strangelove.*

United States and Canada scrambled aloft, and missile bases throughout the nation went on a low-level alert. . . . Pentagon officials said there had been several false alarms of this sort over the years, caused by computer failures, natural phenomena and test firings, especially in the late 1950's and early 1960's, when the early-warning system was in its early days. . . . Jody Powell, the White House press secretary, dismissed the criticism from abroad, noting the Administration's preoccupation with the Americans being held hostage in Teheran. "Given the fact that our people are sitting over there" in Iran, he said, "anybody who wants to get angry about a technical error is not going to get a long hearing."

Should a similar "technical error" someday trigger a nuclear exchange, we have no way of judging the full consequences, for we have built a technology with catastrophic potential but can only guess at what will happen when it is used. To cite the most obvious problem: we cannot gauge the long-term effects of the radiation.[8]

Against this immeasurably hazardous future we are trading away civil liberties. More extensive surveillance systems are devised to "secure" nuclear installations, military and civil. High officials lie in the name of national security, and the lowly lie to protect "industrial credibility." Censorship is imposed, and public records are falsified. Melvin Kranzberg laments that Watergate shook our confidence in the Constitution; yet ICBM technology had already critically undermined the Constitution in one area. The need to respond within a few minutes to a nuclear threat from the Soviet Union had rendered irrelevant the provision that only the Senate can declare war. This check and balance in our Constitution is destroyed.

Let us turn from a death-dealing to a life-sustaining technology— medicine—to see if we cannot find firmer ground for optimism. On the surface the facts would appear encouraging. There has been large-scale improvement in human health in the last 100 years, with average longevity increased dramatically. To what can we attribute this? To improved nutrition, environmental sanitation, public health education, personal hygiene, immunization, pre-natal and post-natal care for mothers and babies, the area of most spectacular achievement because childbirth and infancy were associated with very high death rates.[9]

Yet where is the investment in American medicine today? Where is the health care dollar spent? On mothers and babies? On the areas of the poor, nutrition and public health? Certainly not. Public health gets a meagre four or five per cent of the medical dollar, while ninety per cent

[8]Kevin N. Lewis: "The Prompt and Delayed Effects of Nuclear War," *Scientific American*, vol. 241, no. 1, July 1979, pp. 35–47.
[9]Thomas McKeown: *The Role of Medicine: Dream, Mirage, or Nemesis?* (London, 1976) pp. 75–100.

goes to the treatment of individual patients, those already ill.[10] Annually the proportional expenditure on preventive medicine shrinks, while the share mounts for hospitals,[11] burgeoning bureaucracies (hospital employment tripled between 1950 and 1969),[12] with a gargantuan appetite for high technology and drugs, much of the latter mandated by hospitals' exceedingly pathogenic environment.[13] Increasingly, also, hospital beds are occupied by the affluent middle-aged and elderly, assured consumers of the medical product. Special attention in American medicine is given to rich, old men, because men hold the family purse strings. Besides, most doctors, and those who manage hospitals, drug and medical equipment firms, and insurance companies, are middle-aged, rich males.[14] Twenty-eight per cent of the U.S. medical budget is spent on the ten per cent of the population over 65 years of age.[15] If success is to be measured by increased longevity, then this is wasted expenditure: life expectancy for a 65 year old has increased by no more than two years since 1900.[16]

Given our knowledge of the central importance to the general wellness of a society of care for pregnant mothers and infants, nutrition, environmental protection, and health education, we do not seem to be using our money sensibly. The statistics bear out this conclusion. Although there has been a massive increase in U.S. resources devoted to medical care in the last quarter century,[17] death rates have actually increased in that period for young adults, particularly males. At ages 20–24, death rates have risen twenty-one per cent for white males and twenty-six per cent for blacks. The figures at ages 35–39 are seven per cent and thirty per cent respectively.[18] For an adult in America, life expectancy is little better now than it was in 1920.[19]

Are we then spreading health to the rest of the world? On balance I do not think we can legitimately make that claim. We provide direct and indirect incentives to bring the best doctors and nurses *from* the Third World, where they are most needed, to the rich countries—the notorious

---

[10]Victor W. Sidel and Ruth Sidel: *A Healthy State: An International Perspective on the Crisis in United States Medical Care* (New York, 1977) pp. 32 & 46.

[11]*Ibid.*

[12]Leonard Rodberg and Gelvin Stevenson: "The Health Care Industry in Advanced Capitalism," *Review of Radical Political Economics,* vol. IX, no. 1, Spring 1977, p. 111.

[13]Sidel and Sidel, *op. cit.,* pp. 71–78; Ivan Illich: *Medical Nemesis: The Expropriation of Health* (New York, 1976) pp. 31–32; Office of Technology Assessment, U.S. Government: *Assessing the Efficacy and Safety of Medical Technologies* (Washington, D.C., 1978).

[14]Sidel and Sidel, *op. cit.,* p. 82.

[15]Illich, *op. cit.,* p. 82.

[16]René Dubos: *Man Adapting* (New Haven, 1976) p. 230.

[17]Sidel and Sidel, *op. cit.,* p. 28.

[18]Joseph Eyer and Peter Sterling: "Stress-Related Mortality and Social Organization," *Review of Radical Political Economics, op. cit.,* p. 1.

[19]*Ibid.,* p. 4; Dubos, *loc. cit.*

"brain drain."[20] We tout the Western medical establishment as the model for the world, but it is an inappropriate model. It discourages preventive health care systems, and encourages high-cost technology for large urban hospitals in overwhelmingly rural societies. It introduces expensive, in-dustrially-manufactured drugs, often imported, in place of indigenous herbal and organic remedies. Even where there is a shortage of health workers, it has no use for traditional health-care specialists, who, in many regions, include women with an irreplaceable relationship with mothers and their babies. It substitutes an elitist, male-dominated, medical hierar-chy. Everywhere self-reliance and cultural self-respect are eroded.

Again, we must acknowledge that this is a systematic product of the maxim that if you have a new technique you encourage its widespread adoption; if you have a new product you peddle it everywhere—and God help the competition. This is true for electronic computers to replace the abacus, or baby formula to replace mother's milk.

Who has benefitted from our high technology? We, the residents of the gilded ghetto—and that, of course, does not include all our fellow citizens even in this fabulously wasteful country. The justification—and it is cen-tral to the Florman and Kranzberg thesis—is that what we have done for ourselves, we shall proceed to do for all the rest; or, alternatively, our technological inventiveness will be their inspiration, provided neither we nor they give way to the doomsaying of the pessimists. This is the biggest, most self-serving lie of all. By no stretch of the imagination could our high energy-consuming technology be made available to everyone on the globe and simple arithmetic will give the proof. Americans, a mere five or six per cent of the world's population, are said to be consuming already forty per cent of the world's energy to feed the appetites of their technological toys, and, we are reliably told, are rapidly depleting the sources of that energy. So there is no future for our technology unless we find new energy supplies. All those currently known with the capability of sustaining high technology, and all those likely to be produced, will increase the poisons we are pouring into the world. We are already drowning in our own poisons; imagine the pollution levels if the world's billions of poor were ever to "come on line" with high technology. It cannot be done. It should not be attempted.

There is another wrinkle: wherever was it imagined we would find sufficient highly-trained personnel to provide sophisticated technology for all the world's new people (200,000 added to the queue each day, as Kranzberg observes)? We have had a little over 200 years since the begin-ning of the industrial revolution, and have succeeded in outfitting with advanced technology, at a generous estimate, one quarter of the world's population, about 1.25 billion. This leaves a current backlog of 3.75 billion

---

[20]Sidel and Sidel, *op. cit.*, pp. 98–104.

people, to which the next twenty years alone are expected (barring catastrophes) to add a further 5 billion.[21] An honest projection would cast doubt upon our ability even to provide the elementary school teachers in numbers sufficient to maintain current rates of literacy, unless we are willing to effect a massive shift of resources away from technocracy.

In Melvin Kranzberg's view, however, the growth in world population is the chief imperative for sustaining the development of advanced technologies. He says that the population problem, aggravated as it is by rapid urbanization, demands a technological solution. Strangely, he appears blind to his own evidence of a correlation in time between the appearance of industrial technology and the explosive growth in population. Was there not a causative link? Nobody, surely, would question the connection between modern technology and urbanization. The movement of vast sectors of populations from rural areas to cities was made possible only by industrial technology. Yet the logic with which we are presented is: let there be more advanced technology to overcome the population and urbanization problems. The argument is back to front: these problems are intimately related to the nature of our technology. Like the tragic Sisyphus, punished aptly enough for his cunning in life, eternally in Hades to roll a stone up a hill, we shall be committed to endless and ineffectual struggle if we devote ourselves to more and bigger technology.

Perhaps Florman and Kranzberg are not suggesting more of the same. Perhaps they are proposing alternate technologies, such as those the New Alchemists have developed,[22] or those advocated by Ernest Callenbach.[23] I would be delighted if that were so. Let me state quickly the principles of these alternate technologies. Decentralized, relatively small-scale units with an integration of functions: food production, heating, living and work space, holistic education, all under one roof or at least all within walking distance; the scale within individual comprehension and susceptible to small-group management. (To achieve this, of course, requires a considerable level of technological sophistication. I would emphasize, parenthetically, that to be a pessimist about our current technology is not, necessarily, to be an anti-technologist.) Using locally available, renewable energy sources; recycling; avoiding violent techniques and toxic substances; respecting non-human life forms, our comrades and collaborators on this whirling journey through the heavens. The principle from nature of optimization to replace our current technological and bureaucratic principle of maximization.

It is this principle of maximization that is the key to my pessimism about our technological future, my doubt that we shall adopt these sane

---

[21]Thomas McKeown: *The Modern Rise of Population* (New York, 1976) pp. 1–2.
[22]Todd, *loc. cit.*
[23]Ernest Callenbach: *Ecotopia: The Notebooks and Reports of William Weston* (New York, 1975).

alternatives. To understand why we operate on such a principle it is necessary to recognize the systemic relationship of high technology to the all-pervasive bureaucratic organization of our contemporary economic, political, and social structures. High technology and our social forms are not free-floating, mutually independent things. You cannot, for example, dispense with big bureaucracy and keep high technology. They are systemically interrelated, two sides of one coin. High technology and massive corporate bureaucracy sustain and reinforce one another, the electronic computer being the ultimate expression, the apogee of bureaucratic technology.

Bureaucracy is a bar to the rethinking and reorganization necessary for the adoption of sane, alternate technologies. In the first place, growth for the sake of growth is the functional principle of modern bureaucracy. Big is always better, small is never beautiful. An organization that is growing has expanding opportunities for promotion, for patronage, prestige, and higher status; more chances to be somebody else's boss. It panders to human vanity: the desire to be a big guy, even if it is only a little big guy among lots of other little big guys. You get no brownie points in a bureaucracy by proposing a reduction in scale in personnel, techniques, or products. You always talk about someone else's program being cut, never your own, even if your organization is no longer fulfilling its original function. Bureaucracies come to exist to preserve their own existence. There is a Tamil proverb: "All is lost when the fence starts feeding on the crop." In our technological bureaucratic society we have many fences feeding on crops. Observing the recent spectacular rise in doctors' salaries and the profits of companies servicing hospitals,[24] would it, for example, be unreasonable to suggest that the explanation for the misdirection of medical expenditures away from sectors that would improve general health, lies in the self-serving practices of the health industry?

The huge investment of capital in high technology and corporate bureaucracy, including the human investment in training, is a major source of resistance to change. Innovation, genuine structural innovation, is suspect to the individual technocrat because it threatens the definition of his occupational role, so important to his sense of personal identity. (The pronoun "his" serves as a reminder that one of the structural forms most jealously guarded is male dominance of bureaucracies.) Innovation also poses a threat to the concentration of power in corporate hands. Imagine the plunge in value of General Foods, Campbell, and Del Monte stocks if American farmers were to organize vegetable marketing and processing cooperatives on a wide scale. Well-directed criticism of corporate bureaucracy and its technologies invites, at the very least, inflated defensive rhetoric (the Florman paper is replete with

---

[24]Vincente Navarro: *Medicine Under Capitalism* (New York, 1976) pp. 135–169.

examples); at worst it brings retaliation, as demonstrated by Karen Silkwood's fate,° and Ralph Nader's perilous early days as lone gadfly to the automobile industry.

If bigger is the test of progress for bureaucracy, there is an equally simple test for technology: different and profitable. If it can be done a new way which brings profit to the corporation, it can be called progress. New products and techniques are necessary for corporate growth—they are the stuff of busy-ness for technocrats—but they should not, of course, demand internal structural change. What havoc they wreak on society at large is quite beside the point. When the agricultural researchers at the University of California, Davis, working with generous funding from agribusiness, produce UC-82, the square tomato that can be harvested by machine, it represents technological progress. No matter that it is smaller, less sweet and nutritious than its predecessors, nor that its appearance in the fields will throw migrant laborers out of work, and render many small farms uneconomic.[25]

BATTLEFIELD!

Win the battles of food product innovation or improvement by reducing time and costs. Your best strategy? Recruit ICI. We'll help outflank time and costs by applying our performance-proven mono and diglycerides, polysorbates, sorbitols, and mannitol. Then we'll help assure victory for your product with technical assistance from our cadre of food specialists. They're trained in CREATE A FOOD thinking and backed by some 40 years' experience with 125 grades of emulsifiers and polyols. We'll even make a special grade to meet your need. We're battlewise and ready to help you take on tough competitors by successfully developing new food forms, achieving special effects, or duplicating properties of existing foods. . . .

ICI AMERICAS INC.
ANT*ICI*PATING NEEDS[26]

With technology, the means become the definition of the ends, in the process redefining the meaning of the word "need." Whoever was aware that humans had a need to eat 125 grades of emulsifiers and polyols instead of natural foods before the first batch was whipped up in a laboratory, sparking a glint of potential profit in the corporate eye? With change synonymous with progress, the current state of the art is always, by

---

[25]Cathleen Williams and Paul Barnett: "Brave New Tomatoes," *Politics and Education,* vol. II, no. 1, Fall 1979, pp. 2–3.

[26]Extract from promotional literature prepared by ICI Americas Inc., Wilmington, Delaware, November 1978.

Karen Silkwood's fate Karen Silkwood (1946–1974) died in an automobile accident one week after she had been contaminated by plutonium at the Kerr-McGee Nuclear Corporation, where she worked. She was actively investigating safety conditions at the plant at the time of her death, and there has been speculation about the circumstances of the contamination and of the accident.

definition, the most advanced stage of technology.[27] The term "high technology" is the perfect illustration.

Here we are face to face with the principle of maximization. There is no concept of the optimal, no way in our scientific, technological culture of defining where we should stop. "Without experimentation and change, our existence would be a dull business," writes Samuel Florman. "We simply cannot stop while there are masses to feed and diseases to conquer, seas to explore and heavens to survey." Where there is the power to do, say our scientists and technologists, it must be done, come Hell or high water. (Hell or heavy water would be the current version, I assume!) Formerly, disaster sometimes called a halt, as in the case of the "Hindenburg." The explosion of the "Hindenburg" in April 1937 killed very painfully and spectacularly a small number of people, with the result that the development of that sort of airship with inflammable gases was discontinued. The problem now is that we cannot afford to wait for disasters to teach us lessons about our high technology. Given the possible scale of these disasters, there may be few survivors.

How did we get into this mess? How could we, as a culture, possibly have been so myopic as to let this happen? The answer, I believe, is to be found in segmentation, the structural form of the bureaucratic system. Modern bureaucracy is hierarchical, impersonal, functionally specialized, seeking always through categorization and the universal rule to avoid the unpredictable or the anomalous. The pressure of modern bureaucracy, including the technological, scientific, and educational bureaucracies, is against whole thinking, holism. We have, in the West, increasingly since the seventeenth century, emphasized the value of segmentation, and the product is specialized ignorance for some and generalized ignorance for most. Boarding an airplane six months ago, I was behind two men with brief cases who were telling each other that in a few years there would be a tiny percentage of the world's population which "knew computers," and there would be the rest, dependent upon them. They were delighted with the prospect. Here is another product of technocracy: elitism—us, with our specialized knowledge, and them, out there dependent upon us.

Cultural arrogance aplenty, but also remarkably limited vision. We seem oblivious to the price our advanced technologies exact. Take the problem of the "disappearing middle," as E. F. Schumacher called it.[28] We often mistakenly assume that when we adopt "more advanced" technologies we still have available to us—as though stored away in the human attic—all those old technologies. We do not. Many are irrecoverably lost, or require great cost to restore. In eastern India in the late 1960s, when dams for new centralized irrigation schemes silted faster than the engi-

---

[27]For a brilliant exploration of this, see Hans Jonas: "Toward a Philosophy of Technology," *Hastings Center Report,* vol. IX, no. 1, February 1979, pp. 34–43.

[28]Address delivered at The University of Michigan, Ann Arbor, March 13, 1977.

neers had projected, the Government's agricultural workers urged the peasants to rely again upon the old, local tanks (artificial ponds) and ditches, only to discover that many had been filled in to provide new paddy land.[29] The current sorry state of America's railroads, and Amtrak's inability to revive them, is a tribute to the effectiveness of airplane and superhighway technology. Remember too that we often uneducate when we introduce new gadgetry. The advertising appeal of Yum Yum Corporation's processed foods as tasting "just like Grandma's," would be negligible if processed foods had not destroyed our ability to cook like Grandma. And where shall we find all the blacksmiths when the oil runs out, and we want to harness the highsteppin' strutter[o] to the surrey again?

High technology destroys middle-level technology and skills; big bureaucracy destroys middle-level groups. Modern Western society is characterized by an absence of strong organizations between the family (itself reduced in size and function by the bureaucratization of society), and big bureaucracy, most notably the state. Clans, guilds, peasant communes, labor brotherhoods, free cities, monasteries and nunneries, orders of knights, all have succumbed to centralized bureaucracy. Our social scientists have given the good housekeeping seal of approval to the process by making it one of the defining characteristics of "modernity," and, by the same token, labeling as "traditional" those societies which retain castes, tribes, councils of village elders, secret societies, trade brotherhoods, and extended families. Most reviled of all in the development literature are those societies that have meshed kinship networks with bureaucracy, producing nepotism, seen as the very seat of corruption and "backwardness."

Such "imperfectly bureaucratized" societies are considered to be structurally weak, yet I would suggest that the vitality and diversity of their middle-level groups gives them an ability to respond to disaster, natural or man-made, far better than can we, in our high technobureaucratic state, where the nuclear family stands isolated and dependent on distant, impersonal bureaucracy. It is we, not they, who are structurally weak. Vulnerable because, in our commitment to a belief in the superiority of bureaucracy, we have destroyed alternative forms of organization.

The systematic destruction of alternatives in almost every sphere is the consequence of modern Western civilization's drive to use its technological and organizational power to dominate. In our determination to dominate nature, from which conceptually we set ourselves apart, we destroy other life forms. Monocropping produces more bushels per acre; so we put

---

[29]Author's personal observations and conversations in West Bengal, 1971–73.

highsteppin' strutter   An allusion to a song, "The Surrey with the Fringe on Top," in *Oklahoma* (1944), a Rodgers and Hammerstein musical set in Oklahoma territory at the turn of the century; the strutter is the horse.

vast acreage into a single variety of one crop, disregarding the basic Darwinian precept that variety provides a species with the best chances for survival in a hazardous, perpetually changing environment. Our vulnerable mono-crops then require technological rescue missions, and we wipe out further species with pesticides and herbicides. Distasteful though it may be to recall, historically we have done the same when other humans have stood in our way. Armed with industrial technology and the bureaucratic state, we cleared the American continent of its native occupants in the last century, just as today for our convenience we clear away the snail darters and the Alaskan wolves. We have no time for "primitives," without our high technology and bureaucracy, and our language is replete with words that characterize them as our inferiors. We do not value their cultural difference from us and from each other. We are as little concerned with sustaining human cultural variety—alternatives for response to a hazardous, changing environment—as we are with maintaining variety in nature. Western civilization is most dangerous because in the interest of growth, the anthropologist, Marshall Sahlins, warns us, "it does not hesitate to destroy any other form of humanity whose difference from us consists in having discovered not merely other codes of existence but ways of achieving an end that still eludes us: the mastery by society of society's mastery over nature."[30]

Horse-Drawn Tools and the Doctrine of Labor Saving

Wendell Berry

This selection comes from The Gift of Good Land: Further Essays Cultural and Agricultural *(1981). For further information about the author, see page 525.*

Five years ago, when we enlarged our farm from about twelve acres to about fifty, we saw that we had come to the limits of the equipment we had on hand: mainly a rotary tiller and a Gravely walking tractor; we had been borrowing a tractor and mower to clip our few acres of pasture. Now we would have perhaps twenty-five acres of pasture, three acres of hay, and the garden; and we would also be clearing some land and dragging

---

[30]*Culture and Practical Reason* (Chicago, 1976), p. 221.

the cut trees out for firewood. I thought for a while of buying a secondhand 8N Ford tractor, but decided finally to buy a team of horses instead.

I have several reasons for being glad that I did. One reason is that it started me thinking more particularly and carefully than before about the development of agricultural technology. I had learned to use a team when I was a boy, and then had learned to use the tractor equipment that replaced virtually all the horse and mule teams in this part of the country after World War II. Now I was turning around, as if in the middle of my own history, and taking up the old way again.

Buying and borrowing, I gathered up the equipment I needed to get started: wagon, manure spreader, mowing machine, disk, a one-row cultivating plow for the garden. Most of these machines had been sitting idle for years. I put them back into working shape, and started using them. That was 1973. In the years since, I have bought a number of other horse-drawn tools, for myself and other people. My own outfit now includes a breaking plow, a two-horse riding cultivator, and a grain drill.

As I have repaired these old machines and used them, I have seen how well designed and durable they are, and what good work they do. When the manufacturers modified them for use with tractors, they did not much improve either the machines or the quality of their work. (It is necessary, of course, to note some exceptions. Some horsemen, for instance, would argue that alfalfa sod is best plowed with a tractor. And one must also except such tools as hay conditioners and chisel plows that came after the development of horse-drawn tools had ceased. We do not know what innovations, refinements, and improvements would have come if it had continued.) At the peak of their development, the old horse tools were excellent. The coming of the tractor made it possible for a farmer to do more work, but not better. And there comes a point, as we know, when *more* begins to imply *worse*. The mechanization of farming passed that point long ago—probably, or so I will argue, when it passed from horse power to tractor power.

The increase of power has made it possible for one worker to crop an enormous acreage, but for this "efficiency" the country has paid a high price. From 1946 to 1976, because fewer people were needed, the farm population declined from thirty million to nine million; the rapid movement of these millions into the cities greatly aggravated that complex of problems which we now call the "urban crisis," and the land is suffering for want of the care of those absent families. The coming of a tool, then, can be a cultural event of great influence and power. Once that is understood, it is no longer possible to be simpleminded about technological progress. It is no longer possible to ask, What is a good tool? without asking at the same time, How *well* does it work? and, What is its influence?

One could say, as a rule of thumb, that a good tool is one that makes it possible to work faster *and* better than before. When companies quit making them, the horse-drawn tools fulfilled both requirements. Consider, for example, the International High Gear No. 9 mowing machine. This is a horse-drawn mower that certainly improved on everything that came before it, from the scythe to previous machines in the International line. Up to that point, to cut fast and to cut well were two aspects of the same problem. Past that point the speed of the work could be increased, but not the quality.

I own one of these mowers. I have used it in my hayfield at the same time that a neighbor mowed there with a tractor mower; I have gone from my own freshly cut hayfield into others just mowed by tractors; and I can say unhesitatingly that, though the tractors do faster work, they do not do it better. The same is substantially true, I think, of other tools: plows, cultivators, harrows, grain drills, seeders, spreaders, etc. Through the development of the standard horse-drawn equipment, quality and speed increased together; after that, the principle increase has been in speed.

Moreover, as the speed has increased, care has tended to decline. For this, one's eyes can furnish ample evidence. But we have it also by the testimony of the equipment manufacturers themselves. Here, for example, is a quote from the public relations paper of one of the largest companies: "Today we have multi-row planters that slap in a crop in a hurry, putting down seed, fertilizer, insecticide and herbicide in one quick swipe across the field."

But good work and good workmanship cannot be accomplished by "slaps" and "swipes." Such language seems to be derived from the he-man vocabulary of TV westerns, not from any known principles of good agriculture. What does the language of good agricultural workmanship sound like? Here is the voice of an old-time English farmworker and horseman, Harry Groom, as quoted in George Ewart Evans's *The Horse in the Furrow:* "It's all rush today. You hear a young chap say in the pub: 'I done thirty acres today.' But it ain't messed over, let alone done. You take the rolling, for instance. Two mile an hour is fast enough for a roll or a harrow. With a roll, the slower the better. If you roll fast, the clods are not broken up, they're just pressed in further. Speed is everything now; just jump on the tractor and way across the field as if it's a dirt-track. You see it when a farmer takes over a new farm: he goes in and plants straightway, right out of the book. But if one of the old farmers took a new farm, and you walked round the land with him and asked him: 'What are you going to plant here and here?' he'd look at you some queer; because he wouldn't plant nothing much at first. He'd wait a bit and see what the land was like: he'd *prove* the land first. A good practical man would hold on for a few weeks, and get the feel of the land under his feet. He'd walk on it and feel it through his boots and see if it was in good heart, before he planted anything: he'd sow only when he knew what the land was fit for."

Granted that there is always plenty of room to disagree about farming

methods, there is still no way to deny that in the first quotation we have
a description of careless farming, and in the second a description of a way
of farming as careful—as knowing, skillful, and loving—as any other kind
of high workmanship. The difference between the two is simply that the
second considers where and how the machine is used, whereas the first
considers only the machine. The first is the point of view of a man high
up in the air-conditioned cab of a tractor described as "a beast that eats
acres." The second is that of a man who has worked close to the ground
in the open air of the field, who has studied the condition of the ground
as he drove over it, and who has cared and thought about it.

If we had tools thirty-five years ago that made it possible to do farm
work both faster and better than before, then why did we choose to go
ahead and make them no longer better, but just bigger and bigger and
faster and faster? It was, I think, because we were already allowing the
wrong people to give the wrong answers to questions raised by the improved horse-drawn machines. Those machines, like the ones that followed them, were *labor savers.* They may seem old-timey in comparison
to today's "acre eaters," but when they came on the market they greatly
increased the amount of work that one worker could do in a day. And so
they confronted us with a critical question: How would we define labor
saving?

We defined it, or allowed it to be defined for us by the corporations and
the specialists, as if it involved no human considerations at all, as if the
labor to be "saved" were not human labor. We decided, in the language
of some experts, to look on technology as a "substitute for labor." Which
means that we did not intend to "save" labor at all, but to *replace* it, and
to *displace* the people who once supplied it. We never asked what should
be done with the "saved" labor; we let the "labor market" take care of
that. Nor did we ask the larger questions of what values we should place
on people and their work and on the land. It appears that we abandoned
ourselves unquestioningly to a course of technological evolution, which
would value the development of machines far above the development of
people.

And so it becomes clear that, by itself, my rule-of-thumb definition of
a good tool (one that permits a worker to work both better and faster) does
not go far enough. Even such a tool can cause bad results if its use is not
directed by a benign and healthy social purpose. The coming of a tool,
then, is not just a cultural event; it is also an historical crossroad—a point
at which people must choose between two possibilities: to become more
intensive or more extensive; to use the tool for quality or for quantity, for
care or for speed.

In speaking of this as a choice, I am obviously assuming that the evolution of technology is *not* unquestionable or uncontrollable; that "progress" and the "labor market" do *not* represent anything so unyielding as
natural law, but are aspects of an economy; and that any economy is in

some sense a "managed" economy, managed by an intention to distribute the benefits of work, land, and materials in a certain way. (The present agricultural economy, for instance, is slanted to give the greater portion of these benefits to the "agribusiness" corporations. If this were not so, the recent farmers' strike would have been an "agribusiness" strike as well.) If those assumptions are correct, we are at liberty to do a little historical supposing, not meant, of course, to "change history" or "rewrite it," but to clarify somewhat this question of technological choice.

Suppose, then, that in 1945 we had valued the human life of farms and farm communities 1 percent more than we valued "economic growth" and technological progress. And suppose we had espoused the health of homes, farms, towns, and cities with anything like the resolve and energy with which we built the "military-industrial complex." Suppose, in other words, that we had really meant what, all that time, most of us and most of our leaders were saying, and that we had really tried to live by the traditional values to which we gave lip service.

Then, it seems to me, we might have accepted certain mechanical and economic limits. We might have used the improved horse-drawn tools, or even the small tractor equipment that followed, not to displace workers and decrease care and skill, but to intensify production, improve maintenance, increase care and skill, and widen the margins of leisure, pleasure, and community life. We might, in other words, by limiting technology to a human or a democratic scale, have been able to use the saved labor *in the same places where we saved it.*

It is important to remember that "labor" is a very crude, industrial term, fitted to the huge economic structures, the dehumanized technology, and the abstract social organization of urban-industrial society. In such circumstances, "labor" means little more than the sum of two human quantities, human energy plus human time, which we identify as "man-hours." But the nearer home we put "labor" to work, and the smaller and more familiar we make its circumstances, the more we enlarge and complicate and enhance its meaning. At work in a factory, workers are only workers, "units of production" expending "man-hours" at a task set for them by strangers. At work in their own communities, on their own farms or in their own households or shops, workers are *never* only workers, but rather persons, relatives, and neighbors. They work *for* those they work *among* and *with.* Moreover, workers tend to be independent in inverse proportion to the size of the circumstance in which they work. That is, the work of factory workers is ruled by the factory, whereas the work of housewives, small craftsmen, or small farmers is ruled by their own morality, skill, and intelligence. And so, when workers work independently and at home, the society as a whole may lose something in the way of organizational efficiency and economies of scale. But it begins to *gain* values not so readily quantifiable in the fulfilled humanity of the workers, who then bring to their work not just contracted quantities of "man-hours," but qualities such as independence, skill, intelligence, judgment, pride, respect, loyalty, love, reverence.

To put the matter in concrete terms, if the farm communities had been able to use the best horse-drawn tools to save labor in the true sense, then they might have used the saved time and energy, first of all, for leisure—something that technological progress has given to farmers. Second, they might have used it to improve their farms: to enrich the soil, prevent erosion, conserve water, put up better and more permanent fences and buildings; to practice forestry and its dependent crafts and economies; to plant orchards, vineyards, gardens of bush fruits; to plant market gardens; to improve pasture, breeding, husbandry, and the subsidiary enterprises of a local, small-herd livestock economy; to enlarge, diversify, and deepen the economies of households and homesteads. Third, they might have used it to expand and improve the specialized crafts necessary to the health and beauty of communities: carpentry, masonry, leatherwork, cabinetwork, metalwork, pottery, etc. Fourth, they might have used it to improve the homelife and the home instruction of children, thereby preventing the hardships and expenses now placed on schools, courts, and jails.

It is probable also that, if we *had* followed such a course, we would have averted or greatly ameliorated the present shortages of energy and employment. The cities would be much less crowded; the rates of crime and welfare dependency would be much lower; the standards of industrial production would probably be higher. And farmers might have avoided their present crippling dependence on money lenders.

I am aware that all this is exactly the sort of thinking that the technological determinists will dismiss as nostalgic or wishful. I mean it, however, not as a recommendation that we "return to the past," but as a criticism of the past; and my criticism is based on the assumption that we had in the past, and that we have now, a *choice* about how we should use technology and what we should use it for. As I understand it, this choice depends absolutely on our willingness to limit our desires as well as the scale and kind of technology we use to satisfy them. Without that willingness, there is no choice; we must simply abandon ourselves to whatever the technologists may discover to be possible.

The technological determinists, of course, do not accept that such a choice exists—undoubtedly because they resent the moral limits on their work that such a choice implies. They speak romantically of "man's destiny" to go on to bigger and more sophisticated machines. Or they take the opposite course and speak the tooth-and-claw language of Darwinism. Ex-secretary of agriculture Earl Butz speaks, for instance, of "Butz's Law of Economics" which is "Adapt or Die."

I am, I think, as enthusiastic about the principle of adaptation as Mr. Butz. We differ only on the question of what should be adapted. He believes that we should adapt to the machines, that humans should be forced to conform to technological conditions or standards. I believe that the machines should be adapted to us—to serve our *human* needs as our history, our heritage, and our most generous hopes have defined them.

Technical Arrangements as Forms of Order

Langdon Winner

Langdon Winner is a political theorist who specializes in social and political issues generated by modern technological change. His first book was Autonomous Technology *(1977), a study of the idea of technology-out-of-control in modern social thought. Winner was born in 1944, did all his college work at Berkeley (Ph.D. in Political Science, 1973), and has taught at the University of Leiden, at the University of California, Santa Cruz, and at M.I.T. He is now a member of the Department of Science and Technology Studies at Rensselaer Polytechnic Institute. The present piece, from* Daedalus *(Winter 1980), has been reprinted in Chapter 2 of Winner's* The Whale and the Reactor: A Search for Limits in an Age of High Technology *(1986).*

Anyone who has traveled the highways of America and has become used to the normal height of overpasses may well find something a little odd about some of the bridges over the parkways on Long Island, New York. Many of the overpasses are extraordinarily low, having as little as nine feet of clearance at the curb. Even those who happened to notice this structural peculiarity would not be inclined to attach any special meaning to it. In our accustomed way of looking at things like roads and bridges we see the details of form as innocuous, and seldom give them a second thought.

It turns out, however, that the two hundred or so low-hanging overpasses on Long Island were deliberately designed to achieve a particular social effect. Robert Moses, the master builder of roads, parks, bridges, and other public works from the 1920s to the 1970s in New York, had these overpasses built to specifications that would discourage the presence of buses on his parkways. According to evidence provided by Robert A. Caro in his biography of Moses, the reasons reflect Moses's social-class bias and racial prejudice. Automobile-owning whites of "upper" and "comfortable middle" classes, as he called them, would be free to use the parkways for recreation and commuting. Poor people and blacks, who normally used public transit, were kept off the roads because the twelve-foot tall buses could not get through the overpasses. One consequence was to limit access of racial minorities and low-income groups to Jones Beach, Moses's widely acclaimed public park. Moses made doubly sure of this result by vetoing a proposed extension of the Long Island Railroad to Jones Beach.[1]

As a story in recent American political history, Robert Moses's life is fascinating. His dealings with mayors, governors, and presidents, and his careful manipulation of legislatures, banks, labor unions, the press, and public opinion are all matters that political scientists could study for years. But the most important and enduring results of his work are his technologies, the vast engineering projects that give New York much of its present form. For generations after Moses has gone and the alliances he forged have fallen apart, his public works, especially the highways and bridges he built to favor the use of the automobile over the development of mass transit, will continue to shape that city. Many of his monumental structures of concrete and steel embody a systematic social inequality, a way of engineering relationships among people that, after a time, becomes just another part of the landscape. As planner Lee Koppleman told Caro about the low bridges on Wantagh Parkway, "The old son-of-a-gun had made sure that buses would *never* be able to use his goddamned parkways."[2]

Histories of architecture, city planning, and public works contain many examples of physical arrangements that contain explicit or implicit political purposes. One can point to Baron Haussmann's broad Parisian thoroughfares, engineered at Louis Napoleon's direction to prevent any recurrence of street fighting of the kind that took place during the revolution of 1848. Or one can visit any number of grotesque concrete buildings and huge plazas constructed on American university campuses during the late 1960s and early 1970s to defuse student demonstrations. Studies of industrial machines and instruments also turn up interesting political stories, including some that violate our normal expectations about why technological innovations are made in the first place. If we suppose that new technologies are introduced to achieve increased efficiency, the history of technology shows that we will sometimes be disappointed. Technological change expresses a panoply of human motives, not the least of which is the desire of some to have dominion over others, even though it may require an occasional sacrifice of cost-cutting and some violence to the norm of getting more from less.

One poignant illustration can be found in the history of nineteenth century industrial mechanization. At Cyrus McCormick's reaper manu-

---

[1]Robert A. Caro, *The Power Broker: Robert Moses and the Fall of New York* (New York: Random House, 1974), pp. 318, 481, 514, 546, 951–958.

[2]*Ibid.*, p. 952.

facturing plant in Chicago in the middle 1880s, pneumatic molding machines, a new and largely untested innovation, were added to the foundry at an estimated cost of $500,000. In the standard economic interpretation of such things, we would expect that this step was taken to modernize the plant and achieve the kind of efficiencies that mechanization brings. But historian Robert Ozanne has shown why the development must be seen in a broader context. At the time, Cyrus McCormick II was engaged in a battle with the National Union of Iron Molders. He saw the addition of the new machines as a way to "weed out the bad element among the men," namely, the skilled workers who had organized the union local in Chicago.[3] The new machines, manned by unskilled labor, actually produced inferior castings at a higher cost than the earlier process. After three years of use the machines were, in fact, abandoned, but by that time they had served their purpose—the destruction of the union. Thus, the story of these technical developments at the McCormick factory cannot be understood adequately outside the record of workers' attempts to organize, police repression of the labor movement in Chicago during that period, and the events surrounding the bombing at Haymarket Square. Technological history and American political history were at that moment deeply intertwined.

In cases like those of Moses's low bridges and McCormick's molding machines, one sees the importance of technical arrangements that precede the *use* of the things in question. It is obvious that technologies can be used in ways that enhance the power, authority, and privilege of some over others, for example, the use of television to sell a candidate. To our accustomed way of thinking, technologies are seen as neutral tools that can be used well or poorly, for good, evil, or something in between. But we usually do not stop to inquire whether a given device might have been designed and built in such a way that it produces a set of consequences logically and temporally *prior* to any of its professed uses. Robert Moses's bridges, after all, were used to carry automobiles from one point to another; McCormick's machines were used to make metal castings; both technologies, however, encompassed purposes far beyond their immediate use. If our moral and political language for evaluating technology includes only categories having to do with tools and uses, if it does not include attention to the meaning of the designs and arrangements of our artifacts, then we will be blinded to much that is intellectually and practically crucial.

Because the point is most easily understood in the light of particular intentions embodied in physical form, I have so far offered illustrations that seem almost conspiratorial. But to recognize the political dimensions

---

[3]Robert Ozanne, *A Century of Labor-Management Relations at McCormick and International Harvester* (Madison, Wis.: University of Wisconsin Press, 1967), p. 20.

in the shapes of technology does not require that we look for conscious conspiracies or malicious intentions. The organized movement of handicapped people in the United States during the 1970s pointed out the countless ways in which machines, instruments, and structures of common use—buses, buildings, sidewalks, plumbing fixtures, and so forth—made it impossible for many handicapped persons to move about freely, a condition that systematically excluded them from public life. It is safe to say that designs unsuited for the handicapped arose more from long-standing neglect than from anyone's active intention. But now that the issue has been raised for public attention, it is evident that justice requires a remedy. A whole range of artifacts are now being redesigned and rebuilt to accommodate this minority.

Indeed, many of the most important examples of technologies that have political consequences are those that transcend the simple categories of "intended" and "unintended" altogether. These are instances in which the very process of technical development is so thoroughly biased in a particular direction that it regularly produces results counted as wonderful breakthroughs by some social interests and crushing setbacks by others. In such cases it is neither correct nor insightful to say, "Someone intended to do somebody else harm." Rather, one must say that the technological deck has been stacked long in advance to favor certain social interests, and that some people were bound to receive a better hand than others.

The mechanical tomato harvester, a remarkable device perfected by researchers at the University of California from the late 1940s to the present, offers an illustrative tale. The machine is able to harvest tomatoes in a single pass through a row, cutting the plants from the ground, shaking the fruit loose, and in the newest models sorting the tomatoes electronically into large plastic gondolas that hold up to twenty-five tons of produce headed for canning. To accommodate the rough motion of these "factories in the field," agricultural researchers have bred new varieties of tomatoes that are hardier, sturdier, and less tasty. The harvesters replace the system of handpicking, in which crews of farmworkers would pass through the fields three or four times putting ripe tomatoes in lug boxes and saving immature fruit for later harvest.[4] Studies in California indicate that the machine reduces costs by approximately five to seven dollars per ton as compared to hand-harvesting.[5] But the benefits are by no means equally divided in the agricultural economy.

---

[4]The early history of the tomato harvester is told in Wayne D. Rasmussen, "Advances in American Agriculture: The Mechanical Tomato Harvester as a Case Study," *Technology and Culture*, 9 (1968): 531–543.

[5]Andrew Schmitz and David Seckler, "Mechanized Agriculture and Social Welfare: The Case of the Tomato Harvester," *American Journal of Agricultural Economics*, 52 (1970): 569–577.

In fact, the machine in the garden has in this instance been the occasion for a thorough reshaping of social relationships of tomato production in rural California.

By their very size and cost, more than $50,000 each to purchase, the machines are compatible only with a highly concentrated form of tomato growing. With the introduction of this new method of harvesting, the number of tomato growers declined from approximately four thousand in the early 1960s to about six hundred in 1973, yet with a substantial increase in tons of tomatoes produced. By the late 1970s an estimated thirty-two thousand jobs in the tomato industry had been eliminated as a direct consequence of mechanization.[6] Thus, a jump in productivity to the benefit of very large growers has occurred at a sacrifice to other rural agricultural communities.

The University of California's research and development on agricultural machines like the tomato harvester is at this time the subject of a law suit filed by attorneys for California Rural Legal Assistance, an organization representing a group of farmworkers and other interested parties. The suit charges that University officials are spending tax monies on projects that benefit a handful of private interests to the detriment of farmworkers, small farmers, consumers, and rural California generally, and asks for a court injunction to stop the practice. The University has denied these charges, arguing that to accept them "would require elimination of all research with any potential practical application."[7]

As far as I know, no one has argued that the development of the tomato harvester was the result of a plot. Two students of the controversy, William Friedland and Amy Barton, specifically exonerate both the original developers of the machine and the hard tomato from any desire to facilitate economic concentration in that industry.[8] What we see here instead is an ongoing social process in which scientific knowledge, technological invention, and corporate profit reinforce each other in deeply entrenched patterns that bear the unmistakable stamp of political and economic power. Over many decades agricultural research and development in American land-grant colleges and universities has tended to favor the interests of large agribusiness concerns.[9] It is in the face of such subtly ingrained patterns that opponents of innovations like the tomato harvester are made to seem "antitechnology" or "antiprogress." For the

---

[6]William H. Friedland and Amy Barton, "Tomato Technology," *Society*, 13:6 (September/October 1976). See also William H. Friedland, *Social Sleepwalkers: Scientific and Technological Research in California Agriculture,* University of California, Davis, Department of Applied Behavioral Sciences, Research Monograph No. 13, 1974.

[7]*University of California Clip Sheet,* 54:36, May 1, 1979.

[8]Friedland and Barton, "Tomato Technology."

[9]A history and critical analysis of agricultural research in the land-grant colleges is given in James Hightower, *Hard Tomatoes, Hard Times* (Cambridge, Mass.: Schenkman, 1978).

harvester is not merely the symbol of a social order that rewards some while punishing others; it is in a true sense an embodiment of that order.

Within a given category of technological change there are, roughly speaking, two kinds of choices that can affect the relative distribution of power, authority, and privilege in a community. Often the crucial decision is a simple "yes or no" choice—are we going to develop and adopt the thing or not? In recent years many local, national, and international disputes about technology have centered on "yes or no" judgments about such things as food additives, pesticides, the building of highways, nuclear reactors, and dam projects. The fundamental choice about an ABM or an SST is whether or not the thing is going to join society as a piece of its operating equipment. Reasons for and against are frequently as important as those concerning the adoption of an important new law.

A second range of choices, equally critical in many instances, has to do with specific features in the design or arrangement of a technical system after the decision to go ahead with it has already been made. Even after a utility company wins permission to build a large electric power line, important controversies can remain with respect to the placement of its route and the design of its towers; even after an organization has decided to institute a system of computers, controversies can still arise with regard to the kinds of components, programs, modes of access, and other specific features the system will include. Once the mechanical tomato harvester had been developed in its basic form, design alteration of critical social significance—the addition of electronic sorters, for example—changed the character of the machine's effects on the balance of wealth and power in California agriculture. Some of the most interesting research on technology and politics at present focuses on the attempt to demonstrate in a detailed, concrete fashion how seemingly innocuous design features in mass transit systems, water projects, industrial machinery, and other technologies actually mask social choices of profound significance. Historian David Noble is now studying two kinds of automated machine tool systems that have different implications for the relative power of management and labor in the industries that might employ them. He is able to show that, although the basic electronic and mechanical components of the record/playback and numerical control systems are similar, the choice of one design over another has crucial consequences for social struggles on the shop floor. To see the matter solely in terms of cost-cutting, efficiency, or the modernization of equipment is to miss a decisive element in the story.[10]

From such examples I would offer the following general conclusions. The things we call "technologies" are ways of building order in our world.

---

[10]David Noble, "Social Choice in Machine Design: The Case of Automatically Controlled Machine Tools," in *Case Studies in the Labor Process* (New York: Monthly Review Press, forthcoming).

Many technical devices and systems important in everyday life contain possibilities for many different ways of ordering human activity. Consciously or not, deliberately or inadvertently, societies choose structures for technologies that influence how people are going to work, communicate, travel, consume, and so forth over a very long time. In the processes by which structuring decisions are made, different poeple are differently situated and possess unequal degress of power as well as unequal levels of awareness. By far the greatest latitude of choice exists the very first time a particular instrument, system, or technique is introduced. Because choices tend to become strongly fixed in material equipment, economic investment, and social habit, the original flexibility vanishes for all practical purposes once the initial commitments are made. In that sense technological innovations are similar to legislative acts or political foundings that establish a framework for public order that will endure over many generations. For that reason, the same careful attention one would give to the rules, roles, and relationships of politics must also be given to such things as the building of highways, the creation of television networks, and the tailoring of seemingly insignificant features on new machines. The issues that divide or unite people in society are settled not only in the institutions and practices of politics proper, but also, and less obviously, in tangible arrangements of steel and concrete, wires and transistors, nuts and bolts.

The Recombinant DNA Controversy Revisited*

Susan Wright

Susan Wright was born in England, took a bachelor's degree in Physics at Oxford, and a Ph.D. in History of Science at Harvard (1975). She is now a lecturer in History of Contemporary Science in the Residential College of the University of Michigan, where she also directs the Science and Society program. She has written widely on science policy issues and is the author of the forthcoming book Molecular Politics: The Development of Policy for Recombinant DNA Technologies in Great Britain and the United States. *The following essay is from* Christianity and Crisis, *Sep-*

---

*This article is adapted from a presentation at Hillsdale College in Michigan and from an article written with Robert L. Sinsheimer, "Recombinant DNA and Biological Warfare," *Bulletin of the Atomic Scientists,* November 1983.

tember 1983 (there entitled "Genetic Engineering: The Real Risks"), with corrections by the author.

Media coverage of genetic engineering has painted a picture of an optimistic and benign future: industrialized bacteria meekly pumping out lifesaving quantities of insulin and interferon; a combination of genetic engineering and fetal surgery ultimately eradicating genetic diseases; self-fertilizing plants ending hunger and famine. But the media picture may be too optimistic, too benign. As research and development (R and D) in genetic engineering accelerates, two questions need critical attention.

1. What hazards to workers, the environment, and the general population will be generated by research and full-scale industrial activities?

2. What are the real goals of new military interest in this field?

Recombinant DNA, or gene splicing, techniques were developed in 1972, in a few California biological research laboratories. Gene splicing is a method of chemically cutting and joining DNA, the hereditary material of living things. Because DNA usually has the same structure regardless of its source, the techniques can be used to remove genes from a donor organism and transfer them into a recipient, where, under appropriate conditions, they can function. For example, in 1978, the human insulin gene was introduced into the bacterium *Escherichia coli* so that the bacterium was "programmed" to make human insulin. More recently, recombinant DNA containing the gene for growth hormone was inserted into fertilized mouse cells. In some cases, the gene functioned, and mice bearing this gene grew to twice their normal size.

In a word, gene splicing offers the potential to redesign life (in genetic terms), to construct new combinations of genes, and new organisms with new functions.

Because it signified different potentialities to different sectors of society, it was clear from the first that this technology would be controversial. Biologists had at hand a set of powerful research tools and it seemed likely that these tools would yield a new understanding of the structure and function of genes. (And, indeed they have.) Industrial and commercial interests foresaw a wide range of applications in techniques that could be used to transform bacteria into miniscule "factories" for producing substances not easily manufactured through conventional processes. It also seemed likely that in the future the techniques could be applied to commercially important plants and animals. Plants might be endowed with their own nitrogen-fixing genes; cows might be endowed with extra growth hormone genes; and surely some task would be found for the giant mice.

It was equally clear that the techniques might generate a broad range of problems. Concerns about health hazards and hazards to the environment were expressed. If microorganisms, or other organisms, were endowed with new functions, might they not find new ecological niches, and with what impact on the rest of the living world? For example, could an *E.coli* bacterium, endowed with the gene for *cellulase,* the enzyme that breaks down cellulose, find a niche in the human intestine? If so, would such an organism cause epidemics of chronic diarrhea? Could a plant endowed with nitrogen-fixing genes, and thus self-fertilizing, become a persistent weed, threatening the survival of other plants? The potential for military application was apparent. If gene splicing could find application in commerce, why not in warfare? For example, could the technology be used for toxin manufacture, or for construction of novel pathogens against which an adversary would have no defense?

Concern also focused on:

—the potential for *human genetic engineering.* If gene splicing could be used to redesign mice, why not human beings? Who would decide whether this would be desirable, and for what purpose?

—the *proprietary status* of redesigned forms of life. Was it ethically acceptable for corporations to patent redesigned genes, or organisms containing such genes, or the progeny of such organisms?

—the *terms of development* of this technology: Whose priorities and values should determine how this potent technology would be applied, and toward what ends? Should the reshaping of life be left to market forces to determine?

Many of these issues were either recognized at the outset or emerged shortly after the first gene-splicing experiments, and as they were aired, it became apparent that perceptions were mixed. Many of those close to the development of the techniques saw mainly the advantages they would yield for science and industry. But others saw a possibly highly destructive impact on society and on the environment. These critics focused on the power of the new techniques and argued that increasing the power to intervene in natural processes had frequently brought the power to disrupt them as well. They pointed to the history of nuclear fission and synthetic organic chemicals. Would the technology of genetic manipulation likewise generate serious hazards? Furthermore, would these hazards be uncontrollable since they would be borne by living organisms that could reproduce themselves? And even if the techniques turned out to be safe when used in research or industry, could they be deliberately applied in biological warfare, or in unethical forms of genetic treatment?

The first response to these concerns came from the community of molecular biologists in whose midst the techniques had been developed. In 1974, at an international conference held in Asilomar, California, leading molecular biologists called on governments in countries where research was underway to assess the risks and to develop controls.

This meeting is interesting as much for what was *not* addressed as for what it achieved: The only issue addressed in depth was the question of the hazards of research. Other concerns were either not raised or quickly dropped from the agenda. Health hazards, and controls to protect against them, quickly became the center of concern. This led eventually to the promulgation of guidelines for recombinant DNA research in most countries involved in this work. In the United States, guidelines were written by an advisory committee to the National Institutes of Health.

In 1976, these guidelines were quite strict. Six different categories of R and D were prohibited; much other research could proceed only under rigorous containment conditions; all research was screened both nationally and locally. There was, however, always a major loophole: the guidelines applied only to government-supported R and D; R and D supported by other sources, such as pharmaceutical companies or companies founded by molecular biologists themselves, was not covered.

Only six years after the promulgation of those guidelines, a dramatic shift of attitude has taken place. (This has been particularly striking in the United States.) Within the scientific community, initial fears of potential harm have been widely (although not completely) dismissed. For the general public, the controversy has all but faded away. Controls have been progressively dismantled. At the present time, there are effective controls for only the most hazardous experiments. For other work—the vast majority of recombinant DNA experiments and processes—there is virtually no provision for oversight or containment.

The new "biobusiness," based on recombinant DNA and other forms of genetic manipulation, is now booming. Production processes using genetically manipulated organisms are functioning, and their first products are being marketed. Most major oil, chemical, and pharmaceutical corporations are investing heavily in the field. A race to achieve technological dominance began to accelerate in 1978, and continues today. It is this side of recombinant DNA technology that is constantly reflected in the press: Commercial applications—usually portrayed as "benefits"—are highlighted; hazards and social problems are played down or—what is more usual—ignored.

But have the problems been resolved? Is it really the case that we can now sit back and wait for the new genetic paradise to come to us, complete with giant mice?

I shall argue no: the problems are still there, some, now, in a more acute form than before. I strongly disagree with the conventional wisdom: that the questions surrounding recombinant DNA activities are "non-issues," or, in other words, that the recombinant DNA issue has been decided largely "on its merits" (that is, it has been "scientifically," and "objectively" resolved).

First, the question of hazards that may arise *inadvertently*—as side effects of recombinant DNA activities—is largely unresolved. Second, the question of *deliberate* construction of hazardous organisms has not been addressed; further, there are now pressing reasons to do so.

The question of hazards arising inadvertently in the course of recombinant DNA research or industrial production has long been the focus of concern and the primary reason for development of controls. At one end of the spectrum are gene combinations which would almost certainly produce a fearsome organism. (For example, introduction of the botulinus toxin gene into *E.coli* would likely pose serious hazard.) At the other end of the spectrum are procedures which everyone would agree are innocuous. (For example, the insertion into *E.coli* of a gene from an organism that naturally exchanges genes with *E.coli*.)

Between these two extremes, there is an enormous number of possible gene combinations and their implications have been marked by a great deal of controversy and very little solid scientific consensus based on good evidence. Would it be safe, for example, to be exposed to *E.coli* bacteria programmed to make insulin, or interferon, or growth hormone? We have little evidence to draw on, certainly nothing that scientists would call "definitive."

Those who claim that the recombinant DNA "problem" has been solved agree that we now have "new evidence" which shows that the procedures are safe, that the original fears were unfounded, and that controls are unnecessary (see Sheldon Krimsky, *Genetic Alchemy,* MIT Press, 1982). Note that the scope of this claim is large: it applies not only to the techniques used today, but to future refinements as well. I would argue that while this "new evidence" is applicable to considerations of hazard, it is applicable only in a limited way in which major issues are left unresolved.

Let me briefly indicate two examples:

1. The "epidemic pathogen" argument. One of the arguments used most extensively to downplay hazards is that the bacterium often used for recombinant DNA experiments (*E.coli* K-12) cannot be converted into an epidemic pathogen (i.e., a disease-causing organism that spreads throughout a human population). There is solid consensus that this generalization is correct: K-12 is a weakly bug (usually), and it is unlikely to survive in competition with the normal gut flora. So it is unlikely to be transmitted from one person to another.

It is important to understand what this argument does *not* say:

First, the argument says nothing about what happens to the individual unfortunate enough to be the first to be exposed to *E.coli* bacteria manipulated to make a harmful substance. It doesn't matter that the bacteria would all die out in 24 hours: by that time, the damage might be done.

Second, the argument does not apply to organisms other than *E.coli* K-12. It does not apply, for example, to the relatives of K-12—the strains of *E.coli* that live in the human intestine, which under some circumstances can survive and colonize the guts of human beings quite effectively. It does not apply to all the other organisms being used for recombinant DNA activities: *Salmonella* (a food contaminant), *Pseudomonas* (an organism responsible for a wide range of hospital-acquired and other infections), viruses, etc. So there is a wide range of possibilities that the "epidemic pathogen" argument does not cover.

2. The "intervening sequence" argument. In 1977, new evidence on the structure of genes of higher organisms showed that most DNA of higher organisms would not be automatically processed by bacteria. This meant that the possibility of accidentally constructing bacteria capable of synthesizing proteins encoded in the genes of higher organisms was remote.

This argument, too, is limited in scope. It does not apply to the whole range of recombinant DNA activities *deliberately* aimed at enabling bacteria to make proteins usually made only by higher organisms. It does not apply to experiments in which genes from bacterial species are transferred into other bacteria, where expression of these genes may occur.

Arguments like these—all partial, with a limited range of applicability—have provided a veneer of scientific objectivity for the position that controls for recombinant DNA activities are no longer necessary. They have been used repeatedly since 1977 to justify progressive dismantling of controls to the point where there are now virtually no controls whatever. I think that detailed analysis of these and other arguments shows that, in fact, the recombinant DNA issue was not "decided on its merits": The decision to dismantle controls was political, not scientific.

A more objective assessment would conclude that in fact we still know very little about possible recombinant DNA hazards, particularly those involved in industrial processes. New biotechnologies will use very large volumes of microorganisms such as *E.coli, B.subtilis, Pseudomonas* and yeast in fermentation processes. Within the workplace, possible occupational hazards include exposure to microorganisms containing recombinant DNA, exposure to the products of such organisms, and exposure to hazardous chemicals used in extraction and purification. Outside the workplace, hazards may be generated by spills and leaks, improper ventilation, and improper disposal of wastes. For example, organisms released in large quantities into surface waters or sewer systems might transfer harmful characteristics to other organisms capable of infecting humans or animals. There is very little hard evidence, at present, concerning such possibilities. But the evidence we do have is not particularly reassuring. For example, it has been shown that even a weakened strain of *E.coli* not only survives in sewage but also survives secondary sewage treatment. But perhaps more importantly in the long run, the direction of recombinant DNA research and development is toward increasing both the variety of organisms used for synthesis of new products and the efficiency with which they can function. Genetic manipulation techniques, if they are to compete effectively with existing production methods, must be made more efficient than they are at present. Thus, if there are hazards, it is likely that they will increase as the commercial potential of recombinant DNA technology is realized.

If the issue of hazards that arise inadvertently is unresolved, few would argue against the possibility of *deliberate* design and construction of a hazardous organism with recombinant DNA techniques. That, one might say, is the ultimate biohazard, and the obvious applications are for military and terrorist purposes.

The question of military application of recombinant DNA technology has always been in the background of the controversy. There are several reasons why the issue needs to be addressed, and why, in the last three years, this need has become pressing. (See Robert Sinsheimer and Susan Wright, "Recombinant DNA and Biological Warfare," *Bulletin of the Atomic Scientists,* November 1983.)

First, the progressive weakening of controls for recombinant DNA technology in the last few years means that it is now permissible to do experiments which were originally seen as so hazardous that they were prohibited. Consequently, a variety of experiments are now being planned to introduce into bacteria genes for some of the most potent toxins known to science. We may expect that the number of such experiments will increase. And while these experiments are being undertaken in the civilian sector for scientific and medical reasons, they may be of equal if not greater interest to the military. Thus an unintended consequence of the weakening of controls is likely to be the provision of a body of knowledge on the behavior of novel biological agents which could find military application.

Second, since 1980, new military interests in biological research in general and in recombinant DNA technology in particular have emerged:

1. Data on support for biological research by the Department of Defense (DOD) and the National Institutes of Health (NIH) show that in the past few years, DOD support has increased substantially whereas NIH support has declined. In 1980–82, defense obligations for all biological research and for biological research in the universities increased in real terms by 15 percent and 24 percent respectively. (The percentages in terms of current dollars are, of course, more dramatic: 36 percent vs. 47 percent.) On the other hand, the corresponding changes for NIH were decreases of 4.1 percent and 3.6 percent respectively. We may expect that biologists will feel increased pressure to seek support from military sources.

2. In FY 1980, the DOD initiated programs of research using recombinant DNA technology. There are at present some 15 unclassified projects underway and an expansion of this program is planned. Many of these projects focus on cloning of genes for pathogenic organisms in order to make vaccines against them. No fewer than six of these projects focus on making the enzyme acetylicholinesterase, a neural transmitter attacked by nerve gas. (The DOD frankly acknowledges that the teams of scientists involved in these projects are competing with one another for results.) All of these projects are justified as "defensive" research (a point of legal importance since, as I will discuss later, the United States is a party to the Biological Weapons Convention).

3. In addition, the DOD has recognized that recombinant DNA (as well as other newer biological techniques) could also present new military problems because of its potential to enhance such factors as the selectivity, lethality, and stability of microorganisms. DOD reports to Congress for FY 1980 and FY 1981 characterize this possibility as a "new threat." And in response to this perception, the DOD contemplates new lines of research, the objective of this research being: "to provide a better understanding of . . . [disease-causing organisms] *with or without* genetic manipulation." That passage suggests that DOD planners contemplate projects using recombinant DNA techniques to change or accentuate the properties of disease-causing organisms: For how else could a "better understanding" of such organisms be derived? Statements of DOD officials have confirmed this interpretation: Under certain circumstances, the DOD is prepared to initiate programs aimed at making novel pathogens.

4. The DOD also anticipates that recombinant DNA technology may be applied for the production of toxins or other toxic agents. A report commissioned by the department in 1981 concludes that "toxins could probably be manufactured by newly created bacterial strains under controlled laboratory conditions."

DOD officials insist that no work on novel harmful agents—either toxins or organisms—is currently in progress.

Finally, there are potential loopholes in the international treaty covering biological research and development for military purposes, the Biological Weapons Convention. The convention bans development, construction, and stockpiling of biological weapons. For many years, the fact that the convention existed, and that it had been signed by the major world powers (including the U.S. and the Soviet Union), served to assuage concern about the development of recombinant DNA technology for weapons purposes.

It is not clear, however, that the treaty covers all aspects of the newer forms of genetic engineering. For example, it is unclear how much "research" is prohibited by the convention's ban on "development," whether this ban covers the construction of novel harmful agents, and whether it would cover manufacture of novel toxins. Furthermore, the treaty makes no provision for verification of compliance.

The enhanced capability made possible by the new technology might provide the incentive to use such loopholes. And that possibility is increased in the present climate of deepening suspicion and deteriorating international relations.

In the face of these problems, what can we do, first, to ensure that the new biology is directed exclusively for peaceful applications; and second, to ensure that those peaceful applications are safe?

With respect to the industrial application of genetic engineering, the situation seems comparable to the development of synthetic organic chemicals by 1950. By that point, advances in chemistry had made possible the invention of thousands of novel substances the impact of which on health and environment was unknown. Only now are we facing the full consequences of that ignorance: the overwhelming costs to human health and the environment of dioxin, PBB, PCBs, kepone, and the thousands of other lethal chemicals we have recklessly released. Can we afford to make the same mistake again, this time with self-reproducing novel organisms?

We need to regulate this field. The costs of regulation will be minute compared to the possible costs of damage wrought by an unregulated industry. We need to ensure that wastes are adequately treated and monitored. We need to monitor the health of workers. And we need meaningful involvement of workers and communities in decision making.

With respect to the military application of the new biology, the situation seems comparable to that in nuclear physics in 1940. Novel biological weapons have not yet been invented; yet it is likely that they could be as the result of determined effort on the part of military establishments. The critical question is whether we can learn from the experience of nuclear physics. The application of that field for weapons purposes, fueled by the logic of protection and counter-protection, has brought us to the brink of nuclear annihilation. Unless we renounce that logic, we run the risk of being swept up into a new weapons race, this time based on biology. Efforts directed toward negotiation and control of biological weapons are surely less hazardous than the alternative of *not* attempting to take this step.

Before the nations begin to build major military dependencies on the new biological technologies, we need to intervene to ensure that these technologies are directed exclusively into peaceful applications. All the nations should be encouraged to sign the existing treaty and to incorporate its provisions into their domestic law. And all nations should renounce secret biological research.

Beyond these steps, the entire subject of biological weapons disarmament needs to be reopened. Collectively, the United States and other nations should seek to strengthen the Biological Weapons Convention to ensure that any research on novel harmful agents is screened nationally and internationally, that all appropriate research is conducted in the open, in internationally approved facilities, and that all such work is directed toward peaceful ends.

I am not advocating that we stop the development of the new biology. I believe that we can achieve wonderful and important results with it. But we do need to ensure that its application is both peaceful and safe. We have to learn from the history of nuclear physics and organic chemistry. Indeed, I believe we have no real choice. We cannot afford to develop the new biological technologies without controlling them.

Gene of the Week

Robert Bazell

Robert Bazell (born 1945) is the science correspondent for NBC News. He was educated at the University of California, Berkeley (Candidate in Philosophy, 1971), worked as a science writer and reporter, and joined NBC in 1976. Among his many contributions to magazines is the following article from The New Republic *for March 23, 1987.*

Would you want to be told, at the age of 20, that your body is likely to undergo severe mental and physical deterioration when you reach your early 50s? Should a fetus be aborted if there is a good chance it will be born to lead a normal, productive life—and then develop Alzheimer's disease at age 60 or 70? These are not hypothetical questions. They are choices that medicine can offer now or will be able to offer soon.

Science reporters seem to have joined a gene-of-the-week club. Suddenly, several laboratories have announced the discovery of genes responsible for various inherited diseases. The list of those for which genes have been located includes Alzheimer's, Huntington's, muscular dystrophy, cystic fibrosis, manic depression, and polycystic kidney. At last our understanding of the molecules that control heredity appears to be leading to an alleviation of human illness. This promise has existed ever since Watson and Crick described the structure of DNA in 1953, but it has been fulfilled much more slowly than many scientists predicted.

Molecular biology indeed will pay off. The family doctor will be able to cure or prevent many awful genetic diseases. But we don't get all the benefits at once. In the first stage, physicians and scientists are able to identify those at risk for the illness but are not able to cure it. We are still in that stage for every disease for which a gene has been located, and this means we are faced with serious ethical dilemmas.

Most recently it was announced that a gene responsible for manic depression had been located. This study is notable not only for its contribution to the understanding of genetic disease but also because it turns much of psychiatry upside down. The nature-nurture debate about the origin of mental illness will continue. But there is no longer any question that at least some kinds of mental illness—indeed, one of the most common types—can be caused by specific physical changes. The research proved that manic-depressive illness, just like brown eyes, can be passed on from parent to child by a dominant gene.

The study was carried out in the Old Order Amish community of southeastern Pennsylvania. This closed community, which adheres strictly to tradition, suffers no more manic depression than any other group of Americans. But the Amish's large, extended families and well-understood genealogy make genetic studies much simpler.

Eventually the discovery of this gene will lead to an understanding of the precise cause of manic depression and probably to better ways to treat it. But now, because of what researchers learned by studying Amish families, they can test blood from an Amish child of any age and determine whether he or she is likely to develop manic depression as an adult. Do they want to do that?

"I'm very anxious not to walk up to a ten-year-old child and say, 'Fifteen years from now there is a high probability you will have a formidable psychiatric illness,' and leave that child with a cloud over his head for a significant part of his life," says Dr. David Housman of MIT, who headed the manic-depression study. But for the sake of research, there are reasons Housman and his colleagues might want to test Amish children for predisposition to the illness.

Their studies found that people who inherit the gene have about a 60 percent chance of developing the illness as adults. It would be useful to know what factors (upbringing perhaps?) determine who gets the illness and who does not. It would be important to learn what interventions—drugs, psychotherapy, or others—would lower the percentage of those with the gene who get the illness. The dilemma is obvious and tough.

Those for whom memories of high school genetics are dimming might want to be reminded that everything we are is determined by the information on our set of chromosomes, half from each parent, which we carry in every cell in the body. The chromosomes are made up of the chemical DNA. Each section of DNA on the chromosome that has a specific function is called a gene. Usually a gene directs the production of a particular protein.

Except for one of the diseases (Duchene's, the most common form of muscular dystrophy), the scientists have not yet isolated the actual gene causing the problem. They have found "markers"—that is, genes located near the faulty gene—so that in studies of families they can find the approximate location of the gene that causes the disease. (Contrary to what one might think, it is more difficult to locate the faulty gene itself than the markers.) With that information the scientists can identify carriers of the gene in families where the disease occurs. All they need are blood samples from at least two other family members, one known to be a carrier of the gene, one known not to be.

Most of that sort of testing has been available for families stricken by Huntington's disease, a severe mental and physical deterioration that occurs in later life and is best known as the condition that destroyed Woody Guthrie. Some younger people in the families where Huntington's occurs have elected to be tested. If they have the gene, they might decide not to marry or have children, so that the gene is not passed on. But others have recoiled in horror from the test. What are they supposed to do for the rest of their lives, knowing what lies ahead? If word of the test result leaks out, what are their chances of decent career opportunities, not to mention life or health insurance?

The next step in the research, after using the "markers" to locate the disease gene, is to isolate the gene itself, the specific piece of DNA that is responsible for the disease. Although so far this has been accomplished only for muscular dystrophy, it is highly likely that scientists will succeed within the next few years in isolating all or most of the genes that have been located. Once a gene has been isolated, the DNA chemists can develop a "probe," a test that can determine whether someone is a carrier of the gene.

The most important use of a probe would be as a means of detecting the defective gene in the tiny amounts of chromosomal material that are isolated from the fetus during an amniocentesis. Then the parents can decide whether or not to have an abortion. Today, analysis after amniocentesis only detects diseases such as Down's syndrome, which produce gross chromosomal abnormalities. But several laboratories are working to develop the prenatal test for muscular dystrophy. Very soon amniocentesis will reveal whether the child will develop any of a long list of genetic diseases during its lifetime.

The recent discovery of a gene that causes Alzheimer's disease was the most important finding about that terrible and widespread condition. As a result, it is quite likely that fetuses might soon be tested for susceptibility. Anti-abortion groups already oppose amniocentesis to check for conditions such as Down's syndrome. Their opposition can only intensify. "People have gotten used to the idea that we would terminate a life that would only last for two or three years," says Dr. Nancy Wexler of Columbia University, who heads the Hereditary Disease Foundation. "The notion that we would stop a life that would be normal for many years raises astounding difficulties."

Eventually the discovery of disease-causing genes, and then their isolation, should tell molecular biologists exactly how these genes work. And this in turn should lead to better treatment, prevention, and cures. But that is further off. Right now the biologists are discovering the genes at a rapid pace. Dr. Wexler estimates that 20 to 25 more will be found in the next year.

Grant applications and medical reporting often describe "breakthroughs just around the corner." But we can't wait even that long to confront the moral dilemmas that molecular biology is presenting today.

Computers
and People

Their extraordinary power and usefulness, and their explosive commercial success, have generated in many people an understandably vast enthusiasm for computers and computing. To them there seems to be almost nothing that computers will not be able someday to do faster and better. Others feel, however, that the bandwagon has already become too big for the circus. They claim, for instance, that computers have been "oversold" in such fields as education and personal finance, and that they offer serious threats to democracy in the form of easy political regimentation and breach of privacy.

Two of the fears most widely expressed are that computers will have a destructive effect on people at work, and, more profoundly, that they will ultimately have a destructive effect on our idea of what people are. The more computers are touted as being capable of performing "human" tasks, it is argued, the more there will be a tendency to reduce what we consider "human" to the level of what computers can do.

The essays in this section raise these two issues particularly. Carl Sagan's essay is a respectable specimen of enthusiasm for computer technology. Joseph Weizenbaum, a computer scientist to whose work Sagan refers, expresses grave misgivings about this sort of enthusiasm. He finds it a symptom of the dangers of our too-great dependence on the cold logicality of science. James P. Smith specifically reviews recent thinking about artificial intelligence, and the issues raised by the idea that human thought is ultimately computable. Finally Thomas B. Sheridan, also a computer scientist, while accepting the growth of computer control systems, outlines ways in which they are alienating to humans, and concludes that we must hold the designers and programmers of computers accountable.

In Defense of Robots

Carl Sagan

Carl Sagan (born 1934) is astronomer, astrophysicist, exobiologist, geneticist, teacher, writer, and humanist. As an undergraduate at the University of Chicago, Sagan earned both a B.A. (1954) and a B.S. (1955), then worked in the laboratory of Nobel Prize-winning geneticist Hermann J. Muller at Indiana University. He returned to the University of Chicago on a National Science Fellowship, completing his M.S. in physics in 1956 and, not yet 26, his Ph.D. in astronomy and astrophysics in 1960.

While doing postdoctoral work at the Institute for Basic Research at Berkeley, he wrote a Science *article (March 24, 1961) analyzing existing data on Venus; in 1967 some of his inferences were borne out by the Soviet Venera IV data. In 1962 he was appointed to the Smithsonian Astrophysical Observatory, and he taught genetics at Stanford, where he worked with Nobel Prize winner Joshua Lederberg on research into the development of life on earth. He then taught astronomy at Harvard until 1968. In the years 1968–1970 Sagan and his colleagues were the first to create amino acids, the building blocks of protein, in the laboratory.*

Since 1968 he has been a professor of astronomy and space sciences at Cornell, where he is also the director of the Laboratory for Planetary Studies. In 1968 he was Oregon's Condon lecturer (an honor previously awarded J. Robert Oppenheimer, among others), and in 1970 he won NASA's Apollo Achievement Award. His theories on Mars (National Geographic, December 1967) were substantiated by the 1971 Mars Mariner data, and in 1972 he received the NASA medal for exceptional scientific achievement. He also worked on the Viking project.

A prolific writer of professional papers and journal articles, he also writes for the lay audience (in the Encyclopaedia Britannica *and* Encyclopedia Americana, *among others), and his books include* Intelligent Life in the Universe *(with I. S. Shklovsky, 1966);* The Cosmic Connection *(1973), for which he received the Campbell Award for best science book;* Mars and the Mind of Man *(1973);* Dragons of Eden *(1977);* Broca's Brain *(1979), from which we reprint Chapter 20;* Cosmos *(1980), based on his immensely popular television series; and, with Ann Druyan,* Comet *(1985).*

> *Thou com'st in such a questionable shape*
> *That I will speak to thee . . .*

WILLIAM SHAKESPEARE, *Hamlet,* Act 1, Scene 4

The word "robot," first introduced by the Czech writer Karel Čapek, is derived from the Slavic root for "worker." But it signifies a machine rather than a human worker. Robots, especially robots in space, have often received derogatory notices in the press. We read that a human being was necessary to make the terminal landing adjustments on Apollo 11, without which the first manned lunar landing would have ended in disaster; that a mobile robot on the Martian surface could never be as clever as astronauts in selecting samples to be returned to Earth-bound geologists; and that machines could never have repaired, as men did, the Skylab sunshade, so vital for the continuance of the Skylab mission.

But all these comparisons turn out, naturally enough, to have been written by humans. I wonder if a small self-congratulatory element, a whiff of human chauvinism, has not crept into these judgments. Just as whites can sometimes detect racism and men can occasionally discern sexism, I wonder whether we cannot here glimpse some comparable afflic-tion of the human spirit—a disease that as yet has no name. The word "anthropocentrism" does not mean quite the same thing. The word "hu-manism" has been preempted by other and more benign activities of our kind. From the analogy with sexism and racism I suppose the name for this malady is "speciesism"—the prejudice that there are no beings so fine, so capable, so reliable as human beings.

This is a prejudice because it is, at the very least, a prejudgment, a conclusion drawn before all the facts are in. Such comparisons of men and machines in space are comparisons of smart men and dumb machines. We have not asked what sorts of machines could have been built for the $30-or-so billion that the Apollo and Skylab missions cost.

Each human being is a superbly constructed, astonishingly compact, self-ambulatory computer—capable on occasion of independent decision making and real control of his or her environment. And, as the old joke goes, these computers can be constructed by unskilled labor. But there are serious limitations to employing human beings in certain environments. Without a great deal of protection, human beings would be incon-venienced on the ocean floor, the surface of Venus, the deep interior of Jupiter, or even on long space missions. Perhaps the only interesting result of Skylab that could not have been obtained by machines is that human beings in space for a period of months undergo a serious loss of bone calcium and phosphorus—which seems to imply that human beings may be incapacitated under 0 g for missions of six to nine months or longer. But the minimum interplanetary voyages have characteristic times of a year or two. Because we value human beings highly, we are reluctant to send them on very risky missions. If we do send human beings to exotic environments, we must also send along their food, their air, their water, amenities for entertainment and waste recycling, and companions. By comparison, machines require no elaborate life-support systems, no entertainment, no companionship, and we do not yet feel any strong ethical prohibitions against sending machines on one-way, or suicide, missions.

Certainly, for simple missions, machines have proved themselves many times over. Unmanned vehicles have performed the first photography of the whole Earth and of the far side of the Moon; the first landings on the Moon, Mars and Venus; and the first thorough orbital reconnaissance of another planet, in the Mariner 9 and Viking missions to Mars. Here on Earth it is increasingly common for high-technology manufacturing—for example, chemical and pharmaceutical plants—to be performed largely or entirely under computer control. In all these activities machines are able, to some extent, to sense errors, to correct mistakes, to alert human controllers some great distance away about perceived problems.

The powerful abilities of computing machines to do arithmetic—hundreds of millions of times faster than unaided human beings—are legendary. But what about really difficult matters? Can machines in any sense think through a new problem? Can they make discussions of the branched-contingency tree variety which we think of as characteristically human? (That is, I ask Question 1; if the answer is A, I ask Question 2; but if the answer is B, I ask Question 3; and so on.) Some decades ago the English mathematician A. M. Turing described what would be necessary for him to believe in machine intelligence. The condition was simply that he could be in teletype communication with a machine and be unable to tell that it was not a human being. Turing imagined a conversation between a man and a machine of the following quality:

INTERROGATOR: In the first line of your sonnet which reads "Shall I compare thee to a Summer's day," would not "a Spring day" do as well or better?

WITNESS: It wouldn't scan.

INTERROGATOR: How about "a Winter's day"? That would scan all right.

WITNESS: Yes, but nobody wants to be compared to a Winter's day.

INTERROGATOR: Would you say Mr. Pickwick reminded you of Christmas?

WITNESS: In a way.

INTERROGATOR: Yet Christmas is a Winter's day, and I do not think Mr. Pickwick would mind the comparison.

WITNESS: I don't think you're serious. By a Winter's day one means a typical Winter's day, rather than a special one like Christmas.

No device of this sophistication has yet been built, although I am not sure how many humans would pass Turing's human test. But the amount of effort and money put into artificial intelligence has been quite limited, and there are only about a half-dozen major centers of such activity in the world. One of the more striking results obtained in a very limited universe of discourse—that of children's blocks—has come from the work of Terry

Winograd, then at the Massachusetts Institute of Technology. Here is a dialogue between man and machine, the machine having been programmed by Winograd:

Q: What does the box contain?
A: The blue pyramid and the blue box.
Q: How many blocks are not in the box?
A: Four of them.
Q: Is at least one of them narrower than the one which I told you to pick up?
A: Yes, the red cube.
Q: Is there a steeple?
A: Sorry, I don't know the word "steeple."
Q: A steeple is a stack which contains two green cubes and a pyramid, for example.
A: I understand.
Q: Are there any steeples now?
A: No.
Q: Build one.

The machine does. It reaches out its mechanical hand, moves the cubes and builds the structure that has just been described.

Q: When did you pick up the pyramid?
A: While I was stacking up the red cube, the large red block and the large green cube.
Q: Why?
A: To get rid of it.
Q: Why did you clear off that cube?
A: To put it on the large green cube.

As another example, a machine psychiatrist has been developed by Joseph Weizenbaum, also at MIT. This is a much simpler program than Winograd's, since it involves nondirective psychotherapy, which, generally speaking, requires extremely simple-minded computer programs. Here is a striking dialogue between a human being and a computer psychotherapist. (There is certainly a selection effect here. Many other such machine/human psychiatric dialogues are not nearly so striking. But I suppose most human/human psychiatric dialogues are not very striking either.) In this interaction, in order to spell out clearly the respective roles of therapist and patient, the computer therapist types upper case while the patient types lower case:

men are all alike
IN WHAT WAY
they're always bugging us about something or other
CAN YOU THINK OF A SPECIFIC EXAMPLE

well, my boy friend made me come here
YOUR BOY FRIEND MADE YOU COME HERE
he noticed that i'm depressed much of the time
I AM SORRY TO HEAR YOU ARE DEPRESSED
he's right, i am unhappy
DO YOU THINK COMING HERE WILL HELP YOU NOT TO BE UNHAPPY
i need some help, that much is clear
WHAT WOULD IT MEAN TO YOU IF YOU GOT SOME HELP
perhaps i could learn to get along with my mother
TELL ME MORE ABOUT YOUR FAMILY
my mother takes care of me
WHO ELSE IN YOUR FAMILY TAKES CARE OF YOU
my father
YOUR FATHER
you are like my father in some ways
WHAT RESEMBLANCE DO YOU SEE
you are not very aggressive, but i don't think you want me to notice that
WHAT MAKES YOU THINK I AM NOT VERY AGGRESSIVE
you don't argue with me
WHY DO YOU THINK I DON'T ARGUE WITH YOU
you are afraid of me
DOES IT PLEASE YOU TO BELIEVE I AM AFRAID OF YOU
it pleases my father to think i am afraid of him
WHAT ELSE COMES TO MIND WHEN YOU THINK OF YOUR FATHER
bullies
DOES THAT HAVE ANYTHING TO DO WITH THE FACT THAT YOUR
BOY FRIEND MADE YOU COME HERE

This astonishing—one is very tempted to say "perceptive"—response from the computer is, of course, programmed. But, then, so are the responses of human psychotherapists. In a time when more and more people in our society seem to be in need of psychiatric counseling, and when time-sharing of computers is widespread, I can even imagine the development of a network of computer psychotherapeutic terminals, something like arrays of large telephone booths, in which, for a few dollars a session, we are able to talk to an attentive, tested and largely nondirective psychotherapist. Ensuring the confidentiality of the psychiatric dialogue is one of several important steps still to be worked out.

Another sign of the intellectual accomplishments of machines is in games. Even exceptionally simple computers—those that can be wired by a bright ten-year-old—can be programmed to play perfect tic-tac-toe. Some computers can play world-class checkers. Chess is of course a much more complicated game than tic-tac-toe or checkers. Here programming a machine to win is more difficult, and novel strategies have been used, including several rather successful attempts to have a computer learn from its own experience in playing previous chess games. Computers can learn, for example, empirically the rule that it is better in the beginning game to control the center of the chessboard than the periphery. The ten best chess players in the world still have nothing to fear from any present computer. But the situation is changing. Recently a computer for the first time did well enough to enter the Minnesota State Chess Open. This may be the first time that a nonhuman has entered a major sporting event on the planet Earth (and I cannot help but wonder if robot golfers and designated hitters may be attempted sometime in the next decade, to say nothing of dolphins in free-style competition). The computer did not win the Chess Open, but this is the first time one has done well enough to enter such a competition. Chess-playing computers are improving extremely rapidly.

I have heard machines demeaned (often with a just audible sigh of relief) for the fact that chess is an area where human beings are still superior. This reminds me very much of the old joke in which a stranger remarks with wonder on the accomplishments of a checker-playing dog. The dog's owner replies, "Oh, it's not all that remarkable. He loses two games out of three." A machine that plays chess in the middle range of human expertise is a very capable machine; even if there are thousands of better human chess players, there are millions who are worse. To play chess requires strategy, foresight, analytical powers, and the ability to cross-correlate large numbers of variables and to learn from experience. These are excellent qualities in those whose job it is to discover and explore, as well as those who watch the baby and walk the dog.

With this as a more or less representative set of examples of the state of development of machine intelligence, I think it is clear that a major effort over the next decade could produce much more sophisticated examples. This is also the opinion of most of the workers in machine intelligence.

In thinking about this next generation of machine intelligence, it is important to distinguish between self-controlled and remotely controlled robots. A self-controlled robot has its intelligence within it; a remotely controlled robot has its intelligence at some other place, and its successful operation depends upon close communication between its central computer and itself. There are, of course, intermediate cases where the machine may be partly self-activated and partly remotely controlled. It is this mix of remote and *in situ* control that seems to offer the highest efficiency for the near future.

For example, we can imagine a machine designed for the mining of the ocean floor. There are enormous quantities of manganese nodules littering the abyssal depths. They were once thought to have been produced by meteorite infall on Earth, but are now believed to be formed occasionally in vast manganese fountains produced by the internal tectonic activity of the Earth. Many other scarce and industrially valuable minerals are likewise to be found on the deep ocean bottom. We have the capability today to design devices that systematically swim over or crawl upon the ocean floor; that are able to perform spectrometric and other chemical examinations of the surface material; that can automatically radio back to ship or land all findings; and that can mark the locales of especially valuable deposits—for example, by low-frequency radio-homing devices. The radio beacon will then direct great mining machines to the appropriate locales. The present state of the art in deep-sea submersibles and in spacecraft environmental sensors is clearly compatible with the development of such devices. Similar remarks can be made for off-shore oil drilling, for coal and other subterranean mineral mining, and so on. The likely economic returns from such devices would pay not only for their development, but for the entire space program many times over.

When the machines are faced with particularly difficult situations, they can be programmed to recognize that the situations are beyond their abilities and to inquire of human operators—working in safe and pleasant environments—what to do next. The examples just given are of devices that are largely self-controlled. The reverse also is possible, and a great deal of very preliminary work along these lines has been performed in the remote handling of highly radioactive materials in laboratories of the U.S. Department of Energy. Here I imagine a human being who is connected by radio link with a mobile machine. The operator is in Manila, say; the machine in the Mindanao Deep. The operator is attached to an array of electronic relays, which transmits and amplifies his movements to the machine and which can, conversely, carry what the machine finds back to his senses. So when the operator turns his head to the left, the television cameras on the machine turn left, and the operator sees on a great hemispherical television screen around him the scene the machine's searchlights and cameras have revealed. When the operator in Manila takes a few strides forward in his wired suit, the machine in the abyssal depths ambles a few feet forward. When the operator reaches out his hand, the mechanical arm of the machine likewise extends itself; and the precision of the man/machine interaction is such that precise manipulation of material at the ocean bottom by the machine's fingers is possible. With such devices, human beings can enter environments otherwise closed to them forever.

In the exploration of Mars, unmanned vehicles have already soft-landed, and only a little further in the future they will roam about the surface of the Red Planet, as some now do on the Moon. We are not ready for a manned mission to Mars. Some of us are concerned about such missions because of the dangers of carrying terrestrial microbes to Mars, and Martian microbes, if they exist, to Earth, but also because of their enormous expense. The Viking landers deposited on Mars in the summer of 1976 have a very interesting array of sensors and scientific instruments, which are the extension of human senses to an alien environment.

The obvious post-Viking device for Martian exploration, one which takes advantage of the Viking technology, is a Viking Rover in which the equivalent of an entire Viking spacecraft, but with considerably improved science, is put on wheels or tractor treads and permitted to rove slowly over the Martian landscape. But now we come to a new problem, one that is never encountered in machine operation on the Earth's surface. Although Mars is the second closest planet, it is so far from the Earth that the light travel time becomes significant. At a typical relative position of Mars and the Earth, the planet is 20 light-minutes away. Thus, if the spacecraft were confronted with a steep incline, it might send a message of inquiry back to Earth. Forty minutes later the response would arrive saying something like "For heaven's sake, stand dead still." But by then, of course, an unsophisticated machine would have tumbled into the gully. Consequently, any Martian Rover requires slope and roughness sensors. Fortunately, these are readily available and are even seen in some children's toys. When confronted with a precipitous slope or large boulder, the spacecraft would either stop until receiving instructions from the Earth in response to its query (and televised picture of the terrain), or back off and start in another and safer direction.

Much more elaborate contingency decision networks can be built into the onboard computers of spacecraft of the 1980s. For more remote objectives, to be explored further in the future, we can imagine human controllers in orbit around the target planet, or on one of its moons. In the exploration of Jupiter, for example, I can imagine the operators on a small moon outside the fierce Jovian radiation belts, controlling with only a few seconds' delay the responses of a spacecraft floating in the dense Jovian clouds.

Human beings on Earth can also be in such an interaction loop, if they are willing to spend some time on the enterprise. If every decision in Martian exploration must be fed through a human controller on Earth, the Rover can traverse only a few feet an hour. But the lifetimes of such Rovers are so long that a few feet an hour represents a perfectly respectable rate of progress. However, as we imagine expeditions into the farthest reaches of the solar system—and ultimately to the stars—it is clear that self-controlled machine intelligence will assume heavier burdens of responsibility.

In the development of such machines we find a kind of convergent evolution. Viking is, in a curious sense, like some great outsized, clumsily constructed insect. It is not yet ambulatory, and it is certainly incapable of self-reproduction. But it has an exoskeleton, it has a wide range of insectlike sensory organs, and it is about as intelligent as a dragonfly. But Viking has an advantage that insects do not: it can, on occasion, by inquiring of its controllers on Earth, assume the intelligence of a human being—the controllers are able to reprogram the Viking computer on the basis of decisions they make.

As the field of machine intelligence advances and as increasingly distant objects in the solar system become accessible to exploration, we will see the development of increasingly sophisticated onboard computers, slowly climbing the phylogenetic tree from insect intelligence to crocodile intelligence to squirrel intelligence and—in the not very remote future, I think—to dog intelligence. Any flight to the outer solar system must have a computer capable of determining whether it is working properly. There is no possibility of sending to the Earth for a repairman. The machine must be able to sense when it is sick and skillfully doctor its own illnesses. A computer is needed that is able either to fix or replace failed computer, sensor or structural components. Such a computer, which has been called STAR (self-testing and repairing computer), is on the threshold of development. It employs redundant components, as biology does— we have two lungs and two kidneys partly because each is protection against failure of the other. But a computer can be much more redundant than a human being, who has, for example, but one head and one heart.

Because of the weight premium on deep space exploratory ventures, there will be strong pressures for continued miniaturization of intelligent machines. It is clear that remarkable miniaturization has already occurred: vacuum tubes have been replaced by transistors, wired circuits by printed circuit boards, and entire computer systems by silicon-chip microcircuitry. Today a circuit that used to occupy much of a 1930 radio set can be printed on the tip of a pin. If intelligent machines for terrestrial mining and space exploratory applications are pursued, the time cannot be far off when household and other domestic robots will become commercially feasible. Unlike the classical and anthropoid robots of science fiction, there is no reason for such machines to look any more human than a vacuum cleaner does. They will be specialized for their functions. But there are many common tasks, ranging from bartending to floor washing, that involve a very limited array of intellectual capabilities, albeit substantial stamina and patience. All-purpose ambulatory household robots, which perform domestic functions as well as a proper nineteenth-century English butler, are probably many decades off. But more specialized machines, each adapted to a specific household function, are probably already on the horizon.

It is possible to imagine many other civic tasks and essential functions of everyday life carried out by intelligent machines. By the early 1970s, garbage collectors in Anchorage, Alaska, and other cities won wage settlements guaranteeing them salaries of about $20,000 per annum. It is possible that the economic pressures alone may make a persuasive case for the development of automated garbage-collecting machines. For the development of domestic and civic robots to be a general civic good, the effective re-employment of those human beings displaced by the robots must, of course, be arranged; but over a human generation that should not be too difficult—particularly if there are enlightened educational reforms. Human beings enjoy learning.

We appear to be on the verge of developing a wide variety of intelligent machines capable of performing tasks too dangerous, too expensive, too onerous or too boring for human beings. The development of such machines is, in my mind, one of the few legitimate "spin-offs" of the space program. The efficient exploitation of energy in agriculture—upon which our survival as a species depends—may even be contingent on the development of such machines. The main obstacle seems to be a very human problem, the quiet feeling that comes stealthily and unbidden, and argues that there is something threatening or "inhuman" about machines performing certain tasks as well as or better than human beings; or a sense of loathing for creatures made of silicon and germanium rather than proteins and nucleic acids. But in many respects our survival as a species depends on our transcending such primitive chauvinisms. In part, our adjustment to intelligent machines is a matter of acclimatization. There are already cardiac pacemakers that can sense the beat of the human heart; only when there is the slightest hint of fibrillation does the pacemaker stimulate the heart. This is a mild but very useful sort of machine intelligence. I cannot imagine the wearer of this device resenting its intelligence. I think in a relatively short period of time there will be a very similar sort of acceptance for much more intelligent and sophisticated machines. There is nothing inhuman about an intelligent machine; it is indeed an expression of those superb intellectual capabilities that only human beings, of all the creatures on our planet, now possess.

Introduction to *Computer Power and Human Reason*

Joseph Weizenbaum

Joseph Weizenbaum is a scientist and engineer who has spent most of his adult life studying artificial intelligence, the structure of computer language, the understanding of natural language by computers, and the social implications of these studies. He was born in Berlin in 1923 but has become a citizen of the United States. Educated at Wayne State University, where he earned his M.S. in 1950, he worked as a systems engineer for General Electric before joining the faculty of the Massachusetts Institute of Technology in 1963. His major publication available to nonspecialists is his book Computer Power and Human Reason *(1976), which, he says, contains two major arguments: "first, that there is a difference between man and machine, and, second, that there are certain tasks which computers ought not be made to do, independent of whether computers can be made to do them." The book's Introduction is reprinted below.*

In 1935, Michael Polanyi, then holder of the Chair of Physical Chemistry at the Victoria University of Manchester, England, was suddenly shocked into a confrontation with philosophical questions that have ever since dominated his life. The shock was administered by Nicolai Bukharin, one of the leading theoreticians of the Russian Communist party, who told Polanyi that "under socialism the conception of science pursued for its own sake would disappear, for the interests of scientists would spontaneously turn to the problems of the current Five Year Plan."° Polanyi sensed then that "the scientific outlook appeared to have produced a mechanical conception of man and history in which there was no place for science itself." And further that "this conception denied altogether any intrinsic power to thought and thus denied any grounds for claiming freedom of thought."[1]

I don't know how much time Polanyi thought he would devote to developing an argument for a contrary concept of man and history. His very shock testifies to the fact that he was in profound disagreement with Bukharin, therefore that he already conceived of man differently, even if he could not then give explicit form to his concept. It may be that he determined to write a counterargument to Bukharin's position, drawing only on his own experience as a scientist, and to have done with it in short order. As it turned out, however, the confrontation with philosophy triggered by Bukharin's revelation was to demand Polanyi's entire attention from then to the present day.

I recite this bit of history for two reasons. The first is to illustrate that ideas which seem at first glance to be obvious and simple, and which ought therefore to be universally credible once they have been articulated, are sometimes buoys marking out stormy channels in deep intellectual seas. That science is creative, that the creative act in science is equivalent to the creative act in art, that creation springs only from autonomous individuals, is such a simple and, one might think, obvious idea. Yet Polanyi has, as have many others, spent nearly a lifetime exploring the ground in which it is anchored and the turbulent sea of implications which surrounds it.

---

[1]M. Polanyi, *The Tacit Dimension* (New York: Doubleday, Anchor ed., 1967), pp. 3–4.

Five Year Plan Soviet economic program designed to increase industrial and agricultural output by setting quotas for five-year periods, first implemented in 1928 under Joseph Stalin.

The second reason I recite this history is that I feel myself to be reliving part of it. My own shock was administered not by any important political figure espousing his philosophy of science, but by some people who insisted on misinterpreting a piece of work I had done. I write this without bitterness and certainly not in a defensive mood. Indeed, the interpretations I have in mind tended, if anything, to overrate what little I had accomplished and certainly its importance. No, I recall that piece of work now only because it seems to me to provide the most parsimonious way of identifying the issues I mean to discuss.

The work was done in the period 1964–1966, and was reported in the computer-science literature in January 1966 and August 1967. To summarize it briefly, I composed a computer program with which one could "converse" in English. The human conversationalist partner would type his portion of the conversation on a typewriter connected to a computer, and the computer, under control of my program, would analyze the message that had so been transmitted to it, compose a response to it in English, and cause the response to be typed on the computer's typewriter.

I chose the name ELIZA for the language analysis program because, like the Eliza of Pygmalion fame,° it could be taught to "speak" increasingly well. Because conversations must be about something, that is, because they must take place within some context, the program was constructed in a two-tier arrangement, the first tier consisting of the language analyzer and the second of a script. The script is a set of rules rather like those that might be given to an actor who is to use them to improvise around a certain theme. Thus ELIZA could be given a script to enable it to maintain a conversation about cooking eggs or about managing a bank checking account, and so on. Each specific script thus enabled ELIZA to play a specific conversational role.

For my first experiment, I gave ELIZA a script designed to permit it to play (I should really say parody) the role of a Rogerian psychotherapist engaged in an initial interview with a patient. The Rogerian psychotherapist° is relatively easy to imitate because much of his technique consists of drawing his patient out by reflecting the patient's statements back to him. The following conversation between a young lady and ELIZA playing doctor illustrates both the Rogerian technique of encouraging a patient to keep talking and the operation of the computer program ELIZA.

Eliza of Pygmalion fame Leading role, that of Eliza Doolittle, in George Bernard Shaw's play *Pygmalion* (1912), upon which the musical *My Fair Lady* is based. Eliza is a Cockney flower seller who is taught upper-class speech and manners by a linguistics professor because he had made a bet that he could pass her off as a duchess if he were given six months to work with her.
Rogerian psychotherapist One who follows the methods of Carl R. Rogers.

The first to "speak" is the young lady. The computer's responses are printed entirely in capitals.[2]

Men are all alike.
IN WHAT WAY
They're always bugging us about something or other.
CAN YOU THINK OF A SPECIFIC EXAMPLE
Well, my boyfriend made me come here.
YOUR BOYFRIEND MADE YOU COME HERE
He says I'm depressed much of the time.
I AM SORRY TO HEAR YOU ARE DEPRESSED
It's true. I am unhappy.
DO YOU THINK COMING HERE WILL HELP YOU NOT TO BE UNHAPPY
I need some help, that much seems certain.
WHAT WOULD IT MEAN TO YOU IF YOU GOT SOME HELP
Perhaps I could learn to get along with my mother.
TELL ME MORE ABOUT YOUR FAMILY
My mother takes care of me.
WHO ELSE IN YOUR FAMILY TAKES CARE OF YOU
My father.
YOUR FATHER
You are like my father in some ways.
WHAT RESEMBLANCE DO YOU SEE
You are not very aggressive but I think you don't want me to notice that.
WHAT MAKES YOU THINK I AM NOT VERY AGGRESSIVE
You don't argue with me.
WHY DO YOU THINK I DON'T ARGUE WITH YOU
You are afraid of me.
DOES IT PLEASE YOU TO BELIEVE I AM AFRAID OF YOU
My father is afraid of everybody.
WHAT ELSE COMES TO MIND WHEN YOU THINK OF YOUR FATHER
Bullies.
DOES THAT HAVE ANYTHING TO DO WITH THE FACT THAT YOUR BOYFRIEND MADE YOU COME HERE

DOCTOR, as ELIZA playing psychiatrist came to be known, soon became famous around the Massachusetts Institute of Technology, where it first came into existence, mainly because it was an easy program to demonstrate. Most other programs could not vividly demonstrate the information-processing power of a computer to visitors who did not already have some specialized knowledge, say, of some branch of mathematics. DOCTOR, on the other hand, could be appreciated on some level by anyone. Its power as a demonstration vehicle was further enhanced by the fact

---

[2]This "conversation" is extracted from J. Weizenbaum, "ELIZA—A Computer Program For the Study of Natural Language Communication Between Man and Machine," *Communications of the Association for Computing Machinery*, vol. 9, no. 1 (January 1965), pp. 36–45.

that the visitor could actually participate in its operation. Soon copies of DOCTOR, constructed on the basis of my published description of it, began appearing at other institutions in the United States. The program became nationally known and even, in certain circles, a national plaything.

The shocks I experienced as DOCTOR became widely known and "played" were due principally to three distinct events.

1. A number of practicing psychiatrists seriously believed the DOCTOR computer program could grow into a nearly completely automatic form of psychotherapy. Colby *et al.* write, for example,

> "Further work must be done before the program will be ready for clinical use. If the method proves beneficial, then it would provide a therapeutic tool which can be made widely available to mental hospitals and psychiatric centers suffering a shortage of therapists. Because of the time-sharing capabilities of modern and future computers, several hundred patients an hour could be handled by a computer system designed for this purpose. The human therapist, involved in the design and operation of this system, would not be replaced, but would become a much more efficient man since his efforts would no longer be limited to the one-to-one patient-therapist ratio as now exists."[3]*

I had thought it essential, as a prerequisite to the very possibility that one person might help another learn to cope with his emotional problems, that the helper himself participate in the other's experience of those problems and, in large part by way of his own empathic recognition of them, himself come to understand them. There are undoubtedly many techniques to facilitate the therapist's imaginative projection into the patient's inner life. But that it was possible for even one practicing psychiatrist to advocate that this crucial component of the therapeutic process be entirely supplanted by pure technique—*that* I had not imagined! What must a psychiatrist who makes such a suggestion think he is doing while treating a patient, that he can view the simplest mechanical parody of a single interviewing technique as having captured anything of the essence

---

[3] K. M. Colby, J. B. Watt, and J. P. Gilbert, "A Computer Method of Psychotherapy: Preliminary Communication," *The Journal of Nervous and Mental Disease,* vol. 142, no. 2 (1966), pp. 148–152.

*Nor is Dr. Colby alone in his enthusiasm for computer administered psychotherapy. Dr. Carl Sagan, the astrophysicist, recently commented on ELIZA in *Natural History,* vol. LXXXIV, no. 1 (Jan. 1975), p. 10: "No such computer program is adequate for psychiatric use today, but the same can be remarked about some human psychotherapists. In a period when more and more people in our society seem to be in need of psychiatric counseling, and when time sharing of computers is widespread, I can imagine the development of a network of computer psychotherapeutic terminals, something like arrays of large telephone booths, in which, for a few dollars a session, we would be able to talk with an attentive, tested, and largely non-directive psychotherapist."

of a human encounter? Perhaps Colby *et al.* give us the required clue when they write:

> "A human therapist can be viewed as an information processor and decision maker with a set of decision rules which are closely linked to short-range and long-range goals, . . . He is guided in these decisions by rough empiric rules telling him what is appropriate to say and not to say in certain contexts. To incorporate these processes, to the degree possessed by a human therapist, in the program would be a considerable undertaking, but we are attempting to move in this direction."[4]

What can the psychiatrist's image of his patient be when he sees himself, as therapist, not as an engaged human being acting as a healer, but as an information processor following rules, etc.?

Such questions were my awakening to what Polanyi had earlier called a "scientific outlook that appeared to have produced a mechanical conception of man."

2. I was startled to see how quickly and how very deeply people conversing with DOCTOR became emotionally involved with the computer and how unequivocally they anthropomorphized it. Once my secretary, who had watched me work on the program for many months and therefore surely knew it to be merely a computer program, started conversing with it. After only a few interchanges with it, she asked me to leave the room. Another time, I suggested I might rig the system so that I could examine all conversations anyone had had with it, say, overnight. I was promptly bombarded with accusations that what I proposed amounted to spying on people's most intimate thoughts; clear evidence that people were conversing with the computer as if it were a person who could be appropriately and usefully addressed in intimate terms. I knew of course that people form all sorts of emotional bonds to machines, for example, to musical instruments, motorcycles, and cars. And I knew from long experience that the strong emotional ties many programmers have to their computers are often formed after only short exposures to their machines. What I had not realized is that extremely short exposures to a relatively simple computer program could induce powerful delusional thinking in quite normal people. This insight led me to attach new importance to questions of the relationship between the individual and the computer, and hence to resolve to think about them.

3. Another widespread, and to me surprising, reaction to the ELIZA program was the spread of a belief that it demonstrated a general solution to the problem of computer understanding of natural language. In my paper, I had tried to say that no general solution to that problem was possible, i.e., that language is understood only in contextual frameworks,

---

[4] *Ibid.*

that even these can be shared by people to only a limited extent, and that consequently even people are not embodiments of any such general solution. But these conclusions were often ignored. In any case, ELIZA was such a small and simple step. Its contribution was, if any at all, only to vividly underline what many others had long ago discovered, namely, the importance of context to language understanding. The subsequent, much more elegant, and surely more important work of Winograd[5] in computer comprehension of English is currently being misinterpreted just as ELIZA was. This reaction to ELIZA showed me more vividly than anything I had seen hitherto the enormously exaggerated attributions an even well-educated audience is capable of making, even strives to make, to a technology it does not understand. Surely, I thought, decisions made by the general public about emergent technologies depend much more on what that public attributes to such technologies than on what they actually are or can and cannot do. If, as appeared to be the case, the public's attributions are wildly misconceived, then public decisions are bound to be misguided and often wrong. Difficult questions arise out of these observations; what, for example, are the scientist's responsibilities with respect to making his work public? And to whom (or what) is the scientist responsible?

As perceptions of these kinds began to reverberate in me, I thought, as perhaps Polanyi did after his encounter with Bukharin, that the questions and misgivings that had so forcefully presented themselves to me could be disposed of quickly, perhaps in a short, serious article. I did in fact write a paper touching on many points mentioned here.[6] But gradually I began to see that certain quite fundamental questions had infected me more chronically than I had first perceived. I shall probably never be rid of them.

There are as many ways to state these basic questions as there are starting points for coping with them. At bottom they are about nothing less than man's place in the universe. But I am professionally trained only in computer science, which is to say (in all seriousness) that I am extremely poorly educated; I can mount neither the competence, nor the courage, not even the chutzpah, to write on the grand scale actually demanded. I therefore grapple with questions that couple more directly to the concerns I have expressed, and hope that their larger implications will emerge spontaneously.

I shall thus have to concern myself with the following kinds of questions:

---

[5]T. Winograd, "Procedures As A Representation For Data In A Computer Program For Understanding Natural Language." Ph.D. dissertation submitted to the Dept. of Mathematics (M.I.T.), August 24, 1970.

[6]J. Weizenbaum, "On the Impact of Computers on Society," *Science,* vol. 176, no. 12 (May, 1972).

1. What is it about the computer that has brought the view of man as a machine to a new level of plausibility? Clearly there have been other machines that imitated man in various ways, e.g., steam shovels. But not until the invention of the digital computer have there been machines that could perform intellectual functions of even modest scope; i.e., machines that could in any sense be said to be intelligent. Now "artificial intelligence" (AI) is a subdiscipline of computer science. This new field will have to be discussed. Ultimately a line dividing human and machine intelligence must be drawn. If there is no such line, then advocates of computerized psychotherapy may be merely heralds of an age in which man has finally been recognized as nothing but a clock-work. Then the consequences of such a reality would need urgently to be divined and contemplated.

2. The fact that individuals bind themselves with strong emotional ties to machines ought not in itself to be surprising. The instruments man uses become, after all, extensions of his body. Most importantly, man must, in order to operate his instruments skillfully, internalize aspects of them in the form of kinesthetic and perceptual habits. In that sense at least, his instruments become literally part of him and modify him, and thus alter the basis of his affective relationship to himself. One would expect man to cathect more intensely to instruments that couple directly to his own intellectual, cognitive, and emotive functions than to machines that merely extend the power of his muscles. Western man's entire milieu is now pervaded by complex technological extensions of his every functional capacity. Being the enormously adaptive animal he is, man has been able to accept as authentically natural (that is, as given by nature) such technological bases for his relationship to himself, for his identity. Perhaps this helps to explain why he does not question the appropriateness of investing his most private feelings in a computer. But then, such an explanation would also suggest that the computing machine represents merely an extreme extrapolation of a much more general technological usurpation of man's capacity to act as an autonomous agent in giving meaning to his world. It is therefore important to inquire into the wider senses in which man has come to yield his own autonomy to a world viewed as machine.

3. It is perhaps paradoxical that just when in the deepest sense man has ceased to believe in—let alone to trust—his own autonomy, he has begun to rely on autonomous machines, that is, on machines that operate for long periods of time entirely on the basis of their own internal realities. If his reliance on such machines is to be based on something other than unmitigated despair or blind faith, he must explain to himself what these machines do and even how they do what they do. This requires him to build some conception of their internal "realities." Yet most men don't understand computers to even the slightest degree. So, unless they are

capable of very great skepticism (the kind we bring to bear while watching a stage magician), they can explain the computer's intellectual feats only by bringing to bear the single analogy available to them, that is, their model of their own capacity to think. No wonder, then, that they over-shoot the mark; it is truly impossible to imagine a human who could imitate ELIZA, for example, but for whom ELIZA's language abilities were his limit. Again, the computing machine is merely an extreme exam-ple of a much more general phenomenon. Even the breadth of connotation intended in the ordinary usage of the word "machine," large as it is, is insufficient to suggest its true generality. For today when we speak of, for example, bureaucracy, or the university, or almost any social or political construct, the image we generate is all too often that of an autonomous machine-like process.

These, then, are the thoughts and questions which have refused to leave me since the deeper significances of the reactions to ELIZA I have de-scribed began to become clear to me. Yet I doubt that they could have impressed themselves on me as they did were it not that I was (and am still) deeply involved in a concentrate of technological society as a teacher in the temple of technology that is the Massachusetts Institute of Technol-ogy, an institution that proudly boasts of being "polarized around science and technology." There I live and work with colleagues, many of whom trust only modern science to deliver reliable knowledge of the world. I confer with them on research proposals to be made to government agen-cies, especially to the Department of "Defense." Sometimes I become more than a little frightened as I contemplate what we lead ourselves to propose, as well as the nature of the arguments we construct to support our proposals. Then, too, I am constantly confronted by students, some of whom have already rejected all ways but the scientific to come to know the world, and who seek only a deeper, more dogmatic indoctrination in that faith (although that word is no longer in their vocabulary). Other students suspect that not even the entire collection of machines and instruments at M.I.T. can significantly help give meaning to their lives. They sense the presence of a dilemma in an education polarized around science and technology, an education that implicitly claims to open a privileged access-path to fact, but that cannot tell them how to decide what is to count as fact. Even while they recognize the genuine impor-tance of learning their craft, they rebel at working on projects that appear to address themselves neither to answering interesting questions of fact nor to solving problems in theory.

Such confrontations with my own day-to-day social reality have gradu-ally convinced me that my experience with ELIZA was symptomatic of deeper problems. The time would come, I was sure, when I would no longer be able to participate in research proposal conferences, or honestly respond to my students' need for therapy (yes, that is the correct word), without first attempting to make sense of the picture my own experience with computers had so sharply drawn for me.

Of course, the introduction of computers into our already highly technological society has, as I will try to show, merely reinforced and amplified those antecedent pressures that have driven man to an ever more highly rationalistic view of his society and an ever more mechanistic image of himself. It is therefore important that I construct my discussion of the impact of the computer on man and his society so that it can be seen as a particular kind of encoding of a much larger impact, namely, that on man's role in the face of technologies and techniques he may not be able to understand and control. Conversations around that theme have been going on for a long time. And they have intensified in the last few years.

Certain individuals of quite differing minds, temperaments, interests, and training have—however much they differ among themselves and even disagree on many vital questions—over the years expressed grave concern about the conditions created by the unfettered march of science and technology; among them are Mumford, Arendt, Ellul, Roszak, Comfort, and Boulding. The computer began to be mentioned in such discussions only recently. Now there are signs that a full-scale debate about the computer is developing. The contestants on one side are those who, briefly stated, believe computers can, should, and will do everything, and on the other side those who, like myself, believe there are limits to what computers ought to be put to do.

It may appear at first glance that this is an in-house debate of little consequence except to a small group of computer technicians. But at bottom, no matter how it may be disguised by technological jargon, the question is whether or not every aspect of human thought is reducible to a logical formalism, or, to put it into the modern idiom, whether or not human thought is entirely computable. That question has, in one form or another, engaged thinkers in all ages. Man has always striven for principles that could organize and give sense and meaning to his existence. But before modern science fathered the technologies that reified and concretized its otherwise abstract systems, the systems of thought that defined man's place in the universe were fundamentally juridical. They served to define man's obligations to his fellow men and to nature. The Judaic tradition, for example, rests on the idea of a contractual relationship between God and man. This relationship must and does leave room for autonomy for both God and man, for a contract is an agreement willingly entered into by both parties who are free not to agree. Man's autonomy and his corresponding responsibility is a central issue of all religious systems. The spiritual cosmologies engendered by modern science, on the other hand, are infected with the germ of logical necessity. They, except in the hands of the wisest scientists and philosophers, no longer content themselves with explanations of appearances, but claim to say how things actually are and must necessarily be. In short, they convert truth to provability.

As one consequence of this drive to modern science, the question, "What aspects of life are formalizable?" has been transformed from the moral question, "How and in what form may man's obligations and responsibilities be known?" to the question, "Of what technological genus is man a species?" Even some philosophers whose every instinct rebels against the idea that man is entirely comprehensible as a machine have succumbed to this spirit of the times. Hubert Dreyfus, for example, trains the heavy guns of phenomenology on the computer model of man.[7] But he limits his argument to the technical question of what computers can and cannot do. I would argue that if computers could imitate man in every respect— which in fact they cannot—even then it would be appropriate, nay, urgent, to examine the computer in the light of man's perennial need to find his place in the world. The outcomes of practical matters that are of vital importance to everyone hinge on how and in what terms the discussion is carried out.

One position I mean to argue appears deceptively obvious: it is simply that there are important differences between men and machines as thinkers. I would argue that, however intelligent machines may be made to be, there are some acts of thought that *ought* to be attempted only by humans. One socially significant question I thus intend to raise is over the proper place of computers in the social order. But, as we shall see, the issue transcends computers in that it must ultimately deal with logicality itself—quite apart from whether logicality is encoded in computer programs or not.

The lay reader may be forgiven for being more than slightly incredulous that anyone should maintain that human thought is entirely computable. But his very incredulity may itself be a sign of how marvelously subtly and seductively modern science has come to influence man's imaginative construction of reality.

Surely, much of what we today regard as good and useful, as well as much of what we would call knowledge and wisdom, we owe to science. But science may also be seen as an addictive drug. Not only has our unbounded feeding on science caused us to become dependent on it, but, as happens with many other drugs taken in increasing dosages, science has been gradually converted into a slow-acting poison. Beginning perhaps with Francis Bacon's misreading of the genuine promise of science, man has been seduced into wishing and working for the establishment of an age of rationality, but with his vision of rationality tragically twisted so as to equate it with logicality. Thus have we very nearly come to the point where almost every genuine human dilemma is seen as a mere paradox, as a merely apparent contradiction that could be untangled by judicious applications of cold logic derived from a higher standpoint. Even murderous wars have come to be perceived as mere problems to be solved

[7]Hubert L. Dreyfus, *What Computers Can't Do* (Harper and Row, 1972).

by hordes of professional problemsolvers. As Hannah Arendt said about recent makers and executors of policy in the Pentagon:

"They were not just intelligent, but prided themselves on being 'rational' . . . They were eager to find formulas, preferably expressed in a pseudo-mathematical language, that would unify the most disparate phenomena with which reality presented them; that is, they were eager to discover *laws* by which to explain and predict political and historical facts as though they were as necessary, and thus as reliable, as the physicists once believed natural phenomena to be . . . [They] did not *judge;* they calculated. . . . an utterly irrational confidence in the calculability of reality [became] the leitmotif of the decision making."[8]

And so too have nearly all political confrontations, such as those between races and those between the governed and their governors, come to be perceived as mere failures of communication. Such rips in the social fabric can then be systematically repaired by the expert application of the latest information-handling techniques—at least so it is believed. And so the rationality-is-logicality equation, which the very success of science has drugged us into adopting as virtually an axiom, has led us to deny the very existence of human conflict, hence the very possibility of the collision of genuinely incommensurable human interests and of disparate human values, hence the existence of human values themselves.

It may be that human values are illusory, as indeed B. F. Skinner argues. If they are, then it is presumably up to science to demonstrate that fact, as indeed Skinner (as scientist) attempts to do. But then science must itself be an illusory system. For the only certain knowledge science can give us is knowledge of the behavior of formal systems, that is, systems that are games invented by man himself and in which to assert truth is nothing more or less than to assert that, as in a chess game, a particular board position was arrived at by a sequence of legal moves. When science purports to make statements about man's experiences, it bases them on identifications between the primitive (that is, undefined) objects of one of its formalisms, the pieces of one of its games, and some set of human observations. No such sets of correspondences can ever be proved to be correct. At best, they can be falsified, in the sense that formal manipulations of a system's symbols may lead to symbolic configurations which, when read in the light of the set of correspondences in question, yield interpretations contrary to empirically observed phenomena. Hence all empirical science is an elaborate structure built on piles that are anchored, not on bedrock as is commonly supposed, but on the shifting sand of fallible human judgment, conjecture, and intuition. It is not even true, again contrary to common belief, that a single purported counter-instance that, if accepted as genuine would certainly falsify a specific scientific

---

[8]Hannah Arendt, *Crises of the Republic* (Harcourt Brace Jovanovich, Harvest edition, 1972), pp. 11 *et seq.*

theory, generally leads to the immediate abandonment of that theory. Probably all scientific theories currently accepted by scientists themselves (excepting only those purely formal theories claiming no relation to the empirical world) are today confronted with contradicting evidence of more than negligible weight that, again if fully credited, would logically invalidate them. Such evidence is often explained (that is, explained away) by ascribing it to error of some kind, say, observational error, or by characterizing it as inessential, or by the assumption (that is, the faith) that some yet-to-be-discovered way of dealing with it will some day permit it to be acknowledged but nevertheless incorporated into the scientific theories it was originally thought to contradict. In this way scientists continue to rely on already impaired theories and to infer "scientific fact" from them.*

The man in the street surely believes such scientific facts to be as well-established, as well-proven, as his own existence. His certitude is an illusion. Nor is the scientist himself immune to the same illusion. In his praxis, he must, after all, suspend disbelief in order to do or think anything at all. He is rather like a theatergoer, who, in order to participate in and understand what is happening on the stage, must for a time pretend to himself that he is witnessing real events. The scientist must believe his working hypothesis, together with its vast underlying structure of theories and assumptions, even if only for the sake of the argument. Often the "argument" extends over his entire lifetime. Gradually he becomes what he at first merely pretended to be: a true believer. I choose the word "argument" thoughtfully, for scientific demonstrations, even mathematical proofs, are fundamentally acts of persuasion.

Scientific statements can never be certain; they can be only more or less credible. And credibility is a term in individual psychology, i.e., a term that has meaning only with respect to an individual observer. To say that some proposition is credible is, after all, to say that it is believed by an agent who is free not to believe it, that is, by an observer who, after exercising judgment and (possibly) intuition, chooses to accept the proposition as worthy of his believing it. How then can science, which itself surely and ultimately rests on vast arrays of human value judgments, demonstrate that human value judgments are illusory? It cannot do so without forfeiting its own status as the single legitimate path to understanding man and his world.

But no merely logical argument, no matter how cogent or eloquent, can

---

*Thus, Charles Everett writes on the now-discarded phlogiston theory of combustion (in the *Encyclopaedia Britannica,* 11th ed., 1911, vol. VI, p. 34): "The objections of the antiphlogistonists, such as the fact that the calices weigh more than the original metals instead of less as the theory suggests, were answered by postulating that phlogiston was a principle of levity, or even completely ignored as an accident, the change in qualities being regarded as the only matter of importance." Everett lists H. Cavendish and J. Priestley, both great scientists of their time, as adherents to the phlogiston theory.

undo this reality: that science has become the sole legitimate form of understanding in the common wisdom. When I say that science has been gradually converted into a slow-acting poison, I mean that the attribution of certainty to scientific knowledge by the common wisdom, an attribution now made so nearly universally that it has become a commonsense dogma, has virtually delegitimatized all other ways of understanding. People viewed the arts, especially literature, as sources of intellectual nourishment and understanding, but today the arts are perceived largely as entertainments. The ancient Greek and Oriental theaters, the Shakespearian stage, the stages peopled by the Ibsens and Chekhovs nearer to our day—these were schools. The curricula they taught were vehicles for understanding the societies they represented. Today, although an occasional Arthur Miller or Edward Albee survives and is permitted to teach on the New York or London stage, the people hunger only for what is represented to them to be scientifically validated knowledge. They seek to satiate themselves at such scientific cafeterias as *Psychology Today,* or on popularized versions of the works of Masters and Johnson,° or on scientology as revealed by L. Ron Hubbard. Belief in the rationality-logicality equation has corroded the prophetic power of language itself. We can count, but we are rapidly forgetting how to say what is worth counting and why.

Cognitive Science, Computers, and the Humanities: Artificial and Natural Intelligence

James P. Smith

James P. Smith (born 1935), Education Editor for the Minnesota Historical Society, is a thinker with a particular interest in problems of science and education. He studied mathematics at the University of Denver, philosophy and scientific method at the London School of Economics, and history of philosophy at the University of Minnesota, where he received his Ph.D. He has taught philosophy at Minnesota and at Hamline University,

---

Masters and Johnson William H. Masters and Virginia E. Johnson, noted for their investigations in human sexuality.

in St. Paul, and worked on the Air Force Bionics Computer Research Program. For nine years he was on the staff of the National Federation of State Humanities Councils. From 1983 to 1986 he was editor of its journal, Federation Review; *he contributed the following review-article to its issue of May/June 1986.*

Consider whether it is easier to walk forward than backward.

Of course it is, right? We take it for granted.

Interpretations of the things we take for granted are playing a critical role in the current controversy about whether computing machines can simulate the intelligence of human beings. To see this, note that, while we can say we know the things we take for granted, we should ask ourselves: when we act, do we act *on the basis of* our knowledge of the things we take for granted? Should we actually say we have knowledge of such things in the same way we *know that,* for example, the place we are walking to is on the next street? Or are they part of our relationship with the world around us, part of *knowing how* to do things?

For Hubert and Stuart Dreyfus,* the difference between *knowing how* and *knowing that* is at the heart of what has gone wrong with the field of computer science known as artificial intelligence. In its strong expression, artificial intelligence (AI) claims that one day we will be able to build computers that can "do any work that a man can do."[1] AI researchers claim that all facts we take for granted can be specified precisely and put into a computer program: all of our know-how can be translated without loss into knowing-that. This means that all our commonsense understanding, all our background knowledge, can be broken down into strings of symbols, which, though long—very long—can be manageably organized and made accessible in computer programs.

For the Dreyfus brothers, this is dangerous and false; in *Mind Over Machine* they describe the dangers and seek to demonstrate in what ways it is false. Computer scientists in AI believe that all human consciousness comes down in the end to reasoning, defined as the processing of information according to rules, or *if-then* statements; they go on to say that even at the preconscious level, even at the level of neurons, cognition is the result of rule-connections and so could be reproduced by an information-processing computer.

The Dreyfus brothers say there is more to our mental life than reasoning, that there are things we know *how* to do that are essentially different

---

Mind Over Machine: The Power of Human Intuition and Expertise in the Era of the Computer, by Hubert L. Dreyfus and Stuart E. Dreyfus (New York: The Free Press, 1986).

[1] Herbert Simon, in *The Shape of Automation for Men and Management* (1965), quoted in *Mind Over Machine,* p. 67. Hereafter, all references to *Mind Over Machine* will be noted in the text.

from things *that* we know. They refer to this ability as *intuition,* [2] and tell a story that, though it is about chickens, illustrates the worth and significance of the word "intuition"; it also sets the stage for a later discussion of their theory of the acquisition of expertise.

As reported in the *American Scientist* (1948), the chicken-and-egg industries were, in the 1930s, facing a serious problem of how to deal with the Leghorn cockerel, i.e., the male Leghorn chick. Managers of egg businesses wanted, naturally, to buy only egg-producing chicks, i.e., female Leghorns, but were finding too many cockerels mixed in their shipments. To satisfy this demand, poultry farmers needed to determine the sex of Leghorn chicks. They sought a mechanical system and experts among American farmers, but found neither. They turned to Japan, where, they heard, there were experts who could sex day-old chicks with an amazingly high degree of reliability. One expert, Hikosoboro Yogo, identified the sex of 1,400 chicks in one hour with an accuracy of 98 percent, and even claimed he could determine the sex of a chick before he looked at the genitals. The technique indeed "sounded like one of the mysteries of the Orient." (197)

The American poultry farmers brought the Japanese experts to this country for demonstrations. Fortunately, the farmers did not insist that the techniques be explained, but simply put trainees to work alongside the experts. After three months of apprenticeship the new hands could do efficient sorting on their own. One eventually claimed he could sense the sex of a chick by touch; he became 99.5 percent reliable in sexing 900 to 1,000 chicks per hour.

The Dreyfus brothers suggest that the Japanese sexors, if asked, would not have been able to relate rules according to which they made their decision, i.e., rules that could be made explicit and taught to trainees. They could display their expertise, which others might learn by participating in the sex-identifying situation and noticing, feeling, smelling, listening, and asking questions, but they could not *explain* it.

Evidently, then, they did not know what they were doing, but they were very good at it.

A brief discussion of some of the ways people might react to this paradox will highlight some important issues and so make clear how a critique of artificial intelligence illustrates issues typical of the humanities and the human sciences.

---

[2] Of course, in a scientifically-oriented culture, "intuition" provokes skeptical scorn as an obscuring waffle-word, signifying nothing measurable. Indeed, critics of Hubert Dreyfus's earlier criticisms of artificial intelligence have been vitriolic in condemning his views about intuition as "unscientific" and "mystical." See Hubert L. Dreyfus, *What Computers Can't Do—The Limits of Artificial Intelligence,* second edition (New York: Harper Colophon Books, 1972, 1979).

One response is to *deny* the paradox and say that if we are doing something intelligent, then necessarily we know what we are doing. That is, even when we are not aware we know it, as in the case of things we take for granted or all the commonsense understanding we have accumulated throughout our lives, we have knowledge of what we do. On this view, all of our intelligent behavior is built on information: factual data organized and applied by rule-like processes, through semiconscious, unconscious, and neurophysiological levels of activity. (This view is, of course, itself slightly paradoxical. When the gentleman asked the wise man what the world rests on, he said it rested on an elephant. And that elephant? the gentleman asked. It, too, rests on an elephant, said the wise man, and so on: it is elephants all the way down.)

It follows that we only know what we are doing when we can explain it to someone else. Many of us have been brought up to accept some version of this principle; every time we try to explain to someone else what is obvious to us and not to them, or every time we justify a writing assignment by saying "only when you can write it out do you understand it yourself," we use the principle. In a stronger version, it hearkens back to Socrates, who said we only know something if we could give a definition of it. In contemporary terms, this stronger version holds that we only know what we are doing when we are able to state the relevant facts and specify the rules that connect the facts of what it is we are doing. This view implies that whatever we know can be verbalized and that "you can't teach what you don't understand and you don't understand something unless you can program it."[3] To the Dreyfus brothers, this idea is a rationalistic prejudice that, though it traces its origins to Socrates and Plato, needs to be "confronted and corrected." (193)

If we *accept* the paradox, in agreement with *Mind Over Machine*, we defy that prejudice and, in effect, assert that we can act intelligently even when what we are doing is not based on knowledge, i.e., even though we are not able to explain what we are doing in terms of facts and rules. We thus grant significance to intuition and acknowledge it as an ordinary feature of human action, a feature that is not "mystical" even though it is not explainable in terms of formal or scientific knowledge. The chicken sexors, for instance, cooperated in passing on their expertise, though they did not report in terms of rules or facts.

If we take this position we invite being charged with foolishly (and/or willfully, even maliciously) ignoring the inevitability of scientific and technological progress, and pessimistically believing that some issues are not rationally solvable problems. We are saying that a human being is more than a "rational animal"; given the Aristotelian lineage of that

---

[3]Dreyfus, *Mind*, p. 150, paraphrasing Frederick Taylor, *Computer in the School* (New York, Teachers College Press, 1980), p. 4.

term and how deeply embedded it is in our way of looking at and talking about human nature, this is a daring thing to say.

It should be plain that the issues here are not merely problems in semantics, of the meanings of words such as *intelligence, language, memory, reasoning,* etc. Nor are they of interest only within computer science and engineering; in what has become almost a cliché, nowadays computer technology affects everything we do, practically and theoretically.

It is not too much to say that our definition of *human* is on the table. Some examples can bring this point home. In his widely acclaimed *Turing's Man,* published in 1984, J. David Bolter put it this way:

> A defining technology defines or redefines man's [sic] role in relation to nature. By promising (or threatening) to replace man, the computer is giving us a new definition of man, as an "information processor," and of nature, as "information to be processed."[4]

Graphic illustrations of how people can come to think of themselves as information-processing machines abound in Sherry Turkle's *The Second Self.* Turkle interviewed more than two hundred children and two hundred adults in her research on the psychological impact of the computer age. She found wide evidence that computer jargon is not just a manner of speaking: "Their language carries an implicit psychology that equates the processes that take place in people to those that take place in machines."[5] To cite but one illustration, Mark, a computer science junior, says:

> You think you're making a decision, but are you really? For instance, when you have a creative idea, what happens? All of a sudden, you think of something. Right? Wrong. You didn't think of it. It just filtered through—the consciousness processor just sits there and watches this cacophony of other processors yelling onto the bus and skims off the top what he thinks is the most important thing, one thing at a time. A creative idea just means that one of the processors made a link between two unassociated things because he thought they were related.[6]

As Turkle puts it, ". . . creativity, individual responsibility, free will, and emotion were all being dissolved, simply grist for the little processors' mills."[7]

---

[4]J. David Bolter, *Turing's Man—Western Culture in the Computer Age* (Chapel Hill: University of North Carolina Press, 1984) p. 13, "Turing's men" are those who accept that view of human nature; Alan M. Turing (1912–1954) is credited with launching the computer age when he formulated the nature of logic machines in a paper, "On Computable Numbers," published in 1936.

[5]Sherry Turkle, *The Second Self—Computers and the Human Spirit* (New York: Simon and Schuster, 1984), p. 17.

[6]Turkle, *Self,* p. 288.

[7]Turkle, *Self,* p. 288.

The Dreyfus brothers find this attitude particularly self-defeating; based on their theory of the ways that people become skilled, "thinking of oneself as a computer and therefore looking for rules can prevent the brain from doing the job, and so can stand in the way of learning." (155)

An accurate appraisal of what computers can and cannot do is important, then, not only to avert the "appalling vision of the future" in which computers are the next stage of evolution, but to protect computer technology from within and without. The Dreyfus brothers claim that time and resources are wasted by following the advice of the extremists among the advocates of artificial intelligence, and moreover, that the exaggerated claims of what computers have done and can accomplish add to a growing anxiety that can surely lead to an excessively irrational resistance and revulsion to technology in general. (204)

We are distracted from the many opportunities awaiting intelligent use of "intelligent" computers by the excessive hyperbole attending the grand designs of the human-replacers. The Dreyfus brothers favorably discuss many of these opportunities. In education, they can serve as electronic blackboards, interactive simulators, and conjecture-testing to "greatly improve sociality and intuition in the classroom." (156) In management, computerized modeling proves useful in handling structural problems such as production, distribution, and scheduling in manufacturing; in coping with novel situations such as reactor siting or hurricane seeding, which do not fall into any domain of human expertise; in helping an inexperienced decision-maker understand a new type of problem; and in dealing with problems that, though unstructured and therefore better handled by human beings, come up regularly enough to warrant using computerized models to make decisions that are "acceptable, routine, fast, and economical." (191)

They also describe some appropriate uses of computers in medicine, and tell about a controversy in computer-aided medicine that illustrates the problems caused for both the medical profession and computer technology by an extremist view of AI. In doing some research at Wright State University in Dayton, Ohio, two doctors developed a bionic-man-like therapeutic technique for exercising the paralyzed limbs of patients whose spinal cord had been injured. One doctor predicts that this research will lead to computer-controlled free walking for paralyzed people. The other doctor opposes such optimism as premature, misguided, and counterproductive. He first said that "We have no idea how the subconscious process that replaces the conscious step-by-step procedure used by beginners works." He then consented partially to the mind-as-information-processor presumptions of his partner: "We might walk by using sophisticated subconscious rules, but how can we find them?" Finally, he suggested a physiology-based alternative line of research: "Or walking might involve some process of direct pattern recognition followed by a learned response." (204) (The Dreyfus brothers would probably be in agreement with an approach based on pattern recognition.)

The critique of artificial intelligence in *Mind Over Machine* is based primarily on a "nonmechanistic model of human skill" (xii), which in itself is a combination of philosophical reflection and empirical research into the way human expertise is actually developed and demonstrated. The Dreyfus brothers discovered that in becoming, e.g., skilled flyers, chess players, and language learners through instruction and experience, a common five-stage pattern could be seen. The stages are called *novice, advanced beginner, competence, proficiency,* and *expertise.* [8] Not everyone passes through all five stages; the model does not include the development of such skills as bike riding and walking, which are learned through trial and error and imitation of more proficient people. It appears that chicken sexors, for example, learn by trial and error and imitation. A brief discussion of the five stages follows.

A *novice* relies on distinguishable facts and features of situations and on rules for determining what action to take. The elements of a situation are defined for the novice so that they can be recognized independently of the overall situation; they are *context-free.* "The manipulation of unambiguously defined context-free elements by precise rules is called 'information processing.' " (21)

In becoming an *advanced beginner,* a learner practices following the rules and identifying the nameable objects, and begins to perceive similarity among a number of examples. Thus an advanced beginner learning to shift gears can distinguish context-free features, such as the speed of an automobile, from those that are *situational,* such as a car's sound. New rules can be formulated, as when a nurse takes advantage of the fact that he or she has learned to distinguish the breathing sounds of pulmonary edema from those of pneumonia. (23)

A learner becomes *competent* when the number of nameable features and steps in the rules is overwhelming; he or she constructs plans for putting the features of the task into some order of importance relative to the sought-for objective. This enables the learner to select certain features for attention and ignore others, as a chessplayer does, when, after concluding the opponent's king can be attacked, ignores weaknesses and losses. In becoming competent, the learner sees a necessity to formulate plans and choose one: unlike the novice and the advanced beginner, the "competent performer, after wrestling with the question of a choice of

[8]Dreyfus, *Mind,* p. 20. "After we developed our five-stage description, a group of research nurses who had amassed considerable data about the acquisition of nursing skill found that our model fitted their data very well. The result of that study may be found in the book *From Novice to Expert* by Professor Patricia Benner." (New York: Addison-Wesley, 1984). See also Hubert Dreyfus, "What Expert Systems Can't Do," *Raritan,* Spring 1984, pp. 22–36.

plan, feels responsible for, and emotionally involved in, the product of his choice." (26)

When a competent performer becomes *proficient,* choices are made less frequently by weighing alternatives and more and more on the basis of patterns—memories, sensations, scenes—that are called "holistic similarity recognition" and are not decomposed into smaller parts. (28) Still, the proficient performer will think analytically about what action to take, though the task at hand has been intuitively organized. "The spell of involvement in the world of the skill will thus be temporarily broken." (29)

A proficient performer can become *expert* through extensive experience and practice with a wide variety and large number of similar situations.[9] (17) A proficient performer groups situations with similar goals and patterns of action, and the work is done without that break for calculation: ". . . not only is a situation, when seen as similar to a prior one, understood, but the associated decision, action, or tactic simultaneously comes to mind." (32) An expert is totally engaged: ". . . *experts don't solve problems and don't make decisions; they do what normally works.*" (31) For example, expert air traffic controllers "do not experience themselves as seeing blips on a screen and deducing what must be going on in the sky." (31) Julio Kaplan, an International Master chess player, played chess even while adding series of heard numbers; the calculations did not interfere with his intuitive grasp of the situation on the chess board. (33)

This summary of the Dreyfus model of skill acquisition, though no more than a sketch, should be enough to indicate a striking fact about the stages of becoming skilled: they proceed *from* consciously analyzing situations and following rules *to* involvement and judgment based on experience with numerous instances. Thus:

---

[9]Though the Dreyfus brothers are highly critical of Plato and Socrates, as the originators of the information-processing model of the mind, it is worth pointing out that for these Greeks, too, persistent practice is needed for learning. In the dialogue *Meno,* Plato presents Socrates as questioning a slave-boy about a problem in geometry in the systematic, step-by-step way characteristic of the analytic approach. The questioning draws the correct answer out of the boy, showing that the knowledge of the answer was already in his mind and could be elicited by precise questioning. Plato qualified his account of the method, however, in two critical ways: first, Socrates asks, "Is the boy Greek? Can he speak our language?", (82A) thereby implicitly including all the background information that goes with being Greek and speaking the language. Next, after the boy has reached the solution, Socrates says, "And now these opinions have been stirred up in him as in a dream; and if *someone will keep asking him these same questions often and in various forms,* you can be sure that in the end he will know about them as accurately as anybody." (85D, W.H.D. Rouse, tr., emphasis added.) Such qualifications are a little paradoxical, because the *Meno* is sometimes taken as an archetype of Plato's presentation of the information-processing premises of the rationalistic theory of mind. See, for example, Howard Gardner's *The Mind's New Science* (New York: Basic Books, 1985); "Introduction: What the *Meno* Wrought."

The evolution from the abstract toward the concrete reverses what one observes in small children dealing with intellectual tasks: they initially understand only concrete examples and gradually learn abstract reasoning. Perhaps it is because of the well-known pattern seen in children, and because the rule-following plays an important, early role in the learning of new skills by adults, that adult understanding and skill are so often misunderstood as abstract and rule-guided. (35)

The import of this model for reproducing intelligence in computer programs is that at the level of expertise, human beings are not able to articulate rules they are following. (Nor would an Athenian expert be able to give Socrates the *definition* he sought.) The expert "is simply not following any rules! He is . . . recognizing thousands of special cases." (108) Thus, when asked to report by what rules he or she is acting, an expert will state rules that are *remembered.* Hence a computer program based on expertise as reported by experts will incorporate interpretations of the rules characteristic of an earlier stage of acquisition, i.e., advanced beginner or competence, not the expert's actual judgmental process.[10] "To participate in the construction of a model, an expert must regress to seeing the world like an advanced beginner, or, in some cases, a novice." (177)

An artificial intelligence advocate will argue, however, that an expert is acting on rules even if he or she cannot articulate them. What is needed is a specialist helper, one who could listen to experts' descriptions of their work and, despite any confusion or seeming illogicality in the descriptions, combine and redescribe them in detailed accounts of the experts' knowledge and the logical steps they take in the process. Such a helper is called a "knowledge engineer." (Discussed in chapter 4.)

For example, in an interview with an expert on cleaning up chemical spills, a knowledge engineer asks, "How can you tell what it [the spilt substance] is?"[11] The expert answers:

> Sometimes you can tell what the substance is by its smell. Sometimes you can tell by its color, but that's not always reliable since dyes are used a lot nowadays. Oil, however, floats on the surface and forms a silvery film, while acids dissolve completely in the water. Once you discover the type of material spilled, you can eliminate any buildings that either don't store the material at all or don't store enough of it to account for the spill.

The knowledge engineer proceeds to formulate sequences of "if-then" statements to capture the explanation, using assigned certainties, e.g., "if

---

[10]To introduce the chapter "Five Steps from Novice to Expert," the Dreyfus brothers quote the seventeenth-century philosopher/mathematician, Blaise Pascal, who in *Pensées* wrote, "Mathematical formalizers wish to treat matters of intuition mathematically, and make themselves ridiculous. . . . The mind . . . does it tacitly, naturally, and without technical rules." (16)

[11]The Waite Group/Mike Van Horn, *Understanding Expert Systems* (New York: Bantam Books, 1986) pp. 78–82.

the spill does smell of vinegar, let the material of the spill be acetic acid with certainty .8." The knowledge engineer checks back with the expert and with others, who will offer refinements and new points, in a cooperative process that may take "from several months to a year."

The Dreyfus brothers see many legitimate uses for such systems, which they believe should be called *competent* systems. One example is called RECONSIDER, a diagnostic prompting system, an "interactive encyclopedia designed to help the doctor determine the patient's disease." (xv) They worry, however, that if we rely too heavily on these systems we can lose sight of the differences between them and human expertise. That is, to the extent we suppose the so-called expertise in an "expert system" is really expert, we will be that much less likely to put the computers to work as tools for human experts, from whom more should be expected. (See xiv, xv.)

The Dreyfus brothers are clear that their critique is directed against artificial intelligence research that insists human intelligence can be simulated in logic machines without loss of flexibility or power.

Logic machines must be distinguished from other devices that are of interest in AI research but do not operate mechanistically, i.e., by dividing the information up into different components. Recognizing the lack of vocabulary for dealing with such differences, they propose to refer to these devices as "holistic systems." (62–3) Included in this category are holographic pattern recognizers, in which "the actual recognition work is accomplished by the interference of two beams of light, with no separate functional components doing any work." (63) Other examples include, perhaps somewhat surprisingly, light bulbs, lenses, screws, and levers. (63) We need not, in other words, uncritically identify all physical systems as *machines*.

Also discussed at some length are programs that purportedly simulate various kinds of intelligent performance, such as natural language interpretation, therapeutic counseling, instruction, chess-playing, solving algebra and calculus problems, spectrographic analysis, geological analysis, and medical diagnosis. Despite the impressive accomplishments of these programs, including the way they simulate parts of the human learning process, the Dreyfus brothers argue (a) their success is only in very restricted domains, so they break down when given more general problems to deal with; (b) they are based on massive, "brute-force," calculations in problem situations in which experienced specialists do not gain expertise (111); (c) they are using different (e.g., "distributed associative") memory structures, so that, instead of manipulating symbolic descriptions according to rules of inference, they are in fact simulating holistic systems. (91)

The possibility remains that new programming techniques will lead to the hoped-for full-scale simulation the founders of AI hope for, but the record so far is one of high hopes but sober reality, discussed in detail in chapter 3. Such efforts, they argue, will always run up against (a) the need to incorporate background information, i.e., commonsense knowledge or know-how, to give a true simulation of intelligence, (b) the need to be able to "keep track of all facts affected by all changes," (89) and, (c) as human beings do, have quick access to all facts in memory. (69)

Research is underway on efforts to simulate the mind/brain system of human beings, with "holographic" techniques (60, 91), neuron-net systems (92), "connectionist" design (95), and incorporating key properties of organic brain materials.[12] The goal of such research is to devise ways to simulate the holistic similarity-recognition that is a key part of the proficient and expert stages of skill acquisition. This "artificial intelligence without information processing" (90) is still at a very early stage of development.

Do the Dreyfus brothers go too far in criticising rationality and the main tradition of Western philosophy? What is offered in its place? These are not unjustified questions, because the language of holistic systems, situations, and intuitive understanding is not only unfamiliar, it arouses suspicions of mysticism and memories of recent excesses in substituting feelings for thought.[13]

In their highly positive picture of the virtues of experts, as they themselves say, "it might seem that experts never think and are always right." (31) After all, if someone makes decisions and cannot explain to others the facts on which the decision is based or what reasoning was used, how are we to distinguish the legitimate authority of expertise from the less wel-

---

[12]See Scott Ladd/The Red Feather Press, *The Computer and the Brain—Beyond the Fifth Generation* (New York: Bantam Books, 1986). Ladd tells a (perhaps apocryphal) story about James McAlear, owner of Gentronix Laboratories in Maryland, that suggests the enthusiasm among some of the scientists working on biology-based computers. McAlear's wife tried to get him to accompany her into church one day, and, on failing, questioned his belief in God. He reportedly said, "Not only do I believe in an almighty God, but I'm probably the only one here who has any idea how to build it." (p. 146). *Also see* "Mindworks," a recent article in *Science 86* (May) by William F. Allman, which describes in accessible detail key projects and controversial issues in neuron-net and "connectionist" research. The eye-catching lead says "For years scientists believed that we think like computers. Now they're changing their minds." Connectionist researchers' criticisms of "serial digital computers," i.e., logic machines, resemble many points made by the Dreyfus brothers, though they are not mentioned.

[13]Hubert Dreyfus, in particular, was the target of many such epithets as a result of his earlier critique of artificial intelligence. He had used the term "alchemy" to describe the program of research of AI; though it was primarily meant as a historical analogy, as in the way astrology preceded astronomy, it aroused the AI community to considerable hostility. For an account of the controversy in the 1970s, see *What Computers Can't Do*, "Introduction to the Second Edition," and *Mind Over Machine*, "Prologue." He has also been likened to the cardinals of the Inquisition who denied the evidence seen through Galileo's telescope; a case could be made that the accusation should be turned around. See the informative article by Frank Rose, "The Black Knight of AI," *Science 85*, Vol. 6, No. 2, March 1985, pp. 46–51.

come form of authority based on position? This line of criticism could be, and has been, extended, inferring that the anti-rational position of the Dreyfus brothers encourages doctrinaire, emotional, and even fanatical politics, the kind of thing we associate with cults.

The Dreyfus brothers are no doubt by now used to this kind of opposition and realize that no matter what they say, a staunch rationalist will resist the alternative views they propose. It is to the mechanistic tendency of rationality, *calculative* rationality in particular, that they object. They are not Luddites.[14] Their many suggestions for effective use of information-processing computers in appropriate contexts demonstrate the balance in their view.

They hope to persuade us that the choice is not between rationality and irrationality but "between justification by calculative rationality, that is, inference drawn from isolated, objective facts describing the problematic situation, and consensus-based intuitive shared understanding, derived from concrete experiences, which defies precise verbalization." (194) They suggest that, as in Japan, "cross-examination of competing experts in an intuitive culture might take the form of a conflict of interpretations in which each expert is required to produce and defend a coherent narrative which leads naturally to the acceptance of his point of view." (196)

Replacing scientific-sounding explanations with narratives is linked to another alternative to calculative rationality, *deliberative* rationality. There can be no question that everyone at some time or other detaches him- or herself from a problematic situation, but there are important differences between the detached stance of the novice, who is running through the features and rules of a situation step by step, and the expert, who is "thinking about *the process and product of his intuitive understanding.*" (167) Deliberative rationality characterizes the advice given by management consultants in contrast to advice offered by management scientists; the former seek to enhance a manager's intuitive judgment, where the latter seek to replace it with a quantitative model. (167)

Ideally, deliberative rationality is the means that experts can use to check themselves. The tendency toward slipping from expertise into rashness can be anticipated: experts can reexamine their strategies, choices, and the similarities of perceived patterns to prior experience, to avoid premature fixing on a course of action or solution.

Finally: the issues raised by the competition between interpretations of intelligence might be summarized by considering a passage from J. David Bolter's *Turing's Man*. He concludes his chapter "Artificial Intelligence"

---

[14]In the late eighteenth century Ned Ludd smashed two weaving machines in a fit of rage. His name was used by a group of mechanics in England in the early nineteenth century who destroyed machinery that ruined their livelihoods. As the Dreyfus brothers point out, the Luddites were not mindlessly antitechnological; computer boosters use "Luddites" as a slur to brand opponents as being enemies of all science and technology. (207–08)

as follows, with what appears to be a reference to Hubert Dreyfus, or at least someone who agrees with Dreyfus:

> One opponent of the movement [artificial intelligence] has argued that the human body with its five senses is fundamental to the capacity for intelligent thought. The argument misses the point. The artificial intelligence specialist is not interested in imitating the whole man. The very reason he regards intelligence *(rational "problem solving")* as fundamental is that such intelligence corresponds to the new and compelling qualities of electronic technology. Today, as before, technology determines what part of man will be imitated.[15]

The opponent did not, however, say that what is wrong is that artificial intelligence seeks to imitate the whole man; the opponent said that "the whole man" is fundamental even for what the specialist seeks to imitate. Though it appears that it is Bolter who has missed the point, he points out very clearly how closely the governing idea of artificial intelligence is connected to the imperative of electronic technology: each seems to be participating in the definition of the other.

The intense zeal with which the debates over artificial intelligence have been conducted is breathtaking. There is clearly a kind of culture built around computers, but at times, those who belong to that culture and those who oppose it have behaved more like committed cultists or ardent nationalists than men and women of science and scholarship. Some have spoken of this intensely defended gulf as an ideological difference, in which the two sides have such strikingly different commitments they cannot give credibility to what the other side says. (In one version of this explanation, the humanists are on one side and on the other are the scientists and engineers; in another version, the romantics oppose the rationalists.)

The no-holds-barred discourse may now be subsiding, but in view of the tone and temperature of the debates so far one has to suspect that more than just a fascination or absorption with computing machines is at stake.

Perhaps a root cause is the impulse for freedom. The uncertainties of contemporary social and political arrangements and the prospect of individuals becoming more and more constrained have given new urgency to our natural desire for freedom. The AI advocate is driven to distraction by the critics because they are unreasonably opposing AI's efforts to advance the fruits of freedom: computers can empower us, release us from necessity, and even free us from certain bonds of nature. The critics, on the other hand, are moved by a deep fear that the kind of freedom to be gained through AI is shallow and ultimately self-defeating: *they* are preserving our freedoms.

Whatever the status of this hypothesis, the AI/computer culture has built into it a momentum toward new definitions and expectations of

---

[15]Bolter, *Turing's Man*, p. 213. Emphasis added.

human nature; they contain what J. David Bolter speaks of as "the attempt to make man [sic] over . . . an attempt to circumvent or reverse the process of nature." Ominously, it might also harbor a deep, unacknowledged drive toward a kind of patriarchy.

> Man the artificer and man the artifact merge, but on the artificer's terms. In bypassing the ordinary sexual process of reproduction, man [sic] achieves a new freedom from nature; computer technology offers a path to this new freedom.[16]

Such disquieting speculations as these could profitably be dealt with in public programs. They should be discussed by many people who, if they can acquire a common recognition that critical issues are involved, can also share in the confusion and the desire to understand it.

Seven Factors in Alienation

Thomas B. Sheridan

Thomas B. Sheridan (born 1929) is professor of engineering and applied psychology at the Massachusetts Institute of Technology, the school from which he received his Sc.D. in 1959. He heads the Man-Machine Systems Laboratory in the Department of Mechanical Engineering, which performs research in robotic and person-computer interactions. He also teaches in the M.I.T. program in Technology and Policy. He has served as president of the Systems, Man, and Cybernetics Society of the Institute of Electrical and Electronics Engineers (1974–1976) and has been associate editor of Automatica *since 1982. He serves also as a consultant to government and to industrial organizations. We print below the concluding sections of an article from the October 1980* Technology Review. *It was adapted from a paper presented at the World Council of Churches' Conference on Faith, Science, and the Future (July 1979 at M.I.T.), and first published in* Faith and Science in an Unjust World, *vol. 1 (1980).*

What computers are good at and what people are good at tend to be different. Computers have good memories and are fast, consistent, and reliable but as yet are not creative or readily able to adapt to novel situations. People have poor memories, are slow, seldom do things the same way twice, and are unreliable, but they are adaptable and creative. Computers are a different race from people. It is a wonderful ideal to design systems wherein these two can complement and wed their talents.

---

[16]Bolter, *Turing's Man,* p. 209.

For those persons who program computers and design them into control systems, this interaction can be fulfilling. For others, however, dealing with computers on computer terms is intimidating. What is the difference between the two groups of people in their relation to the computer? And what makes control by computers so alienating?

1

A first factor is that some people compare themselves with computers and worry about their inferiority and threatened obsolescence. Computers clearly do outperform people when a large amount of data must be processed with great precision in a short time. If doing certain things better than people means "overtaking" them, then there is little ground for arguing against such a situation. But rather than worry about this, we should celebrate those ways in which people are not computers, and let computers take over the jobs where they clearly outperform us. People can still pull a computer's plug, though we may have to work at maintaining that privilege.

2

A second alienating factor is the tendency for computer control to make human operators remote from their ultimate task. Centralized control creates spatial distance from objects being manufactured, banking transactions, or patients in the hospital. Human actions become desynchronized from the final shaping of the goods and services being produced, and the end process or product is no longer directly experienced. Instead, artificial sensors feed the information to a computer that digests it and presents a summary of what the computer thinks the human operators should know.

Excuses are often given by managers: workers are not interested; the system is too complex; too much feedback would be distracting. I believe that, under most circumstances, greater satisfaction and improved performance will result if we attempt to reduce workers' estrangement from their efforts.

3

A third and related aspect of alienation occurs in jobs that have demanded considerable training and skill on the part of humans. The advent of computer control means that skilled machinists, typesetters, laboratory technicians, and aircraft pilots are "promoted" to button pushers and machine tenders. Their sensory-motor skills, acquired over decades and contributing to their sense of dignity and self-image, become obsolete. Moreover, while their skills atrophy, it is presumed they will be prepared to take over the computer when necessary; and they are anxiously aware that when the time comes, they may not be up to it.

Button pushing is not so bad if that is not the only contribution the worker makes. Workers must be willing to learn new skills when possible and in some cases seize the initiative when the opportunities aren't provided. Likewise, management must be willing to provide workers with the authority, responsibility, and accountability to use these skills. This may require relinquishing some control and risking new operating styles as yet quite alien to business-labor relations.

4

Closely related is a fourth factor akin to our system of formal education and C. P. Snow's "two cultures."° This is the greater *access* to information and power by the technologically literate minority as compared with the technologically illiterate majority (which usually includes both machine tender and consumers of products or services).

The technological literati in this case include the computer designers, programmers, and their technical management. Curiously, the normally powerful but nontechnical groups such as financiers, lawyers, and politicians feel increasingly at the mercy of the technical elite. At the middle level of this particular pyramid are the workers who would benefit enormously were they better equipped with formal education and were their managers willing to be a bit more flexible in allowing them access. At the bottom of the pyramid are the undereducated and older segments of the society, who simply cannot keep up, having no understanding of the computer-based society and its concepts of probability, feedback control, and artificial intelligence, and having no access to credit cards, home terminals, and the like. Clearly, if we are to check the growth of alienation in our society, we must improve our educational system so that citizens will be better prepared to participate in a computerized society.

5

A fifth aspect of alienation is *mystification*. An elegant analogy of this attribute of computer control was made by the M.I.T. mathematician and "father of cybernetics," Norbert Wiener. In *God and Golem, Inc.*, written in 1964, he compares Golem, the mythical half-man, half-beast of Hebraic tradition, to the computer. Wiener makes his point metaphorically by relating the tale of the Monkey's Paw, a classic in horror literature.

"In this story, an English working family sits down to dinner in its kitchen. Afterwards, the son leaves to work at a factory, and the old parents listen to the tales of their guest, a sergeant-major back from service in the Indian army. He tells of Indian magic and shows them a dried monkey's paw, which, he says, is a talisman that has been endowed

---

C. P. Snow's "two cultures" Snow believed society was marked by two antagonistic cultures: the traditional literary culture and the newer scientific culture.

by an Indian holy man with the virtue of giving three wishes to each of three successive owners. This, he says, was to prove the folly of defying fate.

"He claims that he does not know the first two wishes of the first owner, but only that the last was for death. He himself was the second owner but his experiences were too terrible to relate. He is about to cast the paw on the coal fire when his host retrieves it and despite all the sergeant-major can do, wishes for £200.

"Shortly thereafter there is a knock at the door. A very solemn gentleman is there from the company that has employed his son and, as gently as he can, breaks the news that the son has been killed in an accident at the factory. Without recognizing any responsibility in the matter, the company offers its sympathy and £200 as a solatium."

The theme here is the danger of trusting the magic of the computer when its operation is singularly literal. "If you ask for £200 and do not express the condition that you do not wish it at the cost of the life of your son, £200 you will get whether your son lives or dies."

It is easy to attribute magical properties to the computer—our pop media encourage us to do so at every turn—but there is great danger in this. The computer, having no cultural empathy with its programmer, does not assume the rich contextual fabric underlying all person-to-person communications. If the computer is connected to a control system with fast and powerful machines, the result of this excessive trust could be disastrous.

Fingers can be pointed in many directions: advertising, military and industrial security—all plain technocratic arrogance fostering the mystique of a computer-control panacea without revealing the limitations. These institutions and individuals see posing as magicians as being in their own best interest. A counterforce is growing, but the strategies for demystification have yet to be worked out.

6

This naturally leads to a sixth factor of alienation: higher stakes in decision making. Because computer-controlled systems are growing larger, more complex, more capital intensive, more centralized, and more tightly controlled, the costs of failure are huge, though the probabilities of failure may be small. We need only think of military systems, nuclear plants, and air-traffic control systems to be reminded. Such systems may run reliably and smoothly, with minor failures automatically circumvented. "Fail-safe" is the ideal, and it usually works, but there is always a low probability of complete breakdown, which may be spectacular. Last June, for example, we came uncomfortably close to the ultimate failure when the North American Air Defense computer gave false indications of an enemy attack and bombers were readied for counterattack.

Reliability analysts know how to cope with the minor failures because they do happen from time to time. For these small malfunctions we have some basis for statistics, even some objective grounds for those offensive quantities such as "statistical deaths" and the "price of life."

The improbable, high-cost events, however, are far more difficult to cope with. It is relatively straightforward to gather statistics on an "unk," or "known-unknown": analysts can identify the unknown variable or situation, though its probability or relation to other variables must be established from observation and experience. They can even estimate their confidence or range of uncertainty. But what gives analysts nightmares is the "unk-unk," or "unknown-unknown": they neither know where their ignorance lies nor which variable or situation is critical. Consequently, there is no basis to judge even the degree of confidence. As systems become more complex, they invariably have more "unk-unks" that torment reliability analysts.

The responsible policy here would be to look as openly and dispassionately as possible at all objective evidence, including statistical deaths, and then feed into the computer-aided decision process those subjective factors that derive legitimately from human culture and intuition. We expect to make important personal decisions, such as the choice of a mate or a career, on mostly subjective grounds. Yet in business and public decision making we seem ashamed of subjectivity, attributing it either to ignorance or dirty politics.

There are encouraging signs within academe and government that this is beginning to change and that a new respect for subjectivity is emerging. As we become more sophisticated with computers, we owe it to ourselves to become more intellectually honest and deliberate about combining the objective and subjective, affirming the value of each.

7

The seventh and final basis for alienation is *phylogenesis*. This is the threat, real or perceived, that the race of intelligent machines is becoming more powerful than humans. The decline of humans' self-image has historical precedents—the computer is simply the most recent factor contributing to this decline. Mazlish, Tribe, and other writers have discussed the computer as a bridge spanning the "fourth discontinuity" between humans and all other nature—the gap separating humans from mere machines—in a series of insults that have eroded our view of ourselves as occupying a privileged position in the universe.

The first insult was that of Copernicus: the human realm is not discontinuous from the rest of the physical universe, it is a minor planet of a star on the edge of an ordinary galaxy. The second insult was that of Darwin: Homo sapiens is not a clear discontinuity in the animal forms. The third insult was Freud's: humans are not above base instincts and drives. The question posed by the fourth discontinuity, inevitably thrust upon us in our encounters with the computer, is whether human intelligence is ultimately nothing more than what a machine can attain.

Within computer-science circles, the question is either taken quite seriously and fiercely debated or else cast aside nervously as irrelevant and silly; no one seems comfortable. Most scholars in this area do not believe technology is capable of exerting any more domination over humans than we design and program into it. If there is a culprit, surely it is ourselves.

Hard work is no longer seen as the path to salvation—letting machines do our mental as well as physical work seems increasingly to be the norm. From the viewpoint of energy or cost efficiency, automatic control is often the obvious choice over human control, whether the task is to pump water in a rural village of a less-developed nation or to control a nuclear plant. Take the case of pumping water. Considering the relative energy efficiency of the human body compared with that of a small gasoline engine (calories out versus calories in) and the relative prices of calories for the two (assuming the humblest of food for the person and order-of-magnitude increases in the price of the fossil fuel), the machine still comes out well ahead.

When humans execute control tasks of great scale and complexity, there exist not only the energy inefficiencies of the human body, but also the enormous inefficiencies of the management, organization, and communication of an army of human workers. By contrast, new microelectronic logic takes very little energy and exhibits fantastic speed and reliability. Communication over large distances is almost effortless, and computers can manage complex physical systems with ease.

By more subtle criteria, however, computer control systems do not fare as well. While it is true that human institutions are not known for their ability to change, they, like their members, are self-conscious, whereas machines are not. Human institutions are continually reexamining their own goals, but computing machines, even the most adaptable and intelligent, are still guided ultimately by their programmed criteria.

Any large-scale technology, once in place, is difficult to alter. The national highway system is an example—one does not easily abandon all that concrete for an altogether different mode of transport. The same goes for nuclear reactors and large industrial plants. Once established, they tend to go on producing, whatever resources they use—whether or not there remains a real need for that product. A kind of technological inertia sets in through its sheer size and complexity compounded by the immobility of human institutions whose interests are served by this production structure and who will do all they can to protect it. The automatic factories are so good at making widgets that we are charmed, and we do all we can to cooperate with the production miracle. Furthermore, we can sell the widgets to one another and spur the economy.

In the face of large-scale computer control, with its centralization and dependence on the technological elite, it is little wonder that the "appropriate technology" movement, with its emphasis on ecological viability and community self-reliance, is gaining momentum. It is a movement to watch, but make no mistake: "AT" advocates are not antitechnology. While they preach "small is beautiful," they also recognize that much of the new microelectronic computer technology, with its low dollar and energy costs, may provide, for instance, an effective route to harnessing the sun. But the institutional base for such "appropriate" technologies is not cottage industry, and therein lies their dilemma.

The ultimate criterion for how computers should be used is subjective and I'm not sure that the technologist sufficiently appreciates this. Humans have always been tool builders and are not likely to stop. We *will* have our computers, but our subjective sense of what is right, beautiful, and consistent with a just and sustainable society, and what contributes most to human fulfillment, ought to dictate our use of these exotic tools with their enormous potential. Productivity in human terms should prevail over productivity in machine terms.

As computer control grows, we will see some alienation and suffering. There is but one long-term strategy open to us—we must ensure that the human-machine interaction will offer humanity and dignity. We must strive to celebrate those things human that computers can never be. In the workplace, we must struggle against workers' growing sense of remoteness from productive efforts by improving feedback and inviting creative participation in new roles made possible by the computer. Similarly, operators and other skilled professionals must be introduced to new, constructive tasks that transcend button pushing. In the area of education, one of our greatest challenges is to prepare future generations to become active participants in a computerized society. We must affirm the role of subjective input into computer-aided decision and control processes, and hold the human designers and programmers of computers accountable, not the computers themselves.

Television
and Reality

Television now takes so large a proportion of our waking time that it has to be counted one of the major features of our lives. The fact that TV is still a relatively recent invention, that it has not always been with us, continues to provoke many questions about the meaning of the revolution in communications that it represents. Is the old culture of print giving way completely to the new culture of the image? What is TV doing for people and what is it doing *to* them? How is it affecting the way we feel and think? How is it remaking our political processes? Perhaps the most fundamental question of all: How is it remaking our world—the way we apprehend reality itself?

In brief compass but in memorable terms, Neil Postman's essay gives a most pessimistic answer: TV, by replacing the word with the image, by presenting all subject matter as entertainment, "is transforming all serious public business into junk." George Will's column commenting on Postman's ideas suggests that some of them are overstated, and he imputes to them a certain intellectualist bias.

The next two essays support the frequent assertion that TV is not only a powerful influence, but that it seriously alters our notion of reality. Jack McGarvey illustrates from personal experience how events come to be regarded by young viewers as being more real on TV than on first-hand acquaintance. Henry Fairlie's classic critique shows how much the TV news program, by the inherent nature of its mechanics and its "vested interest in disaster," can distort (or even create) news that the print medium would report more faithfully.

Robert Pattison, finally, argues that TV is *both* a reality machine and a fantasy machine, and that its special character leaves to viewers a good deal of both freedom and creativity.

Amusing Ourselves to Death

Neil Postman

Neil Postman (born 1931) was educated at the State University of New York at Fredonia, and at Columbia. He has taught elementary and secondary school, and is now Professor of Communications Arts and Sciences at New York University and editor of Et cetera. *He is a prolific—and sometimes controversial—writer in the fields of language and educational theory. His recent books include* Teaching as a Conserving Activity *(1979) and* The Disappearance of Childhood *(1982).*

We print below a speech presented as the keynote address at the 1984 Frankfurt Book Fair and published in Et cetera *(Spring 1985). It recapitulates the theme of Postman's book of the same name,* Amusing Ourselves to Death: Public Discourse in the Age of Show Business *(1985), which occasioned the comments by George Will in the essay following.*

Chancellor Kohl, Lord Mayor Wallmann, Mr. Christiansen, Ladies and Gentlemen:

In accepting the honor of delivering this address, I am obliged to say something about the theme of this year's Book Fair, which, as you know, is Orwell in the year 2000. I trust you will not think me grossly disrespectful if what I say is that the choice of this theme is a mistake. To be precise, it is half of a mistake. There is no doubt that Orwell's prophecies and parables have application to roughly half the governments of the world. If, for example, one were to read both *1984* and *Animal Farm,* and then for good measure, Arthur Koestler's *Darkness at Noon,* one would have a fairly accurate blueprint of the machinery of thought-control as it presently operates in scores of countries, some of them not far distant from where we are meeting.

But the fact is that so far as the Western democracies are concerned, Orwell missed the mark almost completely. This obvious point has provided many civil libertarians with a false sense of pride and accomplishment. They were keeping their eye on 1984. And when the year came and the prophecy didn't, they sang songs of praise for themselves and their countries. And they do still. The roots of liberal democracy have not been torn asunder. Wherever else the terror has happened, we, in the West, have not been visited by Orwellian nightmares.

But, I fear, some of us have forgotten that alongside Orwell's dark vision, there was another vision—slightly older, slightly less well-known, equally chilling. I refer to Aldous Huxley's *Brave New World.* Contrary to common belief, even among the educated, Huxley and Orwell did not prophesy the same thing. Orwell warned that we will be overcome by an externally imposed oppression. But in Huxley's vision, no Big Brother or Ministry of Truth is required to deprive people of their autonomy, maturity, and history. As Huxley saw it, people will come to love their oppression, to adore the technologies that undo their capacities to think.

What Orwell feared were those who would ban books. What Huxley feared was that there would be no reason to ban a book, for there would be no one who wanted to read one. Orwell feared that the truth would be concealed from us. Huxley feared that the truth would be drowned in a sea of irrelevance. Orwell feared we would become a captive people. Huxley feared we would become a trivial people, preoccupied with some equivalent of the feelies, the orgy porgy, and the centrifugal bumblepuppy. As Huxley remarked in *Brave New World Revisited,* freedom lovers who are ever on the alert to oppose tyranny have "failed to take into account man's almost infinite appetite for distractions." In Orwell's book, Huxley added, people are controlled by inflicting pain. In *Brave New World,* they are controlled by inflicting pleasure. In short, Orwell thought we would be marched single-file and manacled into oblivion. Huxley thought we would dance ourselves there, with an idiot smile on our face.

In America, Orwell's prophecies are of small relevance but Huxley's are well underway toward being realized. I speak to you of America not only because I know its situation better than any other but also because America is engaged in the world's most ambitious experiment to accommodate itself to the technological distractions made possible by the electric plug. This is an experiment that began slowly and modestly in the mid-nineteenth century with the invention of the telegraph, and has now, in the latter half of the twentieth, reached a perverse maturity in America's consuming love affair with television. As nowhere else in the world, Americans have moved far and fast in bringing to a close the age of the slow-moving printed word, and have granted to television sovereignty over all of their institutions. By ushering in the age of television, America has given the world the clearest available glimpse of the Huxleyan future, 2000.

To anyone who is unfamiliar with this vast shift in America's symbolic ecology, I offer a few examples. According to the 1983 Nielsen Report on Television, ninety-eight percent of all American homes have a television set. Fifty-one percent have two or more television sets. Seventy-five percent have color television sets. The average household has its television sets on approximately seven hours a day. The average American child watches 5000 hours of television before he or she ever gets to school; about 16,000 hours by high school's end. The only activity that occupies more of an American youth's time than TV-viewing is sleeping. Americans who have reached the age of forty will have seen over one million television commercials, and can expect to see another million before their first retirement check arrives.

Television in America, it would appear, is the *soma* of Huxley's *Brave New World*. But let me hasten to say that America's immersion in television is not to be taken as an attempt by a malevolent government or an avaricious corporate state to employ the age-old trick of distracting the masses with circuses. The problem is more serious than that, and far from being age-old. The problem is not that TV presents the masses with entertaining subject matter, but that television presents all subject matter as entertaining. What is dangerous about television is not its junk. Every culture can absorb a fair amount of junk, and, in any case, we do not judge a culture by its junk but by how it conducts its serious public business. What is happening in America is that television is transforming all serious public business into junk.

As our politics, our news, our religion, our education, and our commerce are less and less given expression in the form of printed words or even oratory, they are rapidly being reshaped and staged to suit the requirements of television. And because television is a visual medium; because it does its talking in pictures, not words; because its images are in color and are most pleasurably apprehended when they are fast-moving and dynamic; because television demands an immediate and emotional response; because television is nothing at all like a pamphlet, a newspaper, or a book; because of all this and more, all discourse on television must take the form of an entertainment. Television has little tolerance for arguments, hypotheses, reasons, explanations, or any of the instruments of abstract, expositional thought. What television mostly demands is a performing art. Thinking is not a performing art. Showing is. And so what can be shown rather than what can be thought becomes the stuff of our public consciousness. In all arenas of public business, the image now replaces the word as the basic unit of discourse. As a consequence, television makes the metaphor of the marketplace of ideas obsolete. It creates a new metaphor: the marketplace of images.

Should you need a precise example of what this means, then consider the following: In America, circa 1984, a fat person cannot be elected to high political office. With your indulgence, I shall repeat this, because it captures the sense of the great Huxleyan transformation now taking place: In America, a fat person cannot be elected to high political office. A fat person makes an unpleasant image on television, and such an image easily overwhelms whatever profundities may issue forth from its mouth. If you have not heard any interesting ideas from American political leaders, it is not, I assure you, that they have none. It is because ideas are irrelevant to political success. In the Age of Television, people do not so much agree or disagree with politicians as they like or dislike them, for the image is not susceptible to verification or refutation, only to acceptance or rejection. In 1984, politics in America is not the Federalist Papers. It is not the Lincoln-Douglas Debates. It is not even Roosevelt's fireside chats. Politics is good looks and amiability. It is fast-moving imagery. A quick tempo, a good show, celebrities. Because of this it is even possible that some day a Hollywood movie actor may become President of the United States.

What is true of politics is equally true of news, which is transmitted to Americans through the device widely known as a "TV news show." Our newscasters, sometimes referred to as "talking hair-dos," comprise the handsomest class of people in America. Their shows are always introduced and concluded with music. While on camera, they talk to each other with chatty informality. Each of the stories they tell us rarely occupies more than forty-five seconds of our time. And in all cases, coherence and continuity are sacrificed in favor of visual interest. A TV news show is only marginally concerned with public information. What is important is its tempo, the celebrity of its performers, the pleasant familiarity of its ambience. A TV news show is precisely what its name implies: A show is an entertainment, a world of artifice, carefully staged to produce a particular series of effects so that the audience is left laughing or crying or stupified. And that is why each evening at the conclusion of a news show, the newscaster invites us to "join" him or her tomorrow. One would think that thirty minutes of fragmented images of disorder and sorrow would provide enough anxiety for a month of sleepless nights. Not so. We join them tomorrow because we know a good show when we see one.

And that is exactly why so many Americans now prefer to get their religious instruction from television rather than church. Church is apt to provide congregants with a serious and austere experience; in any case, not a very amusing one. But television makes religion *fun*. Billy Graham, Oral Roberts, and Robert Schuller are only among the more entertaining of a coven of preachers who do religion regularly on television. Surrounded by singers, celebrities, floral displays, sparkling fountains, exotic locales, and exceedingly handsome people, these evangelists offer a religion that is as simplistic and theatrical as any Las Vegas stage show. No dogma, terminology, logic, ritual, doctrines, or traditions are called upon to burden the minds of viewers, who are required to respond only to the image of the preacher, to whom God, Himself, must take second billing. For God does not play well on television. In an imagistic medium God is scarcely present; only the relentless and charismatic image of a messenger who, to gain attention and large audiences, turns theology into a vaudeville act.

Which, of course, is what has been done to education by "Sesame

Street," our highly acclaimed TV show for children. Both its creators and its audiences now accept without qualification the idea that learning and entertainment are indistinguishable, just as businessmen, in spending millions on those mini-entertainments known as commercials, accept the idea that economics is less a science than an adjunct of show business.

This shift in the form and content of public discourse is not only manifested in what is *on* television but also in what is *off* television. As TV moves typography to the edges of our culture and takes its place at the center, the television show becomes our most compelling model and metaphor of all communication. How TV stages the world becomes our idea of how the world is properly to be staged. Our newspapers, increasingly, are designed to give readers the feeling they are watching television. Indeed, America's newest national daily, *USA Today,* is sold on the streets in receptacles that look like television screens. Our teachers have increased the visual stimulation of their lessons, and strive to make their classrooms even more entertaining than "Sesame Street." In case you have not heard the news, I fear I must tell you that the Philadelphia public schools have embarked on an experiment in which children will have their curriculum sung to them to the rhythms of rock music. Those ministers who are confined to non-electronic, traditional pulpits are often driven to adopting a show business style to prove, as it were, that one does not have to be serious to be holy. Indeed, some wish to prove that one does not have to be holy at all, as for example, Father John J. O'Connor, who put on a New York Yankees baseball cap in mugging his way through his installation as Archbishop of the Archdiocese of New York. Our universities eagerly award honorary degrees to television and movie stars, some of whom are asked to address the graduates at commencement exercises on subjects about which neither they nor the graduates know anything whatsoever. It is of no matter. In a culture in which one becomes a celebrity by merely appearing on television, the distinction between entertainment and anything else becomes odious.

That is why our politicians eagerly make appearances on non-political television shows. Henry Kissinger joined former President Gerald Ford for an appearance on the hit TV show, "Dynasty." Speaker of the House of Representatives Tip O'Neill did a cameo role on the comedy show "Cheers." Consumer advocate Ralph Nader hosted the popular show "Saturday Night Live." So did George McGovern and the Mayor of New York City, Edward Koch, who also played the role of a prize-fight manager on a made-for-TV movie, starring James Cagney. Just as the television commercial freed the entrepreneur from concentrating on the quality of his product and, instead, demanded that he concentrate on entertaining the consumer, the format of television frees the politician from the serious confines of the political arena. Political figures may show up anywhere, at any time, doing anything, without being thought odd, presumptuous, or in any way out of place. I can assure you that no American would be surprised if Geraldine Ferraro⁰ showed up in a small role as a Queens housewife in a Francis Coppola film.

In America, all forms of social life strive to be like television shows or are thought to have potential as TV shows. We are now televising our courtroom trials, most recently and notably a rape trial in New Bedford, Massachusetts, which took audiences away from their favorite soap operas for several weeks. We have also discovered that real-life surgery is, if anything, more engrossing than fictional medical shows. In this connection, perhaps the most significant statement made in America, recently, about the state of our culture was inadvertently uttered by Mr. Bernard Schuler, who became an instant celebrity by allowing Dr. Edward Dietrich to perform triple by-pass surgery on him while on television. Mr. Schuler was uncommonly confident about the operation because, he said, "There is no way in hell they are going to lose me on live TV."

That all the world is a stage is hardly an unfamiliar thought. But that all the world is a TV situation comedy has come as quite a surprise— except to Aldous Huxley. We must, in any case, make no mistake about it. Television is not merely an entertainment medium. It is a philosophy of discourse, every bit as capable of altering a culture as was the printing press. Among other things, the printed word created the modern idea of prose, and invested exposition with unprecedented authority as a means of conducting public affairs. Television disdains exposition, which is serious, sequential, rational, and complex. It offers instead a mode of discourse in which everything is accessible, simplistic, concrete, and above all, entertaining. As a result, America is the world's first culture in jeopardy of amusing itself to death.

And much of the rest of the world appears eager to join us. While America may no longer be loved, American television certainly is. It is estimated that America exports 250,000 hours of TV programming per year, equally divided among Europe, Asia, and Latin America. Even the People's Republic of China has lately contracted with CBS to assist its people in joining in the fun. Contracts with NBC and ABC are sure to follow. One hopes the Chinese understand that this represents a revolutionary political act. The Gang of Four⁰ is as nothing when compared to the Gang of Three.

I do not say this merely to achieve an effect, for, in concluding, I wish you to understand me to be saying that there are two ways by which the spirit of a culture may be shrivelled. In the first—the Orwellian—culture becomes a prison. In the second—the Huxleyan—culture becomes a bur-

---

Geraldine Ferraro   The Democratic vice-presidential candidate in 1984.
Gang of Four   Jiang Qing (Mao Zedong's second wife), Wang Hongwen, Zhang Chunqiao, and Yao Wenyuan. They were imprisoned, tried, and convicted by the Red Chinese government in 1980–1981 for their harsh policies during the Chinese Cultural Revolution of the 1960s.

lesque. The first way is far easier for us to recognize and to oppose. Everything in our background has prepared us to know and resist a prison when the walls begin to close around us. We are not likely to be indifferent to the voices of the Sakharovs° and the Timmermans° and the Walesas.° We take arms against such a sea of troubles, buttressed by the spirit of Luther, Milton, Bacon, Voltaire, Goethe, and Jefferson. But what if there are no cries of anguish to be heard? Who is prepared to take arms against a sea of amusements? To whom do we complain, and when, and in what tone of voice, when serious discourse dissolves into giggles? What is the antidote to a culture dying of laughter? I fear, ladies and gentlemen, that our philosophers have as yet given us no guidance in this matter.

Reading, Writing and Rationality

George Will

George Will (born 1941) served six years as a professor of political philosophy before turning to political writing. He is now a nationally syndicated columnist and a familiar commentator on television. Educated at Trinity College, at Oxford, and at Princeton (Ph.D. 1964), Will is noted among columnists for his erudition, his quirky wit, and the relative independence of his (generally very conservative) ideas. He won a Pulitzer Prize for commentary in 1977. His books include The Pursuit of Happiness and Other Sobering Thoughts *(1979),* The Pursuit of Virtue and Other Tory Notions *(1982),* Statecraft as Soulcraft: What Government Does *(1983), and* The Morning After: American Successes and Excesses, 1981–1986 *(1986). The following is his* Newsweek *column for March 17, 1986.*

Neil Postman of New York University is not amused. He has seen television and has decided it is the cause of the decline and fall of just about everything. He announces this, fortissimo, in his book "Amusing Ourselves to Death: Public Discourse in the Age of Show Business." Postman is professor of "communication arts and sciences." Remember when professors taught philosophy, history, mathematics—stuff like that?

Sakharovs   Dr. Andrei Sakharov (b. 1921), Nobel Prize–winning physicist and Russian dissident.
Timmermans   Jacobo Timerman (b. 1923), distinguished Argentinian journalist and dedicated Zionist. He was arrested in 1977 by the military junta then ruling Argentina and imprisoned and tortured.
Walesas   Lech Walesa (b. 1943?), Polish labor leader and founder of the labor union Solidarity.

Orwell warned about a regime that would control through hate and pain. But what is upon us, says Postman, is Huxley's nightmare, the perfumed oppression of control through pleasure—through "man's almost infinite appetite for distractions." People are rendered passive as the truth is drowned in a sea of amusing irrelevance. People become entertained slaves of technologies that destroy their ability to think. Until the 1840s, information could move about 35 miles an hour—as fast as a train. The telegraph, Postman says, began an information glut that has culminated in a world made incoherent by broadcast journalism.

Postman has decided that a Gresham's law of communication dictates that television and print cannot coexist: books are doomed. He has decided that television will always overwhelm words with pictures, and will debase such language as it uses. "Television," says Postman, "does not ban books, it simply displaces them." Actually, there often is a healthy synergism between media. The writings of Isak Dinesen (Karen Blixen) have a new audience created by the movie "Out of Africa."

Still, Postman's preference for print is sensible. Anyone professionally engaged in mass communications through both print and broadcast—for the eye and for the ear—understands the advantages of print. Postman rightly says the process of reading encourages rationality. A printed page, containing a narrative or argument that unfolds line by line, encourages a more coherent view of the world than does a slam-bang broadcast of quickly changing, high-impact images—flood, fire, terrorism, a congressional hearing, now off to a denture-adhesive commercial, now back to war, the stock market, etc. Reading is active: it requires the discipline of bodily stillness and mental attention. Absorbing television is an essentially passive experience. Were broadcasting to supplant rather than just supplement print, much—civilization in fact—would be lost. But were television to vanish, the people who today read almost nothing would still read almost nothing, or would read the sort of printed matter that would cause Johannes Gutenberg to regret his invention of movable type. Besides, print is doing nicely, thank you.

True, it is not what it was when it had the field to itself. Postman says that in 1776 Thomas Paine sold more than 100,000 copies of "Common Sense" in two months, which is equivalent to selling 8 million copies of a book in two months today. "Uncle Tom's Cabin" sold 305,000 in one year, comparable to 4 million today. And when Charles Dickens toured America in 1842 his celebrity was Springsteenian. Books and authors do not now have such megatonnage. But the reading public is large, growing and remarkably receptive to seriousness.

Postman says we are witnessing the debasing of public discourse by entertainment values. Alas, his book is occasionally evidence for his argument. When he says most newscasters "spend more time with their hair dryers than with their scripts," he is being entertaining rather than accurate. He says that when the printing press was dominant, public discourse was "generally coherent, serious and rational." But before saying that television has "devastated political discourse," he should reread the yellow press of the gilded age or examine the "I drink hard cider" campaign that won the White House for Harrison in 1840. Postman says that most of the first 15 presidents would not have been recognized if they had walked among average citizens. But the run of presidents from 7 through 15 (Jackson through Buchanan) hardly establishes the superiority of an information system essentially without pictures. Postman, who seems to think the 1984 election was decided by a Reagan joke in the second debate, says it is highly unlikely that 300-pound William Howard Taft could be a candidate today. Does Postman mean that in the Age of Television only glamorous people win nomination (Johnson? McGovern? Nixon? Ford? Mondale?)? Who is Postman to call Americans "quite likely the least well-informed people in the Western world"?

Postman's analysis resembles Galbraith's in "The Affluent Society." That 1958 best seller beat up on another of the intellectuals' favorite villains—advertising. It said: the mindless masses (not me or you, discerning readers) are enervated, manipulated victims. Galbraith's book, like Postman's, was published after the voters had had the bad manners to re-elect a conservative president disdained by most intellectuals.

While we are speaking, as I gather we are, about "communication arts and sciences," note that Postman uses jargon ("decontextualize"), uses "disappear" as a transitive verb (a politics of imagery "may disappear history"), confuses "captivation" with capture ("radio's captivation by the music industry") and repeatedly misuses the adjective "massive" ("a massive reorientation"; television's "damage is especially massive to youthful viewers"), which properly applies to things with mass. And the book begins: "We were keeping our eye on 1984. When the year came and the prophecy didn't. . . ." He does not mean "prophecy," he means "that which was prophesied."

Postman is right to insist that media technologies are not neutral in their effects on discourse, and a world that does not read well will not think well. However, he should heed an axiom from the pretelevision age: physician, heal thyself.

To Be or Not to Be as Defined by TV

Jack McGarvey

Jack McGarvey (born 1937) was educated at Clarion State College in Pennsylvania and at the University of Connecticut. He has been a teacher for twenty-four years. For a time he was a teaching administrator at Bedford Junior High School in Westport, Connecticut, developing a middle-school philosophy and curriculum. At present he teaches computer and language arts at Coleytown Middle School in Westport. He is also a free-lance writer whose articles have appeared in such national magazines as McCall's *and* Parents. *The piece reprinted here is from the February–March 1982 issue of* Today's Education.

A couple of years ago, a television crew came to film my ninth grade English class at Bedford Junior High School in Westport, Connecticut. I'm still trying to understand what happened.

I was doing some work with my students, teaching them to analyze the language used in television commercials. After dissecting the advertising claims, most of the class became upset over what they felt were misleading—and in a few cases, untruthful—uses of language. We decided to write to the companies that presented their products inaccurately or offensively. Most of them responded with chirpy letters and cents-off coupons. Some did not respond at all.

I then decided to contact *Buyline,* a consumer advocate program aired on New York City's WNBC-TV at the time. The show and its host, Betty Furness, were well-known for their investigation of consumer complaints. I sent off a packet of the unanswered letters with a brief explanation of the class's work.

About a week later, the show's producer telephoned me. She said that she'd seen the letters and was interested in the class's project. Could she and her director come to Westport to have a look?

I said sure and told her about a role-playing activity I was planning to do with my students. I said I was going to organize my class of 24 students into four committees—each one consisting of two representatives from the Federal Trade Commission (FTC), the agency that monitors truth in advertising; two advertising executives anxious to have their material used; and two TV executives caught somewhere in the middle—wanting to please the advertisers while not offending the FTC. Then, I would ask each committee to assume that there had been a complaint about the language used in a TV commercial, and that the committees had to resolve the complaint. "That sounds great! I'll bring a crew," she said.

I obtained clearance from my school district's office, and the next morning, as I was walking into school, I met one of my students and casually let out the word: "WNBC's coming to film our class this afternoon."

I was totally unprepared for what happened. Word spread around school within five minutes. Students who barely knew me rushed up to squeal, "Is it true? Is it really, really true? A TV crew is coming to Bedford to film?" A girl who was not in my class pinned me into a corner near the magazine rack in the library to ask me whether she could sit in my class for the day. Another girl went to her counselor and requested an immediate change in English classes, claiming a long-standing personality conflict with her current teacher.

Later, things calmed down a bit, but as I took my regular turn as cafeteria supervisor, I saw students staring wide-eyed at me, then turning to whisper excitedly to their friends. I'd become a celebrity simply because I was the one responsible for bringing a TV crew to school.

Right after lunch, the show's producer and director came to my class to look it over and watch the role-playing activity; they planned to tape near the end of the school day. The two women were gracious and self-effacing, taking pains not to create any disturbance; but the students, of course, knew why they were there. There were no vacant stares, no hair brushes, no gum chewers, and no note scribblers. It was total concentration, and I enjoyed one of my best classes in more than 15 years of teaching.

After the class, I met with the producer and director to plan the taping. They talked about some of the students they'd seen and mentioned Susan. "She's terribly photogenic and very, very good with words." They mentioned Steve. "He really chaired his committee well. Real leadership there. Handsome boy, too." They mentioned Jim, Pete, Randy, and Jenny and their insights into advertising claims. Gradually I became aware that we were engaged in a talent hunt; we were looking for a strong and attractive group to be featured in the taping.

We continued the discussion, deciding on the players. We also discussed the sequencing of the taping session. First, I'd do an introduction, explaining the role-playing activity as if the class had never heard of it. Then, I'd follow with the conclusion—summarizing remarks ending with a cheery "See you tomorrow!"—and dismiss the class. The bit players would leave the school and go home. We'd then rearrange the set and film the photogenic and perceptive featured players while they discussed advertising claims as a committee. Obviously, this is not the way I'd conduct an actual class, but it made sense. After all, I wanted my students to look good, and I wanted to look good.

"It'll be very hard work," the producer cautioned. "I trust your students understand that."

"It's already been hard work," I remarked as I thought of possible jealousies and bruised feelings over our choices of featured players.

About a half hour before school's end, the crew set up cameras and lights in the hall near the classroom we'd be working in, a room in an isolated part of the building. But as the crew began filming background shots of the normal passing of students through the hall, near chaos broke out.

Hordes of students suddenly appeared. A basketball star gangled through the milling mob to do an imitation of Nureyev, topping off a pirouette by feigning a couple of jump shots. A pretty girl walked back and forth in front of the cameras at least a dozen times before she was snared by a home economics teacher. Three boys did a noisy pantomime of opening jammed lockers, none of which were theirs. A faculty member, seen rarely in this part of the building, managed to work his way through the crowd, smiling broadly. And as members of my class struggled through the press of bodies, they were hailed, clutched at, patted on the back, and hugged.

"Knock 'em dead!" I heard a student call.

It took the vice-principal and five teachers 10 minutes to clear the hall.

We assembled the cast, arranged the furniture, erased several mild obscenities from the chalkboard, and pulled down the window shades— disappointing a clutch of spectators outside. The producer then introduced the crew and explained their work.

I was wired with a mike and the crew set up a boom microphone, while the girls checked each other's make-up and the boys sat squirming.

Finally, the taping began. It was show business, a performance, a total alteration of the reality I know as a teacher. As soon as I began the introduction, 26 pairs of eyes focused on me as if I were Billy Joel about to sing. I was instantly startled and self-conscious. When I asked a question, some of the usually quieter students leaped to respond. This so unsettled me that I forgot what I was saying and had to begin again.

The novelty of being on camera, however, soon passed. We had to do retakes because the soundman missed student responses from the rear of the room. The director asked me to rephrase a question and asked a student to rephrase a response. There were delays while technicians adjusted equipment.

We all became very much aware of being performers, and some of the students who had been most excited about making their TV debut began to grumble about the hard work. That pleased me, for a new reality began to creep in: Television is not altogether glamorous.

We taped for almost five hours, on more than 3,200 feet of video tape. That is almost an hour-and-a-half's worth, more than double a normal class period. And out of that mass of celluloid the producer said she'd use seven minutes on the program!

Two days later, five students and I went to the NBC studios at Rockefeller Center to do a taping of a final segment. The producer wanted to do a studio recreation of the role-playing game. This time, however, the game would include real executives—one from advertising, one from the NBC network, and one from the FTC. We'd be part of a panel discussion moderated by Betty Furness. My students would challenge the TV and the advertising executives, asking them to justify some of the bothersome language used in current commercials.

This was the most arduous part of the experience. The taping was live, meaning that the cameras would run for no longer than eight minutes. As we ate turkey and ham during a break with Ms. Furness and the guest executives, I realized that we were with people who were totally comfortable with television. I began to worry. How could mere 14-year-olds compete in a debate with those to whom being on television is as ordinary as riding a school bus?

But my concern soon disappeared. As Ms. Furness began reading her TelePrompTer, Susan leaned over and whispered, "This is fun!" And it was Susan who struck first. "You can see how luxurious my hair feels' is a perfect example of the silly language your ad writers use," she said with all the poise of a Barbara Walters. "It's impossible to *see* how something feels," she went on.

That pleased me, for as an English teacher, I've always emphasized the value of striving for precision in the use of language. The work we'd done with TV commercials, where suggestibility is the rule, had taken hold, I thought, as the ad executive fumbled for a response. The tension vanished, and we did well.

The show aired two weeks later, and I had it taped so the class could view it together. It was a slick production, complete with music—"Hey, Big Spender"—to develop a theme for Ms. Furness' introduction. "Teens are big business these days," she said. "Does television advertising influence how they spend their money?" Then followed a shot of students in the hall—edited to show none of the wildness that actually occurred. Next, three of my students appeared in brief clips of interviews. They were asked, "Have you ever been disappointed by television advertising?" The responses were, "Yes, of course," and I was pleased with their detailed answers. Finally, the classroom appeared, and there I was, lounging against my desk, smiling calmly. I looked good—a young, unrumpled Orson Bean, with a cool blue-and-brown paisley tie. My voice was mellifluous. Gee, I thought as I saw the tape, I could have been a TV personality.

Now, I am probably no more vain than most people. But television does strange things to the ego. I became so absorbed in studying the image of myself that the whole point of the show passed me by. I didn't even notice that I'd made a goof analyzing a commercial until I'd seen the show three times. The students who participated were the same; watching themselves on videotape, they missed what they had said. I had an enormous struggle to get both them and me to recall the hard work and to see the obvious editing. It was as if reality had been reversed: The actual process of putting together the tape was not real, but the product was.

I showed the tape again last year to my ninth grade class. I carefully explained to this delightful gang of fault-finders how the taping had been done. I told them about the changed sequence, the selection of the featured players, the takes and retakes. They themselves had just been through the same role-playing activity, and I asked them to listen carefully to what was said. They nodded happily and set their flinty minds to look at things critically. But as the tape ended, they wanted to tease me about how ugly and wrinkled I looked. They wanted to say, "That's

Randy! He goes to Compo Beach all the time." "Jenny's eye shadow—horrible!" "When will you get us on TV?"

The visual image had worked its magic once again: They had missed the point of the show altogether. And, as I dismissed them, I felt something vibrating in their glances and voices—the celebrity image at work again. I was no longer their mundane English teacher: I was a TV personality.

I decided to show the tape again the next day. I reviewed the hard work, the editing, the slick packaging. I passed out questions so we could focus on what had been said on the program. I turned on the recorder and turned off the picture to let them hear only the sound. They protested loudly, of course. But I was determined to force them to respond to how effectively the previous year's class had taken apart the language used in the claims of commercials. This was, after all, the point of the program. And it worked, finally.

As class ended, one of the students drifted up to me. "What are we going to do next?" she asked.

"We're going to make some comparisons between TV news shows and what's written in newspapers," I replied.

"Do they put together news shows the way they filmed your class?"

"It's similar and usually much quicker," I answered.

She smiled and shook her head. "It's getting hard to believe anything anymore."

In that comment lies what every TV viewer should have—a healthy measure of beautiful, glorious skepticism. But as I said, I'm still trying to understand that taping session. And I'm aware of how hard it is to practice skepticism. Every time I see the *Buyline* tape, I'm struck by how good a teacher TV made me. Am I really that warm, intelligent, creative, and good-looking? Of course not. But TV made me that way. I like it, and sometimes I find myself still hoping that I am what television defined me to be.

I sometimes think children have superior knowledge of TV. They know, from many years of watching it, that the product in all its edited glory is the only reality. Shortly after the program aired on that February Saturday two years ago, our telephone rang. The voice belonged to my daughter's 11-year-old friend. She said, "I just saw you on TV. May I have your autograph?"

I was baffled. After all, this was the boisterous girl who played with my daughter just about every day and who mostly regarded me as a piece of furniture that occasionally mumbled something about lowering your voices. "Are you serious?" I croaked.

"May I have your autograph?" she repeated, ignoring my question. "I can come over right now." Her voice was without guile.

She came. And I signed while she scrutinized my face, her eyes still aglow with Chromacolor.

To Stephanie, television had transformed a kindly grump into something real. And there is no doubt in my mind whatsoever that in the deepest part of her soul is the fervent dream that her being, too, will someday be defined and literally affirmed by an appearance on television.

Lately, my ninth grade class has been growing restless. Shall I move up the TV unit and bring out the tape again? Shall I remind them what a great teacher they have? Shall I remind myself what a fine teacher I am? Shall I renew their—and my—hope?

To be or not to be as defined by TV? Does that question suggest what makes television so totally unlike any other medium?

Can You Believe Your Eyes?

Henry Fairlie

Henry Fairlie, born in England in 1924, has written, as he says, "on both sides of the Atlantic." Educated at London's Highgate School and Oxford, he wrote for the London Observer *and was the main political editorial writer for the London* Times *until he resigned in 1954 to free-lance in England and the United States. (In a political column in* The Spectator *in 1955, he was the first person to use the term "Establishment" in its modern sense—to refer to a group of powerful people who somehow control government or society.) Fairlie has also written for* Punch *and the* New Statesman, *and he has been a foreign correspondent for the* Daily Mail. *While still in England, Fairlie did reporting for several television documentaries, but he stopped because, as he explained in an article in* Encounter, *television is an "idiot box," and "if you've seen it on television, it didn't happen."*

Fairlie has lived in the United States since 1966, contributing to such periodicals as the New York Times Magazine, The New Yorker, *the* Washington Post, *and the* New Republic, *where he now serves as Contributing Editor. His books include* The Life of Politics *(1968);* The Kennedy Promise *(1973);* The Spoiled Child of the Western World: The Miscarriage of the American Idea in Our Time *(1976); and, published in 1978, two books expanded from essays,* The Parties *and* The Seven Deadly Sins Today. *The essay reprinted here first appeared in the Spring 1967* Horizon. *Its allusions to current events and programs are of course dated; but its judgments are as valid today as they ever were.*

None of us has ever seen Alexander the Great emerging from his tent. If there had been television in his day and we could look at the tape, would we know him any better, as we think we now know a John F. Kennedy or a Lyndon B. Johnson when we see them, on television news, emerging from a convention?

None of us has ever heard Julius Caesar speak. But if there had been radio in his day and we could listen to the recording, would we know him any better, as we think we know something important about Franklin D. Roosevelt from his fireside chats?°

The answer is far from clear. Of all historical evidence, the public presence of voice or of physical appearance is the most revealing but can also be the most misleading. Yet the problem of historical evidence is raised every night on television news, when we are asked to accept what we see and hear as genuine. It is raised especially by the two most important television news programs in the United States: Huntley-Brinkley on NBC, and Walter Cronkite on CBS. Millions of people have to decide not so much whether they can believe what they are told but whether they can believe what they see flickering in front of them.

"The evidence of their own eyes": but that is precisely what is not available to them. What *is* available is the evidence, first, of the camera, making its own selection, dictating its own terms; and it is the evidence, then, of the small screen—still the best description of television—which in turn dictates to the camera. Can television, by its nature, ever tell the truth?

Amid all the pretentiousness of his theorizing, Marshall McLuhan is right to this extent: the medium is the message. Television does not merely create news. That is an old business, practiced for generations by newspapers. Television creates its own events, something even the most imaginative newspaper reporter cannot do. The newspaperman can only create words, and however powerful they may be, words do not *happen* over the breakfast table as television *happens* in a living room. Thomas W. Moore, ABC's president, came very near to the point when he said: "It is difficult to retain one's perspective when, without leaving the security of our living rooms, we become witness to such startling events as the assassination of an assassin, or a war in progress."

It is because television *happens* in this way that people begin to think that the small excerpts from life which they see on the screen in their living rooms are more "real" than the life which they experience around them. There is a vital margin of difference between saying, "Did you see the report in *The New York Times* of the massacres in the Congo?" and saying, "Did you see the massacres in the Congo on television last night?" The first remark implies only that one has seen a report (which may conflict with a report from another source). The second implies that one

---

fireside chats   Radio broadcasts by President Franklin D. Roosevelt to the nation during the 1930s, in which he discussed his policies for dealing with the Great Depression.

has seen the event itself. However carefully television is used, it cannot avoid this deception.

It is doubtful whether it is ever easy—sometimes whether it is ever possible—for a newspaper or television reporter to report an event. He can report incidents, and it is the nature of incidents that they can, and do, happen in isolation. But the true meaning of an event depends on all of its known and unknown cases, on all of the known and unknown incidents that contribute to it, and in the process, cease to be isolated, and on all of its known and unknown repercussions. The whole of an incident can easily be described; the whole of an event may escape even the historian.

If this is a difficulty that confronts the newspaper reporter from day to day, it is one that the television reporter can rarely overcome. For the newspaper reporter possesses a flexibility that the television reporter does not have. He has flexibility because he can move without the paraphernalia and encumbrance of a camera or a camera crew. He has flexibility because he can reach where the camera cannot reach: the camera can never go "off the record."

The newspaperman has flexibility, above all, because words are flexible and the length of a story is flexible: the one able to qualify, even in the shortest parenthetical expression; the other capable of imposing its own perspective. But however carefully chosen the words of a television reporter, they can never properly qualify a spectacular picture; and however discriminating the apportionment of stories in a television program, they are in length too nearly the same.

Incidents are usually in the open; the whole of an event, often obscure and private. Not only is the core of television the public and the spectacular, but there is an important sense in which television has a vested interest in disaster. From the point of view of a good story, both newspapers and television prefer covering a major strike to negotiations which prevent a strike. But it is possible for the newspaper reporter to make negotiations almost as exciting a story as a strike itself: by word of mouth, he can collect a picture of the coming and goings which are the essence of negotiation and, by his words in print, vividly describe them. But what can television do with negotiations? It can only show pictures of people arriving at a building and people leaving it. However colorful they may be—and the modern business executive is not normally colorful—this does not make exciting viewing.

Violence is the stuff of television, and the question of how to deal with it is the most important one confronting the medium.

To be sure, the same question confronts newspapers; but the impact of violence—whether a boxing match, a riot, or a massacre—is much greater in a moving picture than in a still picture or in descriptive prose. Violence is movement—the raising of an arm, the smashing of it on someone's head—and movement is what television cannot help emphasizing.

In covering violent situations, three distinct characteristics of television conspire to intensify both its special problems and the special temptations to which it is exposed. There is, first, the limitation of time. A lead news story in a paper such as *The New York Times* may take twenty minutes to read; in a popular newspaper or a tabloid, as many as ten. There simply is not this time available in television news. In the reporting of all news, this means concentration to the point of distortion. In the reporting of violence, it means concentration on the violent incident to the exclusion of the whole event.

An outstanding example of such distortion was the police attack on civil rights marchers at the Selma, Alabama, bridge in March, 1965. I was not present myself. But I do not know one reporter who was present, and whose opinion I trust, who does not point out that there was first a prolonged period during which police and demonstrators faced each other, without violence, in an atmosphere of unbearable tension, and who does not agree that the tension had to break in the form of police action.

Television news—except in special features and documentaries—did not, and could not, show this preliminary encounter. Three minutes of film is an extended sequence in a news program, and the time is best filled with action, not inaction. On the other hand, a single phrase in a newspaper story, placed correctly, where it carries weight, can put even an extended description of violence in perspective.

The point of such perspective is not to excuse any eventual police brutality, but to explain it. Without this explanation, whether implicit or explicit, one begins to think that brutality is automatic, that the police will always behave in such a manner; demonstrators begin to think that they can, and should, goad the police; and the police begin to think, since restraint is so frail anyhow, they may as well give way to exasperation from the start.

There is, secondly, television's tendency to produce self-generating news. The problem arose most notably during the disturbances in Watts;° but it has arisen, again and again, whenever there have been similar disturbances in other cities. However spontaneous the original outbreak of violence, an external provocation is added once it has occurred. That provocation is the presence of television cameras in the middle of the trouble spots.

This is especially true on the night after the original outbreak. Then, as dusk gathers, television cameramen and reporters move into the streets looking—literally looking—for trouble, and the crowds begin to play up to them. Their presence is very different from the presence of newspaper reporters, who either roam around, hardly distinguishable, or

---

disturbances in Watts   In August of 1965 there were six days of riots in Watts, a section of Los Angeles, California.

lounge in bars until they hear that action has broken out somewhere down the block. Television, merely by its presence, helps to create incidents and then itself remains part of the happening. There is no doubt that this participation occurred after the first night in Watts, and that it occurred again last summer in Chicago.

But in order to create on the screen the impression of continuing disturbance, of continuing riots, television needs only one incident. One spectacular incident of violence can occupy a two-minute sequence in a news program just as impressively as a series of incidents. Much of the Watts film is a classic example of this: showing that it needs only one defiant boy and only one hot-headed policeman to suggest that a neighborhood is aflame.

In this connection it seems worth pointing out that a newspaper reporter's dishonesty—or imagination—can be a great deal less dangerous and provocative than a television reporter's. The newspaper reporter, after all, need only create—or exaggerate—a story in his own mind. But the television reporter must create—or exaggerate—it in actuality: he must make it a happening.

Finally, in this matter of violence, there is the size of the screen: the limitations which it imposes, the temptations it offers. At the end of last summer, television news showed some alarming pictures of white men and women in the Chicago suburb of Cicero screaming abuse at some Negro marchers. Their hating faces—a dozen of them, perhaps—filled the screen. They looked as if they were a representative example of a much larger crowd. But anyone who was there knows that these particular whites were only a small part of the crowds in the streets; and that the crowds themselves were only a small part of the total white population of Cicero. To this vital extent, television that night distorted badly.

What all this amounts to is not only that people sitting in their homes begin to think that all police are brutal, that all demonstrators are violent, that all disturbances are riots, that all crowds are aggressive; the fact that they usually go through each day without either meeting or themselves displaying violence becomes less real to them than the violence on the small screen.

Anyone who has appeared regularly on television knows that complete strangers think they have actually met him. They smile or nod at him in the street or across bars; they approach him and shake his hand; they even ask him to drop in when next he is around their way, as if they really believe that he has been in their homes. It is this imaginary "real" presence of television in people's living rooms which is the background to the whole problem. Surely much of the feeling of living in a condition of perpetual crisis, and the agitation arising from it, comes from a sense of being a witness to a world which is more actual than the routine world in which one lives.

Television can create, not only events out of incidents, but movements and people. The television news coverage of the Meredith° march across Mississippi, during the couple of days when I accompanied it myself, constantly appalled me. It was near the beginning of the march, when it had barely gotten organized, and when the numbers were few and the individuals composing the numbers were anything but impressive.

All the familiar hazards of television reporting were displayed. A straggling column—it was at the time little more—could be made on the small screen to look like an army. When the cameras were rolling, the marchers pulled themselves together and played the role expected of them. The several civil rights leaders strode in line abreast, at the head of their enthusiastic followers.

The real story of the Meredith march was not this unified demonstration at all, but the fact that it produced the deeply significant clash between different factions of the civil rights movement over "black power." Newspapers felt their way to this story and were, by the end, reporting it fully. It was a story which, for the most part, was taking place in private meetings where the cameras could not reach. But then when television at last caught on to the fact of "black power," it inevitably exaggerated and distorted it. Film is expensive. Getting film ready for a news program is a hurried job. The result is that in reporting any speech the television reporter and cameraman make an automatic, almost involuntary, selection. They wait for the mention of a phrase like "black power," and on go the lights and the film rolls.

But, given the length of the usual sequence in a news program, that is all. The impact is far greater than that of any selection made by newspapers. By constant reiteration on the small screen day after day, the slogan of "black power" was elevated into a movement. It was suddenly there. It had suddenly happened. "Black power" switched the cameras on, and in turn the cameras switched the movement on. It was a classic case of self-generating news.

Stokely Carmichael, of the Student Nonviolent Co-ordinating Committee, could not have emerged so rapidly as a national figure without television. (SNCC is a master at using television.) But he is not the only example of television's ability to create—or destroy—people. No one, I think, questions that Governor Ronald Reagan is the creature of the television cameras, just as previously Actor Ronald Reagan was the creature of the movie cameras. John Morgan, one of the British Broadcasting Corporation's most experienced television reporters, returned from the California gubernatorial campaign last fall, amazed at Reagan's professionalism in

---

Meredith James Meredith, marching to spur voter registration in Mississippi in 1966, was wounded in an assassination attempt on the highway. Martin Luther King, Jr., Stokely Carmichael, and other civil rights workers resumed the march, which ended after 200 miles with a rally of 30,000 people in Jackson, Mississippi.

the television studio, and the use that he made of it to dictate camera angles and even the moments for close-ups.

Much of the poor impression that President Johnson has often made is the direct result of his comparatively poor television "image." The close-up, especially, can distort in the crudest way and make what is simply unprepossessing actually repellent. In fact, in considering the impact of the close-up, one can notice the vital difference between television and the movies; between what is legitimate in the cinema and illegitimate in a living room.

Movies are intended to be, and are taken to be, larger than life. Sitting in the theatre, one does not imagine that what one is seeing is real. The close-up in the movies, therefore, is a legitimate *and understood* distortion. But a distortion it is. We never do see anyone in real life as close in as the camera can go, except in one position and in one activity: when making love. There is no reason why President Johnson, or any other public figure, should have to pass this private test in public. Moreover, not only does the close-up bring one ridiculously close to a face, it shows it in isolation. It removes the general bearing; it removes the whole man.

Perhaps the most striking demonstration of the power of television to create personalities is one that most people will think also demonstrates its power for good. For a comparatively short time three men seemed to bestride the world: John F. Kennedy, Pope John XXIII, and Nikita Khrushchev. Their impact, all over the world, was quite out of proportion to the length of time any of them held office. In a few years they had made as great an impression as Queen Victoria had in sixty years. This was the work of television.

Television news is new, and we have not yet got the measure of it. Its hazards are numerous: some of them are inherent in the nature of the medium, and are likely to be permanent. Others are more technical and, with technical advances, may be removed.

Camera crews are costly, and costly to move about; this automatically imposes a preselection of news far more rigorous than it is in a newspaper. Film costs impose a second automatic selection. Time on the screen is expensive, and this imposes a final selection. Again and again, when I have been making news films with a camera crew, I have wanted to utter over the pictures, "It was not like this at all."

However paradoxical it may seem, the only immediate answer to most of the problems of television news lies not in pictures but in words. Given the powerful impact of the pictures, the words covering them must provide the corrective. Most television reporting just describes the pictures, and by doing so, reinforces them. But the object of words in television news should be to distract from the pictures, to say: "It was not quite so. This was not the whole story." Pictures simplify; the object of words should be to supply qualification and complication. Pictures involve; the object of words should be to detach the viewer, to remind him that he is not seeing an event, only an impression of one.

The manner of delivery—especially of the "anchor" men in the studio—is as important as the substance of the words themselves. There is something very professional and very engaging about the television manners of Chet Huntley and David Brinkley and Walter Cronkite. All of them, in dissimilar ways, cultivate a deadpan approach. In Huntley, it is made to suggest a judicial impartiality; in Brinkley, an ironical detachment; in Cronkite, an unfailing common sense. Each of them by his manner reinforces the impact of the pictures over which he is speaking, suggesting that they can be taken at their face value.

Only now and then, when Brinkley's irony is allowed to break loose into that overnourished flicker of a smile, is the value of the pictures ever questioned. The vital role of the television reporter or commentator is to make watching as difficult as reading, to invite the viewer to make comparisons and judgments from his own experience so that he never reacts by assuming that he is seeing actual life.

That television news can do some things remarkably well, especially in full-length features and documentaries, that those involved in making television programs are conscientious and skillful, does not touch the main problem. Television news holds a mirror up to the world in a way that newspapers never can; and the world is beginning to believe that it can recognize itself in it. Life is not made up of dramatic incidents—not even the life of a nation. It is made up of slowly evolving events and processes, which newspapers, by a score of different forms of emphasis, can reasonably attempt to explore from day to day.

But television news jerks from incident to incident. For the real world of patient and familiar arrangements, it substitutes an unreal world of constant activity, and the effect is already apparent in the way in which the world behaves. It is almost impossible, these days, to consider any problem or any event except as a crisis; and, by this very way of looking at it, it in fact becomes a crisis.

Television, by its emphasis on movement and activity, by its appetite for incident, has become by far the most potent instrument in creating this overexcited atmosphere, this barely recognizable world. The medium, to this very important extent, has become the message; and the message is perpetual stimulation, perpetual agitation, perpetual change. The world it creates is a world which is never still.

Many of our unnecessary anxieties about the way in which we live, about the fearful things that may happen to us, might be allayed if television news began, now and then, to say: "It has been a dull day. But we have collected some rather interesting pictures for you, of no particular significance." Television news has a deep responsibility to try to be dull, from time to time, and let the world go to sleep.

Connect the Dots

Robert Pattison

Robert Pattison (born 1945) is a student of literature and of cultural history. His most recent books are On Literacy: The Politics of the Word from Homer to the Age of Rock *(1982) and* The Triumph of Vulgarity: Rock Music in the Mirror of Romanticism *(1987). Professor Pattison was educated at Yale, the University of Sussex, and Columbia (Ph.D. 1973), and now teaches at Long Island University, Southampton. The following essay from* The Nation, *March 7, 1987, is one of several he has written on the media and on popular culture.*

One hundred and thirty million Americans watched the Denver Broncos' Clarence Kay dive for John Elway's pass in the second quarter of Super Bowl XXI. Did Kay catch it? No, said the referee. Maybe, said the Replay Official, a new character in professional football who owes his existence entirely to television. The Replay Official is part of the National Football League's one-year test of an instant-replay system. On Super Bowl Sunday, the Replay Official, ensconced in his replay booth in front of two TV monitors, two videocassette recorders and a bank of telephones, reviewed the tape of CBS's live feed of the disputed play. CBS also passed along to him a few of the ten other shots its cameras had taken but not aired. The Replay Official still couldn't produce the "indisputable visual evidence" required by N.F.L. rules to overturn a call on the field, and after two minutes of game delay, he deferred to the referee's original decision—incomplete pass. Denver was finished for the day.

But wait a minute. While the Broncos were tasting the agony of defeat, CBS technicians replayed all ten unaired shots of the disputed play. The tape of one camera, unearthed nine minutes after the event, provided footage that convinced those 130 million Americans that Kay *had* caught the pass. The state of Colorado seethed with indignation. "CBS replay wasn't instant enough," the New York *Daily News* complained. Most of the flak generated by the N.F.L.'s instant-replay experiment concerned the incompetence of league and network officials in deploying their technology. On Super Bowl Sunday, *The New York Times Magazine* wondered prophetically whether the visual evidence of instant replay wouldn't hurt football by revealing as never before the inadequacy of the referees. The unchallenged premise of these instant-replay debates is that television can show us reality.

More than any other medium, TV is the vehicle for the presentation of the world as it is. With enough equipment at a Super Bowl or any other event, TV is supposed to show us what really happens. Even if TV is showing an abstract-art exhibit, it succeeds only insofar as it displays the paintings as they would appear if we were actually in the gallery. The title of CBS's erstwhile history program captured a central attraction of television itself: *You Are There.*

About half the programming between 6 P.M. and midnight gives us neighborhood tragedies, international calamities and familiar personalities—real events and real people in known and accessible locales. The other half of evening television, the sitcoms and movies, is as relentless in its social realism as a Stalinist art festival. There are no Cubist sitcoms, no Minimalist cop programs. On TV, only children's programming has the artistic license to show the world as the most timid modern artist routinely does—filtered through imaginative forms. Children's TV permits mauve dinosaurs in surreal landscapes. For the rest of us, TV presents a world whose dimensions accord with our common-sense notions of space, whose motions occur at the same pace we experience daily and whose colors, at great cost, are as close as possible to the colors we think we see in life.

There is no reason to believe that television's insistence on realism is merely a reflection of America's conformist capitalism. Russians, Chinese and Albanians also want TV to show them the world as they think it is. They too consider color TV a step up from black and white because it's closer to an accurate depiction of what truly exists. TV is a reality machine.

But just as regularly as the public turns to TV for sharply defined slices of reality, it denounces the medium as a boob tube and a fantasy box. The same public that believes TV can tell it the truth about whether Kay caught Elway's pass also believes that TV is a technological narcotic, warping our perception of the world as surely as heroin or crack. These contradictory appraisals of the medium do not indicate that the public is confused. They indicate that the public understands TV very well. With TV, the ineluctable reality of objective nature becomes each viewer's private plaything.

The perception that TV is a fantasy machine is well founded. The fantasy begins in the technology itself. The presence of a coherent, realistic picture on the television screen is an illusion of the most complex sort. In any nanosecond of TV viewing, all that appears on the tube is a single dot of light. A succession of these dots tap across the screen at high speed, providing enough dots in a thirtieth of a second to make one complete image. But the picture itself is never present in any microsecond on the screen. The task of making the picture rests with the viewer, whose brain holds the evanescent dots and assembles them into a coherent image, then connects one split-second image to the next, creating the illusion of movement.

Despite its pretensions to realism, all television is is an exercise in pointillism. Its demands on the viewer's brain are far more extreme than those made by the movies, where successive images are at least presented as in life, in one piece.

What TV shows us is a reconstituted reality, broken down into light at the point of origin and reassembled not in the TV set but in the mind. Television gives us two worlds masquerading as one, a seemingly objective world that duplicates reality, and an inherently subjective experience assembled by ourselves and for ourselves. TV's champions invariably praise the objective nature of the medium—television brings us together in a global village of shared information and shared truths. TV's enemies just as inevitably fault the subjective side of the tube—TV isolates each of us in a private dream world. Both deal in half-truths. The essence of the medium is in the interplay between these forces.

The N.F.L.'s rules for the use of instant replay illustrate the schizoid nature of TV. Instant replay is used only to check possession-type plays and plays governed by in-bounds lines. Either Kay catches the ball or he doesn't; either Elway breaks the plane of the goal line or he doesn't. By the rules instant replay can't be used to check calls of illegal motion, clipping, intentional grounding or unsportsmanlike conduct. When Elway sees Lawrence Taylor coming and tosses the ball onto a vacant piece of Astroturf half a field away from his nearest teammate, is he trying to keep the ball at the line of scrimmage for the next play or has the intended receiver simply missed his appointment? The N.F.L. has decreed that in such situations, the referee's interpretation is as good as anyone else's. The N.F.L.'s rules are the rules for television itself. TV re-creates for each viewer a brute reality that all but lunatics can recognize as the world. The Replay Official can only overturn the referee's call when he can present this crude, common-sensical television reality about which everyone agrees. This is what the N.F.L. means by "indisputable visual evidence." But the interpretation of events within this framework of brute reality is beyond the scope of technology, and TV leaves each viewer free to impute whatever meaning he chooses to them.

Its critics claim that the sense of power fostered by TV is mere delusion. Their usual complaint is that once TV has intruded upon the viewer's brain, it builds there not an objective model of nature, but a biased reality meant to coerce its victim into buying, voting or thinking as he otherwise would not. TV, they say, actually transfers power from the viewer to the manipulator behind the screen. Admen, politicians and revivalists spend billions of dollars annually to ensure the steady flow of power and money in their direction.

There's no disputing that the media men attempt this kind of manipulation. But do they succeed? The billions spent on TV hucksterism in an attempt to control the viewers are a tribute to a stubborn and unpredictable mental resistance. The most successful media experts have about a fifty-fifty chance of electing their political clients to office, and the most effective advertising campaigns are not the ones that change people's

minds but the ones that reinforce an interpretation of the world already
held. The sense of power engendered by TV is stronger and more durable
than the critics imagine.

That sense of power grows largely from the artlessness of the medium.
With much justice its critics have accused TV of destroying art, though
the reasons given in support of this charge are usually so much sociological babble. The charge is true to this extent: traditionally art has given
us the world as remade in the imagination of the artist. Art asks us to
accept and interpret the world from someone else's perspective. TV moves
in the other direction to remove the mediation of artistic imagination. TV
is most successful when it re-creates the world of common sense, or rather
when it allows us to reconstitute and interpret this world for ourselves
without the artistic middleman we encounter in a book or a film or a play.
If the cameraman is doing his job, if the producers and technicians are
on the ball, we will know whether Kay caught the pass with as much
certainty as we know the sky is blue or the ground is hard. As for the rest
of the game, the part not subject to instant replay, we are free to interpret
as we will.

The freedom TV gives in its coverage of sports or public events is, with
appropriate modifications, also present in its entertainment programming. Compare the conventions of television viewing with those of theater
or film. A trip to a play or a movie is special. Most of us will sit still for
two hours even if we don't like what we're seeing. With varying degrees
of delight or reluctance we surrender to the darkness and the community
around us. But there's nothing special about TV. It is by nature relentlessly ordinary. The game show *Wheel of Fortune* plays in 210 markets
nationwide and has a larger audience share than *Miami Vice.* Are its
viewers powerless swine who have surrendered their freedom to the
show's space-age Circe, Vanna White? Is the audience for *Wheel of Fortune* sitting in front of the TV with the same mental engagement they
would lavish, if only they were better educated, on a Royal Shakespeare
Company production of *King Lear?* Some probably are. Others are ignoring the set completely. Domestic types are cooking or cleaning as they
watch. Gossips are studying Vanna's wardrobe. The working classes have
drifted off to sleep on the couch. Sardonic teen-agers are howling with
mirth at the whole thing, while in the old-age home grandmothers are
playing along as the contestants buy a vowel to spell out the hidden
phrase, "Much to My Chagrin." The improbable rise to stardom of the
unprepossessing Vanna White is itself proof that the audience acts with
an inscrutable freedom that is rarely appreciated when TV viewing is
reduced to ratings or to sociological analysis. The viewer's freedom may
be no more wisely employed than any other freedom he or she enjoys, but
if he or she wastes time on *Jeopardy* or *Moonlighting,* these choices are
not less free for being uncouth to more sublime tastes.

Audiences gravitate to programming with a crude base in some shared

reality and enough lack of artistic direction to allow for individual interpretation. The closer TV approaches the eccentric creations of unique
artistic imagination, the less successful it becomes. So the critics are right.
TV destroys artistic imagination. It does not follow that TV destroys all
imagination. By substituting crude reality for artistic mediation, TV
delivers its largely unrefined materials to the imagination of the viewer.
TV is certainly not a medium inflicted on its passive viewers but a form
that allows the viewer to take a projected reality and make it his own. The
success or failure of TV depends less than any other medium's on the
artistry of the producer and more on the creativity of the audience. This
is precisely what disturbs its critics, whose premise, stated or not, is that
the mass audience has no creativity.

On the Function of Art

People have been debating what it is that artists do, and whether it is important, at least since Plato's day. Artists have commented variously, sometimes with sublime incoherence, but occasionally with a resonant authority that is theirs alone. We present here a philosopher, a political leader, and ten writers—some of them acknowledged literary artists—all of whom share the conviction that art is important, though for various reasons.

The first three essays are concerned with the relationship between art and truth, art and reality. The philosopher, Susanne K. Langer, stresses the role of art in the rendering of imagination and feeling, of subjective reality: "the arts . . . give form to inward experiences and thus make them conceivable." As if to illustrate this very point, John Berger tries to show how Vincent van Gogh's paintings, indeed the sense of his action of painting them, constitutes "the production of [a] world" that somehow dispels the viewer's feelings of disconnection from reality. In the next essay, the novelist John Updike, not quite satirically, compares the fading old art of writing to the dominant new art of the television commercial, and he reflects modestly on the former art's superior freedom to tell the truth.

The two essays following take up the issue of art as political expression. Can the artist serve political ends and still be an artist? For Communist leader Mao Zedong this is no problem at all; in fact he demands the "unity of politics and art," and specifically asks "revolutionary artists" to expose "all dark forces which endanger the masses of the people . . . while all revolutionary struggles of the masses must be praised." The issue is one that is continually raised by minority groups who object to the portrayal of their members in an unfavorable light. The black writer W. E. B. Du Bois comes out, however, for artistic freedom, preferring "the Eternal Beauty that shines through all Truth."

Anthony Burgess and William Geist take up yet another issue: how do we decide what *is* art? Burgess offers a lively diatribe on the self-appointed artist, and the art without craftsmanship. Geist, almost deadpan, asks us to examine the rationale of the mass-produced "original oil painting;" if the painter doesn't care about it, and if the painting is bought because it matches the wallpaper, is it art?

We conclude with four poems on art—two on art and artifacts and two specifically on the art of poetry—in which the reader may test Henri Matisse's remark that "the best explanation an artist can give of his aims and ability is afforded by his work."

The Cultural Importance of Art

Susanne K. Langer

Originally a lecture delivered at Syracuse University, this essay was first published in Aesthetic Form and Education *(ed. M. F. Andrews, 1958). It later appeared as Chapter 5 in Susanne K. Langer's* Philosophical Sketches *(1962), and it is this text which we reprint below. For information about the author and her writings, see page 118.*

Every culture develops some kind of art as surely as it develops language. Some primitive cultures have no real mythology or religion, but all have some art—dance, song, design (sometimes only on tools or on the human body). Dance, above all, seems to be the oldest elaborated art.

The ancient ubiquitous character of art contrasts sharply with the prevalent idea that art is a luxury product of civilization, a cultural frill, a piece of social veneer.

It fits better with the conviction held by most artists, that art is the epitome of human life, the truest record of insight and feeling, and that the strongest military or economic society without art is poor in comparison with the most primitive tribe of savage painters, dancers, or idol carvers. Wherever a society has really achieved culture (in the ethnological sense, not the popular sense of "social form") it has begotten art, not late in its career, but at the very inception of it.

Art is, indeed, the spearhead of human development, social and individual. The vulgarization of art is the surest symptom of ethnic decline. The growth of a new art or even a great and radically new style always bespeaks a young and vigorous mind, whether collective or single.

What sort of thing is art, that it should play such a leading role in human development? It is not an intellectual pursuit, but is necessary to intellectual life; it is not religion, but grows up with religion, serves it, and in large measure determines it.

We cannot enter here on a long discussion of what has been claimed as the essence of art, the true nature of art, or its defining function; in a single lecture dealing with one aspect of art, namely its cultural influence, I can only give you by way of preamble my own definition of art, with categorical brevity. This does not mean that I set up this definition in a categorical spirit, but only that we have no time to debate it; so you are asked to accept it as an assumption underlying these reflections.

Art, in the sense here intended—that is, the generic term subsuming painting, sculpture, architecture, music, dance, literature, drama, and film—may be defined as the practice of creating perceptible forms expressive of human feeling. I say "perceptible" rather than "sensuous" forms because some works of art are given to imagination rather than to the outward senses. A novel, for instance, usually is read silently with the eye, but is not made for vision, as a painting is; and though sound plays a vital part in poetry, words even in poetry are not essentially sonorous structures like music. Dance requires to be seen, but its appeal is to deeper centers of sensation. The difference between dance and mobile sculpture makes this immediately apparent. But all works of art are purely perceptible forms that seem to embody some sort of feeling.

"Feeling" as I am using it here covers much more than it does in the technical vocabulary of psychology, where it denotes only pleasure and displeasure, or even in the shifting limits of ordinary discourse, where it sometimes means sensation (as when one says a paralyzed limb has no feeling in it), sometimes sensibility (as we speak of hurting someone's feelings), sometimes emotion (e.g., as a situation is said to harrow your feelings, or to evoke tender feeling), or a directed emotional attitude (we say we feel strongly *about* something), or even our general mental or physical condition, feeling well or ill, blue, or a bit above ourselves. As I use the word, in defining art as the creation of perceptible forms expressive of human feeling, it takes in all those meanings; it applies to everything that may be felt.

Another word in the definition that might be questioned is "creation." I think it is justified, not pretentious, as perhaps it sounds, but that issue is slightly beside the point here; so let us shelve it. If anyone prefers to speak of the "making" or "construction" of expressive forms, that will do here just as well.

What does have to be understood is the meaning of "form," and more particularly "expressive form"; for that involves the very nature of art and therefore the question of its cultural importance.

The word "form" has several current uses; most of them have some relation to the sense in which I am using it here, though a few, such as "a form to be filled in for tax purposes" or "a mere matter of form," are fairly remote, being quite specialized. Since we are speaking of art, it might be good to point out that the meaning of stylistic pattern—"the sonata form," "the sonnet form"—is not the one I am assuming here.

I am using the word in a simpler sense, which it has when you say, on a foggy night, that you see dimly moving forms in the mist; one of them emerges clearly, and is the form of a man. The trees are gigantic forms; the rills of rain trace sinuous forms on the windowpane. The rills are not fixed things; they are forms of motion. When you watch gnats weaving in the air, or flocks of birds wheeling overhead, you see dynamic forms— forms made by motion.

It is in this sense of an apparition given to our perception that a work of art is a form. It may be a permanent form like a building or a vase or a picture, or a transient, dynamic form like a melody or a dance, or even a form given to imagination, like the passage of purely imaginary, apparent events that constitutes a literary work. But it is always a perceptible, self-identical whole; like a natural being, it has a character of organic unity, self-sufficiency, individual reality. And it is thus, as an appearance, that a work of art is good or bad or perhaps only rather poor—as an appearance, not as a comment on things beyond it in the world, or as a reminder of them.

This, then, is what I mean by "form"; but what is meant by calling such forms "expressive of human feeling"? How do apparitions "express" anything—feeling or anything else? First of all, let us ask just what is meant here by "express," what sort of "expression" we are talking about.

The word "expression" has two principal meanings. In one sense it means self-expression—giving vent to our feelings. In this sense it refers to a symptom of what we feel. Self-expression is a spontaneous reaction to an actual, present situation, an event, the company we are in, things people say, or what the weather does to us; it bespeaks the physical and mental state we are in and the emotions that stir us.

In another sense, however, "expression" means the presentation of an idea, usually by the proper and apt use of words. But a device for presenting an idea is what we call a symbol, not a symptom. Thus a word is a symbol, and so is a meaningful combination of words.

A sentence, which is a special combination of words, expresses the idea of some state of affairs, real or imagined. Sentences are complicated symbols. Language will formulate new ideas as well as communicate old ones, so that all people know a lot of things that they have merely heard or read about. Symbolic expression, therefore, extends our knowledge beyond the scope of our actual experience.

If an idea is clearly conveyed by means of symbols we say it is well expressed. A person may work for a long time to give his statement the best possible form, to find the exact words for what he means to say, and to carry his account or his argument most directly from one point to another. But a discourse so worked out is certainly not a spontaneous reaction. Giving expression to an idea is obviously a different thing from giving expression to feelings. You do not say of a man in a rage that his anger is well expressed. The symptoms just are what they are; there is no critical standard for symptoms. If, on the other hand, the angry man tries to tell you what he is fuming about, he will have to collect himself, curtail his emotional expression, and find words to express his ideas. For to tell a story coherently involves "expression" in quite a different sense: this sort of expression is not "self-expression," but may be called "conceptual expression."

Language, of course, is our prime instrument of conceptual expression. The things we can say are in effect the things we can think. Words are the terms of our thinking as well as the terms in which we present our thoughts, because they present the objects of thought to the thinker himself. Before language communicates ideas, it gives them form, makes them clear, and in fact makes them what they are. Whatever has a name is an object for thought. Without words, sense experience is only a flow of impressions, as subjective as our feelings; words make it objective, and carve it up into *things* and *facts* that we can note, remember, and think about. Language gives outward experience its form, and makes it definite and clear.

There is, however, an important part of reality that is quite inaccessible to the formative influence of language: that is the realm of so-called "inner experience," the life of feeling and emotion. The reason why language is so powerless here is not, as many people suppose, that feeling and emotion are irrational; on the contrary, they seem irrational because language does not help to make them conceivable, and most people cannot conceive anything without the logical scaffolding of words. The unfitness of language to convey subjective experience is a somewhat technical subject, easier for logicians to understand than for artists; but the gist of it is that the form of language does not reflect the natural form of feeling, so that we cannot shape any extensive concepts of feeling with the help of ordinary, discursive language. Therefore the words whereby we refer to feeling only name very general kinds of inner experience—excitement, calm, joy, sorrow, love, hate, and so on. But there is no language to describe just how one joy differs, sometimes radically, from another. The real nature of feeling is something language as such—as discursive symbolism—cannot render.

For this reason, the phenomena of feeling and emotion are usually treated by philosophers as irrational. The only pattern discursive thought can find in them is the pattern of outward events that occasion them. There are different degrees of fear, but they are thought of as so many degrees of the same simple feeling.

But human feeling is a fabric, not a vague mass. It has an intricate dynamic pattern, possible combinations and new emergent phenomena. It is a pattern of organically interdependent and interdetermined tensions and resolutions, a pattern of almost infinitely complex activation and cadence. To it belongs the whole gamut of our sensibility—the sense of straining thought, all mental attitude and motor set. Those are the deeper reaches that underlie the surface waves of our emotion, and make human life a life of feeling instead of an unconscious metabolic existence interrupted by feelings.

It is, I think, this dynamic pattern that finds its formal expression in the arts. The expressiveness of art is like that of a symbol, not that of an emotional symptom; it is as a formulation of feeling for our conception that a work of art is properly said to be expressive. It may serve somebody's need of self-expression besides, but that is not what makes it good or bad art. In a special sense one may call a work of art a symbol of feeling, for, like a symbol, it formulates our ideas of inward experience, as discourse formulates our ideas of things and facts in the outside world. A work of art differs from a genuine symbol—that is, a symbol in the full and usual sense—in that it does not point beyond itself to something else. Its relation to feeling is a rather special one that we cannot undertake to analyze here; in effect, the feeling it expresses appears to be directly given with it—as the sense of a true metaphor, or the value of a religious myth—and is not separable from its expression. We speak of the feeling *of,* or the feeling *in,* a work of art, not the feeling it means. And we speak truly; a work of art presents something like a direct vision of vitality, emotion, subjective reality.

The primary function of art is to objectify feeling so that we can contemplate and understand it. It is the formulation of so-called "inward experience," the "inner life," that is impossible to achieve by discursive thought, because its forms are incommensurable with the forms of language and all its derivatives (e.g., mathematics, symbolic logic). Art objectifies the sentience and desire, self-consciousness and world-consciousness, emotions and moods, that are generally regarded as irrational because words cannot give us clear ideas of them. But the premise tacitly assumed in such a judgment—namely, that anything language cannot express is formless and irrational—seems to me to be an error. I believe the life of feeling is not irrational; its logical forms are merely very different from the structures of discourse. But they are so much like the dynamic forms of art that art is their natural symbol. Through plastic works, music, fiction, dance, or dramatic forms we can conceive what vitality and emotion feel like.

This brings us, at last, to the question of the cultural importance of the arts. Why is art so apt to be the vanguard of cultural advance, as it was in Egypt, in Greece, in Christian Europe (think of Gregorian music and Gothic architecture), in Renaissance Italy—not to speculate about ancient cavemen, whose art is all that we know of them? One thinks of culture as economic increase, social organization, the gradual ascendancy of rational thinking and scientific control of nature over superstitious imagination and magical practices. But art is not practical; it is neither philosophy nor science; it is not religion, morality, or even social comment (as many drama critics take comedy to be). What does it contribute to culture that could be of major importance?

It merely presents forms—sometimes intangible forms—to imagination. Its direct appeal is to that faculty, or function, that Lord Bacon° considered the chief stumbling block in the way of reason, and that enlightened writers like Stuart Chase° never tire of condemning as the source of all nonsense and bizarre erroneous beliefs. And so it is; but it is also the source of all insight and true beliefs. Imagination is probably the oldest mental trait that is typically human—older than discursive reason; it is probably the common source of dream, reason, religion, and all true general observation. It is this primitive human power—imagination—that engenders the arts and is in turn directly affected by their products.

Somewhere at the animalian starting line of human evolution lie the beginnings of that supreme instrument of the mind—language. We think of it as a device for communication among the members of a society. But communication is only one, and perhaps not even the first, of its functions. The first thing it does is to break up what William James called the "blooming, buzzing confusion" of sense perception into units and groups, events and chains of events—things and relations, causes and effects. All these patterns are imposed on our experience by language. We think, as we speak, in terms of objects and their relations.

But the process of breaking up our sense experience in this way, making reality conceivable, memorable, sometimes even predictable, is a process of imagination. Primitive conception is imagination. Language and imagination grow up together in a reciprocal tutelage.

What discursive symbolism—language in its literal use—does for our awareness of things about us and our own relation to them, the arts do for our awareness of subjective reality, feeling and emotion; they give form to inward experiences and thus make them conceivable. The only way we can really envisage vital movement, the stirring and growth and passage of emotion, and ultimately the whole direct sense of human life, is in artistic terms. A musical person thinks of emotions musically. They

---

Lord Bacon Francis Bacon (1561–1626), English essayist and philosopher.
Stuart Chase Prolific American author of social commentary (1888–1985).

cannot be discursively talked about above a very general level. But they may nonetheless be known—objectively set forth, publicly known—and there is nothing necessarily confused or formless about emotions.

As soon as the natural forms of subjective experience are abstracted to the point of symbolic presentation, we can use those forms to imagine feeling and understand its nature. Self-knowledge, insight into all phases of life and mind, springs from artistic imagination. That is the cognitive value of the arts.

But their influence on human life goes deeper than the intellectual level. As language actually gives form to our sense experience, grouping our impressions around those things which have names, and fitting sensations to the qualities that have adjectival names, and so on, the arts we live with—our picture books and stories and the music we hear—actually form our emotive experience. Every generation has its styles of feeling. One age shudders and blushes and faints, another swaggers, still another is godlike in a universal indifference. These styles in actual emotion are not insincere. They are largely unconscious—determined by many social causes, but *shaped* by artists, usually popular artists of the screen, the jukebox, the shop window, and the picture magazine. (That, rather than incitement to crime, is my objection to the comics.) Irwin Edman remarks in one of his books that our emotions are largely Shakespeare's poetry.

This influence of art on life gives us an indication of why a period of efflorescence in the arts is apt to lead a cultural advance: it formulates a new way of feeling, and that is the beginning of a cultural age. It suggests another matter for reflection, too—that a wide neglect of artistic education is a neglect in the education of feeling. Most people are so imbued with the idea that feeling is a formless, total organic excitement in men as in animals that the idea of educating feeling, developing its scope and quality, seems odd to them, if not absurd. It is really, I think, at the very heart of personal education.

There is one other function of the arts that benefits not so much the advance of culture as its stabilization—an influence on individual lives. This function is the converse and complement of the objectification of feeling, the driving force of creation in art: it is the education of vision that we receive in seeing, hearing, reading works of art—the development of the artist's eye, that assimilates ordinary sights (or sounds, motions, or events) to inward vision, and lends expressiveness and emotional import to the world. Wherever art takes a motif from actuality—a flowering branch, a bit of landscape, a historic event, or a personal memory, any model or theme from life—it transforms it into a piece of imagination, and imbues its image with artistic vitality. The result is an impregnation of ordinary reality with the significance of created form. This is the subjectification of nature that makes reality itself a symbol of life and feeling.

The arts objectify subjective reality, and subjectify outward experience of nature. Art education is the education of feeling, and a society that neglects it gives itself up to formless emotion. Bad art is corruption of feeling. This is a large factor in the irrationalism which dictators and demagogues exploit.

The Production of
the World

John Berger

John Berger was born in England in 1926, attended art schools in London, and became a painter and teacher of drawing before turning to art criticism and writing. He is now one of the most prominent Marxist critics in the art world, and also well-known as a novelist, essayist, screen writer, and social commentator. Criticism of his work, even when it objects to his political ideology and his uncompromising tone and stance, often praises his imaginative power, his artistic insight, and his capacity to provoke thought. His writings include G *(a novel, 1972),* The Moment of Cubism, and Other Essays *(1969),* Ways of Seeing *(1972),* A Seventh Man: Migrant Workers in Europe *(1975), and* My Heart, Brief as Photos (1984). *The essay following was written in 1983 and included in* The Sense of Sight: Writings by John Berger, *ed. Lloyd Spencer (1985).*

I no longer know how many times I have arrived at the Central Station in Amsterdam, nor how many times I have been to the Rijksmuseum to look at Vermeer or Fabritius or van Gogh. The first time must have been nearly thirty years ago, and during the last seven years I have been to Amsterdam systematically every six months to attend meetings of the Transnational Institute, of which I am a fellow.

I come away from each meeting where twenty or so fellows from the Third World, the United States, Latin America, Britain and the Continent discuss aspects of the world situation within a socialist perspective— I come away each time a little less ignorant and more determined. By now we all know each other well and when we reassemble it is like a team coming together; sometimes we win, sometimes we are beaten. Each time we find ourselves battling against false representations of the world— either those of ruling-class propaganda or those we carry within ourselves.

I owe this Institute a great deal, yet the last time I was due to go to Amsterdam I almost decided not to go. I felt too exhausted. My exhaustion, if I may so put it, was as much metaphysical as physical. I could no longer hold meanings together. The mere thought of making connections filled me with anguish. The only hope was to stay put. Nevertheless at the last minute I went.

It was a mistake. I could scarcely follow anything. The connection between words and what they signified had been broken. It seemed to me that I was lost; the first human power—the power to name—was failing, or had always been an illusion. All was dissolution. I tried joking, lying down, taking a cold shower, drinking coffee, not drinking coffee, talking to myself, imagining faraway places—none of it helped.

I left the building, crossed the street and entered the van Gogh museum, not in order to look at the paintings but because I thought that the one person who could take me home might be there; she was, but before I found her I had to run the gauntlet of the paintings. At this moment, I told myself, you need van Gogh like you need a hole in the head.

'It seems to me not impossible that cholera, gravel,° consumption° may be celestial means of transport just as steamships, buses, railways, are means of transport on this earth. To die quietly of old age would be like going on foot . . .' van Gogh wrote in a letter to his brother, Theo.

Still I found myself glancing at the paintings and then looking at them. 'The Potato Eaters'. 'The Cornfield with a Lark'. 'The Ploughed Field at Auvers'. 'The Pear Tree'. Within two minutes—and for the first time in three weeks—I was calm, reassured. Reality had been confirmed. The transformation was as quick and thoroughgoing as one of those sensational changes that can sometimes come about after an intravenous injection. And yet these paintings, already very familiar to me, had never before manifested anything like this therapeutic power.

What, if anything, does such a subjective experience reveal? What is the connection, if any, between my experience in the van Gogh museum and the life work of van Gogh the painter? I would have been tempted to reply: none or very little, were it not for a strange correspondence. Sometime after my return from Amsterdam I happened to take up a book of stories and essays by Hugo von Hoffmannsthal. Among them is a story entitled 'Letters of a Traveller Come Home'. The 'letters' are dated 1901. The supposed letter-writer is a German businessman who has lived most of his life outside Europe; now that he has returned to his homeland, he increasingly suffers from a sense of unreality; Europeans are not as he remembered them, their lives mean nothing because they systematically compromise.

'As I told you, I cannot grasp them, not by their faces, not by their gestures, not by their words; for their Being is no longer anywhere, indeed they *are* no longer anywhere.'

His disappointment leads him on to question his own memories and

---

gravel   Kidney or bladder stones.
consumption   Tuberculosis.

finally the credibility of anything. In many respects these thirty pages are a kind of prophecy of Sartre's *Nausea,* written thirty years later. This is from the last letter:

> Or again—some trees, those scraggy but well-kept trees which, here and there, have been left in the squares, emerging from the asphalt, protected by railings. I would look at them and I would know that they reminded me of trees—and yet were not trees—and then a shudder, seizing me, would break my breast in two, as though it were the breath, the indescribable breath of everlasting nothingness, of the everlasting nowhere, something which comes, not from death, from non-being.

The final letter also relates how he had to attend a business meeting in Amsterdam. He was feeling spineless, lost, indecisive. On his way there he passed a small art gallery, paused, and decided to go inside.

> How am I to tell you half of what these paintings said to me? They were a total justification of my strange and yet profound feelings. Here suddenly I was in front of something, a mere glimpse of which had previously, in my state of torpor, been too much for me. I had been haunted by that glimpse. Now a total stranger was offering me—with incredible authority—a reply—an entire world in the form of a reply.

The ending of the story is unexpected. Rehabilitated, confirmed, he went on to his meeting and pulled off the best business coup of his entire career.

A PS to the final letter gives the name of the artist in question as being a certain Vincent van Gogh.

What is the nature of this 'entire world' which van Gogh offers 'in the form of a reply' to a particular kind of anguish?

For an animal its natural environment and habitat are a given; for a man—despite the faith of the empiricists—reality is not a given: it has to be continually sought out, held—I am tempted to say *salvaged.* We are taught to oppose the real to the imaginary, as though one were always at hand and the other distant, far away. And this opposition is false. Events are always to hand. But the coherence of these events—which is what we mean by reality—is an imaginative construction. Reality always *lies beyond,* and this is as true for materialists as for idealists, for Plato and for Marx. Reality, however one interprets it, lies beyond a screen of clichés. Every culture produces such a screen, partly to facilitate its own practices (to establish habits) and partly to consolidate its own power. Reality is inimical to those with power.

All modern artists have thought of their innovations as offering a closer approach to reality, as a way of making reality more evident. It is here, and only here, that the modern artist and the revolutionary have sometimes found themselves side by side, both inspired by the idea of pulling down the screen of clichés, clichés which in the modern period have become unprecedentedly trivial and egotistical.

Yet many such artists have reduced what they found beyond the screen, to suit their own talent and social position as artists. When this has happened they have justified themselves with one of the dozen variants of the theory of art for art's sake. They say: reality is art. They hope to extract an artistic profit from reality. Of no one is this less true than van Gogh.

We know from his letters how intensely he was aware of the screen. His whole life story is one of an endless yearning for reality. Colours, the Mediterranean climate, the sun, were for him vehicles going towards this reality; they were never objects of longing in themselves. This yearning was intensified by the crises he suffered when he felt that he was failing to salvage any reality at all. Whether these crises are today diagnosed as being schizophrenic or epileptic changes nothing; their content, as distinct from their pathology, was a vision of reality consuming itself like a phoenix.

We also know from his letters that nothing appeared more sacred to him than work. He saw the physical reality of labour as being, simultaneously, a necessity, an injustice and the essence of humanity to date. The artist's creative act was for him only one among many. He believed that reality could best be approached through work, precisely because reality itself was a form of production.

The paintings speak of this more clearly than words. Their so-called clumsiness, the gestures with which he drew with pigment upon the canvas, the gestures (invisible to us but imaginable) with which he chose and mixed his colours on the palette, all the gestures with which he handled and manufactured the stuff of the painted image, are analogous to the *activity* of the existence of what he is painting. His paintings imitate the active existence—the labour of being—of what they depict.

Take a chair, a bed, a pair of boots. His act of painting them was far nearer than that of any other painter to the carpenter's or the shoemaker's act of making them. He brings together the elements of the product—legs, cross bars, back, seat; sole, uppers tongue, heel—as though he too were fitting them together, *joining* them, and as if this *being joined* constituted their reality.

Before a landscape the process required was far more complicated and mysterious, yet it followed the same principle. If one imagines God creating the world from earth and water, from clay, his way of handling it to make a tree or a cornfield might well resemble the way that van Gogh handled paint when he painted that tree or cornfield. I am not suggesting that there was something quasi-divine about van Gogh: this would be to fall into the worst kind of hagiography. If, however, we think of the creation of the world, we can imagine the act only through the visual evidence, before our eyes here and now, of the energy of the forces in play. And to these energies, van Gogh was terribly—and I choose the adverb carefully—attuned.

When he painted a small pear tree in flower, the act of the sap rising, of the bud forming, the bud breaking, the flower forming, the styles thrusting out, the stigmas becoming sticky, these acts were present for him in the act of painting. When he painted a road, the roadmakers were there in his imagination. When he painted the turned earth of a ploughed field, the gesture of the blade turning the earth was included in his own act. Wherever he looked he saw the labour of existence; and this labour, recognized as such, for him constituted reality.

If he painted his own face, he painted the construction of his destiny, past and future, rather as palmists believe they can read this construction in the hand. His contemporaries who considered him abnormal were not all as stupid as is now assumed. He painted compulsively—no other painter was ever compelled in a comparable way.

His compulsion? It was to bring the two acts of production, that of the canvas and that of the reality depicted, ever closer and closer. This compulsion derived not from an idea about art—this is why it never occurred to him to profit from reality—but from an overwhelming feeling of empathy.

'I admire the bull, the eagle, and man with such an intense adoration, that it will certainly prevent me from ever becoming an ambitious person.'

He was compelled to go ever closer, to approach and approach and approach. *In extremis* he approaches so close that the stars in the night sky became maelstroms of light, the cypress trees ganglions of living wood responding to the energy of wind and sun. There are canvases where reality dissolves him, the painter. But in hundreds of others he takes us as close as any man can, while remaining intact, to that permanent process by which reality is being produced.

Once, long ago, paintings were compared with mirrors. Van Gogh's might be compared with lasers. They do not wait to receive, they go out to meet, and what they traverse is, not so much empty space, as the act of production. The 'entire world' that van Gogh offers as a reply to the vertigo of nothingness is the production of the world. Painting after painting is a way of saying, with awe but little comfort: it works.

The Golden Age of the 30-Second Spot

John Updike

John Updike (born 1932) is one of the best-known of American writers. After graduating from Harvard with highest honors in 1954, he spent a year at art school and two years as a reporter at the New Yorker. *Thereafter followed an uninterrupted flow of poems, stories, novels, book reviews, and essays. Updike is particularly admired for his prose style, and for his capacity to write interestingly about ordinary people and ordinary things. He has defined his subject as "the American Protestant small town middle class"; in response to critics who want more sensational writing, he has replied, "what we need is greater respect for reality, its secrecy, its music." Among the best-known of his novels are* Rabbit, Run *(1960),* The Centaur *(1963),* Couples *(1968),* Rabbit is Rich *(1981), and* The Witches of Eastwick *(1984). Updike's writing has earned him a great many honors and prizes. The following is a speech (from the June 1984* Harper's) *which Updike gave to the National Arts Club on receiving the club's Medal of Honor for Literature.*

One does not have to be a member of an arts club to observe that great art comes in clumps, that there seem times when a culture conspires to produce artists. Greek drama in the Periclean era, Dutch painting in the seventeenth century, Elizabethan poetry, nineteenth-century Russian fiction, German music from Bach to Brahms—such episodes seem waves that lift to sublime heights the individuals lucky enough to be born in the right place and time. The energy and interest of a society focus upon certain forms, and the single, sometimes anonymous artist conducts the gathered heat and light into a completed work. A thousand years ago, crucifixes were foci of fervent attention, and for centuries what men knew of the nude male form and of human agony and dignity sought expression through the crucifix carver's hands. Something of the same concentration attaches to representations of Lenin in the communist world; and a visitor to the Soviet Union must admit that its official painters and sculptors do wonderfully well with the expressive possibilities latent in the image of a short bald man wearing a three-piece suit and a goatee—though this visitor's rapture was slightly dulled, twenty years ago, when he was taken through a Lenin factory, a clattering place where identical busts of the sacred agitator came down an assembly line and where bins were filled with items of this manufacture that had failed, because of a chip or grimace, to meet quality controls.

Now, in our own American culture, it seems clear enough where the highest pitch of artistic energy is focused. After trying to watch the heavily hyped Winter Olympics, I have no doubt that the aesthetic marvels of our age, for intensity and lavishness of effort and subtlety of both overt and subliminal effect, are television commercials. With the fanatic care with which Irish monks once ornamented the Book of Kells, glowing images of youthful beauty and athletic prowess, of racial harmony and exalted fellowship, are herein fluidly marshaled and shuffled to persuade us that a certain beer or candy bar, or insurance company or oil-based conglomerate, is, like the crucified Christ or the defiant Lenin in other times and places, the gateway to the good life. Skills and techniques developed over nearly a century of filmmaking are here brought to a culmination of artistry that spares no expense or trouble; it has been the accomplishment of television to make every living room a cathedral, and to place within it, every six minutes or so, though it seems oftener, votive objects as luxurious and loving as a crucifixion by Grünewald or a pietà by Michelangelo. Our entire lives—our eating, our drinking, our traveling, our conviviality and courtship and family pleasures, our whole magnificent cradle-to-grave *consumption,* in short—are here compressed upon an ideal iconic plane; one can only marvel, and be grateful, and regret that except within narrow professional circles the artists involved, like Anglo-Saxon poets and Paleocene cave-painters, are unknown by name.

What of the rest of us, who huddle with our known names on the sidelines, practicing relatively retrograde and impoverished art forms while this great glowing pillar of multicolored flickering rotates at the hot center of our culture? Well, there are some consolations to being in the shade. It is cooler there, and people can't always see what you are doing. As Aldous Huxley pointed out, the inattention of the powerful is one of the secrets of freedom. Those of us who are riding the inky old print media into its sunset have, like the last threadbare cowboys, a certain grimly jaunty independence. We *may* do what we *can* do, and in our friendly limbo are under no obligation to assert that Coca-Cola is beneficial for not only the physical but the spiritual health of the nation, or that Mobil is watching out for our best interests night and day. We are free in our obscurity to try to tell the truth. Or to raise Pontius Pilate's old question, What is truth? We are free from committee meetings, from story conferences; no banker invades our sound stage in his anxiety to protect his investment, no character refuses to speak the lines we give him. We are free to explore and transmit private sensations; to permit that osmotic permeation of the ego's cell walls that empathy and love and altruism as well as art achieve. In a world where virtue and even the word *virtue* are hard to find, the hand-woven fictional or poetic text offers a boundless field for striving toward the excellent and the pure. Quite wonderfully, it can always be better, and only it matters—only it carries. There is a fair amount of folderol in a writer's life, but the proof, finally and deliciously, is nowhere but in the pudding. So, to be brief, I am well content at my desk, and grateful that the world has allowed me to stay at it. This kind award comes as something extra, which I take as a symbol of society's wish to cheer the writer on in his private task, as a caretaker of sorts, these last few centuries, of all of our cherished and threatened privacies.

from *Talks at the Yenan Forum on Art and Literature*

Mao Zedong

*Mao Zedong was Chairman of the Communist party of the People's Repub-
lic of China and one of the most powerful leaders in the world. He was born
in 1893 to a family of peasant origin. He attended teacher's college at
Changsha, graduated in 1918, then held a variety of jobs: normal-school
teacher, political organizer, editor, and library assistant at Peking University, where he read Karl Marx and deepened his own ideas of a Communist
revolution based on the Chinese peasantry. He was one of the twelve founding members of the Communist party in 1921.*

*With many political and military vicissitudes, Mao made his way to the
head of a movement which successfully wrested China from provincial
warlords, Japanese invaders, and, between 1946 and 1949, from its erstwhile ally, the Kuomintang under President Chiang Kai-shek. Mao's regime had moments of relative liberalism, and also of severe repression of
dissidents, as in the Red Guard cultural revolution of 1962. Its achievements were most notable in the areas of applied medicine, health care,
literacy, and agricultural techniques. Maoist ideology emphasized collective decision-making and open criticism and self-criticism during collective meetings. Mao's theories were considered infallible by masses of
Communist Chinese, until his death in 1976.*

*His most important statements on art and literature were made in two
talks at a forum held at Yenan, his headquarters, in 1942. At the time, the
Communists were allied with the Kuomintang in a war against the invading Japanese. Mao was just instituting a "rectification" program, designed
to tighten party discipline and get rid of undesirable elements. We reprint
here a section from the second of his talks, as found in the fourth volume
of his* Selected Works *(1954–1961).*

One of the principal methods of struggle in the artistic and literary sphere
is art and literary criticism. It should be developed and, as many comrades
have rightly pointed out, our work in this respect was quite inadequate
in the past. Art and literary criticism presents a complex problem which
requires much study of a special kind. Here I shall stress only the basic
problem of criteria in criticism. I shall also comment briefly on certain
other problems and incorrect views brought up by some comrades.

There are two criteria in art and literary criticism: political and artistic. According to the political criterion, all works are good that facilitate
unity and resistance to Japan, that encourage the masses to be of one
heart and one mind and that oppose retrogression and promote progress;

on the other hand, all works are bad that undermine unity and resistance to Japan, that sow dissension and discord among the masses and that oppose progress and drag the people back. And how can we tell the good from the bad here—by the motive (subjective intention) or by the effect (social practice)? Idealists stress motive and ignore effect, while mechanical materialists stress effect and ignore motive; in contradistinction from either, we dialectical materialists insist on the unity of motive and effect. The motive of serving the masses is inseparable from the effect of winning their approval, and we must unite the two. The motive of serving the individual or a small clique is not good, nor is the motive of serving the masses good if it does not lead to a result that is welcomed by the masses and confers benefit on them. In examining the subjective intention of an artist, *i.e.* whether his motive is correct and good, we do not look at his declaration but at the effect his activities (mainly his works) produce on society and the masses. Social practice and its effect are the criteria for examining the subjective intention or the motive. We reject sectarianism in our art and literary criticism and, under the general principle of unity and resistance to Japan, we must tolerate all artistic and literary works expressing every kind of political attitude. But at the same time we must firmly uphold our principles in our criticism, and adhere to our standpoint and severely criticise and repudiate all artistic and literary works containing views against the nation, the sciences, the people and communism, because such works, in motive as well as in effect, are detrimental to unity and the resistance to Japan. According to the artistic criterion, all works are good or comparatively good that are relatively high in artistic quality; and bad or comparatively bad that are relatively low in artistic quality. Of course, this distinction also depends on social effect. As there is hardly an artist who does not consider his own work excellent, our criticism ought to permit the free competition of all varieties of artistic works; but it is entirely necessary for us to pass correct judgments on them according to the criteria of the science of art, so that we can gradually raise the art of a lower level to a higher level, and to change the art which does not meet the requirements of the struggle of the broad masses into art that does meet them.

There is thus the political criterion as well as the artistic criterion. How are the two related? Politics is not the equivalent of art, nor is a general world outlook equivalent to the method of artistic creation and criticism. We believe there is neither an abstract and absolutely unchangeable political criterion, nor an abstract and absolutely unchangeable artistic criterion, for every class in a class society has its own political and artistic criteria. But all classes in all class societies place the political criterion first and the artistic criterion second. The bourgeoisie always rejects proletarian artistic and literary works, no matter how great their artistic achievement. As for the proletariat, they must treat the art and literature of the past according to their attitude towards the people and whether they are progressive in the light of history. Some things which are basically reactionary from the political point of view may yet be artistically good. But the more artistic such a work may be, the greater harm will it do to the people, and the more reason for us to reject it. The contradiction between reactionary political content and artistic form is a common characteristic of the art and literature of all exploiting classes in their decline. What we demand is unity of politics and art, of content and form, and of the revolutionary political content and the highest possible degree of perfection in artistic form. Works of art, however politically progressive, are powerless if they lack artistic quality. Therefore we are equally opposed to works with wrong political approaches and to the tendency towards so-called "poster and slogan style" which is correct only in political approach but lacks artistic power. We must carry on a two-front struggle in art and literature.

Both tendencies can be found in the ideologies of many of our comrades. Those comrades who tend to neglect artistic quality should pay attention to its improvement. But as I see it, the political side is more of a problem at present. Some comrades lack elementary political knowledge and consequently all kinds of muddled ideas arise. Let me give a few instances found in Yenan.

"The theory of human nature." Is there such a thing as human nature? Of course there is. But there is only human nature in the concrete, no human nature in the abstract. In a class society there is only human nature that bears the stamp of a class, but no human nature transcending classes. We uphold the human nature of the proletariat and of the great masses of the people, while the landlord and bourgeois classes uphold the nature of their own classes as if—though they do not say so outright—it were the only kind of human nature. The human nature boosted by certain petty-bourgeois intellectuals is also divorced from or opposed to that of the great masses of the people; what they call human nature is in substance nothing but bourgeois individualism, and consequently in their eyes proletarian human nature is contrary to their human nature. This is the "theory of human nature" advocated by some people in Yenan as the so-called basis of their theory of art and literature, which is utterly mistaken.

"The fundamental point of departure for art and literature is love, the love of mankind." Now love may serve as a point of departure, but there is still a more basic one. Love is a concept, a product of objective practice. Fundamentally, we do not start from a concept but from objective practice. Our artists and writers who come from the intelligentsia love the proletariat because social life has made them feel that they share the same fate with the proletariat. We hate Japanese imperialism because the Japanese imperialists oppress us. There is no love or hatred in the world that has not its cause. As to the so-called "love of mankind", there has been no such all-embracing love since humanity was divided into classes. All the ruling classes in the past liked to advocate it, and many so-called sages and wise men also did the same, but nobody has ever really practised it, for it is impracticable in a class society. Genuine love of mankind will be born only when class distinctions have been eliminated throughout the world. The classes have caused the division of society into many opposites and as soon as they are eliminated there will be love of all mankind, but not now. We cannot love our enemies, we cannot love social evils, and our aim is to exterminate them. How can our artists and writers fail to understand such a common sense matter?

"Art and literature have always described the bright as well as the dark side of things impartially, on a fifty-fifty basis." This statement contains a number of muddled ideas. Art and literature have not always done so. Many petty-bourgeois writers have never found the bright side and their works are devoted to exposing the dark side, the so-called "literature of exposure"; there are even works which specialise in propagating pessimism and misanthropy. On the other hand, Soviet literature during the period of socialist reconstruction portrays mainly the bright side. It also describes shortcomings in work and villainous characters, but such descriptions serve only to bring out the brightness of the whole picture, and not on a "compensating basis". Bourgeois writers of reactionary periods portray the revolutionary masses as ruffians and describe the bourgeois as saints, thus reversing the so-called bright and dark sides. Only truly revolutionary artists and writers can correctly solve the problem whether to praise or to expose. All dark forces which endanger the masses of the people must be exposed while all revolutionary struggles of the masses must be praised—this is the basic task of all revolutionary artists and writers.

"The task of art and literature has always been to expose." This sort of argument, like the one mentioned above, arises from the lack of knowledge of the science of history. We have already shown that the task of art and literature does not consist solely in exposure. For the revolutionary artists and writers the objects to be exposed can never be the masses of the people, but only the aggressors, exploiters and oppressors and their evil aftermath brought to the people. The people have their shortcomings too, but these are to be overcome by means of criticism and self-criticism within the ranks of the people themselves, and to carry on such criticism and self-criticism is also one of the most important tasks of art and literature. However, we should not call that "exposing the people". As for the people, our problem is basically one of how to educate them and raise their level. Only counter-revolutionary artists and writers describe the people as "born fools" and the revolutionary masses as "tyrannical mobs".

"This is still a period of the essay, and the style should still be that of Lu Hsun."⁰ Living under the rule of the dark forces, deprived of free-

---

Lu Hsun Pseudonym of Chou Shu-jen (1881–1936), revered author of essays and fiction. He supported the Chinese Communists, though he did not join the Communist party.

dom of speech, Lu Hsun had to fight by means of burning satire and freezing irony cast in essay form, and in this he was entirely correct. We too must hold up to sharp ridicule the fascists, the Chinese reactionaries and everything endangering the people; but in our border region of Shensi-Kansu-Ningsia and the anti-Japanese base areas in the enemy's rear, where revolutionary artists and writers are given full freedom and democracy and only counter-revolutionaries are deprived of them, essays must not be written simply in the same style as Lu Hsun's. Here we can shout at the top of our voice, and need not resort to obscure and veiled expressions which would tax the understanding of the broad masses of the people. In dealing with the people themselves and not the enemies of the people, Lu Hsun even in his "essay period" did not mock or attack the revolutionary masses and the revolutionary parties, and his style was also entirely different from that employed in his essays on the enemy. We have already said that we must criticise the shortcomings of the people, but be sure that we criticise from the standpoint of the people and out of a whole-hearted eagerness to defend and educate them. If we treat our comrades like enemies, then we are taking the standpoint of the enemy. Are we then to give up satire altogether? No. Satire is always necessary. But there are all kinds of satire; the kind for our enemies, the kind for our allies and the kind for our own ranks— each of them assumes a different attitude. We are not opposed to satire as a whole, but we must not abuse it.

"I am not given to praise and eulogy; works which extol the bright side of things are not necessarily great, nor are works which depict the dark side necessarily poor." If you are a bourgeois artist or writer, you will extol not the proletariat but the bourgeoisie, and if you are a proletarian artist or writer, you will extol not the bourgeoisie but the proletariat and the working people: you must do one or the other. Those works which extol the bright side of the bourgeoisie are not necessarily great while those which depict its dark side are not necessarily poor, and those works which extol the bright side of the proletariat are not necessarily poor, while those works which depict the so-called "dark side" of the proletariat are certainly poor—are these not facts recorded in the history of art and literature? Why should we not extol the people, the creator of the history of the human world? Why should we not extol the proletariat, the Communist Party, the New Democracy and socialism? Of course, there are persons who have no enthusiasm for the people's cause and stand aloof, looking with cold indifference on the struggle and the victory of the proletariat and its vanguard; and they only take pleasure in singing endless praises of themselves, plus perhaps a few persons in their own coterie. Such petty-bourgeois individualists are naturally unwilling to praise the meritorious deeds of the revolutionary masses or to heighten their courage in struggle and confidence in victory. Such people are the black sheep in the revolutionary ranks and the revolutionary masses have indeed no use for such "singers".

"It is not a matter of standpoint; the standpoint is correct, the intention good, and the ideas are all right, but the expression is faulty and produces a bad effect." I have already spoken about the dialectical materialistic view of motive and effect, and now I want to ask: Is the question of effect not one of standpoint? A person who, in doing a job, minds only the motive and pays no regard to the effect, is very much like a doctor who hands out prescriptions and does not care how many patients may die of them. Suppose, again, a political party keeps on making pronouncements while paying not the least attention to carrying them out. We may well ask, is such a standpoint correct? Are such intentions good? Of course, a person is liable to mistakes in estimating the result of an action before it is taken; but are his intentions really good if he adheres to the same old rut even when facts prove that it leads to bad results? In judging a party or a doctor, we must look at the practice and the effect, and the same applies in judging an artist or a writer. One who has a truly good intention must take the effect into consideration by summing up experiences and study-ing methods or, in the case of creative work, the means of expression. One who has a truly good intention must criticise with the utmost candour his own shortcomings and mistakes in work, and make up his mind to correct them. That is why the Communists have adopted the method of self-criticism. Only such a standpoint is the correct one. At the same time it is only through such a process of practice carried out conscientiously and responsibly that we can gradually understand what the correct point of view is and have a firm grasp of it. If we refuse to do this in practice, then we are really ignorant of the correct point of view, despite our conceited assertion to the contrary.

"To call on us to study Marxism may again lead us to take the repetition of dialectical materialist formulas for literary creation, and this will stifle our creative impulse." We study Marxism in order to apply the dialectical materialist and historical materialist viewpoint in our observation of the world, society and art and literature, and not in order to write philosophi-cal discourses in our works of art and literature. Marxism embraces realism in artistic and literary creation but cannot replace it, just as it embraces atomics and electronics in physics but cannot replace them. Empty, cut-and-dried dogmas and formulas will certainly destroy our creative impulse; moreover, they first of all destroy Marxism. Dogmatic "Marxism" is not Marxist but anti-Marxist. But will Marxism not destroy any creative impulse? It will; it will certainly destroy the creative impulse that is feudal, bourgeois, petty-bourgeois, liberal, individualistic, nihilis-tic, art-for-art's-sake, aristocratic, decadent or pessimistic, and any crea-tive impulse that is not of the people and of the proletariat. As far as the artists and writers of the proletariat are concerned, ought not these kinds of impulse to be done away with? I think they ought; they should be utterly destroyed, and while they are being destroyed, new things can be built up.

Negro Art (1921)

W. E. B. Du Bois

W. E. B. Du Bois (1868–1963) was a political activist, an intellectual, and a writer who became one of the great black leaders in the twentieth century. He was educated at Fisk University, at the University of Berlin, and at Harvard University, where he received a Ph.D. in 1895. Until 1910, he served as Professor of Economics and History at Atlanta University.

Du Bois was one of the founders of the National Association for the Advancement of Colored People and, as its director of Publicity and Research, he created the periodical Crisis. *For the twenty-five years of his editorship he sought to influence public opinion, especially among his black readers. "Oppression" he wrote, "costs the oppressor too much if the oppressed stand up and protest." He urged his readers to "protest, reveal the truth and refuse to be silenced." The editorial below, originally published in* Crisis, *June 1921, is reprinted from* W. E. B. Du Bois: A Reader, *edited by Meyer Weinberg (1970).*

Negro art is today plowing a difficult row, chiefly because we shrink at the portrayal of the truth about ourselves. We are so used to seeing the truth distorted to our despite, that whenever we are portrayed on canvas, in story or on the stage, as simply human with human frailties, we rebel. We want everything that is said about us to tell of the best and highest and noblest in us. We insist that our Art and Propaganda be one.

This is wrong and in the end it is harmful. We have a right, in our effort to get just treatment, to insist that we produce something of the best in human character and that it is unfair to judge us by our criminals and prostitutes. This is justifiable propaganda.

On the other hand we face the Truth of Art. We have criminals and prostitutes, ignorant and debased elements, just as all folk have. When the artist paints us he has a right to paint us whole and not ignore everything which is not as perfect as we would wish it to be. The black Shakespeare must portray his black Iagos as well as his white Othellos.

We shrink from this. We fear that evil in us will be called racial, while in others it is viewed as individual. We fear that our shortcomings are not merely human but foreshadowings and threatenings of disaster and failure. The more highly trained we become the less can we laugh at Negro comedy—we will have it all tragedy and the triumph of dark Right over pale Villainy.

The results are not merely negative—they are positively bad. With a vast wealth of human material about us, our own writers and artists fear to paint the truth lest they criticize their own and be in turn criticized for it. They fail to see the Eternal Beauty that shines through all Truth, and try to portray a world of stilted artificial black folk such as never were on land or sea.

Thus, the white artist, looking in on the colored world, if he be wise and discerning, may often see the beauty, tragedy and comedy more truly than we dare. Of course if he be simply a shyster like Tom Dixon [*The Clansman,* 1905], he will see only exaggerated evil, and fail as utterly in the other extreme as we in ours. But if, like [Edward] Sheldon, he writes a fine true work of art like *The Nigger* [1909]; or like Ridgely Torrence, a beautiful comedy like *The Rider of Dreams* [1917]; or like Eugene O'Neill, a splendid tragedy like *The Emperor Jones* [1920]—he finds to his own consternation the Negroes and even educated Negroes, shrinking or openly condemning.

Sheldon's play has repeatedly been driven from the stage by ill-advised Negroes who objected to its name; Torrence's plays were received by educated blacks with no great enthusiasm; and only yesterday a protest of colored folk in a western city declared that *"The Emperor Jones* is the kind of play that should never be staged under any circumstances, regardless of theories, because it portrays the worst traits of the bad element of both races."

No more complete misunderstanding of this play or of the aim of Art could well be written, although the editor of the *Century* and *Current Opinion* showed almost equal obtuseness.

Nonsense. We stand today secure enough in our accomplishment and self-confidence to lend the whole stern human truth about ourselves to the transforming hand and seeing eye of the Artist, white and black, and Sheldon, Torrence, and O'Neill are our great benefactors—forerunners of artists who will yet arise in Ethiopia of the Outstretched Arm.

A Deadly Sin—
Creativity for All

Anthony Burgess

The following essay is taken from But Do Blondes Prefer Gentlemen? *(1986). For further information about Anthony Burgess, see page 286.*

I was at the University of Nantes recently, and, after I had spoken of the rarity and sanctity of great art, a haired and barefoot pot-smoker said:

'Nous sommes tous des artistes ces jours.'° There was no noise of disagreement save from myself, and I was easily howled down.

That is a growing view and the consequence of misguided democracy. We all have a right to everything, to speak of the greatness of Shakespeare or Mozart is elitism, and we may all wear tee-shirts proclaiming that we went to Princeton or Harvard. Jangle guitar strings and you are ipso facto a musician, daub ordure on canvas and who will deny that you are a painter?, shout alliterative words of protest and you are bound to be a poet.

Some of the debasing of the term art began with the Surrealists, who regarded creation as a form of free association, letting the unconscious speak. Everybody has an unconscious, and one unconscious has as much claim to be heard as another. So if a dustman or car salesman comes out with 'Purple in vestige recoil cabbages derelict from polar outrage,' he is entitled to our attention as much as if he were Tristan Tzara.°

We have abdicated strict aesthetics as much as strict ethics, and nobody is able to say, we are told, what is not art. I think I know what art is—the disposition of natural material to a formal end that shall enlighten the imagination—but many people would say there are too many indefinable terms there, and all we can be sure of is the disposition part. Change things and you are being creative. Change a living organism to a dead one, and you are creating by destroying. The IRA is in the service of the birth of a terrible beauty.° No terrorist or thug would be displeased by the imputation of an aesthetic motive to his acts.

But, at a milder level, we may say that it is a combination of the difficulty of aesthetic definition and the invention of certain machines that has spread the view of the universal availability of creative fulfillment. We are told that there are great photographers, and I have even been photographed by some of them. But I cannot for the life of me see how mere recording can be creation. Ah, I am told, the creative skill lies in the framing of the eye, the balance of chance components, the disposing of light and shadow. This is a matter of *trouvailles,*° I would say, not creation. Find on the beach a salt-eaten stick that looks like a Giacometti and you are not in the presence of art. Blind chance is no artist.

In the days of skiffle you could buy guitars with programmed tonic, dominant and subdominant chords. You can activate Moog synthesizers which will give you massed violins. You can drive a bicycle with paint on

---

Nous sommes tous des artistes ces jours. "We are all artists these days." (French)
Tristan Tzara French poet and essayist (1896–1963); founder of the Dada movement.
birth of a terrible beauty Allusion to "Easter 1916," a poem by William Butler Yeats. The Irish Republican Brotherhood organized a rebellion against the British on Easter Sunday, 1916.
trouvailles windfalls (French).

its wheels over a canvas. It is not a question of saying this is not art but of explaining why it is not.

We have had in recent years in London state-subsidized exhibitions in which groupings of farm boots, decaying turnips and hardened cow dung have been presented as creative efforts. The same was done, notoriously, with some bloodcaked sanitary towels. This is the new creativity of the collage or montage, and anyone can do it. One essential aspect of traditional art is clarified by surveying the ease with which it can be done. True creativity, we were always told, is difficult.

If the writing of a book still remains the most difficult task in the world, it is nevertheless possible to articulate inarticulately into a cassette recorder and get it all typed up. The ahs and ers and syntactical abortions will, in some views, add up to a precious spontaneity which, to his harm, you don't find in John Milton.

We need some Johnsonian° or Ruskinian° pundit to frighten everybody with near impossible conditions for true creativity. We have to stop thinking that what kindergarten children produce with pencil or watercolour, is anything more than charming or quaint. If you want to be considered a poet, you will have to show mastery of the Petrarchan sonnet form or the sestina. Your musical efforts must begin with well-formed fugues. There is no substitute for craft.

There, I think, you may have the nub of the matter. Art begins with craft, and there is no art until craft has been mastered. You can't create unless you're willing to subordinate the creative impulse to the constriction of a form. But the learning of a craft takes time, and we all think we're entitled to short cuts.

It's time, too, that parasitism were excised from the practice of true creativity—meaning the construction of works of art. There are too many hangers-on who are not satisfied with money but want to call themselves creative as well. I mean publishers' editors, literary agents, the *cadreurs* of French television. Art is rare and sacred and hard work, and there ought to be a wall of fire around it.

Sofa-sized Art

William Geist

William Geist is a newspaper columnist who is best known for his insight into suburbia. He covered the suburbs for the Chicago Tribune *in the*

Johnsonian Samuel Johnson (1709–1784), English author, critic, editor, lexicographer, and conversationalist.
Ruskinian John Ruskin (1819–1900), English author and art critic.

1970s, and moved to the New York Times *to do a suburban column in 1980. More recently he has written about urban New York City, and at the present writing he is about to join the CBS "Sunday Morning" TV show and try his hand at a novel.*

Geist (born 1945) graduated in journalism from the University of Illinois, served as an infantry photographer in Vietnam, then earned a master's degree in journalism from the University of Missouri (1970) before embarking on his career. His writings have been collected in two books: Toward a Safe and Sane Halloween and Other Tales of Suburbia *(1985), from which the present essay is taken; and* City Slickers *(1987).*

Carol Zimmerman's husband becomes one with the couch on this Sunday afternoon of televised professional football, and she leaves home seeking art.

She goes where thousands of other suburban residents go each weekend to find it, to motels throughout the suburban area where "affordable art" sales featuring "sofa-sized" original oil paintings are held during the fall and winter.

"I'm looking for something for over the couch," says Mrs. Zimmerman, of Rockland County, New York, holding a swatch of fabric beside a two- by three-foot landscape, said to be the optimal size over a standard seventy-two-inch couch, "something with blue, brown, and peach." She riffles through some of the thirteen hundred paintings stacked on the floor and banquet tables at the Hilton Inn in Montvale, New Jersey. Others have brought fabric and wallpaper swatches and paint samples to the sale, and some also insist on matching the wooden frames to their wooden furniture.

The paintings, which sell for $30 to $350, are produced by thousands of artists working at a gallop to feed weekend art sales at local motels across the country. Several hundred of the artists work for Richard Gitelman, a thirty-nine-year-old suburban resident who supplies paintings to sales in the metropolitan area and across the country. He is variously described by those in the business as "a czar of affordable art" and "the father of the motel art sale"—as well as "the Henry Ford of art" by virtue of his being responsible for original oil paintings in countless middle-class living rooms.

Paintings arrive by mail from around the world at his Long Island warehouse, where eighty thousand original oil paintings, or "units," are stockpiled. Ten workers sort them by size and category: landscape, seascape, still life, street scene, or portrait. The "product" is then stapled onto stretching frames and packed for shipping to retailers.

"Art is a tough, physically demanding business," says an employee, who has bruises on his arms, cuts on his hands, and a bump on the head to show for a weekend of moving truckloads of art in and out of motels for the viewing of customers lured by newspaper advertisements headlined "Emergency Liquidation."

Leonard Morton, president of a similar firm, Affordable Art Sales Inc., talks proudly of the efficient conveyor belt system he uses to move his paintings around the warehouse before they are finally shipped out in semi-trailer trucks—convoys of art, he calls them.

Mr. Gitelman was in the retail end of the business until he tired of "lugging art." He and two partners held what is believed to have been the first affordable art sale ever in the late 1960s in a New Jersey motel. It was a success and Mr. Gitelman set out across the country holding the sales. "I'd have one hand on the steering wheel, going 110 miles per hour, and another on the phone to the Chamber of Commerce in the next town, finding the best motel to hold the next sale," he says. He has a framed Texas speeding ticket as a memento of those days.

Imitators followed and the sales are now held each weekend during the fall and winter in suburban areas across the country. They have been held in such vast arenas as the Nassau Coliseum and the Houston Astrodome.

Carol Fairclough, who now works in Mr. Gitelman's office, was one of his painters. "She could kick out forty florals a week," he boasts. "She could paint with one hand and cook with the other. The paintings are quality originals, but like anything else, after a while they can do them with their eyes shut."

Most of the paintings on display at this sale are landscapes and seascapes with little detail. While each is an original, many are markedly similar, some virtually identical. Of this, one patron of the arts says, "You can find each painting in a variety of sizes. I like that." Mr. Gitelman says that most of his artists "prefer doing landscapes, probably because if you make a mistake on a landscape, who can tell?"

Of her painting days, Mrs. Fairclough says: "I could never go back to it. It's not artistic, and it's very repetitious. There's very little satisfaction in it. Sometimes I painted all night and all day to keep up." Mr. Gitelman did say that he often told the artists what to paint and what colors to use.

At the Montvale sale, Carole Laga bought a large landscape painting to put over her fireplace. "I like beige," she said, explaining why she chose it. "We have a print there now and we like the idea of owning an original oil painting. We're trying to elevate ourselves."

Anne Silverman says that she goes to the sales regularly just as others go to flea markets and garage sales. "Browsing is a big part of their popularity," she says. "I take my kids along, too. I firmly believe that if you surround your children with culture some of it will rub off."

Critics charge that affordable art is "schlock" and that people are buying it instead of "legitimate art." Mr. Gitelman counters by saying that he is giving people what they want at prices they can afford. "We don't make claims about our stuff appreciating in value and we don't hype it. You take a painting to a gallery on the Upper East Side—where they have to get back their fantastic rents—you hang it on a wall and put a spotlight on it and what do you have? Hype."

Mr. Morton, of Affordable Art Sales, defends his paintings: "They are good oil paintings. They really take a beating. And it's the same paint and the same canvas you get with a $10,000 painting."

Four Poems on Art

William Butler Yeats

(1865–1939)

Sailing to Byzantium

I

That is no country for old men. The young
In one another's arms, birds in the trees
—Those dying generations—at their song,
The salmon-falls, the mackerel-crowded seas,
Fish, flesh, or fowl, commend all summer long
Whatever is begotten, born, and dies.
Caught in that sensual music all neglect
Monuments of unaging intellect.

II

An aged man is but a paltry thing,
A tattered coat upon a stick, unless
Soul clap its hands and sing, and louder sing
For every tatter in its mortal dress,
Nor is there singing school but studying
Monuments of its own magnificence;
And therefore I have sailed the seas and come
To the holy city of Byzantium.

III

O sages standing in God's holy fire
As in the gold mosaic of a wall,
Come from the holy fire, perne in a gyre,
And be the singing-masters of my soul.
Consume my heart away; sick with desire
And fastened to a dying animal
It knows not what it is; and gather me
Into the artifice of eternity.

IV

Once out of nature I shall never take
My bodily form from any natural thing,
But such a form as Grecian goldsmiths make
Of hammered gold and gold enamelling
To keep a drowsy Emperor awake;
Or set upon a golden bough to sing
To lords and ladies of Byzantium
Of what is past, or passing, or to come.

(1928)

Marianne Moore
(1887–1972)

Poetry

I, too, dislike it: there are things that are important
    beyond all this fiddle.
  Reading it, however, with a perfect contempt for it, one
      discovers in
it after all, a place for the genuine.
    Hands that can grasp, eyes
    that can dilate, hair that can rise
      if it must, these things are important not because a

high-sounding interpretation can be put upon them but
    because they are
useful. When they become so derivative as to become
      unintelligible,
the same thing may be said for all of us, that we
    do not admire what
    we cannot understand: the bat
      holding on upside down or in quest of something to

eat, elephants pushing, a wild horse taking a roll, a
    tireless wolf under

a tree, the immovable critic twitching his skin like a
    horse that feels a flea, the base-
ball fan, the statistician—
    nor is it valid
        to discriminate against 'business documents and

school-books'; all these phenomena are important. One
    must make a distinction
however: when dragged into prominence by half poets,
    the result is not poetry,
nor till the poets among us can be
    'literalists of
    the imagination'—above
        insolence and triviality and can present

for inspection, 'imaginary gardens with real toads in
    them', shall we have
it. In the meantime, if you demand on the one hand,
the raw material of poetry in
    all its rawness and
    that which is on the other hand
        genuine, you are interested in poetry.

(1921)

Archibald MacLeish

(1892–1982)

Ars Poetica

A poem should be palpable and mute
As a globed fruit,

Dumb
As old medallions to the thumb,

Silent as the sleeve-worn stone
Of casement ledges where the moss has grown—

A poem should be wordless
As the flight of birds.
   *

A poem should be motionless in time
As the moon climbs,

Leaving, as the moon releases
Twig by twig the night-entangled trees,

Leaving, as the moon behind the winter leaves,
Memory by memory the mind—

A poem should be motionless in time
As the moon climbs.
   *

A poem should be equal to:
Not true.

For all the history of grief
An empty doorway and a maple leaf.

For love
The leaning grasses and two lights above the sea—

A poem should not mean
But be.

(1926)

Gwendolyn Brooks
(b. 1917)

Two Dedications

I
The Chicago Picasso

August 15, 1967

"Mayor Daley tugged a white ribbon, loosing the blue percale wrap. A hearty cheer went up as the covering slipped off the big steel sculpture that looks at once like a bird and a woman."

—Chicago *Sun-Times*

> *(Seiji Ozawa leads the Symphony.*
> *The Mayor smiles.*
> *And 50,000 See.)*

Does man love Art? Man visits Art, but squirms.
Art hurts. Art urges voyages—
and it is easier to stay at home,
the nice beer ready.
          In commonrooms
we belch, or sniff, or scratch.
Are raw.

But we must cook ourselves and style ourselves for Art,
who
is a requiring courtesan.
We squirm.
We do not hug the Mona Lisa.
We
may touch or tolerate
an astounding fountain, or a horse-and-rider.
At most, another Lion.

Observe the tall cold of a Flower
which is as innocent and as guilty,
as meaningful and as meaningless as any
other flower in the western field.

II
The Wall

August 27, 1967

For Edward Christmas

"The side wall of a typical slum building on the corner of 43rd and Langley became a mural communicating black dignity. . . ."

—Ebony

A drumdrumdrum.
Humbly we come.
South of success and east of gloss and glass are
sandals;
flowercloth;
grave hoops of wood or gold, pendant
from black ears, brown ears, reddish-brown
and ivory ears;

black boy-men.
Black
boy-men on roofs fist out "Black Power!" Val,
a little black stampede
in African
images of brass and flowerswirl,
fists out "Black Power!"—tightens pretty eyes,
leans back on mothercountry and is tract,
is treatise through her perfect and tight teeth.

Women in wool hair chant their poetry.
Phil Cohran gives us messages and music
made of developed bone and polished and honed cult.
It is the Hour of tribe and of vibration,
the day-long Hour. It is the Hour
of ringing, rouse, of ferment-festival.

On Forty-third and Langley
black furnaces resent ancient
legislatures
of ploy and scruple and practical gelatin.
They keep the fever in,
fondle the fever.

All
worship the Wall.

I mount the rattling wood. Walter
says, "She is good." Says, "She
our Sister is." In front of me
hundreds of faces, red-brown, brown, black, ivory,
yield me hot trust, their yea and their Announcement
that they are ready to rile the high-flung ground.
Behind me, Paint.
Heroes.
No child has defiled
the Heroes of this Wall this serious Appointment
this still Wing
this Scald this Flute this heavy Light this Hinge.

An emphasis is paroled.
The old decapitations are revised,
the dispossessions beakless.

And we sing.

                                                    (1967)

On Death
and Dying

Our one universal certainty is the fact that some day each one of us will die. Yet the fear of death seems to be equally universal and has found its way into the mythology of nearly every culture. Some admit death, viewing it as part of life, while others try to hide it. Paradoxically, though, the more we hide death, the more we tend to fear it. Today, "the more we are making advancements in science, the more we seem to fear and deny the reality of death. How is this possible?" Elisabeth Kübler-Ross asks this question in response to our growing tendency to separate the dying person from familiar surroundings, to become preoccupied with the technical aspects of the dying body, and to lose sight of the human needs of the dying person. "Is the reason for this increasingly mechanical, depersonalized approach," she wonders, "our own defensiveness?" How many of us, we might ask, have actually seen a dying or dead person?

Faye Moskowitz next reflects on her mother's death from a disease "whose name she was never allowed to utter," and on her own need at age sixteen to deny that it was happening. "I still grieve for the words unsaid," she says. "Something terrible happens when we stop the mouths of the dying before they are dead."

In the final selection, Dr. David Hilfiker struggles with the terrible ethical decisions forced on the contemporary physician who has unprecedented treatments available to him. How should a humane physician treat the "elderly, debilitated patient who contracts an acute illness"? Since "few persons in our society want to think seriously about their aging and death," few prepare for it, and neither professional ethicists nor the law, he tells us, provide helpful guidelines. "The problem," he concludes, "is simply too painful for me as a single human being to face day after day in a conscious way."

On the Fear of Death

Elisabeth Kübler-Ross

Dr. Elisabeth Kübler-Ross, a psychiatrist, author, and lecturer, has had important influence on our ideas about the care of dying patients and their families. Born in Zurich in 1926, she did relief work in postwar Europe and studied medicine at the University of Zurich. After becoming a doctor in 1957, she practiced medicine in Switzerland, and came to the United States in 1958 to do her internship and residency in psychiatry.

Dr. Kübler-Ross, who holds dual American and Swiss citizenship, has taught medicine at the University of Colorado and at the University of Chicago, where she instituted an interdisciplinary seminar on the care of dying patients. After she left the University of Chicago in 1970, she shared her special understanding of the needs of the dying and of their relatives and caretakers in lectures and workshops. Since 1977 she has been president and chairman of the board of Shanti Nilaya ("House of Peace"), a controversial therapeutic and teaching center for patients and their families.

Her books on death include On Death and Dying *(1969), the first chapter of which is printed below;* Questions and Answers on Death and Dying *(1972);* Death: The Final State *(1974);* To Live Until We Say Goodbye *(1978);* Working It Through *(1981);* Living with Death and Dying *(1981); and* On Children and Death *(1985). In addition, she has written for professional journals and has contributed chapters to a number of books.*

> *Let me not pray to be sheltered from*
> *dangers but to be fearless in facing*
> *them.*
> *Let me not beg for the stilling of*
> *my pain but for the heart to conquer it.*
> *Let me not look for allies in life's*
> *battlefield but to my own strength.*
> *Let me not crave in anxious fear to*
> *be saved but hope for the patience to*
> *win my freedom.*
> *Grant me that I may not be a*
> *coward, feeling your mercy in my*

*success alone; but let me find the grasp
of your hand in my failure.*

—RABINDRANATH TAGORE,
Fruit-Gathering

Epidemics have taken a great toll of lives in past generations. Death in infancy and early childhood was frequent and there were few families who didn't lose a member of the family at an early age. Medicine has changed greatly in the last decades. Widespread vaccinations have practically eradicated many illnesses, at least in western Europe and the United States. The use of chemotherapy, especially the antibiotics, has contributed to an ever decreasing number of fatalities in infectious diseases. Better child care and education has effected a low morbidity and mortality among children. The many diseases that have taken an impressive toll among the young and middle-aged have been conquered. The number of old people is on the rise, and with this fact come the number of people with malignancies and chronic diseases associated more with old age.

Pediatricians have less work with acute and life-threatening situations as they have an ever increasing number of patients with psychosomatic disturbances and adjustment and behavior problems. Physicians have more people in their waiting rooms with emotional problems than they have ever had before, but they also have more elderly patients who not only try to live with their decreased physical abilities and limitations but who also face loneliness and isolation with all its pains and anguish. The majority of these people are not seen by a psychiatrist. Their needs have to be elicited and gratified by other professional people, for instance, chaplains and social workers. It is for them that I am trying to outline the changes that have taken place in the last few decades, changes that are ultimately responsible for the increased fear of death, the rising number of emotional problems, and the greater need for understanding of and coping with the problems of death and dying.

When we look back in time and study old cultures and people, we are impressed that death has always been distasteful to man and will probably always be. From a psychiatrist's point of view this is very understandable and can perhaps best be explained by our basic knowledge that, in our unconscious, death is never possible in regard to ourselves. It is inconceivable for our unconscious to imagine an actual ending of our own life here on earth, and if this life of ours has to end, the ending is always attributed to a malicious intervention from the outside by someone else. In simple terms, in our unconscious mind we can only be killed; it is inconceivable to die of a natural cause or of old age. Therefore death in itself is associated with a bad act, a frightening happening, something that in itself calls for retribution and punishment.

One is wise to remember these fundamental facts as they are essential in understanding some of the most important, otherwise unintelligible communications of our patients.

The second fact that we have to comprehend is that in our unconscious mind we cannot distinguish between a wish and a deed. We are all aware of some of our illogical dreams in which two completely opposite statements can exist side by side—very acceptable in our dreams but unthinkable and illogical in our wakening state. Just as our unconscious mind cannot differentiate between the wish to kill somebody in anger and the act of having done so, the young child is unable to make this distinction. The child who angrily wishes his mother to drop dead for not having gratified his needs will be traumatized greatly by the actual death of his mother—even if this event is not linked closely in time with his destructive wishes. He will always take part or the whole blame for the loss of his mother. He will always say to himself—rarely to others—"I did it, I am responsible, I was bad, therefore Mommy left me." It is well to remember that the child will react in the same manner if he loses a parent by divorce, separation, or desertion. Death is often seen by a child as an impermanent thing and has therefore little distinction from a divorce in which he may have an opportunity to see a parent again.

Many a parent will remember remarks of their children such as, "I will bury my doggy now and next spring when the flowers come up again, he will get up." Maybe it was the same wish that motivated the ancient Egyptians to supply their dead with food and goods to keep them happy and the old American Indians to bury their relatives with their belongings.

When we grow older and begin to realize that our omnipotence is really not so omnipotent, that our strongest wishes are not powerful enough to make the impossible possible, the fear that we have contributed to the death of a loved one diminishes—and with it the guilt. The fear remains diminished, however, only so long as it is not challenged too strongly. Its vestiges can be seen daily in hospital corridors and in people associated with the bereaved.

A husband and wife may have been fighting for years, but when the partner dies, the survivor will pull his hair, whine and cry louder and beat his chest in regret, fear and anguish, and will hence fear his own death more than before, still believing in the law of talion—an eye for an eye, a tooth for a tooth—"I am responsible for her death, I will have to die a pitiful death in retribution."

Maybe this knowledge will help us understand many of the old customs and rituals which have lasted over the centuries and whose purpose is to diminish the anger of the gods or the people as the case may be, thus decreasing the anticipated punishment. I am thinking of the ashes, the torn clothes, the veil, the *Klage Weiber*° of the old days—they are all means to ask you to take pity on them, the mourners, and are expressions of sorrow, grief, and shame. If someone grieves, beats his chest, tears his hair, or refuses to eat, it is an attempt at self-punishment to avoid or reduce the anticipated punishment for the blame that he takes on the death of a loved one.

This grief, shame, and guilt are not very far removed from feelings of anger and rage. The process of grief always includes some qualities of anger. Since none of us likes to admit anger at a deceased person, these emotions are often disguised or repressed and prolong the period of grief or show up in other ways. It is well to remember that it is not up to us to judge such feelings as bad or shameful but to understand their true meaning and origin as something very human. In order to illustrate this I will again use the example of the child—and the child in us. The five-year-old who loses his mother is both blaming himself for her disappearance and being angry at her for having deserted him and for no longer gratifying his needs. The dead person then turns into something the child loves and wants very much but also hates with equal intensity for this severe deprivation.

The ancient Hebrews regarded the body of a dead person as something unclean and not to be touched. The early American Indians talked about the evil spirits and shot arrows in the air to drive the spirits away. Many other cultures have rituals to take care of the "bad" dead person, and they all originate in this feeling of anger which still exists in all of us, though we dislike admitting it. The tradition of the tombstone may originate in this wish to keep the bad spirits deep down in the ground, and the pebbles that many mourners put on the grave are left-over symbols of the same wish. Though we call the firing of guns at military funerals a last salute, it is the same symbolic ritual as the Indian used when he shot his spears and arrows into the skies.

I give these examples to emphasize that man has not basically changed. Death is still a fearful, frightening happening, and the fear of death is a universal fear even if we think we have mastered it on many levels.

What has changed is our way of coping and dealing with death and dying and our dying patients.

Having been raised in a country in Europe where science is not so advanced, where modern techniques have just started to find their way into medicine, and where people still live as they did in this country half a century ago, I may have had an opportunity to study a part of the evolution of mankind in a shorter period.

I remember as a child the death of a farmer. He fell from a tree and was not expected to live. He asked simply to die at home, a wish that was

---

Klage Weiber   mourning women (German).

granted without questioning. He called his daughters into the bedroom and spoke with each one of them alone for a few minutes. He arranged his affairs quietly, though he was in great pain, and distributed his belongings and his land, none of which was to be split until his wife should follow him in death. He also asked each of his children to share in the work, duties, and tasks that he had carried on until the time of the accident. He asked his friends to visit him once more, to bid good-bye to them. Although I was a small child at the time, he did not exclude me or my siblings. We were allowed to share in the preparations of the family just as we were permitted to grieve with them until he died. When he did die, he was left at home, in his own beloved home which he had built, and among his friends and neighbors who went to take a last look at him where he lay in the midst of flowers in the place he had lived in and loved so much. In that country today there is still no make-believe slumber room, no embalming, no false makeup to pretend sleep. Only the signs of very disfiguring illnesses are covered up with bandages and only infectious cases are removed from the home prior to the burial.

Why do I describe such "old-fashioned" customs? I think they are an indication of our acceptance of a fatal outcome, and they help the dying patient as well as his family to accept the loss of a loved one. If a patient is allowed to terminate his life in the familiar and beloved environment, it requires less adjustment for him. His own family knows him well enough to replace a sedative with a glass of his favorite wine; or the smell of a home-cooked soup may give him the appetite to sip a few spoons of fluid which, I think, is still more enjoyable than an infusion. I will not minimize the need for sedatives and infusions and realize full well from my own experience as a country doctor that they are sometimes life-saving and often unavoidable. But I also know that patience and familiar people and foods could replace many a bottle of intravenous fluids for the simple reason that it fulfills the physiological need without involving too many people and/or individual nursing care.

The fact that children are allowed to stay at home where a fatality has stricken and are included in the talk, discussions, and fears gives them the feeling that they are not alone in the grief and gives them the comfort of shared responsibility and shared mourning. It prepares them gradually and helps them view death as part of life, an experience which may help them grow and mature.

This is in great contrast to a society in which death is viewed as taboo, discussion of it is regarded as morbid, and children are excluded with the presumption and pretext that it would be "too much" for them. They are then sent off to relatives, often accompanied with some unconvincing lies of "Mother has gone on a long trip" or other unbelievable stories. The child senses that something is wrong, and his distrust in adults will only multiply if other relatives add new variations of the story, avoid his questions or suspicions, shower him with gifts as a meager substitute for a loss he is not permitted to deal with. Sooner or later the child will become aware of the changed family situation and, depending on the age and personality of the child, will have an unresolved grief and regard this incident as a frightening, mysterious, in any case very traumatic experience with untrustworthy grownups, which he has no way to cope with.

It is equally unwise to tell a little child who lost her brother that God loved little boys so much that he took little Johnny to heaven. When this little girl grew up to be a woman she never solved her anger at God, which resulted in a psychotic depression when she lost her own little son three decades later.

We would think that our great emancipation, our knowledge of science and of man, has given us better ways and means to prepare ourselves and our families for this inevitable happening. Instead the days are gone when a man was allowed to die in peace and dignity in his own home.

The more we are making advancements in science, the more we seem to fear and deny the reality of death. How is this possible?

We use euphemisms, we make the dead look as if they were asleep, we ship the children off to protect them from the anxiety and turmoil around the house if the patient is fortunate enough to die at home, we don't allow children to visit their dying parents in the hospital, we have long and controversial discussions about whether patients should be told the truth—a question that rarely arises when the dying person is tended by the family physician who has known him from delivery to death and who knows the weaknesses and strengths of each member of the family.

I think there are many reasons for this flight away from facing death calmly. One of the most important facts is that dying nowadays is more gruesome in many ways, namely, more lonely, mechanical, and dehumanized; at times it is even difficult to determine technically when the time of death has occurred.

Dying becomes lonely and impersonal because the patient is often taken out of his familiar environment and rushed to an emergency room. Whoever has been very sick and has required rest and comfort especially may recall his experience of being put on a stretcher and enduring the noise of the ambulance siren and hectic rush until the hospital gates open. Only those who have lived through this may appreciate the discomfort and cold necessity of such transportation which is only the beginning of a long ordeal—hard to endure when you are well, difficult to express in words when noise, light, pumps, and voices are all too much to put up with. It may well be that we might consider more the patient under the sheets and blankets and perhaps stop our well-meant efficiency and rush in order to hold the patient's hand, to smile, or to listen to a question. I include the trip to the hospital as the first episode in dying, as it is for many. I am putting it exaggeratedly in contrast to the sick man who is left at home—not to say that lives should not be saved if they can be saved by a hospitalization but to keep the focus on the patient's experience, his needs and his reactions.

When a patient is severely ill, he is often treated like a person with no right to an opinion. It is often someone else who makes the decision if and when and where a patient should be hospitalized. It would take so little to remember that the sick person too has feelings, has wishes and opinions, and has—most important of all—the right to be heard.

Well, our presumed patient has now reached the emergency room. He will be surrounded by busy nurses, orderlies, interns, residents, a lab technician perhaps who will take some blood, an electrocardiogram technician who takes the cardiogram. He may be moved to X-ray and he will overhear opinions of his condition and discussions and questions to members of the family. He slowly but surely is beginning to be treated like a thing. He is no longer a person. Decisions are made often without his opinion. If he tries to rebel he will be sedated and after hours of waiting and wondering whether he has the strength, he will be wheeled into the operating room or intensive treatment unit and become an object of great concern and great financial investment.

He may cry for rest, peace, and dignity, but he will get infusions, transfusions, a heart machine, or tracheotomy if necessary. He may want one single person to stop for one single minute so that he can ask one single question—but he will get a dozen people around the clock, all busily preoccupied with his heart rate, pulse, electrocardiogram or pulmonary functions, his secretions or excretions but not with him as a human being. He may wish to fight it all but it is going to be a useless fight since all this is done in the fight for his life, and if they can save his life they can consider the person afterwards. Those who consider the person first may lose precious time to save his life! At least this seems to be the rationale or justification behind all this—or is it? Is the reason for this increasingly mechanical, depersonalized approach our own defensiveness? Is this approach our own way to cope with and repress the anxieties that a terminally or critically ill patient evokes in us? Is our concentration on equipment, on blood pressure, our desperate attempt to deny the impending death which is so frightening and discomforting to us that we displace all our knowledge onto machines, since they are less close to us than the suffering face of another human being which would remind us once more of our lack of omnipotence, our own limits and failures, and last but not least perhaps our own mortality?

Maybe the question has to be raised: Are we becoming less human or more human? Though this book is in no way meant to be judgmental, it is clear that whatever the answer may be, the patient is suffering more—not physically, perhaps, but emotionally. And his needs have not changed over the centuries, only our ability to gratify them.

from *A Leak in the Heart*

Faye Moskowitz

Faye Moskowitz (born 1930) describes herself as a late bloomer: "I got my B.A. from George Washington University," she says, "just before I turned forty. I began writing that year also, just about the time I felt I had something to say. I have since earned an M.A. and have completed my coursework and comprehensives for a Ph.D. in American Literature." After twelve years as a director and teacher in a Washington, D.C., middle school, she now teaches at George Washington University.

Moskowitz has written for Women's Day, Good Housekeeping, *the* Washington Post *and the* New York Times. *Some of her articles have been collected in* A Leak in the Heart: Tales from a Woman's Life *(1985), from which we take the selection below. She believes that the memories and reflections of the ordinary person are precious; that in sharing them we come to understand our correspondences, our connections. "Who," she asks, "will accurately describe our lives if we do not do it ourselves?"*

My mother wrote me one letter in her life. She was in California then, seeking treatment for the disease whose name she was never allowed to utter, as if in some magical way, speaking the illness would confirm it. I found the letter in a dresser drawer the other day, written in the round hand of Americanization school on tissue-thin paper banded at the top with the narrow red edge of gum rubber where it was once attached to a tablet.

March 7, 1947

Dear Faye Chaim and Roger,

How are you kids? I am filling little better. My beck still hurts. Today I was at doctors for a light tritement and Saturday I am going again for a tritement. I hope to god I shut fill better. Please write to me. How is everthing in the house? How does daddy fill. The weather is her wondufull nice and hot. I was sitting outside today. Well I have to say good night. I have to be in bet 9 o'clock for my health. Take care of daddy.

your mother

Regart from evrywone.

On the back flap of the envelope, she had written her name, Sophie Stollman, and the street address of the sister with whom she was staying in Los Angeles. On the last line she had lettered in *Detroit, Mich.,* her home. Now, older than she was when she died, I am shattered by that confused address. Loneliness, homesickness, and fear spill out of those laboriously penciled words, and the poignant error that was not a mistake, speaks to me still.

I suppose I realized from the beginning that my mother's illness was a serious one: I had seen the fearful loss of symmetry where the breast had been, the clumsy stitching around it, like that of a child sewing a doll's dress. I had caught her one morning weeping in front of the mirror as she poked at the rubber pad that kept working its way up to the open collar of her blouse. But I was sixteen years old and worried enough about keeping my own physical balance. One false step and I might fall off the edge of the world. I was afraid to walk the outer limits of her sickness; I dealt with death the way the rest of my family did . . . by denying it.

I buried myself in books, played the "will-he, won't-he" games of adolescence, worried about the atomic bomb, tried to keep my little brothers from acting like children in a house where the sounds of childhood were no longer appropriate. My father and I clung to each other, but the veil of my mother's illness fell between us, too, and we were silent.

She got worse, and the family began to gather. Covered dishes and pots of food appeared, crammed our refrigerator, molded, were thrown out and replaced by still more food. Visitors came and went, swirling like snowflakes in the downstairs rooms, sitting around the kitchen table drinking tea from glasses, talking, talking. Still, they said nothing, and it seemed to me, sometimes, their silence would awaken the dead.

A time came when my mother's wardrobe was reduced to open-backed hospital gowns; our home was invaded twenty-four hours a day by a succession of starched uniforms and the incessant whisper of white nylon stockings. My mother was terrified by hospitals and refused to go, but still we were forced to trust her to the hands of strangers. She lay, as in a crib, imprisoned by iron bars; her own bed, where she had slept, knees in my father's back so many years, had been taken down to make room for a mattress scarcely wider than a coffin.

Alone for a moment, she called to me one day as I tiptoed past her bedroom. (Perhaps the nurse was downstairs preparing the unfamiliar food on which they kept her alive.) I stood next to her, watched her pluck at a fold in the bedclothes, smooth them, try to make the question casual by the homely gestures. "Faygele," she said, finally, "do you think I will ever get better?"

How could I answer her truthfully, being bound as inextricably as she was by the rules of the complicated deception we were playing out? Perhaps I understood in my heart's core that she was doomed, but I hadn't the permission of knowledge; I could only answer, "Of course, of course," and help to wrap her more tightly alone inside her fear. She never asked me that question again.

A few weeks before my mother died, when the sounds coming from her room began to move beyond speech, an older cousin was given the responsibility of articulating to me the name of her disease. I remember he took me to an Italian restaurant where we stirred the food around on our plates, and to a movie afterward.

Cordoned off by heavy velvet ropes, we stood in line under the prisms of rococo chandeliers, and there, surrounded by people I had never seen before, I was told the truth, at last. No room to cry in that glittering lobby, fire spurting from crystal lamps and mica-sparkled placards. So I sat, in the darkness of the theater, watching *Johnny Belinda* flickering on the screen, the salt of buttered popcorn swallowed with the salt of tears.

I was out late with friends the night of my mother's death. Walking alone up the darkened street, I saw my house, windows blazing as if for a party, and I knew what had happened. Word must have already spread, for on the sidewalk behind me I heard low voices and soft footsteps, stripped of purpose now, by her surrender.

In my mother's room, the mirrors, according to the old custom, had been shrouded (so the mourners would not have to confront their grief, some say), and damp, chill February fluttered curtains at the open window. My uncle, in a heavy jacket, sat next to his sister's bed. He would watch her until morning. "No, I'm not afraid," I told him. "Let me sit with her a little while."

She lay, hair bound in a white cloth, and I could feel her body, blood and bone under the sheet, pulling away from me, slipping into stone. The memories crowded around me, witnesses to my guilt: the many times I had resented caring for her, the times I had yearned to flee my house when her pain became an intimation of my own mortality.

I remembered, in the bas-relief of shame, the evening I came home from somewhere, to find her leaning on the kitchen sink, washing a stack of dishes I had left undone. "Shut up!" I had shouted when she spoke to me, angered at the robe and slippers, the cane lying on the floor, the medicine bottles, accouterments of a mother too sick to care for her own. Now we were cut off in midsentence. Now I would never be able to tell her how sorry I was for everything.

I still grieve for the words unsaid. Something terrible happens when we stop the mouths of the dying before they are dead. A silence grows up between us then, profounder than the grave. If we force the dying to go speechless, the stone dropped into the well will fall forever before the answering splash is heard.

Playing God

David Hilfiker

David Hilfiker (born 1945) is a doctor who practices family medicine. He was educated at Yale University and the University of Minnesota Medical School (M.D. 1974). For seven years he was a family practitioner in a small town in Minnesota; he now has a practice in Washington, D.C. He has written medical articles for Vogue, the New York Times Magazine, Mother Jones, *and* Harper's Magazine.

In his book Healing the Wounds: A Physician Looks at His Work *(1985), he draws on his own experience to examine some of the ethical dilemmas faced by doctors today. We reprint here all but the final five paragraphs of Chapter 8.*

The phone rings, pulling me from that deepest sleep which comes during the first hours of the night. I can barely remember who I am, much less why the phone might be ringing. I manage to find the receiver next to the bed and pick it up.

"Hello?"

"Hello, Dr. Hilfiker? This is Ginger at the nursing home. Elsa has a fever."

In the silence my mind is immediately clear. Elsa Toivonen, eighty-three years old, confined to the nursing home ever since her stroke three years ago, bedridden, mute. In an instant I remember her as she was before the stroke: her dislike and distrust of doctors and hospitals, her staunch pride and independence despite the crippling back curvature of scoliosis, her wry grin every time I suggested hospitalization for some problem. I remember admitting her to the hospital after her stroke, incontinent, reduced to helplessness, one side completely paralyzed, speech gone; and I remember those first few days during which I aggressively treated the pneumonia that developed as a complication of the stroke, giving her intravenous antibiotics despite her apparent desire to die. "Depressed," I had thought. "She'll get over it. Besides, she may recover substantially in the next few weeks." She did, in fact, recover from the pneumonia, but she remained paralyzed and without speech. For the last three years she has lain curled in her nursing-home bed, my own grim reminder of the power of modern medicine.

"Dr. Hilfiker?" Ginger Moss's voice brings me back to my tired body.

"Oh . . . yeah," I say. My mind is focused; I just can't get my mouth to work. "Any other symptoms?"

"Well, you know Elsa. It's hard to tell. She hasn't been eating much the last few days, and she's had a little cough. Mary noticed her temp on the evening shift, but she didn't want to bother you."

"So why are you bothering me now?" I want to say. Instead I ask, "What's her temperature?"

"One hundred three point five, rectally."

"Oh . . . all right," I say reluctantly. "I'll be right down."

Driving down the hill, I go through my usual jumble of irrational emotions. First I'm angry at Elsa for having her fever, then irritated with Mary for not having called me earlier in the evening, and finally annoyed with Ginger for not waiting until morning. I'm glad I have this ride; otherwise I'd offend a lot of people. By the time I get to the nursing home, my irritation has subsided, and compassion for Mrs. Toivonen has begun to take over. Ginger is waiting for me in the dark hall just outside Mrs. Toivonen's room, chart in hand. "She looks pretty sick, David."

She does indeed! Wasted away to sixty-nine pounds, chronic bedsores on the bony protuberances of back and hip, she peers at me from behind her blank face. I'm used to all that from my regular monthly visits, but this morning there is no movement of her eyes, no resistance to my examination, nothing to indicate she's really there. Worse yet, there is little more to learn about the history of her fever than what Ginger has already told me over the phone. Mrs. Toivonen, of course, hasn't talked in three years, nor has she understood anything I've said as far as I can tell; so there is no hope of further information from her. My exam is brief as I look pointedly for the most common causes of fever in the elderly—upper respiratory infection, pneumonia, bladder infection, a viral illness. I realize I'm not being thorough, and feel briefly guilty as I recall an article I've read suggesting that nursing-home patients receive less thorough medical attention simply because they are old and feeble. It's true, of course. I know perfectly well that if this were a forty-seven-year-old schoolteacher in the emergency room with a fever, I would be spending an hour checking him out and talking with him. I try to assuage my guilt with the thought that I can't exhaust myself now, in the middle of the night, if I'm going to give decent care to all the other patients who need me in the morning. In my heart, though, I know it's a lousy excuse.

Listening to Mrs. Toivonen's chest, I hear the noises I expected, faint crackling pops indicating irritation in the lungs, probably pneumonia. I complete the rest of the exam without finding anything else and look up at Ginger. "I think she's got pneumonia," I say, and we both stare at Elsa's withered body. I wonder to myself, "What am I going to do now?" Ginger's glance tells me the same question is going through her head. I ask her to call Mark out of bed for a chest x-ray, and I write orders for a urine culture in the morning just to make sure a bladder infection is not causing the fever. While waiting for the x-ray, Ginger and I sit at the nurse's station, writing our respective reports in the chart.

Ginger looks up. "Mabel Lundberg said she hoped there wouldn't be any heroics if Elsa got sick again."

"I know. She talked to me, too." What does she mean by "heroics," though? I suddenly feel irritated again, but I keep my mouth shut. Almost thirty years younger than Elsa, Mabel is the only friend Mrs. Toivonen has, her only visitor at the nursing home. Mabel was a neighbor, and before Elsa's stroke she would help her with shopping, drive her to her clinic visits, run errands, and generally help out. She probably knows better than anyone what Elsa would really want, but Elsa's only relative, a niece I've never met who lives in another state, called some months ago asking that "everything possible" be done for her aunt. "Heroics"—"everything possible": each phrase refers to the same intervention but means something entirely different. We all want "everything possible" done for our poor, bedridden aunt; but at the same time we all want to spare her those terrible medical "heroics" in which doctors "prolong needlessly the agony of the dying." It all depends on the words you choose.

Essentially alone in the middle of the night, foggy from tiredness, I'll make decisions that will probably mean life or death for this old woman. I think back to medical school and university hospital where a thousand dollars' worth of laboratory and x-ray studies would have been done to make sure she really did have pneumonia: several x-rays of the chest, urine cultures, blood cultures, microscopic examinations of her phlegm (which could only be obtained by putting a needle through the neck and into the trachea of this sixty-nine-pound, eighty-three-year-old lady), blood counts, a Mantoux test to make sure she doesn't have tuberculosis, possibly even lung scans to check for blood clots. The list is limited only by one's imagination, each test "reasonable" in its own way once you enter the labyrinth of medical thoroughness. I can almost hear the residents suggesting obscure possibilities to demonstrate their erudition. (And are they wrong? Can any price be put on human life? Is any distance too far to go to discover a rare, potentially fatal, but curable illness?)

There in the middle of the night I consider doing "everything possible" for Mrs. Toivonen: transfer to the hospital, IVs for hydration, large doses of penicillin, thorough lab and x-ray evaluation, twice-daily rounds to be sure she is recovering, other more toxic antibiotics to cover the chance of an infection resistant to penicillin, even transfer to our regional hospital for specialist evaluation and care. None of it is unreasonable, and another night I might choose just such a course; but tonight my human sympathies lie with Mrs. Toivonen and what I perceive as her desire to die. Perhaps it is because Ginger is working, and I know how impatient she is with technological "heroics." Perhaps it is because I've been feeling a little depressed myself in the last few days and imagine I can better appreciate Mrs. Toivonen's perspective, although who knows what thoughts are—or aren't—going on behind the impenetrable mask of that face? Perhaps, I think to myself, it is because I'm tired and lazy and don't want to bother.

In any event, I decide against the "heroics," but I can't just do nothing, either. Everything in my training and background pulls against that course, so there is no way I'm going to be able to be consistent and just go home. Instead, I compromise and write an order in the chart instructing the nursing staff to administer liquid penicillin by mouth, encourage fluid intake, and make an appointment with my office so I can re-examine Mrs. Toivonen in thirty-six hours. My orders make no real medical sense, of course. Such a debilitated lady's pneumonia will probably require the higher doses of penicillin possible only through an IV; Mrs. Toivonen is also likely to refuse the nurses' attempts to give her extra fluids. And my compromise makes even less ethical sense. Am I or am I not treating Mrs. Toivonen? Am I or am I not prolonging her life artificially?

On my way out of the dark hospital, I talk with Mark, who looks sleepier than I feel, and we check the x-ray. I've known all along that the information it can offer me will be questionable at best. With her severe back curvature, Mrs. Toivonen is always difficult to x-ray, and she has chronic changes in her lungs which make early pneumonia difficult to detect. I thank Mark for the x-ray, wondering why I ever ordered it. Driving up the hill, I wonder why the practice of medicine is so often dissatisfying.

As usual, it takes me an hour to get back to sleep.

Mrs. Toivonen survived her pneumonia, more because of her constitution than my treatment, but even my compromise treatment was an important ethical choice. I had decided that the quality of her life was not valuable enough to warrant aggressive medical treatment. Situations like Mrs. Toivonen's are common. In my own practice and in those of other physicians I see around me, the old, chronically ill, debilitated, or mentally impaired do not receive the same level of aggressive medical evaluation and treatment as do the young, acutely ill, and mentally normal. Two physicians studied the response of a nursing-home staff to fevers in their elderly residents and discovered that the older and more debilitated the patients were, the less likely they were to receive aggressive treatment. The nursing aide was less likely to bring a fever to the attention of the supervising nurse, the nurse less likely to call the physician, the physician less likely to examine the patient personally, and the fever less likely to be treated with antibiotics. During my student years I was working with a particularly caring and competent doctor. When the nurses one day on hospital rounds reported that a debilitated elderly patient had a fever, I was shocked to watch my preceptor write an order for aspirin without even investigating the cause of the fever. Without further explanation he lamely apologized to me by explaining that it was "probably just a virus." Only years later did I understand that this physician had developed his own way of allowing certain patients to die by withholding all available care.

Some may believe I acted irresponsibly and unethically in not treating Mrs. Toivonen more aggressively. There has been a widespread perception in medical circles that all patients should receive the maximum possible care for any given medical problem. In medical schools, in conversations between physicians, and—until very recently—in the medical literature, there has been the tacit assumption that all patients (with the possible exception of the terminally ill) receive the maximum care. But it isn't so. We rarely discuss this reality or debate its ethics. Only recently has there been acknowledgment that this extraordinarily common, profoundly disturbing ethical deliberation is a daily part of our lives. Instead, the practicing physician has been left to fly by the seat of his pants.

Some might be tempted to dismiss the entire problem with the simple assertion that all patients deserve maximal care. Consider, however, the following situation. We have in our nursing home a young woman who has been comatose for five years as a result of an accident. Although there is no meaningful chance that she will ever improve, she is not "brain-dead" and is supported only by routine nursing care, consisting of tube feedings, regular turnings, urinary catheters, and good hygiene; she is on no respirator or other machine. If, on a routine yearly examination, her physician were somehow to discover that she was in danger of a life-threatening heart attack within the next few years, few persons, I think, would recommend full-scale evaluation for possibly coronary bypass surgery. The decision not to offer her maximal care might be justified in any one of several ways, but most often the question would simply not arise. It would seem obvious to the practicing physician that this particular patient should not receive such heroic treatment.

I think few would quarrel with the decision to withhold such evaluation and treatment. But once we have allowed that some persons should not receive some treatments that will prolong their lives, we must begin the thorny ethical process of "drawing lines": which patients? which treatments? If this comatose young woman should not get the bypass surgery, then what kinds of treatment might we offer her? How far should we go? Would we perform a major abdominal operation to repair a dangerous ballooning of the aorta, a major artery that would otherwise probably rupture and kill her within a matter of weeks? Would we perform routine surgery to cure appendicitis? Would we give her an IV to compensate for fluid loss if she had diarrhea? Would we give her medicines by mouth to treat an uncomplicated urinary-tract infection? Would we put in a new stomach tube so that she could continue being fed? Each person might draw the line differently, but once it is agreed that a certain heroic treatment will not be offered, that still doesn't tell us what to do.

Because of his technical expertise (and his prestige in our society), the physician ordinarily also inherits the responsibility and the power to make such basic decisions about the value of a human life. The good and compassionate physician will, I believe, try to include the patient and the family in such important deliberations, but the physician's ability to phrase options, stress information, and present his own advice allows him enormous power in determining the nature of the care given. This power becomes, for all practical purposes, absolute when he is dealing with incapacitated patients, especially if family members are far away or otherwise not closely involved.

One might expect that the physician would have some special training or at least some resources to which he might turn when such common problems arise. But aside from his experience, no special training exists, and until very recently, almost no practical resources were available. There certainly has been a great deal published about the termination of life-support measures in persons whose brains are dead, but that problem is both simple and uncommon compared to a situation like Mrs. Toivonen's; the difficulties there are not so much ethical as technical—that is, how one determines for sure that the patient's brain is dead.

There has also been much discussion about care of the terminally ill cancer patient, but that situation is also much more clear-cut than the usual one of the debilitated elderly patient. The cancer patient and her physician can know that the illness will end in death within a certain period of time; therefore, the physician can reassure himself that he is not so much withholding available treatment as "allowing the person to die with dignity." (The professional ethicist may see little distinction between the patient terminally ill with lung cancer and Mrs. Toivonen, but the certainty of the former's death within a very short time compared with the possibility of Mrs. Toivonen's living for years creates an important distinction for the practicing physician.) Also, the relatively rapid course of terminal cancer allows the patient to know, while she is still completely lucid, that the illness is terminal. She can thus participate fully in the discussion of the matter before the decisions are made.

Charlotte Stroh was a sixty-three-year-old woman I had known well for several years when she first noticed the abdominal pain which eventually led to a diagnosis of cancer of the pancreas. After the diagnosis was established, Charlotte had a thorough discussion with the cancer specialist in Duluth. Although he offered her chemotherapy, he told her that it was unlikely to help very much and that there was almost no chance of a cure. Charlotte decided against any such attempts at treatment, since the side effects would probably make her very sick and prevent her from enjoying the last months of her life. She returned home with the intention of living as fully as she could during whatever time she had left.

At our next visit, Charlotte and I discussed her situation. She knew she had only a few months to live, and she knew she wanted to spend as little of that time as possible in the hospital. She was afraid not so much of dying as of the pain that might accompany the process. She wanted to be kept as comfortable as possible, but once she was really sick she didn't want anything to prolong her dying. If possible, she wanted to stay at home.

The terminal phase of her illness came quickly. We saw each other every two weeks, but she had dwindled from her usual 140 pounds to 110 within six weeks, and had become very jaundiced since the cancer was beginning to block the bile duct. Two weeks later she was confined to bed and beginning to have periods of delirium. There was not too much pain, and it could be controlled by regular shots of morphine, which her husband learned to administer. During the last days of her illness she developed a fever, probably as a result of an infection in the bile duct. It would have been possible temporarily to treat the infection or even surgically to bypass the blocked bile duct, but the question had already been settled. Charlotte had made it very clear how she wanted to die; besides, the heroic treatments would have added little to the length of her life and nothing to the quality. Charlotte died quietly at home.

Although much energy has been devoted to the ethics of treating the terminally ill and defining the meaning of brain death, the much more common situation of the elderly, debilitated patient who contracts an acute illness has been left relatively unaddressed. Ethicists, though, have advanced several helpful suggestions. Some recommend that the physician sit down with his patient to discuss, in advance, what the patient might like to have done under certain circumstances. Others suggest a "living will" that would direct the physician to a particular course of action if the patient became disabled. Perhaps the best course—now legally possible in many states—would be to discuss the situation with a friend or family member and appoint him or her "surrogate decision-maker" in the event the patient becomes incompetent. Although these are helpful ideas, they have some serious drawbacks.

First of all, few persons in our society want to think seriously about their aging and death. Apart from offhand comments ("I hope they don't let me linger on like that!"), most people do not want to confront the eventual loss of their powers. Few are likely to make out a living will or pay their physician for the privilege of discussing the possibility of their own incapacity.

Secondly, a patient who has discussed all this with her personal physician may very well be attended by someone else when these issues finally arise. Not only do we live in an increasingly mobile society in which the long-term physician-patient relationship is less common, but the very structure of medical care almost assures a stranger for a physician when the patient becomes seriously ill. Medicine has been broken down into minute specialties. Even hospitals are organized according to the level of specialized care available, from the local community hospital to the regional hospital to the large university center. Patients, especially the very ill, are handed from doctor to doctor, sometimes being attended by many at once, and may even be transferred from hospital to hospital. The patient may never have had an opportunity to discuss with the physician or physicians who will attend her how she would like to be treated at the end of her life.

Furthermore, people's ideas about the quality of life change drastically as they age, especially in the last years of their lives. The twenty-one-year-old who would rather be shot than suffer the imagined ignominy of a nursing home may be only too grateful to accept a nursing-home bed and warm meals when she turns eighty-five. A living will or a frank conversation with one's physician even at age fifty-five rarely would reflect what one's wishes will be at age seventy.

Martin Hooker was not atypical. At ninety years of age, his heart failure kept him very sedentary. With much help from friends and family, he had managed to remain living at home. Yet he was often short of breath and weak, and required frequent hospitalization to rest and have his medications adjusted—his "tune-ups," he would call them. Finally, he developed a disease in the heart's natural pacemaker which, while not aggravating his heart condition, could have stopped his heart at any moment, causing sudden death. I explained the situation to him and outlined his choices. Without hesitation, he chose to travel to Duluth and have an artificial pacemaker inserted surgically. Life for him, despite his severe limitations, was still very valuable. Months later Mr. Hooker developed abdominal pain and yellow skin, which suggested a cancer in his liver, gall bladder, or pancreas. When our preliminary tests in the hospital indicated that he probably did have cancer, Mr. Hooker chose not to have any further evaluation or treatment, and he died within a few weeks. Although I did not know him when he was younger, I doubt whether he could have predicted his decisions even fifteen years earlier.

Most important of all, it is simply too difficult to define in advance all the varieties of illness, suffering, prognosis, and treatment with sufficient precision for the definitions to be much help in the actual situation. A physician may know, for instance, that a patient does not want to be "kept alive unnecessarily if I'm a vegetable and there is no hope of improvement." Unfortunately, the real-life situation will almost surely be much more complex. What constitutes "keeping a person alive"? Is it giving her a warm room and regular meals rather than allowing her to lie at home alone, paralyzed, and with no heat? Is it giving her an IV or routine antibiotics? And what quality of life constitutes "being a vegetable"? Furthermore, in real life there is rarely any certainty about prognosis. Improvement may be unlikely, but it is often possible. So even in the best case in which a self-aware person has talked with her physician or made out a recent living will, the complexities of the actual situation probably will render those efforts of little practical use to the physician, and because of her debilities or the seriousness of her acute illness, the patient herself is rarely fully available to her physician at the needed moment.

Although any of these suggestions would be of some benefit to the physician in deciding how aggressively to treat an elderly, debilitated, and incompetent patient, very few patients actually make any such preparations, and the physician is thrown back on his own judgment. Since he does not know what the patient would in fact want, he cannot make what the ethicists call a "substituted judgment" for the patient and must act instead in the patient's best interest. What the ethicists mean by "best interest" is that the physician should take into account everything about the patient: relief of suffering, preservation of functioning, quality and extent of life, and the impact of the incapacity on loved ones' lives—surely an impossible task for one doctor in the middle of the night.

If the professional ethicists have not yet provided much help in this most difficult situation, the law has been positively confusing. As I understand it, some recent court decisions have suggested that the court must authorize the withholding of treatment in any particular case. Although I would not argue with the attempt to relieve the physician of this responsibility, the facts are that these decisions usually need to be made quickly (within hours or days), repeatedly (quality of life, prognosis, and treatment options may vary from day to day), and with a considerable degree of medical expertise. It is unrealistic to believe that the courts could decide these matters promptly even if we decided they should. It will be interesting to see how the courts finally settle the issue, but I expect physicians will get little help, regardless.

In fact, then, I, as the primary care physician, face this complex dilemma alone. I may try to share the decision with the family, who may know how the patient would decide in such a situation, but most often they have even less idea of what to do than I and are desperately relying on me for guidance. Even when someone in the family does have a definite idea of what should be done, the situation is hardly less murky for the physician. Although our society may believe that a patient has the right to refuse treatment, we do not indiscriminately assign that right to any relative who might think he knows what is best.

I first met Maria Alvarez when her regular doctor, my partner, had to be out of town for the week and I began seeing her at the hospital. Before my partner left, he told me some of the details of her case. Although she was only thirty-eight, Maria was dying of a rare and very malignant stomach cancer. Abused as a child, she was full of anger, which she found it difficult to express appropriately, a situation aggravated by her terminal illness. She had never married, had no family in this country, and had few friends. After she became ill, an older friend, Guadalupe Adriano, began taking care of her and eventually invited Maria into her home as Maria became too weak to care for herself. Maria was also befriended by an order of Roman Catholic nuns for whom she had previously worked as a domestic. They visited her daily whenever she was in the hospital.

According to my partner, Maria had chosen to refuse the radiation therapy that might have prolonged her life because she was ready to die and didn't want to suffer the nausea that the radiation often produces. As her only "family," Guadalupe had been part of the decision too. Both she and the sisters felt that Maria had already suffered enough, and they supported Maria's decision to decline the potentially life-sustaining treatment.

Maria had been in the hospital about a week when I first saw her. She was obviously very weak, had lost a great deal of weight, and had to be totally cared for by the nurses. Her English was poor, so Guadalupe was there that first Friday to translate for us. I introduced myself and asked her how things were going. Through Guadalupe, Maria told me she was still having a lot of pain in her stomach but the morphine shots made her fairly comfortable; she complained, however, that the nurses wouldn't give her the shots often enough. I told her I would check to see how often the shots were being given. I then asked about the radiation treatment.

"Dr. Peters tells me that you've decided against having the x-ray treatment to your stomach."

"Oh, yes, Doctor," Guadalupe answered without translating. "Maria and the sisters and I have talked about it many times. Maria has suffered so very much. There is no need to make it go on longer."

"Well, could you ask Maria now, just to be sure, if she is still certain that she doesn't want it?"

Guadalupe and Maria talked for a minute in Spanish, and Maria shook her head weakly and said, "No, Doctor, no x-rays." I nodded my head, we chatted for a while together, and I left.

Guadalupe was out of town for the next few days, so Maria and I had to get along on our own. Although I had difficulty talking with her each morning as I made rounds, I sensed that the language barrier was not the only problem. Maria was withdrawn but also seemed angry. I couldn't get her to talk about what was bothering her, so I asked Maryanne Doherty, Maria's nurse, how she behaved the rest of the day. Maryanne said that Maria was uncomfortable but communicative. She had been asking questions about the radiation therapy the entire weekend. I walked back to Maria's room.

"Maria, Maryanne said that you have been asking about the x-ray treatment."

Maria looked quickly at me, her eyes flashing with anger. "Doctor, why you not want me to have x-ray? I having much pain. Maryanne say x-ray help stomach pain."

"Who told you I don't want you to have the x-ray treatment, Maria? Guadalupe said *you* didn't want it. It might be a good idea, and it might help your pain."

"Guadalupe say you doctors think x-rays not good for me. X-rays make me sick. X-rays not help. But Maryanne say x-rays make pain better."

"We don't know for sure, Maria. The x-rays will probably help your stomach pain, but they may make you nauseated . . . sick to your stomach. I'll help you decide, but it's your decision, not mine."

It was difficult to talk together since Maria was obviously still angry with me and not sure she could trust me. As I deciphered her story, I began to understand. Guadalupe and the sisters had seen Maria in such pain and discomfort that they had evidently decided palliative radiation treatment was not in her best interest. Since Guadalupe was Maria's main source of medical information, she had—unconsciously, I suspect—slanted that information against the radiation treatment. Until Maria was left alone with the nurses for the weekend, she had believed that everyone was advising her against—no, essentially refusing her—the radiation therapy. Surrounded by the uniform opinions of Guadalupe and the sisters, Maria didn't want the therapy, but when left alone in the hospital to face her illness, she decided she did.

Our language barrier and the absence of a family made Maria's situation different from the usual debilitated elderly patient's, but what it does illustrate is that often the closest and most well-intentioned person is precisely the one who has the most difficulty in knowing what the patient wants. Guadalupe was undoubtedly not purposely distorting Maria's wishes; she was simply grieving deeply for her friend's pain and could not bear the thought of potentially life-prolonging treatment. Maria, of course, was still competent to make a decision by herself; but if she had become suddenly incompetent, Guadalupe—apparently an ideal surrogate decision-maker—would have been leading me astray. For better or for worse, then, the decision invariably comes back to me, if only to evaluate the objectivity of the surrogate decision-maker.

It is not that I believe I *should* be making these incredibly important decisions about life and death by myself. The fact is simply that under our current system of medical care, I do. So what do I do, then? Medicine has developed no rational way to make such decisions about which treatment to give and which to withhold once heroics have been ruled out. Perhaps my most frequent response (and I do not admit this easily) is not to make a conscious decision at all. Aware that Mrs. Toivonen has a fever, I may decide to see her at the end of office hours and then, in the rush of the late afternoon, "forget" to drop by the nursing home until the next morning, by which time she is either getting better or is so much worse that "it won't help to put her in the hospital anyway"; or if I do examine her promptly, my examination will not be so thorough as it might be, and I will decide that the fever is "only a virus" when I really haven't excluded all the likely possibilities; or, as I did this time, I will give some treatment that will probably help but is not as aggressive as it could be.

The problem is simply too painful for me as a single human being to face day after day in a conscious way. How do I decide to let this person die when everything in my being says that life is the ultimate value? How can I make a decision about the quality of someone else's life without even knowing what she would want? On the other hand, how can I inflict the pain of aggressive treatment, impose the suffering of further living, and spend scarce resources of time and money on this life that is so obviously trying to end itself? Since I am operating in a vacuum and have no reliable criteria with which to make a judgment, my choice is ultimately guided by my feelings, prejudices, and mood more than by my reason. Occasionally, feeling the burden of this decision-making to be heavier than usual,

I'll turn to a partner, if time and circumstances allow, and discuss the situation. Almost invariably she or he will agree that my proposed course of action "seems reasonable," which is reassuring and of some help emotionally. However, the value of such agreement between two people of the same age, training, vocation, economic status, and social position (who, in addition, are professionally constrained from directly criticizing each other) is questionable at best.

Although I made these sorts of decisions quite routinely for seven years, the cumulative emotional impact was severe. The underlying irrationality of the judgments gnawed at me; the life-and-death importance of my actions kept me awake at night; and the guilt and depression of never really knowing whether I had acted properly wore away at me; for I knew I was being forced into decisions that only God should make.

Physicians are often accused of harboring a God complex and of being defensive about their decision-making. I would like to suggest that, at least in this circumstance, we have been forced into a godlike role. What other choice now exists? If challenged, many physicians would undoubtedly launch into a passionately logical defense of whatever particular ethical decisions they tend to make in such cases. I can easily understand such reactions. Trained to act in everything with impeccable logic and rationality, physicians naturally find it hard to look at the underlying irrationality of whatever they do in these situations, and such defensiveness is a very understandable emotional reaction to having to make ultimate decisions for which there are no criteria.

Epilogue

from *The Firmament of Time*

Loren Eiseley

Loren Eiseley (1907–1977), anthropologist and writer, was born in Lincoln, Nebraska, and educated at the University of Nebraska and at the University of Pennsylvania, where he received his Ph.D. in 1937. He first taught at the University of Kansas and at Oberlin College; in 1947, he joined the faculty of the University of Pennsylvania, where he remained, in various capacities, until his death in 1977.

Eiseley was a prolific writer who has been described as a scientist "who can also write with poetic sensitivity and with a fine sense of wonder and of reverence before the mysteries of life and nature." He was a leading interpreter of Darwin and evolution, but he also published poetry and short stories, essays and articles, as well as technical papers. His many books include The Immense Journey *(1957),* Darwin's Century: Evolution and the Men Who Discovered It *(1958); an autobiography,* All the Strange Hours: The Excavation of Life *(1975); and* The Firmament of Time *(1960), from which we present a self-contained section of Chapter V.*

If we examine the living universe around us which was before man and may be after him, we find two ways in which that universe, with its inhabitants, differs from the world of man: first, it is essentially a stable universe; second, its inhabitants are intensely concentrated upon their environment. They respond to it totally, and without it, or rather when they relax from it, they merely sleep. They reflect their environment but they do not alter it. In Browning's words, "It has them, not they it."

Life, as manifested through its instincts, demands a security guarantee from nature that is largely forthcoming. All the release mechanisms, the instinctive shorthand methods by which nature provides for organisms too simple to comprehend their environment, are based upon this guarantee. The inorganic world could, and does, exist in a kind of chaos, but before life can peep forth, even as a flower, or a stick insect, or a beetle, it has to have some kind of unofficial assurance of nature's stability, just as we have read that stability of forces in the ripples impressed in stone, or the rain marks on a long-vanished beach, or the unchanging laws of light in the eye of a four-hundred-million-year-old trilobite.

The nineteenth century was amazed when it discovered these things, but wasps and migratory birds were not. They had an old contract, an old promise, never broken till man began to interfere with things, that nature, in degree, is steadfast and continuous. Her laws do not deviate, nor the seasons come and go too violently. There is change, but throughout the past life alters with the slow pace of geological epochs. Calcium, iron, phosphorus, could exist in the jumbled world of the inorganic without the certainties that life demands. Taken up into a living system, however, *being* that system, they must, in a sense, have knowledge of the future. Tomorrow's rain may be important, or tomorrow's wind or sun. Life, in contrast to the inorganic, is historic in a new way. It reflects the past, but must also expect something of the future. It has nature's promise—a guarantee that has not been broken in three billion years—that the universe has this queer rationality and "expectedness" about it. "Whatever interrupts the even flow and luxurious monotony of organic life," wrote Santayana, "is odious to the primeval animal."

This is a true observation, because on the more simple levels of life, monotony is a necessity for survival. The life in pond and thicket is not equipped for the storms that shake the human world. Its small domain is frequently confined to a splinter of sunlight, or the hole under a root. What life does under such circumstances, how it meets the precarious future (for even here the future can be precarious), is written into its substance by the obscure mechanisms of nature. The snail recoils into his house, the dissembling caterpillar who does not know he dissembles, thrusts stiffly, like a budding twig, from his branch. The enemy is known, the contingency prepared for. But still the dreaming comes from below, from somewhere in the molecular substance. It is as if nature in a thousand forms played games against herself, but the games were each one known, the rules ancient and observed.

It is with the coming of man that a vast hole seems to open in nature, a vast black whirlpool spinning faster and faster, consuming flesh, stones, soil, minerals, sucking down the lightning, wrenching power from the atom, until the ancient sounds of nature are drowned in the cacophony of something which is no longer nature, something instead which is loose and knocking at the world's heart, something demonic and no longer planned—escaped, it may be—spewed out of nature, contending in a final giant's game against its master.

Yet the coming of man was quiet enough. Even after he arrived, even after his strange retarded youth had given him the brain which opened up to him the dimensions of time and space, he walked softly. If, as was true, he had sloughed instinct away for a new interior world of consciousness, he did something which at the same time revealed his continued need for the stability which had preserved his ancestors. Scarcely had he stepped across the border of the old instinctive world when he began to create the world of custom. He was using reason, his new attribute, to remake, in another fashion, a substitute for the lost instinctive world of nature. He was, in fact, creating another nature, a new source of stability for his conflicting erratic reason. Custom became fixed: order, the new order imposed by cultural discipline, became the "nature" of human society. Custom directed the vagaries of the will. Among the fixed institutional bonds of society man found once more the security of the animal. He moved in a patient renewed orbit with the seasons. His life was directed, the gods had ordained it so. In some parts of the world this long twilight, half in and half out of nature, has persisted into the present. Viewed over a wide domain of history this cultural edifice, though somewhat less stable than the natural world, has yet appeared a fair substitute—a structure, like nature, reasonably secure. But the security in the end was to prove an illusion. It was in the West that the whirlpool began to spin. Ironically, it began in the search for the earthly Paradise.

The medieval world was limited in time. It was a stage upon which the great drama of the human Fall and Redemption was being played out. Since the position in time of the medieval culture fell late in this drama, man's gaze was not centered scientifically upon the events of an earth destined soon to vanish. The ranks of society, even objects themselves, were Platonic reflections from eternity. They were as unalterable as the divine Empyrean world behind them. Life was directed and fixed from above. So far as the Christian world of the West was concerned, man was locked in an unchanging social structure well nigh as firm as nature. The earth was the center of divine attention. The ingenuity of intellectual men was turned almost exclusively upon theological problems.

As the medieval culture began to wane toward its close, men turned their curiosity upon the world around them. The era of the great voyages, of the breaking through barriers, had begun. Indeed, there is evidence that among the motivations of those same voyagers, dreams of the recovery of the earthly Paradise were legion. The legendary Garden of Eden was thought to be still in existence. There were stories that in this or that far land, behind cloud banks or over mountains, the abandoned Garden still survived. There were speculations that through one of those four great rivers which were supposed to flow from the Garden, the way back might still be found. Perhaps the angel with the sword might still be waiting at the weed-grown gateway, warning men away; nevertheless, the idea of that haven lingered wistfully in the minds of captains in whom the beliefs of the Middle Ages had not quite perished.

There was, however, another, a more symbolic road into the Garden. It was first glimpsed and the way to its discovery charted by Francis Bacon. With that act, though he did not intend it to be so, the philosopher had opened the doorway of the modern world. The paradise he sought, the dreams he dreamed, are now intermingled with the countdown on the latest model of the ICBM, or the radioactive cloud drifting downwind from a megaton explosion. Three centuries earlier, however, science had been Lord Bacon's road to the earthly Paradise. "Surely," he wrote in the *Novum Organum,* "it would be disgraceful if, while the regions of the material globe, that is, of the earth, of the sea, and of the stars—have been in our times laid widely open and revealed, the intellectual globe should remain shut up within the narrow limits of the old discoveries."

Instead, Bacon chafed for another world than that of the restless voyagers. "I am now therefore to speak touching Hope," he rallied his audience, who believed, many of them, in a declining and decaying world. Much, if not all, that man lost in his ejection from the earthly Paradise might, Bacon thought, be regained by application, so long as the human intellect remained unimpaired. "Trial should be made," he contends in one famous passage, "whether the commerce between the mind of men and the nature of things . . . might by any means be restored to its perfect and original condition, or if that may not be, yet reduced to a better condition than that in which it now is." To the task of raising up the new science he devoted himself as the bell ringer who "called the wits together."

Bacon was not blind to the dangers in his new philosophy. "Through the premature hurry of the understanding," he cautioned, "great dangers may be apprehended . . . against which we ought even now to prepare." Out of the same fountain, he saw clearly, could pour the instruments of beneficence or death.

Bacon's warning went unheeded. The struggle between those forces he envisaged continues into the modern world. We have now reached the point where we must look deep into the whirlpool of the modern age. Whirlpool or flight, as Max Picard° has called it, it is all one. The stability of nature on the planet—that old and simple promise to the living, which is written in every sedimentary rock—is threatened by nature's own product, man.

Not long ago a young man—I hope not a forerunner of the coming race on the planet—remarked to me with the colossal insensitivity of the new asphalt animal, "Why can't we just eventually kill off everything and live here by ourselves with more room? We'll be able to synthesize food pretty soon." It was his solution to the problem of overpopulation.

I had no response to make, for I saw suddenly that this man was in the world of the flight. For him there was no eternal, nature did not exist save

---

Max Picard   German writer (1888–1965), author of *Die Flucht vor Gott* (1934), translated as *The Flight from God* (1951).

as something to be crushed, and that second order of stability, the cultural world, was, for him, also ceasing to exist. If he meant what he said, pity had vanished, life was not sacred, and custom was a purely useless impediment from the past. There floated into my mind the penetrating statement of a modern critic and novelist, Wright Morris. "It is not fear of the bomb that paralyzes us," he writes, "not fear that man has no future. Rather, it is the *nature* of the future, not its extinction, that produces such foreboding in the artist. It is a numbing apprehension that such future as man has may dispense with art, with man as we now know him, and such as art has made him. The survival of men who are strangers to the nature of this conception is a more appalling thought than the extinction of the species."

There before me stood the new race in embryo. It was I who fled. There was no means of communication sufficient to call across the roaring cataract that lay between us, and down which this youth was already figuratively passing toward some doom I did not wish to see. Man's second rock of certitude, his cultural world, that had gotten him out of bed in the morning for many thousand years, that had taught him manners, how to love, and to see beauty, and how, when the time came, to die—this cultural world was now dissolving even as it grew. The roar of jet aircraft, the ugly ostentation of badly designed automobiles, the clatter of the supermarkets could not lend stability nor reality to the world we face.

Before us is Bacon's road to Paradise after three hundred years. In the medieval world, man had felt God both as exterior lord above the stars, and as immanent in the human heart. He was both outside and within, the true hound of Heaven. All this alters as we enter modern times. Bacon's world to explore opens to infinity, but it is the world of the outside. Man's whole attention is shifted outward. Even if he looks within, it is largely with the eye of science, to examine what can be learned of the personality, or what excuses for its behavior can be found in the darker, ill-lit caverns of the brain.

The western scientific achievement, great though it is, has not concerned itself enough with the creation of better human beings, nor with self-discipline. It has concentrated instead upon things, and assumed that the good life would follow. Therefore it hungers for infinity. Outward in that infinity lies the Garden the sixteenth-century voyagers did not find. We no longer call it the Garden. We are sophisticated men. We call it, vaguely, "progress," because that word in itself implies the endless movement of pursuit. We have abandoned the past without realizing that without the past the pursued future has no meaning, that it leads, as Morris has anticipated, to the world of artless, dehumanized man.

Rhetorical Index

We indicate below some selections that well illustrate rhetorical and technical procedures traditionally discussed in the study of composition. The listing is meant to be suggestive, not inclusive; most essays employ more than one rhetorical procedure, and many refuse to fit neatly into any traditional genre. We have listed those pieces that particularly illustrate the crucial transition from the more personal to the more analytical or discursive essay as a separate category.

Author and Title Index

About the Editors

CHARLES MUSCATINE is Professor of English at the University of California at Berkeley, where he has taught since 1948. He received the Ph.D. from Yale University and has served as a Visiting Professor at Wesleyan University and the University of Washington. A distinguished medievalist, Professor Muscatine has received Fulbright and Guggenheim research fellowships; is the author of *Chaucer and the French Tradition, The Book of Geoffrey Chaucer, Poetry and Crisis in the Age of Chaucer,* and *The Old French Fabliaux;* has published widely in professional journals; and has served as President of the New Chaucer Society. At Berkeley, he has been Chair of the Select Committee on Education, Director of the experimental Collegiate Seminar Program, and Chair of the Committee on Freshman English.

MARLENE GRIFFITH is on the faculty of Laney College in Oakland, California, where she has taught since 1966. She has also taught at Western College for Women, San Francisco State University, and the University of California at Berkeley. She received her B.A. from American International College in Springfield, Mass., and her M.A. from Berkeley. She has contributed articles to *College Composition and Communication, Twentieth Century Literature, Modern Fiction Studies,* and *inside english;* and two monographs, *Writing for the Inexperienced Writer: Fluency Shape Correctness* and *Writing to Think* to a series published by the Bay Area Writing Project. At Laney, she has directed the Writing Center, was one of the founders of Project Bridge, and has served as co-chair of the English Department.

A Note on the Type

The text of this book was set on the Linotype in Century Schoolbook, one of several variations of Century Roman to appear within a decade of its creation. The original face was cut by Linn Boyd Benton (1844–1932) in 1895, in response to a request by Theodore Low DeVinne for an attractive, easy-to-read type face to fit the narrow columns of his *Century Magazine.*

Century Schoolbook was specifically designed for school textbooks in the primary grades, but its easy legibility quickly earned it popularity in a range of applications. Century remains the only American type face cut before 1910 that is still widely in use today.

This version of Electra, (called Avanta), was set on an Information International Incorporated VideoComp 570 by ComCom, a division of Haddon Craftsmen.

Printed and bound by R. R. Donnelley & Sons, Harrisonburg, Va.